DESIGNING & DELIVERING COST-EFFECTIVE TRAINING

Second Edition

Compiled and Edited by
Jack Gordon, Ron Zemke, Philip Jones
from articles that have been published in

TRAINING
THE MAGAZINE OF HUMAN RESOURCES DEVELOPMENT

LAKEWOOD BOOKS
50 S. Ninth Street
Minneapolis, MN 55402
(612) 333-0471

Production Editor: Julie Swiler
Production Coordinator: Helen Spielberg
Design: Deb Gallagher

With special thanks to: Chris Lee, Beverly Geber, Sharon
Proskin, Klay DeVries, David Lawrence, Wanda
Stephenson, and Kathie Majeski.

*Lakewood Publications Inc. is a subsidiary of Maclean Hunter
Publishing Company. In addition to TRAINING, The Magazine of
Human Resources Development, Lakewood publishes the
Training Director's Forum Newsletter, Creative Training
Techniques Newsletter, The Service Edge Newsletter, and other
business periodicals and books. James P. Secord, president;
Mary Hanson, Philip G. Jones, Linda Klemstein, Michael C. Miller,
Jerry C. Noack, vice presidents.*

ISBN 0-943210-04-6

TABLE OF CONTENTS

PART II: INDIVIDUALLY ORIENTED APPROACHES

CHAPTER 5

IN THE CLASSROOM: ISSUES, IDEAS, TACTICS

ENSURING BACK-ON-THE-JOB PERFORMANCE

EVALUATING TRAINING AND MEASURING RESULTS

CHAPTER 8

TRAINING CLASSROOM INSTRUCTORS

SELECTING AND USING OUTSIDE RESOURCES

STRATEGIES AND TACTICS FOR MANAGING TRAINING

ABOUT THE EDITORS

Jack Gordon has been editor of TRAINING Magazine since 1983. For the second edition of this book, TRAINING's Managing Editor, Chris Lee, and Associate Editor, Beverly Geber, helped select articles for inclusion.

Ron Zemke is senior editor of TRAINING Magazine, editor of *The Service Edge* newsletter, president of Performance Research Associates in Minneapolis, and author or co-author of several books including *Figuring Things Out*, the classic text on needs and task analysis, and *Service America!*

Philip Jones, editor of TRAINING Magazine from 1975 to 1982, is vice president of Lakewood Publications and head of its Information Products Group, which includes conferences, books, newsletters and market research.

PREFACE

Reading a good professional magazine is an excellent way to stay abreast of developments in your field, to pick up helpful tricks of the trade, to gain a broader perspective on the issues with which you must grapple, to be confronted and challenged by people with a variety of arguments about what it means to do the job and do it right.

But suppose you're new to a profession. Let's say you've just accepted an assignment as a manager or instructor in your organization's human resources development (HRD) department. Now you face an immediate need for a full range of basic information, a crash course that covers everything from the theoretical foundations of adult education and training to the nuts and bolts of designing instruction and managing a classroom. You need *all* your bases covered quickly and efficiently. That's a need no monthly magazine can fulfill.

At least, not if you have to wait by your mailbox each month for the next issue to arrive.

Or suppose you're an experienced HRD professional looking for some timely advice about a specific problem. Maybe it's a technical decision: Should I or should I not include a role play in this kind of course? Maybe it's a sensitive political dilemma: Do I go ahead and run the team-building program the CEO wants, or do I keep trying to convince him that the sales department's "lack of teamwork" is a symptom and not a disease? This magazine we're talking about might run just the article you need, just when you need it. Or it might not. Same problem: A monthly publication can't cover every base in every issue.

But suppose there did happen to exist an absolutely first-rate magazine—TRAINING, let's say—that had been analyzing the theoretical and practical aspects of employer-sponsored training and development since 1964. Suppose that TRAINING's editors combed through its back issues—25 years worth, as this is written—with an eye toward selecting and compiling articles that *would* offer the reader a comprehensive grounding in both the theories and the nitty-gritty "how-to's" of the trainer's trade.

The result might be an uncommonly useful book—a combination, as it were, of "History 101: Introduction to Western Civilization" and a series of post-graduate seminars aimed at refining a number of specific professional skills.

That's exactly what this book is intended to be. And if the success of its original edition (spanning the years 1964-1981) is any indication, that's pretty much what it is.

The first edition of *Cost-Effective Training* went through three printings to satisfy reader demand. This new, expanded edition includes selected articles published in TRAINING since 1981. It also includes most of the articles from the first edition. That's why this updated volume is twice as large as the first; we subtracted a little and added a lot.

One criterion we used in selecting these articles was that they must be "timeless". That doesn't mean you won't find some anachronistic references in writings spanning a 25-year period. You will. But they are anachronisms of detail, not of substance. People change jobs, specific training programs are phased out, certain products leave the market. But we think you'll find that the ideas, the techniques and the relationships described by the authors in this book remain as useful and as pertinent today (and tomorrow) as ever. For all the fads that come and go in the wonderful world of HRD, most tried-and-true methods—and a surprising number of hotly debated issues—seem utterly timeless. Indeed, one lesson you may learn from this anthology is that despite all the talk you hear in the training business about this "unique" program or that "cutting edge" approach, very little is genuinely new under the HRD sun.

As for explicit lessons, prepare yourself for a step-by-step journey into the intricacies of the training process, a guided tour provided by many of the foremost experts in the field. Between these covers is some of the best advice you'll ever find about how to analyze the causes of performance problems, how to design and deliver training (or other interventions) to solve them, and how to evaluate the results. You'll get tips from veteran trainers on everything from how to use a flip chart effectively to how to decide whether computer-based training would be a more viable option than classroom training for a particular situation. You'll discover that knowledgeable people hold differing views about the nature and purpose of many aspects of employer-sponsored training. And you'll find very persuasive arguments leading to very different conclusions.

Experienced trainers like to distinguish between "knowledge" (as in understanding and gaining some perspective on a subject) and "skill" (as in the effective application of knowledge to accomplish a task). We believe you'll find this book helpful on both counts.

Jack Gordon
Editor, TRAINING Magazine
August 1988

CHAPTER 1

THE TRAINING AND DEVELOPMENT PROCESS

This book is organized loosely around a mythical process referred to variously as the systems approach to training, the ISD (Instructional Systems Development) approach and the ID (Instructional Development) process. Describing the whole thing in 1000 words or less is a bit like trying to turn *War and Peace* into a magazine article; you get the gist of the plot but miss the action and motivation completely.

For the schematically minded, it's basically a seven step process:

in fact been solved. The program is judged a success if the problem is resolved, and the cost of fixing it is significantly less than the cost of doing nothing.

In the textbook, that's how training gets done: neat, clean, orderly, almost antiseptic. In real life, the process of bringing training into being often looks more like this:

1. Mr. Big gets a stinging letter from XXX Inc.'s best client telling him in no uncertain terms that XXX has the worst-trained salespeople in the field. "We'll be dealing with ZZZ Corp. from now on."

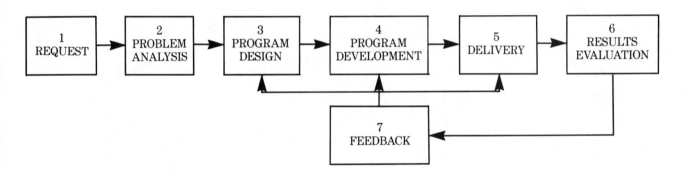

The classic textbook explanation of that process is simple and straightforward:

1. Training department receives request for training assistance, usually from a line manager.

2. Trainer/analyst conducts study to determine causes and consequences of the performance problem that management has identified.

3. If analysis shows problem to be based in a deficiency of skills or knowledge and the resolution to have significant organizational impact, trainer develops detailed statement of learning outcomes, and designs a learning package that will match media and method to the desired learning outcomes and maximize cost/benefit to client and organization.

4. Specialists in various media and method areas come together to develop scripts, create workbooks, design computer-based training programs, etc., as appropriate to meet the learning outcomes.

5. The program is pilot tested, results are evaluated and the program is revised. Simultaneously, a delivery system is designed and tested.

6. The delivery system and learning results are monitored on an ongoing basis.

7. Results are fed back to the design/development/delivery phases as appropriate. Eventually, we test to see whether the performance problem we wanted to solve has

2. Mr. Big sends for training director Terry. "Fix this problem and fix it fast," Big says. "The client says it's bad training, so it's your responsibility. I want to see a total plan for the correction. Tomorrow."

3. Mr. Big calls in Ms. Jones, the vice president in charge of sales. "Boss, this isn't a training thing," she says. "It's motivational. What we need is a good sales contest. Let me get to work on this."

4. Mr. Big's executive assistant, a believer in self-improvement, brings in the latest paperback, *Peak Sales Leadership Excellence Through Team Aerobics*. "Mr. Big, she says, "from what I've overheard, this is really an attitude problem. Our salespeople don't need to know all those details about the product, they just need a better attitude. And this book has certainly changed my whole outlook."

5. Mr. Big calls Terry. "Terry, I've reconsidered this project. I want you to spend today with Jones, who has some things to teach you. But first order a copy of *Peak Sales Leadership Excellence Through Team Aerobics* for every salesperson. Then get someone over to ZZZ Corp. to scout around; find out what kind of people they're hiring. And see me first thing tomorrow morning with a report."

6. Terry, sitting amid the piles of half-finished reports and projects that Big has previously commissioned and abandoned, contemplates suicide.

In theory, the training and development process is a rigorous, straightforward system that combines art and science into an orderly and effective whole. In practice, it can be a frantic, fragmented effort that succeeds occasionally and by chance, sometimes in spite of itself.

The systems approach is nothing more nor less than an operating model, an image of what the thing looks like uncluttered—an ideal. But by aspiring to the ideal, we increase the capacity of the real. The model gives us a guide through the politics and persuasion and compromises that are usually part of the reality of training. The model keeps us aware of what we are trading off and why. At the junction of perfect theory and imperfect reality lies the essence of the business we are in. It is a human and humane business, a business founded on a belief in change and progress. We are in the business of helping others get better and achieve more. We do our job best when we keep our eyes on the model and our hands on the everyday reality.

WHY HAVE A TRAINING AND DEVELOPMENT DEPARTMENT ANYWAY?

No matter how large or small the T&D operation, they all must ask themselves—and answer for others—

BY DUGAN LAIRD

Let's say we're going through the line at a cafeteria. We come to the coffee urn and turn a spigot. Out comes some coffee. Presumably when the liquid went into the machine, it was water—not coffee. When the coffee grounds were put into the machine, they weren't in drinkable, useful form. So the water and coffee grounds are "inputs" to the coffee machine; drinkable coffee is output.

When you get to the end of the line, a cash register "outputs" an itemized bill for your meal—but it can do so only if the cashier "inputs" the prices. Later, as you finish eating, you decide you'd like another cup of coffee. So you signal an attendant, who brings that second cup to your table. The attendant is providing an output in the same sense as the coffee machine or the cashier, except that this output is different: it's a service rather than a product.

Now let's move away from the cafeteria and look at the organization where we work.

When we think of an organization, we just naturally assume that it will have a chief officer. This officer may be called the chairman of the board, or the chief executive officer, or maybe the president. We also expect that there will be some sub-organization-departments with names like "sales" or "manufacturing" or "personnel." In recent years we have also come to expect a "training department," although in very recent years that name has given way to words like "employee development," "organization development," "human resource development," or "training and development."

Why does this training and devel-opment department get there among those other, familiar subgroups?

For a logical answer we might make another common, and safe, assumption about the organization: that its existence, like that of the coffee machine, the cashier, or the dining room attendant, depends upon its having some sort of "output." Such outputs are usually products or services. There are products like machinery, clothing, meals; there are services like fixing machinery, appliances, or human beings...like transporting materials or people...like preparing federal tax returns...like helping the disadvantaged or the aged get along in a nonsupportive society.

Now in order to get such outputs, there must be inputs. For most organizations there are usually at least four. First we think of a technology. That is the precise way the organization does business. The technology might be the recipe that makes one soft drink distinctly different from all other soft drinks. It might be the design that makes one automobile more attractive or more efficient than its competitors. It might include the procedures for mixing and bottling the drink, or for assembling the automobile. The point is this: To get the desired final output, an organization requires work. That work is divided up among positions; and positions are divided into tasks—and tasks are assigned to people.

And there we have our second input: people! To perform their assigned tasks properly, all workers need to

This article is adapted from Chapter 2 of Laird's book, Approaches to Training and Development, *1978, Addison-Wesley, Reading, MA.*

master and apply the unique technology governing their tasks. So here's where training enters the picture.

Preparing people to do their jobs

Civilization has not yet found the way to conceive and maintain a people-less organization. Nor has it found a magic potion which injects technology and skill into people. Training is concerned with the meeting between two inputs to organizational effectiveness: people and technology. Since organizations can rarely secure people who are, at the time of employment, total masters of their unique requirements, organizations need a subsystem called "training" to help them master the technology of their tasks. Training changes uninformed employees into informed employees; training changes unskilled or semiskilled workers into employees who can do their assigned tasks in the way the organization wants them done...into workers who do things "the right way."

This "right way" is called a standard—and one major function of training is to produce people who do their work "at standard." In fact, one simple way to envision how training contributes is to look at the steps by which people get in control of their positions:

Step 1. Define the right (or standard) way for performing all the tasks needed by the organization.

Step 2. Secure people to perform these tasks.

Step 3. Find out how much of the task they can already perform. (What is their "inventory" of the necessary technology?)

Step 4. Train them in the difference...in what they cannot already do.

Step 5. Test them to make certain they can perform their assigned tasks to minimum entry-level standards.

Step 6. Give them the material and the time with which to perform their tasks.

From that six-step process, we can also identify the two remaining inputs: time and material. People can't be miracle workers, creating something from nothing. So we give them materials like fabric from which they can cut dresses...like parts which they can assemble into machines...like parts of a broken machine which they can analyze and repair. In all these cases, management usually makes some statement about the quality; it specifies what the finished product must look like. And it takes time. By stating how many units should be repaired in an hour, or how many dresses sewn in a day, management

3

also sets quantity standards. The job of the training department is to "output" people who can meet those standards, both in quality and quantity.

This description may imply that all training is done after people are hired but *before* they are assigned to their jobs. That's obviously not true. Just look at the rosters of training programs and you'll discover the names of lots of old-timers. What are they doing there?

One legitimate reason for old-timers in training programs is that the organization has changed its technology. And the odds are heavily in favor of its doing so! Some studies maintain that 90% of all scientists who ever lived are alive at this very moment. Other studies show that the so-called "blue collar workers" will learn six brand new technologies in careers from their late teens to their mid-sixties. Another study points out that of all the knowledge taught in high schools today, only 25% was known and accepted at World War II's end in 1945.

Whenever the technology changes, an organization will have incumbent workers who no longer know how to do their jobs the new, right way. When people do not know how to do their job the right way, there is a training need.

People do not usually know how to do their "next job" properly. Thus transfers, or the promotions implied in some career-planning designs, imply potential education needs. Some organizations have training departments which help prepare for the future.

But sometimes we find people in training programs even when the technology hasn't changed, or even when they aren't preparing for new responsibilities.

When people can do their jobs properly, but don't...what then?

That raises the question, "What about people who have been doing their present jobs properly— but no longer do so?" It's certainly true that these people are not meeting the established standards of performance— but will training do them any good?

Not really.

You see, they already know how to do their work; they've shown that in their previous satisfactory performance. Thus the reason for their present nonperformance can't possibly be that they don't know how. And training is a remedy for people who do not know how— not for people who do know how but for some reason or another are no longer doing it.

These other problems are per-

formance problems—but they are not truly training problems, and training is not an appropriate solution. Of course, good training departments don't ignore these other performance problems. The smart training and development officer never says, "Sorry, we can't help you!" when managers report old-timers who no longer perform properly.

Training. The function once known as "training" has had to expand its own technology. It has had to locate and implement non-training solutions for all those performance problems which are not caused by not knowing how. Later on we can look at these "other problems and other solutions" in detail. For now, let's just summarize our answer to the question "Why have a training department?" this way:

1. Organizations get outputs because people perform tasks to a desired standard.

2. Before people can perform their tasks properly, they must master the special technology used by their organization. This means acquisition of knowledge and skill. Sometimes this acquisition is needed when the employee is new to the organization; sometimes it is needed because the organization changes it technology; sometimes it is necessary if an individual is to change places within the organization—either by lateral transfer or by promotion.

3. Training is the acquisition of the technology which permits employees to perform to standard.

Thus training may be defined as an experience, a discipline, or a regimen which causes people to acquire new, predetermined behaviors. Whenever employees need new (the accent is on the word "new"!) behaviors, then we need a training department.

But surely training departments do other things than just fill up holes in peoples' repertoires for accomplishing assigned tasks! Yes. Training people get involved in tasks called "education" and "development." What do those other activities involve?

Not all training specialists distinguish among "training," "education," and "development." They use the three words interchangeably to describe what they do for their organizations. But for those who distinguish, as does Dr. Leonard Nadler in his *Developing Human Resources*, (Houston: Gulf, 1970), training is what we've described: "Those activities which are designed to improve human performance on the job the employee is presently doing or is being hired to do." Education is those human resource development activities which "are designed to improve the overall

competence of the employee in a specified direction and beyond the job now held." To Nadler, development is concerned with preparing the employees so they can "move with the organization as it develops, changes, and grows."

Education. Let's apply these definitions to familiar activities. We can quickly identify some "leadership" and "pre-supervisory" and "personal development" programs as educational activities. People who have been identified as "promotable" often attend such workshops to enhance their capacity for leadership...to receive special orientation in organization goals, policies, or procedures. The "sensitivity training" or T-group syndrome is sometimes used as a vehicle for such education. Assessment centers and career-planning systems often reveal lapses in people's capabilities for future assignments. Education is needed. In these cases, the word is apt, paralleling the Latin origin of "e-ducing," going out from something that is already there. The identified capabilities are used as a basis for an expanded repertoire of skills in the individual. Why increase this repertoire, or inventory? So these individuals can make larger contributions to the organization in their next positions...positions for which they are presumably bound. Such activities are legitimately called "education."

Development. The development activity often takes the form of university enrollments for top executives. They can thus acquire new horizons, new technologies, new viewpoints. They can lead the entire organization to newly *developed* goals, postures, and environments. This is perceived as a way to maintain growth and development for the entire organization, not just for the individual. Yet that's misleading, since the sponsors of such "developmental" activities feel that the organization will grow to meet the future precisely because the individual leaders will grow in their insights about the future...in their capacity to implement change when the future has become the reality of the present.

Certain sociologists believe such development will be desperately needed— and soon! They point out that mankind faces tremendous social change— changes equal to those which accompanied the shift from feudal to modern society in the Industrial Revolution. They point to the post-industrial society now being born. (*The New Yorker*, Jan. 5, 1976.) The blue-collar worker we mentioned earlier is actually a myth. As Tom Wolfe said in *New West* (August 30,

1976), these skilled workers all wear shirts "like Joe Namath's or Johnny Bench's" and earn an annual income higher than most British newspaper columnists. And for the first time, say the sociologists, mankind is aware of these changes as they are taking place.

To a great degree, this is exactly what happens in miniscule when training and development officers use "organization development." They affectionately call this process "OD." It's a change program where change is observed as it happens. It involves launching and managing change in the organizational society. OD is very definitely within the purview of the training and development department.

However, in OD they focus on the organization first— and on the interrelationships of people and units within the organization, on structures and communications— not on the growth of the individual. To be sure, individuals will change— and hopefully in larger, "growthful" directions. Thus cause and effect are inextricably linked: people develop because an organization develops; the organization develops because people grow to new dimensions!

Why have such an OD program? Quite possibly because too many resources (human and material, time and technological) are being invested or squandered in ways which do not produce the desired output. Or perhaps they produce the desired output— but at too great a cost in time, material, or human values. Organization development may question the real "success" of organizations which meet all their goals in ways that make all the human resources feel miserable or unfulfilled in the process...miserable about the condition of their work lives. They agree with Hamlet: "Something is rotten in the state of Denmark!"

How can things get that rotten? There are lots of reasons. For instance, such a thorough organization reappraisal may be necessary because individuals or subgroups have consistently invested their talent, energy, and resources to achieve personal or departmental goals rather than the objectives established for the entire organization. Such reappraisals might be needed simply because communications go sour: key messages are never sent, or they get distorted, or they get lost. Perhaps feelings are never shared; they get "all bottled up" and only the content of doing business is shared. Everything is tasks, tasks, tasks!

Organization development programs use the human beings within the organization as resources in a problem-solving effort which might reassign or reorganize the subgroups, restructure the communications channels or media, reshape individual responsibilities, behavioral modes, or communicative style. It might, in fact, examine every facet of the inter-human and systemic structure in order to find a better way— a way which would permit the human energy to cooperatively produce desired outputs in order to reach organizational goals in ways which prove satisfying and fulfilling to all participant members of the organization.

Nowadays, training departments seek to be ever more relevant to organization goals, to solve performance problems throughout the entire organization—and to do so in a variety

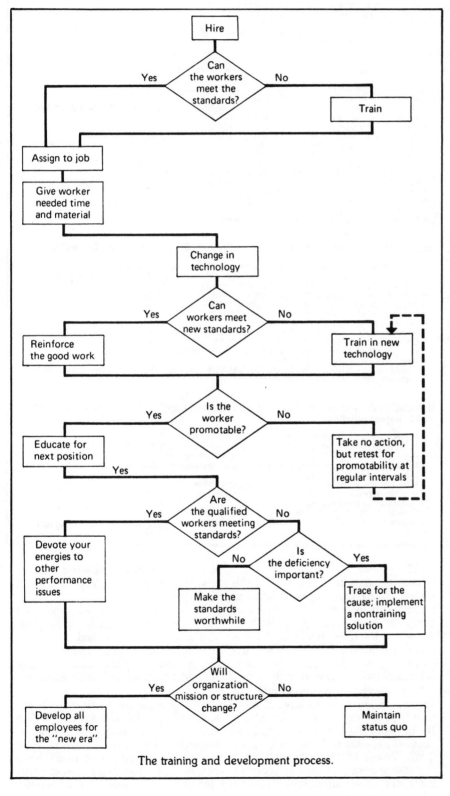

The training and development process.

THE BENEFITS OF TRAINING AND DEVELOPMENT

Most persons involved in training or development would consider themselves indispensable to their organization. Yet as Dr. M.J. Tessin, director of personnel at Kalamazoo (MI) College, reminded us these same persons may find it difficult to explain readily to top management the real value of their contribution.

Says Tessin: "When trainers are asked why money should be spent for training or development, the standard answers are: increases profits, improves efficiency, increases productivity, improves managerial effectiveness and morale—certainly worthwhile goals for any organization.

"But the manager who accepts these answers alone usually is one who already believes in the value of training. As effective trainers, we owe our top management more. We owe them a more comprehensive description of the value of training and development as *we* live it day by day."

So once again, why training? (As usual, we're using the word in its broadest sense, covering all areas of training and development—individual, occupational, and organizational.)

At a recent meeting of the Greater Battle Creek-Kalamazoo Chapter of the American Society for Training and Development (ASTD), Tessin challenged the group to develop an indepth rationale for training. Says Tessin: "I started with a warm-up period of reinforcing self-confidence regarding knowledge of fundamental aspects of responsibilities as trainers. These included: training section objectives, characteristics of good trainers and trainees, some learning principles, barriers to learning, types of training and training methods."

Through audience participation, the group composed a list of answers to the question: Why training—from the manager's point of view? Dr. Tessin synthesized and rearranged the answers into this first-rate outline.

How Training Benefits the Organization

- Leads to improved profitability and/or more positive attitudes toward profit orientation.
- Improves the job knowledge and skills at all levels of the organization.
- Improves the morale of the work force.
- Helps people identify with organizational goals.
- Helps create a better corporate image.
- Fosters authenticity, openness and trust.
- Improves the relationship between boss and subordinate.
- Aids in organizational development.
- Learns from the trainee.
- Helps prepare guidelines for work.
- Aids in understanding and carrying out organizational policies.
- Provides information for future needs in all areas of the organization.
- Organization gets more effective decision making and problem solving.
- Aids in development for promotion from within.
- Aids in developing leadership skill, motivation, loyalty, better attitudes, and other aspects that successful workers and managers usually display.
- Aids in increasing productivity and/or quality of work.
- Helps keep costs down in many areas, e.g., production, personnel, administration, etc.
- Develops a sense of responsibility to the organization for being competent and knowledgeable.
- Improves labor-management relations.
- Reduces outside consulting costs by utilizing competent internal consulting.
- Stimulates preventive management as opposed to putting out fires.
- Eliminates suboptimal behavior (such as hiding tools).
- Creates an appropriate climate for growth, communication.
- Aids in improving organizational communication.
- Helps employees adjust to change.
- Aids in handling conflict, thereby helping to prevent stress and tension.

Benefits to the Individual Which in Turn Ultimately Should Benefit the Organization

- Helps the individual in making better decisions and effective problem solving.
- Through training and development, motivational variables of recognition, achievement, growth, responsibility and advancement are internalized and operationalized.
- Aids in encouraging and achieving self-development and self-confidence.
- Helps a person handle stress, tension, frustration and conflict.
- Provides information for improving leadership knowledge, communication skills and attitudes.
- Increases job satisfaction and recognition.
- Moves a person toward personal goals while improving interaction skills.
- Satisfies personal needs of the trainer (and trainee!).
- Provides trainee an avenue for growth and a say in his/her own future.
- Develops a sense of growth in learning.
- Helps a person develop speaking and listening skills; also writing skills when exercises are required.
- Helps eliminate fear in attempting new tasks.

Benefits in Personnel and Human Relations, Intra and Intergroup Relations and Policy Implementation

- Improves communication between groups and individuals.
- Aids in orientation for new employees and those taking new jobs through transfer or promotion.
- Provides information on equal opportunity and affirmative action.
- Provides information on other governmental laws and administrative policies.
- Improves interpersonal skills.
- Makes organization policies, rules and regulations viable.
- Improves morale.
- Builds cohesiveness in groups.
- Provides a good climate for learning, growth, and coordination.
- Makes the organization a better place to work and live.

Reprinted from TRAINING, February 1978

---

of ways. Thus they are concerned with things other than just training. They seek other solutions to other types of human performance problems.

As a result, their titles are changing. One hears of human performance directors, of managers of organization development, vice president of education and training, director of development, director of human resources development. That last one, human resources development, has a nice ring to it. With its acronym, HRD, it's growing increasingly popular— and is somewhat suspiciously accepted by outsiders who may be asking, "Just how pompous can these characters get?"

True, the new titles and much of the jargon of the training and development technology are still smug and pompous. But they reflect a refreshing answer to the question, "Why have a training department?" Refreshing because it reveals an expansion...a new relevance and new accountabilities.

No matter how big or how small the T&D operation, they all have in common that one important goal: to keep the human resources performing at or above the established standards.

Why have a T&D department?

Because organizations, in order to get their desired output, need someone who is clearly responsible for:

- training people to do their present tasks properly,
- educating certain employees so they can assume greater responsibilities in the future, and
- developing people and entire organizations for futures...sometimes for undefined and undefinable futures.

Why? Because someone must be responsible for human growth if the status quo is to be maintained satisfactorily— and if the future is to be met. Because someone must help people make tomorrow a successful "today."   *Reprinted from TRAINING, October 1979*

HUMAN RESOURCE DEVELOPMENT: A USEFUL BIT OF JARGON?

A look at the development of the term

BY CHRIS LEE

An interesting booklet passed through TRAINING's offices recently: *Sniglets: Or Any Word That Doesn't Appear In the Dictionary But Should.* This handy reference included useful words like charp (the one green, mutant potato chip found in every bag), choconiverous (the tendency when eating chocolate Easter bunnies to bite the heads off first) and ambiportalous (the uncanny ability to always push the locked door in any set of double doors you approach). Useful words all, if still a bit obscure.

Many of the words and phrases commonly used in the training and development profession are every bit as obscure to those outside the profession. Some, like "performance engineering" are almost undefinable even to insiders. Others, like "human resource development" or HRD, as it is familiarly known, roll trippingly off the tongue—even when speakers know not whereof they speak.

To trace the roots of "HRD," we looked back 20 years to the ancestor of today's TRAINING Magazine, *Training in Business and Industry.* And there, in the premiere issue, September-October 1964, was "human resource development." In an article entitled, "Can the growth of training make the training director obsolete?" John Murphy used the phrase to equate an organization's investment in its human capital with its investment in traditional, concrete resources

such as raw materials, factories, etc.

"It's as simple as this," Murphy wrote. "The uncontrolled demands of technology on the skills of the corporation's work force have become so great that a top-management commitment is now required to invest in major, continuing programs of human resource development."

Yes, it does sound as if it could have been lifted from an article written last

> **HRD is somewhat suspiciously accepted by outsiders who may asking, 'Just how pompous can these characters get?'**

month, instead of 20 years ago, but that's another story.

According to Murphy, now director of executive and advanced management education at GTE Corp. in Norwalk, CT, the phrase "fell out" of the context of the article. "I don't remember having seen it elsewhere before I used it," he says. "In context of the article, I needed a business view of the education and training process, some-

thing that would point to resources other than capital and equipment. . . .I'd hate to think I was responsible. . . ."

Since Murphy used HRD—and remember, this was before it became trendy to call the personnel department the "human resources" department—it has evolved into an umbrella term for many people in the business. Others, wishing to avoid any acronym that smacks of professional jargon, stick to "training" and/or "development."

In one of the seminal works in the field, *Approaches to Training and Development* (Addison-Wesley, Reading, MA, 1978), Dugan Laird acknowledges that HRD is a useful term that reflects the widening charter of training departments in many organizations.

". . .Training departments seek to be ever more relevant to organization goals, to solve performance problems throughout the entire organization—and to do so in a variety of ways. Thus they are concerned with things other than just training. They seek other solutions to other types of human performance problems.

"As a result, their titles are changing. One hears of Human Performance Directors, of Managers of Organization Development, Vice President of Education and Training, Director of Development, Director of Human Resources Development. That last one, Human Resources Development, has a nice ring to it. With its acronym, HRD, it's growing increasingly popular—and is somewhat suspiciously accepted by outsiders who may be asking, 'Just how pompous can these characters get?'

"True, the new titles and much of the jargon of the training and development technology are still smug and pompous. But they reflect a refreshing answer to the question, 'Why have a Training Department?' Refreshing because it reveals an expansion. . .a new relevance and new accountabilities."

Still, Laird chose to use the "training and development" label for his book.

For some, the term "HRD" is interchangeable with "training," "development" and job-related "education." As far as these people are concerned, quibbling about distinctions is little more than an argument in semantics. But for others, notably Leonard Nadler, definitions are in order. To Nadler, who takes credit for coining "HRD" in its current form in 1969, all four have different, if related, meanings.

In his 1970 book, *Developing Human Resources* (Gulf Publishing Co.,

Houston, TX), Nadler defines the term HRD as "1) a series of organized activities, 2) conducted within a specified time and 3) designed to produce behavioral changes." Some of the most common activities *within* HRD are training, education and development, he acknowledges, but each has a separate definition.

• "Training is those activities which are designed to improve performance on the job the employee is presently doing or is being hired to do. It can be expanded to include the necessary activities to enable the employee to move to an immediate higher-level position in the organization but still within his same basic area of activity."

• "Employee education is defined as those HRD activities which are designed to improve the overall competence of the employee in a specified direction and beyond the job now held. . . .When the worker is being prepared for a place in the organization different from what he now holds—this is employee education."

• "Employee development is concerned with preparing the employee so that he can move with the organization as it develops, changes and grows. The result could be a new job at a higher level or an expansion of the current activities of the employee into new fields which are as yet undetermined."

More recently, in *The Handbook of Human Resource Development* (John Wiley & Sons, Inc., 1984), Nadler presents a somewhat reworked definition: "Human resource development is defined as organized learning experiences in a definite time period to increase the possibility of improving job performance [and] growth."

To further delineate his definition of HRD, Nadler offers the following explanations:

Organized learning experiences = Intentional learning situations with objectives, a plan and provision for evaluation.

A definite time period = An agreed upon and identifiable point at which a particular phase of learning has been completed.

To increase the possibility of = HRD can provide the learning, but can't guarantee that learning experience will change performance.

Improving job performance = Most organization-sponsored HRD aims at affecting job performance.

Growth = Helps individuals grow so that they will be ready to move with the organization or provides opportunities for personal, non-job-related growth.

According to Nadler, then, HRD encompasses three learning areas: improving performance on an individual's present job (training); preparing an individual for an identified job in the not-too-distant future (education); and general growth not related to any specific job (development).

So there you have it. The next time anyone asks you what *exactly* is HRD, you can either dazzle them with Nadler's definition or refer them to an upcoming version of *Sniglets*. Or you can simply mumble "human resource development" and excuse yourself.

Reprinted from TRAINING, January 1985

ISD: TECHNOLOGY FOR EVERYONE

This 'system approach' to job training was
first designed for the military, but
it can be applied to most any situation
that requires job skills training

BY TOM W. GOAD

It seems that trainers are constantly looking for better ways to do things. For quite a while, a prime source of "better ideas" has been the U.S. military. Because of their enormous need for training and their foresight in budgeting for it, the military services often have been pacesetters in training technology.

A prime example is the Instructional Systems Development (ISD) model. Adopted officially by all the services a decade ago, ISD has been making believers out of nonmilitary training designers ever since. In effect, ISD is a system that already has been paid for and that can work for just about anybody who wants to train someone to do a job. Why not take advantage of it?

What is ISD? It is the model (or process) to which experienced trainers often are referring when they speak of the "systems approach" to job training. A definition adapted from the military version might call it "a deliberate and orderly process for planning and developing training programs which assure that people acquire the knowledge and skills essential to perform jobs successfully."

The following statement from a military publication offers both a nice summary of the philosophy behind ISD and, by implication, a description of the sorts of training situations for which the model is most useful: "...instruction must equip people to do their jobs. More instruction than that is wasteful; less can cause big problems."

The five phases of the ISD process will sound familiar to trainers regardless of their familiarity with the model itself: analyze, design, develop, implement and control (evaluate). Basic stuff, right? Except that in ISD, the phases are interrelated, each feeding into the next and evaluation feeding into all of them, forming a closed-loop system.

Each of the five phases consists of several major steps. The development phase, for instance, includes these: specify learning activities; specify instruction-management plan and delivery system; review and select existing materials; develop instruction; validate instruction. In keeping with the military tradition of exhausting attention to detail, each of these steps is broken into several sub-steps. But ISD is not an all-or-nothing system. The trainer may use only those steps that apply in a given case, and may adapt when necessary.

ISD is a complete model of the training cycle. Virtually anything you might do in the name of training fits somewhere within its five phases (Figure 1 shows some examples). The model is research-based and field-tested, it uses front-end analysis to provide solid data, it considers alternatives, it's criterion-referenced (uses performance objectives), it's thorough—in short, it is an extremely comprehensive tool for designing instruction.

To get a complete picture of everything ISD stands for, you would almost have to go to the reference sources listed at the end of this article. But here are a few highlights of the system's "tools" and features.

Task analysis: One type of task analysis involves determining whether training is needed in the first place. The other type, a key feature of ISD and one for which worksheets are provided in the documentation, creates the basis for training and keeps it closely related to job performance. The designer's options extend to the point of detailing every sub-task that must be performed in order to complete a single action of a given job.

Developing objectives: The name Robert Mager turns up repeatedly in ISD publications, and for good reason: The system is nothing if not "criterion-referenced." A number of tools and examples are offered to help instructional designers develop appropriate learning objectives.

Built-in learning principles: Concepts such as reinforcement, feedback, transfer of training to the job, and categorization of types of learning are integral to ISD technology. Figure 2 shows how the system breaks down four major learning categories into 11 sub-categories. The illustration suggests a major advantage of the ISD model: You don't have to be a professional trainer or educator in order to make sense of it and use it.

Data-gathering tools: The "analyze" phase of ISD involves gathering data. The model provides structure for the process. One form, which can be filled out for each learning objective, includes slots for conditions, standards and test items. The form also requires

FIGURE 1. TRAINING ROLES COMPARED TO ISD PHASES	
Training Roles	**Related Phases**
Needs assessment	Analyze
Training planning	Analyze, design
Curriculum development	Design, develop
Media	Design, develop
Writing/producing	Develop, control
Conducting training	Implement, control
Measuring results	Control

FIGURE 3. DESCRIPTION OF TRAINING TASK CATEGORIES

Learning Category	Sub-category	Action Verbs	Behavioral Attributes	Examples
Mental skill	Rule learning and using	Apply Conclude Deduce Predict Propose Select Specify Solve Determine Repair	1. Choosing a course of action based on applying known rules. 2. Frequently involves "If . . . then situations. 3. The rules are not questioned; the decision focuses on whether the correct rule is being applied.	1. Apply the "rules of the road." 2. Solve mathematical equations (both choosing correct equations and the mechanics of solving the equation). 3. Carry out military protocol. 4. Select proper fire extinguisher for different types of fires. 5. Use correct grammar in novel situations covered by rules.

Source: Interservice Procedures for Instructional Systems Development.

the designer to specify the learning category involved, appropriate media, existing material relating to the objective, and lesson information. The entire ISD process lends itself to automation, and putting it on a computer is almost mandatory for large projects.

Developing and selecting materials: ISD sources are riddled with matrices, flowcharts, hierarchies and other tools to help trainers turn raw data and basic learning objectives into solid instruction. An example is shown in Figure 3. Once materials are organized, writing them also is a matter of following various guidelines. How-to formats are available for such tasks as writing learner workbooks and programmed-learning texts.

Preparation: The system stresses general preparation of the instructor and preparation of training material for the specific course.

Evaluation: ISD provides forms and methods for instructors, learners and outside observers to gather feedback and perform evaluations of two types: first during and immediately after the training course to evaluate the program itself; then after the fact, when trainees are back on the job, to determine the actual effects of the training on their performance.

As should be clear even from this brief sketch, the term ISD refers to an enormous load of training technology. Among its advantages, the model offers plenty of direction (you always know where to go next); it allows the designer to make effective use of subject-matter experts; and it provides a high level of confidence in results.

There are some drawbacks and limitations to ISD as well. In the first place, most ISD applications to date have been for technical training. Although the system appears to have potential for nontechnical applica-

FIGURE 2. HOW ISD BREAKS DOWN LEARNING CATEGORIES

Learning Category	Sub-Category
I. Mental skill	1. Learning and using rules 2. Classifying-recognizing patterns 3. Identifying symbols 4. Detecting 5. Making decisions
II. Information	6. Recalling bodies of knowledge
III. Physical skills	7. Performing gross motor skills 8. Steering and guiding; continuous movement 9. Positioning movement and recalling procedures 10. Voice communicating
IV. Attitude	11. Attitude learning

Source: Interservice Procedures for Instructional Systems Development.

tions, it obviously applies primarily to straight skills-training.

Secondly, the designer must take care that the model's "cookbook" approach doesn't become trainer-oriented rather than learner-oriented.

Perhaps the biggest drawback is that ISD, because of its attention to every detail of the training process, can become extremely time consuming. And time, of course, is the second major luxury (behind funding) that trainers lack. On the other hand, that same attention to detail—and the fact that the designer can choose to ignore sections that do not apply in a given case—can make the most out of the limited time available by ensuring that all critical areas are covered: If you use ISD correctly, you won't have to go back and do it over because you forgot something.

Reprinted from TRAINING, November 1983

SELECTED ISD PUBLICATIONS FOR FURTHER REFERENCE

● *Interservice Procedures for Instructional Systems Development* (5 vols.)
  Vol. I. Executive Summary (AD-A019486)
  Vol. II. Phase I Analyze (AD-A019487)
  Vol. III. Phase II Design (AD-A019488)
  Vol. IV. Phase III Develop (AD-A019489)
  Vol. V. Phase IV Implement, Phase V Control (AD-A019490)
  Describes approved techniques and procedures to be followed in development and conduct of all military training. Detailed steps, substeps, tools, and examples for each phase. (880 pgs.)
  For information on cost and how to obtain, contact: U.S. Department of Commerce, National Technical Information Service, 5285 Port Royal Road, Alexandria, VA 22161.
● *AFM 50-2, Instructional Systems Development*
  Contains description of ISD and how to apply its principles and processes for developing and accomplishing Air Force training. Most material is generally applicable. Defines phases (slightly different from the interservice model but with same tasks), contains some sample tools and has extensive bibliography. (100 pgs.)
  For cost and information, contact: Aerospace Education Foundation, 1750 Pennsylvania Ave., NW, Washington, DC 20006.
● *AFP 50-58, Handbook for Designers of Instructional Systems* (5 vols.)
  Vol. I. Introduction
  Vol. II. Task analysis
  Vol. III. Objectives and tests
  Vol. IV. Planning, developing, and validating instruction
  Vol. V. Evaluation
  Provides guidance for applying the ISD process described in AFM 50-2. Similar to interservice procedures model, but not quite as detailed. Many tools and examples. Extensive bibliography. (400 pgs.)
  For cost and information, contact: BMO/DAD, Norton AFB, CA 92409, ATTN: Chief, Documentation Div.
● *Military Standard, Contract Training Programs (MIL-STD-1379B)*
  Contains brief overview of systems approach to training and steps to accomplish. Also definitions of potentially useful materials and a list of data item descriptions for training. (25 pgs.)
  For cost and information, contact: Naval Publications and Forms Center, 5801 Tabor Ave., Philadelphia, PA 19120.

WHY WE CAN'T AFFORD NOT TO TRAIN

Even at Avis International, some managers don't want to 'Try Harder' when it comes to training rental agents. So they get a little lesson in economics

BY LINDA LASH

One-the-job training. It's a time-honored method of breaking in new employees and, in a hit-or-miss fashion, it works. Many service companies try to save themselves the cost of a formal training program, particularly for entry-level employees. But if you factor in things like mistakes, lost business and employees who quit in frustration because they haven't gotten the training they need to learn their jobs, on-the-job training is about as cost-effective as hiring someone to scratch your back.

At Avis International, we have determined that formal training for the company's new rental sales agents—the customer's first point of contact—is absolutely essential. Avis can't afford *not* to train them.

In order to ensure proper invoicing and sales, financial, marketing and management statistics, data *must* be input accurately at the rental counter. We have found that new rental sales agents who receive formal training are much more likely to enter correct information into the accounting systems. Training these employees also helps Avis comply with the laws of the many countries in which it operates. Rental services must be documented in proper legal form to protect the customer's rights and Avis's assets.

The fact that training cuts the company's expenses in these areas should be fairly obvious. But beyond helping new employees get the mechanics right, training them to do the job properly is terrific motivation. People feel better about a new job when the company has made a tangible commitment to them. People who are forced to try to do a new job with no formal training and perhaps a few hasty on-the-job explanations quickly feel frustrated with their performance and lack of esprit de corps (unless, of course, *nobody* has had any training, in which case they're all in a leaky boat). As a result, they often get discouraged and leave, generating costly high-turnover rates.

All in all, it should come as no surprise that corporate policy at Avis requires new rental agents to go through formal training programs before they're allowed to serve customers.

> ### An improper customer qualification may lead to the headline, 'Rental Car Runs School Bus Off Cliff.'

Yet many Avis managers still resist sending their new agents to formal training. And some training personnel still don't actively demonstrate to those managers why their new employees should be trained.

Why don't managers *demand* training for their new employees, instead of requesting shorter training programs? Why do managers continue to put new employees behind rental counters to "get the feel of it" before they allow them to attend training?

I'll answer those questions, but first let's take a look at how much it costs Avis *not* to train a new rental sales agent.

Sigrid is hired as a rental sales agent at a major London airport. On her first day, the company sends her to an Avis training center for a two-week course for new agents. The objective of the course is to enable her to achieve 90% accuracy in 90% of the transactions she will handle during her first two weeks at the counter.

Sigrid's first four weeks with Avis might cost:

Salary	$800
Benefits (at 40% of salary)	$320
Uniform	$250
Transportation to training	$100
Hotel and meals during training	$900
Errors made in first two weeks on counter (at 10% occurrence rate)	$160
Assistance during first two weeks on counter	$192
TOTAL	**$2,622**

Monique is hired as a rental sales agent for another metropolitan airport in England and, even though a training center is available, her manager decides not to send her to it. She works her first two weeks alongside a senior agent, and thereafter works on her own. Monique's first four weeks at Avis might cost:

Salary	$800
Benefits	$320
Uniform	$250
Errors during two weeks alone (at 30% occurrence rate)	$480
Assistance during two weeks alone	$576
Lost opportunities (complaints, lost accounts and lost up-sales)	$166
TOTAL	**$2,592**

At the end of Sigrid's first month, Avis has spent $2,622 for a capable employee who has a low error rate. She's comfortable with the job and can continue to grow and develop in a career with Avis. Our statistics show that there is a 61% chance Sigrid will

11

remain with the company.

Avis's first-month's investment in Monique is $30 lower at $2,592, but her error rate is too high. She can do most of the job but doesn't have a firm footing in it. Only 22% of the Moniques Avis hires will stay on.

That means we have to hire three Moniques for every Sigrid. Let's look at turnover costs. In an operating unit with 100 Sigrids, we will spend $2,622 × 100 plus $2,622 × 39 for turnover, or $364,458. In an operating unit with 100 Moniques, we will spend $2,592 × 100 plus $2,592 × 78 for turnover, or $461,376.

And that's not the worst of it. Without proper training, Monique could make a critical mistake, exposing the corporation to the considerable expense of a lawsuit, insurance claim or damaging publicity. A large percentage of lawsuits result from untrained rental sales agents who bypass customer-qualification procedures. A missing signature may make a large rental bill uncollectible, and improper customer qualification may lead to the headline, "Rental Car Runs School Bus Off Cliff." While thankfully rare, such occurrences almost always have been handled by untrained agents.

When we staff an entire operating unit with Moniques, these problems expand exponentially.

• One Monique generates a small cost in data-entry delays, but a larger number of untrained agents can generate an expensive backlog. The result: overtime or a need to hire additional staff.

• One Monique may result in a few disgruntled customers who complain or switch to the competition. A lot of Moniques can lose entire corporate or travel-agency accounts. The most profitable rental accounts usually are the first to leave when service deteriorates.

• If there are too many Moniques in the pool of potential supervisors and managers, the company eventually will incur the expense of external recruiting or of promoting unqualified people, who will then perpetuate the problem. ("I learned the hard way, my employees can, too.")

• If Monique is working in a unit planning to automate, she'll be difficult, and therefore more expensive, to train. Untrained agents will be slower to learn a new system, draining away even more supervisory time for on-the-job training.

• A whole unit of disgruntled Moniques can cause expensive problems for management, i.e., unionize, form a workers' council, etc.

When the alternative to training is high turnover, data-entry backlogs, lost business, potential labor problems and few qualified people to promote, how can Avis afford *not* to train its new people?

Here are some examples of objections to training employees that our department has fielded countless times over the years. The answers are backed by documented learning principles and proven cost savings.

1. "I can't afford to let new rental agents go away for two weeks of training. I need them here."

Answer: *You can't afford* not *to let them go to training. For every employee who attends training and then stays on, you'll go through almost three untrained employees who won't.*

2. "Company policy is not to replace a rental sales agent before the agent leaves. Who will cover when someone leaves and the replacement is away at training?"

A: *No one in the Avis system is permitted to replace a rental sales agent before he or she leaves. Many other service companies follow the same practice. When an employee is away at training, the shift can be covered by overtime, by a supervisor or by rotating employees among other stations in the same city. And you don't gain anything here by not sending them to training, either. If a new employee immediately starts out behind the counter, another employee or supervisor must be at their side almost constantly, and two people wind up doing the work of one.*

3. "Training costs money, too. Wouldn't it be cheaper just to train them here, on the job?"

A: *Avis can train all levels of employees for under $10 per student hour. One-on-one training is far more expensive. Before 1969, Avis did use on-the-job training, and the instructor corps was almost twice its present size. Classroom training is just as effective at half the price.*

4. "Let them learn the hard way like I did. You never really enjoy rewards unless you've worked hard for them."

A: *Learning the hard way assures only a 10% to 25% success rate. While that may help to weed out the chaff at medical schools, it's an unacceptable rate for a corporation whose goal is to have the right num-ber of people doing the job the right way.*

5. "If I send them away to training, they'll learn all those time-consuming procedures. This is a volume business here, and we don't have time for all that sales stuff."

A: *Studies show that it takes the same amount of time to rent a car the right way as to do it the wrong way. The difference is that when it is done the wrong way, errors have to be corrected in the back office. Also, "up-selling" a customer to a higher class of car takes approximately five seconds. Without training, it occurs rarely, if at all.*

6. "These are just temporary summer employees. We don't have to train them."

A: *Is an untrained temporary employee any less of a pain than an untrained permanent employee? Customers are the lifeblood of our business. Would you want an untrained temporary surgeon operating on you?*

7. "Training is a big investment. New employees should stay here for a few weeks first and, if they look like they'll work out, then we could send them to training as a reward."

A: *Untrained rental sales agents are virtually useless for the first two weeks. After that, they cause errors and need assistance. If someone is kept on the job for two weeks and then sent to training for two weeks, it'll be six weeks before the station has an accurate, productive employee. Comments from new employees who have had to wait to attend training always include, "Why didn't they send me when I really needed this?" Studies show that untrained hires often decide to leave during the first two weeks because of their frustration at learning the job.*

8. "I like to keep them here behind the counter for awhile. Then when they go to training, they'll understand what's being discussed."

A: *Learning theorists tell us it's much harder to change established behavior than to introduce new behaviors in a new setting. It's easier to train someone who's never filled out a rental agreement before than to train someone who's practiced doing it incorrectly. And the Avis training courses are designed for new employees. It makes as little sense to bring experienced rental agents to them as it does to place intermediate skiers in beginning classes.*

Reprinted from TRAINING, November 1984

TRAINING FOR ORGANIZATION RESULTS

Too often, training departments are evaluated by the quantity and quality of their activities—instead of the outcomes those activities lead to. Here's how to change all that

BY ARTHUR C. BECK, JR.
AND ELLIS D. HILLMAR

What do you mean, I'm not 'getting results'?," asked a participant in a management-by-objectives workshop after the leader suggested that the manager's described work activity did not have results orientation necessary to make MBO most effective. Obviously, there is much confusion about the word "results." To clarify the situation, it is important to recognize that *organization* results are the outcomes—outside the individual or organization—of activities.

Examples of activities would include the number of training sessions/workshops per year, subjects offered or individuals trained per year. Completing the training event represents an "output" for the training function and is often referred to as a "result." The critical question is: What contribution did the training event make to a desired organization outcome or result, such as "managerial skill in problem solving"?

In other areas in the organization, the differences between activities and organization results are:

Activity	vs.	Organization result
Financial reporting	vs.	Informed financial management
Selling customers	vs.	Customer satisfaction
Maintaining machines	vs.	Machines available for operations

The essential difference is that the organization result is outside of the individual or the individual unit. If the trainer is being evaluated only on the number of seminars, number of people trained, design of the seminar, use of audiovisual equipment, conduct of the seminar, and objectives of the seminar, he may not be achieving an organization result, such as "employees performing within standards." In other words, he may do an outstanding job conducting a seminar but fail to obtain results on the job. If the organization result or outcome is not made clear and agreed upon by both management and trainer, the trainer may carry out an activity that doesn't produce the desired outcomes for the organization. When this occurs, it's not surprising that management is unable to see training's contribution to the organization. Thus, when funds are tight, the training budget is one of the first to be cut.

The accounting department of an organization can turn out financial reports efficiently, but if these reports don't lead to informed financial decisions, accounting is not getting results. The sales department can be successful in order volume but not achieve the organization result of customer satisfaction. In some organizations, the sales, production, and customer service groups do not coordinate with each other. Each function operates independently of the other rather than focusing on the organization result, "customer satisfaction," that would require their working together.

In this concept, results are at least one step outside an individual or organization, while activities are inside. Peter Drucker clarifies this in his *Practice of Management:*

> Business performances therefore require that each job be directed toward the objectives of the whole business. And, in particular, each manager's job must be focused on the success of the whole. The performance that is expected of the manager must be derived from the performance goals of the business; his results must be measured by the contribu-

tion they make to the success of the enterprise. The manager must know and understand what the business goals demand of him in terms of performance, and his superior must know what contribution to demand and expect of him—and must judge him accordingly.

The key to understanding and applying this concept is recognizing that the *organizational* goal statements clearly identify the expected "end" condition (organization results), not the "means" (activities) to achieving it. Developing results statements means expressing our performance in terms of the condition that it will create outside of our own group or system rather than describing our own internal job outputs. The final test of individual or organizational achievement is: what difference has it made for someone else?

By emphasizing individuals and what they are doing, we have been conditioned to think in terms of accomplishing the task, not of organization results. The underlying assumption seems to be: If you work hard enough, you'll produce results. Thus, the concern for activities. When a common organization result is not agreed upon by management, subordinates and trainers, a large number of people can participate in training programs, but nothing significantly different will happen in the organization. The trainer may be training for one type of behavior on the job and the manager is managing and rewarding the subordinate for a different type of behavior. This conflict causes confusion, frustration and, frequently, lower performance.

The reason behind it all: Accountability

When we are held accountable for organization results, we will examine closely what we do to be sure those activities are leading to such a result. As trainers, we will determine the result desired for the training function and for individual seminars before we develop the program and design individual sessions. We will spend more time conferring with supervisors and participants and evaluating results on the job after the training is delivered.

Of course, this won't be effective unless organization results are established, valued and emphasized by managers who hold individuals and units in the organization accountable for achieving them. The focus on organization results puts individuals and units in a position to be evaluated on their contribution to the organization's achievement. No longer are they able to confine themselves to their functional activity. They find that being efficient— doing things right—is not enough. It is imperative to be effective— doing the right things well.

This focus on organization results starts with the mission, or purpose, of the organization. Drucker considers the mission outside the organization, and it must be in terms of the customer or client. His needs and wants (both satisfied and unsatisfied) must be considered before examining what the organization is producing and can produce to satisfy them. As trainers, we must know how our contribution is supportive of the mission of the total organization and the unit in which we're located. Often, this mission statement is not visible in results terms (outcomes for the customer or clients). When this is true, efforts should be made to develop a mission statement in results terms that reflects why the organization is in business.

When the training department is asked by management to develop a seminar for supervisors, trainers should ask such questions as: "Why do you want to train supervisors? What do you want to change? What do you want supervisors to be able to do? What will be happening when super-visors are supervising satisfactorily? Are the supervisors aware of what you expect of them? Are their bosses going to hold supervisors accountable for these expectations?" This problem-solving approach will help identify an organization result for training. The identification of this result— supervisors supervising acceptably— will enable both training and management to look at all of the alternatives necessary to achieve the common organization result. These alternatives may include: clarifying the standards and/or criteria for evaluating the performance of supervisors; communicating these standards to supervisors; identifying what skills are needed by supervisors to meet these standards; designing a program for supervisors to develop these necessary skills; and evaluating and rewarding supervisors on the basis of these standards.

This approach provides a meaningful basis for evaluating the training function and its contribution to organization results. Accountability is thus shared with managers and individual employees. This can be a little unsettling to us trainers because we don't have complete control over the outcome. Of course, we have considerable influence on the employees in the classroom, but our job is not finished at the end of the seminar. Only when the employee is performing up to standard on the job can we consider ourselves successful. This approach probably will require new ways of evaluating training seminars, new feedback systems, and more time for evaluations. The performance of trainers in the classrooms and the overall performance of the training department in contributing to organization results must also be improved.

Focusing on organization results creates a variety of enriching opportunities for both individual and organizational effectiveness. Individuals and groups learn to work together to achieve common results after considering several alternatives. Actual performance can be more clearly evaluated so that individuals and groups are held accountable for their contribution to desired outcomes. The allocation and use of human resources are consciously targeted so that individuals know they are working productively rather than just keeping busy.

These changes for the better help the organization deal positively with growth. Creating the outcome that you want and making it happen bring dynamic energy into the organization's management and training process. Reprinted from TRAINING, April 1979

CAUTION: TRAINING IS NOT A CURE-ALL

Don't get caught prescribing training 'pills' for every ache that comes along!

BY ED YAGER

For many years, I was an evening school instructor at a local university. One year I was asked to participate in the annual ceremony during which awards are given for course completion.

As recipients were called to the stage to receive 12-course, 20-course, 24-course and 36-course awards, I recognized many who had attended my classes. Because I was teaching a highly participative communications class, I came to know these class members quite well and established rather close relationships with many of them.

I recalled many of the class members discussing their frustration in not getting ahead in their companies. Many had repeatedly changed employers in an effort to improve their lot. Some of the possible reasons for their lack of success were obvious and some quite hidden. But one theme was consistent. All had been encouraged by their employers—without an honest evaluation of the real chance of success—to get more training and education. I checked the background of one class member of mine and found that he had taken 30 classes over a period of 10 years and was still being promised a supervisor's job.

Suddenly I realized that I was part of this game, too. Do we train for training's sake, I asked myself, or educate for education's sake? I don't think so. Although I do admit that training departments feel their most important responsibility is administering a tuition-refund program and maintaining departments that are evaluated by the number of bodies attending classes.

Management, of course, wants to help employees grow but often lacks the necessary preparation or skills. So a training office is established. And, too often, an equally unqualified person takes on these frustrations on behalf of the managers.

Offices that do employ skilled trainers often overload them with massive programs, leaving no time for individual counseling. They have time only to prescribe—not to diagnose. And the easiest and most efficient prescription is to send the employee to school.

Do we train for training's sake or educate for education's sake?

As an exhibitor at training conventions, I'm amazed at the thousands who shop for films, cassettes, books, projectors, packages and other materials just as if they're shopping for cars or housewares. Trainers are enticed by flashy brochures, badges, balloons, giveaways and attractive models. They come loaded with a list of "topics" and leave with a package or a pill for each. The opening question is usually, "What do you have in....?"

It's in areas like career development, employee selection, management by objectives (MBO) and performance appraisal that authenticity in training is missing. Courses, programs and models are offered to solve everyone's problems— encouraging trainers to ignore human, organizational, social and political issues that every training effort implies. They tamper with style, thought, method, motivation and self-image. And programmed "models" are expected to solve all problems, regardless of environment.

Where is the research? Where are the measures? How do we know what good or damage we do? Have we made "training" a religion in and of itself?

- We teach problem analysis but *we* start with solutions. We assume, for example, that everyone needs a particular course.

- We teach participation, but *we* manipulate our own power with a top manager's signature and call it "commitment."

- We espouse individualism while *we* employ sophisticated audiovisual learning designs and models to demonstrate "the right way."

Proposed guidelines

I propose we establish a new set of principles to govern our training activities.

- Don't prescribe solutions or buy packages unless causes and needs have been demonstrated and analyzed.

- Don't encourage others to attend programs or classes for self-development unless an honest payoff can be expected.

- Don't intervene or impose programs or change on an organization unless ample opportunity is given to consider consequences.

- Study and understand the values of MBO to the organization. Focus on results, satisfy management needs, improve organizational outcomes and measure results.

- Balance human desire to "encourage" and "develop" the individual as a human being with the organization's need for productivity and efficiency.

- Don't assume any program is necessary for everyone. "Across-the-board" training is more for the trainer's convenience than for the organization's good.

- Assume training must pay its own way. Training is not a cost but an investment that must have a measurable return.

- Recognize that commitment is measured by demand and payoff, not by management mandate.

Reprinted from TRAINING, July 1979

A MODEL SYSTEM FOR HRD PLANNING

BY IRVING R. SCHWARTZ

During the 1970's, human resources development (HRD) emerged as a formal functional area in many organizations. Myriad development programs, training seminars and skills modules can be purchased or produced to support this function. But the real trick is to assemble them into a coherent and manifest system.

HRD is a set of management practices concerned with optimizing the interaction of the person, the work and the organization so that the organization as a whole can be more effective in meeting productivity objectives. Interaction of all components should be considered in quantitative terms and in terms of the timing of that interaction, even though some procedures and practices within the HRD area are, as yet, informal.

In the model HRD system accompanying this article, HRD planning begins with a bilateral process: management projects manpower needs, based on corporate policy and strategic planning, while individual employees clarify their career and job goals, defining their own skills, competencies and motives. At the core of the model is a matching process where the self-identified strengths and interests of individual employees, as verified or modified by peer and supervisory feedback, are meshed with corporate needs.

When there's a good fit between strategic planning and career-planning needs, integration occurs. An implied contract is negotiated between the employee and his or her supervisor, sometimes with the help of an HRD specialist or a higher supervisor. This contract spells out short-term expectations for contribution, rewards and development.

A mismatch occurs if an individual's career expectations can't be met within the corporation or if the individual can't measure up to the corporation's requirements. When that happens, termination may be the only solution.

On the other hand, sometimes internal resources are insufficient to meet demand. This condition is frequently found, for instance, in high technology organizations. Then recruitment is necessary to make up the difference.

Organizational development (OD) and career development are shown as contiguous blocks in the model. As systems operators, they're programmed to bring about planned change. OD focuses on organization issues, such as how work gets done by and among groups. Career development more directly affects individual growth through education, on-the-job training and direct supervision.

Output from this process can be measured in three ways. Management's gain is an updated, movable inventory of human resources, available when fast-breaking marketplace demands generate new needs and also available to fill day-to-day productivity needs. From this process, the individual employee gains career vitality—a feeling of success and worthiness that comes with increased self-awareness, free choice and commitment.

The community also gains because HRD can be a "thawing" process that allows the organization to become more porous to work-force mobility. As a corporate citizen, the firm exhibits increased sensitivity to work/family issues, such as dual careers, flextime and job sharing, as well as to its hiring and outplacement practices.

The model illustrated can be used as a frame of reference for planning HRD operations and for monitoring and evaluating existing operations. Furthermore, this model equips employees and HRD professionals with a device to help them analyze job functions and personal competencies within a career-planning framework. When individuals conduct such appraisals, most find validation for their careers and current job assignments. This, in turn, leads to increased self-awareness and encourages a sense of direct responsibility for the collective work that must be done within the corporation to increase productivity.

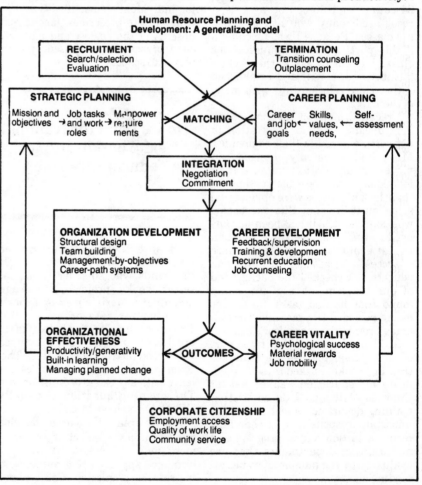

Reprinted from TRAINING, November 1979

TECHNICAL TRAINING: FINDING MONEY ON THE FACTORY FLOOR

Does your company think of technical training strictly as a costly but necessary evil? No wonder your shop has all these problems

BY TED C. HILL

Have you ever known anyone to take a stand against training in a general sense? How about somebody who hates the *idea* of improving productivity? Not likely. Nobody objects to the basic notion that people should be trained to do their jobs as well as possible, or to the concept that an organization's productivity probably could be improved. It's when the subject is a *particular* training program—and its costs—that the griping starts.

Engineers, financial people and a lot of executives will rarely oppose your training plans directly; they'll just wait for the right moment and then nail your hide to the wall with questions about return-on-investment (ROI), cost-benefit ratios and profit centers.

Forget the excuses that some things can't be measured or that the current Management Information System is not set up to give you figures on the things that could be measured; you're still going to get nailed. And maybe you deserve it: The hard-nosed financial types *do* have a point.

Productivity improvement can be approached from two directions: A company can focus on the equipment side, which includes such elements as improved machines, tooling, computer systems and material-handling devices. Or it can emphasize human factors, such as personnel selection, training, methods improvement, morale and so on.

In order to achieve maximum pro-ductivity, an organization must address both types of variables—another maxim that attracts universal agreement. . .in principle. But American management has always been more comfortable with the hardware angle on productivity improvement. For one thing, it's easier to get a firm dollar figure for a machine. And you can see what you're getting—you can touch it and measure its output exactly.

It's much tougher to see and measure the cost-benefit ratio of things like improved employee selection and training. To some folks in the seeing-is-believing camp, what can't be seen must not be real. But the benefits of improving the human side *are* real and they *do*, in fact, show up on the bottom line.

The "thing"-oriented people of this world see technical training as a means of teaching employees how to use a physical device. In other words, they think all production power is built into the device, and to achieve maximum productivity, the employee need only use the device correctly.

No doubt that teaching the uses of new technology and methods is one of training's most important roles, especially in industrial settings. But justifying that sort of training program usually is no problem: It's self-evident that if the new machines are to run, somebody has to learn how to run them. It's a little trickier to show management that training can result in productivity gains that go beyond the improvements offered by better equipment and boost productivity even more.

If the engineering department comes up with a new tooling method that will improve production by 20% and wants a program to train the employees how to use it, should the goal of the training program be limited to a 20% productivity increase? Why not 25%? Fine, but where would the other 5% come from?

Another way to ask that question is, how can training *enhance* the obvious benefits a company gets from the basic communication of "how-to" information about new equipment, methods and procedures? And for that matter, how can technical-skills training be justified when a predetermined mechanical improvement is lacking? Here are some examples based on fully documented training situations.

Cutting training time in half

Suppose (and it's a good supposition) that you want your trainees to learn a skill correctly first, then improve their speed. So you take them through the skill to be learned in a paced, step-by-step sequence identical to one used on the actual job. Your minimum expectancy might be to cut training time in half over the old "stand-here-and-watch-me" school of instruction. Have the bean-counters figure what that is worth in dollars, and watch their eyes light up.

You have to expect, of course, that sales and manufacturing people who want things out the door as fast as possible will not always go for this approach. A sales manager in one company became quite upset when he learned that a machine was being slowed down by about two-thirds in order to train new operators.

In the past, it had taken three months to get a new operator up to production standard, and the firm had a backlog. Within six weeks, doing it the training department's way, the trainees were not only up to "acceptable" speed, but were working as fast as the experienced operators—and the trainees' quality level was the best in the plant. Approximately eight weeks after that, the backlog was gone and the pressure was back on sales to fill the new "excess capacity."

There has to be a better way

While reviewing the first draft of a Bliss die-press manual with an employee, one of our staff people discovered the worker had developed a different die-changing technique that reduced the changeover time by 20 minutes. Encouraged by our interest, he permitted us to use the technique in the training manual. The training program and manual were designed for new employees, but we also distributed copies to all existing die changers. The resulting improvement in productivity completely paid for the program before the first trainee completed the course.

The moral of this story is that most good skills-training programs yield some unexpected methods improvements simply because of the thought that goes into preparing clear definitions of the job skill for a step-by-step instruction manual, job aid or whatever. The process of gathering data, resolving different opinions as to the best method, and careful review of the program's content by employees, supervisors, engineers and managers focuses attention on the details of the task. That sort of concentration by many knowledgeable people tends to result in cost-effective improvements to the way the task is done. It is not at all unusual to pay for an entire training program with the savings from such improvements.

Standardizing set-up procedures

The second-shift operator spends his first 10 minutes changing the machine settings to his own personal favorites even though everything ran smoothly on the first shift. Ten minutes on three shifts, five days a week equals 125 hours of production time per machine per year. Ask accounting what that wasted time is worth in terms of lost profit.

People tend to have preferred and often idiosyncratic ways of doing things. Natural enough, but it creates problems on multiple-shift operations and jobs that require employees to shift tasks frequently. The solution is first to determine the most efficient set-up procedure and then to communicate that method to everyone via training. The benefit is twofold in that you eliminate the constant changing of settings and get everyone to use the most efficient method at the same time.

Taking the mystery out of troubleshooting

Here's one that engineers and supervisors should recognize. The cautious worker has a problem, stops production and seeks help. Some time later, a supervisor, maintenance specialist or engineer arrives, makes a 30-second adjustment and leaves. An expensive, highly skilled person loses valuable time, production drops off slightly and the worker feels like an idiot.

Alternately, the adventuresome employee has a problem and, in an effort to show initiative, attempts to fix it—by making random adjustments and trying different changes. Typically, when inexperienced employees alter a setting without solving the problem, they fail to put it back where it started; instead, they try another adjustment. Coming in to remedy the situation, an expert is forced to reset the whole machine, since so many things are now out of whack. What started as a 30-second problem has become quite a time-consuming affair.

A relatively simple solution is to provide employees with troubleshooting guides. Such guides identify common problems and lay out step-by-step procedures for solving them, usually starting with the most likely causes and working down to the less probable ones. Informing employees about what to do and when to call for help is crucial; from a safety standpoint, it is just as important to tell them what *not* to do.

Troubleshooting guides allow operators to do more minor adjustments and repairs, leaving technical experts free to concentrate on the serious problems. In the end, this adds up to less machine downtime.

Avoiding costly errors

Management at a machine tool company in Cincinnati felt that spending $8,000 on a training program to teach only a few operators how to use a new N/C turning center (a numerically controlled, automated machine tool) was too expensive. Besides, the bosses figured, "These new N/C machines run themselves, right?"

When a new third-shift operator needed to make an offset adjustment to a reamer, he turned the "run" switch to "set up" since the original reamer setting had been made in this mode. This disarmed all of the built-in safety measures in the N/C program. He then restarted the machine, but failed to turn the control switch back to "run." The machine followed the operator's instructions and drove the reamer into the revolving chuck head, causing over $30,000 worth of damage.

Even a very simple training program, combined with some "hands-on" experience, most likely would have prevented this costly error. Preventing "stupid" mistakes is one of the hidden benefits of good skills training.

A skills-training program in a bolt-manufacturing operation was requested partially because written instructions from engineering, and sometimes from supervisors and qual-

ity control, were not being followed. One of several problems turned out to be that many of the terms used meant different things to different people. (What does "length" mean when applied to a bolt? If you guessed measuring from end to end, you'd be wrong.) One of the training solutions was a pictorial list of 59 clearly defined terms. Once this "dictionary" was distributed, many communication problems cleared up.

Most organizations build up their own jargon, using terms that apply to operations or physical items which are unique to particular industries or companies. It's not uncommon for a mistake attributed to employee carelessness or incompetence to be caused by miscommunication among people speaking different languages.

Helping them over the hard part

A bright young employee learns a difficult job quickly and is doing very well. Suddenly, she quits and goes off to electronics school or to another employer. The problem is that although the job was difficult to learn, it became dull to this individual in a very short time. On the other hand, the person hired to replace her cannot seem to master the task in any reasonable length of time.

Solution? A step-by-step training program that permits a person with modest abilities and ambition to learn a fairly complex task. Once the task is mastered, he can settle into a secure and satisfying position which he will be happy with for years. The trick is to find an individual with an appropriate level of talent for the job and to get him over the hard part—learning the job in the first place.

Defining "quality"

While designing a training program for employees who manufacture metal doors, the program developer discovered that there did not seem to be any quality standard concerning small dents in the doors. Given the same size dent, some inspectors scrapped the door, some shipped it and others sent it back for repair.

In many companies, quality standards vary depending upon which supervisor or inspector is on duty, and sometimes according to how close it is to the shipping and invoice date. Gather together everyone who works on the average factory floor: The quality-assurance people will deny that such variations exist, but the supervisors and hourly employees, who always sit in the back of the room, will cheer you on.

TRAINING'S THE PROBLEM . . . OR IS IT?

It's always tempting to grasp at the most obvious solution to an organizational problem. Several employees consistently are making the same mistakes, so what they need is a hefty shot of training, right?

Not necessarily, says John R. Bonar, training and development manager of a medical electronics firm in the Midwest.

As his company's new training manager, Bonar was presented with a situation in which the workers who performed microscopic visual inspections of integrated circuits were rejecting a high percentage of the expensive units unnecessarily. A consensus had developed among the engineering, production and management groups that "more thorough operator training" was the likely solution to the problem. Management assigned a task force, consisting of Bonar and several senior engineers, to investigate the problem.

Believing that inadequate training was just one of a number of possible factors, Bonar's group gathered additional, independent data by interviewing some manufacturing-skills trainers and the visual-inspection operators themselves, as well as their supervisors and managers. They also studied the equipment, the equipment configurations used on the production floor, and the technical specifications for inspection operations, which served as the major training aids for operators. Their findings were revealing.

• The visual inspection of product parts took place in three different production departments, each with its own supervisor and group of trainers.

• Many of the visual-inspection operators had no more than a high-school education and no prior experience in microelectronics manufacturing, but their training consisted largely of studying jargon-laden technical specifications drafted by engineers. Operators were certified as visual inspectors if they could pass a paper-and-pencil test covering the relevant specifications.

• Although most of the production and engineering-support managers acknowledged that visual inspection of parts was one of the most difficult jobs on the production floor, the operators who performed it were paid no more than the rest of the production work force.

• Technical specifications changed frequently and were often communicated haphazardly to the trainers and operators.

• Visual inspections were being conducted on a variety of equipment with different configurations, and without a standard inspection technique.

Bonar's task force presented management with a set of recommendations, grouped according to four main problem areas.

□ *Organizational structure and coordination of information.* Group all of the various visual inspection operators into one operating unit under one general supervisor. Create a new position to coordinate and evaluate changes made in the technical specifications.

□ *Operator job training.* Develop technical specifications in a format and language easily understood by operators assumed to have no more than a high-school education and no prior exposure to microelectronics. Begin a train-the-trainer program for all visual-inspection trainers.

□ *Operator work incentive.* Adopt work incentives for operators that recognize the complexity of the task and the high levels of personal dedication and motivation required to produce consistent, high-quality work.

□ *Equipment and procedures.* Standardize all equipment, configurations, instrument settings and procedures.

□ *Equipment and procedures.* Standardize all equipment, configurations, instrument settings and procedures.

Bonar and his task force were convinced that the entire set of recommendations would have to be adopted in order to improve the situation significantly. As it turned out, however, management acted only on a few of the recommendations.

Most of the equipment and some procedures were standardized. An effort was made to reduce the complexity of the language used in the technical specifications, but engineers did the rewriting, without the assistance of a technical writer.

Bonar and his staff developed a train-the-trainer program designed to improve the trainers' inspection skills. They also developed a system for designing and conducting operator training and certification, which included training specifications, manuals and other aids.

A year after presenting these recommendations to management, Bonar observes that the operators now are more highly skilled at their jobs and that standardized equipment has almost eliminated the earlier inspection inconsistencies. But he also notes that no improvements had been made in the organizational structure or incentive system.

Bonar says the experience taught him four things.

• Study the problem first; there's no substitute for data. "The people most closely associated with the problem often have a clear conception of it and plausible solutions to it. It's essential to solicit their views," he says.

• Things aren't always what they seem. Upon close inspection, a clear-cut "training problem" frequently turns out to be interrelated problems in the technological, communications and management structure of the organization.

• Be prepared to receive less management endorsement than you believe you need to solve the problem—but be willing to work with whatever fragments of the solution are endorsed.

• Partial success is better than no success at all. "There may be other opportunities in the future to chip away at unresolved parts of the problem."

Reprinted from TRAINING, November 1984

As for the problem with the metal doors, discussions with the sales department revealed that it was not the size but the location of the dent that mattered. A fairly large dent on top, where it would never be seen, was acceptable. A small dent at eye level or along the edge where it would disturb the seal was unacceptable.

The repair-department people said that half of the doors sent to them were not repairable and were, therefore, creating double-handling and crowding problems. After quality standards were defined and communicated as part of the training program, the number of doors going to repair was swiftly cut by two-thirds. As the full training program took hold, employees reduced scrap by 90% and achieved new highs in production levels.

Emulating model employees

An automatic screw-machine operator had not had an error charged to him in over eight years. When the company decided to use this employee as a resource to help develop a training program, he was surprised. It was the first time he had been asked for an opinion or an idea in 20 years.

Identifying individuals who consistently produce high-quality work, documenting what they are doing, and then training others to do it that way too, is an appealing and logical approach to reducing scrap and rework. It requires no new equipment, tooling or methods. It only involves converting existing knowledge into a more usable form and spreading it around. It's amazing how much can be saved by this simple training approach. The ROI is usually very high because costs are reasonable and everything saved goes straight to the "bottom line."

Mistakes involving scrap and rework cost a company in three ways: lost time and material from the initial mistake; replacement time and material; and the bookkeeping, scheduling, etc., required to account for the lost item and replacement. Next time you're in accounting, find out what cutting the scrap and reworking the account by 10% is worth.

In other words

The person responsible for skills training in an industrial company has a greater role to play than simply providing the communication link between the hardware and the people. The training function can and should be seen as a profit center—one that contributes a share to the organization's productivity along with the other departments on the team.

Production and finance types are not being unreasonable when they ask for some cost justifications. Considering some of the half-baked training schemes they have seen, managers have every right to be skeptical.

If you can justify a training program in cold hard figures, do so. If you can't, explain the concept and describe the payoff with examples and terms that non-trainers can understand. That way, in the future, when you are forced to say "Trust me," maybe management won't laugh.

Reprinted from TRAINING, December 1984

HOW LONG DOES IT TAKE?

The search for the ultimate answer to a
perennial question turned up an unequivocal,
"It depends"

BY CHRIS LEE AND RON ZEMKE

There are rules of thumb for just about everything. It takes about eight average Australians to eat a hard-boiled ostrich egg and about two hours to boil the average ostrich egg into edibility in the first place. It takes only a single step to begin the longest journey; unfortunately, it takes the average individual 1,760 steps to cover a single mile.

But how long does it take to develop an hour's worth of classroom instruction? To develop an hour of computer-based training? To conduct a needs analysis? To write an instructional objective? To produce a videotape showing the right way to perform a task?

By one estimate, we receive an average of five such inquiries each week here at TRAINING Magazine. Often as not, the inquirers are in desperate search of a rule of thumb, a ballpark figure, some kind of guideline that will help them estimate the staff time that project X will require, the number of dollars project Y will cost or the number of angels that can be crowded onto a double-sided floppy disk. But most of the time the query is about time: How long does it take to do X or Y or Z?

Heretofore, we've had no words of wisdom to impart to these lost souls. But after years of such queries, the light began to dawn that there just might be a story here. So, we have searched the existing literature, tracked down some of the field's most knowledgeable gurus, and left unturned as few stones as possible in hopes of stumbling upon not merely rules of thumb, but the makings for *the* ultimate trainer's job aid: an all-purpose model that would give reliable guidance to those how-long, how-many, how-much questions.

Stop laughing. We knew it was a long shot, but we thought there was a chance we might pull it off. After all, everybody talks about the modern-day precision of the training and development process and the need to be data-based instead of artsy-craftsy if trainers are to take their rightful places in the great organizational firmament, right?

Well, the fact is, there ain't no such animal. "How long does it take?" we howled. Our experts smiled, rocked back on their heels and with a single, resounding voice bellowed, "It depends!"

Given the variables that determine the ultimate investment of time and money in *every* training project, that is, of course, an eminently reasonable answer. Consider the problems inherent in a relatively straightforward project: producing a training film. Ask an experienced filmmaker how long it will take to make a 30-minute movie, and the only sensible answer you can expect is, "It depends." It depends upon the number of pages of script, the experience of the scriptwriter, the necessary locations, the number of actors the script calls for, the weather, the available budget and how many times the technical experts decide to change the script in midstream.

A similar wealth of variables apply when you talk about developing computer-based training (CBT), classroom instruction, learner-controlled instruction, tests, simulations and just about any other activity associated with instructional design or delivery.

For that matter, when it comes to learner-controlled instruction, and especially CBT, we open a whole new can of worms. If it's a genuinely interactive program, with each student being led down different remediation pathways and covering different material depending upon responses to various questions posed by the program, then what do we mean when we say "one hour's worth of instruction"? With CBT, the question has to be hedged: How long does it take to develop what will be, for the "average" learner, about an hour of "contact time" with the program?

Discretion being the better part of authorship, we pulled in our horns and refocused our search on the best rules of thumb we could find.

Roughly speaking . . .

"A rule of thumb," says Tom Parker, author of *Rules of Thumb* (Houghton Mifflin Co., Boston, 1983), "is a homemade recipe for making a guess." It is a guide; it is easy to remember; it is something less precise than a mathematical formula but more useful than a shot in the dark. As Parker explains, "Rules of thumb are a kind of tool. They help you appraise a problem or a situation. They make it easier to consider the subtleties of the topic at hand; they give you a feel for a subject."

Once upon a time, rules of thumb were a way of figuring things out in the absence of facts. It would, of course, be logical to assume that here in the vaunted information age there is hardly a need for such imprecise guidance. Logical, but wrong. The case, contends Parker, is just the opposite: Modern rule of thumbing is alive and well, thanks to the over-abundance of facts, factoids and non-sense in facts' clothing that we all face daily. Rules of thumb are a way to impose meaning on piles of information; they're warm little Mae Wests that keep one afloat in a sea of cold data. With enough experience in almost any field, some people become experts. And experts develop general guidelines that let them judge ideas and possibilities without forming a task force to investigate every single proposal that crosses their desks.

That conviction in mind, we asked the experts, "Despite the compounding variables and exceptions to the rule, what general rules of thumb do you use to estimate instructional development time (i.e., the first three steps of the Instructional Systems Development model: needs assessment, course design and curriculum development)?"

Walt Thurn, manager of technical employee development at Florida Power Corp., is on schedule in year eight of a 10-year plan to implement a competency-based training system for some 2,200 technical employees. But when it comes to a workable ratio for hours of development to produce one hour of instruction, he hedges.

"It's like your 'Training Zone Awards' for budget figures," he laughs, referring to TRAINING's annual "dubious distinction" awards, which this year featured *the* figure you could take to the bank on how much U.S. organizations spend on training and development (anywhere from $10 billion to $450 billion, depending on the source you choose to quote). When pressed for his rule of thumb, however, Thurn says, "I stick with 40 to 1, plus or minus; 20 to 1 to modify an existing program."

If anyone has an exacting standard for development time, it should be the U.S. Army, right? And it does, sort of. According to Charles Jackson, technical director of the Army Armor School at Ft. Knox, KY, the Army's training and development staffing standards govern manpower requirements for the whole training and development process. But, he explains, "It's an aggregate standard that doesn't separate out the phases of development. You have to allocate the

Jackson does have informal, or best-guess, rules of thumb for development time, however. To begin with, "The analysis and design phases are

media independent," he says. By that he means that whether you plan to deliver the instruction via live instructors or computers or videotapes, you spend the same amount of time on needs assessment, task analysis, determining and writing the learning objectives, test design, media/method selection, case design, sequencing and so on. He considers the delivery medium the primary determiner of the total investment in time.

Jackson's rules of thumb for design and development time, according to delivery medium are:

- Programmed instruction (text): 100 hours for each hour of instruction.
- Conventional live instruction (assuming a less-detailed lesson plan that relies on a subject-matter expert as instructor): 40 to 50:1.
- Video (from initial inspiration to edited master): 200:1.
- Computer-based training: 300:1 (time increases with level of sophistication, i.e., simulations will require more development time than tutorials or drill-and-practice programs).

Jackson also conducted a quick check among his colleagues at Ft. Knox, which produced some slightly different rules of thumb. In aggregate, they form an interesting range, more useful, perhaps, than a single-figure estimate:

- Programmed text: 120 to 345:1.
- Conventional live instruction: 80 to 315:1.
- Video: 160 to 345:1.
- CBT: 160 to 420:1.

manpower to [the production phases of] training and development."

Jackson lists three additional variables to consider before you attempt to eyeball development time: the nature of the learning objectives (Do you want to teach concepts or psychomotor skills?), the characteristics of your trainees and the capabilities of your staff.

"My figures are based on actual experience," he says. "I think 40 to 50 hours for [an hour of] live instruction is more reflective of reality. You simply don't do the same analysis for stand-up instruction that you do for programmed instruction." A delivery medium that requires storyboards (e.g., video, film, or multi-image show) or programming (CBT) demands more discipline and, thus, more time, he explains. "If you're forced to put it all on paper, you'll

find more adherence to the systems approach. When you're allowed to deliver instruction live, you're more inclined to whip up a lesson plan or outline for your own presentation."

For classroom training, an estimate from Jerry Vogt, a research psychologist at the Naval Personnel Research and Development Center in San Diego, is in the same ballpark. He pegs development hours at 50 to 100 for one hour of traditional, instructor-led, group-paced instruction. "Fifty is a little low," he adds. "It doesn't include subject-matter experts' time. You could probably add 10% to 20% for their time."

Dewy Cribbs, president of Instructional Science and Development, a San Diego-based vendor of CBT programs that does considerable work for the Department of Defense, begins his rule of thumbing by asking several questions: "What is the media? What is the method or instructional strategy? If it's CBT, is it with or without video, straight drill-and-practice or high-fidelity simulation?"

He also considers situational variables: Is it a new or existing course? Is the procedure standardized? Will he have access to the client's content experts for review and quality control? How much experience do the designers have in this content area? What will the review and approval process be?

"The industry 'standard' for CBT without video is 300 to 400 hours [per estimated hour of instruction]," he says. "But if you consider situational variables and you have enough control over content experts for efficiency (and your designers know the content area), you could be at 150 to 200 hours for a short course."

When it comes to CBT with videodisc, however, Cribbs tends not to talk hours so much as dollars. Interactive video programs entail a team effort—video and pre- and post-production crews—and a variety of other materials, so overall management and coordination of the project become critically important. "Depending on the types of people involved, I've seen $10,000 to $12,000 per hour to as high as $80,000 for one side of a disc (three to five hours)."

If Cribbs' rules of thumb make the prospect of developing CBT look like an attractive option, keep in mind he's talking about hours of development time for an experienced crew of

AN END TO TRAINEE 'HOSPITALIZATION'

Many companies in today's cost-conscious, lean and mean environment recognize the need for training but are uncomfortable sending their employees away for weeks, or even days, of expensive classroom training." notes Carol Haig, assistant vice president and staff development consultant for the Retail Bank of Wells Fargo in San Francisco. The prospect of losing business to competitors because the employees who should have handled it are off at a training seminar leads many organizations to settle for unstructured, on-the-job learning, hoping employees will somehow pick up the necessary skills.

Some employees will succeed, with the help of self-paced materials, computer-based training and interactive video programs. Others, however, require the structure of classroom instruction.

At Wells Fargo, a change in hiring procedures had created an immediate need for training. Branch managers, whose personnel requirements had previously been handled by the district personnel officer, would now have to do their own recruiting and hiring. Some of the managers were at a loss as to how to fill certain positions: for example, tellers who were to work only between 11:00 and 1:00, the bank's busiest hours.

To deal with this and similar training needs, the bank set up "clinics," in which employees participate in short classroom training sessions at their job location. The basic structure of a clinic, which Haig describes as "an 'outpatient' alternative to classroom 'hospitalization,'" consists of a preparatory reading assignment, a formal training session and on-the-job coaching. All three segments are administered, not by a professional instructor, but by a line employee—usually the trainees' own manager.

The clinics are easy and cost-effective to design and present, Haig says. "An experienced developer can design and package a clinic in just a few days. Most clinics require few resources—a content expert and some graphic-design support are usually all that is necessary. That makes development easy on the budget." The clinics' brevity allows flexible scheduling arrangements—incorporating them into staff meetings, for example.

Clinics are most useful, Haig says, when the training need is simply to expand upon existing expertise, as with policy or procedural changes; when the need is immediate and the learners must practice using some actual skills; and in situations where managers are accountable for their employees' learning and job performance.

The first step in designing a clinic is to draw up a topic outline for the entire three-step process. Next, determine what material can be learned during the initial reading assignment. This "prework" phase familiarizes participants with terms and concepts, establishes a knowledge baseline for the class, and instills in the trainees a sense of responsibility for their own learning, Haig says.

In the Recruiting Skills Clinic, developed for Wells Fargo's branch managers, the 10-page prework assignment includes a list of learning objectives, three bits of text on hiring, recruiting and developing an applicant pool, and a set of work sheets based on the readings. "Typically, a 75-minute clinic can support 60 to 90 minutes of prework, so don't be afraid to pile it on," Haig urges. "Getting a jump on the content is what makes the clinic an efficient method of instruction."

The core of the clinic is the formal training session. Go back to the topic outline and pull out any information that will require skill-building exercises and instructor coaching, Haig suggests. Establish behavioral outcomes and determine the most effective way to demonstrate the skills that support them. "In the clinic, exercises incrementally approximate the skills as they will be used in the workplace," she explains. "This means you'll need several short exercises that allow practice of new skills, one step at a time."

The training session should begin with an introduction, in which the course benefits, purpose and expectations are discussed, followed by a "prework debrief," in which participants ask questions about the reading assignment.

Next come the exercises and coaching, which may include small-group exercises, lectures, videotapes or whatever. Wells Fargo's two-hour Recruiting Skills Clinic includes a small-group brainstorming session; presentations by the line trainer on topics such as where to look for sources from which job candidates can be drawn, and how to evaluate candidates; and completion of candidate-search planning sheets.

At the end of the session, the instructor reviews the objectives, checks to make sure the trainees' expectations have been met, and presents the "postwork" assignment. In the Recruiting Skills Clinic, trainees also complete a one-page evaluation sheet.

Postwork is performed back on the job, under the supervision of the line trainer (the trainees' manager). Participants in the Recruiting Skills Clinic are required to contact three new sources of job candidates, using skills and resources they learned about in the training session, and report the results to the manager.

As the managers monitor the participants' job performance over a long period of time, they provide feedback on both the participants' progress and the program's success, Haig says. She notes that line managers like being able to see the results of the skills they have helped their employees build, and being in a position to continue coaching them to attain specific goals.

Reprinted from TRAINING, October 1987

CBT authors and designers. You may assume that CBT will help cut training costs, speed delivery and "modernize" your training efforts. Small problem: When you start adding up the costs of CBT, it can be daunting. And with no experience to draw upon, the road can be a treacherous one.

Greg Kearsley, chief executive officer of Park Row Software in San Diego, warns against attempting an unassisted trek from interest to expertise. "The start-up of a CBT function or capability can be particularly hazardous—and disappointing—if you don't know what to expect," he observes.

Which leads us to Kearsley's law of CBT start-up: Nothing useful will happen for the first three to six months after you decide to go with CBT. It doesn't make any difference whether you go with a vendor or start producing your own in-house.

A corollary: The first course produced by a new CBT development group will be a collection of mistakes. Throw it away.

Seem a bit strong? Kearsley has done considerable research on training media for the U.S. military, as well as a fair bit of CBT authoring, including a microcomputer-based expert system called "CBT Analyst." He makes a persuasive case: "When you are starting a new venture, like a CBT group, it takes people a little time to get on board. Consultants have to learn to think like the company. If you hire a specialist, the same thing applies—the new person will have to get used to the organization and the organization used to him. Net: three to six months before any real productive work gets done."

As for the corollary, Kearsley contends that any first product is going to be bug-ridden and, in retrospect, a little silly. "It's better to avoid making your first effort a high-visibility, bet-the-farm project," he says. A better strategy: Make the first project a pilot—and brand it as such. If you *must* do something of value right away to prove the worth of the investment, Kearsley advises computer-based testing. "You can't go too far afield developing a knowledge test on computer. And there is the added benefit that by adding testing of any kind to a course in any medium, you invariably improve the program."

Kearsley's rule of thumb for developing a CBT program from scratch: He considers 200 hours of development time for each hour of student contact time an ample average. The range: 50 to 500 hours.

Finally, if you prefer your rules of thumb to cover every exigency, here's one from Lynn Guerin, senior vice president of product development at Sandy Corp., a training and consulting firm in Troy, MI, that specializes in high-tech courseware: "There are three dimensions to any development project. You can get it good, fast or cheap, but you only get two out of the three."

From rules to rulers

Those of you who are uncomfortable with the concept of anything so unscientific as a "rule of thumb" are not alone. Several organizations, veterans of the quest for qualitative measures, have searched for more definitive answers about how long things take. And a few have come up with yardsticks that have proven useful for them.

But first, a word from Allison Rossett, professor of educational technology at San Diego State University. She recommends using existing standards as guidelines for building your own data base. "There's lots of data you can collect for your own situation." But she also offers a warning to those who would generalize too liberally from the experiences of others. "The contributing factors vary so much from company to company and industry to industry, you have to approach the entire subject in the context of caveats."

Rule of thumb for considering standards developed by others: The more precise the standard, the more precisely it is tailored to the idiosyncrasies of the organization's own development process and decision making.

That said, let's look at some yardsticks.

The U.S. government took a stab at developing time standards in a 1972 study, "A Training Cost Model," produced by the Office of Personnel Management (then the U.S. Civil Service Commission). Technological changes since then have undoubtedly made its cost estimates iffy, but its development-time guidelines may have a longer shelf life.

As Figure 1 shows, OPM's formula depends heavily on the delivery medium in question, but its blend of medium and content results in a mixed bag of sorts. This study also offers some guidance on an often-forgotten time factor: instructor preparation. For a course of five days or less, budget for three hours of prep for each hour of teaching; for courses between five and 10 days, budget 2.5 hours per teaching hour; and for courses over 10 days, 2 hours.

Another study that offers some guidance was produced by McDonnell Douglas Astronautics Co. in Houston. According to Tacy K. Smith, an instructional designer in flight operations and training, a division that produces training for external clients only, interest in developing a systematic way to estimate courseware costs led the company to conduct an informal survey among CBT vendors.

McDonnell Douglas approached the question in terms of the time required of each individual involved in the ISD process. These figures refer to the time it takes to develop printed

---

FIGURE 1
DEVELOPMENT TIME BY FORMAT

Format	Hours of Production for Each Hour of Presentation
Technical formal courses	5 to 15
Self-contained for handoff to other instructors	50 to 100
Conventional management development	20 to 30
Programmed instruction	80 to 120
Technical on-site	1 to 3
Computer-assisted instruction	Up to 350

From *A Training Cost Model*, 1972, U.S. Office of Personnel Management.

materials that yield roughly one hour of student "contact time":

- Subject-matter expert: 4.8 to 46 hours.
- Instructional designer: 4.8 to 18 hours.
- Technical writer: 3.2 to 14 hours.
- Graphic artist: 8.8 to 92 hours.
- Word processing: 4.8 to 28 hours.
- Review/validation: 1.6 to 6 hours.

If you run a total of these estimates, you'll come up with a range of 28 to 274 hours—a tenfold variation. But McDonnell Douglas also offers some help in narrowing that range. The most critical factors to examine:

- Subject-matter expert. Do you really have a knowledgeable expert to work with? Or will you have to "grow your own" via workbooks, procedures or technical orders? If you must rely on documentation, plan for an increase in development time.
- Content. If the course content involves "state-of-the-art" technology, it is probably still in a fluid state as well. Plan for lots of revisions, and a corresponding increase in development time.
- Delivery medium. For printed text, consider your format early in the development process. Generally, the more structured the format (military standards, for example, require careful adherence to predefined guidelines), the longer your writing and word-processing time. For CBT development, don't forget to account for your own learning curve on unfamiliar courseware authoring systems. Instructional strategy is also a critical factor for any estimate of CBT development time. Increasing complexity, i.e., from tutorial to branching, will increase programming hours, sometimes geometrically.

Martin Smith, district manager of New England Telephone Company's Learning Center in Marlborough, MA, created a job aid several years ago for making rule-of-thumb administrative and staffing decisions. He studied about 70 Bell System development projects that dated from the early to late '70s to come up with the guide shown in Figure 2.

This portion of Smith's guidelines applies only to courses developed for use by a single local Bell company. Any course developed for the Bell System (more than one local company), he explains, went through a much more rigorous process based on AT&T's seven-volume set of precise training and development standards—and all were subject to extensive field testing. Development ratios for these courses were as much as 25 times greater than those in Figure 2.

Smith cautions that this guide was used strictly for getting ballpark figures. It is no longer in use at any former Bell System company, to his knowledge. He also questions the usefulness of any such model in an environment in which fast-changing technology requires constant revisions in training content.

"People love to talk about development ratios," he adds, "but they don't realize that everyone has different definitions of development. And you're comparing apples and oranges if you don't have a common definition."

At Arthur Andersen & Co., precise training development guidelines ensure that everyone *is* speaking the same language. Perhaps it's not surprising that an international accounting firm quantifies the pertinent variables, but Arthur Andersen has plenty of incentive for doing so. For one thing, last year the company provided 3 million hours of training for its 37,000 employees in 45 countries. For another, in 1986 it spent $185 million—9% of its gross revenues—on training. The lion's share of Arthur Andersen's courseware—95%—is developed internally by its staff of 400 training and development professionals—100 of whom are instructional designers.

The firm has created what it calls "schools," 11 categories that differentiate among training projects and aid in development decisions, explains Maurice Coleman, senior education manager at Arthur Andersen's Center for Professional Education in St. Charles, IL. "The list of variables helps you hone in on what it's going to take to develop a course, based on these standards," he says.

School 1, what Coleman terms "the Cadillac approach," requires 215 hours of development time for each hour of instruction. For this type of investment, the standards or decision points include: the agenda and objectives will be stable for five years; the

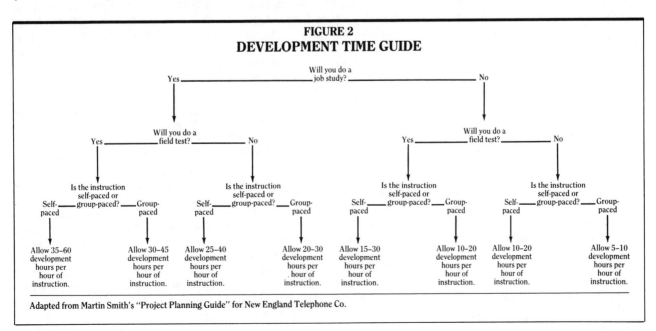

FIGURE 2
DEVELOPMENT TIME GUIDE

Will you do a job study?
Yes — No

Will you do a field test?
Yes — No

Will you do a field test?
Yes — No

Is the instruction self-paced or group-paced?
Self-paced — Group-paced

Is the instruction self-paced or group-paced?
Self-paced — Group-paced

Is the instruction self-paced or group-paced?
Self-paced — Group-paced

Is the instruction self-paced or group-paced?
Self-paced — Group-paced

Allow 35–60 development hours per hour of instruction.

Allow 30–45 development hours per hour of instruction.

Allow 25–40 development hours per hour of instruction.

Allow 20–30 development hours per hour of instruction.

Allow 15–30 development hours per hour of instruction.

Allow 10–20 development hours per hour of instruction.

Allow 10–20 development hours per hour of instruction.

Allow 5–10 development hours per hour of instruction.

Adapted from Martin Smith's "Project Planning Guide" for New England Telephone Co.

faculty pool (in-house experts who teach courses) will be large; 500 or more employees will attend the course each year; supporting visuals—videotape, slides, etc.—will be produced; the course will consist of approximately 30% content delivery, 40% participant exercises and 30% group discussion.

A School 5 course—call it a Buick—has a development ratio of 103:1. The standards: revisions after three to five years; a smaller and less-experienced faculty pool; 500 or fewer participants each year; supporting visuals are not necessary; and the course will be 40% content delivery, 40% exercises and 20% discussion.

The Volkswagen approach, School 11, might be a training meeting that would require 15 hours of development time per hour of instruction. Coleman explains: "It's a forum for local information, for a few people in a single office, that requires little design and development. It would consist of 50% content and 50% participation."

Arthur Andersen's standards also take into consideration the classification and level of experience of trainees and instructors, and the amount of documentation training materials will require. Coleman says the standards come in handy for budgeting purposes, as well as for negotiating with in-house clients. "People often have a Cadillac program in mind, but they can only get a Volkswagen for the price, and roller skates for the development time they're talking about. [Our standards allow us to say,] 'here's what it will cost, here's what you can afford and here's how long it will take: Is that in sync with what you have in mind?' Then we can play that information back and forth until we agree."

Still not satisfied with the level of detail? We uncovered a few more precise models for those who are willing to put considerable time and thought into estimating their development time.

McDonnell Douglas' search for precise cost-estimating guidance turned up a more exacting model, which also is more limited in terms of application. Dee H. Andrews and Charles A. Beagles, both from the Naval Training Equipment Center in Orlando, FL, presented this model at the 1984 Interservice/Industry Training Equipment Conference in a paper ti-

tled, "Estimating Curricula Development Costs: A Model Based Upon the Complexity of the Learning Tasks." It assumes group-paced, platform instruction. It quantifies development time by assigning "work effort points" to 17 instructional design steps in an expanded version of the ISD model.

The estimate of the amount of time each step will require determines its total points. A job analysis, for example, can be assigned anywhere from zero to 15 points, depending on the project. These points are then converted into a development ratio. Andrews and Beagles note, however, that these ratios vary according to the complexity of the task to be learned. For example, their development ratios for courses that teach motor skills, attitudes and verbal information range from 6:1 to 15:1, depending upon the point total for the course; ratios for intellectual skills and cognitive strategies range from 12:1 to 30:1.

Keep in mind that this model assumes group-paced, platform instruction and does not include costs (or time) to develop any supporting media, slides, videos, etc. The authors also emphasize that you may need to increase the ratios, depending on the complexity of the task. In other words, you'll spend a lot of time just coming up with the data you need to use this model to estimate your development time.

"How many hours does it take to develop an hour of CBT? I know you need to know, but if I hear that question asked that way one more time, I'll scream," writes Gloria Gery in *Making CBT Happen* (Weingarten Publications, Inc., 1987). These opening lines from Gery's chapter on cost estimating (subtitled, incidentally, "How long does it take to develop an hour of CBT? How many angels can dance on the head of a pin?") give you a pretty clear picture of how she feels about development ratios purported to be "industry averages."

"Knowing the real contributing factors permits better decision making and courseware than do general development ratios," Gery contends in introducing her cost-estimating methodology. While following her systematic approach to defining your variables requires some up-front time, it's undoubtedly time well-spent if you're serious about nailing down an accurate estimate.

Gery recommends careful consideration of 37 factors that individually and collectively contribute to CBT development time. These factors are grouped into four major categories of variables: courseware, technical, human and other. You must consider whether each factor in each category will require low, medium or high development costs or time. For example, one courseware variable is the nature and complexity of the learning material. If your objectives are recognition, recall or knowledge of the material, you can anticipate low development time and cost. On the other hand, if your learning objectives require synthesis, analysis and extrapolation, anticipate high time and cost.

Once you have made these judgments for each factor and plotted them on a matrix, you'll get a *pretty fair idea* of whether you're talking about low, intermediate or high development time and costs for the project you have in mind. Gery estimates development hours per CBT hour in each range as: high (300-plus), medium (150 to 300) and low (85 to 150).

According to Gery, the key is in synthesizing your individual judgments into an integrated perspective. " 'Left-brain' estimators will likely establish weights and point values for each factor and approach the situation mathematically," she writes. "We right-brained estimators will look at all the graphs, synthesize them unconsciously, and then use our overall judgment about the entire set of interrelationships. The project will 'look like' a certain amount of time. Whatever your approach, recognize that your outcome will be only as good as the quality of the data going into the process."

Gery's advice refers strictly to CBT development, but it's so sensible that we'll give her the last word on this matter of estimating development time for training: "I can't promise you it's a simple matter. . . . Whoever believes that it is believes that 'the check is in the mail,' 'the system is on schedule' and 'it's only a simple programming change.' Develop some realistic perspectives and don't oversell or undersell what's involved. Make very sure you keep records of the time it actually takes for the various activities so you can do a better job next time."

Reprinted from TRAINING, June 1987

TRAINING PROFILES: THE VIEW FROM GROUND LEVEL

During the mid-1980's, TRAINING went 'inside' 41 organizations to take a detailed look at their HRD functions. Here's an overview

BY CHRIS LEE

When it comes to describing human resources development in U.S. organizations, statistics only take you so far. To add shape and color to the wide-angle view provided by our annual *Industry Reports,* we need to zoom in on individual organizations' training efforts in action.

Since 1983 we've been taking these snapshots each month in the form of a "TRAINING Profile," a feature story that examines one organization's HRD practices. How do individual companies divide their own pieces of the $29-billion pie representing the national investment in formal training and development? What strategies do tiny training departments use to stretch their resources? How do large corporate education departments make the most of their staffs and multimillion-dollar budgets?

We've spotlighted banks and telephone companies in the midst of cataclysmic changes produced by deregulation. We've examined mining and construction companies struggling to hang on in roller-coaster markets. We've focused on high-tech manufacturers where the challenge is simply to keep up with the pace of change. And we've looked at public-sector organizations trying to do more with less. TRAINING Profiles have taken us from coast to coast, from urban to rural locations, from organizations with thousands of employees to those with less than 500.

Though we've discovered that the shape of an organization's training and development efforts is as idiosyncratic as its culture—and molded by as many variables—41 in-depth case studies give us a unique vantage point from which to cull trends, observe relationships and, perhaps, offer some insights.

Budgets

Part of the purpose of our Profile series has been to give readers a basis for comparison, a yardstick by which to examine their own companies' investments in HRD. Organizations manage their training budgets in many different ways. In some, training is strictly an expense, a cost of doing business. In others, the training department is expected to recover its costs by charging other departments for its services—or even by selling its services outside the organization.

The most recent example of the latter approach appeared in "A Training Department of Independent Means," a profile of the Mendota Mental Health Center in Madison, WI (TRAINING, September 1986). Training director Myrna Casebolt recovers 30% to 40% of her costs by charging outsiders for training they attend at the center. She said the arrangement presents special challenges, as well as inherent satisfaction: "I love it . . . because I find it more exciting. It makes me more accountable as a training director for a government agency . . . I also like the autonomy. If I screw up, I pay the price; but if I succeed, I reap the benefits."

At the core of each Profile is a breakdown of the subject's training budget, along with other organization-wide demographic and financial information. The training expenditures we report are for formal classroom or individualized instruction, as opposed to informal, on-the-job training. And they are assigned to several defined categories:

- *Salaries*—of in-house training and development staff and the appropriate portion of salaries of employees with part-time training responsibilities.
- *Outside purchases*—off-the-shelf and customized training and development services, programs and materials (including consulting services and tuition refunds) purchased from outside vendors.
- *Raw materials*—blank films, slides, videotapes, processing, printing, packaging, etc., purchased for training programs produced in-house.
- *Hardware*—audiovisual equipment, computers and other hardware used for training.
- *Facilities*—training facilities (buildings, classrooms, etc.) built or remodeled during the current budget year.
- *Overhead*—office rent, administrative and clerical support, etc., charged by the organization to the training department.
- *Off-site meetings*—expenses for off-site training and development meetings, including travel, per diem, facility rental, etc.
- *Other*—miscellaneous expenses.

The average expenditures in each budget category for the 41 profiled organizations are shown in Figure 1. Keep in mind that our Profiles are not a scientific sample from a specific universe of organizations, but rather represent a small number of organizations of various sizes and industrial classifications. If it's meaningful industry norms you're after, look at the big pie graph in this month's report on training budgets.

Given that we're examining a small and extremely varied sample, it is

ORGANIZATIONS PROFILED IN TRAINING

Company	Industry
Amax Magnesium	Mining
Associated Industries of Massachusetts	Services
AT&T Communications	Communications
Bay Area Rapid Transit District	Transportation
Chase Federal Savings and Loan Assoc.	Finance
CMC Corp.	Retail Trade
Congoleum Corp.	Manufacturing
Daniel Construction Co.	Construction
Dean Witter Reynolds Inc.	Finance
Dearborn Police Department (MI)	Public Administration
Deluxe Check Printers, Inc.	Manufacturing
Dunkin' Donuts of America, Inc.	Retail Trade
Florida Power Corp.	Public Utility
General Public Utilities Nuclear Corp. (Three-Mile Island)	Public Utility
Girl Scouts of the U.S.A.	Services
Good Samaritan Hospital	Health Care
Hewlett-Packard	Manufacturing
Honeywell	Manufacturing
Interconics Microcircuits Operation	Manufacturing
Lewis Research Center (NASA)	Public Administration
Life of Virginia	Insurance
Loews Corp.	Diversified Financial
Lutheran General Hospital	Health Care
Mendota Mental Health Institute	Health Care
Motorola, Inc.	Manufacturing
New England Telephone	Public Utility
Norward Energy Services Ltd.	Oil/Gas Extraction
(The) Olde World Cheese Shops	Retail Trade
PACT (Portland Area Center for Training)	Public Administration
Pennsylvania House	Manufacturing
Pinellas County Training Consortium	Public Administration
Rosenbluth Travel	Transportation Services
Rudolph and Sletten Inc.	Construction
School District No. 12, Adams County, CO	Educational Services
Sentry Insurance	Insurance
(The) Southland Corp.	Retail Trade
United Services Automobile Assoc.	Insurance
University of South Florida	Education
U.S. Postal Service	Public Administration
(The) Valley Hospital	Health Care
West Virginia University	Educational Services

more useful to look at budget categories in terms of ranges. Most (20 out of 41) of the profiled organizations allocated 26% to 50% of their total training budgets to salaries for full- and part-time trainers; 11 allocated 51% to 76%; four spent more than 76% on salaries.

The fact that a pair of organizations allocate their training budgets similarly does not necessarily imply other similarities. Two of the four organizations that dedicate better than three-fourths of their budgets to trainer salaries are Southland Corp. of Dallas and the police department of Dearborn, MI. At Southland, the gigantic corporate parent of 7-Eleven stores, more than one-quarter of the $5.5 million pegged for training department salaries in 1984 went to field managers with part-time training responsibilities. These store managers shoulder part of the massive job of training the thousands of new clerks hired each year by the national retail chain. At the Dearborn Police Department, on the other hand, continuous training and education are considered part of an officer's job, as evidenced by the fact that the department employed five full-time trainers for a force of 200.

In most cases, a considerably smaller chunk of the training and development budget is dedicated to outside purchases. Twenty organizations allocated 10% or less of their annual budgets to these expenditures. But there are notable exceptions to that rule. Take Honeywell, for example.

Because the Minneapolis-based manufacturing giant is a highly decentralized company, much of its investment in training and development is made at the division level. We were able to obtain accurate budget figures only for the training provided by its centralized corporate HRD department—approximately a quarter of the corporation's total investment in training. Honeywell's corporate HRD function allocated 32% of its $2.8-million budget in 1982 to outside purchases, and only 27% to trainers' salaries.

The percentage of the budget that goes for raw materials tends to be less than 5%—at least in 27 out of 41 cases. Again, however, several organizations spend considerably more. At the U.S. Postal Service, $7.9 million (10.5% of the training budget) was allocated to purchasing raw materials in fiscal year 1985. And at Life of Virginia, an insurance company based in Richmond, more than a quarter of the $328,000 training budget was spent on raw materials in 1985. In this case, the explanation involves production costs for a seven-module, multimedia sales training program, including a videotaped "final exam" of each agent who completes it.

Hardware is another area where most organizations—32 of those profiled—spend less than 5% of their total training budgets. Given that the investment in "typical" training hardware—flip charts, slide projectors, videotape players, etc.—would be unlikely to account for a large slice of the training budget in any one year, this is not surprising. Anomalies tend to show up only when an organization makes a major (and usually one-time) investment in, say, microcomputers used solely for computer-based training. But on the other hand, some training operations are just plain hardware-intensive. Interconics Microcircuits Operation, a high-tech manufacturer in Hopkins, MN, indicated that nearly one-quarter of its 1985 training budget was allocated to hardware. The explanation lies in the fact that the company maintains its own videotaping facilities; the training department uses personal computers to keep records of trainees and

courses; and actual plant equipment is kept in a training room for hands-on practice.

Although the average (mean) expenditure for training facilities is 4.6%, individual investments in this category tend either to be nearly non-existent or quite large. The reason is simple: If a building or special facility dedicated to training was built or renovated during the year we obtained the organization's budget figures, the breakdown reflects this one-time investment. San Francisco's Bay Area Rapid Transit Commission is a good example. In FY1982-83, BART's facility expenditure was better than $1 million—52% of its total training budget. But that was the year BART used a federal grant to build a new training center that houses its classrooms, offices and media center.

Corporate overhead, on the other hand, is an expense more evenly distributed among the Profile subjects. Although some organizations do not charge overhead to their training departments as a separate item, 26 of our cases allocated between 4% and 15% of their budgets to this general administrative expense.

Expenditures for off-site meetings is another category for which the mean, 15.7%, is somewhat misleading. The range among our 41 subjects ran from 0 to 60%. Most of the orga-

nizations that budget more than one-quarter of their annual training dollars for off-site meetings are those that train a large proportion of salespeople; at least that's true in the cases of Sentry Insurance, Pennsylvania House, Hewlett-Packard's Business Computer Sales Center and AT&T Communications' Sales Marketing Education Center. As usual, however, there's an anomaly in that pattern.

At Deluxe Check Printers, Inc., 29.3% of 1982's $3.6-million budget was targeted for off-site training and development meetings. The rationale is a quarterly "Fundamentals of Management" course. This one-week indoctrination focusing on basic management skills and Deluxe's corporate culture is held at the company's St. Paul, MN, headquarters so that its senior officers can participate in the program. The top managers host a dinner during which the discussion is thrown open to anything and everything trainees wish to talk about. "We've had senior people show up for the dinner during blizzards when the snowplows were barely moving," said Stewart Alexander, national director of training.

Other stats

Training budgets are not the only statistical yardsticks that can measure an organization's investment in HRD. For Profile subjects, we used several different calculations. The averages (means) for each of the following categories are shown in Table 1. While the averages are illuminating, however, remember again the sort of "sample" we're dealing with, and don't make too much of them. Here at ground level, it's the diversity, more than the norms, that flavor the stew.

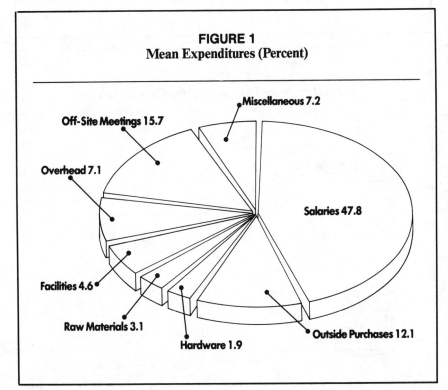

FIGURE 1
Mean Expenditures (Percent)

Miscellaneous 7.2
Off-Site Meetings 15.7
Overhead 7.1
Salaries 47.8
Facilities 4.6
Raw Materials 3.1
Hardware 1.9
Outside Purchases 12.1

TABLE 1
TRAINING Profile Averages

Employee-to-Trainer Ratio	630:1
Man-Hours Per Employee	25.6
Training Budget, As % of Sales, Budget, Assets, etc.	1.0
Training Budget, As % of Payroll	3.3

• *Employee-to-trainer ratio.* These proportions ranged from a low of 40:1 (the Dearborn Police Department, with 200 employees) to a high of 3,460:1 (Dunkin' Donuts of America, Inc., with 41,521 employees). How useful is this ratio as a basis to measure an organization's commitment to HRD? It ignores a lot of important variables, such as the number of employees with part-time training responsibilities, and the organization's use of self-instructional methodologies, outside resources and so on. In the end, it must simply be taken as one of many indicators; an attempt to determine some sort of optimum employee-to-trainer ratio probably would do more harm than good.

We can observe, however, that as an organization's number of employees increases, the number of trainers begins to level out. A certain economy of scale appears to be operating here: Once an organization reaches a critical mass of employees, its full-time trainers just start handling more trainees.

Industry also seems to be an important variable. In the high-tech, public and quasi-public organizations among our profile subjects, employee-to-trainer ratios tend to stay relatively constant—and relatively low. For example, the U.S. Postal Service employs 744,490 people and 1,366 full-time trainers (a ratio of 545:1); Motorola's employee-to-trainer ratio is 125:1; AT&T Communications' is 102:1. Organizations such as public utilities that provide training mandated by government regulation also maintain low employee-to-trainer ratios: At General Public Utilities Nuclear Corp. (GPUN), proprietor of the notorious Three Mile Island nuclear power plant, the 1984 ratio was 49:1.

• *Man-hours of training.* This one takes a bit of explanation. Man-hours of training are computed by multiplying the number of people who received formal training in the course of a year by the number of training hours in which they participated (a one-hour time management course with 20 participants gives us 20 man-hours of training). By calculating the ratio of man-hours to the total number of employees, we get the average number of man-hours provided per employee.

Again, these ratios ranged all over the map, from less than one man-hour per employee to more than 50.

The University of South Florida's HRD function is an example from the low end of the spectrum, with 1.3 man-hours per employee. The headline of that 1984 Profile was a shorthand description of the efforts of a fledgling training department: "U.S.F! H.R.D! Go! Fight! Win!"

Meanwhile, at Florida Power Corp. in St. Petersburg, 2,220 technical employees received an average of 50.7 man-hours of training. The rapidly growing utility recently implemented a performance-based approach to staff development, according to Walt Thurn, manager of employee development, whose battle cry was, "No more training for training's sake!" Instead, a new system of documenting and tracking specific job objectives is designed to ensure that employees get training when and how they need it.

• *Training budget as a percent of total sales* (or, in the case of banks and insurance companies, of total assets; in the case of nonprofit and government agencies, of total budgets). Only six organizations invested more than

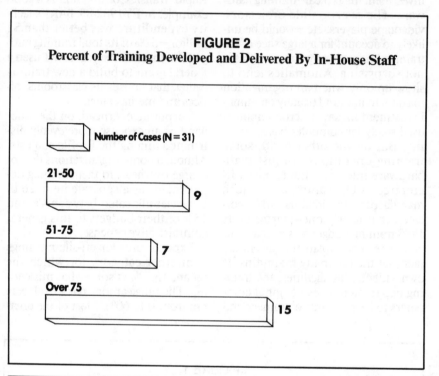

FIGURE 2
Percent of Training Developed and Delivered By In-House Staff

Number of Cases (N = 31)

21-50   9

51-75   7

Over 75   15

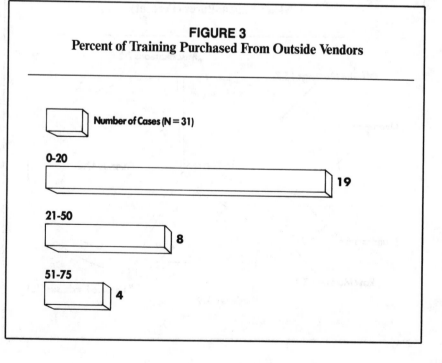

FIGURE 3
Percent of Training Purchased From Outside Vendors

Number of Cases (N = 31)

0-20   19

21-50   8

51-75   4

1% of their total assets, budgets or sales in training. Of those, four were public or quasi-public organizations that are required by law to provide specific training: the Dearborn Police Department, BART, GPUN and Florida Power. The two anomalous high spenders in this category were Girl Scouts of the U.S.A. and Interconics.

● *Training budget as a percent of total payroll.* Since many organizations stubbornly consider their payrolls proprietary information—and some, such as companies that reimburse their sales force through commissions, cannot compute an accurate payroll figure—we have only 28 cases in this category. Those break down as follows: The training budget is 1% or less of payroll in 12 cases; greater than 1% but less than 5% in 11 cases; and greater than 5% in five cases.

Those falling into the top spending category include NASA's Lewis Research Center, which spent $1.1 million—12.3% of its $8.7-million payroll—on training in 1983; GPUN, which in 1984 budgeted $19.6 million for training—16.9% of its $115.8-million payroll; Florida Power Corp., which spent $1.6 million on training in 1984—12.7% of a $12.8-million payroll; and Girl Scouts of the U.S.A., whose $820,000 training budget represented 6.2% of its $13.3-million payroll in 1985.

Where the dollars go

We asked our Profile subjects to apportion their HRD programs among three categories: training "built" and delivered entirely by in-house staff people; training they bought from an outside supplier but delivered themselves; and training they bought from a supplier who also delivered it.

Figures 2 through 4 provide a summary of the mix. As you can see, training developed and delivered by the organization's in-house HRD staff is the most popular choice, with 15 organizations selecting the do-it-yourself route for more than three-quarters of the training they provided.

Dunkin' Donuts is a prime example of a company whose in-house staff develops and delivers almost all—93.5%—of its training. HRD director Bob Harloe's reasoning is fairly typical: Most of the training he provides focuses directly on the company's particular needs—in this case, the nitty-gritty details of how to make donuts, coffee, brownies, etc., plus customized instruction in financial and people-management skills.

Loews Corp. falls at the other extreme: 65.5% of its training is purchased from vendors, and another 10% is both bought from and delivered by outside suppliers. In this case, those logistics reflect the preferences of Alan Momeyer, director of manpower planning and development for the $2-billion conglomerate based in New York City. "I think that internal people often spend too much time developing training programs," he said. "...that's a waste of time when there are so many tremendous programs [available from vendors] out there."

The training managers who, often along with other knowledgeable observers, described the functions, philosophies and strategies of our profiled organizations' training efforts, have voiced many similar themes. Among them: contributing to the bottom line, responding to the needs of their "clients" and evaluating results. Those three motifs, in fact, seem inextricably intertwined. Discussing one leads inevitably to the others.

Leslie Agnello, training manager at Hewlett-Packard's Business Computer Sales Center in Cupertino, CA, put it well: "Training is an overhead function in some companies; [trainers] aren't encouraged to show what their contribution is, and the company isn't sure what it's getting for its money. We think of ourselves as a profit center. We present our contribution to division management, along with the other groups. We are measured on the results we show—more training provided more effectively, skills learned more quickly."

As Agnello pointed out, a training organization that is measured on results must think like a profit center. The trainers at HP's Business Computer Sales Center concentrate on marketing their services to sales reps in the field, creating a situation akin to a client-consultant relationship. Agnello characterized the field-training group as responsive, by design, to the needs of the sales force: "We have a sales connection, not a staff connection, so we're close enough to the field to understand what they do."

"Field driven" is a phrase that popped out when a number of training managers described their departments. And those who use it feel strongly about the philosophy it implies. Ron Crain, manager of training and development at Southland, said: "We don't sit around [the corporate training center] wondering what kinds of training we want to develop. We respond to requests from the field." Another Southland training manager, Roger Cole, manager of program development and field liaison, underscored the point: "If a client wants our services, they have to commit people to a development team.... That's what we mean by 'field driven.' Training programs are developed at the request of the people who make the money. We'll sometimes try to 'sell' them something, but

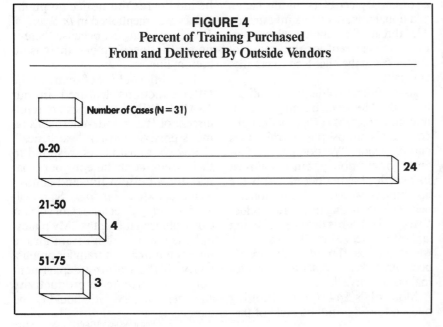

FIGURE 4
Percent of Training Purchased
From and Delivered By Outside Vendors

Number of Cases (N = 31)

0-20   24

21-50   4

51-75   3

we don't ram it down their throats."

There's a caveat attached to that philosophy, but one well understood by any manager responsible for profit and loss: "We need to know desired vs. existing performance and the dollar value attached to solving a given problem," Cole said. In other words, the performance problem a training program is aiming to solve must be costing the corporation money—lots of it.

"We go where the squeaky wheel is, and it should be so described by management," echoed Loews Corp.'s Momeyer. "We don't market internally. We respond to requests. That puts ownership where it really ought to be—with management. They have to tell us what's broken, what needs fixing and what has the greatest dollar implication. Our needs analyses are simple: How much money is it costing us?"

Momeyer implies another concern voiced by many training managers: bottom-line accountability, i.e., is your training saving the organization more money than it's costing it?

That's a paramount concern at Dunkin' Donuts of America, Inc. According to Bob Harloe, a training department that fails to contribute to the bottom line doesn't deserve to survive. "If your programs help to make money for the company, you will stay. It's that simple."

Interestingly, Harloe pointed to *soft*-skills training programs as an example of his department's contribution to the bottom line at Dunkin' Donuts. Like most fast-food retailers, one of the company's major concerns is keeping its turnover rate as low as possible. Its 80% annual rate for hourly employees compares very favorably to the industry average of 300% to 400%, and Harloe claims that training in interpersonal skills is largely responsible. "The soft-skills training—motivating, supervising, interpersonal relating—is essential. . . . When you start tracking tenure, turnover, labor efficiencies and the like, there is no doubt in my mind that there is a real payoff."

Cultural imperatives

In other companies, training is an inherent and unquestioned value, part of the cultural underpinnings that make the organization tick. The HRD function still may be monitored for its economic impact, but it is not regarded as a cost center that must justify its existence on a daily basis.

Training is part and parcel of a career at Deluxe Check Printers, for example. The "Fundamentals of Management" course, considered "a must" for every employee with long-term management aspirations, is an important vehicle for communicating the values of the company. But it is far from the only one: The company carefully grooms employees for promotions via continuous, structured training. The corporate philosophy of promoting from within is visibly reinforced and demonstrated to employees.

Still, the company maintains a close watch on training costs. In 1980, Deluxe determined it was spending $3 million a year on training and development in its 63 plants, an investment it felt could be better managed. It established a national training review committee to examine training activities that affected more than two plants. The decision was implemented judiciously, with individual plant autonomy left intact. "[Corporate headquarters is] only interested in giving some help, some guidance where we can," explained Stewart Alexander. "We can frequently suggest, for instance, that 'such and such a plant faced that problem two years ago and here is how they handled it.' We also screen ideas and designs before management is asked to fund them."

Motorola, another corporation that considers its commitment to training an essential piece of its culture, has an additional impetus for its investment: The threat of technological obsolescence is very real for thousands of employees at the high-tech electronics company.

As A. William Wiggenhorn, director of the Motorola Training and Education Center (MTEC), explained his company's philosophy, retraining is part of the job. "We don't have a full-employment policy, but it's almost like we do. Laying people off is the last thing we would do. If a person has been here for a long time as a productive employee, his chances of being laid off are very slim. But it's a two-way street. The flip side is that we expect him to keep his skills up and remain productive."

Motorola's $44-million training budget, the $8.5-million state-of-the-art training center it opened in 1986, and the fact that its 100,000 employees received more than a million man-hours of training in 1984, provide dramatic evidence that the company acts on its commitment to training. The elusive "support from top management" sought so desperately by many training departments is a simple fact of life at Motorola. CEO Robert Galvin interviewed Wiggenhorn personally for the MTEC job. Galvin also commissioned a five-year training plan, based on an indepth, company-wide study, to determine training needs. "I had never seen a five-year plan for training," Wiggenhorn commented. "And I've never seen another one since."

At BART, by necessity, training also is an embedded piece of the culture. The California Public Utilities Commission requires employees to be certified. They must pass an initial certification process when they are hired or promoted, and they have to be recertified periodically. "I'd stack up our technical training against anyone's," said Alex Braun, manager of training.

As BART ironed out the reliability problems that plagued it in the 1970s, attention began to shift from the technical to the human side of the business. The training emphasis underwent a similar shift, and management development became a priority. Braun explained the governing philosophy that training is designed to reinforce: "We encourage entrepreneurship, even though we're a public agency. Public agencies don't have to be mediocre. You notice no public agency was mentioned in *In Search of Excellence*, but just because there is no profit doesn't mean there is no bottom line."

The philosophies of many of the HRD functions featured in our TRAINING Profiles series are reminiscent of Peters and Waterman's famous prescription for "excellence": Know your customers, respond to their needs, contribute to your organization's bottom line and control your costs while you do so. Sam Gallucci, training director at Congoleum Corp. phrased it bluntly: "My philosophy is that you don't train for the sake of training; you train for productivity. If the training department doesn't contribute to productivity and performance, it shouldn't be there."

Reprinted from TRAINING, October 1986

ORGANIZATION DEVELOPMENT: NEXT TIME, JUST SMILE AND NOD

Just what is OD? Ask a simple question, get a dozen variations on the answer

BY JACK GORDON

Now, don't ask me what Voom is,
I never will know.
But, boy! Let me tell you
It does clean up snow!

"That, roughly speaking, is what much of our literature says is the definition of organization development."—*Marvin R. Weisbord*, quoting from *The Cat in the Hat Comes Back*, by Dr. Suess.

The first time I ran up against organization development, or ever heard the term OD (that's "Oh Dee," not "Odd"), I was a newspaper reporter. My beat included the city government of a Denver suburb. One weekend the city council members took off for a team-building session led by an OD consultant from the University of Colorado. He put them through some mildly unusual exercises: "Everybody close your eyes and try to envision what you want your city to look like a few years down the road." That sort of thing.

I missed the event, but a certain citizen gadfly—one of those peculiar individuals who actually show up every Tuesday night to brood and mutter while suburban city councils debate sidewalk zoning variances—tagged along. And kept his eyes open. He watched, he listened, he went home to his four-bedroom Colonial on Shady Grove Lane and mulled the whole thing over. Then he started screaming that the council had been "brainwashed."

This set one of the council members to thinking. Pretty soon he decided that yes, by God, he *had* been brainwashed, and he started screaming about it too. All very embarrassing for the assistant city administrator, who recommended the consultant, having studied under him at the university. As far as I was concerned, though, OD was terrific. Nobody, including the assistant city administrator and the consultant, could tell me just what OD *was* (other than in such abstract and qualified terms that it didn't come across as being much of anything in particular), but it sure made great press.

Today, of course, having worked for TRAINING magazine for a few years, having heard a lot about OD and having just spent several days researching the subject for this article, I know precisely what OD is. Better still, I know precisely what it isn't, which is the hard part. So if you're new to the training and development game, and people have been firing the term OD at you, and you've been feeling like a donkey because you can't seem to make out exactly what they are and are not referring to, then, boy, are you in luck. You see, OD is . . . well, it's sort of. . . .

It's like this

"Premised upon the notion that any organization wishing to survive must periodically divest itself of those parts or characteristics that contribute to its malaise, OD is a process for increasing an organization's effectiveness. As a process it has no value bias, yet it is usually associated with the idea that maximum effectiveness is to be found by integrating an individual's desire for personal growth with organizational goals."

So says *The Facts On File Dictionary of Personnel Management and Labor Relations*, 2nd edition.

On the off-chance that you should find that less than fully illuminating, some other definitions are listed in the sidebar to this article. But the fact is, many OD'ers resist attempts to corral the beast with a specific definition. That is, what, exactly, do you absolutely have to do in order to be doing OD, as opposed to human resources development (HRD), a quality of work life (QWL) program, industrial engineering, plain old team building or any number of other things?

David Jamieson, a Los Angeles-based consultant currently serving as codirector of Pepperdine University's master's degree program in organization development, offers a useful distinction between OD and HRD, at least. The latter, he says, essentially focuses on "developing the knowledge and skills of individuals." Individuals may be trained in groups, "but whether you're talking about training or job rotation or anything else pertaining to HRD, the focus is on increasing a person's development."

OD, on the other hand, focuses on improving the structures within which people work and the *processes* (a key word in OD) that characterize their working relationships. "You're trying to improve the *context* within which individuals perform," Jamieson says. "You concentrate on how well a group works together. . .and on the work flow between different departments—the interfaces between engineering and support services, say. But you're not focusing on specific, individual skills."

The complication is that training programs—in anything from factory-safety procedures to problem-solving skills to management styles—often are recommended and conducted in the course of OD interventions. Other recommendations might include new performance appraisal systems, revamped job descriptions and so on.

Still, HRD and OD are different animals, Jamieson says. Neither is a "subset" of the other. As for QWL programs, he calls them "a good example of OD—a good approach to take *within* OD."

In an essay included in *Contemporary Organization Development: Current Thinking and Applications* (D.D. Warrick, editor, Scott, Foresman & Co., 1985), Philip H. Mirvis argues that ". . .it is wrongheaded to define OD. Why? Because the phenomenon itself defies precise definition. Marvin Weisbord, a prominent OD consultant, defines it as a secular religion. It has its priests, its rituals, its followers, its moral dogma and, like all religions, its truth is not found in words, but in belief and action."

Indeed, Weisbord's point about "Voom" (from another essay in *Contemporary Organization Development*) is not that OD needs to be more rigidly defined in terms of specific technologies or "competencies" or whatever. Far from it. "Whenever I read about some wonderful new OD technology, or about the 84 skills we're all going to need in the future (a proposition so preposterous I shudder at my own complicity in advancing it), I'm reminded of *The Cat In the Hat*," he writes.

"The last time OD people played around seriously with definitions was about 10 years ago," says Jamieson. "Most of them pretty much gave up." Today's consensus, he says, is that concrete definitions are too limiting and aren't really important anyway.

The same goes for deciding who qualifies as a bona fide OD expert. The Organization Development Institute, headquartered in Chesterland, OH, has developed a code of ethics—currently in its 10th revision—for OD practitioners. And according to executive director Donald W. Cole, it has formally certified about 100 people as "registered OD consultants" (RODCs).

But the institute is only one of several professional groups in the field (others include the OD Network, the OD Division of the American Society for Training and Development and the OD Division of the Academy of Management). Its RODC designation is by no means a prerequisite to practice the OD consultant's craft. Asked whether he was an RODC, George Labovitz, president of Organizational Dynamics Inc. of Burlington, MA, thought for a moment and then replied, "I don't think so."

Roots and values

According to Wendell French (from still another essay in the Warrick book, which I recommend if you want to pursue this subject), the question is moot as to who first coined the term organization development. It seemed to "emerge more or less simultaneously" in the mid-1950s at

---

ORGANIZATION DEVELOPMENT IS . . .

". . .a long-range effort to improve an organization's problem-solving and renewal processes, particularly through a more effective and collaborative management of organization culture—with special emphasis on the culture of formal work teams—with the assistance of a change agent, or catalyst, and the use of the theory and technology of applied behavioral science, including action research."—Wendell L. French and Cecil H. Bell Jr.

". . .a process of planned change—change of an organization's culture from one which avoids examination of social processes (especially decision making, planning and communication) to one which institutionalizes and legitimizes this examination, and from one which resists change to one which promotes the planning and use of procedures for adapting to needed changes on a day-to-day basis."—W. Warner Burke, Columbia University

". . .a complex educational strategy to change the beliefs, attitudes, values and structure of organizations so that they can better adapt to new technologies, markets and challenges, and to the dizzying rate of change itself."—Warren Bennis, University of Southern California

". . .the strengthening of those human processes in organizations which improve the functioning of the organic system so as to achieve its objectives. It is the process of initiating, creating and confronting needed changes so as to make it possible for an organization to become or remain viable, to adapt to new conditions, to solve problems, to learn from experience and to move toward greater organizational maturity."—Gordon Lippitt

". . .an effort planned organization-wide, and managed from the top, to increase organizational effectiveness and health through planned interventions in the organization's 'processes,' using behavioral science knowledge."—Richard Beckhard, Beckhard Associates

". . .the means whereby people can risk changing their old, traditional social norms (hidden feelings and rationalized behavior) to a more open way of relating to each other. . .the breakthrough for people to look at their behavior as something they can change for the better if they so desire. . .the means of creating deeper and more caring relationships between members of a team. . .the force that sets in motion an increasing sense of self-worth, freedom and personal dignity. . .the key for developing a climate in an organization that is good for people." —Bill Crockett, Saga Corp.

". . .planned change with the intended purpose for the organization to become more effective in its environment."—David Jamieson

Thanks to Malcolm Warren for collecting and providing most of these definitions.

Reprinted from TRAINING, September 1986

two or three places (General Mills, Esso and Union Carbide) in the course of consulting work being done by Herbert Shepard, Richard Beckhard, Robert Blake, Jane Mouton and Douglas McGregor.

Regardless of who first called it what, OD's roots are firmly grounded in the 1940s—in the thinking and research of M.I.T. psychologist Kurt Lewin. The landmark year is 1947, the year Lewin died and his disciples founded the National Training Laboratory (now the NTL Institute for Applied Behavioral Science) in Bethel, ME. NTL's founders and early associates—including Ronald and Gordon Lippitt, Leland Bradford, Kenneth Benne, Jack Gibb, Chris Argyris, Warren Bennis, Beckhard, Shepard, Blake and McGregor—were heavily influenced by Lewin's thinking about group dynamics and change processes, and by his concept of "force field analysis," a procedure for identifying the various factors contributing to a problem in an organizational system.

Out of NTL came "laboratory training," an experiential learning concept centered on the T-group (later known as the sensitivity group), which figured heavily in both early OD efforts and in the "human potential movement" of the 1960s. T-groups were essentially "leaderless" (in theory, anyway), and rested on the idea that people learn more from one another than they do from "experts." Their purpose was to get group members to delve into the unspoken rules and processes that governed their working and interpersonal relationships (e.g., "Who is dominant here and why? How does that person's behavior affect my behavior and why?").

A related root from the '40s stretches to London's Tavistock Institute, which Weisbord credits with developing the concept of " 'joint optimization'—the balancing of social and technical systems."

Another of OD's building blocks was "action research," an approach credited to Lewin. Action research is an ongoing data-gathering method in which the people being studied (e.g., to determine their attitudes toward the company, their working relationships with other departments, etc.) actively participate in the study and share its results. The basic idea is that they're more likely to accept and *act*

on the results if they perceive the study as their own instead of some expert's. The survey-feedback technique, a form of action research developed in the '50s at the University of Michigan's Institute for Social Research, became one more important tool.

Those were most of the basic ingredients floating around in the primeval stew from which emerged modern OD, according to most experts.

But there's one more thing: Despite *Facts On File*'s disclaimer, early OD,

---

'No data shows that happy, well-paid employees do anything for a company.'

---

at least, had a very definite "value bias," apparent in both its T-group and action research roots. It was a bias toward workplace democracy, toward a participative approach to management. When quality circles caught on as productivity boosters, for example, they fit very neatly into classic OD patterns. For many early enthusiasts (and some present-day ones) OD was, indeed, a "secular religion"—no less sacred a cause than was the human potential movement to its adherents.

Weisbord argues that its historic value bias is OD's main strength: " . . . the only thing we bring to the party that the other specialties don't is a commitment to democratic processes for achieving desired results . . . . [OD practitioners should support] those clients who know that working *with* other people, face-to-face, is the only way to stop moving the mess from one place to another, the only way out of the 'Voom' game, the only way to make technology serve us instead of the other way around."

Today

OD is essentially about planned change. Malcolm Warren, director of training and organization development for Consumer Value Stores of

Woonsocket, RI, likes to call it a process for "getting people from where they really, really are to where they really, really want to get." But "planned change" covers an awful lot of ground. Is it a commitment to workplace democracy, then, that finally qualifies a company's effort to change in a planned way as genuine OD? Not according to Warren.

There is a sort of schism today in the OD community, he says. One side is values-driven, the other is results-driven. (See Bill Crockett's definition in the accompanying box as opposed to, say, Gordon Lippitt's.) "The National Training Laboratory was values-driven and that's where OD came from," says Warren. "Many people in OD still place a set of values around corporate democracy; they think it's good. I do not. Or rather, I don't approach change with a value set in my mind, although I have one. I come out of the Skinnerian approach to behavior, not the Rogerian, humanistic approach."

For Labovitz, OD's historic Rogerian leanings are something of a problem. "You've got to differentiate between the human potential movement and the OD movement. They've been confused. In a lot of companies, you can't mention OD because the term reminds the CEO of a negative experience he had in a human-potential seminar somewhere." (Remember the Case of the Brainwashed Councilman?)

"In my company, where we package it, we're sort of closet OD people," Labovitz says. "I don't think the word OD is mentioned in any of our literature."

Let's come out and say it. Early OD was a distinctly touchy-feely enterprise. These are the '80s. Touchy-feely is distinctly out of fashion. OD has adapted to the times.

Labovitz prefers to think of organization development as "both a set of techniques and a process for facilitating organizational integration." By integration, he means "the extent to which people share an idea of the objectives of the firm and the degree to which they participate in achieving those objectives . . . . No data shows that happy, well-paid employees do anything for a company. But significant data says that integrated organizations perform better in the marketplace."

Everyone seems to agree that if

you're doing OD, you'll inevitably do some action research, whether you call it that or not. And in "classic OD," Labovitz says, you'll also employ the survey-feedback technique, stage "confrontation meetings," teach problem-solving skills and use other specific methodologies. But must you do those things in order to be doing "real" OD? Labovitz thinks not: "I'm becoming less discriminating in my old age."

Warren demands three things of a planned change effort if it wants to call itself organization development. First, there must be a "unifying goal"—the company wants to be number one in customer service, number one in software engineering or whatever. "It's a single vision and you know what it looks like. . . . OD is goal-directed; it is not an activity pursued for its own sake."

Second, "There must be an analysis of where you're actually at—your 'present state.' There are more than 100 methodologies to do that analysis."

Third, "the focus is not so much on 'what' as on 'how'. . . . OD doesn't decide what product to bring to market. It does decide *how* to bring that product to market."

Jamieson agrees that today's typical OD intervention is more problem-focused than value-focused. Early OD's central thrust was that "participation is good, openness is good, people are important, etc.," he says. That's one reason why team-building techniques have always been a central feature. But while the emphasis on team building "hasn't let up any," the *focus* of most programs today is on concrete problems or challenges—mergers, downsizing, quality improvement, etc.—rather than on, say, openness as an end in itself. What's more, he says, modern OD has expanded its scope. He compares yesterday's typical intervention to today's as "the difference between focusing on the 'system' of a small work team and focusing on the 'system' of an entire division of General Motors."

I promised you at the start of this thing that if you read it, you'd no longer have to feel dumb about not knowing what OD is. Now, you say, you've read it, you still don't understand what OD is, and you're beginning to suspect that the citizen gadfly was right. I've let you down?

Never. Here's the real message: OD is a genuine thing—art, pursuit, set of technologies, call it what you will. The people who practice it have had an enormous influence on contemporary thinking about how to make organizations function effectively. But if it's an art, it's an evolving one. When it comes to what, exactly, OD is and isn't, don't be bluffed. In the words of George Labovitz, "We're making up the criteria as we go along."

Reprinted from TRAINING, September 1986

CHAPTER 2

TRAINING BEGINS WITH ANALYSIS

Training begins with research. We may call it needs analysis, front-end analysis, performance-problem analysis or simply task analysis, but it's always research of some kind, and effective training can't be done without it.

This has been a tough message for trainers to sell to their organizations, though we don't know why. No company with any management sophistication would think of launching a new product or installing a new computer or relocating an office without first doing some research. They'd call it a feasibility study and think of the expense as a simple cost of making a good business decision. Not so when the training department wants to conduct a front-end analysis.

One of the reasons for resistance may be that we ourselves tend to be unsure of what we mean when we toss around our nifty terms.

Take "needs analysis," a term you hear at every training conference you attend. To some it's a synonym for "send out the survey; we gotta do the budget soon." To others the term conjures up images of hours, days and weeks spent sifting through piles of operator-error data, or examining old performance-review forms, or interviewing supervisors and managers, or observing and logging the minute behavioral details of exemplary performers. Each of these images and de factor definitions is "accurate" and correct. Each reflects the fact that—given the organization we are in, the constraints we work under, the jobs we prepare training for, and our own knowledge and skill level—we do the best we can to make sure that our training efforts aim at real and important needs. But every time we read an article or hear a tale about the way some other trainers did their front-end research, we may become a little queasy about our own approach: "Shouldn't I be doing it that way instead of the way I am now?" There are two important things to remember when you get that feeling.

First, the process of figuring out what people are and aren't doing on their jobs, what they should or shouldn't be doing, and what is and isn't interfering with their performance is not an exact science. It is one of training's many art forms. It is science only to the extent that many of the methods we use to do our research are scientific at their base. It is art in the sense that every situation requires a seasoned eye and a deft touch to determine where a given technique will be most useful, or how a certain approach can be made to fit a given situation in just the right way.

Second, an awful lot of people who conduct any sort of performance study become positive, in retrospect, that their particular approach to analyzing problem "X" is the most valid and reliable ever invented. They're usually wrong. In this chapter we look at philosophies as well as practical approaches to analyzing needs, tasks and performance problems. Not every idea will be appropriate or practical for your situation or jibe with your approach to training. So as you assess the entries in this catalog of approaches to analysis, you can boost your return on effort by demanding that each answer one or both of these questions:

In what situation would I attempt to use this approach?

Where could I have used this approach in the past?

PERFORMANCE IS THE PURPOSE

Join the growing number of organizations
that realize training alone
is almost never an appropriate cure

BY GEARY A. RUMMLER

Most organizations are missing an opportunity to increase the contribution of their training functions tenfold. To realize this opportunity, top management must change its expectation and perception of the training function. Actually, this change in expectation and the resultant improvement in the contribution of the training function already has taken place in a number of major organizations.

To oversimplify a bit, you must view the training function not as a keeper of the corporate "schoolhouse" but as a "performance improver." This means changing the mission of the training function from "Number of employees trained" or "training programs produced" to "organization performance improved." Naturally, this will lead to a difference in how management (and the personnel function to which training usually reports directly) evaluates the training function.

Under the current mission of "employees trained," evaluation of the training function is some variant of "heads trained per training budget dollar." This, of course, emphasizes the volume of training conducted, not the value. Under the proposed mission of "organization performance improved," the evaluation will necessarily have to be a variant of "bottom-line contribution per training-budget dollar." This will correctly emphasize the worth of the training, not the amount.

Obviously, such a change in mission and evaluation of the training function will produce changes in how the training function operates.

But the changes aren't going to be nearly as great as you might fear; many training professionals have been moving in this direction for the past five years. Much of the "technology" required for such a change (i.e., analysis of performance problems, measurement of impact on organization performance) already has been developed and adopted.

The key to the change is getting top management to:

1. Expect—even demand—something different and better from training; to view the training director as a business person who must show a return, not as the "dean" of the corporate schoolhouse, somehow exempt from evaluation because of the "high' purpose" of his or her operation.

2. Let the training function operate in order to accomplish this new mission.

I know many training people who have been "bottom-line oriented" for years, but who have been limited in what they could do because of insufficient technology and strategies. However, it is now technologically possible in most cases. For you to comprehend the potential of your training group, you must understand something about this technology, which is generally known as *performance analysis*. The purpose of performance analysis is to view organization performance as a function of the individual *and* the job environment; any modification of performance has to deal with *both* parts. In other words, the human performer is only one of the following five components in a performance system: the job *situation*, or occasion to perform; the *performer*; the *response* (action or decision) that is to occur; the *consequence* of that behavior to the performer; the *feedback* to the performer on the consequences of the behavior.

Schematically, the relationship of the five components can be seen in Figure 1.

In any job, there is a *situation* or occasion where a particular *performer* is expected to make a particular *response* or take some action which results in some *consequence* to the performer. That consequence may be considered positive, negative, or of little value by the performer. Finally, information on that consequence is *fed back* to the performer.

It is imperative to understand that poor performance (i.e., failure to see the desired response) may result from a breakdown in *any* of the five components of this performance system. For example:

The job situation—perhaps it isn't clear that the situation merits the desired action;

2. The performer—perhaps he doesn't know how to perform or is physically or mentally incapable;

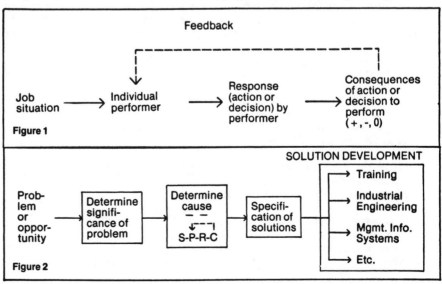

Figure 1

Figure 2

3. The response—perhaps the performer doesn't know he is supposed to make the response or doesn't know how, or it is physically impossible to make it, or the performer lacks the necessary tools or support;

4. The consequence—perhaps the consequence is punishing or nonexistent;

5. The feedback—the performer receives no information about his response—whether it was adequate or inadequate, and if inadequate, how to improve it.

Using the "performance system," let's examine a typical request for training.

The marketing function of a bank has launched a major "sales" campaign in which the branch bank tellers will sell additional bank services, with particular emphasis on personal loans. After six months the campaign seems to have fizzled: The tellers aren't selling. Management concludes that the tellers don't know *how* to sell other bank services, so the training department is directed to retrain or conduct refresher training. In terms of the performance system, management has concluded that the desired action—selling—is not forthcoming because of some failure in the performer component, i.e., tellers don't know *how* to perform. In fact, the breakdown was in the consequence component.

First, there were immediate negative consequences to the tellers for errors in handling money, failure to balance at the end of the day, and taking bad checks. This, coupled with long lines, kept the tellers' mind on the essentials of their job. Second, there was no support from branch management for the personal-loan emphasis. The positive consequences for the branch manager (attracting attention downtown) were for building up a sizeable loan portfolio—which could be done quicker and cheaper by making a $1 million loan to a small corporation; it takes a lot of $3,000 personal loans (and considerable expense per loan) to equal $1 million.

Given these two sets of consequences, 30 weeks of training in "selling services" would have negligible effect on personal loans as long as the *balance* of consequences itself was unchanged.

Had this particular training department utilized the principles of performance analysis, they would have:

1. Questioned the extent of the "problem" reported by management to determine the value of solving the problem.

2. Determined the precise cause or causes of the performance discrepancy, using a framework such as the performance system; and

3. Corrected the cause or recommended the necessary corrections, should they be beyond their capability or organization charter.

Based on 10 years' experience with performance analysis, we can predict that: Training is *infrequently* an appropriate solution; training alone is almost never an appropriate solution: the cause of performance problems is almost always a combination of "faulty" components in the performance system.

A number of training organizations are aware of performance analysis and capable of applying it. However, the organization realities they face are usually: low tolerance for analysis ("You people aren't the R&D Department, you know"), and less tolerance for suggesting alternative solutions to training based on the analysis ("Are you the training department or not? I want training").

The result: The frustration of developing training to solve what is essentially a non-training "problem."

An organization shortcoming

In addition to the problems faced by training, the performance system points up a shortcoming in the organization of most institutions. In short, they are not organized to solve problems. An organization can't really deal with a "problem" until it is classified in *terms of some solution,* be it a *training, communications, wage-and-salary, labor-relations* or *engineering* problem.

Once classified, the problem can be referred to the appropriate department (or solution pigeonhole) for action. Frequently, the recipient department is reluctant to claim the problem, saying "we can have some impact, but this won't solve the problem." The result is a program which produces only marginal results. Why? Because the other faulty components in the per-

formance system have gone undiagnosed and unattended.

The concept of the performance system suggests the need to analyze all performance problems thoroughly, to diagnose *all causes* and, to put together comprehensive solution strategies. This, in turn, suggests two organizational needs. The first one is for some organizational entity—function or department—to be responsible for an accurate, objective analysis of organization performance problems and the specifications for correcting them. The general process followed by such a function might look like that diagramed in Figure 2.

I call this process (and would be inclined to call the function) *performance engineering,* as it goes beyond training or any other single "solution."

The second organizational need suggested by the performance system is that of preparing managers to diagnose or troubleshoot human-performance problems in order to enhance the communication between managers and the "performance engineering" function.

As noted earlier, a number of major organizations are moving toward some form of performance engineering or performance oriented training. Their efforts have assumed a continuum of forms like those diagramed in Figure 3.

If you, as management, want more from your training function, shift the focus from training programs to improved organization performance. Ultimately, the training function should become the foundation for the performance-engineering department. The people in training are philosophically oriented toward improving human performance and, in many cases, already possess the required basic analysis skills.

Unquestionably, the most critical change required to improve training begins when you *demand improved performance* for your training dollar. Only then can the training people do the professional job of performance analysis that is required.

Reprinted from TRAINING, October 1977

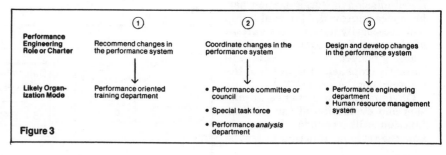

Figure 3

FRONT-END ANALYSIS

Here's an approach to looking
at performance problems
without assuming them to be
training problems

The trouble with a training term that's on just about every tongue is: It's on just about every tongue. Used as a buzz word—"What this problem needs is a little front-end analysis"—the term can confuse as much as it enlightens. It sounds right, but is it really? This kind of question led us quite naturally to ask Joe Harless, coiner of the term front-end analysis, to join us in TRAINING's offices for an interview on the concept. Harless is president of the Harless Performance Guild, Inc. of Newman, GA, and author of the definitive book on the subject.

TRAINING: Joe, we want to begin by asking you straight out, is front-end analysis for real or is it just the Joe Harless *schtick*?

HARLESS: Front-end analysis is not anyone's *schtick*. It's not a *schtick*. It's very real—if you define real as having a definite set of procedures to follow, and data and case histories about its application along with a following of performance professionals who have embraced the procedures and are applying them in their work. If that is what "real" is, front-end analysis is as real a thing as anyone in the business of training could imagine.

TRAINING: Why front-end analysis? Why the name? Why the procedures?

HARLESS: It really began with training packages. We had been developing training packages and were very pleased with them—with their appearance, with the way they taught, with the test data we were getting on them. Our clients were pleased, too.

Despite all this—despite the fact that the trainees were mastering the skills and knowledge taught with our training packages and passed criterion referenced tests at the end—we wanted to see if they transferred those skills and that knowledge to the job. This led us to do follow-up evaluations which in those days we jokingly called rear-end analysis. And surprisingly, in spite of all our expertise in training technology, we found almost as many times as not that the skills were not in fact transferred to the job, that the trainees were not doing what our training packages had taught them to perform.

TRAINING: Why?

HARLESS: That, of course, is exactly the question we began asking and, being devotees of the scientific method, we advanced certain hypotheses. Perhaps the training objectives were not relevant to the trainee's real-world needs. Perhaps the training activities did not simulate the real world as closely as possible (we know that the closer the level of simulation to the real world, the greater the probability that those skills and knowledges will be exhibited).

Perhaps there was something in the environment that prevented the trainees from exhibiting the learned behavior on the job—a manager perhaps, or foreman who disagreed with our methods and would only reward our trainees for performance that was incompatible with what they had learned in training. Or perhaps the trainee had simply forgotten what we had trained him to do.

The scientific method demands that if you pose a hypothesis, you test it. So we began testing these hypotheses. In brief, we found that people don't do things on the job for one of three reasons: They don't know how to do them, they're prevented from doing them in some way or they lack the incentive to do them.

TRAINING: That seems simple enough.

HARLESS: It is. But its implications for the solution of performance problems are profound. That's where the concept of front-end analysis comes in. Rear-end analysis asks, Why didn't training produce a certain kind of performance? Front-end analysis asks, first, What are the symptoms and indicators that a problem exists? Second, What are the performance deficiencies indicated by those data—what is the performance problem? And, finally, What is the relative value of solving that problem?

TRAINING: Value? In terms of what?

HARLESS: In terms of money. Front-end analysis is about money first and foremost. So is training. If not, you're baby sitting or doing psychotherapy. But to continue, I was saying that with a problem identified, a significant front-end analysis question is, What is the potential value—that is, increased profits, reduced loss, etc.—of solving it. And is this potential value great enough to warrant our attention?

Assuming that the potential value is great enough to warrant an investigation, the next step is to ask ourselves, based on the data available, What are the possible causes—not probable causes, *possible* causes—of the problem? I have already indicated that our research indicated performance problems derive from one of three causes: a lack of skills and knowledge, a practical impediment or lack of proper motivation.

Hypothesizing one or more of these causes for a particular performance problem, we take the next step collecting evidence bearing on each hypothesis.

TRAINING: **Can you give us an example?**

HARLESS: Suppose a production line on which high-speed grinding wheels are used is having too many eye injuries. The workers are not wearing their goggles. We ask ourselves why—that's the basic front-end analysis question. And we hypothesize, first, that they are not wearing their goggles because they lack certain skills or knowledge—they don't know they should, they are not aware that their eye injuries can be prevented by the wearing of goggles. Or—our second hypothesis—they are not wearing their goggles because they don't *have* any goggles or don't have enough of them or they're locked up somewhere. Something is preventing them from performing as safe procedures would seem to require. Finally we wonder whether the goggles are uncomfortable or interfere in some way with their work. This would represent a motivation problem, our third hypothesis.

TRAINING: **How do you test these hypotheses?**

HARLESS: We ask for a demonstration. Generally if we want to know

if a person can or can't do something, we have them do it—on the work site or under simulated con-

---

"We found that people don't do things on the job for one of three reasons: They don't know how to do them, they're prevented from doing them in some way, or they lack the incentive to do them. That's where front end analysis asks, first, what are the symptoms that a problem exists; second, what are the performance deficiencies; and, finally, what is the relative value of solving that problem?"

---

ditions if necessary.

TRAINING: **Can't you just go to the foreman and say, Hey, Tom, why aren't the men wearing their goggles?**

HARLESS: You can. We do that—particularly when setting up a performance demonstration is difficult or terribly expensive. But we view this secondary evidence with some skepticism. The informant may have an axe to grind. He may be protecting his territory, covering his tracks, casting blame. So the data is suspect. We'd much rather

look at the performance if we can.

All right. We've isolated a problem and we've come to some conclusion about what the contributing causes of the problem are. Now, before I go on to the next procedure, I've got to tell you about a bias, a rule we follow.

We believe that the nature of the cause of a performance problem dictates the type of solution. Now, that's a simple-minded rule. But it tells you something important. It tells you that if you have a training problem, you train. But if you have a motivation or incentive problem, you don't train. You do some other things. Or suppose you have something wrong with a performance environment—lack of feedback, bad equipment, not enough time. Then you re-engineer the way the job is done or re-engineer the performance environment. You do not train. You don't motivate.

Okay. Having decided what combination of causes is behind a performance problem, and following the rule that cause determines the solution (if it's lack of skills and knowledge, you do some kind of training; if it's environmental, you re-engineer the environment; if it's motivation, you give feedback or attach rewards to the correct performance), you next look at what solving the problem will cost.

Determining cost effectiveness in performance problem-solving involves questions like: How long would it take? How much will it cost? What are the relative probabilities of success? What are the political aspects? We make a detailed analysis of these questions before recommending any particular problem-solving activity or group of activities. And training is not necessarily the solution we come to—not even when we're dealing with skills and knowledge problems. In a remarkable number of cases we have found that you can avoid huge amounts of training with some kind of job aid. So what we're talking about in front-end analysis is not training problems and problem-solving through training, but better, more cost effective ways of producing human performance.

"The nature of the cause of a performance problem dictates the type of solution. That's a simple minded rule, but it tells you that if you have a training problem, you train. But if you have a motivation or incentive problem, you don't train. You do some other things."

TRAINING: You're talking about a different kind of function for the training professional.

HARLESS: Absolutely. This kind of performance analysis has vast implications for trainers. You know, trainers are forever going around looking for respectability. They're always asking, How can we sell management on the idea of training? Well, the answer is you don't. You sell management on the benefits of solving *human performance problems.* You make it clear to management that you are there to *avoid* training when it's not cost effective. That's how you get to be a hero. That's how you get to be respectable. That's how training directors become vice-presidents of human performance or training. That's how you avoid being stuck off in some personnel department somewhere.

TRAINING: But practically speaking, how can a trainer transform

himself into a performance manager?

HARLESS: You apply a little front-end technology to your own situation. Suppose the boss comes to you and says, "I want you guys to produce me a 40-hour course on how to appreciate the beauty of the widget." Okay? Devotees of the performance problem-solving approach apply a little front-end analysis saying, Yes, boss, that's terrific. But do you mind if I ask you some questions—to get some of your wise counsel, etc.? That's another way of saying what front-end analysis is—it's all the smart questions a trainer or manager or consultant asks before he writes training objectives or does anything.

Anyway, the smart question in this situation—and all similar situations—is: What is the performance problem? If it's a performance problem, is it a skills and knowledge problem, an environmental problem, a motivational problem, or some combination of those, and what's the most cost-effective means for solving them? Is the cost worth it? And now—and only now—are we ready to talk about training objectives and detailed goals.

That's how you apply front-end analysis techniques to an existing situation where a problem has developed. In its purest form, front-end analysis deals with new tasks that an organization intends to perform. It deals with anticipating and avoiding performance problems rather than dealing with them after the fact.

Some examples. Your organization is going to convert to a new accounting system. What are the performance implications? You are going to install a computerized management system. What are the performance implications? You're about to make and market widgets. What are the performance implications? Asking questions about performance requirements before you implement a new program of one kind or another can

save you a lot of embarrassing—and expensive—problem-solving activities later.

"Front-end analysis deals with anticipating and avoiding performance problems rather than dealing with them after the fact."

TRAINING: Is that kind of planning and program-shaping activity legitimately a function of the training department?

HARLESS: You're assuming there should *be* a training department. But I say there should be a *performance* department that deals with the analysis of problems as well as their practical solution.

You ask, should there be a performance department *and* a training department? Perhaps so. But my experience is that training personnel—at least in industrial organizations—have the best chance of doing the kinds of things I'm talking about. The word training may be a barrier because the layman, when he thinks of training, thinks of things like writing audiovisual scripts or standing up and giving instructions and so forth. And maybe you need a training department within a performance department to do this sort of thing. But it would seem easier to expand the capabilities of existing training departments rather than to create whole new performance departments from scratch.

TRAINING: You'd expand the capabilities of the training department rather than, say, the personnel department?

HARLESS: Yes, because performance is already the legitimate province of the training department. Modern-day trainers are talking about ultimate performance when they insist on having instructional or training objectives. It's no giant step for them to say that these instructional objectives must be based on performance requirements based on thoroughgoing front-end analysis. The training department is the logical department to develop these performance analysis capabilities. In fact, that's happening. In one of the large hotel chains, a department of performance analysis has been established and the man who heads it up—the vice president of performance—was previously vice president, training.

TRAINING: So you're not against training?

HARLESS: Absolutely not. I'm a devotee of training. But *more relevant training, more cost-effective training . . .* a lot less silly training.

Reprinted from TRAINING, March 1975

ANALYZING ORGANIZATIONAL PERFORMANCE

Perhaps the *most* important job trainers can perform isn't training but determining what training, if any, is required to help solve organizational problems

BY STEPHEN P. BECKER

Trainers are teachers but teachers with a difference. Traditionally, the school teacher's job is to convey subject knowledge to the student who will ultimately graduate. If the student meets the course requirements, the teacher has fulfilled his or her responsibility. When a student is promoted or graduated, the teacher rarely sees him or her again. Schools can be thought of as good-luck and good-bye systems.

Trainers, on the other hand, are employed for the benefit of the organization. Corporations are not in business to educate employees but to make money. And trainers are hired because they can help that happen. Trainers are problem oriented rather than subject oriented because companies are problem oriented. Trainers must decide what, when, where, and whom to train. When trainees leave a program, they don't leave the company, so training is *not* a good-luck and good-bye system. Since there is plenty of feedback about the on-the-job results of training, trainers frequently work with students after instructional programs are completed.

One of the biggest differences between teaching and training is the work the trainer must do before confronting the students. While all teachers are involved in curriculum and material development, it is the unique responsibility of trainers to determine whether or not there should be any curriculum in the first place.

Before they do anything else, trainers must determine what training, if any, is required to help solve an organizational problem.

Let's call this preliminary activity organizational performance analysis (as opposed to human performance analysis or, simply, performance analysis). Performance analysis primarily concerns human behavior and starts with a perceived performance discrepancy between current and desired behavior. Organizational performance analysis starts with a profit and loss statement. Large-system oriented, its purpose is to discover problem indicators or indicators of organizational performance improvement opportunities. It is much closer to the process of industrial management itself, and this is one of its chief values. Looking at the P&L allows the trainer to focus on financial problems that are critical to the organization as a whole. Thus, financial priorities can be established from the outset.

Three important rules

When considering the profit and loss statement, several rules should be followed.

1. Don't do it alone. Include those members of the management team who will benefit from training. They live with the numbers and reap the consequences of the organizational results they achieve. Because there are many things besides training that can affect profitability, managers can

make those things happen only if they fully comprehend the part training will play in the total change effort. I call this the Principle of Training Integration; it means that if training is integrated with other management strategies and becomes a part of the organization's managerial process, then training itself can affect the degree of success. But training in a vacuum, without integration, has little chance of creating organizational change.

2. Consider the two categories of financial trends: Costs as a percentage of revenue may be rising or not reducing, or revenue may be declining

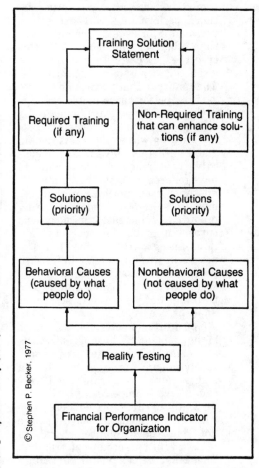

© Stephen P. Becker. 1977

or not increasing. Costs include everything from labor to telephone expenses. Trends can be considered on a weekly, monthly, quarterly, or yearly basis. Generally, other managers will be able to indicate negative and positive trends. Apprised of these, you will be able to point out how training may be able to help change the financial picture. When you identify where the organization is hurting, you won't have to worry about how to "sell" training. If training can be profitable, management doubtless will be receptive.

3. Remember, you're only looking at organizational performance indi-

cators. The numbers don't always mean what they say. The next step in determining if training is required or can help in an organizational performance improvement effort is to conduct a "reality test."

What, you ask, *is* a reality test? Suppose the P&L figures show that the cost of insurance premiums for personal injuries is rapidly rising. Initially, you might conclude that the organization is experiencing more personal accidents. After examining records from the safety department, though, you find that the accident rate has in fact decreased but the cost of each accident has risen sharply. In addition, comparisons with other companies show that your organization's performance with respect to personal injuries is 35 percent better than others in your industry. In this case, the P&L percentage would not be a sound indicator of real performance. The reality is that there is no organizational performance problem.

Now, let's suppose a manufacturing company finds that its inventory costs are growing while other costs remain stable. Further investigation indicates that machine improvements have reduced the cost of raw materials and increased machine output per man. In spite of this manufacturing productivity increase, there was no cutback in production hours. In addition, sales growth remained flat. The net result was an increase in finished goods in inventory. At first, it may seem that this problem is unrelated to training, but, to be certain, further analysis is needed.

You must now determine the causes of the problem. Because organizations are complex, fluid, and dynamic, rarely will any serious problem have a single cause. And rarely will any cause have a single remedy. The way to analyze causes is to determine which are behavioral and which are not. Those that are nonbehavioral will require solutions other than training. Those that are behavioral will require behavioral science solutions which may include training. Even the nonbehavioral solutions can frequently be enhanced by some form of training, though such training isn't essential to implement those solutions.

In our manufacturing company example, you, as organizational performance analyst, could interview the production managers to determine nonbehavioral and behavioral causes. Questions about *why* people do things will lead to behavioral causes. In this case, a key question is: Why didn't the production managers cut back the production hours so that finished goods inventory didn't build up? They could have cut production costs and

not increased other corporate costs by reducing hours—but they didn't. The investigation might produce the following information.

1. The finished goods inventory is stored in warehouses throughout the country rather than in the manufacturing plant. When the goods left the plant each day, the production managers felt a sense of achievement because more was going out at a reduced cost per unit. Their numbers looked great, and nobody told them it was too much. The behavioral solution here would be an improved feedback system.

2. The compensation system paid production management a bonus for quantity produced above quota, providing the quality control standards were met. Here there is a positive reward or consequence for maximum production without regard for the total corporate P&L. The behavioral science solution here might be to alter

---

ORGANIZATIONAL PERFORMANCE ANALYSIS

Improvement Strategy Summary

1. Financial Performance Indicators

2. Results of Reality Testing

3. Behavioral and Nonbehavioral Causes

4. Solutions to Causes in Priority Order

5. Required Training

© Stephen P. Becker, 1977

---

the reward system in terms of the total system.

3. Perhaps it's close to contract-renewal time, and the production managers didn't want to upset the union by reducing hours. In addition, many of the plant management people had little knowledge of union contracts and relations, and thought the union could get whatever their officials wanted. Since the machines had been upgraded, workers were nervous about losing their jobs and morale was low. A reduction in production schedules may have triggered a walkout. The behavioral science solution here might be a training program for the production managers in union relations and contract implementation.

To determine nonbehavioral causes, the questions might concern increasing sales so that finished inventories would move more quickly. Obviously, one way to stimulate sales is to upgrade a sales force, and one way to do that is through sales training. In this case, however, that would be a

long-term solution to a short-term problem. Other solutions might be to reduce the price of goods temporarily or to increase advertising expenditures. To do the latter, a short sales training program could be quickly developed and implemented to help the salesmen utilize the increased advertising support as a benefit in their sales presentations. Thus training would enhance the effectiveness of a nonbehavioral solution to a financially important organizational performance problem. Compared to the cost of advertising, the cost of training as a part of the total corporate solution would be insignificant. And the value of the trainer working with other managers to reach a comprehensive improvement strategy would be significant.

Once all causes and solutions are identified, each solution must be tested against such criteria as probability of success, the cost of the solution, and the time requirements for implementation and payback. It must also be decided if the organization is capable of developing, managing, and implementing the solution. Once test criteria questions are developed and answered, the solutions can be prioritized by the trainer working in conjunction with the management group.

The last step in the process is the creation of a training solution statement. Essentially this is a contract which describes the total organizational change plan and highlights the required training. If training is not required but is desired, that is clearly stated. The statement can be brief— one typewritten page—but it should clearly outline the role the training department will play in improving organizational performance. It should also clarify the parts of the total solution that are the responsibility of other departments.

A thoughtful reader might conclude that this system of organizational performance analysis is nothing more than good management. Well, that's exactly right. Unfortunately, however, few managers are able to think of "cause analysis" in behavioral and nonbehavioral terms; instead they look at the nonbehavioral causes and solutions. Trainers with performance analysis competencies, on the other hand, generally look only at the human behavior cause and solutions. Truly effective profit improvement strategies recognize that *both* are usually present at the same time. If trainers spend more time helping management groups analyze organizational performance, the training that is finally implemented will have greater bottom-line impact.

Reprinted from TRAINING, June 1977

A FINE MESH AT IBM

We all talk about integrating employee training with business objectives, but how many of us do it?
Here's a system that works for Big Blue

BY VAN SYMONS

Why do we educate employees? Is it because new technologies, processes or products require different skills? Is it because our businesses demand greater productivity and innovation? In most organizations, both answers are correct. The need for these types of education is obvious. But what may not be so obvious is whether training programs deliver what the business needs when it needs it.

As educators, most trainers know how to deliver quality instruction. They know how to conduct a needs analysis, quantify the data and set priorities. They may *not* know how to integrate their efforts with their organizations' business objectives and then measure the results.

The integration often is missing because of the way managers describe and direct the education of their people. Typically, a company will hire 100 mechanical engineers when, to meet its business objectives, the company actually needs to develop those mechanical engineers into 50 process engineers, 30 robot-design engineers and 20 package-design engineers.

Education departments keep employees and managers supplied with a vast array of course catalogs that describe available internal and external classes and programs. Since there is

The purpose of the systems approach is to develop a curriculum based on measurable learning objectives and skills. It uses structured techniques to develop the curriculum, train instructors, and audit and measure the effectiveness of programs and changes.

no formal plan for developing the robot, process or package engineers the company needs, managers allow employees to sort through the potpourri of information and select courses that interest them. As a result many people are being trained, but not necessarily the right people in the right skills at the right time.

The education department at IBM's General Products Division in San Jose, CA, developed an approach that helps integrate the education and

business functions. Our first step was to clarify the objectives and responsibilities of management and training. The main goal of a training program is to ensure that employees have the technical skills they need to increase productivity and innovation to meet the company product quality, cost and schedule goals. To fulfill this objective, we must know several things: What technical skills are needed to get the job done? When will those skills be needed? How many skilled employees will be needed? What measurable education programs will increase employee skills to the desired level?

This objective translates into two distinct responsibilities. The training department needs to provide the required curriculum on a timely basis and in a cost-effective manner. Managers are responsible for identifying skill needs, sending the proper people to training, and ensuring that the available equipment and jobs will use the skills of these people.

Against this background, we developed the following techniques and tools to provide a measurable education function that is meshed with the business process.

Reprinted from TRAINING, April 1987

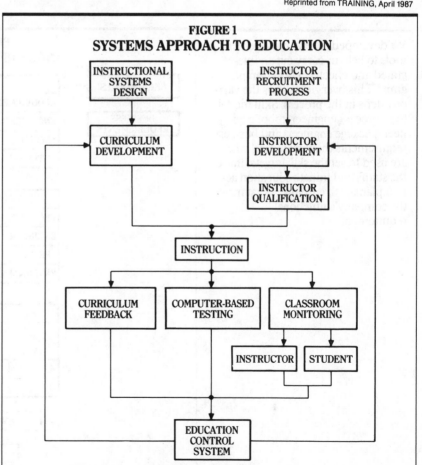

FIGURE 1
SYSTEMS APPROACH TO EDUCATION

A variety of measurement techniques allows us to evaluate knowledge gained and retained, consider changes or alternatives to a program, and identify potential problems and improvements. For example, we use statistical process control, a technique borrowed from manufacturing, to determine the effectiveness of instruction, content and material. Test-score averages are expected to fall within certain ranges if a program is effective.

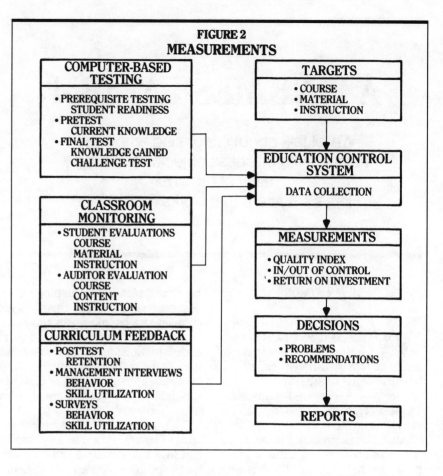

FIGURE 2
MEASUREMENTS

We developed several management tools to help us carry out an integrated and effective education program. This overview shows the various steps in the process. Skill models (e.g., process engineer, robot engineer, package engineer) and business requirements (how many and when) are used to set the skill targets, track the status and initiate education action plans with employees that meet the company's functional requirements.

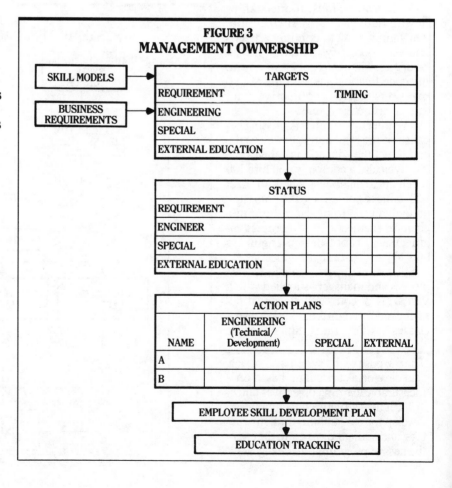

FIGURE 3
MANAGEMENT OWNERSHIP

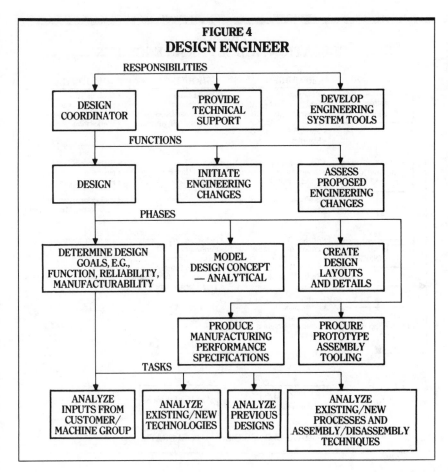

FIGURE 4
DESIGN ENGINEER

This is a typical skill model for an engineering skill. We develop each model using job/task analysis techniques to interview experts from several engineering functions. Each block of responsibilities, functions, phases and tasks includes detailed statements about the specific efforts and skills required. These, in turn, become the basis for establishing measurable learning objectives and skills for each course and curriculum. These models also are used to decide how these skills can be provided—through internal education programs, external programs or on-the-job training.

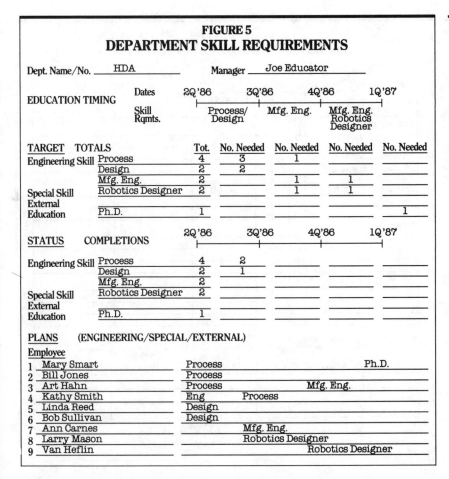

FIGURE 5
DEPARTMENT SKILL REQUIREMENTS

Managers identify the skills their employees will need by completing this form periodically. It allows managers to describe their requirements, track them over time, and initiate specific action plans in terms of who will be trained and when. The special and external education rows identify the number of people who may need special training (e.g., an assignment in another location for several months) or advanced degrees. By combining this data from all functions, the education functions can plan, set priorities and schedule offerings to meet future skill requirements. Experience with this process shows that most managers tend to want all of their people trained far sooner than is practical for either the people or the education departments. Typically, several alterations are required to develop realistic and committed plans.

Managers use this model before they sit down to discuss education plans with their employees. It uses the courses developed from the skills described in Figure 4 to determine the relevant training in view of an individual's responsibilities. Although this model is developed by the education department, managers are free to modify it to fit their specific applications. For example, packaging engineers in a product group may need some electrical, chemical and mechanical skills, but in a frame-design group they may need only mechanical skills. Education requirements for packaging engineers also are influenced by the stage of product design—e.g., initial development vs. production. This model helps managers recognize which skills are required at a given point in an employee's career. It focuses on the concept of required vs. optional skills, and provides a communication tool for management.

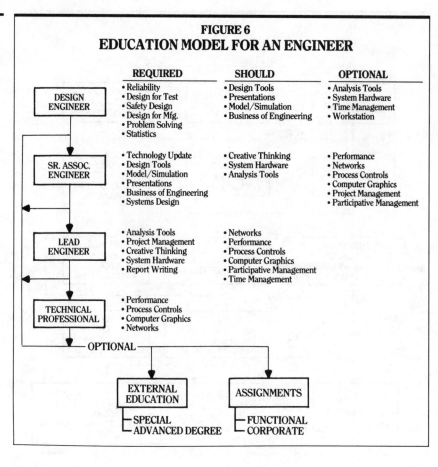

FIGURE 6
EDUCATION MODEL FOR AN ENGINEER

	REQUIRED	SHOULD	OPTIONAL
DESIGN ENGINEER	• Reliability • Design for Test • Safety Design • Design for Mfg. • Problem Solving • Statistics	• Design Tools • Presentations • Model/Simulation • Business of Engineering	• Analysis Tools • System Hardware • Time Management • Workstation
SR. ASSOC. ENGINEER	• Technology Update • Design Tools • Model/Simulation • Presentations • Business of Engineering • Systems Design	• Creative Thinking • System Hardware • Analysis Tools	• Performance • Networks • Process Controls • Computer Graphics • Project Management • Participative Management
LEAD ENGINEER	• Analysis Tools • Project Management • Creative Thinking • System Hardware • Report Writing	• Networks • Performance • Process Controls • Computer Graphics • Participative Management • Time Management	
TECHNICAL PROFESSIONAL	• Performance • Process Controls • Computer Graphics • Networks		

OPTIONAL

EXTERNAL EDUCATION	ASSIGNMENTS
— SPECIAL — ADVANCED DEGREE	— FUNCTIONAL — CORPORATE

During a typical education-review meeting with their employees, managers discuss what knowledge each employee currently has, what courses they might want to "challenge" (they can receive credit for a course by passing a challenge test), and what courses they need to take to meet the skill levels required. Using this information, the manager and employee agree to the plan, and schedule and complete this form. Our experience with this part of the process shows that it pays off: Employees and managers feel they develop a good understanding of what is best for the employee and the company; managers have a chance to encourage and recognize the employee's progress; and both are committed to a realistic and measurable plan.

FIGURE 7
EMPLOYEE SKILL DEVELOPMENT PLAN

Name: Mary Smart   Date: 7/10/85

I. EDUCATION COURSES

COURSE NAME	R[1]	S[2]	O[3]	SCHEDULE Qt/Yr	STATUS	DATE COMPLETE
Engineering						
Statistics 100	✓			1Q'86		
Statistics 200	✓			2Q'86		
Design of Exp. 300		✓		3Q'86		
Process Control	✓			3Q'86		
Creative Thinking		✓		4Q'86		
Extended						
Special						

II. EXTERNAL ASSIGNMENTS

TYPE OF ASSIGNMENTS	PURPOSE	APPROX. SCHEDULE	STATUS

Required[1]   Should[2]   Optional[3]

HOW TO AVOID THE CURSE OF CATCH-22

Sometimes, the cause of your organizations' 'people problems' is embarrassingly simple: Under your policies, they're damned if they do and damned if they don't

BY GEORGE T. LYNN
AND JOANNE BARRIE LYNN

There was only one catch and that was Catch-22, which specified that a concern for one's own safety in the face of dangers that were real and immediate was the process of a rational mind. Orr was crazy and could be grounded. All he had to do was ask; and as soon as he did, he would no longer be crazy and would have to fly more missions. Orr would be crazy to fly more missions and sane if he didn't, but if he was sane he had to fly them. If he flew them he was crazy and didn't have to; but if he didn't want to he was sane and had to.

Yossarian was moved very deeply by the absolute simplicity of this clause of Catch-22 and let out a respectful whistle.

"That's some catch, that Catch-22," he observed.

Joseph Heller, *Catch-22*

Joseph Heller's international bestseller portrayed a situation with which many of us can identify. The book's hero, Captain Yossarian, was caught in the kind of inescapable logical bind that many organizations create for their people time and again.

The manager or human resources development (HRD) specialist trying to get to the heart of an organization's performance problem can often shortcut the process by learning to seek out and pay special attention to such situations. More important, those who can spot these maddening logic traps may be able to work directly with the company's informal value system to effect lasting change.

The Catch-22 concept is not new to the literature of psychology or cultural anthropology. The late Gregory Bateson, one of this century's greatest social scientists, coined the term "double bind" to describe situations in which a person is caught between two conflicting demands. You can't obey both, but disobedience to either results in punishment of some kind. It's a time-honored predicament that goes by several familiar names: being damned if you do and damned if you don't; being caught between a rock and a hard place.

A surprising number of organizations seem to use Catch-22 logic as a matter of course. And Catch-22 situations commonly crop up in many other companies because the process of change keeps shifting the demands placed on the organization by the environment, and the organization passes on these shifting demands to its employees. Sooner or later, people get caught between conflicting forces with no way out. And that means higher stress levels for employees and more performance problems for the organization.

Double binds produce vicious stress because they create a feeling of helplessness; people burn out very quickly trying to do a job in a no-win situation. This higher stress level has been shown in recent studies to relate directly to several negative performance indicators: sick-leave use, high accident levels, poor decision-making and hostility toward co-workers.

What you *don't* need in a Catch-22 situation is more training in "how to cope with stress" or "how to manage your time." The double bind is a management problem, not a training problem. What the organization needs is a bold analysis of norms and policies that create conflicts which make it impossible for people to do good jobs.

Spotting the problem

Before you can do anything about Catch-22 situations, you must be able to recognize them. The demands that produce double binds may originate either in the stated policies of the organization or in its *norms*: its unstated traditions or "rules of the game."

Yossarian and Orr were caught in a *policy* bind. "Policy A" stated that in order to get out of combat, one must be insane with fear of death. "Policy B" said that fear of death is the sign of a rational mind and rational people must stay in combat.

Taken by themselves, each of the policies that combine to set up a double bind may be perfectly logical and functional for the organization. That's important to remember, because it makes the damaging combination hard to spot unless you, yourself, are the one trapped between the two.

How might a Catch-22 situation result from a conflict between a policy and a *norm*? Here's one a lot of training managers might recognize: The policy says, "Be a catalyst for change; give us new ideas." The organizational norm says, silently but unmistakably, "Don't rock the boat; don't try to make us think differently."

The most difficult types of double binds to resolve are those that arise between norms. Conflict in this area goes unrecognized because the conflicting norms are "givens"—untested assumptions which everybody in the organization supports. "Norm A" tells women executives that to get ahead, they have to produce more than men. "Norm B" says that women who produce more than men are "climbers" or "pushy," and cannot be trusted in upper management.

A traditional problem-solving approach is unlikely to be useful in dealing with this kind of normative conflict; its roots go much deeper than a simple misunderstanding of individual responsibilities. The problem is rooted in the organization's bedrock beliefs—in its "culture," to use the current buzzword. So it is very important for the HRD specialist to have a good idea of the origins of the conflict before suggesting a way to solve it.

The employee who gets caught between a rock and a hard place may deal with the dilemma in several ways—stay home sick a lot, stop caring about performance, quit, etc. But one popular way to escape punishment for failing to comply with mutually exclusive demands is simply to fudge performance data to show success where there is none. In other words, if you punish people for telling the truth, they'll lie to you.

In one recent case, employees of a large government agency were required to meet contradictory goals from higher-level regulatory agencies.

One regulator required the agency to open large tracts of government-owned rangeland to ranchers each year. The other required it to preserve the same land intact. The agency's staff members admitted that to get out of this bind, they would "manage" the information they put out on their activities to make each regulator believe it was getting the results it wanted.

Why didn't they just say something? Why didn't they just point out the impossible situation to the two regulatory bodies involved and let *them* fight it out? They were stopped by a powerful organizational norm that said you don't question directives from above, period. And this happens in other organizations: A policy double bind is held in place by a norm that limits inquiry into policies.

In the course of a workshop with an electronics firm, we noted a variation on the government agency's strategy. In this case, the production department was required to speed up the manufacture of a component to meet a new market opportunity. No new people were hired to meet the new goal and quality standards were not relaxed. The employees' ability to deal with the problem was blocked by a norm that said nobody questions production goals established by management; people complained, but no one seriously tried to get management to change its expectations.

The production department escaped its dilemma by speeding up quality checks. This dumped quality problems into the laps of the field-service people, who had to deal with dissatisfied customers.

Thus, one unit in the organization managed to hand off the bind to another unit—a fairly common "solution" to Catch-22 situations. Handoffs also occur *vertically*, of course, when a supervisor assigns conflicting demands from upper management to a subordinate.

People don't resort to these strategies because they're inherently dishonest. They use them either when they fail to see clearly that they're *in* a double bind, or when they do see it but feel helpless to change things.

Tell me a story

The stories told by people in organizations about their successes and failures can be rich sources of information about the organization's practices, policies and values. If you're setting out to unravel double binds, storytelling is a particularly useful technique for gathering information because it allows a management group to admit and discuss the overt contra-

dictions embodied in the binds. *Logical* approaches (responsibility charting, PERT analysis, etc.) may not work as well because they don't set up a discussion of causes that may be largely intangible: traditions and illogical conflict-management styles.

If you suspect that a specific problem—a machinery breakdown, a sudden rise in accidents, the mishandling of a business venture—is a symptom of Catch-22 at work, you can use storytelling to investigate. We recommend a five-step approach.

Step 1: Briefing. Brief the management group on double-bind phenomena, using specific examples (real ones from other organizations, if possible). Ask group members to share examples of double binds from their own experience. Urge them to talk about specific behavior—it's essential that everybody understand what people are *doing* to maintain these double binds. Tell the group that solving the immediate problem is the most vital concern but that in the process, they will learn some important things about their conflict-management style.

Step 2: Writing stories. Ask each person on the team to write a short story (not more than one page) describing the problem. The stories should go back into the problem's history, identify its causes, elaborate on the current state of affairs and suggest probable outcomes if nothing is done. They should be as specific as possible, mentioning names and dates. Adjourn the group after scheduling a follow-up meeting.

Step 3: The master story. Now you write a master version of the scenario, one that incorporates all the individual accounts and stresses the central themes found in each description of the problem. Note overt discrepancies as to what actually happened, including everyone's information. Transcribe the master story onto an overhead transparency or flip chart.

Step 4: Group story analysis. The group meets again. Everyone sees the master story, and additions or corrections are made. Post the amended version for easy reading and ask the group to analyze it for evidence of double-bind conflicts by answering the following questions:

• Are there any conflicting *demands* (policies/norms)? Is this situation a double bind in which people are caught with no way out? Why?

• Who are the major *actors* in the double bind? Who is putting the conflicting demands on whom? What specific people or organizations are requiring compliance?

• What are the *consequences* for noncompliance with conflicting demands?

• What are people *doing* to cope with the situation and how are these actions affecting the organization?

The group might want to get through this stage quickly; its members may be looking straight at the organization's sacred traditions and survival strategies. Nervousness at this point is a good sign that the discussion is on target, however, so press for a complete analysis of the issue before moving on.

Step 5: Planning action/writing agreements. Roger Harrison, the originator of the "role negotiation" technique, has said that if agreements made between individuals to solve problems aren't written as contracts for all members of the team to see, they probably won't succeed. Our experience working with double binds confirms his thinking on this point. We strongly recommend that action plans be written as agreements in this format:

• A statement describing the double bind. This is essentially a summary of the team's responses to the questions in Step 4.

• A clear statement of the preferred situation.

• An agreement explaining what specific *actions* will be taken to deal with the conflict and who will take these actions.

Double-bind action agreements probably will include ways to change priorities, alter work schedules and/or remove penalties for failing to comply with certain demands. A successfully negotiated agreement not only will solve the immediate problem but will promote awareness of the heavy impact of the organization's values on its productivity and morale.

It's important to mention that double-bind analysis should take place *with the people who can change the situation*. If the problem originates within the "power map" of the organization (for example, the informal rules of conduct for promotion established by top management), then this is where the investigation should take place. Support for the change process has to come from the rule-makers, who must demonstrate their commitment in actions as well as words. If the conflicting norms and policies occur in just one subunit, analysis can be done effectively at this level. The issue itself determines who should be involved in the discussion. The double bind must be corrected at its source.

Reprinted from TRAINING, July 1984

MEASURING POTENTIAL FOR PERFORMANCE IMPROVEMENT

This nifty system helps you tell how competent your people already are, and helps determine opportunity for improvement

BY THOMAS F. GILBERT

When we make judgments about the competence of human conduct, we often confuse behavior with performance. Behavior is a necessary and integral part of performance, but to equate the two is like confusing a sale with the seller. Naturally, we cannot have one without the other. But the sale is a unitary transaction, with properties all of its own; and we can know a great deal about it even though we know little—perhaps nothing at all—about the seller.

In performance, behavior is a means, and its consequence is the end. And we seldom have any reason to try to modify other people's behavior in complete isolation of consequences. About the only reason would be to study it. By viewing behavior in convenient isolation we can learn many things about it, ranging from measures of visual acuity to useful information about the perseveration of habits. But those things *by themselves* tell us very little about performance.

Nor do we have much reason to modify people's performance in isolation from its context. Is the performance of killing legal and moral—or is it a heinous crime? We cannot tell this merely by observing the whole performance transaction. We can measure the frequency or accuracy of striking the target; we can measure how many bullets were used. We can even correlate these measures with our measures of behavior. But none of these measures will tell us whether the performance is valuable, legal, or moral.

No sensible person tries to modify other people's behavior just because it is there, or their performance just because it can be done. When we set about to engineer performance, we should view it in a context of value. We should not train someone to do something unless we place a value on the consequence—unless we see that consequence as a valuable *accomplishment (A)*. So, the kind of performance we want to engineer is *valuable performance,* which can be expressed in shorthand as

$$P = B \longrightarrow A$$

Now we have limited our definition of performance to valuable performance. If, for example, we can change the way a hunter handles his gun so that he can hit the rabbits we value, we have engineered valuable performance.

Worthy performance

But is the performance worth it?

Suppose that we really do value the rabbits we have taught the hunter to kill. But the hunter requires an expensive rifle, charges us heavily for his services, and uses a lot of ammunition. Although we may value his accomplishment, we will not find the performance worthy because his behavior costs us too much. Our engineering, then, is a failure. So, what we really want to engineer is not just valuable performance, but *worthy performance*— in which the value of the accomplishment exceeds the cost of the behavior.

All engineering begins with the simple economic purpose of creating valuable results at a cost that makes those results worth it. Worth, then, is the net we have when we subtract the costs from the values: $W = V - C$. Or, we can express worth in another way: as the ratio of value to cost:

$$\text{Worth} = \frac{\text{Value}}{\text{Cost}}$$

Which says only that worth gets greater as value increases and cost decreases.

When we set out to engineer human performance, it is axiomatic that we place value on accomplishments but that the behavior costs us something. We may value the rabbit; but we must pay for the hunter's work, knowledge, and incentives, as well as for his gun and ammunition. We value the crop but pay for the plow and the plowman.

Roughly speaking, *competent* people are those who can create valuable results without using excessively costly behavior.

Behavior vs. accomplishment

Nothing better illustrates the importance of distinguishing behavior and accomplishment than a study of the ways in which we can measure performance. When we think of measuring performance, we usually think of tests. And psychologists have certainly provided us with enough of those. By the traditional view, the way to assess performance is to administer tests of apparent job or school relevance (e.g., mathematics, spatial relations, mechanical aptitude), and then to establish a cut-off score for the selection of employees or the advancement of students.

This traditional view is mistaken in two ways. First, traditional tests, at their best, are only crude statistical instruments, usually poorly correlated with the economic realities of performance. For example, personality tests for salespeople have been cor-

53

related with such supervisory ratings as "interpersonal effectiveness" and "ability to conduct an interview," but never, to my knowledge, with the quality of sales prospecting. Very often those things so easily assumed to be correlatives of actual performance simply are not. As a matter of fact, the best salesperson (by dollar volume) I have ever seen never smiled and had a fish-like handshake; and a leading medical photographer I once knew is color-blind, one-eyed, and severely astigmatic in the one "good" eye.

Second, tests are unfair in that the people who score poorly on them have far more potential for successful job and school performance than we have been able to tap. A test score rates people low on the *assumed* correlatives of the job or school requirements; but it does not identify precisely what must be developed in them for us to make good their potential. Tests are usually too indirect; we need to go more directly to performance. And that is what psychological testing has helped prevent us from doing. That is also why psychological test batteries have been so half-heartedly accepted in industry. They have been better accepted in the schools, but only because the schools have been so little concerned with the worldly use of human performance.

Assessment of human performance has teetered on a dilemma. Here are its horns:

1. We all know that there are great individual differences among people (the statistical "science" of psychological testing is grounded in this assumption).

2. But we know equally well that people are pretty much alike (or there could be no science of human beings, biological or psychological).

Now, I believe both of these propositions, and so does everyone else I have ever talked to about them. But their contradiction is clear and surely needs a resolution. The system of performance analysis described here has emerged from a resolution of this dilemma— from realizing how both of these commanding, yet seemingly contradictory, beliefs about differences in human performance can be true but not contradictory.

Measuring human competence

I believe wholeheartedly: Any kind of performance can be measured—reliably and with considerable precision. We can measure the performance of poets, managers, teachers, physicians, lawyers, research scientists, psychotherapists, composers, and

politicians— not just that of production workers and athletes. The belief that the more complex forms of performance are not subject to measurement and quantification arises simply from ignorance about how to do it. Once you get the knack, performance that you once thought unmeasurable will usually be not nearly so difficult to measure as, say, the radiation of Martian soil or the fertility of farm land. I hope to convince you of this here.

But performance alone is not what I have set out to measure, because per-

---

The engineer's model for worthy performance has an important message for trainers: Competent people create valuable results without using excessively costly behavior.

---

formance alone is not competence. Competence is a social concept, a comparative judgment about the worth of performance. In order to convert measures of performance into measures of competence, we require a social standard. Once we find that standard, competence will be as easy to measure as performance.

We get the competence of any one person, institution, or culture only by comparing the very best instance of that performance with what is typical. Mark Spitz, the Olympic swimmer, was (at his best) only about 20% faster than the average high school swim-contest entrant, which means that the average high school entrant is exceptionally competent. Mark Spitz, of course, was a perfectly competent swimmer, because he was the exemplar. I call this measure of competence, the ratio of the exemplar's performance to typical performance, the PIP (*potential* for *improving performance*); and it doubly serves us. First, it tells us how much competence we already have; second, it tells us how much potential we have for improvement.

I define *exemplary* performance as

the worth of the historically best instance of the performance. And notice that we need not accept mediocrity as a standard. For example, if a greenhorn's acre yields $1,000 in grain at a cost of $500, the typical worth index (W_t) is 2. If the best green thumb yields $2,000 in value at a cost of $250, the exemplary worth index (W_{ex}) is 8. Then the greenhorn's PIP is 4, meaning that the greenhorn has the potential for doing four times as well. (Dollars are convenient units, but the PIP is by no means restricted to them.)

Human competence, then, is further defined by the Second Leisurely Theorem (or the Measurement Theorem), which states: *Typical competence is inversely proportional to the potential for improving performance (the PIP), which is the ratio of exemplary performance to typical performance. The ratio, to be meaningful, must be stated for an identifiable accomplishment, because there is no "general quality of competence."* In shorthand, this theorem states that:

$$PIP = \frac{W_{ex}}{W_t}$$

There is also an interesting corollary: *The lower the PIP of any person or group, the more competitive that person or group is.* Now, the word *competitive* is a delight to some people; to others, it signals unpleasant things. But that is because the cult of behavior has us confuse certain behavioral properties, such as greed, aggression, determination, and the expenditure of energy, with competing. All I mean by competing is performing with comparative competence.

PIP characteristics

You will note that the PIP is a measure of opportunity, the very stuff human capital is made of. The PIP does not assign feeble limitations to people as the IQ does, but takes the humane *and* practical view that poor performers usually have great potential. Also, our measurement theorem does not posit competence mystically inside people's heads, but places it in performance. People are not competent; performance is. People have opportunities, which the PIP can express with precision and validity.

Indeed, the PIP can be measured as precisely and as accurately as we choose. Competence may vary from time to time, but our methods of measuring it need not. I have devised practical methods of measuring the PIP, and they need not be validated against criterion measures, because the PIP, when properly used, *is* the performance criterion. And, naturally, when applied in the world of work, the PIP yields accurate measures of the economic potential for improving performance.

The PIP is principally a conceptual tool, which gives us a basis for comparing potential opportunities to improve performance. In general, the smaller the PIP, the less possibility there is to improve performance and the more difficult it is to reduce the PIP to 1.0. It is easier to reduce a PIP from, say, 4.0 to 1.5 than it is to shrink a PIP of 1.2 to 1.1. This rule is no longer true, however, if two circumstances hold. One is if we have full knowledge of why the exemplar is a superior performer, and we also have *full* control over those variables—that is, when we can give typical performers the training, information, tools, or motivation they require to emulate the exemplar. The second circumstance is even more important: when we can improve on the exemplar. Thus, the PIP is a "dynamic" measure, because new exemplary standards can always be set.

But here is something more to be considered. Even if we gave all performers the information, knowledge, tools, and so on, of the exemplar, some variance in performance would remain—someone would still manage to shine as the best performer. In a "perfectly" competitive world, where we have arranged for everyone to have everything necessary in order to emulate the exemplar, such inherent characteristics as quickness, strength, "intelligence," and ambition will give some people a slight edge. In athletics, that slight edge is the critical distinction, but in the world of work or in the world of schools it would usually be of no special economic significance at all. It is, I believe, virtually impossible to reduce PIPs to 1.0, simply because someone will always discover a better way of doing it, have some natural superiority, or possess an unusual degree of motive to excel.

What I am saying is that, in general, the more incompetent a person or a group of people are, the easier it is to improve their performance. This contradicts the way we often think. But that is because we rarely think as performance engineers. Left to "nature"— to uncontrolled and unplanned events— exemplary performers are likely to improve themselves, setting new standards of exemplary performance. But as a situation becomes more "unmanaged," PIPs will grow— with the result that management has more potential for realizing them. Although large PIPs may discourage the uninitiated, they are a welcome opportunity to performance engineers.

The size of the PIP, of course, only indicates potential for improving performance—not how economically valuable that potential is. To put an economic value on a change in a PIP, we must translate it into what I call "stakes." (Stakes are the money value of realizing the PIP.) A PIP of 4.0 in the speed at which janitors clean a building, say, does not translate into as much economic potential as a PIP of 1.5 in the speed of the production line. Later, I shall discuss the relatively

---

Any kind of performance can be measured reliably and with considerable precision—even that of poets and managers.

---

simple techniques of translating PIPs into stakes; meanwhile, it is important to see the use of the PIP as a conceptual measure, pointing us in the direction of engineering opportunity.

A case in point

A case history, based on real events, illustrates how the use of the PIP can be a solid clue of great economic importance to a performance engineer faced with a really unfamiliar performance system. In this case, we shall see a performance engineer, Frank Roby, face an unfamiliar situation and find opportunities to improve it greatly— opportunities of the kind that experienced management misses every day.

The manufacturing vice president of Surfside Seasonings, Inc., Willis Angel, is dissatisfied with the performance of his plants. He is determined to find some way to improve that performance, and he assigns three groups of people to conduct independent studies to tell him which programs he should invest in. Two of these groups are the corporate training and organizational development departments of Surfside. The third group is a consulting firm specializing in management development. When Angel reads the three reports, he can hardly believe that the studies were independent because their recommendations are so similar. All three reports finger the first-line supervisors of the work force in the processing area as the culprits most responsible for the poor showing in the plants. The once stable, but aging, hourly workers have been largely replaced by young women from the ghetto. All three reports agree that the old first-line supervisors simply don't know how to manage the new breed. A training program in new styles of supervision, and in human relations, will be required; and the management consulting firm offers to develop one for $78,000. For a $400 million business, this does not seem too large an investment in good supervision.

Angel, of course, is impressed by the substantial agreement of the three studies he has commissioned. And the arguments have a certain face validity: The culture of the work force has changed, and there is no doubting that. But the $78,000 training-development cost for an operation that has been losing money gives Angel trouble. He can't quite make up his mind, and he decides to get another opinion. He has heard of a consultant named Frank Roby, a man with a mixed reputation. Some say that Roby is completely without professional qualifications and imply that he is a charlatan. Others insist that although his methods are truly unorthodox, Roby gets results. The word *results* sounds sweet to Angel, so he hires Roby at $750 a day.

Because of Roby's reputation, Angel decides to watch him work. Roby shows up one morning and makes the mandatory tour of a manufacturing plant, seemingly without noticing a thing. He then spends the rest of the day talking with the corporate accountant, the plant production manager, and the chief quality-control inspector. To Angel's surprise, Roby appears in his office at 5:00 p.m. saying that he is ready to deliver his report and suggests that they conclude the study in the nearest bar over Vidalia Specials, a mixture of orange juice and sour mash bourbon.

While Angel begins his adaptation to this curious blend, he asks Roby if he has ever been in a manufacturing plant like Surfside's. "Not exactly," Roby replies, "but I once helped some folks in a chewing gum factory."

So much for Roby's credentials. Angel begins the audition with deep suspicion, but after an hour Roby has completely convinced him that the best way for Surfside Seasoning to waste its time and money is to train first-line supervisors; and that, indeed, the company has an extraordinarily competent corps of foremen in the processing areas. (Mind you, Roby never so much as interviewed a supervisor.) Besides, Roby tells Angel exactly where he thinks the problem is, why it is there, and what can be done about it. He is so convincing that the next morning Angel seeks authorization to spend the $150,000 that Roby said would be required for the program.

Only 18 months later, Angel has sufficient data to prove that the adoption of Roby's program is netting the company a return of several million dollars a year in greatly increased labor productivity, decreased waste, lower employee turnover, and fewer grievances. And Angel finds himself taking all the credit—not that he's that kind of guy. But how could he ever convince anyone that a man could walk into a seasonings plant for the first time and after a day tell you how to turn the plant around— and against all the advice of seasoned professionals?

We can look at just a sample of the data that Roby studied to reach his conclusions: Table 1 shows some production data for three* representative supervisory groups at Surfside Seasonings. (Of course, Roby didn't depend on these data alone, but they contributed far more than anything else to his remarkable conclusions.) In examining these data, Roby could see at once that the potential for improving the performance of the

TABLE 1 COMPARATIVE MANUFACTURING PRODUCTIVITY					
Supervisor A		**Supervisor B**		**Supervisor C**	
Employee no.	Hrly. prod.	Employee no.	Hrly. prod.	Employee no.	Hrly. prod.
1	163	11	194	21	172
2	149	12	138	22	137
3	118	13	137	23	136
4	108	14	131	24	135
5	106	15	110	25	127
6	93	16	89	26	100
7	60	17	61	27	56
8	57	18	49	28	52
9	42	19	48	29	41
10	30	20	41	30	28
Average	92.6	Average	99.8	Average	98.4

hourly employees was considerable, but that the differences among supervisors was small. Even though Supervisor B had the best supervisory performance in the company, getting other supervisors to perform as he does would not improve matters greatly. If the situation were reversed and there were large differences among the supervisors, his conclusions would have been quite different.

The average production is 96.93, and the best employee produces 194 units; so the employee PIP (assuming that costs and quality are the constants) is

$$\text{Employee PIP} = \frac{194}{96.9} = 2.00$$

This employee PIP shows that the average hourly employee has the potential for doubling productivity. But the supervisory PIP is negligible— unusually low, in fact. Roby looked at these variances and then noticed that the job the employees had to do was to operate complex low-tolerance equipment. A lot of learning is required to master it. He also heard people say that it simply took a lot of experience to get maximum production. And he learned that the hourly employees got no formal training— mostly because production managers didn't think that formal training was as good as on-the-job experience. He considered this nonsense, of course, and he advised Angel that $150,000 invested in proper training in the theory and troubleshooting of the equipment could get any new employee producing at about 150 units an hour, reducing the employee PIP to less than 1.3. Roby proved to be right— and the most important information he had was the PIP measures. Management had hidden the data in its books, but not in the form of Table 1.

*In the real case, there were 32 groups. Three are chosen here to simplify the argument.

Frank Roby is a real person, and this is an almost true story. It is true in every important respect except for the time it took— Roby has never met anyone as open minded as Willis Angel; it usually takes weeks or months to build up sufficient appearance of credibility for his advice to be taken seriously. Roby has no magic, no mysterious capacity for insight. Indeed, his methods are so simple that when people watch his behavior, they cannot help but be unimpressed. Roby has learned to observe measures of competence and to make sense of them. Those simple measures can be powerful instruments in our pursuit of competence if we can set aside our behavioral biases long enough to see how they can be used.

Whose performance can be measured?

The Roby example deals with relatively simple performance that can be measured quite easily— in units of production. You might argue, however, that much of the world of human performance is not so simple; and you might reasonably question whether other kinds of performance can be measured to yield neat units like the PIP. At least consider my proposition that any kind of performance can be measured.

Oh, the thrill when we first broke through what seemed to be the dense underbrush of John Donne's poetry. But if Donne was a competent poet, how can one measure that competence? Is there any way to say precisely that Donne is 2.3 times the poet that Herrick is, or 3.0 times Lowell? The obvious answer comes much too easily: There is no way to quantify beauty or spiritual power.

The problem is not *whether* we can measure Donne's performance, but what it is we expect from poetry— what we consider a valuable poetic contribution. Measuring noncreative competence seems to be easier than measuring the competence of creative artists— but only because people can more easily come to an agreement about what is expected of noncreative performance. Anyone's performance can be measured in many different ways, and those measures become measures of competence whenever we can agree on what it is about the accomplishments that we value. It should be sufficient to say that we can measure any kind of performance. And to argue that performance is too difficult to measure is, it seems to me, the luxury view of things. If most people did not live in poverty and abject servitude, this view would be easier to accept. Indeed, in that distant day (should it arrive) when all people have broken the bonds of ignorance and need, and we sit sipping mint juleps on some warm veranda, poetry itself may become the currency of the land, and all the absurd numbers will be safely confined to the computers. But until that time I for one must believe that it is possible to measure performance and competence, even John Donne's, and to make those measures mean something. It may not always be easy, but the stakes are reasonably high. Indeed, if we cannot measure competence, there is very little reason to talk about it at all.

The widespread feeling that many of the important characteristics of human conduct resist measurement is a result, I believe, of the familiar confusion between behavior and performance. There are at least two reasons why behavior is often difficult to measure satisfactorily: much of it is covert and not easily observed; and it is often hard to specify exactly what behavior is required for exemplary performance, because two exemplars may behave in considerably different ways.

If I were to build a scale of poetic competence, be assured that I would not start by observing the *behavior* of poets. Donne's poems speak for themselves— clearly to a few, not too clearly for most. No end of analysis of his behavior would add one scintilla to a proper assessment of his performance. Besides, as I have said, Donne's behavior is no longer available. And behavior is not competence any more than an eight-cylinder engine is a Sunday drive in the country. Once we lock that concept firmly in mind, it becomes much easier to measure human competence.

Reprinted from TRAINING, December 1978

HOW TO CONDUCT A REAL PERFORMANCE AUDIT

You may know what you mean by a 'performance audit,' but do you know what your CEO means?

BY WILLIAM J. ROTHWELL

Performance audit' is a term that means different things to different people. To some, it is synonymous with performance analysis, the step in instructional design that identifies discrepancies between the performance you're getting from someone and the performance you want. To others, it connotes a form of needs assessment that considers the context of the job, the person doing the job, job actions, job results and feedback on results.

The traditional performance audit, as trainers see it, focuses either on instructional outcomes alone or on outcomes within a work environment.

On the other hand, accountants and some management consultants, who are familiar with financial and compliance audits, think of the performance audit in quite a different way. They see it as an extension of more traditional auditing that deals wih broad issues of organizational efficiency and effectiveness. The focus is not on *instructional* outcomes or *individual* competence, but on *organizational* outcomes or on overall *organizational* competence and productivity.

Trainers can learn some important lessons about performance auditing from people outside the field of human resources development. And once they understand this type of audit, HRD professionals will be able to draw their own conclusions about its value and potential application in the training environment.

What is it?

The performance audit is a *comprehensive* examination of an organization or of any activity, conducted by an *independent analyst* reporting to an *interested third party*, that assesses *how well results match intentions* or *how well resource utilization matches results*.

There are two types of performance audits: 1) the management audit, which examines the use of resources and thus addresses *efficiency*, and 2) the program audit, which examines results and thus addresses *effectiveness*.

Performance audits are comprehensive in scope. They recognize an organization's relationship to its environment as well as the relationships among its parts. In short, they accept the assumptions of open-systems theory.

To be credible, audits must be conducted by people who are removed from possible rewards or retributions. For this reason, organization-wide performance audits usually are conducted by independent analysts. And the analysts report to people *other than* those who stand to gain or lose directly by the audit's findings: to third parties such as stockholders or the corporate board in the private sector, or to the legislative branch in the public sector. Audits of a single function such as personnel or marketing may be reported to the organization's chief executive, but are conducted by an external consultant.

Management audits compare the use of resources—land, labor, capital or time—to norms such as organizational policies or procedures, industry averages, common business practice or academic research findings. They emphasize the relationship between the organization's *inputs* and *outputs*. They compare present *conditions* (What is?) to desirable *criteria* (What should be?).

Program audits compare achievements to stated goals, objectives or intentions. They emphasize the relationship between the organization's stated purpose or mission and its achievements in several arenas: financial (return on investment, profit), social (contributions to social justice), economical (market share), geographical (impact on the surrounding community), technical (innovations affecting the industry) and strategic (long-term).

Any form of research that compares a norm to an existing condition or is conducted to improve existing conditions and induce change resembles a performance audit (see Parallels to the Performance Audit for some examples).

PARALLELS TO THE PERFORMANCE AUDIT

● Evaluation research, which compares an existing program to the features of a desired one.

● Action research—the basis of organization development—which compares existing conditions to the goals of the client or change agent.

● Critical research—an outgrowth of Marxist change theory—which identifies key aspects of an ideology (i.e., a value system) and uses inconsistencies between beliefs and practices to induce change.

● Job analysis, which compares an employee's duties and responsibilities to predetermined norms.

● Performance analysis, which compares employee performance to predefined standards.

Reprinted from TRAINING, June 1984

Finally, a key point: Performance audits assume a rational approach to organizational change. That is, their entire justification is based on the belief that decision makers will choose what is best for the organization if only the facts are sound. They do not assume that internal politics or interpersonal relationships will greatly influence decisions.

Conducting the performance audit

Though not all writers on the subject agree on the steps or sequence of steps in conducting a performance audit, most would include the 12 points outlined in Figure 1.

Step 1. Every audit begins with a directive: Somebody in authority *requests* the audit to explore a special issue. In other words, an audit grows out of the stated needs of decision makers or those who monitor the decision makers. The directive clearly defines the type of audit and the issues to be examined.

Step 2. The directive establishes the audit's objectives. The auditors must translate those objectives into an action plan—tasks to be completed and deadlines to be met during the audit project. At this point, the plan is tentative and subject to change as more information is gathered.

Step 3. Selection of the audit staff is a crucial step. The people chosen for the project must know something about the issue to be explored and the audit methods to be used to explore it. Suppose, for example, that the directive requires auditors to answer

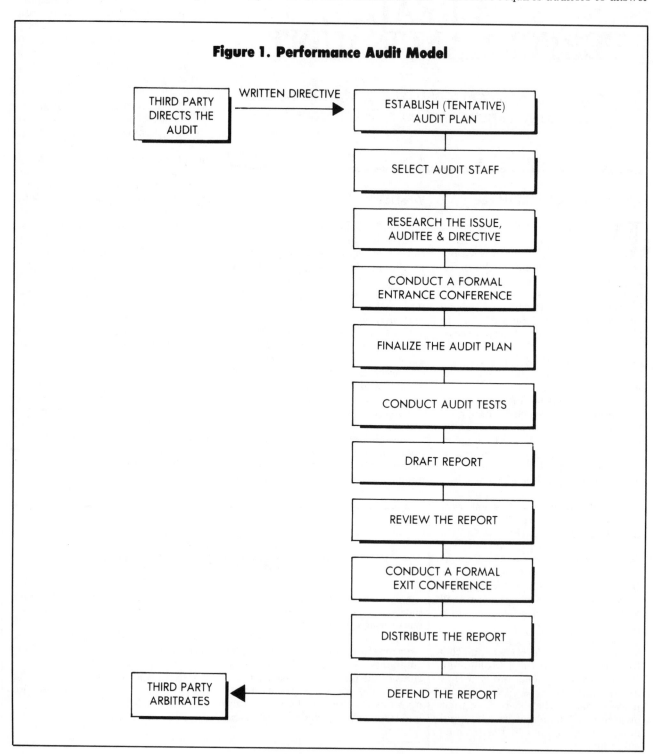

Figure 1. Performance Audit Model

THIRD PARTY DIRECTS THE AUDIT

WRITTEN DIRECTIVE

ESTABLISH (TENTATIVE) AUDIT PLAN

SELECT AUDIT STAFF

RESEARCH THE ISSUE, AUDITEE & DIRECTIVE

CONDUCT A FORMAL ENTRANCE CONFERENCE

FINALIZE THE AUDIT PLAN

CONDUCT AUDIT TESTS

DRAFT REPORT

REVIEW THE REPORT

CONDUCT A FORMAL EXIT CONFERENCE

DISTRIBUTE THE REPORT

THIRD PARTY ARBITRATES

DEFEND THE REPORT

the question: "Is excessive turnover hampering the efficiency of Factory X?" The audit objectives must specify *how the question will be answered* and what is meant by terms such as "excessive," "turnover" and "efficiency." The staff must be competent in examining turnover and in using the methods selected for doing so.

Step 4. The auditors need to research the project thoroughly. They must understand what prompted the audit to be sure their findings will be useful to those who wanted the issue examined in the first place. At the same time, they must research the issue itself. In a turnover study, for

---

Never invest in a full-scale audit to address simple issues or decisions that require immediate attention.

---

instance, they may want to locate reliable figures on national, local or industry turnover, and collect academic studies or other material on the subject. Finally, auditors must learn about the "auditee," the entity to be subjected to the audit. What is its history, structure, general reputation and purpose? Do these circumstances have any special bearing on the issues to be examined?

Step 5. The formal entrance conference is the first direct contact between auditors and auditees. If an entire organization is under audit, the conference is held with the top-management team. If only a part of the organization is to be audited, the conference is held only with the managers and supervisors in that section. The meeting's purpose is to make sure everybody understands the directive and the audit's objectives. At the same time, it gives auditors a chance to hear reactions from the people they'll be auditing and to gather more information on the issues.

Step 6. The auditors reformulate the objectives from the information gathered during background research and the entrance conference. The final plan spells out *what* will be examined, *how* it will be examined (see Performance Audit Tests) and *when* it will be examined. To ensure the plan's validity, auditors occasionally will ask

their colleagues to review it before implementation.

Step 7. Audit tests typically are conducted in the field. Auditors gather information on the "condition" of the auditee or on conditions affected by the auditee. When there is a significant gap between some criterion (What should be?) and the condition (What is?), auditors write a *finding* that stipulates cause, effect, criteria, condition and significance. They also may write a recommendation for dealing with the problem.

The types of tests selected by the auditors depend upon the issue under examination. Most quantitative and qualitative research methods—varying from linear programming to surveys—may be used. In a study of turnover, for example, statistical methods could reveal significant differences between rates in one company facility and others.

Step 8. The auditors draft a report that provides background information on the auditee and the issues. The report also presents important findings and recommendations for improvement. Each finding is supported by documentation that could stand up to rigorous scrutiny by third-party experts commissioned by the auditee.

Documentation is to the auditor what evidence is to a lawyer. Most auditors record any information they collect on work papers. Supervisors, the arbiters of quality control, check

the work papers for completeness and accuracy. Audit reports are written directly from work papers, and all facts are checked and rechecked.

Step 9. The draft report is given to the auditee for review. At this point the auditee may respond to the findings in writing, suggesting corrections, additions or modifications. Auditors can weigh these remarks and accept or reject them. Either way, however, auditee responses are included in the final draft report.

Step 10. The auditors meet with the key decision makers in the organization for an exit conference. Its purpose is to go over the final report, including any changes made as a result of the auditee's review. The exit conference presents an opportunity to make any last-minute changes or to discuss the implications of any part of the report.

Step 11. The final report is distributed to the auditee and to the third party that initiated the audit. The report is self-explanatory; it answers the questions found in the original directive.

Step 12. Auditors, auditee and third party meet to examine the issues, findings and recommendations in the report. The auditors function as plaintiffs, the auditees as defendants, and the third party as judge and jury. Based on the outcome of this meeting, the third party can a) reject the auditor's report, b) accept parts of the report or c) accept the entire report,

---

PERFORMANCE AUDIT TESTS

A performance audit test is any comparison between a normative criterion (What should be?) and the condition of the auditee (What is?). Auditors assume that all is well until the facts show otherwise; they do not try to second-guess management actions or decisions without extremely good reasons. Hence, two matters are of crucial concern: first, the *selection of criteria* that are authoritative, credible and convincing; second, the *selection of appropriate measurement methods* for assessing condition against criteria. Some examples include:

CRITERIA (What should be?)	MEASUREMENT METHODS (How can condition be compared to criteria?)	
• Information collected by government agencies	• Survey research	• Accounting techniques
• Information collected by industry or associations	• Cost/benefit analysis	• Queuing theory
• Information collected by academic researchers	• Linear programming	• Flowcharts
• Legal information	• Systems analysis	• Many others

Reprinted from TRAINING, June 1984

direct the auditee to change methods accordingly and establish some means to monitor those changes.

Clearly, the performance audit stresses the notion that management is *accountable* to others.

Depending on the issues to be ex-

Trainers too often tackle performance issues by the seat of their pants.

---

plored, such audits can require massive amounts of time, money and effort. They should never be initiated for addressing relatively simple issues or decisions that require immediate attention.

How trainers can use the performance audit

Performance auditors make some fundamental assumptions and use techniques that can be valuable to HRD specialists in their own perform-

ance-auditing activities.

Auditors usually limit their efforts strictly to projects at which they are *directed*. The reason? A directive implies that an issue genuinely matters to someone whose opinion counts. In other words, it implies powerful support for the audit. If auditors indiscriminately initiated their own efforts, they would be perceived as self-serving and run the risk that their findings and recommendations would be ignored.

Auditors follow rigorous standards, document their findings and submit their documentation for review by others—but they allow a third party to direct any action based on their results. They want to preserve the integrity of their work and, more important, their credibility.

Auditors may examine *any* facet of an organization's activities. Their playing field is not restricted to financial or instructional matters or even to individuals in a work environment. Hence, they are relatively free to take on issues of strategic planning or organizational culture traditionally ignored by accountants and trainers.

The trainer's role in many organizations is evolving beyond the simple providing of instruction related to specific tasks—evolving toward a broader role of engineering human performance. If that trend widens the

focus of attention to include not only individual competence but *organizational* competence, it is a good sign.

But trainers too often tackle performance issues by the seat of their pants. The predictable result is that a (nominal) performance-based approach to training will be tried, will fail miserably, and will stunt the evolution of this healthy trend.

Trainers can learn valuable lessons from people who approach the performance audit differently. By doing some learning as well as training, they can improve their own techniques and the outcomes of their audits.

Reprinted from TRAINING, June 1984

MORE ON THE PERFORMANCE AUDIT

Gilbert, Thomas F., *Human Competence: Engineering Worthy Performance.* (McGraw-Hill, New York, 1978).

Herbert, L., *Auditing the Performance of Management.* (Lifetime Learning, Belmont, CA, 1979).

Rummler, Geary, "The Performance Audit" (*Training and Development Handbook*, R.L. Craig, ed., 2nd ed., McGraw-Hill, New York, NY, 1976).

"Operational and program auditing: Introduction." A training course complete with videotape and trainee workbooks geared to novices. (CSG, 1979, Lexington, KY).

Standards for Audit of Governmental Organizations, Programs, Activities and Functions (The Comptroller General of the United States, Washington, DC).

SOFT SKILLS, HARD NUMBERS

Things get fuzzy when you try to quantify
a manager's competence:
How decisive? *How* analytical?
And who needs training in which particular skills?

BY RICHARD MIRABILE,
DAVID CALDWELL
AND CHARLES O'REILLY

When we ask whether our training and development efforts are "tied to the organization's strategic plan" or "helping the company meet bona fide business goals" or "aimed at the genuine needs of individuals" or "worth the money," we usually aren't talking about technical training. We're talking instead about "soft-skills" training, and particularly management training.

One reason for this probably is that we're much more precise about designing and delivering technical training than we are about management training. If we want to teach a hard skill such as computer repair, for instance, we find out exactly what a repair technician *needs to know* in order to do the particular job we have in mind. Then we teach those necessary skills—and very little else. We find out what a "master performer" looks like and we break down that performance into specific skills, knowledge and behavior. We can then spot particular areas where a given trainee falls short

of mastery, and concentrate our instruction on those areas. With technical training, we can work with a scalpel.

When it comes to management training, on the other hand, we're still slopping it on with a bucket. We lump together all the organization's second-level managers, for instance, and send them to the same course on time management or interpersonal communication or decision making without ever identifying either the skills a given individual already has or the particular skills that managers in a given department need *most*.

The bucket approach can make sense up to a point—it may give us a desirable consistency of management style, for instance. But it doesn't address the particular training needs of individuals, and it makes it tough to pinpoint the benefits we're getting for our management-training dollars.

It doesn't have to be that way. Pinpointing precise training and development needs in the management ranks may never be as clear-cut as it is in the technical area. But it is a process that can be more rigorous—much more rigorous—than it has been in the past. We can begin a management development program the way we'd begin a technical training effort, i.e., attempt to identify the specific skills and knowledge needed to be a successful manager or supervisor in this organization, and base our training on those needs.

First we can try to identify and de-

FIGURE 1
DESCRIPTION OF COMPETENCIES

Analytical Thinking
Discriminates between important and unimportant details, recognizes inconsistencies between facts and draws inferences from information.

Forecasting
Accurately anticipates changes in workloads, resources and personnel needs, etc., as a result of changes in the work situation, technology or external developments.

Goal Orientation
Ensures that the results to be achieved by the division, units, teams or individuals are clearly defined and understood at all times.

Knowledge of Subordinate Jobs
Thorough understanding of the purpose, general tasks, knowledge and skill requirements of the jobs under one's supervision.

Knowledge of User Support Areas
A basic understanding of the various user areas being supported, their needs and technical requirements.

Multiple Focus
Effectively manages a large number, i.e., 10–15, of different and often conflicting objectives, projects, groups or activities at one time.

Organizational Knowledge
Thorough understanding of organizational policies, procedures and key personnel that enables a manager/supervisor to effectively carry out job responsibilities.

Priority Setting
Identifies and separates those tasks that are most important from those that are less important; maintains a clear sense of priorities and a vision of the larger picture.

Risk Taking
Takes risks when the consequences are difficult to predict but the payoffs are likely to be great, even when proposals may be rejected by superiors or when one's image may suffer if wrong.

scribe a "master" manager (perhaps a hypothetical one) and probe the specific competencies needed to master the job. Then we can look at each individual currently holding the job we're describing, measure the individual against those standards and use the results to decide whether there's a need for training in some specific area. (The results also can help us determine whether a person's strengths would better serve the demands of another job.) It's a six-step process.

1 **Interview job incumbents and their supervisors to find out exactly what it is that managers in a particular department do.** Focus on the job's major tasks, responsibilities, knowledge and skill requirements, time spent in various activities, and any other factors they believe are related to successful job performance. Next, analyze all the interview data and turn it into behaviorally oriented job competencies. Each one should represent a separate knowledge, skill or ability (KSA) that a person needs to perform well as a manager or supervisor in this section of the organization. In other words, conduct a competency-based needs assessment.

Show the first draft of those competency statements to a group of incumbent managers and ask them to edit, revise and—most important—make sure you haven't forgotten

FIGURE 2
PRIORITY RATINGS OF JOB COMPETENCIES VERSUS CHARACTERISTICS OF MANAGER JONES

KSA*	Mean Rating of Priorities	Mean Rating of Jones	Difference
Priority Setting	8.75	6.00	−2.75
Organizing and Planning	7.50	6.00	−1.50
Multiple Focus	7.50	8.00	+0.50
Decisiveness	7.25	6.33	−0.91
Communication Skills — Oral	7.25	6.66	−0.58
Selection	7.25	6.33	−0.91
Delegation	7.00	5.00	−2.00
Organizational Knowledge	7.00	5.00	−0.66
Analytical Thinking	6.75	5.00	−1.75
Motivation	6.50	4.66	−1.83
Fact Finding	6.50	4.33	−2.16
Goal Orientation	6.50	6.66	+0.16
Strategic Thinking	6.50	4.33	−2.16
Team Building	6.50	5.33	−1.16
Forecasting	6.25	5.00	−1.25
Management Efficiency	6.25	6.00	−0.25
Systems Perspective	6.25	6.33	+0.08
Negotiation	6.25	5.33	−0.91
Developing Others	6.00	3.00	−3.00
Risk Taking	6.00	6.66	+0.66
Leadership	6.00	6.33	+0.33
Time Management	6.00	6.66	+0.66
Knowledge of Business Management	5.75	4.00	−1.75
Conflict Resolution	5.75	4.00	−1.75
Flexibility	5.75	6.33	+0.58

*Knowledge/Skill/Ability

FIGURE 3
PROFICIENCY RATINGS — MANAGER'S JOB

Name: JONES

KSA	Proficiency Level Required	Individual Proficiency	KSA	Proficiency Level Required	Individual Proficiency
Accessibility	4.4	3.8	Feedback	4.7	3.3
Analytical Thinking	4.8	3.6	Flexibility	4.8	4.5
Assertiveness/Autonomy	4.4	3.3	Forecasting	4.1	2.2
Coaching	4.4	4.8	Goal Orientation	4.1	4.2
Communication — Oral	4.6	3.1	Innovation	4.1	4.2
Communication — Written	4.8	4.3	Knowledge of Subordinate Jobs	4.4	2.3
Conducting Meetings	4.6	3.0	Leadership	4.7	2.0
Conflict Resolution	4.4	4.6	Motivation	4.6	4.3
Control Systems	4.3	2.8	Negotiation	4.4	2.0
Coordination	4.6	4.6	Networking	4.6	3.8
Decisiveness	4.6	3.1	Organizing and Planning	4.7	3.6
Delegation	4.6	3.0	Organizational Knowledge	4.1	4.0
Development of Others	4.7	4.3	Participation	4.2	4.2
Energy Level	4.9	2.9	Persistence	4.4	3.8
Fact Finding	4.7	3.2			

5	4	3	2	1
Maximum		Moderate		Minimal

FIGURE 4
TRAINING NEEDS FOR MANAGEMENT GROUP
(By Required Proficiency Level)

Item	SMITH	JONES	BANKS	JENKINS	McNALLEY	RENFRO	GALLOWAY	KELLY	Percent Below Level
Organizing & Planning	X	X	X	X	X	X	O	X	100
Problem Solving	X	X	X	X	X	X	O	X	100
Priority Setting	O	X	O	X	O	X	O	O	100
Motivation	X	X	X	X	X	X	O	X	100
Management Efficiency	X		O	X	X	O	O	X	87
Assertiveness/Autonomy	X		X	X	X	X	X	X	87
Delegation	X		O	X	X	X	O	X	87
Selection	X	X	X		O	O	X	O	87
Leadership	X	X	X	X	X		X	X	87
Knowledge of User Support	O	X	X	X	O		O	X	87
Attention to Detail	O		X	X		O	O	X	75
Control	O		O		X	X	X	O	75
Flexibility			X	X	X	X	X	X	75
Forecasting	O		X		X	O	X	X	75
Goal Orientation	X		X	X		X	X	X	75
Oral Communication	X	X		X		X	X	X	75
Organizing & Planning	O		O		O	O	X	X	75
Risk Taking	X	X	X	X			X	X	75
Strategic Thinking	O		O	O	O	O	O		75
Systems Perspective	X	X	X	X		X	X		75
Decisiveness	O		X	X	X	X	X		75
Time Management			Δ		X	O	O	X	62
Written Communication	X	X	X				X	X	62
Conflict Resolution		X	X	Δ			O	Δ	62

KEY: Δ High Discrepancy O Moderate Discrepancy X Low Discrepancy

any crucial job skills. Based on those suggestions, prepare a final list of competencies. (A partial list from a recent project is shown in Figure 1. This particular analysis was done for supervisors and managers of an insurance company's data processing division.)

2 Use the competency statements to describe each individual job. To do this, give the statements to each supervisor and manager along with instructions on how to profile his or her job. Each person needs to judge every competency statement according to how important it is to performing the job successfully. Armed with all these responses, you can then create a consensus profile for each position.

3 You now have profiles describing the relative importance of each skill for successful job performance. But those profiles don't spell out the de-

gree of competence that's needed for *high* performance. Some skills, though necessary, might not require detailed understanding or advanced levels of proficiency. Other skills may demand a higher level of mastery. To pinpoint these differences, ask a group of senior managers to rate the proficiency levels required for each "competency" and use the answers to prepare overall proficiency levels.

Once these three steps are complete, the supervisor and manager jobs can be described as profiles of the specific competencies and the level at which each one should be mastered. (We'll illustrate shortly.)

4 Next, use the competencies to identify the strengths and weaknesses of each manager and supervisor. How? Give the complete list of job profile competencies to each individual, his or her boss, and a peer who works with the person. These three raters

(working separately) look at each competency and judge how characteristic it is of the individual who is being evaluated. The three evaluations are correlated for a mean score.

Figure 2 shows how manager Jones' strengths and weaknesses compared to the priority profile for his job. (The highest possible mean score for any KSA would have been 9.0.) Note that the comparison in Figure 2 does not tell us how Jones' performance stacks up against the required *proficiency* levels that we identified in Step 3. It tells us only what the *high-priority* competencies are, and shows us where Jones is likely to need help first.

5 Now the three raters can go ahead and evaluate Jones' *proficiency* in each KSA area, using the same scale they applied in Step 3 to rate the *desired* proficiency level for each one. With this information, it's relatively simple to identify specific training requirements for an individual manager: We just compare the person's mastery of the specific competencies with the degree of mastery required for the job. Figure 3 shows how manager Jones' proficiencies stack up.

Wherever an individual's proficiency rating falls short of the desired level, we have a training need. And by balancing proficiency shortfalls against the priorities we have assigned to various KSAs, we can create training priority plans for individual managers and for groups. Obviously, the idea will be to concentrate our efforts in those competency areas rated most important to the job profile and where the greatest discrepancy exists between the individual's proficiency and the level of mastery we want. Figure 4 shows what we might learn about a department with eight managers (or supervisors) in it.

6 **This model is also useful for preparing individual career plans.** If we use the same set of KSAs for both supervisory and higher-level management jobs (that is, if the priorities and desired proficiency levels vary from

---

> ## Use the competencies to identify the strengths and weaknesses of each manager.

---

job to job but the KSAs themselves don't), then we can see whether the strengths and weaknesses of particular individuals make them likely candidates for promotion to particular jobs. We can even use correlation coefficients (calculate the overall correlation between the mean scores in Figure 2, for example) to come up with relative rankings of supervisors who would be most likely to succeed as second-level managers. Coupled with other information about the candidates' performance, this data can be very helpful in decisions about placements and promotions.

This competency-based training model is useful for several reasons. It's more closely tied to the business than traditional needs assessments because it uses consensus to determine which skills are needed for a specific position in a particular business, and what constitutes high performance in that job. It's not difficult to do. It yields specific information that's likely to be highly accurate. Moreover, if you're in a fast-changing business, the approach can be modified to project competency requirements for the "manager of the future," thus linking the selection or development of such a person directly to the organization's future business needs.

Reprinted from TRAINING, August 1987

WHEN TRAINERS SHOULD TALK THEMSELVES OUT OF A JOB

The performance improvement business is not for everyone

BY STEPHEN P. BECKER

Many trainers expect too little of themselves. They perform their primary function of developing and conducting educational programs, then toss in a few sideline activities like consultation, counseling, and involvement in organizational politics. But training programs alone will never cause any significant organizational improvement.

Aside from training, there are two major components of performance. The first is the selection and placement of personnel and the second is the motivational environment created by an organization. To understand better why selection and placement is an important component of organizational performance, assume that you're in a company that has a penchant for doing a poor job of selecting and placing its management people. Of course, doing a lousy selection job is never intentional. There are a variety of reasons why this might happen. You could have an incompetent recruiter, a key line manager who is a poor judge of character, or an organizational philosophy which dictates that promotions be based on loyalty which is demonstrated by years of service. You may also be in an industry, company, or location which is not considered attractive to perspective supervisors and managers. Perhaps pay scales are too low.

Whatever the reason, you may find a steady stream of mediocre people flowing into your training programs. You may have produced an excellent training program in every respect, but if your trainees are basically incompetent, you can't realistically expect them to be competent performers after completing your program. To put it simply, if you take a jerk and put him through a great training program, what you'll have when it's over is a well-trained jerk.

Looking at training from this perspective, it would be difficult to justify a lack of involvement in the selection and placement process. Trainers must take some responsibility for making sure the right people get into the training programs and systems. To adopt a position that you will train anybody you are told to, just to show training activity, is not only unethical but bad business as well. The least you should be doing is exercising veto power. You may not have a lot to say about who participates in training, but if you spot a loser or somebody who, in your judgment, is a poor placement, you should yell like hell. This will not only make you feel better, but it's good for your organization.

It may also have some real benefits to the trainee. For example, you have a man who has been hired as a sales trainee. During the first few months of employment you are able to determine that he has little sales ability. Obviously, it would be a waste of money for the organization to continue training this individual. To recommend terminating his employment at this point in time is appropriate. In some organizations, the line managers consider this quite a service.

If you think your job is to train and not to fire, you are wrong twice. Your job is to see to it, as best you can, that your organization is staffed with competent performers who can achieve organizational goals. To do this effec-

---

DON'T CHEAT ON THIS SELF-GRADED QUIZ

Training alone doesn't necessarily result in performance improvement for every employee. Performance is also affected by selection and placement and the motivational environment in an organization. The following self-graded quiz brings this concept into clearer perspective. Fill in the space at the end of the equations with one of three words—poor, OK, or good—to describe the organizational performance you would expect in each of these 12 situations.

Selection & Placement	X	Training	X	Motivational Environment	=	Organizational Performance
Poor		Poor		Poor	=	_____
Poor		OK		Poor	=	_____
Poor		OK		OK	=	_____
OK		OK		OK	=	_____
OK		Good		OK	=	_____
Good		Good		Poor	=	_____
OK		Good		Good	=	_____
OK		OK		Good	=	_____
Poor		Good		Poor	=	_____
OK		OK		Poor	=	_____
Good		Poor		Good	=	_____
Good		Good		Good	=	_____

tively, trainers must have some impact on selection and placement.

Let's consider the value of blowing the whistle on an individual who is being trained for the wrong job. Say you have reason to believe a certain trainee will not be a high, or even average, achiever in the job for which he is being trained. When you make the situation known to the trainee's current manager, his future manager, and the appropriate personnel managers, the chances are good that there will be an in-depth discussion about the individual and his position in the organization. One result of the discussion may be a better assignment for the trainee. Or management may decide to arrange a series of career counseling sessions. Future failure on the job will probably be avoided. In general, the organization and the individual will profit if the training is stopped. To allow this trainee to continue in the program, get a certificate of completion, and start the new job would be irresponsible. If, after all discussions are completed, everybody concerned (including the trainee) decides to allow him to finish the program, then so be it. You did the best job you could—which was a whole lot more than merely conducting a training program.

Another component of performance is the motivational environment in the organization. This environment is determined by the organizational structure, the compensation system, and other systems such as MBO, performance appraisals, job enrichment, and career path planning which are used in managing human resources. It also includes things such as feedback systems, consequences for good or bad job performance, and the types of personal behavior that are normal. The critical cog in the motivational environment is the philosophy and style of supervision and management. The environment can motivate

an employee to do better work, make commitments, want to contribute and learn more, and progress up the ladder as far as he can. It can also produce the opposite result. Motivation is desire. To a great extent it can be increased, reduced, or held constant by the environment in which an individual works.

It doesn't take a lot of imagination to realize that even with outstanding training, a poor motivational environment can produce marginal performance. This may be the case even if the trainees were well selected and properly placed. Their poor performance on the job may have nothing whatever to do with the quality of training. Now if you can buy into this perspective, your job becomes broader than just producing training programs. If you believe the criteria for evaluating training is performance on the job, then you'll have to reexamine the expectations of your own role as a trainer. In essence, you'll have to take some responsibility for improving the motivational environment so your graduates will have a good chance of effectively using the things they learned during training.

This brings us to the real issue. You may perceive yourself as having no influence and no responsiblity for selection and placement or the motivational environment. If this is the case, then don't use performance on the job to measure and evaluate the effectiveness of your training programs and systems. There are plenty of well-trained people who are not performing very well. If you see yourself as having some responsibility for all three components—selection, training, and environment—then job performance is a good way to measure your efforts. It's still not a good criteria to measure training programs because performance is determined by more than training. If training alone could cause the performance of an organiza-

tion to improve, then we'd have it made. But it's just not that easy.

So you have to make a choice. You must choose your perspective. You may choose to be in the training business, which is the narrow perspective. Or you may choose to be in the organizational performance improvement business, which is the broader perspective. One is not better than the other—just different. Once you have made your choice, you will have a better idea of who you are, what your responsibilities are, what to expect from yourself, and what competencies you'll need.

Personally, I choose the performance improvement business. It's much more difficult in many ways. It takes longer to get where you want to go, it requires more behavioral science knowledge and skills, and it demands that you take many more risks on the job. You have to challenge established policy and procedure. You have to try to get people hired, fired, transferred, and promoted. You have to confront executives whose management style is more destructive than constructive. You constantly have to propose new ways of managing. You have to play politics. You have to be right (most of the time). You have to be able to implement your suggestions and be willing to be evaluated by the results.

Being in the performance improvement business is a very ambitious undertaking. Not every trainer should attempt it. In most organizations, nobody else expects you to take on such a burden. The perspective of basing your self-espectations and organizational role on the three components of organizational performance will have to start with you. If you can't resist the challenge, be aware that there is much frustration to be faced along with the excitement. Those of us who are moving from more traditional training to performance improvement may not achieve all our goals, but we have had a heck of an experience.

Reprinted from TRAINING, June 1976

ASSESSING YOUR NEEDS ASSESSMENT

As a reactive process, it's essential.
But a proactive needs assessment
can be even better

BY BARBARA BOWMAN

Motherhood, apple pie and needs assessment. Everyone who's anyone in the corporate education business is quick to avow that a needs assessment is the essential first step in planning a training program: Before you try to correct a performance problem, you have to know what's causing it. The academic literature treats needs assessment as a given in any acceptable methodology. The Instructional Systems Development (ISD) model emphasizes needs identification. The American Society for Training and Development lists "needs analyst" as a critical role of the training professional.

Nevertheless, a 1985 survey of TRAINING Magazine subscribers found that 62% of the respondents do not do a formal, structured needs assessment for all training projects, and that only 47% "spend considerable time trying to discriminate between training needs and non-training needs."

It appears that while human resources development (HRD) professionals universally acknowledge the theoretical benefits of needs assessment, relatively few actually reap them. Conducting a vigorous needs assessment is like exercising, eating well and flossing our teeth: We all

know we *should*, but. . . .

Why do so many trainers neglect needs assessment? Perhaps because they see it as a time-consuming process, little understood or appreci-

---

**Nobody ever says,
'That was a terrific
needs assessment!'**

---

ated by line managers, that yields few tangible results. After all, nobody ever says, "Great job, Perkins! That was a terrific needs assessment!" The response is more likely to be, "Are you still monkeying around doing research? When do we get the program?"

Needs assessment does pay off, however, for both the HRD staff and the organization. Properly conducted, a needs assessment not only identifies training needs, but also builds participant commitment, generates management support, increases the HRD department's credibility and provides data for that other sacred process: evaluation.

The key phrase here is "properly

conducted." By following a few practical guidelines, you can ensure that your needs assessments produce the data you need to plan training, while you build support among employees and managers for the process and the resulting programs. If your needs assessment isn't achieving these results, ask yourself how well it meets these guidelines.

Don't wait to be asked

According to the ISD model, a needs assessment is conducted whenever a line manager requests training or refers a problem to the training department. Certainly such a request requires a detailed needs assessment, but here the training department is acting in a reactive mode. It is the proactive type of needs assessment that so often is neglected.

A proactive HRD staff anticipates educational needs for the next year or more and develops the links between the organization's strategic plan and its training plans. This assessment may have to be changed in response to surprises or problems that alter the strategic plan, but it still serves as the basis for programming during a given time frame.

A proactive assessment can identify a variety of needs: retraining workers whose current jobs are to be phased out; preparing managers for a reorganization; offering stress management training to people whose jobs will be restructured; or anticipating the launch of a new product line. An HRD department that waits to be asked to develop such programs loses the chance to deal with these issues before they become problems.

In other words, a needs assessment does not merely determine whether training should be offered at all, or what type of program would be suitable. The dog must wag the tail, not vice versa: Programs flow from assessment, not assessment from suggested programs.

Communicate the purpose

Once you decide to conduct a proactive needs assessment, explain its purpose to everyone involved. Managers need to know why you're doing it, how the data will be used, what to expect in terms of their own and their staff's involvement, and how to respond to employee ques-

NEEDS ANALYSIS: WHOSE PROBLEM IS THIS?

We all know the commandment that says, "Thou shalt not prescribe training for a non-training problem." We also know that if a department manager or a supervisor tells you that someone in his department "has a training need," you're not going to be able to help until you can determine who needs training: the employee, the supervisor or both.

As trainers at the Gulf Bank of Kuwait, Graham Nugent and Pamela Buckley received frequent requests for help from managers of the bank's 1,000 employees, who represent 80 different nationalities. After an initial, frustrating scramble to be responsive, Nugent and Buckley decided that some preliminary evaluation was in order.

Now, Buckley reports, "When a manager comes to us and points to a subordinate who is 'not performing up to standard,' we operate on the premise that at least three of the fingers on the accusing hand should be pointed in the direction of the manager."

To find out who actually is in need of training in such situations, Nugent and Buckley first meet with the requesting manager for some penetrating discussion. They go over the following list of open-ended questions:

• *Planning and organizing.* How do you establish employee performance goals? How do you establish priority and time sequences for job tasks? How do you ensure that employees have sufficient resources to perform their jobs?

• *Delegating.* When assigning activities, how do you determine whether employees have the knowledge and skills a particular task requires? How do you encourage employees to perform on their own? How do you determine which responsibilities to delegate? When you have to "dump" some of your tasks on employees—and you both know they're undesirable tasks—how do you motivate them? How do you tell them that you'd prefer to see "recommmendations" rather than just problems? How do you balance your supervision between benign neglect and hovering over their shoulders?

• *Motivating.* How often do you discuss your employees' aspirations and ambitions with them? How do you ensure that your feedback is appropriate, timely and focused on improving performance? How do your employees know that you respect them? How often do you schedule time to talk with them? When planning assignments, how do you determine which employees' professional development needs will be served by giving them particular tasks to handle?

• *Directing.* How can clearly defined procedures increase the efficiency of routine tasks? How often do you request status reports when monitoring assignments? How do your employees typically respond when you provide timely and appropriate correction? What guidelines do you follow to ensure that your discussions with employees are confidential and professional? How do you encourage the airing of serious differences of opinion without creating hostility or anxiety?

This discussion itself is a form of one-to-one training for the manager, note Buckley and Nugent. Sometimes, they say, the session helps managers see that it's their behavior that needs to change, not their employees'. But if the manager is doing a good job, they move on to another set of questions:

• *Examine the job.* How is the job described? What is its purpose? What activities does it require? What are the performance standards?

• *Review training needs.* What knowledge and skills does the job require? Was the employee hired with these skills? Has anything new been added to the job since the employee began? Has new technology affected the job requirements? What training has the employee gotten?

• *Assess the individual's performance.* Are performance standards being met? What additional skills are needed? Does the employee have these skills?

Once they've gone over this last set of questions, Nugent and Buckley report, managers have a much better idea of what they want from the trainers, and the trainers have pinpointed where the need lies.

Reprinted from TRAINING, September 1986

---

tions. They also need to know how long the process will take.

To the uninitiated, a rigorous needs assessment may seem interminable; and indeed, gathering and analyzing data is a lengthy process. To maintain the support of line managers, however, develop a precise timetable at the outset and follow it conscientiously.

Employees also need to know the purpose of the assessment and the importance of their participation in order to develop realistic expectations of the process. Communicate what the needs assessment is *not* intended to accomplish as well as what it is. It will not, for example, lead to boosts or cuts in salaries.

When it comes to getting the word out, more is better. Some good ways to keep everyone informed: Give a presentation to managers that outlines the purpose of the assessment; write memos to all employees; attend staff meetings on request to answer questions; publicize your objectives in the employee newsletter; and designate one person in the HRD department to answer questions from employees.

A needs assessment is an ideal opportunity to develop management support for training by soliciting managers' active involvement in the process. The assessment *must* be perceived as the organization's project, not just the training department's project. Several strategies can help you accomplish this: Present the proposal and timetable to management for discussion and endorsement; ask the CEO or another executive to sign the memo announcing the needs assessment; ask managers at all levels for their input during the planning stage; interview key managers early in the process; give middle management an overview of the preliminary results and incorporate their comments into the final report.

It's not a questionnaire

Ever hear a trainer say, "I gave out a needs assessment"? A questionnaire is not a needs assessment. It may be one part of the assessment, but much more is needed.

> ## It must be perceived as the organization's project, not just the training department's project.

An effective needs assessment synthesizes the organization's needs and the employees' perceptions of needs. If the employees' ideas are neglected, you are missing an opportunity to build commitment to programs. A two-year study at Children's Hospital of Wisconsin, for example, showed a significantly higher level of satisfaction with training programs among employees who had participated in a needs assessment than among those who did not participate.

Certainly employees are able to identify their individual needs, but their perceptions alone are not enough. Nor can the HRD department determine what the organization needs. If training is to have genuine impact, if concepts taught in class are to be reinforced on the job, if management is to support programs financially, a broad perspective is essential.

A variety of methods can help you objectively identify both individual and organizational needs. The strategic plan and objectives of the organization, performance appraisals, productivity and quality assurance statistics, minutes of safety and other committee meetings, exit interviews,

customer complaints and plain old observation provide valuable information about the organization's needs. Interviews, questionnaires and focus groups are useful in identifying employees' perceptions of needs.

When you use a questionnaire, include respondents from various levels of management and compare their perceptions of training needs. If opinions vary, fine: You are still receiving valuable data. For example, if managers rate customer relations as a high-priority training topic while employees see it as of little importance, you may have uncovered a failure to communicate organizational goals or feedback from clients. This gives you another potential training need to investigate.

Watch you P's and Q's

In order to protect the credibility of the HRD department, use research methods that are above reproach. Base questionnaires on the results of interviews, not on preconceived notions or a review of the academic literature. Use appropriate sampling techniques to select people to be interviewed and to pretest the questionnaire before you circulate the final version.

Using statistics properly to analyze questionnaire results is a key issue here. Are you using appropriate measures? Applying the correct tests? Considering the correct indicators of significance? Trainers who are not comfortable with statistics may need assistance at this stage of the needs assessment. It will be well worth the investment, especially if the results will be reviewed by managers with expertise in statistical methods.

The HRD staff's reputation and credibility are not based on technical competence alone. Another crucial element is trust. If you hope to collect candid information, assure respondents that their answers will remain confidential and use the data only for the purposes you discuss with them. Managers should have the opportunity to react to findings of the needs assessment and provide clarification or further information before the assessment is complete. They should not receive unpleasant surprises in the final report. In short, apply the same ethical principles in a needs as-

sessment that would govern any organization development intervention.

Is it a training problem?

One classic function of a needs assessment is, of course, to distinguish between problems that can be solved through training and those that require other solutions. You've discovered a disturbing number of customer complaints about certain services? A failure to meet production standards? Widespread resentment over certain management practices? Good. Now find out *why.*

Do the problems stem from a lack

> ## A key use: to find out if a performance problem is, indeed, a training problem.

of skills or knowledge among certain employees (i.e., are they training problems?)? Or do they result from poor procedures, lack of feedback, inadequate supervision or some other factor that training alone won't fix? Once you make that determination, you should neither recommend training solutions for non-training problems, nor sweep training problems back under the rug.

Address these issues and, if appropriate, recommend HRD staff involvement in interventions other than training. In some cases, a simple recommendation for further study may suffice.

Feedback

Now you have conducted a brilliant needs assessment that has produced incredible insights into your organization's needs. But no one will know about it—unless you put considerable effort into a report of your findings.

Prepare your report as soon as the project is completed. Include an introduction that clearly states the purpose of the assessment; the dates during which it was conducted; its specific objectives; an explanation of the methodology and sources of data; analysis of data gathered, including statistical analysis of questionnaire results; a statement of results and the needs that have been identified; and, finally, recommendations. Appendices should include copies of questionnaires and interview formats, observation checklists and other tools used in data gathering and analysis.

Results of the assessment may also be presented and discussed at a management meeting. In fact, the more ways you can come up with to communicate results to management, the better. None of these, however, eliminates the need for a permanent record of the assessment that can be distributed to all managers and routed to key staff.

Everyone involved in the assessment process deserves feedback about its outcome. At the very least, send a letter thanking them for their participation and briefly summarizing the results and the action to be taken. Feedback sessions with groups of managers and employees are even better. Features in company publications are another excellent way to communicate the results to all employees.

A needs assessment is not a one-time endeavor. Employees who spend time on a questionnaire or in interviews will be unlikely to participate a second time if they see no results from the first round.

Once the needs assessment is completed, plan to maintain the data flow begun during the process. Continue to monitor minutes of meetings, exit interviews, production standards and other sources of information so that further needs may be identified as soon as possible. Use needs assessments as an additional source of evaluation. The data can help you measure the overall impact of individual training programs on the organization's and employees' needs. If the programs are meeting real needs, subsequent assessments should show that the problems you're trying to fix have been at least partially alleviated. If not, you have a problem with these programs that needs immediate attention.

You also can use follow-up assessments to evaluate employee satisfaction with training and to correlate this satisfaction level with a variety of variables such as department, shift, job classification, seniority, education, etc. Keep this consideration in mind while you construct the original questionnaire so that you can establish baseline data.

These guidelines will not solve all your needs assessment problems. The process will remain time-consuming and challenging. Managers who are certain they know exactly what employees need will still see it as a waste of time. But these ideas can help you conduct a valid needs assessment that produces results that management will believe and support. And that's accomplishing a lot.

Reprinted from TRAINING, January 1987

HOW TO USE NOMINAL GROUP TECHNIQUE TO ASSESS TRAINING NEEDS

Nominal Group Technique combines features of several traditional needs-assessment methods to collect useful data on training needs

BY EDWARD L. HARRISON,
PAUL H. PIETRI AND CARL C. MOORE

Many trainers are a bit puzzled and uncertain in the early stages of developing management-training courses—mostly because they lack a feel for the organization and the many variables that should be reflected in the ultimate design. We're often faced with selecting an assessment strategy on the basis of the limited data on hand. As Stephen V. Steadham has pointed out (see reading list), we must *learn* to identify the factors that influence the choice of a needs-assessment strategy.

A number of needs-assessment methods are useful in course design, including observation, questionnaires, consultation, print media, interviews, group discussions, tests, records and reports, and work samples. The Nominal Group Technique (NGT)—so called because it uses a group of people who "nominate" problems and issues that deserve attention—combines several of these traditional methods.

Andre Delberg and his colleagues describe NGT as a data-collection method "useful in situations where individual judgments must be tapped and combined to arrive at decisions which cannot be calculated by one person." Trainers have used NGT in a variety of situations—it has even been used as an organizational communications tool and as an organization-development technique. Basically, NGT involves several noninteracting individuals who follow a structured format in developing the desired information. A group facilitator, called a "grouper," leads them through the format.

When you want to generate new information, a significant strength of the NGT is its noninteracting feature. In an interacting group, some individuals often will simply react to ideas rather than produce original ones of their own. In the nominal group, however, the members are not permitted to talk with one another during the initial data-generation stage. Trainers using the NGT allow participants to list their responses

Figure 1
Nominal Grouping Sequence

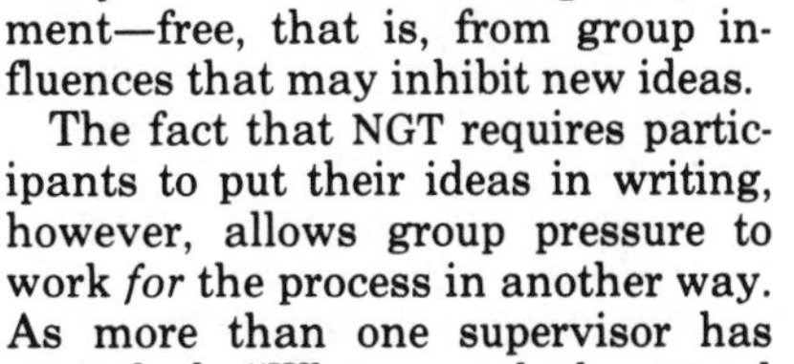

Listing	→	Recording	→
Collating	→	Prioritizing	→

freely in a nonthreatening environment—free, that is, from group influences that may inhibit new ideas.

The fact that NGT requires participants to put their ideas in writing, however, allows group pressure to work *for* the process in another way. As more than one supervisor has remarked, "When you look around and see everyone else writing things down, you feel like you'd better dig in and get busy too."

The structured NGT format includes the four sequential steps shown in Figure 1.

Listing—We define listing as generation of items in writing by the group members. There is no discussion at this stage.

Recording—In recording, the listed items from each group member are noted by the grouper on a flip chart or similar device in full view of the entire group. Again, no discussion is allowed except for explanation or clarification of an item.

Collating—Collating involves clarifying, simplifying and organizing the listed items. Some items may be combined or grouped logically. No discussion, except for clarification, is allowed.

Prioritizing—The grouper leads individual voting on the priority of items. The group decision on priorities is mathematically derived through ordering or rating by each individual member.

Items thus recorded represent the best efforts of each individual. Each member should have played an equal role in the final prioritizing.

Needs assessment

A large company recently asked us to determine the supervisory training needs of several hundred of its first-line supervisors who were located at plant sites in several states. Because of the urgency of the company's desire to implement the program, the needs-assessment phase had to be handled relatively quickly. The amount of time during which company personnel would be available was limited.

We decided to use NGT as the primary data-collection tool. Accordingly, we held nominal grouping sessions with supervisors at several company locations. Approximately 10 supervisors representing cross sections of the firm's operation were involved in each session. (Ideally, of course, a needs assessment also should reflect the views of middle managers, personnel managers and workers under first-line supervision.)

We asked the supervisors in each group to respond to this question: What are the most critical human-resource problems that prevent you from achieving maximum effectiveness? Each supervisor responded in writing on a sheet of paper not seen by other members.

After the participants listed several items, we asked each to contribute one item from his or her list. These were recorded on newsprint where

Figure 2

NGT Results: Prioritized Responses to Question:
"What are the MOST critical human resource problems that prevent supervisors from achieving maximum effectiveness?"

Supervisors — Plant #1
1. On-the-job safety violations
2. Motivating the new, young employee
3. Maintaining high morale in crew during periods of increased production demands
4. Higher management's continued emphasis on production output vs. man-hours worked
5. Opening two-way communication with my crew

Supervisors — Plant #2
1. Communications between crews
2. Violation of safety rules
3. -nPoor attitude among new employees
4. Foreman failing to make clear company policies, rules and conditions of the job
5. Untrained employees

Supervisors — Plant #3
1. Reluctance of men to work as a team
2. Communications, up and down
3. Absenteeism
4. Accidents on the job
5. Lack of harmony between Canadian and American workers

Figure 3

Management Development Course Design Process Using NGT

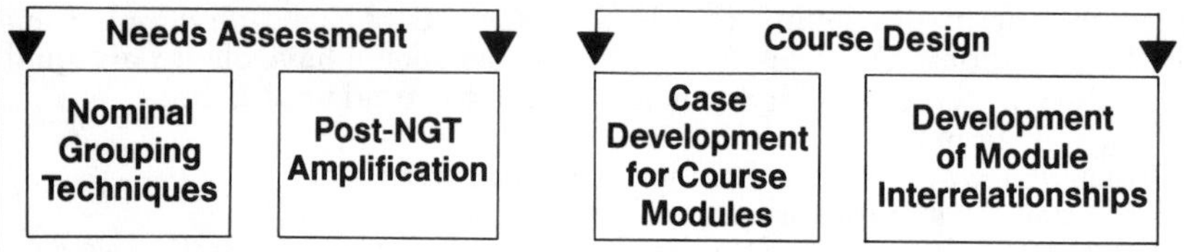

Needs Assessment		Course Design	
Nominal Grouping Techniques	Post-NGT Amplification	Case Development for Course Modules	Development of Module Interrelationships

the entire group could see them. Each supervisor continued to contribute items from his list in round-robin fashion until all of the problems were recorded on several sheets of newsprint taped to the walls of the room. Each trainee group identified an average of 35 different problems.

We led discussions of the problems in an attempt to clarify them. However, we made no attempt to "sell" any particular problem and we discouraged the trainees from doing so.

Group members then were asked to write on a separate sheet of paper the five most critical problems from the many listed, ranking them with No. 5 being the most critical. The rankings were recorded on the newsprint adjacent to each item. By calculating and totaling weights assigned to each problem, we obtained a rank-ordered list. We identified the top five ranked items and confirmed their importance with a brief group discussion. Examples of the final lists from three sessions with different groups of supervisors are shown in Figure 2.

To conclude the NGT session, we added an additional feature to facilitate the development of course material. We asked each participant to

reflect on the problems listed on the newsprint and to recall an incident in which one of the problems had occurred on the job. This post-NGT amplification added specific job-related incidents essential to the later development of course modules. The incidents were described in some detail by the supervisors and their comments were taped.

When we had concluded all phases of the needs-assessment process, the data from each session was classified according to major problem areas, such as planning, communicating, leadership and so on. We provided the data in each of these areas to a member of the course faculty responsible for developing the associated modules of the course. This specialist used the information to create course material specifically tied to the problems and operations of the firm. The tapes from the post-NGT discussion also were helpful in this stage to develop cases. Later in the process, we conducted meetings with all faculty members to discuss the interrelationships between the various modules of the evolving course.

The specific phases of the NGT course-design process are illustrated in Figure 3.

Advantages of NGT

In our experience, NGT in needs assessment:

• Provides reliable data. Individuals in a NGT session generate data through a structured procedure. In contrast to a nonstructured approach that might generate different data on separate occasions, NGT's structure tends to produce consistent information.

• Reduces inhibitions. Subordinates are often inhibited by the presence of their superiors or strong informal peer leaders in interacting group situations. The involvement of first-line supervisors only in the NGT sessions eliminated those inhibitions. And, although the NGT involves silent generation of ideas, the recording phase requires group members to reveal their opinions.

In the first NGT session, we found the supervisors reluctant to speak freely during the opening minutes. In subsequent sessions we added a pre-NGT discussion during which the participants talked casually about matters of topical interest. Then, when the NGT session began, we found the supervisors more willing to discuss sensitive problem areas. We believe the validity of the data is enhanced by this aspect of the approach.

• Increases participation. First-line supervisors often complain about being omitted from decisions made by higher management. The use of NGT in needs assessment provides an excellent vehicle for involving supervisors in the design of their own development programs. This increases their commitment to the program goals.

• Emphasizes job-related problems. The structured process forces NGT participants to focus on job-related factors. The tendency to digress or to pursue irrelevant side issues is inhibited. This tends to result in a thorough evaluation of the items elicited during the session.

Further, using job-related problems produces a more relevant supervisory development course—one closely related to the perceived needs of the participants, who will be more likely to accept the value of a course that deals with familiar and troublesome problems and that incorporates familiar terminology.

The NGT combines ideas solicited from several individuals with an effective method for consolidating and prioritizing them. The supervisory development course that resulted from our application of the technique was, we believe, valid and attuned to the needs of participants.

Reprinted from TRAINING, March 1983

NEEDS ANALYSIS: CONCEPT IN SEARCH OF CONTENT

The trick is applying the right tool to the right problem at the right time

BY RON ZEMKE

The concept of training needs analysis is being subjected to new scrutiny these days. In the textbooks and journals of the late 1950s and early 1960s, trainers were routinely advised that a needs analysis was simply a finding out of what is going on now and a matching of this against what should go on, both now and in the future. The gap between the two gave clues to the amount and kind of training needed.

In a very simple work world, one where jobs are completely and accurately defined and described, where they remain stable for long periods of time, and where job performance is carefully and frequently measured, such guidance may be sufficient. Write when you find that sort of world. For most trainers, reality is jobs so undefined or ill-defined only a personnel rep could love them. It's a world where job details and procedures, indeed whole jobs, transmogrify overnight; where job performance, if evaluated at all, is evaluated in terms so behaviorally coarse as to shed scarce light on the idealized kinds of data the ancient definitions request.

In addition to the problems of finding actual and ideal performances to compare for "gaps," today's trainer is acutely aware of the problems of causation a needs analysis must be prepared to deal with. Work by the likes of Thomas F. Gilbert, Geary A. Rummler and Robert F. Mager has caused the scales to fall from most trainers eyes. The "gaps" between actual and desired job performance can come from a myriad of potential causes. Lack of skill and knowledge are but two.

Today's trainers know that at the very least they must look at such diverse factors as organizational climate, job design, performance feedback, performance consequences and work group politics if they are to avoid misprescribing training as a remedy. What most contemporary trainers picture when they hear the term *training needs analysis* is, at the very least, what Rummler calls a *performance audit*: "A framework for viewing human performance problems and a set of procedures for systematically determining the worth of correcting the problem, finding the causes of the problem, and designing solutions to the problem."

The key word here is *framework*, which is close in contextual meaning to words like *model* and *theory*. It has become increasingly apparent that a needs analysis is less a common-sense problem analysis exercise and more a form of applied research; a structured investigation aimed at finding the significant human-factors components of important organizational performance problems and determining the primary cause or causes of those human performance problems. By definition, the needs analyst has become an individual with a model or theory of how and why people behave as they do who mucks about looking at real-world problems through the prism of that model or theory. The needs analyst or performance auditor is both an impartial and biased observer—a change agent concerned at once with competence, performance, worth and value. The needs analyst is simultaneously concerned with the organization and with people, as well as the dynamic tension of both constituencies' needs.

Needs analysis tools

As the philosophy of needs analysis has deepened and broadened, the tools and tactics have been refined. The practice today is less that of common sense and more of applied research, the tools a growing interdisciplinary amalgam. In the past, a survey asking managers to guess how many of their people could use a time management course was considered pretty state of the art. Today it is considered quaint. Survey technology has become a computer-based science and few would ever again rely on any single measurement technique as the basis for making a training investment. The stakes are too high.

Dr. John W. Gunkler has noted that there are an amazing number of needs analysis procedures and techniques cited in the literature today. He sees a taxonomy of three distinct types:

- **Type O** - Pseudo needs assessment procedures

- **Type I** - Primary data source procedures

- **Type II** - Secondary data source procedures

Under **Type O** he places market research, consumer demand analysis and educational goal setting. **Type-I** techniques are of two subtypes: those procedures that collect data about and from the target population, and those procedures that collect data about the target population from another population. In the former subtype we would find behavioral observations of and interviews with performers in the target population. Procedures in the second subtype would be surveys of and interviews with supervisors or managers of the target population.

Type-II procedures are composed of analysis and interpretation of data *about* the population, and analysis and interpretation of data about previous "treatments." An example of the former would be a Yankelovich-type public opinion study of today's worker. The latter might be an analysis of the courses and grades of people like those for whom we are going to be designing training. Gunkler points out that none of these tools and procedures are unconditionally the best way to do a needs analysis. The trick, he says, is to apply the right tool to the right problem at the right time in the right way.

Dr. John J. Leach points out that the added care and precision being brought to bear on the conduct of training needs assessment is really to help us avoid the common errors of the past, among them:

- failing to distinguish between wants and needs.
- uncritical acceptance of management statement of needs.
- failing to correlate needs with organizational plans and objectives.
- assuming all needs can be met through training.
- underutilizing needs in program selection and development.
- depending on intuition and the literature to explain the meaning of expressed or demonstrated need.
- the tendency of needs assessment to be reactive rather than future-oriented.

Dr. Michael Scriven, an education evaluation specialist, has pointed out that as resources become scarce, it becomes more and more important to be sure that those resources are going where they are most needed and are being used in the best possible manner. By turning more of our attention to the matter of careful needs analysis— in essence the evaluation of what needs to be done— we increase the chances that we will not only be doing good training, but that we will be doing training for good and justifiable reasons.

Reprinted from TRAINING, July 1981

FLOW-PROCESS CHARTS: HOW THEY HELP DETERMINE EMPLOYEE TRAINING NEEDS

Here are step-by-step instructions on how the flow-process chart will make the supervisor's job more effective

BY CHARLES T. UTT

Though a multitude of methods are used to determine training needs, those who work in manufacturing environments have tended to focus on three approaches: organizational analysis, manpower analysis and job description analysis.

However, there is a fourth useful category for training assessment: operational analysis. An important tool of operational analysis is the flow-process chart, an analytical technique used by industrial and management engineers. Many line supervisors use the flow-process chart to improve operations in their areas independent of staff specialists.

This same flow-process chart technique can be used by training specialists to separate methods improvement and operations improvement needs from employee training needs.

There are three basic steps to the process:

1. Break the work flow or process into basic segments or steps.

2. Analyze each basic segment step-by-step through the work-flow process.

3. Try to determine a better method by using: a) methods that are known to be quicker or less time-consuming; b) equipment, jigs, templates and devices that can make the process faster; c) training programs, on-the-job training techniques, instructions, aids, manuals, visual devices and coaching that can improve employee skills.

Obviously you have to understand the process you're analyzing. It's usually most appropriate for trainers to enlist the help of departmental supervisors or other process experts, such as quality control personnel, to develop a flow-process chart.

When the flowchart is completed, all the operations are summarized in chart form. Figure 1 is the summary chart made from doing a flow-process study of a mythical "widget" production line. The study covers the production of 1,000 widgets and a 36.5-hour time period. In addition to time and pieces, the analysts have measured the distance the production of a single widget covers (in this case 400 feet).

Once this baseline data is gathered, the analysts can begin to challenge it and propose changes. There are six factors or questions to the challenge:

1. Does each operation accomplish what it is supposed to do?

2. Why is this operation done? Is it necessary? Can the same result be accomplished without the operation?

3. At what location or area is this operation done? Is it necessary to do it there? Can the operation be improved by changing the location of the operation or changing the location of the employee working on it?

4. At what time is this operation done? Can the operation be changed to another time? Can the sequence be changed?

5. How is the operation done? Is it

Figure 1
Flow Process Summary Chart of 1,000 Widgets

		Present	
		No.	Time
●	Operations	10	20.5 hours
➡	Transports	5	5.0 hours
■	Inspections	2	3.0 hours
◗	Delays	2	8.0 hours
▼	Storages	1	-0-
Distance Traveled			400 feet

Figure 2
Flow Process Improvement Chart for 1,000 Widget Base

		Present		Proposed		Saving	
		No.	Time	No.	Time	No.	Time
●	Operations	10	20.5 hours	8	18.5 hours	2	2.0 hours
➡	Transports	5	5.0 hours	4	4.5 hours	1	0.5 hours
■	Inspections	2	3.0 hours	2	3.0 hours	0	0 hours
◗	Delays	2	8.0 hours	1	7.5 hours	1	0.5 hours
▼	Storages	1	-0-	1	-0-	0	-0-
Distance Traveled		400 feet		350 feet		50 feet	

possible to do it better? Can a different method or layout be used? Is there a better piece of equipment or machine that can be used to improve the operation?

6. Which employee does this operation? Why does this employee do this operation? Is the employee doing the operation the right employee to do it? Would the operation be improved if another employee did the operation?

These challenge questions are traditional in the improvement process. However, this is the time when the trainer on the team would assess employee skill deficiencies or knowledge deficiencies that are detrimental to operations improvement. In essence, the trainer on the team adds a *seventh* type of question to the challenge process:

7. Is the employee performing this function maximally equipped to do it? Does he or she have adequate feedback? Is the operation in some way punishing? Does the employee do the task by the book? Would a job aid decrease errors? Has the employee been trained in all the steps of the operation? Are some employees much better than others at the operation?

Present vs. proposed

Once the challenging process has been completed on all activities, compare proposed changes with the process in Figure 1.

In Figure 2 we can see that two operations have been eliminated for a total savings of two hours. One transport has also been eliminated for a savings of one-half hour and 50 feet of traveling. One delay has been removed with a savings of one-half hour. To process 1,000 pieces there has been a savings of three hours and a travel distance of 50 feet.

Training possibilities

The supervisor and the training analyst also noticed that two out of the remaining eight operations were being done improperly and ineffectively. They believe that an additional savings of one-quarter hour would be realized if they initiated training.

They also noticed that three of the remaining transports can be improved by the use of checklists and a visual aid. No training is required, but only training aids.

When the inspections that remained were observed closely, it was determined that an improvement in the process could be increased by coaching the inspectors. All inspectors had previous training, but poor work habits, from low rates of feedback. Only coaching is necessary to save another one-quarter hour of the remaining inspections.

Analyzing work flow for improvement is an opportune way to review the skills and knowledge of each employee, with an eye on training needs. Not all deficiencies in employee skill and knowledge may be corrected by a training program. In many cases visual aids, drawings, procedures, checklists or merely watching each employee and giving feedback will bring improvement. But it all begins when you take the time to perform a careful flow-process analysis.

Reprinted from TRAINING, January 1982

FIVE BASIC SYMBOLS

This symbol indicates an *operation*. It is used to indicate changes central to material or object. The change can be a process of adding or deleting from the object or assembling or disassembling the object. In nonmanufacturing environments the symbol for *operation* may also indicate a person writing, calculating, planning, drawing, telephoning, receiving, sending or typing information.

This symbol is used for *inspection*. When objects are measured, weighed, reviewed, checked or verified for quality, quantity and specifications, an inspection symbol is used.

This symbol for *delay* is used to indicate idle time. Equipment or machinery waiting for material or supplies is considered a *delay*. An employee waiting for a machine to complete a cycle also is considered a *delay* for the employee. Likewise, an employee waiting for materials, supplies or tools is considered a *delay*.

This symbol indicates a *storage* operation. *Storage* is a delay that is longer than 24 hours. It is usually storage of an object waiting an operation at a later date.

This symbol indicates *transportation* or *movement*. It is used when an object is moved from one place to another, or when a person moves from one place to another.

DETERMINING THE TRAINING NEEDS OF YOUR SUPERVISORS— WHEN THEY'RE SPREAD ACROSS THE MAP

Here's an approach that can make that task seem like a simple procedure

BY PATRICK J. GERMANY
AND C.W. Von BERGEN, JR.

Training competent managers and supervisors is a vital and important task, especially in a growing organization. And we all know the most effective training programs begin with a careful, systematic assessment of needs. Yet how do you assess management/supervisory training needs— efficiently and effectively— in a geographically dispersed organization? Here's how we did it at Western Petroleum Services division of The Western Company of North America, a land-based oil well servicing company employing over 2,000 people in five geographical regions.

Many approaches are available for determining the training needs of supervisors. D. L. Kirkpatrick, in "Determining Supervisory Training Needs and Setting Objectives" (*Training and Development Journal*, 1978) summarizes various methods:

1. Analyzing the supervisor's job.
2. Analyzing problems.
3. Asking the supervisors themselves.
4. Asking the superiors of the prospective trainees.
5. Asking their subordinates.
6. Testing knowledge and/or skills.
7. Observing supervisory behavior.
8. Analyzing performance-appraisal information.
9. Conducting exit interviews.
10. Using an advisory committee.

A combination of several of these methods— an approach Kirkpatrick

FIGURE 1. NEEDS ANALYSIS FLOWCHART

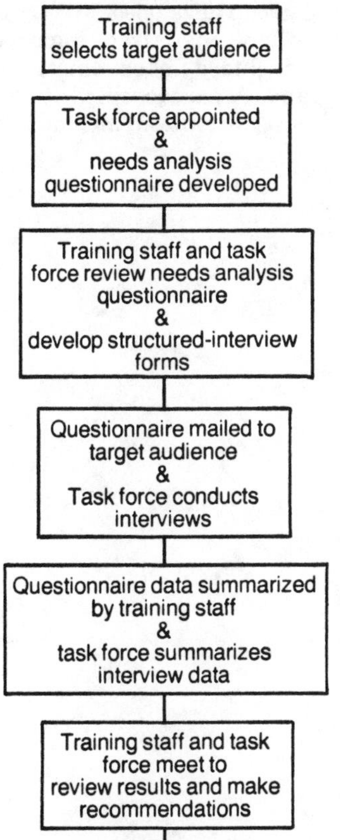

Training staff selects target audience

↓

Task force appointed
&
needs analysis questionnaire developed

↓

Training staff and task force review needs analysis questionnaire
&
develop structured-interview forms

↓

Questionnaire mailed to target audience
&
Task force conducts interviews

↓

Questionnaire data summarized by training staff
&
task force summarizes interview data

↓

Training staff and task force meet to review results and make recommendations

↓

Training staff develops, improves, etc., training programs

endorses— is often the most effective way to determine needs, and it is the approach taken by the training department of Western Petroleum Services.

In 1978, the training staff decided to undertake a supervisory/management needs analysis to determine if existing training programs reflected actual training needs and to identify areas in which additional training might be required. The needs analysis was structured to include numbers 2, 3, 4 and 10 of Kirkpatrick's methods. The staff felt that these items would yield a thorough list of needs without being overly cumbersome and time-consuming.

The target audience in this case was 40 middle-level managers, 55 foremen and 176 first-line supervisors. The needs analysis included developing a questionnaire and appointing an advisory committee (Figure 1). After a review of literature in various training-related publications, a 72-item needs analysis questionnaire was developed by the training staff to measure the importance and frequency of tasks engaged in by supervisors. Respondents were asked to rank the importance of a task on a three-point scale from high to low and the frequency of a task on a four-point scale from often to never.

Help from the task force

While the questionnaire was being developed, the training staff and the regional vice-presidents appointed managers from each of five geographical regions to serve on the analysis task force. The objectives of this group included interviewing key managers and supervisors in each region to identify expressed training needs, reviewing all data accumulated by the training staff and making recommendations concerning any training which might be needed in the future. This group of managers met with the training staff to review the needs analysis questionnaires and to develop a structured interview form. The form (Figure 2) was considered necessary to ensure reliability and standardization among interviewers.

The task force then spent a month interviewing supervisors and their managers. A total of 93 first- and second-level managers were interviewed. The interviews yielded a rank order list of specific areas of needs: Human relations, financial profit & loss/preparing budgets, planning, safety, sales, interviewing, policies/procedures, performance appraisals, communications, sales management.

At the same time the interviews

were conducted, the needs analysis questionnaires were sent to all

supervisors and their managers. The response rate was 82%, with 222 questionnaires returned. The questionnaires were then keypunched and a computerized, statistical analysis was conducted to determine the mean and standard deviation for each item on the scales of frequency and importance. Several of the more important tasks, according to the target group, were: Employee safety rules, planning the work, training employees in policy/procedure compliance, checking on the work of employees, giving instructions to employees, giving safety instructions, problem solving, handling dissatisfied employees, involving employees in decisions, controlling expenses.

The results

The results of the questionnaire and the interview data were summarized by the training staff and the task force, and a second meeting was held to analyze the findings and make recommendations concerning future training programs. One problem encountered at this time was that the results of the questionnaires differed somewhat from those of the structured interviews. For instance, although problem solving was a task engaged in frequently and deemed important by supervisors, the topic was not mentioned in even a single interview. Sales training was mentioned frequently in interviews but the questionnaire, by virtue of its design, did not yield this need. However, the task force was able to deal with these differences by allowing discussion and arriving at a decision based upon the staff's knowledge (derived from the questionnaire and actual training conducted) and the experience of the task force members. For the most part, the questionnaire results were compatible with those of the interviews.

The group developed a list of areas of need, and these were compared to topics included in existing training programs. Areas identified as needing additional attention included training in human relations, finance, planning and safety.

A new program, advanced management, was developed to include the following human relations topics: Orientation for new employees, employee motivation, employee counseling, effective discipline and handling employee and customer complaints. Two existing programs were revised to increase from seven hours to sixteen hours the time spent on planning and finance for supervisors.

No action was taken to add more safety training, since the group felt that existing training in that area was sufficient. The analysis pointed out that more managers and supervisors needed to attend safety training sessions and that more management people needed to attend at least one of the three in-house sales training programs in order to better supervise their sales personnel.

This needs analysis design proved to be an efficient, cost-effective way to evaluate existing training and identify needed programs. One improvement suggested was that the members of the task force serve as content-area specialists, to monitor new and existing training modules to ensure that each reflects a specific training need.

This approach could be used by most moderate to large organizations. It is recommended for those that are geographically dispersed, but it could be applied, with minor modifications, to a large manufacturing organization on one site.

Reprinted from TRAINING, November 1980

DOS AND DON'TS OF QUESTIONNAIRE DESIGN

Try these tips to make sure your next one doesn't bomb

BY DEAN SPITZER

Questionnaires are the most frequently used method of data collection among educators and trainers. Yet few questionnaire designers heed the simple "dos" and "don'ts" that can make a good questionnaire. A few errors in design can go a long way toward invalidating an otherwise well-conceptualized research effort. Therefore, it is especially important for trainers to consider these simple guidelines—along with content considerations—the next time a questionnaire effort is proposed.

"Do" guidelines

• *Begin with a few non-threatening and easy-to-answer items.* This ensures that respondents will continue to complete the questionnaire with a positive attitude. Threatening items at the beginning of a questionnaire can cause defensive— and frequently invalid—responses.

• *Use simple and direct language.* The major cause of invalid questionnaire results is misinterpreted items. Avoid this pitfall by making sure that your items will communicate adequately to your respondents.

• *Make your items as brief as possible.* Filling out questionnaires can be a bore. Sometimes respondents will automatically "turn off" when they encounter tediously long items.

• *Emphasize the crucial words in each item.* If certain words might change the entire meaning of the item if misinterpreted, italicize or underscore them.

• *Leave adequate space for respondents to make comments.* Although unstructured comments are often difficult to analyze, they can provide valuable information that might not otherwise be collected. Plenty of "white space" also makes the form appear less cluttered and more professional.

• *Group items into coherent categories.* This makes the respondent's job easier because he or she won't constantly shift mental gears, become fatigued and make a mistake. Categories don't have to be labeled, but similar items should be grouped together.

• *Provide some variety in the type of items used.* This keeps respondents from becoming fatigued and bored and is particularly important for long questionnaires. Alternative types include: multiple choice, true/false, short answer, open-ended items, ranking items, and items that are contingent upon previous responses.

• *Include clear, concise instructions on how to complete the questionnaire.* Heed Murphy's Law here, too. Be sure that your instructions will inhibit any attempts (conscious or otherwise) to complete the questionnaire incorrectly.

• *Make sure that there are clear instructions on what to do with the completed questionnaire.* The return address should be clearly identified on the cover letter and on the form itself. Should the questionnaire be returned in a self-addressed envelope? What's the deadline for completing it? By the way, deadlines increase questionnaire response rates. Make sure that all relevant information related to the disposition of the completed questionnaire is clearly specified.

• *Provide incentives as a motivation for a promptly completed questionnaire.* This doesn't mean that you should "bribe" respondents, just that you should make every effort to motivate them to respond. Help respondents realize the importance of collecting this information, and how it will be used to benefit them. Sometimes the "visibility" of a questionnaire signed by a highly credible person can promote responses. This device should be weighed against that of an anonymous questionnaire, one that will encourage more candor on controversial items.

• *Use professional production methods.* The more professional your questionnaire looks, the more likely you will get a high response rate. A printed questionnaire is easier to read and respond to.

• *Provide a well-written personal cover letter.* Questionnaires should always be sent with cover letters explaining their purpose and the reasons respondents were selected. Personal letters are best, but if this isn't feasible, have the letter printed to match the type in the address and salutation. Never use a form letter.

• *Include other experts and relevant decision-makers in your questionnaire design.* This helps assure that your questionnaire is comprehensive and technically correct. It will add credibility to the project and will provide you with a head start toward utilizing the completed data.

• *Plan how to analyze and use the data when designing the questionnaire.* Consider the analysis and use of data from the start. What might be a good question can result in meaningless data. Consider the nature of responses as carefully as you design the questions.

• *Be prepared to handle missing data.* Invariably, there will be incomplete responses and missing data on the returned questionnaires. Unless you have a plan for dealing with this missing data, you'll be stymied. Anyone who has used a five-point (or seven-point) rating scale knows that missing data cannot always be treated as if they were 3's or 5's (the midpoints of the scale).

• *Test your questionnaire on representatives of the target audience.* You may be surprised how many serious errors went undetected during the most careful and systematic design process. Perhaps the best way to test a questionnaire (without involving complex statistics) is to watch a few respondents complete it. If they're having difficulties, question them in detail to determine the source. Questionnaire designers frequently find that a single, ambiguous word can invalidate even the best questionnaire item. A little time spent in pilot testing can eliminate lots of problems later on.

• *Number and include some identifying data on each page.* It's possible that the pages of the questionnaire may come apart, causing problems for the respondent. Avoid this by numbering and identifying each page.

Don't guidelines

• *Don't use ambiguous, bureaucratic, technical or colloquial language.* It can confuse or "turn off" respondents. Don't give Murphy's Law an opportunity to sabotage your study. Pilot testing the questionnaire can help avoid this error.

• *Don't use negatively worded questions unless absolutely necessary.* Negatively worded items can easily be misinterpreted or clue respondents into a "desired" response. Most negative items can easily be worded positively.

• *Don't use "double-barrelled" items.* Don't use items that ask respondents to respond to more than one statement or question. Such items can be confusing, especially when the respondent feels differently about each part. Instead, make each item a simple, discrete question or statement. When in doubt, make two items out of one.

• *Don't bias respondents by hinting at a "desired" response.* For questionnaire results to be valid, respondents must not be biased by the way the items have been written. Again, pilot testing is the best way to avoid inadvertently biasing respondents.

• *Don't ask questions to which you already know the answers.* Don't waste respondents' time— and your own— by including items with only one realistic response. The inclusion of such items will bore respondents, needlessly increase the length of the questionnaire and cause more work for those analyzing the data. The only exception to this rule is when you need documentation for the item in question.

• *Don't include any extraneous or unnecessary items.* Make sure all the items on your questionnaire will yield useful data. Otherwise, you may overwhelm or unnecessarily fatigue the respondent. The best cure for this error is to practice tabulating and analyzing the data yourself.

• *Don't put important items at the end.* Items at the end of a questionnaire rarely get the same kind of attention that earlier items get. Save the least significant items for the end.

• *Don't allow respondents to fall into "response sets."* When a great many questionnaire items call for similar responses, there is the tendency for respondents to continue responding in the same way. Item variety will counteract this tendency, as will a conscious decision to vary response formats and probable responses for consecutive items.

Following these simple "dos" and "don'ts" will enable you to design questionnaires that will yield better responses. If you use them, I think you'll find that both your response rate and results validity will increase considerably.

Reprinted from TRAINING, May 1979

THE NON-STATISTICIAN'S APPROACH TO SURVEYS

You don't need a Ph.D.
You do need a good design, a little intuition and the time to do the job right

BY RON ZEMKE WITH DAVE WALONICK

Please," writes a San Diego reader, "enough of these 'how-to-design-questionnaires-that work' articles. Give me some help making sense of the results!" Fair enough. Design is critical to usable results, but compiling, analyzing and interpreting the results of any survey study—be it a training needs survey, program evaluation or market study—*is* where the rubber hits the road. At the same time, it's a mission only the most foolhardy would approach without trepidation and a lot of qualification of what's said.

For where statistics are concerned, there tend to be so many "ifs, ands or buts" that it is virtually impossible to propose a set method of analysis that doesn't inspire the ire of a gaggle of statistical mavins. To forestall some of that criticism, and to give some insight into the logic of our approach, indulge us a few minutes while we share our ground rules and assumptions. *Then,* we'll rush in where angels fear to tread.

Our approach to analyzing survey results starts with the planning and design process, and turns on three propositions:

1 Effective survey research begins with legwork, not "pencilwork." The most widely used and roundly abused information-gathering technique is the survey study. A survey or questionnaire study, when carefully thought out and conducted, *can* be a valuable training and development tool; one that yields information about needs, problems, potential problems and organizational obsta-

cles as well as employee perceptions, attitudes and opinions.

But too often, says survey critic Dr. Harry Levinson of the Levinson Institute, the survey or questionnaire study is used to avoid the responsibility of in-depth confrontation of the issues being addressed. Levinson argues that "no single fill-in-the-blank or multiple-choice question or even group of questions can adequately plumb human insight and opinion." He is especially critical of organizational opinion polls, whose questions, he suggests, are usually biased toward the sponsor's hoped-for outcome— and whose results are never as clear-cut as the analysts would have us believe.

Survey research expert Steve Mayer of Rainbow Research doesn't share Levinson's skepticism, but agrees that most survey studies suffer from poor front-end analysis and a lack of plain old legwork. The result, he suggests, is evidenced by items that don't ask the right questions— that don't answer the research question or at least shed light on the problem at hand— and surveys that are too long. Both of these flaws are obvious to would-be respondents and serve to depress survey return rate.

The remedy is plain old-fashioned homework and elbow grease. Interviews, focus groups, site visits and reviews of performance data all help you clarify and define the goal of your study and give you a context for explaining the obtained results. Survey experts Douglas R. Berdie and John F. Anderson, principals in Anderson & Berdie Research and authors of *Questionnaires: Design and Use*, pass along this quick litmus test of preparedness:

Can you state the purpose of your proposed study in 25 words or less?
- *What do you want to know?*
- *Why do you want to know it?*
- *What will happen as a result of answering the research question? (Both plus and minus information.)*

Question: When you have described the goal of the study, ask yourself: "Is this study really *worth doing?"*

If you can't pass this test, you're certainly not ready to begin building a survey on the problem.

2 The K.I.S.S. (Keep It Short and Simple) principle applies to surveys. Everyone of us has looked at a sophisticated climate/attitude survey or Census Bureau beauty and marveled at its complexity. And there is a great temptation to emulate these marvels in the design of our own "homemade" questionnaires. Consequently, we often err by developing survey items that are "tricky" and thus open to misinterpretation and over-analysis, by developing clever response scales when we need not and by going for a larger sample of our population than is necessary. There are three K.I.S.S. guidelines we try to follow when designing questionnaires for ease of analysis and interpretation.

- **Use yes/no items rather than scaled items whenever possible.**

We're all addicted to Likert-like scales. Writing and interpreting "strongly agree" to "strongly disagree" items is lots of beard-plucking fun. We freely admit that sitting around asking each other, "What do you suppose these results really mean?" and making tea-leaf explanations to management about the hidden meanings in a set of responses is a gas and gives our work a patina of expertise and mystery. Unfortunately, we often end up writing items like this one just for fun and power:

I am a supervisor				
Strongly Agree	Agree	Neither Agree Nor Disagree	Disagree	Stongly Disagree
1	2	3	4	5

There is another reason for avoiding scaled items: the temptation to average the results. These 1-through-5 scales *look* like they measure something in a nice ruler-like fashion. But the "distance" between a 1 response and a 2 response is not necessarily the same as the distance between a 4 response and a 5 response. So computing a mean of, say, a 2, 3, 5 and 8, and concluding that 4.5 is the average answer, is a shakey practice.

How do the "big guys," the climate survey people, get away with averaging? Easy: They don't necessarily assume that their scales have equal intervals. They make their interpretations, instead, by comparing XYZ Company's answers to the answers given by hundreds or thousands of other previous respondents. Our homemade surveys don't have that *normed baseline data* for comparison purposes.

Another glitch is length. How long is too long? The research literature isn't clear on the issue so let's go with another commonsense guideline: If *you* wouldn't fill it out, don't expect others to. A survey of more than two or three pages looks intimidating, and is. Heard 25 words or less? Try 25 questions or less.

● **Use the smallest sample possible.**

We all tend to over-survey. But the more surveys we send out, the more we are obliged to get back or account for as "missing in action." For example, suppose we send out 100 surveys and receive 75. Seventy-five percent is a fair to middling rate *but* we can only guarantee our results are accurate plus or minus 25%. A small percentage return makes one doubt the validity and representativeness of the information that is received. We never really can answer the question, "What do the non-respondents look like?" After all, they didn't respond.

It is also feasible to argue that 12 angry truckers can seriously bias a questionnaire on speed limits and I.C.C. regulations if only 20 or 30 "bull haulers" out of 2,000 take the time to respond. Better to send out 30 surveys and work like heck to get them all back. Tables are available to help you select the number of people to survey, and the number of returns you need for your study to be representative. As a weak rule of thumb, figure you need a return of 80% to put a high degree of confidence in your results.

Hand in hand with this sample size idea is randomization. Most statistics are based on the assumption that we have a *chance* or *random* selection from the population under study. Berdie believes this is the most frequently violated statistical principle. Make it a point to sample small and randomly, and to work hard at getting a good return rate.

● **Use the simplest statistic possible.**

Dr. Michael Scriven, a leading expert in educational program evaluation, suggests that any statistical test you can't do with a simple hand calculator may be too complex to yield practical results. We tend to agree, though there are occasions when access to a big computer can be a time-saver.

A BASIC STATISTICS GLOSSARY

You don't need a Ph.D. to analyze and interpret results of a survey study. The bulk of the techniques you need for that trick are descriptive statistics—simple, number-summarizing methods. Few require more than basic arithmetic skill and a probing eye. All statistics do, says Carol Taylor Fitz-Gibbon, is "help you crunch large numbers." That you can do with a hand calculator and a little common sense. The only correlational method we think

you need is a statistic called Chi-Square, which can help you decide whether or not the numbers in your cross-tabs are distributed in a chance fashion. It helps you make those "older employees tend to complain about pay policy more than do younger employees" statements.

Below are the definitions and explanations of the statistics we used in the case study of XYZ Manufacturing.

Mean: The arithmetic average—add up all the scores and divide by N.

Median: The middle score— count up the number of responses and circle the middle one; the one right in the center of the pack.

Mode: The most common score— if supervisors report four absences per employee *most frequently*, then four is the mode.

When these three measures of *central tendency* are almost equal, you have a normal or bell-shaped distribution of scores or answers. When they are quite different, the answers are referred to as *skewed*. When the three central tendency measures are quite different, you should graph the responses to the question to see just how the numbers are skewed.

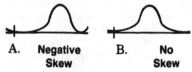

| A. | **Negative Skew** | B. | **No Skew** |

Positive skew: Scores clump up near zero and trail off.

Negative skew: Scores are bunched near the high end of the scale.

If these were graphs of absences, you could say that in Case A there is a general trend among all departments toward high absences. In C, you might conclude that the tendency is toward low absences. In D, you might conclude that there are

two distinct groups of departments: those with high absence records and those with low absence records.

Standard deviation: Whether scores are close to the mean or whether they are scattered about. When a standard deviation is large, the mean doesn't tell you much about the "typical" department, student, etc. When small, most scores or answers are close to the value of the mean and the mean is a good representation of the typical response. The standard deviation is calculated by taking the square root of Σ_x^2 (the differences between the mean and each score squared and summed) divided by N.

Chi-Square (χ^2): Statistical test that

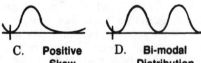

| C. | **Positive Skew** | D. | **Bi-modal Distribution** |

tells you whether the scores in a table (cross-tabs) are uniformly distributed or whether something is influencing the way the numbers fall. Calculating a Chi-square requires arithmetic, some patience and a table of significance. You can find a Chi-square table and detailed explanation of how to derive a representative value in any standard statistics text. A hand calculator helps with the patience.

Reprinted from TRAINING, September 1980

Statistical "tests of significance" are valuable, pure research tools, but they have dubious import for most HRD situations. Instead, use the "Inter-Occular Trauma Test": If the results hit you between the eyes, they probably have practical import. Don't confuse significance with importance. Results can be statistically significant, but trivial nonetheless.

3 **Pilot testing a survey avoids G.I.G.O. and embarrassment.** We pilot test new products, work systems and training programs, so why not questionnaires? There's nothing more embarrassing than a phone call informing you that "there's no box to check for my department" or "I can't figure out how I'm supposed to answer question 7." And how does it feel to receive a return mail survey with four pounds of red-penciled grammar and syntax corrections? According to Anderson, pilot testing a survey often shows you ways to shorten and simplify the final instrument, just as pilot testing a programmed text or workshop shows you where the fat and skinny areas are. And G.I.G.O? Garbage in, garbage out.

With that out of the way, let's take a case study approach to sending out a questionnaire and analyzing the results. The safest way to proceed, the one that will hopefully garner us the least criticism, is to work with a specific survey for a specific case application.

Sam Gumball is training director of XYZ Manufacturing. The energy and power division of XYZ, through the person of the divisional personnel director, calls Sam and orders up a supervisory training program. Sam asks what that program might discuss and is told, "Give 'em everything. They don't know from hunger about management." Sam gives the personnel director the two-minute, "If you don't know where you're going" speech. The latter concedes a little research won't hurt—but make it quick, we've got to do something now!

Because the franchise is broad and the coins are rattling loudly in the would-be sponsor's purse, there is a temptation to do one of those "What sort of training do you think you need?" surveys. Better Sam should send out a course catalog and let the supervisors do the "one from column A and one from column B" routine. We prefer a still more conservative route.

Step 1. Figure out the problem

The best bet is to ignore the panic

and work with the division on identifying specific problems. Find out what problem the requestor—the *real* requestor, not the personnel person— thinks he or she is trying to solve. David M. Schiff, publisher of *Consultants Digest*, a monthly newsletter for HRD consultants, calls this get-together to determine what the client perceives the problem to be an alignment meeting.

The first question to ask in the meeting— once everyone is comfortable and coffeed— is "What's the problem and who is hurting because of it?" Let's assume the alignment meeting goes well and the client is finally able to state the problem concisely:

> Productivity in the battery assembly area is consistently below time-study standards. But beyond that, productivity in the entire plant, and for that matter the entire energy and power division, is lower than we budgeted for this year.

More legwork follows and Sam finds that:

● Production records verify low productivity.

● Supervisors gripe a lot about commitment, morale and the willingness to work of "the kind of people we hire today."

● According to our personnel director, salary reviews and performance reviews are linked (i.e., performance review ratings determine salary increase increments).

● Quality control and production data are closely guarded— for management's eyes only.

Sam now has enough information to develop an idea worth testing via survey. The working hypothesis might be:

> First-line supervisors in XYZ's energy and power division battery plant *do not* provide adequate performance information to the people who work for them. The problem of insufficient performance feedback is especially critical in battery assembly areas, and leads to low productivity and employee morale and turnover problems.

Step 2. Design, pilot, administer the survey

Figure 1 is Sam's survey. It meets our design for analyzability standards and gets at the info Sam needs to finish the needs study for energy and power. This survey has the potential for generating a lot of information, and some simple arithmetic will give Sam plenty of numbers to play with. The previously mentioned Anderson and Berdie book is the best single source we've seen on the "how-to's" of piloting and revising questionnaires,

and on stimulating a good return rate, so we'll move on toward interpreting the response to Sam's survey.

Step 3. Compile and analyze results

The first thing to do is to pull all the responses together in one place so Sam can see the potential relationships between answers. Figure 2 is from Sam's summary table for Part I of the survey, the demographic or "Who are these people anyway?" information that describes the respondents.

Though demographic data is usually just used to cross-tab or make comparisons of the "supervisors with large departments have more turnover than supervisors with small departments" sort, the demographics themselves tell some interesting tales— *if* Sam knows how to look at the numbers.

For instance, by eyeballing Figure 1 we can see that:

1. On the average, most departments are *under* their budgeted manpower. (Item 6 is larger than item 5.) They may be understaffed for the production demands.

2. The standard deviations for items 5 and 6 are large numbers. A standard deviation equal to or greater than 25% of the mean is a large standard deviation. This means that only some units are understaffed. It also suggests we may want to look closely at differences in turnover, absences and so forth, between understaffed and fully staffed departments.

3. Look at the mean, median and mode figures for the first six questions. When these three measures of central tendency are quite different, it tells us that the data is skewed, not normally distributed. Since the means, medians and modes in Figure 2 aren't terribly different, the skew is minimal, with the possible exception of data from question 5.

By the way, notice that these demographics say nary a thing about age, race, sex or eye color. This is a training needs of first-line supervisors study, not an EEOC inventory or a psychological study. A dime will get you a dollar though, that every other time you start doing a survey study some joker will suggest, "Why don't we ask some questions about how they feel about left-handed pirates from Penzance?" Best bet is to cut the jokers from the deck. If the joker is your boss, just try to minimize the amount of garbage he or she insists on stuffing into your study.

Figures 3 and 4 give you an idea of how rich Sam's data really is. All of

FIGURE 1

EXCERPTS FROM THE XYZ MANUFACTURING NEEDS SURVEY

PART I: YOU AND THE UNIT YOU SUPERVISE

1. How long, *to the nearest year,* have you worked for XYZ Manufacturing? _____

2. How long, *to the nearest year,* have you been a unit supervisor at XYZ Manufacturing? _____

3. How long, *to the nearest year,* have you been supervising the unit you now supervise? _____

4. How many years, *to the nearest year,* of supervisory experience do you have; count both years as a supervisor at XYZ *and* years as a supervisor elsewhere. _____

5. How many people are you currently supervising? _____

6. How many people are you budgeted for? _____

PART II: ABOUT THE PEOPLE YOU SUPERVISE

1. How many absence days—both excused and unexcused—did your people take between January 1, 1980 and April 1, 1980? _____

2. How many *overtime hours* did your unit work between January 1, 1980 and April 1, 1980? _____

3. How many *overtime hours* was your unit budgeted to work between January 1, 1980 and April 1, 1980? _____

4. How many people did you hire for your unit between January 1, 1980 and April 1, 1980? _____

5. How many people did you *release* from your unit between January 1, 1980 and April 1, 1980? _____

6. How do you train your new people?

   a. We have a formal—away from the work station—training program. ____yes____no

   b. I break in all the new people myself. ____tes____no

   c. I have a written training routine I follow for new people. ____yes____no

   d. I have one specific person assigned to train in new people. ____yes____no

   e. I assign one of the experienced people to show new people the job. (Who that is depends on who's available.) ____yes____no

7. What is the length, *to the nearest week,* of the probationary period in your unit? _____

8. Of the people you hired between January 1, 1980 and April 1, 1980:

   a. How many people did *not* meet minimum production standards by the end of their probationary period? _____

   b. How many people did you *release* because they did not meet minimum production standards? _____

9. How many of your people fall into each of the following four performance categories?

   a. Usually exceeds 100% of standard. _____

   b. Usually meets, sometimes exceeds 100% of standard. _____

   c. Usually meets 100% of standard. _____

   d. Falls below 100% of standard more often than most. _____

10. How many of your people did you conduct performance reviews with between January 1, 1980 and April 1, 1980? _____

11. The following question asks you to tell us how you feel about the performance review process. Please be as candid as possible in your answers.

A formal performance review should be conducted:	Agree	Disagree
a. Once a year.	_____	_____
b. Twice a year.	_____	_____
c. Every quarter.	_____	_____
d. Whenever a person s performance seems to be slipping.	_____	_____
e. Seldom. They are a waste of time.	_____	_____

PART III: ABOUT YOUR TRAINING AND DEVELOPMENT NEEDS

1. Have you attended a formal supervisory training program within the last five years? ____yes____no

2. *If you have attended* a formal training program, where, when and under what circumstances? (For example, night school, when working for another company, in college, several years ago at XYZ, etc.) _____ _____ _____

3. Please rate yourself in the following supervisory skill areas. Put an "X" in the space that represents your skill level.

	I do this well	I am about average	I could use some improvement
a. Assigning work	_____	_____	_____
b. Keeping workflow going	_____	_____	_____
c. Telling employees how they're doing day to day	_____	_____	_____
d. Controlling absences	_____	_____	_____
e. Conducting performance reviews	_____	_____	_____
f. Training new employees	_____	_____	_____
g. Disciplining employees	_____	_____	_____
h. Controlling line machine downtime	_____	_____	_____
i. Getting people to perform at standard	_____	_____	_____
j. Making employees understand what I want them to do	_____	_____	_____

this information comes from five items in Part II of the survey. Figure 3 gives us a look at overall absence data and a photograph of department-by-department performance. Units with exceptionally high absence records— unit 2 for instance— and units with exceptionally low absences— unit 61 for instance— can be separated out and given special attention in the survey analysis and, if need be, additional study. It's called shrinking the problem to a size you can get your arms around. By looking at the extremes of absence rate, there is a chance that critical differences will emerge.

Figure 4 shows the overtime worked compared to planned or budgeted overtime. Again, it's obvious that while overbudget overtime is out of hand for many departments, there are important differences by department. Unit 3 is much higher in O.T. than are units 1 and 61. It's important to find out why and *how else* these units differ. Unit 3, for instance, is also one of the highest absence rate departments. If unit 3 turns out to be a big loser in turnover, we know that unit 3 is a good anchor point for looking for critical differences in environment, management and other factors that may help account for the divisional performance problems.

Figure 5 shows that all departments tend to be understaffed, which may account for the overtime glut in Figure 3. In addition, some— but not all— units have gone through a lot of people, which explains more about the overtime problem. As the disparity in central tendency suggests, some departments are contributing more than their fair share to the churn.

We won't go any further with the analysis of Part II results, but it is obvious that Sam's survey, as simple and straightforward as it is, has garnered some important information. And Sam's analysis, as simple as it may seem, is developing some subtle implications about the real locus and nature of the problems and their causes.

The tabled data in Figure 6 suggests more supervisors have had no formal training in supervisory techniques and those who have some training received it in a variety of places. Conclusion: A uniform supervisory approach is doubtful. In addition, a large proportion of the supervisors themselves have identified *getting people to perform at standard, telling employees how they are doing day to day* and *controlling absences* as areas in which they need improvement. These are areas that Sam originally hypothesized supervisors

might be weak in.

Though we haven't looked at all the responses to all the questions in the survey, you are getting a pretty good feel for our "look-and-think" approach to survey data analysis.

Cross-tabs

There's only one other operation you need to be able to perform to do a survey-centered needs analysis. That operation is referred to in computer vernacular as cross-tabs. Very simply, a cross-tabs instruction to a computer tells the computer to make a table out of the answers to two or more questions. To do that, the survey information has to be cut into categories. And that, of course, is why surveys are often designed in a "check one of the following" format.

In the absence of a computer, you can do your own cross-tabs by sorting the questionnaires into piles and making your own table. Figure 7 is a sample of two handmade cross-tabs Sam performed on the survey data.

Cross-tab A addresses the question, "Do less experienced supervisors perceive that they have more need-for-improvement performance areas than do other supervisors?" The table tells us quite a bit. First, about one-third of the supervisors fall into Sam's less-experienced (four years or less) category. Secondly, the less experienced supervisors gave a slightly greater proportion of "needs improvement" responses (44%) than we would expect from their relative proportion in the population (34%). Sam can even conclude that less experienced super-

---

FIGURE 2

Part I. Demographics - Training Needs Survey
E and P Supervisors

	Mean	Median	Mode	Standard Deviation
1. Years with XYZ	9	10	8	1.5
2. Years as supervisor	3	4	4	2
3. Years this unit	2	4	3	1
4. Years sup. total	2	4	3	1
5. No. of people supervised	26	19	21	12
6. No. of people budgeted	28	11	25	15

FIGURE 3

Absence Analysis - From Part II Items

Unit Code	Absence Days	Number of Employees	Absences per Employee
01	16	17	0.94
02	30	12	2.50
03	14	11	1.27
60	18	25	0.72
61	8	22	0.36
61	920	1,037	

Mean no. of employees/unit = 17.00
Mean no. of absences/unit = 15.10
Mean no. of absences/emp. = 0.89

FIGURE 4

Overtime Analysis - From Part II

Unit Code	O.T. Worked	O.T. Budget	% of Budget
1	80	85	94
2	120	70	171
3	300	100	300
60	95	80	119
61	70	60	117
61	10,370 hrs.	4,880	212.5

Mean O.T. budget/unit = 80 hrs.
Mean O.T. worked/unit = 170 hrs.
Mean O.T. worked/person = 10 hrs.
Mean O.T. work/person/mo. = 3.33 hrs.

visors tend to say they "need improvement" in some areas more frequently by a ratio of roughly 50% (1.86 ÷ 1.23). So the answer to the original question is an unequivocal "somewhat."

More decisive findings come from the second cross-tab in Figure 7, cross-tab B. This tells us:

1. Supervisors with less than four years experience tend to supervise somewhat smaller departments than more experienced supervisors. No big deal, but interesting.

2. Supervisors with less experience account for a greater proportion of absences (50%) than you would expect based on their proportion in the population of supervisors (34%).

3. Absences per employee are 290% higher in departments run by less experienced supervisors (1.86 ÷ 0.64). Here's the big aha, and the reason we fool around with cross-tabs at all.

This simple cross-tab gives you something to really dig into. Fifty percent of the absences come from 31% of the employees and 34% of the departments. And this 34% of the departments is run by people with less than four years supervisory experience. Question: What are the two-thirds doing that the one-third isn't? What are the managers of the one-third doing about their supervisors' absence rates?

This simple operation of looking at the survey results in pieces started when Sam wondered if the amount of supervisory experience had anything to do with the division's problems. And he was encouraged to do that wondering because he noticed that the standard deviation for the question "How many total years of supervisory experience do you have?" was rather large.

Bottom line: Observation, imagination and a $12.95 calculator

We've been trying to make two points:

• A well-designed survey gives you good information.

• A well-designed survey can be analyzed without a computer or a Ph.D. in statistics.

We recommend three principles. First, look at the information from your respondents— *really* eyeball it long and hard. Next, table it, play with it, ask it questions and look for hints as to where the important relationships are hiding. Use your imagination and intuition. If you've been around for more than a week or two, you've probably developed a genuine "gut feel" or clinical sensitivity to the problems of your organization. Use that gut feel to guide your analysis. And last, but not least, take the time to sit back with your raw numbers, a pocket calculator and do some adding, subtracting, multiplying and dividing.

We won't lie to you. Analyzing survey results is work that is highly clerical, detailed, requires immense concentration, is boring as hell and is almost impossible to delegate. But it is definitely "bread upon the waters" work as well; that little bit of pain-in-the-neck effort *winners* invest up front to reap big results at the bottom line.   Reprinted from TRAINING, September 1980

FIGURE 5

Turnover Analysis - From Part II

Unit	No. of Employees	No. of Employees Budgeted	Percent of Budget	No. Hired This Quarter
1	17	17	100	1
2	12	16	75	3
3	11	16	65	9
⋮	⋮	⋮	⋮	⋮
60	25	27	93	2
61	22	25	88	5
61	1,037	1,098	94	488

No. of employees/unit = 17
Mean of budgeted employees/unit = 18

No. of employees hired this quarter:
Mean = 8   Median = 2   Mode = 2

FIGURE 6

Self-Report of Training Needs - Part III

	Yes	No
1. Have you attended a formal supervisory training program in the last five years?	37%	63%

2. Circumstances

• Several years ago at XYZ Co.	28%
• Other company	11%
• Night school	18%
• College	20%
• Service	13%
• Other (single related courses, books)	10%
	100%

3. Behavior	Do Well	Average	Need Improvement
a. Assign work	12 (20%)	38 (62%)	11 (18%)
b. Keep work flowing	23 (38%)	32 (52%)	6 (10%)
c. Day-to day feedback	7 (11%)	29 (48%)	25 (41%)
d. Absence control	13 (21%)	28 (46%)	20 (33%)
i. Maintain performance standards	13 (21%)	18 (29%)	30 (49%)
j. Make employees understand	28 (46%)	22 (36%)	11 (18%)

FIGURE 7

Cross-Tab A
Years of Supervisory Experience vs. Number of "Need Improvement" Areas

Experience	No./ Percent	Items Checked	Items/ Person
4 years or less	21 (34%)	39 (44%)	1.86
More than 4 years	40 (66%)	49 (56%)	1.23
Totals	61 (100%)	88 (100%)	

Cross-Tab B
Years of Supervisory Experience vs. Unit Absence Rate

Experience	No./ Percent	No. of Absences	No. of Employees	Employees/ Supervision	Absences/ Employee
4 years or less	21 (34%)	462	326	15.5	1.86
More than 4 years	40 (66%)	458	711	17.7	0.64
Totals	61 (100%)	920	1037		

HOW MARKET RESEARCH TECHNIQUES CAN PAY OFF

These tools can help you specify
outcomes, pinpoint organizational problems
and develop better content

BY RON ZEMKE

The word *research* makes many trainers skittish. And for good reason. Many of us have walked away from some version of Dr. Opaque's *Social Science Research: 501* or Dr. Greek's *Basic Statistics: 315* with heads full of Root-Mean Squares, Time-Series Analyses, Between-Group-Variances—and justifiable distaste. These academic encounters of the worst kind have made us gun-shy of doing rigorous research on training problems, Generally, we either fly by the seat of our pants or farm out the job to professors Opaque and Greek or, if we're really unlucky, to the organization's personnel research department.

Enter a new-old kid

Many trainers, however, are discovering that they are extremely comfortable using a class of well-established consumer-research techniques most trainers have never encountered. Market researchers and advertising people have developed a substantial number of tools for finding out what people do in the marketplace. Trainers can use many of these techniques to obtain rich data for such tasks as specifying training outcomes, pinpointing organizational problems and developing training content.

For example, a sales training manager in a major West Coast bank utilized the services of a market-research firm to perform part of a sales training task analysis for calling officers. The researchers studied the buying habits and styles of the clients with whom the bank's calling officers worked. In addition, the firm studied preferred sales behavior and preferred call frequency. Needless to say, this information facilitated the sales training director's search for a new program and the development of a new call strategy.

Need more encouragement? A major automobile manufacturer recently hired a consumer-research specialist to pinpoint the differences between service operations with high and low customer complaint histories. The outcome of the study had predictable implications for service manager selection and training, and surprising ones for dealer and sales rep training, too.

Four for trainers

Probably the consumer-research techniques most useful to trainers are those referred to by James J. Hubbard and Brenda K. Miller, of Wheaton, IL-based Hubbard and Associates, as *primary interviewing techniques*, including Focus Discussions, Intercept Interviews, Personal Interviews, Telephone Interviews and Mail Interviews. Except for the intercept interview, all of these have direct usefulness for trainers.

Focus group discussion. Here, individuals are brought together with a group discussion moderator to discuss some specific aspect of their job, organizational life, or—when used with consumers— some aspect of satisfaction with the products or services delivered by the organization. Focus groups generally range in size from eight to twelve individuals. The moderator's job is to prompt discussion among the individuals in order to learn how the respondents really feel about various aspects of a particular subject. The moderator generally brings to this effort a discussion outline and a background in small group dynamics and good facilitation skills. The moderator's primary role is keeping the discussion restricted to the subject at hand, assuring that no one noisy individual dominates discussion and encouraging all to contribute from their experience. Focus group discussions can last from an hour to over two hours.

As you would expect, there are pluses and minuses for any research technique. On the plus side:

• Focus groups give you easy, fairly reliable access to the ideas and attitudes of a work group. Be they salespeople, secretaries or division managers, focus group participants tend to relax and interact well verbally.

• The group make-up can be carefully controlled and double-checked simply by having the participants introduce themselves and speak about their background for a few minutes.

• Video and audiotaping of the sessions make the extra dimensions of nonverbal behavior and vocal information available to the analyst. Groups rarely object to recording, and transcripts of the session are invaluable for recollection analysis and comparison purposes.

• Focus groups are especially useful for gathering input that can be turned into questionnaires for a quantitative study.

The minuses are pretty obvious:

• The results of a focus group study are *qualitative,* not *quantitative:* there's no way to tell how widespread the group's attitudes and skills are in the populations from which the groups were drawn. And, as Al Anderson, president of Anderson Research, Minneapolis, cautions, "Many times a client foregoes follow-up quantitative study because of the cost and delay. That can lead to over-emphasis of some relatively minor problem or idea."

• Considering the cost of getting interviewees together, focus groups are fairly expensive.

• Just getting representatives from some populations together can be a problem. One researcher, who was conducting a management skills study with district managers of an oil company, relates that one busy manager sent his secretary halfway across the country to attend the focus group meeting for him. Though he certainly demonstrated his delegating skills, his creative solution for being in two places at once didn't add much to the research effort.

Personal interview. This second interview research technique is the most familiar to trainers. Respondents are randomly selected from a carefully defined population, and interviews are conducted near the workplace. Personal, one-on-one interviews can be highly structured beforehand and, when well-planned, can be rather brief. The interpersonal skills of the interviewer are critically important in the personal interview.

On one hand, the interviewer must cover certain ground with every interviewee without seeming bored or giving an "I heard it before" impression. At the same time, the interviewer must "read" the interviewees well enough to know when an interviewee wants to relate something germane to the discussion that is confidential or controversial.

The personal interview has a number of pluses:

• If the interviewer and interviewee can establish a "safe" relationship, a lot of information can be shared in confidence and anonymity and within a short time.

• The interviewer can use rating scales, questionnaires and card-sorting techniques to shape the interview and to relax and stimulate the interviewee.

• If the interview is especially fruitful, the length can be adjusted without having to consider other participants.

• The interviewer can shift and change interview style and question types to meet the style and comfort needs of the interviewee.

There are, however, at least four drawbacks to the personal interview:

• Cost. The one-on-one interview is definitely the most expensive— and slowest—way to gather information.

• Because interviewees may doubt that the interview will be held in confidence— especially if a tape recorder is used— they may not answer the interviewer's questions candidly or fully.

• Often the people selected for interview purposes within an organization are chosen because of their verbal skills or a history of candor rather than because they are representative.

• It is difficult to control the one-

on-one interview to the extent that the structured questions get answered. An interviewer might get carried away with some tangential lead in the interview, and the interviewee may need more time than the interview allows to consider one or more of the interview questions.

A common market-research technique that trainers could definitely use— especially for course evaluation purposes— is the...

Telephone interview. Telephone calls are made to a random selection of the population— be they job encumbents, ex-trainees or consumers— and interviews are conducted, using a structured interview guide. The guides used range from sheets with open-ended questions to questionnaires with specific choices. The typical telephone interview lasts 10 to 15 minutes; about 20% of the people contacted by telephone will give the interviewer 20 to 25 minutes.

There are many pluses for telephone interviewing:

• This is the least expensive live interview one can conduct.

• Interviews can be monitored and evaluated. And, because fewer interviewers are necessary, there's less chance for interviewer bias.

• About 80 to 90% of those called agree to be interviewed.

• People tend to be more candid over the phone than face-to-face. Hubbard and Miller have found, for example, that 70 to 80% of those interviewed over the phone will divulge household income figures— a much higher percentage than other methods yield.

The minuses tend to be minor:

• Telephone interviews tend to be shorter than other kinds of interviews.

• There is no possibility of "show and tell" or for any of the "loosening-up" exercises possible with the face-to-face interview.

• The interviewer must work with a structured interview form that typically requires developmental time and pilot testing.

• Not everyone succeeds at telephone interviewing. Good interviewers must be skilled at "breaking the ice" with total strangers over the phone.

Mail surveys. These usually are conducted on a one-time-only basis with a random sample of the population. A self-administered questionnaire, which is generally shorter than other

interview forms, is required. Incentives can be used to encourage a higher response rate.

Among the pluses are:

• Cost. The mail survey is the cheapest form of information gathering.

• Respondents can complete the questionnaires at their leisure and take more time to think through the questions. Return-mail answers often provide more detailed and accurate information.

• Because of the anonymity of mail interviews, respondents tend to be more frank in their responses, particularly on sensitive issues.

• A large staff isn't needed for administration.

But mail surveys have significant drawbacks.

• The most serious one is the non-response. No matter how many questionnaires come back, one always wonders how the missing people— the non-responders— differ from the responders. Some research indicates that "survey returners" tend to be better educated and more interested in the subject of the survey.

• Respondents tend to read through questionnaires before answering, thus possibly biasing the answer process.

• If the non-response rate is high, cost advantages tend to evaporate.

• Survey studies take a long time to complete since respondent turnaround time pretty much controls the completion date.

• Sometimes, as in the case of the substitute focus group attendee, the wrong person fills out the survey.

• It's difficult to design good surveys and questionnaires.

• Surveys require statistical treatment. If they aren't designed with that in mind, the results of the study cannot be interpreted accurately.

Limits and stuff

Obviously, no single consumer-research technique is appropriate in all situations. For instance, telephone surveys are ideal for post-training information but less so for climate and attitude sampling. And, of course, none of these techniques would suffice for doing a task-analysis study of a job like, say, typewriter repair. But when applied to the right kind of problem, consumer-research techniques can be a superb addition to the trainer's tool box. Reprinted from TRAINING, December 1978

A STEP-BY-STEP WAY TO CONDUCT FOCUS GROUPS

Here's help from market researchers
on how trainers can survey their 'market'
and test their 'product'

BY RON ZEMKE

One consumer-research technique a number of trainers are successfully adapting to their own purposes is the *focus group*. Market researchers use the focus group to find out what consumers like and dislike about a specific product or service and why they buy certain products instead of others. Trainers see focus groups as useful for comparing the attitudes, approaches and even skills of high- and low-performing managers; capturing the cognitive processes, experiences and job approaches of successful salespeople; and ferreting out organizational performance obstacles.

The focus-group technique requires a competent interviewer/facilitator and lots of planning. It is more expensive than survey research, and analyzing the results is a long and often tedious job. But there are a number of benefits, too. A topic can be explored fully, and unusual ideas and suggestions often surface unexpectedly. Specific incidents and quotations useful for developing program content often arise. And focus groups can generate content for questionnaire items for follow-up survey work.

There are three phases in a focus group study: planning, running the group and compiling and analyzing results.

Focus groups are highly susceptible to the "garbage in- garbage out" phenomenon. A concise definition of the problem under investigation and the kinds of input needed for understanding the nature of the problem is critical. The culmination of the planning process should be:

1. a statement of the problem,

2. identification of a specific population of people who should have valuable input and insight into the problem, and

3. an interview outline for conducting the actual focus group discussions.

Running the discussion

Facilitating the actual group discussions can be fun— if the planning has been done well. The following 10 tips and tricks can go a long way toward keeping you out of trouble.

1. Hold the groups on neutral turf. A conference room at a convenient company facility or even an off-site hotel/motel would be appropriate.

2. Give the chosen attendees (groups should number no less than 5 nor more than 12 people) plenty of lead time. Best bet is to send each of those selected for the group a letter specifying the general purpose of the meeting and its time, location and length (preferably two to two and a half hours).

3. Have lots of coffee and goodies available in the meeting room. These and the time spent talking, listening and doing general relationship building can break the ice before your turn on the recorder and start the session.

4. When you're ready to begin, have everyone sit around the table. Explain the purpose of the study, how and why the people were chosen and how the results of the session content will be used. During this introduction, stress the confidentiality of the information. When all questions have been answered, ask permission to turn on your taping equipment.*

5. Begin the session by asking the group members to identify themselves, tell where they work and how long they have been with the organization. This approach: a) loosens the group, b) gives you feedback on how well the participants meet the selection profile, c) gives the participants a chance to get used to the recording equipment, and d) gives your typist/transcriptionist a chance to become familiar with participants' voices.

6. Move from general to specific questions. "How do you approach the job of selling widgets to the Wobegone?" is a nebulous but useful starter. Later, you can ask more detailed questions, such as, "Exactly what *do* you say when you are trying to set up an appointment with someone you've never met?" In fact, the group members will usually volunteer the specifics once they have warmed up on the general questions.

7. Keep your comments nonjudgmental and your probe questions information clarification oriented. Always ask for clarification of technical terms, local jargon and complex ideas.

8. When a group member makes a strong statement or has an interesting but novel idea, find out how others feel about it. In so doing, be sure to "protect" the original speaker.

9. Give everyone in the group an opportunity to contribute to every topic or question in your outline. This entails encouraging some people to talk and tactfully diverting attention away from those who like to talk a lot about a little.

10. When you're sure the participants have covered everything on your outline and have gotten all the "hot topics" off their chests, conclude by saying, "We seem to have covered quite a bit of territory. Is there anything I should have asked or we should have discussed but didn't?" Usually someone has been holding back or waiting for the right question before telling you something important.

Compiling and analyzing results

Once all the groups have been con-

---

*Al Anderson, president of Anderson Research, Minneapolis, MN, cautions us not to scrimp on the quality of recording equipment used. "You'll regret it later if you do," he insists. Use a high-quality recorder, with two good microphones— one for each end of the table— and use new, high-quality tape. Put a heavy table cloth or felt pad on the table: recorders pick up an incredible amount of table noise.

ducted, you'll tackle the difficult part of the study. At this point, you *could* opt for the easy way out and simply listen through the groups' tapes again, make some notes and write up some general findings. But we recommend a more rigorous approach. Experience has proved to us and others we've talked to that enduring the tedium of the following seven-step process pays off in more precise, usable findings.

1. Have all the groups' tapes transcribed. This requires an expert typist and a lot of time: one hour of focus group could easily require five hours of transcribing.

2. As the transcripts become available, the moderator should simultaneously listen to the tapes and edit the transcription for meaning. Often the typist will mis-hear local jargon as legitimate Webster English. Some typists get quite good at typing what they thought they heard as opposed to what was actually said. Some even editorialize from their subconscious, or out of general boredom.

3. Read through the transcripts and make notes about possible key ideas.

4. When you think you have an exhaustive list of the key ideas contained in the transcripts, it's time to man your scissors. Go through a photocopy of each transcript, cut out sections of dialogue and monologue that refer to entries on your initial key ideas list and put them in labeled envelopes— one envelope for each key idea.

5. Once you've cut the wheat from the chaff, so to speak, it's time to fine-sort and cull the kernels. Go through the contents of each envelope, looking for subtopics, usable quotes (you'll want lots of these for the final report) and substantiation of the key idea.

Don't be afraid to change your mind about entries on your key-ideas list. You may have thought that hiring a skywriter was a novel, worthwhile idea; but after reviewing the transcripts of four groups, you realize that only one (eccentric) participant mentioned using skywriting, and even his group considered the idea dubious. So throw out the skywriting envelope or include the quote under another heading— "Unique Marketing Ideas," perhaps.

6. This is the creative writing part. Here's where you have to make flour of the grain and bake some bread. You need a narrative to explain the key idea and its subparts and to hold the supporting quotes together. And you must create this without any fictionalizing or subtle editorializing. For example, if someone in each of four groups makes a mild mention of a disparity between union and nonunion benefits, a summary statement such as, "Some nonunion employees tended to mention and voice at least a little concern, that they receive lower dollar value health care benefits than bargaining unit members" would probably convey the tone of the comments more accurately and appropriately than, "In all groups of nonunion employees, concern over the disparity between union and nonunion benefits was mentioned and pointed to as an example of a job dissatisfier."

7. The final writing task is to condense all your findings into a one-to-two page executive summary. This helps you continue the process of distilling the information you have gathered. And it gives you a summary of the study to show to others as support for recommendations you'll eventually be making. Besides, only you, other trainers and a few corporate masochists will ever read the entire report. The executive summary will satisfy management people who *say* they want to read the report but who really only want a brief idea of what you found.

Double checking. There is an optional Step Eight to consider, one suggested by Darrell R. Griffin, vice president of Research Media, Inc., Cambridge, MA. Griffin suggests that it is sometimes prudent to "test" the findings of the focus group study in one-on-one interviews. Specifically, he recommends finding and interviewing, four or five additional members of the population from which the focus group members were chosen. If the individual interviews yield information similar to the focus group information, you can be quite confident in your findings. If the one-on-one interviews don't confirm the focus group findings, you should consider doing additional work, perhaps conducting a survey study based on the key ideas from the focus group study.

The R.O.I.

Focus group research is a lot of work. A focus group study with four group discussions, each lasting one hour, can require 120 to 150 man-hours of typing, analyzing, writing, cutting and pasting, and hair-pulling to produce a first-class finished study. Is it worth the investment? It depends.

An airline we're familiar with did focus group studies with airline sales reps and travel agents and discovered that company policy and paperwork were inadvertently keeping sales reps from delivering the kind of service they had been trained to deliver and that travel agents wanted. A West Coast financial institution discovered that part of a customer-complaint problem they were experiencing was a result of under-training their telephone reps.

For these two organizations, the return on investment—and effort—was a good one. Focus group research is not a be-all and end-all. But, in the right circumstances and with the right problem it could have a good payoff for you.

Reprinted from TRAINING, December 1978

QUESTIONS & ANSWERS ABOUT DETERMINING YOUR TRAINING NEEDS

Trainers can't determine training needs entirely on their own

BY MARTIN M. BROADWELL

Trainers need help determining training needs from the people who know what the standards of performance should be. Here's how you can get their help.

Q. What can field people do to determine training needs?

A. Let's limit the question a bit and define some terms before going into detail.

The question asks about *training needs,* not *deficiencies,* so we'll limit the discussion to that aspect of an employee's ability to do the job. One thing we've learned through organizational development is that not everything that employees are doing incorrectly can be eliminated by training. (OD wasn't necessary for us to find this out, but it gave us our first strategy for looking at the organization as a whole in some kind of meaningful way, and it helped us put training into better perspective.)

Another limitation. We'll assume that "field people" means the supervisors of the potential trainees. This doesn't mean that all levels of management don't play roles in determining training needs. Rather, it means that if we include every potential role of management this column will become too complicated, and much too long.

We'll deal with the question of what top management can do at a later time. For now we'll limit our discussion to those supervisors who must make a determination on whether or not there is a training need and which employees need the training.

A final limitation. We won't include the part supervisors play in preparing the employees to come to training programs. Here, again, we have a vital issue which is just too significant to touch upon lightly.

Q. What's left to talk about, now that all these limitations have been put on the question?

A. Now we can deal with the *basic* question. "What can a supervisor do to see whether an employee really needs training and how can he determine exactly what the training need is?" First, we must recognize that training is needed when an employee *can't do a job, can't do it well enough* or *is doing it wrong.* These three training needs situations are the only *real* justification for spending training dollars. Any others are hard to justify when the boss asks "Why training?"

Notice that this approach requires the supervisor to look at the standards of the job, rather than

the procedures or job description. The performance on the job becomes the only criterion for determining whether or not the employee needs training. The supervisor compares the standard with the employee's performance. Any deficiency indicates an area where training can help.

Q. Is the "standard" the same thing as a "job description?"

A. No. A job description (or procedures manual) tells us specifically what an employee is supposed to do and how and when he or she is supposed to do it. By a "standard" we mean not only what job and how it is done, but how *well,* how *often,* how *much,* how *many.* We add a *quality* feature to the measurement.

Any good trainer will want to know that his trainees' supervisors have looked at the employees' work in light of quality and quantity, not just procedures. As we often say, monkeys can be trained to do most of our jobs—if we don't care about the time and quality of the work.

Notice now that the supervisor can make training determinations on the basis of the employee's performance measured against a fixed and agreed-upon standard. This standard has been discussed with the employee, with higher management and with the design people in the organization. There is no mystery about how well the job is to be performed. The supervisor can't come up with a hidden standard on things like "attitude" or "customer relations" or "lack of motivation." The standards for these are set as well as the standards for selling widgets or making framuses. The supervisor will pick for training those of his people who aren't meeting these standards.

Q. What if no standards exist?

A. Amazingly enough, many organizations don't have job performance standards, yet still expect trainers to bring their employees up to "performance level." Worse, some trainers find themselves setting the standards without much if any communication with field people. (The classic example is the management training course that teaches *participative* management—because all good trainers know that's the best kind—in an organization where *autocratic* has been and will continue to be the standard.)

When standards do not exist, supervisors can be asked to set standards in a "quick and dirty" way and pass the results along to the trainers. (Actually, the trainer will probably initiate the process during an interview with several of the supervisors.)

What the supervisor does is point out those things the satisfactory employee is doing and distinguish these from what the unsatisfactory employee is doing. The trainer may ask, "Why is it you say that Joe and Mary aren't doing their jobs very well?" Or "Why is it you say Jane or Tom is doing a good job?" The answers to these questions reveal that a standard does exist, even if it isn't written down.

When the supervisors begin to state what they expect of the unsatisfactory employees, we can see what the deficiencies are. We have to be sure to get *standards,* though, and not just *activities.* Just to say that one employee is a good letter writer and another isn't doesn't give us the standard for letter writing. We want the supervisor to say just what it is about the good letter writer that makes the letter good, and what is missing in the bad letters.

Another place to look is appraisal forms. No matter how bad these might be, the supervisor can tell a lot about the performance standards by just looking at what was said to (or about) the employees in the appraisals. As a supervisor I ask myself, "What were the areas where I suggested improvement? What did I say that would help this employee perform better or faster? What did I tell the employee my expectations were?" I look for quantitative and qualitative things. If all I've done is tell the person about their negative attitudes—lack of initiative or poor communications ability for example—I not only haven't got a standard—*I haven't done anything to help employee improve.*

In conclusion, the field supervisor can help determine training needs by finding those things that are measurable and trainable and reporting them to the trainer. He or she should report those things that have a standard which is acceptable to the supervisor, management and the employee doing the work. The trainer may decide not to provide certain training because of cost or difficulty or time, but at least those things that are chosen for training will be deficiencies that exist in the real world, not in the trainer's imagination!

Reprinted from TRAINING, November 1975

BEFORE OBJECTIVES: SOLUTION STATEMENTS

This new twist to a time-tested technique might be just the approach you need to prove that your training programs pay off

BY STEPHEN P. BECKER

Because organizational problems rarely have training solutions, training is most effective when it is only one element in a total improvement strategy. This concept is the essence of the Principle of Training Integration, which dictates that, to be successful, trainers must be concerned with complete solutions.

Such solutions evolve from an organizational performance analysis, not a training needs analysis, which incorrectly assumes that a subject-oriented training program will solve organizational problems. Most needs analyses consist of surveys in which a long list of subjects, not problems, are presented to managers or supervisors who are asked to indicate which are most relevant to them. Courses are then bought or developed and implemented according to those that dominate. Question: When the program is over and everyone has graduated, how will you measure the improvement to the organization?

The answer to this prickly question can be found by writing a training solution statement (TSS), the general features of which are:

• input, the result of an organization performance analysis;
• output or the training plan;
• non-training plans;
• criteria used to measure organizational improvement; and
• schedules for implementing behavioral (including training) and non-behavioral components of the total organizational solution.

A couple of other "musts" for every TSS: Keep it short (a couple of typewritten pages at most) and make sure the trainer writes it.

The first element of this brief document is a list of the names of those who agree to the total plan. Remember the TSS is the result of discussions and agreements arrived at by a group of people, one of whom is you, the trainer. There may only be one other person, a department manager, who is involved, or there may be a group of top managers who are dealing with a key performance problem. In any event, the TSS is a summary of the conclusions reached.

Next, the organizational performance goal or problem should be succinctly stated. There is a difference between a goal and a problem. A goal is something the organization or sub-unit wants to achieve. An example would be increasing market share by 10 percent during the next 12 months. A problem, on the other hand, is a negative deviation from the norm. If, say, costs have increased by 10 percent during the year, the organization has a problem.

If there is a problem, the third responsibility of the author of the TSS is to write both the behavioral and non-behavioral causes. If there is a goal to be achieved rather than a problem to be solved, the causes cannot be stated; instead the trainer writes a rationale. A behavioral cause primarily involves people; a non-behavioral one usually involves non-human resources. Again, the causes of a problem, or rationale for a goal should be brief—one or two sentences.

The organizational measurement criteria should be identified next. Available from standard documents in the management information system, these should be financial or operational. Organizational performance *must* be measured before the next step is taken.

Now the trainer writes the non-behavioral strategies and lists the persons or departments responsible for their implementation. The measurement criteria for these parts of the total solution are included so progress can be tracked. A time table for implementation also must be agreed upon. At this point, the trainer should feel totally—and positively—involved in non-training performance improvement decisions.

Now the trainer writes such behavioral solutions as feedback system development, reward or punishment systems, changes, etc. Here, you may have to abandon your consultant role and become, instead, an educator. As before, measurement criteria and time tables are crucial.

Finally, we are ready to consider training. There are two types: that which is required and that which is not but which would augment or enhance a non-behavioral or behavioral solution other than training.

For example, to increase market share, part of the behavioral strategy (other than training) might be to improve the incentive program for sales personnel. For instance, the planning group may decide to invest in an audiovisual program to explain a new system to the sales force. Such a move may not be required, but it would show sincerity and generate commitment to the goal. Of course, the group realizes that the AV investment is not a required part of the change strategy; it would hardly make or break the entire effort.

Since a TSS concerns itself with a solution for an entire organization or sub-unit, probably more than one training program is needed or desired. Generally you, the trainer, won't have to "sell" training. In fact, you'll look for ways to eliminate it so that you won't work yourself into a froth. For each training program, you should summarize any organizational conditions—estimated total cost, time schedules, priorities, prerequisites, restrictions, etc. If possible, specify how the on-the-job trainee behavior can be measured. While this may not always be practical, you must be able to measure the results achieved by trainees following their training program(s). The method for doing so should be indicated in the TSS.

Every person involved in the original discussions should receive a copy of the TSS. Naturally, not every training solution statement will contain all the preceding elements. Any one of the four major elements—non-behavioral solutions, behavioral other than training, required training, or desired training—could be missing.

Why bother, you may ask, to write a training solution statement at all? Seven sound reasons follow.

1. It gives the trainer a businesslike image and helps attain membership in management.

2. It shares the responsibility for organizational improvement and clarifies accountability.

3. It forces consensus and management unity.

4. It clarifies the training and non-training efforts necessary.

5. It serves as the basis for evaluating organizational achievement.

6. It fosters thoroughness in planning organizational improvements.

7. Solutions tend to be realistic and efficient.

Writing a TSS need not be a Big Deal. You can initiate it by scheduling a discussion with a manager who has a goal or problem. As you discuss it, recommend that others germane to the solution be invited to join you. Help the manager think in behavioral and non-behavioral terms, so he or she will recognize the productivity of the idea. As the meeting draws to a close summarize the conclusions reached.

Every group needs someone to take notes. If you're holding the magic marker, you can ask questions of clarification before you write anything down. Actually, you are engineering a process that is tantamount to providing worksheets with categories to be filled in. Ultimately, you will send what constitutes an action plan to everyone else. And you'll probably evaluate the progress of the goal or solution.

You are, in other words, running the show, while everyone else shares the responsibility. This is what being a change agent really means. You may think you hold a staff job, but that can easily be changed by what you do. Try it. It is, as they say, a piece of cake.

Reprinted from TRAINING, September 1977

FIGURING OUT WHAT PEOPLE NEED TO LEARN

Part of the trainer's job description
should include
the word 'investigator'

BY RON ZEMKE

Task analysis is a classic Alice-in-Wonderland word; it means neither more nor less than the person using it wants it to mean. Steve Becker defines task analysis as "breaking a job down into tasks and into a list of elements for the purpose of describing the skill component of a competency." That's fine for starters, but let's make absolutely sure we are talking about the exact same thing.

We are *not* talking about the process of sending a survey to all the first-line supervisors of Universal Widget and asking them to check, circle or write down all the general-skill or competency areas they, their subordinates or superiors seem to lack. That's needs analysis. Nor are we talking about studying the reinforcers, punishers and organizational obstacles which may be inhibiting the successful repair of a typewriter or computer or whatever. That's behavior analysis. Task analysis is what you and I do when we have faithfully followed all the routes in Robert Mager and Peter Pipe's performance-analysis flow chart and are 99.9% sure that we are stuck with a situation that represents a *bona fide* training problem.

Surprisingly, when it comes to doing an actual task analysis, most of us have a limited vocabulary of techniques. Generally, we fly by the seat of our pants when we try to figure out what people need to know and do to perform their jobs successfully. But we're not alone. Many experts and instructional technology gurus agree with R. B. Miller, who declares that "Task analysis is an art, and as an art is largely dependent for its excellence and utility on the expertise of the task analyst." While that view is a pervasive and persuasive one, it hardly encourages experimentation.

In opposition to the Miller view, Instructional Psychologists Glaser and Resnick see task analysis as a science and, therefore, a growth stock. "Task analysis is the description of tasks in terms of the demands they place on such basic psychological processes as attention, perception and linguistic processing," they declare.

Whether task analysis should be characterized as an art or a science is probably irrelevant to us as practitioners. What *is* relevant is that we learn as many ways to describe tasks and list elements as we can. In that regard, our poking about and asking "How do *you* do task analysis?" has unearthed no fewer than 10 distinct approaches to task analysis. Five of the most interesting are summarized here.

Look-and-see approach

The first and most commonly practiced task-analysis technique is the look-and-see approach. Look and see is a spin-off from the time-and-motion study techniques invented by Frederick Taylor and other advocates of the scientific-management school so popular in the early 1900s.

In its simplest form, look and see is just that—simple observation. The trainer/analyst watches a subject-matter expert—someone who does the job well—and writes down what the SME does. The analyst looks for connections between what is done and what is produced and is especially alert to sequencing—i.e., "Let's see now, which goes on first? The link-washer retaining collar or the spring-assembly compression butt?" After watching the job cycle until every move is pretty predictable, the analyst begins asking questions like: "Why do you do A before B?" and "How did you know that was wrong just then?" The output is usually a prose description of the optimum sequence of events for doing the job and a list of things to do when exceptions arise.

One sophisticated form of look-and-see task analysis is taught and practiced by Dr. William Deterline, Deterline Associates, Palo Alto, CA. Deterline defines task analysis as the "specification of all overt and covert behavior involved in the performance of a job." The analyst's job is to develop a Behavioral Blueprint which consists of three elements; a Stimuli-Responses (S-R) Table, Behavioral Objectives and Criterion Test Items. The development of the S-R Table involves six steps:

1. Record observable behavior of incumbents.

2. Determine the *stimuli* (cues, signals) for the observed behaviors or *responses* (including responses to stimuli which are stimuli for subsequent responses).

3. Classify the S-R elements as: VP—verbal performance; VB—verbal behavior; MP—motor performance; D—discrimination

4. Classify discriminations as *one-way or multiple*. Example: Suppose the task is to pick out a picture of the dinosaur Triceratops when shown pictures of a Triceratops, a Stegosaurus and an Allosaurus. In that case, the task is a single *discrimination*.

If, however, the task is to call picture X a Triceratops, picture Y a Stegosaurus, and picture Z an Allosaurus, then the task is multiple discrimination. This classification makes a difference when one begins designing training.

5. Classify all S-R units as one-way or two-way. If the task is to say Triceratops to picture X, it's a one-way S-R unit. If the task is to say Triceratops to picture X *and* to pick up picture X when the task is to "find the Triceratops," it's a two-way S-R unit.

6. Determine relevent verbal mediators. Example: If ROY G. BIV is a commonly used mnemonic for remembering electrical resistor color coding, it is a relevant verbal mediator. Write it down.

The look-and-see task analysis approach is especially useful in simple motor-skill areas. Such tasks as small-machine repair, prepping scuba-diving equipment, and assembling small parts have been effectively analyzed by the look-and-see approach. It is also useful in situations where simple and moderately complex motor skills comprise the largest part of the job to be learned.

Structure-of-knowledge approach

The second approach, structure of knowledge, is the creation of Military Psychologist Robert Gagne and is based on training research work he and others did during the mid and late 1950s.

In a 1961 paper Gagne presented when he was elected president of the Military Division of the American Psychological Association, he suggested that one should not look to well-known learning principles when developing effective training. "I should look instead to the technique of task analysis," he said, "and the principles of component task achievement, and the sequencing of subtask learning to find those ideas of greatest usefulness."

Later, in his book, *The Conditions of Learning,* Gagne clarifies this approach. To Gagne, the analyst is most concerned with determining "type of learning" that each task would require. This knowledge is useful since the subtasks of the criterion performance must be a given learning type and can be easily identified and separated out.

Suppose Task K, replacing a flat tire, is a chaining task, i.e., there is a sequence of tasks to perform to remove the flat tire and replace it with a non-flat tire. In Gagne's hierarchy of learning types, chains are composed of *stimulus-response learning elements* which in turn are composed of *signal learning tasks.* For example, I must learn that when a tire is flat, the *stimulus* 'lug nut on bolt' is a cue for the *response* 'remove lug nut.''

In *The Conditions of Learning,* Gagne specifies eight types of learning, listed here in decreasing complexity:
1. problem solving
2. rule learning
3. concept learning
4. discrimination learning
5. verbal association
6. chaining
7. stimulus-response learning
8. signal learning

The idea is that all higher-order tasks are composed of lower-order elements. Learn the lower-order elements, and you have mastered the higher-order task. For me to fully un-

derstand the significance of the verbal mediator concept, "the red strawberries are ripe," I must already have, or acquire, a lot of discriminating verbal associations, chains, S-R units and signals. Determining both the *structure* and the subelement structure of the thing to be learned is where the analyst should focus his or her attention, according to Gagne.

The structure-of-knowledge approach is useful in analyzing fairly academic and theoretical subjects, such as math, physics, engineering and computer repair. Anywhere there's a large body of theory and a complex application situation, the structure-of-knowledge approach can be a real expedient.

Critical-incident approach

The critical-incident approach is another military training invention. The inventor, John C. Flanagan, also a military psychologist, was faced with the problem of improving military flight training. Specifically, too many trainees were cracking up the training planes, and someone somewhere in the War Department suggested that perhaps the training wasn't emphasizing the right things. The key word here is emphasis.

Flanagan, who later founded the American Institute of Research, did something deceptively simple. He asked those pilot trainees (who were able to walk away) to describe—in terms of behavior—what exactly they had done incorrectly. That technique of illiciting "war stories" is basically what the critical-incident approach amounts to.

There are, of course, some parameters on the acceptability of those war stories. Critical incidents are facts, not generalizations or opinions. They're about performance which can be pinpointed as either effective or ineffective. Critical incidents need not be major events. However, they're not usually just routine steps a trainee generally does correctly by habit. Consider, as examples, two incidents from a nursing training program Flanagan worked on in the late 1950s.

Effective Incident: A student nurse catches an error on a medication card when she double checked the patient's name.

Ineffective Incident: A student nurse fails to chart consistent elevation of a patient's temperature when the doctor's decision to operate rested on the patient's temperature at 8:00 AM that day.

After the analyst collects many such incidents, a panel of experts sorts

them into groups or factors. The first nursing example—the student catching the medication error—was sorted into a pile of similar incidents which were eventually labeled *Checking.* The second example was sorted into a pile of similar incidents which were eventually called *Observing, Reporting and Charting.*

In a sense, the critical-incident technique is an application to training of Alfredo Paredo's Law of Disproportionate Distribution. Italian Mathematician Paredo originally discovered that 80% of the wealth of Italy was controlled by 20% of the population. The principle has shown to be true in other situations. Twenty percent of a company's salespeople make 80% of the sales; 20% of the sales generate 80% of the profits; and 20% of the effort yields 80% of the output. The critical-incident technique tries to point out what that critical 20% of effort, which yields 80% of the performance, looks like.

Dr. Marvin Dunnette has used the critical-incident approach to develop highly sophisticated and reliable performance-review instruments. He has developed a technique for gathering incidents and developing performance-measurement scales which is fairly simple and most effective in sorting out the 80s and 20s of such large and nebulous jobs as "managing" and "selling." There are roughly six steps to the process:
1. Gather two groups of SMEs;
2. Have them describe specific job incidents and the results produced;
3. Have them analyze these into like factors and name the factors;
4. Have them rank the incidents as good or bad along a seven-point scale;
5. Have them fill gaps in the scales with additional incidents;
6. Have them reconcile differences between the two groups.

Dunnette and others have applied the technique to jobs ranging from grocery check-out clerk to navy recruiting officer.

Process/decision flow chart approach

The process/decision flow chart technique is borrowed directly from the computer sciences. When programming a computer, the task is to break decisions into questions which have simple yes/no answers followed or preceded by equally simple operations. As a training tool, the process/decision flow chart has been honed and perfected by Ivor K. Davies and Ivan S. Horabin under the moniker "algorithm."

The term algorithm, from mathematics, refers to a simple sequence of instructions arranged in logical order and linked by simple-to-answer yes/no questions.

As an analysis technique, the exercise of forcing large, complex and conditional behavioral repertoires into simple instructions and yes/no questions can bring order to apparent chaos. Analysts armed with the algorithm mentality have attacked such seemingly complex and procedure-bound jobs as medical diagnosis, computer repair and the filing of one's income tax.

The procedure for developing the algorithm is a fairly straightforward one sometimes referred to as protocol development. The analyst simply has the SME give a running commentary on what he or she is doing and thinking while performing the task. After a number of these are obtained, an acceptable compromise protocol is developed. One group we know uses the tape recorder extensively. SME's are encouraged to chat with the

FORCE-FIELD ANALYSIS

BY CHARLES UTT

Most trainers are familiar with some form of front-end analysis—determining training needs and requirement *before* a training program is developed and implemented—and *rear-end* analysis—determining the effectiveness of a training program *after* its completion.

Somewhere between front-end and rear-end analysis is another method called force field analysis—analyzing the forces "for" and "against" a change in behavior of an individual or a group.

Consider, for example, a group of busy department heads whose objective is to increase training interest in a program that is unpopular, but still necessary and required. The forces for and against this program were diagrammed by the training director at the start of the program before an effort was made to improve the interest.

Rather than asking "What can we do to raise the level of interest," we can change the question to "What keeps the interest rate as high as it is? What keeps it from going higher?" as we analyze the interest rate as a *balance* of forces. Now it becomes evident that the interest rate can be raised either by increasing the driving forces at the left of the interest scale or by reducing the restraining forces to the right of the interest scale.

Here's how the training director can try to change these forces in order to increase the rate of interest.

The use of this force field analysis technique in training does not guarantee success. Like any other management tool, it assists in planning and building a better training program. But it *can* give some insights to the positive and negative forces which are constantly at work to either help or hinder training programs.

Reprinted from TRAINING, December 1977

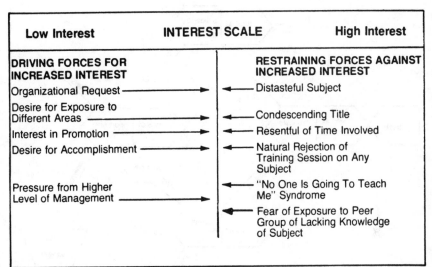

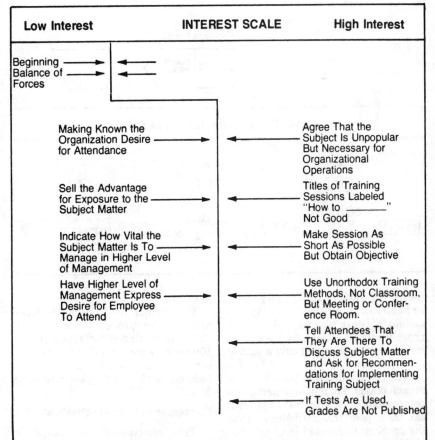

analyst as one would with a student. "Here's what I'm doing. At this point I could do A, B or C. I'm going to do B; here's why..."

Two medical educators, Drs. John E. Rhetts and James H. Moller, used the process/decision flow chart method of task analysis to structure criminations and decisions a bank teller must master to perform the "simple" task of cashing a check. By forcing the information through such questions as "What usually happens first?," "How do you decide what to do next?" and "How did you do that?," an algorithm for check cashing

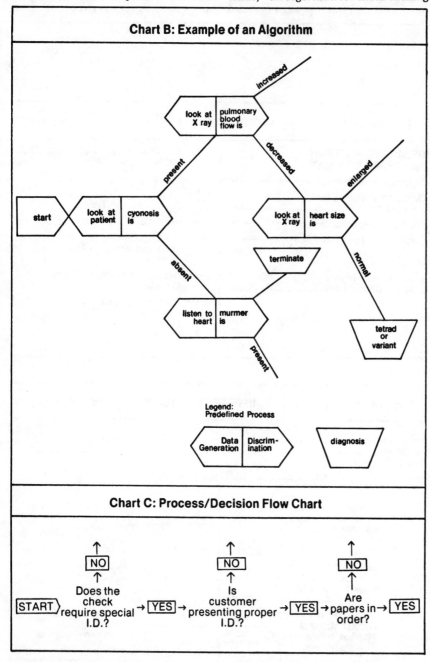

Chart B: Example of an Algorithm

Legend:
Predefined Process

| Data Generation | Discrimination |

diagnosis

Chart C: Process/Decision Flow Chart

niques. Market researchers and advertising people have developed a respected and substantial body of tools for finding out what people do and what they expect from people with whom they interact in the marketplace. Many of these techniques provide rich data for specifying both training outcomes and training content.

For example, we know a sales-training manager in a major West Coast bank who utilized the services of a market-research firm to perform part of a sales-training task analysis for calling officers. The researchers studied the buying habits and style of the clients the bank's calling officers worked with. In addition, the firm studied preferred sales behavior and preferred call frequency. Needless to say, this information became key to the sales-training director's search for a new program and in the development of a new call strategy.

One consumer-research technique a number of trainers are adapting is the *focus group*. The purpose of focus groups is to find out what consumers like and dislike about a specific product or service and why they buy certain products instead of others. All members of the group have had previous experience with the same product, service or problem, and an interviewer seeks responses related to various attributes of the experience.

The focus-group technique requires a good interviewer and a lot of planning. It is more expensive than a survey study. And analysis of results is a long and tedious job. But there are a number of benefits.

A topic can be fully explored and unusual ideas and suggestions often surface unexpectedly. Specific incidents and quotations useful for developing content arise. And a focus group can generate items for verification and use later in a more data-based approach. The focus group is especially useful to the trainer who works with people who have heavy customer-contact responsibilities.

To be continued

We have not, by any means, said the last word on task-analysis techniques. We've probably missed two or three of your favorite toys, and we haven't mentioned two or three of our own favorites.

But the point is clear: When we get to that box in the flow chart that says "do task analysis," there are a lot of possibilities. The trick is to apply the right technique to the right job. If we don't think through our choice of task-analysis approach, we can't figure out what our trainees need to know and do to perform optimally.

the procedures and decisions a general practitioner needs to diagnose pediatric heart diseases. The flow chart would fill the entire page if we let it, so we've included only a part of it in Chart B.

The process/decision flow chart approach is also useful in organizing jobs composed of decisional tasks less critical than pediatric cardiology. Take the problem illustrated in Chart C of sifting through the myriad rules, dis-

pops out.

One trainer we know made a job aide of the process/decision flow charts he designed for repairing the 100 most common faults of a calculating machine. Training time was reduced by 45% and repeat repairs by 30%.

Consumer-research techniques

This last type of task analysis is really a whole class of research tech-

Reprinted from TRAINING, December 1977

HOW TO CONDUCT A SALES PERFORMANCE AUDIT

This analytic approach can uncover problems and help improve sales performance in your organization

BY PAUL HARMON

If you think sales training has changed over the past decade, you're right. Senior managers have embraced the concept of performance-based training, while at the same time a number of high-quality sales-management products have been thrust onto the market. Fierce competition among vendors has launched new and better sales-improvement efforts. All in all, you might expect salespeople to be better trained than they were 10 years ago.

And some are. But all the proven analytic techniques, effective management tools and dynamite sales-training programs in the world are not going to improve sales performance in your organization unless the training fits your needs.

The problem is that more high-quality options result in a more complex decision-making process for sales trainers—and simultaneously increase the possibility of errors. The situation is further complicated by the fact that most sales managers and trainers are forced to rely on the vendor's salespeople to help them analyze their training needs.

Despite the talk you hear about "consultative" selling, it's obviously a mistake to *depend* on most salespeople to recognize and tell you that some other approach would be more appropriate than the one the salesperson is offering. I recently found a financial institution that set great stock in a program designed to teach salespeople to call on clients; but the company was using it to teach officers to sell to customers who walked into branches. A completely different approach is required when a customer walks up and asks to buy a product. The customer *opens* the call and sets the agenda—eventualities that weren't ever considered in the program being used.

What you need is a solid analysis of your sales performance problems *before* you go shopping for remedies. Both external and internal consultants can use a diagnostic tool I call a "sales performance audit" to help their respective "clients" analyze their needs and improve their sales performance.

The sales performance audit

This type of report compares the ex-

pected benefits of alternative options, weighs the cost of tailored vs. off-the-shelf programs, and generally helps sales managers and trainers sort through the available choices. The goal of a sales performance audit is twofold. First, it gives the company a comprehensive overview of its sales organization and the performance problems it is experiencing. This overview summarizes the structure and goals of the existing sales organization; the environment in which the sales force operates; the resources and support services it needs; the skills and knowledge it requires; the motivation, feedback and compensation appropriate for its particular needs; and the management techniques needed to plan, implement, and monitor an effective sales effort.

Second, a sales performance audit identifies and rank orders—in cost/benefit terms—the steps management can take to increase sales. If, for example, an audit reveals that a sales job aid, a feedback system and a workshop in presentation skills are needed, it should also note that job aids are inexpensive, easy to develop and highly effective. Feedback systems fall in the middle range in terms of cost, effort and effectiveness. Workshops, on the other hand, are expensive, take considerable time to develop, and are, at best, only partially effective. The audit should also emphasize that even the best workshop will fail to improve sales performance if an existing feedback system suppresses the behavior the workshop is designed to teach.

In other words, a sales performance audit should include all of those things that performance technologists have learned about changing human behavior, and it should do so in the specific context of your client's sales situation.

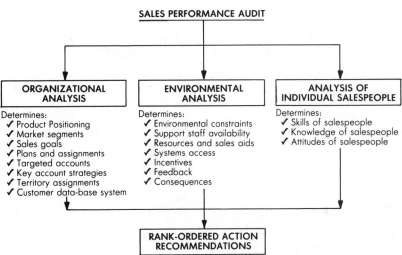

Figure 1. A Sales Performance Audit

Computer consultants will address a sales organization's computer-support problems. Training vendors will recommend sales-training programs. Compensation specialists will always be happy to suggest new incentive programs. Senior managers, however, are becoming savvy buyers—they realize that only performance technologists working in the tradition of Thomas Gilbert, Geary Rummler and Joe Harless are able to pull together a comprehensive picture of an organization's performance problems and recommend effective, logical solutions. This type of performance audit is the vehicle that can focus an integrated analysis and design effort on your sales problems.

Describe the sales organization

To conduct a comprehensive sales performance audit, you'll need to analyze the company's sales organization from three general perspectives: 1) the organization's overall approach to sales; 2) the specific environment in which salespeople function; and 3) the specific skills and knowledge the salespeople possess.

Begin with an organizational analysis (see Figure 1). You can determine the company's overall approach to sales by interviewing managers and examining documentation. Develop a detailed description of how your particular organization handles each of the critical components listed in Figure 1.

Pay particular attention to how information is passed back and forth within your sales organization. Figure 2 indicates typical steps in the market-planning and account-targeting process, but you'll need to probe to determine exactly how your organization handles each of these steps.

Performance problems

To analyze environmental and individual performance problems, begin with a detailed study of the environment in which the sale occurs and the exact activities for which salespeople are responsible.

Study each activity or task by interviewing and observing both typical and outstanding salespeople, and then compare your findings. Assume that the performance of outstanding salespeople is at or very near the best that can be achieved in a particular environment, and focus on the differences between typical and outstanding performers. Obviously, large differences represent areas in which ordinary performers can be significantly improved.

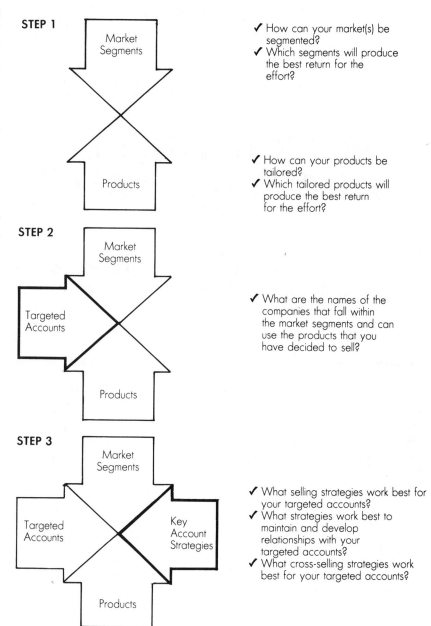

STEP 1
- ✔ How can your market(s) be segmented?
- ✔ Which segments will produce the best return for the effort?
- ✔ How can your products be tailored?
- ✔ Which tailored products will produce the best return for the effort?

STEP 2
- ✔ What are the names of the companies that fall within the market segments and can use the products that you have decided to sell?

STEP 3
- ✔ What selling strategies work best for your targeted accounts?
- ✔ What strategies work best to maintain and develop relationships with your targeted accounts?
- ✔ What cross-selling strategies work best for your targeted accounts?

Figure 2. The Market Planning and Account Targeting Process

Figure 3 lists some of the typical activities salespeople perform. You may uncover significant problems in any of these areas. One study, for example, determined that an organization's major problem centered on the relationships between salespeople and staff people: Good salespeople were able to relate to staff people effectively and quickly obtained the products they promised customers. Poor salespeople ignored staff relationships, were less effective in satisfying customer requests promptly and, consequently, were less-productive salespeople.

The sources of problems

Once you have identified the sales activities, detail the steps involved in each activity to uncover performance problems that occur during each step. For analytic purposes, divide the causes of deficient sales performance into six basic categories (see Figure 4).

1. **Resource/environmental problems.** Resource and environmental problems occur when salespeople lack the necessary tools to do their jobs or when events in the performer's environment prevent adequate performance. To determine if salespeople are blocked by these kinds of obstacles, ask questions such as:

• Does the average salesperson have the resources needed to perform the task?

• Does something or someone in

the work environment prevent the average salesperson from doing the task?

• Do other tasks prevent the average salesperson from selling?

2. Systems and marketing problems. Inadequate systems or marketing support normally result in resource/environment problems. In a large organization, however, these problems often require a rather detailed study of how the computer system works or how a marketing department conceptualizes its function, so this category is worth a separate analysis.

3. Skill/knowledge problems. These usually result from the lack of training, practice, experience and/or information. To pinpoint problems in this area, ask questions such as:

• Does the average salesperson know when to sell?

• Does the average salesperson know how to sell?

• Does the average salesperson know the difference between an acceptable and unacceptable effort?

Pay particular attention to existing training: How is product knowledge packaged and taught to new salespeople? How are salespeople taught to position their products and reposition competitive products?

4. Attitude and self-perception problems. Attitude or deficient self-image problems often look like skill/knowledge problems, but they are more subtle. Look for shadings of tone as salespeople describe their jobs. Metaphorical statements of what sales is about (for example, "sales is war," or "sales is consulting") can say a lot about the employee's overall approach to the job. Just a small change in the way salespeople describe or talk about their tasks can make a big difference in their performance.

5. Motivation/feedback and incentive problems. Are there glitches in your feedback system? Does positive performance produce positive consequences, or are you somehow "punishing" people for doing a good job? Poorly designed consequences are counterproductive, whether they come in the form of verbal or written feedback, incentive programs or whatever. If salespeople do not clearly understand their goals and responsibilities, incentives are usually wasted; people will tend to regard the payments as random events rather than rewards for specific accomplishments.

Questions to ask about feedback and incentives include:

• Does the average salesperson have a clear conception of his or her sales goals and responsibilities?

• Is the average salesperson informed of correct or incorrect performance?

• Does the average salesperson receive any rewards for correct or incorrect sales performance? Any punishment for either?

6. Management problems. Problems that result from inadequate management normally manifest themselves as feedback/incentive problems, although poor planning or the ineffective communication of

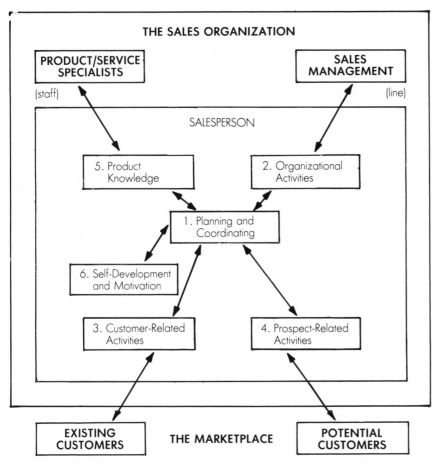

Figure 3. Typical Activities Performed by Members of a Field Sales Organization

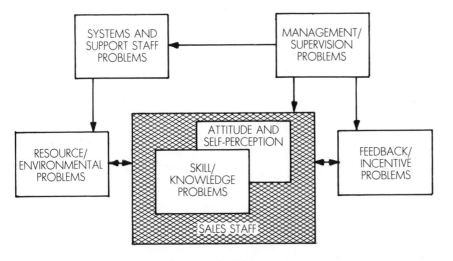

Figure 4. Sources of Sales Performance Problems

goals, priorities or standards can just as easily appear to be resource or skill/knowledge problems. Management continuously must define appropriate goals, standards and procedures, and then work hard to see that performers get timely feedback and appropriate reinforcements whenever they perform in the desired manner. Specific questions to keep in mind include:

• Do managers have a clear understanding of what the average salesperson should be doing?

• Do managers establish clear goals and objectives for the average salesperson?

• Do managers structure tasks appropriately for the average salesperson?

• Do managers train or coach average salespeople when they are deficient?

• Are support people available to assist salespeople in their efforts?

Gather the initial data on a matrix which lists the specific sales activities and tasks to be studied on the vertical axis and the six causes of performance problems on the horizontal axis. Later, when this data is consolidated, it becomes the key to the performance audit report.

At the same time, develop a diagram that gives management a clear picture of how information about customers and prospects is passed between members of the sales organization. It also should show how feedback, incentives, consequences and information about sales goals or targets is passed between managers and sales personnel. This chart is a key tool for planning improvements in the sales organization.

Taking action

After you have identified the problems associated with each of the tasks salespeople perform, combine them into manageable clusters. Rank these clusters according to the improvement that would result if the problems in each cluster were eliminated or at least significantly reduced.

Developing a reasonable list of action recommendations is the toughest part of an audit. Every sales organization has a unique set of problems and a unique mix of resources and management priorities, all of which must be considered as you prepare your recommendations. There's no point in recommending a sales-training program that's too costly for your organization's budget, just as there's no point in recommending changes in re-

porting relationships if you know that senior management will be unwilling to consider them.

When you recommend possible actions, also suggest a specific program—one that can be completed within a given period and price range—aimed at changing a specific sales performance problem in your organization.

Your list of action recommendations should be the result of thoughtful consideration of the problems your particular organization faces, combined with a number of expert judgments about what reasonably can be done to reduce or eliminate those problems.

The sales performance audit, when coupled with performance-engineering techniques, is a powerful approach for trainers and sales managers who want to improve the effectiveness of their people. The audit provides management with an objective source of comprehensive advice on the best means of improving sales performance—and helps avoid costly and ineffective programs. As competition continues to increase, the sales performance audit may well prove to be instructional technology's most important contribution to increasing sales.

Reprinted from TRAINING, August 1984

MEASURING WHITE-COLLAR WORK

Want to create meaningful productivity indicators for white-collar workers? Ask the people who do the jobs to develop the measurements

BY TOM SALEMME

You're not measuring what we actually do." "This job is not routine; it requires the independent judgement of a knowledgeable person." "But we work as a team to produce a single product (or service)." To anyone who has attempted to create and use white-collar productivity measurements, these protests probably sound familiar.

Consider these findings from an American Productivity Center (APC) survey, conducted among 2,000 white-collar workers in 1985:

• Over 50 percent of all respondents were either unsure about or disagreed with the idea that there was a clear way to measure results in their present jobs.

• Only 35 percent of the respondents believed their current performance measures were accurate.

• Approximately two-thirds said they did not receive timely, reliable information about the effectiveness of their organizations.

None of this means that white-collar work cannot be measured. In fact, findings like these mask a genuine concern: Employees fear measures in part because of the way they've been created and used in the past.

So why invest the effort necessary to design an effective measurement system for white-collar workers? For one thing, it provides people with feedback on their performance. Sixty percent of the respondents to APC's survey said they could use feedback to improve their work. Yet most of these people receive little meaningful feedback; it tends to be indirect or negative, offered only when a problem occurs. Feedback—both good and bad—can be a powerful tool for improving performance, but only

Measures should be identified by the people who do the work.

when appropriate measures are used and administered correctly.

For another thing, a measurement system helps evaluate the quality of the services provided by a white-collar work group. Critical service points are directly related to the group's overall objectives. If a department historically has been weak at certain points in its service delivery, then these points should be the focus of attention. By measuring certain factors over time, you can track improvements or collect data that may lead to a new design of the service-delivery system.

Establishing effective measures

Most measurement systems address efficiency (how many, how fast, how cheap, etc.) but ignore the effectiveness (quality, usefulness, etc.) of the final product. Figure 1 contrasts the traditional approach to measurement with one that emphasizes measures of effectiveness.

How do you design good measures for white-collar service jobs? The first step is to answer two basic questions about the work: "Are we providing the correct services to our clients?" and "Are we providing those services in the best possible way?" A good measurement system should focus on a "family" or set of measures that will answer these questions.

Next, decide upon ratios that will measure the rate of work or output in terms of quality, timeliness or usefulness. What you're looking for are measures that will go beyond output and examine the outcome of a service.

Here's an example of a situation that called for service-oriented measurements. A manufacturing division of a large aeronautical firm decided that too many staff hours were wasted because of incomplete and late engineering drawings. Inaccuracies in the drawings led to problems in other parts of the company: wrong parts were ordered, products failed during testing and so on. The design engineering division examined its services and concluded that to improve effectiveness, it had to focus on the quality of drawings and responsiveness to requests from its customers (in this case, the manufacturing group).

To track improvement efforts, the engineering division established the following ratios:

$$\frac{\text{Total specifications met per drawing}}{\text{Total specifications submitted per drawing}}$$

$$\frac{\text{Number of drawing errors}}{\text{Total drawings completed}}$$

$$\frac{\text{Number of drawings released on time}}{\text{Total number of drawings}}$$

These ratios not only measure service output, but also the results or outcomes of services. They answer questions such as: Did the engineering division meet clients' expectations (specifications)? Were the products (drawings) of high quality (error-free)? Were they delivered on time?

Additional sample sets of measurements appear in the box.

Choosing measures

Measures should be identified by the people who do the work. Given clear objectives, employees will have a good understanding of what constitutes an effective level of service. One approach that helps them establish measures is based on the Nominal Group Technique. It consists of the following steps:

1. *Select a group of employees to develop measures.* Pick six to 10 people who are directly involved in delivering the service you want to track. It's best to select employees from several levels in the organization to bring a cross-section of perspectives to the task. A small number of the group's clients or customers also may be invited to participate in establishing measures.

2. *Brief them on the process.* Group members should understand that the proposed measurements will assess the service delivery system. The discussion should center on weaknesses in that system or places where problems have been experienced in the past. Instruct the group to keep these points in mind while deciding upon measures. Make sure that each employee understands the group's service objectives and the language in each objective.

After the group briefing, give a thorough explanation of measurement types. Provide examples of ratios so that the group clearly understands the range of possible measures.

3. *Brainstorm an initial list of indicators.* To get the group thinking in the right direction, post the objectives where everyone can see them. Underline key words and ask the group to identify how the objectives can be measured. Then ask everyone to spend 10 minutes working individually to list as many different indicators as they can think of.

4. *Collect suggestions.* After the group members have created their own lists of possible measures, collect each suggestion in round-robin fashion, asking each participant to give one measure from their lists until all have been collected. Record them on

a flip chart and post the lists around the room.

5. *Clarify measures.* Once the ideas have been collected, make sure everyone understands what each measure means. Participants may want to combine similar measures or put an indicator into ratio form. At this point, the group's objective is to clarify the indicators and make sure they do not overlap, not to come up with a final list of measures.

6. *Vote on suggestions.* Few groups

A measurement system that is not used correctly and constructively will decrease morale and output.

---

can afford to collect data on a large number of indicators. To reduce the number of proposed measures, ask the group to select the top 10 measures, according to how well they meet the original service objectives.

Implementing the system

After the group has identified the measures, ask management to review them according to the following criteria: Are all the objectives covered? Will data from the measures point to real service effectiveness? Can measures from two or more services be combined into one indicator? Do the measures reflect critical points in the delivery system? How easy will it be to obtain the data needed for each

measure?

The final measures also can be weighted to reflect management's priorities. If measures of outcome are weighted more than output, for example, the measurement system will signal employees to emphasize effectiveness in their work, not just volume.

It's important to consider how measures will be used to improve performance. A measurement system that is not used correctly and constructively will decrease morale and output. Management can forestall these disastrous effects by communicating the purpose of the system and addressing questions such as: How will the measurement data be presented? To whom and by what manager? Will it be discussed at staff meetings? How will it be conveyed to employees? How often will the data be analyzed? Who will conduct the analysis? How will the information be displayed?

Management should also agree on how often measures will be reviewed and modified if necessary, and who will oversee that process. Finally, after the measurement system is in place, periodic follow-up should be part of the process to ensure that it is being used correctly by all management levels.

The process of measurement must be thought of as a way to manage performance—not as an end in itself. By focusing on white-collar workers' service objectives and the appropriate methods for achieving them, measurement takes on value. If the measures you select reflect important aspects of the services people are performing, if the system is used for planning and coaching, and if employees are involved in establishing the measurement system, they will respond to it enthusiastically.

Reprinted from TRAINING, July 1987

FIGURE 1
MEASUREMENT SYSTEMS

Traditional Approach	Effectiveness Approach
Measures reflect activities.	Measures reflect services.
One or two measures used to assess a function.	A comprehensive group of measures used to describe all the work.
Measures established by management or outside specialists.	Measures established by employees of a work group.
Measures established for individuals	Measures established for the work group.
Measures used for controlling/ monitoring.	Measures used for planning/ coaching.

say, sales personnel and the behavior "asking for the order" is an important

OBSERVATION*	SALESPERSON		
	A	B	C
No. of ring-ups observed	6	7	6
Small talk (bursts)	7	3	3
Asking "Will there be anything else today?	4	8	2
Suggesting specific "add-on" items	1	3	5
Average "add-on" $ per ring-up	$1.85	$2.10	$5.36

*All observations   90 minutes

THE 'COUNT AND CHART' APPROACH TO TASK ANALYSIS

Behavior counting not only helps you ferret out the subtle differences between effective and ineffective performance. It also helps pinpoint which process differences really count on the bottom line

BY RON ZEMKE

Bottom line, the two major contributions of the Skinnerian school of behavioral psychology are the concepts of reinforcement and frequency. Most trainers are familiar with the concept of reinforcement: a behavior followed by favorable consequences for the performer tends to increase in frequency, while a behavior followed by unfavorable consequences (or *no* consequence) for the performer tends, in general, to decrease in frequency.

Because it is so closely tied to the concept of reinforcement, frequency is often overlooked as a separate and powerful idea. But to the behaviorist, frequency is a distinct and key concept. It also is a highly useful task-analysis concept, be you behaviorist, Gestalt oriented or blithely eclectic. We all use frequency to describe behavior, though we are only marginally aware of it. We refer to one person as quick and another as slow. We describe a third party as fast-talking or tentative or energetic. These are all imprecise references to frequency of speech, particular speaking habits and certain body mannerisms.

The importance of frequency to trainers is the idea that all of us have, without our "behavioral repertoires," behavior that could be judged appropriate or inappropriate in a given situation. For example, none of us

speaks in complete sentences or uses perfect grammar 100% of the time. But a frequency of 80% to 90% "on-target" speech can give the impression that we speak the King's English well. Conversely, an "on-target" of, perhaps, 50% to 60% can give the impression that we speak in a nonstandard or improper fashion. The difference is simply rate or frequency of "correct" and "incorrect" speech habits.

This behavioral-frequency approach to studying performance is the offspring of the first nonlaboratory use of operant psychological principles. In the late 1950s, Dr. Ogden Lindsley utilized the principles developed by his mentor, B. F. Skinner, to develop, first, behavior modification and then a teaching/research technology called precision teaching or precise personal management, depending on the application. The key tools of this system, translated to the task analysis context, are:

• **Pinpointing.** Pick a "large," easy-to-observe and validate, repeatable job behavior(s) to study.

• **Counting.** Count the occurrence of the behavior(s) or "pinpoint" for a specific time period.

• **Charting.** Record the behavior(s) per standard time for the performers.

The "pinpoint" picked should have some known or believed relation to the outcome the trainers will be expected to produce. If we are studying,

part of the *process* leading to the *outcome* "sales made," then "asking for the order" would be an important pinpoint to count and chart when making joint calls with sales reps who have different outcome records. By the way, the idea of counting and timing incumbent performers may seem at first to be a difficult assignment. Not so. With a little practice, most of us can comfortably and reliably watch for, count and time three pinpoints at once and still have time to watch for and record critical incidents, such as unique closing "lines" or cleverly worded objection retorts.

The approach is useful to the study of managerial, sales, line manufacturing and customer-contact skills. And the results can be quite revealing. For example, Dr. C. Aubrey Daniels, Daniels & Associates, and Larry Miller, president of Behavioral Systems, Inc., have determined that supervisors who scold employees four times as often as they praise them are perceived by their employees as *cold*, *hard*, *stern* and *difficult to work for*. Supervisors who reverse this ratio and praise four times as often as they scold are perceived as *warm*, *friendly*, *helpful* and *easy to work for*. Similar relationships seem to exist between customer-contact people and customers' perceptions of their helpfulness and warmth.

The approach has been used to document the existence and impact of specific behaviors in selling. Dr. Thomas Connellan, president of the Management Group, found an interesting phenomenon associated with the pinpoint "makes a verbal closing statement" (asks for the order). In one client study, Connellan found that a salesperson who typically makes four to five closing statements per sales interview accurately perceives that he/she has asked for the order that same number of times. The customer/prospect, however, when asked

STUDY *ORGANIZATION* PERFORMANCE, TOO

The behavioral-frequency method can be applied to the study of performance of not only individuals. It is equally helpful in understanding the performance of a department, store, branch office, agency or any other cohesive work group. The figure at right shows the results of a study of departmental absences.

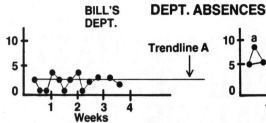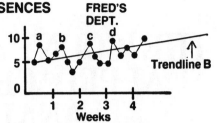

DEPT. ABSENCES

The scenario of this study is fairly typical. ABC Manufacturing is experiencing an uncomfortable absence rate. Factorywide, the rate is over 6%. Personnel and senior management want to institute a new, highly punitive absence-control policy. Tom and Tina Trainer are assigned to communicate the new policy to the troops and to train supervisory personnel to enforce it. But a quick look at the personnel director's data suggests to our hero and heroine that there is quite a difference in absence rates among departments and that a policy change may not be the most effective solution. Tom and Tina separate departments into two groups: those with absence records higher than 6% form

one group, and those with absence records below 6% form the other. Tom and Tina chart one month of daily absences for each department. Typical of the paydirt they hit is the comparison one can make between Bill's department— one with low absenteeism— and Fred's department— one with high absenteeism. Both departments are similar in function, structure and number of employees, so the comparison is a fair one. Two important pattern differences are clear.

One big difference is *trend.* As *trendline A* indicates, Bill's department has a steady rate; that is, the trendline shows no acceleration. Fred's department, however, has not only a higher rate of absences but also

the rate is increasing, as *trendline B* clearly indicates.

A second important difference is that absences in Fred's department have a cyclic nature about them. The absence "spikes" at a, b, c, and d are all Mondays. Bill's department has a similar but much less severe and less predictable pattern of Monday spikes.

On the basis of this analysis, Tom and Tina decide that it would be worthwhile to look closely at differences in supervisory style and methods, as well as differences in physical work environments of the high and low absence departments. They recommend that ABC management delay introducing the new policy until those hypotheses can be checked out.

Reprinted from TRAINING, September 1979

---

his/her impression of how often the salesperson "asked for the order," typically answered "one or two times." Connellan also found that sales reps with higher "ask rates" (seven to nine times per interview) tended to have more sales than reps with low "ask rates" (two to three times per interview).

The behavior-counting approach also helps put the importance or impact of specific behaviors in perspective. For example, the following data were gathered by watching sales clerks ring up purchases in a fashionable, teen-oriented chain clothing store. The purpose of the study was to determine effectiveness of different strategies for stimulating "add-on" items to the sale.

Though these data are stylized, they do represent a real situation and

a real study. The trainer in question changed her retail-selling program to emphasize specific, rather than general, suggestive selling strategies.

The pinpoint-count-chart, or behavioral-frequency, approach has been used successfully to study telephone contact situations, customer relations, performance review and group problem solving. As you might suspect, the behavior-frequency approach to task analysis leads to, or *can* lead to, emphasis on frequency in the training and performance management arena.

One widely discussed use of the behavior-frequency concept in a sales performance and training situation involves an ingenious general agent, O. Alfred Granham, who assigns his new agents a sales point system. Granham's new agents earn "X"

points for making a phone call, "Y" points for taking a client to lunch and "Z" points for making a formal proposal. Granham believes that, by demanding specific performance frequencies of his new agents, they develop the behavioral patterns his studies have validated as leading to successful outcomes for his agency. Does it really work? You can count on it! Granham's Chicago-area insurance agency is one of the most prosperous in the country.

The behavior-counting approach can be one of the most important tools in the trainer's bag of tricks for ferreting out the subtle differences between effective and ineffective performance and for figuring out which process differences really make an outcome difference where it counts— on the bottom line!

Reprinted from TRAINING, September 1979

THE CRITICAL INCIDENT METHOD OF ANALYSIS

The Critical Incident Method is often neglected as a task analysis tool, probably because it seems so simple

BY RON ZEMKE

One of the least used but niftiest little task-analysis techniques around is the *Critical Incident Method*. The inventor of this approach, John C. Flanagan, was a World War II military psychologist faced with the problem of improving military flight training. Specifically, too many trainees were cracking up training planes, and someone somewhere in the War Department suggested that perhaps the training wasn't emphasizing the right things.

Flanagan, who later founded the American Institute of Research (AIR), did something deceptively simple. He asked those pilot trainees who were able to walk away to describe— in terms of behavior—what exactly they had done incorrectly. This technique of illiciting "war stories" is the core of the Critical Incident Process.

In 1954, Flanagan formalized the process and defined it as a method of "...identifying *critical job requirements*...those behaviors which are crucial in making the difference between doing a job effectively and doing it ineffectively."

Critical Incidents are reports or descriptions of behaviors enacted by people in the population being studied. These incidents are recorded and classified as effective or ineffective in achieving the desired job results. The descriptions can take the form of stories, anecdotes, reports, and observations related, verbally or in writing, by supervisors, peers, subordinates or any other observer qualified to judge the performance. The incidents can be analyzed bit by bit, collectively, or both.

There are, of course, some limits to the acceptability of these war stories. Critical Incidents are specific reports of observed behavior from qualified sources, not generalizations or opinions.

Charles E. Watson suggests that critical incidents must address four questions:

1. What was done that led to effective job performance?

2. What was done that detracted from effective job performance or led to ineffective job performance?

3. What, if done differently, would

FIGURE 1. PERFORMANCE INDICATORS WORKSHOP

The Performance Indicators Workshop is based on a set of techniques for gathering together meaningful information for use in developing job description dimensions, behavior-anchored performance appraisals and job performance indicators. The workshop is founded on the premise that *you* are the best and most reliable source of information about the sales force. *You*, because of your unique position in the company and depth of experience, have at your command valuable information about *effective* and *ineffective* job performance. Information about incidents you have observed, evaluated and remembered and things you have seen salespeople do is especially valuable, as are your judgments about the effectiveness of those actions. Let's begin with your recollection of examples of effective performance.

Directions:

1. Think for a minute or two about *specific examples* of effective performance you have seen on the part of salespeople. (Don't limit your recollection just to superstar performance. We're interested in competence, not world records.)

2. Beginning on the next page, write down what you *observed* and what the *outcome* of the performance was.

3. Write out as many of these scenarios as you can remember.

4. Limit your stories to incidents you have observed involving salespeople. Do not include stories about computer salespeople, etc. If you have had an opportunity to observe other learning company salespeople perform, include those stories but label them as such.

Typical instructions to participants in a Critical Incident workshop.

FIGURE 2
WHAT I OBSERVED THE SALESPERSON DOING

This sales rep started the meeting by finding out what each person in the room was responsible for and how each was interfering with Computer printouts or Terminals. During the presentation, he mentioned a benefit of our product that related to each of those responsibilities and areas of need.

THE OUTCOME OF WHAT THEY DID

The Client Team decided to let us design a system plan and make a bid.

Typical incident written by a Critical Incident workshop participant.

have been more effective?

4. What attitudes, values, abilities, knowledge, skills (present or absent) *seemed* to lead to success or failure?

Consider, as examples, two incidents from a nursing training program Flanagan worked on in the late 1950s.

Effective Incident: A student nurse catches an error on a medication card while double-checking the patient's name against the name on the card.

Ineffective Incident: A student nurse fails

to chart the consistent elevation of a patient's temperature when the doctor's decision to operate depends on the patient's temperature at 8:00 A.M. that day.

After the analyst collects many such incidents, a panel of experts sorts them into groups or factors. The first nursing example— the student catching the medication error— was sorted into a pile of similar incidents that eventually were labeled "Checking." The second example— the student failing to chart a temperature—

was sorted into a pile of similar incidents eventually called "Observing, reporting and charting."

Dr. Marvin Dunnette has used the critical incident approach to develop highly sophisticated and reliable performance-review instruments called BARS—Behaviorally Anchored Rating Scales. His technique— gathering incidents and developing performance-measurement scales—is fairly simple and highly effective in sorting the wheat from the chaff of such large and nebulous jobs as "managing" and "selling." The Critical Incident Process, as Dunnette has refined it, has roughly six steps.

1. Gather two groups of SMEs.

2. After observing the amenities, have them describe, in writing, specific job incidents and the results produced. See Figures 1 and 2.

3. After editing,* have the SMEs sort the incidents into factors and then name the factors. See Figure 3.

4. Have the SMEs sort the incidents for "goodness" and "badness" along a seven- or nine-point scale.

5. Have SMEs fill any gaps in the scales with additional incidents.

6. After both groups have finished these five tasks, bring them together to look at each other's handiwork and reconcile differences between the two groups. See Figure 4.

Dunnette and others have applied the process to jobs ranging from grocery store check-out clerk to navy recruiting officer. They suggest that a rigorous statistical test of these scales be made after concluding step six. But unless the scales you develop for training are also going to be used as a performance review instrument, you'd do well to skip the statistical verification part, which can be pretty complex.

In a sense, the critical incident technique is an application to training of Alfredo Paredo's Law of Disproportionate Distribution. Italian Mathematician Paredo originally discovered that 80% of the wealth of Italy was controlled by 20% of the population. This principle also applies to other situations: 20% of a company's salespeople make 80% of the sales; 20% of the sales generate 80% of the profits; and 20% of the effort yields 80% of the output. The critical incident approach to task analysis tries to point out what that critical 20% of effort, which yields 80% of the performance, looks like.

FIGURE 3. SAMPLES OF EDITED CRITICAL INCIDENTS

- Salesperson conducted distracting side conversation during another rep's representation.

- Identified the roles and responsibilities of each person attending before beginning formal presentation.

- Mentioned a benefit of product applicable to needs of each in room during presentation.

A finalized Critical Incident or BARS scale.

FIGURE 4. SALESMANSHIP SKILLS*

Skillfully persuading prospects to join the Navy; using Navy benefits and opportunities effectively to sell the Navy; closing skills; adapting selling techniques appropriately to different prospects; effectively overcoming objections to joining the Navy.

9 — A prospect stated he wanted the nuclear power program or he would not sign up. When he did not qualify, the recruiter did not give up; instead, he talked the young man into electronics by emphasizing the technical training he would receive.

8 — The recruiter treats objections to joining the Navy seriously; he works hard to counter the objections with relevant, positive arguments for a Navy career.

7 — When talking to a high school senior, the recruiter mentions names of other seniors from that school who already have enlisted.

6 — When an applicant qualifies for only one program, the recruiter tries to convey to the applicant that it is a desirable one.

5 — When a prospect is selecting a service to enlist in, the recruiter tries to sell the Navy by describing Navy life at sea and adventures in port.

4 — During the interview, the recruiter said to the applicant, "I'll try to get you the school you want, but frankly it probably won't be open for another three months, so why don't you take your second choice and leave now."

3 — The recruiter insisted on showing more brochures and films even though the applicant told him he wanted to sign up right now.

2 — When a prospect states an objection to being in the Navy, the recruiter ends the conversation because he thinks the prospect must not be interested.

1 —

*Borman, W. C., Dunnette, M. D., and Hough, L. M. *Development of behaviorally based rating scales for evaluating the performance of U.S. Navy recruiters.* NPRDC TR-76-31, Personnel Decisions, Inc., Mpls., 1976.

---

*This is where the trainer earns his or her keep. The war stories are edited down from a full-page description or a five-minute taped diatribe into 25 words or less.

Reprinted from TRAINING, April 1979

COMPETENCY ANALYSIS: LOOKING AT ATTITUDES AND INTERESTS AS WELL AS TECHNICAL JOB SKILLS

The fact that many 'well-trained' employees know what to do and how, but still goof off, points clearly to the need for more in-depth analysis

BY STEPHEN P. BECKER

Before attempting to write specific core learning objectives for any training program, the wise trainer will determine and describe the competencies the learner will need to function effectively. Remember: Training is done primarily to benefit the organization—to provide competent people to perform required jobs. Until now, the closest thing to a competency analysis has been a task analysis—breaking a job down into tasks and into a list of elements for the purpose of describing the skill components of a competency.

But what does the word competency actually mean? I'd like to assert that any competency consists of six parts:

1. **Knowledge:** a cognitive awareness. Examples would be to know generally how an automobile engine works or to know that supervision is getting work done through others.

2. **Understanding:** in-depth cognitive and/or affective comprehension. Examples here would be to comprehend totally the electrical and the mechanical systems of the automobile engine or, as a supervisor, to be sensitive about people's feelings in order to build productive relationships with a work crew.

3. **Skill:** the ability to perform a task or job. Examples are repairing an engine or supervising in such a way that you achieve objectives of productivity, cost control, safety, etc.

4. **Value:** a norm or standard which is a psychologically integrated belief. Examples are that democracy is better than communism; it's best to own your own home; being independent is better than being dependent; participative management is ridiculous—just tell 'em what to do and punish 'em if they don't.

5. **Attitude:** a feeling or mood; a reaction to a stimulus (situation, experience, or people). A salesperson might, for example, be enthusiastic after successfully completing an important sale.

6. **Interest:** underlying motivation, continuing desire, psychological orientation. Examples are that a good elementary school teacher must be interested in small children; a good automobile mechanic must be interested in fixing engines.

A competency, then, is the dynamic interplay of knowledge, understanding, skills, values, attitudes, and interests. I could argue, for instance, that an employee who has the necessary knowledge, understanding and skill but who goofs off unless constantly supervised is not a competent employee. There is an obvious lack in the value, attitude and interest areas. Conversely, I know managers who have the right interests, attitudes, values, and knowledge but who haven't been able to develop the needed affective understanding or skill at supervising people to be considered competent managers. They can perform an individual task in their department, but they cannot de-

© Stephen P. Becker, 1977

velop the skill of managing people.

The key point: When developing training programs, we should describe in writing, as specifically as possible, the desired competency in terms of the six component parts. This should be done before writing any objectives, since it's quite possible that you'll want to draft a number of objectives for each competency component. A job competency can be thought of in terms of a total population. For instance, all customer-service representatives should have the described competency, or all nurses, or production supervisors, or whatever group is being trained. Once the competency is described, you have a clear framework for writing objectives.

Now, of course, you have a problem. You must have some competency at describing competencies. Here are six methods for analyzing competencies.

1. Task analysis—breaking a job down into tasks and then each task into a list of elements. This is an especially good method for describing the skill component of the competency.

2. Plan analysis. If the skill to be performed is a new one—it didn't exist before or the job is changing significantly—then the model may have to be derived from a plan. This would look like a task analysis when completed, and is a common situation when jobs are computerized.

3. Research. Perhaps a review of literature or discussions with others is necessary when developing a training program. This would be common for training programs in MBO, goal setting, job enrichment, etc.

4. Expert judgment. There may be only one or two people in an organization who truly have competency in a certain area. Perhaps the organization needs more people to develop that particular competency. The experts would become a key source of information for developing the competency description.

5. Individual or group interview data. Perhaps there is no one expert; instead, many people contribute to describing the competency.

6. Role play. If, say, you want to develop a program on performance interviewing for supervisors in a specific environment, you could have a number of supervisors role play an interview and then deduce the best points from each in order to create a competency description.

You could probably list more methods now that the process is clearer. The important point is that you take a piece of paper and write something in each of the six competency categories. Once you've done that, you can review it with the sponsors of the training program to get agreement.

Another problem you may have with competency descriptions is not knowing how to design training that will facilitate a change in values, attitudes, and interests. On the surface, it seems much easier to cope with knowledge, understanding, and skills. The way to approach this problem is to structure experiences, case studies, critical incidents, tests, instruments, or discussions that allow the learner to clarify his or her own values, attitudes or interests. In essence, you are reflecting, mirroring, or providing feedback that confronts a person with himself. Once the learner discovers his or her own values, attitudes or interests, that individual can conscientiously decide to change them—or not to.

As long as that learner's behavior is influenced by unconscious values, attitudes, or interests, personal growth isn't possible. Assuming the people concerned are mentally healthy, the process is one of education, not therapy. Remember, too, that many of those who enter the learning situation may already possess the proper values, attitudes, and interests. They are already competent to that degree, but need to master some of the more cognitive objectives to be completely competent.

The greatest value of a competency description is that it forces you to consider all the things that make up in-dividual performance that can be worked with in an instructional setting. Too often, learning objectives are written only for knowledge or understanding and skill, while objectives dealing with attitudes, values and interests are simply ignored. If you can make one statement each about the value, attitudes and interests that a competent person doing a particular function should possess, then you can develop one or more instructional objectives for each. Once you do that, the design of your program will certainly be more complete than it would have been without these "affective objectives."

On the other hand, there sometimes is a tendency to deal primarily with attitudes, values, and interests to the detriment of knowledge, understanding and skill. This is certainly the case, for example, in training programs related to affirmative action. It seems to me that too much emphasis in either direction will produce a program that lacks balance. Any training program should be both useful on the job and personally meaningful to most of the people most of the time. When this is so, both the organization and the individual benefit.

To start a competency description, simply divide a sheet of paper into six parts, and write one component of competency at the top of each. Within each part, write one or more sentences that describes the component. If you find you can't write anything for a particular component (after analysis), leave it blank. For instance, you may be working on a course on motivation and discipline for first-line supervisors. Under the value component you might write: "The supervisor believes positive discipline techniques cause more self-directed and self-motivated performance, and the supervisor believes that negative discipline procedures should only be used as a last resort or when specific acts leave no alternative." If you now find you can't write anything in the category of attitudes, leave it blank. Sometimes values and attitudes come too close to be easily distinguished.

Another key use of competency descriptions is to advertise training programs and to select participants. While it is useful to talk in terms of objectives, it may be more appropriate to talk in terms of competency statements which are a bit broader and usually shorter. They are particularly useful in briefly describing course or program outcomes. In fact, they can be used while objectives are still being prepared.

The training world is just beginning to think in terms of competency. Because it's taken us a long time to recognize the legitimacy of this concept, we trainers now face a challenge: learning how and when to employ it.

Reprinted from TRAINING, December 1977

EMPLOYEE ATTITUDE SURVEYS: HOW TO 'HAND-OFF' THE RESULTS

Finding out how employees feel about the company is relatively easy.
Doing something about it is hard

BY DALE FEUER

If you were coordinating an employee attitude survey, and you happened to overhear this conversation among your coworkers gathered around the office coffeepot, you might just consider getting into a different line of work.

Linda: Did you know we're supposed to have a corporate-wide employee attitude survey next month?

Bob: Yeah. It means we'll all be herded into the conference room, handed No. 2 pencils, and incarcerated there until we've filled in 18 pages worth of little blue circles.

Sandy: Hey, look on the bright side. This will keep everyone in personnel occupied five days a week for the next two years. They'll be so busy tabulating results and cranking out reports, they won't bother us again until 1989.

John (arriving with coffee cup in hand): You kids talking about the big survey? Let me set you straight. The last company I worked for did two of them. Here's how it goes: First you fill out a bunch of forms. Then your managers gather you all together for what they'll call "feedback sessions." A feedback session is where your manager says, "Hmmmm. We seem to have some issues to resolve here," and then the motormouth in your group yaks for about 18 hours while the rest of you doodle on your note-

pads. Then the feedback session adjourns. A week later you get a memo from the CEO's secretary. The memo tells you how wonderful the feedback sessions were and assures you that your hard-working, top management team will absolutely, positively be following up on this enormously valuable input. And that's it. That's the last you'll hear about the whole thing—until four or five years later, when somebody upstairs decides it would be a really great idea to do an employee attitude survey. Then the cycle begins again from scratch.

Sounds a bit cynical for the average employee, you say? Don't be too sure. It's amazing how much disillusionment and skepticism an organization can create by soliciting the earnest input of its employees and then failing to follow up on it. Even more amazing is that most companies will spend at least $250,000 to develop a corporate-wide survey from scratch and another $50,000 for the data analysis and reporting, and never *use* the results to help make the business more profitable. As you can see from the hefty price tags, conducting employee attitude surveys is not cheap, which is why it's typically large organizations, with big human resources staffs and budgets, that have formal survey programs.

Why is it that so many attitude-survey projects seem to run out of gas in

the homestretch, when it comes time to translate the numbers into issues and the issues into actions?

Part of the hang-up is that many companies don't realize just how crucial the feedback phase of the survey process is, according to David Nadler, president of the Delta Consulting Group, Inc. of New York City and author of *Feedback in Organization Development* (Addison-Wesley, 1977). "Traditionally, surveys have been handled by industrial psychologists who've focused on data analysis. Industrial psychologists don't tend to be champions of the feedback process," Nadler says. "Determining how employees really feel may be more important than the data itself, which may not be 100 percent accurate. Effective feedback helps you interpret your results."

Nadler sees a trend today toward more constructive use of survey results. "There is more willingness to do feedback work through special teams, family groups [members of a manager's immediate work team], or training or human resource people," he comments. "This grows out of an increasing concern for quality and efforts to collect data from customers. Data from employees dovetails nicely with data collected from customers. In fact, some studies have shown employee climate to be associated with ratings of a company's customer service."

Nadler points to Xerox Corp., which, in the midst of a massive organizational culture change aimed at raising the company's overall quality consciousness, designed a 27-item survey to monitor the success of the quality campaign. "The reason for the management practices survey is to find out how well the manager is doing in Xerox's effort to become a total quality organization," explains Harold Tragash, director of human resources development and systems at Xerox. "All of our managers go through our Leadership Through Quality training program. The survey was designed to be delivered every six months, after training, to see how well trainees are doing."

Another example of what Nadler sees happening with employee attitude surveys is a relatively new program at Johnson & Johnson. In April 1986, the giant manufacturer of health products and other consumer goods started asking all of its 30,000 domestic employees to rate their individual divisions in terms of how well they are meeting the responsibilities set forth in the Johnson & Johnson credo, a four-paragraph statement of commitment to customers, employees, stockholders and the community. The credo survey, as it's known at Johnson & Johnson, includes items on developing innovative programs, purchasing new equipment, launching new products or services, understanding customer needs, encouraging civic improve-

---

'If line managers don't see the benefit to them, why should they spend the time?'

---

ments, protecting the environment and natural resources, as well as the more standard survey questions about satisfaction with the job, pay and boss.

The use of attitude surveys to ask employees about broader business issues, rather than strictly about their personal relationships with the company, appears to be a recent phenomenon. Even IBM, a company that has been doing employee attitude surveys for more than three decades, only began incorporating questions on the business in the early '80s. According to Windall White, manager of IBM's worldwide opinion survey, the current survey asks employees to rate the company in areas such as innovativeness, efficiency and use of information systems, to name a few.

Companies that have widened their attitude surveys to address business concerns typically do a good job of following up on results for a couple of reasons. For one thing, linking employee attitudes more directly to company goals gives the survey program greater visibility among the top brass. For another, it helps generate interest and involvement among line managers, whose performance is usually judged on the basis of business indicators rather than employee satisfaction levels.

Stephanie Kendall, a survey specialist at Questar Data Services, Inc.

in Eagan, MN, and author of *Employee Attitude Surveys: Communication Line to Higher Productivity* (Alexander Hamilton Institute, Inc., 1986), says that meaningful follow-up activities simply can't happen without the active support of line management. "If line managers don't see the benefit [of the survey program] to them, why should they spend the time? They have all sorts of other things pulling at them. That's why you need to find out what kind of information is going to help them succeed in their jobs."

Most experts today agree that what happens after survey results are tabulated is strictly up to line management, not the survey staff. In most organizations, it is the job of the training or personnel people to be technical resources for line managers who need help in analyzing and interpreting the data, to train line managers in how to do feedback sessions and action planning, and, in some instances, to present overall company results to top management. But unless line managers assume full responsibility for resolving issues under their control, the survey program is destined to be perceived, in Kendall's words, "as just one more program from 'corporate.' "

Kelly Gordon, manager of GTE Corp.'s survey program, explains how she positions her company's employee attitude survey as a management tool rather than a human resources program: "You must establish clients for the data. I send the results immediately out to the functional areas, and I say to managers, 'This is your data, not mine.' Around here [i.e., the organization development department], we like to call this the 'functional pass-off.' "

Built-in support

Before you can hand off the results of your employee attitude survey to line managers, you've got to make sure that those managers feel like part of the team. If you wait until the last minute to include them in the survey process, chances are they're going to drop the ball sooner or later.

Sandy Bauer of Ann Arbor, MI-based Bauer & Associates, Inc., insists that many companies make a critical mistake at the beginning of the survey project that dooms their

later efforts to follow up on the results: Early in the decision-making process, they fail to include people who clearly have relevant information and expertise. "If you drop the survey on these people without ever consulting them, they're going to say, 'What genius up there came up with this?' "

About 1,500 employees, from company presidents to machine operators, had a hand in designing Johnson & Johnson's survey, according to Peter Dinella, director of the

---

Position the survey as a management tool: 'This is your data, not mine.'

---

credo survey program. Likewise at GTE, people from all company levels comprised the survey steering committee. "We even included what we call 'blockers,' " says GTE's Gordon. "These are people who might have a vested interest in not seeing the survey in place."

Xerox's Tragash believes that including people from the upper echelons of the company in the design process is particularly important. "The original authors of the management practices survey were the CEO and his direct reports," Tragash says. "The more senior the client, the more likely that good things will happen as a result."

Asking people for ideas is just one way to get them to buy into the program, Tragash continues. Asking for money is another. If managers have to pay for their surveys, if they have to figure the costs into their budgets, they will be more eager to use the results. "When you put your money where your mouth is," he observes, "the likelihood of utility increases."

Number crunching

While it may be wise to consult a wide cross section of the employee population during the survey-development phase, it doesn't follow that every item on the survey must be analyzed and spit back to all managers. As Kendall puts it, "Not everyone needs to see every result. This can just overwhelm the person who's got to synthesize and feed it back. It's important to simplify the amount of data you get up front."

Give managers only the results that are relevant to their particular work group, Kendall advises. "Often, data is aggregated at too high a level, making it easy for a manager to disclaim it, saying, 'My group isn't like this.'" For issues under local control—teamwork, productivity, quality, etc.—results must apply specifically to an individual manager's immediate work group. The tricky part is slicing the data thin enough to make it useful to managers, yet not so thin that individual survey respondents can be identified by their demographics.

Gordon recalls that after the first administration of GTE's survey in October 1984, she and her colleagues reported results for the company as a whole, which in some instances gave individual managers an easy out when it came to confronting problems. "We haven't changed the questions so much since then," Gordon explains. "What we have changed is the level of feedback. Now there is no way for managers to say that it's not their problem."

At Bank of America Corp., cutting the data has become a fine art. Individual managers can request survey results reports for any group of five or more employees. "Although the process is almost entirely automated at this point, it's still an administrative nightmare," concedes the company's manager of personnel research, Nancy Rotchford. "But the managers love it, because it gives them information they need to manage their units."

Not only do the bank's computer-generated reports give managers the exact breakdowns they request, but they set cutoff points for each category (e.g., career development, compensation, communications, etc.) that tell managers when they need to be concerned. "The cutoffs are part empirical, part armchair scores," Rotchford says. "They are based on what we can expect from looking at previous surveys, external norms, and what kind of ratings we think our managers should strive for."

Just as important as giving managers targeted reports of results is getting those reports out to the field in a hurry. Follow-up efforts stand the best chance of success if issues and concerns raised by the survey process are still fresh in people's minds, before frustration and apathy have time to set in. To speed up the process, some large companies stagger the survey schedule; that is, they tackle one division or unit at a time, allowing results to be turned around faster for each separate survey group.

Some companies are stepping up

Tailored reports: An administrative nightmare, but managers love them.

---

the pace by taking advantage of technology. With the number-crunching computer products available today, lag times of six months and longer between survey administration and feedback of results are becoming a thing of the past. According to Nadler, "Data analysis and report generation can be done quickly and locally, thanks to advanced computer capabilities. Sometimes when we go off-site, we'll bring a computer and a questionnaire. Employees provide the data and we give them a report the next morning."

Going one step further, Xerox's management practices survey is a totally on-line event, from administration to report production. All managers have personal disks onto which their subordinates enter their survey responses. As soon as the last member of a group has entered his answers, the computer locks in the data and kicks out a report, Tragash says. He adds that the computer system also has a 'roll-up' capability, not yet used, that can combine data from various managers' disks and report the overall findings to senior executives.

During the last two years, IBM has been working on getting its entire corporate-wide survey on-line. Where the computerized program has been installed, White says, "it has improved our efficiency tremendously." In these locations, a month-and-a-half wait for results has been whittled down to two weeks.

Training the rookies

So as long as you involve line managers in the survey design and furnish them with relevant results in a reasonable amount of time, successful follow-up is virtually guaranteed, right? Well, not exactly.

Even managers who are highly motivated to do something with the survey findings will be stalled if they don't know *what* to do or how to figure it out. In order for most line managers to conduct feedback sessions and carry out follow-up plans, they need to be trained in group problem-solving and decision-making skills. They need to know how to draw out reticent employees, how to be objective when dealing with unflattering feedback about their management styles, and how to decide whether problems are worth dealing with or not. In terms of action planning, they must learn to isolate areas of concern and describe them in specific, behavioral terms.

There is an obvious appeal in using outside specialists to conduct the feedback sessions and guide the action-planning activities. Presumably, consultants would have the knowledge, the experience and the objectivity that managers lack. But there are disadvantages to this approach, as Bank of America's Rotchford explains: "We considered having external facilitators do the feedback sessions. But the fact that this might cause managers to throw up their hands and say, 'OK, it's not my problem,' outweighed the proposed benefits. In the end, if changes are going to be made, and managers are going to live with those changes, they have to see the decision as theirs."

Bank of America has always put its first-line supervisors in charge of feedback sessions and action planning, but the nature of the training it provides has changed somewhat over the years. At first, supervisors went off-site for either a half or full day of training, depending on how new they were to the follow-up process. Finding it extremely costly to pull such a large number of managers from branches and offices across the state off their jobs and cover travel expenses, the company developed a 45-minute training video and guidebook. In addition to saving time and money, Rotchford says, the video approach allows managers to go through the training with their own results, at their own convenience. "We used to have to start training them even before their employees had taken the survey in order to get everyone scheduled."

GTE also provides managers with a videotape on how to conduct a feedback session. To supplement the tape, members of the corporate staff train 'designated survey coordinators' to go back to their departments and train line managers. Johnson & Johnson has trained its line organizations to run their own surveys—a major undertaking, to say the least, but one that helped build ownership and accountability into the survey process, according to Dinella. As far as he's concerned, training is the primary function of human-resources specialists in the survey process: "They should devote 100 percent of their time to training managers on how to conduct feedback sessions instead of isolating themselves in a cubicle with computers, working out the details of correlations which may mean nothing in the end."

Cultural considerations

Probably the most common obstacle to carrying out a successful survey program from development to follow-up, is the widespread perception that employee attitude surveys will be used as tools in a witch-hunt. Middle managers worry that the real reason for the survey is to give executives a way to identify and ax unwanted managers.

Gordon recalls this problem at GTE. At first, she says, some managers were afraid that the survey results would be used against them. "That's why we have a caveat that information does not have to be shared upward. No one higher than the individual manager has to see the results for that manager."

By not forcing the issue, Gordon says, the company seems to have encouraged many managers to share with their superiors, voluntarily, the feedback they got from their subordinates. "They've said, 'I'd be glad to

---

The real value lies in confirming what managers already sense is going on.

---

share my results. What's the big deal?' "

While managers may not be expected to relay their results up the line in many organizations, they almost always are expected to take full responsibility for following up on those results. Accountability is seen, in fact, as the key to ensuring that the survey program leads to meaningful organizational changes.

"The managers must know that their managers view [follow-up] as an important task," says Rotchford. This may mean that upper managers, including the CEO, tell their people exactly what they'd like to see in terms of follow-up. In many organi-

zations, feedback sessions and written action plans are mandatory. Some companies go so far as to make their survey practices a matter of policy. IBM, for instance, surveys its employees no more frequently than every 12 months but at least every 24 months, with rare exceptions, according to White. All managers, from first-line supervisors on up, are required to conduct department feedback meetings and put action plans in place. And twice a year, CEO John Akers gets a 45-minute presentation of company results.

Whether it's a stated policy or not, people pay attention to things upon which their performance is evaluated. Several sources suggested that organizations with effective survey programs tend to consider managers' follow-up efforts, not their actual survey results, in performance reviews. Often, companies will include a question on the survey itself that asks about what was done as a result of the previous survey's findings.

At IBM, upper and middle managers track the progress of action plans in periodic reviews with the managers reporting to them. However, White is quick to point out, the company advocates a proactive management style, and expects its managers to communicate regularly with employees so that they can take action before problems emerge. Indeed, most experts agree that the real value in the bulk of employee attitude survey data lies in confirming what managers already sense is going on in their organizations. Feedback sessions, if conducted properly and promptly, help clarify the issues and pave the way to effective action planning and follow-up activities.

Reprinted from TRAINING, September 1987

CHAPTER 3

DESIGNING TRAINING AND USING INSTRUCTIONAL OBJECTIVES

In 1962 Robert F. Mager wrote a brief little book titled *Preparing Objectives for Programmed Instruction*. It was based on his research into the common characteristics of that new and daring training tool, programmed instruction. What he found was devastatingly simple. The best programs made a point of telling both trainee and trainer:

- what the learner should be able to *do* at the end of training,
- under what conditions
- and to what degree of success.

He called these statements of desired learning outcomes "behavioral objectives." He renamed them "performance objectives" in a later edition of the book, which was also rechristened as *Preparing Instructional Objectives*.

As simple as "good" objectives look, they can be mighty slippery to construct. It's easy to write mush-mouthed objectives that really don't describe something measurable. For instance, "The student will acquire a developing awareness of the place of the earth in the scope of the universe" is pretty mushy. It's also easy to slide into the error of specifying behaviors instead of outcomes; of confusing ends and means. "The trainee will be able to utilize a 42Q6 weld tester to determine the acceptability of student welds" looks like an instructional objective, but is really just a partial specification of a task or sub-objective. It is not a statement of a desired learning goal or performance outcome.

But objectives do more than just tell us what to measure and how. They are the anvil upon which we shape and hone media and method selections, test learning sequences, exercises and ideas. If you can't write measurable objectives to guide the instructional development process, you haven't finished analyzing the tasks you want learned.

Results-focused instructional objectives do one other thing: They make distinct some key differences between training, education and development. Key to the difference is the specificity of what the learning is for and the immediacy of the pay-back to the organization. Development is a long-term investment. It is a set of activities aimed at giving an employee a series of experiences that enhance, in a more or less general way, the long-term value of the individual to the organization. "Education" implies a shorter-term investment, but it is still quite general. Call education a set of activities aimed at developing the overall competence of the person as a person, and concerned with behavior off the job as well as on the job.

Training, on the other hand, is charged with preparing people to do specific jobs to necessary standards, changing the unskilled to skilled, the unknowing to knowledgeable, the ineffective to effective. Trainers help their trainees exchange old skills for new. Trainers make the highly technical highly learnable. Trainers help people crack the very specific codes of doing a very specific job in order to make a very specific living.

This conceptualization of training makes it a very "accountable" function. While many educators can and often do claim exemption from requirements that they produce measurable results on grounds that the real outcome of their work is not immediately amenable to measurement, the trainer must welcome and relish the measurement process. Measurement against objectives tells the trainer if the learning lasts beyond the training experience. And measurements of the ultimate results—changes in actual job performance—tell the trainer whether or not the whole process was on target.

The articles in this section point out the key role of instructional objectives. They describe techniques for determining and specifying as clearly as possible what is to be learned, and how that learning will be evidenced.

HOW TO DESIGN THE IDEAL TRAINING COURSE

This author practices what he preaches and comes up with a plan for the best possible training design

BY DAVID D. CRAM

Bob Mager and I were chatting one day, grumping over the fact that we knew so much more about good training than we were actually practicing.

"What we need," says I, "is a course on how to do it right."

"What we *really* need," says he, "is a course on how to do it right, *that does it right.*"

As good as his word, Mager developed with Peter Pipe the workshop course *Criterion-Referenced Instruction: Analysis, Design and Implementation,* which provided the model for the ideas discussed in this article.

If you were to set about to design an ideal course, how would you proceed? One way would be to canvass the literature to search out techniques that are known to be effective in helping students to learn. Another way would be to talk to students to find out what pinches—what the common complaints are about the way conventional instruction is conducted. An ideal characteristic is anything that eliminates a pinch or that operationalizes something the literature says is good; and you can isolate a dozen or more ideal characteristics which would be guaranteed to help any instruction. They're all very logical, and obvious once you've seen them. Furthermore, different courses will have different ideal characteristics. That doesn't matter. Our purpose here is to illustrate that if you want to develop what your students will look at as an "ideal course," it is possible to approach the problem head-on and make significant progress.

As we discuss these ideal characteristics, it will help if you can think of them from a student's point of view. So, shift into a thinking mode (brow wrinkled, brain clenched, fist in mouth) and imagine you are a student, dreaming of an ideal instructional system. How would you like to be treated? How would you like the course to be run? What bugs you, and how would you change things, given your druthers?

1. *An ideal course will make it clear to everybody just what the end product skill will be.*

It seems so reasonable! If we want you to be able to pluck a chicken, or sail a steady course, or juggle three balls and a dinner plate, we show you how and make sure that you have the end product visualized. What's more, we stand willing to tell the world what we want.

The same is true if we're teaching you how to solve equations, write grammatical sentences, or design experiments. We have no reluctance to tell you what skill is needed.

We learned a long time ago if we tell the students exactly what it is we want them to be able to do, we often won't have to tell them anything else. But there's more to it than that. When we tell them what we want them to do, we are also making our intentions clear to other instructors, to employers, and most of all, to ourselves. Anyone who has ever struggled with objectives knows what I'm talking about. Many a course has changed direction when the objectives were hammered out in clear terms.

Reasonable? Sure it is. Where we find resistance is where we teach pure information for its own sake, without a clear picture of how it will ultimately be used. You know how it goes:

"We ought to put in a little about the theory of transistors in case they run into a problem where they'll need it." And so saying, we assign a text or a chapter to read, hoping some will stick. But since we don't know what of it will be needed, or when, we can't be too specific about what the student should study.

I'm not saying that we shouldn't teach informational things, but when we do, we should teach them as a necessary part of some skill, and then test the *information* by testing the *skill.*

2. *An ideal course will let everybody know how the objective is going to be tested.*

The more information we can give you about how you are to be tested, the more easily and quickly you can develop the skills. Why do we have such reluctance to let the student know what the test is? Well, when we find ourselves cringing at the thought of giving away the test, we are probably in a *teach about* mode rather than a *teach how* mode. There are very few skills that are taught where we can't let you (the student) know what the skill is and how it is to be tested. It is only when we are teaching *about* (and are using the test as a sample of what the student can say about the subject) that we have to guard the nature of our test.

We're trying to eliminate the adversary relationship between student and instructor, and the quickest way to do that is to be as direct and open about the nature of the test as we can be. We don't want you to be using energy to guess about how the skill will be tested. If we want you to have a skill, and you know what the skill looks like, there is no reason to hide the way in which we will ask you to prove you've got it. (See figure at top of next page.)

3. *An ideal course will take advantage of what you know and can do when you come in.*

This is one of the obviously good ideas, and one that almost everybody will agree with, but it's one of the hardest to implement. We know how irritating and distressing it is to be instructed on how to do something we already know how to do. But how do we avoid that? How do we find out what you can already do, and then how can we utilize that information once we have it?

Well, once the instruction is divided into skills (objectives) and the means of testing each skill is made known, you (the student) can look at objective and test, and decide if you have the skill or not. If the skill is there, you take the test and go on to the next module. If you don't have it or aren't sure, you can turn to the module and judge for yourself whether you need instruction, review, brushup, or practice before going for the test.

Make no mistake, this is hard on the instructor. When students ask to see the test before we've laid our instruction on them, the impulse is to say, "But you can't possibly *really* understand unless you've read Dingle and Queep or done exercise number four," or whatever.

That's a hard tendency to shake, but shake it we must, if we're to take advantage of what the students know and what they can do when they come to us.

4. *An ideal course will give you (the student) as many choices of paths through the instruction as possible.*

You may have noticed in your wanderings through life that people are different from each other and they vary in mood and

interest from day to day. An ideal course would do what it could to allow for variation in path. Very few skill hierarchies have to be taught in a fixed sequence. That is, even though skills may be performed in an unvarying sequence, the parts may be taught in a different order. For example, if you were going to build a table, you would proceed in a certain order, from cutting to assembling to finishing. But if you were to learn the *skills* of table building, you could learn sanding and finishing skills first, or last, or in the middle somewhere.

The tendency to teach in the same order as we perform is strong, and yet a lot of enthusiasm can be dampened when we force students to put off parts that seem interesting so they can learn less interesting things first. One of our objectives for any course should always be the affective one of wanting you to like the subject matter. Now, we can't guarantee that you will like it, no matter what we do, but we can play the percentages. One way to do this is to be ready to capture your interest where it lies rather than to try to force it along an arbitrary path. Of course, sometimes we have to insist on a certain track, but where we don't have to, we're better off not.

5. *An ideal course will provide a range of software.*

One of the dogmas of the audiovisual business is that most of us learn best what we see, but the fact is we learn best in different ways, and the nature—the personality—of a presentation has as much to do with it as anything. We learn from writers we like and find the others hard going. Some of us find books easy to visualize and others need the help of movies. And some topics are harder than others.

When we design instruction for the hypothetical student, we often have to choose a "best method" or "best materials." But most frequently, we look at the situation, make judgments, and then choose one method which will interest and instruct the greatest number of our students.

But think of it this way: an instructor performs a certain number of functions—informing, showing how, providing feedback, counseling, and so on. Some of these functions are easier than others, and some can be done by book, or tape recorder, or TV, or movie. Now if we assume that it's desirable to use living human beings to the highest purpose, then we should have no reluctance in using whatever media are available to replace the live instructor in this dissemination role.

Except for the teaching of very simple skills, no instructional method is likely to be perfect for all students. And for any much-used skill, there is likely to be a host of instructional material available to the student. An ideal course would not use the instructor in a role where a book would do as well, but rather use the instructor where a book would not do at all, for example, in individual counseling.

6. *An ideal course will allow enough time for any qualified individual to finish.*

One of the most counterproductive aspects to our present system is the fact that it is time-based rather than competency-based. The students are started, ready or not, and after a period of time the instruction ceases whether or not the students have mastered the skill. The folly of this practice is made clear when we attempt then to move the students on to new skills which depend on mastery of the old. Of course they can't master the new skills!

We don't make stupid mistakes like that when we teach someone to fly an airplane. The students work on landings until they can do them; the students master navigation before we let them practice cross-country flying. But as soon as we begin teaching *about* rather than *how* we tend to push and prod the slower student to keep up with a time schedule and then cut him or her off when time is up.

An ideal system will give you (the student) assurance that you have the time you need to read, ponder, practice, work out difficulties, look at other explanations, talk to other students—whatever you need to learn to do the skill.

This is important, too: you need to know that you can't get out of learning a skill by simply stalling until the time for learning it is past. The skill sits there waiting to be mastered and the sooner you do it the sooner you can move on to the more complex skills.

The other side of the coin is just as important. You need to know that you are in a system designed so that if your interest catches fire you won't have to sit around and wait for others to catch up.

7. *An ideal course will provide a map to keep you informed about where you are in the system.*

It is a well-documented fact that the closer we are to the completion of a task, the harder we will work to finish. We know this, and yet how many instructional systems take the simple step of providing a course map? *We* know where you are, but we forget that often you have no idea. In a time-based system you know how much time is left in the course, but we're talking about real instruction, where we care about what skills you have. If it's motivating to you to keep track of where you are, then we should provide a way; a course map is such a way. (See figure at right.)

8. *An ideal course will provide opportunity for practice of the skill being taught.*

It seems obvious to say that an ideal system will provide practice, but it's not so obvious at all. There is a strong temptation, when designing instruction, for us to tell you exactly how to perform a skill, what to watch out for, and how to tell when you're doing it right, but not to provide space and time for you actually to practice under guidance. When we're teaching complex skills, comprised of subordinate skills, there is a temptation to overlook practice at the culminating skills and focus all attention on the component skills.

In an ideal system, each skill is learned before it is needed for a greater skill, and that means that practice has to be built in along the way. That way we keep reducing the apparent complexity of

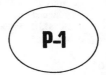

P-1

Prepare Control Documents

OBJECTIVE

Given objectives, criterion tests, materials, target population description and a list of rules for your course, prepare a draft of at least three control documents needed to assist in management of the course.

CRITERION TEST

This unit will be considered satisfactorily completed when (a) at least three control documents have been drafted that will put into practice the course procedures you have listed in Module P-12 and (b) your supervisor, if present, agrees that the rules will be acceptable to your institution.

ADDITIONAL RESOURCES

	RESOURCE NUMBER	
Booklet: *Preparation and Use of Instructional Modules in Driver and Traffic Safety Education*	**55**	Read pages 6–16.
Book: *Modules: The Use of Modules in College Biology Teaching*	**9**	Read pages 19–36.
Tape-filmstrip: "Individualized Instruction: Materials and Their Uses"	**26**	Filmstrip #4, tape, and script (558).

The ideal course includes written objectives for every training module, information about the way it will be tested, and a list of relevant resources. (Shown above, below and on page 78 are pages from the Mager/Pipe course, "Criterion-Referenced Instruction: Analysis, Design and Implementation," © 1974 by Mager Associates, Inc.)

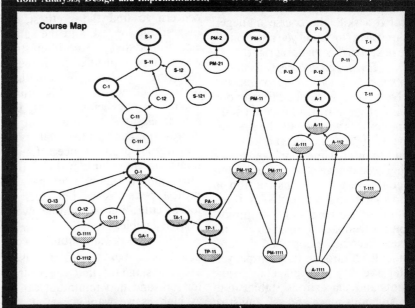

Course Map

The ideal course includes a "road map" to the program's activities. In this example, arrows signify prerequisites; heavier ovals indicate the terminal objective in a series. As modules are completed, they are partly shaded in by the course participant.

complex skills because they are always comprised of things you can already do.

9. *An ideal course will provide feedback to you (the student) on your practice.*

Practice and feedback go together. Without feedback, practice is useless at best and probably counterproductive. You have to know how you're doing or else you can be practicing mistakes which will have to be unlearned later. An ideal system will not only provide practice at a skill, but it will insure that you know immediately if you're practicing correctly or not and if not, why not.

10. *An ideal course will test often and in a nonthreatening way.*

When students dream of an ideal course, one of the things they most often want to change is the brittle, enemy relationship between them and the instructor, brought about by the way we test.

Two things will help: first, we should test often, so that you don't have to accumulate too much before you find out if you're on the right track. Second, we should test in a nonthreatening manner, by warning you accurately what the test will be like, by letting you pick your own time for testing, by giving immediate constructive feedback on the results of the test, and by letting you keep testing until the desired skill has been demonstrated. Once you have demonstrated a skill, the course manager signs you off on it and you move on to the next skill (See figure at right).

11. *An ideal course accepts feedback from the student for self-correction.*

No system is perfect. From your point of view, if you missed a skill, something is wrong with the system. That is, if you bent honest effort (and you did or not) and didn't get something even though you expected to, either the test or the instruction is poor—for you at least. An ideal course would have a built-in provision for feedback to itself so the instruction could be improved as more students go through it. A simple yet effective way is to place a "comments and suggestions" tablet in a conspicuous place and ask any student who voices a suggestion or complaint to jot it down.

The ideal course includes a personal progress summary, in which modules are signed off as each skill is acquired.

Personal Progress Summary

12. *An ideal course compares student to objective, not student to student.*

"Mirror, mirror on the wall, who is fairest of them all?" From *Snow White* to the *Guiness Book of Records* we continually express our concern to find the prettiest, the biggest, the longest, and the smartest. Superlatives are interesting, and I suppose justified in the sense of giving the rest of us something to shoot at, which is O.K. unless you're the one being shot at. Unfortunately, we have allowed an interest in comparative values to obscure our proper concern for the minimum acceptable values. It is interesting to know who has the neatest penmanship, but it is the job of education to see that everybody is legible.

When I say minimum acceptable, remember that I'm talking about a standard that the instructor sets, and that minimum can be as high as we want to set it. But wherever we set it, we should then compare your skill to that min-

imum, and not make the mistake of changing standards based on what some other student did on the final. If we set out to teach you to write, and you learn to write, we should sign you off on writing, without respect to what anybody else did or didn't do.

Certainly, there are times when people want to know who is the most skillful or the brightest or who has the most potential of all the students, and for those times the appropriate measuring tool is one that compares one student with all the rest. But in an ideal instructional system our concern is to teach the skill to an individual. We are successful if you learn it, and if you have trouble we're going to modify our instruction and add to it to do everything we can to build the skill into you. In a system like that, we do what we have to do to make all students succeed, and whether one succeeded better than another is simply an irrelevant concern.

Reprinted from TRAINING, December 1975

THE WHENS, WHYS AND HOWS OF BEHAVIORAL OBJECTIVES

What the research says

BY JAMES M. LEWIS

Behavioral objectives mostly live on action verbs. Only action verbs which specifically mention the overt behavior of the respondent at the end of instruction in concrete, measurable terms contain high nutritive value for learning. Other verbs are junk food. Thus, *turn, twist* and *kick* are good action verbs; *think, feel* and *reflect* are not. There are verbs in the English language rich in meaning, richer in action. Just as they carry a message to a reader, they can also function effectively in an instructional and training environment.

But what of behavioral objectives themselves? What can they be expected to do and not do? When are they appropriate or inappropriate? What alternatives are available, and when should they be considered? Here's an action verb review of what various researchers have discovered about effective use of behavioral objectives which may help you in planning, designing, delivering and evaluating training.

What to expect from behavioral objectives

★ **REJECT** all high hopes that behavioral objectives alone will improve performance in cognitive or psychomotor areas. There is not enough evidence to justify those claims. In fact, of 84 studies, 40 find behavioral objectives have a significant effect on achievement, but 44 studies do not. Similarly, of six studies which have dealt with psychomotor areas, two note a significant treatment effect of objectives while the other four do not.

☆ **ANTICIPATE** strong support for behavioral objectives from trainees in the affective area. Eleven of 17 studies reviewed suggest a significant improvement in student attitudes toward behavioral objectives.

★ **DISREGARD** claims that specific behavioral objectives facilitate greater performance than general objectives. Of 13 studies reviewed, only three report specific objectives lead to significant learner achievement; 10 studies report no significant effect from specific compared to general objectives.

☆ **EFFECTIVE**
★ **INEFFECTIVE**

☆ **ACCEPT** the limitations of behavioral objectives. Empirical studies seem to indicate that behavioral objectives do not increase incidental learning (not related to objectives) and retention. Of nine studies which have attempted to measure this impact, only three have found a significant effect. Again, of 13 studies measuring the effect of behavioral objectives on retention, four cite a significant increase, but nine do not.

In addition, some evidence in the literature suggests behavioral objectives are *not* helpful in certain cognitive skills and operations. First, Merrill (1970) and Yelon and Schmidt (1972) report behavioral objectives do not increase reasoning ability. Second, Hartley and Davies (1976) indicate behavioral objectives are not useful in learning tasks calling for knowledge and comprehension. Third, Olsen (1971) says behavioral objectives do not influence generalization of principles and concepts. Fourth, while Hartley and Davies observe that behavioral objectives are useful in higher level learning tasks calling for analysis, synthesis and evaluation, Zeman (1978) does not find behavioral objectives significantly useful in those same cognitive operations.

☆ **OVERCOME** certain myths associated with behavioral objectives. For example, do behavioral objectives in exact sciences yield better results than in humanities? It is easy to construct objectives in exact sciences. However, they do not show a greater effect in sciences than in humanities. In fact, better results have been observed in courses such as English poetry, reading and education than in biology, economics, math and physics. A second myth is that, in an individualized setting, older learners— college and above— will derive more benefit than younger students from behavioral objectives. The literature indicates academic age is immaterial.

☆ **WELCOME** the additional advantages of behavioral objectives. Koch (1972) finds that using behavioral objectives improves the confidence of learners in their subject matter. Merrill and Towle (1972) report behavioral objectives reduce anxiety.

★ **REFRAIN** from hoping that by using behavioral objectives you will perform well in every aspect of training. While there is evidence to suggest behavioral objectives lead to better lesson plans, there is no evidence to suggest that objectives will automatically improve personal poise and personality, the sequencing and presentation of instructional units, or the application of basic principles of learning.

Using behavioral objectives in instructional planning

☆ **INVESTIGATE** pre-existing subject

121

THE BENEFITS OF COMPETENCE MODELS

BY JOHN D. INGALLS

The training and development field is developing an instrument that may make personnel departments more effective in developing and managing human resources. This instrument, called a competency model, eventually may replace the traditional job description and provide the foundation for a comprehensive and fully integrated human resources system. But, before describing how the competency model can bring about this positive outcome, we must first define the concept of competence within the organization and look at some features of the model itself.

Constructing the model

Competence is the demonstrated ability to perform or accomplish a task, activity or project by oneself or with others. Competence involves the simultaneous interplay of knowledge, skill or ability, understanding, positive attitudes and constructive values. The construction of a competency model calls for the correct identification of the critical competencies required for effective performance in any given assignment, position or job. Specific or general measurement levels are then determined and a matrix is devised that enables individuals and managers to measure increased competence acquisition over a period of time.

More important than the objectivity of the measurements is the identification of a gap between where any individual is in terms of job-related competence and where he or she desires or is required to be to meet individual or organizational performance requirements, objectives or goals. As the gaps are closed by improved performance or increased competence, a valid correlation probably can be made with improved and objectively measurable productivity or cost-reduction goals.

Potential users

The use of competency models is particularly valuable in high-technology organizations where there is a large percentage of "indirect labor" or "overhead." (These accounting terms refer to individuals who are not assigned to directly measurable production machine centers.) Competency models can help reduce effort discretion and allow individuals and organizations to focus on crucially important developmental tasks. The narrowing of discretionary effort with the simultaneous development of increased competence is critical.

Because so many individuals in today's organizations are performing jobs that are not directly measurable in terms of output, new controls are needed to maintain a competitive pricing structure and to prevent runaway cost escalation. And because these new controls must be voluntary and inner directed, it is necessary to appeal both to self-worth and self-interest and to understand the necessary means of fostering human development, personal growth and behavior change, or learning.

Much of the potentially beneficial effect of the competency-based approach may be lost or nullified if the role determination or judgment of competence is left exclusively to any one particular manager. Whether an individual can be proved competent or incompetent is not the issue. What's critical is correctly identifying, calibrating and modeling the essential job competencies for individuals planning their own systematic acquisition of increased competence. When this is done, managers can be effective coaches or counselors of improved performance and be supportive resources to those seeking to develop themselves. And, when individuals are guided through the process of developing their own organizational and individual competency models, both trust in the model and a sense of ownership results. It should be noted that this approach to competency-based learning is based on the theory of adult education, or andragogy developed by Malcolm Knowles and others.

Potential benefits

Competency models produce a number of potential benefits that can link the separate elements of personnel administration into a total human resources management system.

1. Employment and placement efforts become more efficient when positions are filled on the basis of competency requirements rather than on the basis of personality traits, indeterminate prior experience or "fast talk."

2. EEO compliance becomes easier and more effective when people strive to acquire increased competence in relation to their own performance, rather than competing with others. Promotion decisions based on demonstrated competence criteria will usually stand up under legal scrutiny.

3. Many of today's problems with performance appraisal can be resolved when supervisors and subordinates jointly plan for and measure performance development against pre-identified and accepted criteria.

4. Career path selection and planning become more realistic when an individual has a "competency map" to follow. Systematic acquisition of required competencies enables an individual to chart and follow a desired career course.

5. Training becomes more cost effective and beneficial when it provides for the acquisition of specific job-related competencies and is measured by how well individuals are able to improve their on-the-job performance. The competency model makes this measurement possible.

6. Compensation tied to demonstrated performance improvement has long been an ideal. But without competency models, compensation systems must depend on job analyses and intercompany comparisons, which often leave out the personal equation, demotivate the high achiever and contradict the assertion of merit.

7. Opportunity for systematic personal development within a job assignment is probably the biggest benefit because it results in increased on-the-job satisfaction. Also, it allows those who really want to develop to improve their standard of living and their personal worth in the employment market.

Undoubtedly, the eventual replacement of job descriptions with competency models will represent a major step forward for the field of personnel administration.

Reprinted from TRAINING, April 1979

knowledge, since it can be critical in learning with behavioral objectives. Obreiter (1978) says behavioral objectives are more influential with students who have previous subject matter experience than those without it. Varano (1977) reports IQ and previous knowledge of subject matter both influence achievement and retention with behavioral objectives.

☆ **FIND OUT** what learners consider important in a text. Research indicates that judged importance of a text element determines whether objectives will facilitate learning or not. According to Duell (1974) and Melton (1978), if a learner judges an element to be important, it will be learned whether or not it is related to an objective. Objectives in those circumstances may be unnecessary, but provide them if learners consider elements of a text unimportant.

☆ **ADOPT** behavioral objectives techniques if relevant information— needed by the objectives— is given to the students. Seven studies out of nine show that students informed of behavioral objectives (with relevant information) progress through an instructional unit in less time than those not informed of objectives.

☆ **EMPLOY** behavioral objectives in an individualized learning situation. Ritter (1975) says self-paced learners complete courses faster than their instructor-paced counterparts when both use behavioral objectives.

★ **RESIST** the temptation to see grade point averages or aptitude measures as significant factors in performance while using behavioral objectives. Taylor (1976) indicates grade point averages do not influence such performance, while Baker (1976) says learner aptitudes are ineffective for predicting cognitive achievement with behavioral objectives.

★ **STOP** worrying that high academic qualifications or extensive teaching experience are needed to write behavioral objectives. Studies do not indicate that those with higher credentials or broader experience know more about behavioral objectives or express a more positive attitude toward them.

★ **FORGET** about instructors' personality types while accepting and interpreting the meaning of behavioral objectives. Smith (1970) and Hogen (1977) find no relationship between personality types and preference and interpretation of behavioral objectives in actual practice.

☆ **PARTICIPATE** in the decision-making process to use behavioral objectives. If there are staff meetings where behavioral objectives are discussed, your active participation may help you win approval to use them. Stahl (1972) maintains the greater an individual's participation in such a process, the greater the chances of using behavioral objectives.

Using behavioral objectives in instructional design

☆ **DETERMINE** reader comprehension ability. If reading ability is high, behavioral objectives may be less effective— students who can comprehend better perform better any way. Rashkoff (1976) says entry-level high reading comprehension is more effective when learning with behavioral objectives than low-level comprehension, but Petty (1974) reports learners in the upper quartile who are given behavioral objectives do not perform better than those in the same quartile not given objectives. In fact, Keyser (1976) shows that individuals with higher reading ability learn more when *no* behavioral objectives are involved.

☆ **WATCH** the difficulty level of the objectives and the text material. According to Brown (1970), the difficulty level of the objectives influences performance. Keyser (1976) demonstrates that performance objectives are more effective with difficult text than with easy material.

☆ **INVESTIGATE** characteristics which may make objectives redundant in a text. For instance, Duchastel (1979) finds the structure of the text can be as effective as behavioral objectives. Structure, by itself, can orient learning; if the text is well structured, behavioral objectives do not add much effect.

☆ **FURNISH** operational definitions of verbs used in objectives. Zeigler (1974) says definitions plus information on the utilization and importance of the objectives appear to aid achievement.

★ **REFRAIN** from giving details— terminal behaviors, conditions of occurrences, criterion of minimal performance— for each behavioral objective. Janeczko (1971) and Lovett (1971) demonstrate that increasing the knowledge of behavioral objectives does not increase achievement.

★ **AVOID** listing highly specific behavioral objectives instead of general objectives, especially at the beginning of a text. Thinly chopped behavioral objectives are not a written guarantee for performance. General objectives can do the job equally well. In fact, among the 13 studies reviewed, only three note a significant treatment effect from giving specific objectives.

★ **ELIMINATE** giving only partial presentations of objectives prior to instruction. According to Bastress (1971) and Shields (1973), partial presentation of objectives is less effective than a full presentation at the beginning of instruction.

☆ **PROVIDE** an adequate number of behavioral objectives based on the density of the text. Providing too many objectives for a simple task or too few for many tasks should be avoided. There appears to be a relationship between the number of specific objectives to be listed and the density of relevant information in the text. Rothkopf and Kaplan (1972, 1974) report an increase in the density of instructional objectives decreases the probability that an instructional task will be learned. They add that the probability of achieving any given objective decreases as the number of objective-relevant sentences in a text and the number of specific objectives increases.

☆ **DISTRIBUTE** behavioral objectives among the text segments instead of presenting all objectives prior to the text. Games, Johnson and Klare (1967), Kaplan (1974), and Yelon and Schmidt (1972) all point out that such a practice results in greater learning.

☆ **USE** other techniques, such as pretests, directions, questions and advance organizers to support or to provide variety in instructional text. Empirical studies show that, compared with these preinstructional techniques, behavioral objectives are not significantly more effective. Papay (1971), Song

123

(1975), Stalians (1978) and Varano (1977) agree on this point.

☆ **OFFER** specific behavioral objectives at the end of a unit rather than at the beginning. Frase (1968), Keyser (1976) and Rothkopf (1966) say post-behavioral objectives are more effective than pre-behavioral objectives. In addition, such a use of objectives increases incidental learning— learning not related to the objectives.

Using behavioral objectives as you train

☆ **USE** behavioral objectives as guides to your training. Use them in your lesson plans. They may help you concentrate on the relevant elements of the unit and thus facilitate learning. In addition, when you use behavioral objectives you will be cognizant of the expected learner behavior: the relationship between objectives and the concept or skill to be learned.

☆ **INSIST** on learners reading behavioral objectives. According to Engel (1968), assuring that learners read behavioral objectives is a critical factor in objectives-related learning.

☆ **WORK** on the reading ability of students— the ability to focus on items of information required by objectives. Jones (1974) and Stalians (1978) indicate that ability to concentrate on items of information required by objectives influences achievement with behavioral objectives.

☆ **COMMUNICATE** specific objectives to subjects. Such verbal contact with learners may facilitate more objectives-related (intentional) learning. Studies done by Dalis (1970), Rothkopf and Kaplan (1972), and Wingard (1976) show such a practice pays rich dividends.

☆ **PRESENT** objectives during instruction. Kaplan (1974, 1976) finds that exposing objectives during instruction improves objectives-related learning, as well as increasing overt response. And repeat objectives two or three times during instruction. Such a drill may help learners master relevant items. Yelon and Schmidt (1972) show that presenting objectives twice during instruction improves their effect.

★ **AVOID** training people how to use behavioral objectives. Brown (1970), Lawrence (1972), Morse and Tillman (1972), and Sink (1973) find that learners trained in the use of behavioral objectives do not perform significantly better than those not trained. Secondly, avoid asking learners' opinions about whether the objectives are related to the course or not.

☆ **RECOGNIZE** learner personality characteristics while using behavioral objectives. According to Kueter (1970), objectives are less effective with submissive, self-controlled, considerate and conscientious students. Kelly (1972) observes that personality variables (introvert vs. extrovert, stable vs. unstable) influence performance with behavioral objectives.

☆ **USE** other techniques, such as questions and feedback, to support or provide variety. Compared with behavioral objectives, such techniques are proven to be equally effective, if not better. Basset (1973) and Viel (1975) find that providing feedback is as effective as providing objectives. Papay (1971) indicates objectives are less effective than questions.

☆ **TRAIN** learners to take sample test items rather than letting them read a list of behavioral objectives. Such training may reduce test anxiety among learners and may even aid recall of relevant elements. Derr (1978) says students learning through sample test items will be more effective on cognitive post-tests than those learning through behavioral objectives.

Reprinted from TRAINING, March 1981

WRITING OBJECTIVES WITH STYLE

To make sure students get the most out of individualized learning materials, provide clear, concise instructions

BY JESSE M. HEINES

Objectives have long been recognized as the backbone of individualized instructional materials. And we've all heard that these objectives should be stated in terms of overt, measurable student performances or behaviors.

But it is the measurable component of objectives that is the most difficult for instructional designers to write. If an editor takes a general objective (what Bob Mager would call a "goal") and works it into a behavioral mode, the instructional designer will often comment that the edited objective has lost the "depth" of his or her idea and no longer conveys "the true skill to be learned."

But there's another side to the coin. General objectives (Mager's "fuzzies") also do little to provide learning direction. In their course "Criterion-Referenced Instruction,"* Bob Mager and Peter Pipe introduce the concept of stating a "criterion" for each behavior so that instructors can recognize mastery performers — that is, "know one when we see one." This article deals with style in writing objectives and stating the criterion in the form of a sample test item. These test items can serve to clarify objectives and assure that they can be tested. In addition, sample test items illustrate the exact way students will be evaluated.

Over-behavioralism

Sometimes objectives are worded in

*Mager Associates, Inc., 151 University Ave., Suite 400, Palo Alto, CA 94301./1/1

such a way that the objective and sample test item would be exactly the same. In these cases, a sample test item is not required. Usually, however, it is better to make the objective more general to encompass a wider range of skills and then let the test item serve as an illustration of these skills. For example, here is an objective for which no sample test item is needed:

1. Match each function performed by the LQP8-E to the printed circuit board that accomplishes it.

A more generalized objective is:

2. Identify all the functions for each of the LQP8-E printed-circuit boards (PCBs) listed below.

   - Power Amp PCB
   - Print Wheel PCB
   - Servo PCB
   - Logic #1 PCB
   - Logic #2 PCB
   - Transducer PCB

The sample test item for this objective could be

3. Match each PCB to its functions.

Function	PCB
_decodes instructions	A. Power Amp
_outputs ready status	B. Print Wheel Amp
etc.	etc.

Objective 1. is an *over-behavioralized* objective. It focuses on a narrow, short-term behavior ("match") rather than a wider, more useful behavior ("identify functions"). Here's another objective that carries the over-behavioralization problem to the limit:

4. Correctly answer 8 out of 10 questions on the major VS-60 components, features and options.

"Answering questions" is not a real objective of any training course I've ever observed. This behavior is merely an indicator of more complex mental processes. The true objective is closer to:

5. Identify the functions and uses of the CRT display monitor, display processor unit and light pen in the VS-60 Graphics Display Subsystem. You must respond correctly to 8 out of 10 multiple-choice test items on these units to demonstrate mastery.

The second sentence states the objective's criterion. A sample test item for this objective might be:

6. The device that is used to select and manipulate displayed graphic information on the VS-60 is the

   A. central processing unit.
   B. CRT display monitor.
   C. display processor unit.
   D. light pen.

One more point about Objective 4. In most cases, it's not necessary to instruct students to do things "correctly," because it would be ridiculous for them to strive to do things "incorrectly." The term may make sense in Objective 4. because it's possible to answer ten questions and not get eight of them correct. It would not, however, add anything to Item 3. to instruct students to "correctly match each PCB to its functions."

Wordiness

Wordiness is another problem area in objective and test-item writing. I have three suggestions to make in this area.

The first suggestion concerns the phrase "the student will be able to." In general, this phrase should be avoided because it is simply verbiage. Rather, objectives should be written in the second person with the subject "you" understood. Here is an example:

7. Given a block diagram of an LQP8-E, the student will be able to label the interface signals without references.

A simpler statement is:

8. Given a block diagram of an LQP8-E, label the interface signals without references.

An exception to this style involves objectives that are too large or complex to be tested completely. In these cases,

LET'S RESOLVE TO WRITE BETTER TRAINING OBJECTIVES!

BY ELLEN BALL

At this time of year, when people are vowing to quit smoking, lose weight and save more money, it's also appropriate to make one resolution that really *can* stick throughout the year. And that's resolution to write better objectives.

Here, then, is a lesson short enough to fit into a Christmas stocking. An objective's contents, like a present, must fit exactly the person to whom it's addressed. In other words, if you don't want to see your uncle in a purple tie, don't buy him one. Likewise, be sure an objective is important enough to be made part of your training package material. Once you've decided on its appropriateness, write down exactly what you want to see or hear when the person receives the training derived from your objective.

Let's take Uncle Harry's tie. If you bought it, presumably you'd love to see it on him. So, what does he have to do? Wear it, of course. But is there anything else? Well, unless you're specific that he wears *your* purple tie, he might grab another, so you must tell him you want to see that particular one on him. Now, there are a few other things to consider. You've told him what you want him to do, (action) and what to do it with (given). But have you told him you want him to wear the tie in a certain fashion, tied in a double knot, with one end shorter and behind the other and the long edge just above the belt buckle? Criteria that specific can't possibly be misinterpreted.

If you know exactly what it is you want when your objective is met, it's easy to sit down and fill in the blanks— what you want to see, what is needed to do it with and the condition under which you expect it to be done. Maybe the same bottom line of what you'd look like 10 pounds thinner would keep alive your yearly resolution to lose weight.

Reprinted from TRAINING, December 1979

you want students to "be able to" do all the tasks listed, but they will be tested on only a "sample" of them. Here is an example:

9. Given an LQP8-E line printer, be able to remove and re-install the field replaceable units (FRUs). You will be asked to remove and re-install two of the FRUs listed below.
    - Power amp PCB
    - Carriage amp PCB
    - Carriage assembly
    - Shaft carriage
    - Hammer armature assembly
    - Magnetic pick-up
    - Rear carriage bearing
    - Ribbon lift assembly
    - Ribbon lift coil assembly
    - Bail arm (right/left)

Look at the criterion for this objective. It would be too time-consuming to test each student on all 10 of these FRUs. Also, it is probably safe to assume that if a student can replace two or three of these units (a "sample" of the skills), he or she can replace them all. By using a random sample of these FRUs as the test, each student would have to be sure that he or she could replace them all before asking for the test. To guarantee this completely, a different sample should be used for each student. The sample test item for Objective 9. might be:

10. Your instructor will pick two of the FRUs listed in the objective. Remove and re-install the designated parts.

The second suggestion problem concerns long lists of "givens" and starting all or most objectives with the word "given." The first can confuse the reader, while the second can bore him. Look at this objective:

11. Given all necessary tools, test equipment, diagnostics and documentation, perform all necessary adjustments on a functioning, but maladjusted, VS-60.

The "givens" in this objective make it difficult to read because they don't mean anything to the reader until he or she gets to the action, "perform all necessary adjustments." It would be better to break this objective into two sentences with the action stated first. This approach will also allow elimination of the word "given."

12. Perform all necessary adjustments on a functioning, but maladjusted, VS-60. You will be supplied with all necessary tools, test equipment, diagnostics and documentation.

Just as the preceding problems are usually caused by trying to crowd an entire objective into one sentence, you can also cause unnecessary confusion by trying to crowd too many goals into one objective. There is no reason why a goal cannot give birth to two, three or even more objectives as long as they're related. This strategy can often make objectives clearer and allow ideas to be more fully developed.

Finally, be careful that objectives and sample test items don't get bogged down with phrases such as "without references" or "using the XYZ manual." This information can be "factored out" of objectives and placed in a Student Guide. That is, if most tests will be "open book" and allow references, say so in the Student Guide: Unless otherwise noted, you may use any references when taking a test except another person. Thus, you need only specify when references are *not* allowed.

Writing with style

A training organization cannot expect every instructional designer to write in the same style, but it can strive to make its materials look uniform. Such uniformity, especially when standardized in a clear writing style, can assist students by making it easy to move from prerequisite to higher-level courses. An unencumbered style will assure that students "get the message" and that objectives provide clear learning direction.

Reprinted from TRAINING, July 1980

VERIFYING YOUR TRAINING OBJECTIVES

This step-by-step method can help you produce a better match between needs and programs

BY ROBERT W. DOBLES,
PATRICIA M. DROST,
STANLEY S. HAZEN
AND ROBERT C. HINKELMAN

As more organizations send more students to training programs, those organizations rightfully expect to get their money's worth. They expect that the training programs will provide what they need and that it will meet the need in the least possible time away from the job. To determine whether the need is being met, these three questions must be answered:

1. How does "what is" compare with "what should be?"
2. What is being done that should *not* be done?
3. What is not being done that *should* be done? The method described here provides objective answers to these and other questions and provides them in the least possible time.*

The training objective

Before a new training program is designed for a client** or an existing one revised, it is necessary to ask what the program intends to accomplish. Normally, this is expressed in the form of one or more objectives, as described by Mager and Beach: "What kinds of things should the student be able to do at the end of the course that will most facilitate his becoming a skilled craftsman in the least amount of time."[1] In other words, the objectives should be written in performance terms. It must be possible to state what improvement has taken place.

The process

The Verification of Training Objectives process has five steps.

Step 1. Analyze the existing program. The training professional carefully analyzes the content of the existing course by looking for the primary skills or knowledge to be acquired during each session.

Step 2. Write objectives. A set of objectives specifying these primary skills is prepared. Each objective is stated in terms of performance; that is, the objective specifies what the student should be able to do at the conclusion of the course. Each objective should be independent of all others. Our experience has indicated that 25 to 35 objectives are reasonable for a 40-hour course.

Step 3. Evaluate program objectives. The training professional specifies the existing program by recording the time required to teach each objective, the teaching strategy used and the current performance level aim. In addition, he or she prepares interview materials that enable the client to independently rate the objective's relevance for a given trainee and to

*This method was developed at the training department of Eastman Kodak Company's Kodak Park Division in cooperation with Messrs. DeMarle and Shillito of the Management Services Division.

**A client is an organization that sends students to the program and is normally represented by one or more supervisors.

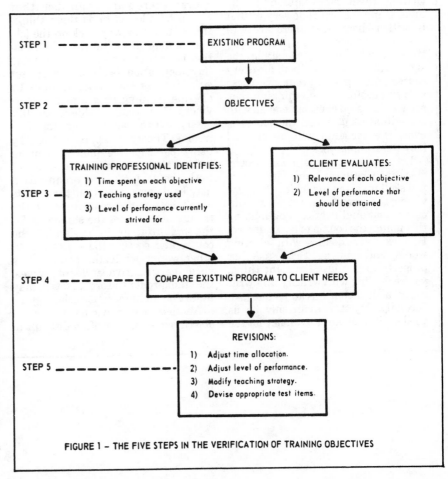

FIGURE 1 – THE FIVE STEPS IN THE VERIFICATION OF TRAINING OBJECTIVES

TIPS FOR IMPROVING YOUR OBJECTIVE TRAINING

BY MARTIN M. BROADWELL

It's a very familiar belief among many people that someday we'll get over this mess of trying to write course objectives and get back to the good old days of just teaching those things we know the students need. In fact, it would be honest to say that there are many who have made the trip back in time to that point. In a sense, they tried the water, didn't like it, and decided to get out of the swim. Others are hanging on, writing objectives for some courses, not for others. And there are trainers who are writing something like objectives, but without going through the full motion of getting a standard, criterion, and condition for each objective. The worst of the lot are those who are out preaching the need for course objectives, but ignoring them in actual practice.

Writing objectives is hard work. Even among those who have been writing them for years, and who understand the principle very well, it is still a chore. And there are still trainers who don't know about objectives or who don't understand the significance of having them for every course. Among this group are those who go blissfully along thinking they are writing good ones, but end up with something like, "When the course is over, the students will understand how the framus works."

Let's look at some reasons why objective writing is hard. First, there is a skill involved in picking the right words, the correct amount of quantification and qualification, and making this match the course to be conducted. Because you're dealing with selecting words and putting them together properly to say just the right thing, you're dealing with writing, and writing is a skill that has to be learned. Secondly, objectives can only be as good as the standards available for the job to be taught. If there is no definitive standard—that is, no one knows exactly what a good job is—then the trainer can't possibly come up with usable objectives. To complicate matters, many trainers end up writing (or trying to write) standards which may never be seen by the people who

Perhaps it's true that nobody writes them anymore. So why is everybody afraid to admit it?

actually have to agree on what the standards are for the organization. While this is less likely to happen in the skills areas than in the supervisory and management ranks, it happens in both. In the skills area, the trainer dreams up a standard of performance for the person to be trained, decides how much of this can be reached in the training course, and creates an objective that may be well written and meets the standard for objective writing. However, no one has seen the new standard, and even if the students meet the objectives of the course there's no assurance that they'll be allowed to do these things this well or this way back on the job.

In management training, the violation is near criminal. Many trainers (my inclination is to say most) set standards for their organizations by offering training programs to supervisors that include objectives like "being able to react to given situations from a Theory Y approach" or "by using participative management in 90% of their actions and reactions." Both the trainers and organization may be disappointed that the results aren't better, not realizing that the trainer actually set the standards for the organization in designing the course and writing the objectives. In other words, while the trainer may write participative style objectives, the standard for the organization may in fact be an autocratic style.

Another reason it's hard to write objectives is that it's often difficult to match training needs with class accomplishment. We find that there are many needs, many things that need to be talked about in class, but we realize it's impossible to meet very realistic objectives in the time allowed. We end up hedging by saying that what we will do is just give an *overview*.

Ambiguous specificity

It is possible to write useful objectives for most courses, even a "survey" course. First, we must admit to ourselves that we are teaching a survey course. Once we do, then it's a matter of writing objectives to match what we plan to have learned by the students. It may be that we end up with a certain amount of ambiguous specificity, if we may coin a phrase. We end up saying that the learners will be able to identify two of the seven reasons why the framus is the market leader, or recognize which sources produce the best results for the majority of the products we sell, but without being able to give any specific data about reasons or sources. We run into this problem in most of our "orientation" courses. We show the new employee the seven thousand different products we make in five hundred different plants in 44 different countries—showing pictures of all the products, plants, and countries—then ask about objectives. The answer is simple. "When the course is over the employees will know that we make a lot of products in a bunch of plants in a lot of places, and will be able to state this in so many words." That doesn't feed our ego very much after we've collected all those pictures, but it's the best we can do for an objective when you get right down to it. We probably could have spent our time better—and orientated the employee better—by telling him where to park, where to go on his break, what clothes to wear, and who the boss really is. That's not very glamorous, but it's probably what the employee *needs and wants*. If we're training towards anything else, why worry about writing objectives anyway?

Reprinted from TRAINING, May 1976

specify the level of performance that should be attained for each program objective.***

Step 4. Compare client evaluation with existing program. The "importance" of each objective, obtained from a computer analysis of the client responses, is compared with the cost of teaching each objective based on the time analysis made at Step 3.

Step 5. Revise existing program. The time allocated for the teaching of each objective is adjusted to more nearly agree with client ratings of relevance. Teaching strategy is modified to accomplish this and also to adjust the specification of performance level for each objective. Test items are redesigned to test each objective at the appropriate performance level.

Role of the training professional

In preparation for the client interviews, the training professional carries out his or her own analysis of the course. After the objectives are written, the total program time is allocated to the objectives. The relative cost of teaching each objective is then calculated. This is the time for each objective divided by the total course time.

$$\%C_{obj.\ \#} = \frac{Time_{obj.\ \#}}{\Sigma\,(Time_{obj.\ \#})\ \text{all objectives}}$$

During the process of obtaining the time for each objective, the strategy used to teach the objective is noted. Typical strategies include lectures, workshop exercises, review sheets, instructor- or student-conducted demonstrations and the like. Each objective is also classified by performance level.

The interview materials

In the interest of having the directions for client interviews presented consistently to group meetings at different times, printed instructions are used. The documents bearing these detailed instructions may take several forms. They may be 3" x 5" file cards, or they may be printed pages in a loose-leaf notebook, both as shown in figure 2. They consist of the following items:

***The rating method is detailed in the following sections: "Role of the Training Professional," "Interview Materials," and "Role of the Client."

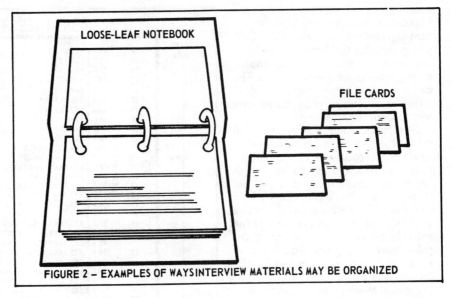

FIGURE 2 – EXAMPLES OF WAYS INTERVIEW MATERIALS MAY BE ORGANIZED

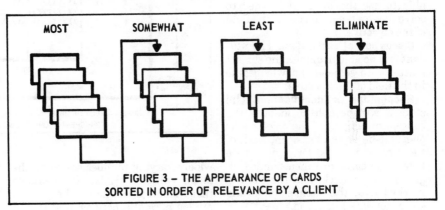

FIGURE 3 – THE APPEARANCE OF CARDS SORTED IN ORDER OF RELEVANCE BY A CLIENT

1. An introductory statement of purpose
2. Directions for a first sorting of objectives cards, by relevance
3. The course objectives, each on a separate 3" x 5" file card
4. A request to add further objectives as needed (Blank cards are included for this purpose).
5. Directions to rank each objective numerically by relevance
6. Directions for a second sorting of the objectives cards, by performance level
7. A second set of cards bearing the course objectives
8. An expression of thanks for the client's participation

Role of the Client

Clients are invited to perform their individual evaluations in groups of about ten people at a time. After the purpose of the exercise has been explained, all the participants are given identical sets of materials. Using the written directions, the client first sorts the course objectives by relevance into the following classifications:

Most relevant
Somewhat relevant
Least relevant
Eliminate

The directions indicate that the classification should be made based on the skills the client believes his or her nominees need for the job.

The clients then add any additional objectives they believe to be important but that were not included in the group provided. The clients write each such additional objective on one of the blank cards and then classify them in the same categories as the objectives cards just sorted.

The client arranges the cards within each classification from most relevant to least relevant. The sorted cards would resemble those shown in figure 3.

Following this, each client assigns to each objective a number or value that indicates its relative importance, using any convenient number scale. Clients are encouraged to select number scales that provide a fairly wide numerical distance between ratings for different objectives. The most important objective in the "Most Relevant" group of objectives receives the highest value, while the least important objective in the "Least Relevant" group receives the lowest value. Any objective receiving an "Eliminate" rating is assigned a value of zero. The cards are then banded together, identified with the client's name and stored for data extraction.

Next, each client is given a second set of objectives cards, identical to the first. Any objectives rated "Eliminate" are removed and coded accordingly. The cards bearing the objectives written by the clients are added to the cards remaining, and the entire deck is shuffled. Clients then sort the cards in the modified decks into three piles representing the required level of performance, as described by the following classifications:

Problem solving. The student will be able to use the material learned to solve day-to-day problems in the field of the objective.

Discussion of explanation. The student will be able to discuss the subject matter with someone knowledgeable in the field of the objective.

Recognition or Identification. The student will be able to identify the concept or activity of the objective as one that he or she has seen. Each of these cards is coded for performance level. The cards are then banded together into a deck, and the deck is marked with the client's name and stored for data extraction.

This concludes the client's role in the evaluation. The entire procedure is usually completed in less than two hours.

Data Produced

As we mentioned earlier, the clients are asked to assign a value to each objective. Arbitrary limits to the number scale were intentionally *not* suggested to avoid influencing the clients' judgment. (For example, our experience has shown that upper limits chosen by clients may vary between 1.0 and 1000.)

For each objective, the geometric mean of the values assigned by all clients is calculated. These mean values are added to find their sum, and each individual geometric mean is divided by this sum. This gives the average percent importance, $\%\bar{I}$, for each objective.

$$\%\bar{I}_{obj. \#} = \frac{G.M._{obj. \#}}{\Sigma(G.M.)_{all\ objectives}}$$

(The use of a geometric mean minimizes the effect of the choice of

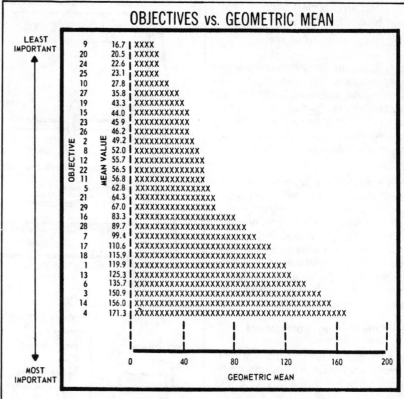

OBJECTIVES vs. GEOMETRIC MEAN

LEAST IMPORTANT

OBJECTIVE	MEAN VALUE
9	16.7
20	20.5
24	22.6
25	23.1
10	27.8
27	35.8
19	43.3
15	44.0
23	45.9
26	46.2
2	49.2
8	52.0
12	55.7
22	56.5
11	56.8
5	62.8
21	64.3
29	67.0
16	83.3
28	89.7
7	99.4
17	110.6
18	115.9
1	119.9
13	125.3
6	135.7
3	150.9
14	156.0
4	171.3

MOST IMPORTANT

GEOMETRIC MEAN: 0   40   80   120   160   200

FIGURE 4 – PLOT OF OBJECTIVE NUMBER VS. GEOMETRIC MEAN ARRANGED FROM LOWEST TO HIGHEST GEOMETRIC MEAN

widely varying number scales on the mean value.****[2]Also, it is known that human perception and cognition are log normal functions; that is, relative values are perceived as ratios in a geometric series rather than as cumulative sums in an arithmetic series.) The geometric mean can be both calculated and plotted by computer, as shown in figure 4. The ratio of respective geometric means is a measure of the relative importance of one objective to another.

Percent cost is determined as described above (see "Role of the Training Professional").

$$\bar{V}_{obj. \#} = \frac{\%\bar{I}_{obj. \#}}{\%C_{obj. \#}}$$

Where $\bar{V}_{obj. \#}$ = average value

$\%\bar{I}_{obj. \#}$ = average % importance

$\%C_{obj. \#}$ = % cost

A Value Index, for each objective, is

****The geometric mean of any data set containing a zero is automatically zero. To avoid this, objectives rated "Eliminate" and thus receiving a zero value were arbitrarily given a value of 0.001.

Figure 5 illustrates how %I vs. %C can be plotted.[1] The position of each objective number on this graph relates directly to the Value Index of that objective. All objective numbers on the straight line shown have a Value Index of 1.0. These correspond to objectives whose percent importance equals percent cost. Therefore, they represent "acceptable value." Objective numbers lying below the line correspond to "poor value," while those above correspond to "good value," as long as specified performance levels are being met.

Analysis of the Data

In a course designed in perfect accordance with all clients' needs, the points corresponding to all the objectives would lie on the straight line. Particular attention should, therefore, be paid to points far below this line. For example, Objective No. 10 appears at the 1.3% importance level, while occupying 11.0% of the course time. This and other objectives appearing below the line clearly indicate areas of concern; that is, cost may be higher than can be justified by the clients' judgment of importance.*

*Care must be taken in interpreting this information. It is possible that objectives far below the line cannot be taught to the required level in the corresponding fraction of the time.

130

On the other hand, the importance of Objective No. 6 was rated 6.3%, while the time devoted to this objective comprised only 1.0% of the course total. As long as specified performance levels are being met for this objective, it is being efficiently taught and is, therefore, a "good buy" in terms of the importance/cost ratio.**

Another comparison can be made, this time relative to performance level. The training professional and the client have both independently determined a performance level; the former as the course is taught, the latter as his needs indicate that the course should be taught. In figure 6, the numbers of certain objectives have been circled for either of two reasons:

1. The cost of teaching is excessive relative to the established importance;

2. Or there is a serious mismatch between the performance level of the course as currently taught and as the client has determined that it should be taught in order to best meet his needs.

Having determined the client's needs in this exercise, the training professional now has guidelines with which to proceed. The time allocated to each objective is adjusted to agree more nearly with client ratings of importance. The specification of performance level is brought more nearly in line with the client's requirements. Both of these help to shape teaching strategy.

Some teaching strategies are more expensive (time-consuming) than others. For example, laboratory experience is very costly in terms of the time required for explanation of procedures, demonstration of equipment and prevention of mechanical pitfalls. The time required for these activities must be considered in addition to the time devoted to the student's actual participation and learning experience. Whether such a time allocation is justified is considered in light of the relative importance of the objective and the level of performance expected of students on the job.

Test items are also prepared in accordance with the client's needs. For each objective, the training professional prepares one or more test items that test the same skill described in the objective and at the performance level specified by the client. If problem solving is the required per-

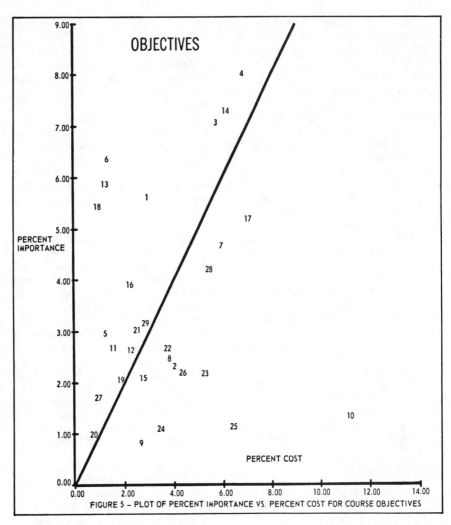

FIGURE 5 – PLOT OF PERCENT IMPORTANCE VS. PERCENT COST FOR COURSE OBJECTIVES

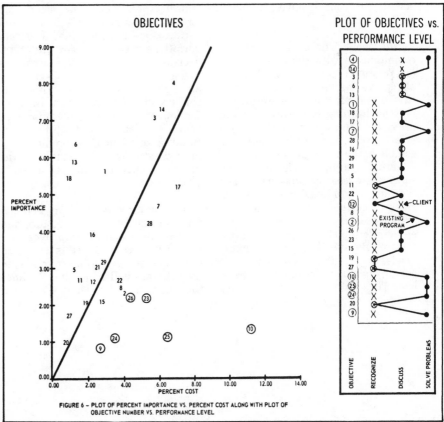

FIGURE 6 – PLOT OF PERCENT IMPORTANCE VS. PERCENT COST ALONG WITH PLOT OF OBJECTIVE NUMBER VS. PERFORMANCE LEVEL

**Here, too, the question must be asked whether *enough* time has been allocated with respect to perceived importance.

131

formance level, the test item asks the student to solve a problem. If an objective is rated at the discussion level, then either an oral discussion or a written essay test item is usually appropriate. Recognition level objectives can be tested by multiple-choice questions or matching exercises or by asking the student to choose the correct word from a list to fill in a blank. *In any case, the test item assesses the skill described in the objective and at the specified performance level.* The relative importance of each objective may also be used to weight the testing; that is, test item(s) for highly relevant objectives may be more extensive than those for objectives of lesser relevance.

In some cases, training professionals are asked to deal with a very diverse student population. If a small fraction of the client population requires an unusually high performance level or attaches an unusually great importance or relevance to an objective or group of objectives, it may be necessary to provide extra time for these students to learn the corresponding skills. On the other hand, an unusually low rating may indicate excusing other students from the session(s) in which the topic receives attention.

Benefits of the Method

The method described appears to benefit everyone involved in industrial training.

1. The client. The client is able to communicate with the training professional in a straightforward and inexpensive manner. The client does this using an objective method of judging training programs in a way previously unavailable. The appropriate people, namely the supervisors, establish the program specifications in terms of training objectives. Decisions are based on supervisors' perceptions of students' needs. Discussions of outlines, tables of contents and/or teaching methodology do not enter into the client verification procedure. By specifying performance levels, the client also participates in establishing appropriate test strategies. These will subsequently demon-

strate that the objectives have been achieved.

2. The student. The students know that the program meets the needs their supervision recognizes. At the start of the program, they are presented with its objectives and with the specified performance level for each. They are informed that they will be tested on each objective at the specified performance level. They are also assured that performance will be tested consistently with the stated objectives.

3. The training professional. The training professional has far more information to guide course design and presentation, in the form of client-evaluated objectives. Creative activities can be more effectively directed toward the most important needs. By matching time allocation to client value judgment, the training professional can design a program that will be more cost-effective. Each topic can be taught to the performance level dictated by the client. In using quantitative information to better meet the client's needs, training professionalism is enhanced.

4. Training management. Training professionals can be held more accountable for student performance. Objectives and performance levels have been specified by the client, and the training professional is responsible for seeing that objectives are met and performance levels attained. Program variations resulting from unilateral decisions by individual instructors are reduced. Teaching strategy among instructors and overtime may change, but the objectives, the performance level and test item for each remain constant. A better understanding of client need produces improved program efficiency and the real possibility for a net reduction in program time.

5. The company. A company benefits from an employee training program only if the program improves employee performance. It is expected that improved performance following the program will more than balance the cost of training. This expectation

can be met only if program objectives match client needs. The better and more economically client objectives are met, the greater is the contribution to plant efficiency, potential employee growth and overall company profitability.

Summary

Training objectives are not new, nor is designing training programs around such objectives. What has been missing is a method for determining with assurance whether training programs match the training needs, as expressed by rated objectives.

Starting with the content and objectives of a program, the training professional now can calculate the time devoted to teaching each objective. The program user rates the importance and level of performance of each objective. The degree of match between importance and time is a measure of program efficiency. Any mismatch between importance and time indicates both that program revision should be considered and where those revisions should take place. The level of performance rating gives the training professional guidance for test design. The student, the student's supervision, the training professional, training management and company management can all be assured that training is being conducted and measured in the most effective manner.

Objectives for new programs can similarly be written and analyzed to give the training professional guidance concerning emphasis and time distribution. A program outline can then be written from a more informed point of view.

FOOTNOTES

1. Mager, Robert F. and Kenneth M. Beach, Jr., "Developing Vocational Instruction," Fearon Publishers, Palo Alto, CA, 1967, p. 29.
2. DeMarle, David J. and M. Larry Shillito, "Delphi Forecasts Aid Renewal," Proc., Soc. of Amer. Value Engineers Regional Conference, Detroit, MI, 1974, p.3.
3. Demarle, David J., "The Application of Subjective Value Analysis to Training," Proc., Soc. of Amer. Value Engineers Regional Conference, Detroit, MI, 1972, p. 5.1.
4. *Ibid.*, p. 5.5.

Reprinted from TRAINING, December 1979

THE TRAINING WHEEL: A SIMPLE MODEL FOR INSTRUCTIONAL DESIGN

Complex instructional technologies that work wonderfully in theory sometimes prove unwieldy in practice.
Here are some streamlined design suggestions from a pragmatist

BY ROSALIND L. ROGOFF

Systems models for developing instructional materials abound. The base ones, such as the Instructional Design Institute and Instructional Systems Development models, have been around for years and have been thoroughly embellished.

These models may be fine for theoretical study in graduate courses on instructional technology. As a trainer in industry, however, I find that a simpler, more pragmatic approach works better.

I have boiled down the systems approach to create a commonsense instructional-design model consisting of four simple steps (see figure). The model is in a circular format, rather than the usual series of boxes, so I call it the Training Wheel—but you don't need a bicycle to use it. Directions for use are simple: Start at 12 o'clock; turn clockwise; spin around as many times as it takes to get where you're going.

Step 1. Find out who, what and why

If you're acting as a teacher or trainer or instructional designer, your job is to figure out how to teach something to somebody. Therefore, the first question you need to answer is: What are you going to teach to whom, and why?

Here we're taking three "Ws" from journalism—"who," "what" and "why"—and relating them to the instructional-design process. Everything else you do hinges on how well you answer this question, and on how well you relate your later instructional objectives and methods to the answer.

You might consider the question to be a combination of needs assessment and audience analysis. Although most models show these steps separately, in real life you usually start a project knowing *something* about who or what you will be teaching. And in any case, the "who" and "what" are inseparable:

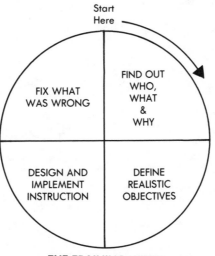

THE TRAINING WHEEL

Start Here

FIX WHAT WAS WRONG

FIND OUT WHO, WHAT & WHY

DESIGN AND IMPLEMENT INSTRUCTION

DEFINE REALISTIC OBJECTIVES

You can't create instruction without a student and a subject.

The "why" component is often overlooked, yet it is very important. If the student doesn't know why he is studying the subject, and you don't know why you are teaching it, what's the point of developing the instruction at all?

Let's say you are a subject-matter expert assigned to teach people how to operate a word processor. You know all there is to know about this particular machine; now you need to find out who has to be taught to use it. Are they secretaries, technical writers or managers? In what different ways will each particular group use the word processor, and why? Obviously, these differences should influence how you design your instruction. If you want to motivate managers, you must come up with a "why" that will justify their investment in time and energy.

On the other hand, you might know a lot about the audience but not much about the content of the training. Let's say the accounting department asks you to develop training materials for all newly hired auditors. In this case your first step is to identify the specific tasks that new auditors are expected to perform, and how quickly they are expected to do these tasks at a minimum level of proficiency. Since this is the job they have been hired to do, the "why" of the training is obvious.

Step 2. Define realistic objectives

It is crucial to define realistic, logical objectives. Simply writing an objective that fits Robert Mager's well-known criteria is not enough. The objectives, and any methods you develop to evaluate them, have to relate to what you found out in Step 1 (i.e., the "who," "what" and "why"). An objective such as "trainees will be able to list the five goals of cost accounting" is almost worthless if what the employees need to be able to do is audit expense reports.

A lot of silly objectives are imposed on training because of the perceived need to make everything measurable. Don't be *too* afraid of what Mager called "the fuzzies." A fuzzy goal that fits your "who," "what" and "why" makes a better objective for designing training than a measurable performance objective that measures something nobody needs to know or do.

Start out with fuzzy goals and gradually whittle these nebulous targets into performance-oriented shapes. Develop exams and other evaluation materials in conjunction with the objectives. If you cannot come up with a way to measure every objective, don't despair. In many training situations, formal evaluation procedures may be optional.

What? Not evaluate? Sacrilege! Why bother to define objectives then?

Because objectives, however fuzzy, are the end result of the "who," "what," and maybe even the "why." Objectives are the road maps that direct your instructional methods to their logical destination. Proving that you reached this destination may be more a matter of instinct than precise evaluation.

Often instructors use evaluations to prove that their training methods worked—everyone passed the test. But if the student is being trained in a job skill, his subsequent ability to perform the job is the real evaluation. Keep in mind that it is more important for the student to feel that he has *learned* something than for the instructor to prove he has *taught* it. In a real-world situation, students and their supervisors will let you know exactly how well the training worked for them.

Step 3. Design and implement the instruction

Prepare the curriculum. Write the textbook. Teach the course. Show the videotape. Do the whole song and dance. But remember to keep the "who," "what" and "why" foremost in your mind while you design the training.

Don't show a videotape just because you have one that sort of fits the subject. Don't design a lot of fancy graphics just to dazzle the class. If the course materials you develop don't support your objectives, they are superfluous.

But, you say, the students need some background in the history of the company in order to put what I'm teaching them into context. Fine. If it's a neces-

---

If you end up ducking eggs and tomatoes, you know your course needs a great deal of fixing.

---

sary part of the "why" component of Step 1, go back to Step 2 and write an objective for it. Your objective in this case is more likely to be affective than cognitive, but you do have to pinpoint exactly what students need to know about the company and why.

Sometimes the dryest, dullest presentations are the most effective for a particular training situation. I came from a film and TV background, so it took me a long time to realize that although punching up a course with visuals is fun, entertainment does not equal good training. If students need to learn how to fill out an "audit summary report form," showing pictures of the form, describing it and talking about its evolution will not teach them to fill it out as well as an exercise in which they actually *do* fill it out. Dull, yes, but effective.

Step 4. Fix what was wrong

Using the evaluation measures you developed in Step 2, find out which elements of your design worked and which didn't. Fix the things that didn't.

Ask for trainees' opinions. Give them a questionnaire. Send another questionnaire to their supervisors. Observe some former students working on the job. And use your own instincts. Sometimes you can just feel when things are wrong.

If you end up ducking eggs and tomatoes, you know that your course needs a great deal of fixing. In formal design models, this process is known as evaluation, feedback and revision. In "pre-systems" days, it was called trial and error. I call it time to take another turn around the Training Wheel.

Reprinted from TRAINING, April 1984

MEASURE TRAINEES AGAINST OBJECTIVES BEFORE YOU TRAIN THEM

Find out what trainees know before they enter your classroom

BY J.B. CORNWELL

After 20 years in the training business, I still can't forecast exactly what trainees can and can't do when they arrive at the beginning of a training course. And I've never met any other trainer who could either.

Until recently, I've always designed courses to meet exactly the needs of a "target" trainee. Of course, the methods used to define the capabilities of this mythological trainee are limited by available time and resources. Limited, that is, to something less than the "learner population analysis" described in the literature on how to be a rich, successful trainer.

Finally, I've come to accept the fact that a "target" trainee isn't going to take the course— but an *actual* trainee is. Actual trainees tend to differ from target trainees in at least two important ways:

• They don't know (can't do) some things that target trainees know— things we expect them to know before they start the course.

• They do know (can do) some things that target trainees don't know— things they're supposed to learn while taking the course.

In order for a course to succeed, it's imperative that we plan for, detect and respond to these two facts of training life in appropriate ways. With that in mind, I'd like to offer some practical suggestions for handling those critical differences between "target" trainees and their flesh-and-blood stand-ins.

The first type of difference has to do with prerequisites. To illustrate, I'll relate an example from my own experience as designer of an electronics troubleshooting course.

In designing this course on how to maintain a particular model instrument, I defined the "target" trainee as one who could competently operate the oscilloscope issued to service reps by our company. I blithely assumed the target trainee would be an experienced service rep. Most actual trainees did match that prerequisite. But some did not. And of those who didn't, some could operate other types of oscilloscopes and some couldn't even *spell* oscilloscopes. Because I hadn't planned for that, the course was a disaster for those trainees who didn't meet my somewhat unrealistic prerequisite.

What I learned from that experience was to define very specifically what trainees needed to be able to do before attending a course, decide what to do if they couldn't and check for differences before the course started. That check is *prerequisite testing*. The contingency plan (what to do if they can't) could range from simply refusing them admittance to the course to preparing and administering a prerequisite course, with lots of options in between.

Prerequisite testing shouldn't be limited to classroom-type courses. As a matter of fact, it's even more essential for learner-managed (canned, AV or programmed) courses because a live instructor has the power to adapt the course, to some degree, to the unique differences in learners. Learner-managed materials rarely have that flexibility regarding lack of prerequisites, although well-designed learner-managed materials are flexible in many other ways.

Objective statement

The starting point for sound prerequisite measurement is a clear, precise statement of what learners should *be able to do* at the beginning of the course. This statement should be structured the same way a terminal objective statement is. For example, a "can do" prerequisite statement should be indistinguishable from a "can do" objective statement. The following statement could be either a prerequisite statement or an objective statement, and a valid method of measuring is implied.

Conditions
Given: An Ajax model 3324H oscilloscope and Whizmation 314X micro computer

Action
The learner will be able to: determine pulse amplitude and duration at test point J

Criterion
Accurate within: three millivolts and one microsecond, in five minutes or less.

Knowledge statement

Knowledge prerequisites and enabling prerequisites can be similarly stated. Don't overlook the fact that in training, as opposed to education, knowledge is of value only because it *enables* people *to do* things. It is, therefore, appropriate to state knowledge prerequisites as ability to do something. Your prerequisite concern may be with vocabulary; understanding of theory, concept or principles; or knowledge of facts. In each case, you should state an action by which your learner can convincingly demonstrate the needed ability. For example:

Condition
Given: A demographic profile and cases from Ajax company showing cases of EEO non-compliance

Action
The learner will be able to: identify the cases of non-compliance and state the criteria for compliance in each case

Criterion
Accurate within: four out of five times within 10 minutes.

It is popular and convenient to state prerequisites in terms of educational experience (courses taken or academic credentials) and/or job experience (so many years in such-and-such job). That is a quick, easy way to exclude many learners who would otherwise be confused and frustrated by your course. But it may not exclude all of them, and it may exclude many who need and want the course and who would be successful in achieving the course objectives. Those are the risks you take to save the time and effort required to define and measure abilities.

Measurement systems

Assuming that you decide that the benefits of defining prerequisites in terms of abilities and measuring them are worth the effort, the next step is designing your measurement system. One of the chief benefits of the prerequisite statement procedure is that the results tend to inhibit us from writing meaningless prerequisite tests that don't really measure anything important and don't usually include skill demonstrations.

Each prerequisite ability statement should be measured by one or more measurement items, which should meet the requirements Robert Mager sets forth in *Measuring Instructional Intent, or Gotta Match?* (Fearon Press). Ideally, that means that the learner will be called on to do exactly what the prerequisite statement says he or she will be able to do, within the criterion stated. In some cases, you may choose to have the learner do something else, something that is a reliable *indicator* that the learner has the ability described. The percentage of prerequisite abilities tested by indicator abilities will be inversely proportional to the degree of your commitment to accuracy in measurement. If you choose to compromise for good reasons, go ahead and compromise. Certainly compromised systems for prerequisite statements and testing are more valuable to you and your learner than none at all, as long as you both acknowledge that compromise is taking place.

Prerequisite testing

Taking a test is usually a powerful learning experience. Assuming that a test is comprehensive— that is, it measures everything it intends to measure rather than a random sample—allowing the testee prior knowledge of the content increases the probability that he or she will perform successfully. It is, therefore, advantageous to administer the prerequisite test as early as several weeks prior to the course. This allows you to determine any shortages, fix them, and re-administer the test in time to allow the learner access to the course. Though it's a bit more challenging to design a self-administered test than a monitored one, it's worth considering. This "early" testing strategy will reduce the need for emergency contingency plans, minimize learner confusion and embarrassment and enhance learner confidence, motivation and success.

But what do you do when a learner fails the test? Actually, there are several possibilities. At one extreme, you can say, "Too bad. Come back when you can pass." At the other extreme, you can tailor and deliver an individualized remedial learning system to provide the needed abilities. Between these extremes, you can recommend and/or provide specific courses, books, programmed packages, practice exercises and other learning activities that will generate the needed abilities if the learner invests the appropriate time, interest and energy. I strongly recommend that you avoid setting entry standards for your course unless you intend to enforce them. And don't admit a learner who has failed the prerequisite test to your course; there's enough inconsistent, flabby management in this world without trainers copping out, too.

Once the prerequisites are under control, we should address the second way actual learners differ from target learners: They know (can do) some things target learners lack, things you intended them to learn in the course. The ability statements on these items are your course objectives, and the measuring system is your objective achievement test, final exam or whatever system you use to confirm and reinforce learner success in your course.

Pretesting to set objectives

In spite of the popular traditions we learned in grade school, it's a good idea to show learners the final exam at the beginning of the course for several reasons. On the whole, people tend to hit mainly what they aim at. The more accurately they know what they need to be able to do at the end of the course, the more likely they will be to learn it successfully. A second reason is summarized in a motto popular in the service business: "If it ain't broke, don't fix it." In order to avoid learner boredom and non-productive expenditure of time and money, don't teach them how if they can do it already.

The administration of the final exam, or any test to determine if the learners can already perform some of the objectives of the course, is *pretesting*. As with prerequisite testing, you need contingency plans— what you will do about learners already knowing what you plan to teach.

If a learner can pass the final exam *before* the course, the most appropriate action is probably to issue a certificate of completion and send her or him away. If that isn't possible—say, for example, a contract calls for this person to take the course— you can enlist her or him to be an associate instructor. More commonly, you may simply choose to delete or bypass portions of the course that most learners know, with allowances for assistance to the minority. When in doubt, summarize and ask questions. If portions of the course have gone over the heads of some learners, you should be able to detect this and make appropriate adjustments.

Summary

In summary, we gain significant control of efficiency and quality in delivering training when we do three things: specifically define our target trainee in terms of prerequisite abilities and learning needs (learning objectives), measure those abilities by prerequisite testing and pretesting, and respond to differences in planned ways.

Reprinted from TRAINING, January 1981

SPEED LEARNING BY PRESENTING OBJECTIVES IN 'TEACHABLE' PARTS

Breaking down performance objectives into bite-size pieces eliminates frustration—both yours and your trainees'

BY LESLIE P. LIMON

Assume you are a trainer responsible for teaching a group of employees the basics of using flowcharts. You have just presented your trainees with a sample problem to flowchart, and, as you monitor the activity, you sense that most of them are bogging down. Some can't decide which cell shapes to use. Others have put all the operations in their graphic but have failed to include decision points. Suddenly it occurs to you that you hadn't even considered the possibility that the trainees might not understand the significance of diamond-shaped cells versus rectangular ones. Furthermore, you can see that you apparently hadn't emphasized strongly enough the need for decision points. Since the trainees' frustration level is already high, you'll have to do some agile back-pedaling in order to fill the gaps and restore their self-confidence.

Occurrences such as this one are not uncommon during the course of a training program. In fact, they are key factors in program failure. But, with proper planning, you can reduce their likelihood or even eliminate it. An important step is to realize that your performance objectives by themselves will not carry you through a training session. To be successful, a performance objective must be broken down into teachable components, individual behaviors that, when recombined, will produce the desired behavior.

The term *performance objective,* as used here, refers to the behavior required of a trainee by the end of a session. It represents the final destination of a learning sequence, and trainees should be allowed to work toward it logically and systematically. A planning process that includes the analysis of the objective's components will ensure that this is done, because it establishes checkpoints that ascertain whether or not the trainees have prior knowledge of the subject. It also prevents the trainees from progressing to Point B before they have mastered Point A.

How do you determine the teachable components of a performance objective? First, you should try to look at the skill or procedure to be mastered as though you, too, were learning it for the first time. This can be a difficult strategy to follow, expecially if the task is already second nature to you. To break down global concepts into smaller ones, remember that a procedure is a sequence of finite steps and must be treated accordingly. Keep in mind, too, that all learning should involve the same basic hierarchy: identification of a concept, understanding the concept, applying the concept, and using the concept to perform analytical tasks.* Let's use the flowcharting class as an example to see how the first three stages of this hierarchy apply.

Assume that the objective of this particular session is "Given a sample procedure or problem, the trainee will develop a flowchart illustrating the accomplishment of the procedure or the solution of the problem." This objective involves a concept— a flowchart— and a skill— "translating"

prose into a graphic form. The flowchart itself can be broken down into its components: terminals, operation and decision cells, sequence arrows and connectors. The "translation" consists of analyzing the prose, determining the decisions that are to be made and their sequence, determining the operations that must be performed and their relationships to each decision, and formulating a way to set it all up in graphic form.

Now that the elements of flowcharts and flowcharting have been isolated, the next step is to map out the sequence of skills to be performed. These skills also will be expressed in behavioral terms. At the most basic level of simple identification, trainees should be able to articulate what a flowchart is and how it applies to their daily work needs. We can express this behavior as follows: "The trainee will define the term 'flowchart' and give examples of its application to daily tasks." Other verbs commonly used in formulating a teachable component at this level are *tell* or *state.*

The implementation of this step requires a minimum amount of time, as little as five minutes. Trainees might write a definition and examples on a slip of paper and then read some of their answers aloud for discussion. This activity not only sets the stage for the rest of the lesson but also gives trainees a chance to think about areas of their work that will require the skill. In addition, this activity would highlight any misconceptions trainees might have about flowcharting; thus, the trainer could deal with these at the outset of the session.

Also at the level of knowledge (identification), trainees must demonstrate that they can recognize specific components of a flowchart when they see them. The verbs *label, distinguish* and *select the appropriate*...describe ways trainees can indicate recognition. For example, we might say, "Given a flowchart containing only empty cells, label the cells 'operation,' 'decision' or 'terminal' according to their shapes."

The next teachable component requires trainees to demonstrate some understanding of the components' interrelationships. Trainees should be able to distinguish an appropriate operation or decision from an inappropriate one. To accomplish this, you'd say, "Given a procedure or problem and an incomplete flowchart illustrating it and given a choice of possible operations/decisions for each blank cell, select the appropriate operation/decision for each." If the trainee can do this, he or she understands the correspondence between the prose and the analytic design of the graphic. This doesn't mean, however, that the trainees are expected to generate this correspondence independently. They will accomplish that task in the next stage of the learning process—application of the concept.

The application component of a training session should receive the most emphasis, since it relates directly to the desired behavior of a trainee and thus facilitates transfer of the skill to the job. During this stage, trainees need essentially the same skills as those described in the performance objective. In describing how these skills are to be performed, you'll probably use the same verbs that appear in the performance objective itself; that is, if your performance objective calls for the trainees to write, the application stage will also consist of writing activities.

The important thing to remember is that application begins in a controlled environment. As the controls are gradually dropped, the trainee begins to exhibit the desired behavior independently. A requirement to write something, for example, might begin in the application phase as an activity to fill in something that is incomplete or to respond to specific questions.

In our flowcharting lesson, we would want to provide structured practice in the actual development of the graphic before asking a trainee to work it out independently. Here's a logical follow-up activity to the selection exercise in the previous stage: "Given a procedure or a problem and an incomplete flowchart derived from it, fill in the blank cells with appropriate operations or decisions." If the trainee can do this, it means that he or she can generate parts of a flowchart independently, as long as other parts have been filled in to provide guidelines. This activity can be repeated as often as necessary or until the trainee can accomplish it easily.

The culmination of this phase, of course, is the performance of the desired behavior itself; in this example, that means generating an entire flowchart from scratch, given a particular procedure or problem. Even this can be accomplished gradually, beginning as a controlled activity and ending as an independent one. You can present a problem to the group as a whole, giving trainees an opportunity to work out a flowchart together under your guidance. This gives you an excellent opportunity to see where students still have problems and enables you to correct any misconceptions they may have before they begin working on their own.

Earlier, I mentioned a fourth stage— analysis— as part of the learning hierarchy. This stage involves using learned skills and concepts to accomplish analytical tasks, such as synthesis, invention or evaluation. While it's often desirable for trainees to attain this level, it's not always crucial to the successful completion of a training session. Furthermore, the strategies required for implementing this stage are beyond the scope of this article.

In summary, you can easily break down performance objectives by isolating each concept to be mastered and each skill to be performed. The trainee deals with these skills and concepts on at least three different levels: knowledge or identification, understanding and application. At the level of identification, trainees are asked to state meanings or functions, define and give examples. At the level of understanding, trainees demonstrate recognition of the interrelationships of elements by distinguishing similarities and differences, by selecting appropriate alternatives from a list, and so on. Finally, at the level of application, trainees begin to perform the desired behavior on their own. In a skill-based environment, you should bring trainees through the level of application, since this is where learning is transferred from the classroom to the job.

As a course developer, you may feel that a lesson structured this way will be stilted and tedious. Keep in mind, however, that the skills you are training others to perform are as unfamiliar to your trainees as they are familiar to you. If you maintain a lively pace throughout the lesson, completing its early stages particularly quickly, you will challenge, rather than bore, your trainees. Because each phase in this learning process requires trainees to *do* something, to perform some activity that demonstrates mastery of the skill at that level, you'll create an environment where trainees are responsible for their own learning. And this sense of responsibility increases trainee motivation and heightens interest.

Finally, the step-by-step approach I've outlined here helps eliminate learner frustration by preventing situations in which learners confront tasks they aren't yet ready to accomplish. When you can say to your trainees, "Now that you've done X, you should be able to accomplish Y," you are programming their behavior by directing it toward success. As a result, your trainees will not only have a better grasp of their own progress but they'll also gain self-confidence.

---

*Bloom, Benjamin S., ed. *Taxonomy of Educational Objectives: The Classification of Educational Goals, Handbook 1: Cognitive Domain.* New York: David McKay Company, 1956.

Reprinted from TRAINING, April 1980

THE COMPETENCY MODEL ALTERNATIVE

Learner-direct learning is an approach fast gaining credence with adult learning theorists

BY MICHAEL MAGINN

Tucked away in Canada's Maritimes, on Prince Edward Island, is a community post-secondary school called Holland College that should interest trainers everywhere. The style of instruction is competency based. Learners direct and select their own goals and learning credence among adult-learning theorists. Why, one wonders, does this educational alternative work on remote Prince Edward Island, when attempts to introduce milder forms of instructional change in more urban and cosmopolitan sections of the continent so often falter.

The answer may lie in Holland College's approach to instructional development. In essence, the administrators and faculty of this hardy community college have taken pains to assure that grandiose sounding systems, methodologies and mechanisms of teaching are adapted to the needs of students, who are offered freedom of choice with associated responsibility for achievement. There are no cookie-cutter systems or cookbook models in use at Holland College. Instead, there exists an approach to competency-based instruction which reflects a carefully developed philosophy of adult education that is unanimously supported by all staff members.

"At the beginning, back in 1969," said Dr. Don Glendenning, president of Holland College, "we found that there were a lot of perceptions about what a community college should be. We went through a period of introspection and consensus before we developed a philosophy we could live

HOLLAND COLLEGE SELF-TRAINING AND EVALUATION FORM

ACCOUNTING TECHNOLOGY

4 C	CAN PERFORM THIS SKILL WITHOUT SUPERVISION OR ASSISTANCE AND CAN LEAD OTHERS IN PERFORMING IT.
4 B	CAN PERFORM THIS SKILL WITHOUT SUPERVISION OR ASSISTANCE WITH INITIATIVE AND ADAPTABILITY TO SPECIAL PROBLEM SITUATIONS.
4 A	CAN PERFORM THIS SKILL WITHOUT SUPERVISION OR ASSISTANCE WITH PROFICIENCY IN SPEED AND QUALITY.
3	CAN PERFORM THIS SKILL SATISFACTORILY WITHOUT ASSISTANCE AND/OR SUPERVISION.
2	CAN PERFORM THIS SKILL SATISFACTORILY BUT REQUIRES PERIODIC SUPERVISION AND/OR ASSISTANCE.
1	CAN PERFORM SOME PARTS OF THE SKILL SATISFACTORILY, BUT REQUIRES INSTRUCTION AND SUPERVISION TO PERFORM THE ENTIRE SKILL.
0	HAS SOME KNOWLEDGE AND LIMITED EXPERIENCE, BUT NOT SUFFICIENT FOR PARTICIPATION IN A WORK ENVIRONMENT.

OPERATE ACCOUNTING SYSTEMS	IDENTIFY SOURCE DOCUMENTS	RECORD BASIC ACCOUNTING ENTRIES IN BOOKS OF ORIGINAL ENTRY	BALANCE BOOKS OF ORIGINAL ENTRY	POST AND BALANCE SUBSIDIARY LEDGERS
	MAINTAIN PARTNERSHIP ACCOUNTS	MAINTAIN EQUITY ACCOUNTS	MAINTAIN SHARE CAPITAL STOCK RECORDS	MAINTAIN BRANCH ACCOUNTING RECORDS
UTILIZE BUSINESS MACHINES AND COMPUTERS	OPERATE ADDING AND CALCULATING MACHINES	OPERATE OFFICE EQUIPMENT	OPERATE DICTATING MACHINES	TYPE VARIOUS STYLES OF LETTERS, FORMS, AND FINANCIAL STATEMENTS
PARTICIPATE IN MANAGERIAL FUNCTIONS	SELECT AND ESTABLISH FILING SYSTEMS	DESIGN FORMS	AID IN IMPLEMENTATION OF SAFEGUARDS FOR ASSETS	EVALUATE STORAGE, DISPOSAL AND SECURITY OF RECORDS
PREPARE AND ANALYZE FINANCIAL REPORTS	PREPARE INCOME STATEMENTS	PREPARE BALANCE SHEETS	PREPARE STATEMENT OF RECEIPTS AND DISBURSEMENTS	PREPARE DEPARTMENTAL STATEMENTS AND REPORTS
APPLY BUSINESS MATH AND STATISTICAL CALCULATIONS	USE SHORT METHODS TO MAKE RAPID CALCULATIONS	CALCULATE AND USE FACTORS, MULTIPLES AND FRACTIONS	CALCULATE AND USE PERCENTAGES	CALCULATE SIMPLE AND COMPOUND INTEREST
MANAGE GOVERNMENT TAXATION AND LEVY	UTILIZE INCOME TAX GUIDE	CALCULATE AND REMIT PAYROLL DEDUCTIONS	INTERPRET AND APPLY UNEMPLOYMENT	PREPARE WORKMEN'S COMPENSATION FORMS

with." That philosophy, which forms a framework for all programs developed, entails the following:

- Skills required in an occupational field shall be identified by persons in the field.
- Students are responsible for their own progress, and instructors are accountable for student progress.
- Learning shall be stressed instead of teaching.
- The instructor shall assess, diagnose, prescribe and tutor but not be the sole conveyor of information.
- Programs shall be individualized (personalized) to the full extent that resources allow.
- Holland College will schedule resource rooms, materials and instructors instead of students.
- Evaluation shall be as realistic and meaningful as possible, in keeping with evaluation in the work environment.
- Students shall be able to enter and leave a program at any time.
- Credit shall be given for previously acquired skills.
- Ratings are based only on performance.
- Students shall evaluate their own performance prior to confirmation by an instructor.
- Students shall be able to continue their learning program in a systematic way after leaving the college.

These principles are embodied in Holland College's Self-Training and Evaluation (STEP) approach to instruction. The objective of STEP, according to Dr. Glendenning, is to help learners assume responsibility for planning and achieving their own development goals while acquiring the skills needed to enter the job market. Essentially, the STEP approach is an open-entry system where students can select objectives to work on from a course blueprint, develop the necessary skills with advice and counsel from an "instructor," and evaluate his or her own performance. This self-evaluation is matched with the industry criteria-based evaluation given by the instructor.

The principles of student freedom and responsibility have guided the faculty in designing two critical and troublesome areas of instructional development: curriculum selection and evaluation. Here's how Holland College does it.

Curriculum selection. The Holland College approach to selecting subject matter involves the active and intense involvement of practitioners. "If we're developing an office-skills program, we'll ask secretaries to help us analyze the tasks they face daily," said Jack Sand, professional development coordinator at Holland College. "If, say, it's photography, we'll get photographers from town."

These subject-matter experts meet at Holland College for a three-day brainstorming session to determine the skills required for a new employee in the field. "The first step is to develop a list of competencies that covers the whole subject," said Sands. "Often that means teaching our subject-matter experts to think in terms of behavior and performance rather than knowledge and understanding."

The next step is to identify specific skills within each major area of competence required for a new hire. In electronics, for example, the subject-matter committee lists areas of competence required of all electricians, such as "use tools and equipment," "troubleshoot, isolate, and replace defective units," and "identify, select and handle electronic components." Each of these broad competency areas are further broken down into specific skills. For instance, troubleshooting would include such skills as "analyzing voltage and current measurements to isolate faults," "isolating faults to component level," and "checking components by patching."

At this point, a skill chart is made for each student and arranged in order of difficulty, from simple to complex. The student chooses his or her own starting point, depending, of course, on course content.

The reference materials for each particular skill are kept in files at learning centers devoted to each area of study. These files contain directories of helpful resources — commercial and homemade — as well as instructions for evaluation. Laboratories equipped with machinery and tools the students can use as they learn the skill are also part of the learning center.

Evaluation. Since courses are essentially designed by industry, performance of students is also evaluated according to industry standards. "The Mager approach to writing criteria standards for objectives is quite valid," said Dr. Glendenning, "but we don't necessarily use that approach here.

Behaviors are stated on our skill charts, but when it comes to stating the criteria for acceptable performance, we avoid all the detail."

Glendenning says he is not opposed to writing criteria statements for acceptable performance for each skill, but "it's just a gigantic task for us, given our resources, time and the framework we work in. Instead, we've found an evaluation route that's workable for us."

The route taken by Holland College is a simple numerical scale representing the kind of quality, quantity and amount of supervision required of the worker. Each rating is awarded on the basis of the student's performance compared to job requirements in industry. The rating scale covers the whole range of skill ability, from no experience at all to highly skilled performance in seven steps. (See accompanying chart.

The evaluation method in Holland College's STEP system reflects the freedom-and-responsibility theme of their philosophy. Students evaluate their own performance when *they* are ready; instructors are asked to observe the skill being executed and offer an evaluation based on industry criteria. If there's a discrepancy, students and instructors discuss *why* that difference has occurred.

Holland College applies its philosophy of learning in training its own instructors and in evaluating staff performance. "We have to use this system daily; we have to take our own medicine," said Glendenning. Accordingly, all evaluations of performance throughout the Holland College system use the scale. To Glendenning, the administration of a competency-based program would be remiss if it didn't practice what it preached.

"The key to implementing a program like this," said Glendenning, "is to see that the staff and faculty are properly oriented and committed to the idea. We also have to orient students, but without the faculty believing in the approach, it would be difficult to make it work. We spend a good deal of time helping staff develop their skills toward that goal."

So, at Holland College, students and faculty are given the opportunity to learn, one from the other. The college provides the setting and the resources for learning to take place, and the student provides the rest.

Reprinted from TRAINING, August 1978

JOB COMPETENCIES: CAN THEY HELP YOU DESIGN BETTER TRAINING?

A growing number of trainers use the concept
of competencies to help them
determine what trainees need to learn.
But precisely what makes a competency is
still up in the air,
as you'll find out from several experts.

BY RON ZEMKE

Competency-based training: Is it a new and revolutionary approach to determining what goes into a training program? Or is it a repackaging of well-known and widely used methods and approaches, with a couple of twists and a high-browed new name?

If you're unsure of the answer, you are not alone. For all the rhetoric about the benefits of competencies and competency-based training, few working trainers are exactly sure what the experts mean when they start praising and promoting competencies.

When TRAINING asked the competency-building experts for detailed elucidation, the reason for the confusion became clear: Competency, competencies, competency models and competency-based training are Humpty Dumpty words meaning only what the definer wants them to mean. The problem comes not from avarice, but instead from some basic procedural and philosophical differences among those racing to define and develop the concept and to set the model for the way the rest of us will use competencies in our day-to-day training efforts.

It begins to appear, however, that the quest for the best approach and the jockeying for position among the inventors is producing a valuable process. In job arenas as diverse as nursing and nuclear engineering, train-

ers and personnel specialists are hailing competency models as a breakthrough in work and performance criteria assessment.

An Alabama hospital administrator reports that the development of nursing competencies has resulted in "our first real success at career development for the profession." Explaining that until competencies were mapped, nurses were stymied in mobility by the parameters of the specialities they acquired in school.

A trainer in the nuclear power industry reports that competency statements help him save training time while improving excellence in training outcome. "They help you clearly communicate the responsibilities and the knowledge and skill demands to operator trainees," she says.

And a Texas-based franchising operation has found competency descriptions useful in explaining to heavy-hitting salespeople why the bottom-line achievement isn't enough for promotion to management. "We can graphically show them where they differ from managers in important skills and skill levels." All of which hints that there may be something very much worth pursuing on the competency model bandwagon.

Interviews with the experts unearthed three distinct approaches to developing competency models: the Modified Task Analysis Approach, the Critical Trait Approach and the Situa-tional Approach.

Modified task analysis

This approach is basically the task-listing/task-analysis technique most trainers know, but with some minor niceties added. It is also the approach most widely used in vocational-technical schools. William E. Blank, author of the *Handbook for Developing Competency-Based Training Programs* (Prentice-Hall, 1982), describes competencies as "... specific, precisely stated student outcomes ... that have been recently verified as being essential for successful employment in the occupation for which the student is being trained."

Blank contends that competency-based instruction (CBI) is really nothing new, and has, in fact, existed for some time under a multitude of different names. On his list of CBI cognates are such venerable training tags as Mastery Learning, Systems Approach to Education, Criterion-Referenced Instruction (CRI), Self-Paced Learning and Instructional Systems Development.

In this approach, panel experts judge which tasks are most relevant. Moreover, the task-analysis effort attempts to capture attitudes as well as motor skill performance and related knowledge.

Arthur E. Worth, of Worth Developing in St. Petersburg, FL, also advocates this method. He, too, sees it as similar to known systems approach procedures. "My approach to competency development is very similar to Robert Mager's CRI process," Worth says. The main differences are accounting for work environment conditions and applying a modified "80/20" (Pareto) analysis thinking.

"We start by getting a description of where time is spent," Worth says. "Then we scrutinize the high-value, high-frequency behaviors. In competency modeling we are after a functional analysis rather than a complete description of all possible job tasks."

Worth subdivides competencies into three classes:

• **Administrative competencies:** skills used to maintain an organization's cohesiveness. They often involve implementing policies and procedures necessary to different parts of the organization.

• **Technical competencies:** skills used to produce a product or service. For those jobs high in motor/manipulative skills, these are relatively straightforward. In jobs requiring many cognitive skills, the distinction between technical and administrative competencies becomes less clear.

141

• **Personal competencies:** people interaction skills. They describe how a person interacts with others while using administrative and technical competencies.

Critical traits

The best-known advocates of this approach are the people at McBer and Co., the Boston-based consulting firm co-founded by renowned Harvard psychologist David McClelland. The McBer approach to competency development

---

In job arenas as diverse as nursing and nuclear engineering, trainers and personnel specialists are hailing competency models as a breakthrough in work and performance criteria assessment.

---

takes its procedural and conceptual lead from McClelland's work on isolating the personality traits of entrepreneurs, and the parallel work of Robert White, who isolated a trait he dubbed competence and defined as "an underlying characteristic of a person which results in effective and/or superior performance on the job."

The McBer approach focuses on the individual performer, not the job. "To us," says George O. Klemp, vice president of McBer, "competency is a description of the qualities an individual brings to work or life pursuits that make him effective."

Using this method, McBer researchers identify two pools of performers: superstars and average or below-average doers. They then try to uncover the critical traits, behaviors and general personal attributes that discriminate between members of the two populations. As Klemp puts it, "A personal attribute in this context can take many forms—it can be a kind of knowledge, an ability, an interest, a trait, a motive, even a self-concept—but the only way that such an attribute becomes a competency is in relationship to performance."

Although most psychology texts define a trait as "a relatively permanent and enduring quality that a person shows in most situations," McBer researchers hold that view to be anti-

quated. According to James A. Burruss, a McBer vice president with a heavy training background, "A finished competency description contains more than traits. It usually includes skills and abilities as well as motivation patterns and traits. But it is our view that even traits can be modified and developed."

Burruss also notes that McClelland's work on Need-For-Achievement (N-ach) motivation in entrepreneurs showed that the N-ach trait could be increased by teaching would-be entrepreneurs to think differently; to think like known successful entrepreneurs. The McBer process for capturing competencies has been dubbed the Job Competence Assessment Method (*JCAM*), which produces a *competency model* composed of three elements:

• A list of the competencies critical for outstanding performance.

• Definitions of the competencies in terms of observable behaviors.

• Descriptions of how each competency relates to the major tasks and functions that make up the job.

This method involves interviewing high and low performers about the "critical events" in their jobs. Prior to the interviews, a panel of supervisors and managers generates a list of behaviors, attributes and traits they have observed in high performers. These initial competency "guesstimates" are used to focus the interviews. Later, transcripts from the interviews are subjected to a rigorous thematic analysis, much as interviews from a projective personality test, such as the Rorschach or Thematic Ap-

perception, would be.

The process is much like that used to develop the Behavioral Anchored Rating Scale (*BARS*). Its strength is that it isolates critical features of high performers. A weakness is that traits or behaviors which don't vary between high and low performers fail to appear in the final competencies. Finally, needs for technical job knowledge tend to be lost in this process since such "entry level" knowledges and skills tend not to distinguish high and low performers, especially in higher level job classifications.

Situational competencies

Exemplified by the work of Patricia McLagan, of McLagan and Associates, Inc., in St. Paul, MN, this approach is a sort of "form follows function" route to developing competency models. McLagan, who is conducting a widely anticipated trainer competency study for the American Society for Training and Development, believes "you can't prescribe one look for a competency model or one method for developing them.

"If you are developing competencies for a given job, a job family, a profession or for a job that doesn't exist, you have four different situations that dictate how you must proceed," McLagan continues. "High-level jobs are very abstract and require special approaches. Lower-level jobs are much more concrete and the competency models for them look like task analyses."

All of which leads McLagan to a

ADMINISTRATIVE

CA3. Evaluates performance of department personnel and provides feedback

    3.1 Collects all relevant data on performance from all appropriate sources.

    3.2 Involves employees in advance preparation for performance reviews.

    3.3 Utilizes competency list for the position to evaluate skill level.

PERSONNEL

CP15. Conducts performance appraisal interviews with employees effectively and on schedule

    15.1 Asks for employee comments on job performance without developing defensiveness in employee.

    15.2 Uses actual job behaviors to illustrate positive and negative aspects of reviews.

    15.3 Listens and reflects understanding of employee concerns about negative aspects of his/her performance.

    15.4 Utilizes competency list to facilitate discussion of skills.

TECHNICAL

T7. Describes and develops building maintenance procedures

    7.1 Describes the minimum and optimum requirements for maintaining a facility in operating condition.

    7.2 Develops preventative maintenance procedures, as needed, for the facility.

    7.3 Identifies the number of personnel required for maintenance.

Figure 1. Sample of a competency model for a Performance Appraisal Responsibility using the Modified Task Analysis Approach (courtesy of Worth Developing).

JOB FUNCTION	COMPETENCIES	BEHAVIORAL INDICATORS
1. Anticipating problems, identifying opportunities	a. Conceptualization	■ Identifies patterns among events, facts, or observations
		■ Uses simple examples to communicate complex ideas
	b. Initiative	■ Takes action before being asked to do so
		■ Persists to overcome obstacles
2. Translating new ideas into practical application	a. Entrepreneurial Drive	■ Looks for efficient ways to get things done
		■ Expresses concern with high standards and performance improvement
	b. Risk Minimization	■ Works to minimize risk
		■ Resists changes that threaten order
3. Managing subordinates	a. Socialized Influence	■ Shares ideas with and solicits ideas from others
		■ Sells ideas in terms of others' interests
	b. Low Need for Affiliation	■ Gives criticism (as well as praise)
		■ Confronts conflict

Figure 2. Sample of a competency model of an Operations Manager developed using the Critical Traits Approach (courtesy of McBer and Company).

	LEVELS OF EXPERTNESS		
	BASIC	INTERMEDIATE	EXPERT
COMPETENCY	1 2 3	4 5 6	7 8 9
User Relationship Building. This competency involves understanding the users' situations, acknowledging their viewpoints, speaking their language, helping them understand the data systems viewpoint, and establishing trust and credibility.	■ "Uses *user language* instead of data processing codes when talking to a user." ■ "*Responds* to user phone calls quickly."	■ "Advises the user in advance of an event that may go wrong and leaves the user *feeling that's OK,* we'll cope together." ■ "Explains the expected effects of a requested change on the rest of the system such that the user *believes the explanation* and changes the requests."	■ "Prepares a joint feasibility study which the user *feels as committed* as the systems expert." ■ "Openly talks about a major and multi-faceted systems problem that has arisen because of user-instigated problems. *Gains the user's support* in correcting the problems and in finding the solutions."
This defines the competency	*These examples illustrate the types of behaviors which can be used to communicate and assess various levels of expertness in the competency area.*		

Figure 3. Sample of a competency statement and expertness rating scale for one (of twelve) competency in a Data Processing Competency Model developed using the Situational Approach (courtesy of McLagan & Associates).

somewhat more complex definition of competency and competency model:

• **Competency:** A capability of an individual which relates to superior performance in a role or job. It may be a knowledge, skill, intellectual strategy or a cluster of all three that may apply to one or many work units. The level of generality (scope) of a competency statement depends on its intended use.

• **Competency model:** A list of the highest-leverage competencies for a specific role, job or job family, within a

One of the most powerful uses (of competencies) is self-assessment.

given time frame. The number and level of generality of the competencies depend on the model's intended use.

Because of her belief in the "situationalness" of competencies, McLagan is reluctant to prescribe a step-by-step process to develop them. But her general approach is "somewhat anthropological in nature. We use a number of data-gathering methods and try to triangulate on the critical competencies." McLagan's associates "work with the people who determine the parameters of the job and who can tell us what the job produces that is of value to the organization."

The result is called a Model of Excellence, used to identify top performers (McLagan terms them Key Producers). Subsequent interviews with these employees help determine critical competencies.

McLagan emphasizes that she seeks master performers—not organizational stars. "The fast trackers aren't necessarily good models," she says. "They sometimes behave oddly, even unethically. Often those aren't behaviors you would want to promote and encourage in the organization; they could shake an organization apart if practiced on a broad scale."

McLagan also is apprehensive of using generic or personality trait names in competencies. "We are trying to communicate the key themes that explain excellence in behavior in the organization," she says. "So the terms we use create a language about performance for people to use in the organization. That language has to be acceptable and comfortable to the users. The competency model has to be written within the users' scope of thinking."

Common enthusiasm

Although the competency builders TRAINING interviewed use different approaches to capturing competencies and developing models, they share a common enthusiasm for the benefits of using them in an organization. One of the most powerful uses is self-assessment, according to both Worth and McLagan.

As an example, Worth cites a hospital plagued by a staffing shortage in the recovery room. Measuring themselves against competencies Worth had developed, nurses from outside the unit determined what skills they needed to work in the recovery room.

Klemp and Burruss say that competencies will help "break the personal development logjam," but also see them as highly valuable in the selection process. Competencies offer something very concrete for interviewing and judging candidates, they suggest.

Other uses for competencies include individual career development, self-assessment, performance assessment and review, curriculum planning, task-team assembly, organizational development, strategic and manpower planning, and job modeling for jobs that don't yet exist but that will be needed in the future.

Perhaps the advocates of competency-based training and development make too many claims of and for their brainchild. Then again, they may not have even guessed the potential. Only time will tell. One thing is sure: The competency concept may be the most exciting and potentially promising idea to hit the training field since behavioral objectives. And that takes some doing.

Reprinted from TRAINING, May 1982

CHAPTER 4

SELECTING
AND USING MEDIA
AND METHODS

This is the longest chapter in the book. It was also the most difficult chapter for us to assemble—that is, to structure the articles we chose into a meaningful whole. Originally we had planned to divide the material into two chapters, one on designing instruction, the other on matching media and method to the design elements. You know what? We couldn't do it.

You know why? Because you can't really look at design without simultaneously considering media and method. True, you can say some general—very general—things about the kinds of objectives different media and methods seem to fit: "If you're teaching an interpersonal skill, use behavior modeling and some form of practice" . . . "Consider job aids when (a) there is a complex procedure that doesn't need to be memorized or (b) a procedure isn't used often." But even those little bits of wisdom are more meaningful within the context of an explanation of what job aids are or what behavior modeling is and how it works. So we've ended up with a different sort of framework than we had first intended.

We have split the articles into two sections: group approaches and individually oriented approaches.

The first section includes articles on behavior modeling, role plays, games and simulations, teleconferencing and the like. These same approaches may be applicable to some individualized situations, but generally they are better suited to the classroom.

In the second section, we look at computer-based training, learning contracts, job aids and the like. Again, these techniques can have classroom applications, but they tend to be most useful in the individualized mode.

Many of the articles were tough to pigeonhole for the simple reason that these aren't pigeons that like to stay in their holes. For example, film and video are obviously "group" media, right? Sure, except that when you see the things being done today with microcomputer-linked videodisc systems, the "obvious" suddenly isn't.

Things get just as slippery when it comes to the question of what method works "best" to deliver which type of instruction in what sort of situation. The variety of perspectives you'll find among the authors in this section may prove as valuable as the 'how-to' advice they offer about using particular equipment and techniques.

ON-THE-JOB VS. CLASSROOM TRAINING: SOME DECIDING FACTORS

Once you get a handle on the cost-related variables, choosing the right training strategy becomes a little easier

BY STEPHEN L. MANGUM

Nobody ever said that making decisions about which training techniques to use was going to be easy. In fact, there usually are difficult preliminaries to go through before you reach that decision point. For instance, what skills should the new employee be expected to bring to the job, and what will be taught after hiring? What level of proficiency do you require and how soon after hiring must that level be achieved? How much damage can an untrained employee do to your operation if thrust into the actual job too quickly? Only after settling issues such as these can you begin to tackle questions of strategy.

Only then can you ask whether skills should be taught with an on-the-job approach or in a classroom setting, whether an outside training provider should be brought in, whether a single method is preferable to a variety of techniques. Not that these are straightforward questions at any stage of the game, but there are fundamental differences between training techniques that should help you make a wise decision.

As with so many business decisions, the dilemma over which type of training to use boils down to a comparison of costs and benefits. The best combination of training techniques is the one that teaches all the skills necessary for the job at the lowest possible cost. That's why you need to understand the costs associated with different training approaches.

On-the-job (OJT) vs. classroom-based training is a good example of this type of cost-benefit decision. (For our purposes, the term "classroom-based training" will be stretched to include computer-based training and other types of "formal" instruction that take place apart from the actual job environment.)

To begin, you need to recognize that, not including trainee wages, at least three categories of OJT expenses exist. First are costs that vary only by number of trainees, with per-trainee costs remaining fairly constant. These costs include training supplies such as manuals, machinery instruction guides and the like.

Next are costs that vary on a per-trainee basis as the number of trainees increases. Supervisory participation in OJT takes time away from production activities. Assuming that more trainees take more supervisory time (in addition to slowing production, increasing the error rate, etc.), costs to the organization go up with the number of trainees. When supervisory involvement in the training function occurs during a slack production period, however, supervisory input into OJT can be obtained at a lower marginal cost.

The same logic applies to capital costs—the third category of OJT costs. Using production equipment for training purposes during slack production periods incurs a very low marginal cost, while using the same equipment in times of peak production becomes a substantial expense.

One basic difference between classroom-based and on-the-job training is the higher start-up costs of classroom-based training. The fixed costs may include the expense of building or renting training facilities, of developing courses and of purchasing equipment to simulate the work environment in a classroom setting. Some of these costs are avoided with OJT because the equipment and facilities used for production and for training are one and the same.

Classroom-based and on-the-job training differ with respect to variable costs as well. In OJT, per-trainee costs increase with the number of trainees as supervisors are taken away from their production responsibilities for longer periods of time to support the training function. In contrast, most classroom-based instructors do not have a direct production role, so per-trainee costs in this case will usually decrease as the number of trainees grows. Likewise, capital equipment in classroom-based training serves no direct production role and is used strictly for training. Therefore, per-trainee capital costs are likely to decline as the number of trainees grows.

Rules of thumb

These observations of cost differences between on-the-job and classroom-based training suggest some guidelines for choosing among alternative training techniques:

• When you are training a large number of individuals, the fixed costs of classroom-based training are spread across many trainees. In such situations, all else being equal, classroom-based training tends to become more economical than OJT.

• When training involves expensive equipment and the demand for skilled workers is uncertain, OJT becomes the more attractive option. Since classroom-based training can require lengthy lead times and the installation of equipment, low demand could spell substantial losses.

• When simulating the work environment is a high-cost proposition, OJT is probably your best bet. If inadequate job performance can damage equipment, reduce productivity or harm workers, you should always choose a training technique that minimizes the likelihood of such performance failures. When a simulated vs. an actual work environment in training is more likely to produce poor performance, resulting in negative consequences, go with OJT. On the other hand, if errors by an untrained or half-trained person can be *disastrous*, expensive simulations (such as the ones designed for airline pilots and nuclear power plant operators) begin to make a lot of sense.

• When supervisory positions involve slack time and/or capital equipment is used at less than full capacity, OJT may be more cost-effective than a classroom-based program, all else being equal.

Cases

Let's take a look at a few actual training situations that lend support to the principles stated above. By studying these cases, you can see how training strategy decisions are affected by changes in the relative costs of alternative training techniques.

The servicing division of the American Express Co. decided to computerize its data management systems and relocate to a different area of the country. It was faced with the need to train a large number of people right away, and expected its need for personnel training to continue far into the future. These conditions suggested a mix of computer-based instruction and classic classroom training, since the fixed costs could spread over the large number of expected trainees. Further, the large number to be trained, the radical change in procedure and the relocation implied an insufficient number of trained supervisors—conditions increasing the costs of pursuing OJT.

In a similar situation, widespread technological change prompted a computer manufacturing firm and a public power utility to shift to large-scale classroom-based instruction. The great many employees in need of training and the lack of expertise among existing supervisors about the new technologies prompted management to choose classroom training over OJT.

In a nonunion mining operation, the continuous introduction of new miners triggered formalized training practices. Hiring practices had to be altered because new machinery required different skills. Management at the mine asked the vendor of the new equipment to provide skill upgrading for current employees as part

of the purchase agreement. Even the layout of the mine itself had to change due to the fundamental alterations brought about by the new technology. Again, the amount of training to be done and the lack of qualified OJT supervisors justified the fixed costs of classroom-based training.

Another intriguing example is H&R Block, the well-known tax-preparation and consulting company. H&R Block offers a course in tax preparation to the public for a fee sufficiently large to offset the costs of the classroom training. To the best students from that course goes an offer of further training and permanent positions in the firm. In this instance, the classroom-based strategy provides the added benefit of an inexpensive selection procedure.

In the case of a unionized mine, an expansion of operations stimulated

---

The dilemma over which type of training to use boils down to a comparison of costs and benefits.

---

widespread recruitment and training efforts. Because of the large number to be trained and the simultaneous introduction of new technology, the mine attempted to institute classroom-based training. The company set up an above-ground training center designed to simulate underground mining conditions. However, a realistic simulation proved to be too costly, and management turned instead to quasi-OJT, setting aside a portion of the underground mine for training. In a subsequent recession, the volume of miners to be trained became too small to justify such "classroom" activity, and the training section of the mine was returned to active production. Necessary training was accomplished totally on the job.

In another example, Skaggs, a national drugstore chain, historically had relied on OJT for training its cashiers. The nature of the skills needed on the job and the flow of trainees suggested that OJT was the proper strategy. However, in response to an increasing perception that OJT was alienating customers who had to wait in lines due to inept trainee cashiers, the chain has recently moved cashier training to off-the-job training centers. The purpose, of course, is to minimize the costs of inadequate job performance. For similar reasons, a gas company began sending maintenance workers to a training center *before* introducing them to supervised OJT as a way of preventing accidents for which the company might be liable.

Faced with the choice of providing its own accreditation training or sending its personnel to a tax-supported educational institution for training, a hospital in a major metropolitan area opted for providing its own training because of the standby nature of many hospital jobs. Taking this approach, personnel could receive training during slack periods but still be available in case of emergencies. In-house training also was less expensive.

Northwest Energy, a pipeline company, also decided on in-house training during work hours. Experienced personnel were available to supervise training since their work responsibilities required only occasional monitoring of systems and full-time involvement only in emergency situations.

Obviously, none of these examples provide an immutable blueprint to follow in making OJT vs. classroom decisions for your organization. But they do point out a number of the factors that come into play in making such decisions. Things such as production schedules, safety considerations and new job requirements *count* when it comes to planning how employees will be trained. These efficiency factors have to be weighed right along with effectiveness factors.

Reprinted from TRAINING, February 1985

THE SNAKE-OIL SYNDROME (AND HOW TO FIGHT IT)

Step right up, folks, and see the management-training technique of the ages. Works on hives, gout, career development, coaching and promotions

BY H. ADRIAN OSBORNE
AND STEVEN D. NORTON

The old snake-oil pitchman of years gone by was able to thrive because the people who gathered around his wagon wanted desperately to believe that his nostrum would cure everything from acne to warts.

Human resource development specialists, on occasion, latch on to a single technique for measuring and predicting the performance of managers, and grasp it to their breasts with that same sort of fervor. The commitment to this single approach grows into a "snake-oil" mind set: The technique becomes a cure-all for every ill. Vendors of HRD products and services have been known to encourage such perceptions.

How do you counter the snake-oil syndrome? By recognizing the importance of selecting a technique in light of the particular goal you're trying to accomplish.

Table 1 lists five popular techniques and evaluates their usefulness in five typical applications for personnel management. The evaluations are somewhat subjective, being based on our interpretation of the findings in the research literature coupled with our own experiences. Whether the reader agrees completely with each evaluation is not as important as an acceptance of the premise that no single technique can serve effectively in all five areas.

Do it right

First, let's recognize it as a "given" that the results gained by any of these measurement techniques will be affected drastically by the way they are implemented. Errors on the part of the HRD specialist, the client or both can produce dismal results regardless of whether the right technique is being used to attack the right problem.

Assessment centers, for example, require good simulations and good training provided by a specialist; but if the client supplies second-rate assessors and facilities, the center will be second-rate. Psychological assessment requires a technically skilled psychologist; but if the client fails to provide realistic information on the demands of the target jobs and accurate feedback on the performance of those who are selected or promoted, the accuracy of the psychologist's recommendations will be greatly reduced. Rating forms require careful development (based on a job analysis) to ensure their validity; but proper rater training and management support for accurate ratings are essential, no matter how good the forms.

Performance standards and joint goal setting have been the subject of great controversy and confusion. We are avoiding the term "management by objectives" in this article because while it originally referred to joint goal setting for the purpose of improving the management process, it has come to be applied to any use of performance standards for determining rewards and punishment. As others have noted, the emphasis has sometimes shifted from *management* by objectives to management by *objectives*.

As the table indicates, both performance standards and joint goal setting are useful in certain applications. Unfortunately, managers often feel that they can combine the advantages of the two techniques by setting performance standards unilaterally, then deluding themselves with the idea that the standards were arrived at through a bilateral effort with subordinates. This pretense is a common thread in the failure of a lot of so-called "MBO" programs.

Another common problem is that standards tend to be set in areas that are easy to measure (like quantity of production) so that managers are rewarded for de-emphasizing things that are difficult to measure (like quality and customer relations). Setting performance standards properly requires an intense effort by a group of individuals with detailed knowledge of the operations being measured. Joint goal setting requires extensive training of both supervisors and subordinates.

Applications

Even if they are implemented flawlessly, none of these techniques is useful in every application. But the following discussion does presume that each technique is being handled properly.

• *Career development.* Although assessment centers were originally developed solely for the purpose of predicting managerial success, they have proven extremely useful for career development. Psychological assessments, on the other hand, have always included some form of career-development feedback; but while the type of information they provide is helpful, it often is not as helpful to the individual as that provided by an assessment center.

Joint goal setting is useful for career development when it provides a forum for the careerist and the supervisor to discuss the link between the personal goals of the former and the long-term requirements of the organization.

• *Coaching.* Rating forms have the potential for being the best foundation for coaching because they *should* focus both the supervisor and the subordinate on specific examples of the subordinate's behavior. Their use in personnel actions tends to hamper this application, however, because too often the attention of the subordinate is on *changing the rating* rather than on *changing the behavior*.

Assessment centers and psychological assessments both provide good material for coaching when the results are fed back to the supervisor of the assessed individual.

• *Planning.* Both performance standards and joint goal setting are very useful for planning, but they produce somewhat different results. If performance standards quantify all of the important outcomes (rather than being open to "gaming") and are linked to pay, managers will be highly motivated to plan to achieve those outcomes. Joint goal setting, on the other hand, tends to emphasize the quality of the *management process* and is more useful than performance standards when it is difficult to quantify all of the important outcomes.

• *Pay.* If they are really "airtight," performance standards are very useful for negotiating salaries and benefits. But when joint goal setting is tied to salary, there is an inherent conflict of interest between the subordinate—who wants to play it safe by setting "easy" goals—and the supervisor, who wants to raise the productivity of the entire unit so that he will receive his own pay raise. (The federal government's recent experience with merit pay is yet another case study in the problems that arise when you try to mix performance standards with joint goal setting.)

Rating forms may *appear* useful for pay administration because ratings on individual scales can be added up to give an overall score for an individual. But in addition to the supervisor's common tendency to give inflated ratings, rating forms may be unsuitable for pay administration because they are most useful when they focus on behavior, rather than on measurable results—and pay raises typically are given for results. For example, if cost reduction is an important goal, it usually makes more sense to compare the rate of reduction among managers than to compare a supervisor's rating of each manager's "ability" to reduce costs.

• *Promotions.* Research generally has shown assessment centers to be the most valid predictor of managerial success. They may not always be cost-effective, particularly when the candidate pool is spread over a wide region, but they work.

Psychological assessments share with assessment centers the advantage of freeing the supervisor from the task of identifying the less-promotable subordinate and then living with the resulting dissatisfaction. For a variety of reasons, however, their track record is not as consistent as that of assessment centers.

Rating forms can be useful for promotion decisions *if* they are related to the target jobs, and *if* supervisors will identify the less-promotable subordinates. Even if assessment-center results are available, there usually is a need to give the candidate's supervisor some say in the promotion process. So, rating forms are difficult to avoid.

At first glance, performance standards look like the ideal tool to use for promotion decisions. The problem is that while almost all low performers are low in potential for promotion, not all high performers are high in promotion potential. The greater the difference between the candidate's current job and the target job, the greater the need for information above and beyond a record of how well the candidate has achieved his or her performance standards. The classic example is the outstanding salesperson who becomes a terrible sales manager.

Base promotions on the candidate's achievement of jointly set goals, and you run into the same problem as with performance standards. In addition, the subordinate again will want to "play it safe," as when joint goal setting is used to determine pay.

A warning

Since each of the techniques described here is expensive to implement properly, it is tempting to adopt or try to develop one technique for several applications, or to take a technique being used successfully in one application and expand it to others. If a joint goal-setting system is proving successful for planning, one wants to believe that the same system can produce acceptable personnel decisions. Unfortunately, the result is more likely to be poor personnel decisions *and* poor planning.

But—and it's a big "but"—there has to be a balance between the danger of adopting a single technique for too many applications, and the danger of overwhelming the line supervisor with a blizzard of time-consuming personnel programs that may damage the supervisor's relationship with subordinates and prevent *anybody* from getting any work done.

In other words, the arguments we have outlined here, like any other approach to organizational problems, can be clasped too firmly to the breast, followed with too blind a devotion ...and turned into snake oil.

Reprinted from TRAINING, May 1983

TABLE 1. TECHNIQUES FOR MEASURING MANAGERIAL PERFORMANCE: APPLICATION TO PERSONNEL MANAGEMENT

TECHNIQUES	CAREER DEVELOPMENT*	SUPERVISORY ACTIVITIES Coaching**	SUPERVISORY ACTIVITIES Planning***	PERSONNEL DECISIONS Pay	PERSONNEL DECISIONS Promotion
ASSESSMENT CENTER Trained assessors observe candidates perform simulations and rate them on dimensions	VERY GOOD Provides objective information from neutral parties	GOOD Provides specific areas for coaching	NOT RELEVANT	NOT RELEVANT	VERY GOOD Most valid predictor of managerial success
PSYCHOLOGICAL ASSESSMENT Psychologist interviews candidates and administers tests	GOOD Similar to assessment center, but less job-related	GOOD Similar to assessment center, but less job-related	NOT RELEVANT	NOT RELEVANT	GOOD Not as valid as assessment center
RATING FORMS Set of rating scales on which supervisors rate work behaviors, methods or skills	FAIR May not be relevant to personal goals	VERY GOOD Scales should reflect true job demands	NOT RELEVANT	FAIR Pay is usually for outcomes, not behaviors	GOOD If raters are trained and scales reflect target jobs
PERFORMANCE STANDARDS Standards set by management for the purpose of measurement. Usually apply to more than one job	FAIR May not be relevant to personal goals	FAIR Standards focus on outcomes, not behaviors	GOOD Focus is on outcomes stressed by organization	VERY GOOD Focus is on outcomes stressed by organization	BE CAREFUL Target job may require different behaviors and different outcomes
JOINT GOAL SETTING Goals set jointly by supervisor and subordinates as a focal point for the management process	GOOD Career development goals may be included	FAIR/GOOD Goals can include behavior changes	VERY GOOD Focus is on identification of obstacles to achievement	BE CAREFUL May lead to setting "safe" goals	BE CAREFUL May lead to setting "safe" goals

*Identification of long-term personal goals and how to pursue them.
**Day-to-day discussion of behaviors and methods.
***Periodic discussion of progress toward goals or outcomes.

BEHAVIOR MODELING: THE 'MONKEY SEE, MONKEY DO' PRINCIPLE

The learning by imitation concept is deceptively simple. But countless training programs still don't use it

BY RON ZEMKE

Monkey A sees Monkey B dig up a red root and eat it. Monkey B smacks his lips, jumps about excitedly, begins digging again. Monkey A "gets the picture," does some digging of his own, finds a red root, eats it, likes it, and digs for more. Simple as it may seem, this scenario captures the essentials of an emerging approach to the development of training. This new approach, based on the principles of social-learning theory, is known as behavior modeling.

Behavior modeling and social-learning theory

Few trainers have more than a vague familiarity with behavior modeling and its parent, social-learning theory. Part of that unfamiliarity has to do with origins. Social-learning theory is a by-product of investigations by Albert Bandura, James Aronfreed, and others into the development of moral behavior in children. The specific question they investigated was: "If people tend to behave in ways that lead to satisfaction in any situation, why do they often appear to forego rewards in order to behave in ways that are socially acceptable, even in private?" The learning model they evolved to answer this question — social-learning theory —emphasizes two simple mechanisms: *conditioning* and the *observation of models*.

Conditioning, a la Bandura, is essentially Skinner's reinforcement-of-behavior concept but with a strong emphasis on interpersonal attention, approval and affection as powerful reinforcers. As children, we learn to repeat behavior that gains parental approval, and we learn to avoid actions that bring withdrawal of affection and/or punishment and disapproval. The approval and disapproval of others remain powerful rewards and punishments throughout our lives.

The social-learning approach recognizes the importance of internal events, such as thoughts and memories, on the control of our behavior but insists that all behavior is at least indirectly controlled by external cues. As we become adults, we learn to reward and punish ourselves "internally" in imitation of previously encountered "external" reward and punishment. Once we've been burned by a hot stove, chances are slim that we'll touch one again, regardless of "social" pressures.

Modeling or observational learning is the way we learn from others' experiences. It takes place in two steps: acquisition and performance. In the first step, we see others act, and we *acquire* a mental picture of the act and its consequences. After the mental image is acquired, we *perform* or try out the act ourselves. This is, of course, where conditioning principles come into play. If we find the consequences of imitating the model rewarding, we're likely to act that way again.

Obviously, you and I don't imitate and try out every behavior we see others engaged in. In fact, adults seem to apply quite a few restrictions to whom and what they will parrot. We are most likely to try out a new behavior if we see someone prestigious, powerful and competent doing it. (How many of us, for instance, dusted off our old tennis racket and ambled onto the court because a significant role model — some personal idol or strong influence — encouraged us through example?)

But our expectations and experiences with reward and punishment in similar situations also mediate the chances that we'll try the modeled behavior. A five-foot-five, 35-year-old male, watching Bill Walton play a magnificent game of basketball, may not be encouraged by the example to play a little one-on-one. But a five-foot-five, 15-year-old female might be.

A growing number of trainers are learning that the social-learning-theory approach leads to a radically different framework for designing training, one that is particularly useful to those who train others to do complex motor-skill tasks and those who train others in interpersonal communication tasks. The use of modeling in the technical-training context has long been recognized. Anyone who has tried to write or even read repair instructions for anything more complex than a rubber band appreciates modeling and learning by imitation. In technical training, the score has always been: talk about it = 0; see diagrams of it = 10; watch someone do it = 1,000.

The big news now is that interpersonal skills, such as those needed to sell or conduct effective performance reviews, can be effectively taught and learned using modeling and social reinforcement. Trainers at IBM, General Electric, AT&T, Levitz Furniture, and others are finding that supervisory, sales, and customer-relations skills are learned faster and more effectively when taught from a modeling base.

Bandura suggests that the social-learning theory is a successful training design tool because it mirrors critical features of the real world in the training experience. In fact, Dr. Bandura bluntly downgrades the efficiency of learning from textbooks and lectures, and from word descriptions of things learnable from direct example.

The marked discrepancy between textbook and social reality is largely attributable to the fact that certain critical conditions present in natural situations are rarely, if ever, reproduced in laboratory studies of learning. In laboratory investigations, experimenters arrange comparatively benign environments in which errors do not create fatal consequences for the organism. By contrast, natural environments are loaded with potentially lethal consequences for those unfortunate enough to perform hazardous errors. For this reason, it would be exceedingly injudicious to rely on differential reinforcement of trial-and-error performances in teaching children to swim, adolescents to drive automobiles, medical students to conduct surgical operations, or adults to develop complex occupational and social competencies.

There are several reasons why modeling influences are heavily favored in promoting everyday learning. Under circumstances in which mistakes are costly or dangerous, skillful performances can be established without needless errors by providing competent models who demonstrate the required activities. Some complex behaviors can be produced solely through the influence of models. If children had no opportunity to hear speech, it would be virtually impossible to teach them the linguistic skills that constitute a language. When desired forms of behavior can be conveyed only by social cues, modeling is an indispensible aspect of learning. Even in instances where it is possible to establish new response patterns through other means, the process of acquisition can be considerably shortened by providing appropriate models.*

Dr. William C. Byham, president of Development Dimensions International, a Pittsburgh, PA-based training company that uses behavior modeling in its program designs, suggests, "Modeling is the way we've all learned from day one. Our whole developmental history is one of modeling the behavior of others. Look, I talk to a lot of successful managers and quiz them about their success. To a person, they claim that the most important experience in their career was working for an exceptional manager at some time — usually early — in their career. They seem to be saying they had a manager who was a good model and mentor. Unfortunately, that's an experience most of us won't have. And that's why I'm so high on giving people good models to learn from instead of textbooks and lectures."

In short, then, social-learning theory and research strongly suggest that, when conditions are right, a trainee can learn rapidly and effectively from exposure to a model performing the desired behavior.

Applying modeling and social learning to training

The first interpersonal-skills training using behavior-modeling techniques in industry was conducted in 1970 at General Electric by Mel Sorcher. The objective of this first course was to reduce the turnover of hard-core employees by helping them adapt to and cope with a job in industry. Both hard-core employees and

*Albert Bandura, *Psychological Modeling* (New York: Lieber-Atherton, Inc., 1971).

their first-line supervisors were trained in taking and giving constructive criticism, asking for and giving help, and establishing mutual trust and respect. The actual training was light on human-relations theory and attitude messages and long on visual examples— films of people *doing* good interpersonal relating— and role play. Basically, the training was exceptionally successful.

Six months after the original training, 72% of the 39 hard-core employees who had been trained and who worked for supervisors who had been trained remained on the job. Only 28% of the 25 hard-core employees who had not been trained and who worked for untrained supervisors did not leave. More important, Goldstein and Sorcher synthesized the important elements of the modeling-training approach, and it has been used widely in the development of interpersonal skills ever since.

Question: So what's the big deal? Don't we, more or less, use modeling in all our training? Most of us show movies — that sounds like modeling —and most of us give live demonstrations. That, too, sounds like modeling. And lots of us use practice and role playing, and that sounds like social reinforcement. So why all the hubbub?

For starters, simply exposing trainees to film and video images of people doing things isn't modeling. A recent stopwatch study of 15 commercial training films revealed that, out of 420 minutes of film, the largest block of time (235 minutes or 56%) was devoted to explaining the skills. Twenty-two percent or 92 minutes were titles and transitions, 13% or 55 minutes showed people doing the skill *incorrectly,* and only nine percent or 38 minutes showed people doing the skill correctly or modeling the behavior. That is an average of 2.6 minutes of correct-skill demonstration per film. Producers of training films would not be surprised at these numbers since they conceptualize their job as dramatizing and communicating an idea rather than providing a source of skill models.

The moral is that simply putting your message on film doesn't qualify the product as a source of behavior modeling experience. Even showing trainees a film or videotape composed solely of examples of people doing the behavior or demonstrating the skill correctly isn't a learning shoe-in. By analogy, you and I can go to a tennis tournament, watch Connors and Evert play perfect tennis and not learn anything new about the game. *Unless* we attend with the conscious intent of "going to school" on Conner's footwork

or Evert's backhand, we won't come away with any new backhand or footwork models.

In training based on modeling and social learning, care is given to facilitating three processes in the trainees:

- Attention — making sure the trainees attend to the pertinent aspects of the behavior being modeled;
- Retention — helping the trainees remember the original observation points in the form;
- Reinforcement and motivation —using practice and positive reinforcement to translate observational learning into skilled performance.

Development Dimensions' Byham suggests that these three processes are promoted by adhering to a specific sequence of events in the training:

1. *Overview.* The instructor discusses the objective and importance of the skill module.

2. *Critical steps.* The instructor describes the specific behavior or critical steps of the activity to be learned.

3. *Positive model.* A film or videotape shows an individual effectively utilizing the skill.

4. *Critique of the film.* The instructor and participants discuss the things done correctly in the film, with particular emphasis on how the model utilized the critical steps.

5. *Skill practice.* Trainees practice the skills in pairs, with one trainee acting the supervisor, salesperson or whatever and the second acting the employee, buyer and so forth. At least one other trainee observes the practice, using a prepared guide.

6. *Skill practice feedback.* After the practice session, the trainee receives feedback from observers and the instructor that emphasizes things done correctly. Where the behavior could have been more effective, alternative positive behaviors are suggested.

7. *Transfer.* Participants write out, practice, and receive feedback on situations they will face back on the job.

Byham also passes along the following tips and tricks for those who contemplate building a program around modeling concepts.

- Do a good needs analysis. Solving the wrong problem is *still* the trainer's number-one pitfall.
- Determine the specific situations where the new behavior is expected to manifest itself.
- Determine the minimum critical steps of the activity or skill to be mastered; don't complicate matters by listing too many critical steps.
- Spend up to 50% of the training time on the trainees on-job problems. (Development Dimensions courses typically devote 10 minutes to viewing

the filmed model in a three-hour training sequence.)

• Keep the feedback sessions positive. The goal is to create a series of success experiences for the trainees.

• Develop the training group into a mutual support group.

• Don't expect a one-shot training program to yield a big behavior change. Work on one skill at a time over a period of weeks. Give trainees time and space to try out the new behaviors and come back for consultation with the rest of the group and the instructor.

Research on the effectiveness of behavior modeling in clinical and school settings is persuasive. Most assertiveness training is done through modeling, and has an impressive composite track record. But how effective is the approach in our world, the normal adult learning context? There is an equally impressive accumulation of studies that say the approach is effective in business and industry.

We have already mentioned Sorcher's work and the book based on his and Goldstein's successes. Robert F. Burnaska, also of GE, reports that a course developed to improve the interpersonal skills of the managers of professional employees was equally successful. A one-month follow-up comparison of 62 trained and 62 untrained middle managers showed that trained managers were better at *performance problem discussion, work assignment discussion,* and *giving recognition to an average employee* than were the untrained managers. In addition, a five-month follow-up found trained managers even better than they were at the one-month follow-up.

At AT&T, Joseph L. Moses and Richard J. Ritchie developed a behavior - modeling - oriented supervisory-relationships training program following the Goldstein and Sorcher model and evaluated the results, using an assessment-center approach. A team of specially trained individuals observed and evaluated 90 trained and 93 untrained first-level supervisors performing a variety of simulation exercises. Two months after the program, both groups were given cases of excessive absence, an alleged discrimination complaint, and a case of suspected theft. In all simulated situations, the trained group utilized "appropriate skills" and handled the situations significantly better than did the untrained group.

Preston E. Smith of IBM office products division reports that modeling training of *meeting effectiveness skills, discussing opinions survey results,* and *customer complaint handling* has paid off handsomely for his organization.

Trained managers were rated higher on employee opinion surveys after training than before. In addition, customer-satisfaction ratings and sales-quota results were higher for branches managed by trained managers.

Lest we seem about to leap too quickly onto the behavior-modeling bandwagon, let's review three *facts* about the technique. First, the behavior-modeling approach comes from a learning model — social-learning theory — that has an impressive set of credentials. Second, a number of trainers are finding that the application of modeling principles is further reducing their dependence on the "spray and pray" approach to training. Third, good, solid evaluations are verifying the effectiveness.

But, as the folks at "Ma Bell" remind us, "The system is the solution." And no new training program or technique can overcome bad products, poor market positioning, or a management team that fights change. With this in mind, we should avoid setting expectations for behavior modeling that it can't fulfill. But we also should be glad we have an innovation, a new tool, that helps us perform better professionally. Who knows what will happen if we begin to model the professionalism we profess.

Reprinted from TRAINING, June 1978

WHAT YOUR TRAINEES CAN LEARN BY SIMPLY WATCHING OTHERS

Behavior modeling or imitation learning was a virtually unresearched and unknown topic prior to the 1941 publication of *Social Learning and Imitation* by Miller and Dollard. Their studies lead them to view imitation learning as a special form of the behavioral conditioning process. Essentially, the trainer must provide a sample of the behavior, the learner must respond in a way that matches the sample, and the imitation must be positively reinforced. In Dollard's and Miller's view, the "model" simply informs the learner where to go or how to behave for reinforcement. The learner does not acquire new, previously unexhibited behavior from the model. Though much of Miller's and Dollard's interpretation of results and theorizing has been questioned recently, they deserve credit for priming the pump, for beginning to research the question, "How and what do people learn simply by watching others?"

Groundbreaking and impressive modeling research has been conducted by Dr. Albert Bandura of Stanford University. In a typical experiment, Bandura, Ross and Ross showed nursery-school children a motion picture of an adult displaying "aggressive behavior" toward a large, inflatable rubber clown — the kind that bounces back for more because of a bottom full of sand. Boys and girls who watched the film behaved aggressively toward the clown themselves, closely mimicking the adult in the film. They lifted and threw, kicked and hit, and beat the clown with a hammer exactly as the adult had. Bandura has repeatedly found that most children will, with little or no prodding, thus imitate the novel behavior of a model.

In addition to establishing that modeling does occur, Bandura has investigated the ways in which it can be increased or decreased. He has found, for example, that children are more likely to imitate the behavior of a model they see rewarded than one they see punished. In one experiment, three groups of children watched films of a model who yelled at and punched a Bobo doll. In the film one group saw, the model was punished by an author-

ity for punching the doll; in the film a second group saw, the model was praised for his aggressive behavior; in the film the third group saw, the model received neither praise nor punishment. When put into a situation similar to that of the model, the children who had seen him praised were much more likely to imitate him than those who had seen him punished. Bandura hypothesized that the children identified with the model and experienced reward or punishment vicariously as they watched the film. Therefore, when given a chance to act as the model had, they tended to behave as if they themselves (instead of the model) had earlier been praised or punished for hitting the doll.

Bandura's approach to understanding the modeling phenomenon is more complex and cognitively oriented than Dollard's and Miller's. To Bandura, models influence learning in an information-transmitting fashion. The observer acquires a symbolic representation of the modeled activities rather than a group of stimulus-response associations. Because there are cognitive or mental, as well as behavioral, components to modeling, Bandura suggests that there are four processes governing the modeling phenomenon: *attention, retention, reproduction,* and *reinforcement/motivation.*

The attention process

The principle here is that a person cannot learn much by observation if he or she does not attend to, or recognize, the essential features of the model's behavior. The learner must be sensitized to look for the things we want them to learn or they will learn something else — or nothing at all. Research suggests there are the following natural factors which shape the attention patterns of learners:

• *Similarity of model and learner.* The people with whom one regularly associates influence the types of behavior one will repeatedly observe and learn thoroughly. Opportunities for learning aggressive behavior are most prevalent for children of the urban poor than for offspring of the rural Quaker.

• *Functional value.* Behavior which has an intuitive value for the learner in the learner's environment is more likely to be attended to. Subway-map reading doesn't have a high functional value to a Los Angelino.

• *Interpersonal attraction.* Models who possess interesting and winsome qualities are sought out, whereas those without such characteristics tend to be ignored or rejected, even though they may excel in other ways.

• *Media attractiveness.* Models presented in televised form are so effective in capturing attention that viewers learn the depicted behavior regardless of the presence or absence of incentives for learning.

Retention processes

If one is to reproduce a model's behavior when the latter is no longer present to serve as a guide, the response patterns must be represented in memory in symbolic form.

• *Mental images.* There is an almost automatic mental imaging function, but for practical use these "mind pictures" should be associated with common symbols, such as words. As Plato suggested, a bowl may be only a poor example of the concept bowl, but the concept name bowl invariably pulls forth an image of a specific bowl one has had experience with.

• *Verbal coding.* Observers who code modeled behavior into words, concise labels, or vivid imagery learn and retain the behavior better than those who simply observe or are mentally preoccupied with other matters while watching the performance of others. Consciously counting Mark Spitz's strokes per lap will help a

swimmer retain and retrieve a mental image of Spitz's swimming style.

• *Rehearsal.* People who mentally rehearse or actually perform modeled patterns of behavior are less likely to forget them. For example, mumbling your "opening lines" over and over to yourself makes them automatic.

Motoric reproduction processes

To actually *do* the behavior, the learner must put together a given set of responses according to the modeled patterns. The amount of the model which can be exhibited depends on acquisition of component skills.

• *Parts must equal whole.* A learner could have all the parts but not succeed with the whole. A young child might watch and be able to exhibit all the components of driving a car but still run the family Hupmobile through the garage wall.

• *Skill level.* Even if all components are learned, can be identified and talked about, performance of the whole will be poor until all the components are practiced and fitted together in a whole. A would-be tennis player can learn a lot by watching others play, talking about it and banging balls against the house. *But,* until one goes on the court and hits with another person, honing and fine tuning to the level of the model can't take place.

Reinforcement/motivation

A person can acquire, retain and possess the capabilities for skillful execution of modeled behavior, but the learning rarely will be activated if negatively sanctioned.

• *Positive incentive.* When positive incentives are provided, observational learning, which has been previously unexpressed, is promptly translated into action. Reinforcement influences not only the demonstration of already learned behavior, but it can affect the level of observational learning by influencing attending, coding and rehearsal phases.

• *Anticipation of reinforcement.* If the learner sees the model reinforced positively or avoiding punishment, learning is enhanced.

• *Familiarity with subskills.* If the learner has all the subskills and also has names or a coding system for them, seemingly complex skills can be modeled verbally — a factor most technical-manual writers rely upon heavily.

• *Multiple models.* The more models the learner is exposed to, the less likely he or she is to learn only one way of behaving. Learners exposed to three or four models exhibit behavior that is an innovative mix of all of the models seen. This would seem especially im-

portant for learning interpersonal skills that are personality dependent, such as selling or interviewing.

• *Outcome for the model.* How the model is treated influences both the probability of the learner learning the behavior and the learner's attitude toward the model and the behavior the model exhibited. This concept has been especially useful in helping people de-learn phobias.

During the last decade, there has been copious research on modeling applications. And at least some should interest the training and development professional.

• Problem-solving strategies—both linear and creative — seem to be enhanced by a combination of process rules and extensive modeling of the processes.

• Rule following and positive attitude toward procedures and rules seem to be enhanced through discussion and viewing of filmed vignettes of people successfully following rules and procedures.

• Interviewing skills can be quickly and effectively learned by watching a videotape of a model conducting an effective interview.

• When watching a model of supervisory skills, trainees also tend to learn and assimilate the leadership *style* of the model.

• Self-disclosure in a closed group increases when the facilitator models self-disclosure and makes a high number of self-disclosing statements.

• Assertive behavior can be effectively learned watching a videotape of a low-assertive person becoming assertive with the help of an assertiveness trainer.

• Complex motor skills can be learned by watching a film of a correctly performing model *or* a film of someone learning to perform the motor skill.

• Tolerance to pain can be learned from watching a model endure what the viewer perceives to be a painful experience. (Especially useful for those who must conduct or endure long meetings or seminars.)

• And, finally, one researcher has determined that we are what we watch. Specifically, he found that those who watch "All in the Family" most frequently are most tolerant of and in sympathy with Archie Bunker's attitudes and views. The researcher does not suggest a causal relationship but if some Sunday morning you notice the "Gilligan's Island" rerun you're watching is one you've seen three times before — and you're still enjoying it — it might be time to consider the effect behavior modeling is having on you.

Reprinted from TRAINING, June 1978

HOW TO SET UP, RUN AND EVALUATE PROGRAMS BASED ON BEHAVIOR MODELING PRINCIPLES

Trainers everywhere can adopt this step-by-step approach, which works so successfully

BY TERENCE O'CONNOR

At St. Luke's Hospital Center, 108 supervisors have improved their skills, thanks to behavior modeling. The program is so successful that some of us have spent our vacations offering the technique at other organizations. Employees of an international insurance company, a multinational shipping firm and more than 20 health care institutions have benefited from our classes alone, and dozens of large and small consulting firms now offer supervisory training that utilizes behavior modeling techniques.

You've probably read other recent testimonials to the concept of learning by imitating the behavior of models. Numerous publications ranging from TRAINING (June 1978) and *Business Week* (May 8, 1978) to the *Journal of Nursing Administration* (April 1978) have explained how and why the process works. But these and other articles generally have steered clear of the nitty gritty details of how you go about setting up, running and evaluating a training program that revolves around behavior modeling. I would like to do just that.

First, I suggest that you read *Changing Supervisor Behavior*, by Arnold P. Goldstein and Melvin Sorcher; this is the theoretical framework for the technique. Next, read one of the many good books that stress improving communications through increased empathy, respect and warmth. One particularly good one is *Human Relations Development—A Manual for Health Sciences*, by George Gazda, Richard Walters and Williams Childers.

A further review of the literature shows the variety of situations that respond to behavior modeling. At St. Luke's, we use seven frequently:

- greeting the new employee
- introducing a new policy or procedure
- improving poor work habits
- improving poor performance
- the discipline interview
- performance appraisal
- reducing conflict between two subordinates

Your organization's records and needs analysis may indicate other situations that require the employee to make a positive individual commitment to alter his or her behavior. Analyze how your best supervisors handle these situations. Compare them with your worst supervisors. From these extremes of behavior, you can identify key points (usually five to seven) in the best supervisors' communications process for each situation.

Generally, these key points include:

- greeting the employee warmly and appropriately
- identifying the situation being discussed
- soliciting the employee's suggestions for improvement
- writing down those suggestions the employee chooses as most likely to be effective
- setting a follow-up date to review the situation
- expressing confidence in the employee's ability to handle the situation properly

For each problem situation, adapt the key steps to reflect the language of that interaction.

Develop a script for a model interview between supervisor and employee, for each situation. The script should model the supervisor's behavior, not the policy or procedure—hence the term "behavior modeling." Because the model stresses the process of the interview, not the content, it requires a certain brevity and pace that are not necessarily realistic. The model will be attacked in class if it contains too many references to organizational policies and documentable facts.

In the script, the supervisor should cover each key step in sequence. He should not move onto the next step until the prior one has been completed. The listener should hear the supervisor control the interviewer's pace. The subordinate should do most of the talking, but the supervisor stays in command.

Now, videotape your model interviews. (Using videotape recording and playback equipment is, of course, optional but it makes the next step much more effective.)

Don't worry if your players don't follow your scripts. What's important is that the model follows the key steps for each interaction. If it does, then encourage your actors to use their own words and mannerisms.

At St. Luke's, we began with supervisors from one department. We have since done groups from many departments and, on occasion, from more than one institution. We also mix experience with inexperience. Members of the group, however, must have difficulty with the same interactions.

At this point, our needs analysis is not complicated. Of our prospective participants, we ask, "What do you want to do better?" In a separate meeting, we ask their managers, "What do you want them to do better?" Each group will use words like "morale" and "motivation"; get them to speak in terms of specific interactions, and you will find a remarkable degree of agreement between the two groups. You may have to bridge some minor gulfs, but the two will tell you quickly which of your models you will use— and if you will have to make more.

I prefer to do this needs analysis orally, rather than by questionnaire.

This lets me probe below the generality and also lets me explain what I'll be doing. But you can use printed surveys before the meetings, if you wish.

Groups size in our classes has varied from four to twenty. The bigger the class, the longer each session lasts. We find 10 is the best size. Classes are at least two hours long and meet once a week. The participant receives a notice of time, place and topic for each class but no preliminary reading.

The first class is devoted to explaining in detail the program's specifics. The camera is turned on, and the group is seen on the monitor, but nothing is recorded. When the group is comfortable with the TV, we turn off the equipment. The remainder of the class is spent reviewing the duties of a supervisor, the importance of communication skills and the techniques of effective listening. Because the class is to learn behavior, not theory, the latter is never mentioned.

Each week thereafter, we cover another interaction. The format of each class is similar:

- Distribute the key steps, read them aloud, answer questions about them (10 minutes).
- Show the model tape for that interaction (10 minutes).
- Talk about the model (5 minutes).
- Have the class in pairs, rehearse the model behavior; after 10 minutes, reverse the pairs, so each person is the supervisor (20 minutes).
- Turn on the television and record a pair rehearsing. At the end of the rehearsal, ask the "supervisor" for his review; then solicit remarks from the "employee." Play back the tape. Allow comments from anyone in the room (30 minutes).

Who goes on the tape? Everyone plays the supervisor at least once. Who goes first? Ask for volunteers. No volunteers? I pick the least aggressive person in the room to star as the supervisor first.

What order for the interactions? Start with the least threatening, and end with the most threatening. Do at least five; the key points are basically repetitive, and five weeks are needed for the rehearsals to be learned effectively.

What is the pass-out material? Only the key steps for each week. Participants should refer to these as they rehearse and be encouraged to have them handy on the job. We also have these key steps in a check-off form and may distribute this to encourage the class to follow the televised rehearsals.

At one time, participants also received brief outlines of situations to use as they rehearse. But we discarded these because few were used. Or, if they were, the actors got involved in our written words and not their oral ones. It's best to let them use their own styles of communication to cover key points effectively.

Who acts in the model tapes? Anyone who is believable. At one time, we used actors from each department as we trained in it, but this had little effect and wasn't worth the effort.

What about tests? The final class is a test, both written and behavioral. Participants arrive alone, complete the written test (on communication skills, not theory) and choose one of three situations. After a few moments to prepare, a tape is made; the instructor usually plays the employee. Total time is about 30 minutes.

Who works the TV equipment? No one. In reality, the trainer turns it on to play the model and then puts on the tape that records the rehearsals. Operating time takes no more than two or three minutes.

Evaluations can take the form of written tests, rehearsal tapes and/or the final test tapes. At St. Luke's, we rely most heavily on the final test tapes. Participants are graded on: control of the interaction, ability to move the employee to a positive response to the problem and ability to follow the key steps.

Outside the classroom, statistical follow-up reveals that problems *do* respond to the program. For example, new employee turnover decreases when participants study orientation of new employees.

Validation? In December 1977, we requested nine randomly chosen graduates (10% of our total), trained from January 1975 to June 1977, to visit our training department. Arriving singly, each was given a typed description of a problem: One of their employees had a pattern of recent Monday lateness. After a few moments preparation, each indicated a willingness for the interview to begin. A trainer played the employee.

Some "testees" were stern and disciplinary, and some were paternalistic and helping. Each revealed his own personality and used his own communications style in the interview. Each graded high in interactive control, employee contribution and following key steps. Even those who had participated three years earlier and who had received no overt reinforcement from training scored well.

For before-and-after comparisons, these interviews were compared with the first taped rehearsal interview of each "testee." Nontraining administrators scored each pair of interviews. In each case, "after" scored higher. Retention of skills, even after 35 months, was significant.

At St. Luke's, where the technique is called "behavior rehearsal," we stress rehearsal rather than the model. It is rehearsal time that allows the participant to make mistakes in the classroom, not the work room. Rehearsal lets each person explore how best to play the role illustrated by the models.

Reprinted from TRAINING, January 1979

QUESTIONS TO ASK BEFORE USING BEHAVIOR MODELING

The technique is attractive,
and the uses seem almost limitless,
but it is not guaranteed
cost-effective or appropriate

BY JAMES C. ROBINSON
AND DANA GAINES ROBINSON

Since behavior modeling began as an experiment with a few supervisors at General Electric in 1970, it has grown into a learning technology that will be utilized in the training of more than 500,000 supervisors, managers and employees this year. Certainly, the numbers are impressive. But the pragmatist should ask, "How do we know that behavior modeling is the most effective learning experience for every one of those 500,000 learners?" The answer is, "We don't know and probably never will know."

Nevertheless, we must ask that question each time a decision is made to use behavior-modeling programs in our organizations. We all have a responsibility to our organizations to use behavior modeling (or any other learning technology) *only* when it is the most effective and cost-beneficial approach to a given problem. Only through careful deliberation can we determine when and under what circumstances behavior modeling should be used.

After several years of experimenting, we have developed a seven-step decision-making process (see table 1) that will enable organizations to examine any training situation to determine whether behavior modeling is appropriate. To illustrate how each step leads toward the ultimate decision, we will use a hypothetical organization, the Homespun Insurance Company. Homespun has 3,400 employees, with the majority located in a major city. There are 200 first-level supervisors in the organization.

Given: Possible training need exists

The decision-making process starts when a possible training need is identified. This training need can pertain to employees, supervisors, managers, top management or any segment of the organization. It usually refers to a current performance deficiency (for example, not achieving a current job expectation) or some future problem (for example, learning to market a new product).

In the Homespun Insurance Company, the possible training need involved the ability of first-line supervisors to put an employee on probation without causing the employee to leave the organization. In the previous year, supervisors justifiably had put employees on probation 48 times; 20 of these employees eventually left the organization. Because rehiring and retraining for the 20 open positions had been costly to Homespun, the company hoped that a training program might reduce the expense.

Decision #1: Could he/she do it if his/her life depended on it?

The decision is to determine whether the performance deficiency is a result of a lack of skill and knowledge or due to other factors. When the performance deficiency is a result of something other than skill or knowl-edge, management should seek non-training solutions— which often involve changing the conditions in which the person is expected to perform— rather than training that person to do something he or she already knows how to do. According to Mager and Pipe, if a person has a genuine skill or knowledge deficiency, then the primary remedy must be either to change the skill level (teach the individual how to do it) or to change the job responsibilities. If, on the other hand, the person is able to perform the job, the solution lies in something other than enhancing skills and knowledge. "Teaching" someone to do what he or she already knows how to do isn't going to change that person's skill level. Instead, the remedy is to change the conditions in which the person is expected to perform.

Supervisors at Homespun obviously were struggling to conduct effective probationary conversations with employees. In almost every instance, it was in the company's best interest to have a poorly performing employee correct performance deficiencies. Supervisors, however, felt so pressured by these disciplinary conversations that their primary objective was to "get it over with." Consequently, the supervisors did not clearly delineate the performance standards expected of the employee. In addition, the discussions often provoked defensive reactions from the employees. To further complicate the matter, the supervisors were not consistently following corporate policies when placing employees on probation. But the crux of the problem was that many supervisors lacked the skill to conduct such conversations effectively.

Decision #2: Is it a skill deficiency?

The second step in the decision-making process is to determine whether the deficiency is one of skill or one of knowledge. Behavior modeling is a feasible method of teaching skills; some other process, however, would be more appropriate for cognitive learning. Since the performance deficiency often involves a combination of skill and knowledge, behavior modeling frequently is used in conjunction with another type of learning experience.

For example, if we were to design a program to teach student pilots to fly aircraft, we would confront a situation in which the students would have to learn several things. First, they must learn the theory of flying so they would know why an aircraft leaves the ground at given speeds. They also

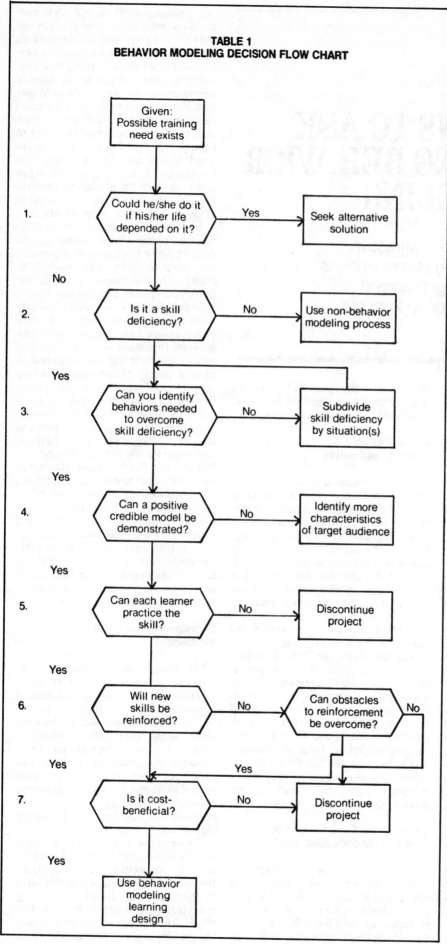

TABLE 1
BEHAVIOR MODELING DECISION FLOW CHART

Given: Possible training need exists

1. Could he/she do it if his/her life depended on it? — Yes → Seek alternative solution

No

2. Is it a skill deficiency? — No → Use non-behavior modeling process

Yes

3. Can you identify behaviors needed to overcome skill deficiency? — No → Subdivide skill deficiency by situation(s)

Yes

4. Can a positive credible model be demonstrated? — No → Identify more characteristics of target audience

Yes

5. Can each learner practice the skill? — No → Discontinue project

Yes

6. Will new skills be reinforced? — No → Can obstacles to reinforcement be overcome? — No

Yes

7. Is it cost-beneficial? — No → Discontinue project

Yes

Use behavior modeling learning design

would have to develop the skills of applying power during takeoff; of controlling the aircraft's rudders, ailerons and elevators; and of reading the instruments during takeoff. We would utilize a non-behavior modeling process for the theory of flight, while we might consider behavior modeling to teach the new pilots how to control the aircraft.

At Homespun, the training need did require skill *and* knowledge training. Supervisors needed knowledge about corporate policies and documentation requirements regarding probation. They needed skill training in *how* to conduct an interview that would maintain employee self-esteem and minimize defensive reactions. Supervisors also needed help in learning how to participate with employees as they attempted to solve performance problems jointly. These are skills that could be acquired in a classroom.

Decision #3: Can you identify behaviors needed to overcome the skills deficiency?

Although we might assume that we can readily identify the behaviors to be learned in *all* skill deficiency situations, many times one set of behaviors is not enough because the skill must be used in a number of significantly different types of situations. For example, in attempting to train salespeople to build rapport with clients or potential clients, we may find that one set of behaviors is not sufficient because there are many different types of potential clients. Potential clients may, for example, be categorized as: a) reluctant, b) openly hostile, c) needing help in solving a problem, d) friendly, but uncertain of specific needs; each of these requires a different set of behaviors.

The first general rule for determining if behaviors can be identified is that behaviors that are very similar in several different situations need *not* be subdivided by situation. Secondly, if a specific behavior is a make-or-break behavior (as is the case of building rapport with an openly hostile potential client) and if it doesn't occur in other situations, you must describe separately the behaviors needed to handle this situation.

A review of the training need at Homespun indicated that it would be advantageous to train supervisors to do the following:

1. Provide the employee with specific, descriptive behavioral feedback (for example, "You've been absent

from work five times in the past two months.").

2. Solicit the employee's reasons for the problem and a commitment to solving it.

3. Outline, in specific detail, the terms of the probation.

4. Set a date for a follow-up discussion.

5. Express confidence in the employee's ability to overcome this performance problem.

Decision #4: Can a positive, credible model be demonstrated?

If you're going to use behavior modeling, you must demonstrate a model of the specific *positive* behavior to be learned. For example, in developing a model to teach a person how to operate an automobile, we wouldn't model an accident, which would be negative behavior. Instead, we would show the model taking action to avoid an accident; defensive driving would be positive behavior. Also, the learners must view the model as credible. They must feel that the model "could have happened in real life." If the learners don't perceive the model as positive and credible, we must identify more characteristics of the target audience. Knowing these will enable us to develop a model with behaviors that would be positive and effective in that environment, while remaining credible to those learners.

A positive model for the Homespun supervisors was provided in a film in which two office workers were shown discussing the employee's probation. The supervisor followed the appropriate skill behaviors, while the employee expressed some hostility and defensiveness in order to demonstrate a credible situation. The trainees focused on how the supervisor worked through the defensiveness to a problem-solving orientation.

Decision #5: Can each learner practice the skill?

In a behavior modeling program, each learner must have an opportunity to practice the new skill. In most cases, it is possible to provide practice opportunities. In certain situations, however, it might not be cost-beneficial to do so. Imagine, for example, that someone advocated that all airline passengers boarding transoceanic flights practice using flotation equipment in water before flying. The purpose would be to ensure that everyone could float with the flotation device when fully

clothed. Those who couldn't do this would be provided with feedback and coaching on how to use the flotation equipment.

Obviously, this would be a costly skill practice. Although it's possible to provide every passenger with an opportunity to skill practice in this manner, it's not probable that it would be done. After all, passengers would have to arrive at the airport early, and flotation equipment and water tanks would have to be available, with lifeguards present. Some provision would have to be made for drying the passengers' clothes or providing them with an extra set. The decision to be made here is whether the benefits outweigh the costs.

For the Homespun supervisors, the opportunity to skill practice could be provided in a classroom situation, where groups of six to eight trainees could try out their new skills in realistic situations based on their office environment. Even better, they could be asked to describe a situation they had to deal with on the job. While two supervisors skill practiced, the remainder of the group could observe and take notes. Following skill practice, they could provide feedback on supervisors' proficiency in handling the situation.

Decision #6: Will the new skills be reinforced?

The learner should be reinforced for using the new skills, both in and out of the classroom. Classroom reinforcement is quite easy to achieve; properly trained instructors can manage the group dynamics so that there is social reinforcement. But on-the-job reinforcement is often more difficult. First, you must do an analysis to determine whether sufficient reinforcement exists to assure sustained use of the new skills on the job. Because sufficient reinforcement is not present in most cases, you must discover the barriers to reinforcement. Only then can you decide whether these barriers can be overcome.

There are several possible barriers to reinforcement:

• **Peers—** If the peers of a newly trained supervisor are not using the skills, that supervisor is unlikely to continue to use them. Conversely, if a supervisor sees many of his or her peers using the skills, the tendency will be to give them a try. The best way to provide peer reinforcement is to train all peer supervisors in the same skills.

• **Workers—** If workers don't respond favorably to the supervisor's

use of the new skills, the supervisor will quickly stop using those skills. To ensure favorable worker response and, therefore, work reinforcement, supervisors must be trained to handle various types of employee reactions.

• **Managers—** The manager of the supervisor frequently does not reinforce the supervisor. Actually, managers can reinforce supervisors' use of the newly learned skills in three ways. As a coach, the manager can offer supervisors suggestions on how to handle specific on-the-job situations. As a reinforcer, the manager can recognize and praise the supervisor when the latter uses the newly learned skills on the job. As a positive model, the manager can show the supervisor that the skills are worth using on the job.

• **The Organization—** Many times, the organization doesn't reinforce the use of the skills. In that case, you must examine the rewards and punishments within the organization. Unfortunately, some organizations not only don't reward the use of newly learned skills, they actually punish those who practice them. For example, it may be punishing for a salesperson to handle a customer complaint effectively, because the time lost could be used to make other sales leading to commissions.

In Homespun, it was felt that the newly learned supervisory skill of effectively conducting a probationary interview could be reinforced in several ways:

1. All supervisors were to participate in the training.

2. During the actual discussion with the employee, the supervisors probably would find employees much less defensive than previously. While not guaranteed, it seemed probable that having supervisors approach probationary conversations in such a manner would produce positive problem-solving results.

3. All managers were shown how to reinforce the newly learned skill and how to coach the supervisor whenever a situation warranted probationary action.

4. Finally, the personnel department would reinforce the skill. Since all documentation of probations passed through this department, employment personnel would be coached to give positive feedback to supervisors as the quality of this documentation improved.

Decision #7: Is it cost beneficial?

The real issue is whether there will be a positive return-on-investment from the proposed training. In this determination:

$$\frac{\text{Value of the training}}{\text{Cost of training}} = \text{Return-on-investment}$$

The value of the training is determined by computing the value of correcting a skill deficiency, preventing a problem from occurring or maximizing an opportunity. The cost of the training typically includes front-end analysis, development or purchase of the training materials, the salaries of the learners while they are in the classroom, the salaries of the instructors and the cost of overcoming the barriers to reinforcement. Return-on-investment is computed by dividing the value of the training by the cost of the training. If the return-on-investment is positive and within the organization's guidelines, behavior modeling should be used as a learning experience for the specific training situation.

For Homespun, it was determined that a complex analysis was not required for this training need. Rather, a break-even analysis was conducted on the cost to Homespun of employees leaving the organization. In the previous 12 months, 48 employees had been placed on probation—mostly for lateness and absence. Of these, 18 employees were finally terminated, and two voluntarily resigned at the time of probation. The average annual salary of these individuals was $9,200. Therefore, the cost to Homespun for these employment terminations could be computed:

Loss in productivity during the 90-day probationary period	$1,300
Recruiting/hiring costs for replacement	135
Training costs and lower productivity during a four-month training period	1,530
Total cost per termination and replacement	$2,965

Also analyzed were the specific costs of training: for example, materials and classroom time, for learners and instructors. The training materials could be purchased from a supplier. In fact, the materials for this training need were part of a multi-modular program Homespun purchased to meet other supervisory training needs. The program cost included student materials for 200 supervisors ($700) and one modeling film ($400). In addition, one instructor had to be trained, at a pro-rated cost of $100. Therefore, total expenses were fixed at $1,200.

The average annual salary of supervisors to be trained was $14,000. The proposed training program required three hours away from the job. The cost of salaries was computed to be $20 per supervisor, or $4,000 to train all 200 supervisors.

The instructor in this example earned $20,000 per year. Therefore, hourly costs of $10 had to be applied against both the three-hour class time and the one-hour preparation time required. A total of 33 classes would be required to train all 200 supervisors. Instructor costs totalled $1,320.

Forty managers at Homespun needed training in a one-hour program so that they would know how to reinforce the newly learned supervisory skills. The proposed program was to be conducted five separate times, with eight managers in each class. Their average annual salary was $22,000 or $10.50/hour. These costs were computed to be $420 for the managers to attend and $50 for the instructor to teach.

Total training costs were:

Training materials	=	$1,200
Salaries of learners	=	4,000
Salary of instructor	=	1,320
Reinforcement training	=	470
		$6,990

The financial benefit to the organization for each employee who was retained was $2,965. Since it was impossible to project what percentage of the 20 employees who had left the organization could have been retained, a break-even analysis was done which showed:

$$\frac{\text{Cost of training}}{\substack{\text{Value of retention} \\ \text{per employee}}} = \frac{\$6,990}{\$2,965} = 2.4$$

According to this break-even analysis, if three or more employees were retained because of the training received by their supervisors, the program would pay for itself. Because of this, Homespun decided to implement the training.

Summary

Behavior modeling may soon begin to be used with senior managers, in matrix organizations, with service employees and in patient care, to name just a few. In addition, it will be used to teach more sophisticated skills, such as goal negotiation, opportunity identification, fact finding, planning, conflict resolution and team building.

Despite its attractiveness and almost unlimited possible uses, we in the training profession are still responsible for making sure that behavior modeling is used *only* when it will be effective and cost-beneficial. By judiciously using the seven-step decision-making process described here, you'll be able to make the correct decision about behavior modeling for each training situation. If you decide behavior modeling would be ineffective in a given situation, then move on to another technology. If you decide behavior modeling shouldn't be used because it is not cost-beneficial, you also should select another approach.

If, however, the decision is, "Yes, behavior modeling is effective and cost beneficial," then the real fun starts as you begin to design an effective behavior modeling program.

Reprinted from TRAINING, December 1980

BUILDING BEHAVIOR MODELS THAT WORK— THE WAY YOU WANT THEM TO

You may already use training programs based on behavior modeling.
But do you know what distinguishes an effective modeling film/video from a loser?

BY RON ZEMKE

Learning by watching. That's the core idea underlying the concept of behavior modeling. Trainers and researchers are becoming increasingly aware of the power of instructional programs purposely designed to take advantage of this "monkey see—monkey do" principle.

Researchers at Stanford University and at the University of Washington recently have demonstrated that training programs based on behavior modeling can be used to teach leadership skills in a relatively short time, that the behaviors learned actually transfer to the job, help supervisors and managers do their jobs better, and continue to be effective, used and useful long after the training. Similar findings are beginning to emerge for sales and customer relations skills training as well.

The behavior modeling concept is an integral part of social learning theory, the product of critical research by developmental psychologists Albert Bandura, James Aronfreed and others. Social learning theory asserts that we learn much—if not most—of our behavior vicariously, by watching others and retaining and remembering both what they did and the apparent outcome of that behavior.

Taking on a new behavior, say the social learning theorists, requires two steps—acquisition and performance. In the first step we see others act. We *acquire* a mental picture of the act and its consequences. Then we *perform* or try out the act ourselves. This is, of course, where conditioning principles come into play. If we find the consequences of imitating the model rewarding, we're likely to act that way again.

Obviously, you and I don't imitate and try out every behavior we see others engaged in. In fact, adults seem to apply quite a few restrictions to whom and what they will parrot. We are most likely to try out a new behavior if we see someone prestigious, powerful and competent doing it. (How many of us, for instance, dusted off our old tennis racket and ambled onto the court because a significant role model—some personal idol or strong influence—encouraged us through example?)

But our expectations and experiences with reward and punishment in similar situations also mediate the chances that we'll try the modeled behavior. A five-foot-five, 35-year-old male watching Bill Walton play a magnificent game of basketball may not be encouraged by the example to play a little one-on-one. But a five-foot-five, 15-year-old female might be.

There seem to be a wide range of behaviors amenable to learning through this "monkey see-monkey do" paradigm. We've all seen young children mimic the way adults dress, walk, talk and treat one another in embarrassingly fine detail. By the same token, most of us can recall a dance step or two, a questionable driving habit or personal peccadillo we learned by scrutinizing the behavior of teenage peers.

Adults, too, learn from watching those about them. Salespeople or supervisors at ABG Corp. will tend to sell or supervise more like one another than like the supervisors or salespeople from XLM Corp. And when a salesperson or supervisor from XLM moves to ABG, his other behavior usually changes to match the behavior of new colleagues, sometimes with foresight and conscious intent, sometimes totally unaware.

Trainers and researchers attempting to apply the social-learning/behavior-modeling approach often find it leads to a radically different framework for designing training, one that is particularly useful to those who train others to do complex motor-skill tasks, as well as those who train others in interpersonal communication tasks.

Though the particulars of a modeling-based program vary from designer to designer, and depend largely on how each interprets or values the research particulars, few would disagree that it's important to facilitate three processes in the trainees:

• *Attention*—making sure the trainees attend to the pertinent aspects of the behavior being modeled.

• *Retention*—helping the trainees remember the original observation points and key behaviors of the model.

• *Reinforcement and motivation*—using practice feedback and positive reinforcement to translate observational learning into skilled performance. These key points tend to translate into a five-step program design.

1. **Present overview.** The instructor explains the objective and importance of the skill module.

2. **Describe critical steps/key behaviors.** The instructor describes the specific behavior or critical steps of the activity to be learned.

3. **View the model.** Trainees watch a film or videotape—a "modeling display"—in which an individual effectively utilizes the skill.

4. **Do guided practice.** Trainees engage in practice of the skill, in pairs, with one trainee acting as supervisor, salesperson or whatever and the second acting as employee, buyer and so forth. At least one other trainee observes the practice, using a prepared guide.

5. **Receive skill practice feedback.** After the practice session, the trainee receives feedback from observers and the instructor that emphasizes things done correctly. Where the behavior could have been more effective, alternative positive behaviors

161

are suggested.

'Modeling displays'

One thing is abundantly clear about a behavior modeling-based program: the "modeling display" on film or tape is a critical part of the program. Unfortunately, the trainer attempting to build or buy a modeling-based program will find little research-based guidance for specifying or evaluating a modeling display.

As one prominent researcher confides, "The research in that area is really just beginning. We only know a few of the general guidelines and not very many specifics at all. We're not even sure what questions the practitioners *need* answers to."

In other words, the design of modeling displays is more art than engineering, and will remain so until researchers have a chance to catch up with practice. But leading practitioners are coming to some conclusions on the basis of their experience at building, testing and revising modeling displays.

And as you might expect, there are both agreements and disagreements among them about what to consider and control when attempting to build a behavior-modeling display that teaches what you want taught.

Interviews with a number of experienced modeling display builders turned up dozens of variables and considerations that go into making film or videotape models. And while the experts disagree on a number of critical issues, there are a few points of consensus:

1. The behavior to be learned must be shown clearly, positively and directly.

2. Trainees must be able to *identify* with the person shown doing the behavior to be learned.

3. Distractors—technically, stimuli which could distract trainees from attending to the key learning points and critical behaviors—should be shunned.

4. The behavior must be presented in careful steps; it should be "programmed" from simple to complex situations and from easier to more difficult-to-handle problems.

5. Modeling displays should not be confused with information or entertainment films.

6. Trainees expect high-quality video, comparable to broadcast-quality; low-quality displays distract.

Though the experts agree on these major guidelines, they disagree on others. Nor do they see eye to eye on applying the things they *do* agree on. There are four of these disagree-ments you should personally resolve when designing your own modeling display, or assessing a commercially available one.

1 Dressing the set. Odd as it may seem at first, there is quite a bit of disagreement about the visual background the model appears in. The basis of the disagreement is a difference of opinion in the balancing act one must do, attempting to create *identification* and *credibility* in the display while avoiding distractions.

Bernard L. Rosenbaum, president of MOHR Development Inc. in Stamford, CT, emphasizes using as realistic a set as possible, even to the point of filming or taping in the actual work environment.

"Every bit of research I've seen indicates that the more people can identify with the setting, the more likely they are to learn," says Rosenbaum. "Of course, you want to avoid distractions. It won't do to have a noisy cash register in the background of a modeling display showing a retail sales supervisor working with a retail clerk.

"When the trainees can say those are *our* people, in *our* environment, handling *our* problems, they can't take their eyes off of the screen." For example, in a recent sales management module, MOHR shot the pre-call in a diner and the post-call part in a car, Rosenbaum explains: "Those are the places where the client's pre- and post-call coaching takes place, so that is the environment we showed."

Dr. Donald Tosti, vice president of Forum/Operants, Inc. in San Rafael, CA, and Robert Carleton, director of Forum/Operants, take a line directly opposite Rosenbaum, preferring to use very barren, almost stark, settings. To Carleton the issue of set design is related to the "focal point" concept in advertising.

"Do everything you can to make the viewers focus on what you want them to be focused on," says Carleton. "The more you put in a set, the more chance there is of distraction. Just as surely as you put a vase of flowers on a desk, someone in the audience is going to holler out, 'Hey, when do I get flowers on *my* desk?' And that is just the opposite of what you want."

Tosti holds a psychologist's view: "You have to guard against eliciting responses—behaviors—incompatible with the behavior you want learned. If you think something has the potential of being a distracting stimulus, leave it out."

"In technical training," Carleton adds, "we cover the parts of the machine that are relevant to the learning point. It's the same here. We've never had anyone distracted by the *lack* of irrelevant details, but we've certainly seen distractions occur because of the presence of irrelevancies."

Danny Hupp, program development manager for Pittsburgh-based Development Dimensions International DDI, takes a middle position, calling for approximate but not identical settings. "The environment must be positive and believable but it must not intrude," he says. "Offices must be credible and plausible but not identifiable.

"When I dress a set, I want it to give context to the scene and then disappear when the interaction starts. People are overpowered by a set that is wildly wrong, and also by a set that is too close to home. You don't want them trying to guess whose office it really is. Funny posters, book titles, all that could distract from the learning, should be out."

Dr. John H. Zenger, president of Zenger-Miller in Menlo Park, CA, tends to agree with Hupp's view. "When the environment is too close to home, participants seem to nit-pick," he says. "During the testing of a hospital program we were producing, the nurses spent time challenging the way the actors wore their hats and the way they opened the autoclave. Being too realistic was a distraction."

But Zenger also cautions that realism is both "a learning and a marketing issue," adding that "sometimes the buyer's comfort level dictates the exact behavior and environment. You can work with that initial resistance but you also have to be sure you are arguing valid learning points, and the research isn't nearly that specific."

2 Perfect vs. coping performance. A second strongly held set of positions involves the perfection of the behavior examples you show. The bone of contention is believability.

Some experts say a perfect and smooth performance is alienating—or at least lacks identifiability—while a less skilled or coping performance may encourage trainees to try the skill. "Watching a Borg or a Connors play tennis doesn't affect us duffers," Zenger observes. "We *know*—or at least believe—there is no way we could serve like that. On the other hand, seeing a fellow duffer improve his serve substantially does persuade us and encourage trying to improve."

Rosenbaum is most emphatic

MORE HINTS ON SUCCESSFUL MODELING

Successful behavior modeling requires advance identification of desirable, manipulable and selectively reinforceable behavior, according to University of Missouri management professor Phillip J. Decker, a leading empirical researcher on the subject, and Rusti C. Moore, education and training director at Barnes Hospital in St. Louis. The duo recently shared with TRAINING a few hints on developing behavior-modeled training.

The skills that behavior modeling will attempt to teach must be outlined in a set of "learning points" that are not only written concisely for study by trainees but serve to introduce and guide demonstration portrayals of the skills. The learning points should be based on a thorough job analysis to discover "the correct and successful method" of doing the modeled behavior, the researchers say.

"An easy way to develop learning points is to ask supervisors (of your target population) to identify successful and unsuccessful employees," says Decker. "You can then interview or observe the successful employees to see how they do the focal task and double-check by interviewing or watching the unsuccessful employees."

Decker and Moore say that rule-like learning points that state general principles applicable in various contexts enhance generalization of the behavior learned from models. But if used, they must be accompanied by several models, each showing a different way of accomplishing the rule.

Models used in the training program should be from the trainee population and should have some status or informal leadership abilities, although it is best not to use supervisors. The easiest way to develop models on videotape is simply to present the learning points to the models and let them rehearse performances until perfection to the certified-correct form. Decker and Moore use no scripts or actors; they try to keep each model presentation as succinct as possible.

The role playing by trainees that follows presentation of a correct model "is more real to the participants and less threatening if we split the participants into groups of three or four," Decker explains. "Each then has a chance to role play more than one time. And each group of three or four participants is led by a subtrainer who gives the feedback and controls the role-play situation."

Again, no scripts are used. "We let the participants come up with their own problems that they have to deal with on the job," Decker says. "The only constraint is that the learning points must be used to solve the problem." Trainee observers offer comments on the quality of the solution; the trainer gives feedback on learning points.

Role plays are videotaped by each of the practice groups and, with the help of subtrainers, skills are reinforced and practiced well beyond the point of being able to reproduce the desired behavior correctly.

"Reinforcement for the new behavior on the job is critical and should be built into any behavior-modeling workshop," Decker and Moore advise. Part of the behavior modeled in a carefully designed program must be targeted at supervisors; they must learn to reinforce correct behavior when it is used on the job, even when the behavior is initially unsuccessful in its objective.

Although the requirements of small groups and videotape make behavior-modeled instruction expensive, Decker and Moore say results often are measurably impressive: behavior-modeled skills usually have productivity components. They also claim that "trainees' attitudes or beliefs about the behavior will come in line with the new behavior" and that modeled training "eliminates the problem of trying to change deep-seated attitudes" before training can succeed.—R.S.

Reprinted from TRAINING, January 1982

---

about the importance of showing a coping performance. "The research says that believability suffers when the performance is too well-mastered," he notes. "You have to like the people and believe you could do as good a job as you see them doing."

Hupp agrees that perfect models are inadvisable. "You can have a positive model without perfection," he says. "The audience must be able to say, 'I think I can do that with a little practice.' If the model is too good—for instance, if the model displays a clinical psychologist's skill at explaining feelings—that alienates the viewer. How could a trainee *expect* to develop that skill level?"

Tosti and Carleton acknowledge that too much skill in the model is probably alienating, but also believe the display must show mastery, not just coping. "You have to be attentive to the verbals and nonverbals; the voice tone and pacing have to be appropriate, positive and believable," says Carleton.

Tosti adds, "If the model is counter to the experiences of the audience, if trainees say 'No, that couldn't happen in our company,' you have a problem. But at the same time, we are careful not to introduce a 'hard times' example—a supervisor, say, working with an employee who is giving him a bad time—too soon."

To counter the "not-like-me" or discounting phenomenon, Tosti suggests having trainees construct responses using the key learning points before they see the model do the behavior. "When they write their own theme and cue lines, the model is a supplement or adjunct and the discounting phenomenon is irrelevant," he says. "The model is being held up as a referent, not a display of perfection."

Zenger recommends simplicity as an antidote to an over-perfect performance. "There is no way you can make a model too simple," he says. "Keep it simple and it won't seem something that the trainees can't do.

Actually, what happens is they find when they try the skill practice that it *isn't* all that simple and they concentrate on mastery of that model that seemed so simple at first."

3 Real vs. neutral content. The experts disagree on whether to use real company problems or neutral issues. Tosti and Carleton go for neutral topics: "We use problems like installing new phones or assigning overtime. Dealing with company issues turns training into a company meeting. That distracts from the process and what you want them to be learning."

Rosenbaum acknowledges that with too much company content in the modeling display, "you begin to do content rather than process training." Just the same, he insists there is important motivation to be gained from viewing "people in real settings coping with significant, enduring company issues. Transient or insignificant problems detract from the identification."

Hupp, who supports showing conflict and difficult problems, cautions against controversial topics such as sexual harassment or politics. He also recommends avoiding graphic descriptions of the problems. "In the old TA terms," he insists, "you run the risk of hooking the critical parent or playful child with problems that distract from learning the process."

4 **Negative vs. positive examples.** Another aspect of display building that separates our experts is the use of "bad guy" examples. Rosenbaum is very emphatic. "In no instance have we found it helpful to show people doing the behavior incorrectly," he says.

Hupp, however, disagrees: "The reality principle requires that we should show people that all problems don't have sugarplum resolutions, but I am cautious about recommending the use of negative models. It's difficult enough to set up a really positive but realistic display."

Neither Zenger nor Tosti rule out negative examples entirely. "The research isn't clear," Zenger says cautiously. "There is some evidence that the negatives may be better remembered in the long run than the positives. If you believe in the power of modeling, it is logical to reserve the use of negatives for situations where it is absolutely necessary."

Tosti makes a critical distinction: "A behavior model is composed of a series of critical steps that lead from problem to solution. Sometimes learning to discriminate between more effective and less effective behavior requires showing both good and bad examples.

"But that is different from showing a complete good/bad contrast model," Tosti continues. "Our experience suggests showing a contrast model at the end of a program doesn't hurt, but it can be very problematic to show one at the beginning of a program, before they can accurately judge the performance on their own."

The list goes on

These are but four of the critical issues to consider when building and evaluating behavior modeling displays. There are other points of contention, such as using trained actors as opposed to "real" managers, whether explanations and concepts should or should not be included on the tape or film along with the model, how long a modeling sequence should be, whether scripting or ad-libbing is better and the relative merits of custom and "off-shelf" modeling displays.

But one thing is abundantly clear: developing behavior modeling displays is a very different technology from traditional training film development. "The advantage of using the behavior model paradigm is that it increases the likelihood of transfer to the job," says Hupp. "Dressing people up in fairytale costumes and having them act out metaphorical stories may be entertaining, but it's not modeling."

Zenger takes even a stronger view: "If you think a subject is so dull—and the students so lowly—that only an entertainer will make an impression, so be it. But if you assume your trainees are adults, eager to learn to do a better job, you need not resort to motivational tricks. I prefer the latter assumption. Behavior modeling programs are based on it, and we've got pretty good data to prove that they work."

Reprinted from TRAINING, January 1982

USING MODELS, MOCK-UPS AND SIMULATORS

Among other advantages these training aids let the learner control instruction

BY JUDSON SMITH

What do a 20-cent orange and a $200,000 computer have in common? Not much, it seems—unless the computer is painted orange. But, in training terms, both are simulators.

The orange has been used for decades to help medical personnel learn how to give injections without painfully pincushioning human subjects. And the computer is used to simulate real-life situations that would be economically unfeasible or hazardous to untrained personnel.

Both fit into the category of "simulator," since they approximate the real-life situation being learned. But one, the computer, is an active simulator, since it can be programmed to respond with feedback if the learner makes a mistake. The orange, on the other hand, won't squeal with pain if a shot is administered incorrectly, so it is a passive simulator, often called a model or mockup.

A model closely approximates some object, usually reduced in scale. A mockup, on the other hand, is often a same-size or larger device used to illustrate basic concepts or procedures by roughly approximating the real thing. The orange, then, is a mockup, since it has neither the texture, shape nor size of a human limb; it is simply a device used to illustrate the basic skills required to give an injection.

Given those broad definitions, the area of models, mockups and simulators covers a lot of ground and includes many items of interest to trainers. Rather than microscopically analyze each item, let's focus on appli-

cations and generalities of interest to all trainers.

The airlines are big users of mockups and simulators. From the basic stage of designing new aircraft, often done using precise models under carefully controlled wind-tunnel conditions, to the final steps of putting a qualified pilot and correctly scheduled passengers on board, models, mockups and simulators find extensive use.

The basic rationale is economic. "When you consider both the student-hour cost of a 747 pilot who makes $80,000 per year and the cost of dedicating an aircraft to training," explains Dennis Sullivan, director of instructional systems and training for the Canyon Research Group, "you can see why most airlines have invested in sophisticated simulators."

Through the use of such systems, Sullivan reports, actual airplane flying time has been reduced from an average of 13 hours to 1 hour for captains transitioning to newer aircraft. It's been calculated that it costs about $4,000 per hour to train an airline pilot in the cockpit. A full-scale simulator, on the other hand, runs about $400 per training hour. And, once initial programming costs are absorbed, computer simulation runs only about $40 per hour.

One such simulation, programmed on Control Data's "Plato" system, is in daily use at American Airlines' Flight Academy. The Plato terminal (Programmed Logic for Automatic-Teaching Operation) links by telephone to a Control Data computer in Minneapolis. The flight crew member, seated before a television-like console, types in requests for specific pro-

grams, and Plato displays required information on the screen.

In a typical program, the pilot is taken through an unfamiliar instrument panel, control by control. He or she is asked to identify each knob or meter by touching a sensitized probe to the object depicted graphically on Plato's screen. Right answers earn congratulations from the machine and the right to continue on to another control. Wrong answers start a learning process designed to teach the pilot how to identify the control and its purpose.

In the rarified atmosphere of aircraft operation, these simulations save not only money but lives. According to FAA figures, more pilots are killed in training flights than in actual operations. By using cockpit mockups and computer simulations, the airlines have reduced training accidents to almost zero.

A scaled-down version of computer simulation is now also being used by some private pilots or pilot candidates for the same safety and savings reasons. Companies such as Analog Training Computers and Pacer Systems now produce desk-top simulators that let learners "fly" at their own pace and at much less cost than if they were learning in the air with a rental plane and a Certified Flight Instructor.

These General Aviation simulators include mockups of a generalized instrument panel, plus computerized learning tools. The trainee plugs in tapes that either simulate actual take-offs and landings, for pretraining before flight to unfamiliar airports, or take the learner through a programmed course to teach new skills.

The advantages of such flight simulators are obvious. A cockpit, buffeted by wind and moving onward at several hundred miles per hour, is no place to develop a new skill or become familiar with a new airport— not when failures could easily lead to fatalities.

The airlines, however, must prepare for such failures. They do this with mockups and simulators, as well. At the American Airlines' Flight Academy, one building is solely devoted to the training of cabin crews. Within are exact replicas of airliner interiors, coupled to a computer console. The instructor can simulate any air emergency, including fires and ditching at sea (using a large pool). Although such emergency procedures are rarely required, it's good to know that all flight crews have experienced similar situations in training.

One major airlines estimated that

the millions of dollars it had invested in a training facility would be recovered in about five years. The company did it in two because of the increased cost of fuel and the release of aircraft back to revenue flying.

Training in the airline industry is highly controlled by government regulations, and airlines must continually send pilots and flight crew members back for updating. The success of simulators has many airlines considering doing *all* such updating or new-equipment training without using revenue-producing aircraft. They feel it is not only less costly but also far more effective and safer.

Airline ticket offices aren't nearly as hazardous as airliners, but computer simulation has still proved valuable in saving time and training effort in this area. Using the Boeing Computer Services' Scholar/Teach 3 system, for instance, TWA teaches personnel how to use their programmed airline reservation system and other air freight or load control systems.

BCS' ST3, like Control Data's Plato, gives the trainer several advantages over other learner-controlled instruction techniques. For one thing, these systems aid in training program management because they automatically monitor student enrollment and progress, as well as assigning students the correct curriculum. ST3, for instance, lists, by student, the answer given to each question in a given program. And a response report categorizes all student responses as "correct" or "incorrect," giving the training staff a measure of the course's effectiveness.

If a course, or section of a course, proves ineffective, most computer simulator programs allow "authors" to revise easily. In most cases, the computer command language is similar to basic English, and computer graphics can be generated easily with a sensitized pencil so updates and revisions can be incorporated at any time.

Of course, these same computer simulators can just as easily train personnel in more down-to-earth fields. Because mistakes during on-the-job training of technicians involved in nuclear or electric power plants can be just as disastrous as pilot error in an airliner, many companies use computer simulators to familiarize personnel with the operation and repair of generating stations and power grids. On Plato, for instance, an operator who mistakenly throws the wrong switch is suddenly confronted with a screenful of jagged lines and explosive words, a graphic demonstration of what would happen in reality if that switch were thrown.

Computer simulators are typically more versatile and less costly than models or exact mockups, but sometimes the subject being studied demands hands-on training with realistic devices. Many medical skills would fall into that category.

The example of the orange, familiar to any nursing student or intern, is still an accepted method for learning how to give an injection. But modern plastics and semiconductors have replaced the more traditional methods of supervised practice on patients for many other medical procedures. Insertion of catheters, for example, is a tricky procedure at best and not one to be undertaken by a novice. With the aid of a plastic model, medical people can now practice this technique on a "subject" that looks, feels and responds as would a human being.

Full-size replicas of the human body are also frequently used by health-care trainers. "Resusci-Anne," one of the most famous, is a willing victim on which procedures related to heart attacks are practiced. Other manikins can be stripped down, layer by layer, to uncover the inner workings of the body. Industrial trainers and educators also use these anatomical models to illustrate the effects of smoking, alcohol or other health hazards in an all-too-graphic way.

Some industrial machines are just as complex as the human body, and it is just as difficult to get under their "skin." For this reason, technical trainers often find plexiglass models extremely useful for explaining the inner workings of a device. Although such models are usually one-of-a-kind and, therefore, quite expensive, they provide every trainee with "x-ray eyes" to clearly view otherwise invisible parts and processes.

In the field of electronics, mockups and simulators are especially valuable. Submolecular particles just aren't visible as they move through wire or create differences of electric potential within solid semiconductor materials. By converting the actual circuit to a large-scale "equivalent circuit," electronic instructors are able to explain the mystical relationships between elements in a concrete, traditional manner.

It's fairly easy to understand why the U.S. Maritime Administration uses CAORF (Computer Aided Operations Research Facility) to simulate on a computer the conditions a tanker captain will face entering New York Harbor. It's just as obvious why oranges make better practice targets for student nurses than would a human being. Speaking of practice targets, it also makes good sense for law enforcement officers to learn firing techniques against "quickdraw" simulated bad guys. But the use of models, mockups and simulators for most training applications are not quite so obvious.

Take something as basic to most large businesses as typing. Why use a simulator or mockup of a typewriter keyboard when the real thing is readily available? First of all, because a typewriter is a fairly complex device, consisting of several basic parts. When the keyboard is separated into number keys, alphabet keys and punctuation keys, trainees can learn in bite-sized steps rather than having to confront the entire board at once. By mocking up the carriage assembly, the trainer can point out features and be sure the entire class knows where he or she is pointing. Finally, typewriter repairs cost money, and it's all too easy for new typists to scramble the keys or strip the gears; by first learning correct procedures on a simulator or mockup, trainees can correct mistakes without damaging expensive equipment.

Seeing the whole picture

The same theory holds true for every training procedure. When technical equipment is broken down into component parts and operators are trained on each part, the whole picture becomes clearer. By using large-scale mockups of small devices or small-scale replicas of large equipment, the trainee can grasp the total more easily.

Training time is valuable time, both in terms of the trainer's work and that of the employee away from production while learning. Devices such as computer simulators are usually learner controlled, so the trainer is freed from routine repetitive teaching tasks for individual counseling or instructional design. And the trainee who can schedule learning time to suit his or her own work schedule takes as much or as little time as required to learn effectively.

So, models, mockups and simulators make good sense for many training applications. They can save time and reduce hazards, let the learner control instruction and provide hands-on experience without pain, danger or lost production time. At the very least, they provide another form of learning reinforcement; at the most, they can help trainers illustrate and explain things that otherwise would be difficult or dangerous. So their worth is undisputable. The real challenge is to design or purchase models, mockups and simulators that fit an individual department's needs.

Reprinted from TRAINING, December 1978

CAN GAMES AND SIMULATIONS IMPROVE YOUR TRAINING POWER?

From the ancient game of chess to modern business simulations, people have learned through make-believe. Today, more than ever, trainers are making play work

BY RON ZEMKE

Human beings are inveterate game players. Give two kids a stick and a stone; they'll invent a game and start drafting teams. And though often overlooked, everyday experience continually confirms that adults are no less taken with game playing than are children.

One need only walk into any airport game room and observe the executive types standing on line to do battle with video game Martians or to scamper video chickens across video highways dodging oncoming video semitrucks to be convinced of the propinquity. If that's not proof enough, consider where NBC, CBS and ABC would be without the Super Bowl, the Stanley Cup or the Battle of the Network Stars.

Despite our seemingly inexhaustible natural enthusiasm for play, until recently few people had tried to harness that motivation and use it to promote learning. Games designed for learning first and leisure second are, in fact, relative newcomers. True, military strategists from Hannibal through Haig have honed their craft on war games.

Moreover, chess, one of the oldest board games known, supposedly developed in India as a learning aid for testing and sharpening the wits of peacetime generals. And, yes, when Lord Wellington pronounced that the battle of Waterloo was won "on the playing fields of Eaton," he both flattered the skills of his officers and gave glowing testament to the value of games in the education and train-ing of the English military mind.

But not until the mid-1950s did the first serious business game see light of play: It was developed by the American Management Associations' then manager of finance, Frank M. Ricciardi. On a visit to the Naval War College in Newport, RI, Ricciardi observed the extensive war game simulations being played by officers/students. It made an impression.

Part of what he saw was the potential contribution the war game/simulation concept could make if applied to advanced business education. On May 2, 1957, after a year of developmental work, real, live managers played Ricciardi's "business war game" for the first time.

Twenty company presidents took part, playing in teams of four. Each team was given a mythical company to manage and assigned the task of capturing the market. Each team made decisions for the company on a quarterly basis for 12 rounds, the equivalent of three business years. All decisions were fed into a computer, which calculated outcomes. This new data was then used in the next quarter's decisions. The game concluded with a critique session; each team compared results and discussed the strategies they employed. Even today, this format is still widely used in business gaming situations.

Game theory and computers

News of the AMA game spread. Within a year, games became an in-tegral part of the teaching technology at the "best" business schools coast to coast. Key to this rapid acceptance and proliferation of the management game concept was the fortuitous coming together of two technologies—the electronic computer and general game theory.

Invented in the 1920s by Hungarian-born mathematician John von Neumann, game theory is the quantitative study of decision-making behavior, especially under conditions of uncertainty about the intentions of people with whom one is in conflict or competition. Just prior to WW II, von Neumann fled Nazi Germany for the U.S., took a post at Princeton University and there, in collaboration with fellow refugee and economist Oskar Morgenstern, wrote *The Theory of Games and Economic Behavior.*

This 1944 classic rigorously examines the concept of strategy, as well as the logic people apply to game playing. It was also one of the first works to treat decision making as an understandable, rational process. The advent of the computer in the 1950s simplified the process of applying the math von Neumann and others were working with, while making the principles of gaming easily available for practical game building and playing. In short, a new training tool was born.

Now that gaming simulations have reached age 25, what do the experts know about them? Quite a bit, as it turns out. For starters, they have a much better idea of what is a game—and what is not. According to A.J. Romiszowski, a British instructional media specialist, the game is distinguished from its nearest cousins, the *role play* and the *case study,* by one important factor: competition. "Some games may be simulations, others may not," he says, "but all games have an element of competition ... [which] may be natural to the reality being studied ... or it may be purposely introduced into the learning to make it into a game."

Gaming simulations have two sides while problem-solving simulations only one. Author and researcher R. Garry Shirts, splits the distinction even more finely, detailing seven categories of activities that are and are not games, contests, simulations and bits of all three:

☐ **Simulations**—This applies to anything that models reality. Models of physical, social or industrial-social systems, as well as mathematical formulas, are high-grade simulations. Role playing, film, literature, painting and sculpture are lower class cousins, but simulations nonetheless.

☐ **Contests**—Not all contests are games nor are all games contests. The difference is that a *contest* may be waged in the "real world," as in an election. A contest also may be a one-on-one struggle between person and environment or goal.

☐ **Games**—To Shirts, a game is an activity in which people agree to abide by a set of conditions—not necessarily rules—to create a desired state or end. General "play" activities reside in this category.

☐ **Non-simulation contest games**—This is what Romiszowski called the game; it is a set of activities in which the playing conditions are designed to create competition and winning. Especially missing here is the element of simulation. Sports, gambling and board games such as Monopoly are contest games but not simulations.

☐ **Non-contest simulation games**—In this category are activities that simulate reality but do not pit players against one another in win-lose fashion. Children playing store or "ring-around-the-rosy" are involved in simulation games. (The latter game dates to the Black Plague and is, in fact, a simulation: Lines such as "All fall dead," communicated useful information.)

☐ **Non-game simulation contest**—While testing two methods or procedures is a non-game, it *is* a contest and a simulation. Simulating the flow of product from two different warehouse designs and determining which is most effective and efficient is a non-game simulation contest.

☐ **Simulation game contests**—This is the categorical home of most educational simulations and games. Here, activities are contests, in that they are concerned with the allocation of such scarce resources as money, time and influence. They also are simulations because they model reality, and games because the participants agree to abide by a set of conditions. In addition, participants frequently agree to follow inefficient practices and rules, such as communicating with one another in writing only.

Trainers have developed and experimented with gaming simulations in a variety of settings, from general management through quality control. And as you would expect, they work better in some situations than others and are more appropriate for some learning objectives than for others. In their book *Gaming-Simulation: Rationale, Design and Applications*, Cathy S. Greenblat and Richard D. Duke suggest a number of strengths and weaknesses of the gaming simulation:

• Games are useful at helping trainees "see the forest for the trees;" games seem to be most effective in helping trainees grasp interrelationships among the parts of a system, understand others' viewpoints of a situation and develop their own perspective. They are less useful in teaching specific facts or skills. Games should be viewed both as communication tools and pedagogical devices, because they deliver holistic, not linear, views of nonlinear or simultaneous events and systems.

• Games are effective at teaching the processes simulated as well as the rules and restrictions of the system or subsystem.

• Games are effective at teaching the relative tradeoffs, costs, advantages and disadvantages of different strategies and alternatives.

• Games can teach the language of the system or subsystem being simulated, as well as the specific facts associated with the problems being worked on.

University of Pittsburgh researchers Omar Khyyam Moore and Alan Ross Anderson have studied the conditions surrounding successful use of games and simulations. From their work emerge four principles for designing a learning environment that optimizes trainees' experiences with a gaming simulation.

• Learners should be given the opportunity to operate from a number of perspectives. They should not be merely the recipient of information, but also should be an agent, referee and a reciprocator.

• Activities should contain their own goals and sources of motivation; there should be some reason other than passing the course. Moore and Anderson term these "autotelic activities."

• Trainees should not be dependent on authority; they should be allowed to arrive at answers by themselves. Therefore, activities should be structured to require decision-making

and problem-solving rather than recall of others' solutions.

• The environment should be responsive to the learners' activities. Not only should they receive feedback, but also should be encouraged to evaluate their own progress.

Frank H. Rosenfeld of Douglass College, Rutgers University, examined the evaluation literature on gaming simulations and found that while proponents' claims sometimes go a bit beyond actual results, there are many positive aspects. He summarized his review in five propositions:

1. Simulation games generally seem no less effective as teaching/learning devices than more traditional methods; they may be even more effective. (Better for cognitive skill acquisition, but not as good for fact and figure learning.)

2. There can be vast differences between participants' perceptions of effectiveness and their actual effectiveness. (Initial enthusiasm doesn't always translate to behavior change over time.)

3. Simulation games can result in unanticipated outcomes, including negative attitudes and lower self-esteem of participants. (Those unable to cope with ambiguity and uncertainty seem most affected negatively.)

4. Variations in the characteristics of the game players and the simulation environment can produce variations in the effectiveness of the resulting teaching/learning. (Variables such as sex, age, IQ and educational background all affect the outcome of a game, as can levels of detail and abstraction in the actual game.)

5. Teaching/learning effectiveness varies widely from game to game. (The more specific and "real world" the game, the more likely it will have learning benefits. But in general, games that are effective at teaching technical specifics are less effective in teaching problem solving and decision making, and vice versa.)

The "bottom line" is that games are more than play. They can be fun, fascinating and a vehicle for real learning, when used in the right context and applied toward the right kind of learning objectives. Gaming simulations won't replace all your lectures, role plays or skill practice sessions. They *will*, however, bring a valuable perspective to the skills being learned and give your trainees a leg up on the training-to-back-on-the-job-transition ladder.

Reprinted from TRAINING, February 1982

USING GAMES TO HELP MEET YOUR OBJECTIVES

If the right game is matched to the situation, both trainees and trainers can be winners

BY LINDA STANDKE

The training session has started and the instructor has announced that part of the program involves playing a game. There is a box of Tinker Toys placed in front of you. According to the directions, you are a supervisor who has been asked to build a four-sided object with "something hanging in the middle." You've only a few minutes to get your subordinate (the person sitting next to you) to accomplish the task. Do you get involved in the doing rather than the directing? How does your subordinate feel about your assignment methods and leadership style?

The outcome would reveal not only a lot about you and your leadership style, but also set the stage for a discussion about appropriate supervisory behavior and the effects of non-specific directions on the final work product. And, if the setting was one where the emphasis was on interactive learning in a positive atmosphere, with good guidance from the trainer, then you probably would have enjoyed the experience and remembered the point of it back on the job.

It's for reasons like these that more and more trainers are using games to achieve their training and development objectives.

What makes a game a game?

Before we review how and why to consider using games in your training, it's important to define our terms. What we're talking about when we say games runs the gamut from board games ("Fair Play," a distant relative of Monopoly, but with affirmative action EEO as the subject) and card games to computer simulations and even some types of role plays and in-basket exercises.

Complicating things further are the various game classifications. For example, the management development branch of the International Labor Office classified games by subject covered, type of competition required (between participants, between the actual self, or between the players and the environment), and how results are processed and fed back to the participants. Others classify games by nature of model (abstract or based on fact) and by purpose (for training or for research).

For the trainer's purposes, perhaps the most useful way of classifying games is whether or not they attempt to simulate reality. For understandable reasons, simulation games, ones where game rules and roles are drawn from real-life, tend not to have predictable outcomes. Non-simulation games, by contrast, involve temporary suspension of real-life rules and roles and the substitution of game rules and roles.

So what's the difference between a role play and a simulation? In a simulation, trainees generally respond to a situation by assuming a role using their own values, attitudes, beliefs and behavior patterns. For example, a trainee might be assigned the title of manager in a simulation where his or her subordinates are nonproductive. Although the label of manager would be assigned, the trainee would be given a part to act out as a manager. This type of role play is generally less effective than simulation in encouraging growth, because, unlike simulation, it doesn't promote abstract thinking and encourage players to react

with their *own* feelings. Pat Eady, principal in Experiential Learning Methods, Inc., Detroit, and developer of numerous games, points out that people don't learn from their experiences but rather by thinking about them. By their very nature, simulations induce reflection on seldom-analyzed situations.

Why use a game?

Experience is the teacher. One of the advantages of simulation games, as opposed to several other interactive instructional design formats, is the extent to which they encourage trainees to explore their attitudes and values. It's very difficult, for example, to escape the feelings and emotions that accompany the tension between players of Value Options, a card game designed by New York City-based Mobley, Luciani and Associates. This game questions and explores values in light of their applicability to the choices day-to-day events force us to make. Played over a two- to four-hour period, Value Options has three critical stages. The first requires participants to upgrade the value cards they randomly receive. This is accomplished either by trading cards with other players or by trading and picking up cards from a large table. At the conclusion of this "upgrading" phase, each player holds at least two cards that reflect his or her values.

The second stage, called community building, requires individuals to form themselves into groups based on shared values. These groups then report on what commonality pulled them together.

The last and final stage, depolarization, requires each participant to pair up with someone holding a value that is in opposition to his or her own. These two individuals then work toward establishing a new value statement both parties can agree with. These stages crystallize the processes involved in making a value choice, recognizing its implications, and finding either common interests or compromise with participants holding different values.

Games can help trainees grasp total course content. An advantage of using a game at the beginning of a workshop is that it can give trainees a chance to experience the whole before discussing the parts. For example, starting a cross-cultural training session with a simulation game such as Bafa' Bafa', is a great way to prepare people, being transferred abroad, for the frustrations, joys and insights that come from contact with a foreign culture. Participants usually spend an hour playing the game and then up to five hours discussing how stereotypes are formed and perpetuated. Further discussion examines these stereotypes in a non-threatening and constructive manner.

Games can help "test" performance, either before or after the learning experience. Playing a game at the beginning of a course allows the trainer to identify those skills which already exist and those which need to be strengthened. Playing the game at the end of the course enables the trainer to assess the instructional experience— how well the trainee can transfer training knowledge to on-the-job skills. Incidentally, game experts tend to agree that the closer a game's structure simulates reality the more likely and extensive the transfer of training.

What's the correlation between game success and work success? "The closer the situation is to real-life, the more valid an observation you can make," says Francine Foster, vice president of Creative Learning Systems, San Diego, and one of several game producers interviewed by TRAINING for this article. "A good simulation is a compressed reality. Typical behaviors can be highlighted because of the highly structured situation. This, then, becomes a powerful diagnostic tool when assessed by a qualified outside observer." The trick, though, is in making sure the trainees realize the objective. Lynn O'Mura, a product manager at Detroit-based Creative Universal, marketer of the well-known Performulations workshop that includes the use of Tinker Toys, believes the trainer or facilitator must not only monitor the rules, but also be aware of what the transfer relationship is between the game objective and the job skills— and help the trainees see that relationship, too. "People can't walk out after the game feeling the same way or doing the same thing they did when they walked in," she says. "If they do, it has only been an enjoyable experience for the trainees and a dog and pony show for the trainers."

Starting and ending the game

Without the right beginning, even the best of training games is bound to end badly. For one thing, some people just don't like games and may not be willing to go all the way through one before learning the moral. Others find it hard to believe that playing with, let's say, Tinker Toys, can have anything useful to teach them about being better managers. The way you introduce and begin the game therefore, is crucially important.

Erica Keeps, Detroit-based consultant and long-time game user, offers some pointers, based on her experiences as corporate training manager for Hudson's, the Detroit-based retail chain. She utilized Performulations as part of a workshop on improving subordinates' performance. This simulation involves Tinker Toys and blindfolds— not typical management tools.

"What we found is that if the Tinker Toys are out on the table as people are coming into the classroom, someone will start playing with them. It's usually been so long since they've had an opportunity to play, that they really get into it. By the time the class starts, elaborate models have been built, usually with the help of the person sitting next to them. Then we announce the session by welcoming trainees to Tinker Toys-101. This breaks the ice."

Sometimes getting into a game involves carefully planned rounds or phases that not only allow role switching and the practice of different solutions to the problem, but also set some psychic distance between players. This is particularly important when the game is being used in a team-building effort and the group is feeling some tension or hostility just by being together in the same room.

Generally, effective games end logically— for example, when the time is up, the goal is achieved, the task is completed, or the competition is eliminated. Or do they? Many game users believe that the most important learning doesn't even start until the playing ends and the debriefing begins. Talking about what has just happened is crucially important, explains Foster, not only to bring the learning into consciousness, but also to take advantage of peer pressure toward positive change. Join, the name of one of Creative Learning Systems' games designed to boost effective teamwork, uses a two-step debriefing model. Debriefing guide cards are used to help each team debrief themselves and then the leader debriefs the class en-masse.

What makes a game good?

Most people find games enjoyable because they provide relief from real-life pressures and usually contain an element of chance, the latter because of the game's structure and/or the unpredictability of other people's responses. Then, too, games users TRAINING contacted agree that the most enjoyable and effective games they've used tend 1) to be sophisticated enough to hold player interest and 2) not to be so detailed as to thwart natural response. (The structural elements of a successful game are covered in the accompanying boxed article.)

Frequently, good games have at least two agendas, the first being the rules, roles and goals that are announced to the participants. The other agenda, usually not mentioned to the trainees until the end of the debriefing, is the moral lesson the trainees are supposed to learn. Take, for example, a game called Desert Survival used at Hudsons. Players are told that their plane has crashed in the desert, that the only item on their agenda is to survive and that only certain items are available to help them. In the first part of the game, players must decide how to survive individually. Then the game is replayed with groups. In both cases, answers are compared with those of a group of experts. Pat Eady, developer of the game, has found that invariably teams "survive" better than do individuals.

The announced mission is, of course, simply to survive. The "hidden agenda"— the lesson participants invariably learn only at the end—is that teamwork pays off and boosts their chances of survival.

When is a game not a game?

Like any other training medium, games are not a panacea. Used with the wrong group at the wrong time, a game may do more harm than good. Used appropriately, they can be an enjoyable and effective teaching technique. As Erica Keeps reminds us, though, it's important to remember not to expect a game to do much more than make participants aware of the consequences of their actions. A game, she points out, does not set up strategies for change.

Reprinted from TRAINING, December 1978

THE NAME OF THE GAME IS FRAME

Framegames provide an easy-to-use structure for developing interactive training exercises

BY HANK HUTSON
AND DIANE DORMANT

As a trainer, you take pride in your resourcefulness. You adapt, borrow and create successful training activities to fit the needs of the moment. You customize training designs to meet shifting priorities and tight schedules. And where do you get these activities and designs? Often from your own past experiences. Every trainer has a personal kitbag of training tools developed over the years. A Framegame is just such a tool. And, since it is a highly effective, efficient, and versatile tool, we hope you'll add it to your kitbag.

Framegames are interactive training techniques that can be pressed into service without fuss or fanfare. Framegames provide structure which is open for your own content. You can use them in various ways— icebreaking, team-building, idea-generating, problem-solving— and you can easily load or insert content that is relevant to your training topic.

The concept of a Framegame is apparent in its two root words. A frame is an open structure made for enclosing something. In a Framegame, the open structure is a game. And, as in other games, there are rules, play-like rather than real-world events, and contested outcomes. But the "something" to be enclosed— i.e., the content of the Framegame— is left to you. Framegames are content-free until you put them to work. Bumper Clumper is an example.

You can readily see why Bumper Clumper is a Framegame. It has rules and it is a simulated rather than a real-world exercise. (Obviously, no one is going to derive a set of training directives from such a procedure alone.) Furthermore, Bumper Clumper is a contest, although not a very serious one. Individuals vie for "best" cards, and groups vie for the most amusing or profound slogan.

As for Bumper Clumper's "content-free" quality, note that the kicker statement "Training should..." could be written to suit any topic about which the participants have knowledge or opinions: "Affirmative action should...," "Management should...," "Our department should...," "Our competition should...." Participants should be reminded that negative statements are acceptable, too: "Affirmative action should *not*..." and so forth. The possibilities are as rich as your imagination and, in our experience as trainers, the outcomes are always lively.

Bumper Clumper, like most Framegames, is simple to load with content, easy to lead and highly flexible. It can be used at the beginning of a seminar to get things off to a roaring start, after lunch as a "wake-em-up," or at the end of a session for evaluation. Again, the frame and the game are there— all you need to do is plug in the content.

Let's look at another Framegame.

Bumper Clumper

Possible Uses: Icebreaker; initial focus on training topic; perception check of attitudes and opinions; evaluation exercise

Participants: Desired minimum of 15 (could be as few as 5, as many as 200)

Time: 20-40 minutes (depends on number of participants)

Materials: Index cards (about 5 per participant), flip chart paper, markers, masking tape

Rules:
1. Pass out 3 cards to each person.
2. Instruct participants to write one opinion on each card to complete a statement. (Example: "Training should...") These can be opinions held by the participants themselves or by others.
3. Take up cards and mix with handwritten "sweeteners." (To make the procedure failsafe as well as to enrich it, prepare extra cards ahead of time, twice as many as there are participants.)
4. Redistribute 3 cards to each person. Instruct them to prioritize cards in order of their perceived importance. Meanwhile, the trainer should arrange all leftover cards, right side up, on a large table.
5. Instruct them to improve their hands to better represent their own thinking by exchanging cards with those on the table. They must always have a total of 3 cards.
6. Instruct them to improve their hands by exchanging cards with each other. (Optional rule: participants must hold hands to make exchanges, and once they take a hand they have to make an exchange.) Participants should try to see as many cards as they can.
7. Instruct them to form coalitions. Say, "Now you know something about what others value with regard to the topic. Let's see if you can find kindred souls who will agree as a group on a total of 3 cards, discarding all others."
8. Ask each coalition to make a "bumper sticker" (using markers and chart paper) based upon the 3 chosen cards which communicate the group's position.
9. Ask them to join in a large group show-and-tell. Each coalition should select a representative to read the 3 cards and to present the bumper sticker to be displayed on the wall. Discussion or reactions may follow.

R.S.V.P.

Possible Uses: Way to elicit problems or solutions in a group with common concerns or expertise.

Participants: Any number of small groups formed into circles (5 persons in each group is a workable number)

Time: 20-40 minutes

Materials: Index cards (5 per participant), letter envelopes (1 each)

Rules:
1. Pass out blank envelope and 5 index cards to each person.
2. Ask each person to make a personal mark on the back of the envelope (e.g., a letter or squiggle) for later identification.
3. Say, "On the front of the envelope, write a question or pose a problem for which you want an answer or solution." (Of course, the question or problem should lie within the training topic selected—the content of this Framegame.)
4. Instruct them to pass the envelopes to the right.
5. Say, "Read the envelope, write an answer or solution on an index card, and insert the card in the envelope."
6. Instruct them to pass envelopes to the right again and, without looking at the card in the envelope, repeat step 5.
7. Continue the process (Steps 5 and 6) for several turns.
8. Instruct them to place the envelopes face down in the center of the table and retrieve their own.
9. Ask them to read and prioritize the cards.
10. Ask them to take turns sharing favorite responses, adding new thoughts, posing additional questions.

The Great Debate

Possible Uses: Final evaluative event in a lengthy training session; a safe way to elicit negative as well as positive comments.

Participants: At least 18 preferred (as few as 12 or as many as 75 possible)

Time: 20-30 minutes

Materials: As many index cards as persons. Sets of 6 cards are marked with plus or minus in 3 different colors. (Example: One card marked with a red plus, one card with a red minus, one card with a blue plus, etc.)

Rules:
1. Pass out one card to each person.
2. Explain procedure: "You are going to debate such-and-such along three dimensions. Those of you who have a red plus on your card will go to one corner of the room and list the positive aspects of the topic along the dimension indicated for red. Those who have a red minus will go to a different corner and list the negative aspects of the same dimension. (The same for the blue dimension, etc.)"
3. Write dimensions and related colors on a flip chart or blackboard.
4. Allow 10 minutes for preparation, then ask each of the groups to choose a spokesperson.
5. After all have returned to their seats (or seated themselves with their debate group), call for the debate. Ask for the negative side of a dimension first, the positive second. Each spokesperson makes a one-minute presentation. End with the safest and/or most fun dimension.

R.S.V.P. is content-free, and it can serve many purposes. For example, it has been used to generate alternative solutions to world food problems, to management problems, to sales problems. It can be used to anticipate possible results of proposed courses of action. Because of its anonymous procedures, people can "green light" or "bad mouth" in relative safety.

Another value of R.S.V.P. is to provide a mechanism for people to solicit responses to a question or problem of specific concern to them. An alternative strategy is for the group or the trainer to select a set of general problems (perhaps five) ahead of time and to write these on the envelopes for each table. All tables then are working on the same set of questions, and fruitful large group discussion can follow.

Framegames are easy to use and they can result in motivating, effective sessions. Framegames are not,

nor are they meant to be, heavyweight techniques to be taken very seriously. But they are once-over-lightly exercises that can serve several purposes, not the least of which is to have fun. (What's wrong with that?) Perhaps the best use of a Framegame is to set the stage for another training technique that is designed to carry a more substantial instructional or decision-making load.

Remember to keep Framegames in proper perspective. As the facilitator, be ready to change a rule or invent a procedure on the spot. Be flexible about time. Don't let things bog down.

The Great Debate, like other Framegames, has been used in many settings with a wide range of topics and dimensions. At TRAINING '79, we used it as a concluding activity for our Framegame workshop. The topic was TRAINING '79 itself and we used four dimensions: facilities, ideas/content,

people and New York. You can imagine the foolishness sparked by that fourth dimension, but the other three dimensions provided a forum for some useful evaluation of the conference.

If you try them, you'll like them—and want more. A good source for additional Framegames is Harold D. Stolovitch and Sivasailam Thiagarajan's book, *Framegames*, published by Educational Technology, Englewood Cliffs, NJ. Also, once you have the notion of a content-free frame, you begin to look at all structured activities a bit differently. For example, John E. Jones and J. William Pfeiffer's two series—the *Annual Handbook for Group Facilitators* and *A Handbook of Structured Experiences for Human Relations Training*, published by University Associates, La Jolla, CA—are rich in activities which can be simplified and adapted to new content.

Reprinted from TRAINING, April 1981

GAMES MANAGERS PLAY

How's this for an addition to your list of
management-training options:
The make-believe company that comes in a box

BY JACK GORDON

At Monsanto and Union Pacific and SmithKline Beckman Corp., groups of managers are agonizing over the national light-bulb situation. Their in-baskets are stuffed with memos about car windshields. They attend meetings at which the hot topic is an unsettling development in the optical-fiber market. They work at their desks, dictating memos and using their phones. They lobby their superiors, delegate to their subordinates, promote their ideas, pick holes in other peoples's ideas and slog their way toward consensus. It goes on for days. Everyone is deadly earnest.

And none of it has one damn thing to do with Monsanto or Union Pacific or SmithKline Beckman—except that, in a way, it does. They're playing a game called Looking Glass.

At Combustion Engineering in Connecticut, at Holiday Inns in Memphis and at Phillip Morris in New York, teams of managers huddle around personal computers, plugging in figures to signal decisions that will have a dramatic effect on a company for years to come. Will they schedule additional shifts on the factory floor or invest in expanded plant capacity? Should they accept a 3% return on sales this year in exchange for rapid growth or grab a 6% return in 1985 and settle for a slower five-year growth rate?

None of it has a damn thing to do with combustion or motels or tobacco. The companies whose futures these managers are fiddling with exist only in a computer program called the Strategic Management Game.

In other companies, and at public seminars around the country, junior and senior managers from all sorts of organizations are sitting around tables jockeying for market shares in a board game that looks like a cross between Monopoly and roulette.

In a sense, there's nothing really new about any of it. For more than two decades, for instance, graduate students in business schools across the country have spent weeks at a time running elaborate, seemingly realistic companies that come to life only when somebody turns on a mainframe computer.

In the business world, there's nothing new about role plays or in-basket exercises or the use of experiential learning concepts to train and evaluate managers. The activity in a number of company assessment centers bears a strong resemblance to the activity in Looking Glass. And as far as outright games are concerned, how many management trainers have never heard of Desert Survival or Lost on the Moon or Performulations?

What's in a game?

In another sense, however, there is something new on the management gaming scene. Mostly, it's a matter of availability. For the past six years or so, increasing numbers of American managers have been exposed to games and simulations whose cost, complexity of structure, length of play, broadness of purpose and "fidelity" in terms of simulating a real business environment place them in an entirely different category from the cheaper, simpler and less ambitious card-game-and-Tinkertoy-type exercises of the past.

Joseph Wolfe, a professor of management at the University of Tulsa and president-elect of the Association for Business Simulation and Experiential Learning (ABSEL), puts it this way: "Desert Survival and Lost on the Moon are short little experiential exercises; they teach you a little lesson about leadership or decision-making. Looking Glass is a full-fledged, organization-building simulation."

The games we're talking about here also are in a different category from the simpler, more narrowly focused simulations built into some management-oriented computer-based training programs that allow learners to practice the specific skills being taught: risk-taking, decision-making, negotiating, etc.

In many ways, the entries in this semi-new category of "games" are entirely different from one another as well. Looking Glass was developed by the Center for Creative Leadership in Greensboro, NC, and has been on the market since 1979. In the words of Mike Lombardo, one of its creators, it is a sort of "living in-basket." Computers play no part in the simulation itself, although the game administrator uses one afterward to measure a variety of results, including the financial performance of the simulated company and the quality of decisions made by participants.

The same is true of the Financial Services Industry (FSI) simulation. A closely related program developed by the New York University School of Business with help from the Looking Glass team, FSI was released only last year. It is geared specifically to financial and service companies.

Neither Looking Glass nor FSI can accurately be called games, since neither pits individuals or teams against one another.

In other cases, both computers and competition play central roles. The Strategic Management Game (SMG), released in 1981 when some instructors from the University of Pennsylvania's Wharton School of Business formed the Strategic Management Group of Philadelphia, is a hands-on microcomputer simulation used in a seminar format. A similar approach is taken by Planning & Control Inc. (PCI) of New York City, which offers several computer simulations and a variety of materials and services for the seminars intended to accompany them. A few companies, including Hewlett-Packard, have created their own intricate, computerized management simulations for in-house use.

The Sony Management Game (called the International Management Game when it left Japan and was released for public consumption in 1982) is a table game that uses plastic chips, cards and a roulette-like game board. Sold by the Sony Management Systems Co. of New York, it, too, usually is marketed with a seminar package.

To somebody like Wolfe, for whom the subject of experiential learning is almost a vocation in itself, the Sony product barely qualifies as a simulation. "A glorified board game," he sniffs, and one with little direct "transferability" to a real work situation. Indeed, its level of realism may be lower than that of advanced computer simulations, and definitely ranks far below that of Looking Glass or FSI. But in terms of cost ($600 per person in an open seminar; $8,000 to $12,000 for delivery to up to 42 players in a particular company), time frame, scope and intended purpose, Sony's game shares some of the characteristics that set the breed apart from less ambitious experiential exercises.

First, its playing time, in the structured seminar format, is measured in days, instead of in minutes or hours. Second, instead of "teaching you a little lesson" about a particular soft-skill subject—decision-making, time management, communication, intercultural awareness or whatever—it immerses players in a range of issues that add up to a broad-based crash course in general management.

The Sony game teaches strategic planning and financial analysis. Players make decisions about hiring, purchasing, manufacturing, marketing, sales and other functions. The Strategic Management Game, which can be played at five different levels of complexity, plunges participants into financial planning, introduces them to specific marketing concepts (product life cycles, product portfolio management, etc.), and makes them adopt strategies for running operations ranging from manufacturing to health care.

Looking Glass and FSI are both geared more toward pinpointing and analyzing the behaviors of individuals and groups than toward teaching specific "hard-management" subjects. But again, strategic and tactical planning are very much part of the

---

The most involving ones teach participants, on a gut level, how an organization works.

---

packages, and trainees must make all sorts of decisions that affect the operations and profitability of "real" companies.

In short, these "games" propose to teach subjects traditionally handled mostly by business schools and avoided by all but a handful of company training departments. More to the point in the "What's new?" area, in-house trainers who did tackle this type of material certainly did not expect to find it in commercially available packages.

A central selling point of all of these simulations, including Hewlett-Packard's in-house model, is that they purport to teach managers in specific functional areas how to see their organizations from a top-management perspective. They force players to *experience* the ways in which a decision by the marketing department, for example, can affect the production or R&D departments. The most involving ones, say their proponents, give participants a gut-level awareness of how a business organization works—how the parts make up the whole.

"Involvement," sometimes to an intense degree, is another common characteristic. Looking Glass and FSI, especially, according to vendors and users alike, become so real to participants that they tend to forget the whole thing is a game. "For about the first half-hour," says Karen Hartman, one of FSI's developers, "FSI is a role play. After that, the players *are* the company. They become completely wrapped up in their roles."

There is at least one measure, aside from the obvious ones, by which some of the new games differ from others. You might call it "open-endedness" vs. "direction." In the Sony game, which stresses Japanese-style management principles, and in PCI's computer simulations, there are definite "correct" choices to be made every step of the way. Sony's board game and PCI's software are loaded to "pay off" for participants who do things the way the seminar instructor just said they should be done. First you get the instruction, then you play the game.

With SMG, some strategies discussed in the seminar are programmed to work better than others, but there's no such thing as a single "correct" approach to the game. "There are right *answers* to a given problem, but no right *answer*," as Strategic Management Group president Joseph Gekoski puts it.

As for Looking Glass, the only information participants generally get before they are tossed into the simulation is some basic orientation. The facilitators tell you diddley-squat about how you *should* play; they just want to see how you *do* play.

Is there a trend in the making? The vendors certainly think so. "Simulation training is being accepted by senior-management people," says Hartman. "They're going to training departments and saying, 'Look into this.' Simulations have proven themselves as useful tools. Now it's a question of how they can be successfully implemented."

ABSEL's Wolfe agrees that it's an idea whose time has come. He not only believes that American companies are becoming increasingly enamored of these broad-based business simulations, he thinks he knows why.

"It ties in to the rediscovery of the individual manager," he says. Spurred by the national fascination with Japanese management prac-

LESSONS FROM LOOKING GLASS

BY JACK GORDON

As far as "packaged," commercially available training programs go, the Center for Creative Leadership's Looking Glass simulation and New York University's FSI appear to form a category of their own (see main story). To the best of our knowledge, nothing else on the market can be described as a blood relative to either.

Both, however, are kissing cousins to the in-house assessment centers run by some companies for their own managers. Mike Lombardo, one of Looking Glass' creators, insists that it is not a training program at all, but rather an "evaluation tool." Indeed, the original impetus for its development was an urge to learn more about what it is, exactly, that makes managers effective or ineffective. So after several years of involvement with the "living in-basket," Lombardo ought to have a few insights, right? Judge for yourself.

In Looking Glass, he says, "40 or 50 problems exist at once for a manager. The most typical thing we see is the shotgun approach: The manager worries about 12 problems simultaneously. You get lots of activity and no results.

"Also typical is the very bright, analytical type who figures out the right problem to concentrate on and the right answer to the problem, but then can't sell it to the boss, the management committee, the company president or whomever. A lot of people are really skilled at dealing with subordinates. That's where a lot of training has focused in recent years, and it's had its effects; I've been impressed. Yet when it comes to dealing with peers and superiors—to cajoling, horse trading, influencing people over whom they have no control—they're weak. They're also weak on dealing with other divisions [within their companies]—putting together coalitions and so on."

When it comes to lateral relationships, persuasiveness and "selling up," he continues, "They know how to say the right words about it, but they don't *do* it." For example, many managers know the axiom "If you don't have the right answer, for God's sake don't bluff; say, 'I don't know.'" But in the heat of the moment, Lombardo says, he hears amazingly few "I don't knows," and sees an awful lot of bluffing.

Looking Glass participants work out a "learning contract" with observers before the simulation begins—a few behaviors to which the observer agrees to pay special attention. Often, Lombardo says, managers will have the right perceptions about their strengths and weaknesses, but for the wrong reasons. For example, "One guy said his subordinates told him he was lousy at defining problems. I found he was very analytical—he picked the right facts and so on. But the problem I saw was that he spoke so softly, in a monotone, that they had to get right next to him to hear him. He projected a know-nothing demeanor. Their perception that he didn't provide direction was right, but for the wrong reason."

Another case: "We had a guy who was perfect. A superman. Extremely capable, polite, helpful, made decisions—everything you could want in a manager. We couldn't think of any way we could help him improve anything. But it turned out that people were intimidated by him. Their skills were so inferior to his that they didn't like him. And [in a debriefing session] they told him so. He said he had the same problem on the job.

"I learned from that one," Lombardo says, "that some people are so facile at problem-solving, they make connections so quickly, that they're always three or four steps ahead. They confuse and demoralize other people. So our advice to this guy was about the need for equity in group situations. He needed to be perceived as less godlike. We told him to start asking some questions he already knew the answers to. 'Play dumb a little.'"

Reprinted from TRAINING, July 1985

tices, the enormous success of *In Search of Excellence*, the stress on promoting from within the ranks and other factors, U.S. management thought has come to focus on "entrepreneurship, freedom from bureaucracy and the importance of the individual." According to Wolfe, "It's no longer a matter of someone getting an MBA and sort of automatically becoming a vice president.

"The whole gaming thing," he continues, "brings it down to how people operate and how they work together—to what is unique about people. . . .A good simulation will allow you to see a person's real behavior—it's better than a psychological instrument."

Computer versions

There is a continuing debate about the future of computer-based training—about the primary roles CBT will continue to play in the national training and educational picture once the hype dies down, the smoke clears, we stop being dazzled by computers and start seeing them as tools with specific strengths and limitations. A lot of people believe that the primary benefits of CBT will come in two major areas. One involves expert systems, software programs that act as consultants or diagnosticians "in a box." The other involves complex, highly interactive simulations.

In business schools and even in a few companies, mainframe-computer management simulations date back almost 30 years. "I'm a traditionalist," says Wolfe in response to the proposition that programs such as SMG represent, in some sense, a new phenomenon. "In 1957 the American Management Association put out the first big [computerized] management game. Executives ran the 'Mose Company,' which had two manufacturing plants, shipping, regional sales areas and so on. In the early '60s, IBM created a users group that built simulations for various industries. It was mostly an effort to show more uses for computers, but the simulations were pretty good. All we've done since is make them better, faster and more convenient."

What is new, Wolfe points out, is the personal computer. It is the PC, he feels, together with that "rediscovery of the individual manager," that is responsible for the sudden leap of computer-simulation training into a significant number of companies.

175

The personal computer, Wolfe says, "makes the technology more available and far less expensive. The PC makes it easy to create games and to grab [adapt or download] classic games from mainframe computers."

Among those who perceive a boom in management-simulation training is Judith Polk, marketing manager for a seven-year-old Carlisle, MA company called Simtek. Over the past few years, Polk says, business has taken a pronounced upswing. For fees ranging from $60 to $100 for a one-time test run, Simtek's mainframe will feed a computer-based business simulation to anybody with a microcomputer and a modem. The company's *International Business Games Directory* lists 35 games, with varying degrees of complexity. Most involve four or five "decision periods" lasting about an hour each (a typical decision period represents one year in the life of the simulated company) and are intended for use in a one- or two-day seminar.

The offerings include games developed for Simtek as well as some that have been in circulation for years and are available from other sources. Their levels of specificity vary widely. On the industry-specific end, the directory lists computer-based simulations with names such as "The Oil Industry Game," "The Home Laundry Game" and "The Grain Elevator Management Game." More generic titles include "The Accounting Simulation," "The Financial Management Game" and an old standby, "The Executive Simulation," a manufacturing-based game that, according to Wolfe, is derived from a model developed at UCLA in 1958 and is available in a personal-computer version.

The games embroil participants in issues and concepts ranging from pricing to product-line management, from commodity markets to employee fringe benefits, from bidding strategies to market segmentation.

True to the norm in the simulation-vending business, which is nothing if not customer-driven, Simtek's pricing structure varies according to its delivery options, which vary all over the map. Customers can have the game fed to their terminals by the mainframe computer for a fixed rate of $60 to $90 per trainee, including instructor guides, student manuals, etc. Or they can opt for a time-sharing rate. For an extra charge, Simtek will supply experienced administrators and trainers to conduct the game. Or, for a minimum fee of $10,000, an organization can license a game's software and run it on IBM, DEC or Honeywell equipment. If the client wants to talk customized computer simulations adapted for use by a particular company, Simtek will listen—also true to

---

'It all ties into the rediscovery of the individual manager.'

---

form for the industry.

The proliferation of microcomputers undoubtedly is a major force driving the simulation boom. "We've been in business for seven years," says John Censor, president of PCI, "and up until three years ago we had to leave the word 'computer' out of our sales literature. It made a lot of our human-resource colleagues uncomfortable. Now it has finally become acceptable to say 'computer-based training' out loud."

Four of PCI's five simulations are geared to managers in specialized functions: sales and marketing; financial operations; manufacturing; and "project managers," a group that might include trainers, engineers, data-processing managers and so on, Censor says. The fifth, called Executive Decision Making, cuts across a number of functional areas. The typical simulated period is six months. The average cost, with PCI facilitators running the game and seminar, is about $600 per trainee for a three-day program.

Probably best known among the packaged microcomputer simulations is the Strategic Management Game. SMG's Gekoski describes it as "like Monopoly for Yuppies." But there's a little more to it. Aside from the standard and "premium" versions of the basic game, which simulates five years in the life of a company that makes generic consumer products, there is a manufacturing version, a service version, a health-care version and a wholesale-distribution version. The games and their

wrap-around seminars also can be run in a variety of different ways, depending on whether the client wants to stress finance and accounting, strategic marketing, "executive microcomputing" or other subjects. The seminar versions have been run with as few as 12 players and as many as 200, always with three or four players to a team.

The cost of seminars, with facilitators supplied by the Strategic Management Group, runs between $100 and $200 per participant per day, and the standard seminar lasts three days. For $350, SMG also sells an "Individual Learning Version" of the basic game, which is played by one person on a microcomputer and has a simulated time span of up to 25 years.

The basic idea, Gekoski says, is to "simulate a year in the life of a top manager in a day." And the overall point involves balancing the consequences of short-run vs. long-run thinking. "If you drive up profitability in the short run by failing to invest in things like research and new-product opportunities," he explains, "it can hurt you in the long run."

On the other hand, Gekoski says, "We've had Japanese businessmen play. They tend to take exactly the opposite perspective from U.S. managers. They think in terms of 20 years and are willing to sacrifice profits for the first five. That's going too far overboard. The game's stress is on acceptable margins of return consistent with long-range plans."

At Hewlett-Packard's international headquarters in Palo Alto, CA, an in-house simulation called DivSim, for Division Management Simulation, has been up and running for three years. But the impetus for its creation came earlier.

"Just after the '75-'76 recession," says Bill Nilsson, HP's manager of corporate training and development, "I got a note from our CEO. He sensed a need among some of our functional managers for a better understanding of the steps they could take to respond to downturns in the economy." Not long afterward, at a conference in Geneva, Switzerland, Nilsson ran into an intriguing mainframe simulation. Developed in Scotland, it was used to teach economics to high-school kids. "They could run a country's economy—vary government spending, interest rates, the money supply, and see what happened."

Nilsson enlisted the Scottish economist who had designed the thing ("There's less difference than you think between a country's economy and a manufacturing company's."), turned the draft version over to HP's own people for modification and customization, and eventually had himself a very slick computer model of the Hewlett-Packard Corp.

Four teams of seven players compete to ring up the highest marks on a complicated scoring system that considers factors such as profit generation and the shape the company is in at the end of a simulated five-year period in terms of assets, human resources, R&D projects in the works, etc. Each team has a general manager and six functional managers who head divisions corresponding to HP's. Since one of the game's main purposes is to teach functional managers how the pieces of the company fit together and affect one another, nobody is allowed to play his real-life role.

"In a high-tech industry," Nilsson says, "you grow up in one function. If you grew up in marketing, you don't have a thorough understanding of the problems of your counterpart in manufacturing or R&D. The point is to teach the interrelation of functions."

Or rather, that's one point. Because Hewlett-Packard has a no-layoff policy, it's also vital that managers understand "the other levers they have control of when the economy goes sour." In DivSim, the economy—and demand for HP products—can go as sour as the trainer wants it to. And the lessons are many. For example, Nilsson says, there's the one about "placing orders in anticipation of need vs. real need. If you're backlogged on inventory when the economy goes down, you can really get whipsawed."

The cost of it all? "Five or six person-years of time," Nilsson estimates, and an investment of more than $200,000.

Living In-Baskets

Looking Glass was conceived in 1976 when the Navy asked the Center for Creative Leadership to develop a simulation of a "typical" organization for research purposes. "The purpose was to try to find out what it is about effective managers that makes them so," explains Mike Lombardo. "Is it leadership? Decision-making? If so, how and why?"

To design the simulation, he continues, "We needed to know things like, who do managers have to deal with? How does government impinge upon them? How does foreign competition affect them? We tried to get a sense of what our choices were, then narrowed them down to typical, ge-

---

'People are adaptable as hell. This "creatures of habit" stuff is nonsense.'

---

neric problems that you could present to most managers and they'd say, 'Yeah, I deal with problems like this.'

"Then we talked to lots of senior managers and asked, 'What problems are lying on your desk right now?' They told us about everything from customer complaints to people quitting to billion-dollar deals. The trivial and the vital.

"We settled," he says, "on a glass company."

The company has three separate divisions with different levels of "market volatility." The highly volatile high-tech division makes things like optical fibers and is affected by all sorts of market forces; a very stable division makes light bulbs and window glass; and the intermediate consumer group (auto glass, bottles, etc.) ties its sales to consumption rates in various markets.

"Put a manager in any one of the three," says Lombardo, "and he'll adapt to the environment he's in. The first thing we learned was that people are adaptable as hell. This 'creatures of habit' stuff is nonsense."

The Looking Glass simulation usually involves 20 participants and runs for two full days and one evening. Lombardo calls it "six hours of experiences with 10 hours of feedback." Although learning is very much the point, it is much more an evaluation exercise than a training exercise; it is intended to pinpoint the strengths and weaknesses of individual participants—to set the stage for later train-

ing in a variety of specific skills.

Each player goes into the simulation having made a prior "learning contract" with a trainer/observer. The contract involves specific behaviors the learner wants the observer to watch for. For example, "I'm afraid I don't show much confidence in myself. I don't persist in my points, I'm hesitant to make decisions, I don't come across as having faith in what I'm doing." (See accompanying story, "Lessons From Looking Glass.")

The players, typically managers from the same organization who don't ordinarily work together, get an introduction to the glass company, including a slide show about its various products and an annual report. Then each is assigned (by prearrangement with the client) to one of the company's 20 top-management roles (president, vice president of the high-tech division, etc.). They go to their offices, each equipped with a desk, a phone and a full in-basket.

"After that," Lombardo says, "people can do whatever they choose. . . . We had one guy who sat down and wrote 56 memos. Never talked to anyone, never left his desk. We didn't interfere. We figure that's typical behavior for this guy."

There are "ghost roles" for trainers who man the switchboards and can provide additional information about some problems and events. The players can call meetings, confer with one another, build coalitions or whatever. There *are* "correct" ways to play, Lombardo says, "but 'correct' involves picking the right problems to work on and working on them the right way."

It is largely the freedom of choice allowed participants that differentiates this simulation from traditional assessment-center approaches (see "Training Terms" department in this issue). "Looking Glass is a type of assessment center," Lombardo says, "but for developmental purposes only. In an assessment center, everybody goes through exactly the same experience; everybody has the same title, so all meetings are between equals; you have interviews and in-basket exercises that you *have to do*. In Looking Glass, everybody has a different role; everyone is not equal. And you're not told what to do. There are plenty of problems that generate all sorts of action, but the action isn't forced."

As usual, the price tag for this one varies according to all sorts of factors. A five-day course at the Center for Creative Leadership's Greensboro headquarters normally costs $1,750 per participant, including meals. Companies have licensed the simulation to use for in-house management development programs for fees running into the $40,000-$50,000 range, including trial runs by the center's personnel, training of staff facilitators and so on.

New York University's FSI simulation is structured very much like Looking Glass. For about $15,000 (delivered by FSI staff at the site of the customer's choice), the standard three-day package places 25 participants in the top roles of two financial companies—"Metrobank" and a securities firm called "Investcorp." FSI was designed specifically to appeal to managers in financial industries, but NYU is trying to interest customers from a broad range of service companies.

Like Looking Glass, FSI focuses on evaluation, but it has more specific instructional goals. As Lombardo puts it, "Looking Glass is not designed to teach you how to run a glass company. It deals with general management, not specific content. FSI teaches you how to run a financial company."

The First Union Corp. of Charlotte, NC has been running Looking Glass for six years (under a licensing arrangement), and used the Metrobank portion of FSI last fall. As First Union's five-day Looking Glass program is constructed, the emphasis is almost entirely on self-assessment. Specifically, the idea is to help managers at all levels learn to deal more effectively with change—the changes wrought by deregulation being a major issue in the banking business these days.

"The question we're always being asked," says Sally Johnston, the cor-

---

'We had one guy who sat down and wrote 56 memos. He never left his desk.'

---

poration's vice president of training and development, "is, 'What can bankers get out of a manufacturing-company simulation?' Actually, one of Looking Glass' greatest benefits to us is that it's *not* about banking. The players have to learn another business, and very quickly they're forced to fall back on [generic] management skills. It isolates the ways in which they'd manage *anything.*"

The purpose of putting 12 manag-

ers through the Metrobank program, Johnston explains, had more to do with training than with evaluation. "Most of them had already been through Looking Glass," she says. "At least the way we used it, FSI was for training."

Both simulations, she feels, are "well researched and well supported." Both have impressed the participating managers. However, she warns, for either of the simulations to be successful, "you need trainers with very strong group-process skills. Every run is different. Groups take different tacks. The trainer can't try to squeeze the same training or debriefing into each group session."

That comment leads us back to ABSEL's Joseph Wolfe, who shall have the last word about these general-management simulations, computerized and otherwise. While the word "facilitator" gets tossed around by a lot of trainers who do little more than stand at the front of a classroom and deliver canned lectures, the value of many complex simulations can be tapped only if the people running them do indeed break from the standard "instructor" pattern.

Simulations, Wolfe says, "change the role of the trainer. It's *hard* to be a facilitator. Instead of doing your thing, you have to study [each individual] and come in at *his* level."

Reprinted from TRAINING, July 1985

DISCOVERY LEARNING: OF NEW MATH AND ANDRAGOGY

The idea is that students learn better when they actively participate in and manage their own learning

BY BEVERLY GEBER

Let's imagine you're a teacher who wants to instruct a class of fifth-graders on U.S. geography. Having just heard about the discovery learning method (let's also say you've been out of the country for awhile), you decide to try it.

You give your students a blank map of the North Central states; it contains only tracings of rivers and lakes, along with notes about the location and type of natural resources. You ask them where the principal cities, railroads and highways would go. Not only do you ask them to locate cities, but you make them justify their decisions to the others in the class. After an hour of raucous discussion, you snap open a detailed map of the United States. Immediately, one student shouts, "I was right! There *is* a big city at the end of the pointing-down lake." That student has just "discovered" Chicago on the shores of Lake Michigan.

In describing that late-1950s' experiment, which contrasted discovery learning with traditional expository learning, psychologist and discovery learning advocate Jerome S. Bruner argues that the group that used discovery learning rationally induced that cities spring up where there are water, natural resources, and items to be processed and shipped. Students in the other group were passive recep-

tacles for arbitrary knowledge. Bruner says there's no contest: Students who manage their own learning and use their existing knowledge to "discover" new information retain knowledge longer and learn *how* to think.

The term discovery learning may have lost some of its cachet since its euphoric phase in the 1960s and early '70s, discredited by some failures to apply it in the school system. But the ideas behind it live on in the training world. Its basic principles keep surfacing in various forms: critical thinking, problem-solving strategies, small-group process, inquiry learning, on-the-job training, even andragogy.

So, a little history. Bruner was discovery learning's main guru and head cheerleader. He argued that children learn best when they couple their existing knowledge with problem-solving techniques to "discover" new information through trial-and-error. His book, *The Process of Education* (Random House, 1960), examined the discovery method in mathematics and sciences, giving rise to the dreaded "innovation" that flummoxed parents for an entire decade: "New Math."

New Math is a perfect example of discovery learning. Its proponents argued that it made no sense to force children to memorize multiplication tables and algebraic formulas by rote. Instead, they proposed "set theory," which tried to explain the number

system by using the concept of groups, or sets. Since school-age children were already familiar with the idea of sets—sets of building blocks, sets of crayons—the concept was supposed to bridge the gap between the real world and the abstract world of mathematics. In other words, children would find patterns in new information that would correspond to mental templates they were already using.

The discovery model of learning was quite different from the expository instructional models common to the 1950s, in which teachers stood before the students and dispensed information like gumballs. It was deductive learning, a planned progression of information in which the general principles were taught first; specifics and hands-on experience came later. For instance, students had to learn the principles of Spanish grammar before they could speak or write the language. Discovery learning reversed the traditional model: It was an inductive process that offered hands-on experience first, on the assumption that theory makes more sense if you have some experience with the specifics.

To Bruner, the most important part of knowledge was the *process* of getting it. He objected to the expository method that treated knowledge as a *product*. He argued that when you teach students how to think and force them to decipher knowledge on their own, it becomes an invaluable learning method they can use all their lives. Moreover, it might take them longer to grasp a piece of information, but when they do learn they retain information longer.

Once that knowledge is learned, Bruner argues, knowledge transfer can be accomplished across all sorts of boundaries. For instance, if a child can learn the economic concept of balance of trade, it's easy to use that knowledge to understand ecological balance, or political balance of power. Once students can process information in this way, they know how to learn when the teacher isn't around.

So taken were educators by the discovery learning theory that vast numbers of schools were trying the concept in the late '60s and early '70s. Popular wisdom among educators back then was, "Children are naturally curious and they want to learn. Give them freedom and they'll do it on their own. Teachers should play a minimal role." All sorts of modular scheduling, independent study and laissez-faire teaching techniques broke out in the schools.

They were modified, of course, as soon as educators rediscovered that some students were only curious to learn how to slip out of school to visit the nearest doughnut shop. As teachers today supposedly know, one theory of learning doesn't work en masse for all students.

Discovery learning had its critics even during its heyday. Some argued that "guessing" an answer was not an appropriate way to learn a complex task. Others said the method is too inefficient and time-consuming to impart knowledge the teacher could give in five minutes. Still others say it was too easy for wrong conclusions to be reached if the teacher was careless in preparing materials. Later, after the students started heading out to doughnut shops, all the critics seemed to come out of the closet with the same rallying cry: "Back to basics!" Since then, learning by discovery hasn't gotten much press as a learning discipline.

But its concepts keep cropping up because it does work—for some kinds of knowledge and some kinds of students. As a matter of fact, the HRD field, imbued as it is with the concept of andragogy—or adult learning—owes much to the ideas of discovery learning (which, ironically, started out as a *pedagogical* theory).

Malcolm Knowles, perhaps the foremost expert on andragogy, says that adult learners are self-directed problem solvers who learn best when they can relate new information to past experience. That's not a bad definition of discovery learning.

Some modern-day trainers still use the term discovery learning to describe their methods. Fredric H. Margolis, a Washington, DC, independent

---

'New Math' is a perfect example of discovery learning.

---

training consultant, uses it to describe training in which he identifies the kind of problem solving an employee would need to do in a job, then designs a training program that lets those skills blossom.

For instance, when he's teaching loan officers how to evaluate loan applications, he designs a program in which the officers work in small groups to analyze a true-to-life application; later, the instructor leads a discussion that tries to describe why certain methods and judgments are more desirable than others.

"I use [discovery learning] synonymously with andragogy. The reason I don't use the word andragogy is that many of my clients wouldn't understand it," Margolis says.

Actually, it's not just andragogy that owes a debt to discovery learning. All kinds of HRD practices conform to the basic discovery learning idea that students learn better when they actively participate in and manage their own learning. Think about on-the-job training. Or small-group discussions. Or case study work. Even computer-based training. At core, they all embrace the concept that participation helps increase retention of the knowledge.

Maybe those practices aren't "pure" discovery learning, which has a decidedly sink-or-swim flavor. Maybe they could more accurately be called "guided discovery," a concept introduced many years ago to mute the extremist approach of discovery learning zealots. In guided discovery, instructors play a stronger role, giving clues and information along the way as the student tries to discover knowledge. Doesn't that come close to describing the role of trainers today?

Reprinted from TRAINING, March 1987

THE DISCOVERY METHOD

Developed from the scientific research on
learning behavior in older adults,
the Discovery method is probably the most
carefully studied innovation in
learning technology since
programmed instruction

BY R.M. BELBIN

The Discovery method refers to a style of teaching that allows the pupil to learn by finding out principles and relationships for himself. It stands in contrast with the traditional style in which the pupil memorizes what he has read in his books or what the teacher has taught him.

The trouble with general phrases like "finding out for oneself" is that they can be quite misleading. The Discovery method is not at all like "sitting-by-Nellie," for example.

Discovery is planned method

First of all, the Discovery method is a planned method. Its success depends on how well the training designer thinks out the progression of problems which the trainee is required to solve, relates this progression to the capacity of the trainee, and ensures that learning is based on intrinsic rather than extrinsic factors.

By intrinsic one means that the keys to progression in learning are provided within the immediate situation. The trainee does not need to rely on previous knowledge and experience, nor does he depend on outside assistance (i.e., extrinsic factors). The teacher may help the trainee, but only if he requests help. It is better that he should use the intrinsic information rather than that he should be shown or told.

With the trainee finding out through a planned progression of steps and no longer relying on the teacher, it might be said that the Discovery method

bears a closer comparison with programed learning than with "sitting-by-Nellie." But programed learning is a very broad term. It usually refers to a way of presenting information bit by bit to trainees and then testing them regularly to help them to consolidate what they have learned. This has nothing in common with the Discovery method. A systematic presentation of instructions and information does not accord with the idea of Discovery learning.

But while programed learning is sometimes operated along lines that are diametrically opposed to Discovery learning, it can also be designed to incorporate the basic concept of a Discovery learning approach. The essential differences lie in the type of sequences chosen and in the type of problems.

In applying the Discovery method, the initial stage is demanding. One requires a good deal more than a listing and analysis of all that has to be learned. First the training designer has to identify the crucial concepts and remove all other nonessentials so that the training material can be appreciated in its most simple form.

But the second stage is the most difficult: The training designer has to get inside the learning situation and decide what are the principal obstacles to understanding. It is very hard to envisage these obstacles in advance with any accuracy. The more the expert knows, the more out of touch he is liable to be with the learning problems of those who are starting from scratch. The training designer must observe the problems of trainees and understand the reasons behind them.

Step three is the stage at which our training designs are fashioned. There are innumerable alternatives. The selection of our methods will depend on the information we have gathered about trainee problems and on our knowledge of learning generally.

Stage four is the testing of the pro-

In the Swedish project, the job of scribing was selected for the experimental study. Scribing is a part of the manufacture of, usually, single metal objects in which a worker transfers the object's profile to a metal blank with a sharp tool. The trainees chosen for the study were taken from a larger group undertaking a basic course for metal industry employees in two training centers. In all, 45 trainees participated in the project, 32 of them in two control groups, one trained by an instructor and the other by a programed self-study course. The remaining 13 were trained by the Discovery method. All of the trainees were divided into groups of younger workers under 30 years of age and of older workers 40 and older and into groups of more and of less than average ability as measured by a special test. The experiment ran for a week. Both control groups received three days of instruction, the Discovery group two days. On the fourth day a reproduction test was given in which all trainees scribed a nonadjustable spanner wrench from a drawing similar to one they had drawn under instruction. On the final day another test was given in which five new items were scribed. This final test was completed at only one of the training centers. The best results in the reproduction test were achieved by the younger workers in the able group who had learned through programed instruction and by the older workers in the able group who had been taught by instructor. Among the other groups, those who had been taught by instructor fared better than those who had learned by the other methods. The picture changed, however, when the criterion of learning changed to refer to comprehension, or the ability to apply knowledge to a different task. In the final test, the instructor-trained groups lost their advantage and were displaced by those trained by Discovery methods. These results suggest that the "best" training method may depend on the nature of the test and on the age and level of ability of trainees.

gram with real trainees in pilot trials. It is more than a formality. I can hardly remember a case in our training program where this has not led to some modifications or additional finishing touches.

Let's take a look at a concrete illustration of the Discovery method. To find out the potential of the Discovery method for retraining older workers in industry, the Organization for Economic Cooperation and Development which is based in Paris, sponsored an industrial experiment in four countries. British Railways provided the project in the United Kingdom. Other projects were carried out in Sweden, Austria and the United States.

The demonstration project in the United Kingdom involved the training of 83 steam locomotive drivers (aged between 29 and 62) in electrical theory in preparation for their transfer to driving diesel-electric trains. Forty-nine of the drivers were "older" learners aged 40 and over, of whom 31 were trained by Discovery methods and 18 by traditional methods; then, we had a group of 34 under-40s, with 16 trained by Discovery methods and 18 trained by traditional methods.

Give controlled experience

The idea was to give the trainees controlled experience so as to allow them to discover principles of electricity for themselves. Trainees worked in pairs. I will confine the illustration to one of the test boards they used, Board

Three. This carried a battery, an ammeter, a switch, three pairs of motors connected as three series pairs in parallel, isolating links for each pair of motors and the accessory circuitry to simulate the elements of the power circuit of a diesel-electric locomotive. The ammeter was calibrated to simulate current consumption in an actual locomotive. In brief, we had motors, which we could isolate, linked in a circuit with an ammeter to give us current readings.

The trainees were directed by the instructor to make various changes to the apparatus and to make observations of the consequent meter-readings and of the behavior of the apparatus. From time to tome conclusions had to be drawn and some simple statement completed. The instructor was available to help out with difficulties, but he gave no information. His response to questions was usually to ask a further question, to rephrase his directions and so on.

From this set-up, the trainees could "discover" a number of things:

- Closing the switch caused all the motors to rotate.
- Isolating one pair of motors caused a current fall of one-third.
- Isolating two pairs caused a current fall of two-thirds.
- Shorting out one motor of a pair caused a spectacular overload.
- Isolating the pair, including the failed motor, ensured a return to safe working at reduced power.
- Attaching the magnetically oper-

ated contact of the adjacent Board Two to appropriate points in the power circuit of Board Three enabled the motors to be stopped or started by an independent control system.

This helped the trainees to understand the principles which were derived from experience of the events. When you conduct one of these sessions, you see that learning is something qualitatively different from what we normally find in the classroom. The trainees working in pairs on the tasks tended to engage in excited discussion. They confirmed each other's readings, checked and rechecked the behavior of the equipment, argued and pointed out discoveries, some quite simple ones. Many of their comments were illuminating in that they revealed a complete lack of electrical knowledge, like: "I never realized the current had to go all the way round," and, "I now see why you have two wires in a piece of cord." Not exactly a great discovery, perhaps, but pretty important by their standards.

Although we did not conduct any formal interviewing to determine whether the trainees felt they were learning more under this method, we did hear a lot of appreciative remarks, like, "If kids do things this way at school, they ought to learn fast." An older man said, "Less of a strain than watching the blackboard; you take your own time." This was an interesting remark, because a common complaint was that "the time went like lightning." I think the methods created an infectious enthusiasm about learning. It even spread to two instructors who were not invited but who came in to observe the new methods. They said, "A pity all the learning couldn't be done this way."

As to results, briefly, the Discovery group trainees learned more, and did so in half the time. The part of the electrical program which was relevant to our examination was covered in sessions lasting 90 minutes on the traditional program and 45 minutes with our new experimental Discovery program.

'Learning' judged by tests

We judged "learning" by giving trainees three tests at the end of their three weeks' training. The first dealt with simple and straightforward electrical aspects of diesel-electric locomotives: To score a mark, the trainee had to give the correct electrical term in answer to the problem posed. The second test was concerned with basic knowledge of electrical circuits and of their properties: This time the trainee

The project in Austria was hampered by a number of limiting factors. It took place at a training school operated by the Ministry of Social Affairs for men, especially building workers, who were out of work during the winter months, when the severe weather ordinarily causes a cessation of building work. The plan was to run two consecutive five-week courses with about 20 trainees in each course, of whom half would be over and half under 40. The trainees would be matched in terms of aptitude and intelligence. Actually, the weather was unusually warm during the winter of the project so that fewer men applied for the course and more dropped out than expected. The need to fit both courses into the winter season meant there would be no interval or breathing space between the courses. Only three days were available for formulating the design of the discovery program, which had to be applied without a manual and so was dependent on oral communications and notes. In the circumstances, the performance of the Discovery trainees showed a "fair measure of achievement." The Discovery method did not produce any evident gains in the practical work of the course, but it did produce significant gains on the theoretical parts of the final examination. It was the theoretical side which had posed the greatest problems for the older trainees. The improvement may be characterized as having raised the level of the poorer performers. The practical implication of this would indicate that with appropriate training methods, trainees can be brought into programs for which they would otherwise be thought unsuitable.

was presented with questions offering a choice of answers, one of which he had to select. The third test dealt with the application of electrical knowledge in the diagnosis of electrical faults: Here the testing involved a combination of the other two testing techniques.

It is true that the range of existing knowledge stretched from complete ignorance to a reasonable understanding. But most of the trainees had only an elementary appreciation of the subject. The test scores naturally show a spread, but we are most interested in the media score. Any difference here is much less likely to be affected by differences in the individual composition of the groups. On all three tests, those trained by Discovery methods showed improvement except for the second electrical test with the younger men, where the results are similar to those obtained by the control group. In principle, these general improvements in scores might have been due to chance, but the probabilities were calculated and reveal that the improvement was real.

The fact that the older trainees in the Discovery group exceeded the performance of the younger trainees in the traditional group on one test and were at least as good on the other two tests does not mean that age is not all that important. The point is that although older trainees generally don't do as well in training programs, the use of a method of training that suits them compensates for the loss of learning efficiency that is due to age. Given a suitable method, the old will do as well as the young trained by that method and could do better than the young trained by traditional methods.

Role of 'Hawthorne' effect

The evidence seems encouraging, but it may raise the questions of whether the superior results gained by the Discovery group could not be attributed to the "Hawthorne" effect. The answer would appear to be no, for our experiments were not like introducing a new and stimulating set of conditions to a stable working group. For each of our trainee groups, these were the *only* conditions they knew. All the fuss surrounding the experiment may have stimulated them into doing well, but it could have stimulated the control group too. I don't think it was a question of novelty and of one group being insufficiently stimulated. They were all keen to learn.

The Swedish project illustrates another major advantage of the Discovery methods. Here we had 45 trainees, a fair proportion of whom were lumberjacks from the North. The project was concerned with scribing (being part of a general course in machine shop engineering). Scribing is the process of "scratching" the profile of a part to be cut on a metal blank. The work has of course to be done very accurately; it is a case of reading and interpreting drawing and using technique and understanding in choosing the right procedures.

Training is task-centered

Trainees were taught to scribe a spanner from a drawing. Three different groups were trained by a traditional instruction method, a programed instruction method, and a Discovery method. On the intermediate test they had to scribe the same spanner without any help; in this the traditional instruction group figured best. But in the final transfer test at a later date, the trainees had to scribe new figures from drawings. This time the Discovery group did best, both in speed of performance and quality of work. I mention this case to illustrate the advantages of thinking about job training rather than task training. A great deal of training in industry is task-centered rather than job-centered. This is a typical problem in industry. We train people in task A, but eventually we want them to do task B. So we devise a training program round task B only to find that task B is shortly to be transformed into task C. If trainees become proficient in task A, does it means that they will be able to switch to tasks B and C when they come along? Should we measure effectiveness of training by how well they can do task A or by how easily they can transfer to tasks B and C?

It is quite possible that the immediate signs of progress in training are misleading. It is easy for a trainee to go through all the correct motions under close guidance, just as it is for him to give some verbal indication that he has "understood." But once he is on his own, there may be a real drop in his performance, especially if the circumstances are not quite the same as in training.

Industry is continually running up against people who progress in training but who disappoint afterwards. It can be quite alarming. This reminds me of a training scheme for process operators in a chemical factory that I heard about. All the trainees were shown charts of the process, had it all explained to them, and then were tested for their knowledge of procedures. Shortly after one of them went onto the job, one of the vats exploded. It could have led to a serious accident. Apparently, he had been told never to let the thermometer reading rise above a certain critical figure. He removed the thermometer just in time.

Can develop understanding

How can one tell in advance that a trainee is so completely lacking in understanding? Industry is often under

In the United States, color and number cues on machines in the machine shop were part of the training in the project which was set up in New Haven, Connecticut, under the auspices of Community Progress, Inc., in their West Street Skill Center. The Skill Center was well equipped and comprised a machine shop, electrical section and a data-processing room. Trainees were assigned to one of the three specialist courses for a period of 26 weeks, after which an attempt was made to place them in a job appropriate to their training. Because there wasn't enough time to prepare material applying the new experimental methods to the three full courses, appreciation courses were arranged for the trainees outside their main work. Four days a week were spent in the principal training activity and the fifth day in a short course in another training activity. The whole program was designed to operate in two stages of six months each separated by a one-month gap. In all, 242 trainees divided into 21 separate groups participated in the three different areas of activity. The outcome of the demonstration indicates that application of the Discovery method improved performance scores in both machine-shop work and data processing by between a third and a half. The electrical results did not reach the same measure of superiority as in the other two training areas, perhaps because the instructor approached his subject in a way that was singularly free from the shortcomings of the traditional method. As to the trainees themselves, within a month of the conclusion of the first stage, over 75 percent of the trainees completing the program had found suitable employment, most of them in jobs with better pay and prospects than they had ever had before. Three months later 70 percent were still on the job. Informal estimates of those working in the State Department Employment Service had predicted an ultimate placement of not more than 20 percent.

pressure to accept people for training who might not be regarded as ideal material, especially in the case of redeployment within a firm following a no-redundancy agreement. But understanding can still be developed. However, this question of how you assess whether a trainee has understood is vitally important. If there is too much direct guidance and instruction during training, it becomes very difficult to ascertain whether a trainee has understood or not, since his actions will broadly follow his instructions.

If you use the Discovery method from the outset, however, it can become evident whether a trainee is understanding. A feature of this method is that it gives little direct instruction. Even though the trainee uses cues, hints and the answers he receives in relation to his questions, he is still short of information. Any lack of competence to grapple with the task set is soon revealed, because he will have difficulty in proceeding. He is so dependent on his own resources that there is no way in which he can cover up.

If we assume, then, that Discovery learning works, how can we account for its advantages? First, I should define *where* it has advantages before I say *why*. The evidence suggests that the best results relative to other methods are achieved with middle-aged and older learners and on task that demand the development of concepts and understanding. It would seem that in this field adults don't learn too well by passively following what they are told.

Secondly, adults are often handicapped in learning by the difficulty they experience in eradicating errors and misconceptions. But because the Discovery method reveals the trainee's progress and level of understanding to the instructor, his performance is easier to control.

Thirdly, learning from experience is easier for adults than learning from words; there is no stress on memorizing, hence this sort of learning is remembered.

There are, of course, disadvantages. A Discovery program needs to be designed for a limited group if it is to offer an appropriate challenge.

Another point is that because the Discovery approach is more concerned with fundamental understanding, the benefits are less evident in the short-term than in the long-term.

The Discovery method is a means of teaching which avoids expository instruction. The trainee is presented with tasks which engage him in the search for and selection of clues on how to proceed. The effectiveness of the Discovery method depends on the design of these tasks which have two aims: To provide an intrinsic means for unassisted learning and to provide the experience upon which insight into key relationships can be developed. If the method has something to contribute to industrial training, it does because, in our belief, it takes account of the natural way in which man uses his learning capacity.

Reprinted from TRAINING, November 1973

MAKING ROLE PLAYS PAY OFF IN TRAINING

If you've been encountering resistance to this technique, try this nine-step approach

BY WILLIAM F. MOLLOY

There is hardly a trainer today who hasn't been involved in a role-play situation. Yet, despite its initial popularity, role playing has become a threatening concept for many people. Even those who have never actually participated are frightened by stories of negative experiences. By developing a structured success format with controlled feedback, however, you can reduce initial resistance to role plays and make most effective use of this training tactic.

Role playing as a human relations training method came into its own when Dr. Jacob L. Moreno first introduced the methods of "psychodrama" and "sociodrama" prior to World War II.

Role plays subsequently were used to improve human interaction skills by having individuals carry out simulated discussions or assume a specified character whose behavior was to be imitated. It did not take long for the approach to spread to a variety of learning environments in an attempt to improve a wide range of human interactions.

But while the effectiveness of this training technique has not been seriously challenged, many role-play situations suffer from a lack of sound planning and preparation. This is a significant factor in the negative impact of role-play training on most supervisors and managers. In role play, they find themselves placed in situations in which they see themselves as doomed to failure and exposed to unbridled criticism from others. Such experiences can create a high anxiety level which not only inhibits learning, but seriously endangers an individual's self-esteem.

This need not be the case. An examination of present role-play approaches reveals several common characteristics which could be changed to produce a more meaningful learning experience. The key evolution is toward the development and practice of a specific skill. Here is a nine-step approach for making your role plays effective skill practices.

1 Start with specific behavioral objectives

Most role plays tend to be free-flowing, directionless discussions. Participants usually are given some general background information and asked to act out a solution to a problem, but no clear guidelines are provided on exactly what to say or do.

To target your role plays on specific skills, you should give learners specific behavioral objectives. One useful form is a progression of "critical steps." Participants are directed to conduct their discussion following a predetermined series of actions, a format which assures they will adhere to useful skill-building procedures within the framework of a realistic discussion.

Careful focus on a specific set of behavioral objectives reduces the anxiety level of participants, since they know exactly what is expected of them. It also probably represents a definite contrast to their past role-play experiences. One of the few studies conducted on role plays indicates that players tend to focus their observations more on their personal feelings than on the content of the situation. To alleviate this anxiety, focus participants' attention on the specific set of behavioral guidelines.

When participants must concentrate, not on their personal or professional anxieties, but rather on following critical steps in a logical sequence, they will be more confident in their actions—they will know what to do.

2 Make use of a positive model

Traditional role plays often do not provide participants with a complete understanding of the desired behavior. Without a model to follow, role players not surprisingly can be expected to do poorly and receive negative feedback. Effective skill practice, on the other hand, should be preceded by a positive model of the desired behavior. For example, participants might view a short modeling film showing an interaction that works. From this positive model, they see they can be effective by using the behaviors they observe.

3 Employ your own skills coaching for success

Many role plays provide a brief description of the situation, but leave participants to their own resources to interpret the data and develop a course of action. The introduction of coaching into this setting can greatly increase the likelihood that your learners will have a success experience.

Prior to beginning the exercise, take some time to thoroughly explain the object of the role play, the guidelines to be adhered to, and your own expectations and perspective. This coaching allows you to clarify issues and become aware of any misunderstanding of the material. It also helps participants focus their attention on the critical steps to be covered.

In your coaching, make sure you make use of this important opportunity to detect and alleviate any anxieties or apprehensions your participants may have. By coaching individual participants, you help ensure the success of the exercise to follow and provide a supportive model for others in the group.

4 Take special care to manage feedback

While most role-play manuals provide several general principles the trainer should follow, they do not sufficiently manage the feedback to participants. This management task is a crucial test for the instructor. A significant part of your role is to provide observations and insight to both target skill mastery and build participants' confidence. It's a delicate balancing act: you must manage feedback from observers to focus on how effectively the critical steps were used while maintaining participants' self-esteem.

Feedback can be enhanced by the guidelines observers are asked to follow. For one, insist on recording the exact conversation that takes place. Requiring observers to limit their feedback to the exact words used during the interaction eliminates the coloring of personal feelings and unconscious biases.

Secondly, instruct observers not to generalize or summarize. Instead of reporting, "He was not firm enough," or "She was hostile," make your observers list specific remarks: "Well, George, it's up to you if you want to start work at 8 a.m. or 8:30," or "You think I'm the cause of the problem, don't you?" Such remarks are fed back to the participant for each critical step followed to reinforce the use of the desired behaviors and illustrate how effectively the progression was followed. For example, "Pat, you effectively asked for the cause of the problem when you said, 'Can you help me understand why you're late getting those reports in?'"

5 Protect participants' self-esteem

Most role-play situations are followed by open feedback sessions. During these sessions, it is not uncommon for observers to make comments about the role play just witnessed, regardless of whether those comments are appropriate to the objectives of the exercise. This kind of feedback can have a negative impact on participants, especially if it is perceived as an attack on the individual's self-esteem.

For effective learning to occur, it is imperative that participants gain confidence in their ability to handle the situations being practiced. Feedback can never be allowed to overshadow the maintenance of an individual's self-esteem, and you must intervene immediately in feedback sessions, as well as in the actual skill practice if necessary, to protect your participants. Role-play exercises are not arenas in which people may be subjected to excessive negative feedback.

6 Broaden the experience with alternative positive behaviors

Feedback in most role plays often focuses on purely negative behaviors. It is not uncommon to hear observers say, "You blew it," or "You were really insensitive." This not only threatens self-esteem, but fails to provide specific behavioral information which could show the participant another way of handling the situation.

Observers should be encouraged to suggest alternative positive responses to role-play situations. This not only helps the participants in the exercise itself, but also helps the group focus on specific positive behaviors rather than general negative statements. An example of a statement offering an alternative positive behavior: "George, it would have been better had you said 'Mary, your production rate was down 5% last week,' rather than 'Mary, you're getting lazy.'" Such feedback provides the participant with an alternative set of words that might be more effective. It also sets the tone for observers to focus on a participant's positive, rather than negative, actions.

7 Prepare yourself to fulfill the role of instructor

Traditional role plays tend to let participants "sink or swim," followed by a discussion of the reasons for their fate. Such discussions can be expected to ramble when conducted without a trained moderator. Successful role plays require the presence of a specially trained instructor whose job it is to structure a positive experience for those involved and enhance the transfer of their newly acquired skills to the job.

As an instructor, you should be prepared to offer a number of services to your participants. You should be able to coach them to successfully handle role plays according to the critical step progression. You should be capable of guiding the participation of observers so discussion focuses on positive, growth-oriented outcomes. And you should be prepared to intervene in exercises that become disoriented or threaten to break down. While such intervention is obviously only for extreme situations, participants who begin to stray from the critical steps or flounder for direction need your protection. Participants should be prepared for the eventuality of your intervention before beginning the role play, and everyone involved should understand that there is no implication of failure or need for diminished self-esteem if such action on your part is necessary. Knowing when and how to rescue your trainees from an unproductive

exercise may be the most demanding challenge you face in conducting role plays.

8 Customize role play to reflect realistic job settings

Quite often, role plays provide only general environmental descriptions to participants. When they deal with purely hypothetical issues, they fail to duplicate the real-life situations which can occur on the job. To be productive, then, you must make your role plays as realistic as possible.

One way to do this is to ask learners to prepare descriptions of situations they commonly encounter. The background they provide you in advance will help you create exercises which will benefit them. The more job-related the skills you practice, the greater the likelihood your participants will use those skills back on the job.

9 Focus attention on the process

Since role plays usually lack specific behavioral objectives, role players often have long discussions about familiar things. Not surprisingly, these sessions can bog down in detailed discussions unrelated to the *procedures* participants are trying to learn. For instance, when two supervisors in an electronics plant are asked to conduct a role-play discussion centered on motivating a poor performer, it is not uncommon that 90% of the discussion will focus on technical matters.

To practice and develop a skill, on the other hand, your learners need to focus on the process, rather than content of the discussion. Since the purpose of role playing is to acquire new skills, attention must be directed toward the desired behaviors, and not the setting in which discussion takes place. For this reason, the critical step progression needs to be well-defined and zealously followed to bring the discussion to a successful conclusion.

While role play has suffered from some negative stereotypes, there are many situations in which it can be an extremely positive and rewarding experience. By structuring the experience to emphasize skill practice, you will help alleviate the resistance and anxiety raised when role play is mentioned. And by utilizing the basic principles of role play in a more skill-oriented environment, individuals will have an opportunity to maintain their self-esteem and learn new solutions to problems.

Reprinted from TRAINING, May 1981

VIDEOTAPE ROLE PLAYS WITHOUT TRAINEE TRAUMA

If your trainees haven't been part of a video role play
before, here's one
way to make sure that their first
experience is successful

A trainee's first experience with video role play can be traumatic. It's bad enough to make mistakes in front of one's peers . . . but to have them reviewed on instant replay is torture few people can endure. Many trainees never get full benefit from video-assisted instruction because they are too self-conscious to act as themselves in front of business associates.

Norman Tice, manager of sales training for Johns-Manville, has found a way to eliminate much of that self-consciousness. "The classroom is structured for 30 participants for day-time instruction," Tice explains. "We use six monitors controlled by a ¾-inch cassette deck to play back tapes. At night, four of these monitors convert to self-contained automatic role-play vehicles."

At the end of each workshop day, participants schedule themselves in pairs for half-hour cycles of role play during the evening hours. Usually all four units are engaged at the same time, but the participants aren't distracted because they're so involved in their own work they don't notice the other teams. Also, the monitors play through small remote speakers on the role-play table.

The key to this system is a table-top remote box that simplifies videocassette operation. There are only two knobs on the box, one for speaker volume and one labeled start. The person acting as sales rep pushes the start button to activate the camera and tape machine. The machine records automatically for seven minutes, then rewinds and plays back. After viewing the segment, the teams switch places and repeat the procedure.

Tice has found that the system works much better than set-ups where the instructor and/or equipment operators are present. "The participants evaluate themselves," he explains, "and tend to be more critical than any instructor would be. Also, we give them specific evaluation criteria during daytime sessions. The result of all this advanced planning," he adds, "is that participants get all the benefits of role play with little of the trauma associated with performing in front of an audience of peers."

Reprinted from TRAINING, July 1978

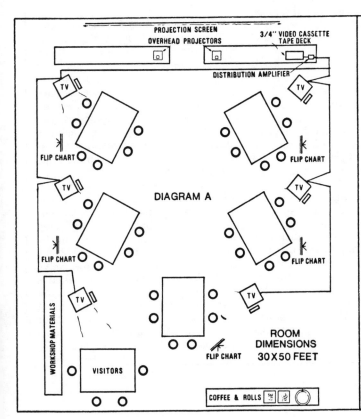

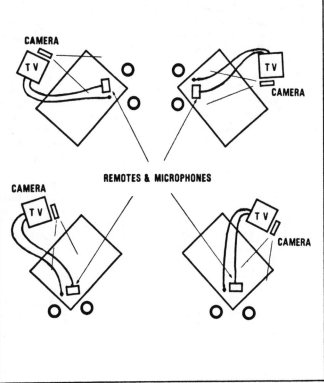

EFFECTIVE *INFORMAL* ROLEPLAYING

BY MARTIN M. BROADWELL

The word "roleplaying" is used with great abandon these days. But what, exactly, does it mean? Quite simply, it is a way to teach a new behavior, specifically in relating to another individual. Through roleplaying, we simulate troublesome relationships in the classroom, so we can practice before we get back to the job and face certain individuals in live situations.

There are many good how-to books about roleplay, so this isn't an attempt to educate, in a few paragraphs, the training world in this technique. But I think there are some missed opportunities to use roleplaying in informal ways. Let's consider these fast, simple, effective training devices after we mull over the question: Just what happens in a roleplaying situation?

Does the roleplayer play the real person, the imagined person, or the desired person? Probably some of each, but we don't know for sure. We do know, however, that roleplaying is more effective than having the instructor stand up and tell the students how they should act, hoping they'll make the transition on their own, without practice. At least with roleplaying, the students must actively participate. We've seen that the student in a roleplaying situation often can produce the proper actions and reactions, which he may have learned from a lecture, a movie, or a tape but has never actually experienced before.

Roleplaying often provides good feedback for the teacher, because it indicates how well certain concepts were grasped. No, it's not a guarantee that the new behavior will be transferred to the job, but it is an indication that such transference might occur. And that alone justifies using the technique. The more feedback we have in the class, the better the chance of transfer back on the job.

Feedback gives students a chance to react, to decide if they like the new model of behavior we're trying to foster. A parallel situation is when a trainee repairs or assembles or produces something in the classroom. While there's no guarantee that his or her success will be repeated on the job, we are better able to predict it will be. In other words, classroom feedback helps us gauge our success in imparting knowledge or, at least, information.

Informal roleplaying

Informal roleplaying requires no structure, no written material, no stagesetting, no preplanning. We're talking about a situation that lasts for only a few minutes. It may occur between one student and the teacher, between several students and the teacher, or between several groups of students. Let's look at some examples.

The students are working on a short case study designed to assist them in dealing with an eager, ambitious employee who is often wrong but always fired up. The objective, among others, is to help the students describe the specific feelings of such an employee and to describe specific actions to overcome inherent hazards in dealing with him. Joe Miller is our ambitious young employee with the wrongheaded ideas. He has worked hard on a proposal that he thinks is great, but we can see it's not practical. Miller's solution has been suggested before by others, and has been tried and proved untenable. Now the class, working in small subgroups, must decide how the supervisor should deal with the young man.

After the third group has reported, it's obvious that the students favor opening with a statement like, "We'll just lay it on the line with you, Joe." In other words, we hear that each group is going to be pretty hard on poor, misguided Joe. But we're trying to teach a different approach. We could ask them, "How do you think Joe would react to this?" But if we're strong on roleplaying, it would be better if we just said, "Let's suppose I'm Joe. Now tell me what you have to say." Add that any class members can talk to Joe if they want to. The participants may have a little trouble getting into the supervisor's role at first, but we can make it easier for them—by keeping in character, offering information, maybe even raising a question that provokes a response. The goal is to get the group itchy to talk to Joe. We continue until the students see that they may have been heading down the wrong path. Not everyone will participate; nor will everyone learn the lesson. But a few will get some "ah-ha's," so it's worth it for them.

Interpersonal relations

This same informal approach will be effective in situations other than supervisory or management training. For example, let's say we're training a group of nurses on hospital procedures. In the course of the training, several trainees have commented on the difficulty they're having with the staff at the radiology lab. "Everytime we go for a report on the work we've given them, we have to listen to a lot of guff about how hard we're making their jobs for them," they complain. Here's a good opportunity for an informal roleplay situation. When one of the nurses says something about the difficulty with the lab, an astute trainer might say, "Hey, why don't I play the part of the lab receptionist, and you come to me with a request." Thus the nurse/trainee gets a chance to practice how he or she will deal with the recalcitrant lab personnel the next time a sticky situation arises.

Conclusion

With a little imagination, we can solve some of our tougher problems by letting the group participate in informal roleplaying. For instance, in a sales relationship, we can say to the group, "Count off by twos; the ones are the unhappy customers, and the twos are the harried sales clerk. See if you can figure out a way to approach the customer without increasing the anxiety, and, better yet, overcoming some of the tension."

Remember: every time a person plays a role appropriately, there should be positive reinforcement. A good argument for the teacher playing one of the roles is that there can be such immediate reinforcement for "good behavior." We'll know we've made this technique a habit when a coworker comes in and asks, "Are you going to get off Friday for the opening of deer season?" And we say, without missing a beat, "Tell you what, you be the boss, and I'll come in and say..."

Reprinted from TRAINING, July 1977

USING TESTING INSTRUMENTS IN YOUR TRAINING EFFORT

More and more trainers use various feedback instruments to help trainees gain insight. Read on to discover what this trend can do for you

BY RON ZEMKE

Sometime in the last two weeks—the last month, at the outside—you have tested some aspect of your self-concept against some form of instrumented feedback. It may have taken the form of the most recent *Reader's Digest* "Marriage Happiness Quotient" quiz. It could have been in the guise of an advertisement challenging "Do you have what it takes to start your own business? Take this simple test and find out." It could even have been some form of a "What is *your* management style?" inventory passed out in a seminar or workshop.

Regardless of where or how you encountered it, if you took the quiz, scored your answers and compared your score to the preprinted norms, you have a feel for the personally involving dynamics of instrumented feedback and the attraction such self-generated, comparative information holds for you as an individual. As a trainer, you also undoubtedly have some feel—and respect—for the power such feedback instruments can have when carefully wired into an artful course design.

As one experienced trainer recently told TRAINING, "You can feel the electricity in the room when you take out the feedback envelopes. For the participants there is the excitement—and anxiety—of getting a very personal report card. For me, the trainer, it's like being master of ceremonies for the Miss America Pageant and the million-dollar drawing for the New York State Lottery rolled into one."

The capacity of these seemingly simple paper-and-pencil devices to rivet trainee attention to task has made them a favored tool of many trainers. Test publishers and vendors have seen the interest grow and have responded in kind. Today, whether you want to give feedback on management style, stress level, communication skill or career advancement capacity, you can almost certainly find a commercially produced instrument that will successfully query it for you.

Powerful and popular as it is, the use of instrumented feedback in training is a fairly recent phenomenon. Credit for the introduction of instruments to organizational training and development efforts is generally ceded to Robert R. Blake and Jane S. Mouton of Scientific Methods, Inc. in Austin, TX, creators of the Managerial Grid® seminar. Their use of self-rating scales and other innovative methods in management and human-relations training contexts in the late 1950s and early 1960s—referred to as *instrumented team learning*—created a fury of debate and a flurry of imitation.

As simple as it may seem today, the process of letting participants rate themselves and their behavior against an ideal model or theory of management behavior was quite an innovation, and a severe break with the then-popular T-Group and sensitivity training approaches to human-relations training, as well as with traditional lecture approaches to management development training.

Jay Hall, president of Teleometrics International, The Woodlands, TX, was one of the first to see the unique promise of instrumented training.

Early on he extolled the virtues of instrumented over unstructured group learning procedures. Blake and Mouton's instrumented innovations broke new ground, according to Hall, for a number of reasons.

1. **They bridged the theory-process gap.** Because of the arousal of personal involvement commensurate with filling out an instrument, training sessions can be made lively and meaningful experiences for participants. Learners look forward to, rather than dread, theory portions of training. Such exposition brings closure, instead of boredom.

2. **They brought structure to process.** Training can have structure and predetermined focus (i.e., a teaching goal) without destroying many of the key involvement, discovery and action-learning attributes of small-group and laboratory training.

3. **They facilitated transfer of learning for participants.** Through the use of instruments, participants are encouraged to think about the theories and concepts in a systematic, structured and personal way. Understanding is more readily grounded in "back home" application possibilities.

4. **They facilitated rapid spread of new ideas in employees' organizations.** Because participants become personally involved and well-versed in the concepts and principles, every learner is a potential trainer. The communication barriers that often exist between those who "went to" and those who "stayed home from" the training are broken down because trainees have learned the language and concepts in a personal fashion. In addition, graduated trainees, equipped with instruments and explanation sheets, can themselves conduct reasonably successful training sessions, since the instruments contain the essence of what is to be learned.

5. **They led to decreases in the cost of training.** Because instruments are easy to use, in-house trainers can hold sessions without depending on expensive expert outsiders. One or two trained facilitators can handle larger-than-usual groups using instruments. The instruments themselves are usually low or moderate in cost.

In essence, Hall was suggesting that the development and spread of instrumented training would be key to demystifying process-based training, freeing training from the bonds of the expertise trap and putting the control of learning into the hands of learners. And so it has. That is quite an achievement for a few scraps of paper with questions printed on them.

Though 20 years of experience

with instrumented learning have indeed demonstrated many of the benefits Hall predicted, experience has demonstrated that Murphy's Law can also apply to using instrumented feedback. Instrumentation makes training easier but by no means foolproof. Experienced instrument producers and users TRAINING interviewed gave this advice.

Do a needs assessment first. Donald Michalak, principal of Michalak Training Associates in Tucson, AZ, who says he hasn't run a training program without instruments in years, nonetheless cautions against "just grabbing a questionnaire to have one and using instruments for the sake of using instruments." If instruments are to be used, he cautions, there must be a relevant organizational need for participants to be concerned with the concepts and feedback they will be encountering.

Instrument developer George F. Truell, of George Truell Associates in Williamsville, NY, voices a similar warning. "It is important that you have your objectives clearly in mind when you consider using instrumentation," he says, adding, "You have to know exactly how you want the people to feel or what you want them to know before you go off shopping for instruments."

Focus on participants, not the instrument. Michalak also suggests that trainers can err by knowing both too much and too little about the model or theory the instrument is based on. "There is no reason trainees need to know who Joe Luft and Harry Ingham are to benefit from the Johari Window concept," he says. "At the same time, the trainer must thoroughly understand the implications of the model. The emphasis should be on helping individuals analyze and change their behavior or confront it as O.K., not on teaching abstract concepts and theories. Too many trainers oversell the potential of feedback but in practice stop short of actually helping trainees."

Another well-known instrument developer, John Geier, president of Performax Systems International in Minneapolis, MN, also cautions against settling for awareness alone. "When instruments were a new thing," he says, "we thought awareness led automatically to change. But now we know that the real facilitator challenge is to bring about real, lasting change. The trainer has to be comfortable coaching people in new skill development and must also know when to recommend organizational change such as installing an ongoing feedback system."

Don't drown—or threaten—participants with data. Truell cautions against giving too much data before its time. "There are degrees of readiness," he says. "Some data is no threat to trainees, some is very threatening. A self-inventory of Maslow's hierarchy of needs isn't very threatening. But a survey that has a lot of subordinate data in it is pretty threatening and has to be set up carefully and well."

David Merrill, president of TRACOM Corp. in Denver, CO, cautions against using instrumented feedback for multiple purposes. "Data from instruments must belong to the participants exclusively," he explains. "If you turn personal growth information into assessment information, you lose the growth opportunity—and the trust and credibility you were trying to develop. Descriptive data can be used effectively for assessment—as in an assessment center—but all parties must agree to that usage beforehand."

Learn to tell the wheat from the chaff in instrumentation. An almost universal set of cautions concerns "knowing-a-good-one-when-you-see-it" or selecting the right instrument for your situation. Truell suggests the would-be user look carefully at two things: the underlying theory and developmental data base.

"You need to be sure that the concepts and ideas the instrument represents fit with your environment," he says, "but that's not enough. The instrument has to be useful for and by your population. For instance, a number of instruments lean heavily on Carl Jung's four typologies. But the questions on each are asked in a different way. Some have very sophisticated wordings, others do not. If you are working with first-line supervisors, an instrument developed on college sophomores may be all wrong even though the concepts and theories may be right."

Geier suggests that it helps to know the people who have developed the instruments, and their reputations. "The credibility of the people who put the instrument out, their training and professional skills are important," he says, adding, "A well-schooled charlatan can fake the statistical and measurement jargon. But a history of good work, good studies and decent research can't be based on a bluff."

Merrill advises taking a balanced view that accepts both personal reactions and measurement questions when assessing a learning instrument. "First determine whether the instrument *describes* or *predicts*," he says, "then, if it describes, ask if it describes what it says it describes." To Merrill, this is especially important to consider when looking at self-perception-only instruments. "My bias is that we can be too easy or too hard on ourselves and not be able to see it," he says. "I prefer that corroborative data come from a source external to the learner as well as from the individual receiving the feedback. This is the simplest form of validity, but a good one."

Secondly, Merrill suggests that the information must have growth potential in it. "Input that condemns or puts down, rather than gives people ideas and opportunities for growth, isn't terribly useful for training," he notes. "Growth potential must be there."

Don't exaggerate the importance of the instrumented data. Oddly enough, most of the experts TRAINING consulted advised trainers not to oversell the importance of the data being given back to the participants. "People shouldn't take the results of any single instrument too seriously, ours included," says Laura L. Horian, director of marketing at Human Synergistics, Inc. in Plymouth, MI.

Her view is strongly applauded and echoed by other instrument publishers and promoters. Merrill, for example, says it from the measurement expert's viewpoint: "Training people are becoming very measurement-wise consumers. They are asking the right questions about validity, reliability, data bases and norming procedures. But an over reliance on measurement technology can overrule common sense and lead to giving an instrument too much credibility and importance. The purpose of instrumentation is to stimulate growth, not to make people throw their hands up in despair, accepting their lot as forever fixed. Most instrument makers are like me, they want people to see their growth potential, not feel pigeonholed."

MTA's Michalak, who uses many but doesn't produce instruments, puts it this way: "I use instruments to help people learn to ask questions that improve their productivity and performance. I tell people not to take the feedback any more solemnly than they would the Sunday supplement 'happy marriage' quiz. The value is in the discussion, not in the scores." Not a bad perspective for anyone to accept as a touchstone. The real data, the important growth information is inside the trainee, not in the simple instruments used to spark awareness of that potential.

Reprinted from TRAINING, November 1982

ASSESSMENT CENTERS: A METHOD WITH PROVEN METTLE

Assessment Centers provide an opportunity to see how people respond in simulations that resemble what they might need to do in a job

BY CHRIS LEE

Douglas Bray lays out a succinct rationale for the technology: "It's easier to increase skill in someone already skilled than in a klutz."

Bray should know. Recently retired as the director of basic human resources research at AT&T, currently chairman of the board of Pittsburgh, PA-based Development Dimensions International (DDI), he is generally acknowledged as the father of the assessment center. During his nearly 30 years at AT&T, Bray conceived and led the pioneering Management Progress Study (MPS), an eight-year project initially undertaken in 1956 that followed the growth and development of 400 AT&T managers. Its purpose was to pinpoint the cognitive, motivational and attitudinal characteristics that have an impact on managerial careers.

In order to do so, Bray and his colleagues at AT&T put the men (all *were* men) through a three-and-a-half day assessment center. A wide range of techniques were used, including paper-and-pencil tests, an in-basket exercise, projective tests, clinical interviews, and participation in group problem-solving and leaderless group discussion. Each year for the following eight years, data was collected on the men to determine their career progress. When the results were released, the assessment center method proved its mettle: 82% of the college men and 75% of the noncollege men who were promoted into middle management were correctly identified by the assessment center

staff; the assessors also were right about 94% of both college and non-college men who were not promoted.

Bray's MPS is a unique piece of industrial research in that the data remains "uncontaminated": The assessment results have never been given to either the individuals assessed or company officials. Yet the results so impressed AT&T's management that operational (i.e., "working") assessment centers spread rapidly throughout the system; centers have been established nationwide and thousands of managers have gone through them.

Roots

Although AT&T's assessment center project is perhaps the best-known and remains the model for industrial applications, the methodology actually is rooted in military selection programs. The pre-World War II German military used the multiple-assessment approach, which remains a key concept of current assessment centers, to select officers. In *Assessment Centers and Managerial Performance* (Academic Press, Inc., New York, 1982), George C. Thornton III and William C. Byham write: "The German military psychologists launched the multiple assessment of leadership capabilities. Many features of current management assessment center programs can be traced to this source, including multiple assessors, complex situational tests and a desire to measure characteristics more complex than atomistic traits."

According to Thornton and By-

ham's historical account of the development of the assessment center, the British and American militaries also contributed to the technology during the World War II era. The British developed a better definition of leadership, used group-testing techniques such as leaderless discussion groups, conducted the first validation studies and provided the first evidence of predictive validity. The American Office of Strategic Services (OSS) used assessment centers, under the guidance of Harvard psychologist Henry Murray, to select candidates for positions ranging from secretary to cloak-and-dagger specialist. The OSS contributed elaborate situational exercises and better observation procedures to the evolving methodology, say Thornton and Byham.

Today the assessment center method is used by thousands of organizations in the United States and abroad to evaluate employees' supervisory and managerial potential, their developmental needs or both. William Byham, president of DDI, puts the present count of assessment centers in U.S. organizations at 2,000—up from just 20 in 1970—and adds to that total several hundred more operating in Japan, South Africa and Australia.

Seventy-five percent of assessment centers in this country are used to evaluate three types of positions, Byham says. "The greatest use is for first-level foremen in industrial settings, followed by sales managers (to avoid the old problem of turning your best salesperson into a mediocre sales manager) and supervisors in clerical situations."

Standards

Different organizations use assessment centers quite differently, of course, and many pick and choose techniques, depending upon the application they have in mind. But to be considered a true assessment center, according to the Standards and Ethical Considerations for Assessment Center Operations, prepared by a task force of interested parties and published in the February 1980 issue of *The Personnel Administrator*, a center must have several characteristics.

• Multiple assessment techniques, including at least one job-related simulation exercise—group problem-solving, in-basket exercise, interview simulation, etc.

- Multiple assessors, who receive training before participating in a center.
- Judgments based on pooled information from these multiple assessors and techniques.
- A separation in time between the behavioral observation and overall evaluation.
- Dimensions of performance that have been identified by a job analysis.
- Exercises designed to provide information on these dimensions.

A traditional assessment center normally operates as follows: A group of six to 12 candidates are sequestered with three or more assessors (who may be line managers, members of the personnel staff or psychologists) who have been trained to observe and evaluate behavior. Managers who act as assessors are usually two or more levels above the participant in the organization, but do not supervise the participant. They observe the participants' behavior in management games, leaderless group discussions, role-playing exercises and other activities. Some organizations also combine simulation techniques with background interviews and tests.

The idea, as Byham says, is to "use behavior to predict behavior. It is organized around dimensions that are related to job success—leading, delegating, planning and so on."

Next, the assessors must integrate the data they have gathered through their observations. After the simulations, they meet and report their ratings for each participant on each exercise. They make independent judgments on overall ratings before meeting with one another to reach a consensus or prediction of management success.

Assessment Designs International, a Winter Park, FL consulting firm, has come up with its own relatively succinct definition of an assessment center: "A process in which individuals have the opportunity to participate in a series of situations which resemble what they might be called on to do in an actual job. They are observed in situational or simulation exercises, that is, work samples, while assessors who are well trained in observation and documentation methodology evaluate their performance in a fair and impartial manner."

One of the key points in the

process, says Steve Cohen, executive vice president of ADI, is training line managers as assessors. "It's critical," he says. "It takes time, but one of the benefits is that they learn about evaluation and documentation."

Assessor training, Bray agrees, is one of the method's greatest strengths. But it also is perhaps its greatest weakness. "When you have real-life managers making decisions, the organization pays attention. With outsiders or personnel types acting as assessors, management tends to be less believing. The downside is training them to do it."

Assessor training, he says, normally lasts from two to five days; he considers five days of training optimal. "The major problem with assessment centers is staffing. The organization has to make a commitment to free up the people for training as well as going through the [assessment/evaluation] process."

The payoff

Although the demanding nature of assessment centers makes them an expensive proposition for organizations, many obviously consider them worth the investment. At Montgomery Ward and Co., Inc. in Chicago, Patrick D. Jimerson, director of corporate training and development, has been using assessment centers for several years to determine the developmental needs of buyers and store managers—at an up-front cost of $100,000. "The most immediate return on your investment is not what you do [with the participants]," he says. "That may not pay off for a year or more. But the assessors learn what they need to be doing back on the job to be more effective. They start to practice the behavior they see as high performance."

Most organizations use assessment centers for selection, development or some combination of the two. According to ADI's Cohen, the trend has been away from using the method strictly for selection, partly because of the expense involved. "Since the mid-'70s, [organizations] have been gravitating toward using them for development." He estimates the breakdown among ADI's clients to be 50% for selection purposes, 20% for development purposes and 30% for a combination of both.

Bray considers the move toward

using the assessment center method for development "a lot of cultural noise. People like 'development' better than 'selection,'" he says. "There's a lot of talk about using it for development or trying to use it for both. Some people use assessment centers for selection and then try to use them for development after people have gone through the process. There's nothing wrong with that but, in a sense, the company is not getting its money's worth."

Jimerson feels that assessment centers are best positioned as developmental tools. "If people feel that it is something that reinforces their strengths, rather than gives away their weaknesses, they won't feel as though they've been thrown to the wolves." One way to do this, he says, is to involve the managers and employees who are going to be assessed in the process of building an assessment center, i.e., analyzing jobs and coming up with objective dimensions for those jobs.

This way, too, he adds, people will be more likely to accept the results. "If I'm going to run, say, a computer center for three days and I *know* I did badly on part of the simulation, I can support a decision [to hire someone else] if I can see how I ranked according to objective criteria."

Bray takes a philosophical view of participant reactions. "People adjust to everything in life. If you've got 10 employees and one is going to get promoted, nine are not," he says. "It's better to get the news clearly and objectively than by slow water torture—anticipating a promotion every six months and not getting it. That's more demoralizing."

Cohen agrees that participants ordinarily accept their evaluations. "We get very high participant reactions. They may not like the results, but they can't argue with the process. The assessment center is the most effective single tool to evaluate potential and the most legally valid."

Jimerson feels that people like to be measured against a norm or standard that is at least quasi-objective. "I say 'quasi-objective' because until we have something magic, like [Star Trek's] Dr. McCoy's tricorder, that measures performance *objectively*, the assessment center method is a good tool."

Reprinted from TRAINING, July 1985

CASE METHOD TRAINING: WHAT IT IS, HOW IT WORKS

Want to get back to basics in training?
Here's a method that dates back to Socrates

BY HELEN KELLY

We aren't talking hardware or software here, but rather an application of the ancient Socratic technique of teaching people how to think—how to ask pertinent questions, how to sort and select relevant information and how to use a systematic approach when making decisions. In the last century, Harvard University took up the venerable technique and called it the *business case method.*

The case method, which typically incorporates a business case as the primary teaching tool, may be familiar to you as the method of choice for training senior managers in seminars often conducted by external consultants.

The case method is a *system of instruction* built on the premise that people are most likely to retain and use what they learn if they reach understanding through "guided discovery." Along the way, trainees refine analysis skills, develop the will to take risks in the face of uncertain outcomes, and come to know their own strengths, weaknesses and talents.

The primary tool of the case method is the *case,* usually written under the supervision of a content expert by a case-writer (who may be the same person). It serves as a springboard for trainers and learners to explore specific objectives.

A case should not be confused with a *case study* or *critical incident.* The differences involve the amount of information, the way the information is organized and the intent. A case study is a chronological history of a decision, usually including the outcome and often a pedagogical analysis of the decision. In addition, a case study is inclusive, like a news story. A case is more like an editorial, which directs the reader toward a way of thinking about an issue.

A case study is historical; a case is usually written before the decision has been made. The objective of a case study is to teach by example. The objective of a case is to learn by taking risks, by making judgments in an environment of uncertainty where multiple options are realistic, and by planning action.

A critical incident is like a case in that it is a "What-should-we-do?" issue, but it presents only the barest of surrounding circumstances and is usually a question of interpersonal relationships, not of impact on the organization.

Format and content

In content, a case is a presentation of *one specific decision* that a manager must make at a specific moment in time. Traditionally *case issues*—as the decision questions are called—have been ones faced by top management. Should a fast-food chain add a new food item? How should a company solve its absentee problems? Should the company diversify, merge, acquire a competitor? Should an American or a foreign national manage the new overseas operation? What should a college's or a bank's marketing strategy be when enrollment or new savings accounts are down? In the last few years, cases have been written around issues of sales strategy, supervisory roles, worker training and human resource planning.

In format, a case is like a play that opens in the middle of the story and uses flashbacks to describe the action that led up to the opening scene. After the decision issue is stated, the rest of the case lays out the documentation and data that was available to the manager at the time the decision had to be made. (Usually, the documentation and data are selected by the case-writer according to the teaching and content objectives for which the case is written.) There should be no answers, outcomes or even leading questions.

During a case-method session participants are asked to recommend the next move by considering the information available and their own experience. They work as a team during the session, though each has come thoroughly prepared with a decision, rationale and action plan. Sometimes role plays are added by the instructor; sometimes additional information or research is available for those who want it; sometimes case participants have access to a computer for forecasting or analysis. But typical sessions are straightforward: Here's what the manager has to decide, here's what was known at the time, here's what others in the organization were thinking about. What should the manager do and why do you think so?

The instructor's job is to select the right case for the training objectives, the audience and the industry, and to guide the participants. Trainees must discover—with the guidance but not the wisdom of the case instructor—the consequences of the issue at hand, the facts relevant to the decision, the options and consequences of each option and the realistic action best meeting the problem.

The case certainly is old-fashioned. It lacks obvious grace and may appear passive. A bare-bones case costs almost nothing. But appearances are deceiving. A closer look reveals the method as a way to rely on yourself and grow as you and your trainees become proficient at learning how to learn and apply skills. Properly conducted, each case builds basic process (thinking) skills, develops objectivity and improves observation. The best cases allow for creative approaches, help trainees build confidence, lend dignity to the training responsibility and allow trainer and trainee to explore new roles in a "safe" instructional setting.

Expanding the range of the method

Despite its academic and esoteric appearance, the case method is mastered by many trainers, with some practice, in a relatively short time. In fact, trainers usually find that they already possess most of the skills; they simply have to learn to put them together in new ways. As for the trainees, most will be intimidated at first, feeling vulnerable when asked to explore their abilities and to feel their way when no right answer exists. But after just one case session, trainees generally enjoy the feeling of being in control when no "right" answers exist.

The case method typically has been used to train senior managers in key functions long believed to be the profit and productivity builders. But boundaries have expanded. Profitability can be tied to the degree to which supervisors can delegate, plant managers can understand participative management, salespeople can listen, team leaders can "relate" up and down, and senior managers can encourage creativity, insight and educated trial-and-error.

Who benefits?

The organization as a whole can benefit from the case method because it helps identify and prevent problems and contributes to better organizational communication. When case-method training is done well, managers at all levels become better oriented to problem analysis, decision making, position taking and evaluating options. They are better equipped to identify potential problems and recommend realistic actions to prevent minor issues from growing into major headaches.

Under the case method, trainees receive immediate feedback as ideas and interpersonal styles are tested and solutions and options surface. The case method is democratic and

inspires self-confidence; because no right answer exists, everyone's educated guess has a fair shot.

The opportunity to practice taking positions and recommending action in an environment of uncertainty can desensitize even lifelong fence-sitters. Those with real expertise in a field can shine. Those who tend to monopolize conversations are discouraged by the case instructor, and often—less gently—by their peers. Narrow-channel runners are exposed to alternative interpretations; those who normally must make decisions alone have an opportunity to ask questions. Experience comes to the

---

The case method is built on the premise that people are most likely to learn if they reach understanding through guided discovery.

---

fore and imagined solutions are examined in the twilight area between role playing and reality. People become involved. They forget about organizational position barriers. They get excited and show their personalities.

Best of all, because the case method demands that participants put information together to draw conclusions, people with intuitive, creative or unusual approaches may be heard by others in the organization for the first time. Sometimes they surprise even themselves.

Trainers who use the case method often begin to find their jobs more interesting and challenging, with real possibilities for accomplishment. The instructor interacts with most of the participants, can sense who is getting lost and can either offer help on the spot or note those who seem to need more specialized training in interpersonal or questioning skills.

Problems of case-method teaching

The case instructor has a high-impact, low-profile job; for most trainers this may mean some adjustments. And the trainer must work as hard as the trainees at using the thinking skills required for good leadership.

Most of the 5,000 or so cases that have been written to date focus on functional management issues. They often involve complex financial data and they may be quite long and highly technical. This is because the issues are so broad, often entailing, theoretically, consequences across an entire organization.

Cases in the areas of human resources development (HRD) and management (HRM) are being written, although not many are well-developed. Some cases representing sales training also are being designed; they tend to be shorter and more tightly focused. Not enough of them exist.

However, because the case format is relatively standard, with some instruction you or a team of trainers could write a set of cases for your own organization, focusing on decisions to be made by your trainee and manager groups. Such *operations cases* usually prove to have long-term benefits because they can be used repeatedly for many levels of management and supervisory training. or you could use one as an evaluation tool. You may select a previously written case that seems to fit your instructional objectives, but ask a colleague who likes to teach by the case method to participate. The latter approach is a good way to develop your internal communications system and excellent practice for team training. You may write a case issue and have a group of trainees build the case. Options and alternatives are plentiful and fruitful.

Whichever route you select, however, go in with your eyes open. Although just about anyone can learn how to select a good case and develop competence in writing and teaching it, not everyone likes case teaching and not everyone learns best under the case method. Like any technique, it's a tool, not a panacea.

Reprinted from TRAINING, February 1983

QUALITY CIRCLES: THE SECOND GENERATION

Just a few years ago, they were all the rage, the saviors of American business. But disenchantment with QCs as magic bullets has not made them vanish. It's made them change

BY BEVERLY GEBER

The image wasn't exactly that of Moses descending from the mountain with the Ten Commandments. Not exactly. But the advent of quality control circles in this country offers some interesting parallels.

Visionaries made the pilgrimage to Japan, the economic Holy Land. The quality circle, or QC, was the most visible and concrete element of an incomprehensible way of doing business that seemed as foreign to us in the mid-1970s as a set of miraculous tablets must have seemed in the desert.

So the true believers returned from Mount Fuji with The Answer to the entropy of American business. Some of them, of course, never meant to carve it in stone for presentation to the masses. But desperate American business executives, with some help from zealots and fast-buck artists, snatched the concept and elevated it from good idea to panacea.

Throughout the nation, top managers spurned the golden calf of business as usual and sang hallelujah for quality control circles. There were stories—possibly apocryphal—of CEOs seeing a snippet about quality circles on the nightly news and demanding a company-wide QC program the next day. In many cases, critics now argue, they were taking one element of the Japanese participative management style and trying to graft it onto a directive American management style. But who can blame them? This was the first flush of a major-league fad. This was the magic cork that would plug the "productivity gap."

With all the euphoria that gripped management, with all the promises that quality circles would revolutionize American business, with all the *expectations* that they would, it was inevitable that QCs would tarnish. As anyone who has any experience with the Ten Commandments knows, it's a lot easier to make promises than to do what you say you'll do (or won't do).

Eventually, stories about hugely successful QC programs began to be replaced by stories about failures. To be sure, some organizations have been able to make the idea work and keep working. Ford Motor Co. still maintains its circles and touts its products with the line that "Quality is Job One." But other companies couldn't make the Japanese model pay off. Employees blamed management. Management declared that circles don't work here because American workers aren't as docile, dedicated or compliant as Japanese workers.

After the shakeout, some companies that suffered uncomfortable growing pains while developing quality circles ended up throwing out the name but keeping part of the concept. Some use "task forces" that operate sporadically to solve specific problems, usually posed by management. Some companies created all-encompassing employee involvement programs that require everybody to participate in regular meetings to set quality goals and check progress. Some simply threw out the entire scheme, along with full-time circle facilitators and program managers.

Not very many kept the original Japanese model.

(Re)made in Japan

As quality circle historians are fond of pointing out, the basic idea actually originated in the United States. W. Edwards Deming was the prophet, ignored in his own land, who exported the idea to Japan. In searching for the fastest way to rebuild their country after the devastation of World War II, the Japanese concentrated on quality improvement and drew Deming across the Pacific to teach them about statistical quality control methods. He was so revered for his contributions that the Japanese established the Deming Prize, an annual award for quality control.

Another American, J.M. Juran, instructed the Japanese in managerial aspects of quality control during the 1950s. But it wasn't until 1962, more than a decade after the quality initiative began, that the Japanese began quality control circles. By 1984, the Japanese Union of Scientists and Engineers (JUSE) had registered 192,101 circles with 1.6 million members.

In Japan, quality control circles were instituted mostly in large manufacturing firms as a way to educate workers about quality control and bring them into the effort for quality. Basically, circles are groups of eight to 12 employees doing similar work who have been trained in statistical quality control procedures. They're charged with spotting quality problems in their departments and ferreting out solutions. Participation in circles generally is voluntary, although there may be management or peer pressure to join. Underlying the process is the assumption that each employee is a quality control manager; in that sense, quality circles are a natural outgrowth of Japanese participative management.

In 1974, quality control circles

boomeranged back to the United States, finding homes initially at the Lockheed Missile and Space Co. plant in Sunnyvale, CA, and at Minneapolis-based Honeywell Corp. By 1977, Lockheed had about 30 circles and was reporting savings of $3 million in three years. Honeywell, too, reported great success with its program. (See accompanying story for a current report on quality circles at those pioneer companies.)

But those programs remained lonely pioneers for a few years until American managers realized they were quickly losing ground to the Japanese. Sky-high gasoline prices sent droves of buyers to smaller, more fuel-efficient Japanese cars. A lot of those buyers, delighted with the bonus of better dependability, stayed with their Toyotas even when gas prices stabilized. The electronics field, too, was swamped by superior Japanese products. Other industries began to feel the heat of the Rising Sun on their necks.

Wanted: Savior

So it was that in the late '70s, the search was on for a way to reverse the trend. Americans weren't averse to learning from their competitors, and quality circles seemed an easy fix, a way to glean the essence of the Japanese success without indulging in the time-consuming quality development process the Japanese had been working on since the end of the war. By 1981, an estimated 2,000 to 3,000 quality circles were operating in the United States and the concept had become a card-carrying Movement. Executives by the boatload endorsed them wholeheartedly. Reporters slobbered over them incessantly.

Wayne Rieker, the Lockheed Co. executive who helped introduce quality circles to the United States, had formed his own consulting firm on quality circles by then. "Things were so hectic," he recalls now. "In 1981 and 1982 it was unbelievable. And I'm sure we started some circles in companies that weren't quite ready for it."

A 1982 study by the New York Stock Exchange showed that 44% of all companies with more than 500 employees had quality circle programs. Other pollsters and experts estimate that more than 90% of the *Fortune 500* have tried QCs. Many still use some of the circle elements. Some, such as Martin Marietta Corp.'s Michoud division in New Orleans, have remained successful while sticking close to the basic pattern; the Michoud division won an award last year from the International Association of Quality Circles (IAQC).

But today, though QCs are operating in plenty of companies, the bandwagon has pretty well ground to a halt. Quality circles never enjoyed the exponential growth their fans were predicting just five years ago. IAQC, the acknowledged dean of quality circle organizations, reports 6,000 members, a number that hasn't changed in

---

After the shakeout . . . not very many kept the original Japanese model.

---

two years.

The fad may be dead, stabbed by the usual culprits of time, reason and reality, but a basic question remains: Are quality circles still valuable and workable?

Experts disagree. Edwin E. Lawler III, a professor at the University of Southern California's School of Business, says quality circles have very limited applications. And even if organizations are moving toward participative management, he adds, quality circles aren't a smart first step. Robert Cole, professor of Sociology and Business Administration at the University of Michigan, defends circles, arguing that they have been unfairly maligned because they weren't done properly at most companies.

One company that has first-hand experience in the rise and fall of QCs is RepublicBank Houston. Its program began in 1982 with six circles and grew within two years to 20 circles with two full-time facilitators. Today, RepublicBank has just two circles and no full-time facilitators.

Candace Watson, customer service and training officer, blames the economy and lack of commitment for the circles' decline. When the economy worsens, she says, executives don't like to spend money on salaries for facilitators, especially when they can't document dollars-and-cents savings to justify the expense. Also, the program lost its political momentum with the departure of an executive who was an early supporter.

Still, Watson remains an advocate. "I don't think you have to measure the results to make sure it's worthwhile. If people are happier, we think we'll end up winning because we'll have less turnover and absenteeism," she says. "I've seen the development of individuals who have stayed with that process, development in their thinking and evaluation [abilities]. You take whiners and make them into problem-solvers."

Touchy-feely vs. bottom line

Many supporters take that sort of human-relations approach to justifying quality circles. Wayne Rieker, president of Rieker Management Systems, Los Gatos, CA, disapproves: "I've deplored over the years the human resource flavor [of arguments used to 'sell' QCs]. A lot of people just didn't teach the techniques the Japanese taught. In terms of management support, it's a real problem. How can you expect them to support it if there are no cost savings?"

Sacramento County in California was one of the first local government entities to establish quality circles. The program was funded by a one-year federal grant to see if QCs would work in the public sector. Sacramento County training officer Craig Smith says the county's 11 quality circles produced about $65,000 in documented savings in 1982, which just barely offset the expense of staff salaries and production time lost. When the grant expired, county officials let the program lapse.

Officials there sometimes had a difficult time pinpointing monetary savings. For instance, one of the circles came up with an idea to cut down on the number of people who would wait in lines in the main welfare office, only to be told by the clerk behind the window that they were in the wrong line. They put up signs in five languages directing people to the correct area.

"It improved service and reduced the stress for everybody involved. But how do you put a cost on that?" Smith asks.

It's definitely a problem trying to quantify the success of quality circles in service industries. Maybe that's why that growing sector of the economy sports fewer circles. According to the 1982 New York Stock Exchange survey, quality circles were more likely to appear in the manufacturing sector than in service organizations by a 2-to-1 margin.

But that doesn't mean QCs can't produce quantifiable savings. In fact, most experts now agree that quality circles *must* produce quantifiable results if they are to please management and continue to exist.

Ron Hutchinson, managing consultant with K.W. Tunnell, a Philadelphia consulting firm, says he has seen a lot of quality circles fail because the bottom line was too nebulous. "If you can't quantify in dollars and cents, you must have some other measuring system. It's absolutely necessary to follow quality circles with statistical management procedures. It's the difference between the touchy-feely kind of quality circles and the kind that have hard-core value to management."

In manufacturing, you can measure increases in the number of widgets produced, decreases in unnecessary inventory and so on. In the service industry, you can use surveys and other sampling devices to measure changes in how customers perceive the organization's quality of service. If quality circles produce little more than an unsubstantiated claim that more "involved" employees are more productive employees, most experts warn, they're doomed to fail.

Case in point

When Honeywell first launched its quality circles—adhering to the original principle that employees should be able to figure out their own problems to solve—workers suggested things such as painting walls, putting salads in the cafeteria and stocking the vending machines with granola bars. The company eventually concluded that these sorts of suggestions weren't enormously valuable, says James Widtfeldt, associate director of Honeywell's quality management systems.

"The crucial thing missing was, 'What does this have to do with the business?'" Widtfeldt says. "This touchy-feely stuff didn't work."

So at Honeywell, quality circles metamorphosed into a new shape. "Employee involvement teams" now

work on problems and issues that have a direct relationship to the company's business imperatives. The program is no longer voluntary and team members don't always set their own agenda; management often gives them problems to solve.

Having observed the change from human-relations-style circles to the type linked to specific business goals, Widtfeldt says his thinking on quality circles has turned completely around. "The reason for getting together in the past was vaguely defined and based on the principle that satisfied people were productive people," he says. "Now I think that productive people

---

Second wave: Please don't call it a quality circle!

---

are satisfied people."

Rieker and other consultants are adamant that QCs must save money and must perform in close harmony with the company's business objectives if they are to succeed. Otherwise, they are simply a fad and eventually will suffer the fate of all fads.

Champions

Another time bomb that helped kill some quality circles is the champion syndrome, in which one person, typically an executive, is the only strong enthusiast for the project and pushes it past a dubious group of peers and line managers. If that person leaves, the program often withers too. Ironically, that's what happened at Lockheed, the quality circle innovator, when Rieker left to start his own consulting business.

Says Lockheed training coordinator Howard Tamler, "Management really didn't support the idea of hourly workers making decisions that went beyond their job descriptions. When Rieker left, a lot of people who had been going through the motions stopped."

Tamler isn't faulting Lockheed management but the case highlights one of the most omnipresent villains in the downfall of quality circles—certainly the one mentioned most frequently by consultants and

trainers alike. The villain? Management.

What does management do wrong? It tries to take a participative management concept, support it only with some lip service by executives, and slap it into a context where participative management does not really exist.

In a 1985 essay in the *Harvard Business Review*, Lawler described some easy ways in which quality circles can disintegrate. For instance, many programs were implemented without the involvement or support of middle management. In effect, they operate as a sort of parallel structure to management, rather than being embedded into the fabric of the organization. When circle members report their recommendations, they usually report to the very middle managers who are most threatened by quality circles.

When QCs come up with better ideas for getting things done, Lawler says, middle managers feel as though their jobs have been usurped. This makes them resentful and suspicious. Later, it's the circle members' turn to feel resentful if management rejects too many ideas, dawdles over answers, or accepts recommendations but doesn't implement them.

Other thorns on the rose: Workers who get used to the freedom and authority they enjoy in their circles begin to chafe under the same old directive management style on the shop floor. They want to share in the savings their ideas produce. Or they simply run out of problems to solve.

In Lawler's experience, few quality circle programs mutate into something similar but different. Most just dwindle and die, killed by middle-management resistance and waning enthusiasm.

Second generation

This isn't to say that quality circles have no value, Lawler is quick to add. They can be used as a group suggestion program, or as an occasional problem-solving vehicle for specific issues. They may even be used as a transitional device toward a more participative management style, although Lawler doesn't recommend it. Usually, he says, companies begin a quality circle program, realize its limitations, then let the concept dangle while they develop a more participative culture. It's putting the cart before the horse, a mistake the Japanese didn't make.

"Quality circles just nibble at the edges of getting people involved in their work," he says. "The problem is that if they're moving toward employee involvement then they have to restructure their organization first."

The University of Michigan's Cole agrees that there has been many a mismatch between quality circles and style of management. But he is an indefatigable supporter of properly used circles. To Cole, QCs have failed only in the eyes of people who thought they would be a panacea. "American management has the need to feel they're doing something new every day, and I think that's a negative thing," he says. "The Japanese have been doing quality circles for 25 years and they don't tire of it. They vary the approach."

So do Americans, as a matter of fact. And they have varied the approach to the point where one can say that a "second generation" of the QC concept has appeared in this country.

But please. . .*don't* call it a quality circle. The idea that started in Japan as the quality control circle and dropped the word control for import into this country—the better to appeal to anti-authoritarian workers—now goes by other names: employee involvement team, worker participation group, continuous improvement process, and even people express program. The change in nomenclature is intended to better reflect the role of these groups, inculcated as proponents say they are in the fabric of a company's management style. And too, once a fad has entered its repudiation phase, no one wants to be caught espousing it under its old label.

"They're still out there," says Shaun Sullivan, director of operations for Rieker Management Systems. "It's just that a lot of [them] have different names."

Cole conducted a recent study of IAQC members that reinforced the view that quality circles have not died but may be changing form. According to the survey, circle activities are growing moderately or rapidly at 40% of the firms, remaining steady at 27% and declining at 33%. There was more enthusiasm for broader employee involvement programs, which are growing moderately or rapidly at 47% of the firms, remaining stable at 41% and declining at only 12%.

Savvy

Actually, the second generation of the quality circle movement seems a lot like the first, except that in this wave, programs appear to enjoy greater acceptance and operate on a broader scope within the company. Their sponsors also seem a lot more savvy about operating within the American business environment. Instead of spotting problems, mature circles (whatever they may be called) often try to prevent them in a company-wide quality management approach.

K.W. Tunnel's Hutchinson refers to the new breed as "bastardized" quality circles, but he's not being uncomplimentary.

At Northrop Corp., workers are no longer in quality circles; they belong to employee performance and recognition groups. Elaine Eldridge, manager of the program for the company's aircraft division in Hawthorne, CA, says the groups, which are no longer voluntary, involve all workers on the shop floor. They set targets for improvement, keep reports on their progress and compete with other groups to achieve goals. During the biweekly meetings, they also get a chance to identify problems and try to solve them.

Northrop instituted quality circles in the late 1970s but began to reevaluate its program in 1982. "We changed the name in 1985 to be more indicative of what we do," Eldridge says. "It's an overall framework for quality with goals in various areas."

McDonnell Aircraft Co. of St. Louis, part of the McDonnell-Douglas Corp., just this year eliminated its traditional quality circle program. John Snyder, manager of the company's "quality communication circles," says the decision represents a sharp change in plans. The company started the program in 1981, and by 1985 it had 227 quality circles with about 3,000 members. McDonnell planned to have nearly 800 circles within a few years. Instead, the company now has two-thirds of its 27,000 employees involved in "natural work groups." Snyder says the change was made so the company could achieve faster gains in quality. Since the U.S. government will probably need only two more fighter planes developed by the end of the century, he explains, McDonnell had to improve its quality quickly and significantly to compete more aggressively for such a limited amount of business.

In Sacramento County, which scrapped the formal quality circle program after just a year, workers in certain departments with sympathetic administrators have begun to coalesce into work groups that routinely gather for problem-solving sessions.

The fever for changing quality circles has even overtaken Rieker's consulting firm, which used to concern itself mostly with quality circles and now deals in "total quality management." Rieker doesn't consider this a substantive change, simply a more holistic approach: "We haven't lost our emphasis on quality circles, but they're just part of the solution." Now, he says, before he will set up quality circles, he studies the corporate culture and makes sure executives and managers are ready to accept the idea of unrelenting quality control and some form of participative management.

Actually, no doubt, many "second generation" programs are just quality circles in a new suit of clothes, the better to please fickle executives. But many others really have changed from peripheral, voluntary brainstorming sessions into self-managed work groups. And it was probably inevitable that Americans would tinker with things.

Says Honeywell's Widtfeldt, "We have taken what we thought was a Japanese miracle and reframed it in a way that makes sense for us."

Reprinted from TRAINING, December 1986

A SECOND LOOK AT NLP

Neuro-Linguistic Programming has a shaky
reputation—through the fault
of its own acolytes.
But isn't that a needle gleaming
in the haystack?

BY MARILYN DARLING

Just when you thought you'd heard the end of the subject, one more seemingly normal acquaintance becomes enamored with Neuro-Linguistic Programming—NLP, as it is known to those who love and hate it. Some of its adherents can remind you of cult worshippers. As soon as you mention those three magic letters, their eyes brighten, color flows into their cheeks and you know that if you stick around, it could turn into a very long evening.

NLP. It's been associated with everything from fixing a jury to firewalking. What is it that gets otherwise normal people so excited? If you ask believers about it, you're likely to get odd descriptions of how people's faces change color several times a minute, or baffling claims about how you can divine a person's thoughts from the way she moves her eyes. You may hear stories, told with a sense of mystic awe, about Richard Bandler and John Grinder, who developed NLP in their mountain hideaways in Santa Cruz, CA: how they can cure a phobia in 10 minutes just by touching people at exactly the right moment.

Or, worse, the NLP enthusiast may ask you a ridiculous question like, "How do you *know* how to spell your name?"

And then he'll *watch* you.

NLP has been evolving since the mid-1970s. Unfortunately, practitioners and fans sometimes get so wrapped up in the tricks and techniques—eye movements, hypnosis, gaining rapport and such—that they communicate (and maybe understand) fewer and fewer of the underlying theories and discoveries that lend NLP its potential value. This leaves most of us without a frame of reference to understand and evaluate it. With NLP, it's tough to become an intelligent critic, let alone an informed consumer.

What, if anything, does NLP have to offer to the training and development field? This article does not include any illustrations of how to read eye movements. It won't teach you how to put anyone in a trance or how to walk over burning coals. I will try to describe how NLP came about, and how it is used—and misused—in the business context.

Modeling

Bandler and Grinder's early work was done strictly in therapeutic settings. But the communication issues and processes they uncovered often are encountered in the business setting.

While studying math and computers at Stanford University in the mid-70s, Richard Bandler became fascinated by the gestalt therapy concepts of psychologist Fritz Perls and family therapist Virginia Satir. He studied their techniques and began to hold gestalt sessions. He invited John Grinder, a professor of linguistics at the University of California, Santa Cruz, to attend some of them.

They made a deal. If Bandler could teach Grinder how to *do* what he did, Grinder would try to describe what Bandler was doing linguistically. From that beginning, they began to "model" communication and behavioral-change techniques using linguistics. Among the people they modeled at work were Satir, Perls and medical hypnotist Milton Erickson.

Why was modeling necessary? For the same reason that a skilled trainer who has studied an expert is often more successful at teaching the expert's skills to others. When skilled people try to explain or teach what they do, they discover that many of their skills are completely unconscious. Or they find it difficult to put into words some of the nuances that make them successful. Or they try to teach others in the way they learned, assuming that if it worked for them, it can work for everyone.

For any combination of reasons, exceptionally skilled people may be unsuccessful at passing on their gifts. Bandler and Grinder believed it possible to break down everything that makes up a "talent" into observable, describable relationships and bits of information, making it easier for others to learn the talent.

They discovered that the gifted therapists they studied were successful not so much because of any one technique that worked magically over and over, but because they had learned how to observe and listen to their clients very closely. Bandler and Grinder concluded that gifted communicators are masters at living in other people's worlds and at learning how to use people's own experiences and resources to help them change.

What sort of information were they picking up? Modern linguistics starts from the premise that "the map is not the territory." In other words, any particular way of looking at the world does not tell us everything there is to know. Because we are not the thing we observe, our "maps" have gaps in them—gaps that we often fill in ourselves in order to make sense of things by generalizing from our past experiences. This *distorts* our maps of the world.

For example, for many years we used a standard IQ test as *the map* for intelligence. We observed that minorities in the United States tended to score lower on those tests than members of the majority population. It was logical to conclude that the minority population was less intelligent, as a whole, than the white majority. Because of this faulty map, "genetic differences" were used for years to justify separate and unequal treatment.

Bandler and Grinder used a series of linguistic rules to develop a process they called the Meta-Model, a technique that could be used to listen for the "gaps" clients revealed in their attitudes and perceptions, and to generate a series of questions that could be asked to fill in those gaps. This technique exposed distortions and generalizations in people's attitudes and behavior—distortions that had been maintained unconsciously but were no longer useful, or were being applied in the wrong contexts.

For example, the Meta-Model could be used as follows to break a misperception. Note the focus on the specific words and phrases the "client" is using:

"My boss hates me."
"How do you know he hates you?"
"Because every time I make a suggestion, he looks at the ground and mumbles something."
"Every time?"
"Well, at least recently."
"How recently?"
"Oh, say the past two weeks."
"Did you know that he's been under the gun for the past couple of weeks to submit next year's budget?"
"No, I didn't."
"When you look down at the ground and mumble when someone makes a suggestion to you, does it always mean you hate them?"
"No, I guess not."

"The next time that happens, why don't you ask him if it would be better to talk about your idea at a different time and see if he takes you up on it."

As they refined their ability to codify client experiences more precisely using spoken language, Bandler and Grinder began to look for other sources of information based on nonverbal behavior, including visual clues (eye movements, changes in skin color, breathing, muscle tension) and auditory clues (pitch, volume, pace). They claimed that these techniques, pulled together, helped explain how expert therapists were able to gather a staggering amount of information about clients.

Knowing what their experts saw and heard helped Bandler and Grinder establish a framework—which could be taught—for how interventions were selected or modified for each client.

Many, if not most, of the informa-

A MINI GLOSSARY

BY MARILYN DARLING

NLP has "stolen" many ideas from the fields of linguistics and cybernetics. Some examples:

Nominalized experience. "Nominalization" is a linguistic term that refers to turning a process into a name or an event. Once a process is named, it can be bound and categorized. Saying, "I have a *fear* of high places," serves to bundle together a group of sensations that result from certain perceptions and memories into a thing that exists on its own. "Attitude," "talent," "intention" and "phobia" are all words we use to compartmentalize our experience into a sort of shorthand as a way to understand and talk about it.

Unfortunately, two things happen when we name or "nominalize" our experiences. First, listeners understand the words we use based not on our experience, but on theirs. Second, once the experience "exists" on its own, it is seen as somehow separate from us and inaccessible to change. NLP practitioners try to bring nominalizations back into direct experience so that the original experiences or processes can be examined more closely and, if a conflict exists, modified or eliminated.

Ecology and well-formed outcomes. Within the context of NLP, human beings are viewed as "ecological systems." The concept of ecology is integral to the field of cybernetics—the study of systems. When a change happens in one part of the system, it affects other parts as well. This is what people mean when they caution, "Be careful what you wish for because your wish may come true."

Changes produce side effects. People quit smoking and gain 20 pounds. I know a man who attended a poorly run assertiveness-training seminar only to find that the result of his "new" self was increased tension headaches and the loss of several close friends. He had no contextual cues as to when *not* to be assertive.

Ideally, NLP practitioners can accurately predict what side effects a change might precipitate because they gather more specific information about how a client's internal systems function now, and because they help the client define a very specific objective or outcome. They can actually observe, test for and mitigate unintended changes.

The law of requisite variety. This law of the field of cybernetics states that the element in a system that exhibits the greatest variety of behavior is the controlling factor in the system. In the realm of human communication, the law holds that the person who demonstrates the most flexibility—the largest repertoire of options in response to a given situation—is the person likely to control or be successful in that situation.

As Bandler and Grinder put it, "When what you're doing isn't working, try almost anything else until you get the outcome you're looking for." This could be called the Golden Rule of NLP. The point is that when speaking English to someone who doesn't understand the language, yelling the same thing louder will not get your point across. There are a few implications in that one for training, aren't there?

Reprinted from TRAINING, January 1988

tion techniques that make up NLP are not unique to NLP, and have not been billed as such—at least not by Bandler and Grinder. Because a number of techniques have been modeled directly from Erickson, Satir, Perls and many others, experienced therapists, trainers and consultants may recognize the ideas of their favorite schools of thought being described within the NLP context. Other techniques are not discouraged in NLP, they are valued. What NLP *tries* to do is test and remove any inappropriate limitations, so that the core ideas can be applied in any situations where they would be useful.

Quick change artists

The possibilities sound wonderful: a clearer understanding of goals, a deeper, more complete perception of the people around us, and the ability to teach "unteachable" skills.

So what's the problem? Because I've observed NLP from a distance for several years, it strikes me that for a system of thought that appears useful to so many fields in so many ways, NLP hasn't lived up to its claims. There should be no phobias left. Everyone should have perfect pitch. Most, if not all, of the world's ills should have been vanquished by now.

I think one of NLP's biggest weaknesses is that Bandler and Grinder—as well as many of their students—show an unnerving tendency to overstate their case. They have made bold and sometimes unsubstantiated claims—phobia cures in 10 minutes, lifelong perfect pitch, etc. And they repeat mythic tales of power and wonder. I remember Bandler and Grinder announcing at one point that they were learning how to walk through walls—or at least how to make large groups of people believe they saw them do it.

If such claims were true, NLP should be universally acknowledged as one of the century's greatest discoveries. In fact, it languishes in relative obscurity, largely ignored by the academic and business worlds.

The real crime here is against one of NLP's own guiding principles: "Know thine audience." Outrageous claims drive people away in hordes (Tony Robbins' trendy NLP-based fire-walking seminars seem to be an exception, at least so far). Concentrating on building a reputation

through example and keeping NLP's basic premises in mind would do a lot to give the techniques the hearing they deserve.

The philosophy espoused by NLP is a challenge. Not all "certified practitioners" have been able to "get it." It is relatively easy to memorize techniques, even to become skilled enough at a particular "trick" to impress people. But it takes time, effort and dedication to test and break deeply ingrained limitations. The limitations and ulterior motives of some practitioners have been translated into the NLP message.

Take rigidity, for example. It's possible for NLP to become as rigid as any other tool because of a trainer's need to be "right." In fact, as NLP gets passed down through the generations, as it were, its techniques are becoming compartmentalized—treated rather like a cookbook of change, which on a creativity scale of one to 10 would rate somewhere below zero. The techniques become inflexible and unadaptable as a result.

There is now a prescribed "phobia cure" which is different in some concrete way from the "insomnia cure." The methods often are taught in a step-by-step process without the framework that allows them to be used creatively in other situations.

Bandler and Grinder warned their students not to let any technique take on a life of its own. Each one should always be evaluated for its usefulness in effecting a desired change. Yet novices can stumble into a cookbook course in NLP and end up learning some particular set of techniques that may or may not be applicable to their needs. They are likely to walk away slightly bewildered and totally unimpressed.

Compounding the problem is a jargon jungle that gets darker and denser with each new technique. "Fourtuples," "Meta-Model," "swish patterns," "submodalities" and, indeed, "Neuro-Linguistic Programming" itself, are terms that trip lightly off the tongues of NLP practitioners. While some of them serve as useful shorthand, they also create a Berlin Wall between the learned and the curious.

For these reasons (and because of people who promote NLP as a weapon to use in clawing your way to the top), NLP has moved at a snail's pace in the training and development world.

If all this doesn't scare you away, if you're still intrigued by the possibility that beneath the manure there lies a pony, then we should answer the question, "How might I use NLP in training and development?"

Change

Two of the most obvious uses to which NLP can be put in business are: 1) creating personal and group change and, 2) discovering and teaching the skills of various experts.

Although NLP grew from therapeutic soil, advocates argue that its change process is equally applicable to evaluating and facilitating group dynamics, to training (especially when an organizational change is involved) or to self-development. Here is a bare-bones outline of an NLP approach to the task of creating change in a group environment.

1. *What exactly is the change desired?* Define precisely the goal a group or business wants to reach. Define it in terms of how it will look and feel. Define the goal so that its soundness can be tested, so group members will be motivated to reach it, and so they'll know when and if they've arrived.

2. *What's stopping them?* Determine exactly when the group members' internal limits (defined as information, actions or beliefs that demonstrate discrepancies between their "map" and the actual territory) get in the way of their desired actions, objectives or growth.

3. *What purpose do these limits serve and how are they applied?* Find out why the limits are there and what decisions and actions they affect.

4. *What works and when? What should be tossed out?* Break down the limitations into valid and invalid discriminations, based on their value in facilitating action or growth in particular contexts.

5. *What would work better, and when should it be used?* For information, actions or beliefs that you find to be invalid, substitute (using any of a variety of techniques) different information, a different viewpoint or a different way of getting something done.

6. *On the whole, does the group function better as a result of this change effort?* Test the group's new information, actions or beliefs to make sure they are working to the group's

benefit in the proper situations, and that no unanticipated changes have been made that might harm the group's ability to function in other areas (referred to as an "ecological check").

The NLP change process focuses on getting to a desired objective by removing all obstacles, including limiting perceptions.

But while this may look like a fairly straightforward procedure—easy to talk about, if not easy to *do*—there is no right way to get from step one to step six. Bandler and Grinder would say, "If it works (and it doesn't upset the ecology of the system) use it." NLP techniques add value to the process by fine-tuning the group members' observation skills and by teaching them how to respond with flexibility to the situation.

Skills

The process of discovering and teaching unique skills offers some of the most exciting potential for using NLP in business. The best teachers a company could ever hire, in terms of passing on skills that are uniquely suited to its business objectives and environment, are on the company's payroll already.

Unfortunately, top performers seldom have the time or the ability to teach others what they know; at least, they rarely seem to make efficient and effective teachers. NLP's claim is that a skilled practitioner can work with (or "model") top performers to understand the conscious and unconscious elements of the skills that make them successful—and can teach those skills to others.

NLP practitioners are using these modeling skills across the country to teach such talents as singing, composing, speed-reading, creative writing and leadership. By using NLP skills, they say, people inside your company can teach things like project management, public speaking or

---

**Gifted communicators
are masters at
living in
other people's worlds.**

---

sales and customer service—and do it as well as, or better than, an outside consultant.

The basic NLP skills that are fundamental to understanding individual and group learning processes also can be applied to any training process. These skills simply ensure that the "message sent" is the "message received" and that the style trainers use to present the material meets the learning needs of the audience. Obviously, neither of those objectives are by any means unique to NLP. NLP just offers a certain approach to achieving them.

Is it manipulative?

Can NLP techniques be used to manipulate people to do something against their best interests? Sure. More than once? Less likely. Can the same be said of a great many other psychological techniques? Of course.

We are all persuasive to some degree. Ministers are some of the most persuasive people I know. And as the Jim and Tammy Bakker debacle demonstrated, their persuasiveness can be used for all sorts of ends. But as recent events also demonstrated, what goes around comes around.

The concept of a person's or a group's *ecology*—its integrity as a system—is considered by ethical NLP practitioners to be a critical aspect of any change or training effort. If the ecology is not honored, the change won't stick. It's like sales: The most successful salespeople, over the long run, are those who understand and satisfy *all* of their customers' needs.

What it comes down to is that like so many skills and tools, NLP can be used for many different purposes—some helpful, others limiting and manipulative. Should we throw out NLP because it can be used for the latter? NLP's basic philosophy is both sound and exciting in what it can offer us as a basis for learning and change.

But buyer beware. NLP certification, though conceived with good intentions, does not guarantee a thing. When you go shopping for an NLP expert, you'll have to rely on your own judgment.

Reprinted from TRAINING, January 1988

47 TIPS FOR FLIP-CHART USERS

Everything you didn't even think there was to know about dealing with a flip chart

BY A.E. BLOOMWELL

I observed with considerable pain the valiant efforts of the instructor. He mumbled most of his material to the flip-chart easel and scribbled the rest as fast as he could in small, illegible longhand. As soon as one page was full, he immediately flipped the sheet over with hardly a breath between . . . Even a seat in the front row would not have helped.

I am firmly convinced that a flip-chart easel and pad is the absolute minimum visual aid required for *any* classroom situation anywhere. The flip chart belongs not only in the seminar/workshop arena of the business world, but also in the academic classroom, the lecture hall, meeting rooms of almost any size and beside the pulpit on Sunday.

With a flip chart, the presenter can visualize and highlight key points, and respond to and capture input from the group. The easel is inexpensive, is used in normal room lighting and requires a minimum lead time for preparation. What more could a trainer ask?

Even poorly used, a flip chart can aid a presentation. But the more expert you become with this tool, the more it will help you. Many of the following tips are aimed at beginners, but veteran chart flippers may find a few surprises, too.

Writing on the pad

• Print in block letters 1- to 1¼ inches high. *Practice* is required to print neatly in horizontal lines. It only takes a moment longer to do it neatly; the result looks professional and communicates the message.

• If the group is large and the room deeper than 30 feet, print larger and bolder.

• Don't talk to the easel board while writing. Stop talking momentarily, write quickly and briefly, then turn again to your audience.

• Don't put more than about 10 lines of information on a page.

• Don't fill a page to the bottom. People at the back of the room probably will not be able to see.

• Write only key points, in shortened form, on the page. The whole idea is to help the learner retain information quickly and easily. *Everything* does not have to be written down.

• If you have a complex page of material, prepare the page ahead of time in light pencil. When you are ready to develop the material, trace over the pencil markings with the broad-tip marker. You will appear very knowledgeable—not to mention very neat. This technique can also provide notes for material to be outlined on the easel throughout the presentation.

• A related technique: When you know there will be difficult words to spell or concepts to remember, plan where they will come up. Print the words in small, lightly penciled letters at the top left corner of the required page, eye level and legible only to you. Presto, perfect recall.

• When teaching from detailed notes, build in cues that remind you of key phrases you want to transfer to the chart. Underline the key phrases with a colored pencil, for example.

• Wait at least 20-30 seconds after you finish writing before you flip the page. Allow time for reading, retention and note-taking.

• As soon as you finish discussing the information on an easel sheet, flip the page back and out of sight unless there is a specific reason why it should remain visible.

• *Practice* flipping pages back if you haven't used an easel before. It isn't as simple as it looks.

• Information on an easel sheet is easily retrieved. If you expect to refer to a page again, dog-ear the page or place a tape index tab on the edge of the sheet.

• Don't stand in front of the easel after you have finished writing.

Past important pages

• You can add emphasis and clarity—and make reviewing much easier—by posting key sheets on the wall. Cover the walls with them if necessary.

• Put a brief but descriptive title at the top of each sheet before posting.

• Rip off pages with a "matador tear," using a sharp tug starting at one corner. Don't pull straight down.

• Use one-inch masking tape. Before class, cut tape in two- to three-inch lengths; stick lightly to the edge of the easel board.

• Post sheets on a smooth, hard wall surface as high as possible. Do not post on wallpaper, and beware of finishes that may peel off with the tape.

• Don't write on the easel page after it is posted on the wall. The ink may bleed through and stain the wall.

Prepared pages

• There are three advantages to using prepared easel pages: Printing is very neat and legible; class time is not spent at the easel; and prepared easel pages double as notes for the presenter.

• If you have a succession of prepared pages, use one easel pad for prepared material, a second for material written during the presentation.

• When using a series of prepared pages, leave a blank page between each sheet of material. Pages are thin and can be read through a single sheet. Don't allow your audience to get ahead of you.

• If you have only a few pages prepared for use at the beginning of a session, prepare them in reverse order and flip them back. When wanted, flip them forward.

- If you will be using a large number of prepared pages, lay them flat on a table to one side. Pick up each page as needed and tape on the easel board or on the wall.

- If you are traveling with prepared flip-chart pages, tear them off the pad, roll them up and place them in a cardboard mailing tube. These tubes also provide good protection from careless baggage handlers.

- If you misspell a word during preparation, cut out the mistake with a razor blade. Tape a clean piece of paper on the back of the hole and correct the error.

- If you want to reuse a prepared page or if you want multiple copies of something snazzy, consider commissioning a full-size, computer-generated easel page. Have it laminated with lightweight plastic.

The easel

- A sturdy metal easel with a solid writing surface and folding legs is your best bet.

- A homemade board may be constructed from quarter-inch plywood and one- by two-inch legs.

- Avoid frills (combination chalkboard, enamel or magnetic surface) unless you need those features. They add weight and bulk.

- The total weight of a good, all-purpose easel should be less than 20 pounds. It should fold flat to a two-inch thickness, making it easy to carry.

- If you are tall, consider a model with adjustable legs.

- Tabletop easels are generally unsatisfactory for classroom use. They are awkward and not very stable.

- Consider using several flip-chart easels (up to five or six) across the front of the room if and when: You must develop a continuous, uninterrupted flow of ideas, and you can't post pages on the wall; the room is big, requiring your printing to be quite large; you have a large, complex chart or diagram.

- If you use multiple easels, you probably should eschew overhead projectors, screens and other visual aids. Don't clutter the room with distractions.

- When using multiple easels, remember to position them so that each is visible to everyone in the room.

Easel pads

- The most common pad size is 27-by 34-inches, with mounting holes spaced at 17½ inches. Not all pads and easels have matching punched holes and mounting pins. Check your supply and beware when you buy.

- White paper with perforated sheet tops offers easy reading for the audience and easy tearing for you.

- If your writing tends to stray from the horizontal, shop around for lined pads. Lines generally are one inch apart.

- If you mount a pad to the easel with a bar clamp alone, without hanging pins, the pad will slip and slide and annoy you.

Marking pens

- Use a wide, felt-tip marker, and print boldly. Make it a watercolor marker, because solvent (permanent) inks tend to bleed through the paper and are much more difficult to wash off hands and out of clothes.

- Multicolored markers add variety and interest, but avoid light colors—use strong, bright hues. (An exception is red, which should be used for emphasis only. Even dark red may be difficult to read at a distance.)

- Use colors systematically: one for page heading, one for primary points, another for subpoints.

- When you aren't writing, put the pen down. It is distracting when used as a toy or to vent nervous energy.

- When the pen starts to run out of ink, throw it away. A squeaking pen on the page sends shivers up spines. And the increasingly faint markings as you try to squeeze the last penny's worth of use out of this one-dollar instrument not only are hard to read, they make you look like a cheapskate. Be big about it. Break down and buy another pen.

Reprinted from TRAINING, June 1983

WHEN TO USE INFORMATION MAPPING

The originator of the mapping technique
tells how to decide whether
it fits your needs

BY ROBERT E. HORN

Just what is Information Mapping and how does it work? Information Mapping is a unique method of organizing, writing, sequencing and formatting learning and reference materials. It replaces the paragraph of prose and the frame of programmed instruction with a series of carefully defined, functional Information Blocks. Information Mapping provides a collection of rules for writing and organizing each information block and for visualizing the system.

Information Mapping includes ready-made graphic formats for many of the common types of training materials. These make it easier to scan and skim than virtually any other type of printed materials do.

Information Mapping is, thus, a collection of things: Principles for system design; taxonomies; formats; procedures for writing and sequencing; rules and policies; rationales based in learning theory, educational technology, communications research, and good writing practice; and a formalized set of trade-offs for different situations.

The diagram below shows how Information Mapping works on a specific project. The subject matter and certain specifications for a course go into the Information Mapping system and out come such things as a course syllabus, a reference manual, a learning/reference book, or a programmed-instruction-like sequence. The output depends on the input, the content of the subject matter, the goals of the job, and hence what parts of the total Information

Mapping system are made of.

Information Mapping arose partly from two observations. The first is that people forget. They forget no matter what kind of learning methods or materials are used. The second is that when people have forgotten something, they like to go back and look at the material they learned from. Taking these two factors together, we have in Information Mapping a design for learning materials that performs as well as programmed learning (or better) and which clearly outperforms it as a reference.

How is Information Mapping applied to training?

Information Mapping can be applied to a variety of training situations, such as teaching computer operators to keep up with changing payroll practices, teaching bank clerks to fill out forms, teaching insurance clerks to use computer terminals in branch offices all over the country, and teaching salesmen, maintenance men, supervisors and managers how to operate, maintain and sell new pieces of equipment.

Another problem that Information Mapping can help solve is that of getting uniformity when more than one writer is working on a project. Information Mapping with its careful set of rules for writing different types of material, not only provides uniformity among writers, it provides a lot of common ground between a writer and his editor or manager. Both can look at a particular block and know that is must do particular things and follow particular rules and policies.

Another common problem arises from the need to use subject-matter experts (SMEs), who, more frequently than not, are not trainers or writers. Here Information Mapping helps by providing what amounts to an outline to the SME to "fill in the blank blocks."

This leads to another opportunity. Within a project, even before the final material is produced, the task analyst must communicate with the SME and with his managers and various other technical and managerial people. Information Mapping provides a number of formats for such documents. The advantage is that these documents in Information Mapping format begin to approximate the final appearance of the product (training course, manual, etc.). Too often task analyses are difficult to interpret and review by SMEs because they do not look very much like final products.

An unusual application of Information Mapping is about to be made by an insurance company. Their problem is

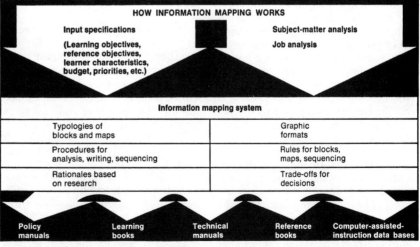

Diagram illustrates how subject matter and certain specifications for a course can be systematized to produce instructional aids of various kinds. As in other systems, the author notes, Information Mapping output depends on input: garbage in, garbage out.

WHEN TO USE INFORMATION MAPPING

If your answer to these questions is yes, take the action listed in the right-hand column.

1. Are written learning materials required?	Use IM.	• Simulate complex situations in business, including interpersonal training and values clarification?	Use other methods, (such as simulation exercises, role plays, case method), which occasionally can be supported by IM documents on the theoretical aspects of the total presentation.
2. Can the data be looked up? Are some reference materials to be made?	Use IM.		
3. Will the materials have to be modified or updated relatively frequently?	Use IM.		
4. Does the importance warrant the cost of preparing written training materials?	Use IM.	• Involve interaction with other people (e.g., such as transactional analysis)?	Use a variety of structured experiential exercises, discussion and counselling models. (Use IM only for theory.)
5. Does (is) part or all of the job/subject matter to be taught—			
• Highly procedural (many decisions and many separate steps)?	Use IM (which incorporates decision tables, algorithms, etc.).	• Require skilled physical tasks (e.g., typing, using tools) or fine perceptual discriminations?	Use various in-person or filmed demonstrations plus usual practice methods.
• Contain processes to be explained (e.g., how a drug works, how a piece of machinery works)?	Use IM (which incorporates a set of blocks designed to teach processes efficiently).	• Attitudinal	Analyze job situation carefully to determine if consequences need to be altered, feedback provided, standards set, job redesigned, organization redesigned, individual transferred, etc.
• Have considerable conceptual material (e.g., definitions, discriminations, generalizations, classifications)?	Use IM.		
• Involve a well-formed method of problem solving or precise analysis?	Use IM (combining procedural and conceptual maps).	Sample planning sheet shown here provides guidelines on whether information mapping applies to a particular training problem.	

that the young people they are hiring can't write very good sentences and can't organize and sequence information logically. This causes lots of difficulties for an organization as word-oriented as an insurance company. The training staff is currently learning how to teach Information Mapping to the newcomers with the hope that it will help them organize their thoughts.

Once the trainees learn to write blocks and maps, the company plans to turn them over to regular English teachers to work on their sentences. The sentences, it is hoped, will at least be in sequence.

Where *doesn't* Information Mapping apply?

There are, of course, specific training areas that mapping does not encompass. Information Mapping should not be used to try to persuade someone to do something. It is designed only to provide people with the *capacity* to act. I should not be expected to provide anyone with the *willingness* to act. This means that it is not designed for advertising or sales literature, legal briefs, debating notes or other types of persuasive writing.

Information Mapping, as it has currently been defined, is also not designed for planning documents. Although I have written a few proposals using a modified block format, no taxonomy of carefully researched sets of blocks or maps exists as yet for such documents. Similarly, historical documents and reports of projects, experiments and case histories have not been treated to the kind of analysis that has

been applied to Information Mapping for the explanatory domain.

We don't recommend using Information Mapping for magazine articles (in which there is a mixture of sequencing, time frames, and levels of abstraction), for short memos (although certain blocks have been incorporated successfully), nor for high-level management briefings (because these are rarely either at the level of technical detail nor at the level of learning or reference that Information Mapping is best used for). In all of these cases, until research and development extends the domain of mapping, other methods will have to be used.

When should Information Mapping be used?

With the foregoing in mind, a trainer might wonder how to determine whether Information Mapping might be useful. The illustration is aimed at helping the trainer reach a decision. He will, of course, have first done an adequate front-end-value analysis to establish that training must be done.

Here's a case to demonstrate the use of the illustration: A multi-national banking company is issuing a new policy on a certain service. Analysts estimate that it will end up in a 50-to-75-page policy handbook. Retraining must also be performed, as many elements of the new service are similar to but not necessarily the same as those of other services. All 125 branches of the bank need to train the following employees—branch manager, cashier, accounting department manager, and a

minimum of two accounting system clerks.

Applying this information to the illustration, we answer *yes* to 1, 2 and 4 and *probably yes* to question 3. In question 5, we answer *yes* to a, c and d. These answers indicate that the task is ideally suited to Information Mapping.

What about cost?

The cost of Information Mapping is at the very least no more than the methods you are currently using and probably somewhat less. This is true whether you figure on a per-page or per-training-hour method. The increased savings come in these areas:

There is an increased efficiency in the writing, task analysis and editing. Some trainers have indicated this has been in the order of five to 20 percent, depending on writer, job and subject. One of the possibilities for savings is that the task-analysis documents can be prepared in Information Mapping formats, which means that as early as the completion of the task analysis you have an abbreviated approximation of the final manual, book, or data base.

There are possible savings in on-the-job look-up time, since mapping is designed specifically for ease of look-up and ease of scanning. There are also the potential savings that come from fewer errors in more easily understood materials.

Savings often occur in the production of a single, combined learning-reference document rather than two or more (typically a programmed-instruction book plus a reference manual).

Reprinted from TRAINING, February 1975

MIND MAPPING: BRAINSTORMING ON PAPER

Use this technique for note-taking, problem solving and writing

BY CHRIS LEE

I've never been quite certain if I'm right-brained or left-brained. Sure, I'm a writer, which might tip the scales toward such right-brain specialties as imagery, wholistic vision and analogous conceptualizing. But on the other hand (or brain), I'm a journalist, not a poet. Most magazine articles depend more on research-fact gathering, interviewing and the like—than on personal interpretation of archetypal symbolism. Once all the facts are collected, the actual process of journalistic writing demands as much sorting, organization and clear expression as creativity. It's a very linear activity.

And if you want to know the truth, I've never been convinced that right-brain/left-brain/whole-brain devotees have discovered any earth-shattering truths about the mind. Granted, brain researchers have pegged certain functions to specific parts of the brain. But a cottage industry of zealots seems to have taken that ball and run with it a hell of a lot further than scientific findings justify.

That bias notwithstanding, I approached the job of researching the definition and practice of mind mapping with what I hoped were equal parts of skepticism and objectivity. I had only the vaguest idea of what it was ("Isn't it what people are doing when they claim to be taking notes, except it looks like they're just doodling?"), so I called Anne Durrum Robinson, a human resource development consultant in Austin, TX. I knew she could give me the basics as well as suggestions for further reading.

She characterized mind mapping—also known as clustering, thought trails and hurricane writing—as "brainstorming on paper. The basic principle is to get information down the way your mind handles it, not in a rigid outline. You're tapping into all your mind's resources before you begin to organize the information. You can use it for any kind of writing—creative, business or professional—or to take notes on reading or lectures."

Robinson says the rules are simple: print (otherwise you may write too much), use key words and create your own symbols for decision points or central ideas.

Mind mapping is fruitful, she says, because it helps you record all your random thoughts without judging them. The idea is to indulge in divergent (nonlinear) thinking until you get a sense of a "felt shift," a direction or trend around which your thoughts are coalescing. Then your judgmental, or convergent, thinking comes into play to refine your ideas. It's a particularly helpful technique for people who are right-brain dominant, she says. "Some right-brained children can't do outlining, but they can do mind mapping."

Now, I was intrigued. As a kid, I was always stymied by outlining. I completed grade-school writing assignments backwards: First I'd write the report and then I'd oblige the teacher with a "bogus" outline completed after the fact. Robinson suggested a couple of books, adding that because they championed something as nontraditional and messy looking as mind mapping, they "curled English teachers' hair." It was a good enough recommendation for me.

The first, Tony Buzan's *Use Both Sides of Your Brain* (E.P. Dutton, Inc., 1974), posits that list-like methods of organization, such as traditional outlining and note-taking, operate "against the way in which the brain works." The linear nature of speech and print notwithstanding, the brain actually deals with "key concepts in an interlinked and integrated manner," he says. Similarly, mind mapping starts with a central concept and branches out to related ideas, enabling the brain to recall, add and review information more easily.

Buzan advocates mind mapping for note-taking, problem solving, writing—"any activity where thought, recall, planning or creativity are involved." Most people will feel some apprehension about developing a "messy" page of scrawled boxes, circles and arrows. But, he concludes, "notes which look 'neat' are, in informational terms, messy. . . . The key information is disguised, disconnected and cluttered with many informationally irrelevant words. The notes which look 'messy' are informationally far neater. They show immediately the important concepts [and] the connections. . . ."

Buzan made sense to me, so I checked out Robinson's other recommendation: *Writing the Natural Way: Using Right-Brain Techniques to Release Your Expressive Powers* (J.P. Tarcher, Inc., 1983), by Gabriele Lusser Rico. Drawing on the work of brain and creativity researchers, Rico developed what she calls "clustering" as a method of teaching creative writing to college students.

She did it by translating psychiatrist Anton Ehrenzweig's conceptualization of the creative search to paper. She explains the discovery process: "I circled [the word] maze in the center of a blank page and clustered, electrified by the connections in my head that spilled and radiated outward from its center. . . . As I continued to cluster, I suddenly experienced a shift from a sense of randomness to a sense of direction in all this welter, and I began to write." As soon as she introduced the "nonlinear brainstorming process of clustering" to a freshman composition class, she says, ". . .my students' writing made a dramatic turnabout, and it has been my approach to teaching writing ever since."

Rico leans heavily on the idea that clustering releases the creative potential of the right brain before the logical left brain gets into the act. She terms the two hemispheres "sign mind" and "design mind" and defines them as follows: "Sign mind is largely occupied with the rational, logical representation of reality and with parts and logical sequences. . . . By contrast. . .the design mind constantly thinks in complex images; it patterns to make designs of whatever it encounters, including language. . . ."

The clustering technique allows you to tap the patterns and associations of your design mind, she says. Then the corpus callosum, a sort of traffic light between the two sides of the brain, "shifts from *stop* to *go*, making right-brain associations accessible to the left brain, which in turn can give them sequential, communicable form."

The second step in using clustering for creative writing is what Rico calls "the trial-web shift." She explains: "You are clustering, seemingly randomly, when suddenly you experience a sense of direction. The moment between randomness and sense of direction is the moment of shift." She likens this "aha!" to the experience of looking through the lens of a camera at a blur that suddenly comes into focus when you adjust the focusing mechanism correctly.

The differences between Rico's clustering and Buzan's mind mapping seem to be more of application and design, rather than mechanics or rationale. (In clustering, the key concepts and associations are circled and linked by connecting lines; in mind

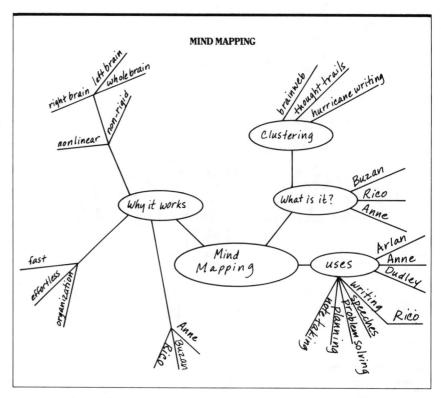

MIND MAPPING

mapping, the radiating structure may include arrows, colors, idiosyncratic codes or geometrical shapes that indicate relationships.) Rico uses her technique for creative writing applications; Buzan employs mapping to solve problems, plan, take notes or "outline" writing of any kind. And that's where it suits the business purposes of mind-mapping fans in the training field.

"I use mind maps to write books, plan projects and develop courses," says Dudley Lynch, president of Brain Technologies Corp. of Fort Collins, CO, and editor of the "Brain & Strategy" newletter. "[The technique] gives you permission to be open, to consider anything in the whole wide world. I call mind maps 'brain webs.' I like that term. I think it's descriptive of how the brain works."

Arlan Tietel, division training manager at 3M's magnetic media division in St. Paul, MN, uses mind mapping and has taught it to employees. "I use it to take notes for myself, I've advocated it in workshops as a method to take notes, and I've used it to construct a leader's guide of the information to be communicated in a

workshop," he says. "I'm not a good note-taker in a linear style, but I used mind mapping at a conference [recently], and I got everything [said] for the day on one page. It's also the only time anyone ever asked me for a copy of my notes."

Why mind mapping instead of an A-B-C outline? "I use it to force myself into a more creative mode—more right-brained than left-brained," Tietel says. "It helps me to capture and recall information."

I constructed the mind map reproduced here after completing the research for this story. It was a first attempt—actually a sort of hybrid mind map and cluster—but most of its branches eventually found their way into this piece. It worked just fine as a substitute for traditional outlining. But so does my own method of jotting key words and phrases on the tail end of my computer file. I add and subtract as I write.

So am I right-brained or left-brained? I still don't know. Maybe I just have an aversion to outlines.

Reprinted from TRAINING, September 1987

JOB INSTRUCTION TRAINING: DON'T OVERLOOK IT

This four-step method is a basic, pragmatic approach to training

BY RON ZEMKE

In the new never-ending quest to "be there or be square," innovationwise, it is easy to overlook the value of the tried and true for the fancy and new. So it is with Job Instruction Training (JIT), a long-whiskered but highly effective and efficient training technique that goes all but unnoticed in today's clamor for high-tech-driven training solutions.

JIT, a form of structured on-the-job training developed during World War II by the Training Within Industry Service of the War Manpower Commission, is credited with a major role in helping American industry meet the challenge of turning thousands of "raw recruits" into a productive industrial work force.

Developed as a quick method for converting supervisors, subject-matter experts and experienced craftsmen into reasonably effective job-skills trainers, JIT is remarkably useful today and has a subtle sophistication often overlooked by the professional educational technologist.

It is true that some training experts, such as James E. Gardner, in his book *Training Interventions in Job Skill Development* (Addison-Wesley, 1981), have complained that the JIT model is too "simplistic" and "mechanistic," and that its application in contemporary settings can "limit trainers' effectiveness and professional growth." But an open-minded inspection reveals a technology with more going for it than one might expect.

The JIT model, referred to as the "Four P Approach" by Herman Brinbrauer, author of *Training for Trainers: Increasing the Effectiveness of the On-The-Job Training Instructor* (Institute for Business & Industry, 1981), is divided into four major steps:

• *Preparation*—of the trainer, the trainee and the training course.

• *Presentation*—tell the trainee what is to be done and show how it is to be done.

• *Practice*—the trainee performs the job steps under the supervision of a trainer or supervisor.

• *Performance*—the trainee is put to work independently, under normal working conditions, with transitional support.

In overview, it's simple, familiar and by-the-numbers: "Tell-Show-Do-Review." But the details are illuminating. Take the *Preparation* step, which relies on the use of two forms to prepare the training program itself: the *Job Breakdown Sheet* and the *Training Timetable*.

The latter is a document that forces the trainer to sequence the training in an orderly, reasonable fashion, while the former is really a precursor of the *Task Analysis* concept that would become a hot topic after the war when psychologist Robert Gagne took the lead in extolling the virtues of task analysis and the critical role it played in wartime military training.

Also included in the preparation step is a considerable amount of advice on working with trainees. Much of it sounds remarkably like the advice one hears today from andragogy or adult-learning theorists. Social-learning experts would recognize admonitions pertaining to good behavior-modeling practices, while the expectancy-theory and behavior-modification people would recognize counsel much like that coming from their specialties.

Some examples: "Give the trainee an overview of what will be learned, how and why" (goal setting, expectancy theory). "Tell the trainee what he

---

HOW TO GET READY TO INSTRUCT

1. Have a timetable.
   • How much skill you expect and when.
2. Break down the job.
   • List the important steps.
   • Pick out the key points.
3. Have everything ready.
   • The right equipment, material, and supplies.
4. Have the workplace properly arranged.
   • As you would expect the worker to maintain it.

HOW TO INSTRUCT

STEP 1: *Prepare the Worker*
a. Put the worker at ease.
b. Find out what he or she knows.
c. Arouse interest.
d. Place the worker correctly.
(Insure a learning situation.)

STEP 2: *Present the Operation*
a. Tell.
b. Show.
c. Explain.
d. Demonstrate.
(One point at a time. Stress key points.)

STEP 3: *Try Out Performance*
a. Have the worker perform the operation.
b. Have the worker explain the key points.
c. Correct errors.
d. Reinstruct as needed.
(Be sure he or she knows.)

STEP 4: *Follow-up*
a. Put the worker on his own.
b. Encourage questioning.
c. Check frequently.
d. Taper off assistance.
(Practice—Key to Performance.)

From Developing and Training Human Resources in Organizations, Wexley and Latham, Scott-Foresman, 1981.

A quick look at JIT.

will gain from the training" (expectancy theory). "Express confidence that the trainee will learn to do the job quickly and well" (expectancy theory, goal setting, cognitive behavior modification).

The same sorts of "Aha's" occur when one looks closely at the "presentation" and "practice" steps. More examples: "When demonstrating the job, sit or stand as [closely as possible] to the exact position the trainee will sit or stand to do the job" (behavior modeling). "Show and tell what to do, how to do it and why things are done the way they are" (behavior modeling, cognitive psychology, adult-learning theory). "Have trainee perform each step telling what he or she is doing and why....Provide feedback on each step, correct errors immediately....Be sure trainee can perform each step successfully before moving to the next step.... Give praise for successful performance" (behavior modeling, social-learning theory, behavior modification).

The performance "P" bears a striking resemblance to quite a bit of the advice we hear today about how to transfer training to the job setting: "Before leaving the trainee alone at the work site, be sure the trainee knows where and how to get help" (adult-learning theory). "Set follow-up schedule, gradually withdrawing support from trainee" (behavior modification, adult-learning theory). "Encourage discussion of work methods and procedures; consider suggestions with real interest. Praise performance and thinking as appropriate but avoid fault-finding" (adult-learning theory, reinforcement social-learning theory).

The do's and don'ts of the JIT approach also are right in step with modern practices. Brinbrauer says he had to do a little updating of the JIT guidelines for his book, but only a little. Among the "Common Instruction Errors" trainers are advised to guard against:

• Talking down to employees as some do to children.

• Attempting to cover too much in too short a time or at one time.

• Failing to determine the trainee's background; assuming prior knowledge.

• Omitting details that the trainer takes for granted.

• Failure to use examples familiar to the trainees.

• Failure to receive or interpret feedback from the trainees indicating understanding, misunderstanding, confusion, etc.

• Failure to follow up on training.

• Inadequate preparation for giving the training.

Dugan Laird, one of the training world's sharpest observers, and author of *Approaches to Training and Development* (Addison-Wesley, 1978), calls JIT "an elegantly simple way to achieve efficient, productive learning." Human resources development researchers Kenneth N. Wexley and Gary P. Latham acknowledge that the JIT approach has a number of good training practices embedded in it and can be very effective as long as several administrative and strategic precautions are observed:

1. Employees functioning as trainers must be convinced that training new employees in no way jeopardizes their own job security.

2. The individuals serving as trainers should realize that their added responsibility will be instrumental in obtaining rewards for them.

3. Trainers and trainees should be paired carefully so as to minimize any differences in backgrounds, language, personalities, attitudes or ages that may inhibit communication and understanding.

4. The choice of trainers should be based upon ability to instruct and desire to undertake the added responsibility. Don't "draft" your trainers.

5. JIT trainers should themselves undergo rigorous training. (The original JIT programs consisted of five two-hour sessions held conference-style for 10 to 15 individuals at a time.)

6. The trainer must understand that the role is not a vacation from the job, and also must be cautioned that trainees are not to be considered "helpers" who can be delegated scut work.

7. Trainees should be rotated among trainers to compensate for weaker instruction by some, and to maximize exposure to a variety of master performers.

8. The organization must accept the fact that trainees will not perform at 100%. Learning must take precedence over production.

9. The trainer must understand the importance of close supervision in order to avoid trainee injuries and the learning of bad work habits.

10. The JIT approach is probably most effective when used in conjunction with other approaches such as programmed instruction, CAI, films and video, etc.

If several of those points sound naggingly familiar—as in "Didn't I hear that in a high-priced, train-the-trainer program last month?"—that's probably because JIT concepts have been repackaged and republished frequently, each time with slightly different turns and twists. But just as new improved Honey Nut Cheerios are still Cheerios, JIT by any other name is still JIT. You can't disguise its basic, pragmatic goodness.

Reprinted from TRAINING, July 1983

HOW GOOD PEOPLE PRODUCE BAD PROGRAMS

You're no dummy, and the producer you hired is no dummy, so where did your promising audiovisual package go wrong?

BY JUDSON SMITH

We have been producing business communications programs for 15 years. We produce bad programs; not often, and never on purpose, but we do end up with some turkeys now and then.

Most professionals who develop such programs—sound-slide shows, video, multimedia presentations for training and other purposes—can make the same statement. Even the most skilled people, working with the best equipment and an ample budget, can labor mightily and turn out a program that's not going to work at all.

How do good people produce bad programs? It's one of those questions like, "What happens to all those single socks that disappear in the dryer?" That is, it's a mystery, and one that may have many answers.

What is a "bad" program? A bad program is one that fails to meet the needs and objectives for which it was designed, one whose objectives were wrong in the first place, or one that meets the right objectives, but is delivered late or comes in at an exorbitant cost.

Notice that we're not speaking of poor photography or typography, of bad narration or incorrect grammar, of illegible graphics or murky video. These cosmetic and creative elements can help make a program good, but assuming a reasonable level of technical competence on the part of the creators, they are rarely the cause of a bad program.

As in so many things, *communica-tion* is the key factor that determines whether a program will be good or bad. Obviously, an audiovisual program must communicate to an audience; if people don't understand the message, they certainly can't learn from it. But communication with the audience is just the final step in a process that must occur at every stage in

The foundation for a bad program often is laid in the first meeting between producer and briefer.

the program's development.

Good communication is especially important among the three most influential people (or groups) involved in producing any program. The first is the "briefer"—the person who provides background data and objectives concerning the program. Then there's the "approver"—the person who has final say about the program's design and content. Finally, there's the "producer"—the person who actually will put the program together, acting either as the "general contractor" for a number of specialists or as the individual controlling most or all of the elements involved in the production.

The foundation for a bad program often is laid in the first meeting between producer and briefer. That

foundation starts to crumble when the approver gets involved in the picture. It happens because the briefer, the approver and the producer fail to communicate.

Sometimes that failure involves a misunderstanding of the intended audience and its needs. Suppose, for example, that you want to develop a training presentation to help salespeople sell a new product—a computerized microwave oven. The briefer and approver both are far removed from the field-sales force. The approver is a salesman who came up through the ranks, but has been in the home office for many years as a vice president. The briefer is a junior executive, punching her ticket by working in the sales department for a year or two.

Both of these people are quite likely to have faulty conceptions of the actual field-sales force. Suppose they believe, for instance, that the reason the new computerized microwave isn't selling is because the sales reps need more training in selling techniques. The briefing with the producer will consist of a discussion of the best way to present a program on basic selling skills.

But now suppose the audience in fact has no lack of basic selling skills. The real problem is more specific: The reps can't be effective at selling a computer-based product because they don't understand how the computer works and can't answer simple questions from nervous customers.

If the producer develops a program about basic selling skills—even a superbly developed presentation—it will be a bad program because it won't address the real need of this sales force.

A ridiculous scenario, you say. All anybody had to do was ask the salespeople about the problem *before* designing a program to solve it. A simple needs assessment, perhaps a few focus-group interviews like the ones used by advertising agencies to unearth consumer needs, preferences and opinions. . . .

Right. It's a problem that should never come up. But it does, and with amazing regularity. Producers in such situations face two problems. First, they must find out what actual need exists. Then they have to convince the briefer and approver that they are wrong.

Briefers and approvers switching horses

One of the classic ways to ruin a program is to make knee-jerk changes in midstream. And this often happens because the briefer, the person in steady contact with the producer, is

211

WHAT TO DO WHEN
YOU HAVE TO SHOOT FIRST

One of the sacrosanct rules for developing video-based technical training is this: Always have the script approved by subject-matter experts before you start the cameras rolling. To do otherwise is to court disaster. You must be sure that all the demonstrations are technically accurate, and that you've neither left anything out nor inserted anything extraneous.

Good advice. Sooner or later, however, most technical trainers run into these lines: Management wants operators trained on quality standards, but there are no defined standards of performance upon which to base the training. You can't independently develop standards, nor can you get the attention of busy engineers and managers long enough to get them to agree on standards, let alone to create thorough documentation.

What can you do? Well, occasionally, you may have to start production without defined standards and develop them as you go. Yes, you do want to avoid this situation like you would an I.R.S. audit, but you may not be able to. "If you want to help solve problems in a timely manner and be responsive to operational needs, you may not always have a choice," says Ted Cocheu, president of Performance Technologies, a Los Gatos, CA-based management consulting and training firm.

Cocheu offers five steps to help you produce an effective technical training video—even under these lousy circumstances.

- *Familiarization.* Although you aren't authorized to define quality standards, you can acquaint yourself with the relevant issues and processes. Talk to the managers about their objectives and concerns. Take a tour of the work area. Ask the engineers to describe the processes to you, and take careful notes. Watch how the operators currently do things.

Now that you understand what skills need to be taught, you're ready to draw up the overall structure and design for the videotape. Have the managers and subject-matter experts (SMEs) review the design and give you feedback before you proceed.

- *Organization.* You'll need some help at this stage. First, you'll need a logistics person—someone who is knowledgeable and has enough authority to obtain the space, tools, equipment and materials to create a set that closely resembles the work environment. By simulating the situation, you'll avoid disrupting the normal work schedule and you'll have more flexibility for lighting and camera angles.

Next, find an operator to perform the procedures in front of the camera. This person should be a highly competent performer who commands peer respect.

Finally, you'll need a SME or two who will stick around while you're filming, define quality standards and make sure the operator follows them. These people obviously must have the knowledge and authority to make decisions and establish standards where none exist.

- *Production.* Film the process according to these authorized standards. Encourage the subject-matter experts to call your attention to any deviations. Do lots of shooting with multiple angles to give you plenty of flexibility in the editing room.

- *Scripting.* Now you're ready to prepare a narrator's script and tie all the visual elements together. Before you start editing, get the managers and SMEs to review the script. If they approve, you're in good shape. If not, you may wind up reshooting a few segments. "Even though your subject-matter experts on the set said to shoot an activity a certain way, they may change their minds once they see it on paper," warns Cocheu. "It's the big chance you take going into production without the proper documentation."

- *Editing.* If the objections are minor, you may be able to work around them by editing certain elements. If you can, have a SME present during this phase, too. If that's impossible, make a rough-cut edit to serve as a preview of the general flow and continuity of the final video.

If you do decide to forge ahead to the final edit, be prepared to face a certain amount of criticism. People always have ideas about how you could have done things differently when they see a process on video for the first time. Ask them if the taped version is technically accurate, and whether the suggested changes would make a significant impact on the program's effectiveness. Their initial concerns may be minor enough not to warrant extensive reshooting or editing.

Reprinted from TRAINING, February 1988

not on the same wavelength as the approver.

We were asked to produce a new training program for a large financial institution. Everything went smoothly—until the day arrived when we were to record the narration. Fifteen minutes before the narrator was scheduled to arrive for the session, the briefer called. The approver had finally read the script the night before and was not satisfied. He wanted major changes.

This led to a domino effect that raised the program's cost and diluted its impact enormously. First, the narrator was paid twice, once for the cancelled session and once for the later session at which he did his job. Second, the final version of the script was written by a committee—a committee of people with little experience in writing "for the eye and ear." Third, the approver chose to make his own revisions to the committee's version. The result was a script that read like an annual report. It could be read well enough, but it could not be well *heard* and understood by an audience.

In addition, we had already shot the visuals for this program and compiled them into several trays. When the approver made his changes, he also changed the order of the various elements, making our compilation useless. We were forced to reassemble the show and to reshoot additional images—at an extra cost of more than $1,000.

The answer to this problem also is obvious: Just make sure the briefer and the approver are in agreement. But that's not always easy. In many cases, the reason you *have* a separate briefer and approver is that the approver is too busy to handle both tasks. In other cases, the briefer is concerned with a specific objective for a program while the approver is concerned with overall policy decisions. In that case, what works for an individual project may not work as part of the corporate philosophy.

A "treatment sheet" can help ensure agreement. This is a document that describes precisely what the project will cost in terms of time and money, how it will be accomplished in terms of both creative and technical approach, and what objectives it will meet. The treatment sheet must be reviewed and approved by both approver and briefer. It then becomes a "contract" with the producer. If producers live up to the terms of such contracts, they are likely to create good programs and probably will es-

the panel discussion was to be transcribed and edited on paper. Natural enough, since they were primarily print-oriented people.

To say that the end result was a bad program is being kind. It was an awful program and an extraordinarily expensive one, costing the clients several times what they expected to pay.

Again, the reason is deceptively simple. The clients thought they could transfer their experience in producing effective print programs into the skills required to produce effective video programs. Further, they hired us for our expertise in producing video, yet ignored our suggestions. To complete the fiasco, when the briefer realized he had a mess on his hands, he still ignored our suggestions and tried to fix the monster by throwing more money and time at it.

Blue skies

A common ailment among producers is optimism. The disease strikes in-house producers and outside production houses alike, and becomes especially virulent when the producer is hungry to do a job for creative or financial reasons. When you're hungry, or when a potential project appears more interesting than the routine of daily work, you want to grab it. To ensure that the project lands in your pocket, it's tempting to paint a rosy picture of what's possible within a given budget and time period. A good way for the client to get stuck with the bill for the producer's optimism is to ignore that contract we talked about earlier.

The same disease afflicts briefers and approvers, of course. In their case, it seems to affect the hearing. No matter how many times the producer suggests that their expectations are unrealistic, the message fails to get through.

A bad program is the probable result of overly optimistic budget and time expectations. But another possibility is that the producer moves heaven and earth to create a good program, working to the point of exhaustion, alienating co-workers or subcontractors, taking a loss on the project, etc. Now the briefer and approver have a successful program, but they also have had their unreal expectations reinforced. As far as they're concerned, this is now the rule rather than a single exception. For an independent producer who doesn't have to work for these people again, that's no big problem. But an *in-house* producer who pulls off such a miracle has just guaranteed that life will be a nightmare from this day forth.

It's what's up front that counts

By the time production actually begins, the seeds for a good or a bad program have been sown and fertilized. It is quite possible—quite easy, in fact—to destroy a well-planned program during the production stage, but production problems tend to be easy to spot and fairly easy to cure. It's pretty obvious when a visual is poorly shot or a music track is ineptly recorded. It's also obvious when the design of a printed piece destroys readability or the type is too small or too large.

What isn't obvious is the case where the visual is technically correct but the message it imparts is wrong, or where the printed piece looks good but fails to help the reader learn and retain the right information.

The major problem in the production phase is that some forms of training media are never seen as entire programs until it is too late to do anything about the glitches. The only cure is to pretest programs whenever possible.

For example, modern word-processing equipment allows the producer to use several different type styles, column widths and page sizes. So it's fairly simple to provide a mock-up of a printed presentation that has a look similar to the final product. In the same way, it's possible to do a "rough track" recording or a "rough cut" editing job for video and audiovisual presentations.

The advantage of this approach is that everyone involved in a project can get a good indication of what the final product will look like. And this makes the problem areas stand out quite clearly.

False economies

A classic production mistake that has ruined a lot of programs is the one where you try to save a dollar or an hour while completing one element, only to wind up spending much more

---

The result was a script, written by a committee, that read like an annual report.

---

fail to deliver the goods according to the contract, briefers and approvers have something concrete to point to when they explain their dissatisfaction and take whatever actions seem appropriate.
cape blame for bad ones. If producers

Who knows best?

Every medium has its own potentials and pitfalls. Experienced producers of training media learn to recognize both, and to eliminate the pitfalls while enhancing the potentials. Briefers and approvers generally lack that experience, but they ultimately control the way in which a presentation is produced. And they often refuse to take advantage of the producer's experience. The result usually is a bad program.

We were hired to direct and produce a videotaped version of a 10-person panel discussion. At the initial meeting, we explained some pitfalls and potentials, based on our prior experience with these uncontrolled—and uncontrollable—programs.

We could have saved our breath. The briefer and approver chose to produce the video presentation as if

---

We could have saved our breath . . . it was an awful program and an extraordinarily expensive one.

---

time and money at a later stage in the production.

A common example of false economy is the use of amateur narrators to save the cost of professional talent. One of our recent clients insisted upon this approach. Furthermore, the client wanted to record the amateur at his office, saving the cost of travel time.

To see why this is a false economy, let's establish a baseline cost for a professional narrator. Say the pro's base fee is $325 and she can record the session in one hour, at a cost of $65 per hour. In addition, let's assume that the pro makes so few mistakes that the editing can be done in three hours, at a cost of $195. The total for a professional voice track, then, is $585.

The same $65-per-hour figure applies for an audio engineer who goes on location to record an amateur, then edits the amateur's work. So the break-even point, assuming the amateur is being paid nothing, is about nine hours.

That seems like a good bet—until you spend an hour searching for a quiet conference room at the amateur's building and another half-hour getting someone to turn off the air conditioning so it doesn't provide a continuous hiss on the soundtrack. Then, of course, it takes three hours for the amateur to record something comparable to what the professional did in one. And it takes the audio engineer two or three times as long to edit the amateur's tape than it does for one recorded by a professional with good breath control, inflection, pauses and consistency.

The actual cost of the recording we are discussing was nearly $700. And the amateur still sounded amateurish. Instead of enhancing the words, he mumbled them, and helped create a bad program.

The same false economies occur in print material. At first glance, it seems obvious that the cheapest way to produce a quantity of copies is with a photocopy machine and that a typist is cheaper than typesetting. But in fact, this is true only for small-volume production, and only if you disregard the salary cost of the person doing the typing and photocopying.

Wrapping it

The last phase of any program is presentation and distribution, and it's the last stage in which a program can go from good to bad. To prevent that, you have to go back to the beginning.

If the initial program design, for example, calls for a booklet that can become a reference volume for employees, it helps if the employees have a place to keep the reference.

We blew a first attempt at a quality-improvement program that included this objective. None of us—producer, briefer or approver—stopped to think about the training environment. So we produced a manual in a standard 8½-by-11-inch format. Trouble was, the employees had no place to put the thing. They worked in a factory, with no desks or shelves. They didn't carry briefcases. So the manuals ended up in lockers or trash cans, and either way the reference material was not available when needed.

So we re-did the manual as a pocket-sized booklet. And this time we included some standard reference material, such as a listing of electronic color codes and common hardware sizes, so the employees would have some reasons to lug the book around.

The same sort of thing can happen with audiovisual materials, of course. And the cure is the same: *Consider the audience and the presentation environment before producing a program.*

That, in fact, is the final solution to many of the problems involved in producing business communication programs. By analyzing all aspects of the project before you begin designing and developing the program, you can spot potential trouble. It's a small investment in time and thought that can pay big dividends when most of your programs begin to soar like eagles instead of flopping like turkeys.

Reprinted from TRAINING, December 1984

HOW TO USE TRANSPARENCIES: A REFRESHER COURSE

Think you know overheads well enough to handle them in your sleep? Think again

BY JANE DUNCAN

Overhead transparencies have been around a long time. During World War II they were considered the latest technology for military and civilian training. Since then, they have been used routinely by trainers everywhere.

So why do trainers often fumble when they use overheads?

Perhaps the maxim, "Familiarity breeds contempt," is operating here. Overheads have been the workhorse of the training industry for so many years that the novelty has long worn off, the rules have been forgotten and the medium is used carelessly.

The truth is that the overhead projector is still the most versatile tool for lending visual support to a presentation. Transparencies can be produced easily and inexpensively and, if used effectively, can add impact to almost any training session.

To improve your use of transparencies, start by observing others in action. Think about presentations where you were a member of the audience. Could you see the screen? Was the printing illegible? Were the transparencies flipped on and off before you had a chance to absorb the material? Was the machine left on without a transparency in place? Did the speaker merely parrot everything written on the transparency? Many presenters make these common errors when they use transparencies, and noting them is a good start toward improving your own performance.

Next, review the basics of effective use of transparencies before you make your next presentation. These rules of design, preparation and delivery are not difficult to follow, but they will add immeasurably to your skills as a stand-up trainer.

Design

Outline your presentation, and indicate suitable places where a transparency will add emphasis. Then design the transparencies to add color, intensity, clarity or additional information.

Too many trainers use the overhead like a reading machine, charges Rosemary Tanfani, a visual communications specialist with Creative Office Products, Inc. of Sacramento, CA. They fill up the screen with information and then read everything. A better approach, she says, is to use just a few key words that add emphasis to a single idea. Here are Tanfani's suggestions for improving transparencies:

• Design each transparency to reflect one idea, expressed in a maximum of six lines, with no more than six words per line.

• Make sure the printing is large enough. Orator typeface just won't do, unless you have a small, up-close audience. Use press-on letters, a Kroy-type lettering system or some other method to ensure good visibility.

• Practice making attractive transparencies. Clip art, accents and attention-getting designs, preprinted borders and cartoon characters can be used to make professional-looking transparencies. Color and overlays can be introduced for more interesting visuals. Keep abreast of new technology for producing graphs and lettering.

Preparation

Now that you have designed a professional-looking set of transparencies, the next step is to organize them. Here are some tips:

• Number your transparencies so that if they are knocked to the floor or otherwise shuffled, you can sort them out easily.

• Analyze your transparencies and decide which of them could be eliminated if necessary. Put a red star (or something) in the corner of the expendable ones, and a matching star in the appropriate section of your lecture notes. There may be times when you need to shorten your presentation, and these specially marked transparencies will give you the flexibility to do so gracefully. It's also useful to carry some extra transparencies that you can use to extend a presentation. Flag these with green stars and corresponding marks in your lecture notes. You may never need the extra ammunition, but it will give you confidence that you can modify your presentation smoothly if time constraints change.

• Practice, practice, practice! Even though you've carefully marked your transparencies and their corresponding places in your lecture notes, it's easy to get confused when the presentation is in progress. Practice using the transparencies until your movements become smooth and natural. Practice how to stand and move without blocking the projected image.

After you have spent hours preparing and rehearsing a presentation, the last thing you need is a bungling meeting chairperson who sabotages all your efforts. Remember Murphy's Law and attempt to keep its operation to a minimum. Test the equipment yourself and make sure it is set up before the audience is seated. When things go wrong, it's you, the presenter, who will be judged, not the meeting organizers.

Too many trainers use the overhead like a reading machine.

Most common problems can be avoided with careful preparation and by assuming responsibility for logistical details yourself. Follow this procedure:

• Arrive early to oversee setup procedures.

• Verify for yourself that everything is ready; don't rely on somebody else's word.

• Carry an extension cord, just in case. Also, carry a kit of other supplies—tape, scissors, tacks, etc.

• Set up and test equipment. Place the first transparency on the light table and check for proper screen placement and image distortion. Lay out your transparencies in order.

• Test the lighting with a transparency on the light table. Keep the lights as bright as possible while maintaining image clarity. The more light you have, the better you can control the audience.

• Have a contingency plan. What if nothing works? You should be able to give a good presentation just referring to your transparencies as lecture notes. Don't leave malfunctioning equipment in place. Put it out of sight

and go on with your presentation without apologies.

Effective delivery

With well-designed transparencies and a carefully thought-out preparation, you are ready to present your material. What you don't need at this point is competition.

Some things are difficult to control. People get up to leave the room. They cough and sneeze. They rustle papers and murmur. But don't compete with yourself by mishandling your transparencies.

When you leave an image on the screen, you are inviting competition. Audience attention is divided between you and the screen. In his book, *Making Effective Presentations* (Training by Design, Inc., New York), Robert B. Nelson addresses this point: "As soon as a visual is exposed, it will attract the attention of the audience. If you are still introducing the topic or the visual, chances are that your spoken word will be missed. When using the overhead projector, you can easily control attention by turning the lights on and off. On individual transparencies, you can cover specific points on a list by sliding a sheet of typing paper between the slide and the machine—then expose your points as you are ready."

Nelson's comments underscore an important rule: Visuals should be used to enhance a presentation, not compete with it.

Here are some other good presentation techniques:

• Don't turn the machine on without a transparency on the light table. This is annoying to the audience.

Learn to transfer smoothly from one transparency to another, or turn the machine off between changes.

• Don't distract your audience by

Visuals should enhance a presentation, not compete with it.

---

walking around waving transparencies in the air.

• Don't look at the screen. Don't keep pointing at it, either. When you do this, you are losing eye contact with the audience. To emphasize something, point to the transparency with a pointer or pen.

• Don't weaken your conclusion by starting to pack up your transparencies while you are still speaking. Turn off the machine and leave the transparencies alone. Then move slightly forward to give your closing remarks. This will focus attention on you and strengthen your close.

By practicing good presentation techniques and using these simple tips to handle transparencies more effectively, you will begin to notice an improvement in your audience's attention. As if by magic, distractions will disappear—fewer people will leave the room, coughing and sneezing will subside, paper rustling and murmuring diminish to a dull roar. You will find yourself in better control of your presentation and your audience.

Reprinted from TRAINING, July 1985

WRITING FOR THE EYE AND EAR

When the words you write must be
heard to be understood, take care that
you present them effectively

BY JUDSON SMITH

Sage advice from every lawyer in the nation is to "put it in writing." When something is written down, it lasts forever—it can be studied and stored and scrutinized. The spoken word, on the other hand, is worthless in court because it disappears as soon as it is expressed. What's worse, chances are whoever hears the words won't have the same sense of what they mean as the one speaking them.

Countless theories about effective communication fill textbooks with data and drawings about senders, receivers, communications paths and the like. But most people who write for the eye and the ear—for speeches, audio recording, films, videotape or audiovisual presentations— never consciously think about these things. Subconsciously, perhaps, their fingers are guided over the keyboard, but a spoken-word writer rarely refers to a thesaurus or dictionary, let alone a text on communications.

Think of verbal media as a foreign language. Can anyone enter a foreign country and immediately absorb, understand and communicate in the native tongue? Not likely. Nor can people instantly interpret and absorb highly sophisticated material presented in a foreign medium. But they can learn— some intuitively know— how to communicate on a basic level by using short words, lots of visual support, finding equivalent English words, and using almost childlike language and structure.

That's the way to write for the eye and the ear. To be understood, keep it simple, use short words, reinforce with visuals and follow some standard conventions, such as uncomplicated sentence patterns. Say what has to be said in a simple declarative sentence with an action verb, few or no polysyllables, and no confusing words.

Remember that people don't really translate what they hear into discrete words. Instead, they group words into "particles of meaning," phrases that convey a thought. In terms of verbal media, most of the particles of meaning that can be imparted well are emotional or feeling in tone, not intellectual. It would be difficult, for instance, for a trainer to illuminate all the details and procedures of a firm's benefit package through an audiovisual presentation, but not too tough at all to create a good feeling about that package if the AV presentation was accompanied by a booklet that explained the plan in detail and could be kept by the employee for ready reference.

Writing begets rewriting

Revision is as important for the spoken word as it is for the written word. Most writers find they must get something down on paper, some barebones skeleton of the finished work, before they actually know what it is they are trying to say and what's wrong with the way they just said it. They have to "get it out of their system" in the first draft, then let it stew a bit.

It's far easier to build a framework that makes sense once the basic thoughts, particles of meaning, words and phrases are down on paper. The first draft often contains some interesting phrasing and insight, but needs support and substance in terms of order and focus. Revision and reshaping is simply a matter of fitting the thoughts into a usable format.

The basic rules, or at least suggestions, that will usually result in a decent product for the eyes and the ears are actually just common sense, but sometimes common sense falls by the wayside in the heat of writing. Here, for the nonsuperstitious, are 13 things to keep in mind as you write.

1 Use active, not passive, voice. Don't underestimate the power of an active verb. Even if the first draft must be passive, go back and recast in active voice. Passive voice says the subject has done something; active voice has the subject doing something. "The apple was eaten by Bill" is textbook passive. "Bill ate the apple" is active, and shorter, and the listener knows who did what to whom (or what) in an order that is easy to understand.

2 Shorten everything. Hemingway was a master at this. He'd write standing up, but edit sitting down. He'd cut everything not absolutely necessary. As a result, his sparse little books cut immediately to the core of the concept he was describing. It's better to die a little death at the typewriter or at the hands of a blue pencil when editing your "deathless prose" than it is to expire in a bomb blast at showtime.

The simplest way to cut a sentence is to go back to English grammar days and parse the sentence out. Find the subject and the predicate. Put those in simple word order and see how much, if anything, is lost. Add only those adverbs, phrases, clauses or other sentence parts that are absolutely necessary to enhance meaning. Cut long sentences into short ones, avoiding dependent clauses (like this one), and see if the writing doesn't read better.

3 Break the rules. If an American school child carries any rules into adulthood, they are probably rules about grammar, such as not using "ain't" and sentence fragments, and not repeating the same word in a sentence. In reality, people don't speak in complete sentences, yet they are understood. Write as you talk. (Like you talk.) Use implied subjects. Don't fear the pause...represented by those three dots. Fragment sentences when the fragment says it all. Actually, the punctuation of anything that is spoken rather than written is purely for the convenience of a reader. Take a look at what is popular in music and in magazines, things people buy because they are current. Popular communications forms are becoming far less rigid and structured. They are often sentence-less. Same for commercials.

4 Don't describe, amplify. The classic example is the travelogue everyone yawns through. The traveler drones on about every nuance of the slide, even if those nuances are seen in the first second of viewing. "One picture is worth a thousand words" is trite and untrue, but there's no reason to speak a thousand words, or even ten, to describe what can be clearly seen. If you are writing "In this slide" or "As you can clearly see," chances are you are wasting valuable time that could be spent explaining what can't be seen.

5 Practice some verbal chauvinism. Anglo-Saxon words are *magnifique*. If, when you write or read a word, you find a translation popping into your mind, use the translation. It will probably be shorter, have a more specific meaning, be clearer in tone and read better.

6 Use repetition. People repeat themselves constantly. Spoken-word writers should, too. Follow that old rule: "Tell them what you are going to tell them. Tell them. Then tell them what you told them." Repetition works.

7 Write to reflect your audience's personality. It's often considered bad form to use loose sentence structure and contractions (such as "it's"), but that's the way people talk. One way to include a proper amount of this informality is to use focus group interviews. If the task is to design an orientation program for factory workers, ask them what they think about the company. Then—within reason—use the words they use in writing your script. If they say, "I like workin' here 'cuz this's a company that cares a bunch, really does good stuff for us workers and like that," don't clean it up so much that your factory worker sounds like a displaced Ph.D. in English. Compromise: "This company cares. It really does good stuff for workers." Chances are the top brass will balk at "stuff," but workers won't.

There's another school of thought concerning cleaning up language, of course. This school says that the company is The Company, and should speak with a voice that is intelligent, reasoned and educated. There's something to be said for this, and your narrator should say it. Don't ask a stentorian-voiced narrator to say "stuff," but don't ask a semi-skilled employee who normally says "stuff" to say the firm offers "a complete

---

PUT 'BELIEVABILITY' INTO VIDEO DRAMAS

While preparing videotape presentations for the Federal Prison System, Ed Harding's crew from Media Concepts, Inc., encountered some interesting training and production problems. Their solutions may help all trainers who must produce believable media packages under location conditions.

Harding's production company was hired to produce videotape materials that would help employees understand the workings of their own correctional facility, including how it connected with the surrounding community and the people inside and out of the prison. They had to seem real enough so that participants imagined themselves part of the work force, but they couldn't be shot at an actual institution.

Until Harding's Philadelphia-based firm was hired, the organization used a print hand-out that outlined a simulated institution. Although it described this fictional prison in great detail, participants had trouble making the transition from their actual position to this mythical place.

So Media Concepts produced a video documentary, complete with an on-camera news reporter doing an investigation on the simulated prison. The reporter interviewed the warden, other staff members and even prisoners. The trainee audience was exposed to people whose names would later come up in their sessions and also got some idea of the situations and conflicts they would deal with during subsequent course exercises.

Television news has a built-in credibility, Harding believes, and is familiar to most people. He felt that trainees would tacitly understand how to watch the program and would internalize the attitudes and information contained within the script.

Since trainees would be coming from institutions throughout the prison system, no actual prison settings were used in the tape. This helped eliminate the "guess where this was shot" distraction. For much the same reason, no actual prison employees were used. Harding went through the Prison System's file of prison photographs and then looked for non-prison locations that resembled actual penal institutions. A military barracks, for instance, served as the dormitory, and the grounds of a college campus looked like the landscape around a federal corrections institution.

Actors from several community theaters played the roles of employees. Here again, Harding used the System's picture file to guide his selection of actors according to existing employees' age, dress, grooming and other characteristics. One of the trainers, coincidentally, bore a striking resemblance to one of the actors used in the videotape. By adding a few small make-up touches, he was able to walk into the meeting room and participate "live" in a discussion of the attitudes espoused by the character played in the program.

As with most location productions, this one encountered disasters and lucky accidents. Harding found that the only way to cure an annoying video noise source was to wrap all equipment and cabling in aluminum foil, using most of a nearby supermarket's supply. The noise source—a local AM radio station—was being picked up by the video equipment because all the television cabling acted as a giant antenna; the aluminum foil shielded out this unwanted signl.

On the good side, a fortunate accident brought the production crew to a local college athletic field on the day after a heavy rain. Groundspeople, who were shoveling the field and sprinkling it with sand to make it playable, looked strikingly like prisoners. The sight of "inmates" in such an activity struck a responsive, realistic chord—at no cost for the "extras" in the scene.

Such unplanned events and meticulously planned set-ups came together in the form of several realistic training programs for the Federal Prison System. Because participants had little trouble believing that the scenes they were witnessing were from an actual prison, the training effect was enhanced. In fact, several trainees expressed interest in being transferred to this mythical institution, because it was so well run.

Reprinted from TRAINING, July 1979

benefit package and many fringe benefits of great value to those of us for whom the package was designed."

8 **Write for one member of the audience.** Talk to one person, probably a composite, who represents the middle level of your audience. Consider several factors, including level of experience within the firm, age and education, sex, lifestyle and profession, geographic or fraternal taboos, and amount of involvement with the media you are using. Avoid colloquialisms and regional references and, if possible, avoid gender-specific structures.

The composite figure for this article, for example, is a training professional, probably a college grad with some post-grad work, in his or her mid-30s, with an urban background. Since TRAINING's readership is national, regional references shouldn't be used, and sexual stereotypes will

not be allowed to pass unchallenged. Chances are the reader has an excellent command of the English language and is used to reading articles (thus a high degree of understanding and involvement with the medium). If you can distill the same sort of profile for every spoken-word writing assignment, it will help improve both style and word choice.

9 **Use a narrative hook.** Look at the difference between an old movie, one that had a captive audience, and a made-for-television movie. In the boob-tube production, the grabber goes up front. If someone is going to get in trouble, it will be in the first few minutes. No suspenseful waiting for the action anymore. Here's a classic narrative hook: "Hell," said the Duchess. "Let go my leg!" It has excitement, royalty, violence, action and sex. You can just see a network executive buying a program that be-

gins with that scene.

In training programs, it isn't usually possible to employ such a strong hook, but it is possible — and necessary — to grab the audience's attention early on. Maybe all it takes is a fast-paced beginning that uses music and some "happy face" shots of employees, or a narrator asking an almost unanswerable question. It is worth a great deal of time and effort to come up with a narrative hook that drags the audience into the presentation.

10 **Don't climb too far up the ladder of abstraction.** This is a device to show the specificity of a noun. For example, "armament" is about as abstract as possible. "Gun" is more concrete, at least ruling out bows and arrows, rocks, slingshots, and other non-guns. And "Colt .45" is very concrete. Remember, keep it simple, clear and concrete.

HERE'S WHY YOU SHOULD CONSIDER VIDEO-BASED LEARNING

Although trainers have used videotape for years as an instant replay device to improve role plays, to bring slices from the real world into the classroom and to train more effectively," says Walt Robson, "some still consider it an all-electronic version of the classroom projector. But videotapes's unique features provide some tangible benefits. The challenge is to develop software that matches the sophistication of the hardware."

Robson, president of Innovative Media, Inc., a San Mateo, CA video production company, offers some classic examples of the misuse of video. He then offers some suggestions for using the medium more effectively.

The biggest problem is using video to make recordings of classroom lectures for distribution to the field. Robson says that training effectiveness may actually decline in this case, since the absence of the instructor eliminates the possibility of feedback. In addition, the instructor's absence

can affect accountability; the trainees may not bother watching a long, boring lecture unless there's an instructor around.

Another problem is videotapes used as "learning experiences" but not integrated into the training design. "The medium is used as a gigantic information dump," Robson says, "but no reinforcement is built into the instructional design."

The problem with video as a tool for improving role plays is that many trainers use the medium *just* for this facet of the course. Trainees aren't given the chance to see positive behavior and to develop good role models. "We believe learning how to swim should precede being thrown into the water," Robson explains.

Given all those incorrect or inefficient uses of video, what positive ways exist to put the medium to work for training? Robson suggests integrating video into every part of the training process.

In a course recently designed by MR Communications Consultants, titled "Presentations That Work," each video module develops principles for in-house and sales presentations through two positive models. "Mary" depicts a person doing an in-house program, while "Jeff" must make a high-level sales presentation. Rather

than watching one, long videotape, the trainees view several shorter clips at appropriate times during training. Each clip reveals principles and processes while stimulating discussion based on the behavior of Mary and Jeff.

During the second day of this course, attendees make a presentation to the class and video camera. Here, again, video is used somewhat differently than in normal applications. The morning session becomes an "on-camera" rehearsal, where the trainee makes mistakes and is evaluated by the class. But the afternoon performance, complete with changes determined by the rehearsal, is usually a positive experience. The trainee forgets the camera and concentrates on influencing the audience.

Robson has found this course to be highly effective; one client determined that presentation productivity increased by 23%. He believes that results such as these will cause more and more trainers to use the medium differently. "The trend is toward using the medium judiciously to make abstract concepts more concrete. It is a pivotal component in discovery-based learning and can stimulate discussion and interaction like no medium we have seen," he concludes.

Reprinted from TRAINING, November 1979

11 **Avoid number problems.** In rewriting, watch for the "him or her, he or she" problem. Don't say, "Everyone should have his or her day in the sun." Instead, say "People should have their day in the sun." Or avoid that cliche entirely. In some cases, varying the gender pronouns not only avoids the trap of "him and her," but also enhances listener attentiveness by keeping the audience a little off balance.

12 **Watch your sentence context.** Avoid unconscious humor and poor use of gerunds. Many writers can't clearly state what a gerund is, but the problem of poor use of gerunds is obvious. "After climbing the mountain, the view was beautiful," is a glaring gerund problem. What's beautiful? And is it only beautiful because it climbed the mountain? Unconscious humor is harder to spot. Suppose you wrote a script for Planned Parenthood that said, "The problem only became apparent after pregnancy." You'd find the word "apparent" seemed fine on the printed page, and even when recorded, but had them rolling in the aisles at every viewing.

13 **When you are done, quit.** This is difficult for every writer, but especially so in writing for the eye and the ear. There is a tendency to dot every "i", cross every "t" and never rely on the visuals to complete the message. But retention studies, not to mention introspective viewing of audiovisual shows, indicate that only a few key messages come out of most spoken-word scripts. If the audience walks away feeling the company is good, and cares, and does good stuff for its employees, an orientation program is probably pretty solid. If the audience thinks safety is a pretty good thing and individuals go back to the shop a little more wary of the machines, that safety program was a success.

The same idea works in written form, too. If this article leaves you with the impression that writing for the eye and the ear is different than writing for the printed page and that, basically, the keys are to write conversationally and simply, then the "particle of meaning" has been passed and it's time to quit.

Reprinted from TRAINING, March 1981

10 STEPS TO BETTER SLIDE SHOWS

Whether you're creating a single-projector slide show or a multimedia extravaganza, keep these basics in mind—and you'll end up with a more effective program

BY JOE FARACE

You know the story. The boss walks in one morning and says, "We need to whip up a training program for 'Project X' fast! The deadline is yesterday." When that happens, the audiovisual support you select most likely will be the single-projector slide show. And with good reason.

Single-projector shows are inexpensive to produce, can be assembled quickly and are easy to update. But their simplicity can lull you into a sense of complacency. The fact that it's only a one-projector show doesn't mean the program can't be interesting.

Producing a single-projector show *is* easier than creating a multimedia spectacular. But the same care needed for more complex projects should be used when producing something simpler. Let's start with the assumption that a one-projector presentation doesn't have to be dull. Here are 10 steps that can make noticeable improvements to your next training program.

1. Analyze the audience

Who, exactly, is going to be viewing this production? Establishing "who" at the outset guarantees that your program will be on target. Be precise in your definition by asking a few questions: What's their educational background? Are they new or experienced? Why am I showing them this presentation?

Consider similar questions that relate specifically to the program you're producing. Look at the demographics of the people who'll make up the audience. You may find that you'll have to produce a few different versions to be really effective.

Write down the answers to your questions, and keep them in front of you while you work on the other nine steps involved in creating an efficient and cost-effective program.

2. Plan before you start

You need a roadmap when traveling in unfamiliar territory. After you've established whom you're producing the show for, you need to decide what you're going to say and how you're going to say it. You need a plan.

The "what" part of your training presentation is its message. To determine exactly what's needed, ask a few more questions: What do I want to accomplish with this program? What specific items *must* be covered? What reaction do I want from the viewers?

The answers to these questions, when combined with the data gathered on the audience, will form the outline of the final script.

How you deliver the message is harder to quantify, but it's important to keep all options open at this point. Don't be afraid to try something that hasn't been done before. The production will only be successful if the viewers react positively to the message.

One slide show I worked on introduced a new system for measuring employee productivity. The purpose was to explain the system so that everyone would understand how they were to be measured and therefore could work to achieve results under the system's terms. A potentially dull subject for a slide show—but since those results would be compared against the achievements of divisions in other states, each divisional manager was strongly committed to making sure that his or her branch would come out on top. In other words, some powerful people had a big stake in this presentation. That's *why* it was created.

The visual concept we used to introduce the subject was a parody of a television game show, with cartoons of typical participants and a toothy host. That's the purpose of the visual design of a training presentation: Capture the viewer's attention with the first slide, and don't let go until the last one.

All of this "who, what, and how" may sound like a lot of work. It will take time, and time is something you have too little of. But developing a verbal and visual plan *before* you begin active production will save both time and money on the final production.

3. Keep it short

Resist the urge to create an epic. "Gone With the Wind" is a good movie despite its length, not because of it. Experience has shown that even the best single-projector slide show will begin to lose viewer interest after about 15 minutes. And when your audience loses interest, your presentation begins to lose its effectiveness.

If the subject demands that your program be longer, consider breaking it into several smaller modules. This usually results in stronger presentations that will satisfy your goals and needs.

4. Write as you talk

Creating the final script for audiovisual presentation is different from writing a training manual. But you've done your research, you know who the audience is and you know what to tell them, so the only problem is *how* to tell them. The purpose of the script is to organize the information in line with the visual design you've chosen for the show. A few tips:

• Use the universally accepted, two-column script format. The right column contains the narrator's words, the left column the visuals associated with them.

• Anything that should *not* be read by the narrator, such as sound effects, should be in parentheses.

• Don't break sentences between

pages or hyphenate words between lines. This will make it easier for the narrator to read your script and give you a better reading.

• If you're using title slides, don't have the narrator read the same words. The visuals and soundtrack should reinforce each other, not repeat each other.

• Finally, write it as you'd say it. Use short, simple sentences (your listeners can't refer to a printed page to reread or untangle complex phrases), and keep it lively and informal—you're *talking* to a group of people, you're not writing a formal thesis for your doctorate. When you've finished writing the first draft, read it aloud. Better yet, tape record your reading and play it back. Does it sound natural—as if you're speaking instead of reading?

5. Create a lively soundtrack

Music and sound effects will help keep the viewer's attention. Music, in fact, can act as "audio punctuation" to your script.

Use the services of a professional sound studio when recording your narrator. The studio's engineer also should be able to help you select library music to complement and enhance the presentation. You'll be surprised to find how inexpensive it is to add music—especially considering its impact on your program. By the way, the fee you pay to use library music includes copyright clearance.

The more unique your program looks and sounds, the more memorable it will be. In audiovisual communications, having the audience *remember* your message is the name of the game.

6. Make the graphic consistent

When discussing title slides with whomever will be doing the graphics, emphasize the importance of maintaining the same "look" throughout the program. For instance, use the same typeface style for all "word" slides. This isn't an invitation to monotony, but you do want the viewers to read the slides, not say "Wow! What a pretty one." The only exception to

this rule would be in the use of the organization's logo.

Keep the overall style consistent. And make sure that the style fits the design of the program. If your message is serious, the graphics should be in harmony with the message. If it's a "fun" program, unleash your imagination. Mixing these two styles within the same show, however, will result in confusion for the viewer.

Any change in the visual rhythm of the presentation will cause viewers to stop and ask why. Too much of that, and they'll miss the rest of the program. Graphics should be used to draw their attention *into* the program and maintain it throughout.

7. Watch out for visual overload

A common mistake is to cram too much information onto a single slide. Here's an area where we can learn from the outdoor-advertising industry. Their rule of thumb is a maximum of eight words per billboard, since that's all a motorist can read while driving by at 55 mph. It's a good rule of thumb for slide shows, too.

No matter how much information you have to deliver, there are alternatives to cluttered slides. Let your narrator say it, or spread the information onto several slides instead of packing it all onto one.

Be careful of charts and graphs, too, and remember that screen size is important here. Are you projecting onto a large, 12-foot screen or using the 10-inch screen of a self-contained projection unit? If you think a visual might be too busy, it is.

8. Use photography effectively

One of the best values in a slide show is being able to use a 35mm slide directly out of a camera. Hiring a professional is a good idea, not a frill: You'll ensure consistency and quality for the finished product. A simple cost comparison will show that the cost per usable slide is quite a bargain.

Provide your photographer with a "shot list." This is a *written* list of all the specific photographs you want. Let the photographer know you'd like

to see a variety of camera lenses and angles used. This will add variety and keep the presentation from becoming routine.

Be flexible enough to allow your photographer to capture the kind of spontaneous event that can add life to your production. The key to this flexibility is communication. The more information you give your photographer, the better results you'll get.

9. Use a variety of visuals

Keep your presentation moving by blending different types of slides—graphic and photographic for instance. In fact, you can combine both on a single slide for some fascinating effects.

Use appropriate graphic slides to emphasize—not repeat—the narrator's words. Dramatic, storytelling photography can show the viewer *exactly* what the script says. By using a variety of visuals you'll keep the program from slowing down and becoming predictable.

10. Distribute the show cost-effectively

While you may have produced the show in slide format, that may not be the most economical way to distribute it. Do the trainees have easy access to sound/slide projectors? How about video playback equipment? The answers to those questions will point at the most appropriate format for distribution.

If they have access to both, prepare a cost comparison between slides and a videotape transfer of the original slide show. Depending on the number of slides and the number of copies required, videotape may be cheaper.

One of the advantages of using videotape copies for distribution is that they're easy to use and difficult to tamper with. If you decide to send out duplicate slide sets, put a few drops of strong glue on the tray ring or dust cover. This tactic will ensure that the slides stay together—in order—if they experience any rough handling during use or shipping.

Reprinted from TRAINING, July 1984

NEW AND TESTED WAYS TO USE SLIDES

Sure, most trainers would like to spend zillions on exotic training media. But sometimes 35mm slides are a perfectly adequate—and affordable choice

BY JUDSON SMITH

Despite the ever-increasing proliferation of video, the 35mm slide remains a popular presentation aid for trainers. Every year brings new methods, making slides easier to use—and more effective. In addition, tested techniques of producing and using slides are constantly refined. Using these new and tested ways to produce and present slides, you can create effective slides on a moderate budget and within tight time lines.

Although presentation is the final step, it should be the first consideration when planning a slide package. Many trainers are finding that slides originally produced for simple one-projector presentations are now doing double- and triple-duty as part of multi-image presentations or videotapes. Because of this, they are now specifying different standards for slide photography.

Perhaps the most important of these new standards involves "TV cutoff." Since television screens have a different width-to-height ratio than slides, it is necessary to "shoot loose" when the final slide may be shown on video. If important information is too close to the border of the slide, it will be lost when the slide is converted to TV format.

In general, plan slides so the outer 20% of the perimeter contains no vital data. (This guideline will prevent problems if slides are used in rear-screen setups with extremely wide-angle projection lenses. Wide-angle lenses sometimes degrade, or darken, the borders of the image.)

Because most multi-image or TV applications of slides involve a horizontal format, such as the 4:3 ratio of width to height for TV, many trainers now produce all slide shows in horizontal format. Although this creates some problems for vertical subjects, such as head-and-shoulders portraits, it makes the finished product more consistent and easier to frame for TV or for most projection surfaces.

When you must use vertical slides, follow the lead of professional producers: They alter the slide in some way, either by making it part of a split-screen effect or using a special masking mount. Both of these techniques have been greatly improved in recent years.

For instance, several firms now manufacture a variety of stock mounts to mask the standard 35mm slide into a circle, quarter-frame, star, oval, center square or other shape. More elaborate mounts also include registration pegs that match up with the film sprocket holes to ensure that the strip of film remains secure within the mount. Knowing about these masking mounts in advance of photography allows you to plan shooting so that important information is highlighted through special screen position or masking treatment.

Special photographic effects have become far easier to create in-house or to purchase than they used to be. Some photo labs have worked for more than 30 years to perfect their special slide effects, and the results of all that experience are lower prices and more consistency in the finished product. In addition, new color transparency films can be processed easily and rapidly, making retakes possible within two hours.

Today's photography equipment also has increased the ease and precision of slide photography. One continuing problem with color slide film has been low "exposure latitude." The exposure must be dead-on or the slide will be useless. Each slide is a final product, not an intermediate step as is the case in negative-to-print photography. Because of the close tolerances required, most slide photographers "bracket," varying the exposure in several shots to ensure that one frame is correct.

As film prices rose, this practice became much more expensive. Just a few years ago it was possible to shoot slides for a dime a frame. Now the price is closer to 50 cents. But just a few years ago the average photographer didn't have the exceptional exposure accuracy now possible with electronic light meters built-in to most 35mm cameras.

The result of new films, new cameras and better systems for double-exposure and slide masking is that trainers can now purchase a workable slide photography system within their budget limits. With this system they can shoot both on-location and studio work with consistency and confidence.

For example, most camera manufacturers offer at least one model that will allow you to cock the camera shutter without moving the film forward. By using this double-exposure feature, you can record multiple images on the same strip of film, either overlapping the images for a superimposition or masking off portions of the frame for each exposure to create a multi-part slide. With some practice, this feature allows you to do simple special effects "in the camera," rather than paying for post-photography special effects.

In addition, several manufacturers sell "macro" lenses that allow you to shoot same-size photographs. In other words, you can fill the film frame with an image of a subject that is no bigger than one frame of 35mm film, such as a short headline from a newspaper. By combining this macro lens with a copystand, you can rapidly create your own title slides and special effects.

The last few years have also seen great improvement in copystands, on which you mount your camera and take photos to size. It's now possible to accurately predict the amount of light falling on the copystand "stage," or platform. This results in fewer poor exposures, and less time spent creating slide presentations. Coupled with a modern film stock that can be developed in less than two hours, you can create a slide program within one business day.

Even if you lack the time or the inclination to produce your own slides, refinements and new processes have made purchasing slides less expensive and easier than ever before. Your choices range from computer-generated slides to hand-created images available from production houses and photograph banks.

There are several standard effects that skilled slide houses can easily create. Most involve one of two basic techniques—moving the camera or subject during exposures and creating masks or overlays from original material, then manipulating the overlays through the use of filters and special lighting. The movement creates "zooms," where the image appears to leap out at the viewer, or "pans," where the image appears to speed across the frame. And the manipulation results in star bursts, glows or neons, and other effects that add color and substance to many subjects.

Many firms invest a few hundred dollars in having their logos or company name treated with these effects, then use the resulting slides in subsequent shows. But few training departments can afford to specially create many title slides for each individual training program.

This problem also has been solved. A growing number of companies offer a wide variety of stock slides, including a range of type slides with words and concepts commonly used for standard business presentations. Because you buy "off-the-rack" instead of custom-made, you pay far less for each slide.

In addition, new presentation methods help you avoid some of the high costs for special effects by creating them on the spot with multiple projectors. For example, a two-projector setup makes it easy for you to superimpose titles and names over slides without the need for an in-camera "burn-in" to put the title and slide together on one frame of film.

Until recently, you had but two choices: Invest in elaborate multi-image programming equipment designed to handle many projectors, or purchase simple systems designed to handle two projectors and a limited number of dissolves. The trade-off was difficult; you had to give up the ability to do many interesting effects, such as flipping between two images or varying the fade-in/fade-out rate for each pair of slides, in favor of saving complexity and cost by using simpler systems.

Now, however, several manufacturers are marketing a scaled-down multi-image programmer that precisely fits the needs of the trainer. These devices control two or three projectors, allowing each to be turned on, turned off, faded or flashed independently. Yet they cost far less than the standard multi-image systems designed to do a similar task for many projectors. Linking such a device to a stereo cassette recorder gives you a highly flexible system capable of adding interesting effects to your training programs.

The same computer technology that has made these inexpensive programming devices possible has made feasible random-access slide presentations for most training departments. Using a palm-sized remote-control device, you now can instantly call up any slide in a tray, in any order desired. This ability is invaluable for applications requiring review of previous material or where several audiences may need to see differing presentation order of slides.

Of course, the most prevalent form of slide presentation has also improved over the years. At one time, it was standard to have an AV cassette recorder capable of putting out one pulse that would advance a slide projector or dissolve control one time.

Now many systems are available with several pulses. You can choose between several dissolve rates or use a separate stop/start pulse to turn projectors on and off when required. Some systems even automatically correct themselves, finding the correct position of audiocassette and corresponding slide if the program falls out of synchronization.

The "revisability" of slide presentations also pays big dividends for training applications. Consider using the same sound track for more than one set of slides. It's an easy leap from that to producing a sound track and title slides, then amortizing the cost over several programs for regional offices.

Another approach is to design a sound track and pulse program so that the slides can be changed without altering the content of the audio and compilation. Of course, every training presentation can't use the same sound track and programming, but designing a "generic" music track and pulsing track can be a budget-saver and a time-saver for many applications.

Multi-image presentations may appear to be out of the budget range for most training uses. But here, too, a generic presentation might make sense. Many firms use multi-image equipment for sales conferences or other large-audience applications that occur infrequently throughout the year. Yet they use single-projector programs for training, reasoning that it would cost too much to create a new multi-image presentation for each training need.

With a little preplanning, though, you might be able to adapt some of the music, programming and slides from these elaborate presentations for your own use. The employee orientation program, for instance, could benefit from multi-image and, chances are, enough slides will be available to make a lively show.

The key here is to locate a multi-image sound track that can be adapted to a new narration, then keep the same slide cues and music, but change the narration and slides. If there's a place within the show where sales reps saw the word "Sell" flash on and off several times, you can substitute the company logo. And if another sales show section used fast-paced slides of new products, maybe that's the place to put face shots of employees.

Initially, your in-house production staff may argue that each show requires a custom audio and cueing track. But give them time to think about it—and about the fact that it further justifies equipment they may use only once or twice each quarter.

Slides have long been used as "point-of-purchase" aids and as trade show exhibit booth draws. Some trainers are adapting this method to their needs, especially for "walk-in" training of the general public. In a health-care setting, for instance, many patients need to receive the same basic information.

Rather than repetitious lectures by physicians or staff, the basic data on procedures, illnesses and injuries can be imparted through a self-directed slide presentation. And the same medium can be used by drug firms, medical associations and other professional users to impart training to health-care professionals at *their* "point-of-purchase."

There's one final way slides can enhance a training program. At the conclusion of your next off-site seminar, try presenting a "candid" slide show. Most cities have at least one lab which will process film within three hours. As a result, it's possible to shoot slides almost up to the last few hours, then have the slides ready for a send-off before the group leaves.

And what all of this means for trainers is simple. Slides are easier to create, easier to purchase and easier to present than ever before. Whether you choose to create slide programs in-house or to purchase programs outside, you now have more cost-effective options available to make full use of this powerful and popular training medium.

Slides, of course, are receiving stiff competition from other media, such as video and computer-aided instruction. Yet they remain a mainstay for many trainers because they are easy to revise, transport and present. For that reason, each year will bring more new ways to use slides, and more refinements to existing methods of producing and presenting this proven training aid.

Reprinted from TRAINING, May 1982

TRAINING SLIDE SHOWS: LET YOU ENTERTAIN US!

You're there to train, not to entertain. Right? Not this time

BY CAROL FEY

What makes a good training slide show? Computer-generated graphics at $50 a slide? Glamorous product shots at $200 per studio hour? Professional models, name voices, dazzling facts?

No, money can't buy it. Even with all of this stuff, a show can still be a dog.

What makes a good show is entertainment. Yes, that is contrary to every educational principle you've learned. Yes, you do hear voices in your head saying, "Come on now, take yourself seriously or nobody will."

Sure. But can't you also picture your audience coming into your conference room for a slide show? The lights dim. Everyone nestles down into a comfortable chair...for an afternoon siesta.

There is a certain stigma attached to training slide shows: They're b-o-r-i-n-g. What it boils down to is that it doesn't matter how seriously you take yourself if your audience is asleep (some members, admittedly, with eyes tactfully open).

Many of us recognize this but stick to our principles, laying the blame on the audience—as if that solved the problem. People are beginning to suspect that an audience can't really concentrate on any one item for longer than, say, 10 minutes. Speculation holds that this is a result of conditioning from watching TV—every 10 minutes or so you get a commercial break. Whether that's the cause or not, the malady appears to be real. If you don't believe it, keep tabs on yourself the next time you're watching someone else's show.

Television also is responsible for the fact that people expect to be entertained by anything "audiovisual." If it's not interesting the moment it begins, we change the channel or turn it off. Combine this conditioned demand for instant fascination with the preconception that training materials are boring, and you get a group of people who expect to "turn off" as soon as a training slide show hits the screen.

As the producer of such a show, you have to do everything in your power to keep the audience turned on. If they're not turned on, they are not receiving your message, and all your efforts are a complete waste of time.

Okay, you say. Maybe I'm convinced that I have to entertain a little if I want to get my message across. But I don't know how to do that. The very thought of trying to be funny makes my head sweat.

Take heart. Entertainment is not limited to humor. Entertainment is anything interesting enough to be enjoyable. Or, put to the acid test, entertainment is anything to which people would subject themselves *voluntarily* just for the sake of doing it.

The bare facts

It can be such a harrowing experience simply to gather all the information—to pull all the facts from all the reluctant subject-matter experts—that when that stage is done we desperately want to believe that the script is nearly written. Transfer it from notes and outlines to something somebody can read into a mike and, boom, the tough part is done. All that's left is to scrounge up some slides that will fit the script. That's it. Right? And the result is this:

"Today we're going to present you some crucial information about our new model XYZ. The first of its many features is the accessory switch. Next to it is the reset button. Over here, although you can't see it, is the adjustment level. In back, under this plate, is the power indicator." And so on, with the visual element consisting of three studio shots of the device.

By this time, the people who were already excited about the XYZ are starting to wonder and the rest are snoring.

Facts aren't enough. When all the facts are gathered, the production process *begins*. To draw an analogy, you have a nice picture, but you'll have to put it in an attractive frame before anyone's going to look at it.

Your slide show's first challenge is to grab the audience's attention. The easiest way to do that is to bring up a topic in which they're automatically interested—the thought of which entertains them. Then you can steer them to what you really want to talk about.

Homework assignment: Watch TV

If you have any doubts about this technique, turn on your television set and watch some commercials. You'll see it over and over again, and you'll have to admit that not only does it work, but people really don't notice it in action. So you probably won't get "caught."

But what commercials do best is create a connection between what people already know and like (or fear—social rejection and bad breath) and a product.

Consider the beer commercial. Beer as beer is pretty dull stuff—a yellow liquid with a bitter taste. If we want to go into the intrinsic features of beer—the way it performs as a substance—we could say: "When first removed from storage, beer will create a white foam caused by the release of CO_2, and will make a sticky mess if you're not careful. If consumed, beer can cause disorientation, euphoria, slurring of speech, clumsiness and headaches. If you want to get drunk, hard liquor is quicker." These are the bare facts. Want to buy a beer? No, you don't. And the commercial producers know that. So the commercial instead shows you things you like and builds an association with the beer: Beer equals a friendly bar in which pretty people and/or your favorite athletes are having a wonderful time, equals don't you wish you were there, equals wouldn't you like a beer?

If you watched 10 television commercials with the sound off and could ignore the final close-ups on the brand names, you'd be hard-pressed to say what most of them were trying to sell you; many associations are created out of thin air. But when you watch normally, the message is clear. And at some level in your mind, you probably don't forget the association between the "grabber" and that brand name.

Here are some ways to create such associations, to entertain your audience enough that it not only will stay awake, but will remember your presentation.

Take a lesson from the kids

Children admit they like pictures better than the words. At least one experiment has found that kids can be shown some cartoons with the correct sound tracks and others with the wrong sound tracks without seeming to notice the difference.

Adults, too, pick up most of the message from the pictures. Going through a magazine, most of us "read the pictures" first and get back to the words later, if at all.

The lesson for slide-show producers is, make sure your pictures say what you want to convey. Assemble your pictures—without the sound—and look at them. What message comes across?

In other words, are the pictures alone interesting? Can someone enjoy just the visual part of your production? If the answer is no, then it is probably a "no" for the whole show. They sleep through another one.

Time the script or the sound track so that you know how long each slide will be on the screen. Then watch your show without sound. If you get tired of looking at a picture, there's a script clue for you: too much script for that slide. Cut the script or add another slide or two. If, on the other hand, there's an urge for the picture to be held longer, lengthen the script or insert a pause or music.

You may find yourself suffering from visual monotony—you're looking at the same thing over and over again. Are the pictures all distant shots? Or close-up after close-up after close-up? Alternate close and distant shots to give the eye a break. Break up a string of "the same thing" by adding an interesting face or a pair of hands doing the job. Better yet, build progressions: distant (a user at a computer terminal seen from across the room), then mid-distant (user's head, hands and the terminal), then close-up (only the user's hands and the keyboard). For illustrations of this technique, take another look at television commercials.

Lack of color can be a problem. A show about metal products, for example, can turn out very grey. Instead of shooting the device on a table, have someone put on a bright, solid-colored shirt and hold it. The picture now will be of the device, the hands holding it and a colored background. The eye will pick up the color without really noticing it's a shirt.

Bad photography is another interest-killer. Without sound, you can no longer pretend that an out-of-focus or overexposed picture will go unnoticed. Fix it.

Create some analogies

The "facts" of your show don't automatically tie into the viewer's world. If the viewers are to focus on your slide show instead of on all the distracting thoughts and worries they bring along, you have to help. Create some analogies, or bridges, between the viewer's world and the slide show.

For example, in a quality-control program you might want to explain the concept of sampling. You could "give them the facts" by explaining sampling at length in QC terms. You'll be correct, but your information probably won't be remembered even if it is understood.

On the other hand, you could create an analogy—"Sampling is like tasting ice cream; one lick, and you know the whole carton is good"—and show a few close-ups of a child eating an ice-cream cone, complete with drips. The analogy, which also builds a pleasant association, won't be unnoticed or forgotten.

Windows on the world

Certainly, one purpose of a training slide show is to give people factual information. But they need another kind of information to go with the facts: experiences.

Let's say the purpose of your slide show is to introduce a new product. A common approach is to explain its features, its importance to the company and so on. Visuals typically will be glamour shots of the product, charts and graphs. Ho, hum. They've seen it before and it all looks alike.

The "window-on-the-world" approach lets the viewer see how the subject fits into the real world. If you're giving product information, show where the device is used and how the lives of customers are enhanced by it. Show where it is installed—on the roof, in the basement or in the computer room. Show somebody installing it. Get a factory shot or two of people making it, complete with close-up, "we care" smiles. There are many places your audience never gets a chance to see—windows they don't usually peek through. Inserting a few windows into your slide show can be as refreshing as opening the blinds in a dark room. Everyone sits up and blinks.

Highlight people

There's nothing most people would rather look at than other people—or, better yet, themselves. Take advantage of this. Show a human every chance you get. And remember that "real" people are more interesting than models.

When you begin a production, you should know pretty much who its audience will be. The best guarantee of attention is to take pictures of some of those people and put them in the show. If you can't do that, find some types who would fit in with the audience.

When illustrating a procedure, show someone demonstrating it, not a chart of points to remember. Have the demonstrator look into the camera to create a sense of contact with the audience. Or, if you must have a chart, don't linger on it any longer than necessary.

One way to create continuity and familiarity with a process or policy is to use one person for all the shots. Early in the show, establish this person as "one of you." On the other hand, a good way to take the monotony out of a broader presentation—an orientation program, for instance—is to have a series of people explain their parts of the total operation. That way you can vary both the faces and the voices, and give the audience a sense of ownership.

Now use your ears

In an effective slide show, the visual element *is* the message. The audio (sound) serves to highlight the visual. But it doesn't hurt to add some variety and spice there, too. Imagine yourself hearing this presentation through a closed door. Do the sounds make you want to see the pictures? Do they make you imagine real places—a crowded department store, a grassy meadow with birds, a factory?

Music adds texture and variety. Opening music sets the tone—circus music, honky-tonk, easy listening—they all tell the audience what to expect; and you can choose to demand attention by delivering the unexpected. Music can be used midway through the production to bring back attention, to emphasize a point or to make a transition. And ending music can help determine the closing emotion. What feeling do people take away: pride, sadness, fun, boredom?

Before you finalize the production, field-test it. Try it out on a group as identical as possible to the intended audience. If the show is intended for sales reps to give to distributors, field-test it with a few local reps and distributors. If it's for secretaries, try it on a few secretaries. Insist on getting constructive criticism, and follow through on the suggestions.

Showing the production to your peers, your boss or your relatives does not count as a field test. But if the neighborhood kids love it, you probably have a winner.

Reprinted from TRAINING, April 1983 .RM48/

SIX MEDIA GUIDELINES FOR MEMORABLE TRAINING

How do you get trainees to remember more than half of what they see?

BY GARY AUSTIN WITT

The true cost of training cannot be measured by the training budget per employee or even in hours of instruction per worker. The only relevant measure is the cost in dollars for training ideas remembered. Training that the employee forgets in two hours or two weeks represents a financial loss as well as an instructional failure.

How much information is forgotten from expensive training films and videotapes? A staggering amount. Learning research shows that, on average, students forget half the information they see within two weeks —and that figure can range upward to nearly 100%.

Why is some media-based training welcomed into the mind like a favorite uncle, while some encounters a closed door? Perhaps for the same reason many primitive airplanes never got off the ground: faulty design. To be welcomed in, understood and remembered, media-based training must be designed for the special problems of its audience.

Learning is not easy. When information comes via film or tape, the difficulty skyrockets, partly because film and tape are transitory media. Unlike readers who can stop, ponder and reread difficult passages, media viewers are stuck on a downhill express. They have one chance to look at the scenery before it is gone forever. But with proper use of media psychology, you can help make that one look memorable.

Media psychology, the study of how people learn and remember mass-media information, is built on a century-old foundation of learning and memory research. The result has

been the emergence of practical guidelines that professional communicators in many areas can use to help ensure that their messages are remembered.

The psychology of using AV media can be broken into six guidelines, designed to help you get the most out of your training media. The central tenet is this: *Provide for the mental needs, desires and limitations of your audience. The easier you make it for them to learn, the more they will remember.*

1 Tailor your media session to its audience. Your tape or film will take the audience on a journey through a foreign land. You are the tour guide. You must decide how best to help trainees remember their trip, relying on your understanding of objectives and audience. The proper design of a media-based training session represents an accommodation between the two.

Every training session has an objective. The first step in designing your media-based session is to write down that objective in very specific language. (Be sure your tape or film has a comparable objective). The objective should not be stated in terms of what *you* want to do or the tape will do (e.g., "Explain how to operate this new drill press"), but in terms of what you want the *audience* to be able to do ("After seeing the tape, the audience should remember which buttons to push in sequence so they can operate this new drill press"). Writing down the precise objective will help you keep the lecture portion of the session on target, eliminate irrelevant material and orient the audience's attention toward that one specific objective.

Once you are focused on the objective, you must decide how best to present your opening and concluding remarks to help the audience achieve the objective. An audience profile will help you do this. You will need to investigate the mental needs, desires and limitations of your audience. Some of the considerations:

• What is the age group of your audience? How educated are they? How familiar are they with the general subject of the tape you will be using? How many specific new ideas are they supposed to learn?

• Is the information simply a list of steps or concrete ideas they must learn? Or is the task more complicated, such as understanding how these ideas interact to form general principles? (Operating a machine is usually done by a series of steps, but fixing that machine usually requires conceptual understanding as well.)

• Are the trainees interested in the subject? Will they have an opportunity to use their new information quickly and repeatedly (such as operating or fixing a new machine)? Or will your tape and lecture be their major opportunity to learn the information (such as a program on assertiveness training)?

• Will the audience have to put up with distractions while watching the tape (interruptions, ringing telephones, excessive heat or cold, crowding, poor sound or picture quality, outside voices or noise)?

Review your tapes or films to make sure they are aimed at your audience and consonant with your objective. If they aren't, and substitutes are not available, you must put even greater emphasis on the remaining guidelines, which explain how to structure your presentations before and after the media event.

2 Tell the audience what is important and why. The introduction to any training tape is the most important element of the session. To maximize learning, people need to know what they are supposed to learn. Learning is like putting together a jigsaw puzzle—you have a better chance if you know what it will eventually look like.

The opening of your media training session should accomplish several things:

• Orient the audience toward the information in the tape. (For example, "This tape will show you how to operate our new ABC machine.")

• Give them a reason for being interested in the material so they will pay attention. ("The ABC machine can make your job easier by reducing the time you must spend collating material.")

• Explain how this new information fits into the audience's present knowledge and procedures. ("The ABC machine is part of the MNO computational group we already use. It operates in conjunction with our GHI machine.")

• Summarize the basic points or steps to be covered in the tape. ("To operate the ABC machine, you must know four separate but related operations. They are, in summary, first ...")

By giving the audience an overview of what the tape is about and why it is important to them, they are able to decide where to store the coming information before it begins to bombard them.

3 Use mental imagery to promote memory. When you forget where you parked your car or put your glasses, you try to visualize where you left them. You're using mental imagery. Mental pictures are one of the most powerful means of recall we know—and one of the most overlooked in training.

Concrete, vivid sentences like "the fat, red-faced cowboy leaped onto the sweating, brown stallion" evoke sharp images. These images are stored in memory just like their pictorial counterparts. Both the actual picture and its word-painted image are recalled far better than abstract words.

In one of hundreds of imagery studies, psychologist Allan Paivio showed three groups of students either pictures (like a cat), their concrete noun labels, or abstract nouns (like "liberty"). As reported in Paivio's *Imagery and Verbal Processes* (1979), one week later the students could recall 80% more pictures than concrete nouns and 100% more concrete nouns than abstract nouns.

Clearly, abstract ideas are difficult to remember. But often the very information we want to get across to the audience is abstract, such as "Work-related despondency is frequently the result of unrelieved mental anxiety." There are two important techniques to help your audience remember such ideas:

• Try to translate abstract facts and ideas into concrete language which will produce strong, cohesive images in the minds of the audience. Use analogies, metaphors, stories, examples; simple, everyday words—anything to help them "see" the information. (For example, "Workers often get depressed or burned-out

because they can no longer carry that heavy sack of on-the-job frustrations.")

• Use visuals to illustrate what you're saying, even ones drawn on a blackboard or pad. The audience will associate your words with the pictures. Later they will more easily remember the pictures, which will, in turn, help recall the ideas they associated with the pictures.

4 Don't overload your audience with information. Most training messages are choked with facts. Your audience can only process so much information at a time. If you pour out a Niagara of facts, many of them never will be adequately soaked up. Like water overflowing the capacity of a bucket, they will just wash away.

Research indicates students usually remember basic ideas and the conclusions those ideas lead to; but they forget many supporting details. The amount of information forgotten is directly related to the rate of presentation—the faster/denser the rate of factual accumulation, the greater the number of errors. For a lean, memorable message:

• Present only the minimum information the audience needs to attain your objective. To grasp the ideas in your objective, the audience must understand certain facts. That is the only information they need. You must cut away anything which doesn't explain, support or help the audience understand the objective.

• Present your objective first, then outline the ideas needed to attain it in a few concrete, specific sentences. Finally, take up each idea separately, adding the supportive details, stories and examples needed to buttress it. This technique helps the audience understand the parts of the message, and also how they connect to form the overall picture.

• Don't rush the pace of your presentation. The audience will learn quicker and remember it longer if they have a few seconds after each new idea to process it fully.

5 Relate new facts and ideas to things the audience already knows. For permanent memory a message must be understood in terms of the learner's present knowledge. It must be firmly associated with old facts and ideas already stored in memory, like connecting new strands of a spiderweb into the whole.

To be effective, therefore, you must proceed step-by-step as you spin out new ideas and show the audience how each is associated with other

ideas new and old. For example, if your session deals with cold-call selling, discuss how new techniques are a logical outgrowth or modification of familiar sales techniques the audience already knows. In a well-designed presentation the audience will realize that the new information flows from familiar higher-order principles in a natural, interlinked progression down to specific applications.

6 Close with an integrated summary of the major facts. After you show the film or tape, it is critical to training success that you summarize the information presented. All the pieces of the jigsaw puzzle have been presented; now you must help the audience step back and see the overall picture.

For a good summary, do the following:

• Review the theme and major concepts just presented. Your summary begins by restating the objective of the production, its theme and the major concepts upon which that theme rests.

• Remind the audience how these concepts fit together, showing graphically and visually how these concepts mesh to support the theme and help the audience achieve the objective. Try to help them see the interrelations as a single mental image. Mention only critical supporting facts.

• Relate the concepts and the theme to the audience. Here, above all, the students should see as concretely as possible how they will be expected to use the material step-by-step on the job.

Together these six guidelines should help you shepherd your audience through the unknown territory of your media message by planning for their specific needs, desires and limitations; telling them what they will see and why it is important; using imagery; chopping out unnecessary ideas; connecting new and old facts together and, finally, bringing them to the mountaintop to look back on all the things they have seen, emphasizing how it all fits together.

A shorthand version of these six guidelines was succinctly expressed by the backwoods preacher (or the Army drill sergeant) who, when asked how he delivered the Word, explained, "I tells 'em what I'm going to tell 'em. I tells 'em. Then I tells 'em what I told 'em."

An effective media-based training session should do no less.

Reprinted from TRAINING, February 1982

A GUIDE TO COST-EFFECTIVE VIDEO

Still think of video as a budget blower? Here are some tips that could change your mind

BY JOHN R. INGRISANO

Just five years ago video was barely beyond the touch-and-go experimental stages and easily could have gone the way of quadraphonic sound or the rotary engine. Production costs were high; quality was low. Playback machines were bulky ¾-inch industrial models, and only a handful of pioneers could tell you what the letters VCR meant. As a training tool, video was just starting to come of age.

Today video is part of the mainstream. It is accepted as an effective training tool, albeit with a reputation among training directors as a budget blower. In fact, although the cost of producing video training has declined significantly over the last several years—to the point where thousands of companies and organizations now are developing much of their own programming—video remains one of the most expensive training media.

The trick is to make it cost-effective, to get the biggest bang for your training buck. Whether your budget is $5,000 or $100,000, you *can* produce quality video programming.

In fact, the size of your budget will make a lot of decisions for you. Can you afford to splurge on the helicopter shot of the home office (à la the opening to "West Side Story"), or do you go with a hand-held camera

walk through the sea of happy faces in the customer service department? Do you shoot on location in the Virgin Islands or produce the entire program in the studio?

Your budget may dictate many of these decisions, but not the quality of the outcome. Hundred-thousand dollar blockbusters can become

Whether your budget is $5,000 or $100,000, you can produce quality video.

expensive bombs, while $5,000 shoestring productions have been known to take top honors at film and video festivals.

The most important thing is to know what the budget is before doing any but the most preliminary planning.

Planning is important in the successful development of any program. With video it is crucial. There are too many variables involved to play it by ear. And any one of dozens of details can make or break your program.

Producing a quality, cost-effective video is 90% planning and organization and 10% execution. Here are

just some of the planning details you should attend to:

• Have clear, written objectives.

• Develop a "critical path" for each program. This is a step-by-step checklist indicating who is responsible for what and when it needs to be done. Everybody involved in the project should have a copy.

• Don't attempt to operate in a vacuum. Meet with those involved both as a group and individually. Hold brainstorming and planning meetings to develop the critical path and subject treatment.

• Check, check and recheck your plan.

Know your medium

There is a trend these days to "put it on video," even if it doesn't belong there. A great idea executed in the wrong medium is an expensive, time-consuming exercise in futility. A program on how to write clear, professional business letters probably would be more effective in print, just as one on listening skills might be better on audiotape. If, however, the subject is body language, a demonstration of effective closing techniques or dressing for success, video is a natural. Just make sure the medium and the message are a good match.

The same goes for the intended use. Video is not ideal for every presentation situation. It is especially ill-suited for large audiences but perfect for small-group or one-on-one training. And regardless of the situation, remember that the final product will lack the big-screen impact of a film or slide show.

Another limitation is that video rarely can stand alone as a training tool. You usually need to develop a viewer's guide or other printed support material.

Finally, thanks to talking-head epics of the company president addressing the troops, video doesn't always get taken seriously. Its home-movie image has soured some people forever.

Once you have settled on the video medium, select an approach that meets your objectives and your budget constraints. A training video is not a text and should not be produced like one. No matter how small your budget, there is rarely an excuse for sticking a narrator in front of a camera to read page after page of a script.

Take the worst of all possible worlds: dull, rote subject matter and a low budget. What might you do? Use a classroom setting, shooting in a studio or in your company's meeting room. An inexpensive blackboard or flip chart can be used to display graphics. Rather than standing a narrator at the front, hire an actor to play a trainer in a classroom simulation. (Don't be afraid to spend a few dollars on quality acting. This isn't the Amateur Hour. More programs lose credibility due to poor acting than for any other reason.)

You might add variety by having two actors play trainees. Perhaps one is a wise-guy know-it-all who plays the foil. This gives the trainer the opportunity to expand upon or reinforce ideas. ("Bob, a lot of people make that mistake. . .especially those who haven't read the manual. But it's not true. Let me explain.") Balance the foil with another trainee, a positive role model with whom viewers—trainees themselves—can identify.

Another approach might be to use a "Six O'Clock News" format, with

---

You may not be an expert in producing video, but you are an expert in watching it.

---

two or more "news people." For instance, one could be the anchor, another the market specialist, a third the features and benefits expert. This approach is inexpensive and it gives the subject matter a sense of urgency.

You may not be an expert in producing video, but you are an expert in watching it. It's called television. If you watch television with a critical eye, you'll begin to notice camera angles and scene changes used by news programs, interview and informational talk shows, educational series and commercials.

As you study the mechanics of each show—how it opens, how it's organized, what you like and don't like—take notes so that you can borrow ideas. There's no better source. Training department archives around the country are loaded with programs based on "60 Minutes," "Wall Street

HIRING IT OUT
BY RALPH PRIBBLE

So you've decided to go outside the company for expert production, and you're now in the market for a video producer. They're out there, in endless shapes and sizes. Whom do you hire? And how do you make sure you'll get your money's worth once the project is in their hands?

It pays to have a plan for dealing with potential producers—before you're brought to the point of answering the question "How much do you have to spend?" Bruce Whitmarsh, a media and instructional design specialist with the University of West Florida, offers some ideas to keep in mind during your search.

• *Public relations.* Your first order of business, Whitmarsh advises, should be a meeting with the production staff. Don't settle for a tour of the facilities with a salesperson. Try to spend a few minutes with the artists, photographers, writers and others. They'll get to know you as a client—and appreciate the fact that you respect them as craftsmen.

• *Objectives.* You'd hardly go looking for a video producer without an audience and an objective in mind. But beyond getting a quality production, have you considered what you're trying to accomplish with it? Whitmarsh says it helps to think of that in measurable, clearly defined terms.

"What do you want your audience to do when your presentation is completed?" he asks. Don't be afraid to ask the producer how 20 projectors are going to help trainees make better widgets when they return to the job or how shelling out for an original music score will get the message across more effectively. If you keep this bottom line as a constant reference point, you and the producer will have a yardstick for measuring the success of your investment.

• *Technical resources.* Everything else may feel right, but does the firm you've got in mind have the ability to produce a technically attractive product? Can it create high-impact, creative images and clear, distortion-free audio tracks? A lot of that will tell in its presentation sample. Are you seeing its best work? If you are, and you spot a few glitches, it could be cause for suspicion.

• *Communication.* You can't possibly write a contract to cover every detail, so it's imperative that you keep talking to each other throughout the entire process. "How well you get along with the production personnel will be reflected in the final product," Whitmarsh says. You're working together, and while you shouldn't try to dictate, it won't hurt to suggest.

• *Conceptual thinking.* Can the producer grasp abstract ideas? A good producer will be able to make your own ideas clearer to you and will take your concept and build a spectrum of options around it. Whitmarsh warns that if the producer isn't able to offer a range of approaches, at least some of which clarify or add to your own ideas, you're not getting your money's worth.

• *Creative resources.* A production house may not have on staff all the talent needed for your production, but does it have access to that talent? If your project needs an original score and an orchestra, can the producer round up top people for that? Suppose the production calls for multiple projectors and the producer lacks the staff to stage it on the road. Does the firm know a good staging company, or can its staff train your personnel to do it?

• *Intuition.* If everything seems to be going swimmingly in the above areas but you still feel uneasy about something, stop. Don't tear up the proposed contract, but at least step back for a moment and discuss your worries with the producer. You both have a lot at stake. "Remember, you're purchasing an idea, a work of art and a training or sales tool all in one," Whitmarsh says. You've got to have a good feeling about it.

Finally, Whitmarsh cautions that while spending a bundle won't guarantee a great video presentation, being too stingy will guarantee a flop. "Expect something for nothing, and you'll spend something and get nothing."

Reprinted from TRAINING, August 1985

Week" and George C. Scott's rendition of General George Patton's address to his troops ("You men and women out there, remember one thing. You are the best-trained, best-equipped sales force in the business. . . .").

The script counts

No amount of production hoopla will make up for weak content, poor organization or an unfocused program. On the other hand, a solid, well-thought-out script can overcome many production flaws. A good example is the 1950s "Twilight Zone" series. Many of the episodes were put together on a shoestring budget. Their production quality was often weak, but the plot organization and writing made the series a hit.

Dozens of books have been written about techniques for developing clear, powerful scripts. There are few hard-and-fast rules, but several suggestions are in order:

• Keep it tight and well-focused, with the program objectives clearly in mind.

• Remember that this is a visual medium. Reinforce ideas visually.

• Provide as much clear production direction as possible. Assume

HOW TO REVIEW A VIDEO SCRIPT

Effective video training programs begin with good scripts. That's easy for us to say. But how do you make sure the scripts you approve turn into good programs? What do you look for?

Mark Bade, a communications consultant based in Glen Ellyn, IL, offers some techniques to help you review your own scripts and work with writers to tailor their scripts to your needs.

• *Reread the treatment or design document before you start reviewing the script.* It may go by any number of names, but Bade is referring to the basic document the writer was supposed to be working from when he or she wrote the script—the one that describes things like the program's purpose, objectives, content and format. It will help you remember what you wanted from the program in the first place.

• *Read the script for the big picture.* Don't worry about details the first time through. Look at the overall content and message. Concentrate on the right-hand side of the script, where the dialogue is: What do the narrator and the characters have to say? Go for general impressions. Does the script serve your overall purpose? Does it meet the specific objectives you and the writer agreed upon? Does it cover the content and adhere to the format described in the treatment?

"If the script properly handles the objectives, content and format, you're ready for the next pass," says Bade. "If not, the writer has some major rewriting to do before you spend any more time reviewing."

• *Review the visual flow.* Start from the beginning again. This time, focus on the left-hand column, where the visual action is described. How has the writer handled the visual flow? Do you get a sense of unity, continuity, smoothness?

The flow should create a mood that contributes to the overall purpose of the program. Note how the writer uses devices and format elements, and how topic changes and transitions are conveyed visually. "Quick, jarring cuts may be appropriate in an inspirational piece, but distracting in a training program," says Bade. Try to imagine what the viewer will see in each scene.

• *Review for detail.* On your third pass through the script, check for accuracy in the language and visuals. Is the language realistic and appropriate to your audience? Look for typos and misspellings; they can create problems in the review and production process. But don't be bothered by ellipses and sentence fragments. That's the way language written to be spoken is supposed to look.

• *Read aloud for sound.* Mark any tongue-twisters, awkward-sounding passages and overly long sentences. Listen to how the most dramatic scenes play. Get a rough idea of the running time of the program.

• *Read for the "hidden audience."* The primary audience—your trainees—is the most important one. But while you're putting the program together for them, it will be seen in various stages of development by other audiences: reviewers, approvers, performers and production personnel.

You may want to have the writer include a "note to reviewers" at the beginning of the script. The note might include a recap of the treatment document, a summary of talent and locations used, explanations of the script format, special concerns of the writer and resources needed for further script development.

To help the narrator and the actors, make sure the writer indicates any special pronunciations (by spelling unfamiliar names or terms phonetically, for example) and marks topic changes. If there will be a voice-over narrator, avoid breaking words between lines (by hyphenating them) and breaking paragraphs between pages. Underline passages to be emphasized and mark voice changes clearly.

For the third "hidden audience," the production people, have the writer provide an outline of scenes, listing the talent, sets and props needed for each. And include the director in the review cycle as early in the game as possible.

There is one other person in the process whose needs must be considered: the writer. As you present your criticisms, try to express them calmly and in a positive manner. Be judicious with exclamation points; they come across to writers as meaning, "How could you be so dumb!" If you spot a chronic problem in spelling, grammar, etc., just point it out once and indicate that it is to be corrected throughout.

One thing Bade advises against is specifying the exact wording you want in a passage. The writer has been working to establish a style and tone for the program, and may have a hard time working your revisions into that style. Your best bet is to state your concerns and let the writer provide the solutions. However, if you think the writer might have trouble understanding your comment or coming up with an alternative, go ahead and suggest—don't dictate—some possible wording.

Finally, if a number of people will be reviewing the script, they'll all want to throw in their two cents worth. To keep the writer from being barraged, designate one reviewer as the "funnel," with the authority to discuss the collected comments with the writer. That will save time and keep the script on track.

Reprinted from TRAINING, August 1985

nothing. Don't worry about being well-versed in production jargon. Although it helps if you know the fundamentals, detailed descriptions and instructions written in English will suffice.

• Keep it short. It's better to do five 10-minute programs (each with a clearly defined objective) than one rambling, 50-minute epic.

Occasionally you may have to go into production without a finished script in hand. For example, the program may require shooting an interview in a talk-show setting, a speech by a company bigwig or outside expert, or excerpts from the annual meeting or company picnic.

Even in these situations, try to have at least an outline based on the theme or objectives of the video. The program itself will be created almost entirely in the editing process. Since you want plenty of material to work with, there's only one rule: Shoot everything.

Decisions, decisions

If you have in-house facilities, you are both cursed and blessed. The curse is that you have no choice in facilities: Good, bad or so-so, you must go with what you have. On the other hand, the clock isn't always running; you can do a lot on a small budget. The people are easily accessible and are familiar with the subject matter, your needs and restrictions.

If you don't have in-house facilities, shop around. Selecting the "right" production house is time-con-suming, but it's worth the investment. Your choice can make or break the program (see accompanying story).

Many production houses specialize. Some produce nothing but high-budget corporate-image programs. Others do only television commercials. The trick is to find the facility that's right for your needs. Some suggestions:

• Check with other people in your field. Word of mouth is sometimes the best way to get the inside track on

---

It's your budget and your program. Retain control.

---

reputation and quality. There may be a specialty house in your field or a broad-based production facility that has handled similar projects.

• Walk in with all the available information on the project. Nobody expects to see a script at the first meeting, but try to be as specific as possible.

• Based on the information available, ask for a reasonable estimate of total production costs. You are unlikely to get a solid quote in writing; few facilities will make that sort of commitment without a complete script in hand.

• Ask to see samples of other work, preferably programs similar to yours.

• Be sure to meet with the director with whom you will be working. Is he cooperative? Does he offer ideas and ask questions? Will you be able to work with this person?

Once you have hired the director and production crew, retain control. You may not have the technical expertise to know when a straight cut is better than a cross fade, but it's your budget and your program. Don't just hand it over to people who don't have the same vested interest in the program that you do. You can ask questions—lots of them—and demand translations if the answers are too technical.

A good director will explain everything and will offer advice and suggestions. Still, because you are responsible for the final product, the final decision is yours.

Your job is not done when the cameras shut down. The real work begins in post-production editing. A good technician can perform minor magic. But you will need to oversee content decisions, help select the best takes on scenes and watch for errors that weren't caught earlier. An on-camera guest who leaves out the word "not," reversing the meaning of a key point, can ruin a whole program—if it's not caught in editing.

These suggestions are not the complete guide to instant success as a video producer. They will, however, make your job easier—and will help you bring your next program in on time, on budget and on the mark.

Reprinted from TRAINING, August 1986

ESTIMATING VIDEO COSTS

When it costs anywhere from $50 to $100,000 per finished minute to produce a videotape, it pays to estimate what you're getting into

BY DANNY E. HUPP

As a nation of television addicts, we all know a good videotape production when we see one. We watch them every day. Everything looks so crisp, so seamless, so . . . flawless. No wonder we take high-quality video for granted.

TV-bred viewing standards become a problem as soon as you decide to produce a custom video for a corporate training program. You'd like it to look and sound just as smooth and professional as what you see on television. But at what cost? Can you produce a low-budget training video that won't be laughed at by the jaded couch potatoes in your audience?

These questions are being asked more frequently now that video is widely used in the classroom. But before you decide if you can afford to produce a training videotape that meets your trainees' expectations, you must be able to estimate costs accurately. Unfortunately, if you've never been involved in production before, that becomes a dicey proposition. Production companies may not be much help, either. Try calling several for estimates. Their answers will vary from, "Plan on $1,000 a finished minute," to "I don't know. Let me see the script first." The second answer may leave you frustrated, but it's the most accurate response.

To understand why, think of the script as a blueprint. No contractor will bid on a construction job until he has seen a blueprint, right? The contractor has to know what time and materials will be needed before he can prepare the budget that will determine his bid. A well-written script is the blueprint that allows the producer to identify the required time and materials—so she has the right to ask for one. Of course, this puts you in a Catch-22: The production company (or your organization's internal video department) won't give you an estimate until you write a script, and you don't want to write a script until you have an idea of how much the video will cost.

To escape this classic trap, a little education helps. You need to know which factors producers consider when they develop production budgets. Armed with this information, you'll find you can write your script to fit your budget, rather than trying to stretch your budget to fit your script.

Experienced producers start by using the script, or a detailed script treatment, to determine the running time of the video, measured in "finished minutes"—the time it takes to view the tape when it's done. The average production cost for videos used in training is about $1,000 a minute. However, the average isn't a useful gauge when you consider that the range varies from less than $50 to more than $100,000 per finished minute.

Recording days

How long will it take to record the script? It depends. Look first at the number of locations you'll use. If the crew can record the entire script in one spot, such as a studio, the production will require fewer recording days and be considerably less expensive than if it needs several locations. I've found that the average cost for one production day is $3,500. Obviously, costs multiply quickly the more time you spend in production.

The script's length also plays a part. Generally, up to 25 pages of script can be recorded in one day, assuming you're using one location and you're not fussing with elaborate camera moves or scene changes.

Talent

The cost of actors usually isn't a major line item in the total budget, unless you're hiring stars. The standard day rate for union actors is $312, including union dues and withholding. On-camera narrators usually receive $535 a day. These prices buy professional talent, which is usually suitable for training films. If your video needs popular or nationally recognized talent, you can easily be talking $25,000 a day. If you want Michael Jackson, multiply that figure by your social security number.

If you're considering saving money by using your own employees instead, proceed with caution. There are hidden costs when you pull employees from their regular duties and try to make actors of them. The obvious costs are salaries. The less obvious costs are the business opportunities that may be lost while they're tied up in production. What's more, there's quality to consider. Most actors study and practice for years; few nonprofessionals will appear natural before a camera. If your script calls for credible, believable performances, hire professionals.

Location vs. studio

Renting a studio costs anywhere from $600 to $1,200. You may be tempted to conclude that it's cheaper to record at your company. But there are hidden costs here, too. First, the

VIDEO PRODUCTION COSTS

Cost Per Minute*	Factors	Cost Per Minute*	Factors
$4,000 to $6,000	Four to six days of production in multiple locations. All one-inch recording and editing. Up to 36 hours of editing. Up to 24 hours of graphics animation. Narrator with national name recognition. Original music.	Under $2,000 (continued)	Up to 24 hours of editing one-half inch to one-inch tape. Up to six hours of special effects. Music from music library.
Under $3,000	Up to four days of production in multiple locations. All one-inch recording and editing. Up to 24 hours of editing. Up to 12 hours of special effects. Professional talent, including extra money for "commercial narrator." Some original music.	Under $1,000	One or two days of production at up to four locations. Up to 16 hours of editing one-half inch to one-inch tape, including two hours of special effects. Up to four professional actors and one narrator.
		Under $500	One day of production at no more than two locations. Two professional actors. Up to six hours of editing one-half inch to one-inch tape with no special effects.
Under $2,000	Up to three days of production at up to six locations. Up to eight actors and one narrator.	Under $100	Production at one location. No editing. One day of production. No professional talent.

*The price estimates represent costs per finished minute for a 10–12 minute video.

recording session is bound to be disruptive to the workers. You can minimize the distraction by recording during off-hours, but scripts often call for normal office activity. A less obvious cost is the extra time you must spend dealing with uncontrollable events, such as the unwanted sounds of office equipment automatically turning on and off, or the numerous retakes caused by employees who walk by and stare at actors during shooting. Difficulties in arranging proper lighting and sound conditions will produce additional delays. Whenever production can be done in a studio without expensive set construction, I encourage it.

Editing

The cost of editing varies greatly, depending on the number of special effects you want. With video, you can flip the image, or squeeze a full screen down to a tiny screen. The screen can show several images at once, and each image can show real-time movement (which costs more, of course, than still frames). You can use computer-generated animation and special graphics.

These aren't all the options. With the current state of the art in the electronics field, you're limited by little more than your imagination. However, each special effect takes time to create, and it may take special computer equipment if it's a fancy one. Production companies charge by the hour for editing, and those charges vary based on the type of equipment your effect requires. The range is roughly $75 to $750 an hour.

Format

The type of equipment affects cost because some sizes of recording tape are more expensive to edit than others. The highest-quality—and most expensive—format used in industrial videos is one-inch tape. (One-inch tape is also used for most broadcast television productions.) Half-inch VHS tape is the lowest-priced format used for recording training videos. Dramatic differences show up after the tapes have been edited and copied for use in the classroom. Videos recorded on half-inch tape look fuzzy. They show shadows around the images and the colors are flat.

Lately, production companies have started using half-inch, high-speed Betacam tape, which nearly matches the quality of one-inch tape. Many television stations use it for on-location reporting. When this tape is edited, it's transferred from the half-inch Beta to a one-inch master by a process called interformat editing. It cuts editing costs from about $400 an hour to $200 an hour. Beta also saves money because it uses less expensive recording equipment.

Although it does seem daunting, it's not impossible to estimate the cost of producing a training video. The accompanying table shows how your cost per minute will increase as you vary certain factors. Considering all these factors before you start writing your script puts you in control. Generally, the question is not, "Can I afford video?" The question is, "What production elements do I need for a video that meets my training objectives?"

Reprinted from TRAINING, January 1988

VIDEO THROUGH THE EYES OF THE TRAINEE

If you're going to put your training on a tape, the pros say, it helps to know something about the audience's unique relationship with the medium

BY TERRI O'GRADY
AND MIKE MATTHEWS

Sometimes,' goes the lament, "there's just nothing good on television." Over the years, we've all complained about the empty programming, excessive advertising and negative newscasts. Yet while people in the '80s may be less than willing to apply favorable adjectives to television, total household viewing is about 6½ hours daily. And as if it isn't enough that people are watching all that less-than-satisfying TV at home, now you're going to use a video program to train them?

"Almost all of us [in the workplace] have been children in America," says Harry Lasker, cofounder of Interactive Training Systems of Cambridge, MA. "We've all been exposed to the medium over the years. The video we use in training has got to have sound production values in order to be watched and not be seen as second-class, ho-hum, even deficient programming."

It shouldn't be surprising that adults have their own well-developed attitudes, values, feelings and expectations about television. They don't leave them at home when they come to work each day, which means they bring them along to your video training sessions, too. Television's recreational format and visual nature can turn all types of communication into packaged entertainment. It's not the sort of medium that's good at providing in-depth information; it shows, rather than tells. And among adults, television viewing is to a large degree a passive activity, where acceptance rather than enthusiasm is the rule.

To use television technology effectively in training, we need to have some appreciation for what is going on in the minds of trainees when they turn their attention to the tube.

Video vision

A picture is a very special type of symbol. We learn to recognize pictures long before we develop more organized language and learning skills, and research shows that we retain picture-recognition ability as a way of learning about the world around us. Film and video play to that powerful method of learning.

"The 'magic' of the medium is that it makes the invisible visible," says Lasker. "It makes the abstract concrete. The technology for creating video images is exploding. With its ability to not only reproduce what we see, but to animate and create visual effects that electronically generate events, video has the potential to transform the way we perceive things."

What we see through video images, however, often is simplistic in form and content. In contrast to written materials, where each reader must analyze and find the meaning, television viewers don't find things for themselves. Everything is "found" for them. Perspective is a function of the camera's eye.

For example, when the camera zooms to one object in the frame, it makes a powerful value judgment: That object is important and everything else we had been seeing is less important. It's the video equivalent of pointing, but with the assurance that viewers can't pick out the wrong thing to look at or get caught looking the wrong way.

When we read of a blue Ford cruising down a dark alley on a rainy night, we are left to fill in the details with our imaginations. Given a written text, no two people are likely to visualize the scene the same way. But when we see that scene on the tube, the details become fixed forever: The car is in profile or head-on, moving left to right or top to bottom, past a lighted window or darkened doorway, in a driving rain or a chilling drizzle, and so on into as much depth as we can absorb. We all get the same image. And the next time we read the story on which the video was based, even months or years later, it's likely to be *that* car, *that* alley and *that* night we call to mind.

The consistency and control of the image is potentially a major strength of video. Compared to other forms of presentation, and barring unforeseen distractions from another source, viewers are always looking at what they are supposed to be looking at and seeing it the way we—the programmers—want them to see it.

Done well, video can bring similar consistency and control to the presentation as a whole. Unlike a live lecture, where variations in the instructor's performance from one day to the next can change the learning experience (even though the material at issue hasn't changed), video can be the same for everybody who sees it, every time they see it, regardless of where or when.

But. . . .

Bite-sized

The problem is we've created our own monster. With so much to choose from, we watch those things that keep us stimulated and entertained, and tune out those that don't. Through our mass media, we are subject to a constant barrage of images and vicarious experiences, all broken down into little bite-sized particles and interspersed with the advertising we've conditioned ourselves to ignore. As a result, even though we're inundated by commercials (in which advertisers invite us, in often ingenious ways, to "learn" about their products or services), research shows that only 7 percent of us can recall the brand name of the last thing we saw advertised.

That should give trainers pause for thought. The first assumption to avoid, offers video designer Septh Bloedoorn, president of Antaeus Ad-

> **When the camera zooms to one object, it makes a powerful value judgement.**

vanced Presentation Technologies of Minneapolis, is the one that says you're dealing with a captive audience.

"Managers and trainers who aren't video-sophisticated will often assume that because their audience has no choice but to sit through their training, they don't have to spend much time thinking about design," he observes. "You can make them watch, but you can't keep them from mentally resisting the message."

Once you have them watching, the next trick is to *keep* them watching. The average viewer, says Greg Martin, president of Buscomm, Inc. of Isanti, MN, "is groomed to expect no more than 12- to 15-minute blocks of information before a break. With video, statistics say you can hold them for 10 minutes if it's good. After 10 you start to have drop-off. After 12 minutes, drop-off is more substantial. At 15 minutes you've lost a major part of your audience. Any longer blocks and you'll get unconscious resistance."

And within those blocks?

"By commercial television standards, the picture should change every three to seven seconds," contends Lasker, whose background includes some work with Children's Television Workshop, the "Sesame Street" folks who pioneered TV-based learning for kids. "If all we're seeing is a picture of somebody talking, we might just as well listen to the radio."

What can you do to try to keep your audience tuned in? Here are four television-tempered techniques to keep in mind.

1. Create images. Video *shows* far better than it *tells*. If your program depends more on the words than the pictures, video might not be the proper medium for it. Conversely, if you can find or create images that trainees can understand and learn from, you can draw on the powerful picture sense that is basic to human learning.

"Film and video have always had great power in behavior modeling," says Lasker. "You can show not only the behavior, but the context in which one will use that knowledge or skill. And with the development of interactive video, users can now participate much more directly. We can literally touch and maneuver. We can explore spatial environments and social events. We can see how things change. In a funny sense, we can be in the show."

Images need not be limited to just moving pictures videotaped from real life. Pictures can be overlaid with graphics or enhanced with special effects. Content summaries can be superimposed as titles on video sequences or built up billboard-style through character generation. Icons and animation can create new images where none existed before.

"One of the reasons we don't understand computers," Lasker maintains, "is because their inner workings are invisible. We can't 'see' what's going on. But with video, you can create images that make the computer accessible to the learner—pictures they can interact with."

2. Set the pace. When Lasker says the image changes every three to seven seconds in commercial television, he isn't recommending that trainers adopt that pace. But the slower and more tedious video training looks and feels to the viewer, the greater the contrast that will be visible

between it and the flashier programming we're accustomed to seeing.

"Common sense tells us the medium of television is becoming more highly paced over time," says Lasker. "The heightened pace can serve to increase attention." It can also, he cautions, distort or trivialize the message of the training involved. The trick is to keep the pace moving, the images changing, without burying the content in the glitz and glitter.

Similarly, overall program lengths must respond to the viewer's needs and expectations. Bloedoorn points out that while people can spend two

> **False assumption: The more it resembles popular TV, the more it will hold their interest.**

hours in a darkened theater watching a feature-length movie on a big screen, they don't do as well in front of the smaller television screen: "Adults need breaks for both physical and mental comfort—to process new information as well as to get the blood moving again. Video show times need to compress down to the kind of times that correspond more to what people can sit through."

3. Call up reinforcements. Educational experts agree that repetition is a key to retention. But it's important to remember that you're working with adults and not children, so reinforcement can come in a multiplicity of ways, some of them obvious, some subtle. Savvy production designers will use graphics, question-and-answer sequences, role plays, background footage accompanied by a voiceover, and even music to help their audiences get the message.

"Music shouldn't be intrusive," says Martin, "but that doesn't mean it can't be effective. The first time we introduce a message, we support it with music that has an upbeat, anticipatory sound and rhythm. It creates an expectation of more to come. In the middle block, where we're maybe repeating a detail or concept, the music is a palette with which the information is being presented. Then when we summarize, we'll use music that hits hard—something that will linger with the information before trailing off into a relaxing tone that signals a break."

Adds Lasker: "Video offers all kinds of special effects aimed at dazzling the eyes while at the same time heightening attention and visual appeal. You can make manageable chunks out of the steps in an interaction by using subtitles, role plays and other illustrations." There are many ways, he says, in which the facts of your case can be put forward visually so as to cover the same information you'd present orally or in a text—but that communicate your message "both with greater potency and with greater speed."

4. Get real. People identify with the people, images and experiences around them. Unfortunately, according to Tom Reeves, a professor in the department of instructional technology at the University of Georgia, many training videos are designed on a false assumption: Since people like to watch TV shows, the more the training resembles popular TV, the more it will capture and hold interest.

"I can't tell you the number of programs I've seen in the last few years that build their training around popular TV show motifs," Reeves says. "For example, I've seen at least six

---

TRANSFERRING SLIDES TO VIDEO

BY JOE FARACE

Why would you want to turn a slide show into a video? The best reason is a simple one: cost. A training program produced as a slide show and transferred to video will cost less than an all-video production. Moreover, since the original format is slides, the video will be easy to modify in the future.

Another reason to consider the transfer process is videotape's convenience and transportability. Compared with multi-projector presentations, it's easier to take video on the road or send it out to field offices. You also might want to use video transfer to create a backup copy of an original slide show.

To ensure a successful transfer, however, you must design the original with video in mind. Here are a few tips:

• Don't assume a full-frame, single-screen slide show will transfer easily to the almost square shape of a video monitor. Even the layout area known as "TV safe" is not really all that safe. Your best bet: Follow the specifications for "safe action area" laid out in the American Society of Cinematographers' technical manual and double check with the company that will be doing the transfer.

• Imagine your slides converted to black-and-white images. Video will do a better job with colors that translate into middle shades of gray. Lighter colors work well for backgrounds; in fact, white is your best choice.

• Don't use extreme lighting ratios for studio or location photography—it won't transfer well. The flat lighting you see in a lot of television productions is designed to fit the limitations of the video medium.

• You don't have to use special TV slide mounts; use whichever pin-registered mounting system you prefer. Cleanliness is imperative, so remember to clean your slides before transferring them.

A training program produced as a slide show and transferred to video will cost less than an all-video production.

Now you're ready to consider your transfer options. There are two basic methods: off-the-wall and optical bench. Your budget and the way you intend to use the videotape will determine which method is your best choice.

In the off-the-wall method, the slide show is projected onto a screen, and a video camera simply records the image. This approach is inexpensive, but offers uncertain visual quality. Some projector lenses concentrate a higher light density at the center of the screen and form a noticeable "hot spot" when the image is recorded on videotape. Some walls and screens don't reflect light evenly to the video camera.

Still, this method will suffice if quality is not critical. When I was an in-house AV producer I used it to create archival tapes of our library of slide shows. It enabled clients to view our repertoire easily.

For most videotape programs, however, you'll probably opt for the higher quality resolution of the optical-bench or aerial-image method. This requires a video multiplexer that captures images by transmitted light rather than reflected light. It gives a cleaner image, with better color saturation and detail.

If you use an outside lab to transfer your slides to video, explain your needs clearly and give the company what it needs to give you the best possible results. Here's a sample checklist from one company that specializes in transfers:

• Are all trays titled and designed for program, channel, etc.?

• Are all slides in correct position in tray and ready for front projection?

• Are the slide mounts all of one type and mold number?

• Are the slides clean?

• Is there a cued script or storyboard included for checking the show's synchronization?

Reprinted from TRAINING, December 1987

different programs that use the 'Twilight Zone' approach; you know, 'You are now entering the Training Zone.' I've seen a lot of production money go into making programs look like they have broadcast value, and not enough money go into the design of the interactions. It's almost like they're sneaking in the training."

Reeves concedes it's a two-edged sword. Uninteresting, unappealing programs can limit learning; people don't want to sit in front of an electronic workbook. Yet trying too hard to copy hackneyed or inappropriate television formulas, he argues, runs the risk of sacrificing substance to style, trivializing the training. The trick is to use the visual power of the medium in a realistic context so trainees will connect the new skills with their own work styles and on-the-job environment.

Lasker believes trainers can have it both ways—good training and good production values—if they learn the strengths of the medium and turn those strengths to their own advantage.

"To do video well requires skill, and it requires money," he contends. "Where many productions fall short is in [the producers'] thinking that just because you've made a tape, you've 'done video.' If you don't do it well, the learner can be so jarred by the second-class nature of the production that it creates noise. It gets in the way of what you're trying to teach."

Reprinted from TRAINING, July 1987

TRAINING BY VIDEO: HOW TO SHOOT YOURSELF IN THE FOOT

This instructional videotape is either
boring or it isn't, eh?
So let's just pop some corn, cut the lights
and see what we think, eh?

BY PETER MARTIN

Last year our training division was asked to help produce a videotape that would teach engineers how to fill out input forms for a computer program developed by another division of our company. The forms contained spaces for the engineer to fill in certain parameters having to do with the diameters of pipes, temperatures of fluids, and so on. The computer program would calculate a heat-exchange index based on these parameters.

We agreed to help and proceeded to make what we thought at the time was a reasonably good industrial videotape. Considering that the potential audience for the tape was small, strictly within the company (and therefore "family"), and seeing that they were engineers, we kept the production informal, rather dry, and very much to the point; no frills, just "need-to-know" information. Since the tape would have a short shelf life (on the order of a year or less), we dispensed with our TV studio in New York and used our home-style, half-inch, local black-and-white setup.

Our "actors" were actual computer programmers, people who knew the subject matter intimately but had no particular flair for acting. All in all, we figured we were producing a perfectly appropriate tape for the audience and subject matter we were dealing with.

When we finished taping and editing, the manager of the computer-programming division asked to view our tape before sending it into the field. Since management was involved, we took pains to show the tape under the most favorable, if somewhat formal, conditions. We reserved one of the company conference rooms with a 23-inch monitor built into the wall, a room that accommodates about 14 people.

The manager and several of his lower-echelon supervisors showed up for the viewing, along with the two "actors," the camerawoman, and me, the director. We darkened the room and told the projectionist (over the intercom—just like Hollywood) to start the tape.

Within five minutes everybody in the place was bored out of his skull. Unfortunately, the tape was 45 minutes long. After 20 minutes or so, just about everyone had had enough.

When we were making the tape, it seemed a fine idea to have the two actors take turns standing beside a flip chart and leading the viewer through the process of filling in parameters on enlarged copies of the input forms. Now all the forms looked alike; in fact, even the two actors began to look alike. We had no trouble arriving at a consensus that this was the most boring production any of us had ever witnessed.

We never did get to the end of that tape. When the programming manager could stand no more, he ordered the lights brought back up and the tape stopped. After a brief discussion we decided to put the tape on ice rather than release it to the field. It was relegated to the scratch shelf in our tape library, where it gathered dust for the next six months.

A funny thing happened . . .

Then, one day, a funny thing happened. An engineer who needed to use the heat-exchanger computer program came by to inquire about a rumored videotape that was supposed to explain how to fill out the input forms for the program. He was having a hard time doing exactly that. Could he, by any chance, view the tape?

We told him the tale of the disastrous preview session. But the engineer countered that something, no matter how bad, was bound to be better than nothing. So after apologizing once more for the product, we set him up in his own office to view the tape. We put our ½-inch VTR on one corner of his desk, and a nice little 8-inch SONY portable TV in the center. Our "audience" sat at his desk with a supply of input forms in front of him. Felt-tipped pen in hand, he turned on the SONY and switched the VTR to "play," while we watched over his shoulder in embarrassed silence.

You may have guessed by this point that the results were fantastic. As the "actors" filled in their forms, the engineer filled in his. If he had to stop to look up some parameter value, he reached over and stopped the player. In front of our wondering eyes, the engineer sat at his desk and filled out forms for 45 minutes, following the directions of our videotaped actors. When he finished, we asked him if he hadn't found the tape boring. He had not. As a matter of fact, he said, 45 minutes seemed a singularly small investment of time in order to accomplish a task that had baffled him for days.

From this experience we learned something about the use of videotapes in training. Why wasn't the engineer bored? Because he didn't *expect* to be entertained. When we set up our preview for the programming manager, we unwittingly prepared everyone to expect entertainment. Look at the viewing environment we had arranged: a large, darkened room with a snazzy, built-in monitor; an audience of several people relaxing in conference chairs; even an intercom to the projection room. In short, the whole arrangement was like a small movie theater, or perhaps somebody's recreation room set up for a Saturday night of television viewing. We had created a theater environment; *of course* everyone expected to be entertained. And of course everyone was disap-

239

pointed, since our tape was not intended to entertain but to instruct.

In contrast, look at the viewing environment six months later when the engineer viewed the tape. He was at his own desk in his own, fully illuminated office. He had his input forms in front of him and a pen in his hand. He was prepared to do some work. And that was the vital difference. In the first case, the tape was shown to the wrong audience under the wrong conditions. In the second, it was shown under "field" conditions to a member of its intended audience and for its intended purpose.

One other lesson is worth mentioning here. With training tapes intended to teach some procedure, it is important, maybe vital, that the learner be able to control the progress of the tape. The "impersonality" of automated learning is compounded by forcing the learner to take what the TV monitor dishes out, and at a rate selected by the monitor, not the learner. Our company found the old one-inch Ampex systems almost useless for training people, because the

trainee always needed a technician to load the tape for him. Even starting, stopping and rewinding presented problems. The machine simply intimidated people. That's why the newer cassette-format machines are such a boon to the training field. It is far from a trivial development that at last the student can control what he does and at what rate.

Within five minutes everyone was bored out of his skull. Unfortunately, our tape was 45 minutes long.

Select the right audience

So what should you do to check out a new training tape? *Don't* show it to the company brass. If all they're going to do is sit and watch, they are una-

voidably primed to expect entertainment. Despite your disclaimers, when you put people in a room and turn on a TV monitor you are competing with television, and the entertainment value of your in-house production is probably lower than that of the worst television program ever aired. You're doomed. And besides, what does the company brass know about either taping or teaching?

Instead, do some low-key effectiveness tests with the type of people the tape is intended for, and have them view your product under actual "field" conditions. Set up an environment that will induce the viewer to expect work, not entertainment. If you bomb out under these conditions, go back to the drawing board. At least you've saved yourself the embarrassment of advertising your failure to management. But if the test results are positive, you can now approach the brass with some objective evidence that you know what you're doing. They have to accept the fact that your product works, whether it appeals to them or not.

Reprinted from TRAINING, April 1985

VISUALIZING TECHNICAL TRAINING PROGRAMS

How to get high-tech skills training out of those manuals and onto a video screen

BY MICHAEL J. BASHISTA

As the technology of the American work place continues to evolve, one of the looming problems facing employers is the question of how best to train low-tech workers for high-tech jobs.

The Center for Continuing Study of the California Economy in Palo Alto predicts that 45,000 to 50,000 new high-tech jobs will be created by 1990 in that state alone. The work will be there. But how does one design effective programs to upgrade and expand the skills of the people who will have to do it?

The need to provide technical training not only to new hires but to experienced employees is nothing new, of course. What is new is the challenge of merging technical training with the delivery media of the '80s such as video and interactive computer systems. With the military, in many cases, leading the way, training departments are turning increasingly to those media as a viable alternative to the classic, often-impenetrable volumes of high-density print.

The bottom line on the effectiveness of visual programs rests, of course, on the ability of the program designer to integrate complex subject matter with the new media. Technical training usually covers operational, maintenance-related and analytical skills. The challenges associated with developing and delivering technical training in a video format are formidable.

In the first place, the raw information the designer needs often exists only in those volumes of mumbo-jumbo he is trying to get away from. Basic questions such as "What is the critical content?" and "What are the important tasks?" may be hard to answer.

In the second place, the learners whom the designer is trying to serve will require a viewpoint—a "map" providing visual clues from which to uncover skills, knowledge and con-

---

Technical training is nothing new; the challenge is to merge it with the delivery media of the '80s.

---

cepts. "Visualization" is the development of viewpoints, symbols, analogies, relationships and vehicles of presentation. Who is best qualified to do the developing? Do you hire a scriptwriter with visualization talent or ask a content expert to write the script?

The best answer probably is, refuse to treat this as an either/or decision: Use both as a team. Working together, the writer and a knowledgeable expert first should complete an analysis of the O.A.C.R.: Objectives, Audience, Content (including tasks) and available Resources. After the analysis stage, the content expert becomes a reviewer while the writer takes over conceptualization and visualization.

Although conceptualization and visualization are two distinct steps in the design process, experience indicates that they often merge: The designer tends to begin visualizing quickly, before completing the concepts. In any case, visuals are based on concepts, and concepts hang on the visuals.

Given the state of special effects, it is relatively easy to use animation, music and camera technology to add "bells and whistles" that spruce up a technical training program. Unfortunately, this usually is a mistake. The writer should take advantage of available technology, but only in the context of the O.A.C.R. analysis. The idea, remember, is to train the workers, not to distract them.

Working from the book

Ordinarily, the analysis will have uncovered the fact that visuals play a secondary or nonexistent role in the written material that you are trying to translate into video. The figures, charts, tables, exploded-view illustrations and complex diagrams are in there, all right, but they probably are comprehensible only to Ph.D. candidates. Beyond the dubious values of these, you may be faced with step-by-step procedures that continue for page after page, with the elucidating comment "See Fig. 7" implying answers to all questions.

In other words, you often will have to design the visuals almost from scratch—and anything involving motion obviously will have to come from you. To reemphasize, the concepts and visuals you design must be based upon your analysis of the O.A.C.R. They must take advantage of the inherent advantages of video—particularly the ability to show motion—even at the additional expense of including special effects and animation *when appropriate.*

Guidelines

The key to visualization is controlled movement. There are three ways to create movement: Move what is in front of the camera; move the camera; or use editing and other post-production techniques, such as music and effects.

Keep the program tight and succinct. Use short sentences and, as a rule of thumb, restrict segments to less than seven minutes. Don't hesitate to incorporate support materials, allowing the video to present only core information.

Pay particular attention to the audio. Narration should not be used as a redundant backup for what the viewer sees ("As you can observe, the liquid rises"), but should amplify and expand upon visual elements. Special sound effects can be effective cues and are useful as punctuation. Silence can focus attention. And music can be a bridge to a preview or review of the material.

Narration should employ the active voice. When possible, avoid the use of "we" or "I" in favor of the implied "you" (not "We remove the element," but "Remove the element"). Too much "we" can make a technical program sound like a kindergarten cooking class. The progressive removal of "we" and "you" as the program continues places more subliminal learning responsibility on the viewer.

Video-based technical training manipulates the same tools found in writing: character, plot, setting and theme.

Typically, individuals who appear in technical training programs are simply credible sources of information: They look the part but do not have complex personalities. Limited on-camera appearances or total voice-overs are the norms, with actual demonstrations usually provided by anonymous yet knowledgeable technicians. Time, money and the abilities of the talent determine the extent of character involvement.

Plot, which might more aptly be defined as "framework," is tied closely to the setting. Some frameworks include "a day in the life of ...," classroom instruction, an on-line tour or a network parody.

The program's theme is based on its objectives. And in just about every technical training program, one of those objectives is to teach people to do a job better.

A video-based course on troubleshooting and diagnostic procedures produced recently required a lot of flow charts and diagrams. A professional on-camera instructor was selected, and the initial proposal called for a newsroom set. The news set became a classroom due to cost and time restrictions.

As the material became more complex, so did the visuals. That created problems of format and detail resolution. To accommodate the complexity, the instructor explained some of the examples using a flip chart. The camera panned other diagrams from a copystand. Split screens, highlighting and wipes (to reveal information sequentially) also were used.

In the March 1982 issue of *Educational & Industrial Television* one producer described another way to show and explain complex diagrams. Using a key, the producer shrank the instructor, permitting him to walk like Gulliver through a land of giant flow charts.

A third video-based training package, this one on troubleshooting and repairing audio equipment, used the subjective angle extensively to eliminate mirror-image confusion. The package was based on printed troubleshooting guides, and many visuals had to be reformatted for the TV screen.

Exploded views and a few brief animated sequences illustrated data flow. To speed up repetitive disassembly procedures, jump cuts were used to create a cartoon effect, with screws and covers appearing to remove themselves.

Unlike the first example, on-camera talent appeared only during the opening two minutes, the segue between preventive maintenance and troubleshooting, and the close. Actual technicians demonstrated the close-up repairs. The lower third of the screen showed abbreviated, printed explanations of the steps being completed.

The audiences for the first and third programs are expanding, which points out a feature of video-based technical training that is attractive to the designer as well as the client: More and more companies are marketing in-house programs to outside clients—sometimes even to the competition.

Reprinted from TRAINING, January 1983

TECHNICAL TRAINING BY VIDEOTAPE

A video veteran reveals nine lessons she learned the hard way

BY TERESA S. STOVER

1 *Make sure video is the right medium.* Videotape is a very valuable medium for all sorts of technical training subjects, but it isn't the solution to every problem. For certain abstract technical material, it can be the worst way to go.

Many processes are not easily seen. They may take place on a microscopic or atomic level; they may be "visible" only in the mind's eye. If you just point a camera at a lecturer and ask him to describe such a process, the main value of the resulting video will be its ability to cure insomnia.

Just the same, good video solutions to abstract training problems are only difficult; they're not impossible, provided you get your creative juices flowing. Think of analogies or physical ways to express an intangible process or thought. I have seen electron flow represented by people wearing T-shirts with negative signs on them as they all moved down a cardboard canal representing the path of current flow. I've seen the atomic sputtering process[1] illustrated effectively with a dramatic billiard break.

Videotape usually works best in technical training when you're doing system overviews, schematic explanations and procedure demonstrations—in other words, when you're dealing with tangible, concrete material that easily can be *seen*. In a system overview, for example, where the goal is general familiarization, you can start with a cover shot of the machine, talk generally about what it does, and then move in to talk specifically about the different operator panels or subsystems.

The most obvious and effective use of videotaped technical training is the procedural demonstration. Nothing fancy here: Set the camera up next to the machine or whatever, tell the actor to do the procedure, and say go.

There are two ways to handle the narration that accompanies the actor's demonstration, and chances are you'll get decent results either way. The conventional method is to write the script in which the narrator lists the procedure's steps *before* the actor performs them. Since the narration is already set up, you must make sure the actor does it exactly that way, or you'll run into problems in the editing room. One solution is to have the narrator read the script *while* the actor performs the procedure. Or, if you're doing the narration and videotaping separately, you can simply read the narration as you watch the actor go through the steps on tape. Read the steps one at a time, and don't go on until the actor has finished that step. This helps greatly in editing.

The other way to tape the procedure is to have the actor (a content expert) perform the procedure the way he usually does it. Afterward, let him explain what was done as you play back the tape. Record this explanation, then turn that transcript into a video script for the narrator to read.

2 *Follow specific objectives.* Once you develop your objectives and they are approved by your client, tape them up in front of your face at your desk. Program your computer to flash them whenever you log on. Read them every day like a litany. Keep yourself on track.

The best training programs start with simple basics the student can relate to and then build on this knowledge to get to the more difficult areas. Our problem as technical course developers is that we start with an undefined mountain of knowledge from engineers and books written by engineers or other technical experts.

This is where the danger comes in. While sifting through this mass of information, it's easy to become preoccupied with subjects that have nothing to do with what we're supposed to be teaching. A colleague of mine once became completely befuddled with formulas for vacuum rates of rise before remembering that her program objectives only included demonstrating the proper way to install an O-ring to seal a vacuum chamber.

While researching, always keep one eye on your objectives for what the students must learn in this particular unit. You don't want to overwhelm and discourage them (or yourself, for that matter). But keep your other eye on the course prerequisites—you don't want to bore or insult the students either. In other words, don't delve so deeply into your research that you forget your objectives. Learn what's necessary; then develop the program.

3 *Get reliable feedback.* It's a sad fact of training life that clients (e.g., line managers) and content experts often do not scrutinize the course ob-

[1] *Atomic sputtering:* The process of using the momentum of ions and electrons from a plasma to bounce atoms off a target material in order to deposit that material onto a wafer for a thin metallic film.

Plasma: Gas that has been introduced into a vacuum system and ionized by applying energy such as DC or RF. The molecules of the gas are excited to the point that they break up into charged atomic particles: positive ions, negative ions and free electrons. Depending on the gas, energy level and equipment, plasma can be used for several applications in semiconductor processing. (We knew you'd want to know.)

HOW TO WRITE A VIDEO SCRIPT

A properly executed script is as important to a video production as a blueprint is to a building project or a map to a cross-country trip," says Donald Gruber, senior training specialist at Baldwin Associates in Clinton, IL.

Planning the script, he says, is the first step: You must collect and organize the information to be presented and choose a basic treatment of the subject, taking into consideration the audience's level of interest in and understanding of the topic.

The beginning of a video program should grab the audience's attention and prepare them for what is to follow, he says. The middle should be designed to hold their attention, and that means avoiding monotony, predictability, "talking heads" and "video chalk talk. . .a talking head that also writes on a board." The close should briefly summarize what was covered. In most cases, the program should be kept to 10 minutes or less.

Gruber advises scriptwriters to "play" moving pictures in their heads so that they can specify every word spoken and every movement made. He recommends following certain basic conventions and using a step-by-step page layout to prepare a script.

To indicate a new scene, assign it a number and type it in capital letters at the left-hand margin. Scene segments, which describe camera moves, stage directions and any change of continuity within a scene, are identified by letters. Indent scene segments a number of spaces from the left margin and type them in upper- and lower-case letters.

When writing dialogue, indicate the character's name in caps and center it over the dialogue. Indicate voice-overs by typing the name of the character followed by "VOICE-OVER" in brackets, all typed in caps and underlined on the right-hand side of the page. "This keeps it separate from the rest of the dialogue and makes it easier to read during a separate audio recording," explains Gruber. Type camera moves and/or action in upper and lower case and set them in brackets.

The scene transitions also are typed in caps, underlined on the left-hand side of the page at the end of a scene. "CUT TO" is the editor's direction to make an instant change from one picture to another. "FADE OUT" and "FADE IN" indicate that one picture will gradually fade away to black followed by the next scene gradually fading in. A slow or quick fade may be specified. A "DISSOLVE" is a transition in which one picture fades out while the next simultaneously fades in, with no black between them.

"Each of these transitions also can be used during a scene segment to achieve a desired result," adds Gruber. "Cuts are used primarily when it is necessary to go quickly from a concept or location after that particular subject has been thoroughly covered. It's like a pause before moving on to the next topic. Dissolves can be used effectively to give the illusion of passing time."

Finally, the writer should review the rough script to check locations for accessibility, believability and applicability, and to visualize movements and camera directions for continuity. For example, if a scene segment calls for a character to move off camera right and enter the next segment, the person should enter from camera left.

"Use of variety in scenes, characters, visuals and dialogue will keep the presentation moving and interesting," says Gruber. "Variety in dialogue and/or camera angles can overcome the inherent dullness of a one-scene program." If the dialogue itself is on the monotonous side, Gruber recommends livening it up with voice-overs and frequent changes in visuals.

Reprinted from TRAINING, April 1985

SAMPLE PAGE LAYOUT

1.   SCENE: A SEPARATE LOCATION OR CONCEPT, SUCH AS AN ANIMATION SEQUENCE, DESCRIBED IN SOME DETAIL.

    A.   Scene segments indicate parts of a scene.

<u>CHARACTER'S NAME</u>

    This represents the spoken portion of your script.

    B.   Whenever you change cameras, you change scene segments.

<u>CHARACTER'S NAME [VOICE OVER]</u>

<u>THIS IS NARRATION RECORDED SEPARATELY AND PLACED OVER THE VISUAL DESCRIBED IN SCENE 1.B.</u>

[Bracket camera moves and/or action that takes place during a segment]

<u>TRANSITION:</u>

   CUT, FADE OR DISSOLVE

jectives or your drafts. They only think to do this once the final version comes out, when changes are costly and time consuming. With videotaped programs, the time and cost factors increase dramatically.

I know of a client, also serving as the content expert, who heartily approved draft after draft of a script. Not until the tape was produced in its

---

Don't overwhelm and discourage them, but don't bore or insult them either.

---

final, edited state did he begin to clamor about the lack of depth and certain inaccuracies. The program was never delivered.

To prevent such situations, demand that your clients and content experts mark up your drafts. Ask them to look at specific items. Sit down with them and go through the script, page by page. Toss in a ridiculous remark here and there to see if they catch it. Do whatever you have to do to make certain they're paying attention.

Another important consideration: Make sure the client either provides or approves your content expert. Don't invest time, effort and money in the project only to discover that your client believes your content expert doesn't know what he's talking about.

Start planning the production only after you are absolutely certain that everyone involved knows exactly what will be seen and said in the tape.

During production, take your content expert along, especially if he is part of the approval loop. He will make sure that the little things, as well as the big things, are accurate. The second videotape I ever made demonstrated procedures for removing, cleaning and replacing targets to a sputtering system.[2] Being new to the semiconductor industry and its passion for contamination control, I allowed shots of the model working without his smock, hood and gloves. I also included taboo shots of him cleaning the target with an abrasive pad that spewed particles on top of O-rings and other parts that were supposed to be free of all contaminants.

If I had taken a content expert along on the shoot, I wouldn't have had to reshoot and reedit half the program.

4 *Know what your client wants.* Different clients mean different things when they pronounce that infamous phrase, "I want a videotape."

The simplest interpretation could be a "point-and-shoot" session of a lecture or demonstration, with very little editing afterwards. Deadly dull, most likely, but it may be what the client wants.

A middle-of-the-road interpretation might be that the client wants to use in-house video facilities and allow employees to serve as the actors.

The top-of-the-line interpretation is what I call the "Universal Studios" approach: You don't take the video equipment into the production area. Instead, you build a production setting into a studio, complete with two or three camera crews, three different types of lighting, a teleprompter, a video engineer, a sound engineer, a lighting grip, a director, the actors from Los Angeles and all that wonderful stuff.

So when your client says, "I want a videotape," ask, "What kind of videotape?" and describe these scenarios. The answer leads immediately to your next question: "How much do you want to spend?" Check with your internal or local video production service for prices for the three ranges of quality.

About a year ago I wrote and produced a 60-minute videotape on the theory and operation of a plasma etching system.[3] I was very pleased with it. It contained a lot of nice elements, including a recognized authority who did the introduction and summary, good video shots, interesting computer graphics and step-by-step procedures. It was well edited and professionally narrated (for free!), and the total project cost $15,000 —quite a bargain, I thought. As it turned out, my department manager thought $15,000 was exorbitant. I had been under the impression all along that we were still in the "money is no object" mode in which we had operated the previous year. I hadn't been told otherwise and I didn't think to ask.

Find out what you can spend. Find out what you must do internally, and what you can hire outside help to do.

5 *Be creative.* No matter how much money is available, creativity and innovation are always important when producing a technical-training videotape. Television has made video critics of us all.

Some of the most boring viewing in the world can be found in technical videotapes. But they don't have to be dull. Put your brainstorming skills to work, either by yourself or with others.

Think of analogies or parallels for your subject matter. To describe a wafer transport system,[4] I came up with the idea that if the wafer were human, it might think of the wafer transport as an amusement park ride. So I had our graphic artist fabricate a wafer cartoon character. This character described each part of the system and what its function was as it rode along on it. Maybe it wasn't "Gone With the Wind," but it sure beat a guy in a white coat standing next to the machine trying to explain what goes on inside. It kept them awake while it taught them the material.

Keep an idea file. Mine has scribbles that refer to soap operas, westerns, spy movies, horror films, science fiction, superheroes and various commercials I've seen with a usable twist. Public television programs and music videos are also good sources of inspiration. The key is to keep your mind open at all times for new ideas, gimmicks and possible hooks for your programs.

When you do come up with an idea, however, consider your audience. Will they understand the gimmick? Will they appreciate it? Or will they find it stupid, distracting or insulting? Who is your audience? End users? Operators? Technicians? Engineers? Production supervisors? Create accordingly.

6 *Write the script clearly.* Good writing is critical. Unwieldy sentences, twisted logic and backward sequencing in a video script will become embarrassingly apparent once the narration is edited into video action.

Keep the sentences short and the language conversational, not academic or literary. This is something

---

[2] *Sputtering system:* A machine designed to do atomic sputtering of silicon wafers or some other substrate.

[3] *Plasma etching system:* A machine designed to use plasma to etch patterns into wafers.

people will hear, not read. Ideas must flow from one section to the next. Put all procedural steps in order. For example, don't say, "Hook the coax cable to the output after disconnecting the RF fuse." How do you do that visually? Instead say, "Disconnect the RF fuse, then hook the coax cable to the output." Read your script out loud, perhaps into a tape recorder.

Find a 'ham' who can breathe life into your technical script.

Listen to it and change what isn't right. Reading it aloud will also help you find grammatical mistakes.

7 *Use good narrators and actors.* Find a narrator who is enough of a "ham" to breathe life into your technically oriented script. One of my first technical tapes was very straightforward, with no gimmick or hook. It simply described a subsystem in a plasma sputterer,[5] and discussed its process, parts and some maintenance procedures. But the narrator I used for the voice-over was versatile in his craft. As I sat in the studio hearing and directing his narration, I was amazed that he could take such a dry script and give it life and substance.

On the other hand, I did another tape in which only the introduction was a voice-over. The rest was done with employees acting out a scene—a senior technician showing a junior technician how to perform a certain procedure on a vacuum system. The "actors" were the maintenance engineers who had served as my content experts and occasionally taught their own maintenance courses. So we're talking about a very simple scene and two people who are experienced in delivering this information to an audience, right? One of the "actors" did very well. The other is the reason why

I have never again failed to audition actors beforehand.

Always audition prospective narrators and actors, whether they're in-house or professional talent. Keep in mind the kind of tone and conversational style you want, and work toward it with your talent. Don't be afraid to direct. They expect and want you to direct them, so they look and sound good on tape. This, of course, makes you look good too.

8 *Plan and organize compulsively.* Preplanning and organization are of paramount importance. Become fanatical about them. Never believe for an instant that *anything* will just "fall together." It won't, and you'll irritate and alienate a lot of people who will vow never to work with you again.

I used to think that the research and writing phases of a project were the easiest, while shooting and editing were the most stressful. The potential is certainly there for this to be so. But the "background" phases also have the most potential for making you look like a fool later.

Since I loathe looking like a fool, and since I am a lazy person who avoids stressful situations like the plague, I have evolved into an organized director. Now the shooting and editing are the easiest parts. I just get the people I'm working with scheduled and prepared. Same with the sets. I gather all the props. I write and study my shot list. I get everyone and everything there on the shoot date. After that, I just relax in my director's chair and tell everyone else what to do. I can't understand why I used to have such bad dreams the night before a shoot. It's the easiest job in the world.

Post-production is even easier. I review the rough footage and log where the shots are on the tape, noting the locations on the script. Then I sit on my editing stool, relax and tell the video technician what to do. He pushes buttons; I drink coffee. Sure, every now and then I have to work up a sweat to make a decision, but that

just keeps me interested.

Plan, plan, plan. Make lists and lists of lists. Orchestrate *everything* well in advance. Then, on the big days, show up and relax. That's all there is to it.

9 *Pay attention to detail.* Don't ever let anything go. If you do, your client will catch it. Then you'll catch it.

Research your objectives thoroughly. Then do the same with your subject matter. Don't treat one area well and then glide over the next.

Nitpick your script. Make sure the grammar is correct, the sentences are short and readable, and the style is conversational.

If you're using graphics, examine each line. Get picky with your artist.

Make sure your talent, whether they be actors, narrators or both, are a known quantity, and that they are exactly the quantity you want. Work with them closely to get the scene or the sentence perfect. It's worth it.

Are the props and set correct and presentable? Is everything you're saying and showing accurate? Do you know it's accurate because you've checked it? If the video is representing your company in any way, is it presenting the company's best side?

If you're not sure of a shot, shoot it several different ways. Then you'll have a choice in the editing room—and you can more easily call in a content expert for verification.

When shooting and editing, strive for perfection. Don't get sloppy and don't adopt an "it'll do" attitude just because it's getting late and everyone's becoming cranky. Shooting and editing for perfection will make everyone involved more pleased with the outcome—especially you. And you'll get the credit.

---

[4]*Wafer transport system:* A subsystem within a given machine that carries the wafer from a loading area to a processing area to an unloading area. It usually works on pneumatics, and is an automatic system serving to decrease human wafer handling, which decreases contamination problems.

[5]*Plasma sputterer:* Remember "atomic sputtering"? A plasma sputterer is a machine that uses plasma to do sputtering.

Reprinted from TRAINING, July 1986

VIDEODISC DEVELOPMENT

Programmers, instructional designers and
AV people all play a role.
If you want a good program, make sure
nobody gets upstaged

BY MAUREEN M. BEAUSEY

We have only begun to tap the potential of interactive videodisc technology as a training tool. The future is surely bright. Yet those of us who work in the field fear that misuse of the videodisc will send it the way of programmed instruction before it has a chance to sparkle. The seeds for that sad outcome are being nurtured today. And they spring from an overly narrow approach to designing IVID programs.

People from various unrelated disciplines are working in the field today. The three heavy hitters are computer programmers, video or film producers and instructional designers. Without question, these experts are all essential for making a good videodisc program. But individually, none is capable of producing a truly superior interactive videodisc training program.

To understand why, we must remember that the number and kinds of tasks involved in IVID design and production are completely different from those of other training programs—whether the training is delivered by computer, video or human being. Before you can create successful IVID programs, you must think about instruction and learning in a radically different, unfamiliar way.

Until now, presentation styles haven't changed much as a result of new technologies. True, we have introduced various types of media into our education systems, but they seldom do more than stand in for the teacher. We show a video, or use slides, or present lessons and tests on the computer. But the media have not changed the system.

Interactive videodisc *can* change the system, but it won't if we continue to do the same things we've always done. Each person now working in videodisc development comes to the field from a specific discipline—and discipline, by definition, implies a set way to approach and solve problems.

To see the problem, just ask, 'What is the heart of videodisc?'

Our disciplines may, in fact, preclude our abilities to approach this new medium in the way it deserves.

To see the problem clearly, you need only ask the question, "What is the heart of an interactive videodisc system?" Programmers probably would argue that it's the computer capabilities. Video production people would counter that it's superior audiovisual capabilities. Instructional designers would have eyes only for the way the information is organized, presented and tested. They would each be right—that's the beauty of this medium. And they would each be wrong—that's the problem with viewing the world through the eyes of a disciple.

IVID training programs are complex creations that require the successful integration of four essential design elements: instructional design, audiovisual design, computer programming design and geographic design. They are all equally important to the medium's success as a training tool.

Instructional design

When an instructional designer plans a training program, she considers such things as the audience and the types of tasks the learner will be expected to perform when it's over. She then creates learning objectives that she will use later to measure the effectiveness of the program and the success of the learners.

That means that the skill or behavior described in the objective must be matched to performance on a test of some kind. If we expect trainees to be able to diagnose and repair photocopier malfunctions upon the completion of a training course, the course must have them do just that. Asking them to list the types of malfunctions commonly found in copiers will not accurately assess whether they learned the skills they need to perform their jobs well.

IVID is capable of complex performance simulations that often can take the place of hands-on practice and testing. Used appropriately, a well-designed interactive simulation can be a better learning tool for a student than a classroom experience. If, however, we simply use the computer to present traditional tests, we aren't using the medium effectively or stretching the limits of the technology. Nor are we giving the student a dynamic learning experience.

Interactive videodisc technology makes possible truly individualized instruction. Unfortunately, few programs actually provide it because it requires sophisticated instructional design. If it is going to be used, individualized instruction must be built into the design of the program; it seldom can be added on later.

User control options are a good way to provide an individualized path for the learner, but in many programs they're limited to exiting from the program or returning to a menu. True user control allows the learner to move around the program with ease, to make decisions, to be in control of the learning event. We grew up in an educational system that prevented students from having that kind of control and bestowed it instead on the teacher. Consequently, we often set up the computer to perform the teacher's role instead of letting the computer perform its best role—"traffic cop" for the student's trip around the courseware.

Audiovisual design

Videodisc is, above all, a visual medium. But an interactive videodisc program is not—or should not be—like a linear video program. If you press a linearly designed program into a videodisc, you've wasted your money and ignored the promise of the medium.

As all good scriptwriters know, the visual portion of a program should be designed first, and the narration should enhance the picture. How often, though, is the narration developed first, with the visuals added later to support it? I've seen videodisc programs that allegedly teach people to use computer software. They usually show shots of a "talking head" interspersed with pictures of computer screens. Why are programs like this inflicted on learners? Why not get the computer screens straight from the source and provide this type of training in a strictly computer-based environment?

If the content of your program is not inherently visual, there is no instructional value in trying to make it appear so. Yes, people remember better when all the senses are involved in the learning experience, but only if the involvement is relevant to the learning objectives. This is not a problem peculiar to training. I recently watched a network news documentary about the effects of alcohol and other drugs on the brain. It was filled with irrelevant video, such as first-person camera views of skiing.

The picture on the screen should support your training objectives and the narration should support the picture. So how can you best accommodate these two critical elements? Plan for the best use of the available space. Each side of a videodisc has 30 minutes of motion, which translates to 54,000 single-frame images and 60 minutes of audio on a disc. However, if you think of those 60 minutes as a single piece, you will probably not plan for your audio as effectively as if you think of it as two separate 30-minute segments.

On conventional videodisc systems, the videodisc plays each time you use audio. Audio track 1 usually (and arbitrarily) plays with the main video path. Audio track 2 can be used to provide narration with computer graphics, introduce a second language, or support remedial training or feedback. The trick is to produce the biggest bang for the buck.

Take the idea of using the second track to dub in a foreign language. In this scheme the same video will play, but in one mode the program will run in one language while in a second

> **An interactive videodisc program is not—or should not be—like a linear video program.**

mode it will run in another. From a programming perspective, that means that each program element must be in the same place in both modes, or you will have to program each version separately. The problem is that different languages use different amounts and sizes of words to express the same idea. To match the video to this requires complex planning (with voice-over narration) and probably will result in a compromise of your visuals because you'll need a longer hold time for the shorter language in any given piece. In addition, you probably won't be able to provide narration over graphics unless you are willing to use more sides of videodisc for the program. This strategy can be used, but it is not particularly cost-effective from a development point of view.

Programming design

All the innovative instructional-design ideas in the world are worthless without a computer program that makes them work well while remaining transparent to the learner.

What makes a good interactive program? Well, how interactive is it? One way to decide is to measure the time each student spends on each disc side. The more often the learner

makes interaction decisions or branches to other parts of the program, the longer the contact with the disc. For example, if a program occupies two sides of videodisc (or one hour of running video) and a student takes 16 hours to complete it, the program has a good degree of interactivity.

But you also need to evaluate the quality of the interaction. Using the computer as a page turner, or using it to present tests that can be taken just as well on paper, does not demonstrate quality interaction. Instead, the training program should be made to simulate the actual work environment.

Given enough time and money, an interactive program can do anything. Of course, you usually don't have unlimited time and money when you're trying to produce cost-effective, timely training. But you can develop good interactivity with the same kind of careful planning you give to the other aspects of the program.

There have been cases where the computer programmers did the instructional design on a videodisc after it was pressed. But that is an expensive and ineffective strategy. It's important to know up front which portions will be coded with a relatively simple authoring system and which parts will be coded with a more complex programming language. That means the programmers or authors must be involved from the beginning.

How do you choose whether to author or program the software? There are advantages and disadvantages to each. Bear in mind these factors: efficiency, flexibility, execution speed, storage of data, responsiveness and power, development time and cost, and difficulty of use for program developers and students.

A program developed with an authoring system will let you build the program without the aid of computer programmers. This saves time and money that you'd spend on the programmer's salary. However, an authoring system limits the instructional and programming strategies available to you. On the other hand, a program developed and written in a computer language will allow almost unlimited strategic opportunities but will require some expensive expertise.

We find that we can author be-

USING COLOR IN CBT DESIGN

Color is more than just a nice touch for your training programs, according to Emily Wright, an artist and instructional designer for Courseware, Inc. of San Diego, a developer of computer-based training programs. "Human beings respond both physically and emotionally to color; thus the use of color can be an exciting and effective way to teach or persuade a target audience," she says.

Wright adds, however, that "the ill-considered use of this powerful tool can also detract from a project. . . ." She offers several guidelines for CBT designers who want to use color effectively in their programs.

● *Integrate color with the instructional or persuasive goals of your project.* "This is perhaps the single most important guideline. . . . The goals of your project will determine the flow of instruction or persuasion, the affective response you wish to evoke and the information and/or skills you wish to transmit to your audience."

● *Choose colors that prompt the appropriate emotional response in your target audience.* Adults in North America find hues of red and blue to be the most pleasing, and tend to prefer tints (produced by adding white to pure hues) to brighter colors, Wright says. She adds that about 12.5% of the male population has some trouble with color perception—either confusing similar colors such as orange and yellow-orange, or perceiving both red and green as gray.

Certain colors tend to evoke specific emotional responses. For example, reds, yellows and oranges are associated with warmth, activity and excitement; blues, violets and greens with coolness, passivity and calmness. Different cultures attach their own symbolism to colors. For instance, what does the combination red, white and blue suggest to you? "You will save time, money and possibly embarrassment if you research the color preferences and symbolic associations of color in the culture of your target population," Wright emphasizes.

● *Choose background or keynote colors first.* Be consistent in your choice of background colors. A black background has more depth than a colored background. Don't switch back and forth unnecessarily—your audience needs time to adjust to these different background depths. "Also remember that while a black background is simple, dramatic and unifying, you must use brighter colors against it for ease of perception." Neutrals such as gray can be effective with a wide array of color combinations.

A color wheel can be useful in planning the flow of colors in a program. For example, you may want to engage the audience's attention with warm, active tints, use cooler hues on screens you want them to examine closely, and finish with warm tones to recall your opening points and suggest a feeling of closure.

● *Choose emphasis colors that harmonize with keynote colors.* People tend to see harmony in two kinds of color combinations: 1) colors that are closely related to each other (e.g., yellow and yellow-green), and 2) colors that are opposite each other on the color wheel (such as yellow and violet).

Use bright, attention-getting colors to emphasize the most important material, softer tints as emphasis colors for secondary material, and so on. Keep in mind that the same color will be perceived differently in relation to different colors. For example, the same hue of blue will look "bluer" against an orange background than against a green one. That means you can use even a limited range of colors effectively.

● *Use color proportions that work well with each other.* "Sometimes two colors combine best when one color dominates a greater screen area than the other," says Wright. "For example, equal areas of pink and orange may seem to clash. This perception may be removed if pink is used to dominate the screen and orange is used as an emphasis color."

● *Choose harmonious relationships between light and dark hues.* Combine a light variation of a color found on a lighter part of the spectrum with a dark variation of a color from the darker part. For instance, light green and dark blue generally combine better than dark green and light blue (green is lighter than blue on the spectrum).

● *Get a fresh eye to review your color choices*—someone who has not seen your program. In fact, get two fresh eyes: a reviewer with some color or graphic art expertise and someone with a lot of characteristics in common with your target audience.

Wright's final advice: "Don't be afraid to experiment. Spend some time just playing around with your color graphics program. This is an important part of developing a good eye for color and will stand you in good stead when it is time to get down to production."

Reprinted from TRAINING, January 1987

tween 60 and 75 percent of most of our own programs, leaving the programmed portions to be done by computer specialists.

Geographic design

A videodisc is, finally, nothing more than a piece of real estate. Like all real estate, its space is finite. How can you use that space to your best advantage?

The ultimate aim of the developer is to produce a program whose workings are imperceptible to the learner. When the learner uses the program, it should respond in a way that *simulates* the contact the student would have with a human or a familiar piece of equipment. The most obvious way to accomplish this is by maximizing the *speed* of program execution.

A number of factors influence speed. One is the method of programming—authoring vs. hard-coding, for example. Another equally critical factor is the amount of disc space that has to be searched before the object of the search is found. Shortening the search time is the primary purpose of geographic, or real estate, design.

Do you have segments that will be called often, like test openers or course maps? Do you have segments that must appear on each side of the disc? How many modules or units will the program contain? Keeping in mind that each side of videodisc contains exactly 30 minutes of space, how will you create a course that provides continuity to the student but still makes the best use of disc space?

You do it by allotting very specific amounts of time to each element of each module—but you can't do that until you know the instructional design. We tell the scriptwriter exactly how much time there is—in seconds—to express or explain a concept.

Because the development of an interactive videodisc program is such a complex undertaking, a structured, systematic approach is another essential element for success. Your design system must allow each team member access to the elements needed without preventing other team members from performing their own tasks. It must be flexible and adaptable, because an interactive videodisc program must allow for changes throughout its development. The system also must provide complete documentation throughout, allowing for alterations and updates. A final suggestion: The best system in the world is completely useless if no one uses it, so make it easy to use.

Taken together, the four elements of videodisc boil down to this: teamwork and a system. Working with dedicated, committed professionals from various disciplines—each of whom has a different vested interest in the program's success—can be a challenging experience for the project leader. Each member of the team, from the instructional technologist to the graphics designer to the computer programmer, has valuable insights to bring to the program, and each person's expertise is essential to the success and quality of the project.

Keep in mind that although any one of the experts working alone cannot make the project succeed, each one alone can make the project fail. Be sensitive to your team—a good videodisc development team is a treasure.

Reprinted from TRAINING, February 1988

THE REDISCOVERY OF VIDEO TELECONFERENCING

For years it's been the medium of choice
for flashy special events.
Suddenly it seems poised to become
a delivery system for
meat-and-potatoes training

BY RON ZEMKE

Has the video teleconference come of age as a training medium? Consider a few signposts:

Today, according to *Marketing Communication* magazine, teleconferencing is a $150-million-a-year business. With a growth rate of 30% per year, it's the fastest-growing segment of the telecommunications industry. And a lot of those "conferences" are actually video teletraining. Associations, universities and an increasing number of corporations have embraced the videoconference as an important instructional medium.

This year, says Emily Rothrock, spokeswoman for the American Hospital Association, AHA will beam a dozen major programs to member hospitals. Rothrock claims that the average AHA telecast is picked up by 250 of the 1,000 member hospitals that have either satellite or microwave receiving equipment. A May 8 teleconference featuring "Excellence" guru Tom Peters was "brought down" by 450 hospitals.

The National University Teleconference Network (NUTN) has an even more ambitious schedule. According to E. Marie Oberle, director of the Oklahoma State University-based consortium of 171 accredited colleges with teleconferencing capability, the network has carried over 100 ad hoc videoconferences (i.e., temporary hookups for special events) in its four years of operation. NUTN programs cover topics ranging from accounting to law to salesmanship. The largest program the network has carried—in terms of number of approved downlinks (earth stations that receive satellite signals)—was a "1985 World Food Day" symposium taken down by 250 colleges and universities in the United States and Canada.

The American Management Association (AMA) got into the teleconferencing business last year via the U.S. Chamber of Commerce's American Business Network (BizNet). The AMA/Chamber videoconferences, dubbed "Seminars by Satellite,™" have so far covered cold-call selling, professional development for secretaries, management skills for first-line supervisors and telephone selling techniques. According to Fay Communications, Inc., the Arlington, VA, telecommunications company that mounted the productions for the AMA, five more programs are slated for the fall and winter of this year. AMA spokesman Ed Ritvo considers the whole thing a pilot project, but observes that "the potential is there for this to become a very important, cost-effective way to deliver training to a large number of people at once." So far, he says, "Seminars by Satellite™" have attracted as few as 10 and as many as 200 downlinks.

Rebirth

The big news, however, isn't that universities and associations are taking video teleconferencing seriously as an information and training medium. Videoconferencing has been around since the '60s. And though colleges have long been interested in the potential of the technology, it is the growth in *corporate* videoconferencing capacity, particularly downlink capacity, that has led to the current boom.

According to Eliott Gold, publisher of "TeleSpan," an industry newsletter, 1984 was probably the turning point for the coming of age of teleconferencing. In that year, says Gold, American companies purchased approximately 100 teleconferencing rooms, about three times the number of installations made in any previous year, at about $250,000 a room. Gold estimates that another 100 rooms were installed in 1985 and that the figure for 1986 will be considerably higher. In 1984, he says, 15 corporations were videoconferencing in a serious way. By the end of 1985, that number had doubled.

For companies that don't want to build their own facilities, rented ones are becoming a lot easier to find. For example, Holiday Inns, Inc. now boasts a videoconferencing network called Hi-Net, which it claims is the world's largest. As of July the network had 900 downlinks nationwide. A spokeswoman for the Hi-Net division says new outlets are being installed in the company's hotels and motels at the rate of 25 to 30 a week. And training ranks second only to new-product introductions as the most common reason why corporate customers rent the Hi-Net facilities.

Holiday Inns don't suit you? Try Hilton. Through a marketing arrangement with AT&T, an obvious presence in the videoconferencing market, a number of Hilton hotels are now equipped with the ultimate in videoconferencing facilities: two-way audio, two-way video. AT&T is marketing the same system, called Vivid™, to corporations.

Judith and Douglas Brush, authors of *Private Television Communications: The New Directions (The Fourth Brush Report)* attribute the lull in interest in videoconferencing in the '60s and '70s to the same factor that now has caused a renewed interest in the medium: cost. Their reasoning: By the

251

mid-'60s videoconferencing already had proven itself as an effective way to deliver important information quickly to large numbers of people in remote areas, and to give them access to experts and expertise. But it was very expensive. The introduction of videocassette technology in 1972 put video teleconferencing into the moonwalk category: novel, worth doing once for its attention-getting value, but in the long run not nearly as cost-effective as shipping out videocassettes or linking people together for a simple audio teleconference.

Today, several technical developments have reversed the cost equation. First, there are more satellites in orbit and available for transmitting private video than ever before. As the Brushes put it, it is now "far less expensive to send a television picture on a 45,000-mile round trip into space and back than 3,000 miles through coaxial cables owned by the telephone company." What's more, since the introduction of satellites capable of carrying a high-frequency video signal known as "Ku-band," corporate videoconferencing enthusiasts can use smaller signal receiving dishes and less expensive receive equipment. Before Ku-band and its paraphernalia appeared, the standard was C-band, a broadcast-quality (read "expensive") technology.

The final development, one just starting to become truly important, is "Codecs"—devices that can code and decode a full-motion, color television transmission and move it from one place to another in digitalized form, much the same way computer information is moved about. The availability of Codecs means that companies no longer have to pay an exorbitant price to make video material confidential. It also means that the same satellites an organization can lease for video meetings and tele-training can be used to transmit all sorts of data to and from remote areas.

Prices of both equipment and airtime have fallen dramatically in recent years—as much as 70% since 1982, according to Gold. He says a coast-to-coast video link that would have cost $2,000 in 1982 prices out at about $700 today. Three years ago a good Codec machine would have weighed in at $200,000. Today, top of the line is less than $90,000. "1986 is

an exciting time for DBS [direct broadcast satellite]," he opines.

As hardware and service costs plummeted, corporations that previously only dabbled in the medium bought permanent facilities—and have become regular videoconferencers. Just a few of the more dramatic examples in 1986 alone:

● In January, when Northwestern Bell wanted to promote public dialogue in favor of telecommunications deregulation, it enlisted ABC "Nightline" host Ted Koppel, *Future Shock* author Alvin Toffler, and a panel of economists and consumer advocates to debate the proposition via two-way videoconference.

● In February Hewlett-Packard Co. introduced a new business minicomputer to most of its 84,000 employees all at once via a videoconference that linked 86 offices in the United States and Canada and 18 sites in Europe.

● In April A. L. Williams Corp., the United States' largest life-insurance marketing agency, installed videoconferencing equipment in 450 of its 5,600 offices and announced plans to link a total of 1,000 offices by mid-1987. The primary purpose of Williams' system is to provide training and information to the 100,000-member field sales force.

● This spring the Public Broadcasting Service (PBS) conducted a 15-week demonstration of its capability to deliver training to the business world. The experiment offered five hours of programming, five days a week, via 21 PBS stations. The content was supplied by a number of corporate-training vendors, such as Time-Life Video and Arthur Young & Co.

● On June 9 Chase Manhattan Bank, N.A. linked 2,500 employees in eight countries for a live, interactive discussion of perspectives on the bank's current and future global strategy.

● On June 25 Texas Instruments sponsored a free, global videoconference symposium on applying artificial intelligence technology in the workplace. Last November TI held a similar teleconference limited to U.S.-only networks. More than 30,000 people in 500 locations took part in that one.

One step at a time

Big events, impressive though they may be, do not a reliable communications channel make. The high-profile, ad hoc videoconference has been around since the first confluence of television, satellites, money and corporate ego. Extravaganzas are the seasoning, not the staple of a videoconferencing operation. The meat-and-potatoes question is whether a medium can swim efficiently and effectively in the mainstream of corporate communication and training. Does it endure and prosper after "Gee whiz!" has given way, as it inevitably does, to "So what?"

Videoconferencing is definitely beyond the "Gee-whiz" stage at places like Hewlett-Packard, JC Penney, Aetna Life and Casualty, Atlantic Richfield, Ford and General Motors.

In 1983 Hewlett-Packard became the first corporation to build its own permanent Ku-band satellite business television network—dubbed HPTV. According to Marika Ruumet, HP's television network manager in Palo Alto, CA, HPTV evolved from a strictly special-event-type schedule of new product introductions and training. "We ran on an ad hoc basis for two years. After a while we saw that renting equipment and conducting special events was no longer cost-effective. Our projected use told us we would buy the equipment several times over through leasing. So we bought our own system." Ruumet calls the whole process a step-by-step and "very logical" progression.

Today HP has more than 90 permanent receive sites and originates 20 hours of programming a week. HPTV also has begun "internetworking," that is, picking up a videoconference originating in another network, then rebroadcasting it. "If you count the feeds we rebroadcast from Chico [Chico State University] and NTU [National Television University], we're running closer to 60 hours a week," says Ruumet.

A "step at a time" also describes JC Penney's entrance into the video teleconferencing business. As explained by Ed Sample, general manager of JCPC's videoconferencing subsidiary, NTN, the company's first steps into teleconferencing sound downright timid. "We were pretty cautious," Sample admits, "but we had a problem to solve and teleconferencing seemed a logical conclusion." The problem was that JCPC's store-level buyers were spending a lot of time and money commuting to New York twice a month to look over new merchandise. Teleconferencing seemed like a great alternative, *if* the same quality of business could be conducted over the airwaves—a big "if" to Sample and his fellow buyers.

"To test the idea, we split into two groups. One group met as we had been, face-to-face in the New York headquarters. The rest of us met down the hall in another room by coaxial cable," he explains. After about six months of mock videoconference meetings, the Penney merchandise specialists compared notes and voted to do a real videoconference test. Today JC Penney is not only a dedicated user of videoconferencing, but a for-profit producer of programs as well.

JCPC has a heavy in-house broadcast schedule serving 110 stores and 50 regional and district offices. In addition, JC Penney Communications, Inc., another subsidiary, has produced videoconferences for a number of the parent corporation's *Fortune 500* neighbors in New York City, among them NBC, ABC, Nippon Electronic Co., Pizza Hut and Procter & Gamble. The new videoconferencing subsidiary, NTN, will begin operation this fall as a supplier of training to small retailers located in shopping malls. NTN not only will produce its own programs but will mount productions for other training vendors interested in videoconferencing.

At ComputerLand a unique experiment is under way to test the efficacy of videoconferencing as a major training and information disseminator. According to Al Maggio, manager of television production for the Hayward, CA-based computer-retail chain, the corporation wants to know if videoconferencing offers benefits that go beyond travel-cost savings, before committing to a costly, fixed system.

Maggio says ComputerLand has installed 1.8-meter dishes at 20 different stores and is comparing results (in terms of product sales and "measures of learning") to 20 other stores that are receiving training and information in the traditional way. The four-month trial period for "CLTV" ended July 31, and as of this writing the results had only begun to be analyzed. But early signs are positive, claims Maggio: "The people in the broadcast stores *feel* they are learning more, and they definitely like working with the medium."

ComputerLand's major reason for exploring a video network is training. "Our primary area of concern was service authorization training," Maggio says. "Our store managers have a hard time freeing up their technical people to go to Los Angeles or Boca Raton to get the training that will allow them to service new equipment." But the side benefits for which the company was searching already have begun to accrue.

For one thing, hardware and software manufacturers have been very enthusiastic about using CLTV to present their latest and greatest to ComputerLand's sales force. "The responses from the computer industry have been overwhelming," Maggio says. "Companies like Compaq, Toshiba and Ashton-Tate all regard CLTV as 'their' network and see it as a great way to reach every ComputerLand dealer simultaneously with their new product introductions, sales training programs and point-of-sale information." A benefit for the stores is the ability to bring their key corporate customers "face-to-face" with the manufacturers who supply the products.

Maggio's scenario for the future of CLTV, should his test prove positive, is of a network that feeds video and data—even computer software—directly to an enclosed learning center in every ComputerLand store, including those in Paris and Tokyo.

Dedicated networks

There are any number of reasons to stage an ad hoc videoconference: reaching corporate milestones, announcing new products or major strategic shifts—the list is endless. Justifying a permanent, dedicated corporate network is something altogether different. It is a major corporate decision. A. Reza Jafari, president and CEO of Satellite Conference Network, a New York City firm that produces videoconferences for associations and corporations, strongly suggests a team approach to making that decision.

"A dedicated network is really an integrated system of audio, video and data. There are implications beyond training. You need a decision team composed of people from training and personnel, marketing, corporate communications and information systems to properly evaluate the feasibility for your organization," Jafari says.

Hewlett-Packard's Ruumet advises adding a good satellite engineer to your panel "to help you do costing and to tell you about problems and trade-offs you will encounter."

Maggio stresses the need for a thorough feasibility study that will identify potential problems early in the

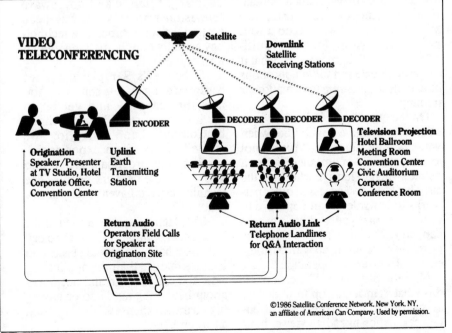

VIDEO TELECONFERENCING

Satellite

Downlink Satellite Receiving Stations

ENCODER

DECODER DECODER DECODER

Television Projection Hotel Ballroom Meeting Room Convention Center Civic Auditorium Corporate Conference Room

Origination Speaker/Presenter at TV Studio, Hotel Corporate Office, Convention Center

Uplink Earth Transmitting Station

Return Audio Operators Field Calls for Speaker at Origination Site

Return Audio Link Telephone Landlines for Q&A Interaction

©1986 Satellite Conference Network, New York, NY, an affiliate of American Can Company. Used by permission.

game. "We found out during our pilot, for instance, that installing the downlinks was much more complicated than we expected. We had to go through a lot of municipal red tape getting the permits and approvals we needed for putting in the hardware, for one thing. And we found that some of the landlords of the properties where our test stores are located were reluctant to approve the modifications we needed to make to premises."

Another important task for the decision team is interviewing network management firms. A video network, like a telephone network, is a complicated arrangement of technology and technicians. It must be managed carefully and correctly if send and receive sites are to communicate with the ease of, say, making a long-distance phone call.

"Working with a network is a fairly complex matter," says Joseph Rizzo, vice president of Private Satellite Network, Inc. (PSN). "Satellite time has to be booked and managed, the uplink has to be managed, system health has to be monitored and technical troubleshooting has to be available for every broadcast. That's our job. But for the corporate network owner, it should be a simple, turnkey operation, like obtaining telephone or electrical service. You shouldn't even notice it 99.9% of the time. You should be able to push the button, and it's there."

But like electrical and telephone service, the network has to be paid for. And as with post-deregulation phone service, a vendor has to be chosen.

Rich Bell, a sales manager with VideoStar Connections, Inc., of Atlanta, another network management firm, suggests that while there are several firms—such as his and Rizzo's—that can manage network operations, there are other criteria to apply. "The would-be private network owner can turn to organizations like ours for help in designing facilities, buying and installing equipment, even in program production. You should ask, 'How much help do I want in those areas?' and evaluate the potential vendors over that whole set of needs," he suggests.

How do you know if a dedicated system is worth thinking about at all? JC Penney's Sample suggests three very basic criteria. When you have a

training program or some other information that has to get out quickly, teleconferencing is worth considering if a) you don't have enough trainers to do the job, b) you don't have the facilities to accommodate people for training, or c) you are spending a disproportionate amount of money bringing people together. "Look, if I can get, say, 12,000 people together for four hours to hear my message from a nationally known expert at, say, $20 apiece, how can I go wrong?"

Private Satellite Network's Rizzo says a videoconference network begins to make economic sense to an organization at about the 15-site level. That is, if you have more than 15 branch offices, factories or whatever, and you're either "suitcasing" training out to them regularly or pulling their people into headquarters regularly, then a business television network may be cost-justifiable. He also adds another, less tangible rationale. "The fact is, the reason so many corporations bring people together for one or two or three solid days of training is that travel is so expensive. But the effect on retention and application of the material is terrible. With business television, you can afford to do your training in more pedagogically sound half-day or even two-hour segments, sort of like high schools and colleges do it."

VideoStar's Bell adds a note of caution. "Every organization is different, so you have to be sure of your objectives for the system to really evaluate its feasibility. If you're going to limited audiences or very small populations with most of your programming, you may not want to do it with private television. Point-to-multipoint, as we call it, means just what it suggests: People at multiple locations have to need the *same* information or training."

On the other hand, Bell urges, consider some positive possibilities when you evaluate the idea. "You're not looking at an intercom; there is also a public switch to receive what's on the air. That gives you access to other networks to consider. And you have to remember that you will have excess capacity. You should consider the possibility of coming up with customers to subsidize your operation."

Now the bad news. The cost of all this—that is, in actual, up-front dollars as opposed to some painless distribution calculation like $10 a viewer hour

amortized across the millenium—can bring Hollywood daydreaming to a quick end. Establishing a permanent uplink runs from $200,000 to $600,000, depending on your current video studio capacity. Receiving sites (with one-way video, two-way audio capacity) weigh in at $5,000 to $6,000 each, not counting monitors, furniture or room construction. Network usage fees can run to $5,000 a day, though the number of hours a day and days a week—as well as some pretty deep discounting that seems to go on—can drastically reduce that figure.

Such wide dollar ranges warrant a reprise of HP's Ruumet's advice to get yourself a good consulting engineer. "A lot of vendors will want you to have much more uplink than you need, for instance, and you won't know that without technical advice. It's worth it."

Getting started in teletraining

Once the decision to go private is made, the fun has just begun. Those who consult on videoconferencing, as well as those who have built a corporate videoconferencing network and lived, have more than a few words of wisdom and warning for the uninitiated. Most of the advice falls under three general headings.

Rule One: Don't Sweat the Hardware. The hardware involved in all this is expensive and the things it does are more than a little mysterious to the nontechnician, but it shouldn't be daunting. Satellite and microwave television transmission has been around for some time. The technology actually does work. Generally it works quite well.

JC Penney's Sample dismisses hardware as a pressing concern: "You hire that capacity and get on to the important stuff." He is echoed by ComputerLand's Maggio: "We started off using an experienced, professional broadcast group and knowledgeable network people. The technical aspects haven't really been a problem."

SCN's Jafari puts a nice coda to the consensual opinion. "The technology is there. It has been growing faster and is more mature than the application side. You can jump in and not worry about becoming outdated or having big upgrade expenses. It's very solid all around."

Rule Two: Do Sweat the Training.
Experienced teletrainers emphasize that a videoconference is only as good as the training it carries—axiomatic, maybe, but there are some complications.

Hewlett-Packard's Ruumet minimizes the differences between videoconference training and training based in other media. "How you format the message is critically important. But that's not any different a problem than you would encounter in any medium we might be talking about."

At the same time, however, she cautions that "your material has to be better prepared [for live teletraining] than for, say, a videotape-supported classroom program. Your objectives have to be more obvious, the graphics better done and your instruction more thoroughly prepared."

Allstate Insurance Co. maintains one of the few two-way video, two-way audio systems in regular operation, a dedicated, 24-hour network that links the Barrington, IL, headquarters to 28 regional offices. Asserts Jerry Abend, a senior training consultant with Allstate, "Anything that can be trained live in a classroom is appropriate for teleconferencing."

He elaborates: "Our two-way video technology has eliminated some of the normal teleconferencing problems. When you are in one of our videoconference rooms, it feels like you're talking to people in the same room—or at least talking to someone in an adjacent room through a silk mesh screen. If you want to show a slide or a tape, you show it on the screen between you. If you want to pass out a piece of paper to the trainees, you put it in a facsimile terminal, press a button and, zap, it shows up next door. If you want to show a small object to your trainees, you put it on a graphics table and project it on the screen. If the trainees have questions, they press a button on the console in their room. The calls automatically cue up, and you go through them one at a time until they're all answered. It really feels as if you are in the same room with your trainees."

As far as meeting-planning skills and logistics are concerned, Abend says, the only special consideration is that "your time is limited to the time you have reserved on the satellite, so you have to start and stop on schedule." Beyond that, most of the planning boils down to "commonsense things that you'd do for any seminar."

Abend admits to only one significant difference peculiar to video conference training, and it's limited to two-way video and audio: "Since you are going over satellite, there is a half-second delay—a lag—that isn't there in normal conversation. So humor, which depends on timing, doesn't always work well. I guess tap dancing on the table would be pretty odd with the lag. But that's about the biggest difference there is."

There are dissenters from the view that teletraining is not a significantly different animal. SCN's Jafari has several cautions for new users. "Teleconferencing is simply not for everyone or every topic. . . . You wouldn't, say, try to put a conference or convention on teleconference. The point there is one of maximum options and networking and looking at new goods. That doesn't belong on a teleconference. And problem-solving training doesn't belong on the medium, not if the point is to be flexible and to work with real problems. The dialogue is very important in that kind of training. You don't have that in a teleconference.

"You must remember that interaction is fairly limited and narrow. You can't establish comfortable rapport between trainer and student. You can't call a break when the group looks tired, or stop the program early or late, or have an unplanned evening session. And if there is a lot of reference material for trainees to work with during the program, they will more than likely get lost and confused. You have to keep these sorts of limitations in mind when designing teletraining."

There is one difference in videoconferencing about which experts tend to agree. While the trainer's presentation skills are an important factor in any sort of live training, in videoconferencing they're vital. Says ComputerLand's Maggio, "The person making the presentation makes all the difference in the world. They have to be very sure of themselves and their material."

JC Penney's Sample elaborates. "You have to recognize that the attention span of a video audience is much shorter than a classroom audience. And the audience expects broadcast quality in both technical *and* performance aspects of the program. Sooner or later, you have to face the issue of whether you go with experts or trainers or actors. I have seen people who are very good in the classroom fail in the videoconference. Grammar, enunciation and a general verbal style that might be perfectly fine in the classroom can be catastrophic on television. My preference is to choose the actor over the trainer, and script the presentation."

Sample is quick to add that this means you must have subject-matter experts available to handle questions and answers on the audio link at another point in the show.

Arthur H. Bell and Tom Housel, both professors of business communication at the University of Southern California, suggest that the "talent factor" has been a major culprit in limiting the acceptance of video teleconferencing in the business community. They write in the *T.H.E. Journal* that normally glib and confident experts and managers are wary of videoconferencing for three reasons:

Image: "We care about the way we come across to our audience. If we don't know what image we're sending, we freeze up. A CEO who charms the socks off a roomful of corporate directors can look—and feel—like a corpse on camera."

Perceived consequences: "We care about the consequences of our words. In business communications we choose our words with an eye toward our listeners. [Vendors] assumed business leaders would speak as frankly on the screen as they do on the telephone. Not so." (Part of the same phenomenon is the worry that any "backyard hacker with a satellite dish" can tune in to sensitive corporate communications.)

Lack of training: "Developers and vendors of teleconferencing equipment forget that, unlike the microwave oven, their new devices are not appliances. . . . Untrained users may feel they've ridden a bull into a china shop."

Pamela Soden of PA Soden & Associates in New York City, says she got a jarring introduction to the phenomenon last November when she took on the role of presenter for the AMA's first video teletraining program, "Management Skills and Techniques for New First-Line Supervisors."

"Reading a script from a teleprompter and looking directly into a camera is completely different from my normal style," Soden says. "And I was restricted in movement because the cameras had to know where I was going beforehand. And you can't just pull out a hip-pocket lecture or exercise that seems right for the moment. You have to be very predictable, but appear spontaneous."

JC Penney takes the performance issue so seriously that it has developed a "How to Be On a Teleconference" course. Anyone who ventures on camera must do so *after* a trip through the training.

Another issue you must resolve for yourself is whether you need trained facilitators at the receiving sites. Some, like Allstate's Abend, say they're unnecessary. "We don't need them. In our system, the instructor at the origin site can handle all that a site facilitator would do."

Ruumet believes the choice is situational. "If you are using a case study, for example, you would definitely want someone knowledgeable and skilled in the room to make sure the case works. At a minimum, you need someone in the room who knows how to run the [videoconferencing] equipment, and can do minimal troubleshooting."

SCN's Jafari believes the local role is critical. "You need to be sure that on-site facilitators are competent and know exactly what is going to happen with the program," he says. "They also have to be good at managing interaction and evaluating—verifying that learning has taken place."

NUTN's Marie Oberle, another strong advocate for the "local component," as she calls it, insists that "the success of any teleconference depends on the on-site coordinator." Who but an on-the-spot assistant can make sure the program responds to local conditions and situations?

Myra Traynor, also of NUTN, suggests that the local person is indis-pensable if the program is a general feed being broadcast on a national, pay-per-view basis. "The local person has to put a good 'wrap-around' together if people are going to get the most of the experts on the conference. The local [facilitators] have to kick the program off, let people know *exactly* what will be going on in the program. They have to manage the question and answer process. And they have to put together a summarizing event—like a local panel discussion—to end the program on a high note."

Rule 3: Take Your Time.
Those who have been the route unanimously recommend the slow and cautious approach in getting into videoconferencing. For one thing, says Hewlett-Packard's Ruumet, the people in your organization—trainees and their managers—won't get comfortable with the new medium overnight. "You need to go slow enough to build acceptance. We wanted everyone on board every step of the way [in moving from ad hoc events to a dedicated system]. You must sell the idea to the organization through your successes."

JC Penney's Sample suggests buying some help. "Work with a concern that can package a whole program for you. You need to work with someone who can manage the expense for you, who will say, 'Here is the bottom-line on that program,' and 'Here is the per-person cost.' "

"If I were consulting with a corporation," says Britt Davis, senior producer/director of teleconferencing for the University of Kentucky's Office of Instructional Resources, "I would offer two pieces of advice: Go slow and bring money.

"Don't jump in with both feet. A lot of people want to begin with 10, 12, even 20 hours a month. That's crazy. It's a learning experience for you and for the organization, and that takes time. You're going to have to build viewer loyalty just the way a broadcast network has to."

So, Davis concludes, "I'd say, a) set clear and limited goals for what you expect to accomplish and, b) work hard at building quality programs and a quality production team."

Will it last?

Videoconferencing has come and gone before. This time, is it here to stay? The people who make their living from the medium obviously hope so, but they can point to evidence that leads one to believe so as well. Training is a key factor. In June alone, says PSN's Rizzo, "Wang did 65 hours, JC Penney did 75 and IBM did 80 something. Two-thirds of that airtime was product knowledge and refresher training. And in just the last eight weeks, Federal Express, Aetna and IBM have taken steps to increase their broadcast capacity."

J.O. Grantham of Oklahoma State University, one of the founders of the National University Teleconference Network, argues that the times are right for the medium. "The explosive growth in teleconferencing activity has a lot to do with the speed needed in the management process today. Managers don't have time to visit sites and see people face-to-face the way they used to. A good system can put them back in contact."

Today, Grantham says, "there is a need for information to be disseminated faster and for access to experts to be more immediate. For the first time, those of us who are providers are talking programming [as opposed to technology] very intensively. Excess capacity, internetworking and the idea of continuing series are important discussions now. I think we're just beginning to see what can be—and will be—done with video teleconferencing."

Reprinted from TRAINING, September 1986

WHEN *NOT* TO USE A CLASSROOM

The advantages of carefully designed
and implemented on-the-job
training are numerous

BY JAY M. SEDLIK

To design and implement training
for execution in the trainee's job
environment rather than in a
classroom at a training center or in
some hotel meeting room, you *must* use
a systematic approach:

• that will allow you to create
training materials that will bring
about desired behavior changes,

• with effectiveness built-in so that
people can do what you are training
them to do,

• that is based on *instructional
development* in which you take all that
is known about learning and apply it
to the design and production of the
training,

• with feedback during development
to validate the prototype materials
against a given standard, and permit
revision of those materials until that
standard is met,

• so that the program as the trainee
sees it works (and you know that it
works in advance).

The result of the effort is an instructional system that enables a client's
employees and his customers requiring training to meet specific job
performance requirements in support
of business goals.

Field-implemented training has
significant cost saving implications as
well. It significantly reduces or eliminates:

• the substantial cost of room, board
and transportation,

• the need for large numbers of
instructors,

• the time period to implement the
training to the entire organization,

• most of the administrative problems associated with scheduling per-

sonnel and facilities,

• problems associated with providing the training to new hires and those
who, for illness or other reasons, are
unable to attend live training.

In the case of sales training, reducing the time out of the territory has a
positive impact on potential incremental revenue per trainee. For technical and support personnel, shortening the time away from the job
increases productivity and reduces
some of the real headaches in attempting to "cover" for people while they're
away.

As the number of courses and
trainees increase, the cost savings and
added benefits become increasingly
dramatic and compelling.

A question of innovation

From a philosophical and practical
point of view, the question of field
implementation of training can be
looked at as a problem in *innovation*
because the attempt is to introduce a
new concept—that training can be
effectively designed for field implementation. We've all experienced
the "reality shock" of being forced to
apply what was learned in the classroom to the real world. Generally we
learn in the classroom what *should* be
done on the job; then we learn on the
job, the constraints and pressures
which force reliance on personal ingenuity to apply what was learned to
the day-to-day job activities. This
experience has contributed to an attitude that separates training from
the real world. Therefore, when one
suggests that training can be done in
the field, one is immediately pre-
judged against earlier experiences

with traditional, classroom-oriented
training which was not designed to be
job-related. Traditional training usually does not have specific, performance objectives; it often is simply
an off-the-shelf program which is
presented to the trainee in the hope
that he can make some connection
between the content and his day by
day, work related responsibilities. It is
typically not *designed* to be implemented in the field as it is not
conceived as "applied" training.

As in any *new* experience there are
often objections to "changing the way
things are done." Even though the
existing methods may not be satisfactory, they are, at least, known.
Perhaps the objections should be
looked at as "misconceptions" rather
than objections because, basically,
they are based on a misconception of
what *can* be done to design field-
implementable training that works
(and is cost justifiable). What follows,
then, is a discussion of seven common
misconceptions and some suggested
strategies and techniques to overcome
them.

The misconceptions are:

1. The trainee's immediate manager
does not possess the skills to administer the course in the field.

2. Field managers will not implement the course.

3. Field managers downgrade the
training by requiring their staff to
take the training home and do it at
night.

4. The field manager will not be
motivated to follow through.

5. There is task interference when
an employee is asked to take a course
of instruction in his job environment.

6. Media and facility limitations
inhibit learning.

7. It is difficult to measure goal
achievement.

Each of these misconceptions may
be considered a legitimate objection
when measured against programs designed for traditional learning. However, each is a "misconception" when
carried over as a pre-judgment against
training which is specifically designed
for field implementation.

MISCONCEPTION 1: *The trainee's immediate manager does not possess the
skills to administer the course in the
field.* **Discussion:** Most courses are
designed for classroom instruction
and if you attempt to transpose a
classroom-oriented environment to
the field you would indeed have a
problem of trying to turn operating
field managers into instructors or
training specialists. However, courses
can be *designed* for field implementation...courses that take the

257

burden of instruction off of the instructor and place it onto the materials themselves. Therefore, the instructor, in this case the field manager, need only guide and assist his staff. He now becomes the manager of a learning process rather than a presenter of information.

The developing technology of instruction and the science of performance management, provide the designer of the training program with the opportunity to develop an effective, individualized training course that can be designed to any parameters existing in the field. For example, there can be minimal involvement of the manager in the formal structure of the course. Or the course could be designed for more frequent interaction between the manager and his subordinate at logical breakpoints in a modularized course. For example, role playing could be incorporated as a one-on-one exercise between the trainee and his manager, or the experience could be simulated, as in an in-basket case study.

If the objectives for the course are clearly defined and behavioral in nature and the parameters for the field environment are specifically defined, then the instructional designer can develop a training course that will apply any number of instructional and media strategies to achieve the course objectives. The field manager's main role as course administrator is to assure that his subordinates are provided the materials, time and support to complete the course. Other objectives are to localize the course to the manager's own style of training and to help establish the validity of the course in the on-the-job environment. By directly involving the field manager in the success of the program, even to a minor extent, the achievement of the effective field implementation of training is brought closer to realization. It provides the field manager with a vested interest in the success of the course, and through the use of performance aids and transfer exercises it provides the field manager with an opportunity to achieve measurable increases in performance on the part of his subordinates in a short period of time.

Strategies/techniques:

1. Design a self-paced rather than an instructor-based course.

2. Use print and/or non-print media to provide interaction and instruction.

3. Instructionally design and validate the course to achieve objectives and cover all points.

4. Build in answers to probable questions.

5. Provide brief, complete and easy to follow administrative instructions.

6. Keep the role of the field manager flexible—he can play a more active role if desired.

7. Relate to work activities through "transfer exercises" that require the trainee to apply what he has learned to his job so the field manager can see a direct, relevant application immediately.

MISCONCEPTION 2: *Field managers will not implement the course.* **Discussion:** If we make the assumptions that the training is needed, and is effective, a field manager who does not implement the training will have a problem in achieving his goals or work objectives. Well designed, effective training based upon real needs will be used when the role of the field manager is clearly defined and he knows it will help him meet the objectives and goals. Because a field manager will avoid a task he does not understand, tasks and instructions must be clear, concise, and relevant.

Strategies/techniques:

1. Produce and distribute only high quality, validated training packages designed for field implementation.

2. Provide motivation and instructions to implement the program in a

field manager's guide.

3. Provide transfer exercises that demonstrate the effectiveness of the training and relate it to solving his day-to-day problems.

4. Use measurement systems described above.

5. Publicize and promote the training packages using initial announcements and actual success stories.

MISCONCEPTION 3: *Field managers downgrade the training by requiring their employees to take the training home and do it at night.* **Discussion:** There's nothing inherently wrong with employees being able to take a training package home—especially when the training is designed in a modular format. Capability of taking the training when and where desired, whether it is home, at the office, or enroute to or from the office is an advantage, not a disadvantage. It becomes a problem when it is sent home as an afterthought and not positioned as an important, job related activity. Training should not become an *overload* to an already busy schedule. Field managers have to be made aware of the objectives of the training and the benefits and value they will accrue by successful completion of the course on the part of their subordinates.

Once they see this value, and if the course is structured to achieve the objectives and demonstrate the value, field managers will assure that their subordinates take and apply the knowledge and skills taught in the field implemented courses.

Strategies/techniques:

1. Position the course as a requirement with written documentation of course completion.

2. Require certification of individual course completion to be entered on the employee's personnel training record.

3. Provide motivation in cover letters accompanying the course and in the field manager's guide.

4. Include an activities action planner as a performance aid that requires the field manager to monitor step-by-step achievement.

MISCONCEPTION 4: *The field manager will not be motivated to follow through.* **Discussion:** Once again, the answer would be that the amount of follow-through activity required of the field manager can be limited in design to precisely what he needs to do in order to assure that his employees complete the course successfully. Again, much of the burden of motivation of the field manager relates to his experience with training packages which he is expected to implement. If a training package is designed so that it, indeed, does motivate and train his men so that they can accomplish their job tasks in a highly effective and efficient manner, it will make the field manager's job that much easier; and if he can be brought to this expectation and it demonstrates and manifests itself, the field manager will become more and more motivated to follow through on course activities. It should be noted that the activities are not merely classroom paper exercises, but they are related to real-life, job-centered activities whose relevance will be evident to the field manager.

Strategies/techniques:

1. Design an easy to administer course.

2. Provide field manager control.

3. Provide transfer exercises with reports built-in.

4. Build motivation into field manager's guide: a) It will make his people more productive; b) Require less time away from the job; c) Help him achieve work objectives; d) Save him time and effort; and e) Give him control.

MISCONCEPTION 5: *There is task interference when an employee is asked to take a course of instruction in his job*

environment. **Discussion:** Part of the problem here is to overcome the attitude that the office is a place for working and the classroom is a place for training. With a well-designed package that excites the learner by providing him valuable information that he perceives as helping him to do his job more effectively and efficiently, an effective field manager should be able to position his staff so that the training is an important and valuable asset to personal growth and company success and belongs, or at least has a definite position, in the on-the-job environment. The field manager must position training as a job-related activity and a specially set aside learning area should be provided that separates the employee from his immediate work surroundings and provides him with the opportunity to work undisturbed on a module-by-module basis.

One of the keys to successful management is, of course, time management. Successful employees and a successful field manager should have control over the time spent during the work week. If the employee does indeed manage his time effectively, he should be able to schedule training within his strategic planning of his work week. This becomes cost-effective for the employee, for the field manager and for the company...in that the hour spent in the field taking a course of instruction can be equated to several hours required in taking that same unit of instruction and achieving similar objectives when the course is offered at a remote site. The elimination of travel time to a remote site and of the group-paced, lockstep form of instruction makes the learner's time more productive.

Effective design can provide a prepackaged course implementable as a series of modules or units of instruction capable of being completed in sessions of 20 minutes to 60 minutes. Generally, a specific course should not be taken over an extended period of time, nor be concentrated in one or two eight-hour days. It can be taken one session at a time, either in the morning before leaving the house for work (in the case of audiocassette, some of the training can be accomplished enroute between the home and office), it can be reserved for the first hour at the office, or morning and afternoon hours of instruction can be set aside when the employee preplans his weekly work schedule.

Strategies/techniques:

1. Design a modular course.

2. Include units of instruction within modules.

3. Position the field manager to the importance of this approach.

4. Establish a learning environment that is free from distractions and day-to-day interruptions.

5. Provide a planning aid for time management so that an employee can include training time along with his work activities for the week.

6. Establish a schedule for course completion to be monitored by the field manager.

7. Require the field manager to assign course as a job responsibility.

MISCONCEPTION 6: *Media and facility limitations inhibit learning.* **Discussion:** Requirements for media and facility utilization can be and should be prescribed during the development of the course. Once field-implemented training is an accepted reality, media and facilities can be structured to enhance learning. One should not pre-suppose that the media and facilities located at a training center are unlimited. Equipment may not be available or functioning. One should not compare the media and facilities in the field to some ideal training center environment. Thus, the instructional design needs to carefully consider the field environment and the availability of reliable equipment to meet the course objectives. Where media equipment is not practical or available, the design should include the use of printed materials.

Strategies/techniques:

1. Most of training could be workbook with audiocassette.

2. For an ongoing field training program, equipment and facilities would be justified and provided just as they would if it were at a training center.

3. A major portion of the training can be done in the normal office (using earphones, if necessary), with audiovisual segments taken at a central location in the building.

4. Initial training of the majority of personnel can be roadshowed and prescheduled so that sophisticated equipment (video, motion picture, slide/tape or filmstrip) could be borrowed from a training center, rented or purchased.

5. The return on investment of field-implemented training would seem to justify the establishment of learning carrels specifically designed and equipped for effective implementation in the field environment.

6. Effective, job-related training is self-motivational and can overcome media and facility limitations.

7. Field training is readily used in an "on demand" basis for refresher

259

training as well as for initial instruction.

MISCONCEPTION 7: *It is difficult to measure goal achievement.* **Dissussion:** Achievement can be monitored both within the course and on the job; however, the measure of effectiveness of training is not simply the achievement differential between pre- and post-tests, but is related to the business goal which led to the need for training. Business *goals* must be translated into measurable *performance objectives.* Therefore, achievement is measured in terms of the performance objectives (business goals) and not just completion of the training program. The employee's on-

---

Use the strategies and techniques suggested here to overcome misconceptions in your organization about nonclassroom or 'field-implemented' training.

---

the-job performance is a far more accurate measure of training effectiveness than a "paper and pencil test." Instruction which is *designed* to be field implemented is "performance oriented" and lends itself properly to direct measures of performance. In addition to the benefit of improved employee performance, there are two notable benefits derived from properly designed training: (1) it is easier to design future training programs

based upon the experience from a course which has been designed, implemented, validated and evaluated in the field, and (2) it is easier to cost justify training which is performance oriented and which achieves the results chosen by management.

Prepackaged courses delivered to the field should have built-in measurement and reporting systems to meet the needs of any monitoring system.

Strategies/techniques:

The field manager can evaluate the trainee's activities sequentially:

1. Measure against specific activity accomplishment *within the course.*

2. Measure course completion module-by-module.

3. Assess the application of transfer exercises to a target (practice) account.

4. Examine account records of the target account.

5. Conduct programmed field manager work reviews against specific performance tasks assigned to the employee.

6. Measure performance against business goals.

Summary

Basically, traditional instruction is designed for the classroom and the objections that have been raised when it is proposed for field use are valid. Designers and producers of performance-based training programs recognize the lack of transfer to the work environment and are committed to the development of performance-oriented training specifically designed for field implementation. This commitment is real because performance management applied to field-implemented training works and is cost effective.

When the burden of teaching is carried by effective instructional strategies within the materials, the field manager need only administer

and guide the trainee's progress in the course and the application to the job. Behavioral objectives clearly state the expected outcomes of instruction, the conditions under which they will be performed and the level of acceptable performance. In addition, the field manager is provided administrative instructions which detail specific tasks and contain the tools and monitoring systems that assure consistent quality of implementation.

All training, whether classroom instruction or on-the-job, requires intrinsic motivation. Participation, interaction, and results are the keys. Field-implemented training involves the manager in implementing the training so that he interacts with the learner.

In a well designed field-implemented course, the trainee actively participates by performing various written and/or manipulative exercises and job-related activities. Because the course is based on measurable performance objectives which have been validated by preliminary trials in the field, the value of the program is thus readily observable by both the field manager and the trainee.

Field-implemented training works. The techniques and strategies used in the instructional design are somewhat different from those used in regular instruction, but the difference accomplishes one very important objective—it gets results.

From outward appearance, the training takes many familiar forms—videotapes, films, slides, filmstrips, audiocassettes and/or print. The difference is the use of systematic approach that applies the technology and science of instruction to specific business and organizational needs...a system that assures thorough research and analysis of the problem, professional instructional design, validated developmental testing, quality production, and a recognition of the importance of implementation.

Reprinted from TRAINING, June 1977

IDEAS FOR RESPONDING TO INDIVIDUAL NEEDS

Something many trainers still neglect: Responding to individual training needs

BY DUGAN LAIRD

Many training and development officers find it helpful to think of two classes of training needs: "micro" and "macro." The difference is very simple, but it has heavy impact on the response made by the T&D department. A micro training need exists for just one person, or for a very small population. Macro training needs exist in a large group of employees—frequently in the entire population with the same job classification. That happens, for example, when all clerks must be trained in a new procedure, or all managers in new policy. A manger in a specialized department, however, may develop a micro training need when some new technology is introduced into that field . . . or when performance as a manager reveals lack of comprehension one facet of good managerial practice!

Once the T&D specialists have determined that a performance problem can be solved through training, the next step is to design or locate an appropriate program. The central issue? "How can we ensure that trainees acquire the necessary behaviors — and that they apply them on their jobs?" The two parts of that inquiry are equally important; acquisition without application is an inadequate response to individual training needs!

If we were dealing with macro training needs, involving numbers of people, we would want to make sure that the investment produced differences in the on-the-job performance of the graduates. Is it any less important when we solve an individual training need? When we meet micro training needs we "put teeth" into career-planning and assessment-center pro-

grams. We also take major steps in the total human resource management of our organizations.

Performance appraisals, assessment centers, career planning — all provide data about individual training needs. And they are all hollow exercises unless there is a relevant and *implemented* educational program as a result of the data gathering!

Of course, T&D specialists complete the normal performance analysis when individual training needs arise. Then they add a few special considerations. What are these special issues for meeting micro training needs? They are Source of Supply and Organizational Control. These two issues require special attention; on other tasks we respond to micro training needs much as we would respond to any other training request. T&D specialists should process *all* training requests with a regular performance analysis. That means considering cost effectiveness. And in doing this they face a special dilemma.

Developing a highly individualized program with existing resources may easily cost more than the new skills could contribute back to the organization. On the other hand, the search for the "precisely correct" outside program can also be very expensive. It can mean searching many brochures, or making lots of phone calls. It can mean gambling on untested programs. It can seem like searching for a tiny needle in an enormous haystack.

The range of micro training needs is fantastic. Top executives, for example, have micro needs all the time: they need crest-of-the-wave knowledge for their unique technology; they need unusual help in solving unusual managerial problems; very often they need perceptive skills so they will antici-

pate future problems which haven't yet become reality! Where does the T&D staff locate that highly individualized program for them? It's at this point that we ask whether we use inside or outside resources.

Existing programs are the first place to check. Do the behavioral or learning goals for the need match or parallel those published for programs already in the curriculum of the organization? If there is a match, the obvious thing to do is to enroll the trainees in the next session. It may also be possible to attend only certain modules of that program or arrange for a "special session." If the established objectives vary only slightly, minor adaptations and tutoring by the regular instructors might be an inexpensive, quick, and effective way to respond.

Self-Study programs are especially adaptable to individual needs. They are thus excellent answers to micro training needs. By omitting certain segments, or by combining several programs, T&D specialists can often "tailor-make" highly specialized programs with minimum effort. Many commercial self-study programs need trimming and adaptation to fit the peculiar needs of an organization anyway. Therefore, it's wise to check the files or stockrooms; perhaps an available self-study program will solve the micro training need.

Special Assignments within the organization may be the ideal way for individuals to acquire desired learnings. This is particularly true when specialists need knowledge of practices in other departments in order to manage "handoffs" smoothly, or when middle managers need insights into how other interdependent departments operate. Suppose the auditing department wants to develop a few managers who are consistently empathic with the functions they audit. Rotation through jobs in other departments may be the most effective and inexpensive way to develop such empathy.

A mere "visit" or *field trip* may be adequate as the solution for simple micro training needs. Such visits can be productive— but they require careful planning. Generic visits ("just to look things over") are seldom very useful — and quite often annoying to the hosts. They easily result in superficial or misleading learnings. A previsit session is needed. The trainee,

---

This article is an abridgment of Chapter 6 of Laird's book, Approaches to Training and Development *(copyright 1978, Addison-Wesley Publishing Co., Reading, MA).*

the immediate superior, a manager from the host unit, plus a T&D specialist should compile a list of the questions which need to be answered at each position. A method of evaluating the visit should also be designed. This can be a simple mechanism for tallying the percentage of questions correctly answered, and a tally sheet for listing the number of times the trainee applied the findings in the first few weeks back on his job.

Task-detailing for self-discipline sounds a bit punitive and pedantic, but it is really an effective way to overcome micro performance problems in employees who are deficient in just one characteristic of their work. Typical of these deficiencies of execution (they usually are D_E's) are carelessness, lack of attention to detail, flying off the handle, missing parts of assignments, tardiness, lack of follow-through, or unilateral decision making. Such personal problems can best be overcome if the trainee is acutely conscious of the problem—and aware that the temporary assignment will give maximum experience...plenty of chances to apply a good level of performance. Thus the phrase "task detailing"; thus the phrase "self-discipline." In such detailing, feedback mechanisms are vital. The trainee must have some sort of log which will show when there was a chance to apply a satisfactory level of performance in the deficient behavior — and how many times the opportunity was seized! Without this quantitative feedback mechanism, the assignment tends to get cloudy and discouraging. Trainees in such regimens should keep their own tallies, discussing them with their immediate supervisors at predetermined intervals. When these special detailings grow out of appraisals, they can be tied in directly with promotion, salary increases, and the next appraisal. Such integration with other processes shows that the problem is worth attention — and that there are happy consequences for overcoming the deficiency.

Coaching offers a very important internal answer to many micro training needs. It can be conveniently coupled with the task-detailing approach. Coaching has many advantages.
• It can be totally individualized.
• It can ensure total validity if the coach is the trainee's immediate superior. (That is the usual and ideal situation.) Since the "boss" is coaching, there can be no doubt about management's valuing the behaviors which are to grow out of the coaching.
• The close, one-on-one communication permits dynamic feedback

mechanisms and reappraisal of the learning objectives.
• Training responsibility is delegated to that point in the organization where it has the most immediate and direct payoff: the relationship between superior and subordinate.
• Manager/coaches tend to learn a great deal about the inventories of the individuals whom they coach — as well as about the whole process of motivation, directing, and communicating with subordinates.

There is, in addition, a subtler benefit from widespread use of coaching in an organization: Managers who have served as coaches represent an empathic population for all T&D activities. As decision makers or requesters of T&D services, they know more "of the ropes" about learning— why it is important and how it works. They are certainly useful resources in meeting future micro training needs.

None of these programs from within the organization is complete without an ongoing planning and evaluating mechanism. That is another reason for

the active involvement of T&D specialists when any such solution is implemented for a micro training need. In every case, the trainee, immediate superiors, "hosts" (if job rotation, special assignments, or visits are used) and a T&D specialist should:
• set goals;
• define the activity;
• describe the way in which the learnings will be applied back on-the-job; and
• establish criteria and a mechanism for evaluating the experience.

This implies creating a post-program feedback form on which trainees tally and analyze their on-the-job applications of the new skill. Such feedback forms not only give data for evaluation; they help maintain the new behavior as well!

Seminars and workshops offer one of the more frequent answers to the T&D officer's quest. Their sponsors range from independent consultants through professional societies to colleges and universities. Their length ranges from a single day (even a few

---

Questions to ask about the workshop or seminar

	Yes	No
1. Does the brochure publish learning objectives or "expected outcomes?"	—	—
2. Are those outcomes stated in behavioral terms?	—	—
3. Are the behaviors observable, measurable, reasonable?	—	—
4. Is a topical outline included in the announcement?	—	—
5. Does the brochure specify what types of employees should register? (Nature of position? Level of position? Experience assumed?)	—	—
6. Does the outline provide some time for participants to raise issues and ask questions?	—	—
7. Does the time schedule look flexible? (Could it possibly be completed? Can it adapt to the unique needs of individual participants?)	—	—
8. Is there provision for "process feedback" so participants can let leaders know to what degree their needs are/aren't being met?	—	—
9. Does the brochure mention the learning methods which will be employed?	—	—
10. Do those methods involve "action training"...chances for your trainees to get involved in something other than just listening and watching?	—	—
11. Is there workshop time so your trainees can contemplate ways to apply the learnings back on the job?	—	—
12. Does there seem to be an opportunity for your trainees to access the leaders in small group or one-on-one conversations?	—	—
13. Are the leaders well known to you or to the managers in the department in which the micro need exists?	—	—
14. Have the leaders published on this subject?	—	—
15. Have the leaders worked for or consulted with corporate or bureaucratic organizations, or is their background entirely academic?	—	—

hours) to several weeks. Unfortunately, their quality ranges through an even wider spectrum!

How do T&D officers locate such events? Usually they need only open their mail! Membership in any professional society (ASTD, NSPI or ASPA) will get your name on mailing lists which are then going to be sold to sponsoring agencies. Furthermore, attendance at any event by a single sponsor will guarantee future mailings — frequently multiple, because their computer lists get cross-fertilized! If these methods haven't already produced more mail than there is time to read, phoning the associations or writing nearby universities (or the American Management Associations) will ensure lots of brochures in the future.

How do alert T&D officers select the really "right" answer to the particular micro training need they face at the moment? For openers, one might ask the questions in the accompanying box.

A really reliable seminar or workshop should score "Yes" on at least 10 of those questions. It certainly should score "Yes" on five of the first six questions if it is to meet the unique learning needs of your trainee.

If the program has been offered previously, T&D staff members can check with those who have used it. But be sure to ask the users how they're *using* the program — not how they liked it. Answers to the latter question will be contaminated with data about the food, the meeting site, the trip to and from the program, other participants. A useful list of questions to ask previous participants at seminars and workshops would include some of these:

● Did you or your participants institute any new policies and procedures — amend or cancel any old ones— as a result of attending?

● Did participants come home with any product they could immediately put to use?

● What specific problem was solved as a result of attending this seminar?

● Have you calculated a dollar payoff from participation?

● If the need still existed, would you send people to this program today?

● Did others who attended really reflect the audience appealed to in the advertising — or did they admit just anyone who paid the money?

● Should our participants make any special preparation?

● In what ways did your partici-

LEARNER-CONTROLLED INSTRUCTION PRODUCES BETTER THINKERS

BY JOHN ROSENHEIM

Instead of telling trainees how to do something, send them to the right resource and provide the questions they'll need to ask," says Phil Bade, general manager of Universal Training Systems (UTSC's) management development division. "This method retains the main advantages—haphazard trial and error and receiving too much or too little information in the wrong order. Trainees learn the 'survival skills' first, so they'll be productive as soon as possible."

Universal's Learner-Controlled Instruction (LCI) is being successfully used by International Harvester Credit Corporation (IHCC). New field service representatives (FSR) learn about dealer operations, taking inventories and other aspects of their job. Sixteen months after the program was implemented, a survey of 90 FSR supervisors indicated that FSRs were learning more effectively in less time than before.

"Eighty-two percent of the supervisors reported that new FSRs' competency was greater when they were assigned to their zones," said Chuck McLaughlin, manager of business planning and human resources for the financial services group of IHCC. "The supervisors felt trainees performed better after completing this program. It used to take two to three years for FSRs to become as productive as many new FSRs now are after five months."

LCI "causes trainees to think," says Bade. "They're required to make analyses, judgements and comparisons, not just asked to absorb information. They're learning actively, not passively." Quickly learning essential job skills is also good for trainees' morale, he adds. "Many trainees have just come out of school, so they've had enough lectures and textbooks. They want to feel they're actively contributing to the organization right away."

Even if a trainee isn't working out, it's better for both employee and company to discover it as soon as possible, Bade explains. "At first, several clients were startled when turnover apparently went up soon after starting LCI programs. But then they discovered turnover wasn't increasing; it was just occurring sooner."

Universal's LCI involves three steps. "First, we program the trainee into a resource. It might be a co-worker, the company files, a policy manual, a customer, the local bank— whatever's appropriate. Then, we equip the trainee to gather information from the resource. Finally, someone knowledgeable in that subject area makes sure the trainee really did learn," Bade says. "Progress is based on competency. Learners proceed when they can demonstrate they've mastered a topic. They aren't bound by arbitrary schedules or forced to accommodate someone else's learning speed."

Trainees benefit because some of their resources are people they'll be working with later on. Human resources can include clients, distributors, suppliers and dealers, as well as company personnel. For example, field representatives for restaurant supplies were assigned to interview the manager of their favorite restaurant. Later, they interviewed cooks, dishwashers, and other food-service employees to learn first-hand about equipment features and customers' needs.

"Trainees who learn how to fill out a form from the person who processes it or learn about dealers' financial records from a dealer will understand how their own work fits into the whole picture," Bade says. "They'll be able to make other people's jobs easier. And when they encounter difficulties, they'll know where to look or whom to ask to get the answers."

LCI isn't a cure-all, Bade cautions. "It wouldn't teach concepts very well— human relations or communications, for instance. But it's proved very effective in teaching specific job skills. What's more, several clients have told us their employees perform better because of the discovery method itself. LCI teaches trainees how to ask the right questions and how to gather and analyze information effectively. And these skills prove very valuable on the job."

Reprinted from TRAINING, March 1980

THESE TRAINEES DEVELOP THEIR OWN TRAINING MATERIALS

BY JUDSON SMITH

William King, director of sales training for Acme Visible Records, Inc., has devised a simple aid to solve a common problem faced in sales training: How to help the trainee make an immediate transition from theory to practice and how to apply his or her new skills back in the "real world."

King gives each new sales representative a "Personalized Sales Presentation" booklet at the beginning of the training session. The booklet covers the sales process, step-by-step, with abundant white space for trainees to supply their own answers to tailor the process for an actual prospect.

"Throughout the training, we stress how the techniques we are discussing can sell *this* prospect, the one each trainee will soon call on in the 'real world,'" King explains. "Since the branch manager, who has also attended the program, is required to followup and join in the next call on this prospect, the manager also can use the trainee's notes to preview the upcoming call."

King finds that the booklet facilitates the transition from classroom to selling interview. In addition, comparison of each trainee's booklet illustrates two main training themes—that selling techniques are universal, but that each prospect is unique and must be sold as an individual.

"Our follow-up shows that more than 70% of the prospects have been sold or moved closer to the sale by trainees using the booklet," King concludes. "Frequently, participants tell us they've changed their whole approach after seeing it in writing. But the most important aspect of this approach is that it personalizes the entire sales process and relates it to a real-world prospect." (Based on the unpublished manuscript King originally wrote for his colleagues in the National Society of Sales Training Executives.)

Reprinted from TRAINING, May 1980

---

pants get special individualized time and attention from the leaders?

When previous participants are unable to identify unique assistance or specific applications, the program is questionable. (Of course there's one fallacy here: Users can be incompetent too—so check with more than one.)

University programs take a variety of forms. They may be short seminars. They may be "one-night-a-week" programs offered through regular channels or through extension services. They may also be full-time investment of the trainees' time and energy during a period of release from normal work responsibilities.

How can T&D officers assure investments in university programs? To begin with, they can check the programs for relevance and quality in the same way they check seminars and workshops. But beware. A glittering array of renowned authorities on the faculty does not guarantee that those luminaries will actually teach your people! Astute T&D officers check, and get a commitment about:

• The amount of time the learners will be exposed to each faculty member — and the nature of that exposure.

• The size of the class.

• The nature of the testing. (Will your trainee be held accountable for the learnings?)

When there is no commitment to make learners accountable for their learnings, some action by the T&D director may be indicated. Perhaps a conference with the trainees and their immediate superior can identify the specific ways in which learnings are to be applied on the job. This is expected in any enrollment anyway; but perhaps this conference can let the trainees see it as an added signal that the enrollment is a responsibility as well as an opportunity.

Sometimes these "contacts" between learners and employers can remove the stigma of the theory-only testing which haunts university testing systems. Sometimes they may be made quantitative. Here is a simple example: The micro need is for improved public-speaking skills. The oral tests in the night-school program may effectively hold the learner accountable — but bear no real-world impact. A "contract" could make the trainee accountable for locating and delivering four public speeches in the six months following the night-school program.

The contract can and should be a simple document in which learners and their superiors indicate acceptance and comprehension of the learning objectives. There can be a place for the learner to estimate achievement or nonachievement of each objective. There can also be a place for the learner to tally the occasions when the behavior was applied. The document is useful when trainee and superior review the impact of the training — and it's useful for the T&D officer in evaluating the program. That evaluation, by the way, shouldn't be done just in terms of the present micro training need; a copy of the document should be retained as a data source for future, similar needs.

Self-study is another medium for meeting micro training needs. Most self-study programs are available as books or packages, sold through publishers or commercial vendors. Such packages usually involve some equipment: audiotapes, filmstrip projectors, or teaching machines. The sophistication of the presentation is relevant to the decision only if it involves unavailable equipment or unreasonable costs. More important is the appropriateness of the presentation to the learning goals.

In evaluating self-study programs, the usual questions arise:

• Are the behavioral (learning) outcomes clearly defined? (This may not apply to books, but it should be a minimum test for accepting any programmed text!)

• Is the scope of the content clearly specified?

• Are there indications of the "normal" time required for completion? (Beware of averages; look for upper and lower limits.)

• What do previous users say about their use of learnings from this program?

Professional conferences and conventions provide another source of learning to meet micro training needs. They are seldom structured as behaviorally oriented learning systems. Thus they often become "head trips," intellectual bazaars at which people discover new trends in their fields. As such, they can be an effective way to bring state-of-the-art and wave-of-the-future knowledge into an organization. At other times, they clarify state-of-the-art concepts which had previously been only fuzzy phantoms that worried management — but not in sufficiently concrete form to do the organization any good. Hopefully, people who attend conferences and conventions will bring back ideas which they will try out, or at very least share with their peers.

Conference attendance involves some preparation so delegates can: 1) distinguish between "rubbing elbows" and "bending elbows"; 2) make intelligent decisions about which sessions to attend; and 3) realize their obligation to apply or share the acquisitions when they return to the organization.

To meet these requirements, the T&D officer can take certain steps. First, there can be an obligatory chat between delegates and their superiors. (If managers are properly trained, the T&D staff doesn't need to be present!) At this chat the boss and the delegates can make initial decisions about which sessions look most promising in terms of applications within the organization. They can even discuss the relative qualification of presenters, treating each event as if it were itself a workshop or seminar. The analysis is far less profound, but the same primary issues apply. Second, the T&D department can see that not all the delegates attend the same conference. Within any discipline there are usually several societies, each offering its own convention. Gentle prodding by the T&D officer can see that members of that discipline divide their attention among the conferences. Finally, the investment can be protected by establishing a policy that short follow-up reports or briefing sessions must follow attendance at all conventions. This should not be arduous or punishing. It may be a staff meeting, or merely a copy of the report required by their own management.

All of these policies or activities, introduced into the organization by the T&D officer, send the important signal that attendance at conferences and conventions is an investment — not mere fun and games. They also imply that such attendance isn't a mere, thoughtless ritual; it happens because it's a response to a real or potential micro training need.

In actual practice, many micro training needs come to the attention of the T&D officer because managers arrive saying "I have this problem," or "Can you help me with funds to send some of my people to...?" Intelligent T&D officers reinforce such initiative. They also subject it to gentle analysis. That analysis tests the validity of both the request and the suggested program. It asks, "Will the people learn something *new*? Will the program supply what they need to learn? Will the learnings actually be put to use on the job? If not, will the experience permit intelligent rejection of the technology in the program?"

In other words, astute T&D officers put special stress on steps 3, 8, and 9 of

the control process in Figure A. Step 3 deserves special attention. Especially important is the presence of three parties in the joint planning. The T&D department is obviously involved —but just as important is the active involvement of both the trainee and the immediate superior of the trainee! Without their inputs there is no real assurance that the learnings will be

useful to the organization, that they will be properly reinforced after they have been acquired— or even that the trainee understands the purpose of the training!

Even if the T&D officer is not informed or involved in all the decisions, the control system is needed— and it is the responsibility of the T&D officer to see that managers at all levels com-

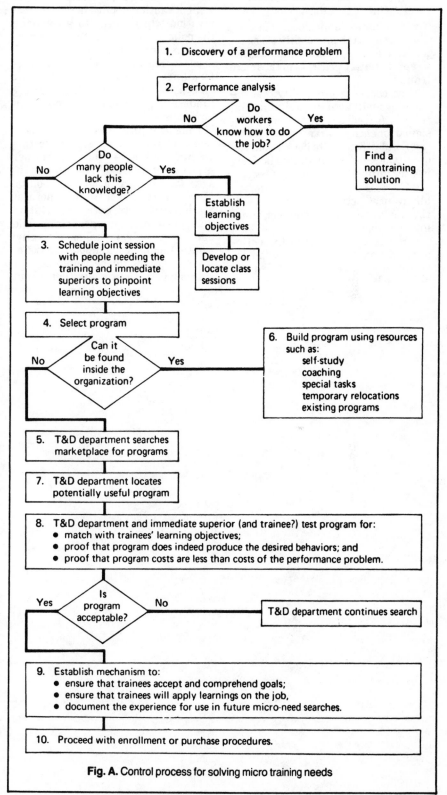

Fig. A. Control process for solving micro training needs

prehend and apply the system whenever they solve a micro training need.

It's not a question of control for the sake of control. It's not a policy designed merely to keep the T&D officer informed of what's going on — although that is not an insignificant item. The reasons for a centralized, systematic decision process are many. They go like this: A control system for meeting micro training needs:

- Eliminates duplicate searches.
- Increases the probability of selecting an effective, appropriate solution — appropriately priced — to the micro training need.
- Increases the probability that the learnings will actually be applied on the job. A feedback device can be designed for each program.
- Establishes a data bank about the quality of vendor's products and services for future micro training needs.
- Keeps the immediate superiors of all trainees actively involved in setting goals and following up each training investment.
- Makes a statement to the entire organization that training is an investment which must be justified and evaluated.

- Provides data to monitor the actual dollars being spent on training, education, and development.
- Keeps the T&D officer informed about the genuine training needs. From this data, trends may emerge; and the organization learns when micro training needs have become macro training needs.

The theme of those advantages is application and accountability. A word of caution applies here. The reservation which needs to accompany the policy is an admonition, "Be gentle." In other words, the T&D staff needs to tread lightly when giving performance analysis or cost-benefit analysis — especially when denying funds or approval for ill-conceived proposals.

Take a typical case. A manager comes to you and says, "I have this training problem — and this seminar is just what we need." Now that manager may be wrong on both points. Maybe there isn't a training need at all. Even if there were, the solution may be totally inappropriate. The manager may be mistaken — totally! But that manager is supporting training — and should be reinforced for such support! Gentle questions about the nature of the deficiency, and gentle questions about the appropriateness of the proposed solution, and gentle questions about how the learning will be applied on the job — all these are in order.

The alternatives to such gentleness are frightening. T&D officers who are too rigorous, too hard-headed, will soon observe some unhappy consequences. First of all, they will get fewer requests for their consultative services. Second, they will grow increasingly ignorant about the many employees who attend special training. That is to say: client-managers who want training will find a way to get it — whether they get the proper training through the proper channels or go the "bootleg route." These are the days of assessment centers and career planning and appraisal programs. Such systems are meaningless unless accompanied by proper individual training and development plans. The T&D officer wants to be a major factor in the design of those individual programs...and above all, a major factor in the follow-up which gives such programs their real impact.

Reprinted from TRAINING, June 1978

LEARNING CONTRACTS: HELPING ADULTS EDUCATE THEMSELVES

Contracts not only provide a vehicle for individual development, but also prove that learning has occurred

BY STEPHEN P. BECKER

Back when well-known adult learning theorist Malcolm Knowles was a professor at Boston University, and longtime TRAINING contributor Stephen Becker was one of his graduate students, the two had plenty of opportunities to talk about training and development. Not so anymore, with Dr. Knowles a professor of adult education at North Carolina State University and Becker a training and development practitioner near Boston.

So it was especially fun a few weeks ago to lock Knowles, Becker, and a tape recorder into the same room for a day, and to ask them to discuss adult learning theory and its applications in human resources development.

Part of their discussion revolved around Knowles' concept and use of learning contracts. Here is the essence of that conversation, followed by Becker's own ideas about how learning contracts can be applied to management development.

The first principle of learning contracts is: They are a vehicle to move the learner from where he is to where he wants to be. The only real motivation for learning is the learner's desire to develop some competency. And the best basis for the development of a learning contract is a competency model.

Malcolm told me that he has, along with other faculty members and students, developed a model of competence for performing the role of adult educator. Twice a year, he does a self-rating, based on the model which involves two steps. The first step is to determine the relative importance of each of the competencies to the role he wants to perform. The point is to determine which competencies are critical at this time. This is done by creating a six-point scale for each competency to indicate the level of competency. An "R" on the scale indicates the required level of competency, and a "P" indicates the present level. If the "R" is placed at 6 and the "P" at 2, then the gap is 4. This way, a learner can determine his or her own learning needs. It's a self-directed learning-needs analysis.

Step two is to double check subjectivity by talking to several peers for an hour or two. The purpose is to check the ratings by raising such questions as, "What was the basis for rating a required competency at 5 rather than 3?"

Using peer resources thusly is part of what Malcolm means when he talks about using human resources proactively. He says: "In the adult years, the richest resources most of us have for learning are the people around us everyday. But our experience with schooling has taught us that to make such use of peer resources is cheating. So one of the critical skills that adults must acquire to be self-directed learners is to make use of peer resources."

Assuming that six or seven competencies need further development,

© Stephen P. Becker

Malcolm plans a learning contract for himself that is personally critical at this point in his development. He translates the learning needs into learning objectives and then writes a learning contract, which has these four columns:

1. learning objectives
2. resources and strategies to accomplish each objective
3. evidence to be collected of having accomplished each objective
4. criterion means that will be used by, say, peers for getting that evidence validated.

In six months, Malcolm will convene a new panel of peers to assess the evidence of his contract. Then, at the same session, they will help him do a new needs assessment.

He uses this same process with all students in all his courses. He feels extremely committed to learning contracts as a method for helping adults educate themselves. He states: "For me, the learning contract has solved so many problems in terms of providing evidence of what really has been learned. A good learning contract will provide much more useful evidence of what the learner has learned than a final exam possibly could."

While learning contracts have applications in courses and short-term workshops, it also seems clear that they are valuable in career, management, and executive development. That's because these kinds of educational activities tend to take a longer period of time — perhaps months or years— during which the learner may enter into a series of contracts with himself, an advisor or consultant (a trainer, a boss, or a peer), or even some kind of support group consisting of peers.

The process would include the following eight steps:

1. Within the framework of the person's total life, career goals would be established that are realistic and within the scope of the employing organization. The goal must be one toward which the person feels motivated.
2. Once a goal is available, key sub-goals would be identified.
3. The competencies for each of these sub-goals would be clarified and listed (a competency model).
4. The required and present level of individual competency would be identified.
5. After analyzing the gaps, learning needs to be worked on during a specific period of time would be selected.
6. A learning contract would be written for a specified period of time.

267

7. While the contract is active, there would be several checkpoints to provide on-going support and encouragement.

8. At the end of the contract time, there would be a formal session to examine the evidence of achievement and help plan a new learning contract.

And, if you subscribe to principles of behavior management or modification, this is when some kind of positive consequence or reward could be introduced.

Let's consider a practical example. Think of the department manager in a high technology activity or industry. There are four primary reasons why this manager got the job. First, he or she had an excellent technical education. Second, the person's performance of technical work was also excellent. Third, the organization was growing faster than it could recruit management people with technical backgrounds in that industry. Fourth, the manager wanted and asked for the job.

Now, of course, the job tasks change for this individual. No longer does he or she function as an individual contributor, responsible only for the work assigned. Now all kinds of managerial work — planning, controlling, budgeting, motivating, listening, interviewing, selling, disciplining, cost cutting, etc.— must be done. Yet, the manager is totally unprepared for these activities.

Here's an ideal time to utilize learning contracts as a strategy to develop management competencies. The manager involved could, with help, identify competency areas he or she felt were important; this decision is based on both personal desire or motivation and perceived organizational need. For instance, if the organization was having trouble with numbers-oriented activities, such as costs, cash flow, production analysis, etc., and the new manager also was weak in that area, then competencies related to numbers might represent the greatest need at this point. If the numbers competency was strong and the organization was experiencing problems in the area of employee relations, then the manager might see the development of his or her human resource competencies as the highest priority.

Here's when a learning contract could be written, using such resources and strategies as tutorials, reading books, taking courses, observing a peer, participating in a short workshop or seminar, and/or attempting to do certain activities while being observed and then evaluated. In fact, there is no limit to the available resources and strategies; this is a time to be creative and innovative so that the learning job gets done efficiently.

Needless to say, neither Malcolm Knowles nor I believe that learning contracts are the be-all, end-all for management development for individuals. It's possible to have a well-written learning contract that just doesn't work. If this happens, there are two things to keep in mind. First, we are basing the learning contract on the development of competency — in this case, management competency. A competency is the dynamic interplay of knowledge, understanding, skills, values, attitudes, and interests as they relate to the individual, the job, and the organization. If we want to get a person to behave like a manager, we must remember that he or she requires more than just knowledge and skill. Malcolm put it concisely: "A person's behavior will change only when a new behavior is supported by both the skill involved in that behavior *and* the attitude and the value lying behind the behavior."

Second, for a learning contract to work, the manager or perspective manager has to be motivated. He or she must honestly want to become a competent manager. Before a learning contract is written, therefore, it pays to probe the motivations of the individual involved. This is where the "art" of the trainer can really be utilized. By counselling, listening, and asking non-directive questions, you can allow the manager to convince you and himself that he wants to manage. If he does, learning contracts can be enormously valuable.

Finally, it's not the learning contract that succeeds or fails. It's the manager who will do so. As trainers, our task is to help control the process so the chances of success are high.

Reprinted from TRAINING, April 1978

MASTERY LEARNING: NOBODY FLUNKS

Trainees can master the material in most training programs.
Just let them do it at their own pace

BY RON ZEMKE

In the early 1960s Frederick S. Keller, a highly respected Columbia University professor of psychology, created a teaching technology he called the Personalized System of Instruction. PSI was based on the idea that a subject—like introductory chemistry, physics or psychology—could be learned better and faster—*mastered*—if the students were allowed to advance at their own pace rather than be subjected to the classic lecture-exam system. It was a radical idea to drop into a staid university environment.

Under the PSI procedure, subject matter is broken down into a number of small, easily mastered units. Each unit consists of a set of learning objectives and key learning points, and a list of study options—a book chapter to read, a film to watch, an audiotape to listen to, an experiment to perform, whatever. Students are then on their own to work through the material until they feel they understand the key points and can meet the learning objectives.

At that point they demonstrate mastery over the material by taking a unit test administered by a course proctor—a more advanced student— who also acts as a one-to-one tutor should the student need help with the unit. The student takes the test, the proctor scores it on the spot and the two review it immediately. The proctor probes for weak points and listens to the student's defense of alternative answers to test questions. If the student's test score is below a specified mastery level, the student can take a second or third or fourth test on the material.

Mastery is the point, period.

Two critical points in this process: First, the student does not go on to other material until mastery over the current material is demonstrated; second, no grade penalty is assessed for failure to reach mastery in one try. Mastery is the point—period. Sometimes a final examination is included as part of the course, but in those instances the exam items are a composite of the unit-test items students have already seen.

This may not seem like a big deal, but in 1963, when it was introduced at Columbia University and the University of Brasilia, it was considered quite revolutionary. In 1967, when Keller was inaugurated as president of Division 2 of the American Psychological Association, he delivered a provocative paper entitled "Good-bye Teacher. . ." which caused quite a bit of controversy. The use of phrases like, "A new kind of teacher is in the making. To the old kind, I, for one, will be glad to say 'good-bye!' " didn't make a lot of people in the education establishment terrifically happy. PSI eventually became known as "The Keller Plan," and a cookbook account of the process was published in 1974.

A few years removed from the excitement, it is easy to see PSI and the Keller Plan as simply one example of a general approach to training and education that has been dubbed "mastery learning." Diomidis Stamatis, a Southgate, MI-based training consultant and Ph.D. candidate at Wayne State University, describes mastery learning as both an instructional procedure characterized by "the attainment of adequate levels of performance on tests that measure specific learning tasks," and an instructional model based on a bit of social philosophy that assumes "nearly every student can learn everything in the training at a specified level of competence, given [that] the learner's previous knowledge and attitudes about the subject are accounted for. . .the instruction is of good quality. . .and adequate time on the task is allowed to permit mastery."

Or, as Keller put it in "Good-bye Teacher. . .", "I have learned one very important thing: The student is always right. He is not asleep, not unmotivated, not sick, and he can learn a great deal if we provide the right contingencies of reinforcement. But if we don't provide them, and provide them soon, he, too, may be inspired to say, 'Good-bye!' to formal education." Great—nearly inflammatory—stuff in the early days of the equal opportunity movement of the '60s.

Today, in cooler times, Stamatis points out that many of the mastery learning concepts were, in fact, worked out as early as 1918 by curriculum-development pioneers J. Franklin Bobbitt and W.W. Charters. The Winnetka Plan, developed by Carleton Washburne in the early 1920s, and work by Henry C. Morrison at the University of Chicago Laboratory School in 1926 share many of the features of present mastery-learning models as well. Rather than Keller's work, however, Stamatis cites the work done by John B. Carroll in 1963, and later studies by Benjamin Bloom, as catalysts for the revival of interest in mastery learning.

Whomever you credit with paternity, roughly eight assumptions underlie mastery learning:

1. Most trainers and learners *can* master the material in most training programs. In short, people can learn almost anything—with proper instruction.

2. Learning, not instruction, should be the focus of training. When trainees fail to learn, the training, not the trainee, is at fault.

3. The goal of training (in the working world) is to prepare people to do a job, not to flunk people out.

4. Individual differences between students are a minor concern.

5. Given enough time, most people can master most information. Mastery, not time to attain mastery, is what's important.

6. Training outcomes can be specified in behavioral, observable terms that can be agreed upon as representing mastery of the content.

7. Subject matter can be broken into discrete units that can be mastered in a logical order.

8. Motivating the learner is a key responsibility of the trainer.

William E. Blank, who equates mastery learning and competency-based training, emphasizes that in mastery learning the instructor manages a learning environment rather than instructing or managing the learner. "Most management concerns in traditional programs deal with managing instruction. In competency-based, individualized programs, the primary concern is with managing learning, and there is a world of difference between the two." By that he means the emphasis in mastery learning isn't on the lecture, the classroom performance of the instructor or the big examination. Rather the focus is on developing learning objectives, assessing the entry level of learners, preparing alternative materials the trainees can use to instruct themselves, developing diagnostic procedures and prescriptions, and preparing methods for trainees to demonstrate mastery.

If all this sounds a little less tidy than bringing in a group of trainees, sitting them down at a horseshoe-shaped table, lecturing at them for a few hours and sending them home "instructed"—it is. But to those who have introduced a mastery design into their training, it is irresistible.

Arlene Tietel, project administrator for supervisory development programs at 3M Co. in St. Paul, MN, has based several programs on the mastery model. She points to benefits such as trainees' increased performance in training and easier management of a curriculum. "But," she cautions, "it takes a 'champion' to keep the system in place and working. It's easy to let it erode back to a platform-peformance sort of thing."

For Further Reference:

The personalized System of Instruction, J. Gilmore Sherman and Robert S. Ruskin, Englewood Cliffs, NJ: Educational Technology Publications, 1978.

The Keller Plan Handbook, F.S. Keller and J.G. Sherman, Menlo Park, CA: W.A. Benjamin, 1074.

Handbook for Developing Competency-Based Training Programs, William E. Blank, Englewood, NJ: Prentice-Hall Inc., 1982

Reprinted from TRAINING, May 1985

SELF-STUDY: BOON OR BUST?

There are plenty of advantages to letting trainees go it alone, but accountability is the key to ensuring that they go someplace worthwhile

BY MARGARET MORGAN BYNUM
AND NATE ROSENBLATT

Depending upon whom you talk to, self-instruction is either the best thing that's happened to training since the invention of the multiple-choice quiz or a doomed concept.

Even when they accept self-study's basic premise ("People are inherently motivated to learn and don't need a teacher/authority figure standing over them to see that they do"), detractors point out that it's a generalization that tends to run afoul of the real world: "Yes, but that doesn't mean they're motivated to learn what *you* want them to."

We'd like to settle the issue once and for all by stating unequivocally that self-instruction works wonderfully in the business world. Or, it fails dismally.

Before we go any further, let's define what we mean by "self-instruction." We're talking about courses of study—work-related training or self-improvement programs—in which learners are expected to master the material on their own, working without direct supervision, usually at their own pace. While computer-based training is the type of self-instruction making headlines these days, most self-study programs rely on audio- or videotapes, books, manuals and so on, often including written examples and practice exercises in some form. The list of subjects is unlimited, goals often are personal and vague, and time restrictions tend to be left up to the individual taking the course.

Companies use self-instructional programs to extend the scope of their training departments, cut costs, avoid conflicts of class scheduling or site selection, and eliminate problems with employees who are reluctant to "expose" themselves in a group context. Believers are convinced that they can provide outstanding training on an individual basis.

The bad news is that a depressingly low percentage of self-study courses are completed.

The key is accountability. Without accountability, self-study provides dismal results; with it, self-study can be one of the greatest assets in a training department's arsenal of resources because of its flexibility and generally lower cost—which means more people can be trained. Accountability provides the "proof orientation" which creates an environment in which self-study is accepted and even sought. It supplies the motivation not only to complete a program, but to take the extra necessary step: *applying* newly gained knowledge on the job. Accountability provides support for drooping self-control. It's the secret ingredient that changes self-study from a bust to a boon.

There are some obvious—and some not so obvious—advantages of programs that can be distributed to trainees for completion according to their varied schedules.

• *Logistics.* Self-instructional courses can solve logistics problems. When employees are scattered in branch locations around the country (or around the world) it can be an overwhelming problem to transport them to a central site at a universally convenient time. The unexpected always governs the schedule. With self-instruction, the time and place are always right.

• *Cost-effectiveness.* Self-instruction, as a rule, is far less expensive than classroom instruction. That becomes evident when you consider even fleetingly the cost of an instructor, food, lodging, conference-room rental and transportation. The cost of trainees' time away from the job isn't exactly a small item either. Good group training is often worth every penny it demands, but it *is* expensive.

• *Privacy.* Self-instruction eliminates the fear of being "exposed" as ignorant, slow to catch on, uncomfortable in groups, etc. A lot of people, particularly on the management level, shy away from needed training because they are unwilling to allow their weaknesses or inadequacies to be observed by anyone else. Some fear that knowledge of their shortcomings will prevent promotion, so they camouflage inadequacies with skills they find easy to learn.

• *Flexibility.* Training directors can enroll as many people as necessary in self-instructional courses without any particular strain on the company's facilities or its training staff. And programs which do require instructors, of course, can be conducted at the same time self-paced programs are being completed.

• *Individuality.* Self-instruction can answer particular needs. If there are only a few requests for specific skill training, they can be handled on a self-study basis without tying up classrooms. Combinations of available programs can be tailored to specific, individual needs.

First steps

Those are some powerful selling points for self-study programs. But they'll probably collapse like a house of cards if you simply hand out study packages, wish the trainees well and wave good-bye. Their completion rate will be abysmal, they won't learn what they're supposed to, and the whole exercise may be a waste of time and effort.

Before we get to accountability, there are a few general rules of thumb about running effective self-study programs. The first involves advertising. Too many training departments purchase good self-study programs and keep them a secret: The only people in the company who know the programs exist are trainers, who scratch their heads and wonder why nobody seems interested.

An attractive, concise catalog of available courses and their potential applications is a necessity, both for those who recognize their own needs for self-improvement and for those who are responsible for recommending programs to others.

As for those who need to be "sold" instead of simply informed, the objective of any advertising is, of course, to promote the use of the product. Posters near time clocks and in lunch-rooms, paycheck stuffers and in-house newsletters all can attract potential participants. They also help sell the general concept of self-instruction.

Once their interest has been aroused, participants must know what is expected of them. Prior to beginning a program, they should be given a course syllabus that will let them know how much time they have to complete each part, how much written material they are expected to produce, and some methods for *applying* what they learn. A recommended schedule of study provides a valuable framework and allows them to make decisions with open eyes. Without these guidelines, participants make unfounded assumptions about the program—a major contributing cause of low completion rates.

Finally, if at all practical, it's a good idea to bring together everyone taking a course to acquaint them with the goals they share and the objectives the author envisioned. "Everyone" may mean three executives who feel they need better negotiating skills or five secretaries who want to brush up

EXPERIENTIAL TRAINING: LEARNING FROM DOING . . . AND FROM HAVING DONE

Experiential or experience-based training is designed around the twin precepts that a) adults, by virtue of the fact that they've been around for awhile, can learn new lessons from their own life histories and, b) they learn best when what they learn can be related to concrete, personal experiences.

Although it's one of those phrases that tends to mean whatever the trainer wants it to mean—consultant Dugan Laird has observed that "The terms [experiential and experience-based] are not yet terribly well defined"—it is safe to say that in a broad sense, experiential training is a *participative approach* to training design in which learners "do things" and interact with one another rather than sitting and listening while someone lectures. The goals of the activities—especially those encountered early in a session—are to "unfreeze" participants' thinking so they can look objectively at themselves and to give them a fresh experience that can be used by the instructor to help them "relate to" the concepts, ideas or principles that will be discussed or explained later in the training program.

The "fresh experience" is key to what most trainers mean when they talk about experiential training as a specific technique, rather than a general training "style" in which the instructor draws upon the experiences of participants by asking questions, encouraging discussion, and so on. For example, Herb Cohen, author of the best-selling *You Can Negotiate Anything*, often begins a negotiation-skills workshop by asking participants to role play a hiring interview. One person plays the personnel director, the other an engineer being courted by the company. The two are instructed to come to an agreement wherein the engineer is hired and both parties are pleased with the arrangement. Some pairs come to an amicable agreement, some fight, and some break off negotiations altogether.

Later, by referring back to the exercise during the workshop and having participants talk about their *experience* in the role-play situation, Cohen brings a sense of reality, immediacy and credibility to his explanation of the negotiation process. Students are supposed to say to themselves, in effect, "Hey, these ideas must be right! We (or 'those guys across the room') had exactly the experience the instructor's theory predicted."

Donald F. Michalak and Edwin G. Yager have attempted to capture the experiential learning approach in a flow diagram they refer to as the Participative Training Model.

During the *experience phase* trainees can be exposed to a number of trials and tribulations—games, pretests or instrumented feedback—involving peers, superiors, subordinates, customers or even loved ones. The point of the experience phase is to have trainees *do something* that they can refer to during the training to help them grasp—on a personal and perhaps an emotional level—the concepts explained in the program.

Michalak and Yager suggest four rules for selecting and/or structuring an experience for trainees: 1) Experiential exercises should precede the course's content phase; 2) initial experiential exercises should emphasize *process*; that is, they should "require the trainees to become involved in situations entailing the same skills, processes, ideas or attitudes that will be developed in the learning session or skill session that will follow"; 3) the opening exercise should not lead to failure; 4) this first experience "should not be related specifically to the trainees' jobs; it ought to be general in its approach."

It isn't all that easy to build—or even to find—exercises that meet these criteria. As a result, some rather widely traveled experiential exercises are floating around. Open a session on creative thinking with the "Nine Dots," or a team-building session with "Lost on the Moon" or "Desert Survival," and odds are that several of the participants will have seen the exercise before; some will know the solution from memory. And that, of course, defeats the purpose of the exercise.

Michalak and Yager caution that the experience is not an end in itself, but part of the six-step process described in their model. The episode in which the trainee participates is meant to create an awareness of the need to change. The experience generally can't and shouldn't be expected to contain all the elements necessary to produce lasting changes in behavior. They point out that in addition to the experience, it is necessary to provide:

• *Content*—information, ideas, theories or facts the trainees can use as a model against which to analyze their on-the-job behavior and the training experiences.

• *Analysis*—trainees must be guided to some new understanding of their experience, in some sort of query fashion.

• *Generalization/Influence*—trainees need to look at the experience, the content and the analysis, and determine how this new knowledge can be used; what are the implications of the new data back on the job?

• *Practice*—trainees are more likely to use new information or exhibit new behavior back on the job if they experiment with it first in the safe harbor of the training environment.

• *Transfer*—Michalak and Yager caution that new knowledge and skills

on spelling and punctuation.

This meeting also can be used for pre-testing (when appropriate), planning schedules and signing course contracts. Course contracts represent commitments by participants to comply with stated requirements of both quality and quantity. And yes, putting it in writing is important.

So is sharing the experience. Some organizations bring participants in at the program's midpoint to discuss problems, questions, course content or possible applications of what they're learning.

Behavior changes are more likely if the group assembles again at the completion of the course for post-testing (when the content lends itself to testing mastery) and evaluation. A file of trainees' assessments of the course's benefits—and the ease of applying them—serves both the program coordinator and future participants.

Accountability

One surefire method for guaranteeing a high completion rate is a tuition-reimbursement arrangement under which the employee pays the company for the program when signing up for it. Then, upon successful completion (workbooks submitted, improvements in test scores, proof that new skills are being applied on the job or whatever has been agreed upon), the company reimburses the employee.

To make this approach work, the organization must be very specific about what is considered "satisfactory completion" and must be firm in maintaining consistent quality. "Almost complete" and "a little late" are not acceptable for professional credit.

---

will not automatically be exhibited back on the job. All of the classic obstacles to "training transference" apply, as do the classic techniques for getting around those obstacles.

Again, the "activity phase"—the role playing, the exercise, or whatever—is what usually distinguishes "experiential training" as a more or less specific *technique*. In a more general sense, however, the term (and its companion, "experiential learning") refers to the adult-learning concept from which the exercises draw their rationale. If a group of school children play "Desert Survival," they're simply playing a new game. When adults play, the idea is

that they will relate the new experience to the wealth of information they already possess and, with the trainer's help, will benefit much more from the exercise than would the children.

In other words, the purpose of including such exercises in training programs goes beyond the simple desire to introduce variety or active involvement into the learning environment.

Adult educators such as Robert J. Kidd, Malcolm Knowles and K. Patricia Cross, have long emphasized that adults' experiences, their daily interactions with their environment, are an important part of what they bring to a learning situation. It is this wealth

of life experience that experiential training techniques are trying to tap. As Knowles puts it, "To a child, an experience is something that happens to him....But to an adult, his experience is him....An adult is what he has done....Because an adult defines himself largely by his experience, he has a deep investment in its value. And so when he finds himself in a situation in which his experience is not being used, or its worth is minimized, it is not just his experience that is being rejected—he feels rejected as a person."

At the same time, experience *by itself* is often a poor teacher. Harry Miller implies the trainer's role perfectly when he says, "All of us learn poorly, lopsidedly and wrongly from some experiences and not at all from others, because we do not know how to compensate for human frailties, how to frame the kinds of questions which can be asked about an experience to make it more meaningful, or how to look for connections and interrelationships which might be relevant to interpret experience."

A word of caution: Some suggest that making experiential training *work* is a feat akin to catching lightening in a bottle. And indeed, it's a dicey challenge; when an experiential session bombs, it really bombs. But when it works, it is as exciting a training process as there is.

Reprinted from TRAINING, September 1983

Further Reading

Cohen, Herb. *You Can Negotiate Anything* (Lyle Stuart Co., Secaucus, NJ, 1980).

Knowles, Malcolm S. *The Modern Practice of Adult Education* (Association Press, New York, NY, 1970).

Laird, Dugan. *Approaches to Training and Development* (Addison-Wesley, Reading, MA, 1978).

Michalak, Donald F. and Yager, Edwin C. *Making the Training Process Work* (Harper and Row, New York, NY, 1979).

Miller, Harry. *Teaching and Learning in Adult Education* (MacMillan, New York, NY, 1964).

Smith, Robert M. *Learning How to Learn* (Follett Publishing, Chicago, IL, 1982).

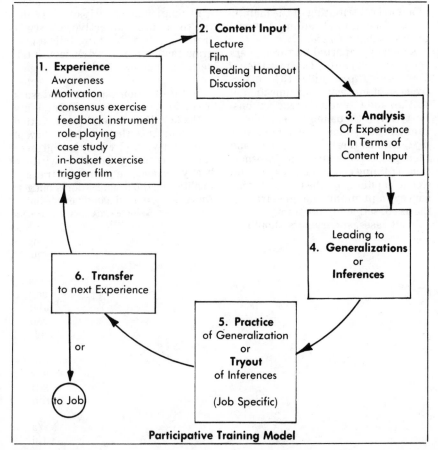

Participative Training Model

In some cases, program publishers will provide an objective set of "completion evaluation" criteria for a fee. Besides saving the training department's time, this avoids getting trainers involved in a possible rejection of submitted material and any resulting resentment. The American Institute of Certified Public Accountants, the Institute of Electrical and Electronics Engineers and the National Management Association are among those who use publisher evaluation as a basis for awarding continuing-education credits.

Motivators

Here are some other accountability techniques.

• *Job advancement*. The use of a self-paced course as a prerequisite for a desired program or promotion can be a powerful incentive. Working together, trainers and managers can develop a grid of short- and long-term self-instructional objectives to meet clearly defined departmental or corporate needs.

Examples of companies that have done this successfully include New York Telephone, which required that all executives who signed up for an accelerated MBA program take a reading-improvement course before receiving permission to attend the program, and Carpenter Technology, which required its representatives to take a course before they were permitted to attend the annual sales meeting. And the meeting itself was a prerequisite for moving up within the ranks of the firm's sales and marketing hierarchy.

• *Performance reviews*. Periodic performance evaluations provide supervisors and managers an opportunity to diagnose reasons for substandard work and to recommend study programs. Again, a contract clarifies the situation by defining specific courses and time frameworks. By signing, the employee indicates an understanding of the terms and a commitment to complete the programs as outlined. By becoming an element in regular performance evaluations, the continuing-education program becomes a positive part of career planning. And self-study is the logical way to offer this individualized training.

• *Supervisor involvement*. The selection of training *possibilities* is a function of the training department. But involving supervisors in choices about their subordinates' training programs is a basic necessity for two reasons.

First, supervisors recognize immediate needs within their own areas of responsibility and expertise. Alert supervisors or managers are aware of individual attitudes, group reactions and lagging productivity. They are invaluable in predicting the level of knowledge at which a subordinate will begin the course, and in developing task analyses, subject-matter analyses and instructional objectives for *selecting* courses—particularly self-instructed courses.

Secondly, supervisors can provide priceless feedback on which training programs seem to pay off in terms of better job performance and which don't—feedback that is as valuable for self-study courses as for classroom programs. When included in the planning stages, supervisors become part of a team contributing to the maintenance of a library of self-instructional programs that get *used*.

A survey, reported on three years ago in the *Journal of Organizational Communications*, judged the effectiveness of internal communication in 40 U.S. and Canadian organizations. Forty-five thousand respondents ranked their immediate supervisors *first*, both as their major sources and their preferred sources of information. Training coordinators would do well to capitalize on the results of this survey in planning and encouraging the use of self-study programs.

In all cases, supervisors should be notified by the training department that their subordinates are taking a self-instructional program, and course participants should know that their supervisors are aware of their involvement. The supervisor should be responsible for monitoring the course, or at least encouraging its completion within the time frame.

But there are other possibilities. Trainers also should distribute course objectives to managers and supervisors. Only then can they anticipate performance changes and recognize them as applications of skills acquired in the program. This involvement also helps differentiate between training objectives (e.g., how to), performance objectives (e.g., acceptable standards) and end results (e.g., *improved* performance).

• *Evaluation sheets*. Some record of participation and the results observed by the supervisor is necessary, of course. Two records are helpful, one to track individual progress and one to help the supervisor and the trainer in evaluating the popularity and usefulness of various programs.

As a matter of fact, follow-up and evaluation by the supervisor after a course has been completed is a vital key to success; follow-up by the trainer is a poor substitute. More record keeping, even by a full-time coordinator, is of little value.

Evaluation by participants is essential to maintain an active self-study training effort. Nothing kills a program faster than word-of-mouth advertising that it's a turkey.

Self-instruction can work and work exceptionally well. But accountability is the key. With careful planning and administration, the self-study concept can offer virtually limitless growth for the training function with no heavy demands on personnel, training facilities or the organization's budget. And that is, indeed, good news.

Reprinted from TRAINING, November 1984

FACT AND FICTION ABOUT INDIVIDUALIZED INSTRUCTION

Most instruction that is labeled 'individualized' really isn't

BY MICHAEL MAGINN

Individualized instruction? You've got to be kidding," said the executive when the training director proposed a new product training course. "That stuff puts everyone to sleep. Herd those new hires into the training center for a couple of weeks and give 'em a little spirit."

And so it goes. It's no secret that individualized instruction is still not fully accepted or understood by many decision-makers. The question is why such a widely used, versatile method of instruction has a tainted reputation in management circles.

What do you say in response to an executive who objects? You might counter with "But individualized instruction is perfect for this new course. The content is filled with details and facts, and you know how incredibly well *that* goes over in a classroom. It's perfect for home study. And as for our technical manuals ... well, if I were that fat, no one would pick me up either."

You'd be making a good point. For detailed information that needs to be retrieved or accessed from time to time before it is transferred to memory, individualized instruction is the key. Relegate to the classroom those nebulous process skills like getting along with your manager, answering customer objections, and persuading your crew to hand in time reports when they're due. These are best taught by role playing, group discussions, case studies, and the like.

"There's nothing *that* wrong with classrooms," says the executive. "I learned a great deal in them."

"And there were many others," you add, "who were lost because the structure and logic of a group lesson were dropped, never to be picked up again. Individualized instruction allows slower students a chance to succeed, a chance to take their time to get the Big Picture. Builds character, self-discipline, too, especially if you tie in some visible reinforcement system when the course is complete. At least, that's the feeling you get from talking to the current proponents of this method," you comment, "even those in the public schools."

"Thunderation on the public schools," your boss exclaims, rising slightly out of his seat. "That stuff is still the best cure for insomnia. Who learns from that programmed gibberish anyway?"

Why do executives protest so much?

Mistaken Identity

One of the by-products of the enthusiastic wave of instructional innovations which emerged in the early 1960's was programmed instruction. Using principles based on operant conditioning research, B. F. Skinner's disciples designed instruction which rather rigidly adhered to three cardinal principles: 1) student participation, which meant "emitting" an active response to a stimulus (usually a blank word to be completed in a sentence); 2) immediate feedback as to the correctness of the response (usually found in a response column under the familiar cardboard answer cover-upper); 3) small, bite-sized chunks of information which contain the one stimulus required for the simple expected response. Crowder subsequently developed a format for branching programmed instruction which used a scrambled text approach, leading students who answer multiple-choice questions to remedial or "Whoops, wrong answer" pages.

Needless to say, properly designed programmed instruction, either linear (Skinnerian) or branching (Crowderian), are effective means of instruction. However, because of the time required to produce instruction true to the rather strict principles of Skinner or the ever-entangling network of Crowder's scrambled pages, fill-in-the-blank counterfeits became popular. Hundreds of "programmed instruction" companies were formed by entrepreneurial educators. Unfortunately, many of the products were less than perfect. Most of them were designed by erasing the key words in a sentence and rewriting them in the page margin. Ideally, good programmed instruction, validated on a specific population, takes about 100 hours of design time for one hour of instruction. Since few organizations can afford that type of process ... well, corners were made to be cut.

What curdles the disposition of many middle-aged executives at the whisper of individualized instruction is the memory of *programmed* instruction which they probably studied in the training programs for their first jobs, back in the early 1960's when PI was the rage. Often, what people remember about PI is boredom, rushing to finish, reading reams of hard-to-read materials, and feeling vaguely like a pigeon in a box.

So, when you hear an executive object to "individualized instruction," find out if it is "programmed instruction" which causes the bad memories.

"Well, if it's not PI, what is it?" asks the manager.

What is Individualized Instruction?

To be sure, programmed instruction (linear or branching) can be used by individuals studying by themselves. However, these forms have evolved greatly over the past decade and a half, incorporating some new techniques and methods indicated by educational research. Today, linear and branching programs can be considered antecedents to a whole category of self-study methods which are systematically planned, contain elements of good instructional design, and which attempt to motivate the student as he learns.

In state of the art design for individualized instruction, more than one medium is often used. The programmed instruction era found a plethora of instruction usually delivered by written materials or (ugh!) teaching machines.

Today, many educators agree that "programming" visual materials alone is difficult at best without some type of supporting medium. For example, a videotape containing narration or case dramatizations can present the elementary concepts behind sophisticated and detailed material. A workbook, designed to interweave between video segments, provides reinforcement, explication, and expansion as well as problem-solving exercises, formative evaluation, or diagnostic tests. This same format can be used with audiotapes and workbooks presenting conceptual information on audiotape immediately followed by a corresponding workbook section filled with structured detail. For other types of learning, audiotapes can provide "talk-through" instruction for a student sitting at the console of a computer or at an engine lathe.

This type of instruction, no matter what the format or medium, should contain the "Basic Three" elements of Skinnerian PI mentioned earlier (active participation, immediate feedback, and small steps or "chunks" of information) in addition to many other principles shown effective by research. Some examples: 1) *Repetition,* the single device that over 75 years of educational research has clearly identified as foolproof; 2) *Direction of students' attention* to certain parts of a visual or to elements of a spoken passage; and 3) *Preparing the learner for instruction* — telling him what you're going to tell him. The alternatives to frames and branches are limited only by the imagination and resources of the training manager or instructional designer.

The myth of individualized instruction as a cheap, fill-in-the-blank method is no longer valid. In fact, as long as the design elements of effective instruction can be built into a program, there is no reason why humor, drama, and other motivating devices can't be used as long as they don't interfere with the instructional content delivery. However, it would be wise for the individual trainer to assess his or his staff's ability to write comedy or drama. Amateurish attempts at humor can be disastrous.

Return on Investment

"Okay," your executive says, "I didn't understand everything you said, but it sounds good. You're the expert. How much is it going to cost?"

Congratulations. Your executive is about to invest a considerable amount of money and resources. You should be prepared to indicate how he will be *saving* money in each of the following areas:

• **One-time expense.** The development of a carefully planned self-study course involves a single expenditure which can be amortized over the projected life of the program. Bringing students to a training center, providing an instructor, and paying for logistical support, travel, and lodging expenses entails a recurring cost *each* time the course is given.

• **Number of students.** Reproduction costs for audiotapes, workbooks, and even filmstrips and videotapes— already relatively inexpensive— become more reasonable as the quantities increase. With group or lecture instruction, the number of students is usually restricted, which means the course may have to be offered more than once.

• **Standardization.** The content is always the same. The only difference will be the experience the student brings to the course and the rate at which he progresses. The problem with group study or even the popular "road show" lectures given at branch offices by a singularly gifted teacher is that it is different each time it is given. While some may feel this "tailors" the instruction to the audience, valuable material is lost to digressions, time pressures, personality problems, etc.

• **High Access to Information.** Because the student usually retains the self-study materials he uses, he will be able to retrieve the *entire* course for review or for use on the job at any time. Also, class scheduling problems (i.e., having personnel in the field waiting several months for a course opening) are eliminated. Individualized instruction allows for flexible scheduling.

• **Time Savings.** Probably the most encouraging research finding involving individualized instruction from an economic point of view is that use of this medium saves a great deal of training time—sometimes up to 50 percent. And, these time savings translate into redirection of man-days for both students and instructors. Put another way, less training time means less time away from the job.

• **Portability.** Certain types of individualized instruction can be taken home by the student or used at a work station, which provides for greater flexibility in implementation. In some cases, this may even be motivational for the student.

"Well, now, Boss," you say with a breath. "Just how lucky can you get? All that time and money saved through a simple format change. Plus, the student gets a chance to work where he wants, at the speed he wants, and he can go through the course until he's got it."

If your executive is like many, he'll have learned his lesson, tailored, as it was, to his individual instructional needs.

Reprinted from TRAINING, January 1977

ONE-ON-ONE TRAINING: A SOLID BET FOR SKILLS

Classrooms may be fine for some topics,
but for teaching tasks
and procedure the personal approach
is hard to beat

BY JEROLD W. WILEY

When it comes to teaching a person to operate equipment or do a specific procedure, often the best method is working alone with the student, one-on-one. Like other training techniques, this has its own special strategies, some of which are more effective than others. One-on-one training is a delicate but often highly productive challenge to your interpersonal skills and instructional expertise. The better you understand the forces at work, the more effective your action can be.

As a one-on-one instructor you must deal with far more than you might imagine. For one thing, you directly influence your students—either negatively or positively—and you foster certain attitudes in them. If you are unhappy with your job or continually gripe about everything, you'd better believe that your student will pick up on these attitudes. Negativity can easily demotivate students, causing them to take a "what's the use?" attitude. They will remember your approach and attitudes long after you're through with them. There is a "snowball" effect. Whether good or bad is up to you.

There are three distinct elements in one-on-one training: preparation and briefing, the training session itself, and debriefing and follow-up. It's easy to lose sight of the first and last, but if you neglect them you imperil all your time and effort.

Preparation and briefing

Before the training session ever begins you should review the student's records. If the student is just entering the one-on-one phase, make sure the necessary documents and basic data are ready. Beyond the first session inspect the record, looking for trends. Notice if the student has made the same error repeatedly and keep this in mind during the training session.

Review the events or specific procedures slated for the training session: It's essential that you be very familiar with what the student will encounter, and it gives you a chance to identify potential problem areas and prepare for them well before they arise. You may want to devise optional situations to help the student work through trouble spots.

Before the training session you must also sit down with your student. Although in some cases a group briefing is enough, more often you should do this one-on-one. Pay attention to four essential points:

1. **Go over the basic elements of the training session.** Discuss new procedures and explain the significant events to watch for. This is crucial in the early stages but becomes less so as the goal of proficiency overtakes the amount of new information presented.

2. **Answer questions about the training to come.** This is not a time to play "I've got a secret." The student should arrive at the training session with correct and complete information. Explain a procedure or concept to the *student's* satisfaction.

3. **Discuss problem trends noted while reviewing the student's records.** Try to find out why the student has had problems in this particular area and offer suggestions to help out. Discuss the possibility of using additional training to correct deficiencies.

4. **Explain how you will conduct the training session.** Under what circumstances will you interrupt to demonstrate new procedures? Will you stop the training if safety conditions warrant or to point out a serious error? Finally, tell the student not to be concerned if you take notes: It doesn't always mean that you are pointing out errors; you might be making positive comments about an exceptional performance.

The training session

Your student should leave the briefing and go into the actual session with a feeling of confidence and a desire to meet the challenge. To be effective, the training session itself should seem like the real thing—there should be ample opportunity to learn by doing. Of course piloting a flight simulator and flying an airplane aren't the same. But even in that kind of situation you shouldn't let your concentration wander from your student. In real-world training you might have to take the controls if there's trouble. Take a low-key approach—be there to answer questions but don't breathe down the student's neck.

In the early sessions you will be more actively involved in the training process. The first time you will demonstrate how a procedure is done. You will move the controls, punch the buttons or turn the knobs. Take each procedure step-by-step and don't rush it. An excellent demonstration at this point could save a lot of grief or anxiety later on. Show the relationship of new tasks to old ones. Explain what you are doing and why you are doing it.

After the demonstration let the student do the task while you coach, if necessary. You may need to go through it several times. Remember, a mistake or error at this point isn't the end of the world. Correct mistakes on the spot; it will help the student remember "how to" instead of "how not to."

If the student has unusual problems, redemonstrate the task with the learner alternately watching and doing. Remember to remain patient and calm, because the trainee may be flustered by now, especially if new to the job. Be positive, offer support and motivate your student. If you establish good rapport at this stage, later training should be a cinch.

When the student shows proficiency in one task, move to the next. With each new task the student will gain confidence, knowledge and proficiency. New tasks will become variations of the old ones. As that happens it isn't necessary to demonstrate the task. Just point out the appropriate controls or describe the procedure and let the student perform it. As with the basic tasks, call attention to any errors immediately.

As the student improves you will be more of an observer than an instructor. In this role, it is imperative to keep good notes. If your student makes a small mistake that doesn't really affect anything, you probably shouldn't interrupt; just make a note of it and cover it during the debriefing. For a serious error, however, you probably should interrupt and make a correction right then. Don't lay down an all-inclusive rule though, because it may be best to let the student continue, especially if the error will be apparent later on.

It often helps to use a question or series of questions to make a point. If you see an error, you might interrupt and ask, "Why did you do that?" or "Are those the correct indications?" This will force the student to review his or her actions

and perhaps see what's wrong—and what it takes to get it right. It also helps the trainee save face while admitting the error.

Praising correct actions is always important, especially during the early stages of training. It will encourage more correct actions. Don't forget that how you say something is at least as important as what you say. Although you may need to be firm in a critical situation, never yell at your student; there is no excuse for being rude and loud. You can win the student's respect by being a professional human being rather than by being a know-it-all. If your object is to put down the trainee by proving how much you know, you're in the wrong business.

Debriefing and follow-up

When the training session is finished, it's important to debrief your student, which essentially involves sharing your notes of mistakes and successes. You can either work from beginning to end or you can cover the errors first and the proper actions next. Either way, the student should leave the debriefing knowing exactly which actions are correct. Remember, identify the incorrect act and tell the student how to do it right. Better yet, have the student explain the proper procedure. If you can use the equipment during debriefing, do so.

In some cases just pointing out the incorrect act may not be enough: You

need to explain the ramifications of continued improper acts. Students normally respond if they can associate the reasons behind doing something a certain way.

Of course, you have to watch out for the trainee who questions everything. This one will drive you crazy with questions about the simplest procedures or unrelated matters. Your best defense is to say you would be willing to discuss the other areas later, but now is the time for the debriefing of this training session.

If the student's pretraining records indicated a problem trend, bring it up now. If you noticed the same error in your training session you may need to think about remedial training. If the deficiency is serious enough, you might have to discuss the problem with your supervisor. On the other hand, if the student did not make the same mistake, make sure you recognize that and offer encouragement.

As soon as possible after the debriefing, record your impressions on the student's training record. Do it while the thoughts are fresh in your mind and you can still decipher your notes.

Being a one-on-one instructor can be very challenging, a rewarding way of helping a student learn. As a highly motivated and competent instructor, you can help your student become a highly motivated and competent operator.

Reprinted from TRAINING, August 1981

MENTORS AND PROTEGES: HOW TO BUILD RELATIONSHIPS THAT WORK

Organizations can develop management talent by hooking up promising young rookies with seasoned veterans

BY MATTHEW J. HENNECKE

The good sense and practicality of the experienced and knowledgeable person teaching the inexperienced and uninformed person was probably never better expressed than by Sophocles in his Greek tragedy *Antigone:*

> *The ideal condition*
> *would be, I admit, that men*
> *should be right by instinct.*
> *But since we are all likely*
> *to go astray, the reasonable*
> *thing is to learn from those*
> *who can teach.*

Unfortunately, in many organizations veteran managers and executives who best represent "those who can teach," do not or will not teach. As a result, many companies are destined to write tragedies of their own in red ink, with poor leadership playing a lead role.

Why is it that seasoned managers who have the greatest knowledge of the organizational machinery, the most perceptive grasp of the market or the sharpest insight into the company's mission are often so hesitant to become mentors?

There probably are two main answers. First, many would-be mentors are aware of the potential problems associated with mentor/protege relationships and are justifiably (though often overly) cautious. For them, the risks outweigh the advantages. Second, many *potential* mentors are simply not sure how to become mentors. They are interested, but need some guidance.

Who is the obvious candidate to provide that guidance for potential mentors and to outline a pathway through the obstacles and drawbacks of the mentor/protege relationship? The organization's HRD specialist, of course. Mentoring, in fact, is a classic example of a form of human resources development that usually takes place outside the direct purview of the HRD department, but which can benefit greatly from that department's guidance. And from a political point of view, the HRD director fighting for greater visibility and recognition for the training department could do worse than to offer its expertise to mentors—who tend to be the organization's movers and shakers.

What can the HRD department tell potential mentors about the pitfalls that may lie in wait and how to avoid them? The following list of problems and solutions is far from exhaustive, but it covers some of the major drawbacks associated with the mentor/protege relationship. Perhaps the best way to keep things in perspective is to address the issues as if you, the reader, were the potential mentor. What would you worry about?

Potential problem 1: Selecting a protege

The first major risk encountered in the building of a mentor/protege relationship involves the selection of your protege. Some organizations remove the burden of selection from the mentor—and avoid the problems caused by those not selected—by assigning *all* new employees above a certain grade level to preselected mentors. The catch is that such formalization often reduces the intimacy of the relationships, which many argue is of singular importance to mentoring. Formalized mentoring programs are often difficult to administer, and there seem to be as many documented failures as successes.

As in any other selection process, there is always the risk that your initial judgment of a person will be inaccurate and that your protege will fail to meet your expectations or the organization's. If this occurs, you may feel torn between a desire to end the relationship and a desire to justify your initial decision by continuing it—especially if others are aware of your attempt at mentoring.

Solution: Prevention clearly is the best cure. Choose your protege carefully, paying special attention to *demonstrated* skills and abilities. By taking the time to observe and evaluate the potential protege, you will reduce the chances of selecting a poor performer.

What should you look for? Generally, proteges should fit the following general profile:

- Optimum age: 22-39 (but be wary of violating age-discrimination laws).
- One or more years with the organization.
- Demonstrated skills and abilities; consistent high performance.
- High level of technical or managerial competence.
- Willingness to learn and take direction from others.

Suppose that despite your careful selection, the relationship fails to work out. Obviously, a decision to drop a protege should not be made hastily; in fact, your continued guidance and help may be the stimulus this person needs to become a successful performer. But if you feel you must end it, the most graceful and painless method is to reduce the frequency of meetings with the protege gradually, thereby allowing the relationship to die a natural death.

Potential problem 2: Employee/colleague resentment

Suppose that employees not selected as proteges resent the relationship you form with the chosen one and create problems for you, the protege or the organization. What if your colleagues or peers, who feel you may be mentoring their replacements, also resent you, your protege and the idea of mentoring in general?

Solution: Keeping a low profile on your mentor/protege relationship will do much to reduce the likelihood of trouble from both groups—the protege's colleagues and your own. If they don't know about the relationship, they can't resent it. This does not mean that you and your protege should meet clandestinely; the point is that there is no reason to broadcast the fact that you are the mentor of some rising star. Mentoring relationships should be private and low-key.

You might go a step farther and refrain from using the terms "mentor" and "protege" in connection with your relationship. Be satisfied with "developing" your protege, and be willing to develop others who may be interested in learning from your experience.

Potential problem 3:
The mentor vs. the supervisor

In many cases a protege's mentor is also his or her supervisor, so there is no danger of conflicting advice or alliances. When the mentor is someone other than the supervisor, however, things can get sticky. A few possibilities: a) The protege may try to use the mentor in an effort to gain some advantage over the supervisor; b) The supervisor may feel that his or her authority and control are being undermined; c) The mentor may make demands on the protege that conflict with the demands of the protege's supervisor.

Solution: Effective communication will reduce if not eliminate the possibility of conflict between mentor and supervisor. By emphasizing to the protege that your role as mentor is to counsel and advise, and not to second-guess or overrule the supervisor, you can squelch from the start any ideas the protege may have about trying to play you and the supervisor against each other.

As a mentor, you also might want to communicate openly and frequently with your protege's supervisor. Explain your role and assure the supervisor that his or her authority will be maintained.

Finally, don't make demands on your protege that conflict, or appear to conflict, with the demands of the supervisor. This includes demands on the protege's time. Meet frequently with your protege, but remember always that your student must continue to perform effectively in his or her

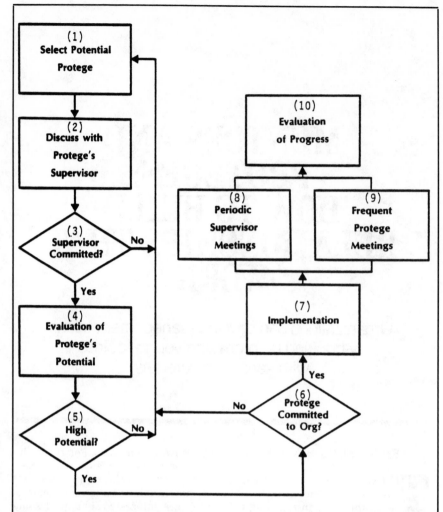

Flowchart demonstrating author Hennecke's "fairly formal" strategy for initiating and maintaining a rewarding mentor/protege relationship. For details, see "Mentoring: How to begin."

current job.

Potential problem 4:
The crown prince/princess syndrome

In its broadest sense, the Crown Prince syndrome involves the potential resentment of supervisors, colleagues and other employees; but specifically, it refers to the possible perception of the protege that since he or she has been "chosen" as a rising star, there is no further need to perform on the job at the same high level that prompted your selection in the first place.

Solution: Again, the best approaches to this problem are preventative and involve communication. First, don't refer to your association as a "mentor/protege" relationship. For some, the terms "mentor" and "protege" are misunderstood to mean "king" and "heir apparent." Secondly, there is nothing wrong with discussing this issue with your protege early in the relationship. You can empha-

size that your assistance and counsel have a requisite: continued performance on the job.

If at any point in the relationship performance levels do seem to be declining, discuss the matter with your protege. But do not automatically assume that the decline is due to the mentoring relationship. Bear in mind that other factors are possible.

Potential problem 5:
Cross-gender mentoring

A mentor-protege relationship can be almost invisible in an organization, except when the pair happens to be of opposite sexes. Then there's a strong risk that the sexual issue will arise in the minds of onlookers.

This possibility concerns both the mentor and the protege, and is further complicated by the possibility that both parties' spouses may resent the close relationship, especially if the pair travels together.

Solution: This may be the most dif-

MENTORING: HOW TO BEGIN

BY MATTHEW HENNECKE

In many ways mentor/protege relationships are like other close relationships: They often begin spontaneously, with little or no preplanning, no step-by-step instructions, no manual. Nevertheless, a certain amount of strategy comes into play in the development of rewarding mentoring relationships.

The chart on previous page demonstrates a fairly formal strategy tailored especially for the mentor who wants to invlove the protege's supervisor in the relationship.

If the mentor is already quite familiar with the protege and needs no current or ongoing performance information from the protege's supervisor—or if, for some reason, you prefer to leave the supervisor out of it—a less-formal approach will serve just as well. And, in fact, first-time mentors probably are well advised to choose a protege they know fairly well.

If the mentor is the protege's supervisor, the less-formal approach obviously applies as well. But most of the steps in the flowchart must be completed regardless.

Step 1: Select potential protege

On a sheet of paper, jot down the names of individuals in your organization: a) with whom you are acquainted or with whom you come in contact on a regular basis; b) who are newer to the organization and younger than you; and c) who are considered "comers" in the organization.

Review the list and narrow it down to one or two individuals you would most like to help develop. Be sure to save your list because, as the flowchart indicates, you may have to eliminate your first choice.

Step 2: Discuss intentions with protege's supervisor

You probably should not refer to your intended developmental assistance of the supervisor's subordinate as "mentoring." Merely explain that you would like to get the subordinate involved in some additional developmental activities—separate from the ones the supervisor should already have initiated. Assure supervisors that:

• Their authority and control over the subordinate will not be undermined.

• The additional development will not create a time problem for the subordinate

• You will follow up periodically to answer questions, listen to concerns and discuss the protege's performance levels.

Step 3: Is the supervisor committed?

Without supervisor commitment it might be difficult to initiate and maintain a mentoring relationship, especially if you have discussed your intentions with the supervisor and he or she is against it.

If the supervisor dislikes the idea, you may wish to select another potential protege. Obviously, such a retreat is unfair to the potential protege, but so is a mentoring relationship that makes an enemy of the supervisor.

The supervisor may have a good reason for opposing the relationship. Perhaps a special project or some other circumstance makes mentoring temporarily inappropriate. If such is the case, yield to the supervisor's judgment. If, however, you feel the supervisor's reasons are inappropriate (jealousy, fear, etc.), you may wish to get the supervisor involved in some kind of management training or counseling program. In either case you should probably select another potential protege.

Steps 4/5: Evaluation of protege's potential

Determining "high potential" is probably the most subjective aspect of mentoring, but it is a necessary step. You want to give your knowledge of the organization to those who will be able to appreciate and grasp the implications of the information you provide and use that information effectively as they advance in the organization.

The best way, perhaps, to determine whether the protege has "high potential" is to focus attention on *both* the protege's demonstrated performance and his or her behavior. The supervisor's involvement is important here because he or she probably is in the best position to evaluate the protege's talents.

Step 6: Is the protege committed to the organization?

This question will help you and the supervisor focus attention on the career goals of the potential protege. Obviously, if the protege does not intend to stay with the organization, your time will be better spent developing someone else.

Step 7: Implementation

The preliminaries are out of the way and now you are ready to initiate contact with the person or people you have selected. So as not to create concerns in the mind of the protege or suspicion in the minds of others, you should increase your contact subtly. Mentoring relationships are not formulated overnight.

Begin to involve your proteges in some of your decisions and in the company's plans. Solicit their opinions on tough decisions. This provides a means of evaluating their grasp of issues and concerns, and also stimulates their thinking along organizational, rather than departmental or functional, lines. Let your proteges do important research for you, submit proposals, conduct meetings, act as sounding boards, challenge your thinking—anything that will help them begin to develop a holistic sense of the organization.

Steps 8/9: Meetings

Steps eight and nine appear together on the flowchart because they are ongoing in nature. Frequent meetings with your protege are essential if you want to develop an intimate mentoring relationship. Early in the relationship you will probably have to initiate most of the contact. Later, as the protege begins to feel more comfortable about the relationship, he or she probably will begin seeking you out for advice and counsel.

It is a good idea to meet periodically with the protege's supervisor to discuss progress and performance. Check to make sure your protege's performance levels are not declining

Step 10: Evaluation of progress

After you get comfortable with the relationship (it may take several months), and the continued development of your protege falls into a steady routine, ask yourself some questions:

• How do you feel about your mentoring relationship? Why?

• How do you think your protege views the relationship?

• Does the relationship seem to be all give and no take, or are you benefiting from it as well?

• Is your protege better able to handle organizational challenges now than when the relationship began?

• Do you really want to continue this relationship? Why?

If you find you still are enthusiastic about your new role as a mentor, you may want to consider selecting another protege to develop while you maintain your first.

Reprinted from TRAINING, July 1983

ficult problem you can face as a mentor. Obviously, the most clear-cut solution is to refrain from becoming the mentor of someone of the opposite sex. However, this "simple" solution can cause other problems. Senior management, which probably represents the best pool of potential mentors, is still largely male in most organizations. Cross-gender mentoring is one effective way to rectify that imbalance. And if mentor/protege relationships are recognized as a method by which your organization develops management talent, it is clearly discriminatory to "lock out" one sex from such relationships.

A 1981 survey by Lawton Fitt and Derek Newton found that rumors and innuendo *could* be minimized when mentors and proteges involved in cross-gender relationships were careful to keep those relationships strictly on a business level. The best solution, in other words, may simply be professional conduct by both parties.

Another possible solution is for you to become the mentor of more than one protege and to meet with them in a group for regular coaching sessions. This can practically eliminate sexual innuendo, but the intimacy of a one-on-one relationship will be minimized as well.

Potential problem 6:
Poor advice

The advice and counsel you give to your protege is based on your best estimation of where the organization is going and how the protege can best develop to help the organization get there. Because the direction and missions of some organizations are as subject to change as the weather, it is possible that even the most perceptive mentor will give some poor career advice to the protege.

Solution: Encourage your protege to seek advice from a variety of sources; avoid confining your protege's growth potential to your own limitations. Remember to explain the *basis* of your advice and counsel, and urge

---

SHOULD SUPERVISORS BE MENTORS?

BY MATTHEW HENNECKE

Surveys have indicated that nearly half of the managers and executives who become mentors have their own subordinates for proteges. So as you go "shopping" for a potential protege, don't overlook candidates from among your own ranks. That supervisors or managers would become the mentors of their own subordinates seems only natural, and probably should be encouraged.

But there are two major arguments against having your own subordinate as your protege. Both should be considered before you make a decision you may regret.

First, it is difficult to become a subordinate's mentor without creating resentment among other subordinates. Second, because you, as a supervisor, probably administer rewards and punishments to your subordinates, the intimacy associated with mentoring relationships might not be easily achieved.

You are in the best position to judge the degree to which these potential problems may apply in your case. But do take an objective look at your situation before you attempt to become the mentor of one of your direct subordinates.

Reprinted from TRAINING, July 1983

---

the protege to seek other opinions before making any major decisions.

Potential problem 7:
The protege may advance beyond you

The whole point of this relationship is that your counsel and coaching will be instrumental in helping your protege advance in the organization. What if the protege ultimately advances beyond you? For most mentors this "relationship shift" is at least disconcerting and often an outright insult. After all, you were the one who developed the protege in the first place. Why weren't you promoted? And if there is a risk that your protege eventually may wind up with the job you want, why should you cut your own throat by becoming a mentor in the first place?

Solution: Analyze your feelings about this potential problem and decide whether you can accept the possibility before you become a mentor. The greatest compliment that can be paid to a mentor is for the organization to recognize a protege by promoting him or her to increasingly challenging positions. Would you be able to think of it in that light?

The list goes on

Any number of additional problems may arise in the course of a mentor/protege relationship. To mention a few:
- Mentors may try to mold proteges in their own image.
- Mentors may exploit the relationships for fame and fortune.
- Mentors may damage their own performance—or their own careers—through excessive devotion to the needs of their proteges.
- Proteges may become greedy or demanding; or they may display clinging admiration, self-denial or arrogant ingratitude.
- Unhealthy competition may develop between mentor and protege.

The vital point for the HRD specialist to get across to potential mentors is that the advantages to mentor/protege relationships outweigh the potential pitfalls—not vice versa. None of these problems is unsolvable, and most need never arise. Almost all of them can be anticipated and headed off by simple, honest communication that establishes the ground rules and clarifies the concerns of the mentor, the protege and the organization.

Reprinted from TRAINING, July 1983

JOB AIDS: IMPROVING PERFORMANCE WITHOUT FORMAL TRAINING

Job aids may be the most practical, flexible and cost-effective training medium for complex jobs

BY PAUL C. NASMAN

The training situation we find in branch banking and bank operations is similar to many other "soft skill" industries: pressure to complete the job, high turnover, rapid change, shortage of qualified supervisors, and a centralized training department responsible for remote locations that may number in the hundreds.

The reality in this situation is training on the job. Supervisors and officers are too busy solving problems to function as mentors, and no one can afford more than a few minutes away from his or her work. But the training must be done. In banking, the consequences of error can be enormous, ranging from a rejected item to a lost customer to the improper transfer of millions of dollars.

Job aids, essentially step-by-step task summaries, may be the most practical, flexible and cost-effective training media banks can develop. And California banks are finding that such aids meet many training needs.

Traditional approaches impractical

"In most cases, it's best to look at job aids before going to manuals," says Gayle Coates, vice-president in charge of Wells Fargo Bank's retail bank training department at its San Francisco headquarters.

Coates points to two major trends that have redefined the nature of retail banking jobs, making traditional classroom training impractical and challenging the wisdom of developing instruction manuals to teach branch employees their jobs.

First, the introduction of computers and data processing has fragmented job functions into specialized tasks that are more related to computer routines than they are to each other. The employee who formerly learned one job function from beginning to end now must perform a combination of tasks from various job functions. Many of these tasks are detailed, and accuracy is always a prime ingredient. Moreover, employees in different branches often perform different combinations of tasks, making it difficult to develop comprehensive training manuals for specific jobs.

Secondly, banking services have multiplied in number and diversity, with new services being introduced all the time. A bank may have more than 20 kinds of time deposits and checking accounts, each governed by a different set of regulations, and various other services, such as coupon redemption, travelers checks, credit cards and overdraft protection.

Consequently, bank employees have more to do and more to remember than they used to. Some transactions may not occur frequently, but employees must be able to handle all of them and follow correct procedures when they do occur.

Confronted with these realities, training departments must decide how to teach each task — up front in a comprehensive training program, on the job as each task comes up or not at all.

Wells Fargo developed a "Student Loans" job aid, illustrating how job aids in general can solve this training dilemma. Many of the bank's retail branches receive applications from students for state-guaranteed loans during two application periods twice a year. The application forms, though not complex, must be completed accurately by branch personnel. Errors or omissions cause the application to be returned to the bank for correction, and the loan deadline may be missed.

The consequence for the student is not getting the desired loan; the consequence for the bank is losing a future customer. Because state student-loan regulations are constantly changing, bank personnel, especially in branches that receive only occasional student applications, were often uncertain how to proceed.

To correct this situation, the retail bank training department developed a checklist job aid summarizing all the requirements for completing a student-loan application and following through the application process. The job aid ensures that bank personnel, even in branches that process only one or two applications a year, will be able to handle the application process right the first time.

As the regulations governing the loan program change, the training department can easily revise the job aid. Branch personnel no longer have to sort through circulars that drift in announcing changes in the loan process. And loan officers are confident that they are following the correct procedures.

Complex tasks made simpler

Anyone who has worked in a bank has probably experienced the frustration of trying to find information in a two-foot-thick policy manual. And once the sought-for information is located, translating it into clear directions on "how to do the job" is yet another matter. A well-designed job aid, in contrast, selects the information necessary to complete a specific task, organizes this information into a step-by-step format and communicates it in clear, concise language comprehensible to the employee who must perform the task.

Another Wells Fargo job aid, "Teller's Cash Activity," illustrates how this directness makes a job aid an effective teaching tool. Teller's cash activity, the daily reconcilement of actual cash to general ledger cash amounts, is an essential activity in any retail bank. It also is a difficult job to teach a new person. At Wells Fargo, experienced branch employees used to explain the process to the trainee. But even though an experienced person could perform the job readily, he or she often had a difficult time explaining the process clearly.

The problem was complicated by the fact that the function itself was not well-defined; each branch had a different way of arriving at the same results, often by taking shortcuts or doing several things at one time.

Wells Fargo tackled the problem by organizing teller's cash activity into several basic tasks and using a job aid to outline step-by-step procedures. Although the suggested procedures did not necessarily represent how experienced people actually did the job, the job aid successfully simplified the procedures so that trainees could learn and understand them as they performed them.

"A good job aid forces you to simplify," states Coates, and she maintains this is something seldom done in the course of writing a manual. Developing the "Teller's Cash Activity" job aid required the bank to look at all the pieces of a complex process and reformulate them in straightforward terms. In effect, this job aid helped to create procedures for a function that previously had not been well thought out.

The extensive use of job aids appears to be cost-effective. Coates estimates the cost of providing job aids to Wells Fargo's 400-branch system at less than five cents per job aid, after initial development. This low distribution cost justifies sending complete, updated sets of all job aids to every branch twice a year. This reminds branch officers that the job aids are there to help them and supplies each branch with a current set for reference. The branches then can order additional job aids through the bank's supply department.

Indeed, job aids are assuming a significant place alongside the standard operating manuals in many banks. Wells Fargo sends out complete sets of their 30 or so job aids in a display box to be used right along with their procedures manuals. In fact, says Coates, "Someday we're going to have job aids on all the detailed jobs covered in the manuals."

Another large California bank is currently developing job aids for all the major functions in their branch banking offices, too. These job aids will be integrated into the bank's existing procedure manuals, serving both as official procedures documentation and the potential core of clerical and management training programs.

As part of this project, the bank surveyed the reactions of supervisors and trainees to a test batch of job aids. The vast majority of trainees felt the job aids helped them understand the work they were doing. The trainees followed the job aids easily, and they learned the jobs well enough to feel comfortable doing them without assistance. Supervisors pointed to coverage of essential functions and features, reduction of training time and usefulness in cross-training as key benefits of the job aids.

These creative solutions illustrate job aids' inherent flexibility. They can serve as training support, reference material and control documents. They are cost-effective for both continuous use and occasional reference. Their simplified step-by-step, task-by-task design makes them ideal for complex or rapidly changing procedures. And their compactness serves well for overview or summary documents. Job aids may well be the most useful tools in the bank trainer's kit.

WELLS FARGO BANK
TELLER'S CASH ACTIVITY

OVERVIEW

The Teller's Cash Activity (TCA) reconciles the actual cash in the Branch with the figures listed in the general ledger cash accounts. In the six-step reconciliation process, you balance the TCA RECAP sheet to the Daily Statement of Condition. Each of these steps is a <u>bank requirement.</u> As a reminder they are printed in red.

Step 1: Prepare a TCA RECAP sheet.

Step 2: Clear POD correction totals.

Step 3: Clear teller's pay totals.

Step 4: Balance the Trial Journal and Balance Sheet to the TCA RECAP.

Step 5: RECAP and balance total cash on hand in the branch to the total on the Statement of Condition.

Step 6: Process appropriate clearing adjustments and customer deposit errors through POD.

STEP 1

Prepare a Teller's Cash Activity (TCA) RECAP sheet. (The SOM states that this RECAP must be run at the end of each day's activity.)

OVERVIEW

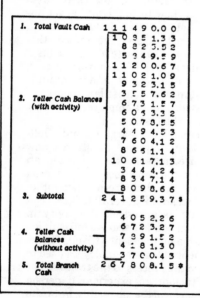

The RECAP sheet summarizes the actual cash on hand in the branch. The remainder of the TCA process involves reconciling the totals of this RECAP sheet to the figures listed on the Trial Journal and Balance List.

1. List the total vault cash.

2. Add to this each teller's actual cash balance (<u>only</u> for the tellers who had cash activity for that day) using the Teller's Balance Sheet as the data source.

3. Subtotal the amounts in 1. and 2.

4. Add to this subtotal each teller's actual cash balance for tellers who <u>did not</u> have cash activity for that day.

5. Total the amounts in 3. and 4.

Quick to read, easy to use. This Teller's Cash Activity job aid organizes a critical cash accounting procedure into six basic steps. (Only the first page is shown.)

Reprinted from TRAINING, December 1979

PERFORMANCE AIDS: HOW TO MAKE THE MOST OF THEM

What do mileage charts, do-it-yourself manuals, checklist, schematic diagrams and conversion tables have in common?

BY JOEL RAKOW

What do you do when paper jams in your friendly photocopy machine? Stomp and curse? Call the repair service? Or read the instructions mounted on the inside? If you choose the latter you must rely on a performance aid—the words and pictures developed to walk you through the quick-fix process. But the aid you see inside the copier is only one of many types of performance aids (this one's called a *proceduralized aid*) that trainers use to convey information.

Most training professionals know performance aids can substitute for formal training in some instances. Aids also are effective memory joggers for infrequently performed tasks —like fixing the copier.

Less obvious, though, is the fact that there are several different types of performance aids, each with various formats and each with specific training applications. How can a performance aid work for training problem X? What type of aid is appropriate? What format should it have—a checklist, a chart, a sample form? And, how will it be used? Answers to these questions will help you select and use performance aids more imaginatively and effectively.

There are five basic kinds of performance aids, as shown in Figure 1. This "Aid to Performance Aids" identifies the common types of performance aids and describes the attributes of each. Typical formats for each type of aid are listed along with

guidelines for selecting when to use each type.

It is important to recognize the difference between an aid's format and its type. Different formats determine how an aid is used on the job, even for an identical task. For example, a checklist of the necessary steps for a task could be used either before or

after completing the job as a refresher or a reminder. By contrast you'd rarely use a computational worksheet at any time other than while performing the task. Nonetheless both formats fall into the cueing category; they signal specific action without providing step-by-step instructions.

On the other hand, the difference between types of aids is crucial to job performance. Each type of aid functions in only one way during training.

The type of performance aid determines what information is provided for the trainee while the format determines how the trainee will use the aid on the job. In either case, which type you choose and, perhaps to a lesser extent which format, greatly affects the success of your training program.

Example style performance aids are common in many areas of everyday life. They can be found in the appendices of many dictionaries, and in brochures from banks, insurance companies and other businesses which require customers to complete information forms. A straightforward form letter serves as an example aid for the sales representatives of a major computer firm. It not only illustrates the format and general tone of an introductory let-

FIGURE 1. AN AID TO PERFORMANCE AIDS

TYPE	ATTRIBUTES	TYPICAL FORMATS	WHEN TO USE
Example	Illustrates responses required to complete a task	Forms filled in with correct information or sample of document (letter, etc.)	When format or location of information is important
Cueing	Signals a specific action without providing step-by-step directions. Also, directs attention to specific characteristics of objects, procedures, situations or information	Checklists, worksheets, using photo-diagrams, arrows, underlining or circles, task lists	When each step in a several-step procedure is relatively simple, but an error will result if a step is out of sequence. Also, with lengthy or seldom-used procedures
Association	Relates unknown information to existing or already known conditions or information	Conversion tables, graphs, code books, reference documents	When information must be transformed for use in predictably different environments or when the conversion process is not important
Proceduralized	Provides pictures and text in a programmed sequence that both illustrates and describes each step in a procedure	Do-it-yourself repair books for cars, bikes, appliances and so on	When training for skills in the manipulation of objects, materials or equipment
Analog	Provides information that cannot be presented directly	Schematic drawings, organization charts, flow charts, formulas, equations and symbolic logic	When correct job performance requires conceptual knowledge of organization, structure, relationship or flow

ter, it also uses a number indexing system to describe several key objectives of such a letter and to locate where the objectives are satisfied.

Cueing aids are also fairly common. In their least developed form they can be shopping lists, "to do" lists or any simple checklist. Figure 2 shows a cueing aid designed to lead sales representatives of a major soft drink company through a fairly complex pricing computation. The form was designed because the sales representatives needed to evaluate the figures of different retailers who independently set their own prices. To use this form they simply filled in the blanks and performed the calculations.

Association aids are great if you must organize large quantities of information such that specific information can be isolated. Examples of association aids include metric conversion tables and mileage charts that list the distance between several cities. Figure 3 is a similar association aid that helps a major communications firm market its products to the hospital industry. It identifies several communications activities that exist in a hospital admissions department. For each activity the sales representative can find opportunities for improvement, specific communication needs, possible solutions, the impact of the solution and suggestions for calculating that impact. Aids like this not only help train new sales representatives, they make it easier for experienced reps to develop sales strategies .

Proceduralized aids are becoming increasingly popular, especially in do-it-yourself repair manuals. In many cases, such aids can completely replace the need for training. Although expensive and time-consuming to develop, they can have long-term cost benefits. Many manufacturers

supply such aids to reduce their customers' demands for education and support.

Some companies modify this format by producing audiocassettes that contain a large part of the instructional content. Used in this way, the instruction manual stands alone as a cueing aid, simply signaling each step in the operating procedure. This design eliminates extraneous information when the trained operator needs only reference and not instruction.

Analog aids are familiar to most of us in the form of organizational and flow charts or schematic drawings. These aids represent large quantities of verbal or conceptual information that's difficult to communicate effectively. Although it is possible to communicate verbally everything such a chart represents, it would be extremely difficult. Using this kind of diagramming both to plan and communicate has led to many technological advances. For trainers, analog aids are excellent in both front-end analysis and instruction.

Each type of performance aid provides special advantages over others. It makes good sense to spend plenty of time choosing the best one for your application. Think about what kind of information you need to present and how it will be used. The aid you pick will have a substantial impact on job performance.

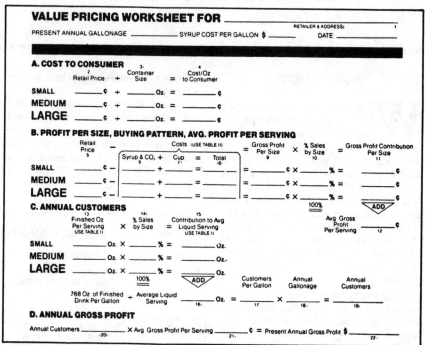

Figure 2.– *This worksheet exemplifies a cueing aid. It signals the calculation of each component in a seven-step process.*

Figure 3.– *This association aid relates information about the primary communication activities of the admissions department in large hospitals to the sales needs and resources of sales representatives for a major communications firm.*

Department Operation Analysis Chart: Admissions

PRIMARY ACTIVITIES	IDENTIFY RESPONSIBLE PERSONNEL	PROBLEMS OR OPPORTUNITIES FOR IMPROVEMENT	COMMUNICATIONS NEEDS	POSSIBLE SOLUTIONS	POTENTIAL IMPACTS	RELEVANT COST/REVENUE FACTORS NECESSARY TO COMPUTE TANGIBLE BENEFITS
• Receive admission requests from Doctor's offices and information requests from patients.		• Doctors (patients) encounter difficulty reaching Admissions through hospital switchboard or due to busy indication from admissions	• Ability to receive and originate calls from (to) patients, doctors' offices for Admissions	• Direct Inward Dialing • Hands-free Headsets • Directory Listing • Additional Lines	• Improves public image.	• Do not quantify.
					• Easier access to Doctor/patient relieves switchboard.	• Quantify by conducting a Traffic Study Analysis.
• Fill out admissions forms for patients prior to admission.		• Admissions Clerks spend time unnecessarily in correcting errors on patient's admissions forms created when patients fill out forms and return them by mail.	• Communicate directly with patients to reduce errors and administrative time involved in check-in procedures.	• Pre-admission telephone procedures	• Improves efficiency of the Admissions department.	• Do not quantify.
		• Admissions personnel are delayed in contacting patients due to difficulty in dialing outside calls, both local and long distance.	• Ability to receive and originate calls from (to) patients, doctors' offices for admission and P.A.T. information.	• D.O.D. • Additional lines • Touch-tone®	• Easier access to Doctor/patient relieves administrative time.	• Do not quantify.
			• Foreign Exchange Lines			• Examine account records.

Reprinted from TRAINING, September 1981

HOW CROSS-TRAINING PROVIDES ON-THE-JOB SKILL DEVELOPMENT

Don't undervalue this simple and relatively inexpensive means of assuring a constant supply of well-trained people

BY JACK J. PHILLIPS

I wish John and Karen could swap jobs," daydreams a harried supervisor. *"Then if one was out, the other could fill in temporarily. But right now, we're too busy. A job swap would hurt our performance. I'll try to arrange it when things slow down a little."*

That supervisor's reaction is shared by many who have considered job rotation. The results, unfortunately, may also be predictable. Let's say John is an ambitious employee who has potential to move up in the organization. He's been on his job long enough to master it. A challenge is what he's looking for, but no promotion is available for him now. Karen, too, can handle her job completely. And she would also like to move up.

The swap refused, John (it could as easily be Karen, or both) soon becomes disappointed with his career opportunities and begins searching for another job, eventually leaving the company for what he hopes will be a better opportunity. Now the supervisor is forced to put Karen on John's job and hurriedly replace her with someone new. Performance goes down until both Karen and her replacement are trained.

Who loses in this situation? Maybe everyone. The company loses a valuable employee. Productivity suffers. And John—and Karen—may be dissatisfied with their new positions. The problem could have been avoided if the supervisor had let Karen and

John swap jobs. This would have kept John with the company. Both he and Karen would have felt a sense of achievement from their new responsibilities. And both would have become more valuable employees for mastering another job in the organization.

Too often supervisors and managers get caught up in day-to-day performance and lose sight of the long-range development of their staffs. Every organization is looking for effective, inexpensive development programs. On-the-job training is one of the most effective opportunities for employee development, and job rotation is just one form of cross-training.

Cross-training involves preparing employees to handle different jobs within the work unit, department, division or company. Almost any job has potential for cross-training, but some are better suited than others. Among the best cross-training prospects are:

Critical jobs. Every organization has jobs which are critical to operation, key jobs upon which productivity and continuity depend. When someone is absent, these positions must be filled with trained replacements. An example would be a production scheduler responsible for arranging the work of many other employees.

High-turnover jobs. In some situations, turnover is simply a given. These jobs are usually important and must be filled quickly. Many banks, for instance, experience high turnover among tellers. It is mandatory to

have replacements ready to fill in and keep things running smoothly when there is an absence. Cross-training is an excellent way to prepare a number of people to take on the teller's job.

Jobs held by mature employees. Positions held by employees nearing retirement may be good candidates for cross-training. The job will need to be filled someday and it's best to groom a trained replacement before that day comes, especially at a time when it's increasingly difficult to predict precisely when someone will retire.

High skill jobs. Jobs requiring months or even years of preparation are good cross-training prospects. An organization cannot afford to have an interruption in performance while this extended training is taking place, and it cannot count on finding qualified applicants in the job market. Cross-training prepares someone to step in before a replacement is needed.

Cross-training methods

There are many ways to accomplish cross-training within an organization. To begin with, there's the job rotation option we began with. This involves rotating two or more people at the same time, with each taking on new responsibilities. These can be permanent transfers or transfers for a specified period. The inspection department of one manufacturing firm, for example, has several supervisors who manage the employees inspecting the work at different stages in the production process. These supervisors are rotated systematically to give them exposure to different kinds of inspection problems. A large agricultural company recently rotated its employment and training managers, giving each a new challenge in the opportunity to learn the other's job.

An internal lateral replacement involves filling a vacancy through a transfer from within the work unit or department. Filling from within allows the individual to gain more experience and knowledge, and without the orientation time involved when bringing in someone from the outside. The team can continue functioning while a new arrival works in at a lower level. The promoted employee will be unfamiliar with some duties of the new job, but may already have most of the skills needed to handle it.

Part-time or temporary job rotation allows two people to swap activities for part of the week, or to train one another in certain duties of their jobs. This could also involve a temporary fill-in on a cross-training or rotational assignment. Under this arrangement, one or more individuals are periodically learning a new job or parts of a job. For example, one organization temporarily assigns district sales managers to corporate sales management jobs when a headquarters office manager is on vacation. This not only provides cross-training for district sales managers, it also improves the cooperation and working relationship between field and headquarters.

There are also cross-training methods involving only one employee at a time. As a part-time arrangement, one employee can learn parts of another job on a scheduled basis, usually a set number of hours per week. This has the added benefit of providing some assistance in areas where it's needed. In one organization a training specialist spends four hours a week cross-training in the wage and salary administration department. The training specialist handles routine duties and selected projects to prepare for possible assignment in another area; the wage and salary department gets the bene-

fit of some additional manpower.

Under a partial responsibility shift, additional responsibilities become part of an employee's duties. Acquiring the new skills, it should be noted, may require a corresponding reduction in other responsibilities. The

---

Cross-training also builds stronger trust between employees and their supervisor.

---

engineering staff of a large construction contractor routinely exposes project engineers to areas where they haven't worked before, enabling them to move up when a vacancy occurs.

Finally, if budget and organizational forces permit, an extra em-

ployee can be allocated for continuing training status. This may involve keeping one person in the unit or department to learn as many jobs as possible, or rotating several employees into the training slot over a period of time. The "extra employee" is in preparation for the next opening, whenever it occurs. There is some flexibility in this approach because the extra employee can be involved in cross-training or used to relieve others who are involved in cross-training activities. One manufacturer has an extra supervisor for every major production department, usually a newly promoted supervisor who fills in whenever someone is on vacation, jury duty or short leaves of absence.

Cross-training provides several advantages, both to organizations and to the supervisors who initiate the activity. A supervisor has more flexibility to make job assignments when more than one person can do the job. This flexibility keeps an operation running smoothly. Preparing employees to assume other jobs obviously helps them develop, but since cross-training is "on-the-job," the supervisor may be more comfortable with that development. If employees perceive this as a chance to develop themselves, they in turn will be more satisfied, challenged and, in many cases, more highly motivated.

Cross-training prepares the replacements that will eventually be needed to fill critical jobs and those that require long periods of training. It can even let the supervisor develop a replacement for his or her own job, avoiding the anguish of a promotion deferred because a trained successor is not available. With proper planning the efficiency and effectiveness of the department also should improve, at least on a long-term basis.

Finally, through cross-training activities the supervisor can identify those employees who are most deserving of promotion. With this invaluable opportunity to see how people perform on other jobs, promotion decisions can be made more accurately—and confidently.

In addition to the advantages to the organization, the individual involved in cross-training also can benefit significantly. Taking on new assignments with new responsibilities provides a challenge— employees don't go stale from being stuck in the same routine. Cross-training promotes lateral growth from learning more about other positions in the company. In addition, employees may be given a chance to develop skills and abilities not called for in their current jobs.

Cross-trained employees become

SETTING GOALS KEEPS YOUR CROSS-TRAINING STRAIGHT

People work best when they have goals, especially goals to which they are personally committed. As with any other activity, cross-training must be established with clear goals in mind—for the individual and for the entire organization—set by those who understand the importance of effective goal-setting. Typically this means long-range planners and seasoned human resources development practitioners.

But most organizations can be expected to have managers who are still wrestling with their day-to-day jobs. While some will never attempt cross-training (or other OJT activities) unless required to do so, many can be convinced of training's ultimate usefulness. Without commitment to cross-training goals at this organizational level, even the best-designed efforts will start off in deep trouble.

Goals may be set in many ways, but there should be clear targets for each activity. For example, a commitment might be sought to have perhaps 20% of all project engineers in a depart-

ment involved in cross-training at any given time, or to have 10% of all first-line supervisors rotating into new assignments every two years. Goals can also be formalized at the department or division level: 10% of all employees in this or that region will participate in cross-training activities this year.

Alternatively, goals can be set by type of cross-training activity: job swapping, temporary fill-in, partial responsibility shift. Whatever goals are proposed, they should be realistically aligned with the organization's mission and presented to management for formal acceptance and support. Keeping this support, it should be noted, will very likely entail regular progress reports. By properly communicating an understanding of cross-training's benefits to both individual employees and the organization as a whole, such efforts can play an important role in making sure vital skill positions are backed up by trained people throughout the work force.

Reprinted from TRAINING, July 1981

more valuable members of the work group, and cross-training raises self-esteem and respect from other employees due to the fact the employee is contributing more. It also builds stronger trust between employees and their supervisor, particularly when the former are given additional responsibilities.

And last there's the aspect of career development. Too often employees feel lost within the organization with no hope of building a career. Cross-training is one response, and will be even more effective if well-planned, well-executed and part of an overall career development plan.

Any organization considering cross-training activities should review the disadvantages. First and foremost is the budget stress likely. Costs may increase, at least initially, particularly if an extra person is hired for cross-training. On the other hand, long-range cost may be another story— cost avoidance should be one ultimate benefit, but it may be hard to identify in simple dollars.

At first, because someone is learning a new job, cross-training will probably reduce efficiency. Long-term, however, efficiency should improve. The time element may be the key reason more cross-training doesn't take place. It does require extra time on the part of all involved. When an organization is already fully utilizing all resources, it's understandably difficult to find time to do any cross-training.

A potentially dangerous aspect of cross-training is the possibility that employees may build false hopes of moving up in the organization. For instance, your efforts might reveal that an employee doesn't have the ability to be promoted. As a result, the employee may never move up. The training may also be premature if no opening occurs within a reasonable amount of time. Skills may consequently rust as interest wanes. Certainly some cross-training can be undertaken just to give an employee an additional challenge, however. The employee may be in the highest job he or she can ever hope to occupy. Cross-training will not be detrimental if you thoroughly explain— and the employee understands— the reason for the activity.

Predictably, some employees may resist cross-training. They may have unrealistic fears about taking on new assignments with new responsibilities, or they may feel they will be replaced if someone is trained to do their job. A thorough understanding of the purpose and benefits of cross-training can help overcome this resistance.

> **Crossing-training should not impose additional hardships on the employees involved in the activity.**

A VIEW OF CROSS-TRAINING

Cross-training is supposed to be one of those win-win schemes: The more skills employees learn, the more challenging the job, which leads to a happier employee, who is more productive, which results in high profits for the employer. It certainly sounds good on paper, but how many organizations are successfully using cross-training.

Michael Maggard, a professor in the College of Business Administration at Northeastern University in Boston, wanted to find out. So he sent questionnaires to members of the American Society for Training and Development. He admits that his results are inconclusive because of the small number of responses he received (116). However, he believes his survey can be viewed as a "preliminary analysis" of cross-training practices and attitudes.

Of the respondents, 88 percent said that at least 10 percent of all employees were cross-trained. The average number of employees in a department that used cross-training was 15. Maggard also asked the respondents about the best level of cross-training and found that, on average, the respondents preferred to cross-train 50 percent of the employees.

The respondents were evenly split between manufacturing and service industries; Maggard found no difference between the two groups' propensity to offer cross-training.

When it came to hard dollars, Maggard found that only 63 percent were willing to spend money for cross-training, even though 88 percent employed cross-trained people. Maggard surmises that some of those employees were cross-trained by circumstance rather than design. For example, an employee who moved to a different job could be considered cross-trained. Among those who did invest in cross-training, the average amount they were willing to spend was $1,995.

When asked to rank the reasons for having cross-trained workers, increased efficiency was the top choice by far. Three reasons vied for second place: absenteeism, job enrichment and scheduling flexibility. Maggard notes that of the eight reasons he offered, those relating to efficiency drew 76 percent of the first-place votes. Reasons unrelated to efficiency—job enrichment, promoting employees and increasing salaries—drew 20 percent of the responses.

Nearly three-quarters of the respondents said they do not pay cross-trained employees more money. The remaining fourth said cross-trained employees receive extra compensation ranging from 5.5 percent to 8.1 percent. When asked if cross-trained employees should be paid according to the number of jobs they can perform, 47 percent said yes.

Reprinted from TRAINING, November 1987

Establishing a program

For cross-training to be effective, it must be done in an orderly, planned manner. Here are a half-dozen guidelines for establishing cross-training:

1. **Explain first.** Cross-training efforts should be explained completely to the individuals involved and to the general work crew. Without this, there may be unnecessary anxiety on the part of those involved. In the absence of proper explanation, you can be sure the rumor mill will generate a reason for the efforts.

2. **Show the benefits.** It is best that the entire work group see the positive potential of cross-training. It's particularly necessary for those directly involved; they should be willing to participate. Employees should never be coerced into cross-training.

3. **Set clear goals.** Cross-training should be planned and executed in accordance with both long- and short-range goals. Without a specific plan, it is unlikely that the training, no matter how well-intentioned, will benefit the organization or the individuals involved.

4. **Stay on schedule.** Whatever the form of cross-training, it should keep to a realistic timetable. For instance, if an employee is to be involved in four hours of cross-training per week, the schedule should be established and the time actually spent should be documented.

5. **Minimize down-time.** Cross-training should be scheduled to provide the least disruptive impact on the overall efficiency of the work group. For instance, cross-training should not be undertaken during peak periods in a seasonal operation.

6. **Protect employee morale.** Cross-training should not impose additional hardships on the employees involved in the activity. Unfortunately, longer hours or less pay are often the by-products of cross-training. Cuts in pay can be demotivating, even devastating. Yet this can happen if an employee on an incentive bonus system is transferred to a job that doesn't offer a bonus. If more responsibilities are added, the job should be upgraded or a salary increase granted. Caution should be taken to prevent cross-training from becoming simply an additional workload.

Cross-training can be an effective and inexpensive method of developing employees on the job. For most organizations, the advantages should outweigh the disadvantages. But it must be supported and encouraged at all levels, particularly by top management. Goals and timetables should be established and progress should be monitored and reported. Managers must see the long-range benefits of such activities and must be motivated to pursue cross-training methods of their own. These methods vary considerably, but there is a cross-training vehicle suitable for every supervisor and every manager which will lead to greater development within the work group and the organization.

Reprinted from TRAINING, July 1981

COMPUTER-BASED LEARNING: DECIPHERING THE ALPHABET SOUP

As the use of computers grows, so does the jargon. Here's a vocabulary list

BY ANGUS REYNOLDS

While computers have become increasingly important in many of our organizations during the past few decades, we only recently have begun to make significant use of them for human resources development (HRD)—that is, for learning. Although a few of us have been doing this for some time, the number of organizations using computers for learning still is relatively small. It is growing, however, at an exponential rate.

The reason for this growth is that increasing numbers of training and development professionals are becoming aware of, and interested in, computer-based learning (CBL). Two major contributing factors are the ever-decreasing cost of CBL and the wide attention which personal computers have attracted recently. Suddenly, great numbers of HRD professionals are finding themselves exposed to large doses of new jargon. If you have not yet been thrown into the alphabet soup to sink or swim, you probably will be soon.

If we aren't careful, we will make our work more difficult. As we begin to use computers for learning, we also are beginning to pick up and toss around some of the terminology that has been well established and understood by CBL users up to the present. That terminology is becoming muddled.

The current "veteran" users of CBL are destined to become only a tiny fraction of the eventual users of the terminology. It is important that we take at least as much care in the use of CBL as we take with other professional jargon.

The use of computers for learning was pioneered by university research. This origin spawned the term "computer-based education," or CBE.

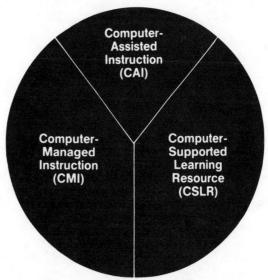

Figure 1 Computer-Based Learning

When industrial organizations began to use computer-based learning, they substituted the more comfortable term "training" for the academically oriented "education." The result is CBT. Other organizations decided to use "instruction," resulting in CBI. This proliferation of terms may appear confusing but is easy to deal with because all three terms mean essentially the same thing. Real confusion—the kind that hampers communication—sets in only when we misuse terms that genuinely differ in meaning.

Only four basic terms need concern us: computer-based learning (CBL); computer-assisted instruction (CAI); computer-managed instruction (CMI); and computer-supported learning resources (CSLR).

Computer-based learning

This is the "umbrella" term. It is synonymous with CBE, CBT, CBI and—someone is bound to come up with it—CBHRD. It *includes* the activities described by CAI, CMI and CSLR. My favorite definition is one given by Donald Bitzer of the University of Illinois, who has been called the "father of CBE." Bitzer says that CBE (CBL) occurs "anytime a person and a computer get together and one of them learns something."

The term "computer-based learning" is becoming increasingly popular, reflecting today's emphasis on learner-centered thinking. It also is appropriate in all settings: academic, business, industrial and even the home. Regardless of their particular biases for one term or another (my own bias is evident), the aliases under which CBL travels create few problems for knowledgeable people, who realize that the names are interchangeable.

Computer-assisted instruction

This term is emerging as the main source of difficulty. CAI refers specifically to use of a computer in the actual instructional process. It is not synonymous with CBL. The various forms which CAI can take are called modes. The modes of CAI are:

- Tutorial.
- Drill and practice.
- Instructional game.
- Modeling.
- Simulation.
- Problem solving.

Some trainers use CAI rather than CBL as the general descriptive term, and this is largely responsible for the confusion. The main reason for the improper use of CAI is that many trainers assume the term covers the whole field. Usually, they are unaware of the existence of CMI.

Computer-managed instruction

CMI is well named. It is, indeed, the management of instruction by a computer. The fact that it is not as familiar as CAI does not reflect on its inherent worth or the frequency of its use. It probably reflects the fact that there is less romance in managing instruction well than in teaching with an exotic technology. The distinction is that CAI always directly involves learning. CMI does not. The modes of CMI are:

- Testing.
- Prescription generation.
- Record keeping.

CMI is a powerful technique. An organization frequently can produce a bigger result with a smaller investment of resources in CMI than in CAI. In many cases, CMI may be the best way to initiate computer-based learning in an organization. In the practical world of human resources development, CMI often can be used as an effective—and cost-effective—approach to projects and performance problems.

Computer-supported learning resources

This is the component of CBL least often seen. For those who are comfortable with the term, CSLR is usually a "data base." This means that CSLR is a pool of information, which does not, itself, teach. It provides information which we can use to learn. For example, a library is a noncomputer learning resource. A CSLR is used in the same way as a library, except that a CSLR is supported by a computer program. The program facilitates the retrieval, examination and manipulation of the data.

Used correctly, the jargon associated with the "CBL biz" can help convey specific meanings and keep a lot of tongues from being bitten. Next time you are talking computer-based learning, don't be intimidated. Just remember which terms are interchangeable—and which aren't.

Reprinted from TRAINING, January 1983

STANDING CLOSE TO THE DOOR AT THE COMPUTER CELEBRATION

A jaundiced look at the Computer Revolution

BY DAVID G. GUEULETTE

Computers are wonderful. Computerization of life is no longer an option, it is a fact of life, not unlike sex and death. In our work, acronyms like CAI, CBT, CMI and "MODEMs" and terms like "micros," "minis" and "hardware-software interface" have found their way into our jargon . . . The first "computer literate" generation is in junior high; capabilities for which there are no current applications are discovered almost daily, and computer stores are gobbling up space in neighborhood shopping malls as the size and price of small computer systems, continue to shrink. It's all terrific, but . . . some of you may have noticed I'm wearing sneakers with my tuxedo and standing close to the door at this celebration of automation.

Claude S. Lineberry, former president of the National Society for Performance and Instruction wrote those words in the April 1982 issue of the *NSPI Journal*. His reservations about the Age of Microcomputer echo the qualms of many others in the field of instructional technology who were wary of the celebration of television, teaching machines, film and other media in earlier days. The revolutions promised by each wave of "advanced technology" never changed our educational systems or our lives in quite the ways promised by the advocates and salesmen of the new devices.

Lineberry is especially concerned with the fact that instructional software is not keeping pace with advances in the hardware field. He notes that ". . .bad instruction is bad instruction, no matter whether it is on paper, film, video or a computer display."

"The computer is not the answer," he concludes. "It is the question."

This is only the tip of the iceberg that may lie in wait for trainers and educators who sail uncritically and unawares into microcomputer-infested waters. In the geyser of enthusiasm that has accompanied the Computerization of America, a lot of drawbacks—present and potential—tend to be overlooked, downplayed and ignored. Here are a few negatives to consider alongside the positives in an evaluation of the microcomputer's role in instruction.

Cost and servicing

Costs of personal microcomputers have dropped to very affordable levels and seem to have stabilized, despite inflation, compared to the costs of other teaching media such as film projectors, tape recorders, and video recording and playback systems.

One must remember, however, that a microcomputer can serve only one person at a time—at best two or three. Therefore, the cost-per-trainee can be quite high, especially if courseware costs are figured into the capital outlay. Those costs can be excessive compared to broadcast-television courses, which can be seen by many learners and shared across a broad geographic area.

Compared to traditional media like 16mm films or filmstrips, microcomputer systems are expensive both in terms of initial equipment and subsequent software purchases. And while hardware costs have fallen, *software* costs are going up. The key strength of the microcomputer—its unique ability to provide individualized and interactive instruction—is also its financial weakness. One wonders at the apparent certainty of so many forecasters that tomorrow's adult learner inevitably will choose expensive, optional electronic systems instead of the less-expensive offerings of public schools or specialized educational television courses.

Despite glowing reports in the press, professional journals and manufacturers' ads, truly effective applications of microcomputers in public schools have not been particularly extensive, let alone universal. While school administrators have been willing to buy and support a few systems to demonstrate their concern with modernity, they have been far from aggressive in their efforts to acquire microcomputers as a primary means for delivering instruction. The pervasive "wait and see" attitude reflects both experience with earlier ballyhooed systems such as teaching machines and television, and reluctance to invest large sums in new and costly equipment. By and large, school administrators still tend to think of classroom computers as "frills." They continue to rely on print materials—and human teachers.

Microcomputers are elaborate, interrelated and dependent systems. As such, they are vulnerable to failures. They are easily damaged by extensive use or abuse. Ancillary components such as tape recorders, cassette tapes and television monitors also are subject to breakdown. A lot of red flags have gone up among system users concerning the need for frequent and costly servicing or maintenance.

The familiar expression "downtime" translates into "the computer doesn't work"; and "downtime" seems to be a chronic condition for many systems. Heavy use of the equipment often is necessary to reduce overall per-person costs of microcomputer instruction, and courseware often requires lengthy stays at the keyboard. Heavy use invites potential maintenance problems, just as with any other mechanical device. And some people who have tried to use microcomputers for individualized instruction report that the isolated and sometimes frustrating interaction between student and machine encourages abuse and, thus, expensive repairs.

Dealers who are quick to promote and sell microcomputer equipment are often tardy in responding to service requests. The state of the art of microcomputer chips and circuitry is

CONFESSIONS OF A FORMER CAI AGENT

BY JEFFREY W. PARIS

I was recruited fresh out of graduate school. In keeping with the agency's recruit profile, I came armed with a master's degree in instructional technology and an unwavering belief that machines could ultimately free man and create a better world for all concerned. Indeed, I was a typical case, a recruiter's delight.

I spent three years spreading the gospel of computer-assisted instruction (CAI) to companies of all shapes and sizes. When we tasted success, it was truly sweet. Unfortunately, such moments were few and far between.

Lest you mistake my feelings for bitterness, let me state up front that it is not for myself I lament. I have survived to enter the mainstream of corporate training. But for my fallen comrades-in-arms, I feel compelled to come forth and set the record straight.

We were sent into the field with a mission: Infiltrate organizations and convince them to convert their training activities to CAI. Our modus operandi was straightforward: Get a foot in the door and keep it there long enough to evaluate a curriculum or two and produce a cost-benefit analysis showing the potential savings of CAI. To say we came on strong is being polite. Inspired by the righteousness of our cause, we exhibited the zeal of your average airport religious proselytizer. Just ask any training manager who sat still for half an hour.

Even blind faith falters after a while, however. And when it did, a pernicious truth began to crystallize in my mind, which was ultimately responsible for my leaving the agency.

At about the same time my crisis of faith began, an agent whose own career was on the wane dropped a gem of wisdom on me. He called it the "three-wave theory." In brief, he likened change in an organization to the marines attempting to establish their presence on a beach. The first wave to descend from the amphibious vehicles gets mowed down. Twenty percent of the second wave makes it to the beach, paving the way for the third wave to saunter onto shore and plant a flag.

The third wave of CAI agents is now at the flag rack making preparations for the final assault that will lead them over and around the strewn bodies of my dearly departed comrades.

Which brings me back to the pernicious truth.

The agency knew our efforts were doomed to failure. At least kamikaze pilots were aware that they weren't coming back. We of the first and second waves were sent out to fight a war we couldn't win. We were expendable! All along, the agency knew that our real mission was not to sell CAI, but to act as a public-relations front to pave the way for the third wave. *We* didn't know it, but I must say, we did a bang-up job.

Every corporate trainer throughout the land has heard of CAI, not to mention CMI, CBT, CAT, CBI and more. They still may get the acronyms mixed up, but at least they recognize them. And we of the first and second waves can be proud of that. Some left the agency with the sense of ignominious defeat that often accompanies unfulfilled expectations. But we did our jobs and did them admirably. We gave everything we had. In the end, there was nothing left to give, no place to go.

Now it is time for the third wave to do its thing. But its thing is not what the agency was selling. What's more, companies have not converted their voluminous training curricula to CAI. Simply stated, as the hype faded into the sunset, CAI has come to be viewed for what it is: a source of interactive instructional intelligence to guide learners in appropriate instructional applications. Computers can be attached to videodisc and tape players to add yet another dimension of realism to self-paced training—interactive video. In the future, trainers will use the computer's artificial-intelligence capabilities to allow employees to solve real-world problems as part of their training process.

The computer's indisputable contribution to training is its artificial intelligence. It can direct, present and manage the learning process. The agency's biggest mistake was in not recognizing this and, in fact, taking the approach that CAI can be "productized." That is to say, the agency configured a certain set of hardware, wrote courseware for it, gave it a cute name, and asked corporate training departments to embrace it. The "product" had a price tag that few organizations wanted to embrace.

Now that we're well into the third wave, the last laugh will be on the agency, which I predict will soon be defunct. After all, if a trainer can buy a PC and an authoring system, there are no secrets left for the agency to guard. And guess what? We former agents can come in from the cold, and have the time of our lives developing courses on these fantastic "little" systems that the agency used to dismiss as "toys." Or better yet, we can sell our services as CAI consultants.

Take comfort, fellow agents, we won after all. The ironic thing is that, in spite of the tremendous marketing effort put forth on behalf of CAI, the medium will have made it when it is no longer packaged and crammed down people's throats. Moreover, we will know CAI has come of age when it is no longer called "CAI." It will be thought of as just part of a training system, much in the same way an automobile engine may contain microprocessors but not bear the name "computer-assisted combustion engine."

As we are inclined to say in California, the key to CAI proliferation is to mellow out and let it happen. War is really heck.

Reprinted from TRAINING, October 1984

new; in rural areas, especially, it can be difficult to locate repair people who are accessible and affordable.

The replacement of basic components is sometimes mandatory—and these are the expensive items in computers. One often hears horror stories about microcomputer breakdowns and subsequent problems involving the cost of repairs.

Perhaps the most frequent and frightening service problem is the loss of a program or courseware due to equipment malfunction. Microcomputers have a reputation for erasing or destroying programs, not only on cassettes but on disks. Since programs are expensive—regardless of whether you buy them or produce them in-house—replacement and downtime can be disruptive and costly.

Because microcomputer systems are relatively new, there is little reliable, long-term information about life expectancy of the equipment or software, or on probable maintenance costs under real-life operating conditions. As with modern color televisions, it is sometimes less expensive and troublesome to discard malfunctioning microcomputer equipment and to replace it. In this sense, the equipment is consumable and thus very expensive as a throwaway medium.

Programming and programs

The fact that solid typing skills are necessary to develop programs efficiently—and to interact *at all* with some typical courseware—may seem a minor issue. In fact, it can be a significant problem. Not only does poor typing or keyboarding hinder the effective development or use of programs, it also tends to create immense anxiety toward the machine system.

Microcomputers absolutely require keyboarding skills, at least at a minimal level. It is difficult, if not impossible, for a person who does not type to master programming. Nontyping users can respond, if slowly and often incorrectly, to commercially prepared courseware, but the "hunt and peck" approach to the keyboard is not efficient and delays short-term, shared use of the equipment. Too much time is lost in correcting typing errors even in elementary canned programs. For this reason, many potential users will avoid the machines; they will be left out of the "Age of the Microcomputer."

Some contend that microcomputers soon will be able to respond and interact with spoken, idiomatic English, thus eliminating the need for keyboards. But this breakthrough is far in

the future, if it is possible at all. A 1982 article in the *Los Angeles Times* outlined the problem thus: "...Computers, on the other hand, have no knowledge of the world. As a result, except in limited cases, prodigious efforts by computer scientists to get machines to extract the meaning of ordinary written English sentences have been unsuccessful." And this is for written English. Spoken English, with its many dialects, idioms and supportive gestures, is far more complex. As the *Times* article put it, "The

---

Promises of easy learning, and dramatic, overnight business success simply have not materialized.

---

language is simply too vast, there are too many meanings attributed to words, and with those meanings go varieties of symbolic properties." The dream of language-reactive microcomputers is just that—a dream. The likelihood that units with such capabilities will be a force in the market anytime soon is remote.

Use

Microcomputer programs and equipment are generally limited to intellectual and highly logical instruction. With a few notable exceptions (such as pilot-training and driver-training simulators), computers lack the ability to teach hands-on skills effectively, and few programs are able to convey affective learning objectives or to encourage intuitive or serendipitous learning.

Recent research on the use of computers for learning has indicated that as much as one-half of the population has the sort of cognitive structure that resists learning from the highly linear and orderly process of the computer. These people tend to be extroverts who rely on "random," often intuitive learning; they gain far more in a typical classroom situation than when forced to sit in front of a video screen for extended periods of time.

Additional research probably will tend to support the argument that computer-assisted instruction is not the most effective way to transfer knowledge and skills to everybody—or even to most people. Adults, especially, may be at a disadvantage in relation to young people in a computer-

ized-learning environment, since today's children are growing up in a world in which computers are becoming increasingly familiar—even if only in the form of video games—and nonthreatening.

On the other hand, within a few years we may look back in amazement at the popular claims that exposure to video games is paving the way for our children to evolve naturally into computer-literate authors/programmers, and that video-game technology will evolve into highly effective instructional courseware. After all, watching television and videotaping TV shows does not lead automatically to the production of television programs. And just as commercial television has continued to cater to the mass-entertainment market, the billion-dollar software industry of the '80s probably will continue to concentrate on entertainment rather than quality instruction.

Comprehensive elementary, secondary and adult curricula are not widely available on microcomputer programs. As H. Beder observed in *Lifelong Learning: The Adults Years*, "...there are programs to do this and programs to do that, programs to do about anything—except what you want to do."

It is also a fact that existing instructional programs are often difficult to understand and use. "At present," said a 1981 *Time* magazine article, "complexity and cumbersomeness bedevil the software industry, creating an obstacle to even greater acceptance of microcomputers. Everybody is saying their software is easy to use, but it isn't."

Conscientious instructors inevitably consider programming some of their own courses, but this approach is also fraught with complexities. Programming, even BASIC, can be difficult to learn and is easily forgotten if not used constantly. Programming requires knowledge of the subject area, typing skills, a logical mind, patience, considerable time, sufficient expertise in a programming language, and access to equipment. Neither learners nor instructors usually write their own textbooks; it is unlikely that they will write their own microcomputer programs.

Outlook

FOR SALE
TRS-80 Microcomputer, with 16K memory, has been sitting on desk for the last six months.

This classified ad from the DeKalb (IL) *Daily Chronicle* suggests some of the frustration that has accompanied the cheering during the Microcomputer Revolution. The promises of easy learning and dramatic, overnight business-management success simply have not materialized. The potential of self-directed learning and trainer-produced programs has not yet been realized. Barriers to the production and use of programs are many. Breakthroughs in equipment that is *really* easy to use and program, language-activated computers, widespread availability of top-quality instructional programs and a general positive attitude toward sitting in front of a machine for long periods of time—all of these developments are far in the future.

Microcomputers will emerge and expand their role in training and adult education, but they will not find the pervasive role suggested by equipment possibilities alone. The medium is beset with numerous technical problems, a lack of useful programs, and difficulties for users and programmers.

It is probable that more buyers will join the ranks of the disillusioned. Microcomputers will be neglected or misused in many homes and offices. The history of television suggests the probable direction of this new medium: entertainment, overuse for trivial purposes, regimented mass delivery of low-quality programming and passive interaction with the medium.

Microcomputers are being used everywhere today—in schools, businesses and homes. But trainers and educators only recently have begun to explore the use of microcomputers for learning. Before we rush into this rapidly developing area, we must take a cold, hard look at the microcomputer's advantages and limitations. Above all, more balanced information is needed so that we can make more informed decisions about how, when, where and whether to employ this complex and often contradictory technology.

Reprinted from TRAINING, June 1983

HOW TO DESIGN INTERACTIVE TRAINING PROGRAMS

Thinking of taking the plunge into interactive computer-controlled training? Here's a beginner's guide to help you get your feet wet

BY JUDSON SMITH

We're seeing many advertisements and some case studies concerning "interactive" training programs, but we are not seeing much information about the basics of *producing* them; that is, how trainers should design and develop programs that take advantage of the capabilities of computers and/or computer-driven video systems, and the capabilities of "interactive training" itself.

Partially, this is because each medium used for interactive instruction has different parameters and production techniques. But there are some common denominators, and they are the topic of this article.

Let's begin with some definitions. You won't find these particular descriptions in any dictionary and you may not find much agreement among trainers concerning precise wording. But we have to start somewhere.

A "passive" training program is one in which the audience has nothing to do but receive information imparted by words, pictures or some combination of words and pictures. An "active" program relies almost totally on audience involvement: "on-the-job" training or some other situation in which the trainee learns how to do something by doing it. An "interactive" program, then, is a combination medium: Sometimes the learner participates, sometimes the learner receives information.

In earlier incarnations, interactive programs used mechanical teaching machines or programmed texts. Today we think of interactive programs as involving computer-assisted instruction (CAI). But the concept is the same—people tend to learn better when they can combine the reception of information with hands-on application within a short period of time.

In an era when more and more training is designed to help people move efficiently into the computer age, interactive computer-assisted programming can do double duty—it develops familiarity with computers while imparting instruction. (In fact, many of the best interactive CAI programs developed to date are designed to teach the use of computer hardware or software.) And interactive systems allow trainees to *control* their own learning, while freeing the trainer to design new programs or handle individual problems.

Flexibility

The crucial factor in the design of any interactive program is flexibility. The program must anticipate the needs of trainees, and meet those needs in a variety of ways that also satisfy the requirements of the organization sponsoring the program. Because of this, the design of most interactive programs becomes a group effort, taking advantage of the varying perspectives and objective analyses of many people.

Most instructional design work begins with a needs analysis. But interactive design requires a far more extensive analysis than other media. You have to dissect the training objectives very thoroughly, and make sure you provide material that will appeal and inform at various competency levels.

For instance, a supervisory training program produced as a manual or in an audiovisual format may begin with some basic skills necessary for supervisors and end with a few case studies showing how those skills are applied. An interactive program on the topic should allow people who are already aware of basic supervisory skills to skip ahead to the case study, yet still ensure that those basic skills are reviewed and understood by all trainees. In other words, you don't force trainees to go through all the basic material, but you do design the case study so that no one can complete it correctly without understanding those basics.

Also, almost all interactive CAI programs should include careful instructions for users who may be unfamiliar with the equipment involved. One computer may require you to press the "Break" key to stop what you're doing and start over again, while another may ask you to press a combination of keys to reset the system. Without understanding the commands and the language of the system in use, the trainee could find it impossible to "erase" a mistake and begin again.

To prevent this problem, many computer programs include a special "help" function that can be called up at any time. This signal usually fills the display screen with a list of commands and explanations of what they will cause the system to do. This is especially important for training applications because a major problem facing many trainees is fear of the machine; if the system acts up, they may literally pull the plug and walk away.

Menus

Most of the material needed to run interactive programs is included in a "menu" of some kind, either written on paper or provided within the computer's memory system or both. The menu, in turn, often is found on a "directory" that lists the various titles included within the program. So a crucial part of your job is making sure that those titles are as descriptive and interesting as possible.

This is important because most interactive programs aren't monitored or "proctored" by the trainer—that would defeat the purpose. If the student is to be kept involved and interested, the program has to do the job on its own. So each menu selection trainees choose should grab their attention immediately. Many designers begin each segment with some question or problem that will intrigue the learners.

You also must balance the length of each segment so that trainees don't become bored with the process of answering questions or determining solutions to problems. An interactive program becomes like a patchwork quilt; each individual segment stands alone, yet becomes part of a larger pattern. Only rarely will a trainee see the overall pattern, or need to see it. Instead, the learner should concentrate on small combinations of segments that form a minor pattern in your "grand design."

Branches and conditional statements

These minor patterns are called "branches." Most good interactive programs include many branches which are nonlinear in nature; that is, the program unfolds more like the give-and-take of a press conference than an orchestrated speech. When correctly designed, interactive programs can be just as effective as press conferences in giving the participants the information that is most important to them.

The key to effective design of an interactive branching program is the "conditional" or "If, then" statement, the standard form familiar to anyone who has taken a course in basic logic: *If* all birds have feathers, and this is a bird, *then* it has feathers; if one thing is true, then the other follows; if one thing happens, then the next thing will happen.

In interactive program design, the "If, then" statement often takes the form of a multiple-choice question. If a participant chooses a certain answer, then a certain sequence of events is set in motion. Perhaps the participant chooses answer "C" when asked a question concerning the proper way to determine the postal cost for fourth-class, bulk-rate mail. If answer C is correct, then the participant is allowed to move to the next learning segment. But if answer C is wrong, the participant may be sent back to the beginning of the previous segment or to some special branch within that segment that provides the information required to answer the question correctly.

The "If, then" statement is a standard form for most application languages used in interactive systems. In other words, the computer "understands" what you mean and what to do when you phrase something as "If, then."

But not all training objectives can be met with simple "If, then" formulas. So some instructional authoring lan-

guages allow the designer to set ranges and limits. For example: "If the student answers 'C' once, then go to remedial branch; if the student answers 'C' twice, then go to main branch and repeat entire segment; if the student answers 'C' three times, then go to list of suggested readings."

In some cases, these "If, then" statements can refer to prior knowledge of the student stored in the computer's memory: "If the student has an 80% average so far, then allow him to continue even if this answer is wrong."

Although an interactive program can't observe and analyze all the subtle hints a human trainer can use to track the student's understanding, the "If, then" statement does permit some "diagnosis." Just as a physician fre-

---

Flexibility is the crucial factor in the design of any interactive program.

---

quently will diagnose an ailment through a series of questions, searching for an overall pattern, so can a well-designed interactive program rely upon the answers to a number of questions to produce a pattern that indicates not only lack of comprehension, but also the specific problem area.

Once that area is spotted, "If, then" statements can be used to send the trainee to a "remedial branch" containing instruction designed to remedy a specific problem.

These "If, then" statements aren't reserved for computerized interactive systems, of course. You probably use them frequently in most training sessions. It's the standard thinking pattern you'd follow, for instance, if you realized that your explanation of a certain concept or technique was not getting through to a group of trainees: "If they're all having problems understanding Maslow's Hierarchy, then I'd better look for another way to present human needs."

You might then provide a "remedial branch" to your normal program that defines what a "need" is or uses several examples of common needs that could be placed within a hierarchy.

When using interactive systems, however, you must rely upon active input from the participants to deter-

mine comprehension. The computer can't read the nonverbal cues or other subtleties you use.

The challenge for the instructional designer is to create program materials that *isolate* the information and competencies required of trainees. It may be that each answer to each question should lead the trainee to a different program branch. This is more difficult than it sounds because you must provide enough information to cover the topic without presenting so much extraneous material that you bore the audience.

If you're using a computer-controlled interactive system, you can refine the "If, then" statement even more, and ensure that participants receive the precise information they need about a topic. You do this through the use of "And, or" logic statements.

Computers use devices known as "logic gates" to process information. These are electronic circuits that act like switches, similar to electric light switches. An "or" gate is like a light circuit that can be turned on or off from two locations; if either light switch is flicked, the light goes on. If a signal is received at either one *or* the other of the inputs to a computer "or" gate, a signal results. A computer "and" gate, by contrast, requires that the same signal be received at both inputs. In other words, if input A *and* input B are present, then a signal comes out.

If you intend to design an interactive program and then give it to a programmer to place on the computer, you don't need a comprehensive understanding of computer language. But you do need to understand how these "and" and "or" gates can be used to define various program elements.

They are called "gates" for a reason: They either let something through to a "pathway" or prevent entrance. The major benefit of computers as aids to interactive learning is not their "intelligence," but their patience. The computer will patiently check each possible gate until it finds a pathway—and do it in less than the blink of an eye.

You can block passage to another level of instruction by requiring that certain parameters be met. And the parameters can be quite sophisticated. For instance, you can demand that the trainee provide the correct answer to three questions within a certain time span or be sent back for remedial instruction. That command may require the computer to make dozens of comparisons and decisions, including reference to a timer circuit: "*If* questions 1 *and* 2 *and* 3 are answered correctly *and* the three correct answers are given within 12 seconds, *then* go to the main branch; if question 1 *or* 2 *or* 3 is answered incorrectly, *or* the three answers aren't given within 12 seconds, *then* go to a remedial branch."

A sample interactive program

Suppose you've identified two basic things that supervisory trainees must understand. First, they must grasp a basic concept, such as why it is better for a supervisor to allow employees to make suggestions about the best way to do their jobs than it is to demand that employees follow a rote procedure. Second, they must understand at least one of two specific ways to *encourage* employee suggestions.

You can state this need in a very general form: *If* the trainee understands the basic concept *and* understands method one *or* method two of encouraging participation, *then* the trainee has successfully accomplished this section of the course. With this basic form, you can create program material that addresses the basic competencies required. And you can create questions and answers that test understanding and provide branches to follow if that understanding is faulty in some way.

Now assume you are using a video-disc-based interactive system that has a built-in computer capability. Because the videodisc has massive storage capability, several programs might be included on the same disc. So the trainee is first sent to a directory, perhaps by pressing the "D" key on a keyboard, to call up a listing of all programs on the disc.

If this is the trainee's first encounter with the system, perhaps he or she will then call up the directory listing titled "How to Use." (Or you could make "How to Use" an automatic part of every program, shown as soon as the disc is inserted into the machine. In this case, however, you'd want to provide a means for participants who have seen the program previously to skip or abort the introduction and go on to another listing.)

You also may require each participant to use a specific password to call up programs. There are two reasons. First, individual passwords give you a means to identify each trainee. In some systems, for instance, the same computer that delivers the instruction is used to aid the trainer by monitoring and recording each participant's responses so the trainee's activities and answers can be reviewed. Second, the use of passwords can limit access to various programs, preventing trainees from jumping ahead of the sequence. For instance, a trainee might

have to answer one or more comprehensive questions at the end of one program before the computer releases the password that permits entrance to the next level.

Suppose you begin with an introductory segment that outlines basic concepts and terms. The segment ends with a test. Trainees who complete the test successfully are allowed access to the next segment. Those who

fail obviously require more comprehensive training. This is where the "And, or" statements built into the computer program help you identify specific problems and correct them with specialized training segments.

Combinations

The challenge is to set up the program in such a way that the answers

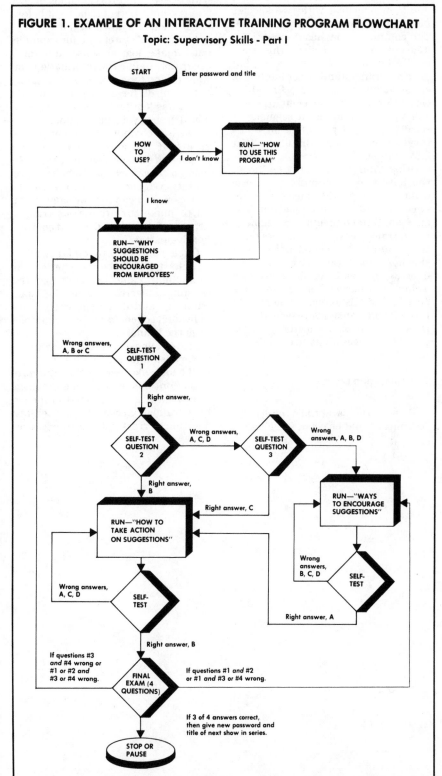

FIGURE 1. EXAMPLE OF AN INTERACTIVE TRAINING PROGRAM FLOWCHART
Topic: Supervisory Skills - Part I

299

chosen by trainees to *combinations* of questions tell the computer which specific segment of material needs to be covered in more depth. Using both "and" and "or" statements allows you to be very precise in this endeavor.

For instance, suppose that a trainee answers question 1 correctly, showing that he or she understands the basic concept being covered (supervisors can benefit by encouraging employee suggestions), but misses questions 2 and 3, which deal with two specific methods of encouraging suggestions. The computer now has three distinct items of information about this trainee: He or she knows the basics, but does not understand either method of encouraging suggestions. Based on this information, the computer can call up a new program segment or recall the specific part of the introductory segment that discusses that information.

Using "And, or" and "If, then" logic, you have told the computer that the trainee must provide the correct answer to question 1 *and* question 2 *or* question 3 to complete that segment. *If* the trainee correctly answers questions 1 and 2 or question 3, *then* he or she moves on. If the trainee misses on question 1, then he or she doesn't get a chance to answer 2 or 3. Instead, the basic concept is explained more fully. If the trainee answers 1 correctly, but misses 2 and 3, the methods of encouraging suggestions are explained more fully.

Potentials and pitfalls

By now, the potential of interactive learning should be clear. It allows you to design programs that directly and precisely address the individual problems of each trainee while still meeting the course objectives. Perhaps you also can see the potential pitfalls in interactive-system design: If you don't ask the right questions and don't provide the right answers, your program is a useless mess—and there is no human instructor present to make adjustments or solve problems on the spot. With interactive programming, design is everything. It's got to be right before the student sits down with it.

An "If, then" statement, for example, must make logical sense and must accurately define the information you want understood. If your logic is faulty ("If all birds have feathers, and this object has feathers, then this object is a bird"), so is your instruction.

One way computer programmers ensure that the application programs they create make logical sense is by using a flowchart—a symbolic representation of the steps involved in the program. You can use the same method to make sure that your training program follows a logical and comprehensive pattern.

Once you start to create such a flowchart, you'll see where the term "branching" came from. The central training objectives form the main trunk up and down the page, while individual concepts, ideas or examples form the branches.

Figure 1 shows what a flowchart for a very simple interactive program might look like. Notice that this program contains at least one potential design flaw: unremediated branches. Until trainees answer the first self-test question correctly, for instance, they keep returning to the same introductory section. If the problem is that the instruction in that section is faulty or if the trainee simply doesn't "get it," he or she just keeps reviewing the same material until guesswork and the process of elimination produce the right answer—or until the trainee quits in frustration. The program might need more remedial branches. It definitely needs a point (perhaps after the trainee has failed a self-test twice) at which the trainee is told to stop and seek help elsewhere.

Remember the basics

All the computerization in the world won't make your job any easier. You still have to design the program carefully to take full advantage of the precision possible with interactive learning. And you still have to be creative to make the program as flexible as possible. And you still must chart out the learning path with extreme care to make sure that you have no logic flaws in your plans.

That's a lot of work, and it's work that isn't always necessary to meet simple training objectives. But for those programs where learner control and flexibility are important, interactive systems containing well-planned programs have enormous potential.

Reprinted from TRAINING, December 1983

DOES COMPUTER-BASED TRAINING PAY?

A study in a controlled environment allowed
these trainers to answer
a perennial question.

BY ROBERT P. DELAMONTAGNE
AND PATTY MACK

Trainers often feel that when they try to measure the value of a particular training approach, it's an exercise in frustration. So many factors other than training can affect job performance that data interpretation becomes little more than a crapshoot.

Computer-based training (CBT) is no different. "Proving" the value of CBT becomes an iffy proposition when you're faced with the same old problem of data contamination. And presumably because CBT is a recent technological development that requires an upfront investment in hardware and software, many organizations adopt a wait-and-see attitude. The question yet to answer: Can CBT deliver significant results?

We recently had the chance to study the impact of a CBT program in a setting that let us control the effect of outside factors without a lot of statistical fancy footwork. This CBT program was developed for aseptic-packaging filler operators at Houston-based Coca-Cola Foods. (Aseptic packages are small drink boxes with long shelf lives.)

Personnel Management Systems, Inc. of Princeton, NJ, designed and developed the software. It consists of seven hour-long modules that use graphics and picture digitization.

The scope of the study

From October 1985 through February 1986, we measured the impact of this program on line operating efficiency. We gathered data from four large U.S. plants. Three of them used the CBT program; one plant served as a control group and did not use the software.

Data collection methods

We collected data only during the five-month study period. It came from designated CBT coordinators at each plant who sent the information to the industrial training department. We compiled the following data:

1. Year-to-date (YTD) operating efficiency for each shift at the start of the study (October 1, 1985).
2. Daily efficiency for each shift for each day.
3. A positive or negative comparison of each shift's daily efficiency with the fixed YTD figure (average shift deviation).
4. Description of the causes of any negative deviations (i.e., maintenance, systems or operator error).
5. Data from the control plant, including the original shift supervisors' production reports and computer printouts on daily line/shift efficiency.

Statistical Design

We eliminated from the study all shifts that had negative deviations (daily efficiency was less than YTD). This reduced the chance of data contamination from outside forces, such as machine breakdown, which were beyond the operators' control. We also eliminated shifts that were unusually efficient for artificial reasons (i.e., adding additional operators, running only a few production lines, increased maintenance support, etc.). In the end, three-fourths of all shifts were included in the study.

The average shift deviation removed most of the negative factors that could affect line efficiency; it also let us analyze what would happen to production when the operators had full control of the aseptic-packaging fillers.

Study findings

Our five-month study yielded the following results:
- The average shift efficiency for the three CBT plants increased 0.4% as compared to a 0.9% decrease in the control plant, totaling an average difference of 1.3% (see Figure 1).
- The CBT plants experienced a high turnover of aseptic operators during the months of January and February due to transfers into other areas. When these two months were

> **The environment allows us to control outside factors without a lot of statistical fancy footwork.**

removed from the analysis, the CBT plants experienced a 0.7% average increase in efficiency while there was a 1.5% decrease in the control plant—a total difference of 2.2%.

Conclusions

We drew several conclusions from this study:
- Computer-based training had a significant positive effect on operating efficiency in the plants.
- The 1.3% difference in average

FIGURE 2

	YEAR 1	YEAR 2	YEAR 3	YEAR 4	YEAR 5	TOTAL
MINIMUM EXPECTED INCREASE — 1.3%						
Cost	$ 80,000	$ 10,000	$ 10,000	$ 10,000	$ 10,000	$120,000
Savings*	$130,000	$130,000	$130,000	$130,000	$130,000	$650,000
Net Savings	$ 50,000	$120,000	$120,000	$120,000	$120,000	$530,000
MAXIMUM EXPECTED INCREASE — 2.5%						
	YEAR 1	YEAR 2	YEAR 3	YEAR 4	YEAR 5	TOTAL
Cost	$ 80,000	$ 10,000	$ 10,000	$ 10,000	$ 10,000	$ 120,000
Savings*	$250,000	$250,000	$250,000	$250,000	$250,000	$1,250,000
Net Savings	$170,000	$240,000	$240,000	$240,000	$240,000	$1,130,000

*Based on production projections.

efficiency during the five-month period represents a "minimum expected gain" from the CBT training program.

We consider this the minimum because 30% of the aseptic operators didn't complete all seven training modules during the study period, reducing the full impact of the program. The high turnover rates in January and February also decreased operating efficiency during the last two months of the study.

As more of the aseptic operators complete the program and turnover decreases, we estimate a 2% to 3% gain in annual operating efficiency. These gains represent significant cost savings for Coca-Cola Foods.

We believe this research is particularly valid because measurements were based on machine output. Aseptic-packaging machines can produce a specific number of packages in a given period. Either the machines produce packages or they don't. If mechanical problems are eliminated, that leaves the operator and the machine. Either operators can run the machines more efficiently after the CBT program or they can't. Rarely can so many variables be controlled as part of the study design. And rarely can training's effect on behavior be as neatly isolated and measured as in this particular situation.

Does it pay?

For computer-based training to be a good investment, it must offer a

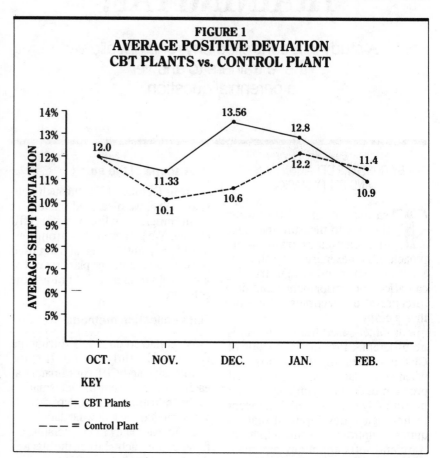

FIGURE 1
AVERAGE POSITIVE DEVIATION
CBT PLANTS vs. CONTROL PLANT

KEY

——— = CBT Plants

— — — = Control Plant

high return over time on the initial investment in machines, software development and staff time. The measured impact must be large enough to justify funding when other projects compete for the same funds. Figure 2 shows the anticipated financial returns from Coca-Cola Foods' CBT program.

The results of this study support the use of CBT and lend additional evidence that it is a highly effective means of instruction. Does computer-based training pay? In this instance it did.

Reprinted from TRAINING, March 1987

CBT FANTASIES: THE GROUND BECKONS

The potential of computer-based training
tantalizes do-it-yourselfers.
A former zealot compares CBT to video and
offers some advice:
Examine your premises

BY DAN SIEMASKO

Let's make a computer program that teaches sales skills through simulations. Then let's develop the software for a safety orientation that tests basic knowledge and remediates until the learner knows everything we want him to. Then we'll create a program that explains the new company benefits by incorporating an employee's actual records..."

The dreamers among us have imagined every conceivable application for computer-based training (CBT). Trainers who anticipated keyboards and screens at every desk in the organization began to see themselves as the beneficiaries of a communication revolution comparable in scope to the introduction of the printing press. Fantasies soared as we gazed beyond the mundane level of most early CBT, preferring to concentrate on the ultrasophisticated programs we imagined ourselves creating. Some still believe that the sky's the limit.

But the ground is beckoning.

According to *TRAINING Magazine's Industry Report, 1986* (October), 32.1% of all organizations with 100 or more employees were using computer-based training in 1986, compared to 28.2% in 1985. That's not exactly a staggering growth rate. And according to the 1985 report, CBT users are much more likely to buy packaged programs than to build their own. [*The same is true in 1986, according to our research—Ed.*]

What happened? Maybe too many of us expected too much to come too easily. Maybe we had too little experience with the *actuality* of CBT before our dreams took off. We tend to forget that we have to start at the bottom.

The good news is that producing effective CBT is much like developing any other effective training package. The bad news is that CBT is so different from traditional media that many of our old habits interfere, making us look as if we're trying to get to the moon by strapping booster rockets to Oldsmobiles. The CBT we create won't fly until we learn the medium's special aerodynamics.

Authoring heaven

I thought I would sidestep an embarrassing takeoff. All I did was read; every article or book on interactive media inflated my loftiest visions of a world in which CBT reigned supreme, and seemed to secure my place in authoring heaven.

Two years ago I found the cash for an authoring system. In a rush of excitement, I opened the package (which involved breaking the cellophane—an act that committed me to God knows what). Then, for some reason or other, I had to put it down for a moment. The package sat in my office, untouched, for almost another year.

Last year I finally found the time to digest the manuals (at home; it's impossible to find enough time to learn CBT programming on the job). On weekends I experimented. During the week I railed against my disappointing progress—while I worked with traditional, established training media.

After two long years, I completed a 10-minute program. It's frustrating to sense such great potential in microchips and to produce page-turning text, boring drill-and-practice exercises, lopsided tutorials that fail to anticipate every interaction, and half-finished simulations that demand more time than I can give.

Along the way, however, I learned to keep my frustration in perspective (see accompanying story). Today I look for articles by those who have experience, those who know whereof they speak. A lot of what is written about CBT (or computer-assisted instruction, or any of the other synonyms by which the medium is known) is still weighted in favor of glowing success stories—some convincing, some not. But many recent articles express caution. More and more, I've come to appreciate Claude S. Lineberry's classic phrase from the April 1982 issue of the *Performance & Instruction Journal:* "I'm wearing sneakers with my tuxedo and standing close to the door at this celebration of automation."

Ron Zemke described the state of the art as I've found it to be—a state I've contributed to—in "Evaluating Computer-Assisted Instruction: The Good, the Bad and the Why" (TRAINING, May 1984): "To date, the history of computer-assisted instruction has been notable for some yawning gaps between promise and performance—grandiose claims backed by an often-mediocre actuality. . . .

"Actually, the question 'Does CAI work?' is a *non sequitur.* It's like asking, 'Does a book work?' 'Does a film work?' or 'Does a trainer work?' The only meaningful answer is, 'It depends.' A better (but wordier) question is, 'Under what circumstances does what kind of CAI work to teach what to whom, and how well does it work compared to something else?' "

Apples to rutabagas

Zemke suggests that we compare

one specific with another. His advice: Imagine a realistic application for CBT in your purview of activities and compare it with how well you get that instruction done now in other ways.

Let's take this advice as the basis for a little investigation. I happen to have a 30-minute videotape on performance appraisal that we produced

---

The CBT we create won't fly until we learn the medium's special aerodynamics.

---

in-house for our supervisors. How might it compare with a theoretical CBT program I believe I can author myself with PILOT, using straightforward text and simple graphics?

Like the videotape, the CBT program would be designed to introduce first-line supervisors to the company's performance appraisal system and present the basic principles involved in doing a good appraisal. The computer program also would cover setting objectives, rating performance, and preparing for and conducting the appraisal interview.

My training challenge seems suitable for a CBT solution: stable subject matter aimed at a large, widespread audience. In fact, a recent development points out a nice advantage of CBT: Our company changed hands, so the videotape—though less than a year old—is already obsolete, numerous references to our former parent being embedded forever in the audio and video of the shelved cassettes. By comparison, a CBT program could have been modified quite easily.

In addition to training our 1,000 supervisors in performance appraisal, we could sell the program to the public—if it was generic enough—just as we do with some of our videotapes. On that count CBT and video are equal.

Comparing the two isn't easy. A straight grid analysis is impossible, but I finally identified four criteria:

- Which is more attractive?
- Which is more compelling?
- Which is more convenient?
- Which is more appropriate?

REALITY 101 BY DAN SIEMASKO

A preflight checklist for computer-based fantasy pilots:

Takeoff Instruction #1: Computer-based training is a new medium that requires new ways of thinking. So, yes, dreaming is part of the package. We have to imagine useful CBT programs before we build them.

We know about video's possibilities. We have yet to learn CBT's. CBT developers will be haunted for a long time by questions for which video producers have stock answers: How difficult is it to produce? Is it worth it? Have we taken on too big a mission with this project? Does this program have to be all things?

And CBT poses additional questions of its own: How intelligent does it have to be? How much control should you give the learner? Do drill and practice, testing, tutorials, simulations and games cover the full range of the medium's possibilities?

Producing a CBT program calls for some revamping of the traditional client/writer/producer relationships. The main contributors to an interactive program are the instructional designer, producer, computer programmer, content expert and client. New politics will evolve to go with this new set of players.

Takeoff Instruction #2: CBT is hard work, especially for experimenters. Program development time—authoring and debugging—can run between 200 and 600 hours for each hour of courseware. That's probably 600-per for beginners and 200-per for pros. [*Estimates of CBT development time vary widely. Many run in the 60- to 100-hour range for experienced programmers.—Ed.*]

David Hon, founder of IXION, an interactive software company based in Seattle, offered some advice to beginners in "That which looks easy..." (*Video Manager*, September 1985). To those who imagine that interactive programming is no harder to create than video, he warns, "Alligators breed twice as quickly when they are interactive."

Just remember that doing CBT for the first time is clumsy. If you're like me, you'll cringe at every sign of amateurishness, swear at every glitch, agonize over the time spent on each repair and apologize at every showing for what you weren't able to accomplish yet. But that's how we learn to fly.

Takeoff Instruction #3: Start small. Since neither the medium nor our skills are highly evolved, our first products are likely to be pretty scrawny.

Homemade CBT progresses one humble step at a time. Until you sense that you're competent to move to the next rung, stick to the basics. How do you eat an elephant? One bite at a time.

What's more, there's something to be said for programming without the full flurry of bells and whistles. "We find that the users usually like the simplest productions best," write Diane Gayeski and David V. Williams in *E-ITV* ("Interactive Video—Accessible and Intelligent," June 1984).

Gayeski and Williams promote "homegrown" programs, adding that interactive programs need not be expensive to be effective. In fact, they claim that short, tailored programs are *more* effective than generic productions with huge budgets. "Because the viewers' attention is held by the quality of the interactivity rather than by the program's production values, special effects are not necessary; in fact, they are often undesirable."

Reprinted from TRAINING, December 1986

Attractive?

Video is more interesting to view. It can be as jazzy and dynamic as commercial television. Video has been around awhile. It's established. We know the wonderful things we can do with it. Not so with CBT, which is

in the pioneering stage, its potential only to be imagined.

Video has audio. Unlike CBT, video puts people in motion. Viewers can identify with the actors who model situations, attitudes and outcomes. Our performance appraisal videotape is filled with realistic interactions between supervisors and subordinates.

CBT, on the other hand, relies on text and graphics. It doesn't require actors, producers, crews or sets. We don't have to look for locations, props, music, graphic generators, etc. For the kind of basic courseware we're talking about here, the program designer supplies just about everything needed.

Video moves by itself. In most CBT programs, even those with a little quiz thrown in from time to time, the trainee basically just reads and presses a key to "turn the page," which can be tiresome, if not downright boring.

Video can be artsy. The CBT program probably will be less so. Our video dramatizes situations, creates an atmosphere and presents human encounters that the viewers can laugh about. But this is not to say that CBT has to be dull. The appeal of a program in any medium depends on the creativity of its designers and producers.

Our videotape was designed for group viewing, with built-in discussion breaks so that trainees could discuss their experiences. Although both video and CBT can be viewed individually, CBT's interactive and intimate qualities preclude group viewing.

Finally, CBT does not (and should not) produce a "show" in the sense that a slide, filmstrip or video program does. An interactive medium, by definition, calls for ordinary conversation. As Rudy Bretz points out in *Media for Interactive Communication* (Sage, Beverly Hills, 1983): "In interactive communication, whatever the medium, there is never a show, for one very good reason: There is no audience. There are only participants. . . . The model for interactive communication is real life."

Compelling?

If I intend to surpass videotape's training effectiveness with CBT, I'm going to have to make the most of what the medium has to offer. That means taking advantage of its interactive capabilities, as well as its ability to allow trainees to control their own learning.

Of course, many trainers remain unconvinced of video's effectiveness, and understandably so. Videotape is one-way communication that doesn't allow for the flexibility of live instruction. Like most mass media to date, it also is linear, passive, formal (often authoritarian) and impersonal: "Here comes a 30-minute canned message from our director of human resources on how to do performance appraisals. Sit there and watch it."

Good CBT focuses on the learner's last response, creating a more conversational exchange. The computer program puts something on the screen, poses a question and waits for a response. The screen reacts to the learner. The learner and the program bounce back and forth in a seemingly spontaneous, informal, involved interaction.

> **To date, mass media are linear, passive, formal and impersonal.**

The computer also creates an environment of privacy. In effect, the learner is alone with the program developer, which is no more threatening than being alone with the author of a book. While our videotape on performance appraisal addressed certain issues generically, e.g., the tendency to rate everyone average or to allow one event to inflate or deflate overall ratings, CBT could be used to personalize a similar training program.

I envision a computerized program that would respond to private inquiries. Perhaps the courseware would be programmed to ask appropriate questions about an individual's work.

Suppose a supervisor is preparing to rate the performance of a secretary who functions mainly as a typist, receptionist and phone-call handler. The program would ask specific questions about this worker's performance and react instantaneously with a marker on a scale at the bottom of the screen. For example: "How would you describe this person's typing efficiency? Fast and flawless, fast with few problems, fast with too many problems, slow but flawless, slow with some problems, or slow and careless." The marker would react to the supervisor's response, moving the scale up for credits and down for certain shortcomings.

This program would explicitly illustrate the impact of value judgments in a situation close to home. It would serve as a specific exercise for the supervisor who says, "I need help evaluating this employee."

Videotape, too, is designed to be responsive to audience needs. But video's value is fixed—embedded in the program during scripting, once and for all. CBT programs that present choices and wait for decisions take on new dimensions for users: Participation involves, interactivity motivates and feedback provides a sense of achievement.

Convenient?

Compared to live instruction, both CBT and videotape programs offer flexibility in terms of when and where the program can be delivered: One need not wait for a subject-matter expert or for a quorum of people who need the training to justify running a class. One need not schedule the course at a special time or place.

CBT programs don't have to be geared to the slowest students, as videotapes tend to be. But to serve trainees with a range of abilities, the designer must develop multiple routes to the same learning objective.

Although developing CBT that adequately anticipates the responses of trainees can be an arduous task, it has the attraction of being a do-it-yourself project. As CBT designer/producer, you don't have to work with video scriptwriters, producers, directors, talent and crews. Nor do you have to share the credit. The result will be your creation—and that's not just self-serving, it's also project-serving. It's the best kind of motivation to get you through the tedious scripting, programming and debugging stages.

A videotape requires a player and monitor. CBT demands a computer terminal, which may be more accessible if employees have personal computers at their desks. Assuming PCs are in place, people can learn on their own turf—which may or may not be a plus. Employees still have to set aside the time to take the CBT course.

In *Microcomputers For Adult Learning* (Follett, 1982), David G. Gueulette points out a drawback to CBT that is often downplayed or ignored: "The key strength of the microcomputer—its unique ability to provide individualized and interactive instruction—is also its financial weakness."

Since the computer can serve only one person at a time—at best two or three—the cost per trainee can be quite high, Gueulette explains. The cost of hardware continues to drop, but computers are still expensive. And don't forget the cost of servicing.

Appropriate?

Will CBT serve the organization's ends better than videotape? Like "Does CBT work?" the question is a *non sequitur:* It depends. The answer lies in the application, a better question being: How appropriate is CBT for this specific training task? After all, an interactive medium may not be worth the effort for certain types of instruction.

On the other hand, Greg Kearsley contends that "there are situations where there is no acceptable alternative to CBT." In *Authoring: A Guide to the Design of Instructional Software* (Addison-Wesley, 1986), he writes:

"Computers have unique features that should be exploited in the design of instructional software. They should not be used to mimic the things that other media do better. Screens should not be designed like printed pages and animation should not be used as a substitute for video sequences. Most important, instructional software should be highly interactive. Otherwise, why bother to use a computer?"

Paul H. Selden and Norman L. Schultz ("What the Research Says About CAI's Potential," TRAINING, November 1982) return to the theme that delivery media have to be judged

on their own merits: "We are not dealing with a single, abstract choice: 'CAI' or 'traditional.' Rather, trainers should see in CAI the potential for improving particular courses. Each potential use must be addressed on its own merits. . . . As always, it is the trainers' responsibility to make the best use of the tools they have to work with."

When we compare CBT to print, still frame (slide shows and filmstrips), motion (video and film), audio or live instruction, we have to consider the characteristics of each

---

Video's value is embedded in the program during scripting—once and for all.

---

medium, make a choice and then adapt our means of expression accordingly.

Or is that the wrong way to put it? Perhaps we are faced not with "a choice" but with a smorgasbord of choices. Perhaps different tasks can be assigned to different media: Video can take care of the generic aspects of the topic, while CBT covers individual work, and live instruction or texts provide the transitions between the two.

Indeed, one wonders why we persist in thinking of delivery options as either/or choices. The training industry in general seems to be moving beyond the simplistic notion that there must be some single "best" medium

to deliver all the instruction on a given subject. Arthur Young Business Systems, for instance, packages its self-teaching software courses, such as "Teach Yourself Lotus 1-2-3," with a video segment, a tutorial diskette and a reference guide. That strategy demonstrates just one way to integrate various delivery options.

Lest I be accused of advocating that we chase yet another wild goose, let me add that throwing together three or six or 20 different media to teach a course is no more a guarantee of optimally effective training than is the search for a single "perfect" delivery option. Just the same, I'm not going to answer the implied question posed by our comparison of CBT and video for the performance appraisal course. I don't have a clear-cut answer. I doubt there is one. Which would you choose: CBT? Video? Both? Neither?

Meanwhile, new training missions come up. The marketing director wants to teach salespeople how to use a new computer-based catalog; the personnel vice president asks for an automated system that would answer employee questions about the company's benefit options; the sales manager imagines computer presentations that will help customers evaluate the features and benefits of products. We're going to have to introduce each of these dreamers to the ground.

Someday we'll have plenty of genuine experts in do-it-yourself CBT, and articles like this one will be museum pieces. Writers who do take this cautionary tone will be addressing other dreamers: "You thought laser brain-imprinting was going to be a piece of cake. . . . "

Reprinted from TRAINING, December 1986

COMPUTER-BASED TESTING

You can avoid potential risks by testing the waters before you train

BY HAROLD WOLFE

Here's the good news: Your company's interest in computer-based training has led to the purchase of an authoring system license and a commitment to develop CBT. The bad news: You've never developed CBT before, you're uncertain where the medium can be used to greatest advantage, and management expects results—fast.

In this case, even the good news has the potential to produce unhappy consequences. For instance, since management is making quick CBT development a priority, your project will be scrutinized closely and at a high level. You realize that while some of your company's managers pay lip service to "the need to exploit the instructional power of technology" and all that, there is not a risk-taker among them. The corporate culture is cautious to a fault; rewards are nil for daring and failing, and nearly as scarce for daring and winning. All in all, the situation could spell big trouble for you.

Let me switch from a hypothetical to a real-life situation. I was recently called in by a corporation in which CBT advocates had finally won—after several years of struggle—the blessing for a project. Why such prolonged corporate resistance?

The story goes that the executives once had been infatuated with the idea of CBT. They had a new computer system that would be used by nearly every department to automate the paper flow and service every account. In other words, the system computerized the corporation's bread and butter. CBT seemed to be the ideal medium for teaching their

tens of thousands of employees to use the system. (It's a computer, isn't it? And CBT runs on a computer, doesn't it?) So they bought an authoring system and assigned someone to develop instructional software.

They selected a programmer who had been an instructor at district headquarters. (Excellent! The man is a techie, so he'll understand the new computer system and easily learn to use the CBT authoring package. He's been a teacher, so he knows all about instructional design.)

The honchos weren't exactly unrealistic; they gave him a whole year to complete the job. So for one year, this man worked alone in his cubicle, churning out screen after screen of instruction as if his (corporate) life depended on it. He had no graphic designer. His only sounding boards were other instructors at district headquarters. Like himself, they were subject-matter experts with no background in instructional design. At the end of the year the executives convened to view the results, and. . . .

Well, let's just say the verdict was unanimous. The message reverberating through the corporate halls that day: "CBT is not a viable form of instruction." It took several years to break through that ironclad consensus.

Testing the waters

If that scenario sounds at all familiar, then your reluctance to leap into computer-based training is justified. However, if your mandate is, "produce CBT," you don't have much room for negotiation.

So the question remains, how do you best apply CBT without embar-

rassing yourself and undermining the medium's credibility? The most sensible advice I've seen came from Greg Kearsley, chief executive officer of Park Row Software in San Diego. As he told TRAINING Magazine ("How Long Does It Take?" June), "It's better to avoid making your first effort a high-visibility, bet-the-farm project." Instead, he suggested, "You can't go too far afield developing a knowledge test on computer. And there is the added benefit that by adding testing of any kind to a course in any medium, you invariably improve the program."

Computer-based testing is a good trial balloon for several reasons. It's a low-risk application because you're confining the use of a new medium to a portion of a course that entails relatively limited development. It allows you to start using your authoring system quickly by creating a test, or converting an existing test, that will become a component of a course that's already in place. Most authoring systems have good, easy-to-use question capabilities with an array of options that build in some interactivity. Another plus: You can evaluate CBT's effectiveness and its reception among learners without investing massive amounts of valuable time.

A major bank's experience is a good example. All of the bank's account officers are required to attend a series of week-long courses on its major product areas, such as trade finance and commercial loans. They are expected to know the features and benefits of each product line, the customers for whom the services are designed, and how and when to refer customers to the correct product expert.

Faced with the task of delivering lots of information to a large audience, the bank wants to automate instruction as much as possible to save time and money. Before making a major investment to convert this series of existing courses to CBT, however, it decided to test the waters by converting the criterion exams for the courses to a computerized format.

Learning by doing

Developing a computer-based test will introduce you to your authoring system and its various capabilities and options. Gradually, you'll learn various screen-design considerations, absorb the rudiments of branching and discover techniques for shortening your development time.

You're under pressure to produce a seven-hour simulation with multiple review loops, tutorials and a myriad of lesson tests along with a final exam? Keep your wits about you. Present your case for a pilot, Beta test, prototype or whatever jargon is acceptable in your company. You'll not only do yourself—and your trainees—a favor, you're actually likely to create something useful in a relatively short time.

Even this limited approach to initial CBT development does not eliminate risk—any new endeavor involves risk. You are bound to make mistakes, and therein lies the beauty of taking a cautious approach. Later, with hours and hours of CBT development behind you, you can smile at your first clumsy efforts and think, "I really didn't need to use all 32 colors in the first 10 screens" or "I can't believe how dumb those feedback jokes were." But you'll be able to give yourself credit, too; if you employed a sound strategy and the program did its job, then you earned your salary. On top of that, you prepared yourself to develop that 12-module course that's saving the company 10,000 trainee days a year, not to mention instructor costs, travel expenses, etc.

Testing as added value

Still skeptical? "No Guts, no glory" is your motto? Then consider the fact that computer-based testing is by no means a stepchild of the CBT industry. Frequently, testing is the only CBT element in a course—a small, but extremely valuable enhancement. Companies have various reasons for taking this approach. Some are in your situation—eager to try CBT, but in need of a low-risk, low-cost introduction that allows them to assess the medium realistically. Others are looking for a more secure means of capturing student scores than with pencil and paper. Still others want to leave the bulk of the course in the hands of a live instructor, but wish to add CBT (perhaps along with other media, such as video) to beef up a particular segment or simply provide a change of pace.

Consider the strategy employed by a major pharmaceuticals company.

Its novice sales representatives, whose backgrounds range from microbiology labs to used-car lots, sell the company's drugs to doctors. They must learn the rudiments of Latin, medical terminology and the unpronounceable names of their products as well as those of their competitors. After extensive study on their own (essentially homework), the reps attend a week-long product-knowledge course in which they are immersed in the medical jargon they need to know.

Total immersion may work for Berlitz, but retention of any new language fades without application. That's where this company decided computer-based testing could be a valuable tool. The test, which serves as a comprehension check, also gives the students an opportunity to apply what they've learned about their competitors. Questions are built into scenarios in which they "meet" a series of doctors, and answer queries about the features and benefits of their products as compared with their competitors'.

Aside from providing a welcome break from intensive lecture sessions, the computer-based test provides the learners with drill-and-practice and a score. To make the score particularly relevant, it is given in terms of the dollar bonuses the rep actually would have earned for real sales. The scoring system allows both learners and instructors to track progress.

Flying the pilot

Don't be afraid to make mistakes; this is a pilot project. Stretch yourself to use all the question-and-answer capabilities of your authoring system. Combine questioning strategies so that the test does not become predictable. Test the limits of your system's response analysis. If your test naturally breaks into several units or a series of lesson tests, try different feedback strategies. For example, you might try giving immediate feedback conditioned upon particular responses in some segments and strictly upon scores in other segments. Then give cumulative feedback and scoring at the end of the test.

One caveat—and it's a big one—in mixing strategies: Don't confuse the users. Remember that your objective is to test their knowledge of course

content, not their ability to decipher your instructions. Take care that users won't stumble if they're asked to respond differently than in the previous lesson, or when confronted with different types of feedback. Use your office mates as guinea pigs before you send the test out the door.

Use your initial project as a chance to identify other people in your company who can help you develop or critique your efforts. If you use writers to implement your design, you'll soon find out which ones come up with creative approaches and which ones are more likely to crank out mechanical, unvaried material that will be deadly in large doses. Find out who is intrigued by branching and lesson variables and who will welcome the opportunity to do more authoring.

Keep a log of the project. Track development time by function (design, writing, entry, etc.) so you'll be able to estimate time for future projects. Record efficient techniques; the better you document your process, the better you'll be able to duplicate it—or improve upon it—for your next project. Eventually, you'll be able to create design checklists, format specification guidelines and evaluation sheets to help your authors do the job right the first time.

As you work on your first CBT project, don't hesitate to call or write your vendor. When you licensed your authoring system, you bought a service, not just a piece of software. If you have a question about your system, you're entitled to an answer. You'll need good customer service from your vendor if you're going to continue to explore your system's capabilities. If you don't get the support you need to begin with, you might want to start shopping around for a replacement.

If you find a bug in the program, the vendor wants to know about it. Companies that sell authoring systems are constantly issuing new releases, enhancing their programs and adding capabilities. You are the true test of their product. Like you, they must stay abreast of the latest advances in instructional technology. With good communication, you can educate each other. Then, some day, when you decide to create the ultimate CBT program, you'll have a trusted, knowledgeable partner for the project.

Reprinted from TRAINING, November 1987

PC TRAINING: GIVING USERS WHAT THEY NEED

Teaching people to use personal computers?
Sources for training abound.
But which alternative is right for
your company?

BY MICHAEL J. COPPOLINO

The proliferation of personal computers on desk tops throughout American organizations has created a situation akin to having thousands of small, independent data processing departments. PCs can be linked together in a network, connected to a mainframe computer or operated as free-standing devices, but one thing remains constant: a growing need for good training at every level.

Before leaping into the fray, however, give your organization's decision makers a clear picture of the learning process. A brief explanation of the levels of learning outlined in Bloom's "Taxonomy of Learning" (a classic reference) will help you discuss training needs with various departments. As you organize personal computer training, keep in mind the five major learning categories: knowledge, comprehension, application, analysis and synthesis. This outline should help you explain that each learning step is prerequisite to the next; each is part of the next. Knowledge gained from reading a manufacturer's technical manual generally does not produce comprehension. That comes more readily from a training manual, disc tutorial, interactive video course or introductory class.

Similarly, traditional classroom training will not instill a clear grasp of application concepts. That must come from hands-on learning—working with real problems on real equipment. And sometimes, even that is not enough. Many computer users need deeper analysis skills, the kind that are necessary for preparing complicated spreadsheet instructions or for programming data-base management software.

Finally comes the ability to synthesize—to put all of this learning together in new and creative ways to make the employee's job easier

Who, what and how?

From the organization's perspective, effective PC-user training incorporates three important objectives: properly trained users, cost-effective and timely training, and convenience. Who actually does the training and how it is delivered are not the primary considerations. They are questions of means, not ends.

In most organizations, human resources development (HRD) departments traditionally have handled the training needs of administrative workers. In the early 1960s, when corporate data processing (DP) really came into its own, it represented a mysterious and technical specialty. It was an exception to the norm, and often HRD did not become involved. DP taught its own—and generally anyone with whom its services and systems came in contact.

Then came the personal computer. Often it arrived through the back door, and the DP department wasn't even aware of its presence in the corporation. As DP people began to lose control of corporate information resources, their attitude often was, "We'll be damned if we're going to teach people how to make our job more difficult." What's more, DP had no budget for training the users of those "overgrown calculators."

As a result, PC training has been variously handled by HRD, DP or the department using the computers, with a unanimous lack of agreement on how to provide the most effective and efficient training. However, in a growing number of companies the Information Center has provided the missing link, taking over administration and coordination for much of the PC training.

Although training choices abound, no PC training method is a clear-cut favorite. Each has advantages and disadvantages. Some choices are dictated by employees' needs and motivation. Others are based on corporate policies and resources: Some companies make PC training available to any employee who requests it; others require employees to have a computer at their desks prior to providing any training; and still others leave the decision up to department managers.

When?

Introductory PC training is often provided prior to or during the installation of personal computers in a company or a department. A well-rounded introduction to microcomputers is appropriate to allay employees' misconceptions or even fears. The need for someone who will answer questions, laugh with the class when they discover that their fears were groundless, and give encouragement to tentative beginners argues strongly for an instructor-led class instead of a self-taught course with a TV screen or printed materials.

Hands-on practice also is a good idea. There is no substitute for the experience of making mistakes: Sitting down and plunking away at the keys is the only way to learn to play the piano, and the same principle applies to using a PC. This does not mean that classes can't be based upon or supplemented with computer-simulated tutorials. Once the computers are installed, training can be broadened to include programs that require a variety of skills, such as using a spreadsheet, word processing or data base program. This is also the time to address the specific needs of the company: how to use telecommunications, CAD/CAM software (for engineers) or system administration of local networks.

Remember that whenever training involves equipment of any sort, the machines must be available to the trainees soon after they complete the course. If computers are unavailable or access is delayed, introductory training becomes largely a waste of time.

Once computers are firmly established in an organization, training requires a less-structured approach. Advanced and intermediate users establish networks that replace some formal training. In this environment, seminars held perhaps once or twice a year will help sharpen skills or demonstrate new or enhanced program capabilities.

Even experienced PC users appreciate the opportunity to learn new techniques, shortcuts and applications by rubbing elbows with other users. For years companies have been sending DP personnel to user meetings for precisely this reason. Personal computer users are no different, except that they are not professional bit twiddlers and probably will benefit even more from periodic reviews.

PC training tools

A variety of methods are available and each has its advantages and disadvantages. As the accompanying table indicates, one place to start is by matching the level of learning desired with the source best able to provide it.

1. *Product documentation.* Most experienced users of the major spreadsheet programs feel that publisher-supplied program documentation is not an effective, efficient way for beginners to learn. Why? The original manufacturer's documentation usually is an encyclopedic reference rather than an instructional tool. It has to be; it must contain virtually all of "the answers." Thus, both new and experienced users tend to be "anti-documentation."

2. *Tutorial books, videos and diskettes.* The self-tutorial is an economical solution for training just a few or very large numbers of employees when money is not available to send

---

FIGURE 1
PC TRAINING TOOLS

Source	Level of Learning
1. Documentation provided with PC products	Knowledge
2. Tutorial books, video, diskettes	Knowledge, comprehension
3. Computer stores	Knowledge, comprehension
4. User-group training classes	Knowledge, comprehension
5. Outside seminars	Knowledge, comprehension, application, analysis
6. Custom third-party training	Knowledge, comprehension, application, analysis, synthesis
7. Internal, technical experts	Application, analysis, synthesis

---

them to instructor-led seminars. Tutorials are best used for motivated learners, for reviewing seldom-used features and in conjunction with instructor-led training classes. One major disadvantage: For the majority of employees, "I can't find the time" may well become the universal excuse for not completing the tutorial.

The quality of tutorials varies, so any time invested in research will pay

---

Match the level of learning desired with the source best able to provide it.

---

off later. Computer publications are a good place to start; many regularly review tutorials, just as they do software. A good tutorial should allow trainees to make mistakes. What they learn through trial-and-error will invariably pay big dividends when they are on their own.

3. *Local computer stores.* An increasing number of retail computer stores are offering training. Many require their salespeople to do the training; some, recognizing the inefficiencies inherent in that system, are contracting with outside training organizations or hiring their own internal trainers. Professional training companies train people because it's their business; they must do a good job to succeed. Retail stores must sell to succeed. If they have a professional training arm—licensed, if appropri-

ate—then they, too, are training for the sake of training, though usually with the motive of luring people back for more software and hardware purchases. The advantage to the user is the "deal" inherent in the computer purchase. The disadvantage lies in what often is a generic, broad-brush approach to the training.

4. *User group training.* Many cities have computer-user groups—loosely organized clubs of PC users with common interests. These groups tend to be either highly technical or broadly based. However, they often provide training classes in specific products, sometimes taught by professional trainers. More often, though, the lecturer at these groups is simply someone who uses the package. Regardless of the trainer, this type of instruction can familiarize people with the basics of what a package does and how it does it.

Your company might be able to take advantage of user-group offerings, but remember the importance of sufficient practice and computer time. Your employees must be allowed to get their time in and to make their own mistakes. Generally large classes lack one or the other of these components. More importantly, few such courses are scheduled all year round. The Boston Computer Society is one notable exception, offering both scheduled classes and experts to teach them.

5. *Outside seminars.* To introduce a few employees to a new software program, perhaps before the program is purchased, or to train the first users (or the first trainers), seminars can be

AUTOMATING YOUR OFFICE

Who bears the responsibility for customer training in office automation (OA)? A few years ago the answer would most often have been: "The vendors; they know their products best." Increasing, however, buyers are saying they'd rather do it themselves.

Why the shift? According to Barbara Braverman of Computer Thinking, a Rochester, NY, consulting firm, and Thomas J. Castle of the Rochester Institute of Technology, "vendor training is sales-oriented and focused on the attributes of a product line." Training offered by local universities, on the other hand, may be too technical or unrelated to corporate needs.

For buyers of office systems who want to tackle the training job in-house, Braverman and Castle offer a four-pronged strategy (see accompanying figure). Their model was developed on the basis of 20 OA training and consulting projects. The training strategies, designed for groups of eight to 10 trainees, are as follows.

● *Executive briefing.* This approach includes "hands-on" experience as well as a discussion of issues related to automating the office. The session is geared to participants' interests: For example, trainees from the finance department will work with spreadsheets containing budget and ratio and net present value analyses.

● *Office automation training.* This strategy involves both decision makers and the professionals chosen to implement the system. By analyzing case studies and discussing various approaches to implementation, decision makers can harmonize OA development plans with corporate goals. The people who will be charged with introducing the system design an implementation plan and learn how to minimize the employee anxiety that inevitably accompanies automation.

● *Computer-user skills training.* This type of training should go beyond keyboarding skills to educate trainees in the functions of the computer and the ways in which it can af-fect the entire company. Since computer systems confront users with continuous problem-solving challenges, Braverman and Castle advocate including a dose of problem-solving skills, along with training on how to operate the equipment.

● *Advanced computer-user skills training.* Recent studies show a 30-month backlog for new applications work in the average corporate data processing department, say Braverman and Castle. Advanced skills training can cut down on this backlog by teaching nontechnical professionals how to analyze their own information needs and develop their own solutions on microcomputers.

Reprinted from TRAINING, September 1986

FIGURE 1
OA TRAINING STRATEGIES MODEL

Strategy	Audience	Objectives	Outcomes
Executive Briefing	Decision Maker	Awareness of potentials and pitfalls of OA.	Decisions are made on whether further investigation is necessary.
	Implementor	Ability to analyze operations and determine if OA is appropriate.	Activities are identified which can benefit from office automation.
	OA User	Awareness of the various ways in which the computer influences the work environment.	OA activities are incorporated into daily work routines.
Office Automation Training	Decision Maker	Ability to associate potentials of OA with strategic plans of corporation.	Goals of OA are established.
		Understand the impact of technology on personal and professional lives of employees.	OA task force is established and provided with goals and guidelines for the OA project.
	Implementor	Understand the impact of technology on personal and professional lives of employees.	OA objectives are developed.
		Understand systematic approaches for implementation of OA system.	OA tasks are identified and resources are specified.
		Ability to perform job functions involving use of the computer.	Computer functions are tested.
		Ability to define management information needs and design appropriate systems.	Management information systems are developed.
Computer User Skill Training	OA User	Ability to perform job functions involving use of the computer.	Ongoing computer functions are completed.
Advanced Computer User Skill Training	OA User	Ability to generate new applications of software for company needs.	New applications are identified and implemented.
		Makes appropriate recommendations for hardware and software to solve business problems.	New OA projects are proposed.

an ideal, albeit expensive solution. For groups of 10 to 20 people, however, they are neither cost-effective nor convenient. For large groups, you'll probably be better off with training designed by or customized for your company. Particularly for people who are uncomfortable with computers, familiar examples and specific applications improve the likelihood of a successful class.

6. *Custom third-party training.* Many large American corporations are using third-party trainers and sending employees to outside seminars. Vendors specialize not only in training, but also in software and hardware products, so they are well equipped to understand training problems and potential pitfalls. Also, outsiders may add credibility to the training program.

Outside vendors can be an expensive and unnecessary solution to your PC training needs, however, if you have skilled internal people available to conduct needs analyses, design instruction and teach courses. The cost of using outside firms is sometimes exorbitant, but negotiating can bring it down to less than $100 per person per day, depending on the number of instructors, who supplies the equipment, the duration of the contract and so on. If insiders are willing and able to do the job, PC training probably should not be contracted out. After all, no one knows your business like your own people do.

7. *Internal technical experts.* The PC training resources your company already has might include information center staff, DP professionals and corporate trainers. They offer cost efficiency and knowledge of the company's day-to-day operations. A lot of time and money can be wasted getting an outside expert up-to-speed on sophisticated or unique corporate applications.

Other employees who have an interest in teaching and are adept at presenting technical information also should be tapped to conduct training on topics such as introduction to the PC, DOS utilities and software applications. Even if teacher types are unavailable, end-user workshops that address sophisticated or unique business problems can be conducted or facilitated by internal experts. Networking and micro-mainframe connection questions also can be best answered by internal experts closest to the operation.

To write, edit and test quality course materials, figure approximately 25 hours for each hour of classroom time. Unless PC course developers—and ample time—are available, consider using packaged or customized courses instead of developing your own. And even if you *can* develop your own training, shop around a bit before you do. If the program you're going to design already exists "on the shelf," there may be no point in reinventing the wheel.

Reprinted from TRAINING, October 1986

HOW AWARDS AND INCENTIVES CAN HELP SPEED UP LEARNING

Incentive programs can be combined effectively with learning activities so that training is reinforced and learned behavior is also practiced

BY ROBERT C. EIMERS,
GEORGE W. BLOMGREN
AND EDWARD GUBMAN

The trainer who is interested only in training will have little interest in incentive programs. However, the trainer who assumes the broader mission of improving organizational and individual *performance* may find incentives an invaluable adjunct to his or her programs. The reason is simple. *Performance* of any task—on the job or off—is a function of two factors, ability and motivation. This may be stated as a simple behavioral equation: Performance = Ability x Motivation. It is important to note that these two factors are related in a multiplicative fashion. To be knowledgeable or skilled at performing a task is not the same as performing it. Nor will desire alone produce actual performance. Management places little value on "trying to" or "knowing how." It's performance that counts.

Several years ago we became interested in the possibility of combining the reward elements of incentive programs with training activities. Our first opportunity to test this interest came in the banking industry, and we have subsequently run a number of programs with both large and small financial institutions across the US.

The results of these programs have been dramatic. In one large bank, over $500 million in new business was produced in a 120-day period, at a total acquisition cost (including the cost of all training and awards) of less than one-half of one percent. While it is difficult to compare the results of similar programs applied to different banks in different markets, our data suggests that performance programs combining motivation and training produce vastly superior results when compared with traditional bank incentive programs dealing only in motivation. The results of two different programs run by the same bank give the reader some idea of the difference (see table).

While our data for these programs does not enable us to actually separate the independent effects of the training and motivation, several processes seem to account for their success. Some, although not directly related to reinforcement, have important implications for performance-oriented learning.

1. Employees are given an incentive (an award) for learning. What is learned becomes worth knowing. The employee can see that skill acquisition will lead to real awards, so even the learning process itself is reinforced. By correctly completing quizzes, employees can immediately earn award points. These are easily cost justifiable because of the enormous program results.

2. Newly acquired skills, such as listening, questioning, or presenting, are reinforced. They have a clear, tangible reward. This reinforcement occurs not in the classroom (correct answers) but on the job or in the marketplace (correct behavior) where the "connections" among behavior, environmental cues, and reinforcement are more realistic.

3. It is peer-oriented training. With the exception of the design of some training material and the initial training of team leaders, there are no experts or training authorities involved in the program. No doubt this somewhat decreases the effectiveness of the teaching process, but it may be more than compensated for by various factors. Learning seems to be enhanced when the learners are also given responsibility for the training. Just as the do-it-yourselfer may devote special care and interest and derive a unique sense of self satisfaction, do-it-yourself training may have some unexamined merit.

4. American industry runs on individual needs for achievement. A group (team) setting for learning introduces group needs for achievement, which we believe are qualitatively different from individual needs for achievement. Among its advantages: it can be created through the formation of teams. By contrast, it is relatively more difficult to effect an individual's need for achievement.

5. Training is, or should be, tied to organizational objectives. Too often, however, the learner is unaware of these objectives; or, if aware, fails to identify with them, thus undermining the personal relevancy of the training. In contrast, when these same objectives are reformulated at the team level, they acquire a personal relevancy, ensuring the meaningfulness of connected training activities.

The ways the trainer effectively can apply incentives are limited only by imagination and organization needs. Whatever the application, the basic

	Incentive Program	Incentive Program with Training
Training costs and promotional material	$ 501	$ 11,773
Awards costs	22,874	54,990
Total costs	$ 23,375	$ 66,763
New business generated	$2,582,202	$11,160,263
Cost as % of new business	.905%	.598%

GIVE AWARDS BEFORE, DURING AND AFTER TRAINING

BY RON ZEMKE

Nearly every employee, sooner or later, attends some sort of training session ostensibly designed to help him or her improve some aspect of job performance. Whether that training actually effects an on-job behavior change depends at least as much on things peripheral to the training as it does on the training itself.

According to a number of trainers and trainees we polled, one of these important peripherals is the matter of RECOGNITION. According to our respondents, there seem to be three critical times to provide recognition to the trainee. Surprisingly, perhaps, the first of these is before training begins.

Pre-attendance recognition. This is really what a salesperson would refer to as positioning.

The best positioning is to take the prospective trainee through the *who, what, when, where, why and how* of his or her selection for this training and to do it well in advance—at least four weeks in advance—of the actual training. The ideal result of this sort of positioning meeting would be the trainee understanding that selection for training is a recognition of both his or her potential worth to the organization and worth as a person.

End of training recognition. Some trainers tend to overlook the importance of recognizing successful completion of a training program in some tangible way. "We [trainers] are pretty blasé about training as a peak or significant event," suggests Sales Trainer Brent Caryle, "but the training event is significant to the trainees and successful completion should be formally recognized."

Another perspective has to do with the end-of-course award as a reminder or stimulus. According to Bob Giorgi, a long-time trainer and manager of National Indirect Distribution, General Electric's Mobile Radio Division, "The end of training diploma or plaque should function to remind the person of the skills he or she acquired in the course. That means it has to end up somewhere the person can see it. And *that* means it has to be classy, just the right piece of merchandise. I want my trainers looking around for a nail to hang it or a shelf to put it on, not wondering where to bury it."

Recognition of accomplishment. People come back from a training program turned on to trying out their newfound skills. But many times they are greeted back on the job as if they had been out with a cold. A "the work's been piling up. Get caught up" atmosphere prevails. Most of our respondents suggest that turning the corner from training room to bottom-line benefit is a two-step process.

The first step is another positioning step; recognition that the trainee has had a learning experience and that he or she has developed a new potential which needs some room to be exercised and experienced. Some managers hold an hour or two debriefing with returning trainees. Some require a written report. Many are beginning to go the route of sitting down with the returnee and developing an action plan for trying out new ideas and exercising new skills.

The second recognition step of the "making it happen back on the job" process is the recognition of accomplishments. According to Duane Christensen, vice president of corporate communications at Maritz Motivation, Inc., recognition and reward for using just-learned skills tells the trainee that his or her performance does matter to others and improvement is important enough to be specially recognized.

Christensen and others favor tangible, desired rewards such as merchandise or travel awards because of the validity or earnestness they bring to the recognition of accomplishment. But Christensen also stresses that there are intangible aspects to tangible awards: "There seems to be a more lasting kind of reward that people get. It's the recognition they receive, the 'psychic income' that results when work is well done and goals are achieved. This is a very real thing, although it's tough to put your finger on the lasting impact of the psychological return one gets."

principles of a well-designed incentive program remain constant.

1. The behavior which is to be rewarded must be clearly defined.
Any confusion about behavioral standards quickly leads to perceptions of unfairness by the participants. One way to demotivate people quickly is to let them perform certain behaviors and then have them find out that they don't get rewarded because they didn't understand (or you didn't communicate) exactly what was required.

In this sense, target behaviors must not only be measurable and properly defined, but they must also be communicated effectively to program participants. The measurement system assessing performance must also be publicly communicated. The more accurate, specific and behaviorally oriented the measurement system, the less subjective the behavior-reward process will be and the more successful the program will be.

2. Awards should be given as soon as possible after the desired behavior occurred. Bonuses given at the end of the year for a job well done in the beginning, for example, simply lose some of their impact in the intervening months. Why not reward outstanding achievement right away? This strengthens the connection, in everyone's mind, between high performance and management's willingness to reward it. Whereas salaries and other forms of compensation may be rather inflexible in this regard, due to organizational policy and administrative practices, recognition awards and/or merchandise can be given almost immediately.

3. When it comes to awards, one man's meat may be another's poison.
We all know that people do things for their own reasons, not for those of someone else. We also know that no two people are exactly alike in terms of what they value. To maximize the behavioral return on incentive investment, trainers and incentive planners must provide as broad a range of awards as possible. When this is done, participants can then select the award or set of awards that has particular appeal to them. Simple logic dictates that the more highly the reward is valued by people, the greater the likelihood that they will perform the desired behaviors and maintain them over time. Programs that offer only one type of award tend not to influence each participant personally. Broad reward menus, such as merchandise catalogs, typically create greater interest and, consequently, greater effort.

4. Awards should have memorability.

One disadvantage of giving cash awards, for example, is that they are

PUT THE PERSONAL TOUCH INTO YOUR RECOGNITION AWARDS

Putting an existing employee recognition program on track or founding one in a growing organization requires feedback best obtained by a "recognition audit," says Robert L. Mathis, professor of management at the University of Nebraska in Omaha.

A proper audit, Mathis says, basically asks simple questions: What are the objectives and methods of the existing or proposed award program? What kind of program do employees think is needed? Which employee groups need and deserve recognition? When should recognition come and what should be recognized?

The first thing to nail down is the objective, says Mathis. Personnel officers need to decide whether longevity, continuous performance (safety, perfect attendance) or outstanding accomplishment (productivity) is to be rewarded. And in setting the award criteria they should rely on a work-force profile.

If a profile reveals a large percentage of young, female, blue-collar workers with more than five years of service, for instance, "one should design a program and offer some awards that will appeal to that employee group," he explains. Similarly, if the analysis discovers that a significant number of workers quit after two or three years, a two-year service recognition award should be established as a step toward the traditional five-year plateau.

Mathis recommends a short, anonymous-response survey to establish criteria for sensible (and tasteful) awards or to assess the effectiveness of existing recognition programs. In a nationwide survey of attitudes toward corporate recognition programs sponsored by Balfour Corp., a manufacturer of customized awards, Mathis found "a definite gap between employees' needs for recognition and employers' understanding of those needs.

"Employees generally felt their contributions were not truly recognized by their employers," he continues. "Also, many expressed dissatisfaction with award presentations. This feeling clearly stemmed from the lack of personal, sincere presentation of awards."

More work on publicity about awards and award programs through newsletters, bulletin boards and local news media is advisable, Mathis suggests. Formal luncheons and banquets should be maintained, he says, but encouraging supervisors to hold impromptu presentations at work sites makes award ceremonies much more personal.

Supervisors who acknowledge accomplishments immediately and in the presence of the employee's peers also aid in promoting the program, Mathis says. The most important part of the event is a personally delivered message of appreciation that focuses on the employee's contributions to departmental and organizational goals.

"What must be stressed is that the thing given, while important, is less important than the manner in which it is given," he says. "All activities connected with a recognition program should stress the personal touch if awards are truly to convey high praise and symbolize real acknowledgment of accomplishment."

Reprinted from TRAINING, March 1983

---

apt to be melded into household budgets and used for groceries and dental bills. Merchandise, travel, and recognition awards, on the other hand, typically have a more lasting impact, and continue to evoke pleasant associations for the recipient over the years.

5. Effective awards have emotional appeal. They arouse an individual's awareness of his needs and wants, thus motivating him toward achievement and satisfaction of those needs. We have often heard merchandise catalogs described as "wish books," for example. They have a capacity for evoking pleasant images and fantasies of desired life styles. Because merchandise, as well as travel, has such broad and strong emotional appeal, it tends to inspire increased levels of employee performance.

6. Awards should be accompanied by social recognition. Fanfare may be "corny," but you cannot underestimate the value of presenting an award with enthusiasm and dignity. When the company president, for example, presents an award, its impact is doubled. This shows the recipient that his or her efforts are being noted and appreciated at all levels.

Newspaper publicity, even if it is only a "house organ," also enhances the value of an award.

Most trainers recognize and understand the value of verbal reinforcement, recognition and other forms of encouragement. An incentive program provides a valuable opportunity for trainers to tie these social rewards closely to the tangible rewards. Excessive reliance on material awards is just as limiting as their exclusion. Verbal reinforcement is both free and powerful. Recognition and encouragement can be used after the program ends to strengthen the newly learned behaviors. Simple feedback is a powerful motivator, and the results from a behaviorally oriented system of measurement are of special importance. A good performance program taps a vast range of human motivations.

7. Award programs need to be administered fairly if everyone is to participate. Different levels of performance deserve to be rewarded at different value plateaus. When the rewards are too difficult to achieve, effort becomes minimal. Conversely, when rewards are too easily attained, participants are not pushed to excel, to stretch themselves, and generate significant performance increments.

8. Awards must be won if they are going to serve any purpose at all. Winning an award is an energizing process; it creates good feelings about oneself and about the company. Don't be stingy in your award programs. Awards represent an investment in your employees and their performance, an investment which typically pays off handsomely in terms of increased morale and employee effectiveness.

In too many instances, incentives are applied as part of a contest. This typically creates a situation where there are a few winners and many more losers. A number of people approach contests with a negative mental set; their expectations for winning are slim. To avoid this problem, make sure that the program incorporates opportunities for *everyone* to earn according to the amount of effort they're willing to expend or the results they achieve. This dramatically increases participation. An element of competition definitely enhances a performance program, but experience shows that grand awards for winners are best employed as bonuses, rather than as substitutes for programs that allow everyone to earn and win.

9. **While awards can be used to motivate behavior and facilitiate learning, this fact in itself creates real danger.** Just as government excesses in printing money can create economic problems, trainers who print diplomas and buy plaques haphazardly can destroy the motivational value of their awards. Just as "printing press" money loses value, "cheap" awards come to have little motivational value.

10. **Awards stimulate motivation, but we have frequently found that motivation alone is not sufficient.** Performance is actually a function of two factors—motivation and *skill*. Thus, it is often effective to supplement incentive awards with training.

One more point should be made regarding the use of incentives to reinforce behavior. Too often we reward only the *outcome* of the desired behavior, rather than the behavior itself. For example, incentives are often used to reward increased sales. This does increase motivation levels, but the behavioral outcomes are not always under the control of the participant. Whether a person closes a sale is at least partially determined by the customer. If the behaviors leading to the positive outcomes— such as increased prospecting or more sales calls— are rewarded, then we strengthen the desired behavior

change. Once this change becomes part of the individual's behavioral repertoire, the desired outcomes will occur naturally and frequently.

The team concept

In general, the use of teams adds a powerful motivational element to any incentive program. Teams satisfy basic social and affiliative needs. Enthusiasm is generated, and, more often than not, this enthusiasm is contagious. Awards based on team performance serve to generate a healthy sense of good-natured competition, which often motivates people who otherwise might not have participated on an individual level. Group achievement, especially when natural work groups are involved, tends to generate lasting organizational benefits, such as improved communication skills, teamwork and leadership training.

Goal-setting

Trainers who truly want to maximize the benefits of using incentives should build a goal-setting component into their programs. This applies to individual goals and to team goals. Research shows that people who set goals tend to perform at higher levels than people who do

not. Furthermore, data indicate that individuals who publicly commit themselves to achieving various measurable objectives tend to achieve their objectives more often than those who do not make such a commitment. Thus, it makes good sense for performance program participants to develop their own behavioral contracts, noting the awards they will be shooting for and the specific steps they will take in order to achieve those awards.

The need for improved performance doesn't begin and end during any particular time span. When training is combined with incentives, the goal is to provide a healthy "push" that moves participants toward improved performance and permanent behavior change. The wise incentive user knows that when a performance program ends, performance might well return to pre-program levels. For this reason, it's important to take action to ensure more lasting behavior change. Periodic "booster" skill-building sessions are helpful. So is the continued use of social rewards and feedback. Additional programs, albeit smaller and segmented for specific groups, also can be employed to take advantage of the momentum generated by the effort and success of the initial program.

Reprinted from TRAINING, June 1979

CHAPTER 5

IN THE CLASSROOM: ISSUES, IDEAS, TACTICS

Every few years comes a flurry of proclamations that the day of the stand-up trainer is over. It may be related to sunspot cycles. At various times programmed instruction, audiocassettes and closed-circuit television were the leading nominees to replace classroom training. Today, microcomputers, interactive videodisc systems and satellite teleconferencing are the favorites to play pallbearer. To paraphrase Mark Twain, rumors of the impending death of the human instructor are greatly exaggerated.

The epitaph writers miss the boat on a couple of counts. One reason for their eagerness to be rid of the live instructor is that they confuse public speaking with classroom training. There are good public speakers who are good trainers, and good trainers who can deliver a swell banquet speech, but the two sets of skills aren't necessarily interchangeable.

A second misconception common among the "down with stand-up" crowd has to do with the nature of learning. Books, videotapes and computers, no less then overhead projectors and chalkboards, are aids to learning. They are important mechanisms in the learning process, but they are not the process itself. The instructor-learner relationship is a social, not a technical interaction. Person-to-person teaching is as much an emotional experience as a rational one. Instructor-based training has an impact that an operator manual or a computer-based learning experience can never achieve—albeit that impact is not always positive.

The better we get at building learning aids, the more we learn about how special human interaction is in the train-ing process. In *The Imperial Animal*, Lionel Tiger and Robin Fox observed that the human animal has a propensity to learn and a propensity to teach. They believe this combination is what makes the teacher-student relationship such a satisfying and frequently sought-after one. To try to replace it completely with automated, machine-mediated learning is to misunderstand the key elements of learning. The effort attempts to take a primary social relationship and make it over into a technical transaction. This recalls an observation by English lexicographer Ben Johnson, who was not so much impressed that the dog could be taught to walk on its hind legs as puzzled that anyone would want it to.

The classroom professional is a continually curious character. Always looking for new ways to make a point, continually refining techniques that allow trainees to "discover" the answers on their own, ever on the lookout for tips that keep the process flowing—the prototype of the life-long, self-directed learner. The methods described in this chapter run from alpha to omega in the modern classroom trainer's interests. Tips for keeping interest high. Tricks for making materials more useful. Hints for getting out of the way of the trainees' learning processes and learning-style preferences.

Most of the techniques and ideas you'll find in this chapter come from real trainers who have time and again faced the problem of what to say after you say hello. No lofty theories, nonsense issues or abstract advice here. Just things that work.

REACHING FOR RAPPORT

These trainees are different from the last group—and very different from you. Before you can teach them anything, you must win their acceptance and respect

BY MARTIN M. BROARDWELL
AND P. CAROL BROARDWELL

Corporate trainers will forever find themselves before classrooms of people who are different from them in age, experience, education and learning ability. And the trainer won't always be at the top of any of those categories: not the oldest, the most experienced, the best educated or the most informed. To compound the problem, most trainers eventually will find that today's group of students will be totally unlike yesterday's, and next week's group will be different still. Success under these circumstances depends upon learning to adapt rapidly and establish rapport quickly.

For the past year, we have been team-teaching groups of supervisors and would-be supervisors whose ages and educational backgrounds varied as widely as their occupations and industries: accounting, pulp milling, poultry processing, computer programming, nursing, banking, heavy manufacturing—you name it. Sometimes we'd teach one class in the morning and face a radically different group in the afternoon. Yet the subject matter—supervisory skills—remained basically the same. Because of the limited time we were able to spend with each group, we had to dive into the material immediately, yet make the experience meaningful

to the trainees. We think we learned some things about how to do that.

Meet them ahead of time

It's important to see the people we're going to train in their own environment. And it's important that they see *us* on their turf. Our presence sends a message: We respect you enough to come out here and see what your job is before we try to tell you how to do it better.

The idea is to see how they dress, how they talk and what their working conditions are like. Do they work outside in mud, heat and rain, or in cooled offices with music piped in? Talk to them. Ask them questions— and listen to their answers. This visit will set the tone for training. It's here that we'll learn about their likes and dislikes (both personal and job-related), hang-ups, language and experience.

Since we all know that we will never have to do their jobs, we don't have to learn *everything* about what they do—certainly not how to do it. But even if we're doing supervisory training, which means we'll be talking primarily about managing people and not about the specific tasks these people are performing, we're usually talking about supervising *skilled* people. In most cases, the supervisors will have risen through the ranks or had experience in the areas where

they now supervise. If we're going to develop cases, role plays, action mazes or other job-related activities, we need to call things by their right names. We don't have to go into detail, but we still must know the language and the job enough to use off-the-cuff examples. What better way to get a feeling for the job than to visit the job site?

One thing we are *not* trying to do with this visit is to become experts in their field. We dare not come away with any grand pretenses about the deep understanding we have gained about what they do. Primarily, we're getting to know *people*, not things. The most important thing that comes from the pretraining visit is a feel for what the potential students think about the job and attending our training session. So our real task is one of asking the right questions and listening like crazy.

Our expertise is training. If we listen carefully, our expertise will come out much more quickly when the session starts. Being able to give even one example ("I was in the plant the other day talking to one of the supervisors and this employee came up and. . .") will help us establish this rapport much more quickly. Here again, good questioning helps. Rather than getting into a discussion about whether or not training will help at all, we need to ask questions such as, "If we can only help in one or two areas, where would you suggest we start?" and "If what we want to accomplish is to make the job easier, can you give me some hints as to where the training time can be best spent?"

We don't need to talk to large numbers of people when we visit the job site. Presumably, a needs analysis has already been done; we don't need another one. We just want to see and be seen. We want the experience of being where the work is and the right to say we've touched it and smelled it.

Now that we've been on their turf, we're ready to move onto ours—the classroom.

Dress like you, not them

The jury may be out forever on the effect of clothing styles on training results. But obviously trainees don't really expect us to enter the classroom with muddy shoes—not if we have carpeted floors in our offices.

ORCHESTRATING YOUR BODY LANGUAGE

You've got a group in from the field next week for a problem-solving session, and boy, are you going to put on a show for them. You've got your new multimedia slide show ready; your flip charts and markers are greased and ready to roll.

But have you thought about another important visual aid?

The most versatile communication tool at your disposal is your own body. If you ignore what it's doing (or not doing) while your voice tries to run the show alone, you may be working against yourself by not getting across as much as you could.

So say Sharon Lafferty and Ed Cunliff, director of nursing education at Bethany General Hospital in Bethany, OK and HRD director for the State of Oklahoma Teaching Hospitals in Oklahoma City, respectively. They believe that trainers can improve their presentations enormously by paying more attention to where and how they sit, stand or move around in relation to the class.

A speaker should remain centered before the audience, they advise, thereby telling participants that they're all of equal importance. If your visual aids of necessity dominate the center foreground, try to divide your time on both sides of them.

Moving around in front of an audience, perhaps to selected points, gives a number of cues to listeners. Coming from behind a podium, for example, might mean, "We're going to be less formal now and questions are welcomed."

You also can use movement to help you manage an audience, the trainers advise. Move away from a disruptive group to cue them to ease up; conversely, unresponsive groups may be drawn into the discussion if you confer status on them by standing near them.

Lafferty and Cunliff believe that too few presenters capitalize on the wealth of expression in their eyes and faces, and recommend learning to use smiles and other appropriate facial expressions to convey positive feelings about the group. In other words, your face should show that you're excited about the prospect of working with them. "Attitudes are catching and if your face says you'd rather be sailing, then do the class a favor and go," they say in a paper sent to TRAINING.

As basic as it may seem, they also feel that eye contact is often neglected. Avoid looking over the audience's heads or focusing too long on one individual. Instead, sweep the room slowly or by blocks; making eye contact with unresponsive groups may invite them in.

And, of course, watch gestures. Thoughtful use of the hands, such as a "gathering in" motion to draw responses, a simple "okay" sign or even applauding your group, will contribute to the positive feelings they get from you.

Pay attention to your stance. Do you lean casually against props, perhaps appearing uninterested? Or maybe you're fond of the Patton look, with feet planted wide, chest out and arms crossed, probably giving participants the message that you feel superior to them. Try leaning forward slightly to hear questions, standing with arms comfortably at your sides or with one on the podium, or try sitting down with some groups to emphasize informality.

While most people think they're stuck with what they've got, if your voice is not an effective tool, you *can* improve it. Lafferty and Cunliff suggest you tape yourself making a presentation and ask a trusted friend to listen with you. Although almost all of us are disagreeably surprised by the sound of our own voices on tape, check to see if yours is high-pitched, nasal or monotone. Does your volume fade off at the end of sentences? Do you use too many annoying "you knows?" If so, you could be a more effective presenter. The speech department of a local college is an excellent place to seek help.

Reprinted from TRAINING, January 1985

At the same time, a perfectly tailored, three-piece suit may not be appropriate. It isn't very practical (or clever) to wear high heels and a white woolen suit into a makeshift classroom in a warehouse filled with sacks of seed and fertilizer. But that doesn't mean we should show up with dirt under our fingernails and a baseball cap, even if the students do. (One advantage of visiting the work site before the training is not only to see how they dress, but for them to see how we dress.)

Dressing down is easier than dressing up. If we come in wearing a suit or coat and the trainees show up in shirt-sleeves or uniforms, it's simple to remove the coat. But actually, there is little evidence in our experience to show that dress has been an obstacle to learning. Even when there is a giant mismatch, the difference soon becomes irrelevant as we get into the training.

Come early, stay late

We should be in the room and comfortably established before the trainees show up. This is our domain and we need to be comfortable in it. They are now going to have to adapt to our sights and sounds, as we adapted to theirs when we visited the work site.

The process is the same, whatever the group: a big, friendly greeting followed by personal introductions of other trainers, people in the class, company officers who may be sitting in—whomever. Now is the time for questions, casual conversations and some serious putting-at-ease of the students. If we handle ourselves well, we will put ourselves at ease, too. They need to see that we aren't ogres or aliens, and we need to see the same about them.

The questions are fairly standard ("Where are you from? What do you do? How long have you been on the job?"), but the listening is crucial. Because we listen to their answers, we are able to respond: "I remember seeing that. I've been there. That's about the time I started with my company."

This informal getting-acquainted period also gives us a chance to sense the mood of the students with regard to the organization or the training. Hearing them gripe about the fact that they aren't drawing overtime pay for attending this after-hours session or about how this class interferes with their heavy work load will tell us something. By coming early and *listening*, we get valuable insights we wouldn't get if we strolled in at the last minute.

By coming early, we can have everything set up: books out, videos cued, easel paper in place. This puts us at ease, and lets us play the gracious host. Even if we are going to be introduced by the plant manager, we still want to meet the people. The

---

Disarm the malcontent, relieve the anxious, convince the slow learner there's nothing to fear.

---

worst thing to do is mess around up front or behind the easel, or spend the time talking with a co-teacher or the introducer. We want the trainees to know our voices and we want to know theirs. It may seem like idle talk to them, but it's our way of letting them know they are welcome and setting the tone that this is going to be a useful and satisfying experience. Use the time to disarm the malcontent, relieve the anxious, and convince the slow learner that we're all in this together and there is nothing to fear. These 20 or 30 minutes will be some of the most valuable moments we'll spend with the trainees.

When the class is over, we must stay and talk to anyone who's willing. If we've convinced trainees that we can help them, some will want help quickly. We should be there to assist. We should be prepared for questions that invariably start with, "I've got a problem I'd like to get your opinion on. . ." or "What do you do with an employee who. . .?" The empathy we show may be worth more than the solution we offer; the mere fact that somebody listens and cares can be incredibly important. Also, we may be able to make this into a case for the

next session, changing the story to protect the contributor, and getting the person's permission to use it, of course.

Adjust to the situation

We may not always find ourselves conducting this class in the best of environments. Sometimes the room may be full of equipment or junk: computers, sacks, supplies, tools, models used in safety or skills training. It may not have the best audiovisual equipment or good study tables. The furniture may be makeshift or uncomfortable, the lighting may be poor and distracting noise may penetrate the walls.

This is another reason to arrive early. Getting there early gives us a chance to accept the bad, improve what we can and perhaps alter some of our exercises.

There is no advantage to badmouthing the facilities, the equipment or the size of the room; it's not the trainees' fault that we aren't satisfied. While we may feel better getting it off our chest, our complaints won't improve anything. Better to make the best of it. Now it's *our* expertise that's at stake. Can we adjust? We've asked the trainees to adjust, coming to this class when they don't really want to, or at a time that's inconvenient, or at a place they don't even know is poorly designed for training. Our best bet is to think positive and act positive. We don't have to say this is the greatest instructional environment in the world, but we don't have to say it's the worst, either.

Mix and mingle

No matter how little we feel we have in common with the group, we need to mingle with them, not only during breaks and at lunch, but sometimes even during small-group work. We shouldn't be the center of attention, but we can listen and comment as we like.

During breaks, we get a chance to discuss the job, the training or whether they like fishing. We are always looking for something we have in common with them; preferably, it relates to the job but not necessarily. We are all adults, with cares and avocations and families and car problems. The more commonalities we discover, the better off we are in es-

tablishing rapport.

Use their examples and problems

We must use the students' experience to move the teaching forward, especially when we don't have enough background to carry the load. Careful listening allows us to reflect on something that has been said, a problem that was raised or an example used earlier. And the right kind of questioning often allows the students to provide input without the teacher having to confess any ignorance:

We must use the students' experience to make the teaching forward, especially when we don't have enough background to carry the load.

"That's a common problem on this type of job. Who has an example to share with us?"

As we circulate during small-group activities, we hear examples or stories we may want to repeat later: "Sue, I think you were telling your group about a similar problem in your shop. How about sharing that example with us all?" If we have a question at break, we can even say, "Do you mind if I pose that question to the whole group? It really highlights the exact problem I want to discuss."

Modify exercises to fit students

Our ability to be flexible and make quick changes in the exercises will be one of the keys to our success in establishing rapport quickly. Again, it's best to get to know the students ahead of time. But we'd better be prepared for such situations as discovering that the paper-and-reading-intensive course we've designed won't work for some supervisors who can barely read or write.

This kind of thing cuts in the other direction, too. The case that last class loved so much—the one about the problem of motivating the maintenance people—may not go over with the high-tech types who supervise the engineering programming group. We'd do better to describe a situation or write it on the easel than to use one that's ready to hand out but just doesn't fit.

Respect what they say, but challenge when necessary

Perhaps the worst way to try for rapport is to play the patsy and agree with every opinion they voice. We can gain their confidence without acquiescing to everything anyone says or does. We have a responsibility to express opinions, to disagree, to challenge when we think the matter should be debated. (We have no right to be sarcastic, to force our opinions onto people or embarrass a participant.)

Remember, they didn't come just to be agreed with. They came to learn something and they expect us to know something. They'll appreciate us more if we take a stand when taking a stand is called for. The stand, however, is always based upon the organization's viewpoint, not our personal biases. If we're talking about company policy or procedure, we're always on safe ground. If we're expressing our own opinion, we should identify it as such and give our reasons.

At the same time (admittedly this gets tricky), we don't want to come across as mere parrots for the organization. If we're taking this company's money in salaries, fees or expenses, we are obligated to teach the material the company's way and not to undermine its policies. But we can't be effective unless we behave like three-dimensional people with likes and dislikes, opinions and biases. Bad-mouthing the company, even if it weren't unprofessional, won't build much respect or rapport. And the classroom is not the place to change policy. But we can suggest to people who seem to have a valid gripe that they use available avenues to try to get the changes made.

Trainers can go into situations in which the students are quite different from themselves and still establish rapport reasonably soon. It takes concentrated effort and an understanding of the instructor's role. The instructor must care about the students and their learning—that is, we must balance a concern for people with a concern for the task at hand. This concern must show. It will show if we make a constant effort to find out who the students are, what their learning needs are, and how we can relate to them with language, examples and exercises that are real to them.

The trick is to do this without trying to become all things to all people. We need their respect as well as their acceptance. Respect comes when we prove that we not only care about their learning, but have something worthwhile to teach them. This happens best if we can establish rapport with them quickly.

Reprinted from TRAINING, September 1987

THE TRAINER AS A BEHAVIOR MODEL

Trainees often acquire new patterns of behavior by watching the trainer

BY BERNARD L. ROSENBAUM
AND BARBARA BAKER

You have the best intentions in your desire to motivate people to hear. So you study adult-learning principles and build into your training experiential exercises in order to encourage self-directed learning. But when you conduct the training session, participants don't accomplish the learning objectives to the degree that you expected. Perhaps that's because *your behavior* in the actual interpersonal situation of teaching didn't support your intentions.

There *are* specific trainer behaviors that support adult-learning principles and that help you, the trainer, accomplish your training objectives while building the participants' self-esteem. In Managerial Grid language, this is 9,9 training (maximum concern for the participant and maximum concern for learning), and it is highly motivating to the learner. These trainer behaviors are soundly based on five principles of motivation that apply to all areas of interpersonal communication. And because they are behaviors, they can be demonstrated, taught and applied in a way that no theory can. Once your training philosophy and intentions support your teaching behavior, you'll become both effective and believable.

When you think about your own experiences as a participant in a training session, you probably find that you often can remember more about the instructor than you can about course content. Behaviors modeled by an instructor can have a powerful impact on group and individual performance. Participants are likely to discount the quality and usefulness of course content when in-structor behavior erodes participant self-esteem. Particularly in training courses that teach *motivation*, the trainer must be *motivating*. Instructor behavior that is at odds with course content produces feelings of discomfort within a student, which he or she tries to relieve by discounting the quality and relevance of course content and by engaging in other defense mechanisms that restrict learning.

Five trainer behaviors that increase motivation to learn

1 Maintain and enhance the self-esteem of participants. For most participants, the motivation to learn can be increased by creating a classroom environment that boosts the participants' confidence in their own ability to learn. Research has demonstrated that people are motivated to learn at a level consistent with their perceptions of self-competency. By maintaining and, when possible, enhancing the self-esteem of participants, the instructor creates a classroom environment that boosts students' confidence in their ability to perform. The motivation to learn is thereby increased.

Research clearly supports this conclusion. Individuals who are told they are incompetent to achieve a specific goal or task will perform worse than those who are told they are competent to achieve the task goals. And individuals and groups of low self-esteem are less likely to achieve goals they have set for themselves than individuals of high self-esteem. The more failures a person has, the less the person will aspire to in the future and the less the person will be motivated to obtain. As a matter of fact, there is a significant positive relationship between self-concept of ability and grade-point average.*

Fortunately, there are specific trainer behaviors that do maintain or even enhance the self-esteem of participants. The trainer who is aware of these would do the following:

- Listens to ideas.
- Praise ideas of participants.
- Acknowledge participants' ideas.
- Turn questions back to the group.
- Write down participants' ideas on a flip-chart.
- Refer back to previous comments by using the speaker's name.
- Point out positive behaviors and their effect.
- Reinforce group compliments of an individual and elaborate upon them.
- Ask for examples from the group's own experience.
- Share his or her own experiences.
- Admit to being wrong.
- Avoid arguments and making "right" and "wrong" judgments.
- Show enjoyment of the class.
- Spend additional time with people during breaks and before and after class.
- Focus on the learners' concerns rather than on his or her own preoccupations.
- Express confidence in the group.
- Ask questions that the learner probably can answer.
- Give complete reasons for directions.
- Share information.
- Keep notes and live up to follow-up commitments.
- Give constructive feedback and build behaviors through positive reinforcement.
- Begin sessions on time.

2 Focus on participants' behavior and not on personality or attitude. When an instructor focuses on the personality traits of a participant, the odds of eroding the participant's self-esteem are increased. One way to improve classroom communications is to focus on specifics and behaviors rather than on personality, attitude or subjective interpretations. The instructor who says, "I'd like you to pay special attention to this," is not modeling this principle as effectively as the instructor who says, "I'd like you to take notes." "You're not being cooperative" and "You don't seem to have a very positive attitude" can be replaced with "You haven't handed in the last two assignments on time." Partici-

*A. Korman, *Industrial and Organizational Psychology* (Englewood Cliffs, NJ: Prentice Hall, 1971), chapter 3.

pants respond more productively when their behavior is discussed than when references are made to their personality or attitudes.

The following suggestions should help you concentrate on behavior, instead of drawing attention to more personal attributes.

- Ask for specific examples.
- Use examples when presenting an idea.
- Ask, "How so?" or "How would you say it?"
- Rather than solicit general comments, ask participants to demonstrate their points of view.
- Ask for evidence. When participants offer praise or criticism, don't accept generalities. Press for specifics.
- When offering praise, explain why.

3 Actively listen to show understanding. Active listening is a communications technique that enables trainers to establish rapport with participants and stimulate open and frank expression of feeling. It aids the trainer in clarifying participant comments and enables the participant to be heard and understood. In active listening, the trainer accepts what is being said without making any value judgments, clarifies the feelings being expressed and reflects this back to the participant.

In the following instances, active listening is particularly important. When a participant makes an emotional statement— "I don't see how we're supposed to get our work done and also attend this class,"— you might respond by saying, "You're feeling stretched pretty thin and are worried about getting your job done." When a participant is being uncooperative, you might say, "You're bored and think this course is a waste of time and not really relevant to getting your job done." And when a participant doesn't seem to understand what you or what another participant has said, your comment might be: "You're a bit confused and uncertain about John's point-of-view."

Other times when active listening responses would be appropriate are:

- When participants keep changing the issue being discussed.
- When a participant is rambling or grandstanding.
- When a participant's remark is important to the group's learning.
- When a participant disagrees with a suggested procedure.

- When a participant is being supportive.

4 Use reinforcement to shape learning. Participant behaviors that are rewarded tend to be repeated and strengthened. Unlike some other consequences of a behavior (e.g., punishment), positive reinforcement is not accompanied by negative side effects. Skillful trainers are able to identify and reward small units of learning and gradually build that learning into the desired outcome. Trainers who rely on overt and/or covert forms of punishment to induce learning tend to generate a defensive reaction that minimizes transference of the training from the classroom to the job.

Reinforcing learning is a three-step process. First, identify the specific, observable behavior that facilitates the learning process (e.g., answering a question, asking a question, participating in an exercise, completing an assignment).

Next, explain what helpful effect that behavior had on the learning process for the participant and for others (e.g., the question helped to clarify an issue, the participation in a role play allowed everyone to learn more).

And finally, indicate your positive feelings about the behavior (e.g., "I really appreciate your comments, thanks for helping me out").

And remember these hints, which serve as verbal and silent reinforcers to your participants.

- Refer back to a participant's ideas or examples.
- Use people's names whenever possible.
- Nod your head when you agree.
- If a particularly cogent remark is made, don't repeat it to make it "yours."
- When a participant's comments or responses are only partially correct, acknowledge the accurate elements before correcting what's wrong.
- Paraphrase or write on flip-charts in the participant's words rather than your own.

Keep in mind that while the learning is in the acquisition stage, it is difficult to overdo specific and sincere positive reinforcement.

5 Set goals and follow-up dates and maintain communications. Set training goals that are challenging,

but achievable, measurable and accompanied by specific deadlines. Well-stated, measurable training goals are effective in improving learning. A growing body of research has demonstrated the motivational properties of goals. Moderately difficult and specific goals lead to higher level of performance than do no goals at all or "do your best" goals.

- "Contract" for specific, on-the-job applications of learning.
- Set specific follow-up dates with participants.
- Clearly indicate what level of proficiency you expect and by when.
- Periodically report on progress toward the goal.
- Keep trust and credibility high by maintaining your follow-up dates.
- Evaluate movement toward the goal against established reference points.

Teaching effective behaviors to trainers

As we've pointed out, trainees often can acquire new patterns of behavior by watching the performance of the trainer. They can abstract common features from a trainer's behavior and transfer them to the job. This is particularly true when the trainer is highly competent, has considerable status and has some influence over resources the trainee desires. That's why certain line managers can make highly effective trainers.

Behavior modeling is a powerful way to provide trainers with skills that facilitate learning. Videotapes are constructed to show trainers successfully teaching others. These tapes (behavior models) show specific trainer behaviors in a variety of situations and problems. Trainers view the models; identify with the situations, which represent their own experiences; rehearse the modeled behaviors under the coaching of a "master trainer"; and are able to transfer the skills to their next training class. This process necessitates spacing the training sessions so that trainers can apply newly learned skills between training sessions.

We believe that it is essential for trainers in Supervisory Skills Training (SST) programs to be able to model everything they are teaching. After all, a significant difference between training that is transferred to the job and training that remains in the classroom is the effectiveness of the trainer as a behavior model.

Reprinted from TRAINING, December 1979

MAKING THE MOST OF THE FIRST 20 MINUTES OF YOUR TRAINING

How you begin your training session
determines whether you have trainees or
just warm bodies in the class

BY DON M. RICKS

The instant a training course begins, a roomful of relaxed talkative adults is suddenly transformed into dutiful pupils. A mere hint that "it's time to begin" can trigger deadly silence, as faces assume attentive expressions and pens are poised expectantly over notebooks. The instructor's stomach lurches uneasily. He has successfully welcomed people at the door, shaken hands, caught names, passed out jokes and strokes; he has, in fact, established credibility as a Human Being. Now he must prove himself, according to the group's expectations, as a Teacher.

This is a promising moment. Regardless of how long the course will last, the trainees can achieve their highest l.v.p.s. (learning volume per second) during the next 20 minutes. Now is the instructor's chance to mold them into a group of active, working learners. Every face in the room says, "I'm ready—start talking." And the temptation to do just that is tremendous. Yet if those first 20 minutes are devoted solely to instructor talk, they may be wasted; worse yet, they may inadvertently lock both the instructor and the group into a nonproductive learning relationship.

Let's look at a typical opening process and the effects it creates. After a joke or two (the participant's reaction: *These instructors always begin with something humorous to try to loosen us up.*) and an uncomfortable round of self-introductions, the instructor attempts to establish the credibility and importance of the course. *(Why does he think I signed up in the first place?)* Then comes an elaborate explanation of the objectives

and methods of the program. *(Okay, okay, let's get on with it.)*

As attention begins to lag, the instructor tries to create some interaction by inviting questions. *(My gawd, he expects me to ask him something!)* Failing that, he tries asking *them* some questions. *(The course hasn't even started yet. How am I supposed to know what he wants me to say?)* When someone does venture a query, the instructor pounces on it as an excuse for a detailed explanation of several related points. *(All I wanted was a "yes" or "no.")* Beginning to panic, he assures the group that the course will be very interesting. *(Oh yeah. When?!)*

A class community

By now class members have solidified. They have assumed avoidance postures, waiting for something to happen that will resuscitate them. In a desperate attempt, the instructor shifts to a more dramatic, and louder, style. *(What happened?)* A contrived joke may bring a couple of chuckles ...and several blank looks. *(Was I supposed to laugh at something?)*

Now the instructor, having delivered his introductory remarks but failing to establish rapport, is stuck. He can only proceed with the instructional material, hoping to loosen up the class along the way. The magic words — "Well then, let's get to work"—spark a flurry of movement, a scraping of chairs. Again the pens are poised, ready to take notes.

What has this instructor accomplished during the first crucial 20 minutes? He has conveyed to the course participants that they will play Pupil to his Teacher for the duration.

Pupil is a role they assume effortlessly; each has had from 12 to 20 years preparing for the part. As for him, the easiest thing to be, when standing in front of a group, is a Teacher. So both are forced into compulsive behaviors. He is authoritative, patient, and wise. They are passive, compliant, and dependent. He makes lists on the chalkboard, tosses out humorous comments, and speaks important words. They laugh appreciatively and write down everything. If he's a Good Teacher, they will be impressed by how much *he* knows about the subject.

The problem with such introductory lectures is not that they cover the wrong materials but that they happen at all. In fact, an instructor should not have time to lecture at the beginning of the course. There are too many other worthwhile things to do. Here are four that should rate high priority with all trainers.

1. Neutralize the incipient Teacher-Pupil relationship.
2. Begin to form a class community.
3. Encourage trainees to discover and start to correct any nonproductive learning agendas they may have.
4. Encourage them to formulate definite in-course and post-course objectives for themselves.

The potential Teacher-Pupil relationship has to be disrupted immediately, even before it has begun to function. The canny instructor will use the opening as a time to start reacting to his students, not vice versa. By creating opportunities for the trainees to talk, he can validate their own knowledge and experience, their own potentialities for contributing to the course. He should remember that, at this point, it is more important for people to *feel* right than to *be* right. So he should treat contributions and responses as opportunities for showing approval, not as excuses for displaying his own abilities to correct or explain.

Unless the group is very large, the instructor should make eye contact with, and direct at least one comment or question to, every individual in the room. Thus he will avoid having some people wait for "something to happen to me." And he will prevent that uneasy feeling, a couple of days down the road, of discovering a stranger in the course, someone he hadn't noticed before.

The instructor can also start building a class community immediately. During the first 20 minutes, everyone should make direct eye contact with, talk with, and even touch at least half a dozen other group members. They should also be made to move at least once. Their first instinct was to claim a territory and establish a defensive perimeter; but if they leave their seats and relate to their neighbors on neutral territory, "block party" style, they will be better prepared to work together.

By seating people in small groups of five or six and by briefly addressing each group as a separate entity, the instructor can accomplish a great deal. People will begin to like members of a manageable social unit within which a lone individual can exert influence. Moreover, they will speak up more freely, because they will feel supported by their own team; in confronting the authority personified by the teacher, they will feel they have allies.

A few minutes of personal agenda work at the beginning of a course can produce a marked improvement in the post-course performance results. Trainers can safely assume that everyone in the room is there for the wrong reasons. Some people bring *irrelevant* agendas: "Sue got sick, so I'm sitting in for her"; "Now that I've finally signed up for this course, maybe my boss will get off my back." Others come with *inappropriate* agendas: "I'm here to evaluate this course for use by others"; "I want to find out what I've been doing wrong"; "According to the outline, this course touches on one or two of the topics I'm interested in." And far too many attend with seemingly reasonable, but *non-functional*, agendas: "I'm here to learn the course content" (not "to improve my performance"). "I'll *try* to improve" (not *"will* improve"). "After I look at the whole program, I'll pick out and learn the parts that are directly relevant to my situation."

So an instructor can use a brief agenda exercise to make people aware of their subliminal reasons for attending the course. Here again, the temptation to talk—or, rather, to preach—is strong. But by helping adults discover a) that they may have come into the course with a nonproductive mental set, and b) that more positive alternatives exist, an instructor can indirectly shift attitudes.

Post-course objectives

Establishing an explicit sense of individual objectives is a critical function of the introduction. Most people have two generalized objectives when they enter the training room. First, they want to *perform well* (i.e., make "correct" responses) in the course. Second, they intend to *learn the materials* (i.e., the concepts and information) they assume the instructor will cover. Usually they have only a vague notion of post-course objectives. They know that what they will learn should help them do a better job—but in some uncertain way and at some undefined future time.

Not only are these objectives too general, they may be counterproductive. In a course which is intended to improve performance rather than increase knowledge, the trainee determined to "can the content" will frustrate both himself and the instructor. He who thinks his purpose is to "do well" will expend his energies trying to figure out the correct answers rather than adopting more effective ways of performing.

The instructor should therefore prepare for the transition from the training room back into the "real world" on the first, not the last, day of the course. Moreover, he should emphasize that the course consists of what *the students do*, not of what the instructor does. Again, questioning is the most effective technique. Some-

thing as simple as, "Which should be better—the last letter you wrote before the course or the first one you will write afterward?," can initiate dialogue. Students will discover that their objective in the course should be to change how they write, not just to learn about good writing, and that the real proof of their performance will be a demonstrable improvement in the documents they later produce on the job.

Ostensibly, a course opening serves to introduce trainees to the instructor and to outline the course's content. Actually, such an introduction contradicts two principle premises of modern training: that trainees themselves are the active agents in their own learning processes, and that the instructor should serve as a well-informed guide, not a talking textbook. The instructor's initial task then should be to bring people to a point where: 1) they can work together comfortably in an unfamiliar environment, 2) they will draw freely upon the special resources the instructor provides, and 3) they have set some positive goals to achieve.

The objectives and techniques of the course introduction, therefore, should be the most carefully planned and executed of the whole program. Technique, of course, is not nearly as important as attitude or the role function the instructor brings to the training room. If an instructor considers himself an expert, the group will treat him as an expert depending upon him to make the training happen. But if the trainer sees himself as assisting others in accomplishing their learning goals, the trainees will be better able to work in cooperation with him. Similarly, the instructor who enters the room expecting to enjoy the trainees—not hoping to *persuade* them to enjoy him—will discover that establishing rapport and getting results are easy, even pleasurable, tasks.

Your course introduction is the most important part of the training. If it isn't well planned, your trainees will tune you out—wasting both your time and theirs.

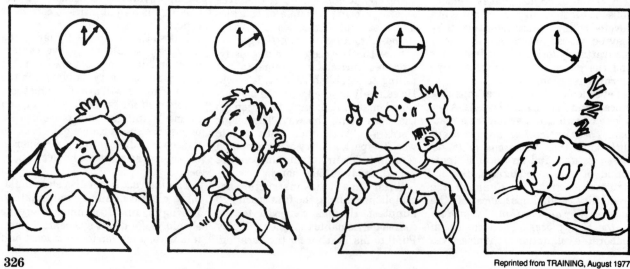

Reprinted from TRAINING, August 1977

MOTIVATING AND MANAGING LEARNING IN THE CLASSROOM

Make sure your trainees want to learn what you have to teach

BY J.B. CORNWELL

How can I motivate my students?" "What can I do about students who don't want to learn?" "How can I show students the value of my objectives so they want to learn?"

Sound familiar? Those questions and variations on them are among those most frequently asked by classroom teachers/trainers seeking to become more effective.

Unfortunately, there are no simple answers. Students are human beings. Because of their individuality, no technique will stimulate all of them—even in the unlikely event that your presentation is ideally suited to them all.

But there is at least one way to ensure that students will want to learn what you offer and will invest considerable effort doing so.

Let's assume, though, that, in the planning session, you have accurately identified the performance needs of your students and have formulated specific objectives that describe performances the students will agree they don't have.

Learner assessment

Think about the experiences you have had with good salesmen. No, not the con artists who made you feel you'd been had. I mean those who sold you something you really wanted and made sure it fit your needs. Many car and insurance salesmen fit that description. When you finish this paragraph, put the book down, close your eyes, and relive the whole experience. Then come back.

One of the things that first-rate salesman did was find out what our needs were. The car salesman asked questions about the size of the family, how much driving we do, how much money we wanted to spend and some questions about our attitudes toward cars. Then he checked his conclusions with a statement-question sort of like this one:

> Well, let's see now. You've got one six-year-old, you live a block from work but you take long, driving vacations and you tow an 18-foot ski-boat. It seems to me that comfort and prestige are more important to you than price and economy. Is that correct? Okay, then I think our Superdynamic Flowmobile V12 Formal Sedan with towing package, stereo, power dimmer switch, and robot remote gas pump detector would fit the bill. Have you looked it over? Would you like to test drive it?

Do you see what he was up to? Doesn't it seem likely that he was testing what he knew about you, what he thought he knew about you and the conclusions he drew from that *before* he started filling out a sales contract? As a matter of fact, you probably responded by correcting some wrong assumptions he made. For example: "No, actually reliability and low maintenance costs are very important to me. What do you have in a six-cylinder, standard-shift, two-door sedan?"

When did the salesman start getting your full cooperation? Wasn't it when he offered you a car with the features *you* wanted, that met your needs the way *you* saw those needs? That's what I thought.

When, then, do you suppose a teacher is likely to get full cooperation from learners? I suggest it will be when the learners agree that the objectives fit what they see themselves as needing.

If we thoroughly analyzed the needs of our learner population in the early stages of the design of our presentation, we would have a reasonably accurate set of assumptions about what they want and why. However, even if that analysis of a generalized population includes asking direct, to-the-point questions about what the learners want and why, we must establish— verbally— the connection between self-perceived needs and our product.

For example, imagine yourself in either role in the following situation. You are about two hours into a presentation on behavioral objectives:

Presenter: Karen, from watching you these past few minutes, I've decided that you're bored to tears with this program. Am I reading you correctly? But I assumed that, with your new job in training nurses' aides, you'd be really turned on by behavioral objectives.

Karen: Oh, I *was* turned on— until the program started. It's just not what I expected. I don't see how it relates to my situation. Behavioral objectives may be useful for training production workers and technicians, but my problems are different. I'm dealing mainly with attitudes.

P: What had you expected to learn?

K: I expected to learn how to do a better job of changing attitudes. What I'm getting is how to set objectives for and evaluate skills.

P: How do you determine whether or not you've changed attitudes?

K: That's pretty intangible. I have to go on gut feeling and on feedback from the nurses and patients.

P: You said you came here to learn how to do a better job of changing attitudes. Assuming you went back and did a better job, how would you know? What evidence would convince you that you were doing a better job?

K: Well...I don't know.

P: Does this seem logical to you: Attitudes describe how people feel about things? What they do and say is evidence of how they feel. The only indicators we have of what people feel is what they say and do—in other words, their behavior. Do you agree so far?

K: To tell you the truth, I never thought of it that way. But yes, that makes sense.

P: Well, suppose you nailed down some observable behaviors that are acceptable evidence of the attitudes you are trying to produce. Would that

WHY DO WE WANT TRAINEE INVOLVEMENT?

BY MARTIN M. BROADWELL

A couple of things often give the new classroom instructor the feeling of "losing control": Turning the group loose for a discussion and breaking the group up into some kind of subgroup assignment. But we know that an instructor has to be truly exceptional to reach learning goals without actively involving the students. This raises a number of questions: What kind of involvement do we try for? Is just any kind of involvement good? Is it the involvement that causes the learning? What are some of the ways of getting useful involvement?

Why involvement?

Considerable argument is offered both for and against involvement. Many experienced trainers who advocate it claim it makes a course more interesting and helps numb the "pain" of learning. No doubt about it, the involved student may find an otherwise dull course more interesting. Involvement seems to make time go faster and relieves the boredom of a monotone lecture. It forces students to concentrate on the subject at hand. But involvement based on this premise is incorporated to overcome something negative. Instead, it should be built into the design *of our training program* to accomplish something positive.

Other instructors try to add a respectable amount of participation to a classroom setting in the form of showing a few slides or a movie or occasionally using an easel and chalkboard. This, they believe, adds credence to the classroom activity. Because it is expected and because all the "right" books suggest it, they dutifully—and mechanically—try to get the group involved by using often uninspired tools and techniques.

Some instructors rely on involvement to fill up class time when they run short of material. With no particular objective in mind, they decide to toss out a couple of discussion questions and make a subgroup assignment that will keep students busy. They might try to justify their "efforts" by saying that the students "always like this exercise" or "this question really ties them in knots." But this hardly represents the use of involvement as a learning tool.

The best design

Basically, the only reason for generating meaningful involvement is that it *can be* the best teaching method available to accomplish the learning goals we're seeking. This reason applies to any technique we use—anytime. And it should govern our approach to all course designs.

Involvement itself is certainly not synonymous with successful teaching; nor is just any kind of involvement guaranteed to be satisfactory. When we feel the urge to add involvement, we shouldn't satisfy that urge by, say, arbitrarily assigning a role play. We should assign role play only when that type of involvement is most likely to elucidate a certain point we need to reach a certain, *specified* objective. The same reasoning should dictate the use of other techniques, too.

Added benefits

In addition to being a good technique for reaching an objective, involvement gives us a chance to get feedback from students, feedback that is related directly to the goal we're striving for in the activity itself. If we're doing a role play to teach salespeople how to close a sale, we receive feedback in precisely the areas we're concerned with. By hearing the efforts to overcome objections or close the sale, we know where the trainees' strengths and weaknesses are in the subject we're teaching.

Furthermore, the feedback produced by the involvement usually is transmitted back to the students, too. In the example above, the sales trainees can see how their approaches work (or don't work) and can make any necessary improvements. They don't need an instructor to tell them what's wrong with their presentations, especially if they've seen themselves role play on a videotape.

Feedback through involvement also allows us to measure the success of our objectives, especially those we hoped to attain at the end of a class period. Any kind of involvement will have students doing something, saying something, working on something that is the result of things that have been taught in class. By simply observing the involved and participating students, we can match what we see against what we wanted to see (our objectives) and decide whether or not we've met our goals.

What kinds of involvement?

Involvement is, simply, any kind of student activity that is observable. (We'll avoid the obvious fallacy in this definition—the case where students are *mentally* involved." In its simplest form, it's a student answering "yes" or "no" to a question or writing an answer in a blank. In its most complex form, it might be a student doing individualized instruction with virtually no aid from the teacher.

The best way to stimulate involvement activities early in the teaching game is to pick those that provide some kind of built-in controls for the teacher. An example of a controlled involvement activity would be a subgroup assignment with rigid restrictions. Such activities may sound fixed, inflexible, and unimaginative—and they are. But they should be, because the novice instructor usually isn't ready to allow much latitude. That will come. First, the instructor must learn to handle the involvement technique itself.

Having each student make lists of reasons, name two problems, or give one written solution to a problem are other ways of stimulating involvement. We can have the students teach a portion of the material, especially in an area where one of the students is an experienced resource person. We can have them work on forms or find things in manuals. There are good, practical forms of involvement. If they are chosen because they are the best for the student at *this time* to *this subject*, they probably will be successful. If they're viewed as a means of getting through the training day as quickly and painlessly as possible, they may still be as successful. But obviously not for the right reasons.

One problem with involvement: It is easy to get caught up in the *doing* of it, without considering the *purpose* behind it. Therefore, the instructor, be he novice or old hand, always ought to ask, "Is this really a *meaningful* activity?" Excessive reliance on involvement techniques presents another problem—using them just because it's easy to do so. Adult learners need a reason for doing things in class. Many will play our game for just so long before asking themselves. "Why are we doing this?" Naturally, they aren't happy with the answer: "Don't worry, you'll see it all clearly a little later." A little later, we may find ourselves with fewer and less capable students. And for good reason.

Reprinted from TRAINING, May 1977

make it easier to measure how well you are doing?

K: It sure would! Writing behavioral objectives that describe those behaviors would be the first step toward improving my course. I guess I had the cart before the pony. Could you go back over the key points on describing conditions?

If the presenter had begun by establishing the connection between Karen's perception of what she needed and the objectives of the program, Karen wouldn't have been bored two hours later. All too often, "Karens" leave our presentations feeling frustrated. How, then, do we establish this connection? How do we get the learners to agree that we perceive their needs accurately?

Here are a couple of helpful approaches:

1. **Presenter:** As I understand it, everyone here is a new instructor. Is that right?
   Learners: (a murmur of assent, some affirmative nods)
   P: Okay, our survey indicated that most new instructors felt they needed to be able to tell how well they had done. In other words, a method to measure how good they are. Does that seem desirable to you?
   L: (another murmur of assent)

2. **Presenter:** The title of this presentation is "Writing Behavioral Objectives." Behavioral objectives specify what we are going to achieve so that, when we are finished, we can accurately measure what we have achieved. Now, I would like you to tell me how this subject might fit your situations and what you would like to get out of today's session. Why don't you start out, Mike?

In both cases, a climate is established for serving the learner. (Of course, we must adjust the presentation to accommodate any real needs that we had perceived inaccurately.) We have probably successfully accomplished this step in the opening of our presentation if, after the presentation, the learners answer "Absolutely yes" to the question, "Did the presenter accurately perceive what you wanted from the presentation?"

Commitment to objectives

Let's return to our professional salesman for a moment. Do you recall what he did after you agreed on what you wanted and needed? Did he give you a detailed description of his product, its features and benefits? Actually, that's the next step in a traditional sales presentation: after the salesman has "qualified" his prospect (clarified what the prospect wants and needs and received the prospect's agreement about it), he describes the product in detail.

We should do something similar. We'll describe our product in detail, or state our behavioral objectives and the things that will happen during the presentation.

If we work from notes, our notes at this point will tell us to state the objectives—"After this presentation you will do such and such, under such and such conditions, to such and such standard"—and describe the presentation—"To accomplish this, we will do the following...."

Is it now clear to the learners what the objectives of the presentation are? What evidence convinces you of that?

Have you ever heard this little ditty? *I know I said what I thought I said.*

LEARNER ASSESSMENT (SAMPLE)

PROGRAM

The purpose of this questionnaire is to provide the presenter of this program with insights into your current skills in knowledge or about the subject. By knowing what new skills and knowledge you would like to get from the program, what personal goals you are pursuing that this program can contribute to, and some personal characteristics about yourself, the presenter will be better able to serve your needs in the presentation.

This form will be held in the strictest confidence and will be destroyed after the program.

Name_____ Age_____ Gender_____

Years of formal education_____ Title of current position_____

Briefly describe the responsibilities of your current position.

How do you expect the results of this program to improve your life and career?

What is the most important thing you expect to get out of this program?

How long have you been working in the type of job you now have?

Complete the following sentences.

I hope that this program will_____

I hope that this program will not_____

LEARNING CONTRACT (SAMPLE)

In the matter of the training course, _____, objectives and outline attached, and in consideration of the expense and effort invested in making this course available to me, I agree to do the following:
1. Appear in the classroom at the scheduled time(s).
2. Be alert and in as good physical and mental condition as possible.
3. Give my undivided attention to the presentations and projects scheduled.
4. Complete all projects assigned according to scheduled completion times.
5. Achieve the objectives listed on the attached.

Signed, _____ date _____
    Student

In consideration of the above, I agree to devote my full attention and energy to assisting _____ and other students enrolled in this course in achieving the objectives listed on the attached..

Signed, _____
    Instructor

I know you heard what you thought you heard. The problem is: You didn't hear what I said.

The point is, you heard my words, but you didn't hear my meaning. Let me try different words: Listeners don't always understand the speaker's words the way the speaker intends them. The only sure way we have of confirming understanding is to have our meanings fed back to us.

Are you still convinced that your learners understood the objectives? How will you convince yourself?

You might ask some of them to explain how they will apply the objectives to their jobs. You can watch the others for nonverbal feedback to see if they agree.

Once the learners clearly understand what the objectives are, we must be sure that these are also the learners' objectives. Just because they agree that we understand their needs, doesn't mean that they automatically agree that our solutions to those needs are worth the effort. The car salesman doesn't assume that we will buy his car just because we agree that we want and need a new car.

The question we must now answer for the learners is: What do I have to do to get it? (Remember asking the salesman how much the car cost? Is there any chance that you would have signed the sales contract before you knew?) What the learners have to do is cooperate during the presentation. So tell them what is going to happen and how—and get some feedback.

Now it's time to close the deal. When salesmen use that term, they mean getting the prospect to commit himself or herself to a contract. What the learners will do is give an overt (outward) sign that they are going to pursue the same objectives that you are during the presentation. The overt sign may be a nod of the head or a statement, such as "Yes, that's a worthwhile objective that will help me get where I want to be. I'm going to put forth the required effort to achieve it."

To the casual observer, the closing of the contract may be too subtle to notice. It may be just a casual transaction, like this:

Presenter: Well, that's our objective, and that's how we plan to achieve it. It will require your cooperation and effort. Can I count on that?

Learners: (Heads nod. But one learner stares blankly at the presenter.)

P: Do you need time to think it over, Sam?

S: Not at all. I just didn't think it mattered whether I wanted to cooperate or not, and I was wondering why you bothered to ask. No one ever asked before.

P: How do you feel about being asked this time?

S: I'm not sure. I don't know whether you're trying to avoid wasting your time on learners who don't want to put forth any effort or avoid wasting my time on things I don't want to learn badly enough to work at.

P: Would you accept both reasons, plus the fact that having made a conscious, outward commitment increases the probability that you actually will work at it?

S: Hmm. Maybe that's manipulation and maybe not. Either way, my desire is in motion; let's go.

Okay, so that wasn't such a casual transaction. But would have been had Sam just nodded, or if the presenter hadn't read his nonverbal feedback. Learners don't always respond exactly as we would like them to. What would you do if a learner says, "No. I don't think it's worth the effort"? Tell him to get his keester out of your classroom?

Well, we might do that, but it's not our classroom. It's theirs, the learners'. I'm there to fill their needs. I'd ask the learner how much effort it *is* worth. I don't think it's likely that a student would say "None." But if he did, I'd ask him what he proposes to do during the presentation. I'd also give the rest of the learners a chance to offer their comments.

Once we've closed the contract with the learners for mutual effort toward achieving the objectives, we are ready to begin the planned learning experiences.

At this point, we've completed the opening of our presentation. The strategy and sequencing of the opening are the same as in the classical sales presentation:

1. *Qualify the learner*. Get agreement from the learners that you accurately perceive their goals and needs.

2. *Describe the features, benefits and price of the product*. Describe the objectives of the presentation and the things that will happen during it. Get feedback to confirm their understanding.

3. *Close the contract*. The purpose of the first two steps is to get a valid contract. Get an overt commitment from the learners to work at achieving the objectives.

You have probably opened your presentation effectively if, after the presentation, your learners answer "Absolutely yes" to these questions:

1. Did the presenter accurately perceive what you wanted from the presentation?
2. Were the objectives clear to you from the beginning of the presentation?
3. Has the presentation provided you with solutions to your real needs?

Suggested exercises for trainers/presenters

For one presentation you make:

1. Have all your learners complete a learner-assessment form that you design or a variation on the same learner assessment sheet in this article. Or, if you cannot directly collect learner perceptions of their needs, list those needs as you perceive them.

2. List learner needs that will be served by your presentation.

3. Opposite each need listed, enter one or more objectives of the presentation that will serve that need.

4. Write down your plan for getting agreement from your learners that their needs have been accurately assessed and that the objectives will solve those needs.

5. Write down your plan for establishing that the learners understand what the objectives are and what will happen during the presentation.

6. Write down your plan for getting commitment from the learners to invest effort toward the objectives.

7. Use your plan the next time you make that presentation. If you have decided to ask for a written contract from your learners, use the sample learning contract provided here or some variation on it.

Reprinted from TRAINING, December 1978

DEALING WITH AGE AND EXPERIENCE DIFFERENCES

Protect the ego—theirs and yours—when your class has varying levels of experience

BY MARTIN M. BROADWELL

Perhaps few things plague the training director and the classroom like the presence of experienced employees sitting next to those who are brand new, either on the job or with the organization. There are some solutions but you may have to change your traditional teaching methods to get the best results.

Remember the first public speaking class you were ever in? One of the first things you were told was "know your audience." This is equally good advice for the instructor: "Know your students!" Just because you have people of different age groups or with different years of experience does not—*in itself*—mean that there is a difference in knowledge or skills level among your trainees. One of the things that bothers me a great deal is to be conducting some management or supervisory training (whatever the difference is) and have some old-timer say, "I've heard all that before." I've finally found the appropriate response to that. I simply ask (smiling all the time), "Great, are you suggesting that you've not only *heard* all this but that you're also *doing all of it* now?" I have yet to hear anyone say that they are, in fact, practicing all the things I'm trying to get across, though I suspect there are some who think they are, but are afraid to come out and admit it with peers (who know better) right there in the room. You might also request that the "hearer of it all before" help out with practical examples whenever possible. In other words, enlist the help of the experi-

enced person as a means of selling your own points, and as a means of at least neutralizing any opposition.

This, then, is one of the basic rules of handling the variance: Use the experience to your advantage, rather than have it used against you to your disadvantage. This means sometimes catering to these experienced people in ways your own ego might not like. You may have to give them recognition, ask their opinion, give them talk-time when you'd rather not, and avoid cutting them down when you'd like to. For consolation, remember that these people who do have experience carry a lot of weight with those who don't, and the newer employee may take their word over yours. If this is the case, it's best to have the words *agreeing rather than disagreeing*.

Protect the Ego

The experienced supervisor or skilled employee probably feels somewhat out of place in the classroom with the newer employees. In a way, it's a put-down to be there. It's sometimes shattering to find that the organization thinks he needs training in areas where he's been working for a long time, and then to discover that he's in a class with a bunch of wet-behind-the-ears beginners. One of the problems for the instructor is that this assault on the ego may promote some frustrations which exhibit themselves in behavior that is undesirable to the instructor. Herein lies the secret to successfully using these people: Protect their egos, not your own. In their frustrations, they may challenge you.

Take the challenge, but in an adult way, trying to find the empirical proofs for what you are saying, not by drawing your sword and trying to cut the person down with an "I told you so!"

If the person is wrong, make the let-down easy, firm, and pleasant. If the person is right, make the thank-you sincere, and the experience a *learning* experience for the whole class. Be careful, though, not to carry this ego satisfaction too far. You can't devote the entire class period to just keeping the egos salved. You have to get in some learning, too. This takes some skill at observation, and it takes some admission that you may not be very good at observation—especially in the early stages of the class meetings.

Let's take an example. You start the class and immediately get a challenge from an older or more experienced student. You debate hurriedly in your mind and decide that this person may become a problem if you don't get him on your side in a hurry. You give the person some attention early in the session. This works well for you, because the students comment, you're looking for participation, and all this is working well. Soon, there is another challenge from this same employee/student, and again you respond in a way to build up the person, giving satisfaction, allowing for discussion, agreeing where you can. Again, there is a challenge from this same person. By now, you're probably feeling dominated by this person who has successfully challenged and won on several occasions, and you would like to hear from the others, who seem to be holding back. A monster is beginning to take shape, and you don't know whether to kill it, run from it, or feed it.

You must set some standards on how much interruption you'll tolerate, how much participation you want from others, then use your teaching skills to meet these standards. This doesn't mean you should go back to putting down the student. It does mean that at some point the student must conform to the rules and procedures of the classroom.

Remember, you reinforced this early participation, diagreement, knowledge-sharing, and the student was responding to your encouragement. It would be improper if you now embarrassed him. The easiest thing to do is withdraw reinforcement. When the person speaks out, listen to him, but don't enter into a discussion about it. If it's a question, hear it out, decide if it is pertinent. If so, then answer it, or reflect it to *someone else*. If it's not pertinent, then say something like, "That's interesting and something to think about later. Right now, we've got to deal with...", and go on with your agenda. An extreme procedure is to look at the employee, listen, but not respond at all...just go on to the next point. It's a bit frustrating, but not necessarily embarrassing, if you don't dwell on the looking and listening too long. There's always the alternative of, "We can talk about that after class, if you like."

New People Have Ego, Too

Most of these techniques are designed to protect the older, experienced students. But what about the younger ones? Obviously, they have rights and feelings, too, and you should be equally concerned about them. You should find out what they know, what they don't know, what they need to know, how they feel about being in the class with older employees, what pressures they feel, and what they think about why the organization sent them to this course with the older, more experienced employees. Again, your power of observation comes into play, and you must be equally careful not to move too fast, or draw conclusions too quickly.

These employees are apt to be conscious that they're not as experienced as their co-students. They won't be able to answer the questions as readily, nor be willing to answer them even if they think they know the answers. Again, you must be willing to change your traditional teaching methods. You might even confront the class with the question, "How can we handle this inequity in distribution of experience and knowledge?" You may have to create a makeshift lesson plan right there in the class. Try asking for volunteers to teach certain material in an "aide" capacity. Or you can give some quick knowledge tests to find out

---

Your own ego might not like these techniques, but they can help resolve this age-old classroom problem.

---

who can handle what material. This isn't a threat, it's just a quick means of helping out the students and using their resources.

Another technique is to allow the trainees to move at their own pace, if possible. If you know ahead of time that you're going to have a level difference, you can design with this self-pacing in mind. Otherwise, you can do some of it right in the class. "Those of you who feel you have a working knowledge of this may want to move on to the next step." Or, "Those of you who feel comfortable with this material can be of assistance in helping the others in small-group work." This technique shows consideration for the newer employees, gives them the advantage of the resources in the room, and still deals favorably with the older egos.

Finally, we should protect these less experienced employees by teaching to them at their level, rather than aiming over their heads just because there are a few more experienced people in the class. Some of us have a tendency to talk to one person if we don't watch ourselves. We ask a question, get an immediate answer from one of the students, go on for a while, ask another question, get the correct response from the same student, and before we know it, the rest of the students are sitting around wondering what they're doing in the class in the first place!

We should work on systems that get feedback from all the students; we should respond to the questions of the newer students in meaningful ways. At the same time, when one of the newer employees comes up with a right answer, by all means we should reinforce this immediately and sincerely. If we do, we'll soon have them all working together toward the same objective, helping each other and us, too, in getting to that goal.

Reprinted from TRAINING, July 1976

LEARNING TO LISTEN TO TRAINEES

Real listening requires three sets of ears, each specially trained

BY RON ZEMKE

If you're like most trainers, you place a high value on your ability to communicate. For every 20 minutes you spend holding forth in the classroom, you spend two and a half hours in preparation. You undoubtedly spend additional time, money and effort improving your speaking and writing skills. Many trainers take night courses in speech and communication, and every Toastmaster Club numbers teachers and trainers among it membership.

But how much time and effort do you spend developing your *listening* or *"receiving"* skills? Cathrina Bauby, author of *Understanding Each Other*, talks about person-to-person communication in terms of the "dialogue skills of listening, questioning and acknowledgment." Classroom communication is nothing if not an active, unpredictable process of dialogue. Were it otherwise, the role of instructor could and should be relegated to the boob tube.

Listening requires practice, too

Most of us assume that listening is a natural ability we all possess. Certainly, hearing is inborn for most of us...but effective listening is not. Marshall McCluhan has quipped that, while we have no idea who discovered water, we can be pretty sure that it wasn't a fish. Listening and hearing are like that. You and I are so immersed in the daily stream of survival communication that we seldom realize that real listening goes beyond simple decoding of the literal meanings of the words we hear. Communications experts suggest that words and their dictionary meanings are only one-third of any speaker's message. Voice tone, body language, and even the tense and person of the words we choose convey that other, vital two-thirds of the message. To be effective in the classroom, we must be keenly aware of the three types of listening—selective listening, active listening, and "eye" listening.

Selective listening: listening for facts

"What's he trying to say?" "Will she ever get to the point?" "Did I miss something, or did he forget to get where he was going with that?" Ever ask yourself those questions? If so, then you've experienced selective listening problems. If we listened only to trained public speakers all day, listening would be no problem. The "pro" invariably follows the sequence of introduction, thesis, body, and conclusion. The army used to call it the bull's-eye formula: Tell 'em what you're gonna tell 'em, tell 'em, tell 'em what you told 'em. Few of us speak in that organized fashion. Especially off-the-cuff. Especially trainees.

Compounding the general disorganization of conversational or daily speech, the *rate of hearing* mitigates against effective fact comprehension. The average speaker delivers approximately 140 words per minute. Researchers have found that the average listener can comfortably comprehend messages delivered at 300 w.p.m. You and I tend to fill the "dead space" by watching cars go by, inspecting the speaker's shoeshine, and talking to ourselves sub-audibly ("Will he *ever* get to the point?"). Small wonder that we are occasionally "out to lunch" when the trainee finally formulates the main point of his or her question, or that we sometimes fail to correctly sort and classify the speaker's facts and opinions.

According to Chris Hickey, product manager for Xerox Learning Systems' "Strategies for Effective Listening," we can double the effectiveness of our listening by developing the process skills of separating fact from opinion, distinguishing between main points and supporting arguments, and building mental outlines as we listen to people. A simple enough concept, but one that requires time and practice.

Active listening: listening for feelings

If some messages are difficult to understand because the speaker is disorganized and has trouble making himself "perfectly clear," others are difficult because the message isn't contained in the speaker's words at all! According to Psychologist Thomas Gordon, author of *Parent Effectiveness Training* and *Teacher Effectiveness Training*, not all communication is self-evident and easily understood. The sentence "What time is it?" *may* be a request to know the time; but if the speaker is hungry and the dinner hour is at hand, "What time is it?" might actually mean "When do we eat?" The technique needed to decode these subtle messages is Active Listening.

According to Psychologist Carl Rogers, you and I could be superb at semantics—able to follow and untangle the most convoluted of scholarly arguments—and still be totally inept at understanding what people are "telling" us. Why? Because the symbols themselves—words—have nothing to do with the main message. Want proof? Simple. Say the following phrase aloud, emphasizing the underlined word, and you'll see how different a message the same words can convey:

We're not going to have a test today?
We're *not* going to have a test today?
We're not going to have a *test* today?

Active listening was created by Rogers for training therapists to work with patients. The method consists of "listening for feelings" and reflecting back your guess at the speaker's emotional state. With advance apologies to Rogers and Gordon, here's approximately how active listening works.

Charlie Trainee storms into your office, screaming at the top of his lungs: "I wouldn't work for this chicken outfit another 10 minutes if my life depended on it." You, a calm, cool trainer schooled in active listening, reply: "Charlie, it sounds like you're upset. And I know you wouldn't be upset without a good reason. Tell me about it."

"First they screwed up my housing allowance, and now my plane tickets are all wrong. They just don't care about us trainees."

"You don't think the company cares about your problems?"

"I've got to get home before seven on Friday night. It's our fifth anniversary, and my wife is planning a big party."

"You really want to leave here earlier than you're scheduled for now."

"And how!"

"Let's call travel and see what we can do."

Easy? No. Effective? Yes. Try it and see, the next time a communications problem presents itself. But, first, take a look at Gordon's work. To Rogers' active listening skill, he has added the skills of identifying problem ownership and "I"-message delivery to form a vocabulary for the developing technology of listening for feelings.

Eye listening: the body speaks

The third part of listening isn't listening at all; it's looking. Watching what people do with their bodies, how they stand, move, and hold themselves, gesture, make eye contact and the like, in relation to other people—this is what is meant by non-verbal communication.

One aspect of non-verbal communication concerns cultural norms. In *The Silent Language*, cultural anthropologist Edwart T. Hall suggests that you and I can communicate effectively only to the extent that we share three things he calls Key Cultural Isolates. These are time and its meaning, space and its use, and common experiences. While Hall was working for the State Department, he noticed that Americans overseas who failed to perceive and honor the ways different people use time and space accomplished little. Simple example. Americans tend to keep business associates literally at arms length; four to seven feet is the distance we normally maintain for talking to business-only acquaintances. But in the Middle East, business is often literally transacted nose to nose. American business people dealing with Middle Easteners often feel they are being attacked, and, conversely, the Middle Eastern business person is uncomfortable with Yankee stand-offishness.

A friend of ours, who spent four months in Iran for a computer manufacturer, began to fear he smelled offensive when he returned to the States. He couldn't figure out why people stood so far away from him. The problem? He had adapted so well to a different norm for using space that space use in his own culture actually felt uncomfortable.

Another example: eye contact. Blacks and whites in our culture have slightly different eye-contact rules. In general, whites avoid eye contact when speaking but watch the speaker closely when they are listening. Blacks tend to do the opposite. This leads to "He/She isn't paying attention to what I'm saying" interpretations of normal, subculturally sanctioned listening behavior.

The second part of non-verbal communications is actual body language or Kinesics, as Psychologist Ray Birdwhistell dubbed this art/science in the 1940s. The listener or speaker who twists and turns in his or her chair while engaged in dialogue probably finds the conversation unpleasant. Rubbing one's nose may simply be a response to an itch, but some body linguists contend that it might mean the speaker is nervous, disapproving, or even dishonest.

Here are some other gestures to watch for from your trainees:

• *Arms folded across chest.* This could mean the individual is implacable, seemingly unbudgeable. His mind may be as tightly locked as his arms.

• *Sitting on the chair edge.* This is tricky because its precise meaning is ambivalent. It could be either that the individual has warmed to you and your ideas and is ready to cooperate *or* that he is turned off and is anxious to end the meeting.

• *Leaning back with hands behind head.* This suggests arrogance, aggressiveness, a propensity to dominate.

• *The poker face.* It successfully masks all feelings and reactions and confounds observers.

• *Excessive blinking.* It may indicate nervousness, apprehension about being backed into an uncomfortable corner. It may spell guilt.

• *Coughing and/or throat-clearing* See blinking.

• *Steepling* (bringing the fingertips of both hands together to form a steeple): This generally indicates self-confidence, a sense of certainty that what one says is correct.

If we have ears to hear

Our trainees want to communicate with us. They want us to listen and hear. But, as the CBers say, we can't hear if we don't have our "ears on."

Real listening requires three sets of ears, each specially trained—one set for hearing facts, one for hearing feelings, a third for seeing what you hear.

Reprinted from TRAINING, July 1977

THE QUESTION OF QUESTIONS

Trainees ask a lot of tough questions.
Some are just plain tough.
But others are tough only because you
fail to 'switch gears'

BY W. NORMAN SMALLWOOD,
MURRAY HIEBERT
AND P. JEFFREY FLOOD

Q: A question is a question is a question—isn't it?

Think back to the last half-dozen training sessions you presented. Try to remember a particularly difficult program. Can you recall a moment when one of the participants raised an especially difficult question? A question that, in hindsight, you wish you had responded to differently?

Why do certain responses work while others do not? Because questions come in a variety of shapes and sizes. Some are straightforward content questions, some seek to clarify a point and others are designed to trip you up. These different kinds of questions require different kinds of responses.

Q: Can you be more specific?

Virtually all questions fall into one of two categories. They are either *content* or *context* questions.

Content questions ask for a specific response *within the framework of a discussion*. A participant might ask a trainer: "What do you mean by 'prioritization?'" This question can probably be answered in a direct manner and satisfy the intent of the questioner.

Context questions challenge the assumptions or generalizations inherent in the content of the discussion. Let's assume you are discussing decision-making and employee motivation. Two examples of context questions related to these topics would be: "How am I supposed to find time to involve my subordinates in decision-making?" and "Isn't using this motivation model a little too manipulative?"

Note that these questions don't directly concern participatory decision-making and motivational models. They are more related, perhaps, to time management and ethics of supervi-

sion. Context questions cannot be responded to with content replies. The questioner has stepped outside the boundaries of the content you are discussing, or is questioning the boundaries themselves. No amount of paraphrasing or rehashing of the basic content will satisfy the questioner.

Many questions which are inappropriate to replies at the content level are of the "dilemma" or "paradox" variety. How would you explain the following paradox?

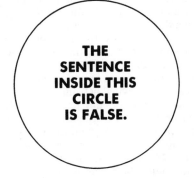

THE
SENTENCE
INSIDE THIS
CIRCLE
IS FALSE.

If you try to explain the sentence inside the circle—that is, respond to the content—you are almost certain to fail. On the other hand, you could move your analysis outside the circle and respond to the paradox. Responding to the *context* requires that you move outside the framework or boundaries presented.

Q: Can you give me a more concrete example?

Let's say you're conducting a program on time management for 20 first-line supervisors. One of the points you are emphasizing is the importance of planning—setting objectives, milestones, target dates and review procedures.

One of the participants is very skeptical. "What you're proposing is extra work and that's the last thing I need. Our section is just keeping its head above water as it is. And what's the

point? Even if we did manage to finish one project earlier because of planning, the boss would just advance the deadline on the next project. It's a vicious circle."

The content of your discussion is the importance of planning. You are presenting this content in a specific context—the context of time management for first-line supervisors. The participant's question goes beyond the context of the discussion: It really concerns the questioner's work load and the section supervisor's attitude toward deadlines.

Q: So how do I deal with this question?

You must address the context of the question.

Your opening response might be: "So you're saying that planning is time-consuming and that time is one thing you're always short of. And you're also concerned that even if planning works, the end result will be an increased work load from your boss...."

Now you've acknowledged the context of the question—it's not really about planning, it's about work loads and management pressure. A possible follow-up would be: "I can't solve your time-management problem with the techniques we're discussing. The real issues, from what you've said, are your overwhelming work load and a lack of understanding by your boss. Let's talk about those problems for a minute...."

Now the issue has been placed in a different context. You could lead a discussion on the participant's work load, or on communicating with superiors. The important point is that the initial question was "loaded"—it was virtually impossible to answer from within the framework of the original discussion. Now you've moved the framework of the question. You may or may not be able to solve the trainee's problem, but you have resolved the dilemma created by the question.

The key is to step back from the specifics of a question and to determine what is *implied* by the question. If the question challenges the premise of your argument, you can use a number of responses to satisfy your questioner.

Q: Are there different kinds of context questions and different responses for each?

Context questions come in several varieties. For example, the participant may be attacking the validity of the ideas you are presenting, or perhaps your credibility as a trainer. Maybe the participant is frustrated or confused by the implications of your ideas, or is trying to tie together several concepts related to the topic.

But your first step in responding to context questions should always be the same: active listening. Clarify the question, then prepare the questioner for your response—because you're about to change the context of the question.

Q: What do you mean, "change the context?"

To answer that, we have to backtrack on the concepts behind "content" and "context" questions. In *Principia Mathematica*, Bertrand Russell and Alfred Whitehead developed an idea they called the "Theory of Logical Types." The theory states that people constantly are faced with hierarchies of logical levels, the next higher level involving a statement which includes the lower level. Here is how Paul Watzlawick describes the implications of the theory:

"There are, then, two important conclusions to be drawn from the postulates of the Theory of Logical Types: 1) logical levels must be kept strictly apart to prevent paradox and confusion; and 2) going from one level to the next higher...entails a shift, a jump, a discontinuity or transformation—in a word, a change—of the greatest theoretical and...practical importance, for it provides a way out of a system." (Watzlawick, Weakland and Fisch; *Change: Principles of Problem Formation and Problem Resolution*; W.W. Norton, 1974.)

If you examine the two types of questions we've been talking about, you'll see that context questions are a "higher level" version of content questions. And because you're moving to a higher level, you have to prepare your questioner for this change of context.

Q: And how do I do that?

Again, active listening is the first step. Once you've acknowledged the context of the question, you have several alternatives to use to preface your response. For example, you could discuss the question itself: Ask the participant why this is a concern. That could lead into a discussion of specific examples of the concerns raised.

Conversely, instead of limiting the context, you could expand it: Ask what the implications of this question are, or what subsequent questions it may raise. If the question is a paradox, you can identify it as such, or create a counter paradox. Also, you could respond from a completely different context—a metaphor or humorous anecdote may be appropriate.

Q: So there are two steps, active listening and changing the context. Can you outline an example in detail?

Recently, our organization invited a famous futurist to discuss his views on current trends in society. During the presentation, he expressed his perception that Western thinking has traditionally used mechanistic views to analyze the world, and his opinion that this mode of thinking is less useful than more holistic models to explain current and future events. He reinforced his argument by describing a shift in employee values from an external to an internal orientation. After the presentation, he invited questions. One manager asked: "Isn't this 'values switch' a lot like a pendulum? Over time, aren't we tending to switch from one value system to another and back again?"

Let's analyze the futurist's dilemma. The content of his presentation concerned the overemphasis on mechanistic perceptions of the world. The manager's question implicitly challenged the content—especially since the pendulum comparison is itself a mechanistic one.

Here are two possible responses:

1. Use the pendulum analogy with some modifications: "Yes, the pendulum is swinging from an external to an internal value orientation. However, I visualize the pendulum *itself* moving in a different direction...."

2. Explain how the question itself is mechanistic: "I can understand why you visualize this shift in values as a pendulum. There are examples of certain values swinging from one perspective to another and back again. But let's look closer at the idea of a swinging pendulum. A pendulum is a machine—it is predictable and measurable. If I know certain things about the pendulum—such as its mass, length and velocity—I can predict exactly where it will be at any given time. This is the kind of model that the new value system is rejecting. Mechanistic, measurable models are being rejected in favor of...."

Note that these responses acknowledge the question (active listening), and prepare the questioner for the response (changing the context).

Here are some examples of typical context questions—questions which cannot be answered within the *implied* context. As you read the list, try to imagine what active-listening responses you might give and what bridging responses you might use to change the context of the question.

• Do you think your model of active listening is helpful in my situation?

• Do you expect me to believe your process is realistic?

• I'd use this model, but do you see us being rewarded for that?

• How can I set my objectives when my boss hasn't shared hers with me?

• Isn't this business of writing clear objectives a sort of trick management will use for trapping me at appraisal time?

Q: When I boil down all the ideas in this article, it seems to me that you've just come up with some fancy terms for dealing with tough questions. Am I right?

It depends on what you mean by "tough." If we asked you to give us the square root of 1,522,756 (and we stole your calculator), that would be a tough question, wouldn't it? But with your calculator, you'd come up with the answer very quickly (1,234 for those who were about to drop this magazine). So the question wasn't all that tough—not if you have the method of handling it close at hand. It was strictly a *content* question.

But how would you respond if we asked you, "Why bother including square-root tables on a calculator when people rarely use them?" You couldn't answer in terms of calculators; you'd have to respond in terms of the uses of square roots, how difficult they are to determine *without* calculators and so on. This is a tougher question than the first one, because it requires that you switch to a different *context*.

So if you consider content questions as easy and context questions as tough, then yes, we have come up with some fancy terms for simple ideas. But most people don't realize *why* certain questions are tough to answer. We think the terms we've used are more descriptive. They can help you distinguish between tough *content* questions, which are tough because you don't know the specific answer, and tough *context* questions, which are tough because you have to change the frame of reference in order to respond to the question.

Q: What you're saying sounds valid, but how often do you have time to respond to questions the way you'd like to? Especially when you're in front of a group?

It's easy to think of good responses to questions an hour after they have been asked. But with some practice, you can apply the concepts of content and context to enhance your effectiveness as a trainer and the understanding of your trainees. An excellent trainer can manage both types of questions, answering at the content level when appropriate, at the context level when necessary or, in some cases, at both levels.

Reprinted from TRAINING, December 1983

WATCH WHERE THEY SIT IN YOUR CLASS

Where someone is seated can give you clues to the interpersonal forces at work

BY KENNETH SHORT

A few years ago, in an informal group of about a dozen people, a friend of mine sitting to my right about three places around the circle disagreed with me on a particular issue. The exchange between us became so intense (yet friendly) that my friend got up and moved to a seat directly opposite mine in the circle.

The issue under discussion has long since been forgotten. But my friend's movement started me observing something about the dynamics of groups that has proven both fascinating to me and amazingly consistent.

My observation is that in any group with a designated leader (DL), what might be called *dynamic leadership tension* tends to develop between the leader and the person sitting directly opposite him or her. It is as though the person sitting directly opposite becomes, even unwittingly, a counterweight. This person tends to respond in one of three ways: He or she either leads support for the leader, leads the opposition to the leader, or withdraws and leaves a curious leadership vacuum. In essence, this person becomes the Alter Leader (AL).

Whether in opposition or support, the alter leader is usually more aggressive than others in the group in challenging ideas or raising important questions that may further the inquiry. In fact, far from being an unrelievedly negative presence, this person may be quite helpful, thus creating a sort of leadership tandem with the designated leader. In groups with two leaders, the leaders often

will position themselves directly opposite each other to accomplish this tandem effect, whether consciously or unconsciously.

Dynamic leadership tension creates a *charge of influence* on other members of the group which is directly related to an individual's proximity to the DL and AL, both to the right and the left. This is not, incidentally, inconsistent with research findings in regard to why persons tend to like or dislike each other. In his *Handbook of Small Group Research* (Free Press, New York, 1962), Paul Hare indicates that persons who are near to each other in residence or on a job become friends more often than others.

Within the charge of influence that develops, persons closer to the DL tend to become more supportive of him or her, while those closer to the

AL more often than not lend their support in that direction. Further, those immediately to the right of the DL, and those most immediately to the right of the AL, tend to offer more unquestioned support to the corresponding leader to their left. Those to the left of either the DL or AL offer support, but with less intensity—in a more "left-handed" way. Charge of influence support, both to the right and the left, tends to wane about halfway between the principals in the dynamic leadership tension.

Recently, while leading several groups of nursing supervisors in training activities, I described this theory. In one group, innocently but predictably, the first person to respond was the person sitting directly opposite me.

"I don't agree with that," this nurse said at the first response point.

"You've just proved my point," I replied.

Her good-natured reaction evoked laughter, but the incident advanced both productive discussion and the theory. It was as if awareness to what had happened in that exchange created a sensitivity to the dynamic, and also insight as to how it might be used.

In another group, a charge nurse said she had been having trouble with the person who stood across from her in daily report. We talked about the possibility of the DL in a conflict situation moving to where the AL would

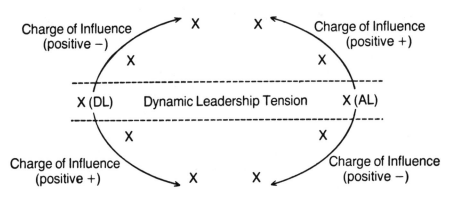

Figure 1

be physically to her immediate right. This has the effect of making the AL the DL's potentially strongest supporter (but, of course, sets up a new AL across the group).

We also talked about the phrases we commonly use in our day-to-day dealings with others. For instance we say, "I'm not in a position to do any-

337

thing about that now," or "those two really squared off against each other," or "he's my right-hand man," or "that certainly was a left-handed compliment."

The charge nurse decided to test the theory in report. For the next week, she moved to her adversary's left. The dynamic did indeed change. At first, she reported, it was almost more than the group could handle. Persons had taken the same positions for so long, and were so comfortable with what had come to be predictable tensions (albeit loaded with conflict), that even a small change was a threat. "All hell broke loose," she noted, "but it worked."

Leadership tension tends to develop across diameters. If, in a fairly mature group—one that has developed a comfortable level of trust and cohesion—the leadership shifts to a point other than the DL, the dynamic leadership tension also moves to cross between the newly assumed position of leadership and its alter leader. I have seen this dynamic operate in community committees, church groups, business meetings, classrooms, speaker-audience settings and counseling sessions. You probably have, too.

It is important to use the theory of dynamic leadership tension in positive ways. If you are a leader, for instance, this means you position yourself and your supportive strength to advantage, not to be manipulative or inconsiderate, but as a strategy toward productive results. If you know what to expect from different positions around the group, you can use the dynamic and avoid being trapped into agruments or other destructive activities. If your AL is not supportive, it is well to watch your eye contact in that direction. There is sometimes a tendency for a small group leader to look at that particular person in a way that suggests the leader's authority or approval must be won from that position. This can be defeating. The DL needs to consciously direct eye contact to all members of the group.

Should too much tension be generated in the group between the DL and AL positions, temporarily shifting the leadership role to a person on the DL's supportive right via a question or other device will change the direction of dynamic tension for at least a time and relieve the pressure. A creative leader will think of other ways to use or reduce tension so the group may function effectively rather than get bogged down in polarization and division.

If you have problems in your work group, check out this theory of dynamic leadership tension. If nothing else, get your group together, watch the positions people habitually take, then plan to use the dynamic in a creative way. Begin with your own supportive presence in the group and help build positive self-images among its members to develop a more harmonious working relationship.

Everyone is at one time or another a member of a group. If you can learn how dynamics tend to work within a group, know what to look for, and are aware of the potential forces you may create or contribute to, you can become a more effective and contributing group participant.

Reprinted from TRAINING, April 1981

STIMULATING AND MANAGING PARTICIPATION IN CLASS

Wallflowers and motor-mouths can change

BY J.B. CORNWELL

How do I get learners to ask questions and participate in classroom discussions? What can I do about wallflowers who won't speak up? How can I control that "motor-mouth" so that other learners can participate and I can stay on schedule? These questions represent one of the eternal challenges to the classroom presenter. I'd like to explore that challenge and offer some practical solutions. But, first, let's consider some why's.

Why have participation? Why not lecture?

It would be inaccurate to say that adults cannot learn at all from listening to lectures. But it's certainly true that we are more likely to learn—and learn more— from what we say and do in guided discussion than from what we hear in lectures. Evidence is abundant, as a matter of fact, that if we can't participate in learning, many of us actually nod off.

Most experts agree that all adult learning is self-directed. As adults, we want to test, to try out new ideas and concepts, which we accept only after some sort of validation exercise. We have taken control of our own lives and aren't as pliable as we were as children. If that's so, then why do some learners resist participating?

I once asked a trainee why he didn't speak up in class very often, and he replied, "Mainly because I don't want to look foolish. But also because I don't have much to add to what others have to say. I don't want to waste class time just saying that I agree with someone." "You don't have any

questions?," I asked. "Oh, yes. But if I'm patient, someone else usually asks them." "Why do you think you may look foolish if you speak up?," I persisted. "I guess it's always been that way. If I ask a question, someone puts me down. If I say what I think, I may be ridiculed. I don't need that. I'm not as smart as a lot of people, and I don't have their way with words. Why should I stick my neck out?"

Apparently, this individual had been "trained" to believe that speaking up is more likely to result in his being embarrassed than rewarded. He also felt that his ideas weren't of value to the group and that even valuable ideas must be well-articulated to be acceptable.

Obviously, teachers and trainers in this person's past had inadvertently fostered this unfortunate non-participation. As a result, entrenched habits would have to be unlearned and a whole new set of experiences collected before this trainee could voluntarily participate in discussions or ask spontaneous questions.

On the other hand, many learners are so anxious to participate that it is as much of a challenge to limit them to their share of time as it is to get others to open up and say what's on their minds.

Why do some learners want to talk all the time?

It seems to me that the learner who tends to dominate conversation is usually an alert, aggressive, confident person who likes attention. Frankly, I tend to be such a type when I'm in a learner role. I think that's because I'm also a trainer, and I feel I should help the presenter. But it's

also because I like to be noticed. My past experiences have caused me to believe that participating brings rewards— recognition and respect, as well as new knowledge—rather than punishing embarrassment. I think that most over-participators are seeking both recognition and knowledge.

It's important to note that it's irrelevant whether nonparticipators and over-participators have accurate self-perceptions. What is important is what we *believe* to be true and how that affects our participation in the classroom.

As I see it, then, there are three major categories of learners:

1. The typical learner, who wants to participate in order to learn more. Our only problem here is keeping the door open for participation and keeping the discussion aimed at the objectives of the session.

2. The non- or under-participator, who may be inhibited for any one or any combination of reasons.

3. The over-participator, who is probably seeking to show off a little as well as to participate for better understanding.

Typical learners are not going to participate just because they want to. They are going to evaluate the learning environment to decide if a particular session demands participation or a look-and-listen attitude. They may not do this consciously, but they do it.

Key words in describing a learning environment are *formality* and *focus*. A formal room arrangement— seats lined up in neat rows facing the front, a podium for the speaker to keep notes on (and hide behind), a raised platform at the front, screens and easels clustered by the podium— usually says "lecture." Most, if not all, the features of a formal environment tend to focus attention at all times on the presenter and, therefore, inhibit participation.

On the other hand, with a totally informal environment—no podium or platform, chairs arranged around tables, visual-aid paraphernalia scattered about— there is no one central point of focus created by the physical characteristics of the room.

In the formal environment, each learner has plenty of opportunity to feel alone. He is only one of many focusing attention on the presenter. And if he decides to ask a question or offer a comment, he must wrest attention away from the presenter and go "on stage" in front of all those people— a very threatening prospect to a shy person. But if he's seated at a table with three to five other people, he'll feel less alone and will be able to converse with them to gain some support for his idea or question.

Obviously, the climate influences how much anxiety a learner feels about the possible punishing results of speaking to the group. In both verbal and non-verbal messages to the learners, the presenter establishes this climate early on. As the presentation proceeds, the presenter either will reinforce that initial climate or cancel it.

The most obvious way for you, the trainer, to initiate a participative climate is to come right out and say that you planned for the session to be a group discussion. Say that you want people to question the ideas and concepts you will introduce and ask them to relate each idea to a problem or situation on the job or relate an experience that shows the idea in action.

to talk and then keeps us talking. Most important, she listens to what we say and shows respect for our ideas as well as our feelings."

● "His sessions sound like a cross between interview and a counseling session with a 'shrink.' He doesn't offer a single fact or opinion of his own. Instead, he gets us to talk about the subject by offering provocative comments, stories and questions. Finally, he summarizes what we've said."

● "She walks over to you and watches you intently while you are talking, at close range, as though just the two of you were having a conversation. She leans toward you while she nods and says 'yes' or 'right.' Sometimes, she even puts her hand on your shoulder or arm as though she

getting feedback and making adjustments — just as though he had interacted directly with the presenter.

So much for the basics. Now let's see how those problem learners, the wallflower and the motormouth, can become more productive participants.

The wallflower is a learner who resists participating. Whether this non-participator actually has been trained to keep quiet or simply is a shy person, he or she is more likely to speak up when the threat of embarrassment is nonexistent. As the presenter, you can reduce this threat in several ways. Watch the trainee's face to see if it registers clear understanding of what is going on before asking him or her a question. And always ask questions with no "wrong" answers; after another learner has said something concise and accurate, ask the wallflower if he or she agrees. Always express approval of inputs, particularly those offered by wallflowers. Remember, you have two kinds of learning going on: the objectives of the session plus the spontaneous participation of all learners.

The motormouth is a learner who over-participates, usually from a simple case of aggressiveness and/or excessive enthusiasm. Here, there's always a risk that an adversary relationship will develop between the motormouth and the presenter. This begins when the presenter ridicules the learner or his or her ideas. Even though the other learners usually lose patience with the motormouth before the presenter does, they usually resent the presenter berating or belittling *any* of their colleagues. When that happens, the climate collapses. The savvy trainer might ask other learners to comment on motormouth's input. If those inputs interfere with the success of the session, someone eventually will say so.

A more subtle technique is to use some body language on motormouth. Move about the room so that you do not directly face him or her, and, at the same time, use some of the techniques already discussed to draw other learners out. If that doesn't throttle the motor down to an acceptable level, try holding out your palm at him or her in the classic policeman's "stop" signal when he or she tries to interrupt.

Obviously, I haven't offered any pat answers to complex problems here. Nor did I intend to. My intention has been, rather, to describe and discuss the types of learners and learning environments all trainers eventually will encounter and to emphasize the importance of spontaneous, productive participation.

Reprinted from TRAINING, May 1979

HELPING TRAINEES PARTICIPATE: KEEP THE OTHER GUYS TALKING

Leader Statement	Leader Attitude	Leader "message" to group
I see. Yes, yes.	Neither agree nor disagree; noncommital but positive	I'm interested in what you're saying.
In other words, you think... If I understand you correctly, your decision would be...	Be sure you understand what he means.	I've listened, I understand, I have the facts.
You feel that... You are upset about...	Be sure you understand how he feels.	I've listened; I understand how you feel; your feelings are important.
The group seems to feel that... The key ideas you have expressed seem to be...	Summarize group contributions.	This is what you have expressed; it is important.

Many presenters ask learners to describe problems to which they seek answers during the session. This approach initiates a participative climate and gives each learner a chance to try participating.

How the presenter responds to those initial participations will set the climate for the rest of the session. If he or she is warm and receptive to these inputs, participation will continue. But if he or she is cool, argumentive, unresponsive or in any other way fails to reward participation, he or she probably will end up doing the rest of the talking.

Here's how some learners I interviewed described trainers who successfully stimulated participation:

● "She says, 'Yes. Say more about that,' and nods her head and says, 'Right, right, and how do you feel about that?' I guess she just invites us

were reassuring or protecting you."

● "He reaches toward us with his hand open and palm up. Sometimes he beckons with it as though asking us to keep talking. He signals to the one who's talking and keeps the others from butting in."

Many trainers believe that, in groups of more than 20, participation is not practical. Perhaps wide-open, free-flowing participation isn't, but I think that limited participation is possible and just as beneficial as in smaller groups. Participation in a large class should be limited to small-group discussions, with each table or group of four to six discussing and deciding upon an issue. Then a spokesperson for the group can present their ideas to the larger group. Thus, each learner is involved in the learning — testing understanding,

GETTING THEM TO OPEN UP

Dear Reader: We guess you've just about had it with ponderous dissertations on adult learning theory. Here's something in a lighter vein

BY DUGAN LAIRD
AND FORREST BELCHER

Dear Know-It-Alls:

I keep reading that it's important for trainers to get people to "open up" in the classroom. Once and for all, why? I'm a modern person, and I can accept nudity on TV and the movie screens if it's appropriate and tasteful, but this insistence on emotional immodesty in a training session strikes me as embarrassing and unnecessary. People are in a classroom to add to their knowledge or skills, not to strip themselves bare. Sometimes trainers act like amateur psychologists. What do you say to that?

A Skeptic

Dear Skeptic:

We agree with some of your points. There are indeed faddists and unqualified "psychologists" whose zeal for open expression of emotions in classrooms has been totally inappropriate. We don't like this any more than you do.

On the other hand (Do you feel we're getting ready to zap you?), under some circumstances, openness is critical. For one thing, learning means making a change—and for most adults change is awkward, stressful, threatening. Feelings and emotions are real factors in the learning dynamic. If those emotions are bottled up, the experience might more accurately be called a "learning static." We need openness as a release mechanism for the inherent tension of a learning environment. Maybe that's why Carl Rogers makes such a strong point about the need for instructors to inquire about and respond to the *feel-*

ings as well as the *thoughts* of students.

Secondly, suppose you're working in an organization where emotions run rampant in three directions: high, deep and widespread. The lack of openness in some companies is so serious a problem that training specialists are asked to conduct workshops in which people learn to express and hear and accept and adjust to the emotions of the work place as well as to the tasks themselves. Thus, the very objective of the training is to learn and practice openness and to develop mechanisms for maintaining it on the job.

Do these explanations clarify? Confuse? Convince?

The Know-It-Alls

Dear Know-It-Alls:

Oh, your answer was clear all right, if a bit glib. But it raised two more questions in my mind. One, shouldn't deep feelings be controlled as a sign of maturity? Two, can't we protect the anonymity of people who raise emotionally loaded issues through something like a classroom "suggestion box"?

Skeptic

Dear Skeptic:

You raise two good points, which we'll answer in reverse order. First, is anonymity necessary? Certainly people are entitled to protection from reprisals for things they say in the classroom. But one of the goals of any organizational team should be, we feel, open sharing of those feelings which accelerate and those which impede the achievement of group results. In a classroom workshop, as a way to help

people feel comfortable about opening up, you might *guarantee* that nothing said in the session will get back to the work place. By the end of the training, people should be comfortable sharing feelings as well as ideas. Suggestion boxes strike us as a bit immature—an artificial way to hide from ourselves. We like an environment in which each member of the "society" is honestly and openly responsible for his or her own ideas and feelings. This doesn't mean that you drop your defenses completely and run around babbling everything you know and feel. But you *can* enrich relationships and accelerate learning by mature and genuine openness.

That brings us to the second point: We feel emotions to be natural, inevitable and totally adult. Emotions aren't a burden, they're just there. By being open, we often can convert potential conflict into synergistic joint effort. Finally, we believe there is no such thing as "too much" or "inappropriate" emotion—only the need to make the inevitable emotion manageable and constructive.

The Know-It-Alls

Dear Know-It-Alls:

I've been following your correspondence with "Skeptic" and it makes me inquisitive. You talk as if feelings centered mostly around relationships and process. I am concerned with such classroom issues as asking questions, responding, willingly sharing ideas and work-place problems. Don't people have emotions about things like these? And what about policies, procedures and people in the work place? Aren't we emotional about these things, and don't these emotions have to come out in class? I am as I say,

Inquisitive

Dear Inquisitive:

You're absolutely right. Thanks so much for pointing this out. The fact is that asking questions, sharing work-place problems—almost any sort of talking—involves a lot of feeling and emotion.

The Know-It-Alls

JOHARI WINDOW		
	WHAT INSTRUCTOR KNOWS	WHAT INSTRUCTOR DOESN'T KNOW
What Participants Know		
What Participants Don't Know		

TIPS FOR HANDLING TROUBLEMAKERS

Maintaining effectiveness in the classroom isn't only a matter of enforcing civilized deportment—keeping the humor out of the toilet, banning spit wads, encouraging the postponement of knitting projects until break time, and so forth.

Rosemary Lambie, an assistant professor at Virginia Commonwealth University's School of Education in Richmond, reminds us—and the trainers she teaches under a federal grant—that being a stand-up trainer often demands quick-witted parrying of irrelevant, rambling, distracting or otherwise unproductive discussion arising from the subject matter.

Feel you need some help in this area? Lambie is glad to oblige.

• To counter demands for off-the-cuff solutions to specific (and often esoteric) problems, simply refuse to offer suggestions or opinions outside your own field of expertise. "Let trainees know from the beginning that you do not have all the answers," says Lambie. Save problem-solving specifics and cases for discussion at the end of the session.

• Maintaining focus on the subject at hand is easier if trainers "define the reservation" for themselves with notes and an outline, and define it for trainees by presenting an overview in perspective before plunging into detail.

• Prepare "several surprise activities that can be pulled out at any point at which there is a lull or problem with attention." The purpose of this recommendation, Lambie says, "is to have plans for getting trainees moving and talking." Announce and stick to a schedule of breaks, and don't allow *your own* break time to be taken up with questions and requests for documents, articles and so on.

• Confront troublemakers by asking what their objections are and giving them a chance to air their feelings. Prepare a pretest and use it to spot those who already know the course content. Draft the know-it-alls into the work of presentation.

• Realize that "10% of any population is negative," says Lambie. "Out there in that sea of faces there will be some who will not respond." Dealing with cynicism, a related problem, is easier if you avoid preaching or arguing, Lambie adds. Just say, "You might be right," or "I see your point," and move on.

Reprinted from TRAINING, March 1984

Dear Know-It-Alls:

Your stuff about "openness" is all well and good, but I become frustrated and angry when I read theory without any practical advice attached. You've told me *why* to be open; what about *how*? How do I achieve openness in classes and workshops? Get down out of the clouds and into the real world!

A Realist

Dear Realist:

Okay. Here are some preliminary steps for helping people open up in the learning environment.

First, be open yourself. Identify your feelings as they occur, and describe them to your class in "here and now" terms. It is appropriate (even productive) to say things like, "I'm getting nervous about the time we're spending on this subtopic, Bill," or "I am really pleased when you demonstrate your willingness to look at both sides of a hot issue like this, Clare." Open instructors can express anger and sadness, as well as pleasure. The really important thing is to lower your own defenses and take risks—that's what you're asking your participants to do. You might even break down and admit to being wrong about something.

Second, use "open questions," which, as their name implies, invite sharing and analysis (nonjudgmental analysis, please) of feelings. "How do you feel about this?" "What are you feeling right now?" "What feelings and emotions are affecting us in this activity?" Even the more direct and confrontive question, "Why are you here?" can encourage an open expression of feelings. Note that open questions never have "correct" (externally verifiable) answers; whatever the respondent says is presumed to be an accurate statement. You can't disagree with a person's feelings, and it certainly doesn't help much to tell the person who answers an open question, "Well, you shouldn't feel that way."

Third, select low-risk open questions and model low-risk openness. Why embarrass people with questions like, "Are you really being honest with yourself about this?" or, "Let's face it, none of us really want to change this procedure, so let's get rid of our hatred for the managers who forced it upon us. How do you feel about that, Charlie?" No. Simply state very early in the proceedings that this is a classroom and therefore a workshop where everybody has an opportunity to try out, test and experiment with new behaviors. One new behavior involves the right to express opinions and feelings that are subject to sudden amendment. That right is backed by a guarantee that no negative consequences whatsoever will follow any such expressions.

Fourth, give gentle, positive reinforcement to every early sample of openness on the part of participants. Phrases such as "Thanks for sharing that with us," or "I see," or "I feel good about knowing your feelings on this issue, Jane," make good reinforcers.

Well, Mr. Realist, there are four ways to secure openness. How do you feel about using them in your next workshop?

The Know-It-Alls

Dear Know-It-Alls:

How do I feel about using the ABCs of openness in my next workshop? Talked down to, that's how I feel. Doesn't everybody do the things you've been talking about? Surely you can come up with some more advanced tips. Just call me your

Experienced Realist

Dear Experienced Realist:

It's always a bit embarrassing to cover material which seems extremely basic. Sometimes we fear we start sounding "preachy." But we'll defend that discussion because we think less-experienced trainers might not stop to think about these extremely important behaviors. And more experienced trainers often verbalize these points while failing to practice them. Their egos, along with their needs for control and authority, sometimes get in the way.

Once you have established an open environment—or if these simple methods don't seem to be doing much good—there are some structured activities which encourage openness.

Present models for openness. The Johari Window is a good example—and it's easy to draw one on a flip chart (see illustration).

You can discuss what each of the four "window panes" mean and why we are reluctant to open up the side of ourselves that is "unknown to others." Often, just by talking about

A HIERARCHY OF VALUE

I f the main objective of most training programs is to change behavior, improve skills and impart job-related knowledge, it seems indisputable that trainers should use a consistent method and a common vocabulary to set goals and conduct evaluations of training needs and trainee accomplishments.

So argues training consultant Margery L. Pabst of Development Dimensions International's Houston, TX office. She says her behavior-oriented hierarchy of learning stages (see chart) can serve instructional designers as "benchmark" indicators—the closer a training program comes to enabling the learner to *use* information and skills on the job, the higher its value and prospect of success.

LEARNING STAGES FROM SIMPLE TO COMPLEX	
Level, Stage	**What the Learner Does . . .**
Imitation	The learner . . . imitates, matches, recites, retells, copies
Selection	The learner . . . locates, selects, seriates, orders
Classification	The learner . . . groups, classifies, compares, contrasts
Definition	The learner . . . names, states, supplies, labels, describes
Construction	The learner . . . builds, writes, changes, draws, modifies
Application	The learner . . . uses

"The focus is on the process of learning and the accomplishments of the learner rather than on the content and materials of each individual training program," says Pabst. Although any such list should reflect "increasing levels of skills sophistication," she allows that the choice of terms is arbitrary: "It is the principle of consistency that is advocated here."

Reprinted from TRAINING, March 1984

the *processes* of openness, we move toward open behavior.

The Johari Window is only one example. You also might want to consider the Dalton Change Model or even Lewin's Force Field Analysis. Such abstract models may lack any real pay off, however, if not accompanied by some instrument trainees can use to gather data about themselves (their views and feelings) and probably to share that data with others. The instrument might be a simple agree/disagree scale. Here's a sample from a communication course:

Or, you might use a forced-ranking exercise:

By answering such questions, learners gain certain insights about themselves. That in itself helps promote personal openness. Sharing the collected data with the group contributes to greater social openness. If the environment needs to be protective, let the revelations be posted so there is no possible way for individual respondents to be identified. Or begin the sharing process in very small groups (two people), then proceed to foursomes and so on until you achieve an "open society."

Even if you don't use this expanding method, you'll find it helpful to let the sharing begin in small groups. This permits people to participate in groups with different constituencies, and they get practice in being open with ever-shifting populations. This matters because it's one thing to be open with a specific group of people and quite another experience to be open with several different groups. Do these techniques make sense to you Experienced Realists?

The Know-It-Alls

Dear Know-It-Alls:

Yes, you make sense. I understand the devices you are using and how they are administered. But doesn't all of this take a lot of time?

Another Experienced Realist

Dear Experienced Realist:

Yes, gathering and sharing this sort of data does take time. But remember, being open can be pretty uncomfortable—even threatening—which makes it a difficult lesson to learn. Like all difficult learnings, openness takes time. If we believe in teaching it, we must be prepared to *invest* the necessary time.

One way to accelerate things is to clarify norms and expectations. Make a contract with the class at the earliest possible moment. As trainer, you might say: "Here's what I'm willing to do as an instructor. I'm willing to start on time, to answer your questions, to listen to how you feel about our processes, to give you all my energy. In return, here's what I'd like from you: I'd like you to be here on time, to express your feelings about what's

	Strongly Agree	Tend To Agree	No Real Opinion	Tend To Disagree	Strongly Disagree
1. Managers should always tell employees everything they want to hear.					
2. Managers should always have an open-door policy when communications break down.					
3. When communications break down, it's usually the sender's fault.					
4. And so on.					

Here are five qualities which are important to effective management. Rank them in the order (1 for most important) you give each quality. You may not allow any ties.

RANK

PATIENCE _____

HONESTY _____

SENSITIVITY _____

RESPONSIVENESS _____

CONSCIENTIOUSNESS _____

happening as well as your ideas about the content, to share your experiences and to participate willingly. Do we have a contract?"

In such contracting you are of course "modeling openness." This is the first step, and you must take it very early. You can also probe the participants' feelings about this contracting process and reinforce their expressions of those feelings. Thus, the dynamics of openness begin immediately—openness is seen subtly as a natural part of this learning experi-ence. If the responses are sluggish, of course, you'll need extra time for data gathering.

We're getting the feeling that we may have told you more about the "Why and How of Openness" than you really care to know. We'd like to close by quoting Sidney Jourard's testimony from *The Transparent Self*: "People become clients of psychotherapists because they have not disclosed them-selves in some optimum degree to the people in their life." And again, also from Jourard, "Self-disclosure is a symptom of personality health."

We believe that at the end of any learning experience people ought to feel better about themselves, about the tasks they're asked to perform and about the organization for which they perform those tasks. That's our honest opinion, and we feel good about having expressed it. See how open we are?

That's why they call us ....

The Know-It-Alls

Reprinted from TRAINING, February 1984

PARTICIPATORY TRAINING: SEPARATING FANTASY FROM REALITY

It's hailed as a heaven-sent alternative
to the boring lecture.
So why does this session feel like hell?

BY JANET HOUSER CARTER

The brochure for your favorite annual convention has finally arrived. It's the one you've anxiously awaited since you heard that this year's gathering would be in Las Vegas. You open the program to the session descriptions, already formulating justifications and "derived benefits" in your head. As you scan the listings, one session jumps out at you:

"An analysis of current trends in high-tech training systems. The presenter is an internationally recognized authority in the field, whose experience includes 15 years in human resources development positions and four years of work and research with technology-enhanced training delivery in Fortune 500 *companies. In this participative session, we will explore together the uses and implications of various interactive systems for efficient and effective training. Four hours."*

Sounds good, eh? Beware: That pleasant-sounding line about a "participative" session might be a danger signal. Suppose that, just once, the brochure contained an actual description of how this particular session will run:

"An analysis of current trends in high-tech training systems. The presenter, who claims to have devoted considerable study to the subject, will not burden participants with her own thoughts or findings. Instead, she will solicit lists of answers from the group, which will be composed mostly of people who, like you, are here because they don't know very much about computer-based training or interactive video, and were hoping to learn something from someone who does. Each response, no matter how dumb or irrelevant, will be written on a flip chart with a squeaky magic marker. Flip chart pages will then be taped to the walls and thereafter ignored, unless they fall to the floor. Four interminable hours."

Now, you may be a big fan of participative learning—in principle. But for this session? During its time slot, I'd look for you at the blackjack tables. And so would the person who's presenting it—which is why she actually wrote Version 1 of the program description, instead of something closer to Version 2.

Participatory training (PT) has been a fact of life in adult education since the advent of andragogy. It has been lauded as the only true way adults learn, as the universal antidote for dreary training sessions, as the most professional form of training and as the only interesting way to teach.

Truth be told, PT is no panacea. It is, in fact, a teaching strategy with a narrow range of effective applications. Applied correctly, planned well and implemented by a skilled trainer, it is all of the good things it is purported to be. Used poorly, it's a silly waste of time that can do more harm than good.

Unfortunately, the overuse and gross misuse of PT techniques have led to uncounted sessions such as the one described in our "honest" convention brochure, and to an understandable suspicion of any training session touted as a "facilitated experience." Further, suffering through sessions where PT is used inappropriately has led some trainers to abandon this valuable teaching strategy altogether.

PT is simply that: a teaching strategy, one more tool at the disposal of the trainer. As with any strategy, it must be applied to the right subject, with the right students, in the right situation and using the right teaching skills. It's easy to get caught up in the euphoria about participatory techniques without first identifying the purpose for them and without determining whether PT is the *best* strategy for accomplishing your objectives in a particular situation. The first step in reevaluating the usefulness of participatory training is to separate the fantasy from the reality.

The fantasy

It's terrifically appealing, this vision of the Socratic teacher, interacting with the learners and coaxing from them—through purposeful and extremely intelligent questioning—complex analyses and "Aha!" insights. The students revere the instructor; "awe" is not too strong a word to describe their regard for his wisdom. They are well-prepared, having done their assigned prework, so each question prompts a flurry of eagerly waving hands. Each answer is more insightful than the one before. When class is finished, half the students cluster around the instructor, hoping for one more drop of wisdom. The rest stand to the side, animatedly arguing points raised during class. The course evaluations are ecstatic: "Best teacher I ever had!" "Made learning fun!" "I really got something from this class!"

From the instructor's point of view, the fantasy is even more appealing when compared to traditional forms of training. No more lengthy lectures to prepare, no audiovisual equipment to requisition, no bibliographies to wade through—just some thought about the questions likely to be asked. Then you sit back and wait for the kudos to roll in.

The reality

In fact, the participative session may not work out so well. Your first questions will elicit only blank stares. No trainee will be dumb enough to make eye contact with you; that's asking to be called upon to answer a question. When responses do begin to flow, they rarely will be insightful or analytical. Most (partly due to the nature of your questions) will be self-evident banalities. Some will be downright dumb.

The students will not regard you with awe. In fact, it isn't unusual for a trainee to confront a trainer outright about the latter's apparent lack of preparation and effort. You'll be uncommonly lucky if half the students are actually prepared, and luckier still if more than three are willing to respond without being called upon or "pulled out." If they aren't required to stay, many will get up and leave. Two loudmouthed trainees will stay after class and waste your time for another hour while the remainder gallop for the exit the moment the minute hand reaches 12.

And the evaluations? Two will be glowing. Eight will be cautiously lukewarm. ("You can learn *something* in any educational experience.") Three will be scathing.

Separating the two

That description of "reality" is not inescapable, of course. But the training world's infatuation with the idea of participatory learning has led us to tell one another that the difference between the fantasy session and the one we keep running into in the real world hinges entirely on the trainer's facilitative skills. The fantasy *within* the fantasy is that it's all a matter of classroom management: A trainer with the proper "group competencies" will run an excellent PT session regardless of the course content or the circumstances; a trainer without these competencies will preside over a flop.

That's bull. Facilitation skills are indeed part of the answer—but only part. To be successful, participative training also demands intense preparation, the right circumstances, the right learning objectives and the right

trainees. It demands that we understand each aspect of the participatory learning experience and that we exercise restraint in the application of PT. It demands that we separate fantasy from reality.

Fantasy #1. Students universally like participatory training, find it more interesting than lectures or other teaching methods, and feel it makes classroom time pass more quickly.

If they aren't required to stay, many trainees will get up and leave.

Reality. Participatory training actually only lends itself well to students with a relational, verbal learning style—roughly 50% of adult learners. Most trainers agree by now that there *is* validity in the concept of individual learning styles, and that those styles really do influence the way people learn. Yet we continue to overuse teaching strategies aimed at a narrow range of possible styles.

Excessive reliance on PT is no more justifiable than excessive lecturing. The analytical learner, who prefers the formal training situation with the instructor viewed as an information-giver, will be frustrated and uncooperative in a totally participative session. And analytical learners make up nearly half of the adult student population. Using PT for an entire session, then, will tend to alienate about half the trainees in an average classroom.

Fantasy #2. PT is an effective, stand-alone technique that successfully exposes trainees to one another's experiences and encourages the exchange of experience-based knowhow.

Reality. PT is not an effective, stand-alone technique unless a host of criteria are met. The fact is, relatively few audiences are ripe for participatory training. The students must be well-prepared. A mix of trainee exper-

tise should be present so they can learn from one another, and the instructor must be aware of the strengths in the audience. The group members must be aware that the course is to be participatory, and they should have done some "homework" beforehand so the discussion doesn't deteriorate into vague superficialities. The purpose of the training session ought to be to discover differing viewpoints or creative solutions, and the subject matter must lend itself to that purpose.

Even when all of these conditions converge—an unusual situation at best—the fact remains that no single technique is likely to stimulate all students in a given classroom.

Participation is a specific strategy, intended to be built into a course design to meet specific objectives. The only reason to use PT is that you've decided it will be the *best* teaching method to meet some of those specific objectives. And just as we would not conduct an entire course using nothing but case studies, brainstorming or role playing (all effective participatory techniques when used correctly) neither should we rely solely on class participation for effective learning.

Fantasy #3. PT sessions require less preparation time and are easier on the instructor.

Reality. We have a standing joke in our department whenever a guest speaker is late for a workshop session and we're afraid we'll have to wing it. "No problem," the stand-in instructor will say. "I'll just go in there and say, 'I believe you can all learn as much from each other as you can from me, so turn to your neighbor and start talking.'"

It's true that some PT classes—the bad ones—are easier on the instructor. Effective PT sessions, on the other hand, require much more prep time than does a lecture. In a lecture format, the instructor prepares specific information to be imparted to the students and prepares for a predictable set of questions or clarifications. When you're planning a participatory session, however, you have to prepare for any contingency that may arise. The progress of topics and questions must be designed to arrive at a predicted conclusion. You must be skillful at leading groups and have a working knowledge of group dynamics. PT

THE CONVENTION ZONE

BY JANET HOUSER CARTER

Unwilling to fly on Friday the 13th, I arrived at the conference a day late and missed the keynote address. So as I sat in the afternoon session, I used my peripheral vision to scan my neighbor's morning notes. What I saw nearly made me groan out loud.

At the top of the page, neatly printed, were the date, title of the speech and speaker's name. Next came the heading, "I. Examples of excellence in educational service," followed by an expectant colon. The rest of the page was covered with those curlicues, mazes and three-dimensional boxes that I recognized from the pad of paper next to my telephone back home.

Had I been a pessimist, I would have taken this as a sign to catch a cab to the airport posthaste and return home, where I could at least raid the refrigerator. But enough of the trainer lingered in the student to stick it out. Surely the keynote address was intended to inspire rather than to instruct. Surely the advanced sessions would be highly informative. Surely I could take better notes than that.

Surely not. The primary yields turned out to be a doodle pad of my own, guilt, more guilt and, finally, one decent idea to take home.

The first session, an overview of futuristic trends and general strategic directions, was one that had prompted my decision to attend. The instructor had impressive qualifications (meaning they were better than my own), the session's title was a grabber, the objectives were well-written and, of course, measurable. My expectations were dashed after only 12 words had escaped the speaker's eminently credentialed mouth: "I'm not going to teach you, I'm here to facilitate your learning."

You know the rest of the story. The session opened with a general question to the audience: "What are the major trends you have identified?" That was followed by, "And what do you see as happening in the next five to 10 years?" Then the climax: "What strategies will help us survive?"

Unfortunately, the students in this room were no more knowledgeable than I. At least a third of them deserted, an urge I resisted only out of compassion for the "facilitator" (that, and the knowledge that my only alternative was "networking," an option I rate somewhere below getting a Pap smear). Soon I, too, had a notepad full of squiggles.

The remaining sessions were better, but by minimal measure. The major problem was the way I felt when I left them—in a word, guilty. The session on "competency-based education" opened with a comparison of CBE and traditional training, a word much maligned at this conference. ("Training is what you do with animals; we *educate* people." These educators obviously had not seen some of my students.) The point of it all was that every minimally worthwhile *education* department relies solely on CBE. I made mental note of the fact that at least two of my company's programs were competency-based. However, the vast majority fell into the category of "traditional training" and were, therefore, unfit for human consumption. Guilt.

The next session, on organization development, opened with—you guessed it—a comparison of OD and traditional education. (By then, I wasn't using the word training. I subdue my sarcasm when surrounded by zealots.) It turns out that every minimally worthwhile education department relies solely on organization de-

velopment. Three of my programs definitely fall into the category of OD. As for the rest. . . . More guilt.

Networking, once I forced myself into it, was even more demoralizing. Every education department in the nation is doing more, with greater administrative support and a larger budget, than mine.

Major guilt. I always feel good about my department—how far we've come, our accomplishments, etc.—until I get around other training directors. Either I've entered the Twilight Zone or these people are hedging a bit. I suspect the latter. That's what I have to tell myself.

After four days of self-awareness, encounters, roundtable discussions and small-group work (which always makes my leg jerk), the conference came to an end. Eventually, I managed to assuage my guilt by coming up with the novel idea (at least to me) of "situational education." This theory, untested of course, is similar to that of contingency management: No single approach to education applies to all situations and programs. You have to match the way you're teaching or facilitating or developing to the needs of the learners and their particular situations. Some of my programs will be competency based, some will be OD and some will be (I'm willing to admit it) training.

By the time I left the conference I had reduced my guilt to a tolerable level.

The one decent idea to take home? It occurred to me while daydreaming during one of the sessions at which someone had the foresight *not* to give us doodle pads: Surely there's got to be some benefit from this experience. I'll write it up and send it to TRAINING Magazine. They'll understand.

Reprinted from TRAINING, November 1986

usually requires overpreparation: You may have to shift into another teaching style if the participation plan bombs, as it sometimes will even if you're doing things right.

If the instructor is not prepared to guide the group to conclusions, the results can be disastrous. The session may end up to be no more than guided networking, producing only

lists of alternatives that are practically useless in the absence of any analysis or critical review. Instructional goals are lost and the entire experience seems purposeless.

Participatory training *is* easier on the instructor physically. The teacher doesn't have to talk for the entire period and may even be able to leave the room for a break during group exer-

cises or case studies. These may be prime considerations for trainers familiar with the aching feet and backs that accompany marathon workshops.

Fantasy #4. Participatory training fosters cooperativeness among participants rather than competition, and gives students an opportunity for a little ego gratification.

Reality. Every instructor who has used participation in the classroom knows the dreaded affliction of the motor-mouth monopoly. Chances are that any class will have at least one; some groups are "blessed" with several. Participation does give students the opportunity to feel good about themselves and their accomplishments. Trouble is, only a few will take advantage of the opportunity—and the rest will suffer while they do.

A PT session often becomes an open forum for patting oneself on the back, for exchanging war stories or for an elaborate game of one-upmanship. Instead of progressively analyzing a situation, participation becomes a mere recitation of accomplishments.

Fantasy #5. There are no dumb questions or dumb answers, only opportunities for clarification. The trainer should consider this when planning the session, and either ask questions with no wrong answers or express approval for any response whatsoever.

Reality. I'm sorry, but I believe there are such things as dumb questions and dumb answers. I have asked and answered a few myself. I once had a student ask me, after a lecture on infant crib death, if I knew of any babies who had survived the condition. At that point, I knew someone had seriously misled me on this "no dumb questions" business.

Further, I don't believe we are doing adults any favors by pretending that truly dumb questions and answers have merit. Acting as if an obviously wrong answer has value is patronizing to the student, insulting to others in the class and detrimental to the trainer's credibility.

This doesn't mean we have to ridicule or embarrass students. But how about saying simply, "No, I don't think so" and moving on to the next volunteer? That's sufficient to keep the class moving without humiliating a trainee. We certainly don't need to record the dumb answer on our flip chart or contort ourselves like Romanian gymnasts trying to find some whisper of value in it.

A word is warranted, however, regarding the *way* in which we solicit answers. Asking a nontechnical question that has only one correct answer

is setting the class members up to fail. How many times have we all endured the interminable guessing game of trying to figure out exactly which word the instructor wants us to spit out? Participatory questions should be phrased in general terms and aimed at guiding students to general conclusions, not specific answers.

Fantasy #6. Participatory training lends itself to any topic.

Reality. PT works especially well only with particular types of topics. And it's downright contraindicated for some. It is best suited for subjects that encompass multiple, divergent viewpoints and are open to rational argument. It is with these topics that participation and dialogue are most valuable. Subject matter requiring creative solutions or consideration of several options is also well-suited to participation. Again, participatory training is effective only when there is a particular reason for the participation, and that reason is tied to the objectives of the class.

PT is *not* suited for highly technical subjects, for teaching skills that require memorization of precise procedures or for teaching material in which there is only one right answer. Participatory training is a waste of time when the learning objectives involve only knowledge or memorization. It should be reserved for the "higher-level" goals of analysis, evaluation and synthesis.

Fantasy #7. I can use participatory training effectively.

Reality. This one is no fantasy. Despite all these cautions, participatory training *can* be an effective and rewarding strategy when used judiciously.

But remember: PT is best used with adult learners who are predominantly relational in learning style; as one specific technique to achieve specific goals and objectives (as opposed to a universal panacea); by an instructor who is well-prepared and skilled in group dynamics; with topics that are open to argument, analysis and higher-level learning objectives; and with diverse groups whose members are prepared to participate.

Paradoxically, the one situation in which you are likely to find a diverse, verbal, knowledgeable group—a

professional convention—is also a place uniquely ill-suited to participatory training as a sole technique. Generally it's impossible to ask that students be prepared for class; the characteristics and strengths of the group are usually unknown; and the time period is so limited that by the time the instructor *does* recognize the expertise in the group, the session is over. Also, convention audiences often are too large for strictly participatory training (PT usually is ineffective in a group with more than about 20 members). Yet a convention—particularly a training convention—is the one place where you'll find PT running rampant.

At the risk of tarring some hard-working and very capable people with too broad a brush, I'd venture to say that one reason for this is that so many presenters are consultants and would-be consultants who get themselves onto the faculty for the exposure value. In itself, that's perfectly legitimate: Some feel that exposure value comes from conducting an excellent session, and an excellent session might include PT. But for others, exposure value starts and ends with getting your name in the brochure and your face in front of a group: Once your proposal has been accepted by the sponsors, why do any research or put any real effort into preparing a solid presentation when you can just stroll in and spend the whole period hiding behind the sacred cow of participatory training? As I said earlier, *bad* PT really is easier on the trainer.

Our misguided convention speaker, then, would have a better chance of keeping you out of the casino with the following:

"An analysis of current trends in high-tech training systems. The presenter will summarize recent trends and predict future directions. Students will then be asked to participate in determining strategies for surviving and thriving in the future environment. Please attend this session only if you enjoy discussion-centered learning and are willing to review some literature prior to the class. Enrollment limited to 20. If you attend under these conditions, you will almost certainly enjoy yourselves and learn a great deal, as will the presenter. Four hours."

Reprinted from TRAINING, June 1987

HANDLING THE 'I'D RATHER BE SOMEWHERE ELSE' TRAINEE

These strategies and techniques are useful for those 'problem' trainees

BY MARTIN M. BROADWELL

More often than not, there will be a certain number of students in every training classroom who simply do not want to be there. This does not necessarily reflect on the ability of the trainer or the subject matter being covered in the class. Many factors, some beyond the control of the instructor, can influence a student's "I'd rather be home" attitude.

Take for example the case of the trainee whose income is derived from commissions on sales. During the time he's in the classroom, he's making only his base salary, while someone else may be getting his sales. His customers might even be lost to a competitor. It's not enough to say that the organization ought to correct such inequities. As long as this situation does exist and the trainee is required to attend training sessions, there is going to be a problem.

There are other problems which relate to the student's perception of the course content. Some may see little or no relevancy in the material. This doesn't mean that the material is, in itself, bad or irrelevant, but it does indicate poor communication. The trainee's supervisor should be encouraged to take the time to discuss why the training is necessary, point out the advantages, and spell out deficiencies in the trainee's performance.

Some students may have feelings of inadequacy that can make them wish they were back on the job instead of sitting in a classroom where the material seems too complicated and confusing and the discussions beyond their reach. On the other hand, other students might consider the material too basic or trivial. This can make them feel uncomfortable about attending a class they consider beneath them because, obviously, *someone* thought they needed it.

Other factors are completely out of the instructor's control. A student may have personal, non job-related problems such as a sick spouse, a troubled child, or an important meeting to attend after hours.

Rather than argue the relative merits of sending such students back to their jobs, let's discuss the options for handling the problem at the training site. First, we can use the basic motivating tool we should use with every student to get them interested and keep them involved—try to show what's in it for them.

Typically, companies attempt to sell the importance of a training program on the basis of what it will do *for the organization*: "Our sales were off last year by 10 percent. This training course will help get them back up where they ought to be," instead of, "This course will help you increase your sales by 10 percent." Or a supervisor will say, "We can cut down on employee turnover if you'll learn more about human relations," instead of, "You won't have to spend so much time training new people with the skills you'll learn from this course." The solution is obvious: a training course should be presented to a student to appeal to *his* needs.

Another way of maintaining interest is to apply the recognition or status principle of motivating. If the employee/trainee has certain skills or special knowledge, the instructor can use these to enhance the course: "Anne has some good experiences to share with us, I'm sure. Would you tell us what you do when you find this happening in the real world, Anne?" In this way, the trainer gets good input from the students, uses their credentials to build credibility, and motivates the trainees at the same time. We shouldn't force this activity, of course, but neither should we worry about the results. If the employee is experienced and the experience doesn't relate to what we are teaching, then we'd better examine our curriculum!

Another useful technique is to ask the "problem" trainee to discover the relevancy of the training for himself—to determine just how the course can help him back on the job. Even if the employee is one of those who feels inadequate, looking for relevancy on the job will be a source of encouragement. It's a subtle way of helping him find the reasons for being in the class in the first place and discovering the weaknesses that explain the boss's reason for thinking the course could overcome this performance deficiency.

If more than one person feels they don't want to be in the course, this self-examination technique may be good for the whole class. Stop and let them brainstorm about the value of the course objectives. This will also get the committed students working, as the class as a whole tries to bring some reality and reason to the course. It may be that we can see some areas where we can change our direction and make the course more meaningful for everybody. This is a measure of the flexibility a good instructor must have to be successful.

We've not mentioned one of the most obvious things that can be done. Have a talk with the trainee in private and see if there's anything you need to know about the person that can make the course more valuable to him or her. A simple statement such as, "How's it going?" may be all it takes, if you follow the rules of good interviewing from that point on. If you don't get results at first, you may have to expand the questioning to be a little more specific, even to the point of saying, "I sort of get the feeling that I'm not making the course as mean-

WAYS TO ENCOURAGE YOUR TRAINEES TO ASK QUESTIONS

That winds it up for today. Are there any questions? No? OK, folks, see you Wednesday morning for our next session which will be on modulation principles."

The instructor puts his notes into his attache case, wipes the chalkboard clean of the 17 equations and three circuit diagrams he managed to squeeze up there during the last hour, and thinks smugly to himself, "Well, not one person asked a question so I guess they got it all! Not bad! I wasn't sure I'd be able to cover all those points, and I guess I did rush a little toward the end, but by golly, I covered them. And not one question!"

A far fetched story? Hardly. On the contrary, and unfortunately, that situation is often more the rule than it is the exception. "Look at some of the factors involved," says Milt Badt, training supervisor for Western Electric Co. "It is 11:56 AM when the instructor asks for questions. The presentation had been scheduled from 9:30 to 12:00. Five out of the 10 students in the audience of 30 who would have liked to ask questions do not, because they are hungry, tired, bored, and perhaps a bit snowed, and want to get the heck out of there. Two who wanted to ask questions simply do not, lest they incur the wrath of the others who want to leave. And three others are not about to ask under any circumstances, because each one thinks they must be the only one in the class who didn't understand the point, and they don't want to appear foolish."

Of course, much of what Badt was getting at is just as true of a nicely scheduled question period during the middle of a meeting. Just the simple question, 'Are there any questions?' can be said a great number of ways. And of that number of ways, there are some that will turn students off and make them reluctant to ask any questions at all.

How can an instructor encourage questions? Here are Badt's suggestions:

• Use phrases like: Don't be afraid to ask questions. Raise your hand, or just speak up. Please interrupt me. If you have a question, chances are others have the same concern, so you'll be helping more than just yourself by asking."

• Remember there is no such thing as a stupid question. Look for and mention the merit in every question whenever possible. This will make the asker feel important and encourage others to speak up.

• Repeat the question loudly and clearly so that everyone in the room can hear it as well as the answer.

• Don't say, "If there are no questions on that we'll get on to the next topic, since I'm running a little behind schedule." Allow time in your presentation planning for the asking of questions— at five- or 10-minute intervals if the going is rough. Don't lecture for more than 15 minutes without calling for questions.

• Allow some time for trainees to respond. Don't ask for questions and immediately resume your discussion.

• Pay attention to the back of the room, where it's easy to overlook a raised hand. And, don't ask for questions while your eyes are glued to your notes or while you are writing on the board.

• Don't ask for questions in such a way that your voice implies, "If anyone was really too dense to get that, speak up now and I'll see if I can get it through your skull." If you think that way about your audience, your tone of voice will betray you.

• Don't call for questions within two or three minutes of a scheduled coffee or lunch break.

• If you have a printed schedule, insert several 10 or 15 minute question and answer sessions right into the format. However, you must still encourage questions during this time by using the applicable do's and don'ts.

Reprinted from TRAINING, May 1978

I WISH HE HAD COVERED THE XYZ POINT WITH MORE DETAIL. BUT I'M PROBABLY THE ONLY ONE THAT DOESN'T UNDERSTAND IT!

I'D LIKE TO ASK WHAT THE XYZ POINT MEANS. BUT I'M PROBABLY THE ONLY STOOP HERE THAT DOESN'T KNOW!

MY HAND'S BEEN UP FOR TEN MINUTES. BUT HE IGNORES ME!

LAST TIME HE MADE ME FEEL LIKE AN IDIOT! DARNED IF I ASK ANOTHER QUESTION!

ASK A QUESTION AT THREE MINUTES TO TWELVE? NO WAY!

ANY QUESTIONS? NO? GOOD! NOW, BLAH...BLA...BLA

—by Marilyn Leak

ingful to you as you would like," or, "Is there some way I can help you get more from the sessions? Your responses have indicated that the course isn't meeting your needs very well." You shouldn't try to put the trainee on the grill, nor make veiled threats. You want the employee to know you're sincerely concerned about maximum learning for every student.

It would be less than admirable if we didn't mention some ways to avoid the problem in the first place. Basically, the problem resulted because of poor communication. Somewhere along the way, the course objectives failed to be communicated to the trainee, his supervisor, or both. An instructor will do well to make a practice of asking himself, "Is there enough information about the course available to the bosses and potential trainees to let them know not only what we're going to cover but also what behavioral changes we're hoping to make? Essentially, what are the promises we're making? What will the employees be able to do when they get back to the job that they can't do now? What deficiencies are we aiming at?"

The important things to avoid are being so vague about course objectives that all employees will believe they need to attend and making so many promises that no one wants to be left out. We should give enough information so supervisors can sit down with their subordinates and decide—on an intelligent basis—who needs to attend and who doesn't.

These techniques cannot eliminate the problem entirely. Instructors will always have a few discontented students, but there's no excuse for building problems into the system by poor design and poor communication. Good trainers will remain alert and sensitive to symptoms, causes, and possible cures, and they *can* learn to deal with the "I'd rather be home" student constructively.

Reprinted from TRAINING, November 1976

SURVIVING—AND MANAGING—THOSE HOSTILE PARTICIPANTS

Every trainer eventually runs into an audience determined to resist

BY CARL E. PICKHARDT

A trainer is always a target. Even when training within the organization to which you belong, your leadership position temporarily separates you from the group with which you are working. Every group makes a participant/leader distinction: The participants are *we* and the trainer or trainers are *they*. As an outside trainer this distinction is even more strongly felt: "You are a stranger; you are not one of us."

Participants do, however, assign you two roles as a trainer. You are an *authority* coming in to exert training control, and you are an *expert* coming in to enable the development of skills and understanding participants do not already possess, or possess in lesser degree than yourself. Having given you these two roles, participants have now identified you as a target, and some will feel impelled to move to destroy your effectiveness and legitimacy in each area.

Why? Because in all organizations there is always a certain amount of free-floating dissatisfaction, anxiety, frustration and anger which accrues from the daily pressures of organizational life— people feeling pushed, blocked and let down in their work relationships. There is a desire to express these negative feelings, but in a "safe" setting which will not jeopardize standing at work. The training situation can provide this outlet. The rules of social conduct which ordinarily govern work relationships are temporarily relaxed. The trainer becomes a safe authority target upon whom participants may displace frustrations with their superiors; someone they can with relative impunity challenge, criticize and punish. They may in addition compete with the trainer, elevating their own self-esteem by putting the "expert" down. Some may feel built-in resentment toward the trainer as well: "It's easy for you to talk about our problems since you don't have to live with them." That the trainer is free from the toils of the participants' problems can serve as an irritant itself.

Trainers are in a real sense paid to be scapegoats— to provide opportunity and target for this pressure release. We must accept this reality and learn (and this *does* take experience) not to take participant hostility personally. Any time you are going to work with a group which you know in advance is operating under undue pressure, you can expect basic attacks on your two roles. They will attack your *expertise* ("You don't know so much," "I knew all this before," "I know more than you"). And they will attack your *authority* ("You can't control me," "I'll do what I please," "I have more power than you").

Hostility expressed

They will come at you in a variety of ways.

• There is *hostile withdrawal*— participants who refuse you both verbal and nonverbal response. "If you can't reach us you will fail to teach us," they seem to say.

• There is *hostile diversion*— participants who initiate their own social interaction independent of that which you are orchestrating for the larger group. "If we can secede from your control, we can encourage others to do likewise," they seem to say.

• There is *hostile attack*— participants who directly challenge your authority, oppose your directions or criticize your message. "If we refuse to go along with you, that rejection will undermine your confidence and destroy your poise as a leader," they seem to say.

Participants particularly resourceful with their hostility can use all of these in combination. For example, they first set up a *diversion* to invite your response. Then, as you move to recontrol that situation, they *attack* you from out of their support group. And finally, when you try to deal directly with their objection, they *withdraw* into stubborn silence and will not respond.

What does it mean?

When participant anger is expressed in any of these three ways, it is always *a statement of protest*. The participant, beneath the overlay of hostility, is indirectly saying: "I don't like being placed under your leadership. I don't like being in this training situation. I don't like what you represent. I don't like what you are saying. I do not like what you are asking me to do."

Further, participants do not commit themselves to public protest unless they are trying to elicit a particular trainer response to their challenge. They may want to punish you, and indirectly those responsible for the training, until you defend or apologize for your presence. They may want to push you until you give up your agenda and give way to theirs. They may want to provoke you into a fight to allow them to vent frustrations hitherto suppressed and usually forbidden.

The choices of a trainer wishing to honor protest are to reflect back the concern you think that protest may be masking ("Would you like to talk about your dissatisfaction at being here today?"), to apologize, change the agenda or absorb the ventilation of grievances. The major problem in honoring participant hostility in these ways is that it does delay and divert you from fulfilling the training assignment. There is, however, one

LEARN TO READ NON-VERBAL TRAINEE MESSAGES

BY CHARLES R. McCONNELL

You're about to begin a lengthy workshop with a group of relative strangers. A good start depends on early identification of some willing talkers for a participative activity. How do you find your participants?

You might begin, as I did for years, by asking for volunteers. You may even get some — eventually. Do you politely but firmly repeat the request until somebody breaks the ice? Perhaps, although this requires valuable time and risks generating resentment.

Although I still voice a friendly request for volunteers, I no longer repeat the query to the group as a whole. Instead, I'm guided by their reactions. The instant the request is made, most of the eyes in the room shift away from the speaker. Chances are, most of those who avoid eye contact don't want to volunteer; they may also be afraid of being selected against their will. Occasionally — but not often enough to depend on — somebody will volunteer and your worries are over. Usually, however, you're left with silence and perhaps a third of the people still looking your way.

Concentrating on the one-third, direct the request for participation toward them. Keep it good-natured, perhaps joking ("I really need the help, folks; I don't know enough to go it alone.") Try something like: "I haven't met any of you before, but most of you know each other. Maybe you know of some willing talkers among you? People who like to argue?"

Watch the reactions. Smiles, a spurt of physical activity as people settle in more comfortably, and — most important — obvious glances toward a few particular individuals. You're also likely to hear comments about those with a reputation for garrulity.

A group of 30 people who know each other will usually yield two or three such central figures. With these few, you're on fairly safe ground for a direct, friendly request. You'll usually get your participants.

You may also accomplish some desirable extras with this process. In finding your central figures, you've probably also identified the group's informal leaders. And you may well have given your listeners the ice-breaking opportunity needed to create a loose, friendly atmosphere early in the session.

The process isn't infallible, but it works often enough to be worth trying. Although there's some verbal interchange involved, many of the key indicators are nonverbal: looks averted or returned; smiles; glances and physical reorientation toward certain people. As leader, you must "listen" to your group's wordless messages.

When we hear about the necessity for interaction, we tend to think of it mostly in terms of verbal exchange. Just as important is the kind of interchange that involves your response, whether verbal or otherwise, to your audience's silent signals.

A note of caution: There are few, if any, nonverbal signals that consistently have the same meaning, and none with precise meanings. A few scattered displays of any particular signal may or may not be significant.

The key lies not in the *what* of some nonverbal signals as much as in *how often* you see them. However, the occurrences needed to suggest a signal's significance vary according.

The classic folded-arms pose provides a good illustration. This position frequently indicates resistance, the listener protecting himself by forming a barrier against you and your ideas. But it can also indicate other things. Two or three sets of folded arms in a group of 30 people may mean, "At the moment I'm most comfortable this way," or "I feel slightly cold." But if a large number — say, 10 or so — fold their arms, you may be generating resistance in your audience. You might respond by changing the direction or tone of your presentation.

I recently had to present a controversial plan to a 13-member board of directors. About 10 minutes into the talk, I found myself looking at nine pairs of folded arms plus a few frowns. I frantically wondered what I was doing wrong and how to change it. Almost desperately, I condensed part of the material, skipped a few notes, and, with some impromptu transitional comments, went into another part of the presentation. Things improved. Most of the frowns disappeared and many of the arms unfolded. Only later did I realize I'd prepared a lopsided presentation, concentrating all the "bad news" in one part — and thus turning off the audience.

The frown, of course, is an obvious nonverbal message. The sudden appearance of a few scattered frowns while you're talking suggests disagreement and lack of understanding. Several responses are possible. You can back up and restate your last point. You can pause and ask for questions, perhaps mentioning that your last remark seemed to cause some concern. Or, if you feel you've established some rapport, you might zero in on a specific frowner and ask if you can clarify anything.

A number of simple signals can suggest boredom. The hand-over-mouth can mean a stifled yawn. Glances at watches, frequent recrossing of legs, fidgeting, and eyes wandering around the room can also mean a bored audience. These often increase alarmingly as the end of the allotted time period approaches — especially if the group feels the session is going to run overtime.

What do you do when signs of boredom appear? Something different. Move about if you can. Change your speed of delivery and vary your vocal tone. Don't depend on your material to put itself across. The best material can flop if the delivery is lifeless. But even dry material can find life through an animated presentation.

Watch also for people who habitually nod or shake their heads slightly as they agree or disagree with what's being said. A few of these give you some idea of how you're going over. You can also get helpful information from those whose eyes give them away. The "skyward glance" — eyes rolled upward under raised brows —may signal anything from "Heaven help us!" to "Now I've heard everything!" The other, likely to signal skepticism or disbelief, is the "conspiratorial cut"—the sharp corner-of-the-eye look that flashes between adjacent listeners.

Communication, including that which takes place between a lecturer and a group of listeners, is always a two-way street. Generally, new instructors and speakers require considerable time and exposure to become sensitized to their listeners' nonverbal messages. Most of us start by working on what we have to say and later learning to improve the way we say it. Eventually we consider the shifting needs and moods of the audience which are often communicated by wordless messages of posture, motion, and expression.

Learn to "hear" these silent communications. Some of the signals will be swift, subtle, and almost elusive. But some will leave little doubt as to their meanings. One of the latter made a lasting impression on me. Some years ago, my boss sat through one of my first classes, which was woefully dry and running overtime. My boss looked directly at me and yawned widely, then looked down and shook his watch as though it had stopped. I got the message.

Reprinted from TRAINING, May 1978

case where some diversion may have survival value for you as a trainer.

When hostility triggers fear

In all relationships anger is the great intimidator. For this reason one cannot adequately talk about the management of anger without including some discussion about the management of fear. It is an unpleasant reality of the trainer's life that on some occasions the expression of participant hostility will trigger within you some fear. This is normal. And although beginning trainers are most vulnerable to this response due to inexperience, even the most seasoned trainers are not entirely immune to this anxiety.

When, in response to participant hostility, you experience sufficient fear to distract you from your training focus, your first priority must be to

---

> **"Trainers are paid to be scapegoats— to provide opportunity and target for participants' pressure release."**

---

accept that fear and move to reduce it as quickly as possible. Why? Because fear undercuts the three major self-supports upon which your leadership as a trainer depends: your confidence, concentration and momentum. You suddenly question if you can do the job, your mind wanders away from your training purpose into worry, and you lose the assertive and responsive momentum upon which the illusion of your training authority depends.

Like all teachers, trainers have three major needs when working with a group: to be liked, to be in control, to be effective. When these needs are frustrated the trainer can become afraid. The participant who attacks you can trigger your fear of rejection. ("They do not like me.") The participant who creates a diversion can trigger your fear of authority loss. ("I cannot control them.") The participant who withdraws beyond your reach can trigger your fear of failure. ("I am not being an effective trainer.") Training is risky. Potential anxieties are built in, and under pressure from

participant hostility they may become actualized.

Coping with fear

The most efficient way to reduce trainer fear is to close the distance with the hostile participant. Although our instinct at these times is usually to move away (to flee) or to defensively attack (to fight), both of these responses only increase our own anxiety and communicate it to our attacker. Behaviorally, closing the distance means:

1) physically moving closer to the hostile participant;
2) making direct eye contact;
3) courteously soliciting information about the nature of their protest;
4) dialoguing in a positive and supportive way about their concerns.

Even if the participant will not respond to these last two overtures, going through these active motions can still serve an anxiety reducing function for you. The purpose of these four moves is to reduce your fear of the hostile participant by reasserting your initiative in the relationship, by gaining more information about them, by establishing through dialogue a working connection with them that you can manipulate. Having moved to regain self-control, you are then ready to consider your options for gaining control of participant hostility in a group.

Responding to participant hostility

One way to conceptualize participant hostility is as a *resistance* to the training progression through which you are leading a group. In your choice of responses it is always well to consider that the harder you press against that participant resistance the more likelihood there is that the resistance will increase. This is an isometric principle. (Isometrics is the conditioning procedure where, by pushing hard against a fixed resistance, you increase the tension in the relationship.) This applies to managing interpersonal resistance. The harder you push against the resistant participant, the harder their resistance is likely to become, the more energy you are going to have to spend in maintaining that relationship, and the more fatiguing it will become to you over time. Trainers need to conserve their energies and should follow the path of least resistance whenever possible, particularly in response to participant hostility. The following five categories of trainer response

begin with the lowest and move to the highest amount of trainer resistance applied to manage the situation.

Option 1: Avoidance. There are three major strategies to be considered here. The first is to literally ignore the hostile action or remark and proceed with your program as though nothing untoward had occurred. Sometimes simply denying protesting participants the reinforcement of your response is sufficient to shut them down. A second set of strategies has to do with avoiding direct contact with the hostile participants while attending to their disruption. Here you solicit peer influence to shut them down. For example, you deliberately lapse into silence after the hostile outburst. If the majority of the participants want you to continue, they will move to quell their disruptive peer. A third set of strategies has to do with providing an indirect response to the participant. You appear to be avoiding the protest, but actually you are interpreting its intent and then responding to meet the underlying concern expressed. For example, a diversion builds in a group to your left, but you avoid looking at them. However, because you interpret their protest as a restless desire for an intermission, you go on a few minutes and then, apparently independent of the protest, announce a break. Notice that with none of these strategies do you actively engage the resistance.

Option 2: Acceptance. This strategy is a very direct one. When hostile participants push against you, move to find out the purpose of the protest and then give them their way— accept their resistance. Some people feel that a trainer sacrifices authority by "giving in" this way. However, allowing some latitude for participants to alter the content or conduct of the session to suit their needs can actually increase their sense of ownership involvement in the training. For example, a participant who is dissatisfied with a training agenda which puts his concern last may well be brought back into cooperation by altering the order of items to be addressed. Of course, acceptance of resistance is counterproductive when the participant's only intent is to disrupt the proceedings.

Option 3: Adapt. The strategy here is a manipulative one. What you want to do is to engage with the participants in such a way that you ultimately use the force of their resistance against them or for yourself. Thus when they protest and strongly disagree with what you are saying, you immediately switch sides and say, "You're right, that's a good point." Then you take their argument away from them; you begin arguing for them against the position you had previously taken. Having thus championed their argument you have defused their resistance. Sometimes this is sufficient for your purpose. At other times you may, now that you control the thrust of their argument, want to turn it back into the direction you were originally heading.

Option 4: Stand fast. This strategy is at once a very simple, but a very energy-expensive response to make. What you are doing is standing fast in your intent to do what the participant is protesting. You will not give way. You will not discuss. You will not negotiate. Perhaps the training was designed to include an evening session, and several participants are vociferously complaining. You simply stand there and let their resistance wash over you and wear itself out. Then you proceed with the program as contracted. Withstanding this onslaught of negative emotions can be abusive to the trainer, which is why providing a firm resistance against which the hostile participants can

level their protest is an energy-costly option.

Option 5: Push back. This is the most energy-costly response to participant protest. They push against you. You push back. When two resistances push against each other, of course, you have created the social formula for conflict. What you hope to gain by resisting is to overcome the participants' resistance, persuading them to back off. The problem with pushing back, however, is that if the participant doesn't back off you have just created a fight. In almost all cases, that is a no-win situation for the trainer. If you "win" the fight, participants tend to array against you out of sympathy for their defeated peer. If you "lose," then participants tend to have reduced respect for your training authority.

Pushing back is always a gamble. As a bluff it can pay off if the protest subsides and there is no conflict. Sometimes the stakes are even great enough where fighting back with a hostile participant can be worthwhile for the trainer. For example, you may have a participant so forcefully hostile that others are both intimidated from cooperating with you and afraid to stand up to and stop their peer. At

this point, if the program is to be salvaged, you are the only person there to beat this opposition down, restore order and reestablish the training framework. Obviously, pushing back is the option of last resort when dealing with a hostile participant.

Surviving hostility

When encountering participant protest, the most critical concern for a trainer is to maintain your "cool"— the capacity to calculate and choose wisely under pressure. Fear provokes impulsive responses not reasoned choice. The five management options just described are available to us *only* so long as we retain our power of reason. Thus the key to trainer control of a hostile situation is keeping fear down and all management alternatives open.

As trainers we need to accept the inevitability of participant hostility. We need to learn to deal with our fear when upon occasion it becomes aroused in a hostile situation. We need to keep our cool in order to preserve our power of management choice. We need to know and use the full repertoire of these choices. And we must not take participant hostility personally. It comes with the job.

Reprinted from TRAINING, September 1980

BREAKING THE PATTERN OF LEARNED HELPLESSNESS

Of dogs and elephants and burned-out managers: Here's how to restore an environment for training success

BY MARK J. MARTINKO

Every experienced trainer has had it happen. You spend hours of painstaking preparation designing a program to improve managerial effectiveness. Then, halfway into your presentation, someone sighs and says, "It won't work here. We tried that before and it didn't work. That's okay for a manufacturing company, but we're different."

At that point you know you're in for a rough day. You may ask yourself why it had to happen to you. You may label the person a malcontent or write off the individual as another incompetent, burned-out manager. Or you may try to engage in direct confrontation (which you almost never win). But if you are a little more introspective, you may come to the conclusion that there are some very good reasons for that skepticism or frustration—or both.

Learned helplessness is the notion that experiences with prior, uncontrollable aversive circumstances interfere with later learning. The concept was first developed in experimental animal psychology, but studies also have confirmed helplessness behavior in humans, and the theory of learned helplessness now has been adopted as a possible explanation for depression. This same theory appears relevant to the helplessness behaviors exhibited by managers and employees in work organizations.

The early research was conducted with animals and is particularly instructive in the definition and understanding of learned helplessness. In the late 1960s, Martin Seligman and his associates immobilized dogs in a harness and repeatedly shocked the animals. At first, of course, the dogs reacted very aggressively to the shock—howling, whining, defecating and urinating profusely. After a series of trials, however, these behaviors diminished and the reaction became passive; they became resigned to their fate.

Later in the experiment the dogs were released from the harness. At this point they could escape the shock by crossing a small barrier. Instead, the majority of the animals remained passive, exhibiting few escape behaviors. Even when a conditioned dog was able to terminate the shock by crossing the barrier, it usually did not continue escape behaviors on subsequent trials. In sharp contrast a control group of naive dogs quickly learned to escape the shock on almost every trial. The conclusion of the experimenters, supported by subsequent studies, was that when organisms (including humans) are exposed to inescapable punishing conditions, they eventually learn that their behavior is ineffective and makes no difference. As a result, their behavior becomes passive and ineffective, even when circumstances and conditions change.

Since the early studies, a great deal of research has been done on the helplessness phenomenon. In general it has been found that helplessness can indeed be induced in human subjects, and many of the dynamics of this process are similar to those found in the animal literature. The effects of helplessness have been found to generalize across tasks, yet a complex discrimination process is also involved. (Human subjects, for example, may exhibit helplessness for one experimenter, but not another.)

Considerable research has also been devoted to the process of immunizing and alleviating helplessness conditions. Prior success experiences, for instance, usually result in human subjects resuming normal response patterns when the period of exposure to inescapable punishment ends. Helplessness has also been alleviated through attributional training, where individuals learn to attribute their failures to their own lack of effort rather than a lack of ability or

Just as an elephant is conditioned *to think it's the rope, not the tree, that restrains him, people learn to assume they can't change things. For your training to break through, you have to find where the resistance really is.*

circumstances beyond their control.

Research on the existence and effects of learned helplessness in work organizations has not yet been done, but the theoretical foundation developed in animal and experimental human psychology can help explain many of the passive and hopeless behaviors exhibited in organizations— behaviors often in evidence during the training of experienced managers. It may be that many of the managers who reject training as inapplicable or unrealistic are actually voicing their learned helplessness. How many efforts at innovation with techniques such as management by objectives (MBO) or organization development (OD) have withered and died due to lack of support— or even punishment— of managers? Small wonder that after repeated efforts are met with indifference, resistance or reprisals, many managers eventually conclude that their efforts make little difference; they believe they are helpless to improve their organizations.

The elephant syndrome

In conducting OD interventions, there always seems to be a point in the process where the participants tell me they feel almost totally helpless to control or influence their situations. At that point I talk about "the dogs and the elephants." The dogs, of course, are those in the experiments of Seligman and his associates. The elephant story, on the other hand, I first heard from one of my students.

As the story goes, when the natives of Asia and Africa depended on the elephant as a major source of transportation and labor, they developed an intriguing technique for restraining the animals. When a mature elephant was first captured, it would be tethered to a huge baobab tree. After days of struggle, shaking and trying to pull the tree down, the elephant learned helplessness, becoming passive and ceasing its efforts to escape. From that time on, it could be restrained simply by driving a small peg into the ground. At the first sensation of tension on its tether, the elephant would stop and passively accept a condition it could easily have escaped.

What does this suggest for trainers? It suggests that many helplessness reactions can be recognized and at least partially alleviated by understanding the conditioning process that may have been involved and designing the training experience accordingly. There are several methods which can be employed for this.

Success experiences. A number of studies have demonstrated that prior success helps subjects return to normal response patterns even after experiencing helplessness conditions. This suggests that particular care be taken in orienting new managers so they experience success before they become involved in situations in which they are more likely to experience failure. Also, in introducing new concepts or techniques to experienced managers, role play and simulation exercises designed for success may effectively immunize these managers from experiencing helplessness when difficulties are encountered.

More recent evidence on the effects of success experiences in the alleviation of helplessness suggests that this approach needs to be used with some care. Some studies, for example, demonstrate that subjects who experience continued success may have problems later learning to respond appropriately to failure. On the other hand, subjects experiencing equal levels of success and failure may be more persistent in responding appropriately when failure occurs. This learned persistence is heavily dependent on an individual's own internal explanations for success or failure.

Attribution training. The concept behind attribution training is that behavior is a function of internal beliefs about the reasons for success or failure. Behaviors differ depending on whether success is perceived to be a function of chance, other people, personal ability or effort. Similarly people's perceptions of the probability that they will be successful also influence their performance. A number of studies have fairly conclusively demonstrated that feedback emphasizing the attribution of failure to lack of effort often improves performance.

Within a training environment, helplessness reactions might be modified by training subjects to attribute the results of their actions to factors other than luck or people and conditions beyond their control. Questioning and discussing attribution values may be particularly effective. Ask skeptics *why* they think a technique will not work, *who* will block their efforts, *why* they feel they cannot control outcomes. Confronting trainees with their attributions— and the assumptions on which they are based— may also be an effective strategy.

Watch for the feelings of helplessness participants consciously and unconsciously communicate. Many may be legitimate; be sure to recognize them as such. Many, however, may come from a failure to recognize that circumstances and conditions can change. Are your trainees tied to pegs instead of trees, or accepting shock passively when it can be avoided?

It should be recognized, however, that attributing failure to lack of effort may be unrealistic and even unhealthy in many circumstances. In some of the research on psychologically depressed people, for example, it has been found they sometimes attribute failure to themselves even when circumstances are not under their control. Care should be exercised to ensure that attributional training accurately reflects the real environment.

Modeling. Many people learn vicariously through observing the experiences of others. As such, a third strategy for alleviating feelings of helplessness during training is to provide trainees with a description of the success experiences of another manager they respect. Films and examples provided during training may accomplish this objective, or another manager within the organization might offer a short presentation of his or her personal experiences with the topic being discussed. If this manager operates in the same environment as the trainees, it will be very difficult for them to continue to maintain they are helpless because of *their* circumstances.

Structuring/shaping. Here the managerial technique is broken down into discreet steps, with success at each step being reinforced. By breaking down the procedure into successive stages, trainees can clearly see that they bear the responsibility for success almost completely within each particular phase.

The theory and research regarding learned helplessness appears to generalize very readily to organizational situations, particularly training environments, but the state of knowledge advanced by research in this area is still somewhat uncertain. There are, to be sure, many unanswered questions and theoretical controversies regarding helplessness phenomena. As such, care must be exercised in generalizing findings to situations outside controlled experimental settings. To the extent that theory combined with common sense can provide us with helpful suggestions and insight, however, recognizing the causes and ways of dealing with learned helplessness may facilitate our efforts to create healthy work environments.

Reprinted from TRAINING, August 1981

HOW TO SURVIVE THE FIRST CLASS TAUGHT

Some tips for the new trainer

BY MARTIN M. BROADWELL

No matter how much preparation you do, no matter how well you know your material, no matter how many times you practice, no matter how much instructor training you have..sooner or later you have to face the class for the first time. You've never taught before. You've been a good supervisor and you know the job well. As a reward for that, you've been chosen by your organization to teach a portion of the course that is designed to train employees in your area of expertise. The recognition of your job talents is flattering, but the motivation fails to veil the panic that soon prevails—and grows as the day of the first class session approaches. For all the *job* expertise, you doubt your expertise in front of the class.

"Don't worry. We'll give you instructor training." That made you feel better—until you had the training, and your worst fears were realized: You really don't have much native talent in this newly appointed skill! More panic. You develop your materials, practice with them, struggle with these fancy gadgets called AV equipment. The overheads keep moving to the left when you want to shift them to the right. The film comes out backwards with "The End" appearing upside down and reversed. At least you're consistent, since that's the way the slides project, too. The course is scheduled, participants' names arrive, then the fateful day is upon you. The students actually show up. Your prayers for a small catastrophe like an earthquake, hurricane, flood, or the end of the world failed to materialize, so you're really going to go through with it. And you wonder: "Could this have been avoided?"

Why does it happen?

If you can identify with the above scene, then you may have wondered why the first days of instructing are so frightening and what could have been done to avoid it.

There are four main reasons why we get ourselves into this panic condition, and these are obviously intertwined. First, there are many things to be remembered, and all of them are unfamiliar to us—the schedule, the equipment, the topics, the breaks, the teaching skills, the handouts, the procedures for running the exercises, role plays, games. "Let's see, the slides come before the break, right after the first quiz..."

Second, there is that almost indefinable thing called "stage fright"—the fear of getting up in front of the group, the feeling that you can't talk, can't move, can't think. It strikes people of high estate and low, educated and not, the well informed and the unprepared.

Third, there is the matter of insecurity. No matter how well you prepare yourself, you still have those moments of wondering if the class knows more about the topic than you do. As you look at the simple subjects, you begin to tell yourself, "surely they know all about this!" Then you look at their credentials and realize they're coming right off the job, and you wonder, "What if they ask a question about...?"

Finally, the first teaching assignments are often frightening because you have no comfortable habits to fall back on. When you're on the job, you're almost always comfortable; and when you aren't, it's the exception rather than the rule. In the case of the teaching assignment, you're rarely doing anything that you do habitually on the job. Even when you're *talking* about the job, it's in front of the group, in unfamiliar surroundings, trying to remember all the things that the teaching part of the job requires. And when you finish one part of the assignment, the next part isn't going to be any different, so there's nothing to look forward to.

What can you do about it?

Before we go further, let's insist—in the face of many witnesses—that it doesn't have to be that way, nor is it that way for everybody. If you're thinking about doing some teaching, this isn't intended to frighten you off. It's meant to show you that it can happen, it's normal, but there are some things that can be done to overcome much of the anxiety. There are also some things you can do wrong if you aren't careful.

First of all, let's discuss what can happen if you allow nature to take its course and just do what comes natural when these signs of fear and insecurity come upon you. Let's consider the matter of "so many things to remember," for instance. Usually one of two things happen. Either you try to put it all in your head, with no notes, or you write everything down and use a wheelbarrow to cart the notes around. Both extremes are self-defeating. In the first case, you get into an awkward situation of wandering around the classroom trying to look nonchalant while you kill time by fumbling with the equipment, hoping you will remember what to do next. Invariably you do forget something and have to decide whether it's better to go back and pick it up out of sequence, admit your error (or try to cover it up), or whether you should leave the gap in the teaching session, messing up the learning pattern as well as the time scheduled. If you have too many notes, you find yourself wedded to the speaker's stand, since you can't carry all those notes around. And you're constantly getting lost in the pages. What's the answer?

The answer isn't more or less notes, it's *better* notes. Not just notes, but well organized notes, showing activities of both the teacher and the student. Perhaps on the left page is the teaching action, on the right is the

COOPERATIVE LEARNING

A recent study indicates there are two good reasons to encourage your trainees to train each other: They'll probably learn more, and they may develop a spirit of cooperation, rather than competitiveness, essential to the success of your training program.

Students in a University of Washington social psychology course were grouped in pairs and told that their final grades would be determined not by individual achievement but by the average of both partners' grades. Each peer-monitoring group, as they were called, was expected to study together, and the partners were to motivate each other as much as possible. Although they weren't told this, students with low GPA's were roughly matched with students having high GPA's. Despite initial grumblings— that the arrangement wasn't voluntary, that each student s grade could be adversely affected by his or her partner's — the results were gratifying. The number of As and Bs in the peer-monitoring group (as opposed to the control group, a separate class conducted in the traditional way) increased substantially. In fact, no student in the peer-monitoring class got a D or an F; 87% of the students performed above the 80% grading criterion established ahead of time (no curves allowed) for a B grade.

Contrary to early fears that score averaging would pressure students to spend more time preparing for this course while letting others slide, students in both the peer-monitoring and control groups spent about the same amount of time studying. As an added bonus, students in the peer-monitoring class were more interested in the subject matter and felt more motivated to learn the material; at the end of the quarter, they also rated the class more highly than did the control group.

No student in the peer-monitoring group got a lower grade as a result of the score averaging than he or she would have received had grades been based solely on individual performance. On the other hand, some students got higher grades than they would have under the old system. In addition to performing better on tests and generally learning more, students made new acquaintances (unusual in large lecture classes), cooperated with each other, and became more aware of the need to work with and help each other while becoming more tolerant of others' values and approaches to life.

What do these results have to do with the trainer faced with a three-day seminar or a continuing in-house program? Since cooperative learning strategies such as this one seem to get better results than the "every man for himself" approach, it might be time to try the peer-monitoring system. And, since this system produces cooperative behavior in college classrooms, notoriously dog-eat-dog and overly competitive, it may also be good for the trainee whose final payoff depends on the performance of his or her group as a whole. In other words, the good old buddy system, which kept us from getting lost in the woods at summer camp or wandering off during field trips, may be just as useful today in your training program. — From *Journal of Educational Psychology*, 1977, Vol. 69, No. 2.

Reprinted from TRAINING, May 1978

---

learning action. There can be a row or column for time, visuals, method, and key points. Looking at the whole page, the teacher can tell at a glance everything that should be going on. An open notebook offers tremendous space for guidelines for an hour or so of instruction. On the other hand, note cards are bothersome, limited in space, and tend to get out of order.

What about stage fright?

Can you overcome the fear of getting up in front of an audience? What are you likely to do wrong if you just let your "natural" self come forth? Almost without exception, you'll overprepare, end up with hurried notes up the side of the paper, get in front of the class, and lose your way immediately. Usually this is done while leaning on (or should we say "choking") the speaker's stand. The more you fear the audience, the less you look at them; and the more notes you have, the less you look at the audience. Put them together and the students may never know what the teacher looks like.

What's the remedy? There's no substitute for preparation. Mostly, the solution is mental, but there should be some teaching skills thrown in for good measure. Regardless of what you may think, there's little chance of the students eating up a perfectly good instructor, especially if the teacher is knowledgeable in areas where the students have shortcomings. Remember, they're there because they have a job performance deficiency of some kind, not because they're addicted to teacher meat. The teaching skill here is to build in a design that gets the students working, talking to each other, coming to the teacher for help, building a dependency on the teacher's ability to facilitate their learning. The other things you do, like lecturing, using quantities of visuals; solving their problems for them, build the wrong kind of dependency. They become dependent on the teacher for information, not facilitation.

What about insecurity?

This, too, is mental. You worry that they might ask a question you won't have an answer for. Again, preparation is a key factor. If you know the job, the material, the policy, and the procedures, you aren't likely to get many questions you can't answer. If you do, then answer them the same way an experienced instructor does— "I don't know, but I'll find out."

Many instructors fall back on comfortable habits. The things you're likely to do include rambling, falling back on tales of the job like it used to be, giving background information in great detail, or, even worse, developing some incorrect habits. If you have "success" in overcoming stage fright by looking at the screen even when there's nothing there (screens don't bite), this "reward" may cause you to develop a habit of screen-looking all the time. If you find satisfaction in cutting down students (now they don't ask those silly questions), then you're likely to continue doing this. The solution: Intentionally develop some good habits. Say to yourself, "I'm going to try to redirect every question for the next hour, even if it's awkward," or, "I'm not going to draw a single conclusion during the period between break and lunch until after the students have had a chance." Watch yourself carefully and, when the period is over, see if you kept your promise. If you do this often enough—and you may have to write reminders all over the place—you'll end up with some good habits that will give you the right kind of rewards. The trick is to determine what habits you want and practice until "doing what comes natural" means habitually doing the correct kind of teaching.

Reprinted from TRAINING, September 1976

REMINDER: LEARNING IS A SELF-ACTIVITY

When teaching is confused with learning, payoffs for effective training techniques are often overlooked

BY MARTIN M. BROADWELL

If I were asked to give a novice instructor just one basic belief about teaching and learning, this would be it: Learning is a self-activity. The concept is, simply, that the learner is all important *to the learning process* because the learner controls the switch that lets learning happen. That may not be very scientific, but I suspect experienced teachers can relate to it pretty well.

When I used to teach mountain folks, I discovered that I usually learned more than they did. I first began to think about learning as a self-activity when I heard these folks say things like, "You can't larn them nuthin' " or "Somebody done a heap of larnin' on that boy." Obviously, they were substituting the word learning for teaching.

We more "sophisticated" types do that, too...but in reverse. We hear teachers say, "I taught them about statistics today" or "I taught a class how to complete the 2304-A form." We've even heard a class, unable to work a problem or recall data from a previous teaching-learning situation, chastised thusly: "Don't you remember? I taught you that yesterday!"

Learning is a personal thing. There is no such thing as a "group-learn" situation, though most of the formal training we do is in the group mode. We may teach in a classroom where there are a number of people, but whatever learning takes place does so on an *individual basis*. It is rare indeed when the whole class gets a simultaneous "ah-ha!" from something the teacher has done or said. Even those who have been involved in T-group or sensitivity activities don't claim that everybody in the group learned the same things at the same times.

This is no startling revelation, of course, but we tend to forget it in front of a group. Because the group all heard and/or saw something at the same time, we generally assume the students all "learned" that particular something just as, and when, we presented it. For the new instructor, this assumption can be a serious problem.

Individual needs

What does it do for an instructor to believe that learning is a self-activity? It makes the job a lot harder, that's what. It means we must think of our students as individuals and recognize that they learn at different paces, have different needs, and bring to the class different amounts of desire to learn.

Acceptance of the premise should affect our design efforts, too. Acknowledging that our students are different, we'll begin to think more in terms of individualized efforts in teaching them. We'll become discouraged with certain existing group efforts, and find ourselves intrigued with things like programmed instruction, teaching machines, the open classroom and other individualized instructional concepts. We become advocates of anything and anybody that suggests the students should learn at their own paces, set their own goals, and direct their own learning.

Then comes the realization that there's no way the whole world of instruction can be converted overnight to this form of teaching-learning effort. Result? We become somewhat discouraged and plenty frustrated.

Hopeless situation?

Next, we discover that others have been down this road of thinking before. Then we realize that these seasoned instructors are still engaged in what looks like plain old classroom teaching. Has their enthusiasm for individualized instruction dwindled? Or have they decided that, as a "cause," it is hopeless? We look at ourselves and our newfound convictions and eventually most of us decide we must continue to conduct business-as-usual.

Of course, different individuals react to these revelations in different ways. Many find themselves quite popular when they advocate the need for students to learn on their own. With their egos, stoked by this popularity, they devote more time to *talking* than *doing*. On the few occasions when they are involved in a teaching situation, they usually revert back to the old standby of lecturing, tossing in a sub-group exercise or two to keep it looking honest. Even in this incongruous situation—lecturing to a group—they often lecture on the need to cut down on lecturing.

Fortunately, change is at hand. Superior instructors are beginning to look at things differently in terms of the design and conduct of training programs. Those who are dissatisfied enough to desire lasting change are realizing that this change comes most easily and least painfully from within the system, rather than without. They begin by conducting programs that use *some* of the techniques that encourage self-pacing, self-choosing, and self-learning. They may even experiment with the open classroom or do some programming for self-study. Best of all, they become keenly aware of *individual students needs*.

This crucial awareness of individual student needs focuses all attention on the learner. It starts with the needs analysis—determining where the deficiencies are—and progress through

A GLOSSARY OF TRAINEE TYPES

Certain kinds of people turn up regularly in training courses, and as trainers we need a set of terms that we can use in describing them. At least that's the reasoned opinion of Don Ricks, president of IWCC Ltd., a Calgary, Alberta-based consulting firm specializing in writing training. Ricks, a frequent contributor to TRAINING, proposes the development of a glossary of Trainee Types that would provide trainers everywhere with easily remembered terms for categorizing people on the basis of their in-class attitudes and behavior. A word or phrase could be used to make the key identification, and a short motto could define the distinguishing characteristics.

Someone Else. "I don't need this course. I'm just here to find out if someone else should take it."

Learned. "Does your approach take into account Bruconowski's theory concerning the intermultiplicity of organizational relativities?"

Reader. "According to the last five books I read on this subject..."

Over The Hill. "I only wish I had taken this course while I was still young enough to learn something."

Lookout. "I'm on the lookout for Male Chauvinist Pigs."

Me. "If you and the others keep talking all the time, how are you going to listen to me?"

Hide. "Maybe if I look inconspicuous, you won't ask me any questions."

Conditional. "I'll learn if..."

Vacation. "It's good to get away from the office, even if it means sitting through a course."

Bird Dog (Male). "Charlie told me that a lot of horny chicks show up at these courses."

Bird Dog (Female). "Suzie told me that..."

Wow. "Lay another good one on me, teacher. I'm hanging on your every word."

Critic. "Unless I argue about everything, no one will know how smart I am."

Smiley. "You know I'm learning, because I smile and nod every time you look at me."

Mask. "You may be getting through to me, but I'll be damned if I'll let you know it."

Signed Up. "I didn't come here to do anything, I just signed up for a course."

Blue Eyes. "I'm trying to concentrate, but you're so distractingly sexy."

Like Me. "Learn? I'm too busy trying to make you like me."

Sub. "Don't look at me. I'm just sitting in for someone who couldn't make it."

Belligerent. "Nobody had better try to teach me anything."

Live and Let Live. "You just stand up there and do your talking, and I'll sit here and do my listening."

We Always. "But that's not the way we always do it."

I Always. "But I always thought that you were supposed to..."

Last Time. "But the last time our instructor said..."

Never 1. "That's great in theory, but it would never work in the real world."

Never 2. "That's a good idea, but my boss would never go for it."

Reprinted from TRAINING, November 1977

the training process to the evaluation of the training results. When we examine the trainee's work world to decide what training, if any, is needed, we look at individuals, not groups. We may use individuals as samples of group needs, but we still insist on looking at individuals, not total populations. We see what a specific person is able and not able to do. We talk to specific supervisors about specific people, not groups of supervisors about nebulous groups of deficient employees. Once we've decided what training is needed to overcome the discovered deficiencies, we carry this same individuality over to our training design. We think about what the individual students will be doing at any one time. We think about pairing and grouping in sub-groups from the individual up, rather than from the large group down.

In other words, we take individuals and form groups or teams, rather than taking the whole group and breaking it down into some convenient arrangement of teams or sub-group, without regard to anything but numbers.

When the training is completed, we return to the work world to look at individuals and draw conclusions about the entire population based on what specific individuals have accomplished. This represents quite a departure from the days when we amassed quantities of data with total surveys and then made the applications to individuals within the group.

Conclusion

Has this new-found bit of information about learning as a self-activity changed us so that it's blatantly obvious we're operating under another flag? Of course not. But because *we* know we're thinking differently and actually doing differently, we sleep a little easier, teach a little better, and sympathize a lot more with those who are struggling with the questions that once haunted us. Perhaps, since we've agonized along the same road, we'll even give them some encouragement.

Reprinted from TRAINING, April 1977

USING SMALL GROUP ACTIVITIES IN THE CLASSROOM

Success or failure can depend on group size and seating arrangements

BY PATRICK SUESSMUTH

Every instructor is familiar with the advantages of dividing a class into small groups for problem solving, case study, discussing or exploring a situation, answering a specific question, model building, developing ideas for further study, and even preparation of projects. Students learn best when they're actively involved in the learning process, and small groups tend to encourage this involvement in a number of ways:

● Non-talkers feel freer, less threatened by being wrong in front of large numbers of people if they do speak out.

● Each participant has a greater level of self-commitment to what has been said, hence a higher probability of following up the idea with action.

● Individuals are far less likely to be ignored in a small group.

● Individual tutorial type of learning, with its greater effectiveness, is more closely approached.

How big should the group be?

My experience has shown that the following size groups will produce roughly the results indicated:

GROUP SIZE

2 only—Not really a group; suitable for one-to-one situations.

3—The barest minimum that forms a group, but limited in its capacity to generate ideas and develop thoughts. Not enough people to be effective in most situations.

4—Reasonably effective.

5 or 6—Best results are usually achieved from groups this size.

7—Reasonably effective, but starting to get a bit large.

8 or 9—Group structure starts to break down as subgroups form or splinter discussions occur. Satisfactory results can still be attained, but may take longer.

10 plus—Very unsatisfactory unless your purpose is to illustrate problems of groups. Any group of eight or more will create situations where participants get in each other's way and negatively affect group achievements.

How should students be seated?

The most effective group seating arrangement is a tight circle, although it sometimes takes a bit of doing. Tell a class to form groups and they almost always will sit in a straight line. Even when told to form circles, they don't do it well; often all they do is form into a half-moon shape. The best formation is one in which all group members' knees are touching; this means the group members are facing each other and are close enough for easy communications and maximum group cohesiveness.

Tables can impede group effectiveness. The last thing we need is a table between group members. The table, though serving as a writing and working surface, also serves to 1) set up sides and 2) add one more barrier to communications.

What is your role in various types of groups?

There are six ways that groups are usually structured, and your function is different in each:

1. Task group. This type of group is established for a specific purpose such as building a list of points, doing a project, solving a case study, etc.

In this type of group structure the teacher's role is totally outside the group. He listens in unobtrusively and periodically to be sure the students understand the task and have the

Task group-teacher relationship.

resources needed. He also provides any feedback required.

2. Discussion group. This type of group gives the students a free and uninhibited opportunity to discuss a topic of importance; discussion groups usually occur at the end of group tasks when a free flow of feelings and reactions have been generated by the task performed.

The teacher should be careful not to impose his presence too obviously upon a discussion group; one of his main functions is judging when to cut off the discussion. The only guide to this judgment is the discussion itself. Usually lively at the start, when all participants are intensely involved, the discussion will gradually wind down as more and more people drop out. At this point, the instructor should step in and end it.

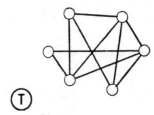

Discussion group.

3. Brainstorming group. This is usually a larger group (6 to 12 students) and rarely used by trainers. If you decide to hold brainstorming sessions, be sure to first train the students in brainstorming techniques. Consult

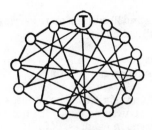

Brainstorming group.

Alex Osborn's books which are available in most libraries.

4. Tutorial group. There are two types of tutorial groups. In the first, the instructor presents material directly to all members of the group at once. Most of us probably react negatively to this approach as it resembles the lecture-type format we are trying to

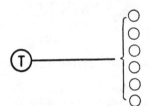

Tutorial group—Type 1.

avoid by using small groups. But it is undeniable that by using this form of tutorial group we can take a more personal approach and be sure our information gets across to all of the students.

The second type of tutorial group is not really a group situation as such. In this setting the group works on a task and the instructor assists the students individually. Normally one doesn't consider this as a separate way a

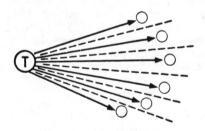

Tutorial group—Type 2.

teacher and group can interact, but it arises in any of three ways. First, a student may ask for help voluntarily. Second, the teacher may spot a person needing help or straying off the task. Third, the teacher may set up a task that specifically requires each student to work alone and need, at various points, help from the instructor.

5. Explorer group. This has the purpose of developing students' skills in asking questions leading to a suitable exploration of the subject at hand. In its basic form, the teacher is central. Students ask questions of the instructor as they progress through the material under investigation, usually in three stages.

Stage one consists of the students asking the instructor questions about the situation. In other words, the students are analyzing the situation to

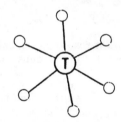

Explorer group—teacher central.

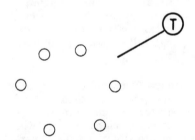

Explorer group—teacher divorced.

be sure they have an accurate idea of what they are trying to do. In stage two, students search for facts relevant to the situation at hand. In stage three, the students formulate and test various solutions to the situation.

Obviously the teacher is central in stages one and two, but he should take a passive stance in stage three. Ex-

plorer group activity can be used with verbal case studies, films, problem situations, or anytime students must search out further information in order to reach a valid solution.

Another format is to have the instructor divorced from the group though readily available to answer questions. The divorced arrangement usually leads to better questions being asked. Its disadvantage is that it restricts the flow of questions and often causes key points to be overlooked.

6. Discovery group. This type of group usually focuses on a problem which takes the form of "What can we do to...?" The instructor is part of the group and the group's findings repres-

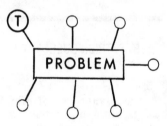

Discovery group.

ent discovery for him also. The instructor's role at the start is one of challenger. He responds to student comments with statements such as "Prove it!" "Why that?", "Are you sure" or "What do you mean?" In later stages, after the facts have been established, the instructor's role shifts to passive support in order to enable the group to reach its own solution and its own commitment to action.

Most instructors find the discovery group the hardest type of group activity to manage. This is because all solutions must come from the group and not from the instructor; the instructor must muzzle himself, even when he has a good solution he would greatly enjoy revealing to the group. The teacher can support various students, but only to assure that the whole group heard a particular point the student has made. The instructor supports listening—not student ideas or thoughts.

Reprinted from TRAINING, June 1976

HOW TO BREAK THE NEWS THAT YOU'RE BREAKING THEM INTO SMALL GROUPS

'Group stuff' in structured training sessions is not by nature an odious experience; it's all a matter of setting the stage

BY FREDRIC H. MARGOLIS
AND CHIP R. BELL

Most professional trainers know that active, relevant, focused experiences foster learning. That's why they usually try to engage the learners in some kind of structured activities. Whether role play, game or small-group discussion, structured learner involvement enhances skill building, insight and deeper understanding.

Despite this, some trainers argue that "group stuff" doesn't really work. Learners tend to resist all activities that go beyond passive listening, and this has led some instructors to abandon their use of structured activities. What these trainers fail to acknowledge is that the problem may not be with the "group stuff" per se, but with the way it is designed or presented.

Trainers need to introduce their programs in a manner that encourages rather than directs, one that creates clarity instead of confusion. And coming up with truly effective task instructions (the words the trainer uses to introduce an exercise) demands precision and thoughtfulness.

First, it is vital to begin all task instructions by giving participants the rationale for doing the exercise or task. This helps to keep learners motivated throughout the program. Beyond this, we have identified a four-step process for giving task instructions.

The sequence of steps follows the logic of learning and the logic of motivation. It does not, however, follow the logic of administration. And here's why not.

We have all been through training programs in which the leader starts out by saying something like, "I'm going to divide you into small groups." Leading with a statement like this generally causes participants to look around immediately for people they'd like to work with and to dread the exercise before they even hear what it will entail. Participants often have an aversion to working with small groups, perhaps because it requires a different kind of effort from sitting and listening. Naturally, they react to an abrupt introduction to group activity by thinking, "Who will be working with me?" or "Why am I doing this?" or "Oh, damn!"

By opening with a statement of rationale, this sort of resistance is easily circumvented. Learners can see right away why the task is going to be appropriate and valuable to them. Then when you describe the structured activity to be performed and the applicable conditions or constraints, participants begin to see that small-group work is a useful tool for learning, not an irritating, irrelevant exercise. A premature description of the task, on the other hand, can result in overt rejection of the task or superficial acceptance in the form of "playing along" with the teacher.

Many trainers find this sequence difficult to follow at first. They want to sneak in extraneous comments.

This is not a good idea. Try to follow the recommended sequence as closely as you can. While you should use personality and your unique approach to present program *content*, giving instructions is different. Here it is imperative that the proper relationship between the participants and their work be established. This will happen if you give each step of the instruction in the advised order, either reading from your notes or from a short outline you have prepared.

Step 1: Give the rationale

The introduction or rationale answers a fundamental question for the learner: "Why should I enter into this task or experience?" Only when the participants see a personal benefit from doing the task will they be ready to take part.

The rationale does not answer the question, "What should be done?" That question is addressed in the next step, the actual description of the task. The rationale for the task should always be consistent with the learner's point of view, as it is in the following example:

"When interviewing, you may or may not choose to reveal certain things about yourself or the organization. What is important is that you feel comfortable and competent in revealing certain information to interviewees. This largely comes through experience. The more we risk, the better we get at taking risks. In a moment, you'll have an opportunity to practice revealing certain kinds of information."

Notice how the same basic message is less appealing when it comes from the organization's perspective:

"When interviewing, you may or may not choose to reveal certain things about yourself or the organization. At Acme, we believe you should know in advance what you will reveal before you begin an interview. In a moment, you will have the opportunity to practice revealing information."

The rationale should communicate a personal and professional reason for the task or exercise; it must make emotional and logical sense. It should be neither a justification of the training program nor a statement about organizational needs.

The best way to tell whether the rationale is making sense to participants is to look around at the group while you are stating it. If you are hitting home, you will probably see attentive looks or some heads nodding. On the other hand, if you see stony faces and glazed eyes, you've proba-

A MEETING
PLANNER'S PRIMER

This article is adapted from Chapter Two of "Managing the Learning Process," Fredric H. Margolis and Chip R. Bell, TRAINING Books, Lakewood Publications, Minneapolis, MN, 1984.

Begin at the beginning. You want to arrange a training meeting. Why should you consider going off-site? On-site programs generally are more economical, and they usually are easier to set up and manage. Familiar surroundings also can aid participants in feeling comfortable and secure.

But on-site locations do have their drawbacks. Executives can drop in, potentially adding a note of anxiety. Participants are more likely to be interrupted by phone calls. While familiar surroundings contribute to a sense of security, they also make it more difficult for participants to separate themselves mentally from the pressures of their daily work. On the other hand, conducting a program in a conference room on Mahogany Row may produce more formality and provoke less candor than you desire.

Off-site locations give participants the opportunity to get away from the constraints of the work place and to focus on the topic. Casual dress and, therefore, behavior are more likely off-site. The change of environment can enhance the growth you are trying to foster.

The disadvantages of an off-site location? You must coordinate the event from a distance. It takes energy and time for participants to acclimate to the new environment. You may have less control over the surroundings off-site. Some of us have begun our programs in the Holiday Inn's Acorn Suite only to be interrupted halfway through by the Apex Company Sales Rally in the suite next door, complete with laughter, frequent applause and a brass band.

Whatever your decision—on-site or off-site—do put some thought into it. Don't spend the company's money on a hotel meeting facility across town for no reason other than a vague feeling that "it might be kind of nice to get them away from the office."

Basic requirements

The site you select conveys the expectation of a certain environment, atmosphere or mood. A rustic retreat projects a different ambience than the boardroom on the 99th floor. Whether it's classroom B, the Acorn Suite or the engineering department's conference room, a good training site meets the following criteria.

- *It is comfortable and accessible.* If the site is austere or primitive, participants will waste energy worrying about being cold, hot or wet. If the site is remote, they may arrive exhausted from the drive or, worse, be unable to find the place easily or, worse still, be unable to find it at all.

- *It is quiet, private and free of interruptions.* External noise or interruptions, such as people being pulled out of the program for phone calls, will drain your momentum and break the participants' train of thought. Watch out for construction work in progress (inside or outside the facility), loud typewriters next door, intercoms and so on.

- *It has ample space.* This is a major consideration in site selection because both cramped conditions and vast, empty arenas inhibit success. The site should be sufficiently roomy for you to move easily among small groups and for your visual aids to be seen clearly by all participants. Too large a room poses different problems; it's difficult to create an atmosphere of togetherness and the acoustics may be bad.

How do you decide how much space you'll need? Basically, the room should be large enough to accommodate the tables and chairs required (more on that in a moment) and still allow you adequate space to move around as you deliver your presentation. Participants also need enough room to work comfortably, store their belongings and move around occasionally.

What if you aren't able to get an appropriate room but you have to run the session anyway? Here are some common headaches you'll run into and tips for curing them—more or less.

The enormous cavern: Set up in an end or corner of the room, marking a boundary with some sort of divider if possible.

The room with pillars or other obstructions: Set up as best you can to ensure that all participants can see each other, the visual aids and you.

The room filled with distractions: These may include elaborate audiovisual equipment, couches, huge paintings, stuffed owls and so on. Remove what you can and cope with what you can't remove. Every trainer has a story moose head or a frieze of mermaids competing for the learners' attention.

Seating arrangements

A good rule of thumb is that form follows function. First identify the learning goal, then select the form which best contributes to reaching that goal. Seating not only serves a utilitarian role—a place to rest one's body—it also serves a psychological role by enhancing the positive social climate in which learners gather.

We believe the fan-type seating arrangement is most conducive to delivering andragogical designs (that is, to teaching adults). Figure 1 shows table groups of five, but the variations are endless. The fan-type arrangement has three main advantages: All of the participants have a good view of the trainer and any audiovisual aids; they can switch easily from listening to a presentation, to working with their table groups, to engaging in a full-group discussion; they can communicate with each other easily, even across the room, because everyone's view is relatively unobstructed.

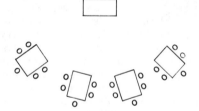

Figure 1. Fan-type seating

Other arrangements also are effective—if the learning goal involves something other than analysis, synthesis and judgment. If the goal is mostly knowledge acquisition or awareness, with straight presentation and audiovisual methods predominating, traditional classroom-style seating

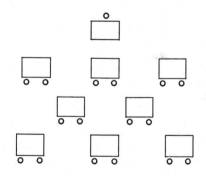

Figure 2. Classroom-type seating

is fine—i.e., with table groups all facing the same direction, as in Figure 2.

If total-group discussion will predominate, with a limited presentation and little or no small-group interaction, a conference-table arrangement can be effective (Figure 3).

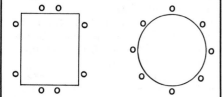

Figure 3. Conference-type seating

If the program requires both presentation and total group discussion, the horseshoe arrangement in Figure 4 works well.

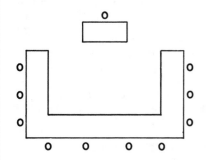

Figure 4. Horseshoe arrangement

Participants should know whether a meal will be provided before, during or after the training program. If you are conducting two three-hour segments with a meal scheduled in between, plan to serve a light one. Sessions that begin right after a heavy meal often have their share of nodders.

Reprinted from TRAINING, June 1984

bly told people what they will do, rather than why it is important to them.

Step 2: Explain the task

An effective task explanation is designed to convey the idea that the individual or group will inevitably produce a product. The task statement always incorporates active verbs. Some training designers wouldn't be caught dead without their dictionary of active verbs for writing learning objectives; we think active verbs are just as essential in describing the tasks participants are to perform. And more precisely, we're talking not just active verbs but "active active" verbs: Ask them to list, identify, solve, rank

and so on. Avoid asking them to discuss, go over, review, think about or talk about.

In addition to describing the product, the task statement usually includes some qualifying phrase, such as "list the most important," "list the five most important," "list those that you have used." Such qualifiers are critical because they enable your task statement to zero in on the exact objective you have determined is appropriate for that learning.

In summary, your explanation of the task accomplishes two things: 1) it describes a product, and 2) it usually contains some qualifiers useful in defining the expected quantity and/or quality of the product.

In the task description example that follows, look for these elements. Also, there should be a natural connection between the rationale and the task. Usually there is a transitional sentence; sometimes it is located in the rationale, sometimes in the task. As you work on your skill in giving instructions, try making the transition from the introduction/rationale to the task statement smooth and complete.

"To help clarify these points, identify and list the most important reasons, in your opinion, why feedback based on performance standards can help employees do their work more effectively."

Step 3: Define the context

The definition of context explains how the participants will accomplish the task. The context for the task involves three things: 1) the size of the working unit (individuals or groups), 2) the composition of the groups, and 3) the amount of time the participants have for the task.

Group size is determined by the nature of the task. The more technical the task, and the more it requires individual or personal thought, the smaller the group should be. Tasks requiring the exploration of ideas and group creativity usually work best with groups of four or five.

Depending on the total number of participants in your training session, you may have to adjust this number. If the group does not divide exactly, you may have a few groups of six. When this happens, be particularly attentive to these groups. Six people often subdivide into two groups of three or even pair off when the work begins. If the total group size is relatively small, then you may want to use small groups of four instead of five. Activities designed for groups larger than six are uncommon, unless the content of the program is group dy-

namics. Occasionally, you'll want to use small groups of three—usually when the task is somewhat technical yet requires the exploration of ideas, or when the task requires two people to do something with a third functioning as an observer.

Most training designs, whether for packaged programs or those developed in-house, recommend a particular size group for each activity, based on a number of carefully considered factors. Stay with the recommended small-group size. Don't adjust the size of the groups solely because of the total number of participants in the room. Often the most significant learning happens in small groups. Therefore, the *size* of the small groups is far more important than the total number of small groups working on any given task.

The composition of the small groups is just as important as their size in accomplishing learning. To understand the effects of group composition, consider the concepts of homogeneity and heterogeneity: Groups can be composed of people who are alike or different, according to objectives of the task.

Homogeneous groups are composed of people who know each other, who have the same level of experience, who are on an equal standing in the hierarchy, who work in the same plant or at the same type of job. Heterogeneous groups include people who are strangers, who have varying degrees of experience, who are from different levels in the hierarchy, who have different leadership styles, who are from different plants or work at different jobs.

Group composition plays a key role in establishing a good learning climate at the start of the session. As a general rule for the first (climate-setting) activity, you should put people together with those they know least well. Why?

• It exposes people to new ideas from new people.

• It helps people avoid habitual patterns of behavior (such as joking around with good friends) that might delay or interfere with learning.

• It keeps people from evading the task or accomplishing it in a perfunctory way.

• It helps people meet others with whom they may want to work or build a support system.

• It decreases potential competition among those who work together.

At the end of a session, you should usually assemble people who work together to enable them to discuss what they learned and explore ways they might apply this learning to their own work situation.

Many purchased programs suggest the composition of groups that is appropriate for each task. However, you should feel free to make adjustments. Consider the group that will be attending the training session. Think about what will help different members learn the most. Review some of the groupings we have suggested, and then arrange your own groupings according to what you know about the people who will be present.

One caution: Avoid forming the groups yourself. Instead, state the criteria for group composition, and allow participants to organize themselves into task groups based on those criteria. If you set up the groups, participants may feel suspicious about the reasons you put certain people together. If you simply state the criteria (and if the criteria make sense), then people will naturally group themselves appropriately. And you avoid taking a stance that elicits resentment or the feeling that you are manipulating participants.

The amount of time you give participants to accomplish a task is important for reasons that may not be obvious at first. This part of your task instruction is more an indication of how to do the task than a precise measure of how much time to take.

Participants understand the nature of the task better when they know approximately how long they have to accomplish it. If, for example, you were to ask people to list as many reasons for something as possible and you told them they had five minutes to do so, they would know you expect a quick brainstorm. If you gave them 25 minutes to accomplish the same task, they would know that the task involved exploring, considering, digging and examining different aspects of the issue. In a way, specifying the amount of time adds a helpful qualifier to the task by focusing energy in a productive way.

In most purchased programs, the amount of time to be stated in the instructions is indicated in the trainer's

notes. Be aware of the fact that the prescribed time is basically a qualifier that helps the learner understand how to approach the task; it can be adjusted.

Step 4: Explain what is to be reported

The process of reporting information people have generated in small groups adds greatly to individual learning. The goal is not simply to report (that is, regurgitate) to the total class what went on in the small groups. Instead, the goal is to *extend*

Describe the rationale from the learner's point of view, not the organization's.

---

and *amplify* learning beyond what was gained in the small groups. Some trainers refer to this as "processing"; others tag it "sharing." We call it "reporting." Regardless of the label, keep in mind that the intent is to help learners expand, integrate and generalize learning from their individual or small-group work.

When you reach the fourth step, you only have to tell participants what they may be responsible for reporting to the total group when their small-group work is completed. There is no need to explain how you will direct the reporting phase. For example, you might simply say:

"Appoint a spokesperson in your small group who should be ready to share the list your group has generated."

You don't have to mention that your plan is to ask for only the top three items of each list generated. Just give

participants a notion of what they are responsible for, not details on how you will conduct the reporting.

Most often, what is to be reported is identical to the task product. Sometimes, however, the product of the task is not reported, particularly if it involves personal information that is difficult to disclose. When this is true, be sure to include a clear statement about what is expected—or not expected—to be shared. For instance, you might tell participants:

"You will not be asked to share exactly what you write with the others at your table. It will simply be an aid to group discussion."

Occasionally the product produced is different from what is reported. This will occur in certain management-skills areas such as leadership and group dynamics. For instance, the task may require a small group to assemble a Tinkertoy tower and then have participants report on how the leadership of the group was performed. Or, a group may be requested to put together a complex puzzle without talking or touching pieces other than their own and then report on their feelings during the task. Such cases, however, are the exception rather than the rule.

Practice makes perfect

Giving clear, precise instructions—in a guiding, not a controlling, way—is one of the most difficult tasks for trainers to master. It requires practice. Practice the sequence described here, and you'll find the task becoming easier for you, more informative for the learner, and more effective in accomplishing the goals of the program. The cardinal principle to remember is: Give the rationale for the activity before you describe the task, how it is to be done and what will be reported. We believe this is the closest thing to a surefire formula for helping learners participate more productively in the activities of a training program and to draw the greatest learning from them.

Reprinted from TRAINING, March 1984

FIVE WAYS TO GET TRAINEES TO OPEN UP AND GET MOVING

Group energy doesn't just happen. It takes careful planning and activities

BY JUDITH H. STEELE

"I'm John Smith, manager of the uptown office," drones the gentleman in the first row.

"I'm Mary Jones, supervisor in the accounting department," recites the woman next to him in a flat voice. The trainees continue introducing themselves in singsong voices and sit back lethargically as the trainer mounts the podium to deliver a humdrum lecture.

Of course, you'd never allow this tedious scene to unfold in *your* training classroom. You're aware that exposing trainees to one another's experiences sparks the exchange of vital job know-how. And, you also want your adult learners to generate their own problem-solving group energy. But group activity doesn't happen automatically. It takes more than noble intentions to get employees, from various branches or departments of the organization, to begin talking, sharing, and working together.

To make it happen, build group activities into your training agenda. Set an active tone early and reinforce it throughout. Ensure that your group "jells" near the beginning of training, and you can turn placid trainees into adults willing to take charge of their own learning.

Here's how you can translate your training ideals into workable classroom activities that harness group energy:

Introduce people creatively

Remember those uninspiring trainees who could barely blurt out their names and job titles? Anxiously muttering their lines, they were stymied by lifelong exhortations to be modest— and by low training expectations. The grim results: a tense, "first day of school" feeling in the room, and little useful information for trainer or trainees.

Next time, try it another way. Channeling trainees toward their favorite topics— themselves— builds group energy fast. Make trainees abandon comfortable cliques and team up with new partners. Allow time for pairs to interview each other, venturing beyond the basics toward self-disclosure.

When your trainees introduce their partners to the class, watch your talented, multifaceted group come alive. No longer do stiffness and humility dull the atmosphere. Trainees publicly boost each other, announcing that Mary "has quite a bit of useful experience in sales," or that John "solved a stubborn office problem last month." They are also quick to point out common threads of experience that help bind the group: "Like John was saying before, Sue finds meeting the public the most challenging part of the job."

As an open-minded, open-eared trainer, encourage this process by making your own comments throughout the introductions. Your trainess will follow your cue and begin talking directly to each other. Here's the chance for you to pick up some subtle messages about your trainees. Have you spotted your classroom characters: Mr. Garrulous, Ms. Humorist, or Mr. Technicality? Seize this opportunity to review your plans, so you'll be able to gear your training to these newly revealed experience levels and personality traits.

For a more structured beginning, ask trainees to list facts and qualities which best describe them. Then, when they compare their lists with partners, the differences and similarities will spark lively discussions, and provide a vehicle for colorful introductions.

Give trainees something to talk about

Do your trainees start the day as stonefaced, inert bodies? Break their passivity *before* they can fall back on their old, tight-lipped school behavior. Introduce the unexpected— a stimulating topic or an unusual format that your trainees can relate to course content.

A Polarity Worksheet exercise is one way to ensure that trainees don't doze through your class. These sheets contain an equal number of small boxes at the top and bottom. Each box on top has two captioned pictures illustrating polar opposites— a "noisy" lion and a "quiet" mouse, for example. Trainees select the pictures that best suit their self-definitions and draw them in the corresponding empty boxes below. If they balk at committing themselves to either pole, that's something to talk about, too, when they complete the sheets and introduce themselves to partners who have drawn different pictures.

Make sure your trainees are aware that there aren't any "right" or "wrong" answers—and no one is being judged for artistic talent. Avoid amateur psychological interpretation. Instead, relate the exercise to the rest of your training. Stress how a variety of personal styles can result in effective managers or salespeople and watch your trainees mirror your acceptance of human differences.

For your training session in Life/Work Planning, you might try Movie Screen Worksheets. These handouts contain outlines of three empty screens. Instruct trainees to "freeze the action" on the movies they're making about their own lives. On the first screen, they draw characteristic scenes of themselves at work. On the second screen, they zoom in on leisure time. The third screen might be X-rated— it's for a personal fantasy. Now everyone's active, involved, and focusing on the training objectives.

Keep trainees moving

Add movement to your training activities by, for example, breaking up familiar seating patterns several

HOW TO HANDLE THE CLASSROOM SHARPSHOOTER

Every classroom trainer is, at some time in his or her career, confronted by the inevitable "sharpshooter"—the wiseacre who loves to put instructors on the spot by demanding an answer to what is usually a loaded question. In addition to being potentially embarrassing for the trainer, such questions can do considerable harm to a well-planned presentation, distracting the rest of the class from the important business at hand.

New instructors, especially, are vulnerable to this nemesis of the classroom. So how can you help your new trainers respond appropriately to sharpshooter questions? Milt Badt, an experienced instructor and senior engineer with Western Electric Co., believes preparation is the key. Badt offers the following list of defense mechanisms which, although basic, may serve to help the new instructor face his or her first sharpshooter with equanimity.

- Don't be afraid of the sharpshooter. If he were already an expert on your topic, he probably wouldn't, or shouldn't, be enrolled in your class.
- Don't bluff and don't be afraid to say "I don't know."
- Don't get drawn into a long dialogue or argument with the questioner because this will take time away from the material you are expected to cover.
- Smile. A pleasant smile is perhaps as disarming as anything else you may do or say.
- Let the sharpshooter off the hook easily (if he traps himself— and he probably will). You'll gain his respect and that of the rest of the class.
- State loudly and clearly, "That question has merit!" Then attempt to find some merit, in your own mind, in the particular question asked and state what that merit is. Chances are, there is somewhere, buried within its treachery, some real value to the question. Find it and you may surprise as well as disarm the sharpshooter.

As with every technique of instruction, developing it takes practice. Undoubtedly, your new trainers would eventually find the best method for them, but it never hurts to be prepared.

Reprinted from TRAINING, April 1978

---

times during the day. But your adult learners deserve more than an updated version of musical chairs. For example, when your trainees disagree on a topic, have them regroup according to shared views. When each group's recorder reports back to the entire class, new "converts" have the opportunity to change group affiliations.

To help trainees keep from gathering mental cobwebs, shift the size of the working groups during your training sessions. Alternate trainer input with trainee input, individual work with group work. But tailor the movement to your training content. Clusters of two or groups of 10 may suit your purposes at varying times.

Group shifting does more than just energize your training. It also caters to the diverse personal learning styles of your trainees, some of whom might, for example, clam up in large groups but participate freely in small ones.

Ask, don't tell

If your trainees seem reticent and unresponsive, it could be *you've* been overworking. Next time, don't try to do all the work by yourself! Tap the resource buried in your trainee's rich body of experience. Resist the temptation to always "tell" your trainees with texts or lectures.

If you're about to hand out a list summarizing MacGregor's management theories, stop and reconsider. Change "telling everyone" to "asking everyone" with a thought-provoking questionnaire or survey. Ask trainees to rate their own degree of agreement or disagreement with the tenets of each management theory. Devise a method to graph individual and class results. Rather than a vague discussion on which theory is "correct," trainees can now decide which parts have meaning for their own jobs. Adrenalin is up— and so is active learning.

Don't say it, do it

If you want to prove to trainees that participatory communication networks make for more effective management than hierarchial ones, you could cite numerous studies. But with a simulation, your trainees will feel the effects firsthand.

Seat the group in rows, each row being a team, hand each team member a packet of prearranged playing cards. Together, each team holds an entire deck, except for one missing element— like clubs or nines. The game is to find out what's missing, and your goal is to show which manager-subordinate communication system does this best.

Play this in three rounds, with different card packets for each. In the first, no one— including the decision-making manager seated at the end of the row—can speak to anyone except the occupant of an adjacent chair. For the next round, vary the rules by allowing the manager, seated mid-row, to speak individually to anyone in the group. Subordinates, however, can talk only to the manager. Finally, play without any assigned manager and with no limits on communication.

Treat this simulation as more than a diversionary game. Have "managers" and "subordinates" discuss their reactions to the exercise. Ask them to compare the efficiency and effectiveness of each of the three rounds. Pay special attention to the emotions of the "subordinates." Find out which structure fostered the highest morale.

Rounding out your training agenda with group energy activities like these will make your sessions lively, controversial, and, most important, productive. With everyone in your group participating, you'll not only help adults take charge of their own learning, but win points as an effective trainer, too.

Reprinted from TRAINING, November 1978

HOW TO INVOLVE LEARNERS IN YOUR LECTURES

The secret of getting—and keeping—audience attention in a teaching lecture is involvement. Here are 18 ways to create more of it

BY PAT BURKE GUILD

Despite a current emphasis on participative teaching techniques for adult learner, the lecture still prevails as a popular instructional method for both trainers and students. It has proven itself a tool not easily abandoned.

Giving up the lecture is not, of course, an all-or-nothing issue. Some people *do* learn well from lectures—especially from good lectures. The lecture's advantages are many: It can effectively convey information; it can be the best way to communicate with a large audience; it can arouse strong feelings—enthusiasm, loyalty, excitement. But the lecture does have some built-in problems: Many people don't learn well passively listening, no matter how dynamic or entertaining the presentation.

Trainers who want to ensure active student involvement in learning, however, can build a repertoire of participative techniques around their lecture skills. But before adding new techniques, know what the lecture can and cannot do.

The lecture is best used to convey general knowledge and information. It cannot deal with values, beliefs and attitudes or teach specific skills. True, a lecturer can talk about these things, but from a learner's point of view, it's all talk.

Regardless of subject matter, a good lecture requires careful organization and a clear and sincere delivery. In order for students to learn from a lecture, the speaker must outline, identify and repeat the most important concepts; illustrate them appropriately; and summarize them at the close. At the same time, a good presenter must communicate ideas confidently and enthusiastically. Good speaking skills are important, but an effective teaching lecture helps learners focus on the content, not just the speaker.

Be guided by the old Chinese proverb, "I hear and I forget, I see and I remember, I do and I understand." When you increase learners' involvement in lectures, you also focus their attention, clarify the content, make the ideas relevant to individual situations, assist retention and create a sense of "investment" in your presentation. Ultimately, students *learn* more.

1. **Use visual aids.** Make your lectures less abstract—and provide a break from constant talk—with visual illustrations. Many people need to see something, even after hearing it, to really learn it. Consider using charts, graphs, diagrams, the blackboard, models, films, filmstrips, slides, overhead transparencies, videotape, a storyboard or actual materials used in the work procedure.

2. **Encourage and use questions.** Questions are at the very core of the learning process. Actively encourage questions by asking for them, taking them seriously, listening to them carefully and incorporating their substance into future teaching. At the same time, ask questions frequently to help participants synthesize ideas, to hear their opinions and concerns and to evaluate their knowledge and understanding.

It's a good idea to set parameters for questions, however, with instructions such as: "It's OK to interrupt"; or "Hold all questions until the end."

3. **Guide note taking.** Each learner will have a personal style for taking notes, but offer some guidelines anyway. Is the information found in a book or in a handout? Is it important to note specific details? Do exact figures and labels matter? Will there be a test on this information? Or, you can actually structure the participants' notes by providing an outline.

4. **Encourage discussion.** Discussions are directed conversations among participants aimed toward a specific learning objective. They vary from informal conversation to structured talk with specific goals and tasks, time limits, prepared agendas and/or moderators.

You can begin a presentation with a discussion to obtain the learners' ideas and opinions; break the lecture with discussion to clarify issues or to reinforce and summarize content; and/or follow a lecture with discussion for all of these reasons.

You can start a discussion by posing a statement, a question or a problem. Or you can use a film, demonstration or exercise. Any number of other methods provide a framework for productive discussion.

Discussion methods range from small "buzz" groups of four to six people, to "partner chats" between two individuals, to the "fish bowl" in which a group of six to 10 discusses a topic while the other participants listen in an "outer circle."

5. **Involve learners through written participation.** Before, during and after a lecture, ask learners to respond in writing to a question, idea or opinion. This written response can be kept private, shared with the group or turned in to the instructor. The idea is to help participants clarify their thoughts and to personalize the content of the lecture.

6. **Use values-clarification exercises.** Values-clarification exercises help participants become aware of their own values, beliefs and attitudes, consider alternatives and consequences, examine the match between theory and practice, and share their values with others. Most exercises need an atmosphere of trust, and thus work best with small groups who meet over time. Some exercises, however, are very effective "ice breakers" or "dis-

369

cussion starters," and can be used with large groups. Values-clarification exercises are particularly effective in courses which involve attitudes and behaviors.

Values Clarification: A Handbook of Practical Strategies for Teachers and Students (Hart, 1972), Sidney Simon, et al., describes 79 exercises designed to help clarify values. One familiar and easy-to-use exercise is "values voting." Read questions such as "How many of you feel that a supervisor should not be friendly with employees?" or "How many of you would like to work a four-day week?" After each question is read, ask participants to take a position by a show of hands.

7. **Use role play or simulation.** Before, during or after a lecture, set up a simulated situation and select learners to play roles. You can structure the situation around a specific problem and carefully defined roles, or it can be fairly informal. A discussion may follow to examine the effectiveness of the actions taken and to suggest alternatives to them.

8. **Structure a lecture to solve a problem.** State a problem *before* your lecture to involve the learners in seeking a solution. When a lecture is structured to respond to a given problem, learners begin with a need and purpose for the information given—and become more active listeners.

9. **Use brainstorming.** The purpose of brainstorming is to stimulate ideas, so state the topic or problem to solicit suggestions and record them without making value judgments. By brainstorming before or during a lecture, you create a sense of involvement for participants and, at the same time, you get a chance to assess learners.

10. **Prepare supplementary handouts.** Lecture handouts help learners follow the main ideas, summarize the content, extend the ideas and apply the information.

11. **Illustrate with a case study or critical incident.** These usually contain a problem that must be resolved in some way. Both are designed to help learners apply theories and ideas, make decisions and analyze situations. Used along with a lecture, both involvement techniques encourage learners to develop a "mind set" that will help them apply the concept later.

The incidents you use can be taken from a wide range of sources: your own experience, textbooks, literature or the newspaper. But to make the content of the lecture more meaningful, select incidents that relate to the learners' previous or expected experiences.

12. **Give informal tests.** Brief "tests" can help both the learner and the trainer measure the success of the instruction. Self-corrected quizzes (with answers posted, or on the back of the quiz) can help participants measure their understanding and retention of information or review the subject before the lecture begins.

Be clear about the role of such "informal" tests in the final grading process. If they "count," learners must know how and when.

13. **Conduct interviews.** Participants can interview the lecturer or vice versa to summarize and test knowledge, to clarify issues or to illustrate applications of the information. The interview can take place before, during or after the lecture, depending upon the learners' familiarity with the topic. An interview of a learner should not be a public test, but rather an opportunity to share opinions and experiences and to plan practical applications of the information.

14. **Encourage directed listening.** Before the lecture, direct learners to listen for particular information. Directed listening can also form the basis for group discussions: Form groups before the lecture and give each one a specific listening assignment (e.g. the "how to" or "the why").

15. **Make a concept diagram.** During or after a presentation, ask learners to illustrate the main concepts of the lecture in a diagram. To do this, they must be able to identify the main ideas and show their relationship, which demonstrates how well they understand the concepts. When you intend to use a concept diagram as an involvement technique, tell learners *beforehand* to encourage active listening. Accept a variety of diagrams as "correct"; the learner is reporting relationships, not parroting the lecture.

16. **Ask for "I learned..." and "I wonder..." statements.** This simple sentence-completion exercise gives you an easy way to assess the learners' understanding. The statements may be written during a lecture or at the end, and may be private for the learner, given to the lecturer or shared with other participants.

17. **Team lecture.** Work with another presenter to keep the presentation from getting monotonous.

18. **Guide follow-up.** Give suggestions for next steps—further thinking, reading, other resources, practice and action.

Many participative techniques are simple, yet they can make a significant difference in the students' learning. By focusing the audience's attention on the content of a lecture, you can quit talking at learners and actively involve them in their own learning.

Reprinted from TRAINING, April 1983

HOW TO TURN BYSTANDERS INTO ROLE PLAYERS

Face it, many of your trainees are embarrassed and uncomfortable with the idea of role playing.
How do you get the reluctant ones out of the audience and into the action?

BY DUGAN LAIRD
AND RUTH SIZEMORE HOUSE

If you're training people to change their behavior in some way, sooner or later you'll probably be getting down to cases—to the case methods, that is.

By offering learners the chance to address specific examples of a principle or a theory, the case method tends to allow more meaningful learning than is possible through discussion alone.

When learners simply analyze a prepared "case," however, they remain outside the experience, "looking in on life." To give trainees a deeper level of experience, instructors often use role plays. In a role play, of course, learners *enact* the situation rather than merely talk about it. In a significant way, role plays let learners escape the environment of the classroom in order to behave as they would in another place and at another time—for example, on the job, tomorrow morning.

Thus case studies lead naturally to role plays, especially in situations where learners need to:

• Try out new behaviors the trainer is recommending.

• Try out behaviors which they themselves see as potentially useful.

• Practice new behaviors in order to make them habitual.

• Experience difficult situations from the viewpoints of other people.

• Test a theory in a practical "behavioral laboratory."

Let's examine that last point. For example, in a discussion during a case study, a trainee might say, "Well, I'd just let Edith know who's boss around here." That may be an excellent idea under the circumstances set up by the case, but announcing what one would do does not mean one actually knows how to do it, nor that one *could* do it in an actual situation. The role play provides a chance to illustrate that fact.

As the instructor, you might simply say, "That's an interesting approach. Let's try it out. I'll be Edith, and you say what you would say to let me know who is the boss around here."

Nobody has moved "on stage," no lights were dimmed, no curtains were raised—but all the same, a role play has begun.

That's an important point: Role playing can be spontaneous and very informal. In fact, the most effective role plays usually are informal and untheatrical. The more students use their imagination and the less they depend upon props, the greater the learning. And the less sound and fury with which you introduce the idea of role playing, the less resistance you'll run into.

A number of trainers prefer to use the term "reality practice" rather than "role playing," feeling that the former term better explains what role plays are about. They also feel that calling it reality practice helps them deal with the fact that a lot of people don't like to role play.

Why wouldn't trainees like to role play? There are a number of reasons.

But there also are a number of things the instructor can do to overcome them. Here are 13 tips on how to use role plays effectively.

1. Use the multiple format. This means simply that instead of asking one set of players to move to the front of the room and do the enactment, you give roles (and/or observer sheets) to everyone in the class. As soon as they have had time to read their respective roles, they can complete a number of simultaneous enactments in small groups. By wandering around the room, you can gather data to lead a profitable feedback analysis—and you'll know when to stop the role plays.

Multiple plays serve a dual purpose in that they put *everyone* into the action and, at the same time, eliminate the intimidating effect of "spotlighting" one group of players at the front of the room. Even if you intend to introduce "spotlight" plays later, multiples are an excellent way to begin.

2. Give specific checkpoints to all observers. These probably should be listed on printed "observer sheets," which are useful regardless of whether you use the multiple or the "one-scene-in-front-of-the-class" format.

Sample questions for a sales-training session might look like these: How did the customer handle the initial complaint? (Quote specific words.) What did the salesperson's nonverbal behavior say to the customer? (Cite specific postures, gestures, facial expressions.) What was the first verbal response to the salesperson? How did the customer react to these words? At what point, if any, did the customer's behavior begin to change? Would you describe the customer as more irate, less irate or totally satisfied at the end of the conversation?

Observer sheets for a supervisory-training session would include similar questions: What words did the supervisor use to put the employee at ease? How did the supervisor word the denial of the employee's request? How did the employee respond? (Note both verbal and nonverbal behaviors.) What vague phrases on the part of either player inhibited understanding? Did you note any cases where one person interrupted the other? (Jot down words to remind you of these occasions.)

3. Keep the number of characters to a minimum. Two or three is best; five is probably too many. Other learners can be given an active role through observer sheets. Since the role play needs to focus on the details of specific behavior, neither you nor the observers should be trying to analyze what every single person does in a "mob scene"—

leave that to Cecil B. De Mille. If there are too many characters, too many people will try out too many things and nobody will get meaningful feedback. The amount of data generated by the role play will be unmanageable and the learners will be lost.

4. In writing role plays, be sure the characters have distinct and conflicting objectives or ideas about how to solve a problem. Reality practice must involve the opportunity to "work things out." If all of the characters are in harmony, there can be no confrontation. This is especially important in interpersonal-skills training: Differences of opinion or values are necessary to stimulate true interaction.

This variety of viewpoints is something like the "ambiguity" sought in case studies. Further ambiguity is inherent in the role play because the differences can be resolved in as many different ways as there are players for any role. The fun of the interaction (as well as of the learning) comes when those differences are evaluated in the analysis which must follow every enactment.

When using role plays to "imprint" a procedure or to provide practice, give the players a "job aid"—a list of specific steps they should take. Here, ambiguity lies in the way they execute the separate steps, not in the steps they select to solve the problem.

5. During the enactments, wait for the "second lull." That strange-sounding advice refers to the fact that when people role play they typically will start off slowly, then build in intensity until they have passed a crisis in the interaction. Then things will "fall off" in what amounts to the "first lull"—a period of introspection, analysis...and learning.

After the lull they will reenter the role play with some new insights and new plans; noise levels will rise along with the intensity of the role playing.

Then there will be a second lull. Wait for this second lull before you halt the enactments and begin to analyze the results.

6. Always follow a role play with an analysis. Players deserve feedback on how others perceived their solutions and the way they executed those solutions. Everyone in the group is interested in how other people handled the situation, and all want ideas on how they could improve their own performance.

7. When possible, let players repeat the enactments. This allows them to polish behaviors that gave them problems

---

Nobody has moved 'on stage,' no curtains were raised—but all the same, a role play has begun.

---

the first time and/or to try out behaviors they didn't think about until the feedback session.

8. Change responsibilities so observers become characters. Everyone gets a chance, if not in the same situation, at least in parallel situations.

9. In emotionally charged confrontations, let the characters reverse roles. This does not require a new case or an elaborate new set of instructions. Just step into the role play and tell the players to "switch." By shifting suddenly from the "boss" role to the subordinate role, for instance, a trainee can gain new insight and develop some empathy about what it's like to be on the receiving end of the orders and condi-

tions he himself just finished laying down.

10. Let learners write up their own role plays. This allows them to describe roles in conflicting situations they face in their own work. It tends to make the role playing more realistic, more relevant and, therefore, more credible.

11. Introduce the role play by relating it to a specific learning objective.

12. Reinforce the way role players solved the problem, not the way they played the roles. This above all is the key to administering role plays effectively.

You aren't running a community theater here, so beware of comments like, "Charlton Heston better watch out." Far better to say, "Did you notice how well Barry controlled his desire to interrupt?" or "What were some of those excellent open questions Sharon used to get the applicant to reveal his past prison record?"

There should be no Oscars for role playing—only reinforcement for the best execution of appropriate behaviors.

13. "Rotation" and "doubling" are two optional methods you might want to try to increase participation in your role plays.

In rotation, any observer who wants to try a different approach may replace any player during the enactment—just walk up, tap the player on the shoulder or whatever, and step into that player's role. The action continues. In doubling, added players may enter the action, standing or sitting beside or behind the original player so that several people simultaneously are enacting one or both of the roles in the situation.

Using these techniques, you can eliminate the bystanders to a classroom interaction. And "learner participation" won't amount simply to busy-work: It will be part of a purposeful and responsible learning process.

Reprinted from TRAINING, April 1984

OVERCOMING ROLE-PLAY RESISTANCE

'Hey, let's role play!'
'Hey, let's don't and say we did!'
What's a poor trainer to do?
Here are some ideas

BY SUSAN HAKE SURPLUS

The fastest way for a trainer to turn an otherwise cooperative group of adults into a sullen mob is to say, "Let's role play." Something rises out of the group's unconscious (memories of fourth-grade recitation?) and brings participation to a standstill.

The role play, which actually is nothing more than a form of practice or rehearsal, is a powerful instructional tool for enabling learners to try on new skills and to integrate them into on-the-job behavior. But adult learners in a classroom setting tend to be about as receptive to the notion of role playing as children are to castor oil.

Here are some guidelines to help in the diagnosis and treatment of what we may as well break down and call the Role-Play Resistance Syndrome.

Causes

Are they catching the syndrome from me?

When you get negative reactions to the role-play segment of a program, ask yourself how you really feel about the technique. Your responses may be a clue to the problem. "I hate making people feel uncomfortable"; "I dislike role play myself, but I never let on to the trainees"; "Role play adds interest, but I don't think it changes behavior."

The trainer's discomfort in using the device is contagious. Consciously or unconsciously, the nonbeliever sets up the failure of the role-play experience by apologizing for it, by joking about it, by cutting short the preparation or rehearsal times, by ignoring or shutting off negative trainee comments, or in less tangible ways—through subtleties in voice tone, eye contact or enthusiasm level.

Any one of these behaviors says to the participants, "I know you're not going to like this."

Are trainees born with the syndrome?

No. Reluctant role players are made,

Reluctant role players are made, not born.

---

not born. We start out as social animals, trying on behaviors that are conditioned by success or failure. The syndrome may begin as a result of past embarrassments or of unpleasant episodes in previous training classes. Since egos are involved in these negative experiences, the experiences may need to be addressed directly before a resistant role player can be motivated to participate.

Treatment and prevention

Regardless of the syndrome's causes, the symptoms can be diagnosed fairly easily. These can range from the subtle (the looks on their faces) to the glaringly obvious (refusal to participate seriously—or at all). Once the symptoms appear, they must be treated quickly; and treatment is trickier than diagnosis.

Recognize and address symptoms openly.

When we ignore the reluctance of trainees to role play and simply plod ahead into the activity, a critical teaching opportunity is missed. We miss the chance to acknowledge that a learning barrier exists and to demonstrate that such barriers are common and curable.

Use *probing questions* and *reflective statements* to determine *why* this group is resisting: "What do you dislike about role playing?" "You feel that role play doesn't teach you anything?"

When the causes of resistance are on the table, trainers can deal with each objection by discussing and demonstrating the benefits of role-play activities. Trainers also can *structure the role-play setting* to minimize its threatening aspects. For example, start with "multiple" role plays involving small groups or individual pairs of participants to avoid "big audience" anxiety.

Use *analogies* to describe the discomfort that precedes the learning of new skills. For example: "Think back to when you learned to drive a car. Think how it felt to concentrate all at once on steering, shifting, signaling, accelerating. Think of how integrated that process is now—how all of the skills fit together. That same integration, from discomfort to confidence, will happen as you practice these new skills."

Model the desired behavior. Trainers can demonstrate the role play either formally (through a videotaped model, perhaps) or informally (by playing the required role first with one of the participants). Your lead-in might go something like this: "I'll do the first role play as a manager. Follow the list of skills we're learning to see if I've demonstrated each one. Then you suggest how I might have handled any part of the role differently."

Observe the role plays closely and *reinforce* examples of effective behavior. Use video or audiotapes to allow participants to critique their own behavior, following an outline of the new skills. In your own comments, stress the specific positive behaviors demonstrated by each trainee: "You were very effective in summarizing the employee's three complaints without using any judgmental words."

Stress the *problem-solving benefits* of role playing. Encourage participants to role play actual subordinates or actual problems which might be resolved by using the new skills: "Before we practice this technique, take a few minutes to outline an actual employee-performance problem. Be specific. List a concise statement of the problem and two or more examples of the problem behavior and instances when it occurred."

"Flag" success

If the role-play segment of your program is successful (it was well-prepared and well-conducted, and they "got into it"), try to ensure that the participants *recognize* that success. This not only will help transfer the new skills to the job setting, but will

---

Recognize and deal with role-play resistance—before you have a full-fledged rebellion on your hands.

---

make life a lot easier for the next trainer who wants these people to role play—and that trainer might be you.

How do you communicate that recognition? Point out to the participants the specific skills they developed in the role-play activity. Encourage them to use the learned skills *immediately* back on the job, just as they practiced them in the role play. Involve the participants' supervisors in observing, reinforcing and rewarding the use of the new skills back on the job. ("Rewarding" can mean something as simple as noticing and mentioning.)

Changing behavior, as trainers well know, is a slow and arduous process. Breaking down role-play resistance is a critical part of that process, and well worth the trainer's time and effort. The payoff is participation—and through participation, effective training.

Reprinted from TRAINING, December 1983

HELP TRAINEES BELIEVE THEY NEED TO LEARN

When it comes to motivating trainees, trainers can learn from good salespeople and ad copywriters

BY MARTIN M. BROADWELL

Perhaps it's fair to say that people learn for the same reasons they buy toasters or don't buy mixers—because they have a need of some kind (or perceive themselves as having a need). One has only to read the newspaper ads or watch the sales efforts on the TV screen to see that much advertising is aimed at taking advantage of the "need" syndrome. The idea of getting more for less, better for the same price, avoiding the last minute rush and price increase, taking advantage of a one-time offer—all are designed to appeal to an individual's impulse to gain a reward or avoid punishment.

But good salespeople and ad writers don't just wait for the potential customer to figure out some need. They go out and create a need where it doesn't exist.

It's not often you have a salesperson come to the door of your office, lay a product on the desk or table and say, "Here it is. Wanna buy it?" But think how many times some trainers walk into the classroom, lay the books on the table and say to the students, "Here it is. Wanna learn it?"

Let's take it a step further. Imagine your reaction when the seller tells you, "You'd better buy it. You're gonna need it someday." If you're the naturally patient kind, you'll respond only by suggesting rapid departure. If you're less patient, you might aid that departure somewhat. When using this approach in the classroom, then, is it any surprise when the patient stu-dents simply sink into a coma and the less patient ones begin a concentrated harassment program?

This may be an ideal time for each of us to look at every program and decide what there is in the course for the students. For those who have given up on real discernable objectives, what are you using to offer the students a reward or to help them avoid punishment? How are you creating the need? For those who still struggle with objectives, are you sharing them with the students? Are they perceived by the students as fulfilling their needs?

Whose needs are you meeting?

Here's an experiment you can try in your teacher training classes. Ask half of the group to list reasons why an organization spends money on training. Obviously, training costs money. There's the cost of the facilities, the trainers, the materials, the transportation, the trainees' salaries, etc. Money has to be approved, and the expenditures therefore must be justified. Have the subgroup list the justifiable reasons for getting approval for training dollars. While half the group works on that assignment, have the other group answer this question: "Why would a learner ever bother to learn anything?" It takes some effort, some motivation, some expenditure of time, and some commitment to learn most things. Why would a learner want to make the effort?

When the subgroups report, you'll probably have two completely different lists. On one side you'll see things like, "To improve efficiency, provide more services, increase profits, save money, meet competition, keep up with changes, keep a backlog of promotable people, and reduce accidents." On the other side you'll find things like, "To keep my job, make more money, get ahead, make the job easier, fear of the boss, self-satisfaction, and curiosity."

There are reasons for the differences. Training programs are established for organizational reasons. People learn for self-oriented reasons. It doesn't have much appeal to tell employees they're being trained so they can produce more for the same wages, or that the organization wants them to be more efficient so it can get more goods or service without adding people or increasing costs. Remember, the employees are hoping to make their jobs *easier*, and more production or service sounds like *harder* work. We might kid ourselves and say that what's good for the organization is good for the trainee. That's often correct, but it seldom computes that quickly in the employee's mind.

What this suggests is that we don't use the information we have to motivate the students. We have the things that would turn the students on, motivate them, create within them a need for the learning to take place. We know (or should know) what's in it for the trainees. We know that we're training because there is a deficiency in job performance. We know what happens to employees who can't perform up to standard. We know what happens to employees who *do* perform up to standard. We know that safety has a direct bearing on the employee's pocketbook. We know that we're going to need a certain number of people with certain skills next year, or five years from now. Since we know these things, we ought to share them in such a way to get maximum motivation.

So can we motivate trainees? One way is to use a good sales approach. Create a need for the material—the learning. Create a desire for the objectives on the basis that there is something in it for the students.

Are you doing that now? Well, there are ways of telling. When was the last time you heard a trainee say, "That's okay, but we don't do it that way back at home"? Or, "That's interesting. I hope I get to use that someday." Or, "This is all well and good, but I can't use it until my boss has been here. When are you gonna send him?" And what is your reply? If it's "you'd better learn this or you'll be sorry," you'd better make a resolution to stay out of the selling business. You'll never make it by threatening the customers. As for making it in the training field, well...

Reprinted from TRAINING, February 1977

LEARNING FROM EXPERIENCE IS A GOOD LEARNING EXPERIENCE

BY ANDRE NELSON

Talk about your bright-eyed, bushy-tailed, wet-behind-the-ears trainers! You should have seen me 15 years ago. There I was, just out of college, an anointed training officer in a correctional agency in one of the largest states and burning with zeal to prove myself.

But where to strike first? There were so many areas in need of my expert attention. Where could I look good and do good at the same time? Safety! Everyone is in favor of safety! Who wants to go to work alive and come home dead? Safety would be a perfect first triumph. I devised an elaborate program. My very own first training effort had films, statistics, lectures by safety experts and my own, very personal BS&T. The result of all this frantic activity? Apathy and resentment on the part of the trainees and a monthly accident rate which completely ignored my admonitions and kept right on inching up.

Of course, the presentations were boring. Safety is boring, isn't it? (It's like Latin. "Take Latin. It *must* be good for you, it's so awful.") A year of safety training, given once every two months, produced no changes in the accident rate. The solution? Cut back to safety training once a year. That'll show 'em. Besides, safety is such a nebulous subject that it wasn't my fault if the trainees were too obstinate to take advantage of my efforts in their behalf. That was the flimsy rationalization I used to salve my conscience.

Just recently, a chance comment made by one of our maintenance people jolted me out of my complacency about safety training. I think what I learned is of value to any trainer in any context. While my office was being remodeled to make room for some television equipment, one of the maintenance men, a welder, sat down wearily next to my desk. As he sank into the chair, he grimaced in pain, straightened out his leg, and grunted, "Man, it hurts all the way to my hips." Knowing he was an avid sportsman, I asked if he'd been hurt while hunting.

"No," he said, "I was on a ladder and fell. Landed on my left hip and side and strained and stretched muscles way down to my ankle. Boy, I sure hate to get up before that group again. This will be the second time in two months."

I was bewildered. Ed is a bull of a man, whom nothing seems to faze. To me, he always seemed about as sensitive as a Patton tank, and certainly the first to guffaw at any safety suggestion. His favorite phrase, when I was launching my safety program was, "Shove off, sonny. I've done this longer than you have years, and I'm still healthy."

I was more than mildly curious about what sort of meeting *he* would be reluctant to address. And *why*, I wanted to know, would he be talking to people about an accident.

It seems that a few months after I gave up my formal, stylized safety training approach, the chief of plant operations had, on his own, initiated a very different kind of safety program. He referred to it as a "tailgate" session, patterned after the informal safety sessions some public-utilities maintenance crews hold around the tailgate of a truck before the start of a work day.

The CPO had been holding informal safety-training sessions for half an hour once every month. During this meeting, every member of the maintenance crew who had an accident during the previous month would stand up in front of the group, describe his accident and suggest ways he could have avoided it. His peers were free to offer corrective suggestions, and, invariably, a discussion regarding that accident and similar ones would develop.

As Ed had confided to me, no crew member relished having to stand up and admit he had injured himself through his own carelessness. There was no breast beating or pleading for forgiveness, just a frank recital of an accident and what had caused it. And the causes the maintenance crew isolated were reasonable and avoidable —trying to take a short-cut to do a job, using improper equipment, or simply daydreaming on the job.

By any measure, this simple program initiated by the CPO has been an ongoing success. The men accept it as necessary, but once they appear before the group they don't wish to repeat the performance. The accident rate, which previously averaged three per month (one usually a disabling injury), has now dropped to less than one a month. And there has been only one disabling accident in a year!

As a novice training officer, I had failed—failed to realize that those for whom I set up safety programs had much more to contribute than I gave them credit for. The CPO, on the other hand, knew something I had forgotten. Safety isn't only rules, regulations and procedures. It's people working in certain ways. And who could have a greater vested interest in going to and returning from work alive and whole than the workers themselves? They are indeed the most valuable resource a safety program could hope for.

Reprinted from TRAINING, July 1978

THE POWER OF THE QUESTIONING APPROACH

Socrates can provide a powerful model for classroom trainers

BY PAUL J. MICALI

There is nothing new, modern or revolutionary about the Socratic method. The man who perfected it, Socrates, was a Greek philosopher who lived around 450 B.C. His method consisted of asking a series of well-planned questions, through which the prospect's thinking was guided to the only correct conclusion possible—the ultimate truth. When Socrates did the selling, the prospect did most of the talking. As questioner, it was Socrates' role to evaluate his subject's reaction and determine the next question to fire out. He became so good at this that he rarely missed a sale.

Typically, trainers of our day spend a great deal of time and effort prompting salespeople, for example, to use the Socratic method. Why, then, is it so difficult for trainers to use it themselves? Trainers are far from college professors who can be content with lecturing, lecturing and lecturing some more. Adult learners have habits which have changed since their college days, if indeed they went to college. And the material is quite different, both in content and application. As Jay Beecroft, formerly of 3M, puts it, "Education is a simple process; training is not. Educators give people knowledge. Trainers help people put knowledge to use."

The power of the question

In contrast to the lecture style of presentation, the Socratic method promises training that is impactful, that comes across with much more emphasis. And if it has positive results with adult learners, its use also serves to enhance the trainer's style and performance.

The Socratic method forces a trainer to prepare more fully. It is fundamental that you can't ask intelligent questions without first thinking them over carefully. It is also fundamental that you cannot jam too much material into too short a span of time and expect it to be absorbed. In both cases, the trainer is compelled to do a more thorough job—admittedly at some cost in time and effort.

In addition to enhanced planning of material and scheduling, there is the benefit of increased learner participation. By listening carefully, the trainer gets a feel for the intelligence level and overall preparedness of the audience, general morale and attitudes toward training, and attitudes toward superiors and the company. All of this makes it possible to adjust a presentation to not only fit the special needs of the group but also to correct any negative attitudes. And trainers may well learn as much from the answers they receive as they impart to their audience.

Participation also promotes tremendous rapport between trainer and trainees. For the latter, there is a myriad of benefits to be derived from the Socratic method. The best of trainers cannot keep an audience alert for hours on end single-handedly. The questioning approach avoids boredom since it is fueled by both trainer and learners. If trainees know that questions are the rule, they may arrive better prepared for learning, since there is an incentive to read over material very carefully in advance. In addition, the open forum promotes the feeling that personal views can be expressed and won't be criticized, which is always satisfying. The talkers get to talk. The quiet ones get drawn out. The experience is all the more productive for the enthusiastic participation encouraged in attendees.

When wrong is right

Most trainers will concede the advantages of the Socratic method, but many will also offer a laundry list of disadvantages. The time schedule may not permit its use, they will argue, or the material may be new to attendees. Some trainees may be embarrassed by revealing themselves as novices or unprepared, and others will surely contribute the wrong ideas. And what to do with all those sophisticated visuals if time is to be spent in question and answer interplay?

In their simplest form, these arguments indicate a very real problem, though maybe not the predictable one. The Socratic method is ostensibly simple—conduct a training session by asking questions and handling the responses in such a way that the correct answer is ultimately arrived at. The tricky part is handling the answers properly, especially handling the wrong answers properly.

Those who oppose the Socratic method argue that it doesn't make much sense to entertain a bushel of wrong answers until the right one is finally arrived at, or—at last resort—is given by the trainer. It's a waste of time, they claim, since the wrong answers are of no value anyway. Not so. In learning, it is important to understand the wrong way of doing something along with the right way. In fact, when the wrong is innocently voiced, it gives the trainer a golden opportunity to explain *why* it is wrong to the benefit of the entire group.

It's almost like handling objections. Done well, there is much to be gained; done poorly, much to be lost. And it really goes beyond that. The trainer must be able to answer *all* questions—right, wrong or irrelevant. Some answers aren't answers at all. They may represent an attitude, egotism, wise-cracking, or some other personal agenda. The trainer must

WHY IT PAYS TO MAKE A GOOD FIRST IMPRESSION

BY RON ZEMKE

In their book, *Contact: The First Four Minutes,* Drs. Arthur and Natalie Zunnin claim that first impressions are lasting impressions. That is, the first four minutes we spend with someone we've just met can, and usually do, set the tone for an entire relationship. According to the Zunnins, we decide whom we will or won't buy from, hire or fall in love with in those first few critical moments of contact. Whether you're a salesperson, a job seeker or a cruising single, that can be a pretty startling realization. Obviously, it's important to know how to put your best foot forward in a first-contact situation.

Recent research by Drs. Brad and Velma Lashbrook, Wilson Learning Corporation, may shed some light on the dos and don'ts of that first-contact period. The Lashbrooks, working from the "counselor" model of buyer-seller relations, have been studying the factors that led prospective buyers to feel *comfortable* with salespeople.

Working with 605 salespeople, the Lashbrooks tested the idea that "a certain degree of social penetration (interpersonal comfort) is necessary for a buyer-seller relationship to develop to the degree that two parties can engage in a decision-making process." Their procedure was to have the salespeople in question distribute an interpersonal relations questionnaire, called the Interaction Feedback Profile, to their customers and prospects at the culmination of a sales call. The customer or prospect filled out the form and mailed it directly to the researchers.

At the end of the six-month data-gathering period, the researchers factor analyzed the data to tease out the elements that most affected customer comfort in the buyer-seller situation. Their findings indicate that variations in three perceptual factors—*competence, trust* and *propriety,* or "interactive integrity"— account for almost half (45%) the variation in level of customer comfort reported by the buyers in their study. That is, when a buyer perceived a seller to be *competent* (technically qualified to help solve a problem), *proper* (the right kind of person to be working with) and *trustworthy* ("win-win" motivated), then the buyer was most likely to report that he or she felt *comfortable with the salesperson.*

The Lashbrooks report that their data also suggest an order in which these three factors come into play. Apparently, the most impact on comfort occurs when the seller establishes the "normative" factors—competence and propriety—and then the "psychological" factor— trust. Establishing these client perceptions, they further suggest, may require more than one sales call.

Though their data analysis is a maze of complex factor analyzers, oblique rotations and regression modeling, the results are pretty clear. If you believe in and teach the "win-win" counselor or consultative approach to selling, your trainees should be aware of the critical impact of first impressions and should know how to make good ones.

According to the Lashbrooks' work, that good first impression requires the would-be seller to answer three questions for the buyer:

● Is this person enough like me to understand and deal with my problems? Do we have enough in common to work together (*propriety*)?

● Does this person have the knowledge and skill to help me solve my problem (*competence*)?

● What is this person's intent toward me? Does he/she really *want* to help me solve my problem (*trust*)?

When the buyer can answer all three questions positively, it means that the seller has established his or her *interpersonal integrity,* the buyer is comfortable with the seller and the problem-solving dance can begin. Be it buyer-seller, employer-employee, trainer-trainee or person-to-person, good relationships start with putting your best foot forward. A sincere effort to make the other person comfortable is clearly a step in the right direction.

(Originally reported in "Applying the Concept of Interactive Integrity to the Sales Setting," an unpublished research report by William B. Lashbrook and Velma J. Lashbrook, Wilson Learning Corporation, Research Dept., Eden Prairie,MN.)

Reprinted from TRAINING, May 1980

---

remain in control, but in a positive manner, not by becoming pompous, irritating, insulting, abrasive or in any way terrifying. He or she must reflect the smoothest of salesmanship, appeal to reason where appropriate, and resort to tact and often humor in sidestepping delicate or difficult interchanges.

The acid test of a trainer's ability to set up and effectively maintain a Socratic dialogue is when a trainee offers a wrong idea. If wrong answers are handled properly, much is to be gained by all in attendance. In fact, wrong answers should never be discouraged, whether by ridiculing in any way the people who come up with them or isolating them from their peers as somehow less smart or less qualified to be a part of the group. This is intimidating as well as embarrassing to the individual, and ultimately counterproductive for the group.

The fact is that wrong answers are far from harmful to the cause. On the contrary, if trainees hear six wrong answers before the right one is finally nailed down, they (including those who offered incorrect responses) will understand the reasons behind the right one even better. It is naturally important to be judicious regarding how much time is spent on wrong answers. In any training, time is always a significant factor whose value is measured by the trainer.

What can be said regarding results obtained with the Socratic method? By many measures, trainees learn and retain more, though how much more is hard to quantify. In one case, however, the average test score of a group of 40 sales trainees after a two-day Socratic style seminar was 22% higher than the average score of a similar group of 85 who attended the exact same seminar in lecture format.

Reprinted from TRAINING, March 1981

STAGE FRIGHT: BREAK THE BARRIER

A little pep talk for new trainers (and others) who worry that they just aren't cut out for speaking to groups

BY ANTONI A. LOUW

It's said that the thing business people fear most, the dread that outranks even fear of death in polls on the subject, is public speaking—making presentations to groups. So congratulations on your new assignment to the corporate training department. Guess what you're going to be doing a lot of.

Few trainers consider presenting to be the best aspect of their jobs, especially early in their careers. Conducting a classroom session can be a lot like pitching a marketing plan or a new product proposal to a group of senior executives. Sometimes presenting seems to consist of ducking and diving between hidden agendas and conflicting interests, often in full view of competitive peers, prospective clients and critical superiors. It's an ordeal to be suffered through.

Does it have to be that way? Of course not. Presenting needn't be painful. It can be an extremely rewarding experience once you know how to feel comfortable in front of a group, how to field questions and how to give yourself more successes than failures. Most presenters suffer because of barriers they themselves construct. If you can discover your own barriers and break through them, you're on your way to enjoyable and productive presenting.

Faking it

The first barrier is the inability to create a "presentation presence." This public presence replaces the private person that you are in a one-to-one situation across the lunch table.

Why present a training session or a product or a marketing plan as if you were giving a funeral oration or a dissertation on strategies of macroeconomics? Why not open up, let yourself be more forceful, *show* what you feel for the subject? "It's not me," you protest. "I wouldn't feel natural. I'm not an extrovert by nature, I'd be trying to be somebody I'm not. I'd be faking it."

Really? Chances are you're the same person who spends Sunday afternoon in front of a television, if not in the stadium bleachers in front of thousands of people, waving your arms and bellowing war cries when your team scores. You're the person who, when your daughter makes her first successful solo bike ride, cheers and carries on for the whole neighborhood to hear. Yet when asked to liven up a little, to show more energy, to be more expressive, you insist, "It's not me."

Everybody has an expressive side, and it's your expressive self on which you must capitalize. You let your audience know how sold you are on your subject by showing them, not by telling them.

It's your responsibility as a speaker to persuade your audience to listen. A renowned authority might sit in front of a large audience and talk in a monotone, very deliberately, with no perceivable change of pace, and still enthrall the audience. But until you become famous and have people listening to you because of *who* you are, you'll have to *develop* listeners in your audience. If you're not a "who," then you have to depend on how and what—how you deliver your message, combined with what you are saying—to hold their attention.

Another protest you might make is that it doesn't look professional to be overexpressive or to gesture with wild enthusiasm. I remember being told this in high school and at college when I was majoring in communications. It seems to be commonly accepted. But look at it from the audience's viewpoint. Think of the times you have listened to a speaker, a professor, an orator. Which ones motivated you? Which ones instilled enthusiasm? Which ones did you limp away from, feeling listless and bored, not remembering a thing? How many times have you sat there on the verge on nodding off and muttered, "This guy may be brilliant, but I wish he'd put some more life in his speech."

It's true that "wild" enthusiasm can be overdone, but you really have to work at it. Enthusiasm and expressiveness are never out of place in teaching or persuading. They're a must.

Suppose you're unusually inhibited or a severely stoic type: Even in one-on-one situations you're uncomfortable communicating enthusiasm to others. "No, I do not jump for joy when my team wins. It takes a lot to excite me. When I get good news, I don't necessarily feel greatly elated."

Maybe it's your upbringing, maybe it's the way you perceive social requirements, maybe it's rigid thinking about how one should behave in front of people. Whatever it is, it may not be a barrier in your everyday life. But when you put on your presenter's hat, it becomes one.

Have you ever spent considerable time and effort looking for a very special present for a friend, and received a lukewarm "thank you" for your trouble? You probably went away thinking that the present hadn't been appreciated. Actually, it may have been treasured, but you lacked the necessary crystal ball to see the low-key recipient's emotion.

Your audience doesn't have a crystal ball either. They too can recognize your emotion only if you show it. People need to be *shown* as well as told in order to be convinced.

Successful presenters are those who bring life to their presentations and instill in audiences an interest in the content. This became obvious to me when I had the opportunity to see two different presenters deliver the same material. Both had developed an outstandingly logical sequence to their delivery; but it was the one with the enthusiastic delivery who received the most applause, acknowledgment and agreement from the audience. This presenter also looked more natural, enabling the audience to relate to him as a person. Afterward, I went backstage and asked him how he was able to look so comfortable and sincere in front of 500 people. His simple answer: "I *like* talking to people."

So what can you do if you don't "like talking to people?" Try to discover the values and behaviors you have subscribed to, through choice or environmental conditioning, that now prevent you from enjoying the exchange of communication. If you can recognize them, you can work on overcoming them. You'll find yourself livening up, beginning to speak with more enthusiasm and generally looking more energetic.

Here's another related barrier: "I know the audience is already predisposed to a different viewpoint, so why should I break my back trying to persuade them?" Ever hear of a self-fulfilling prophecy? Put life, energy and enthusiasm in your presentation and you can cut through fixed ideas, biased viewpoints, predisposed thinking and other inflexible attitudes. It's a real challenge, but remember that the audience *is* there and *will* listen to a dedicated presenter.

The way a presentation is structured plays a vital role in breaking through audience barriers. But that's only half the battle. The other half is won when you show that you truly believe in what you are saying, and that you're convinced your listeners will benefit by at least considering alternatives.

It's hard to accept change. People have to want to change. They have to be motivated to consider other alternatives. So motivate them. Show that you believe in your presentation.

Who's impressing whom?

So much for barriers having to do with enthusiasm. The second major kind of self-imposed obstacle to the presenter is the pressure that goes with *who* is in the audience. How many times have you seen people stand up and deliver sterling presentations to their peers, but then fall apart in front of the boss or the board of directors? Why?

One answer is labeling: We tend to label certain people as unapproachable. We are inclined to revere those who have achieved power or public recognition: actors, politicians—and senior managers. But wait a minute. Doesn't this person also laugh, cry, eat, sleep, feel lonely or frightened from time to time?

You may have heard the classic advice to nervous and intimidated speakers about imagining the audience members sitting on the john. The point is that nobody can seem threatening to you in that position; the simple bonds of being human draw us all to a state of equality. But do you know who is credited as the originator of that scatological advice, the person who found the image necessary to reduce his nervousness? Some inadequate pip-squeak, maybe? Not exactly. It was Winston Churchill. And the audience he was talking about was the British Parliament.

A third barrier to successful presenting is the universal fear of making a mistake or of making a fool of yourself. The purpose of giving a presentation is either to inform or to persuade. The purpose is not "to avoid making a mistake."

I have never seen a perfect presentation. You probably haven't either. And you won't. Approach a presentation from the perfectionist's viewpoint and you focus on making errors. Focus yourself instead on correcting them. The hallmark of good presenters is not that they don't make mistakes. It's the ability to recover well.

Recognizing the possibility that you might make a mistake lets you devote your attention to the issue at hand: delivering the presentation. "But if I'm talking to the board of directors I can't *afford* to make a mistake," you say. Well, can you afford the time and effort and worry you're putting into avoiding the possibility? Wouldn't your time be more productively spent in determining what makes the audience tick? Can you afford *not* to spend your time designing examples that assist in your delivery, and visuals and props that emphasize the key issues of your presentation? Can you afford *not* to prepare yourself to answer questions that will inevitably come up during or after the presentation?

When you start to break through these barriers, you lose a shield you have raised between yourself and others, a shield that is very easy to hide behind. You built it initially as a solution to the problems of communicating.

As you lower the shield you may feel exposed and vulnerable, open to attack. It's simple to say things like, "You can only be affected by things you want to affect you." But in dealing with intricacies of emotion and personality, answers aren't really that simple. For the fledgling presenter, the real solution is to experience how much more successful communication becomes in the absence of barriers.

One way to relieve the anxiety caused by letting go of your protective barriers is to concentrate your attention and concern on the audience members themselves rather than worrying about how you're coming across to them. The latter attitude is introspective; it puts the focus on you. The former is extroverted and puts the focus where it belongs: on the people you're trying to teach or convince.

Your final protest may be, "I don't want to be conditioned. You're trying to package me like merchandise." Hey, if you stand like a zombie, use poor gestures to emphasize key issues and speak monotonously, you're already conditioned.

You can *uncondition* yourself. You can unwrap the communications straitjacket you're wearing. Remember the first time you drove with a stick shift? Did it come easily or automatically? Did it seem completely natural to press the clutch, steer, watch the rear-view mirrors, the cars in front of you and your speed, all at the same time? Chances are you felt clumsy, foolish, stiff and embarrassed at first. Those feelings are an integral part of learning to drive. They come with the learning territory. Recognize this stage. Use it; don't reject it.

You don't have to compromise your view of who you are. Presenting is something you *do*. It's a learnable skill like any other. You may have to change your *approach*, but you don't have to change your life. However, you'll notice that your audiences will change. They'll support you more often and more enthusiastically. And you, the presenter, will reap the rewards and go home smiling.

Reprinted from TRAINING, August 1986

HOW TO PREPARE FOR PRESENTATIONS

Whether you're a first-timer or a seasoned presenter, this guide will help you organize, illustrate and deliver effective presentations

BY DAN E. ANDERSEN

You are undertaking a very important mission: As an expert in your field, you are going to deliver a presentation. From the time you step into the spotlight, you will set the pace. You will control the audience.

But remember, your audience has limited time to absorb your ideas. If your presentation is not coherent and simply communicated, you will lose them.

How do you hold an audience's attention? Regardless of the type of presentation you are giving—speech at a professional organization, panel discussion at a trade show or pitch for the training department before your company's executives—the bottom line is the same: Be prepared.

The objectives of such a presentation—the keynote speech at a training conference, say—obviously are different from those of an actual training session. The criteria according to which you will prepare—and against which you will be judged—differ as well. But most of the following guidelines apply to almost any situation in which you are the one at the front of the room delivering information, presenting opinions or seeking to persuade an audience.

Define your objectives

The first step in preparing any presentation is to define your objectives. What do you want to accomplish? What changes do you want to take place in the attitude or behavior of the audience? Do you want them to perform a task? Recall some information? In other words, what is the most important aspect of your presentation?

You must grab your audience's attention from the very beginning. You know what you want to say; now determine the sequence. Organize your thoughts by getting them down on paper in a complete outline. The first step is what might be called a "Brain Dump": Dump everything you know about the topic onto paper, and then see how it all fits together. What is the most logical sequence to follow? Figure 1 illustrates a typical "Brain Dump" outline.

This type of topic-cluster outline enables you to see how all the pieces fit together, and how you can logically assemble your data to flow properly. You can now prepare a more standard topic outline using single-line statements that cover all of the items from your cluster diagram.

Each entry in your outline should be a statement of what you intend to say. Along with those statements, you may find it useful to jot down questions such as: How are objectives defined? What needs to be done to develop written material? These will guide your writing approach later.

You also should be considering what illustrations you will need to support the text. Make a complete list of illustrations and note which are photographs, which are drawings and which already exist.

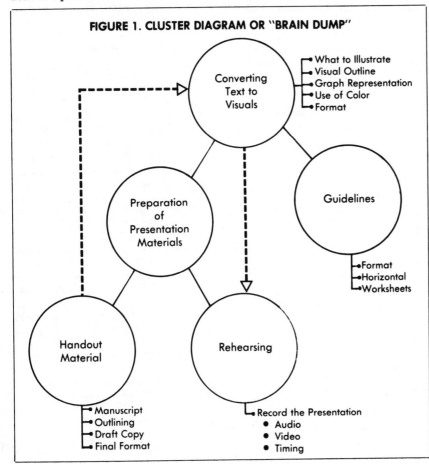

FIGURE 1. CLUSTER DIAGRAM OR "BRAIN DUMP"

Converting Text to Visuals
- What to Illustrate
- Visual Outline
- Graph Representation
- Use of Color
- Format

Preparation of Presentation Materials

Guidelines
- Format
- Horizontal
- Worksheets

Handout Material
- Manuscript
- Outlining
- Draft Copy
- Final Format

Rehearsing
- Record the Presentation
  - Audio
  - Video
  - Timing

FIGURE 2. EXAMPLES OF VISUALS AND FORMAT

GOOD SLIDE

BAD SLIDE

FIGURE 3. CONVERT DATA TO GRAPHICS FOR QUICK UNDERSTANDING

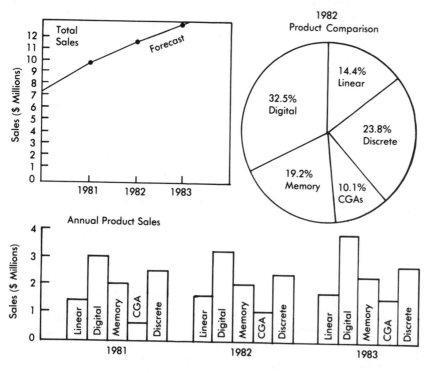

Developing the written message

The written text and your oral presentation are two different things: They call for different methods, different illustrations and a different language. The written text is, however, the key document in this project. It not only defines your message but establishes the basis for preparing your visual material. The text must be able to stand on its own.

The first draft is your working copy—your first attempt at getting down in writing the approach you feel best supports the subject. Read through the material as though you were seeing it for the first time and ask yourself:

• Does it accomplish my original objectives?

• Is it clear and easy to understand?

• Do the illustrations support the text?

• Is the sequence or organization logical?

• Does the material emphasize the important points?

Type the draft copy double-spaced without inserting the illustrations. You want to be able to read through the text and view the illustrations as you go to make sure each works with the other. Once you have read through the material a couple of times and feel comfortable with it, have a clean draft typed and illustrations prepared.

Preparing the final test

You can follow several approaches for your final copy. If you plan to distribute copies to the audience, you can either use standard typed text pages or have the material typeset.

For ease of reading, typed text pages should be double-spaced on standard-sized paper with 1-inch margins on the top, bottom and right side, and a 1½-inch margin on the left. All illustrations should be limited to the same area of the page. The result will be a clean, readable manuscript.

If you are going to have your draft typeset, the best format is two columns. It is much easier for the reader to follow and will allow you to use both columns for your illustrations.

The best illustrations in the world will lose their impact if not prepared with care. Keep in mind that inked drawings with typeset notes reproduce well; pencil drawings with hand lettering do not look finished, and may not reproduce well.

Converting text to talk

Now the bad news: The language

and style of your printed materials are not suitable for direct oral translation. How many times have you lost interest in a presentation that dragged on and on? How many times have you been exposed to illustrations, text, charts and other material too complicated to understand, not to mention too small to read?

Your presentation is not an exercise in remedial reading. It is an opportunity to inform, convert and excite your audience. Slides and overheads are excellent media for stimulating your audience's attention and helping you get your message across. A well-prepared and executed presentation can deliver your message with punch and clarity. Figure 2 shows the difference between a good visual and a bad one. It also shows which format and type size to use.

Stand-up presentations have their own set of rules for successfully moving ideas from the presenter to the receivers. You have an implicit agreement with your audience: They already may have sufficient proof of your technical proficiency, the adequacy of your research and a preconceived idea of the topic. They expect to hear you talk about your topic, discuss your techniques and justify your conclusion. You can be more general and less analytical in speaking to your audience than in your formal paper.

What appeals to the eyes in print must now also appeal to the ears. Since you do not talk the way you write, you must tailor your speech for the ear. Your sentences should be simpler and shorter. Words and main points should be repeated to aid memory and understanding. Emphasized words will be remembered. Words come to life with your voice, your gestures and your personality. Use them all to your best advantage.

The most successful and informative presentations are an effective mix of verbal and visual elements. To effectively communicate complex and detailed concepts, you need pictures, graphs or diagrams on a large screen. To the ear, you owe logical explanations that support your objectives. To the eye, you owe information about shapes, colors, surface qualities, motion and space.

What to illustrate

Visuals can effectively expand the limitations of words by displaying complex ideas quickly and by summarizing lengthy, detailed explanations. Figure 3 shows a graphic example of tabular data that is more easily absorbed visually. In short, good visuals should:

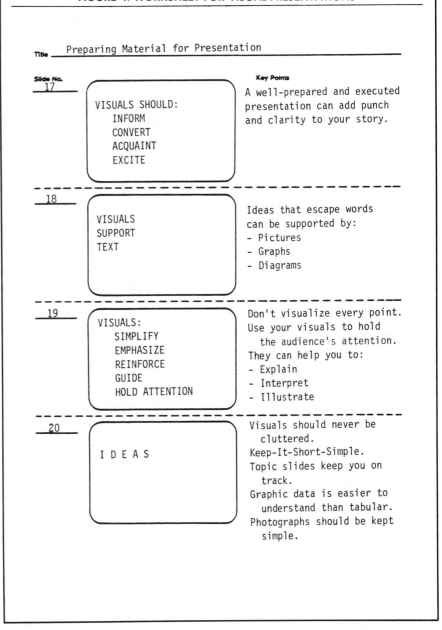

FIGURE 4. WORKSHEET FOR VISUAL PRESENTATIONS

Title: Preparing Material for Presentation

Slide No. 17

VISUALS SHOULD:
INFORM
CONVERT
ACQUAINT
EXCITE

Key Points: A well-prepared and executed presentation can add punch and clarity to your story.

Slide No. 18

VISUALS SUPPORT TEXT

Ideas that escape words can be supported by:
- Pictures
- Graphs
- Diagrams

Slide No. 19

VISUALS:
SIMPLIFY
EMPHASIZE
REINFORCE
GUIDE
HOLD ATTENTION

Don't visualize every point. Use your visuals to hold the audience's attention. They can help you to:
- Explain
- Interpret
- Illustrate

Slide No. 20

IDEAS

Visuals should never be cluttered.
Keep-It-Short-Simple.
Topic slides keep you on track.
Graphic data is easier to understand than tabular.
Photographs should be kept simple.

- Simplify complex data.
- Emphasize major points.
- Reinforce key ideas.
- Guide you through your talk.
- Hold the audience's attention.

Illustrating every point is as useless and boring as underlining or italicizing every word in a sentence. Use visuals to reawaken, redirect and create interest for your audience. Good visuals also can help you explain and interpret the ideas you are communicating.

Most people have trouble understanding—and remembering—complex ideas, numbers and abstractions that are verbalized. To make this type of information memorable, write out and illustrate comparisons between quantities and relationships. When you add visuals to your spoken words, you add understanding to what you are saying.

How to make up a worksheet

Worksheets are among the most effective tools you can use to outline your talk. They allow you to match

TIPS FOR USING GRAPHICS

1. **Word Slides**—Never allow copy to clutter a visual. Try not to use more than 15 words.

2. **Key Items**—Orient and focus the audience on key thoughts with "topic slides."

3. **Trend Data**—Use continuous line graphs to show trends clearly and effectively.

4. **Comparisons**—Use bar charts to depict comparative magnitudes; use pie charts to show relative portions of a whole.

5. **Symbols**—Use symbolic diagrams of circuits or mathematical expressions to graphically depict complex concepts.

6. **Flow and Relationships**—Convey flow and interrelationships with simple diagrams, not photographs.

7. **Photographs**—Keep photographs simple and clean. A dramatic view of an object adds impact; a close-up that shows details is more effective than an overall view.

8. **Tabular Data**—Avoid tables that require interpretation. If you must use tables, include only the items you will mention.

9. **Rule of Six**—Don't present too much information at one time. Research shows that the mind identifies and recalls up to six items easily. Omit every number or word that does not contribute to rapid understanding.

10. **Readability**—Resist the temptation simply to use the illustrations from your written material. Some illustrations that work fine within a text are far too complex to be effective visuals.

11. **Visual Contrast**—Make your visuals more legible by using contrast in brightness and tone between illustrations and their backgrounds. Different colors will create the most striking contrasts.

12. **Arrangement**—Don't include too many items on a single visual—use several simple illustrations instead.

13. **Duplicate Visuals**—Make copies of any visual you will use more than once and insert a copy in every position (each slot of a slide-projector tray, for instance) in which it is to be used. This eliminates the need to hunt for it and delay your presentation.

14. **Keep it Horizontal**—Use a horizontal format only. People in the back of the room may not be able to see the lower portion of a vertical image (see Figure 2).

---

ideas and illustrations simultaneously. Each sheet provides an area to describe your illustration and write down the key point you need to illustrate. Insert a sketch in the illustration panel or the details of how to make the illustration (see Figure 4).

Your first draft of the worksheet will reveal additional visuals you'll need to make smooth transitions and develop continuity. It acts as a road map by showing you where to expand or cut material.

Rehearsing techniques

It's time to talk your way through your presentation. Your face alone can instantly communicate thousands of bits of nonverbal information. Your delivery will depend on how you see yourself—you reflect how you feel. If you are alert, enthusiastic and confident, your audience will sense it in your face and posture and hear it in your voice. So stand up straight. Be honestly eager to share information and to convince your audience.

To find out how you sound, record your complete presentation, play it back and listen for words you are having trouble with or that are hard to understand. Replace them with words that come through loud and clear. A video recording, for obvious reasons, is even better.

Your worksheet, or script, is only a guide. Don't read it to the audience. *Talk* to the audience as you would if you were talking to a friend over coffee. Practice with your slides until you can practically ignore your script. Keep your worksheet with you as you give your talk, however, and you won't need to turn away from the audience to look at the screen.

Time yourself. You will want to pace your rate of delivery according to your audience's familiarity with your subject. When the information is likely to be new to your listeners, talk slowly. As you get into the subject, you can speed up a little.

The success of any presentation is a direct result of the amount of work that went into preparing it. Know your audience. Thoroughly review both your written and visual material. Rehearse your presentation. If you are prepared, your confidence and experience will come across in the tone of your voice and every gesture you make.

Reprinted from TRAINING, December 1983

BUILDING PRESENTATIONS: A TOP-DOWN APPROACH

You know your way around the topic but how do you get in?

BY TOM W. GOAD

The room is almost dead quiet. But because something is missing, a buzzing fly begins to sound like a B-52 practicing touch-and-go landings. The chair is really quite comfortable, but something continues to be missing, so the small lump in the seat grows to the size of a cantaloupe. All the necessary supplies are available—the pad of paper, the sharpened pencils—except the one thing that is determined to persist in the flagrant obstinacy of remaining most unmistakably and infuriatingly missing.

It's not that the assignment isn't clear. The assignment is all too clear: Develop a presentation on your training department for next Monday's staff meeting.

"You know the drill," the V.P.-operations said an hour ago, "tell 'em why you're on the payroll."

So here you sit, and the harder you try, the blanker the paper becomes. That's what's missing. The words on the paper.

Sooner or later, everyone who writes is going to sit in that room and stare at that blank sheet of paper. Whether you're preparing a presentation for the boardroom or the classroom (or, for that matter, writing a magazine article) the toughest part is likely to be getting beyond the first idea, committing the first words to paper and, once they're there, assuring yourself that they're the right words. Presentations must be cohesive, comprehensive and complete—not always an easy combination of goals.

The "top-down" approach is one proven method for producing, if not necessarily the presentation of the decade, one that meets the needs of the moment. We're all familiar with the top-down method. Organizations, particularly the military, use it to disseminate orders and information. Top-down, structured programming is a highly efficient way to design and develop complex computer software packages.

The method has a key advantage for presentations as well. It keeps you focused on your original objectives.

Think of the process as an "iterative" one—a term popularized by the computer age, but a concept long familiar to instructional developers. Each iteration—each attack at the problem—adds a bit more substance to the top layer, filling out the framework of the presentation.

Storyboards

To begin, assume that your topic (even if poorly defined at this stage) can be broken down into a handful of main points—a half dozen or less. If

---

FIGURE 1. STORYBOARD WORKSHEET

Frame No. _____ Presentation Title _____

Subject _____

Theme Sentence _____

_____

_____

Amplifying Information: Illustration (description/sketch/reference):

GIVE THEM TIME TO THINK

BY THEODORE J. KREIN

I continually find myself in training programs crammed full of content. It's like the developer wants to be sure I get my money's worth. It would never do, presumably, for me to feel cheated. Unless my hosts figure I'm attending the program to enjoy the location—such as Anaheim or Aspen—they seem to want to keep me very busy. Maybe they want to keep me off the street. Far be it from me to question such noble motives.

But, alas, I usually attend a seminar because I'm hoping it will add to my meager repertoire of knowledge and skills. And the tightly packed program often fails to meet that expectation. Why? Because in their zeal to give me a lot for my money, the developers neglect to provide some means for *processing* all the input. Without sufficient processing time, I will leave the program with a reeling feeling. My learning will be minimal, and my retention probably will be nonexistent.

Now, I am not against pushing the limits of training hours per day. Nor am I arguing for a leisurely schedule. I am campaigning for focusing the program content on fewer ideas and treating each in a manner that will help to ensure lasting learning.

For example, if the program description promises that I will achieve a modest level of basket-weaving skill, I expect to do more than talk about basket weaving. If I am to learn how to apply macroeconomic concepts to strategic planning, I want more than a lecture on the subject. I'll need to spend a fair amount of time interacting with other participants, sharing experiences and, I hope, applying this newly acquired knowledge to some personally relevant situations. In other words, I want some practice. And I want to process the data so that I can turn it into useful information.

All that requires time and effort. Determining how much new material is appropriate and how much of the time should be spent processing that material is seldom easy. But it can be done.

For starters, here are a few questions we can ask as we begin the challenging task of designing a training program:

Who is my audience? Is this a novice group? If so, I'll need to be extra careful not to put more into the program than the audience can cope with in the allotted time. Is this an experienced group? If so, then I must be sure to reach them at their level and to take advantage of their knowledge and experience. For either audience, I must design the delivery approach with their experience in mind, relating the new unknowns to the old knowns.

What should the program accomplish? Ah, objectives! If I spell out my objectives in terms of performance (What will they be able to *do* when they leave?), it will be much easier for me to figure out which activities will be required to achieve those objectives. If my objectives are fuzzy and relate to subject matter rather than to performance, it will be very difficult for me to imagine what should go on in the program to achieve them.

How much time will I have? I am never completely comfortable with a time period imposed upon a program before its objectives have been set; that smacks of the tail wagging the dog. But I must be practical and realize that the corporate world does not revolve around training. Given certain time limitations, I must decide whether my objectives can be achieved in that time. I must never fall into the trap of merely shortening the delivery (and processing) time to fit the schedule. Ten pounds of training requires a 10-pound bag. If I've only got a five-pound bag, the idea is to throw out some objectives, not just stuff them all in faster.

What kind of processing is appropriate? If a program is to include a lecture, and my objective is for trainees to be able to apply the knowledge gained from that lecture to practical situations, then I must provide some means for them to manipulate that knowledge. Case studies that require analysis and problem solving are one possibility. Small-group discussions that let participants share their own ideas and experiences are another. Whatever I do, the technique I choose becomes an enabling objective, the purpose of which is to help achieve the main objective: to help participants *internalize* the knowledge. Thus it becomes a part of their knowledge base—something that stays with them long after the class is over.

The next time you attend a training program, take a critical look at whether there is a good balance of input and processing, a balance that promotes maximum learning and enables participants to achieve the objectives. The next time you set out to create a training program, try to achieve that balance.

Reprinted from TRAINING, August 1987

FIGURE 2. LESSON GUIDE FORMAT

Part 1: General Information	Part 2: Lesson Outline

Part 1: General Information

Course title: Computer-System Operator Course

Lesson title: Computer-System Introduction

Lesson number: SYSOP-01 Latest revision date: 5/8/82

Learning objectives: Name major uses of the system
Identify who is responsible for various operations
Name major components of the system

Target audience/job classification: All clerical and management personnel; potential system operators

Prerequisites: none

Student preparation: none

Student materials: brochure, handout set for this lesson

Instructor materials/preparation:
1. visual-aid set for this presentation
2. overhead projector and screen

References: System-user manual; standard accounting-practices manual

Evaluation and follow-up/outside assignments: review operator manual (potential operators only)

Lesson length: thirty minutes

Comments: This lesson can be used on a stand-alone basis to familiarize nonoperators with the system.

Part 2: Lesson Outline

Lesson: Computer-System Introduction **Time:** Thirty minutes

Lesson Outline	Comments, References, Handouts, Visual Aids
A. Welcome learners	
1. point out that some will be present only for the first two hours	
B. State objectives	T01
1. major uses	
2. responsibilities	
3. components	
C. Overview	
1. background material	
2. nomenclature	
3. knowledge of total system	
4. following lessons will look at details	
D. Major components	T02
1. input devices	H01 (handout)
a. user terminals (CRTs)	T03
b. magnetic tapes	T04
2. processor/memory	T05
3. mass storage devices	T06
4. output devices	T07
E. Responsibilities	T08
1. supervisors	
2. operators	T09
3. service technicians	
4. users	etc.

your mental engine stalls, try the journalistic technique of asking who, what, where, when and why. Throw in "how" and "if" if you need them. Asking questions is a solid way to organize a presentation. If you can answer them to your own satisfaction, chances are the answers will work for your audience as well. And anything that suggests why or how the recipient may benefit from the information you're presenting is a plus for you.

Write down these ideas, main points and questions. Even if you're able to come up with no more than time divisions (beginning, middle, end), write those down. If you think you can arrange the pieces in appropriate order, go ahead and arrange them, but be ready and willing to make alterations later.

Using a storyboard format, such as the one shown in Figure 1, can make the next step easier. Make a separate storyboard for each of your main points. Those points become the "subjects" of their boards. Once you're looking at a specific subject, amplifying information most likely will come to mind and can be added to the form; a single word may trigger an avalanche of ideas.

Even if your presentation will have no visual aids, the "illustrations" section can help expand your ideas. Use it to list examples, jokes or whatever.

Writing a "theme sentence" will help make the point of each board as clear and concise as possible. If you can't express the point in a single sentence, you're probably trying to force too many ideas (or too "big" an idea) onto one storyboard.

Once you've spent some time with the main storyboards it should become obvious where expansion must take place. Triggered by the theme sentences, amplifying information and illustrations (particularly if your presentation will include visuals), the

first few boards should now explode into many storyboards. Fill them out accordingly. This can be repeated until you have a stack of boards, in an order that flows logically, each with at least a first draft of a theme sentence and possibly with some amplifying information and a likely illustration. This is the first draft of your presentation.

Scripts

The next step may vary depending on your needs. For an informal talk, the storyboards may be sufficient, although even then you probably will want to polish them a bit. If you're preparing a "canned" presentation (videodisc, sound/slide, film, TV) or a more formal one, you'll want a more finished script.

Begin with an introduction that lays out the purpose of the presentation, its benefits to the audience and an overview of its content, perhaps backed by an illustration (the company logo?). After that, your storyboards become enormously useful, regardless of whether you're working up only a detailed outline or the actual words to be spoken.

Your boards contain ideas for the illustrations you'll be using and outlines of the text that will accompany each illustration. If visuals are to be produced, the final storyboards can be used as worksheets by the graphic artists and photographers who deliver the final art. Be prepared to take the script through several iterations, however, especially if the presentation is to be recorded in any way. Read it aloud and keep asking, "How does this sound?"

Another format, useful for repeated classroom presentations, is the self-explanatory lesson guide shown in Figure 2. Again, your storyboards are the first step.

Let me be the first to say that nothing in this approach is new. The top-down method of attack is common sense. Television and movie writers have used storyboards for decades. Script and lesson-guide formats are available from many sources. But the reason the approach *is* used so widely is because it offers so many advantages.

- It allows the presentation to "build itself," each iteration making it more definitive.
- You need only a few ideas to begin.
- You remain focused on the main objectives.
- The approach is modular, and thus easily changed.
- The methodology is "field-tested."

The top-down approach is nothing more than a tool. It won't deaden the sound of buzzing flies or take lumps out of chairs. But it will help transfer what's in your head—and it *is* there, whether you realize it or not—to some well-organized words on that pad of paper. The method works.

Reprinted from TRAINING, June 1984

USING THE PARABLE TO MAKE A POINT

The world's great teachers have had
the ability to illustrate their messages
with simple but moving stories.
You can, too

BY LILITH REN

It earned Socrates the reputation of master teacher. It brought Abe Lincoln influence through persuasive power. And it's a crucial factor in a trainer's success. All of us can use it because it is a simple, trainable technology.

"It" is the ability to thoughtfully construct stories, or parables, that underwrite the training outcomes we want. For centuries, stories, anecdotes, jokes and other kinds of parables have been used to communicate important information, attitudes and skills. From Homer to Uncle Remus, storytellers trained while they entertained.

A parable is a bridge that can link my experiences and opinions to yours. Granted, my experiences and problems will never match yours, point for point. We see things differently, so what's true for me may feel off base to you. However, if in my communication with you, you recognize enough similarity between the situation I share through my parable and the situation you face, then you'll find ways to adapt my communication to your particular situation. This process, like all communication, is both conscious and subconscious. Consequently, the more subtle the suggestions I offer, the more likely it is you'll want to incorporate my ideas. Parables carry subtle messages. That's why they're particularly powerful.

Remember those "magic" speakers who've won your respect and atten-
tion with their right-on opening anecdote? It was more than just amusing. Holding clearly in mind their desired training outcomes, they could create and tell a story that danced right past your questions of credibility and began creating a mind-set for learning. The difference between using a story and letting it use you is aligning its underlying messages with your training goals.

Recently I was training a group of managers in effective communication. My partner and I were there because our needs assessment showed people were creating conflict by not sharing their opinions. I opened our first session with an adaptation of Dr. Jerry Harvey's "Abilene Paradox," an anecdote about family members who suffer the needless discomfort of a hot trek to Abilene because no one wants to speak up assertively. As I spoke, I watched my audience bob their heads in fascinated recognition. I had them. Or so I thought.

To our dismay, no one wanted to apply their new communications skills back on the job. "This stuff is great," we'd hear them say, "but my office is beyond all hope." Frustrated, I turned to my co-trainer and we discussed our work. What went wrong? Was it us? Was it them? It was neither. It was a poorly planned parable that sabotaged our previously effective design.

Learning from my mistakes, I opened the next course with a reworked parable. This time as the story ended, the family's new communication patterns led them to new
levels of teamwork and personal satisfaction. And this time we began to hear coffee-break tales of, "You know, this really works. Yesterday, I said to the boss...."

The parable has influence, whether we use it to warm up a group, motivate behavior change, deal with "yes buts," or point out an everyday application of theory. The parable also has power when we apply it outside our presentations. Imagine using this technique to help sell a proposal or next year's training budget. And you can see the possibilities of using informally delivered, but cleverly planned, parables to coach an individual toward more effective behaviors. Or, as the legendary sage will so often do, use a parable to get your point across while skirting an awkward question.

Well-planned parables sweeten advice with amusement and warm it with rapport, making it far easier to swallow. There's a very subtle— and very real—difference between giving advice and influencing via an effective parable. Part of this difference lies in the parable's ability to entertain. A parable will amuse your listeners while clearing a path through to their more creative, innovative subconscious. The better to hear you with...and problem solve.

The most crucial factor in the parable's power is your ability to construct it carefully, and with an eye to depth. Here's a seven-step process for effective parable engineering.

1 **Identify the problem.** We sabotage ourselves most often by telling jokes, stories and anecdotes before we think about the behavior we want to shape. To become more skilled at using parable power, first identify the problem clearly and define it in terms of behavior within the listeners' control. For example, increasing the division's budget may be out of their realm. Redefining department priorities isn't.

2 **Analyze the structural supports.** It's vital to clarify the structure of the situation. Looking at the perceived problem, what's the sequence of events to date? Specifically, when and where does this situation take place? Who are the characters involved? Most importantly, how do they relate to each other?

- **Hierarchy**   who reports to whom
       who supervises whom

- **Method**   who's a peer
       do they relate via writing
       face-to-face conversation
       non-verbally

- **Effect of** what happens physically
- **their relating** what happens emotionally
  to them
  to others

3 **Find the balance point.** What's blocking the desired behavioral outcome? More importantly, *how* is that happening? Of course, be sure you identify a factor the recipients of your parable can effect. Throughout this clarifying, you'll discover "what" and "how" are more useful than "why."

4 **Script a parallel situation.** The analytic groundwork completed, you've a solid foundation on which to build a strong, effective parable. With a keen eye to this blueprint of the problem, change the names, costumes and settings to something more entertaining. A work team becomes a family with parents and children; in-laws or neighbors represent other departments or regulatory agencies. Or use animals in a forest, with the boss disguised as a fox or good-hearted but misunderstood troll. Keep your casting parallel to the data you collected in steps one through three.

To select relevant settings, cue in to common figures of speech your listeners already use. If they talk about "strategies" and "the big guns," create a war story. If it's "teamwork" and "first stringers," use sports as a backdrop. A note of caution: To make parables relevant, let listeners do their own detail work. "Those memories were strong whenever she saw him" will be more meaningful than "She felt furious about those memos whenever she saw him in the cafeteria." Listeners will provide the relevant details from their own experience.

5 **Provide a pragmatic alternative.** You've pinpointed the desired outcome. Now the question is what could the recipients of this parable be doing *instead* of what you see them doing now to reach the desired outcome? The alternatives you see can be changes in actions and/or attitudes. The essential thing is to encourage them to develop an alternative that *parallels and replaces* whatever ingredient it was you saw triggering their present problem.

Our clients aren't dumb. Sometimes the alternative to their problem is obvious to them. If the situation allows, check to see if they've already tried it. If so, what happened? Often, they'll recognize the way out of their quagmire, but feel they can't take that first step. That's why it's paramount you recognize *how* they stop themselves before giving advice wrapped in a parable.

6 **Point the way out.** The means to the end you've identified is the "connecting strategy." This is how you help them move from present situation to desired outcome. As you shape the parable, add something its characters either do, see or hear that helps them see the light and feel ready to act differently.

7 **Illustrate through a role model.** The connecting strategy dovetails into one or more of the following actions for the character who represents your listener(s):

- Character experiences old situation in a new way

  "He began to see ways to use his angry feelings..."

- Character engages in a new behavior and/or reacts with a new attitude
  "...they became important signals that reminded him to share his views clearly so they could begin to negotiate..."

- Character achieves desired outcome
  "...listening thoughtfully and speaking assertively until their horse-trading ended in mutual satisfaction."

Your finished parable will clearly show it's not the events, behaviors or emotions involved that are the problem. The problem is *how* characters are perceiving and using them.

Parables increase in power when built with skill and subtlety. David Gordon's *Therapeutic Metaphors* is a good book to look over as you develop more command.

There are two other tips useful in telling more powerful parables. First, build direct instructions into the parable. This is accomplished when you use active verbs rather than passive nouns and construct sentences that include direct suggestions. "Your *belief* in this system is something we need if it's going to be *workable*," translates to the more potent "We need to have you *believe* in this system if we're going to *make it work*."

When you use this kind of phrasing you can add more emphasis by using voice tone to underline phrases with instructions and desired outcomes, adding gestures for further emphasis and drawing listener attention to a phrase by inserting the word "you" or their name. ("If you like this idea, then, Terry, follow up on it.")

Second, most people pay attention to one kind of input. Some focus mostly on what they see. Some tune into sounds and speech. Some are generally in touch with what they feel and their sensory environment. By identifying those who are mostly seers, listeners or feelers, you gain a new key to establishing quick rapport. Listen to the verbs people use:

- Visual language: *focus on, picture, look for*
  "She scanned the situation for a new point of view."

- Auditory language: *tell, discuss, word of mouth*
  "Sounds like keeping your ears open for new ideas might work."

- Feeling language: *getting in touch, solid, joyful*

  "He was reaching for a new way to handle it."

Clearly, this can be a powerful tool in one-to-one communication. It can also be useful when training groups. For instance, to reach a larger number of listeners with your parable, choose words that guarantee you're understood by all three kinds of listeners.

If you discover an individual or work team paying attention to only one kind of input, teaching them to pay attention to another category can contribute to the connecting and empowering strategies you choose.

Like others who value their craft, as trainers it's rewarding to experiment with one more tool or technique that adds to our art. Honing the power of the parables you tell is just such a technique. With it, we make our entertaining more training and vice versa.

Reprinted from TRAINING, May 1981

USING MENTAL IMAGERY TO ENHANCE LEARNING

How well do your listeners 'see' what
you mean? Boost the effectiveness
of your training by understanding the link
between what the senses say
and the brain retains

BY RON ZEMKE

Mental imagery, the ability we all have to "see" in the "mind's eye" an object, person or place not actually present, has been regarded as a powerful training tool since the time of Socrates. There is nothing especially spooky about it either. Dr. Joseph Shorr, director of the Institute of Psycho-Imagination Therapy in Los Angeles, maintains all of us use this ability to construct pictures in our heads all the time, sometimes consciously, sometimes not. He contends that regardless of the kind of wishing, thinking, reasoning or problem-solving we're involved in, we use some form of mental imagery to help us get the job done.

Skeptical? Try this: Picture yourself standing in your bedroom...now see yourself in your kitchen...now on an airplane endlessly circling O'Hare...now floating on an air mattress in the blue Caribbean...now reading...now on the telephone. In a flash you can be on a sandy beach, in a log cabin or at a special party. And you can slide effortlessly and at will from scene to scene. Similarly, you can *choose* to experience these scenes as vivid and real or in a more detached, distant manner; it's up to you. There are differences in the clarity and vividness of individuals' images, but if you simply relax and close your eyes you will most probably have mental pictures.

A supple, subtle tool

This apparently intrinsic ability we all seem to have in some degree has a long history and many uses. The ancient Greeks taught a memory system based on the pairing of outlandish or unusual mental images with the object or idea to be remembered; a system popularized and refined this century by the likes of Dale Carnegie, Harry Lorraine and Robert Montgomery. Let's say you have to remember a list of three things to bring home from the market—a head of lettuce, a pound of ground round and a box of bagels. One memory system has a set of rhyming pegs for lists: one-gun, two-shoe, three-tree and so forth. To use these pegs you literally make a link between the items on the shopping list and the pegs. Coupling might go like this: "One-gun— I see a face on a head of lettuce and a bullet going through it. The face has little x's for eyes. Two-shoe— I see a football shoe kicking a meatloaf through the goal posts. Three-tree— I see a Christmas tree decorated with bagels." Believe it or not, making these connections verbally and then seeing these absurd scenes in your mind's eye, your imagination will put your shopping list neatly into short-term memory. And there's plenty of research that says it works.

But this "names-faces-dates-places" use of imagery may only scratch the surface of ways directed mental imagery can be used to enhance learning. Preliminary research suggests grade school students who are instructed to make a mental picture of the ideas in a story learn— and remember— new vocabulary more quickly and also tend to develop conceptual understanding of new words more quickly. *Brain Mind Bulletin* reports that a special imaging-based learning procedure developed by Synectics Education Systems, Cambridge, MA, has been shown to significantly affect reading and aural comprehension scores.

Other studies have shown that children who are told to make a mental picture of new spelling words perform better on recall tests; that university students learn lists of pairs of items faster and remember them longer when the word pairs form mental pictures; and that university students instructed to make mind pictures of what they read are able to answer more short essay questions than students who do not receive these instructions.

Overall, imagery as a direct aid to memory seems to work best for lists of numbers and names, and concrete objects. Overt activity with the objects increases the ability to form mental images and to recall the objects. As mentioned earlier, the Carnegie-Lorraine-Montgomery approach to remember names and faces has been researched and verified. A number of good studies have been conducted in England, and other researchers have found that the more bizarre the images used in the mental picture, the longer the name, face or idea stayed on the peg.

Cold call daydreams

For all its uses in remembering words, ideas and concepts, imagery seems to be most powerful in the direct facilitation of behavior change. As far back as Freud, imagery— in the form of free association and dream recall techniques— has played a part in helping people change behavior. Fritz Pearl and other Gestalt therapists have used guided symbolic imagery instructions to help people get at what's bothering them and to help them seek out answers to problems. In one Gestalt technique, the Empty Chair, people having trouble confronting others are taught to construct an "image" of that person sitting across from them in a real empty chair. Their conversations with the empty chair have been known to become so real to them that more than a few have taken a poke at the imaginary adversary.

Yale psychologist Jerome Singer says we all use spontaneous daydreaming to solve current problems, prepare for future events, ward off tension, relieve boredom, dispel fear and dissipate anger. He points out studies which show self-esteem and even bottom-line success can be affected by the way we image ourselves and the goals we are trying to achieve. Many sports figures, says Singer, report that they spur themselves on by imaging the act of winning. Philadelphia Eagles quarterback Ron Jaworski, for example, is known to spend time floating in a 20% saline solution isolation tank imaging the week's game plan.

Psychologist Frances Meritt Stern reports using imagery to help people slim down better and faster in her book *Mind Trips To Help You Lose Weight*. She also reports that executive stress can be managed by the use of short, pleasant mental imagery episodes, or what she calls "mini-vacations in your head." Likewise, salespeople who are having call reluctance or "phono-phobia" can reprogram themselves with carefully constructed success images.

What's the difference between the structured imagery that psychologists are pushing today and the 1950s sales motivator's cry of "What mind of man can conceive, man can achieve" and "Your success is only as limited as the dreams you dream of yourself"— or even Professor Harold Hill telling the children of River City they need only "think" the music to learn to play the instruments? For one thing, reality. For another, research.

For years the power of positive goal images was a popular platform topic. But people found that, just as with management by objectives, simply being able to picture a goal was not enough. There has to be a plan and a method—and a realistic chance—before attainment takes place.

One of the most frequently cited examples of the use of imagery in direct behavior change involves junior high students and free throw shooting. Three groups of boys were asked to take 10 shots from the foul line. Then one group was instructed to practice in the gym for 20 minutes every day. A second group was instructed to practice shooting free throws "in their heads" for the next week while a third group was given no instruction at all. A week later the practice group and the imagery group

both outperformed the control group. And, surprisingly, the imagery group outperformed the practice group.

But notice two things: First, the imagery practice group was working with a very specific discrete behavioral act: shooting free throws, something they had some prior experience with. Secondly, they were instructed to image those specific behaviors, not some wild fantasy such as playing in the NBA and making the free throw that won the game. In short, imagery seems to change behavior when the imagery used is concrete, behavioral and realistically attainable by the individual doing the imaging.

Fascinating literature is developing on the usefulness of this form of behavioral-specific, positive mental imagery. Among the more intriguing findings:

- Specific positive, pleasant mental images can be used as positive reinforcement for a variety of behaviors, from doing math problems to making cold canvass sales calls.
- New skills such as speaking before a group, acting assertively and eating with your mouth closed can be successfully practiced through mental imagery *if* a minimal amount of real practice is also interspersed.
- Directions to imagine a stressful event can actually trigger a physiological stress response. Conversely, instructions to picture a pleasant or peaceful event or place can reduce physiological stress responses.
- Debilitating fear of snakes, heights, open spaces and people named Big Al have been cured or eliminated by the use of mental imagery and a one-step-at-a-time procedure called systematic desensitization.
- Goal rehearsal of pass throwing, ground-ball catching, back hand hitting, slalom skiing and other athletic endeavors has proven successful in increasing performance for a variety of athletes, amateur and professional. (Researchers in this area generally conclude that if you are already good at some physical activity, the practice of goal rehearsal can make you better.)
- A number of medical problems— the so-called psychosomatic disorders— can be alleviated with imagery. Hypertension, dermatitis, ulcerative colitis, spastic colon and tension headaches have all reportedly been cured through the use of guided mental imagery. A few medical researchers are reporting that teaching patients specific "healing" mental

imagery seems to be useful in the treatment of cancer.

In addition, Dr. Albert Ellis, creator of rational-emotive therapy, has used imagery instructions to change the "self-talk" people use to assess, evaluate and guide their behavior. Research surgeon Wilder Penfield has found that electrical stimulation of the brain can cause an individual to see vivid images of things past and hear vivid echoes of sounds long ago faded. The late Dr. George Kelley suggested that the way people visualize the outcomes of anticipated events often shapes that outcome. Your imagery, adds Dr. Arnold Lazarus, can spawn an optimistic or a pessimistic life view. Thus, sadness and despondency can also be overcome using specific self-image, self-esteem enhancing imagery.

Lazarus believes we can even inoculate ourselves against future shock through imagery. His advocated technique is rehearsal through projected imagery. "To avoid future shock," he says, "it is important not only to think about events that are likely to occur in time, it is most important to picture them as clearly as possible, and to vividly imagine oneself dealing with these situations."

If you've just become a parent, you might want to inoculate yourself against the woes of parenting by imaging the good and bad things you are likely to encounter in years to come. For example, if it seems reasonable to you that there may be a shoplifting incident to deal with in the future, you will be better prepared to cope with it if you anticipate it now. That beats the heck out of the usual surprise, panic and blame that so many of *our* parents experienced when we failed to meet their expectations— images, if you will, of the perfect child.

We've only briefly touched on the many uses researchers are finding for the power of structured and unstructured mental imagery. Many of these uses have direct application to our work as trainers and human resources development specialists. Some techniques can be used to make the classroom experience faster and easier. Others can help incumbents handle the rocks and ruts of daily duties. Some can even help us make our lives and jobs more effective and fun. And *that* is an image worth imagining.

Reprinted from TRAINING, January 1981

TEACHING LISTENING AND QUESTIONING SKILLS

These useful tips are applicable for trainees as well as trainers

Training in how to listen is fast becoming a key element in many supervisory training programs. That's not surprising, especially when you consider that without listening there can be no communication. And, of course, communicating is a major part of any manager's job.

Recent phone calls and inquiries from TRAINING's readers reflect increased interest in the area of listening. Many readers are asking us how trainers in other companies are teaching listening skills. We decided to ask Raymond A. Higgins, director of sales training and development at Armour-Dial, Inc., who has been teaching listening and questioning skills for 20 years. He calls these skills "the most needed (and often neglected) tools of any manager, supervisor, sales representative, parent, or training director."

Higgins bases his courses on the counseling tools developed by Carl Rogers. These techniques, often taught to professional counselors, are also part of the repertoire of most successful managers.

The problem, as Higgins sees it, is to put "handles" on the tools, to name them and present the techniques in such a way that trainees can grasp their significance and then practice using them. Asserts Higgins, "Sure, you can 'enlighten' managers on the tools available and they may even 'understand' them to the point where they can fill in the proper response on a written quiz or voice-back an 'example' in response to a staged tape recording. But we try to get them to 'learn-it-in-the-muscles' by practicing a la 'bedlam' with each participant-manager trying to implement his solution to his real-life problem with a subordinate, peer, or boss."

In keeping with his "learn-it-in-the-muscles" principle, Higgins formulated his programs which progress through the following 10 steps.

1. Use the participants' real-life problems, rather than hypothetical cases. Each manager is required to submit one written case history of his or her most difficult problem in getting work done through people. This is their "price of admission" and the workshop revolves around these problems, which are numbered and reproduced in each participant's workbook. Before the class begins, the instructor chooses one-third of the problems for the first problem-solving session and divides the trainees on the seating chart into groups of three, each triad composed of one individual whose problem is being discussed.

2. Provide a framework for good problem analysis. "The best and simplest format I've found," says Higgins, "is an oldie (a generation before Kepner-Tregoe) by Dr. William J. Reilly, first published as *The Twelve Rules for Straight Thinking* (Harper Bros.). Reilly had defined how the mind works and how it ought to work, and believe me, they are not the same!"

Early in the workshop, Higgins gives a short, 15-minute lecture—that's right, a lecture—on the "straight-thought" process and progressively builds the steps with "slap-ons" on the hook and loop board. As he explains it, the process is comprised of four components: 1) factual and analytical observation, which includes gathering facts like what, when, where, and who, and opinions; 2) definition of the *real* problem; 3) examination of possible solutions; and 4) conclusion(s).

Following the lecture, the class is split into the triad work groups and a case assigned to each. Since the participant who wrote the case is in the group analyzing it, there are no assumptions or suppositions necessary. After an hour of analysis, the class is reassembled and each group, in turn, reports on its assigned case, following a four-page form which lists: major contributing causes, their definition of the problem, at least three possible solutions, their conclusion, and why they chose it.

3. Participants set up their own practice of implementing their solutions. As each triad concludes its reported decision, the instructor asks what first step to implementation would involve a face-to-face confrontation with a person involved in the problem. A role-play situation form is then prepared by the triad and serves to help identify the personality and probable reaction of the subordinate.

4. Conduct "bedlam" practice of the confrontations. This is, in effect, a sort of "practice" session, intended to get a reading on how well the participants perform before they are introduced to the interviewing skills. The managers assume various roles and are videotaped while trying to solve the problems they've discussed.

"I used to give the input on 'Listening-Questioning' before any practice," comments Higgins, "but not any more! Our participant-managers—especially those district managers from supermarket chains—are grown, mature, successful managers. Each is directly responsible for eight to 14 stores and 40 to 60 million dollars in annual business volume. So I let them practice first. Then, during the videotape playback, I have always found several situations where the interviewer was doing most of the talking and/or was not getting true acceptance. Stop the tape!"

5. Present the "Listening-Questioning" tools. The instructor, using visuals and examples, explains each of Carl Rogers' tools. Higgins likes to start by hanging a face on the hook-board with the caption, "God gave us two ears and one mouth!"

6. Pass out the billfold-size card which lists the six guidelines on how to listen and the six guidelines on how to ask questions. If your class runs anything like Armour-Dial's, most managers have been taking copious notes. But don't bank on them retaining what you present without a "keeper." As the

SIX TIPS ON HOW TO REMEMBER TRAINEE NAMES

Dosen't it feel good when someone remembers your name? Dale Carnegie said our names are the sweetest and most important sounds in any language. Most salespeople agree . . . just notice how many times a car salesperson or other "hard sale" representative calls you by name. Sometimes training is a "hard sell," too, and there's no sense making it harder by pointing to trainees or identifying them as "you with the blue shirt" or "the blond woman in the back row."

George Bell, Westborough, MA, memory expert, offers this advice for remembering names:

1. Pay attention to the name. Hear it the first time, or ask the person to repeat it.

2. Repeat the name yourself. Bell says this will improve recall by 30%.

3. Use the name in conversation. Repetition will engrave the name in your long-term memory.

4. Observe the face. Most of us can remember faces better than names, so really study the face and choose one outstanding detail.

5. Associate the name to the face. Form a mental picture, using an active image. Get the Bell to sway, the Byrd to fly, Waters to gush.

6. Use the name when saying good-bye. This final reinforcer also assures you that you know the name.

Of course, some names are easier to associate than others. Bell suggests symbolic phrases, such as an *ant* on a *honey*comb filled with *pellets* and *grain* for Anthony Pelligrino. And use symbols that immediately call up a name, such as a *walking slingshot* for David Walker.

Trainers have a special problem since they must often absorb 30 or 40 names at once when walking into a training session. Bell advises trainers to arrive early, so you can meet people as they enter by ones or twos. If possible, get a list of names in advance so you can devise replacement symbols more easily. During Bell's own memory classes, he has students fill out information cards. While the students complete a memory test, he picks up the cards at each desk and associates the name with the face.

To train others in how to remember names, Bell offers a three-part plan. First, explain the six points listed earlier. Second, provide worksheets so students can practice converting names to replacement words. Third, show slides of faces and gradually increase the number of faces students are asked to name.

Reprinted from TRAINING, January 1979

managers are tucking the cards away into their billfolds, Higgins dares them with "next Monday morning, just before walking into that first store, I challenge you to pull out the card and review both sides. See if you don't accomplish more!"

7. Put the triads back to practice. This time, they are supplied with two easel cards—one on listening and one on questioning. These are placed on the desk facing the interviewer. Back in bedlam practice, you'll probably notice a dramatic lessening of "telling" and complete involvement in two-way communication. Every once in a while, you may even notice an interviewer's eyes drop down to the easel cards, then back to eye contact with the "subordinate."

8. Have one observer in each triad keep score. The observer takes notes on how many of the listening-questioning tools are used and then conducts a private critique within the triad after the interview is concluded. Following the critique, the participants change roles and go back into practice until all three managers have been in all three roles.

9. Replay randomly videotaped excerpts from the "after" practice. During the replay, the instructor points out specific listening-questioning skills as they appear on the screen.

10. Move on to more practice on handling difficult personalities. You may want to use this step as the first exercise of the second day of your

---

How To Listen

1. **Remain neutral.**
   Do not give advice, agree or disagree, criticize or interrupt.

2. **Give your complete attention.**
   Let him know you are listening. Nod your head — "uh huh, I see what you mean."

3. **Ask about his statements.**
   Dig out information, invite him to tell everything. Say: "In addition to that is there anything else . . .?"

4. **Restate his main points.**
   Let him hear his exact words restated by you. This prompts him to stick to the facts and to think intelligently.

5. **Put his feelings into words.**
   State what his feelings seem to be. When he hears them voiced by you he evaluates and tempers them.

6. **Get agreement.**
   Summarize what you have both said — encourage him to suggest the next step or course of action.

 ARMOUR·DIAL,INC

How To Ask Questions

1. **No third degree.**
   Use questions to help the other person think — never to degrade or to spy.

2. **Ask "W" questions.**
   What, Why, When, Where, Who and How are the key words that will secure facts and information.

3. **Ask questions that make him go deeper.**
   Ask for evidence, examples or explanations to discover reasons behind his thinking.

4. **Ask "suppose" questions.**
   Introduce a new idea, break a deadlock or bring up an overlooked point with: "Suppose we . . . ?"

5. **Ask him.**
   To encourage others to think or to avoid committing yourself, return the question or relay it to another qualified person.

6. **Ask questions that get agreement.**
   Offer several solutions in the form of a question.

---

workshop, as Higgins does. The session opens with a discussion of close-mindedness and how to overcome it. Naturally, the listening-questioning tools come into play again as practice continues. Higgins also introduces some new techniques for dealing with such characters as "The Hot Shot," "The Old-Timer," "Mr. Excuses," "Mr. Belligerent," "Mr. Lazy," and "Mr.

Nervous."

Raymond Higgins and Armour-Dial have reported excellent results using this workshop format. You might try it on your next group of supervisory trainees and find that it works as well for you, too. And, remember, as Mr. Higgins cautions us all, "It isn't what you *tell* a man that counts—it's what he *accepts*."

Reprinted from TRAINING, July 1977

TEACHING TRAINEES HOW TO THINK

Yes, you can help others to develop their brainpower. How? By treating thinking' as a teaching subject. Here's a model to help you do just that

BY KARL ALBRECHT

Training trend spotters should note that mental fitness may well be to the '80s what physical fitness was to the '70s. The notion that you can increase your total brain power by comprehensively developing your entire range of practical thinking skills is taking hold. And it's the impetus behind a wave of interest in cognitive processes, thinking games and puzzles, and practical thinking skills and strategies.

For at least two generations, educators and trainers as a group have displayed a singular lack of interest in the skills of applied thinking as primary areas of teachable human capability. The focus has been almost exclusively on teaching *what* to think, rather than *how* to think. Considering what we now know about ways to teach the skills of thinking, and the many concepts, methods and techniques available, the thoughtful trainer might well ask why we have never considered Thinking as a subject in itself— as a legitimate topic of teaching and learning, just like history, English, mathematics, typing, music, carpentry, physical fitness or management.

This question invites some interesting speculations about the way we teach and the way we learn. How many of us have fallen prey to the same subtle messages transmitted to students by the structure of our academic curricula: the notion that each person comes into the world with a certain basic capability for thinking

and learning, and the only thing a teacher or school can do is help that person acquire a storehouse of information? How many of us unconsciously consider thinking ability more or less innately fixed and assume that, except for a bit of fine tuning, we can never significantly increase that ability? Years of preoccupation with IQ testing and other evaluative schemes for identifying "high-potential" people, and for indirectly slotting the rest of us as "low-potential" people, have probably contributed to this semiconscious belief. We have never seriously considered Thinking as a subject, and thus have never seriously approached the wide range of practical thinking skills as teachable and learnable.

A new trend

Today, we see growing interest in total brainpower in a variety of areas. More and more periodicals are reporting new developments in research on brain functions and cognitive processes, and articles on memory research, attention, cognitive styles, neurolinguistic programming and the like are increasingly popular. Business seminars dealing with problem solving and decision making, creative idea production and innovation are burgeoning. Consider, too, the rapidly increasing sales of electronic thinking and learning games based on the revolutionary microprocessor chip, books of thinking puzzles and various other thinking games for children as well as adults. Finally, there's been a

slow but steady growth in the number of courses in primary and secondary schools and colleges that deal directly with the development of useful thinking skills.

These and other recent happenings suggest a significant increase in the priority given to thinking skills in some educational institutions, as well as in industrial training programs. We already have plenty of resources in this area and a large foundation of concepts and techniques. Now we must put them together into an overall structure of recognized value. In other words, we must make a subject out of Thinking.

Define Thinking

What does it take for something to qualify as a subject? What common elements do we find among music, computer programming, welding, public administration, sales and physical therapy when we consider them as teachable subjects? From the standpoint of human resources development, we can call something a teachable subject if it meets the following criteria.

It has a recognized body of knowledge. In this case, we're dealing with knowledge about knowledge— more specifically, about how the brain takes it in, organizes it, stores it, manipulates it and acts upon it.

It has a vocabulary. This helps to describe the body of knowledge.

It has a conceptual structure. This enables us to study and apply the elements of knowledge.

It includes a competence model. This categorizes those greatest objectively identifiable skills we can learn and teach, and is perhaps of interest to the trainer.

Training methods exist. We must have techniques that one person can use to help another person master the elements of knowledge and acquire the basic skills. We already have a variety of these, and we need to organize them and systematically associate them with the various elements of competence.

Resource materials exist. The trainer and the learner need support materials they can use in their respective roles. Again, we have some of these, and we need to organize them and develop more of them.

Clearly, we can meet all six of these defining criteria for a subject called Thinking. But of what does Thinking consist? I consider 10 associated concepts fundamental to the subject. Each one serves as a kind of "bucket" in which we can capture some portion of what we know about Thinking. We can analyze each of these concepts, understand it and help others understand it.

1 **Total brainpower** — the sum of a person's *acquired* thinking skills and so-called innate brain capability. This concept avoids the misplaced emphasis on IQ and focuses attention more appropriately on what a person can do to deploy available cognitive functions effectively.

2 **Thinking about thinking** — becoming more aware of our thought processes, monitoring our mental procedures as we approach situations, and deliberately using mental strategies or techniques that help us deal with situations more effectively.

3 **Using a vocabulary of key terms** — accepted terms like mental flexibility, problem solving, logical thinking, making inferences and deciding help to "capture" key concepts for study. Other less-known terms include option thinking, thinking on your feet, suspended judgment and such whimsical creations as decidophobia, opinionitis and mental arthritis. By teaching people to describe thinking processes with these useful terms, we can help them become conscious of those processes as they build specific skills.

4 **Mental flexibility** — deals with the ability to adapt, suspend judgment, change your mind, tolerate ambiguity, think and speak nondogmatically, and remain open to new and potentially worthwhile experiences. We can contrast mental flexibility with mental rigidity in specific, behavioral terms — what a person says, how he or she uses words, how he or she forms and defends opinions.

5 **Divergent and convergent thinking** — two highly contrasted and equally important modes of thought. In the divergent mode, one searches, explores, questions, examines multiple factors, identifies additional features and components of a situation, checks various points of view, generates more and more options and generally *expands* his or her field of attention. In the convergent mode, one zeroes in on a narrowly defined item or solution that meets rather specific criteria, casting out options, reducing the range of possibilities, evaluating, eliminating, choosing and generally *narrowing* the field of attention. By learning to recognize both divergent and convergent modes of thought, and to choose one or the other according to the situation, one can deploy stored knowledge effectively and deal with situations in versatile ways.

6 **Option thinking** — refers to the skill of generating a variety of choices and reviewing them before making a decision. Many people will jump at one familiar or attractive course of action in a situation, or will consider at most only two. An effective option thinker makes a habit of alternatives.

7 **The role of language in constructing thoughts** — eliminating dogmatic or absolute phraseology, minimizing either/or (black/white) descriptions, and describing concepts in flexible and adaptive terms can increase your mental flexibility. You also can maintain a positive frame of mind by changing negative language habits. For example, you can exclude from your speaking and thinking vocabulary those terms that have negative emotional connotations and use positive or neutral terms instead.

8 **Brain lateralization** — a complex and subtle aspect of brain function. We can develop fluency in visual and spatial thinking, enhance intuitive processes and increase reliance on holistic pattern processing as adjuncts to our more familiar linear-sequential processes. We'll probably find that the *interplay* between the brain's right and left hemispheres has more influence on total thinking ability than the individual lateralized functions that have been getting an inordinate amount of media attention recently.

9 **Problem solving and decision making** — by teaching people to pay attention to the *process* of solving a problem, rather than merely wrestling with the *elements* of the problem, trainers especially can help people significantly increase their mental effectiveness. A stepwise problem-solving model can play an important part in developing this "process awareness."

10 **A new view of creativity** — abolish the word "creativity" as an abstract noun and replace it with an action-oriented description of what a person *does*. Current usage has apparently contributed to a common view of creativity as something you're born with, like your kidneys or your hair color. Psychological testing has, in my opinion, discouraged people from acknowledging and using the skill of idea production which re-

sides in every normal human brain.

A competence model for Thinking lends structure to the subject and establishes some relatively objective target skills we can learn and teach. This aspect of the subject has lagged further behind than any other. Psychologists have given names to many micro-skills that play a part in a person's thinking processes but, to the best of my knowledge, no one has developed a categorical framework — a "Christmas tree" on which to hang the various mental functions and skills in relation to one another.

We can develop such a framework by classifying some fairly basic brain functions into larger-scale thinking skills. Out of the many overlapping terminological categories of brain functions that psychologists recognize, we can synthesize a useful working list of 10: concentration, observation, memory, logical reasoning, forming hypotheses, generating options, forming associations, recognizing patterns, making inferences and spatial/kinesthetic perceptions. These 10 categories can then be matched against six general areas of mental competence, or functional thinking skills, that amount to the effective deployment of basic brain processes.

While psychologists might prefer a more dignified and academic-sounding nomenclature, I've chosen some rather unorthodox vernacular names for the six categories I've identified. In designing your own training program in Thinking, I think you'll find these terms useful.

Fact finding includes all those thinking skills required to get useful information into your brain. It manifests the investigative attitude, a habit of perceiving and thinking that values evidence, new information, possibilities, relationships and points of view. Your skill at fact finding determines your basic storehouse of knowledge, which plays a fundamental part in the rest of your practical thinking capability. The more you know, generally speaking, the more effectively you can think.

Crap detecting, a charmingly blunt term attributed to Ernest Hemingway, refers to what psychologists euphemistically call "critical rationality." It means the skill of examining the structure and context of the message, as well as its content, and identifying ulterior messages, motives and logical fallacies. It involves an attitude of noncynical but nongullible examination. It also extends to the skills of questioning the status quo and constructively challenging basic beliefs and practices. A thinker who has his or her crap detector turned on and tuned in becomes very difficult to manipulate.

Thinking on your feet means effective adaptation in challenging situations. It involves psychological preparedness, having some useful "standard tactics," scanning the situation, identifying key factors, keeping your eye on the ball (that is, your real objective in the situation), communicating assertively, reviewing the options of a situation and avoiding getting drawn into unproductive digressions from your objective.

Idea production describes what you have left when you strip away the psychological mumbo-jumbo from what behavioral scientists vaguely label "creative thinking" (or the now-forbidden term creativity). Producing ideas simply means consciously combining two or more existing ideas to make a new and novel one. If the new idea turns out to be useful, so much the better. The skill of idea production rests on the attitude that *all* ideas may have potential value and the belief in idea-making as a far more valuable process than idea-killing.

Problem solving and decision making is a comprehensive skill which integrates many cognitive processes into an important personal capability. By developing a consciousness of the *process* of thinking through one's problems, one can anticipate problems, attack them more thoroughly and systematically, make more reliable decisions, and follow them through to results. In this way one becomes a more effective and productive problem solver, both in personal life and in business.

Happying, a term that admittedly involves a bit of grammatical license, means the active process of coping with your world in ways that enable you to maintain a highly positive frame of mind and to achieve those outcomes you value. Happying differs from "being happy" in that the former focuses attention on what one does. We can consider feeling happy a by-product of effective living and, therefore, a barometer of effective thinking, including the emotional dimension of our functioning. In this respect, happying means *doing* what-

---

TRYING THESE TIPS AND TRICKS
FOR INCREASING CLASSROOM BRAINPOWER

BY KARL ALBRECHT

Once we have a grip on Thinking as a potentially well-structured subject, many techniques for the trainer and the learner suggest themselves. Over several years of conducting seminars on various aspects of brainpower, I've collected and developed a variety of such techniques. If you review some of your own training resources with the subject of Thinking in mind, you'll probably find that many of them fill the bill quite well.

In working with groups, especially in management team building, I've had a great deal of success in using a structured problem-solving model. Getting everyone in a task group to adopt a common "process" model, to post it on the wall in the form of a large diagram, and to refer to it whenever they run into difficulties enables them to proceed more rapidly and achieve more effective decisions. It also eliminates the well-known "group-think" phenomenon, in which a few participants with strong personalities run away with the process, and uncommitted members get dragged into premature closure by a false impression of consensus.

Visual aids that demonstrate perceptual processes can help people understand how they take in information and organize their thoughts. The Uncritical Inference Test (published by the International Society for General Semantics in San Francisco), is a very useful little story-listening exercise that helps people identify their tendencies to jump to conclu-

sions from insufficient evidence. You can also find plenty of thinking puzzles and games that challenge and develop various cognitive skills, such as sequential thought, logical inference-making, information organization, hypothesizing and idea production.

I frequently use a thinking challenge as a warm-up or ice-breaker. Once the participants have had a chance to solve it (I usually pick one most people can handle with a little effort), we review it together and become more aware of the kinds of thinking processes we employed to work it out. By collecting and analyzing these thinking games, you can identify the kinds of mental skills they challenge and develop, and catalog one or two for each of the kinds of skills you want to teach.

I've even used magic tricks to demonstrate thinking principles, such as the ways the brain forms and uses mental sets. The surprise effect of a magic trick comes from the sudden demolition of the mental set— an assumption the magician invited you to adopt, and which organizes your expectations and perceptions thereafter. The concept of a mental set plays an important part in understanding mental flexibility, and a few startling demonstrations make people aware of this normal feature of the brain.

In addition to problem-solving models, thinking games, magic tricks and practical illustrations, the trainer can also employ group dis-

cussion of specific thinking strategies and, of course, a certain amount of well-organized lecture. You can also use idea-production groups to give people experience with free-wheeling divergent thought. In this technique, participants in teams of four or five work against perhaps a five-minute deadline to produce the largest possible numbers of ideas that deal with some selected topic (for example, ways to improve the design of an ordinary piece of furniture). Following the skill-building experience, they can apply the idea-production technique to specific, practical problems of their choosing. The time limit, the element of competition and the emphasis on getting large numbers of options combine to get people out of their habitual convergent modes of thought and into productive divergent modes.

From the standpoint of specific resources designed for the learner, we can use games such as Master Mind, a two-person logical thinking challenge that makes skill-building enjoyable. The Creative Education Foundation, Buffalo, NY, offers a number of publications, and more and more consulting firms are producing training materials in this area. We also have a smattering of books on the subject, mostly on selected subtopics like logic, idea production and decision making. To the best of my knowledge, my recent book, *Brain Power*, is the first to attempt a comprehensive treatment of Thinking.

Reprinted from TRAINING, March 1981

ever it takes to make you happy.

To extend this competence model, inventory the various micro-skills, such as sequential thinking, recognizing logical fallacies, asking divergent questions, identifying blocking assumptions, brainstorming, analyzing options and random association of ideas, and catalog them under their respective competence categories.

Thinking in training

To design an effective training program on Thinking or to use a cognitive module as a part of some larger program aimed at an objective (such as positive customer contact), we first must explore the learning need. Suppose we find, for example, that our managers want to foster innovation among their employees but don't seem to know quite how to go about it. We might introduce them to the competence category of idea production and teach them skills under this category which they could then teach to their employees. We might focus especially on teaching the managers to use the cognitive skills of suspended judgment and divergent thinking as they listen to suggestions, concerns and new ideas from their employees. This will probably improve the communication process and encourage staff members to generate more new ideas as they see their efforts affirmed and rewarded.

Or suppose you've been asked to train a staff of counselors in the use of logical reasoning techniques that might help their clients deal with problems more effectively. In this case, you might focus on the area of problem solving and decision making, and teach them the skills of using a stepwise model as a communication aid in discussions with their clients. You could show them how to trace the process of personal problem solving—the basic dynamic of counseling—through the sequence of steps of a structured problem-solving model and help them develop thinking diagrams and other techniques for sharing the model with their clients.

These examples show that an overall competence model for Thinking, while not perfect or even all-inclusive, can provide us with a means for organizing our approaches and focusing our resources for learning and teaching. Many situations will call for multiple skills. In some cases, we'll need all six of the macro-skill categories. In others, we will need to combine thinking skills with skills from other subjects. The competence model will serve its purposes well if it enables us to isolate a useful skill and train others to acquire it.

Learn what you teach

It's intriguing to speculate on the possibilities for approaching mental fitness just as explicitly as we approach physical fitness. Can you visualize, for example, a facility equipped as a mental gymnasium? How would you design one? What would it include? What can we do with the microprocessor? Will it finally make the long-awaited teaching machine a reality? Can it develop basic cognitive skills such as memory, concentration and logical reasoning?

As facilitators of learning, trainers generally can teach best what they have learned well themselves. To the extent that you have developed a high level of personal competence in Thinking, you can design effective training experiences for others. However, with an open-ended subject like Thinking, in which we find such a diversity of skills, learning never ends. You need not wait for some far-off day when you can confidently claim the status of "thinking expert" in order to begin to help others learn these important skills. Equipped with a workable competence model, a collection of training methods and resources, and an open-minded attitude that enables you to acknowledge which of your own skills you need to develop further, you can start now to train yourself and others to increase total brainpower.

FOR MORE INFO

Interested in more brain training theory and practice? You might find one or more of these texts a good guide.

Books of brain stretching exercises

Albrecht, Karl, *Brain Power;* 1980, Prentice Hall.

Bry, Adelaide, *Directing the Movies of Your Mind;* 1978, Harper & Row.

Buzan, Tony, *Using Both Sides of Your Brain;* 1976, E.P. Dutton.

Edwards, Betty, *Drawing on the Right Side of the Brain;* 1979, J.P. Tarcher.

McCarthy, Bernice, *The 4 Mat System: Teaching to Four Learning Styles Using Right and Left Mode Techniques;* 1981, EXCEL Publishing.

Books on brain theory

Naranjo, Claudio, and Ornstein, Robert E., *On the Psychology of Meditation;* 1977, Viking Press.

Restak, M.D., *The Brain: The Last Frontier;* 1979, Doubleday.

Sagan, Carl, *The Dragons of Eden;* 1977, Random House.

Smith, Adam, *Powers of Mind;* 1975, Random House.

Reprinted from TRAINING, March 1981

SPLIT-BRAIN PSYCHOLOGY

How the science of learning affects the art of training

BY RON ZEMKE

The idea that there are personal differences in the way individuals process information in the course of learning new concepts and principles is decidedly old hat. What is "new hat" is a relatively recent set of findings that locates these functional differences in the physical brain.

In the early '50s, neurosurgeon Wilder Penfield found that electrical stimulation of the physical brain caused old images, tastes, smells and thoughts to surface in the consciousness of the brains' owners. In the 1960s, another neurosurgeon, Joseph Bogen, was looking for ways to relieve severe epileptics of their seizures. Then-current brain function theories led him to experimentation with the surgical severing of the corpus callosum— the bundle of nerves which joins the two hemispheres, or right and left sides, of the brain— in some of his patients. Researchers subsequently found some interesting things about the functioning of these "split-brain" patients. While blindfolded, they could answer questions about objects held in their right hands but not in their left hands. Patients reported that they "knew" what the answers were but couldn't verbalize them. This jibed with the physiological theory that the neural pathways from each side of the body cross over and connect with the opposite side of the brain—information from a person's right hand is relayed to the language center in the left hemisphere of the brain and vice versa.

These experiments and a few more became the basis for claiming that the two halves or hemispheres of the brain, right and left, have distinct and separate functions. The ensuing hoopla was something to behold. In the popular press, the right hemi-sphere of the cerebral cortex became known as the "right brain" and was said to be the seat of everything artistic, emotional, aesthetic and, eventually, Eastern and "good." The poor old left hemi became the "left brain" and was tagged as logical, linear, controlled, analytical, ordered and, of course, Western and "bad." The true believers encouraged us to throw off our left brain thinking and being and ways of training and put the old right brain in charge. Sprinting quite a bit in front of the actual research, these zealots claimed that split-brain psychology could explain virtually every heretofore unexplained sweet mystery of life. Among the notable quotes and claims:

- Marshall McLuhan proclaimed "bureaucracy is left hemisphere and the generation gap of the 1960s a conflict between right-brain kids and left-brain parents."
- Because so many artists are left-handed— right-brain dominant— many held that truth, beauty, justice and love must have their origins in the right brain.
- A prominent media research psychologist claimed that newspapers and magazines are left-brain media while television is a right-brain medium.
- The right brain was claimed to synthesize patterns from diverse-looking data, the left brain given the job of analyzing the nature and lawfulness of such patterns.
- Invention was said to be a right-brain act, while production was relegated to a simple, left-brain function.
- Managing was claimed as a right-brain dominated process, while planning was relegated to the left.

Balance came back into the picture when the researchers cleared their throats and asserted that the concept of hemispheric specialization wasn't intended as a social statement and that balance is a much more important concept. Among the modifying facts ignored by the faddists were these:

- Most of the early research on brain hemisphere specialization was purposely conducted on a unique group: right-handed males, right-eye dominant, with no left-handed relatives.
- The right side of the brain is *not* idle or out of gear when you're writing a letter or doing something linear. It simply is *less* active than the left side of the brain. Every mental operation requires many parts of the brain to be active.
- Japanese researchers found that patterns of hemispheric functional specialization in Japanese brains are quite different from those of Western brains. This East/West difference holds for Japanese raised in the West and Westerners raised in Japan. These researchers are evolving a theory that suggests *language and culture* may play a role in assigning functions to specific brain locations.
- The brain has more than a right side and a left side. Because of its multitude of lobes and bundles and special function areas, the brain can just as easily be "split" from front to back or top to bottom.

Now that the zealots have moved on, those trainers and researchers who busied themselves panning for significance in the continuing stream of serious brain research are beginning to pluck up some useful nuggets. One of these hardtack hardies is Judith Springer, president of Bethesda, MD-based Athena Corporation. According to Springer, the study of the brain is just beginning to have learning and training payoffs.

Part of that payoff comes from the shedding of misconceptions. Take the great right brain/left brain dichotomy. According to Springer, "Physiologists have said all along that we in essence have *three* brains: the Reticular Activating System, sometimes referred to as the Dinosaur Brain; the Limbic Cortex, or Old Mammal Brain; and the Cerebral Cortex, or New Mammal Brain. It takes all three of these physical structures for us to be who we are, *not* just the cerebral cortex as some would have you believe."

The first system is the attention mechanism. When we focus on something in the environment, when we are simply conscious, we owe our thanks to the Reticular Activating System. We are part of that broad group of attentive organisms and not trees or shrubs because of it. The Limbic Cortex is the reason people and dogs and cats have emotions and aren't simply funny looking fish or paramecia. It is the home of the values that go with the facts and concepts we know. It may even be the seat of our feelings of internal and external locus of control. It's really an uncharted area that is just being learned about. And the Cerebral Cortex is where all the language and logic and associated "intelligence" functions seem to be.

Just knowing this set of facts, says Springer, gives us new insight into a couple of common training problems: "One of the things we've told each other, and researched a great deal, is this matter of a proper learning atmosphere. We've proven we need it, but the reasons have been nebulous. When the limbic system is aroused, when some other matter is affecting it, or when the learning environment is perceived as unsafe or the values implied in the training are counter to the values of similar material the person has learned, then forget it— no new learning will take place. We've all had our kids say, 'I don't like Mrs. Smith and I can't learn geography from her,' and understood it intuitively. Now there seems to be a reasonable, understandable basis for it. It's in the brain."

The new brain learnings explain why the darndest things can be so controversial. "Nothing we learn is free of values," says Springer. "All of the brain has to be functioning for an idea, fact or experience to sink in, and that means awake, attending, judging, and processing. Every fact, every thing in memory has to have some feel, some emotional loading, just to be there. Remember the electrical stimulation experiments? Those patients remembered with their whole brain— sounds, colors, feelings, shapes, people, words, thoughts— all came rushing back as a set when the electrodes were activated." Small wonder some trainees are terrified by new learning experiences.

Springer sees the most immediate applicability of the developing new brain knowledge on the personal level. "Bernice McCarthy of EXCEL and Ned Herrmann of GE are both working on brain psychology-based style assessment instruments that can be used to help students on a one-to-one basis. But that is only helpful in a general way when you're working a classroom. It says for sure that during a speech you have to have attention-getting and keeping devices, and you have to present material in both linear-logical and pictorial ways. All those things about pacing and leading an audience make sense when you realize you are working with an organism that paces and tracks stimuli all the time."

Springer also has some tips for the management of one's own working/processing modes. Feeling melancholy or blue? "When people are sad, upset, unhappy, they slouch and look down to the right," she says. To get them— or yourself— up, do what happy and excited people do: "Sit up straight or, better yet, stand up and look up, not down."

Need to be analytical and linear when you are really feeling creative and holistic? Have to stop dreaming and start writing? "If you are both in an emotional place and being very right-brain, try using some art to pull out and get linear. When you're feeling emotion, you have to go from limbic to right hemisphere and then across, so to speak. The connections between the limbic system and the right cerebral cortex are stronger, so it's hard to go directly to a left-cortex dominant activity from the limbic. Start with art. Look at some colorful abstract pieces; study them. Move on to more and more geometric sorts of shapes, paintings with less and less color and more regularity. Work your way toward an Escher painting. See if you can't figure out how he tricks your eyes with those impossible staircases or waterfalls or fish turning into geese. If you're really having trouble getting into a concept, try to flow-chart it or diagram it visually. In just a matter of minutes you'll be perking along in a nice analytic, linear mode. Try it, you'll see."

Reprinted from TRAINING, March 1981

16 WAYS TO SAVE TIME IN THE CLASSROOM

What can you do to cover all the material without running into overtime—and without sacrificing effectiveness?

BY EMILIA SZAREK

Time is money—a concept as true for training as it is for any other aspect of business. While trainers would like to think that learning is their trainees' only goal, however long it takes, the facts of the working world do not permit the luxury of unlimited time away from the job. Hence the classic challenge: How do you cram the maximum amount of learning into the shortest feasible time slot?

Classroom training is especially vulnerable to time overruns, particularly during application and practice activities, although instructors tend to stretch out their presentations as well. The trouble is that a simple extension of the time allotted for either presentation or application generally will guarantee only that trainer and trainee will consume the extra minutes or hours: More time for a training activity does not necessarily equal more effectiveness. The time frames listed on well-designed, prepackaged training programs, for instance, usually are sufficient, realistic and consistent (for actual classroom time, but not for "session time"—see sidebar), and the trainer's extension of the schedule seldom pays off in terms of better-informed trainees.

The problem often lies with the trainer's management of the classroom process. Learning and efficiency *can* go together. I believe that if we employ a few basic techniques to save time in the classroom, we actually can improve the effectiveness of our programs as well.

It boils down to a list of basic questions. What can you do to improve classroom efficiency? Given a well-designed training package, how can you prevent or control time overruns?

> **A few basic techniques that save time in the classroom, can improve program effectiveness as well.**

What can you do to ensure adequate time in the classroom for group or individual application and practice, and still stay on target with schedules?

There are two areas where you can employ several time-saving measures to promote classroom efficiency: *during your preparation* for the training, and *during the actual classroom presentation*. Here are some techniques that have worked for me.

During your preparation

1. *Do your homework*. Take a cue from the Boy Scouts and "be pre-pared." A trainer should never step into a classroom without having studied the material backward and forward. If your trainer's guide does not have predetermined time frames for each segment of the lesson, figure them out yourself. You should know in advance of the class how long every segment and example in your lesson should take, so that you can properly pace yourself and your trainees.

Don't forget to plan time for non-training activities such as breaks, lunch, location changes, etc. Also, be sure to acquire in advance all hand-outs, supplies, equipment and references, even if you are not sure you will use every one. I've seen trainers blow an hour or more by leaving the room to get materials they should have walked in with.

2. *Establish time priorities*. Even experienced instructors frequently spend too much time on relatively lightweight portions of their lessons, usually because they become fascinated with the training content, or because they get sidetracked by questions. Sometimes it happens because they have not assessed in advance the relative importance of each segment of the lesson.

Obviously, you should spend more time on the most vital segments than you spend on the less important or lighter ones. If you have determined priorities for the elements of your lesson in advance, you can sense in the classroom when you are spending too much time on a topic. Many instructors never realize that they have "overstayed their welcome," but trainees do.

3. *Anticipate questions and problems*. Think like a trainee. Prepare both the presentation and application sections of the lesson as though you were the trainee hearing and reading your words for the first time. This technique helps generate the kinds of questions or problems the audience is likely to have with your instructions. You can then adjust your presentation in advance to prevent the problems.

Many of the questions that come up spontaneously in the classroom are useful, and you may want them to arise. But others can be time-wasting interruptions, especially if they involve the instructions or materials. Don't discourage questions from the group, but prepare the clearest presentation possible and be ready to deal quickly and smoothly with issues that do come up.

4. *Develop visuals*. A picture is still worth a thousand words—even if it's a picture *of* words. We all know that visuals provide interest, sharpen attention and increase retention. They

401

are also faster than spoken words. You can often show people what to do more quickly than you can tell them.

Well-designed "word visuals" employ at least two features: conciseness and abbreviation. Designing them can help the instructor think and speak more succinctly. One useful technique is to prepare by picturing your entire lesson in the form of good word visuals. This steers you toward brevity and pertinence in your oral presentation.

5. *Take responsibility.* When you are given a good training package and adequate preparation time, you become responsible for all the events and results that occur in the classroom—for accomplishing the training goals. This means taking responsibility for meeting both the learning objectives and the time frames. Trainers who are unwilling, unprepared or unable to take the necessary actions to meet all of these goals should not step into the classroom.

During your presentation

6. *Take charge.* Since you're responsible for the results of this session, don't be timid about managing it. Establish control at the beginning; you'll find it easier to maintain later. And control, of course, need not be confused with authoritarian dominance. Controlling the training means managing the actions of the group to accomplish the desired outcomes. It means leadership, not dictatorship.

One of the best ways to establish control is to inform everyone at the outset of the framework for the training session. Provide clear statements of such things as the purpose and objectives, what will be discussed, what *won't* be discussed, how questions will be handled, how breaks and lunch are to be observed, and so on.

7. *Start on time.* Start at the announced time, at the beginning of the session and after every break—even if some people are missing. It helps establish your credibility and control, and it helps make the trainees take responsibility for their actions. Furthermore, it is not fair to the on-timers to delay their participation because of a tardy few.

Remember, though, to *announce* specific starting times. Never simply tell a group to "take a break" and watch them walk out the door. Always let your audience know two things: how much time to take, and the *clock time* when the session will begin again. When you say "Let's take a ten-minute break. We will reconvene at 11:20," nearly everyone will immediately look at his watch.

8. *Develop a lively pace.* The pace of your delivery is important not only for meeting the time objectives but also for maintaining interest and attention. While there is no special formula, it's probably better to err by moving a little too quickly than too slowly. If your pace is too fast, the group will let you know. If you're dragging, you may not find out until it's too late (unless they actually start snoring).

9. *Teach to the "average" trainee.* Gear your explanations and your time frames to the "average" individual, rather than to the fastest or slowest.

While most instructors know better than to focus their presentations on the sharpest trainees, many do teach to the slowest without realizing it. This happens when you use classroom time to go over and over a point with the group for the benefit of one individual. It also happens during application and practice sessions when you wait until everyone has worked all the examples before going over the answers. After the planned time has expired for a training activity, begin your review session *on time* even if some people have not finished. If you

HOW TO ESTABLISH TIME FRAMES FOR TRAINING

BY EMILIA SZAREK

When you are working with a training package that does not indicate time frames for presentation, application and practice sessions, or when you design your own training with these activities, you will have to estimate the amount of time to allocate to each segment of the lesson. The intervals you determine should be adequate, realistic and efficient. How do you compute the amount of time to apportion to each activity? Here are some techniques that should help.

1. **Let management decide.** This is more often a fact than a choice, because management often determines independently how much time you have. The trick is not to try to squeeze into the "always-impossible" time frame all of the training you would like to do, but rather to identify realistic and necessary outcomes that can be achieved within that time. An understanding of learning objectives—and skill at writing them up for management approval—really pays off here.

2. **Process each activity yourself.** Clock yourself while you work through the problems and exercises exactly as you want the trainees to do them. Then double that time. The doubling is necessary because you know the answers, you know how to arrive at the answers, and you know all the tricks and shortcuts to the problems. Your trainees will have to figure it all out by making mistakes and thinking about it. It will probably take them twice as long as it does you. There are other benefits to this approach as well. Your processing of the activities will help you detect problems with your training design, your presentation strategy and your instructions for the exercise.

3. **Start with "too long" and work backward.** If you are having a hard time estimating how long an activity should take, figure out how long is too long, and work backward. Continue to shorten the estimate until it feels right. Suppose you have three problems you want the trainees to work. You can start by deciding that one hour is too long. So is 45 minutes. One-half hour would be plenty. Twenty minutes is adequate. Ten minutes is too short. Twenty minutes, then, becomes the time frame for the activity.

4. **Add up all the parts, and then some.** Work through all of the exercises and examples and compute the time for each. To time presentation or lecture segments, "walk through" them mentally, guess at the time they should take, then add a 25% to 50% cushion. For instance, if you "walk through" a lecture portion and guess it should take 20 minutes, add an extra 10 minutes to your estimate. This allows for questions, interruptions and other natural classroom phenomena. Once you compute time frames for each piece of the lesson, add all the pieces and round up to the next quarter-hour.

This gives you the sum of the parts, but not the total time to allot for the *session.* Even if you are working with a packaged training program that lists recommended time frames, the designation on most packages refers only to classroom instruction or learning time. When you are responsible for determining and labeling the time frames, be sure to include your estimate for breaks, lunch, travel and so on. And *distinguish* this miscellaneous time from actual training time so that trainees can select from a variety of scheduling options. For example, a training course requiring 12 hours of classroom instruction might be scheduled for 1½ eight-hour days, two six-hour days or three four-hour days.

Reprinted from May 1983

wait for everyone to complete every example, you are teaching to the slowest person in the room.

10. *Give clear and thorough directions.* You know how important this rule is for enabling the group to execute tasks properly, but you also should recognize it as a time-saver. Give clear and thorough directions and the group will go right to work. Give few or poor instructions and people will waste a lot of time talking and trying to figure out what to do. Your directions should always include exactly what you want the trainees to do; how you want them to do it; what results, outcomes or products are expected; and *how much time they have* to do it. A specific time frame tells the trainee how to pace himself, especially if he has a series of problems to complete within that interval. In nearly every case I have observed where the instructor failed to give this information, trainees took at least 50% more time on the activity than they really needed—or than the activity justified.

11. *Observe progress and provide assistance.* This applies mainly to application and practice segments of the lesson. It is difficult to provide individual assistance when training very large groups, but it should be routine procedure with groups of 35 or under. Yet you continue to find trainers glued to their notebooks in front of the room while their trainees struggle through a series of practice examples.

By observing and assisting the trainees during the exercise, you can pick up a lot of valuable information. You can see how trainees are pacing themselves. You can assess how well the design is working. You can see if your directions were clear. You can tell if the whole group is on the wrong track. If so, get the group's attention and provide a few hints to put them on course. The whole class may have blown 20 minutes moving in the wrong direction, but you won't find this out if you remain rooted behind the lectern.

12. *Provide periodic time signals.* Once the trainees get involved in their assignments, they lose all track of time. You must cue them at appropriate intervals so they can tell how they are pacing themselves. An announcement at the halfway point is usually a good idea, and a signal a few minutes before the end is standard. Long exercises may need more frequent signals.

If trainees are doing a series of problems, you might also indicate at certain intervals which problems they should be working on by now. It is often a good idea to explain in advance which examples they should work first and which they can do if they finish the others early.

13. *Adjust application and practice activities.* Even the most efficient trainer may sometimes find it necessary to trim some of the material to make up for lost time. One technique is to alter the way exercises are processed by the group. With a series of problems, you can speed things up by having trainees work on only the ones you feel are most important. Or do several problems together as a group, and have the trainees do the others individually. Or assign half the group to work on odd-numbered examples, and the other half on the evens; there are a lot of ways. Remember, though, always to give trainees the correct solutions to whatever problems you ask them to work.

14. *Don't get sidetracked.* Following a tangential topic down the "Road of No Return" is probably the most common classroom time waster. It usually results from a trainee's questions about similar or related issues. Tangents can be more exciting than the basic subject matter in many cases, and you don't even realize what's going on until you are well along some ir-

---

HOW TO SWING THE BIG LUMBER

Most trainers know the elated feeling that comes from conducting a really satisfying program—one of those workshops where everything seems to go right and the trainees' evaluations resound with praise and enthusiasm. But even then, it only takes a few sour comments to deflate the bubble a bit. They say you can't please everybody, but wouldn't it be great, just once, to do exactly that?

You may never pull it off. But your chances will improve, advises David Dalton, a management consultant in Newburyport, MA, if you keep four things in mind: first, second, third and home.

In baseball a runner can't score without touching the bases in the correct order. Neither, says Dalton, will you go over big as a trainer without building in three "bases."

First base: Participants must need the training and know that they need it. Second: They must believe the instructor can teach it and let him or her do it. Third: The instructor must be able to teach it.

You've got to cover all three before you'll ever get home.

Here are some stumbling blocks that can trip you up on the way to first, according to Dalton: Someone else thinks the trainees need the training and orders them to go, without convincing them of a real need; they attend merely out of curiosity or because a friend signed up; they attend strictly in order to justify a raise or promotion; they're there for a diversion; they misunderstand the seminar's objectives; or, it's the wrong course for their needs.

To help you get to first base safely, Dalton suggests that you:

● "Market" the course only to people who you know (or at least think you know) have a need for what you offer.

● Promote not what you offer, but what you have the answer to or the remedy for. In other words, sell the ends, not the means.

● Offer long- and short-term evidence of a need for what you offer.

● Cite specific results and changes that you think you can achieve.

● Answer unspoken questions and provide demonstrations.

To get the class past the first bag, Dalton continues, "the participant must have faith in the instructor as an expert and trust him or her as a person." Everyone wins people over in different ways, but keeping a few things in mind will help you get to second base.

● Be yourself and not who you think they expect you to be.

● Don't hide from anyone or behind anything.

● Don't try to go beyond your experience or convictions.

● Never answer a challenge by flaunting your credentials or experience.

Getting to third base—qualifying yourself to teach the subject and then doing it—requires you to:

● Be convinced the topic is valid.

● Be able to demonstrate, even be an example of, your program's results.

● Be able to prove the value of learning what you offer.

● Use methods that engage the participants' thoughts, feelings and will.

Reprinted from TRAINING, October 1986

relevant path and wake up to discover that the time you needed for the lesson is gone.

The most effective way to handle this is to prevent it from happening in the first place. Your opening remarks at the beginning of the class should always identify the depth and scope of the discussion, and should include the kinds of issues that *won't* be discussed. Then, when those tangent issues arise, you can remind the trainees about the contract made at the start.

In other words, don't fall prey to the trainer's compulsion to answer every question that comes up no matter how unrelated the issue. Stick to the training objectives. Defer individual needs for discussion outside the classroom.

15. *Manage the overzealous trainee.* You aren't a trainer for long before you become all too familiar with the eager-beaver trainee who nearly "what if's" you to death in front of the class. Over-eager trainees with their endless hypothetical questions eat up valuable time and usually generate tons of tangential issues. Rarely do these people contribute to the group's understanding of the topic. On the contrary, they usually confuse the issues and the other trainees.

It is the trainer's responsibility to deal with the problem, and there are several approaches. Again, your agenda-setting session at the beginning of class can help: Remind the individual of that contract to stay on course and of the issues you said would not be discussed. You can also restate the point you had been making when interrupted and refocus the group's attention on that. If the trainee seriously wishes to explore a number of hypothetical situations, make an appointment to discuss them with him individually after class. Finally, you may have to confront the trainee directly and privately, explaining your responsibility to the group and that his behavior is obstructing progress toward the required training goals.

16. *In closing, be brief.* Most training courses have some final segment referred to as Closing, Summary, Conclusion or Wrap-up. Always keep this brief. Remember that these remarks are meant only to highlight, not to reteach, the important points. Your concluding statements should take no more than three to five minutes. The trainees know the session is over and they are anxious to leave. Overkill here will not only take longer, but will diminish whatever upbeat impression was left with the group.

Reprinted from TRAINING, May 1983

404

CLASSROOM TIPS

MEMORY TIPS YOU CAN'T FORGET

Most of us agree with the youngster who said, "Memory is what I forget with." We also know memory is particularly important in training. As the old hand told the new trainer who had just finished a reading presentation, "How do you expect us to remember your talk if you don't?" Yet no matter how poor we say our memory is, we have an inexplicable ability to remember certain items. For example, the executive who can't remember an appointment for the next day can recall the scoring inning by inning at last week's ball game.

What information IS memorable? We most *remember* pleasant experiences, motor skills, and material that is worth remembering, talked about often, used frequently, given time to sink in, and stretched our learning capacities. We most *forget* names, dates, numbers, facts we don't believe, material not understood, "crammed" information, unpleasant experiences, our failures, times when we are sick, and times when we are mad.

We can turn those *most forgotten* items into *most remembered* items by using three simple procedures taught by Ken Cooper, a training consultant who teaches listening and memory techniques at the Civil Service Commission's regional training center in St. Louis.

Pay attention to what is important. We can't recall something never noticed in the first place. When meeting someone, we usually forget the most important thing—the person's name. While our body is shaking hands, our mind is elsewhere. The successful executive has learned what is important in his or her job. To find out what you are missing, carry a small notebook around for several weeks.

Concentrate on the important facets of your job. Most people talk about one-fifth as fast as you can think. This means that about 80 percent of the time they're talking your mind can be distracted by literally millions of bits of information presented to your brain every second. If you use your mental "idle time" to listen and observe reactively, you will think about what you are hearing and seeing. Evaluate it, analyze it, turn it over in your mind. Look for flaws, truths, similarities, or usefulness. Make certain you shift your attention and concentration to another subject only because you have exhausted the current one's value, and not because you have been lured away through distraction.

Organize what is important. A minister was shocked when a member of his congregation told him after a shortened sermon, "Where was your last point? You promised us four at the start of your sermon and I only counted three!" The member was trying to organize the sermon while listening. While most people believe that memory gets worse with age, memorization actually becomes easier the longer we've lived. The more we have experienced and learned, the more easily new information can be organized with respect to something we already know, or some similar fact or event.

Reprinted from TRAINING, November 1977

BETTER LEARNING THROUGH LAUGHTER

Stories in the form of case studies, first person and apocryphal examples, and what-if illustrations are widely used in training and education. There has even been research done on the pedagogic power of children's stories from "Hansel and Gretel" through "Cat in the Hat." Child psychiatrist Bruno Bettelheim's book, "The Uses of Enchantment," is the touchstone for understanding the meaning and importance of fairy tales and myths in the educational process. While teachers may hotly debate the implications of teaching reading to rural and suburban school children using textbooks featuring tales of growing up in the big city, the use of the story per se goes unchallenged.

But another form of storytelling, the use of jokes, funny stuff and humorous tall tales, is far from accepted among trainers and adult educators. Just as PBS Sesame Street has been attacked as too much fun to be of educative value for children, the trainer who sounds too much like a Tonight Show guest host aspirant is often condemned as instructionally irrelevant.

Dr. Herb True, a psychologist turned "edutainer," believes humor is vital to a successful adult learning experience. True believes humor releases the tensions in a group and helps defuse any ill will trainees may have about their attendance in the program. "But," writes True in his book *Humor Power,* "applied as a communications system, humor does more than release tensions and evaporate hostility. It opens up channels to others, shows us how to communicate clearly, and reminds us when we aren't communicating."

Without evidence, the question of how humor affects learning is essentially a defensive debate between those who tell stories and those who don't. Fortunately, the controversy over Sesame Street has begun to stimulate research into the effects of humor on the learning of children and adults. Though many issues are unresolved, preliminary findings are interesting and instructive. Five examples:

1. Researchers at Tel Aviv University have demonstrated that students retain more information from lectures that have interspersed "humor breaks." Specifically, the researchers played routines from a recorded comedy album between segments of a lecture and found that these humor breaks somehow facilitated learning of the material in the lecture segments.

2. Researchers at a major U.S. university found that key learning points followed by a humorous story were better remembered than key learning points not followed by a humorous story. In addition, when the joke or humorous anecdote was in some way relevant to the key learning point, the greatest degree of retention was registered.

3. Media researchers at Indiana University have found that children learn and retain videotaped information when humorous, "entertaining" material is interspersed between "serious" content segments. In fact, when multiple segments of serious and humorous material are used in a long video sequence, learning of the serious content becomes progressively better. That is, the content of serious segment 2 is better learned than the

content of serious segment 1, segment 3 better learned than segment 2 and so on, suggesting that the humorous segments have a cumulative effect on learning.

4. Brain researchers have found that humor creates remarkably intense attentional reactions. One researcher, Dalf Zillman of Indiana University, believes humor somehow stimulates the reticular formations in the brain, and that related diffuse projections to the cortex of the brain bring about a kind of vigilant behavior in the learner. The attention and vigilance stimulation seems to make the learner more receptive to information storage.

5. Humor has a positive effect on instructor as well as instructee. Trainers who regularly use humor in their training report they do so to help build rapport with trainees, to underline key learning points, and to relieve test anxiety among students. But these reasons may be secondary, since these same instructors report that the laughter of students decreases *trainer* stress and anxiety and gives feedback of student attention.

The research has yet to suggest the effects of telling one too many shaggy dog stories to a room full of highly motivated learners, ready for and *expecting* a straight, facts-only presentation. And until this and similar questions of parameter are resolved, we need to proceed carefully in the serious matter of making learning better through laughter.—R.Z.

Reprinted from TRAINING, May 1981

GRAFFITI PROVIDES USEFUL FEEDBACK

Emily Hitchens first observed the use of graffiti as an evaluation tool while working as a psychiatric nurse. The technique allows patients to ventilate their feelings and opinions in a public, yet anonymous, way. Hitchens adapted the use of graffiti to help her deal with a difficult group of students.

"One of my lecture classes was notoriously angry and difficult," she reports. "They'd been together through three years of college and were now second-quarter seniors in psychiatric nursing with a long history of lateness, talking in class and giggling during lectures." Hitchens

tried most traditional methods of extinguishing this behavior, but found that none helped. "The class seemed to be at odds with itself," she explains, "and it seemed to me that they needed more than just a traditional course

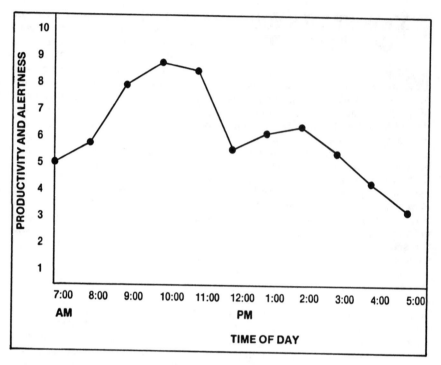

CHART PRODUCTIVITY BEFORE CLASS STARTS

Everyone has ebbs and flows in his or her daily productivity and alertness cycle which drastically affect performance. There are "day people," who love to tackle the rough jobs in the morning. And there are "night people," who are dynamos after dark but who have a hard time perking up before noon.

You can schedule a lesson plan to best fit the alertness and productivity cycle of your class by using the following simple exercise developed by Kenneth Cooper of KCA Associates, St. Louis, MO.

Have each student divide a piece of paper into one-hour increments, from 7:00 AM to 5:00 PM. Instruct the students to rate their productivity and alertness for each hour of the day, using a scale of "10" for most, and "1" for least. Tell them at least one "1" and one "10" must appear on their rating. Next, divide the hourly totals by the number of students in the class. This gives a composite class productivity and alertness rating. It also shows how much less effective students feel

evaluation form by the end of the term."

During the last class period, Hitchens told the students that she would leave the room for ten minutes while they filled three large blackboard

they are in early and late overtime sessions.

This class in the example has a majority of "day people," whose best hours are from 9:00 to 11:00 AM. Before lunch, there is a drastic drop in performance which is never quite recovered. The rating picks up slightly after lunch, and then drops off sharply as fatigue sets in.

The trainer now has a clear picture of how best to schedule the day. Detailed lecture or lengthy material should be scheduled in the morning. As lunch nears, it would be advisable to allow for short breaks every 40 minutes or so, instead of longer ones every hour. If there is a large amount of workshop or interactive time in the course, it might be beneficial to break early for lunch and minimize the hunger plummet in class effectiveness.

After lunch, the trainer has approximately one hour of suitable lecture time available. Breaks should be more frequent as the afternoon wears on, and classroom activities should allow the students chances for increased participation and physical movement to help overcome fatigue.

Reprinted from TRAINING, December 1977

panels in graffiti style, under the headings of "course content," "methods of presentation" and "class participation." After discussion, all the panels would be erased.

The first two panels, she states, contained traditional comments expected in any course evaluation. But the third, "class participation," was entirely negative, peppered with words such as "rude," "inconsiderate," and other bad assessments of class morale and conduct.

This last panel provoked a long and revealing discussion among class members. Hitchens facilitated the conversation with questions such as "What can you do about this in the future, for next term?" "Though the discussion was brief," she concludes, "I believe it was a catalytic one. Afterwards, they all clapped and rushed up to erase the board. In the future, I will use the technique of graffiti evaluation even earlier in the term so the participants have more time to learn new behaviors."—J.S.

Reprinted from TRAINING, August 1979

STAND UP, SPEAK OUT, AND LOOK 'EM IN THE EYE

Speech teachers since the time of Aristotle, Cicero and Quintilian have been telling us that it's not so much what you say but how you say it that drives the message home. And according to Dr. Steven A. Beebe, University of Miami, numerous studies do indeed support the contention that certain speech-delivery techniques can both increase speaker credibility and enhance listener learning.

For some time, speech textbook authors, relying upon both research and personal experience, have instructed that *eye contact, varied vocal inflection* and *appropriate posture* are key to speech effectiveness. Likewise, audiences, when surveyed, almost always identify a *monotonous voice, stiff posture* and *lack of eye contact* as the three most distracting behaviors of public speakers. While each of these variables has been tested separately by speech and communication researchers, little is known about how they combine to affect an audience during the same presentation.

Dr. Beebe combined and manipulated these three influencers in the same speech and tested both the credibility they lent to or detracted from the speaker and the effect they had on

speech content comprehension. Specifically, Beebe had a student give the same seven-minute speech—a talk about computer-generated music—to eight different groups of 16 students. Each time the speech was delivered, the speaker used a different combination of two *vocal inflections,* either varied or limited; two *body postures*—formal (upright body, face forward, feet together) or casual (body leaning, stance open); and two levels of *eye contact*—constant or none at all. Beebe tested this mix and match of effectiveness influencers on audience comprehension and speaker credibility.

Comprehension, or learning, was tested using a 20-item, multiple-guess test. *Speaker,* or *source,* credibility was measured using a set of nine, seven-point Semantic Differential scales that previously had reliably measured and defined source credibility as a combination of speaker *dynamism, believability* and *likability.*

Though somewhat complex and open to more than one interpretation, the results of Beebe's study were decidedly interesting and instructive to those of us who make a living "holding forth" to others. For starters, Beebe found that *eye contact* definitely is the most powerful influencer of both comprehension and

by Marilyn Leak

DON'T FLIP YOUR FLIP CHART

The so-called Rip-Off—Stick Up method was brought to our attention by Milt Badt, a senior engineer with Western Electric Co., who has worked as an instructor and a trainer for several years while assigned to the Bell Telephone Laboratories and Western Electric field locations. Badt learned it from Mr. Alec Mackenzie, author of *The Time Trap,* and well-known lecturer on time management. Says Badt: "It's simple. Sketch or write as usual, using a felt-tipped marker, crayon, or other stylus. Speak clearly, stand back, use a pointer for emphasis, let the message sink in for a moment, look at your audience, and answer any questions. But then, before you pro-

ceed, pick up a strategically placed roll of masking tape, tear off two small strips of it, return to the flip chart, and *rip it off.*

"Then, instead of having folded the chart over the back of the easel, take the chart you've just ripped off, and with the two small pieces of masking tape *stick it* to a convenient surface where the audience can look at it if they want to.

"Think about it. 'Hiding it from view' is *exactly* what we do when we flip a chart over the back of the easel. And how frustrating it can be for the trainees who didn't quite get those extra 10 seconds to let it sink in, or to make notes, or who wish they could remember some detail from a previously flipped chart.

Reprinted from TRAINING, May 1977

credibility. Constant eye contact promoted significantly more learning among listeners than no eye contact, regardless of the other variables it was combined with. Beebe speculates that strong speaker eye contact helps focus the audience's attention on the speaker and signals message importance. Constant eye contact also seems to enhance the dynamism and believability factors of credibility scale.

Apparently, body posture has little influencing power compared with eye contact and vocal inflection. But a combination of constant eye contact, varied vocal inflection and casual body posture work together to decrease speaker believability slightly but simultaneously increase speaker likability.

Perhaps the most interesting result is the effect of contradictory delivery cues upon speaker credibility. For example, when the speaker combined constant eye contact with limited vocal inflection, she was perceived as incredulous; Beebe suggests this may have been because of an inconsistency between the verbal and nonverbal cues being sent. In short, whenever the speaker employed contradictory delivery cues, regardless of which cues they were, her believability was lower than when the cues were consistent.

A few years ago, maverick Canadian communication researcher Marshall McCluhan flatly proclaimed that the media *is* the message. Though he was referring primarily to television, his concept also applies to the classroom instructor and public speaker.

If you want them to hear what you're saying, believe it, comprehend it, and like you all in the bargain, then stand up and speak out and look 'em straight in the eye.—Dr. Beebe's research was originally reported to the 1978 Speech Communication Association in a paper titled "Effects of Eye Contact, Posture and Vocal Inflection Upon Credibility and Comprehension." (R.Z.)

Reprinted from TRAINING, August 1979

CHAPTER 6

ENSURING BACK-ON-THE-JOB PERFORMANCE

On at least one level, the difference between education and job-related training is pretty simple. In education, when the course is over and the grades are handed out, the job is finished. In training, the job isn't done until the "problem" is solved. Educators give people knowledge; trainers help people put knowledge to use.

So it behooves us to do everything we can to insure that skills and knowledge acquired in the classroom are transferred into performance at the job site. And there are an incredible number of things that can interfere with the process.

Supervisors are notorious for saying, "All that stuff you learned in training? Forget it! I have my own way of doing things." Sometimes co-workers make it tough to do things a new way, especially if it is a more effective way; nobody likes a rate buster. Then too, the organization can be guilty of not having the right tools and materials available when the trainee gets back to the job. Training people to read and use computer reports 18 months before the company actually converts to the new computer system is an open invitation to a sudden need for "refresher" or update courses about the time the system goes up.

Sometimes a word to the wise can forestall most of these problems. Unfortunately, they are often beyond the trainer's control.

But while we can't dictate factors such as supervisory support for new methods, we can certainly influence them. And there are factors within our control: the classroom, training materials and program design. As the authors in this chapter attest, there are significant things we can do to ensure transfer. Take the matter of the trusty old management development course. It's fun to hit them with Theory X-Theory Y, motivators vs. hygiene factors, positive feedback, warm fuzzies and maybe a little "whole-brain" theory. Students marvel at your vast knowledge, and there is a little something for everyone in this smorgasbord of management ideas. Unfortunately, there is also pretty good evidence that the "10 Great Management Theories" approach is just 10 times more confusing than a well-engineered "one-theory-and-nine-applications" approach.

If the real goal is to give people the skills to do well on the job, then the training, the job environment and management support must all point arrows, big neon ones, in the same direction.

These factors, of course, can't be assumed. Supervisors have more to do than ensure that returning trainees have a comfortable re-entry. So they, too, need some support—and training—if they are to help justify the investment the company makes when it trains their subordinates.

Training programs related to promotions, changes in job assignments or responsibilities, new product introductions and the like have a built-in plus for transfer because you're catching people at a prime learning time—and their supervisors are often primed for a returnee with new and better skills.

The toughest transfer problems arise when the training focuses on changes in standard operating procedures. First of all, no one is getting better—or getting ahead—as a result of the training. So trainee and supervisor are both disposed to be disgruntled by the mandated training. Second, there are old procedures to unlearn back on the job. Old habits die slowly; change the wastebasket from the left side of your desk to the right, and you'll throw paper on the floor for 60 days. The trainee who must go back to the old job site and accomplish the same or similar goals in new ways needs a great deal of support if you really want the new ways to be used.

Here's a rule of thumb: Spend as much time engineering the system for ensuring that new skills will be used back on the job as you spend designing the actual training. Don't panic. As you will see in this chapter, there are numerous ways to design your programs to facilitate the transfer of learning.

FIVE KEYS TO SUCCESSFUL TRAINING

Why do perfectly good training programs fail
to improve skills on the job?
Here are nine causes and five ways to combat them

BY DEAN R. SPITZER

It makes no difference if you're teaching new welding techniques in a vestibule off the factory floor, or communication skills in the executive suite. From the classroom instructor's point of view, training succeeds if the trainees demonstrate that they have mastered the material being taught. But from the point of view of the training department—and certainly of the organization—a program that is successful under that definition can be a complete failure. It fails if the trainees don't apply their new skills on the job, and it fails if they *do* apply the skills but their performance doesn't improve in a way that benefits the organization significantly.

Like a lot of people in the training business, I have studied the reasons why training fails and tried to figure out how to make it more likely to succeed. I keep reducing the causes and cures to fewer, more inclusive categories, always in search of a more elegant solution. At this point, my list of causes has been pared down to nine items, and the list of cures (success factors) to five.

Why training fails

1. *Limited training resources are not focused on the most promising projects.* Training resources often are wasted on projects that are doomed to failure, either economically or politically.

2. *The real reasons for training are not clear.* Training often is an inappropriate response to a performance problem that cannot be solved by increased knowledge and/or skill.

> **We all have
> the tools
> to ensure that
> training succeeds.**

3. *Training alone is never powerful enough to lead to long-term, verifiable performance improvement.* While training often will improve performance in the classroom, it is rarely potent enough to overcome the resistance to change inherent in the work environment.

4. *Training is aimed at the symptoms, rather than the causes, of performance problems.* Attempting to eliminate the symptoms will not solve the problem.

5. *Critical non-training factors are ignored.* The success or failure of even the most effective training depends on a multitude of factors.

6. *Management support is lacking.* This is usually because trainers have failed to mobilize it.

7. *The central role of the supervisor is not recognized.* Aside from the person (trainee) who actually does the work, no one is more important to the success or failure of training than the trainee's supervisor. As the primary manager of the work-performance system, the supervisor's attitudes and involvement are critical.

8. *Too few employees are trained, and the ones who are trained are chosen poorly.* When this is the case, untrained employees will quite likely reconvert trained employees to the same old ways of doing things.

9. *There is little or no preparation or follow-up.* Drop an employee into a training program and plop him back on the job; little will change.

Training success factors

Training is not destined to fail. We all have the tools to ensure that it succeeds. What it takes is the systematic use of five training success factors: value, focus, power, mass and duration.

1. *Value.* Every organization is full of training needs or "performance improvement opportunities." Trainers respond to them either reactively or proactively. The reactive trainer jumps when a manager says "train"; the proactive trainer is constantly on the lookout for the most valuable opportunities to improve performance in the organization.

At least 90% of the training requests I receive are inappropriate for one of two reasons: Either a disproportionate amount of resources would be required to achieve minimal results, or the training is doomed to fail because of the negative attitudes of participants or supervisors. These are low-value performance improvement opportunities. A high-value opportunity exists when there is a large performance gap among employees in the same job or task, and when closing this gap can mean significant increased revenues or reduced costs for the organization. Look for these opportunities in your organization. They may not be obvious, but when you find them they will produce the greatest impact.

2. *Focus.* Performance improvement (a much more appropriate term than training) should focus on all rel-

411

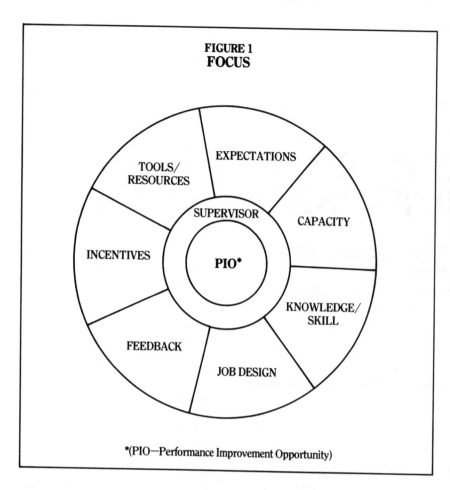

FIGURE 1
FOCUS

EXPECTATIONS
TOOLS/RESOURCES
SUPERVISOR
CAPACITY
INCENTIVES
PIO*
KNOWLEDGE/SKILL
FEEDBACK
JOB DESIGN

*(PIO—Performance Improvement Opportunity)

FIGURE 2
POWER

IMPROVE TOOLS & RESOURCES
CLARIFY EXPECTATIONS
PERFORMANCE-BASED INCENTIVES
EXPECTATIONS
SELECT TERMINATE REDEPLOY
TOOLS/RESOURCES
INCENTIVES
PIO*
CAPACITY
KNOWLEDGE/SKILL
FEEDBACK
TRAINING
JOB DESIGN
IMPROVE FEEDBACK
IMPROVE JOB DESIGN

*(PIO—Performance Improvement Opportunity)

evant performance factors. Most training programs aim at improving only knowledge and skills; they ignore the other crucial aspects of work performance (see Figure 1).

Lack of knowledge or skills is only one factor that can cause problems. Others include unclear expectations, lack of capacity, poor job design, inappropriate feedback, lack of positive incentives and inadequate tools or resources. The supervisor, whose cooperation is a prerequisite for addressing any of these factors successfully, is at the hub of the wheel.

> **It is virtually impossible to achieve long-term performance improvement with a one-shot training program.**

The supervisor usually controls the employee's immediate work environment and, consequently, factors such as performance standards, job knowledge, work procedures, information about workers' effectiveness, performance appraisal, promotion, and supplies and equipment.

Truly effective performance improvement interventions (a.k.a. training programs) require performance improvement consultants (trainers) to focus their efforts on more than one of these factors. Focusing on knowledge and skills alone and failing to involve the employees' supervisors virtually guarantees that the project will flop.

3. *Power.* Performance improvement interventions must be powerful enough to overcome all the forces in the system that resist change. Since lack of knowledge and skill is not the only cause of the problem, training alone cannot solve it. You need to take a multiple approach (see Figure 2).

If the problem is due in part to unclear expectations, then an effort must be made to clarify these expectations. If employees lack the basic capacity or background to do the job,

A MODEST PROPOSAL FOR CONTINGENT REWARDS FOR TRAINERS

BY DEAN R. SPITZER

I received a phone call recently from a woman who was inquiring about a position I was helping to fill in the training department of one of our mills. Among her first questions was, "What's the salary?"

When I explained that the starting range was $30-35,000, she was horrified. Neither she nor her job-hunting friends would be interested in a job that paid so little. When I told her that my own salary was within that range, she seemed genuinely shocked. (Her present salary was $36,000.)

I had already been through this conversation with several other callers. Some of them even seemed to consider the starting salary range an insult. Perhaps this latest call was simply the straw that broke the camel's back, but as our conversation progressed, I became increasingly defensive. I argued that Kimberly-Clark could hardly be advised to pay me top dollar for things I had achieved elsewhere—and in the past. I argued that in the human resources development profession, especially, compensation should be based on results. I don't know whether I convinced the caller, but I succeeded in convincing myself. The conversation forced me to think about some important issues. I sat down at the typewriter and began to work on this little essay.

I think we in the "performance technology" field are losing some of our professionalism. From a group of people who speak so convincingly about contingent rewards (for others) and the wisdom of "paying for performance" (the performance of others), I hear entirely too much talk about salaries and consulting fees. If we really believe in contingent rewards, why shouldn't we be compensated accordingly? Why shouldn't our salaries be based on the results we achieve? If we are truly convinced of the efficacy of our technology, our skills and the underlying principles of contingency management, there appears to be no other viable system of rewards for performance technologists.

Would you be willing to put your money where your interventions are? Would you be willing to accept performance-based rewards: no money for no results, substantial compensation for outstanding results? We talk a good game, but are we willing to do what we constantly ask our employers and clients to do: bet money on our skills and technology?

I can't think of anything that would enhance the credibility of our field like this modest proposal. I think it would be wonderful to receive, say, 10% of any savings directly attributable to my intervention in lieu of a salary. I can't think of anything that would motivate me more.

Instead of being paid to run seminars, to develop self-instructional packages, to write CAI programs and to produce videotapes, how many of us are being paid to produce bottom-line results, verifiable changes in performance, cost savings, increased sales and high levels of customer satisfaction? And how uncomfortable would it make us if our paychecks depended on these results?

Some will object that HRD people have little or no control over many of the factors that determine success or failure in performance-improvement interventions. We complain that trainees are under our control only for limited periods of time and that any number of things can cause their new skills to deteriorate once they return to the job. But how much do we do to try to control the factors that impact performance on the job?

With follow-up and reinforcement technologies, we *do* have the tools to make a much more meaningful impact on performance than we currently achieve. We *can* gain management commitment to bottom-line results. I think we'd be amazed at how few of these constraining forces would prove insurmountable if our paychecks depended upon their circumnavigation. I think that minds would boggle at how much we could achieve if we were being paid for results.

I have great confidence in my skills and my technology. I have the same confidence in many other trainers. I know we can produce real impact on organizations. But we are becoming soft and greedy. We're being co-opted by a system that rewards activity rather than results—exactly the sort of system so many of us preach against. In the process, I am afraid that we lose a sense of urgency about making things happen—and perhaps we lose some credibility as well. External consultants have some of this urgency and are, sometimes, paid for results. Internal "consultants" should operate under the same conditions. How can we talk with credibility to others about contingent rewards and performance engineering from the security of a salaried position?

I will accept a contingent salary anytime. In fact, before accepting my current job, I considered putting myself on the market under those terms. "For hire: in-house performance technologist on a contingency-fee basis." I never did, but now I wish I had. Maybe soon I will. I don't know whether there are any organizations flexible enough to accept such a challenge. How would other employees react? What would the personnel department say? How could the bookkeeping be done?

Even if you think this idea is off-the-wall, give it some thought. If you *could* work on a contingency basis, would you? The answer may tell you a lot about your own self-confidence, motivation and belief in the things you teach—and preach.

Reprinted from TRAINING, December 1983

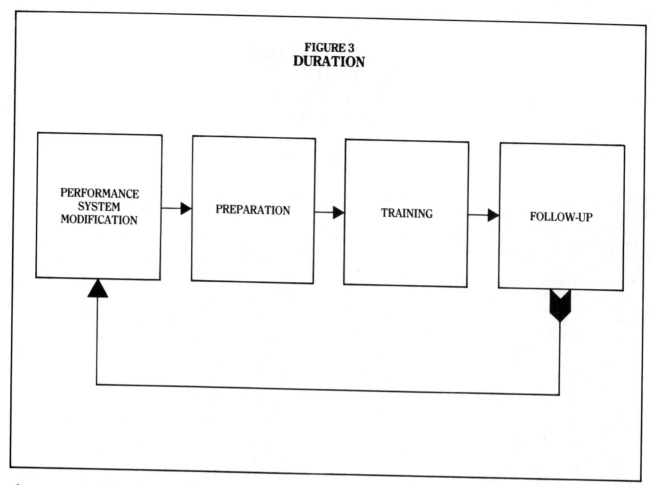

FIGURE 3
DURATION

PERFORMANCE SYSTEM MODIFICATION → PREPARATION → TRAINING → FOLLOW-UP

then new people might have to be selected or existing employees fired or reassigned. If lack of skills or knowledge is part of the problem, then training may be an appropriate part of the intervention. If the job is poorly designed, then work procedures may need revision. If employees are receiving little or inappropriate feedback, then feedback mechanisms and systems may need to be improved. If incentives are inadequate to motivate employees, then new performance-based incentive systems might have to be developed. If information or material resources are lacking, then better information or equipment might have to be found.

4. *Mass*. The concept of mass in training relates to the proportion of employees in any job category that are trained. If only a small percentage of the employees doing a particular job attend training, then the untrained employees are more likely to convert the trained employees back to the old ways of doing things than vice versa. A support system is usually essential

for trained employees to maintain their new knowledge and skills over time. In other words, innovation loves company.

As critical as the proportion of trained employees is the credibility of those trained. Key "opinion leaders" may have a significant impact on the success of any attempt to change work variables in the performance system. If enough opinion leaders in a given job are trained, however, you will attain critical mass, i.e., a positive environment for change.

One excellent way to increase the critical mass of any training effort is by having supervisors train their subordinates. This method also will be likely to build supervisory support for continuing use of the new skills on the job.

5. *Duration*. I maintain that it is virtually impossible to achieve long-term, verifiable performance improvement with a one-shot training program. New skills take time to become part of the trainees' repertoire, and no habit (poor performance can

be viewed as a bad habit) can be changed without a significant commitment of time, as well as effort.

The concept of duration includes four distinct steps (see Figure 3). First, all non-training factors in the performance system (e.g., unclear expectations, poor job design, etc.) are appropriately modified. Second, employees are prepared for training by supervisory contact, preview sessions and/or preliminary reading. Third, training sessions begin; ideally, they are timed to allow for on-the-job application. Fourth, the trainer coordinates follow-up activities that also involve trainees' supervisors.

Using these five success factors systematically can help you overcome the nine major causes of training failure. If you start a training project with a high-percentage performance improvement opportunity, and consider its value, focus, power, mass and duration, your limited resources probably will be well invested.

Reprinted from TRAINING, June 1986

28 TECHNIQUES FOR TRANSFORMING TRAINING INTO PERFORMANCE

This was going to be called 'Things We Know for Sure About How to Transfer Classroom Learning to On-the-job Behavior.' Guess what?

BY RON ZEMKE
AND JOHN GUNKLER

It happens all too often. The training program was a smashing success: The trainees raved about it, results from the written test told you that 90% of them had mastered 90% of the objectives, and they responded like old pros on the performance tests. But at a meeting over a new project a few months later, you are stunned when a regional field manager lances a verbal right cross off the side of your ego. "I don't know why you think you're so qualified to build training for the managers," he says, "when you haven't proved you can teach the service techs anything yet." That, of course, is the first word you get that repeat repairs, while down a little, are still high, misdiagnosis is still a problem and service managers *now* are up in arms about time standards.

In short, the operation was a success but the patient died. The training "worked" but the problem—whatever it was—didn't get solved. Somehow, what the trainees learned didn't transfer to the workplace, and into their day-to-day performance repertoire.

Though much has been written, little has really been said about this perplexing problem. That may sound harsh, but we recently did a pretty thorough search of the literature and found that the most frequently recommended remedy is, "*Do good training.*" This pronouncement usually comes in the guise of such seemingly sage advice as, "A thorough and properly done front-end analysis will differentiate between poor performance caused by a lack of skills or knowledge, and those performance problems that arise despite the fact that the individual performers are fully qualified, trained and motivated to perform," or, "To ensure that trainees will go back to the job and perform as well there as they did in the training room, you must make a special effort to be sure that they see a payoff for exhibiting the new behaviors in the old setting," or, "Reinforcing the performance and providing feedback ensures that the new skills are adequately learned."

Boiled down, we are simply being told, "If you do it right in the first place, dummy. . ." and little more.

We certainly don't dispute the wisdom of the "*Do good training*" solutions scattered throughout the literature. It seems patently obvious that one must provide the very best, most job-relevant training possible if there is to be any hope that the skills and knowledge in question will be manifested in the trainee's on-the-job behavior.

Having sworn allegiance to the greater glory of doing good training, however, we must add that we see the "*Do good training*" admonition as begging the question. It also frustrates and tacitly insults the many trainers who have done all the good things they were supposed to do to deliver a good program but who, nonetheless, find themselves with a skill-transfer problem. We are reminded of the Little League father who, having given junior his best spiel about "eye on the ball, shoulders square and swing level," can only resort to repeating the lecture, volume up and nostrils flaring, when the kid proceeds to drop the shoulder and whiff the ball.

This brings us to the point where we are supposed to tell you either that we have just invented a miracle technique for overcoming the problem of learning transfer, or that we have discovered an abandoned cache of heretofore unpublished research by Gunneer Enslab, a mad Norwegian learning scientist who solved the whole thing once and for all in 1967, but who was run down by his estranged wife while waiting for a No. 2 bus on the first leg of his journey to visit the noted publisher/editor Ole Olsen.

Truth is, we haven't done either. We know of nothing you can rub on, administer, do or say to your trainees that is guaranteed to make transfer from training to the job a lead-pipe cinch—and that includes threatening to fire them if they don't go back and do it the way you just taught them to do it. Nor have our labors at literature review been that fruitful. In fact, relatively little research worthy of the name has been done on the problem. Are you listening, thesis-topic seekers?

The fact that there is only a modest amount of help to be gleaned from published research does not mean, however, that the cupboard is bare. For buried in the cracks and crevices of the training and development literature and related paper, there *is* quite a lot of practitioner-tested help, if not 100% scientifically validated formulas, for troubled training programs.

Our review kicked up 28 specific things trainers can do to increase the odds that skills, knowledge and behavior acquired in the training setting will be used back on the job. For conceptual clarity, we have lumped these suggestions into five broad, and not entirely exclusive, categories:

- Pretraining strategies.
- Good training strategies.
- Transfer-enhancing strategies.
- Post-training strategies.
- Finessing strategies.

Before we look at each of these "clusters" and the techniques that comprise them, there are a couple of caveats we need to deal with.

This five-part taxonomy is simply an attempt to take some of the sprawl out of the mass of ideas out there and impose some kind of order on them. You may decide, for example, that "job aids" are misplaced in the finessing category and are more properly considered part of post-training strategy. Okay by us. In fact, it is more than reasonable to consider a given idea or technique as useful in a multitude of transfer contexts. Since there is no great body of research to call upon for guidance, we pigeonholed the scientific techniques where they either seemed to make sense to us, or where someone else has suggested they belong.

To some extent, our classification scheme is arbitrary. We prefer to think of it as flexible. The only real point in explaining all this is to allay the remote possibility that someone might read our classifications as more authoritative than they are. So please be advised that when we classify a particular technique as, say, a pre-training strategy, we are not implying that there is some hidden reason why you should never consider the same technique for post-training use.

A final point before we get on to specifics concerns the exhaustiveness of this listing: It isn't. We are under no illusion that we have uncovered all the possible ways a trainer might go about increasing the probability that a skill learned in the classroom is used back on the job. This is not the ultimate "Everything you could ever want to know about transfer of learning" article. But it is a pretty good cut at the territory, even if we do say so ourselves.

PRETRAINING STRATEGIES

These are things you can do to or for trainees, before they begin the training, to help ensure they get the most out of the training and that the skills and knowledge they acquire in the training actually will have a chance of being supported back on the job. Some are things upper management can do to increase the probability of transfer. Others are things the trainees' supervisors can do. Some put the burden squarely on the trainees, while still others are things the trainer can do to prepare the trainees to make the most of the experience they are about to undertake. The common theme: All of these activities take place *before* the trainee ever steps into the training room or logs in on a computer terminal.

1 **"Hoopla": Making the training a high-visibility event.**

The goal of "hoopla" is to convince (dare we say "sell"?) everyone who influences on-the-job use of the information and skills the training addresses that it is important to the or-

ganization that this training "takes." A situation that cries out for hoopla is the introduction of computerized executive workstations. People all around the organization are going to have to exchange old work habits for new and, regardless of how good the training is, there is going to be storm and strife a'plenty before everyone settles into the new way of doing things.

The temptation will be to resist the change, or at least foot-drag on it, as long as possible. Introducing a new customer-relations strategy, bringing a new product on stream, or simply asking managers to begin to manage in a different way are all occasions that can produce the same tendency.

These are also situations where the hoopla strategy—turning the spotlight of executive attention on the training—can help ensure that the training doesn't die or lie dormant after final papers are in and grades passed out. Though specifics will vary

from situation to situation, the thrust is the same: Someone "high up" in the organization champions the new way of doing things, sponsors the training to teach people how to do the new things in the new way, and insists on the importance of everyone pitching in and helping the newly trained people implement the new way of doing things. The laser beam of the high-up's attention has to be focused on two critical audiences: the trainees-to-be, and the supervisors and managers of the trainees-to-be.

There probably are a limitless number of ways to implement the hoopla strategy, but the simplest is the *Executive Memo*. Be it from the chairman of the board, the president of the company, the chief operating officer, the head of the division or the manager of the department, someone the trainee and the trainee's supervisor fear and respect sits down and pens a semi-personalized missive that acknowledges that the trainee is about to undertake

---

TRANSFER OF LEARNING: THE LABORATORY PERSPECTIVE

"The empirical studies of transfer of training have provided a wealth of practical suggestions for enhancing the value of training in the world of work."

If you bought that, please consult the authors immediately for a once-in-a-lifetime opportunity to buy over-water real estate in a borough of New York City.

The truth is, as you cynics have guessed, that once again the laboratory has let us down. Not only is there little clear-cut evidence that doing particular things will help transfer learning to the job environment, there isn't even much consistent theory behind why transfer does and doesn't occur. We can't even find agreement about how to define "transfer of training." Some researchers want to restrict its meaning to something akin to response generalization—the occurrence of a discriminated (trained) response to stimuli different from those to which the response was trained.

Others want "transfer" to refer only to the effects of prior learning on learning something new. And while it may make sense at times to measure transfer by measuring how readily something else is learned, it is the effects of training *on performance* that are of primary concern to trainers.

Given that prejudice, we define "transfer of training" as: the effects

of training on the subsequent performance of an operational task.

By "operational task" we mean, simply, anything a person must do in the performance of his or her job.

There are a couple of things to note about this definition. First, because we specify "subsequent performance," the *retention* of what is learned in training will be a factor in transfer. And since retention depends, in part, on how well something is learned originally, the quality of original training will play a large role in how much transfer of training occurs.

This is one reason why much of the advice we find on improving transfer of training boils down to, "*Do good training.*"

We would like to believe that "good training" means training that transfers to on-the-job performance. For many, however, the result of "doing good training" is simply improved end-of-training performance. At least, that is the implication of using end-of-training performance as the measure of training effectiveness.

In this article, we try to focus on things you can do to improve subsequent performance of an operational task. Many of these things (not all of them) also will tend to improve end-of-training performance, and so may also fall under the "do good training" rubric.

Reprinted from TRAINING, April 1985

an endeavor that has considerable significance for the organization and for the addressee personally.

The participant version of the executive entreaty is then sent to the trainee, timed to arrive prior to the beginning of training. Thanks to the wonders of modern word processing, the message can be as personalized as you deem appropriate to your organization.

As a fallback, the letter from the top can be day one, page one of the training materials. The preferred approach, however, seems to be to get the letter to the trainee before the program. Timing the letter to arrive a week prior to the training will give the recipient a sufficient period to verify that this training is indeed as important as your semi-personalized, word-processed letter claims, and to ponder the implications.

The supervisor version of the letter should cover the same ground as the trainee letter, with two additions. The supervisor should be encouraged to work closely with the trainee to see that he or she has all the support needed to apply the new knowledge and skills, and reminded to discuss the importance of the training to the trainee prior to the beginning of the program.

2 "How do you rate?": The trainee self-assessment strategy.

We seem never to tire of those little quizzes about sex, diet, happiness and health that appear in *Reader's Digest*, the Sunday paper and any number of consumer magazines. They touch that same streak of curiosity that has made Trivial Pursuit a runaway bestseller. Wouldn't you love it if people got *that* excited about your training? Can't promise that, but you can take a leaf out of the Blake and Mouton/Pheiffer and Jones/Jay Hall bag of tricks and exploit this insistent little bit of human nature as a pretraining strategy.

The use of simple self-tests and self-assessment instruments prepares trainees for training by giving them a look at the content and some insight into what they do and do not already know about it. The hard part is developing a pretraining quiz that is meaningful, interesting and nonthreatening—yet doesn't lead the trainees-to-be to think they know enough to skip the training if they do too well on it.

One approach is to make the instrument an obvious tease. The "tease" part has more to do with the way you position the questions and present the feedback. If you ask trick or deceptive questions, you run the risk of giving trainees the impression that your training, not to mention any subsequent testing you may do, is filled with "gotchas."

Consider this question: "Which of the following is *always* illegal to ask during an employment interview? a) Are you married? b) How old are you? c) Have you ever been taken by an uncontrollable urge to sell life insurance? d) Whoa! Nothing is illegal to ask a prospective employee, but some questions *can* put you at risk."

That's the sort of thing that might be appropriate on a self-administered pre-course quiz for a selection-interviewing course. The feedback could say something like: b) "That's right! You really *can't* ask a person his or her age in an interview. But do you know why? Sorry, for the answer to that one you are going to have to show up July 23rd for the workshop, 'Interviewing Skills for Supervisor IIs.' "

The tone is deliberately relaxed and informal. The goal is to avoid a pre-quiz that feels like a career-threatening *test*. As a rule of thumb, one question per major objective is appropriate unless the subject matter is so technical and specific that the trainee won't be able to make heads or tails of it.

3 "Send my boss": Familiarize management with the content of the training.

Pouring through a stack of trainee smile sheets, you have undoubtedly run across the comment: "It was a fine course and I am glad I was chosen to come. But they really should have sent my boss, since he needs this program as badly as anybody."

So send the boss. If the doers are supposed to go to training and learn a new way of doing things, the boss had better know that new way as well. Boss training doesn't have to be identical to the training subordinates receive, but it should cover the same objectives and familiarize the boss with everything the employee will be learning in depth. This also is the time to give bosses a few techniques for supporting the trainees when they return to the job.

WARNING: Do not call your boss training "training." Call it "Executive Overview," "Managerial Familiarization," "Supervisory Briefing" or any label that will work in your organization. Be sure to cover the role the boss plays in setting expectations for employees going into a program, and a couple of ways to conduct an "expectations setting" meeting. Also, send them out the door with a handful of materials they can use both to refresh their memories and to conduct that meeting.

4 "Can we talk?": The pretraining supervisory-expectations discussion.

In a sense, this is the visibility strategy driven as far down the organization as possible—to the trainee's immediate supervisor. But there is a difference. The visibility strategy is aimed at drawing attention to the importance of the training as a whole, while the expectations discussion is focused on exactly what the trainee should, in the supervisor's view, expect to get out of the training.

To push it just a bit further, the supervisor is telling the employee exactly what the *supervisor* expects the trainee to get out of the training. The difference is primarily a matter of style. The discussion can cover a number of topics. Among the most commonly mentioned are: What the training will cover; why the trainee was chosen to participate (or was okayed for participation); why the training is important to the trainee and the organization; the supervisor's assessment of the trainee's strengths and weaknesses as they relate to the content and objectives of the program; specific projects or problems related to the content and objectives of the program that the supervisor would like the trainee to work on during the training sessions; and how the supervisor will help the trainee apply the new skills and knowledge when he or she returns from training.

Obviously, the supervisor's skill in setting expectations and familiarity with the program the trainee is going to attend become important considerations here. Both imply that the supervisor must be trained in the subject the trainee will be tackling, as well as in the fine art of setting expectations with an employee.

5 "Homework": Assigning pre-course study and projects.

Pretraining study and projects were fairly common a few years back and are regaining popularity. In the mid-1960s trainees frequently were expected to work through a programmed text or self-study course prior to attending a program. This was an especially popular technique with technical-training people, who could assign basic content as pretraining study, and concentrate on troubleshooting, repair procedures and the like during the face-to-face or "lab" training. It was—and is—a common practice to require trainees to pass a criterion test on the pre-course material before they attended the "hands-on" part of the course. The advent of inexpensive computer-based training has

417

prompted a rekindling of interest in the approach.

A variation on the theme is the pre-program project. Here, trainees are sent worksheets or guidelines that direct them to gather specific pieces of data on their departments; to interview a boss, subordinate or customer on a specific topic; or in some other way to pull together information for use in the program. If the program is on project management, for example, the pre-course assignment might be to bring details of a project the attendee is or will be managing. The onus is on the program planner to give attendees enough guidance so that they will be able to ask the right questions and collect enough information for the project actually to become a personal case during the program.

GOOD TRAINING STRATEGIES

Call the following points "making the systems approach work," "the principles of good practice" or simply "the basics." It *is* important to attend to the fundamentals of good analysis and design if you hope to be in the business of providing training that solves significant organizational problems. You can't afford to do otherwise. But also bear in mind our earlier comments about the holes in this approach to "solving" the problem of learning transfer. "Good training" safeguards alone will not guarantee transfer from training room to playing field.

All that said, we can take some steps in the analysis, design and development phases that *will* increase the probability of transfer.

6 "Soil sampling": The work-environment assessment strategy.

The good book says that all training begins with a thorough needs assessment. Dana and Jim Robinson of Partners in Change, a Pittsburgh, PA consulting firm, suggest that a work environment assessment is critical to finding and attacking transfer problems before they have a chance to arise. The assessment, they suggest, should focus on potential barriers to transfer centered in the learner, the boss and the organization.

More specifically, *within the learner*, the search is for compatible and incompatible values and beliefs about the job, the way it should be performed and the employee's view of his or her own ability to change, successfully, the way he or she does the job. The Robinsons contend that if the employee's values and views are in conflict with the new way things are to be done, or if the individual does not believe he or she can master the new ways, resistance to training *and* use of the new skills will exist, and transfer will be doubtful.

Within the boss, the Robinsons suggest, the analysis should center on managers' and supervisors' willingness to act as coach/counselor to employees trying out new skills, as well as the willingness and ability of bosses to reward newly trained employees for demonstrating the new skills in the workplace. Without these two support elements in place, transfer becomes a much more dubious possibility.

Looking at the organization, they continue, means looking at several factors that traditionally have been associated with thwarting the development of new skills. Among them are the consequences to employees for trying out new things; the organization's physical and temporal barriers to performing new behaviors; policies and procedures that may work against exhibiting new skills; and the presence or absence of systems that give feedback to newly trained employees on the results of performing in a new way.

The assessment can be carried out in written-survey, face-to-face or small-group interview form. The strengths and weaknesses you consider when you use these methodologies for needs assessment and evaluation purposes apply here as well. Interpretation problems are inherent in paper-and-pencil surveys, while face-to-face and small-group interviews run into problems of trust and fear of disclosure.

7 "Why are you here?": The goals and expectations opener strategy.

It's nice to know where you are going before the plane leaves the ground. Airline cabin-crew people routinely remind us that, "This is Flight 467 to Juneau, AK. If you aren't interested in going to Juneau with us this afternoon, it would be a good idea to deplane at this time." The same principle applies to training. It is a good idea to make sure everyone has a clear idea of exactly where you are taking them before you begin. This is especially helpful with very long courses that will cover a lot of information and with programs that cover knowledge and skills that are somewhat foreign to the trainee population.

Two common "opener" approaches are:

• *The expectations opener.* Here the trainer begins the session with an exercise designed to elicit trainee expectations. In their book *Games Trainers Play*, Ed Scannell and John Newstrom suggest dividing trainees into teams and having them answer the simple question, "What two or three things do you most want to learn from this course? What do you want to be able to do or know as a result of this training?"

The trainer records the expectations on a flip chart. When all the expectations have been voiced and recorded, the trainer discusses which ones the course is and is not designed to meet. If a wide disparity exists, the trainer might have to modify the program or commit suicide to atone for a faulty needs assessment.

• *The statement of objectives opener.* This one is fairly self-explanatory—and even has some data to back up its effectiveness. Several years ago, author-consultant Robert Mager and friends conducted a number of studies on instructional objectives. In one of the studies, a group of engineers was given a set of detailed instructional objectives and some sample test questions. The engineers then went off and taught themselves as they saw fit. The result was that they learned faster and as well as those who were taught in several traditional ways. A second study found that in classes where a written list of objectives was handed out to students, their performance on criterion tests was superior to that of a no-objectives group.

The point is that if you simply hand out the objectives of the training at the beginning of the program, you increase the chances that they'll learn what you want them to learn.

8 "The more we are together, the more...": Training groups and teams.

There are two schools of thought about training intact work groups. One side says, "The group that learns together earns together" and so on. Team-building enthusiasts are particularly fond of working with natural work groups and teams intact. Blake and Mouton's Grid® training is based partly on the premise that people sort out their on-the-job differences during the training.

The countering view is that social relations get in the way of the training. People fear they will look foolish to peers, give the wrong answer to a question or have their performance during the learning period confused with—and evaluated against—their performance on the job.

When the issue is transfer, option 1, training intact work groups, wins. "I have found that unless there is a 'support system' back on the job, deterioration of job skills is very likely," contends consultant Dean Spitzer of High Impact Training, Alameda, CA. "We tend to forget that work is a group activity, not an individual activity. I like the concept of 'critical mass.' This means that there is a threshold number of employees that should be trained in any one job or unit in order to provide the necessary support for application of new skills."

9 "A picture is worth. . . .": The behavior-modeling strategy.

The data is overwhelming: Programs that use behavior-modeling technology in their design have a better success rate with respect to transfer of skills to the workplace. Start with the research of Stanford University social psychologist Albert Bandura, move on to the very impressive work of Arnold Goldstein and Melvin Sorcher at General Electric, and end with the research of Henry Sims and others who evaluated the transfer effects of a large behavior-modeling-based supervisory training program for a California manufacturer, and you come to the same conclusion: Behavior modeling increases transfer.

Now for the bad news. First, some things cannot be effectively modeled. Behavior modeling *is* doing; it *is* behavioral. Secondly, turning on a video camera is *not* the same as developing a behavior-modeling-based program. In fact, videotaping is only a small part of the applied behavior-modeling process. The trainer's demonstration skills, the trainee's success in practice attempts, and back-on-the-job consequences also play a big role.

10 "First you punch in, then you. . . .": Teach daily work habits.

Sometimes, we get so wrapped up in trying to teach "the big picture" and the "underlying theory" of a job or an operation, we forget one important detail—what the employee is supposed to do back on the job.

Robert Kushell, president of Dunhill Personnel Systems in New York City, has observed that, "Much is taught [to managers] on business theory and practice, [but] I know of no training ground where executives can learn the basic work disciplines: how to plan and organize their time effectively; how to develop the specific, small-scale goals necessary to the success of their long-range plans; and how to assess their productivity level accurately." That same criticism can apply to types of training other than

executive and management development. The nitty-gritty how-to's of the workaday world aren't that much fun to teach, but they are critical to *know*.

11 "Borscht is better": Keeping theory to a minimum.

The "Every Theory in the Known Universe" survey course may be great in undergraduate business school programs, but it makes for terrible working-world training. J. Regis McNamara, a professor of psychology at Ohio University, calls it the "chicken-soup or the-more-ingredients-the-better theory of training." Dean Spitzer asserts that if anything in training comes close to resembling an experiment designed to prove that forgetting exists, this is it. When concept after theory after concept are shoveled in, the poor trainees are left to make up their own minds about what applies to their jobs—that is if they can remember any of the theories, concepts and ideas and if they can resolve the conflicts between them.

If you want transfer, Spitzer and McNamara agree, the idea is to focus on a few, related, consistent concepts and make sure they are learned well.

12 "Let me see you do it": Evaluate performance.

You've heard this lecture a dozen times before: "Evaluate the outcome of your training—not just how the trainees felt about it." But you've probably never heard evaluation referred to as a strategy for *transferring* learning. It requires you to a) test trainees' performance at the end of training to see if the stuff was, indeed, learned; and b) observe and retest performance back on the job to see if they can still do it and *will* do it in the real world.

This strategy produces several potential benefits. First, if transfer *does not* occur, you have some idea where the breakdown is—if not the explicit causes. Secondly, if trainees are to be performance tested, your training will be shaped in that direction. And finally, if trainees are told that their performance will be tested not only at the end of training but on the job as well, they will be alerted to the fact that on-the-job performance is an important outcome.

TRANSFER-ENHANCING STRATEGIES

We're hanging the "transfer-enhancers" label on those procedures

and strategies that are included in programs not for the purpose of improving immediate end-of-training results (indeed, some of them can even detract from those results), but rather to improve later, on-the-job results.

13 "One more time!": The use of overlearning.

Overlearning, or having trainees practice beyond "mastery," is sometimes justified. Especially when the training includes some motor skills, overlearning can be quite effective after trainees go back to the job. Even if the motor-skill component is small (such as when we teach managers to praise their employees), we know that overlearning can enhance transfer. Why? How can it possibly do any good to train people beyond the point where they can exhibit adequate end-of-training behavior?

Part of the answer is, we don't know. We just know it works—sometimes. In the laboratory, for instance, certain kinds of tasks show more transfer as the degree of original learning goes up (even beyond mastery). Research by Gordon Mandler conducted in the 1950s showed increasing generalization of both simple motor and simple verbal responses with overlearning. In interpreting such research, it helps to conceptualize performance as situation-action combinations. That is, in most training, people must learn *what* to do and *how* to do it (the "action"), and *when* or *under what circumstances* to do it (the "situation"). Overlearning can apply to either "situations" or "actions."

There is some logic in believing that overlearning of actions may be helpful primarily in the motor component of the action. Part of the reason seems to lie in the nature of motor skills. The movements we make continue to become smoother, more natural and easier even after we achieve criterion-level accuracy. No one who has ever practiced shooting a basket or hitting a baseball will dispute that. The "grooved swing" is more likely to be right, more often, in the real world. So one reason for overlearning actions is to improve the consistency of on-the-job performance and its correspondence to end-of-training performance.

In order for overlearning to occur, trainees must be given plenty of time during training to practice what they have learned. This alone makes it unlikely that overlearning will be used very much. In our experience, it is a rare training design that allows even enough time to reach criterion performance.

14 "Step into my LINK trainer": The use of lifelike situations.

Simulations, or lifelike situations, are a standard way to bring "realism" into the classroom. The justification for simulating a real-life environment comes from arguments about what facilitates transfer of training. To the extent that the "identical elements" theory of transfer holds water ("the greater the similarity between the training and operational environments, the greater the transfer of training"), simulations are wonderful ways to enhance transfer.

As usual, however, it's not that simple. Most of the research you see cited was done on the learning of simple new responses to simple situations—paired-associate learning, serial learning and recall, recognition of simple items, etc. But a lot of practical training is actually concerned with what researcher Charles Noble refers to as "human selective learning," that is, taking actions you already know how to do at the appropriate times.

So, what can we say about "identical elements"? First, what seems to be important is that the "right" elements be identical between training and operational settings. But what are the "right" elements, you ask? Well, there's the rub. For example, if you simulate the work setting right down to the smells, then discover that the most important aspect of the job involves attending to sounds, where are you?

Donald Holding, an early researcher into motor skills and feedback, formulated a "principle of inclusion" that states: "If the training task includes most or all of the requirements present in a subsequent transfer task, then transfer performance will be high; but if this inclusion is not present, then transfer performance will be low."

In some simulations the designers seem to forget that it is people who are involved, and so don't provide for any modeling of affective responses. But people who are confronted by an angry customer on the job may be afraid or angry themselves, in response. And if the simulation doesn't take those emotions into account, its fidelity (and therefore usefulness for transfer) may be low.

15 "Imagine that. . . .": Mental imagery and rehearsal.

Clinical psychologists have used mental-rehearsal techniques with patients for years. And they work. Visualizing a feared object, such as a snake, and slowly decreasing the imaginary distance between yourself and it, really

does reduce the fear of snakes.

There is also pretty good evidence that mental visualization can help increase motor skills performance. One often-quoted piece of research (which means we've never been able to locate the original study) involved three groups of kids aspiring to improve their basketball skills. Each shot 10 free throws from the foul line. For the next week, one group did nothing, one group went to the gym and practiced shooting free throws, and the third group sat in a room thinking about—visualizing—themselves shooting free throws. Guess what? The mental-rehearsal group did almost as well as the "practice shooting" group on a retest two weeks later.

The visualization technique has

DO MANAGERS HELP 'TRANSFER' TRAINING?

Nobody is likely to argue the point that for training to be really effective, supervisors and managers must do certain things to help trainees transfer their new skills back to the job. But according to research conducted by Mary L. Broad, assistant deputy director of career development, education and training at the Defense Communications Agency, management is letting down its end.

Broad asked for the opinions of 105 past presidents of local chapters of the American Society for Training and Development (ASTD) regarding what management actions best support the transfer of training from classroom to job site and how widely those actions are being taken in American organizations. Broad found that respondents tended to report five general categories of important management actions.

● **Upper management involvement.** Authorizing release time for training, changing work hours to allow participation, providing physical facilities for training, and previewing the programs to be taught.

● **Pretraining preparation.** Managers participate in needs assessments, arrange for training to be conducted on company time, notify employees of their selection for training and authorize in-house development programs for trainers.

● **Support during training.** Releasing employees from normal duties during

training, awarding certificates and so on for successful completion of training programs, and arranging to keep normal duties from interrupting training.

● **Job linkage.** Managers assign returning trainees to work with experienced people, arrange for trainees to use new skills immediately upon return from training, meet with trainees to plan the use of new skills on the job, assign trainees to supervisors who are good models and who encourage use of the new skills.

● **Follow-up.** Supervisors involve trainees in work-related decisions based on new learning, hold regular conferences with trainees back on the job, acknowledge and reinforce use of the new learning on the job, and require trainees to report on the usefulness of what they learned.

Unfortunately, the respondents who rated these management activities as important to the success of a training program found management remiss in providing them. Overall, managers were rated highest in the "upper-management involvement" and "support during training" categories and worst at providing job-linkage and follow-up activities. The following table tells the tale best.

Adapted from "Management Actions to Support Transfer of Training," *Training and Development Journal,* (Vol. 36, No. 5).

Reprinted from TRAINING, May 1983

General Activity	Percent of Respondents Who Rate Activity Important*	Percent of Respondents Who Have Observed This Activity Taking Place**
Upper management involvement	80	59
Pretraining preparation	86	57
Support during training	83	62
Job linkage	81	36
Follow-up	83	38

*Mean of response for all specific behavioral items in this general activity category.
**Mean of responses of observations of all behavioral items in this category.

been used successfully in a number of interpersonal-skills training areas—supervision, public speaking, sales, customer relations and so on.

16 "Thar she blows!": Building trigger mechanisms for back on the job.

When the lookout spotted Moby Dick and the cry went out, the crew sprang instantly into action, each member doing exactly what he had been trained to do. There was no problem of transfer of training. All that was needed was the "trigger"—the lookout's cry.

Any good training is aimed at imparting not only knowledge and skills, but the conditions under which specific skills are to be used back on the job. Once again, it is often useful to conceptualize jobs as consisting of condition-action sets: "Under X conditions, do this; but under Y conditions, do that; and under Z conditions, do nothing at all." Then it becomes clear that the trainees' ability to discriminate one job situation from another, and "hook up" the appropriate set of behaviors to the situation, is critical to transfer of training. One way to help trainees hook up their skills with the right situation is to teach them "trigger mechanisms" that either exist naturally or have been added on the job.

If you design a machine to flash a red light when it needs oil, that red light is a potential trigger mechanism. If you then train a person to know what that flashing red light means, and how to do what needs to be done, i.e., how to add oil, the light acts to enhance the likelihood of on-the-job performance.

But signs flashing "low oil pressure" and "add toner" are not the only kinds of trigger mechanisms. There are also natural situational triggers. Many come directly from customers. When the client asks, "Can I have the payments automatically deducted from my checking account?" salespeople can learn to respond appropriately (in this case, by assuming the sale and asking for an act of commitment).

The training task, in the case of natural triggers, is to teach people to recognize trigger situations. Naming the triggers often helps. In a sales situation, for example, we might classify a whole set of trigger behaviors on the part of prospects as "buying signals," and try to teach salespeople how to recognize them, and to respond correctly when they do recognize one.

A simple technique is to put triggers on signs or posters, reminding people to "Catch someone doing something good today," or whatever. When trainees see the poster they will be re-

minded of (triggered to perform) newly acquired skills. That is, you *hope* the poster will trigger them; hanging wall posters all over the plant doesn't guarantee anything. But one reason commonly given by trainees for not using skills they possess is, "I forgot." Triggers in the form of reminders can help overcome this kind of barrier to transfer of training.

17 "Where's PAPA"?: The Participant Action Planning Approach.

The Participant Action Plan (PAP) can be, well, a rather perfunctory exercise: "All right, class, I'd like each of us to stand up in turn and tell how we are going to use what we learned when we go home."

Just the same, when done well, the PAP can be very effective. Robert Youker of the World Bank in Washington, DC, enumerates 11 benefits of the approach: It encourages transfer by acting as a sort of MBO for the training program, increases commitment by verbalizing it, provides for practicing the skill, helps anticipate problems, encourages contingency planning, gains commitment to action, sets up an expectation for follow up, provides an opportunity for reinforcement, helps set up a supportive environment, sets up a "system" for organizational change and provides an opportunity for evaluation.

Dean Spitzer suggests the first item on the trainee action plan should be to meet with the boss to discuss the training just completed. He goes so far as to suggest the trainer send a copy of the PAP to the supervisor with a note explaining what it is and how it works.

POST-TRAINING STRATEGIES

Post-training strategies generally focus on defeating poor transfer through some form of augmentation. Refresher courses, beefed-up feedback and special attention from the returning trainee's supervisor are typical strategies. Post-training strategies and procedures are sometimes very expensive, and always very visible.

18 "Love notes": The follow-up letters strategy.

Follow-up notes to the trainee and the trainee's supervisor after the training can produce significant gains in skills transfer, suggests Thomas Connellan of Performance Feedback Associates in Ann Arbor, MI. Actually, the pro-

cess he advocates starts at the *outset* of the training, with a letter to the trainee's supervisor while the training is still in progress. This letter asks the supervisor to set up a meeting with the individual on his or her return from training to discuss what was learned, how the individual will use the new skill or information on the job and what support the person needs from the supervisor. The letter also asks the supervisor to schedule a second meeting three to five weeks after the first to discuss progress.

A second letter goes from the training department to the trainee two months after the training. This one asks the trainee to assess the two meetings with the supervisor, and the support received from the supervisor since the end of training.

19 "Can we talk—again?": The post-training chat.

The post-training discussion between the supervisor and the returned trainee should center around the trainee's end-of-training action plan—if there is one—with the supervisor taking a reactive role. If no PAP or list of action items has been generated, the supervisor's role becomes a more active one.

With the supervisor in the driver's seat, the discussion should center on:
• What did you learn?
• How will it be useful to you?
• What can you do first?
• By when?
• How can I help you?

20 "Practice, kiddies, practice!": The rehearsal-room strategy.

Very old joke:
Tourist to beatnik: "Excuse me, sir, how do you get to Carnegie Hall?"
Beatnik: "Practice, man, practice."
The ingredient most frequently shortchanged in training is practice. Knowing about something is quite different from being able to do it—ask any armchair quarterback.

But often practice is kept to a minimum for very legitimate reasons, especially in off-site training. When lack of in-training practice is questioned, considerations such as safety, cost, time and logistical problems in setting up realistic practice situations are usually blamed, along with the ever-popular, "They always groan about role play. It's the least-liked part of the course, anyhow."

The real reason for not providing practice usually boils down to the matter of dollars. It is very expensive to take people away from their jobs to train them, and allowing them to practice what they are learning is frequently viewed as somehow being of secondary importance to cramming one more piece of new "stuff" into the program and, hopefully, into their heads.

One way around the problem is through planned rehearsal. If the training is being held near the trainees' actual work site, setting up a laboratory is a possibility. This approach works nicely for word-processing and microcomputer skills. We've also seen labs for public-speaking skills. Here, an executive with a speech to make or a press conference to hold goes to the lab, turns on a videotape machine, gives the speech or makes his announcement, and then reviews the tape. Only graduates of the initial training gain laboratory privileges, and part of the training is in the use of the laboratory. In the case of trainees who are from remote areas, it may be possible to set up a situation where off-line and out-of-production equipment is designated for practice work.

21 "As you remember....": The refresher training strategy.

The follow-up or refresher session is a much-overlooked option for promoting transfer. Arty Trost of Organizational Dynamics in Sandy, OR promotes the refresher session as a way of dealing with things the trainees are encountering on the job that were not considered in the training. The refresher session also gives the trainer a way to gather case material and caveats for subsequent rounds of training.

Trost emphasizes that the "follow up does not provide new material; it refines and polishes skills learned in the original training session and encourages continued use." Timing of refresher training seems to be related more to convenience than to any optimum we discovered. Periods from four weeks to four months are commonly recommended as the proper interval between training and refresher. In practice, we've seen refresher programs mounted as long as a year after the initial training.

22 "Hey! Nice job, Gladys!": The supervisor-as-coach strategy.

Several of the strategies already mentioned allude to the supervisor as an important figure in the successful transfer of new skills to the workplace. If the supervisor doesn't care for the new ways or doesn't encourage the employee to use what was taught in the training, then nothing will be different back on the job. Every train-

er's nightmare (and perhaps the single most effective way to guarantee that learned behavior will *not* be transferred) is the one where the supervisor sits the just-graduated trainee down and says, "You know all that crap they taught you at the training center? Forget it! Around here we do things my way."

Experience suggests that while this does happen, it isn't as frequent as the nightmare might imply. It is more often the case that the supervisor isn't aware of his impact on the employee's behavior—it *can* be hard to believe sometimes—and that even being aware, he isn't 100% sure of the best way to apply that influence to promote the use of new skills. So teach him.

Advice varies on the skills this training should build, but there are some common themes. The supervisor-as-coach should:

• State expectations of the trainee with regard to the content of the training.

• Set goals for using new skills.

• Give trainees feedback on their progress toward using the new skills on the job.

• Encourage and praise the trainee's use of the new skills, progress toward mastery, and efforts to apply the new skills and knowledge on the job.

• Be available to coach and counsel the trainee in applications problems.

• Act as an appropriate model of how the skills are applied.

23 "This group gets the gold star, this one the....": The count-and-chart approach.

The results of feedback on performance can be pretty dramatic. Connellan cites instances in which simply specifying the performance level and providing precise sequential feedback on performance, along with a little reinforcement, have decreased absences, increased sales and reduced error rates dramatically.

These very basic behavioral tools work for individuals, small groups and whole departments. They can work as a follow-up to training. The only "trick" is to be sure that the performance being counted and graphed on a regular basis—daily if possible—occurs frequently enough that it *can* be counted and that *progress* toward a goal can be perceived and reinforced.

Post-training goals like "Be promoted by June" or "Start acting like a better person" are difficult to track or keep frequency counts on. In broad terms, they are goals but not performance objectives or standards.

The supervisor and the employee will have to come to grips with the problem of "indicators"—behaviors and performance that have a tangible relationship to the goal.

A twist on the chart-and-count trick is the keep-a-diary gambit. Cutting a post-training goal into behavioral measures with a meaningful frequency to track can turn out to be worse than trisecting the angle. If that's the case, try a critical-incident diary. Returned trainees end each workday with journal entries that recount their last eight hours' most memorable and heroic efforts to apply "management by walking around," "participative decision-making" or whatever it was that they learned during the training program.

FINESSING STRATEGIES

In some instances, transfer of training is a problem only because we train people at times and places distant and different from those where they're going to perform. Suppose we didn't do that; we wouldn't have so many transfer problems! The trick is to finesse the problem by not expecting the skills to be learned sufficiently—or at all—away from the job. The core idea is to bring the training as close to the job as possible through one of several strategies.

24 "Problem? What problem?": The job (re)design method.

Probably the clearest case of finessing the transfer-of-training problem is the one where you can figure out a way not to do any training at all. No training, no transfer-of-training problem. Simple, huh? Well, sometimes it actually is. As Robert Mager and Peter Pipe (and countless others) have suggested, sometimes the best way to help people do their jobs better is simply to *change the job*.

For example, if people on a production line are required to lift heavy objects to a workbench and are having trouble doing it without injuring themselves, we *could* put together a training course on "lifting heavy objects safely." But on the other hand, we could arrange it so the heavy parts are delivered to the workbench by conveyor so that no lifting is required.

We were impressed by a sign on a piece of machinery in a Caterpillar Tractor Co. plant a few years ago. It said: "This machine does the work of three people." At first we were mostly impressed at the chutzpah it took to flaunt that fact in front of the employees. Then we discovered that the signs were a positive factor in the work setting. Why? Because the three people the machine replaced had the worst jobs in the factory; workers were delighted they didn't have to worry about doing those jobs anymore.

In other cases, where jobs will not be eliminated, they still may be changed and made simpler. Automation may replace the need to perform certain of the most tedious or precise tasks, leaving an easier or livelier set of tasks for the worker. Or technology can be used to enhance the skill, speed, power and precision of a worker. This is precisely what any good tool does. Granted, sometimes this means we must train the worker to use the tool. But typically, it is easier and more efficient to learn to use the tool than to learn to do the job as well without it.

25 "Let's try that move out on the dance floor": The interim-project approach.

One way to get the training environment closer to the work environment is to bring the work environment into the training. And one way to do that is to include instances of "live work" (actual performance of job tasks in the work setting) as part of training.

If application of skills actually can be made in the work setting under work conditions, then you have finessed the transfer-of-training problem because no transferring is necessary (or, more accurately, learners actually make the transfer during the training). The trick here, as it is in simulations, is making sure that the application of skills occurs under work conditions. Otherwise, all you've done is set up a "simulation" that happens to use the physical environment of the workplace.

What researcher Shirley Harmon calls the "interim-project approach" is multiple-phase training that consists of three parts: the original training workshop, an on-the-job application project and a summary report workshop (to discuss the application project).

At first glance, this technique appears to be your basic "follow-up project" or Participant Action Planning Approach in another cloak. The difference is larger than it seems. Structuring training so that the project, or live work, falls between two meetings with a facilitator or instructor is more likely to benefit trainees than just sending them home with a project in

their hands. With the interim-project approach, the designer can exert more control over how much and what kind of feedback and reinforcement trainees will get after they do their projects, and not count so much on supervisors and managers to handle those tasks.

There always seems to be an awkwardness and embarrassment when trying skills for the first time—awkwardness that makes it difficult to deal with someone up the reporting chain. It often works better if participants can hear about struggles, failures and successes from each other, and can work out explicitly with peers how it felt and how they think it will be next time.

Extended, spaced or "multiphase" training can often benefit from an opportunity to apply the training on the job between training sessions. To make this worthwhile it helps to provide some structure (much like competence-building activities do) for the application—rather than just exhorting the participants to "Go try this stuff out." And it usually helps to devote some time at the beginning of the next training session to reporting application experiences, and giving feedback and some kind of reinforcement to those who tried out their skills.

26 "Experience is the best teacher (we're just lousy students)": Competence-building activities.

When we ask people who are unusually good at doing something where they learned to do it, they usually answer, "from experience." Almost nobody, in the long history of humankind, has ever said, "From the Frizblit Training Course!"

Discouraging, isn't it?

So, if people learn from experience, just *what* do they learn? If you practice a bad forehand swing, over and over, will you learn anything? You bet! And you'll have the hardest-to-improve forehand at the racquet club. What people learn from experience is full of good stuff (to the extent that they are good performers), but it is also full of silly stuff, superstition, irrelevancies and just plain bad habits.

John Wannamaker, the legendary Philadelphia department store magnate, was once asked, so the story goes, how effective his advertising was. He replied, "Half of it is no damn good!"

"Then why don't you get rid of it?"

"Because I don't know which half it is," was Wannamaker's answer. We suspect that what excellent performers do is like that: Half of it is no damn good, or at least irrelevant to their

successful performance, but they keep doing it just because they learned it from experience—along with the crucial stuff.

What's the trick? How can you turn plain vanilla "experience" into anything like an efficient competence-building activity? You have to impose some structure. It can take these forms:

- Designate specific on-the-job "experiences" as learning opportunities (e.g., the third customer who approaches you next Tuesday; or every fourth phone call you make next week).
- Set explicit and specific learning expectations for each designated experience.
- Have the learners keep track of *what they do* and *what results they achieve* (and sometimes, how they feel about it), using a form that also serves as a job aid to remind them of what they are trying to do and accomplish.
- Construct a way for a second party to monitor and reinforce what is learned (through regular meetings with others who have been trained, or with an instructor, mentor or boss).
- Provide a simple record-keeping system so participants can track their own progress.

27 "Just put this template over your keyboard and. . . .": Using job aids.

One of the most venerable methods of finessing the transfer-of-training problem involves the use of informational job aids, or performance aids. (We say "informational" to distinguish them from physical tools that aid performance.) The theory is simple: Rather than requiring people to do things they aren't good at (such as storing masses of data in their heads), you provide "external memory" in the form of checklists, look-up tables, reference manuals, flowcharts, computer data bases, labeled machine parts, templates to put over their keyboards or telephones, etc. Then you don't have to train them to remember all that stuff; you just have to train them to use the job aid.

How difficult will it be for people to use the job aid? How much training in using it will be needed? You may be designing the thing to avoid training—but giving trainees something they won't or can't use properly isn't worth your while. Typically, some training in the use of job aids is necessary.

It's almost universally true that if you can replace training with a job aid, it's a good idea to do it. Exceptions include occasions when it's most effective if skills are run off automatically (so that stopping to look at something would interfere), or when looking something up would simply take too much time, or when there is so much information to be conveyed that for efficiency people had better remember at least what they use most often.

28 "Good old OJT": On-the-job training.

Yes, this hoary old creature rears its ugly head. And you thought OJT was what you were in the business of replacing, right? It's true that some OJT has a deservedly bad reputation. Typically, it's the kind that was put in place because no one wanted to (or could) design or pay for decent training. So OJT became synonymous with "Let's just throw 'em in the water and keep the ones who learn to swim."

But there are situations where the best way to learn a job is by doing it, especially when doing the job poorly during a "break-in period" doesn't have dire consequences, or when it is simply too costly or complex to adequately simulate on-the-job conditions.

There are situations where poor initial performance means nothing more than doing it more slowly than highly competent people do it. If such a job can readily be learned by observing others and practicing, it may be more economical to let trainees work slowly for awhile than to take them off the job entirely for training.

In other circumstances there are prerequisite, low-level portions of a whole job that must be learned before higher-level performance can occur. Apprenticeships often begin this way, with the apprentice doing the "dirty" work that takes little skill, then progressing up to higher-level tasks. Again, if much can be learned by observing, giving a trainee something easy to do while observing the more complex parts of the job may make sense.

In situations where the amount of practice required to achieve competent performance is much greater than the amount of instruction, it may be more efficient to provide the instruction in small doses on the job, letting the trainees add new skills one at a time. Many jobs that require motor skills are like this.

On-the-job training is an implicit part of all other training. We know that we don't teach trainees everything. So how do we justify sending them out to work? By explicitly or implicitly counting on OJT to finish the job.

Here are a few recommended "rules" about using OJT. For those who will supervise apprentices during their OJT, "training" must be an explicit objective of their position; supervisors should be measured, monitored (at the very least during performance reviews), and singled out for rewards based on their achievement of those training objectives.

Likewise, we think that "learning objectives" should be an explicit part of the job of the apprentice during OJT; the apprentice should be measured, monitored (more frequently than quarterly) and rewarded for achievement of learning objectives. Further, the achievement of learning objectives during OJT should receive at least as much attention from supervisors and the rest of the organization as does the performance of other job duties.

So there are the 28 techniques, strategies, methods—call them what you will—we have cataloged by combing the literature of psychology, educational research, and training and development. What did we leave out? Probably quite a bit. But like old John Wannamaker, we don't know which half.

Reprinted from TRAINING, April 1985

REFERENCES

Bilodeau, E.A. and I. McD. Bilodeau (eds), *Principles of Skill Acquisition*, Academic Press, Inc., New York, 1969.

Briggs, G.E., "Transfer of Training," in Bilodeau and Bilodeau, pp. 205-234, 1969.

Brown, M.G., "Understanding Transfer of Training," *NSPI Journal*, pp. 5-7, March 1983.

Connellan, T.K., *How to Make Sure Your Training Takes*, Performance Feedback Associates, Ann Arbor, MI, 1978.

Duncan, C.P., "Transfer After Training with Single Versus Multiple Tasks," *Journal of Experimental Psychology*, 55, pp. 63-72, May 1958.

Georgenson, D.L., "The Problem of Transfer Calls for Partnership," *Training and Development Journal*, 36, pp. 75-78, Oct. 1982.

Harmon, S.J., "Management Training and Development: An Interim Project Approach: Optimizing the Transfer of Training Back to the Work Situation," *Training and Development Journal*, 28, pp. 16-18, June 1974.

Holding, D.H., "Transfer Between Difficult and Easy Tasks," *British Journal of Psychology*, 53, pp. 397-407, 1962.

Johnson, S.L., "Effect of Training Device on Retention and Transfer of a Procedural Task," *Human Factors*, 23, pp. 257-272, June 1981.

Joinson, D., "Using Checklists as an Aid to Transfer of Training," *TRAINING Magazine*, 14, pp. 50-51, June 1977.

Katz, S. and R. Bollettino, "Transfer of Learning," *NSPI Journal*, pp. 27-29, July 1981.

Kent, R.H., "Transfer of Training Without the Boss," *Journal of European Industrial Training*, 6, pp. 17-19, Spring 1982.

Kushell, R.E., "Teaching Daily Work Habits and Patterns Aid Transfer," *TRAINING Magazine*, 16, pp. 54-57, Nov. 1979.

Mager, R.F. and P. Pipe, *Analyzing Performance Problems or 'You Really Oughta Wanna,'* Fearon Publishers, Inc., Belmont, CA, 1970.

Mandler, G., "Transfer of Training as a Function of Degree of Response Overlearning," *Journal of Experimental Psychology*, 47, pp. 411-417, Sep. 1954.

Mandler, G. and S.H. Heinemann, "Effect of Overlearning of a Verbal Response on Transfer of Training, *Journal of Experimental Psychology*, 52, pp. 39-46, June 1956.

McNamara, J. Regis, "Why They Don't Do What We Train Them To," *TRAINING Magazine*, 17, pp. 33-36, Feb. 1980.

Noble, C.E., "Outline of Human Selective Learning," in Bilodeau and Bilodeau, pp. 319-353, 1969.

Osgood, C.E., "The Similarity Paradox in Human Learning: A Resolution," *Psychological Review*, 56, pp. 132-143, Fall 1949.

Osgood, C.E., "The Nature and Measurement of Meaning," *Psychological Bulletin*, 49, pp. 197-237, June 1952.

Robinson, D.G. and J.C. Robinson, "Breaking Barriers to Skill Transfer," *Training and Development Journal*, pp. 82-83, Jan. 1985.

Robinson, J. and K. Hultman, *How to Make Sure Your Supervisors Do on the Job What You Taught Them in the Classroom*, Development Dimensions Intl., Pittsburgh, PA, 1981.

Spitzer, D.R., "Why Training Fails," *Performance and Instruction Journal*, pp. 6-10, Nov. 1984.

Stern, F.M. and R.E. Zemke, *Stressless Selling: A Guide to Success for Men and Women in Sales*, Prentice-Hall, Inc., Englewood Cliffs, NJ, 1981.

Trost, A., "They May Love It But Will They Use It?", *Training and Development Journal*, pp. 78-81, Jan. 1985.

THE SYSTEMS VIEW OF HUMAN PERFORMANCE

A refresher course on how to look at performers in context—and the implications for training when you do

BY GEARY A. RUMMLER
AND ALAN P. BRACHE

Most attempts to improve human performance in organizations are doomed to failure from the start. Training initiatives aimed at getting workers to turn out higher quality products? Doomed. Motivational schemes to boost productivity? Doomed. Programs intended to improve customer service, to cure production problems, to introduce more efficient sales methods? Doomed.

Sorry to be so gloomy. But most of these efforts fail, and they'll go on failing because they proceed from the fundamentally false assumption that people perform in a vacuum. Any time we try to improve an individual's *output* solely by changing the *input* of knowledge or information or skills to that individual, we are making the naive assumption that the person exists in a performance vacuum, isolated from and immune to the rest of the organization. We are ignoring the performance environment. That environment—that "system"—has an enormous impact on the way people do their jobs and on the results the organization achieves.

Take a typical improvement initiative—a request for training. The senior vice president of insurance operations in a large casualty-property insurance company sends a memo to the training director. What the VP wants is "a one-week refresher course for 500 claim representatives on han-

dling claims, with special emphasis on scoping damage." By "scoping damage," the VP means figuring out the nature and extent of the loss a policyholder has suffered, and estimating what it will take to fix it. A claim rep is "scoping damage" when she looks at a half-burned house and says, "The foundation is probably OK, but it will need a new roof."

A typical response to the vice president's request is: "Fine. Now let's see, shall we develop this course ourselves or shop for a packaged program on the market?"

If the training department does respond that way, it has fallen victim to the fallacy of the performance vacuum: It's assuming that a training input will automatically lead to a valuable performance output. So what? Well. . . .

● We don't know what, if anything, is broken, so how will we know if we've fixed it? How *can* we know, unless we ask what shortfall in the organization's performance has prompted this request for training?

● Assuming there is some particular shortfall, we don't know its extent. So how can we estimate the value we'd gain by fixing the problem? Maybe investing the same dollars in some other area would give the company a bigger payoff.

● Again, assuming there is some organizational shortfall, we don't know that it's caused by a human performance problem. And if it is, we don't know whose performance is deficient, so how do we know if we're

trying to "fix" the right people? Is the claim rep the critical performer here?

● We don't know what, if any, duties the claim reps are failing to perform, so how do we know we should focus on scoping damage?

● If there is a deficiency in that particular activity, we don't know what's causing it. So how do we know that training is the right cure? What about all the other factors that affect the claim reps' performance—and the "scoping damage process" itself?

No, if training is to make a real difference in the organization, we need an alternative to the vacuum view of performance. There is such an alternative view. It springs from two fundamental premises. First, every individual operates within the context of a performance *system*. Second, improvements in individual and organizational performance will happen only if we understand and manage the variables in that system. With those thoughts in mind, let's begin at the beginning.

Performance, part I

Every person in an organization has a job. The point of the job is to produce various outputs that the organization values for some reason. For instance, a correctly settled claim is an important output for an insurance company.

But every performer exists within a particular human performance system. Will we get the output we desire from a performer? That's determined by the five components of the performance system (see Figure 1).

The performer (1) is required to process a variety of inputs (2), such as a form, a sales lead or a phone call. For each input, there is a desired output (3)—inquiry answered, form processed correctly, etc. For every output produced (and for each action required to produce an output) there is a resultant consequence (4)—some event occurs that affects the performer. This event is interpreted by the performer (often uniquely) as either positive or negative. A basic behavioral law holds that behavior is influenced by its consequences; people ultimately will do things that lead to positive consequences and avoid things that result in negative consequences.

The final element in the system is feedback (5). The performer must re-

425

ceive information about the outputs he or she is producing. Are they satisfactory or deficient in some way? How do they help or harm the organization as a whole?

As Figure 1 suggests, individual performance will be a function of several factors relating to the components of the performance system:

• *Performance specifications:* Have we adequately specified and communicated the performance we want?

• *Task interference:* Have we removed barriers to effective performance by good job design and by providing any necessary resources?

• *Consequences:* Do the things we do to the performer support the desired output?

• *Feedback:* Does the performer know if his output is on target and, if not, how to get it on target?

• *Knowledge/skill:* Does the per-

former know *how* to produce the output we want? And even if she knows the procedure or the formula, does she have the expertise to *do* it effectively?

• *Individual capacity:* Assuming that the other five factors are adequate, does the performer have the basic physical, mental and emotional capacity to produce the output we're after?

It's critical to understand that consistent performance is a function of all six of these variables, not five out of six. For instance, you can have a group of capable, well-trained workers who know exactly what is expected, face minimal interference and get regular feedback. But if they receive (or perceive) negative consequences when they perform as desired, we will not continue to get the outcomes we want. A classic example

is the outstanding worker who, precisely because he is outstanding, keeps getting loaded up with extra work by his supervisor. If the only noticeable consequence of being outstanding is that you get saddled with more burdens than your comparably paid peers, you'll probably stop performing so well.

This "systems" view gives us a useful framework for troubleshooting performance problems. Instead of saying, "Let's train them," we ask, "Where has the performance system broken down? Which components are inadequate? What do we need to 'fix' in order to fix this problem?" The systems view also helps us design new jobs, new responsibilities and new organizations by urging us to ask, "What components do we need to put in place to support the new output we want?"

Performance, part II

We have now placed the individual in a "loop" of inputs, outputs, consequences and feedback. But the performance environment is not that simple. Each performer most likely is part of a hierarchy of performers, and that hierarchy is part of a function.

For example, a claims representative in our insurance company is part of a hierarchy consisting of a claims supervisor and a claims office manager. This hierarchy is part of the field-claims function.

Each function is expected to produce certain outputs. These are determined by the larger organization, based on its customers' needs. The function's outputs are the results of key business processes to which the function contributes.

For instance, the claims office (field-claims function) must produce a number of outputs, not least of which is "claims settled." This output results primarily from the "claims-handling process." Other business processes that operate within the field-claims function include the "policyholder-inquiry process" and the "claim-filing process." Several jobs might be required to support each process.

The business processes dictate the performance or outputs required of all people in a hierarchy. This is a key point, and not necessarily an intuitive one, so we'll illustrate it.

In our view, the first performer in

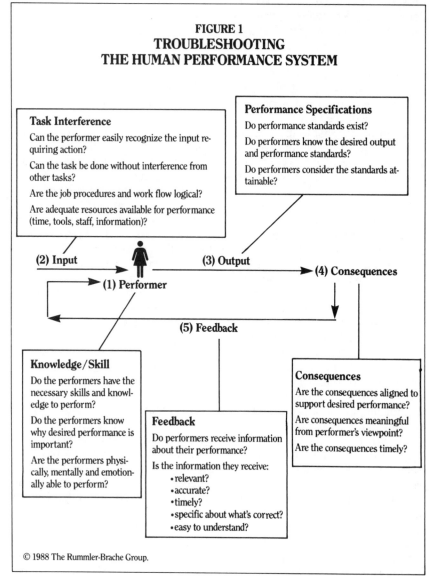

FIGURE 1
TROUBLESHOOTING
THE HUMAN PERFORMANCE SYSTEM

Task Interference

Can the performer easily recognize the input requiring action?

Can the task be done without interference from other tasks?

Are the job procedures and work flow logical?

Are adequate resources available for performance (time, tools, staff, information)?

Performance Specifications

Do performance standards exist?

Do performers know the desired output and performance standards?

Do performers consider the standards attainable?

(2) Input **(3) Output** **(4) Consequences**

(1) Performer

(5) Feedback

Knowledge/Skill

Do the performers have the necessary skills and knowledge to perform?

Do the performers know why desired performance is important?

Are the performers physically, mentally and emotionally able to perform?

Feedback

Do performers receive information about their performance?

Is the information they receive:
• relevant?
• accurate?
• timely?
• specific about what's correct?
• easy to understand?

Consequences

Are the consequences aligned to support desired performance?

Are consequences meaningful from performer's viewpoint?

Are the consequences timely?

the hierarchy, the claims rep, exists to work with the claims-handling process to produce that process's desired output: "claims settled." The specific outputs of the claim rep's job are determined by the requirements of the steps in the claims-handling process.

At the next level of performer, the claims supervisor exists to ensure that the claims rep works effectively with the claims process to produce the same desired output: claims settled. The specific outputs required of the claims supervisor are determined by the interaction of the claims reps and the claims process.

And so it continues. At the third level, the claims office manager exists to ensure that the supervisors provide the support that enable the claims reps and the claims process to be effective. At this level, the manager may be concerned with several hierarchies and a number of major business processes, but the principle is the same: The function manager's core responsibilities are determined by the requirements of the function and the business processes therein.

We have now formed a performance "linkage" for the claims function (see Figure 2). It starts with the requirement for a specific output (claim settled) and links to the requirements of a specific process (claim handling). One step in that process is "loss scoped," which dictates what is required of the claims rep (the first-level performer) and of performers on all higher levels. In other words, our expectations of performers must be linked to the business process that underlies the work they do and to the requirements of that process.

Performance, part III

Now we come to the broadest view of the performance environment. We've seen that the individual is part of a human performance system and part of a hierarchy that is related to a business process that is part of a function. But each process and every function is part of a larger organizational system. The inputs and outputs of all processes and functions are tied to and determined by other functions and by the needs of the organization as a whole.

Furthermore, the organization itself is part of a larger economic environment. A company can be seen as a processing system (Figure 3) that responds and adapts to factors such as the strength of the marketplace, competition, regulations and technological advances. At a macro level, every business exists in a larger performance-system context.

If we visualize our insurance company as a system (Figure 4), we see that the claims function is tied tightly to the product development and underwriting functions. The settlement of claims (that is, the "payout") is not just a function of the claim-handling process and the way it is executed by the people in the claims office. The payout also reflects the quality of the

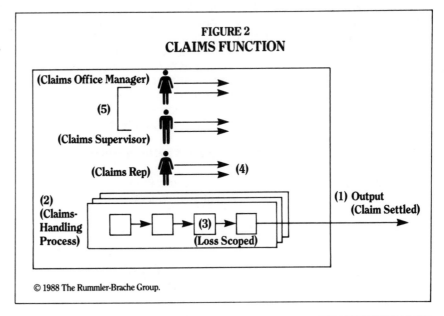

FIGURE 2
CLAIMS FUNCTION

© 1988 The Rummler-Brache Group.

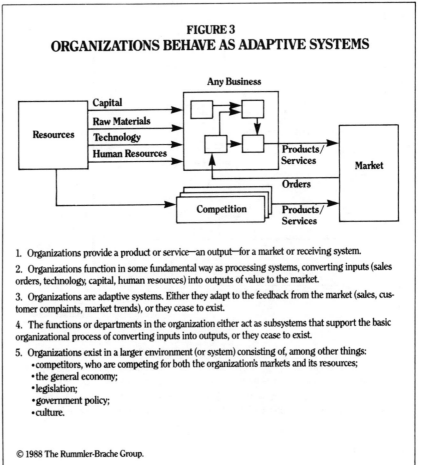

FIGURE 3
ORGANIZATIONS BEHAVE AS ADAPTIVE SYSTEMS

1. Organizations provide a product or service—an output—for a market or receiving system.

2. Organizations function in some fundamental way as processing systems, converting inputs (sales orders, technology, capital, human resources) into outputs of value to the market.

3. Organizations are adaptive systems. Either they adapt to the feedback from the market (sales, customer complaints, market trends), or they cease to exist.

4. The functions or departments in the organization either act as subsystems that support the basic organizational process of converting inputs into outputs, or they cease to exist.

5. Organizations exist in a larger environment (or system) consisting of, among other things:
    • competitors, who are competing for both the organization's markets and its resources;
    • the general economy;
    • legislation;
    • government policy;
    • culture.

© 1988 The Rummler-Brache Group.

policy conceived by the product-development function in the first place, and the rate set by the underwriting function for any given policyholder.

In essence, this systems view of performance breaks down to three levels:

• *The organization level:* The total organization is part of an economic system. It responds to the marketplace, competition, fluctuating resources and so on. At issue is how well the organization is adapting to the demands of this "external system."

• *The process level:* The organization is a giant processing system, converting a range of inputs into products and services for the marketplace. This conversion takes place via a myriad of processes and subprocesses, which must be wired together to form an efficient system. The outputs required of each process are determined by the demands of the marketplace, as interpreted by management. At issue on the process level is whether these are the correct outputs for the business to remain competitive, and whether the internal processes are sufficiently effective and efficient.

• *The individual job level:* Each performer's job outputs are determined by the demands of the various processes. Further, each individual is part of a human performance system. At issue is whether the job outputs have been correctly identified as the ones needed to support the process and whether the performance system will support the employee's efforts to achieve those outputs.

Toward better performance

The idea of those three distinct yet interdependent levels is useful when we try to analyze and improve performance in an organization.

A project intended to improve the performance of an individual or group must start with the question, "What outputs do we want from the job?" To answer, we have to identify the key processes served by the job and understand the demands placed on those processes by the organization. Because we're aware of the components of the basic human performance system, we are interested not just in training solutions but in the feedback and consequences the performers are getting. We're also interested in the feedback the process itself is getting: What consequences does the organization experience as a result of this process being conducted this way? In short, even in a project focusing on the job level, we must consider the larger performance context.

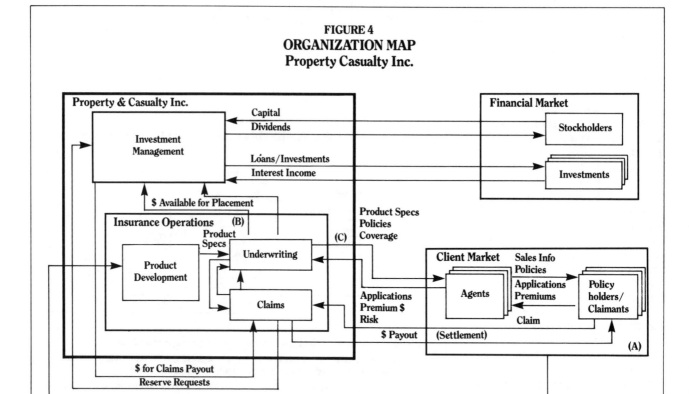

FIGURE 4
ORGANIZATION MAP
Property Casualty Inc.

A. Claims: Calculates the dollar amount of payout based on the specifics of the policy and the actual loss.

B. Product development: Specifies the characteristics of products, including the types of risks covered and under what conditions, the claim-handling process and, in some cases, required minimum payout levels.

C. Underwriting: Evaluates application information (risk) and determines policy price based on coverage requirements and estimated company "exposure" to claims. Underwriting can also reject business that carries excessive risk.

What about a company-wide quality improvement project? This will necessarily begin at the organization level; we'll have to determine the level of quality demanded by the marketplace. But soon our analysis must move to the processes that are key to producing that quality: product design, production, customer billing, etc. What do those processes require? Finally, we'll have to look at the job level to determine the critical outputs we need from various performers and to design a performance system that will support those outputs. In this case, failure to take the analysis all the way down to the job level probably will give us no appreciable increase in quality.

For a project intended to improve a process (filling customer orders, for instance), we would have to determine the organization's demands upon the process, then specify what we'd require of individual performers and what they would require of us. Again, we'd need to operate on all three levels.

This systems view of performance has important implications for the training function. It suggests some things about how we ought to determine training needs, and about how the function in general ought to be managed.

Needs

Let's take another crack at the vice president's request for a refresher course on handling claims and scoping damage.

If we believe in the systems view of performance, we are skeptical. Would such a training program make a significant difference? We have no idea. So we ask six questions (Figure 5):

1. *What performance output (of the function or the organization) is subpar? In other words, what makes you think you have a need for training?*

Our claim payouts are too high, and it takes too long to settle claims.

2. *What process affects this function's performance? What process outputs are subpar?*

Claim payouts are affected by the product development, underwriting and claims-handling processes. Settlement time depends on the claims-handling process. Let's focus on claims handling to begin with.

3. *What process step is breaking down?*

Through observation and interviews with claims reps and their supervisors, we find that "scoping damage" is not a deficient step in the process. However, the first two steps, "claim qualified" and "claim assigned," are often not handled properly. This seriously affects claim payouts and settlement times.

4. *Which performer in the hierarchy affects the critical process step?*

Through observation of claims reps and their supervisors, we learn that qualifying and assigning claims are duties performed by the claims supervisor, not the rep.

5. *What desired output of this key performer is subpar?*

The supervisors are not properly qualifying claims and assigning them to the reps.

6. *What is the cause of the subpar*

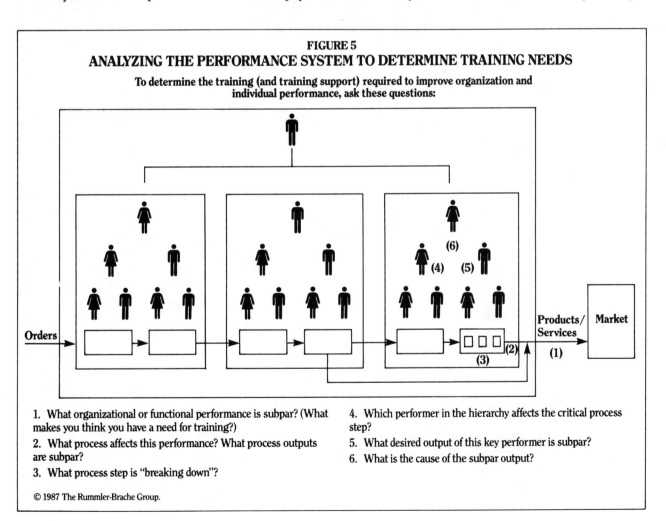

FIGURE 5
ANALYZING THE PERFORMANCE SYSTEM TO DETERMINE TRAINING NEEDS

To determine the training (and training support) required to improve organization and individual performance, ask these questions:

1. What organizational or functional performance is subpar? (What makes you think you have a need for training?)

2. What process affects this performance? What process outputs are subpar?

3. What process step is "breaking down"?

4. Which performer in the hierarchy affects the critical process step?

5. What desired output of this key performer is subpar?

6. What is the cause of the subpar output?

output?

In most cases, the claims supervisors don't know how to qualify and assign claims properly. And in all cases, they get no feedback on this aspect of their performance and perceive no negative consequences for poor performance.

According to the systems view, we haven't identified a significant training need until we have answered those six questions—which is to say, until we have examined the performance system. In this case, we did find a real need for training, but "scoping damage" isn't the topic and claims reps aren't the trainees. We also discovered breakdowns in two other components of the performance system—lack of feedback and negative consequences for poor performance—for which training is not the solution.

Managing it

The systems view of performance has two important implications for managing an organization's training function. The first one dawns on you when you realize that the training function is a subsystem in the larger organizational system, and as such must follow all the system laws. Take another look at Figure 3: The training function exists to meet the needs of its receiving systems or customers (who have to be identified), and it must adapt swiftly to its environment.

The second implication relates to the function's mission. We have described two views of performance, the vacuum view and the systems view. Organizations can choose one or the other. A company that accepts the vacuum view will have a training department that responds to requests for programs (on scoping damage, for instance) by whipping up programs. Regardless of the language it uses in its formal mission statement, we can argue that this training function really sees its mission as "provide skills and knowledge." It will see its outputs, therefore, as "employees trained." The function will be evaluated along feedback loop 1 (Figure 6) in terms of "heads trained per budget dollar." It will get little systematic feedback from its receiving system—the organization's performance environment.

A company that believes in the systems view, on the other hand, will have a training function that responds to requests for training by asking questions. Its mission will be to "improve the organization's performance." Its outputs will be training programs and other performance-improvement initiatives (involving feedback, incentives, job design, etc.). It will be evaluated according to its impact on the organization. It will be able to link its output to the organization's output—that is, to the quality, quantity, value or cost of the company's products and services, and to the efficiency and effectiveness of the performance system.

The choice of missions also will determine the structure of the training function—the processes that drive it. A vacuum-view training function most likely will have three internal processes: course development, course delivery and course evaluation. A systems-view function will require some additional processes, such as: organizational needs analysis (based on the company's strategic, operating and human resource plans); performance analysis; performance improvement initiatives aside from training (for example, design of measurement, feedback and consequence systems).

These processes in turn dictate the kinds of measures required to manage the training function effectively. A function operating according to the systems view will measure its outputs in terms of actual performance improvements noted in individuals, functions and the organization as a whole. It will not be concerned merely with ratings of its training programs.

The processes that drive the training function also determine the kinds of people needed to manage and staff it. A systems-view function requires "performance analysts" and organization development specialists in addition to instructors and instructional designers.

In a nutshell, an organization's view of performance—whether it adheres to the vacuum view or the systems view—will determine the mission of its training function, how it goes about identifying training needs, the operating components of the training function (its units and processes) and how much impact the function will have on the organization's performance.

Reprinted from TRAINING, September 1988

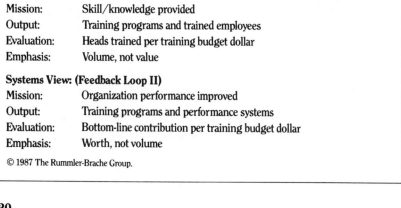

FIGURE 6
ALTERNATIVE VIEW OF THE TRAINING FUNCTION

Vacuum View: (Feedback Loop I)

Mission:	Skill/knowledge provided
Output:	Training programs and trained employees
Evaluation:	Heads trained per training budget dollar
Emphasis:	Volume, not value

Systems View: (Feedback Loop II)

Mission:	Organization performance improved
Output:	Training programs and performance systems
Evaluation:	Bottom-line contribution per training budget dollar
Emphasis:	Worth, not volume

© 1987 The Rummler-Brache Group.

WHY THEY DON'T DO WHAT WE TRAIN THEM TO

When trainees aren't performing what they learned—perhaps it's time to add more elements that increase transfer of training

BY J. REGIS McNAMARA

As the issue of accountability becomes more important in human resources development, the question of what training accomplishes becomes increasingly relevant. Of particular concern is the impact training programs have on individuals back on the job. In other words, how much transfer of training or generalization (terms used synonymously here) took place? Transfer of training effects can be considered to occur when the relevant aspects of behavior altered under one condition or in one setting carry over in some form to non-training conditions or settings. Transfer occurs, then, when trainees do what you trained them to do, where and when you hoped they would do it.

A system I believe can assist trainers in developing programs with more transfer elements in them is based on the Training, Resource, Assessment, Intervention and Network System, or TRAINS. A TRAINS analysis begins with a thorough examination of all elements connected with the training experience.

Training component analysis

The impetus for most training endeavors develops from the assumptions and models used in constructing a training experience. To analyze this component for transfer, the conceptual underpinnings of the training experience should be identified and assessed for their soundness in relation to achieving transfer objectives. A number of concerns related to this issue need be explored. The first question to pose is whether the training is derived from a *unimodal* or *multimodal* orientation. A management training program derived from behavior modification principles would be considered a unimodal system, whereas one that was jointly predicated on humanistic and behavioristic concepts is developed from a multimodal orientation. Unimodal systems are easier to deal with than those derived from a diversity of perspectives and viewpoints because of their greater theoretical integrity; also they usually have generated more extensive empirical evidence addressing the issue of external validity or generalization.

In unimodal systems, questions about what kind of discrepancies exist between the transfer procedures used to conduct a program and those implied by the theory are of particular concern.[1] An important associated issue is how discrepancies, when they occur, might influence the magnitude of desired transfer effects. For example, using a behaviorally based personalized system of instruction, more generalization in the use of concepts is achieved if the concepts are first defined, then elaborated on and finally worked through by learners using a concept formation program.[2] Failing to incorporate these elements into this type of instructional system may compromise generalization. For example, a program designed to enhance the counseling skills of trainees may be consistently derived theoretically. But its ability to change actual behavior in the counseling situation could be limited if the theory was developed to influence cognitive structures and attitudes of the counselee toward others.

Training is an eclectic field, where diverse orientations, philosophies and activities are accepted, and it is not unusual to encounter training programs that combine elements in ways that might seem, from a single perspective, unusual or perhaps even discordant. These multimodal systems pose vexing evaluation problems. When ideas from a social learning model, communication's theory and humanistic philosophy are tied together with the inspirational intuition of a program originator, an experiential tangle can be the end result. This is not to suggest that such a combination does not work from a participant's point of view, because it frequently does. It simply implies that the diverse orientations will contribute unevenly to the production of generalization effects. Whatever benefits might be evidenced from using procedures derived from one source probably will be compromised by adding less effective or counterproductive elements from another source. The synergism resulting from combining diverse theoretical orientations rarely enhances transfer effects, though the *chicken-soup, or the-more-ingredients-the-better, theory of training* asserts the opposite.

Resource component assessment

Social factors and the physical training environment both influence transfer. The characteristics of both participants and trainers are one of these elements. One critical question pertaining to trainers is how much visibility, contact and influence they currently have and potentially will have in the post-training environment. To the extent that trainers are isolated from the rest of the organization, their ability to extend the gains made during training to other relevant organizational settings is unlikely to occur. If this situation exists, then it may be necessary to recruit, on a short-term basis, surrogate trainers from those settings to which the participants will return. By virtue of their continued presence around participants before, during and after training, surrogates are likely to provide relevant social support for the newly acquired behavior in the appropriate organizational setting. Even if trainers are well integrated into other aspects of organizational functioning, a variety of trainers should be employed to increase transfer possibilities.

Personal investment and a feeling of some ownership of training content by significant participating figures in the transfer environment also contribute to successful generalization. When individuals with social and administrative influence participate

431

A TRAINER'S GLOSSARY: BEHAVIOR MODIFICATION

When Benjamin Franklin was a colonel of the Pennsylvania militia, he had a "training" problem. The soldiers weren't attending Sunday services. Rather than lay down the law or chastise the troops, Franklin turned over dispersement of the rum ration to the chaplin. Attendance was no longer a problem. When Franklin's parson began passing out the rum after Sunday services, he was practicing an art referred to variously as **positive reinforcement management, behavioral engineering, operant conditioning, behavior modification, contingency management,** or any of a dozen or so terms meant to describe the process of managing behavior through the systematic use of positive reinforcement.

Parents have always known that a behavior followed by certain consequences (sometimes incorrectly lumped together as "rewards") will continue to be exhibited until it is no longer reinforced. Grandma's law of "work first, then play" is as old as Adam.

What *is* new is the systematic and willful use of a number of "Grandma's laws," old and new, to control many aspects of behavior. The basic premise is that the consequences of a behavior shape the behavior. If the result is aversive, there is less likelihood that the behavior will be repeated; if the results of the behavior are favorable to the behaver, the likelihood of the behavior being repeated is increased. That may seem a complicated way to say good things increase behavior and bad things decrease behavior. But b'mod or operant conditioning isn't that simple. There are five consequences which can possibly follow any behavior. Each has a different effect on the possibility that the behavior will be repeated (see table).

There are some surprises in the table. For example, **punishment** doesn't have a predictable effect on behavior. This invariably is proved by research. Punishment is generally followed by emotional behavior, which neither increases nor decreases the chances that the target behavior will occur again. The only sure way to decrease a behavior is to follow it with an **extinction** procedure, i.e., by doing nothing. It seems so simple. Just pick the behavior you want to see promoted and go promote it. Not that easy. First, what is a reinforcer? Sure, rest for the weary, food for the hungry, activity for the bored, and liquid for the thirsty are all reinforcers, but they are also products of deprivation and we can't fool with **primary needs**.

Fortunately, **secondary reinforcers** are a possibility. When some neutral, non-reinforcing stimulus is repeatedly associated with a primary reinforcer, the formerly neutral stimulus takes on the ability to reinforce. Example: Money is used to purchase things which are primary reinforcers, so money becomes a reinforcer—as long as it still has purchasing power. But even the power of secondary reinforcement is limited, and the guideline for finding usable reinforcing stimuli is often best characterized by the maxim "different strokes for different folks and different ways on different days." Letting the behaver choose his own reinforcer—a process called contracting—is sometimes the only practical solution.

That leads us to a slight procedural problem. To reinforce a behavior, the behavior must occur. In some instances, we can simply wait until the target shows up and then make something "good" happen for the performer. Catch your kids being "good," pass out the positives, and, chances are, they will be "good" again. "Good" in this case defies definition; it's a matter of values and ethics, not technology. This waiting strategy is, alas, useless in many training situations. You can wait forever for your trainee to make his first computer program, but you'll never have anything to reinforce. Instead, you simply will have to reinforce the nearest approximation of the target behavior and then work toward the final target in a stepwise fashion. This is called **shaping**. It is pretty expensive in terms of time to be constantly reinforcing the target behavior. Fortunately, a process called **schedules of reinforcement** helps somewhat. A helpful surprise represented on the table is: A behavior which is only occasionally reinforced *after* it has been shaped into the desired form is more resilient to extinction (going away) than behavior which is reinforced after every occurrence. Don't be fooled, though: The reciprocal cost of getting a desired behavior where none now exists isn't cheap. Reinforcement isn't a something-for-nothing affair. You get when you give. If you stop giving, you eventually stop getting. Remember the story about the two canny rats in the Skinner box? One says to the other, "Look how well I've got this jerk trained. Every time I push the lever he serves up a meal." The only reinforcement system which lasts is the one based on mutual benefit.

Reprinted from TRAINING, June 1976

CONSEQUENCE	CALLED	EFFECT ON POSSIBLE REOCCURRENCE OF TARGET BEHAVIOR
nothing	extinction	decrease in likelihood
something good occurs	positive reinforcement	increase in likelihood
something good withdrawn	punishment	unpredictable
something aversive occurs	punishment	unpredictable
something aversive withdrawn	negative reinforcement	increase

in the development of the goals and objectives of the training experience, they feel more committed to carry through on transfer objectives and influence others to achieve similar results.

Another critical factor to assess is whether there is considerable hostile, negative or unconstructive sentiment among the participants for any particular training experience. If there is, transfer will be minimal. If the critical mass of negative opinion is not neutralized or balanced by careful participant selection during training, then participants will either be uninfluenced by the transfer program or will attempt to undermine it by poor role modeling and verbal innuendo. This aspect is particularly important to understand when the program in question deals with potentially emotional or controversial subjects, such as race relations, social skills training or performance counseling.

Trainers and participants are bound together by the social climate created during training. A persistent problem that compromises transfer effects is the special emphasis placed on developing social and emotional response patterns that are most adaptive within the training program itself.[3] Too often, participants conform to the demands of training, because it is functional to do so. Once these demands are removed, other factors influence a person's response, such as work load, new organizational priorities and so on. Examination of the discrepancy that exists between the social climate created *during* training and that which exists in the primary work setting of the participant is important. Large discrepancies between the two social climates decrease the likelihood of transfer, while small discrepancies increase the possibility of transfer effects.

Similar training and transfer physical environments are also important. Two aspects of the training environment should be considered— the physical space provided for training and the resources contained in the training space. The more common and salient stimuli that exist in the training and transfer environment, the greater the likelihood that generalization will occur. One way to accomplish this is by "vestibule training": on-the-job problems or situations along with their physical characteristics are recreated in the classroom.[4]

Assessment component analysis

All program assessment can be divided into two types— process and outcome. Process-oriented assessments are structured to collect information on what happens to people undergoing a training experience. And outcome approaches focus on the changes (both positive and negative) that happen to the individual and/or organization as a result of training. Both types of assessment are frequently used to evaluate the success of a training effort. Neither of these assessment techniques to promote and better understand transfer effects is used often enough.

There are several issues associated with the selection and use of assessment methodology. A fundamental concern associated with drawing conclusions from assessment is whether the instruments or procedures chosen will reliably detect change back on the job. Since assessment for transfer will, by definition be conducted some time after training and in an environment different from that of training, the procedures used must demonstrate situational relevance and temporal stability. Relevance is established by identifying whether the measures used to assess the beliefs, behaviors or attitudes during training are likely to detect these same characteristics in the transfer setting. The selection of particular dependent measures has differential utility for establishing outcomes related to transfer effects.[5] For instance, both video recordings and direct observations of selling behavior may be made during training. But when these same procedures are used in the field, in the presence of customers, the nature of the selling situation is likely to change so dramatically that an accurate representation of transfer to the field situation could not be made.

In order to strengthen transfer, special assessment procedures must be used. For example, an assessment strategy that can be used for both process and outcome purposes, as well as to promote transfer effects, is a self-monitoring data collection and feedback system. By recording their own behavior each day, individuals are motivated to change and progress, thus, positive change can be maintained in the transfer environment. Keeping track, in a diary, of the number of times employees are praised for their accomplishments reminds the supervisor to use principles of positive reinforcement taught during training. It also illustrates how dispensing such reinforcement affects improvement.

When self-monitoring systems are occasionally supplemented by means of external surveillance systems (which can corroborate or extend the information gathered by self-monitoring), even more sustained maintenance can be expected. One way to accomplish this is by having the employees also keep track of the amount of praise they receive from the supervisor. Periodic comparisons can be made to determine the correspondence between the two sources. The use of more automatic devices, such as television monitors, personal telemeters and electrical or mechanical counters, would also serve the same function.

Finally, we should consider the following factors when using assessment to promote transfer. First, how reactive are the procedures with the characteristic being measured? That is, will the mere process of having the behavior measured produce a predictable change in it? Second, are the cues associated with the assessment in the transfer environment obvious enough to remind individuals about their behavior? And is the feedback from the assessment delivered at appropriate intervals and in a practical way? And, third, are consequences provided to groups or individuals for meeting or failing to sustain adequate performance standards in the transfer environment? This last issue relates to the establishment of performance standards in the transfer setting and the creation of a motivational system that allows individuals to meet these standards. To the extent that much variation in transfer behavior is permissable, individually determined goals and reinforcement systems are acceptable.

Intervention component analysis

The procedures and operations used during training to create generalization are critical to the transfer process. For instance, the diversity, variety and novelty of tasks, responses and problems presented during training assist transfer.[6] Providing an adequate number of informational stimuli, as well as teaching sufficiently varied responses to them, is important. An underused method for programming generalization is to do the training in a number of organizational settings. For example, subgroups can be simultaneously trained in different environments with appropriate sequencing between them until training is completed; or the whole group can serially pass through training presentations in different settings. Both these approaches increase the logistical problems of scheduling and staffing, but they increase the transfer effects by weakening the association between the behavior learned and the environment it was learned in.

Although immediate reinforcement for correct responding is usually the operation of choice to facilitate a learner acquiring a new response, intermittent and delayed reinforcement ultimately assure better generalization. Thus during the latter part of training, both feedback and reinforcement should be delayed over time and varied in their amount so that the learner will maintain a reasonable level of persistence. This thinning of reinforcement and feedback to small amounts and at lengthy or unpredictable intervals approximates the usual state of affairs in most organizational environments.

The use of cues and consequences to bring forth generalized responses and then maintain them in the transfer environment is important, too. Written and verbal instructions form the principal basis for most cueing (or signaling of what comes next) that exists in organizations. The development of a commitment to perform in the post-training environment can be fostered through the use of contingency contracts,[7] while the use of policy control procedures[8] can assure that the postraining behavior may be maintained through administrative means.

Consequences are those events that happen to a person after a behavior is performed. Positive consequences or reinforcement increases the likelihood that the behavior would be exhibited in the future; negative consequences or punishment decreases this likelihood. Those consequences that are useful during training— a passing grade in an examination or a certificate of attendance— may be entirely worthless in maintaining the behavior in the transfer setting. Therefore, it's important to identify payoffs in the transfer setting that are known to motivate employees effectively and to make these conse-

quences contingent on the transfer behavior.

The transfer effectiveness of the procedures used to promote facts, skills and concepts presented during training also must be established. Generalization of factual material involves the ability to recall pertinent information at a later time in different surroundings. An effective way to enhance recall during training is to provide the participant with a set of retrieval cues and plans for the material to be recalled. A mnemonic scheme based on a memorized list of words associated with information to be recalled would be appropriate here. The use of live or videotape models to simulate the behavior as it will occur in the transfer setting is essential for skill carry-over. For concept generalization, an approach combining guided and discovery learning seems applicable. Using these combined procedures, participants are initially taught about the task; later on, they are allowed, through trial and error, to find out the answers for themselves.

Network component analysis

An examination of the arrangement and sequencing among the components in TRAINS is the focus in this part of the system. The adequacy of the linkages established between each component should be explored, with special attention being given to how each component complements and strengthens the influence of the other. The identification and removal of incompatible and counterproductive arrangements is of particular concern. The network analysis puts into perspective the entire transfer effort of the program and determines the effort's consistency and integrity. The network analysis finally attempts to balance transfer needs against other program and organizationally related factors, such as initial program learning, feasibility and

cost/benefit to the organization.

Conclusion

Our knowledge of how to create transfer and generalization effects from training have reached a stage where formal recommendations for the use of such a technology is warranted.[9] The TRAINS system examines factors that have been identified as important in training programs. How widespread and effective the use of TRAINS becomes, however, will depend on two factors. First is the extent to which the ideas contained in TRAINS are incorporated into training programs. The second relates to the support this system receives from research that demonstrates its incremental benefit over other transfer systems and models.

Reprinted from TRAINING, February 1980

REFERENCES

1. Leidecker, J.K., and J.J. Hall, "Motivation: Good theory— Poor application." *Training and Development Journal*, 1974, 28, 3-7.
2. Miller, L.K., and F.H. Weaver, "A behavioral technology for producing concept information in university students." *Journal of Applied Behavioral Analysis*, 1976, 9, 289-300.
3. Miller, F.D. "The problem of transfer of training in learning groups. Group cohesion as an end in itself." *Small Group Behavior*, 1976, 7, 221-236.
4. Luthans, F., and R. Kreitner, *Organizational Behavior Modification*, Glenview, IL: Scott Foresman, 1975.
5. McNamara, J.R., "Ways by which outcome measures influence outcomes in classroom behavior modification research." *Journal of School Psychology*, 1975, 13, 104-113.
6. Gagne, R.M., and L.J. Briggs, *Principles of instructional design*. New York: Holt, 1974.
7. Homme, L., A.P. Csanyi, M.A. Gonzales, and J.R. Richs, *How to use contingency contracting in the classroom*. Champaign, IL: Research Press, 1970.
8. Andrasik, F., J.R. McNamara, and D.M. Abbott, "Policy control: A low resource intervention for improving staff behavior." *Journal of Organizational Behavior Management*, 1978, 1, 125-133.
9. Stokes, T.F. and D.M. Baer, "An implicit technology of generalization. *Journal of Applied Behavior Analysis*, 1977, 10, 349-367.

LET'S GET RID OF THE TRAINING DEPARTMENT

A primer on performance improvement—with a twist

BY JEFF FIERSTEIN

Let's get rid of the training department. I don't mean we should cut out the function or reduce its budget or staff. I mean, once and for all, let's get our labels straight—right there on the department's door and on the company's organizational chart—by putting training in its proper perspective. Let's present it to the rest of the organization the way we present it to ourselves in our textbooks. Then maybe we'll finally start to *do* it the way we keep saying it ought to be done.

Training, we say, is just one possible remedy for performance problems, one tool in the performance engineer's tool kit. Very well. Let's get rid of the training department and make training one function—one division, if you will—of the "performance management department."

The rationale? Training is an intervention whose purpose is to establish, improve or maintain competent work behavior. It's a means, not an end. Employers don't want well-trained employees, they want employees who do their jobs well. Training won't necessarily give them that. It's only one of many things an organization can do to assure competent performance. We need the whole tool kit, not just one tool.

Dugan Laird, in his classic book *Approaches to Training and Development*, offers four additional interventions: feedback, contingency management, job engineering and organization development. A performance management department that used all of these options skillfully and appropriately would begin to make some real impact.

Laird did not depict his performance interventions as different boxes in an organizational chart, but Figure 1 shows what that chart might look like. We're really talking about the functions our performance management department would perform, rather than entirely separate divisions, but the chart makes the point that training is only one of the things we do. Maybe we ought to paint it on the wall—not so much for the edification of the rest of the organization, but as a reminder to ourselves.

How many of our classic failures to achieve lasting performance improvements through training would vanish if we actually became *accountable* for using the whole tool kit? For better or worse (depending on our own knowledge and abilities), our performance management department would have that accountability.

How would each of the department's five divisions operate? The literature on performance improve-ment has been telling us for years.

Division of training

The function of our training division is to give employees the knowledge and skills they need to achieve or maintain competent performance on the job. We only provide training when we are convinced that deficient performance is due to a lack of skills or knowledge—not to some other factors in the work environment. Here are some questions that must be answered each time we face the decision of whether or not to train:

● *Is training the appropriate intervention?* And even if it might be appropriate, is it the *best* intervention we can use for the performance problem?

● *Is the training itself effective?* We'll need a full quality-control function to ensure we're teaching the right things in the right way to achieve measurably improved performance back on the job.

● *How do we transfer training to the job?* This is clearly a performance management problem, not just the training division's problem. Trainees and their managers will have to help plan and execute the skills transfer.

● *How do we ensure that the right performance continues over time?* Another performance management problem.

● *Is the problem worth the training it would take to solve it?* We wouldn't spend $100,000 to fix a $50,000 problem, now would we?

Here are the functions our training division will perform: Identify problem or need; analyze problem or need; select training as the appropriate intervention; develop performance-based objectives; develop instruction; develop performance-based evaluation methods; design (with trainees and their managers) transfer-of-training implementation; deliver instruction; evaluate instructional effectiveness; evaluate transfer-of-training.

Division of feedback

Since the functions of our other four divisions are a little less familiar, let's put our performance management department in a hypothetical organization.

An accrediting agency just completed a licensing survey of Oedipus

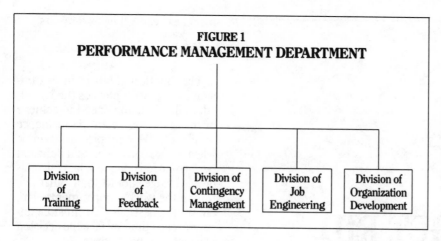

FIGURE 1
PERFORMANCE MANAGEMENT DEPARTMENT

Division of Training | Division of Feedback | Division of Contingency Management | Division of Job Engineering | Division of Organization Development

Memorial Psychiatric Hospital. One area in which the hospital was cited as below standard was that of patient charting. Entries are made on patient charts by a variety of staff members—doctors, nurses and paraprofessionals known as mental health technicians. And it seems that charting is being handled differently in the hospital's various clinical units. For example, some charting is done in a loose, narrative style: The staff members write down general impressions of the patient's condition during a particular time. People in other units favor a more behavioral style, recording on the chart specific things the patient said or did.

The accrediting agency's citation recommended that all hospital staff members who make entries on patients' charts use the same method and that specific standards for quality charting be developed.

Because Oedipus Memorial's administrators felt that this was a training need (they assumed the staff didn't know *how* to keep charts in the correct way), the project was assigned to the training department. Over the next three months, trainers met with representatives from the various units to develop a single charting procedure and quality standards to apply to it. Everybody was then trained in the new procedures and standards, and sent off to perform competently. (After all, the program was competency-based. Ninety-five percent of the trainees demonstrated proficiency—in class—on at least 90 percent of the procedures.)

Three months later, the training department performed an audit of patient charts to see how effective the training had been. Lo and behold! More than 90 percent of the staff had reverted to the old, familiar methods.

What went wrong? A little study uncovered a *feedback* problem. People weren't being told how well they were performing their charting duties. They didn't know if they were keeping good charts, average charts or inadequate charts. And even if they cared, nobody could remember what was considered good, average or poor performance. "It's been a long time since the training program and there was so much to be done managing the units that...well, we've put that stuff on the back burner," the trainers were told.

Within the performance management department, the division of feedback will be responsible for ensuring that all employees receive necessary information about:

• Performance output targets: What and how much are they supposed to produce or accomplish within what time frames?

• Standards of quality work performance: What does quality performance look like, and what levels of quality are acceptable?

• Their actual performance compared to those standards and targets.

• Deviations from or deficiencies in acceptable work procedures.

• Their own development over time (performance planning and appraisal).

• Any changes in targets, standards or expectations.

The feedback division will be held accountable for making sure that newly acquired training doesn't go down the drain because performers aren't receiving appropriate and effective feedback. Obviously, the division can't do this without the cooperation of managers throughout the organization.

Division of contingency management

The function of this division is to ensure that on-the-job consequences of workers' actions reinforce work behaviors—positively and negatively. More simply, the contingency management division ensures that employees are rewarded for doing things back on the job the way they learned to do them in training courses and corrected (or "punished") when they do things the wrong way. If this happens, the skills built in training courses are far more likely to become habitual, rather than to deteriorate over time.

Let's back up a bit. Having learned its lesson from the charting fiasco,

---

Trainers must always keep one eye on the ripple effects— reverberations—of training and performance changes.

Oedipus Memorial established a regular audit and feedback system. Through formal audits, each unit was provided with feedback showing its charting performance compared to the established standards. Each individual employee received similar performance feedback regularly.

However, three months later (six months after the training) the training division did another audit of the unit charts and discovered that the 90 percent error rate on charting had dropped only to 75 percent.

"*Now* what's wrong?" the trainers wondered. "Good training backed by an effective feedback system ought to have given us practically perfect charts by now." Off they went to the units to study the natives in their natural habitats.

The observers noticed that unit staff members spent a great deal of time in the medical records department. Soon they discovered that these people were being sent to the records department to fix the errors they had made in the charts of patients previously discharged. But why were so many coming to medical records so often? Here's what the trainers found out:

• Being sent to medical records got employees off the unit for a "break."

• Fixing charting mistakes had become a social opportunity—an excuse for people to mingle and chat.

• Going to the records department provided a chance to take care of other personal business in the same part of the building (for example, stopping in at personnel to drop off an insurance claim).

• Nothing seemed to happen to people who made lots of charting errors. They got feedback, all right—they *knew* they made a lot of charting errors. But they were treated exactly the same as everyone else. In other words, there were no negative consequences for poor performance.

All in all, it actually paid to make errors in charts. If you did it wrong, you were rewarded with breaks, companionship and a chance to take care of personal business. If you did it right, you lost out on those little benefits—and gained nothing except the knowledge that you were following the officially approved paperwork procedures. It wasn't hard to see how people who did it right might start feeling like suckers.

After much discussion about the situation, Oedipus' management decided it would be smarter to reward desired behavior instead of undesired behavior. So "correct charting procedures" became an item on each employee's performance appraisal form. Administrators leaned on unit directors to get them to lean on their people about charting errors. And the social club in the medical records department was broken up.

Functions of the contingency management department:

• Analyze the job environment to identify and help eliminate negative consequences for desired behavior and positive consequences for undesired behavior.

• Help managers establish performance contingencies (consequences) to maximize positive consequences for desired behavior and ensure negative consequences (and remedial help) for undesired behavior.

• Design a positive consequence

system to transfer and maintain new skills learned through training.

Division of job engineering

During the training program, a few of the mental health technicians were unable to master the charting skills. The obvious cause of the deficiency was illiteracy. These people simply could not read or write at a level nec-

---

**Lo and behold!
More than 90 percent
of the staff
had reverted to
the old methods.**

---

essary to complete the training. They were among the original staff at Oedipus Memorial when it opened 20 years ago as a nursing home. All were competent, valued employees who had worked their way through the ranks into positions that required charting skills. The training department's investigation uncovered an abnormally high rate of charting errors by this group, as well as a high rate of non-performance (they wouldn't make entries on the charts at all or would have others do their charting for them).

It seemed to management that the first logical step would be to send these employees to a basic literacy program to improve their reading and writing skills. Further investigation revealed, however, that a six- to 12-month training period would be required to get most of them up to minimum levels required to perform their charting correctly. This wasn't acceptable, since both patient care and cash flow were jeopardized by the employees' current deficiency (insurance companies refuse to pay for patient care until they're happy with the copies of the charts they receive).

The next logical suggestion was to fire these technicians or transfer them to jobs that required lower-level literacy skills. But all of them were highly experienced employees and were considered good care givers by patients and supervisors. Charting

was a small, albeit important, part of their jobs, and it was the only task with which they had a problem.

Finally, the answer dawned. Change the job: Create a new job category for employees who provide direct care to patients but are not required to do any charting. The real problem here, management decided, was with the job classification system, which demanded that all mental health technicians handle charting duties. In fact, it wasn't necessary for *everyone* to do it. Enter our division of job engineering, which is responsible for changing the way jobs are defined and performed.

Sometimes neither training, feedback nor contingency management can effectively solve a performance deficiency. The job itself may be too complex—or too simple, repetitive and boring—for the desired level of performance to occur. In such cases, job engineering can be applied to enrich, simplify or specialize a job.

Of course, the first question the job engineer must answer is whether the job *ought* to be changed. Sometimes we have simply selected the wrong employee for the job. It is better for the organization to transfer or terminate the employee than to tinker with the job description.

Division of organization development

Performance can be greatly influenced by the structure, processes, culture and goals of the organization. For example, an organization with a highly competitive culture is probably throwing its money away when it sends some employees to a team-building course just because team building is fashionable.

Sometimes it is the organization itself that imposes barriers to improving performance via training, feedback, contingency management or whatever. Suppose a corporation has a number of branch operations competing in the same city for the same clients. Suppose it decides to restructure those operations into cooperative (and specialized) units. Some team building and communication training will be desirable—but it probably won't be effective until many aspects of the corporate culture change from competitive to cooperative. To bring that about, our organization development division will have to identify and implement some systemic changes within the organization.

Trainers must always keep one eye on the ripple effects—the reverberations—of training and performance changes. Improving performance in one area of the organization can have unanticipated effects on others, because an organization is a collection of interdependent *systems*. Training and performance must be consistent with the culture and goals of the organization or, if not, should be part of a larger planned change intended to modify the culture or goals.

The organization development division's job is to:

• Identify the consequences of training and performance changes on the organizational system and subsystems.

• Ensure the congruence of training and performance change with organizational culture and goals or,

• Ensure the congruence of training and performance change with a planned change effort.

A comprehensive approach

The five interventions we have looked at here often are found scattered in organizations. They are seldom combined effectively into one area that resembles our performance management department.

As for those of you who groaned mightily at the beginning of this article ("Oh, no! Not another yo-yo who thinks problems will disappear if we change the labels—like they disappeared when we switched from 'training' to 'human resources development' ")... well, I agree that the crucial step is not to change the name of the training department—although

it wouldn't hurt. We needn't push for a "performance management department" at all, provided we're able to integrate these five functions *somehow* to accomplish the goal of ensuring the impact of training on successful work performance. It probably *can* be done through a cooperative working relationship among the various areas of the organization responsible for each of the functions (for example, human resources, industrial engineering, organization development, training and management).

But this sort of integration ought to be common today in organizations where the functions are scattered. Instead, it's extremely rare. Maybe consolidation is the answer. A performance management department that lived up to its name would be a mighty force indeed.

Reprinted from TRAINING, June 1988

NINE WAYS TO MAKE TRAINING PAY OFF ON THE JOB

If the skills you teach in class don't get
used on the job, maybe you've got
one of these problems

BY RUTH COLVIN CLARK

Ever observe a group of trainees a month or two after they emerged from your training program? Are the skills they learned in class being used on the job? Does your organization have a workable system for following up on its training efforts to see whether they result in better performance in the real world of the workplace?

Even after an excellent class, training frequently fails to pay off in behavioral changes on the job: Trainees go back to work and do it the way they've always done it instead of the way you taught them to do it. The phenomenon is called transfer failure. It happens because skills do not transfer automatically into job performance. In other words, the fact that you have learned how to do something a certain way doesn't necessarily mean you'll do it that way. Since the point of job-related training is to improve performance on the job, transfer failure obviously defeats the whole purpose.

Why does training—solid, effective training—fail to transfer? There are a number of reasons. Here are nine typical situations and some tips on how the problems could have been avoided.

1. Rocking the boat

A supervisor in the documentation services department previewed a training program on structured writing techniques. The program taught an unusual method for formatting written material. The supervisor liked the approach and sent four of his writers to the course. They came back to work and designed a new policy manual using the techniques they had learned. When the department manager saw the result, she promptly vetoed it on grounds that its unique appearance would draw criticism from other managers in the organization. The supervisor pointed out the advantages of the new method, but the department head was adamant. "We haven't turned out anything like that before," she said. "Things have been going smoothly up to now. Let's not rock the boat."

Solution: The supervisor just discovered—too late—that his own department manager, as well as other managers and supervisors, should have previewed the course with him. Front-end consultation and approval by all interested parties would have prevented tail-end failure.

Management advisory committees can be formed to set policy and to help review training courses while they're still in the development stage—or before they are purchased. If a proposed program is scrapped due to lack of management commitment, better it should happen early, before a lot of dollars are invested.

2. Mismatching courses and needs

The manager of a data processing center met a training vendor who demonstrated a very impressive course on prototyping. The DP manager asked the training department to send all employees to the course. However, the techniques applied only to about 25% of the employees who were building new applications. The other 75% were working on maintenance projects that did not require the use of prototyping techniques.

Solution: Match courses to needs systematically. Curricula that reflect the ideas of one or several line managers, working independently and sporadically, tend to be fragmented and counterproductive. Training should flow from two primary sources: 1) a validated analysis of current job tasks and the skills required to perform them and, 2) a model of the future technological directions of the organization, agreed upon by upper management.

To conduct a job analysis, first identify all major tasks and required skills. Then ask a sample of the employees currently in the job (and their supervisors) to rate the importance and complexity of each skill as well as their current proficiency in it. Concurrently, ask top managers to rate the same skills on the basis of their importance in meeting departmental objectives. Training priorities should be based on skills perceived as high in importance by managers and rated low in competency by employees and their supervisors.

This job analysis will only identify *current* skill needs. In any rapidly evolving technological environment you also will need to identify new technological applications to supplement the job analysis. Finally, the people in charge of training should have access to top management's strategic plans for the future so that appropriate training will be in place when needed.

3. Supervisory slipups

The organization offers classes on time management and other generic skills. These programs are in heavy demand, and supervisors sign up their subordinates months ahead of

439

time. When a given employee's turn finally arrives, the supervisor sometimes has forgotten why the individual was supposed to go to that particular class in the first place. Small wonder that supervisors rarely take the time to discuss the training with their people, either before or after the class. Supervisors are counting exclusively on the training department to improve their employees' skills.

Solution: Ultimately it is the supervisor who must be responsible for the work performance of his or her employees. Training is one tool supervisors have to improve that performance. They need to recognize that training only teaches people to do things they don't know how to do: There is no point in sending anybody to a training program unless he lacks a particular skill required by the job.

Instead of abdicating all responsibility to the training department, supervisors can increase the impact of training dramatically by: 1) conducting brief pre- and post-course discussions with employees where they agree on how the skills learned in the program will be applied on the job and, 2) making specific follow-up assignments after the employee returns to be sure that the skills are applied. This is especially important when employees are attending nontechnical training (time management, interpersonal skills, etc.), where the transfer challenge tends to be most difficult.

Busy supervisors will not do these things without a push. The training department should help them by teaching them *how* to handle those pre- and post-course activities. In addition, second-level managers should be persuaded to include planning and implementation of employee training as part of the supervisors' formal job responsibility, to be evaluated in regular performance appraisals. In other words, supervisors must be taught how to play their crucial role in training and they must be held accountable for playing it.

4. Losing track of what training employees need

In the data processing department, supervisors typically have responsibility for 10 to 20 employees at different job levels working on various project teams. In constructing their training plans, supervisors generally refer to the training catalog and use their best judgment to assign training to individuals based on their recent performance. But because the supervisors are dealing with a lot of employees who work on varied assignments that involve a large number of different skills, it's difficult to be consistent and accurate in determining each employee's training needs.

Solution: Help supervisors assess and track employees' skills by providing an automated records system. A variety of such systems are available to run on either micro or mainframe

---

Busy supervisors will not do these things without a push.

---

hardware. They can be programmed to list all job-related skills and provide for a competency rating agreed upon by employee and supervisor. When the individual competency ratings are matched against recommended competencies for the particular job, discrepancies are flagged and training options matched to the job skills are generated automatically. These computer programs help supervisors make systematic training plans based on both the requirements of the job and individual assessments of employee skills.

5. Lack of a "critical mass"

Employees of a sales and product-support division were sent to a course on conducting and participating in meetings. But their attendance was staggered over a one-year period. By the time the last of them had attended the class, 10 months had slipped by since the first students had gone. Division supervisors found it very difficult to implement the techniques in real meetings.

Solution: Train intact work groups. Peer group support is a major factor in determining whether newly learned skills will transfer to the job. People are much more likely to do things the new way if everybody in the work group (or at least almost everybody) is trying to do them that way at the same time. When you train only a few people at a time from any particular group, you never develop a "critical mass" of commitment to the new skills. Without that critical mass, the status quo tends to defeat change. Furthermore, if people aren't called upon to use new skills immediately after they learn them, the skills tend to atrophy.

Whenever possible, train entire working groups at the same time. If it isn't practical to train an entire team, try setting up interdepartmental or even intercompany support networks. User groups have been formed around various computer-software applications. Why not set up user groups for other types of training as well?

6. No help applying skills back on the job

During the structured writing class mentioned earlier, most students did very well on the practice exercises they were given—but they had the instructor's help. When they returned to their jobs, the instructor wasn't there. Many had trouble applying the new techniques to actual work assignments. After a few attempts, some became discouraged and reverted to their previous writing styles.

Solution: Extend training beyond the classroom. If an intact work group is learning an important new skill, follow-up training is essential to transferring the skill. Require program graduates to work on a regular project assignment using the techniques they learned. The instructor or someone competent in the new skills should provide follow-up consultation, visiting the trainees and helping them apply the techniques to their unique job assignments. Or, as an alternative, give the graduates an assignment to work on for two weeks on the job. Then schedule transfer sessions where they meet as a group with the instructor, compare results and discuss problems.

7. The external instructor is gone

That writing class was taught by an outside consultant, and it was not feasible to arrange for her to follow up after the class.

Solution: To ensure continuing con-

TRAINING FOLLOW-UP SURVEY

Course Title _____ Dates Attended _____

Company Division (please circle):

    Sales Manufacturing Customer Service Data Processing Other _____

Course Objective _____

(Section above completed by training department.)

- -

A. At the end of this course, to what degree did you feel that you achieved the objective stated above?

VERY LITTLE		MODERATELY		VERY MUCH
1	2	3	4	5

IF YOU CIRCLED BELOW 3 ON QUESTION A, STOP HERE AND RETURN THE QUESTIONNAIRE. OTHERWISE, CONTINUE.

B. Since completing this course, how *often* have you used the skills you learned in class on your job assignments?

RARELY/ NEVER		OCCASIONALLY (MONTHLY)		FREQUENTLY (DAILY)
1	2	3	4	5

C. As a result of this course, how much improvement have you experienced in completing your job assignments?

LITTLE/NO IMPROVEMENT		SOME IMPROVEMENT		MAJOR IMPROVEMENT
1	2	3	4	5

IF YOU ANSWERED QUESTIONS B OR C WITH A 3 OR GREATER, THEN GO ON TO QUESTIONS D AND E. IF YOU ANSWERED QUESTIONS B OR C WITH LESS THAN A 3, THEN GO ON TO QUESTION F.

D. Describe at least three typical ways that you have used the skills you learned in class and how your job performance has improved as a result.

E. Place a check next to each reason below that might explain why you have applied the skills you learned to your job assignments:

_____ My supervisor discussed with me how my new skills would be used on my job assignments.

_____ My supervisor required me to use the new skills.

_____ I received help from others in my work area.

_____ I was given necessary time and/or tools to apply the skills.

_____ I received training at the right time to provide me with the skills when I needed them on the job.

_____ The skills I learned applied directly to my job assignment.

_____ Other: Please list other factors that helped you apply these skills to your job assignments.

F. Place a check next to each reason below that could explain why you have not been successful in applying skills learned to your job assignments:

_____ My supervisor did not require me to use the skills.

_____ My supervisor did not agree with the skills I learned.

_____ My supervisor was not aware of what skills I learned.

_____ I was not given time/tools to implement the skills on the job.

_____ There was no one to help me implement the skills in my work area.

_____ The skills did not seem to apply to my job assignment.

_____ My job assignment changed so these skills did not apply.

_____ The training was not timed right for my job assignment.

_____ Other: Please describe other reasons you did not apply the skills to your job assignments:

MEASURE YOUR TRAINING TRANSFER QUOTIENT

Here is a generic survey you could adapt to your own training situation. Send the questionnaire to everyone who has completed a given course within the past six months. (Or, randomly select 100 employees who have completed the course.) Even a 50% response rate will give you a good indication of whether the training transferred to the job. Administer the survey anonymously to ensure honest feedback.

Scoring: Add up the number of responses of "3" or above to both question B and question C (i.e., one person who checks "3" to question C and "4" to question B counts as two responses). Divide by twice the total number of questionnaires returned, and multiply by 100. A score of 80% or better probably means that the skills you're teaching are transferring adequately to the workplace. A score of less than 70% suggests that you need to make some changes.

Reprinted from TRAINING, November 1986

sultation beyond the classroom, consider using internal instructors—or supplementing a consultant's classroom training with an internal expert who can serve the follow-up functions. This may mean asking the consultant to spend extra time with the person who will serve as your internal expert.

8. Training as a "day off"

The training department teaches a variety of courses on supervisory effectiveness. Trainees are required to show up for class, but they aren't evaluated on their performance in the course or back on the job. Practice exercises are voluntary and many trainees choose to skip them. Most of the supervisors listen politely in class. Some ask a few questions. But rarely does anyone invest much effort in acquiring the new skills. A day in training is generally regarded as an opportunity to kick back and drink coffee.

Solution: Build accountability into your training. Competency-based training is built on specific, job-related objectives. Learners must be held accountable for reaching these objectives. Instructors should send a summary of course objectives and the trainee's performance in class to the trainee's supervisor. The organization should demand that all training courses be instructionally valid,

i.e., each course should prove that people who take it and invest reasonable effort will attain the objectives.

If the course is just plain ineffective, the issue of transfer to the workplace becomes irrelevant. Likewise, if learners are not held responsible for

---

Train entire working groups at the same time.

---

investing effort in their own training, even the best instruction will not generate maximum benefits. Accountability in training should address both of these problems.

9. Training is not available when needed

Many organizations rely heavily on classroom training, scheduling courses on some fixed timetable (e.g., quarterly) or when there is sufficient enrollment to justify teaching the class. This means that people may be on waiting lists for several months. Knowing this, supervisors will send employees to courses as the classes become available, even though the employees will not be needing the skills in the near future.

Solution: Consider self-instructional

training. When live classes are scheduled on a body-count basis, there is often a lack of coordination between the timing of the training and the opportunity to apply the skills on the job. Self-instructional courses delivered by workbooks, video or computer-based training provide access to information when it's needed.

The drawback to self-instructional courses is that even when they're well-designed (and a lot of them aren't), they demand a high degree of motivation from the learner. There is no instructor to answer to; learners often start the courses but fail to complete them. An obvious alternative is to build or buy self-instructional courses and supplement them with live tutors to help trainees, give them regular feedback, and measure and report their progress.

All of these "solutions" demand a greater investment of time and resources—both finite quantities—on the part of the training department. You may want to consider offering fewer courses, but investing more effort to enhance transfer: Rather than offering six new courses next year, concentrate on one or two critical programs but build in the pre-course planning and post-course follow up that will help ensure transfer to the job.

Reprinted from TRAINING, November 1986

TEACHING DAILY WORK HABITS AND PATTERNS AIDS TRANSFER

Don't stop at theory. Here are specific steps

BY ROBERT E. KUSHELL

With all the talk these days about MBO, very little thought or attention has been given to the daily habits and work patterns that ultimately affect the success or failure of a particular management plan. It's an unfortunate fact that most people have terrible work habits. They may be aware of what has to be done and may even think they are doing it, but a careful audit of their daily and weekly accomplishments reveals that much valuable time has been wasted on nonproductive details.

Although much has been taught and written on business theory and practice, I know of no training ground where executives can learn the basic work disciplines: how to plan and organize their time effectively; how to develop the specific, small-scale goals necessary to the success of their long-range plans; and how to assess their productivity level accurately. As a result, many executives get bogged down in insignificant details and then wonder why certain production quotas or financial goals have not been met by year's end.

It was this premise that encouraged Dunhill to institute an expanded training program for both experienced and professional employment consultants and franchisees opening new branch offices. Years of observation and placement of middle management executives and technical personnel in a variety of industries have given Dunhill executives an understanding of the abilities and talents necessary for success in the corporate environment. It was only one step further to the application of these observations and techniques to consultants in the 250-office Dunhill System itself.

The expanded training program, developed by Dunhill's Director of Training Joel Palmer, consists of a two-week intensive course required of all new franchisees, plus a follow-up, three-day management seminar. Since its inception one year ago, 51 offices from the Dunhill network have seen a 31% increase in total billings resulting from the management seminar alone. One year ago, only eight new offices out of 43 trained had billings during their first two months of operation. This past year, 25 offices out of 48 trained had billings during their first two months. Since most new franchise offices are managed by people who have never worked in this particular field before, the training is obviously effective.

The Dunhill training program focuses on the work habits, disciplines and procedures necessary for success in the recruitment business, but the techniques can be applied, by extension, to almost any industry. The program was developed originally because Dunhill executives realized that, like most franchisors, we were teaching franchisees what to do to run their new businesses but not really giving them the tools to do it. The problem was critical in the case of Dunhill franchisees, who, as personnel recruiters, work on a contingency basis. Fees are only generated when a successful placement is made. Therefore, successful decision-making abilities and effective work habits are crucial to success. But these are considerably harder to teach than the concepts and mechanics associated with the running of a personnel recruitment agency.

Many of Dunhill's franchisees have pointed to the new training techniques as critical to their survival during their first year in business. In fact, the high failure rate of many new businesses in general is often due not to the lack of a bright idea or of motivation but simply because the new businessman may not have a working knowledge of how to run a business efficiently or how to organize his time and work efforts.

Almost all Dunhill consultants come out of corporate life. Although some have been quite successful, this is no guarantee that they will run a successful personnel recruitment business. Sometimes, quite the reverse is true. The underlying assumptions behind Dunhill's training program are that most new franchisees have little true understanding of time and priority, despite their corporate backgrounds; that they have little, if any, formal discipline for daily planning; that they may have difficulty distinguishing between what they like to do and what they must do to accomplish their goals; and that they may have fundamental difficulties replacing old work habits with new.

The training program begins with an evaluation of the long-range goals of the new Dunhill owners and then asks them several questions. Why do they want to operate their own business? What sacrifices do they expect to make? What tangible returns do they expect over the next 10 years? And so on. These questions are, of course, very open-ended.

The next step is for new franchisees to learn how *to establish realistic, shorter-range goals with meaningful benchmarks for success.* This is one of the keys to the success or failure of any business plan. Long-range goals have little place, if any, in the world of the new, unrooted business. The battle is fought and won or lost in the setting and reaching of a multitude of short-range goals.

To establish realistic concrete goals, franchisees calculate exactly how much money they must generate yearly to make their fledgling business a success. They are then asked to break down this figure on a monthly and weekly basis, so that they will have a specific idea of how much revenue must be forthcoming at all times to meet their financial requirements. After this is done, they learn to calculate how much and what kind of preliminary work (phone calling, interviewing, etc.) it will take to generate one job placement (the successful

443

bringing together of candidate and employer) and how to keep this information up-to-date based on fluctuations in the market. These calculations provide franchisees with a series of realistic daily, weekly, monthly and yearly goals.

Once these realistic goals have been set, new franchisees are taught how to *formulate specific, step-by-step plans to carry out these goals*. A series of simple log sheets helps accomplish these ends. A daily log sheet has space for listing each phone call and its results, as well as for a summary of the day's transactions. Weekly, monthly and yearly log sheets summarize important transactions, indicate what has been accomplished and what must be accomplished by which date in order to meet certain goals. These log sheets take no extra time to keep, are easy to read and reveal the status quo at a glance.

Based on the information listed in the log sheets, franchisees are shown the importance of constructing a *realistic, attainable daily plan* for *every* working day, listing what must be done and when. This daily plan is integral to the success of the training program, and trainees are given a specially designed desk diary to help them organize their activities within specific time frames. Standard rankings of daily priorities are preprinted on each diary page so that items can be listed in their order of importance. Items of the highest priority are tackled first thing in the morning. These are the activities that are most critical to accomplishing specified goals.

Learning how to *control task interference* is as important to the new franchisee as is establishing priorities. It is one thing to set up a list of daily tasks that *must* be accomplished and quite another thing to accomplish them. No day is without its interruptions, and these often can be fatal to the success of any preplanning.

Controlling task interference can mean different things to different people. For some, it means making sure the telephone doesn't ring in their office and that messages are taken, unless an important call is expected. For others, it may mean scheduling regular daily appointments with colleagues or subordinate department heads in order to prevent people from wandering in and interrupting with random questions.

The key thing franchisees are taught is that, once a daily plan has been established, it must not be deviated from, as long as it is deemed realistic and attainable. No matter what else piles up on the desk, the

pre-established tasks take first priority.

One specific trick taught in the sessions is to open mail only during "down time" (non-productive work periods such as lunchtime and late in the day). When mail is opened, immediate decisions must be made. Does something warrant enough attention to be included in tomorrow's daily plan? Does something warrant attention at all? This structure constantly forces the new franchisee into a decision-making mode that eventually becomes automatic.

Since the telephone call is the basis for all personnel placements, franchisees are taught to make chain telephone calls during the prime morning and afternoon hours, using other times for less critical tasks. This one simple technique alone is responsible for Dunhill's high rate of placement, compared with similar personnel networks.

Once they have mastered these techniques, franchisees are shown how to *audit themselves every evening* to assess their success. The franchisee meets respectively with each member of his staff to go over the day's activities, asking such questions as, "Was the daily plan completed?" "If not, why not?" "How might better control and handling of 'new' items be accomplished?" "How might problems be made non-recurrent?" "If the plan was completed, what were the results?" "Were they as planned?" "If not, why not?" The franchisee is encouraged to have one of his staff members audit him in return, rather than attempting the procedure himself.

Trainees are taught how to handle the daily audit through special role-playing sessions where they analyze sample problems. Once mastered, the whole technique should take no more than 10 to 15 minutes per session.

In addition to this audit, trainees are taught to construct a new daily plan for the following day before they leave in the evening. This plan must be submitted and approved by their manager before enacted . This is the time to establish the following day's priorities based on the accomplishments of today. What must be done so that weekly goals can be met? If the end of the month is near, how close are those goals to completion? These questions should all be considered when the evening plan is drawn up. Without such a daily plan, the work day becomes a formless mass of confused detail.

In addition to being taught numerous work disciplines, trainees are placed in an environment that exactly

duplicates their future offices. Videotape is used to help them observe work routines and identify problem areas. The actual tasks performed during training sessions are those that the trainee will continue to perform once he has established his own business. Thus, all telephoning during this time is done in the geographic locale where the new branch will be located. To minimize "real-world" shock, the Monday following the last day of training becomes nothing more than an extension of those activities undertaken during the past two weeks.

Once a newly franchised office has been opened, periodic visits by Dunhill staff specialists enable the fledgling entrepreneurs to review what they have learned, ask questions and take stock of their successes. Regional seminars also provide a forum for exchanging ideas and assessing successes.

The basic assumptions and techniques underlying Dunhill's training program can be implemented easily and to great advantage in almost any corporate environment. The guideposts to working effectively are simply: *establish short-range, realistic goals; formulate a plan to carry out the goals; control task interference;* and *audit success daily.*

Many executives have a clear sense of overall goals, but they neglect to break down these goals to their simplest elements and ask such questions as: What production deadlines must be met this week to achieve year-end quotas? What must I do today, this morning, to make that happen? Many executives rely on random notes to jog their memory, but this doesn't structure a day. A simple matter such as scheduling brief end-of-the-day appointments with colleagues can drastically eliminate uncalled-for interruptions and increase working efficiency. Used routinely and conscientiously, the written daily plan and the daily audit are also invaluable executive tools.

The significant increase in the number of placements Dunhill achieved over the past year, coupled with the entire system's outstanding success in the personnel recruitment industry, are not surprising when viewed as the partial outcome of this intensive training program. The *techniques* may seem obvious to some; but it is the *discipline* that most executives fail to exert over themselves and their staff. It is this discipline and the flexibility to implement new ideas that can make the difference between the success or failure of business goals.

Reprinted from TRAINING, November 1979

WHY SOFT-SKILLS TRAINING DOESN'T TAKE

Do our 'interpersonal skills' programs
really build skills?
Do our role plays miss the point?
Have we built a house of cards?

BY JAMES C. GEORGES

Good technical trainers have very high batting averages. They can start with an average group of people and turn most of them into skilled technicians. In fact, the standard definition of a successful technical-training program is one in which 90 percent of the learners master 90 percent of the skills being taught. And that means—as far as good technical trainers are concerned—that trainees can demonstrate skilled performance not just in class but in a real job situation.

Similarly, good tennis or golf coaches can coax dramatic improvements out of just about anybody. Few people would doubt that those coaches are building valuable skills—that their coaching produces visible improvements in the athletes' performances in tennis matches or golf tournaments.

"Soft skills" training, on the other hand, is much more a hit-or-miss proposition. When we teach subjects that fall under the headings of management, leadership, interpersonal communication, problem solving, consultative sales techniques and so on, we have a lousy batting average. In most organizations, we're lucky if 20 percent of the people who graduate from our courses go back to the job and use the techniques we taught

them to improve their "games." The other 80 percent may try out their new "skills" a few times, but they quickly revert to their old patterns.

We warned them, of course, that doing things the new way might seem clumsy at first. We encouraged them to stick with it: "You'll have to practice these skills back on the job to make them your own. Draw up an action plan for integrating them into your behavior. They'll start to pay off for you eventually." We urged their bosses to support them for practicing the new skills, even if their performance suffered somewhat in the beginning.

But in the real world, people simply don't stick with behavior that makes them feel artificial and maladroit, especially if it causes their performance to suffer in ways that *hurt*. Most trainees will drop the new techniques like hot potatoes the moment the idea of a temporary dip in performance becomes concrete—as soon as "My performance may suffer a little at first" turns into "Hey, I'm losing sales with this technique," or "I'm actually *alienating* people by stumbling through this formula."

What's more, it may be that the only reason we have even that pitiful 20 percent success rate is that about 20 percent of our trainees were already skillful performers when they walked into class. Somebody who is

naturally good at giving effective feedback to subordinates, for instance, will be able to take just about any reasonable set of principles we present and make them work. After all, when it comes to soft skills, we *know* there are "naturals" and self-taught masters out there. Almost everything we teach about communication and leadership and so on comes from studying those masters.

Why are we so much less effective at teaching "people skills" than we are at teaching technical skills or at teaching people to play tennis? Perhaps it's largely because we don't really *do* any skills training in "soft" subjects. We just call it skills training. What we actually deliver is knowledge training; we pass along information *about* a particular behavior.

Knowing about how something is done is not a skill. Being able to describe the steps involved in completing a task is not a skill. The ability to perform those steps in a clumsy, disjointed way is not a skill.

It's not what you do but how well you do it that determines whether you are skilled. You have a skill only when you are able to do something *skillfully*.

That seems so self-evident it shouldn't need to be said. But it does. Because when it comes to soft-skills training, skillful performance is the one thing we don't build or teach. Instead, we tell trainees they'll have to achieve it on their own, through practice, back on the job.

Sure. Back on the job—the last place where they can afford to look awkward, uncertain and incompetent, as people do in the early stages of learning to master any new skill.

Steps

When we teach soft subjects, what we really do is "steps" training. It works like this.

First, pick a subject or process and break it down into a series of steps. For example, here are five steps in a rational procedure for problem solving that's older than Plato: 1) define the problem, 2) seek options and alternative solutions, 3) gain agreement on the most acceptable solution, 4) commit to a plan of action, 5) observe the results and follow up with appropriate actions.

Second, discuss the steps in class to see that everybody understands what they are. If possible, show them a videotape (a behavior model) of someone demonstrating the steps.

Then conduct a role play or two so the trainees can practice using the steps. All trainees should prove that they understand what the steps are, and roughly what they look like in practice. The point is not to achieve a smooth, convincing, *skilled* performance. Who has time for that? We're happy if everyone can achieve a forced, artificial approximation of what a human being might look like and sound like while using these steps skillfully in a real situation.

Finally, make everyone promise to practice the steps back on the job until they come smoothly and naturally. Get their bosses to promise to reinforce this practice. If they aren't getting enough support from their bosses, bring the trainees back for more sessions. Show them a different videotape. Stage more role plays. Then sing, once again, the soft-skills training theme song: "Now go back to work and make these skills your own."

What's wrong with this picture? The essential problem is that the steps aren't the skill. Skill is what it takes to execute the steps successfully. That's why program graduates who use perfectly valid procedures fail so often to achieve the results they desire. Whether the subject is sales, supervision or whatever, any logical set of steps is doomed to fail if the person's demeanor is too mechanical, too tentative, too pushy, too righteous, too unconvincing.

Leave the trainees with the impression that the steps are the skill, and you've encouraged them to discard the steps when they experience repeated failures back on the job—as most of them will, at first. People aren't stupid. They protect themselves. A step-by-step procedure that isn't comfortable and doesn't seem to work will not be used. Not even if management "buys into" the training program enough to do a little bit of coaching and reinforcing. Busy managers don't have time (and often don't have the skill) to do *enough* coaching.

Another weakness of that standard "skills training" process lies in those role plays. A few role plays will not build a skillful performance. Most role plays are designed, in fact, only to ensure that the trainees have grasped what the steps *are*. That's why the language and performances seem so artificial. Role plays aren't designed or even intended to produce the sort of smooth, natural performance that would be required in order for the steps to *work* in a real-life situation. Provided the trainees attempt to execute the steps, however clumsily, they graduate from the course and are deemed to have a new "skill."

Nonsense. The only thing they have is new knowledge *about* certain step-by-step behaviors. Good technical trainers would consider it criminal to throw a novice machine operator into a real production process if the novice could perform only a clumsy—even counterproductive—impersonation of a person actually able to operate the machine. But when it comes to people-skills training, that's standard procedure.

Then we all stand around and engage in endless arguments about why soft skills so often fail to "transfer" from the classroom to the workplace. We have a long list of excuses: Management failed to reinforce the new skills, the company's culture wouldn't support them and so on. Sometimes these arguments are true; but if so, the training program should not have been run in the first place.

In truth the No. 1 reason for transfer failure is that most of the "soft" programs we run don't give trainees any genuine skills that they *can* transfer to the workplace.

Real skills

Suppose we conducted people-skills training more in the way that world-class coaches build the skills of athletes, musicians and karate experts? Or the way a good private coach might train a politician or a top business executive to field questions from the news media? Whether you're talking about Jack Nicklaus, Mary Lou Retton, Ella Fitzgerald, Bruce Lee or a presidential candidate, much of the training they received was patterned along these lines:

• First, find out what the learner needs to accomplish. Then present the appropriate skill model in plain language, explaining the "what to do's" in the fewest possible words. These "what to do's" are the smaller elements in the overall model.

• Show examples of the whole skill model. Then show examples of the first smaller skill element. Videotaped behavior models are great, but any clear example would do. Check the trainee's understanding until "Do you know what to do?" is no longer an issue.

• Now shift the emphasis away from the "what to do," that is, away from the "step." Explain that the step is not the skill. The skill lies in how well you execute each step, and ultimately in how well you integrate the various steps into a skillful performance.

• Drill each single skill element. (A drill is not the same as a role play. More on this in a minute.) Keep drilling each element until both learner and coach can see that the learner has mastered it well enough to succeed in a real-life situation—that is, until the learner performs smoothly, competently, consistently and *confidently*.

• After each skill element has been drilled to mastery level, move on to the next element. Finally, combine the skill segments and drill the entire skill model. By the time you get to the whole model, this will be relatively easy to do, since little will be new to the learner and any weak areas will have been strengthened in previous drills. (In a traditional role play, by contrast, the whole skill model is the first thing practiced and critiqued. The learner's performance is riddled with weak areas.)

• Finally, for reinforcement back on the job, do not rely solely upon the trainees' bosses to provide encouragement and additional coaching. Instead, teach the trainees—during the training program itself—how to coach each other. During the drills, trainees should alternate between the roles of learner and coach—just as gymnasts "spot" and critique each other while they practice a difficult move, then a series of moves. This not only helps logistically (one trainer cannot simultaneously coach 30 individuals through the sorts of drills we're talking about) but also improves each person's learning. The old maxim that you learn by teaching is true. Once trainees return to the job, they will be more accessible to one another for coaching and reinforcement purposes than one boss can be to a whole group of people. By all means, get bosses involved. Just don't count on them to provide all the necessary support.

What's the difference between a

IS IT REALLY LEADERSHIP TRAINING?

Imagine being on the receiving end of a typical seminar on leadership. "OK, trainees, we have now covered all the materials. You've learned to parrot the labels we attached to what we told you are the key characteristics of numerous heroes in sports, politics and business. You've filled out two do-it-yourself psychological profiles, so you can now label your own leadership styles. You have been exposed to six different theories of leadership, as articulated by noted researchers and authors. We have fed you a smorgasbord of information culled from some old courses on management and communication that we found lying around—all of it jazzed up with the latest leadership jargon. You have studied situational strategies for exercising influences. You've got notebooks full of helpful reminders about how to do everything from run an effective meeting to conduct a legally defensible performance appraisal.

"Yes, I think that's everything. Now, of course, you'll have to go back to the job and *practice* all of these skills in order to make them your own. Work at it. And good luck!"

Practice these *skills*? Good luck, indeed. Luck is exactly what the graduates of most "leadership development" courses will need. Because they didn't learn the first thing about how to lead.

How do I know? How can you know? It's easy.

First, ask the trained people to give you a specific definition of leadership. What is it, and how do you know when you're demonstrating it?

If you get a vague answer ("communicating a vision") or a lot of different answers, begin to worry.

Second, check the confidence levels of several trained people while they are performing a leadership skill that they supposedly learned. If they perform tentatively or unconvincingly, your concern should grow. They may have understood the concepts, but they didn't learn how to function effectively as leaders.

Finally, the best and easiest test of all: Observe the trained people at work. Do they get more followers after the training? That is, do they succeed in attracting the wholehearted support of others for whatever courses of action they favor?

No followers? Then no leaders! That is the pure and simple measure of leadership.

A distinction often drawn between managing and leading is that leadership commands the follower's head *and heart*. That's true. "Followership" is always a decision based on both intellect and emotion. But this tends to draw us into a wonderland of abstractions, where "leadership" stands for every desirable quality under the sun.

If we really want to talk about leadership as a discrete skill—or set of skills—that can be improved by training, then the point of effective leadership training is: how to get a wholehearted follower, or followers, for any given course of action. Period. That's it. It's not how to be the best person you can be. It's not how to get more productivity out of people. It's not how to be a better supervisor or a better communicator or a more creative thinker. It is how to get from others their genuine "buy-in"—support, enlistment, ownership—for a given course of action. That is likely to *result* in any number of benefits—better teamwork, for example. But teamwork isn't leadership either.

Leadership is some ineffable quality? It's hard to pin it down? It's difficult to measure the impact of a leadership training course? Nonsense! Define leadership as what it is—obtaining followers—and you have a supremely measurable skill. You can always tell if and when you're successful at leadership. You can tell every time you commit yourself to an idea, a project or a course of action, and try to win someone else's support for it. If you got a wholehearted follower, you succeeded at leadership. If all you got was compliance or surrender, you failed. If you got increased resistance, outright opposition or apathy, you failed miserably. No followers means no leadership—not on this issue at this time.

In other words, leadership places you at risk. It's something you can lose at. You often have to compete for followership, and the leader in any situation is the one who ends up with the followers. But the current direction of training tends to make competitiveness a dirty word—that is, when it means something you, personally, do. The *art* is to make all sides win. But we're kidding ourselves if we think we can shy away from winning and still be effective leaders.

You really want to teach your company's people to be more effective leaders? Define leadership as the ability to get wholehearted followers. Stick to that point and build your curriculum around it. There's plenty of valid information out there about how to practice leadership as a skill. Some of it may even be buried in the course you're teaching now.

Reprinted from TRAINING, December 1987

---

drill and a role play?

Take a golf lesson with me. I'll show you a series of steps, covering everything from driving off the tee to putting. The first three steps will be: how to grip a club, how to align your feet and shoulders to the target and how to swing side-to-side so as to strike the ball squarely. Once I've shown you the whole series of, say, 15 steps, we'll want to give you some practice.

The "role play" model for that golf lesson would be for you to go out and play nine holes of golf, bearing in mind the 15 steps I described. I would coach you and critique your performance only after you finished the ninth hole.

To "drill" you, on the other hand, I'd take you to a driving range. You'd work only on the first three of the 15 steps in the total skill model. But in less time than it would take to play nine holes of golf, you'd hit several hundred balls. And you'd get immediate, continual feedback about your performance on every swing. Once we were satisfied with your driving, I'd take you to a putting green. And so on.

Suppose we had only enough practice time for you to play four nine-hole rounds. Shall we go ahead and play those rounds, according to the role-play model? Or do you think you would develop more skill and confidence as a golfer if we devoted the

---

Repetitive drills build real skills— right here, right now.

---

same amount of time to the drilling model, perhaps ending with one nine-hole round? Professional golfers build their ability to drive and putt and escape from sand traps by drilling those skills, not by "role playing" them.

Drills are short, repetitive experiments. And repetitive, coached practice is the best way to develop skillfulness. You can get a lot of drilling done in the time it takes to complete one full role play.

Drills also build confidence, because drilling is the fastest way to master each particular skill element. And confidence comes from the knowledge that you can do something *well* and do it consistently and predictably under a variety of circumstances. Confidence builds "ownership" of the skill. And ownership must occur *during* the training course in order for the skill to transfer to the real job.

Doing it with people skills

How would you drill people to perform a "soft skill" consistently, predictably, smoothly and confidently? Let's take a particular skill element that might be taught in any number of courses, whether the topic is interpersonal communication, effective supervision, sales, negotiation, leadership or how to conduct a perform-

ance review. The element is the ability to maintain self-confidence and poise even in the face of resistance— that is, resistance from the client, the subordinate, the peer or whomever.

Training works best when it's tied to real goals that the trainees really want to accomplish. So have each learner pick a real situation to work with: trying to sell the Mark IV electric widget to a customer, trying to enlist the support of a peer from another department in some project, etc. Tell the learner to make a specific request for the coach's commitment or support (for example, ask the coach to buy the product or to lend his wholehearted support to the learner's project, etc.). The learner makes essentially the same request a number of times, but each time the coach expresses a different type of reaction: refusal, resistance, indifference, hesitant interest, acceptance, enthusiastic support, etc.

Coach and learner immediately discuss and critique the way the learner handled each of the coach's reactions. If they find that the learner has trouble maintaining composure in the face of, say, a challenging or distrustful reaction, then they drill heavily on handling that reaction. The coach challenges and the learner responds to the challenge, over and over again. These are not role plays, but brief, repetitive exchanges. The learner experiments with different ways of responding to the coach's challenges.

The two aren't experimenting in the dark here. They have the recommended "steps" and techniques to work with. But since they're drilling a particular skill instead of working through an entire role play on "giving a performance review" or whatever, they can isolate the learner's specific weak points and work effectively to strengthen them.

You can use drills to build any number of specific skills that might fit into a variety of soft-subject courses: the ability to negotiate or inspire a change in another person's point of view, the ability to end con-

versations at the most productive point or at the point of maximum commitment. Whatever skill element you're teaching, the advantage of repetitive drills over the standard role play is that well-executed drills build genuine skillfulness—right here, right now.

Take another generic skill element: the ability to establish conversational rapport. The true "skill" is being able to do it *without* resorting to artificial feedback techniques. In the real world, credibility is the issue. So the question is not, "Did you remember to acknowledge that you took the other person's point of view seriously?" That's the *step* that you demonstrate in a role play. When you try to use it, unconvincingly, back in the real world, you may well find that you just annoy and alienate people.

No, the question is, "How *believable* were you while you were acknowledging that you took the other person's point of view seriously?" That's the *skill.* And unless you have developed it naturally, you're likely to build it only in the low-threat environment of a training program, and only through repeated drills that focus on your personal believability. You won't build it in a few role plays by doing an awkward impersonation of the woman in the videotape. And you won't build it back on the job.

When it comes to interpersonal-skills training of all sorts—be it for managers, salespeople or anyone else in the business world—plenty of organizations do a perfectly adequate job of imparting valid knowledge about effective behaviors. So why does this training have such a spotty batting average?

Let me say it one more time: Knowing about how something is supposed to be done is not a skill. Skill is the crucial element that turns knowledge into behaviors that succeed in the real world. If the so-called skills you've been building in class seem to vanish when people get back to the job, the first question to ask is whether you were building any genuine skillfulness at all.

Reprinted from TRAINING, April 1988

TEACHING JOHNNY TO MANAGE

Why doesn't most management training 'take?'
Maybe because it has no connection to
real life in the company

BY ALEX MIRONOFF

In most organizations, teaching Johnny to manage has been a difficult, haphazard and often unsuccessful exercise. After years of watching several major corporations struggle with a variety of dubious approaches to management training, I venture to suggest an embryonic solution to the problem.

As a way of analyzing the management-training muddle, let's apply—informally and unmethodically—the Kepner-Tregoe principle of comparing a defective object with a similar object that does not have the defect. In this case, the similar, defect-free object is technical training.

Management training, in most organizations, differs from technical training in two important respects: 1) Management programs tend to be vastly more controversial and entertainment-oriented than technical courses, and 2) They don't work. At least, they don't work very well, considering the amount of money you're pouring into them.

I propose a seemingly simple solution—"seemingly simple" because, like most concepts involving management training, it is much easier to talk about than to apply. I've seen this one applied successfully, however, so I can offer a concrete example. First,

though, let's look at technical vs. management training and observe some critical differences between the ways we approach them.

In search of reality

You could argue—lots of people do—that teaching people to manage is different from teaching them to use a personal computer. You could assert

> **In management training we usually attempt to teach things that do not exist in the organization.**

that managing people is a more complex activity, that people are *really* hard to understand, that management is a "soft" science, and so on. But in fact, PCs also are quite complex. I don't really understand how they do what they do. And I could develop training that treats PC operation as though it were a "soft" science. This last observation gets to the

heart of the critical difference between our traditional approaches to technical and management training.

If we strip away the surface distinctions between technical and management subjects, we are left with the fact that in management training we usually try to teach things that do not "exist" in the organization. We teach ideas and behaviors that participants and top management alike view as nice to know but essentially irrelevant to getting the job done. In technical training, on the other hand, we teach facts, ideas and behaviors that everyone clearly understands from the outset are intrinsic to the successful performance of the job.

Our personal-computer example is particularly apt here. A few years ago, when the hype for PCs was at its zenith, we saw an onslaught of generic "computer literacy" programs. They were designed not to teach people how to use any specific hardware or software applicable to their jobs but rather to teach "bits," "bytes" and random snippets of programming languages to people with no real need or desire to know. In technical training, such programs are aberrations, quickly corrected. Generic computer-literacy courses flourished briefly, then died.

Can you imagine a company today spending vast sums of money to put its people through PC-training courses on hardware or software applications that the company does not have, does not intend to get and may not even believe exist? Is there a single profit-oriented organization in the country today that would consider funding a program such as "Concepts in Personal Computing"? Is there a training director who would dare ask for that funding?

In most businesses today, before trainers teach anybody anything about PCs, the company will have decided how they'll be used, who will get them, what brand will be the company standard, what software will be purchased and so on. Once management has made these decisions and committed itself to a course of action, trainers can teach the relevant concepts, procedures and skills. Employees usually will leave the training program with better capability to use the equipment that, you will recall, already is sitting on their desks and for which they have specific work applications. While we can certainly debate the design or effectiveness of the training program, there is no question about its relevance to the employees' jobs.

The picture is quite different for the typical management training program. First, companies regularly budget for courses with such nondescript titles as "The World of Management," "Effective Business Writing" or "Delegating to Motivate." These staples are routinely developed, purchased or, even worse, farmed out to fly-by-night seminar sponsors in the naive hope that Johnny will somehow see the light and be transformed. He'll stop flogging his people—even though his own manager continues to flog him. He'll stop writing ponderous reports in tortured, bureaucratic language—even though the company considers such language "businesslike" and rewards people for using it. He'll become a better manager—whatever that is.

Second, the people who design management training courses ordinarily go to great lengths to avoid content that suggests there are right and wrong ways to manage. In this scheme of things, weaknesses are merely strengths amplified to a gross degree. Every management style is basically OK—even Attila's. Who knows when the fifth century will make an encore?

By contrast, when we teach PC operation, we show participants the three equally acceptable methods for issuing a particular command—and we tell them clearly that any other method will fail.

Most companies do not realize that they have effectively delegated policy-making in the critical area of acceptable management practices to the training department and to academic management theorists. And this is something that *cannot* be delegated; trainers and academics have no authority to enforce the policies they establish or to reward Johnny for following them. The result is a costly, pointless exercise that raises two questions: Why do organizations persist in supporting this kind of training and what should they be doing instead?

Sticky wickets

Part of the answer to the first question lies in the pervasive assumption that every *civilized* company provides management training. But I believe the plethora of generic programs that have no roots in organizational reality are a direct result of management's discomfort with making decisions about people issues. While managers are used to making decisions about products and equipment (often to a level of detail they would do better to avoid), they seem considerably less decisive in the unpredictable area of handling people. They would rather delegate this onerous chore to someone foolhardy enough to volunteer. Enter the human resources development department.

Having dropped this sticky wicket into someone else's lap, management wants to hear no more about it other than how many bodies were put through the training cure and at what price. Management's tolerance for more of the same then becomes a function of the company's current profit-and-loss picture ("Can we still afford this?"), the occasional trainee reaction ("I got a lot/nothing out of it") and, ultimately, the resulting change in performance ("If this training is so good, how come Perkins still acts like a horse's ass?").

It isn't surprising that so many management trainers spend no more than two to three years in the job—just about long enough for the company to figure out that the training isn't taking and that it needs to be delegated to someone new.

This leads to the second question: What *should* companies be doing about management training? The answer is that they should do management training the same way they do technical training. They should train people only in concepts and skills that complement the existing hardware and software.

In the management realm, "hardware" and "software" refer to an organization's mission, values, policies, procedures, standards of performance—in other words, the sum of all those management decisions that give the organization its unique shape and distinguish it from a mere collection of people, housed together and engaged in some loosely related and—one hopes—profit-making activities.

Absent a clear mandate that defines the management philosophies and behaviors that best serve the organization's mission, trainers are re-

duced to presenting conventional wisdom or the musings of this season's management guru. If that's what is happening, then all of the methodological decisions that trainers agonize about are moot. Lectures, behavior modification, experiential exercises, video, computer-based training—they all make equally little sense or impact if participants do not recognize that the content is a formal, visible standard within the company.

The acid test of a proposed management program is whether it conveys your senior management's actual position on a particular issue. It must be backed up by the personal examples of people at the top, by a plan of action and by a way to measure results.

For example, if you, as the trainer, are asked for a program on effective delegation techniques, your first question should be: What is this organization's policy about delegation?

Nobody in the executive suite can tell you? Nobody has time to talk it through with you so that you can prepare a valid program? Somebody does tell you, but you know from experience that the policy you're hearing about is a fantasy that bears no relation to the way things really work in this organization? Then you may as well forget the training. You have no subject to teach—that is, not if you're looking for any kind of significant, practical, high-impact outcome. If you merely want to prolong the agony, go ahead and design or buy a course on effective delegation. But start planning now for your next career move—or for an exciting future in court reporting.

Case in point

I promised a concrete example of a training program that avoids the trap of being a nice-to-know, in-house version of Management Sciences 101. The example comes from the company I work for.

It came as a pleasant surprise to find senior managers at Provident Life and Accident Insurance Co. who were eager to tackle people issues, and to use the human resource function in general and the training division in particular as vehicles for doing so. I repeat: To *use* the training department, not to delegate the policy function to it.

Last year, the Provident revised the

performance planning and appraisal process. Top management planned the revision and determined the values that would underlie the new process, as well as its essential design features.

The performance planning and appraisal system was tied into revised job descriptions. Every employee would have a written statement that described the accomplishments necessary to perform the job well. These statements would be the basis for the appraisals. Guidelines were prepared for the personnel policy manual that showed how to complete appraisal forms and conduct appraisal interviews properly. Only then was a training program developed to teach managers how to conduct performance appraisals.

All managers and supervisors attended the program during a two-month period. Chairman and CEO H. Carey Hanlin attended the first program and demonstrated his support by telling participants, "... the group that has been least effective are the people at the top. . .and the inadequacy of our performance appraisals begins with me. . .so I'm looking forward to participating in this program, too."

He spoke to virtually every class thereafter. He talked about his belief in the importance of the appraisal process and what he would like to see done differently in both the writing and delivery of future appraisals. On the few occasions when schedule conflicts made a personal appearance impossible, a videotape of his talk was shown.

The program included a comic video based on performance-appraisal war stories from the company's employees and showed typical, unproductive approaches to the appraisal process. Videos showed executives conducting various phases of an effective appraisal interview. Critiques and role plays followed.

We also used the standard "how-to" exercises—how to write performance standards and supporting comments, how to interpret ratings and so on. But throughout the program, we made it clear to the trainees that this was the Provident's performance planning and appraisal system, and one of their major responsibilities as manager was to use it effectively. What's more, they would be held responsible for using it effectively.

The result was a program not in "Good Ways to Coach and Counsel" or in "Principles of Effective Performance Appraisal," but in the specific values, policies, systems and procedures to which the organization had committed itself. Coaching and counseling were covered, but not as freestanding topics. Principles of solid human relations were covered, but as a subset of a company system that already embodied those principles. The program did not even have a properly jazzy name. It didn't need a name.

The course did not include evaluation forms or other internal measurements. The outcome of the program

---

The blame for Johnny's inadequacies as a manager lies squarely with the top management of his company.

---

and the means for measuring its success became the appraisal forms themselves. More than 60 percent of the forms the human resources department received after the program contained significant new information on the employees' performance, while only 15 percent of reviews held prior to the program had had any written comments at all. The comments written in reviews conducted after the program tended to be precise and behaviorally or quantitatively phrased, while prior comments had been unspecific at best and, at worst, personal, judgmental and accusatory.

For once it was possible to decipher what managers were really trying to tell their people. Fewer employees complained about the way managers handled performance-appraisal interviews. When complaints or poorly completed appraisal forms surfaced, human resource staffers—who now had the backing of senior management, as well as program and policy materials—directly questioned the responsible managers. The gap

between training and application had been closed.

What about Johnny?

My underlying assumption is that Johnny really isn't doing a good job of managing. But don't blame Johnny. Chances are he was promoted into a management position after displaying good technical skills and an ability to think and talk in ways that led someone to believe that he had "management potential." Don't blame the training department, either. It probably has exposed Johnny to half-a-dozen courses explaining how ideal managers should think and act in a theoretical world.

The blame for Johnny's inadequacies as a manager lies squarely with the top managers of his company, who neglect their responsibility to define, update, communicate and demonstrate the organization's mission, values and management standards so that Johnny can understand them and the training department can elucidate them.

Training can only elaborate on that which already exists; it cannot create new behavior for an environment that will not support it. The sad truth is that precious few top managers are willing to take a stand on what constitutes desirable and undesirable management practices. Even fewer will go so far as to bring their reward and sanction system into line with their stated positions. That's one big reason why the solutions I'm proposing are easier to talk about than to do.

In a routine planning session with the senior management team of a previous employer, for example, I was amazed to discover that those managers put no stock whatsoever in the concept of situational leadership. Project managers, they maintained, should not be asked to adapt their leadership styles under any circumstances; it might unsettle them and make them even less effective than they already were. Why was I shocked? Because these same people had sponsored about five years' worth of management classes based on the Hersey-Blanchard situational leadership model. Nor did this discovery deter the training group from continuing to present Hersey-Blanchard as the way to go. The situation did not bother the executives much either, since they instinctively understood that nothing happening in training programs could possibly have an impact on the real world anyway.

The odd little marriage of convenience between training and top management at this company continued until downturns forced a purge of all "nonessential" functions. Training went first and the executives followed in due course. What these executives failed to recognize was that they were paid their handsome salaries to make tough decisions about which management norms would best serve the organization's mission. They were responsible for managing the corporate culture. What the training department failed to recognize was that it was neither authorized—nor paid—to make such decisions.

I fear this farce is being repeated in boardrooms across the country. The key questions for these executives

---

**The key question
for executives:
What management
practices
do you believe will
best advance your
organization's mission?**

---

are: Which management concepts and practices do you really believe will best advance your organization's mission? What is your role in ensuring that they are effectively defined, communicated and practiced in the organization?

Even less-than-optimal management approaches—if they are consistently understood, supported and communicated throughout an organization—can be taught and implemented with more effect than highly pedigreed academic theories that have no credibility in the company's ruling circles. If top managers would take the time to think through their beliefs on what management concepts and practices are essential to success in their businesses—just as they do when they decide which types of products and services to sell—training departments would be capable of achieving considerably more success in teaching Johnny to manage.

Reprinted from TRAINING, March 1988

KEEPING SUPERVISORS FROM SABOTAGING YOUR TRAINING EFFORTS

Disregarding the post-training environment is asking for trouble

BY JOSEPH SPINALE

Well-designed training efforts that meet specific objectives and produce the desired behavioral changes can prove to be ineffective or even counter-productive unless the organization considers the supervision style the new trainee will encounter back on the job. The trainer, then, is responsible for defining the parameters of the supervisory behavior the trainee will experience; and this will ensure that the training will result in behavior that meets supervisor expectations.

In order for the trainee to maintain and strengthen newly learned behaviors, these behaviors must be positively reinforced back on the job. In many occupations, the supervisor provides the main source of reinforcement of the newly learned skills. This is particularly true of human relations skills: the trainee may tend to adopt and emulate the behavior of the supervisor, regardless of what he learned in the training situation.

In some cases, supervisors should be pretrained so the necessary climate for maximum reinforcement of training objectives can be established. The nature of the industry and/or the organization, on the other hand, may require that training complement existing supervisory behavior, particularly if that behavior produces desired organizational results. If the trainer fails to consider this situation, the trainee may receive contradictory messages from training and supervision, and the organization may experience alarming levels of turnover.

A recent study, conducted in one of the major fast-food organizations, supports these conclusions. The original intent of the study was to measure the relationship between satisfaction with various dimensions of the job of restaurant manager and an individual's value orientation toward work in general. The hypothesis was that certain occupations provide certain kinds of satisfactions. These satisfactions, in turn, appeal to individuals who value the kinds of rewards and reinforcements available on the job.

Everyone's value system develops through a psychological process which begins in early childhood, and is fairly well established by the time an individual enters the work force. If an organization is able to identify the kinds of satisfactions available in a particular job and the types of individuals who will respond to these satisfactions, then it should improve its ability to fit the person to the job and, thereby, reduce turnover.

A hundred fast-food restaurant managers who were assigned to units in one of nine different geographical regions participated in the study. A different supervisor was responsible for each region or area; in general, there were 10 or more managers per supervisor. Each manager completed two separate questionnaires: one was designed to measure satisfaction with various dimensions of the job, and the other measured aspects of the value system associated with the individual's attitudes about work in general. The resulting data were computer processed and statistically analyzed. (Both questionnaires were factor analyzed and a multiple regression performed between the resulting factors.)

Supervisors are key

Interestingly, the strongest multiple correlation (describing the relationship between all the work-value factors combined and a specific job-satisfaction factor) was satisfaction with supervision ($r = .74$, $p < .01$). Since the study was conducted with managers who reported to nine different supervisors, this result would tend to suggest two things. First, the supervisor apparently is the source for much of the satisfaction (or dissatisfaction) that occurs with this particular occupation. Secondly, it seems that supervisors in this organization tend to behave in some uniform way, since similar management personnel tend to respond to different supervisors in similar ways.

The implications for training become clear when one examines the factors that contributed to this significant relationship. Those managers who tended to be satisfied with the kind of supervision they received were those who considered their jobs a way of life and had settled down in their chosen occupation with career objectives. They had accepted the job for what it offered and were willing to work within its defined scope. Managers who tended to be dissatisfied with supervision, on the other hand, were typically those who valued creativity or the ability to be innovative in their work; they valued achievement in terms of positive feedback and reinforcement from their supervisors.

From a training point of view, these results help explain a phenomenon that the organization's training department had been experiencing for some time. Certain managers who left the week-long management development seminar reported that some of the skills and behaviors they had developed in the training situation were not supported by the policies or actions of their supervisors in the field. When these managers tried to apply these skills in dealing with their employees, their actions were considered suspect by their supervisors. In other cases, certain managers felt compelled to use one set of skills in dealing with their employees and another set when dealing with their supervisors. The resulting confusion and frustration contributed to the high rates of turnover among managers in the period immediately following the management seminar.

In addition, a kind of self-perpetuating cycle was established. Since those managers who were satisfied with their jobs were dealing successfully with the existing supervision style, they generally were able to maintain the most satisfactory relationships with their supervisors. Since the supervisor is largely responsible for determining who is eligible for promotion into supervisory ranks, they usually selected those who were satisfied with the existing situation, required minimum feedback and reinforcement, and were not inclined to be particularly creative or innovative in their work.

This sets up an interesting and chal-

LINK CLASSROOM LEARNING TO ON-THE-JOB EXPERIENCES

BY PAM SMITH

By designing course assignments that link the classroom to the trainee's work environment, Toronto General Hospital transformed a routine in-house supervisory training program into one that is tailor-made for its participants.

TGH's Employee Services and Education Department has been conducting this supervisory skills program (two-hour sessions for 12 weeks) for three years. The course is so effective and popular that TGH now accepts trainees from six other area hospitals.

Central to the course's success is the close and dynamic trainee/supervisor relationship set in motion during the two-hour discussion sessions. After each session, attendees receive assignments that are to be completed in their respective department settings, with the cooperation of their co-workers and supervisor. This arrangement brings the participant's bosses immediately into a teaching partnership with the TGH education department. For TGH's HRD program, this student/mentor relationship has become the key component of this unique program.

A sample supervisory skills assignment is this one on "Problem Solving and Negotiation":

It appears that there have been an increasing number of complaints about your department from within the hospital. Your director believes that it is not so much the way the department is operating as the fact that people seem unclear about the service you are offering. Other departments are making inappropriate requests (in type and frequency) of you and your people. You cannot have more money, more help, or, of course, more time. The director wants to know how you are going to handle the situation. (The manager has delegated the matter to you because, for three or four weeks, he is going to be tied up with the hospital's "Operation Austerity.")

Each week, participants receive similar course assignments and complete them under the tutelage of their superior. The payoff, according to TGH trainers, is that participants and their managers have enjoyed a spillover from this new learner/coach relationship into their day-to-day dealings. In general, both parties have found the trainees role expanding on the job as they demonstrate capacities each week and as their supervisors trust them with more discretion and responsibility.

TGH trainers report that because this strategy has been effective with supervisory training, it probably could be used in other areas, such as clinical or professional development, as long as the key student/mentor relationship could be established.

Reprinted from TRAINING, November 1979

lenging dilemma for the trainer. Training objectives are being met, and managers are developing behaviors consistent with the desires of the organization. Supervisors, on the other hand, are behaving in a way that virtually negates training results, even while giving verbal support to the methods and objectives of the training department. In some cases, effective training actually was establishing no-win situations for both managers and supervisors. Supervisors were not deliberately behaving in ways that would sabotage training efforts, but they were responding in ways that had proved successful for them in the past. They had survived and been successful in the system by adhering to certain methods of behavior. And these entrenched behavior patterns had been rewarded with promotion. While these supervisors gave lip service to what the organization promoted as improved methods of restaurant management, they actually continued to use tried-and-true methods with which they felt more comfortable.

Depending on the objectives of the organization, the trainer in this situation has various options. One obvious alternative is to provide the supervisor with intensive training first, while ensuring that the next higher level of management not only supports this behavior change but reinforces appropriate responses by the supervisor. In addition, the current state of affairs should be presented to the supervisor openly and honestly so that he becomes more aware of the significance of his own behavior.

An alternative approach simply would be to revise current manager training to be more consistent with existing patterns of supervisory behavior. Training effectiveness should increase dramatically in this instance since the trained behaviors will be more naturally reinforced by the supervisor back on the job. In any case, any alternative must be considered in light of specific organizational objectives and in relation to desired job performance levels and results.

The point is, training objectives must always be consistent with the kinds of behavioral reinforcements available from the immediate supervisor once the trainee returns to the job. Obviously, any training effort that promotes behavioral change that is inconsistent with the existing supervision style will subtly be sabotaged and prove to be either ineffective or, worse yet, counterproductive.

Reprinted from TRAINING, March 1980

MAKING SURE YOUR SUPERVISORS DO ON THE JOB WHAT YOU TAUGHT THEM IN THE CLASSROOM

Trainers can ensure that skills learned in the classroom are used on the job

BY JAMES C. ROBINSON
AND LINDA E. ROBINSON

The real measure of success of any type of supervisory training is not the amount of learning that takes place in the classroom but the extent to which supervisors continue to use the new skills back on the job. The new training technologies of the 1970's have proved to be highly effective in improving supervisory skills in the classroom. A disturbingly large amount of evidence indicates, however, that the amount of skill actually transferred to the job is still disappointingly low.*

What can you, as a trainer, do to ensure that the skills you teach will be transferred to the job? Fortunately, a great deal. In recent years, specific methods for increasing the amount of skill transfer in supervisory training have been identified. Because all these methods are within the direct control of the trainer or the line manager, you can use them in conjunction with your supervisory training programs to increase skill transfer.

Prior to training

If supervisory training is to be successful in changing on-the-job behavior, two essential issues must be satisfied before the training begins. First, the supervisors' needs must be identified. Additionally, management must be prepared to support on-the-job use of the new skills to be taught. There-

*Byham, W., and Robinson, J. Interaction modeling: A new concept in supervisory training. *Training and Development Journal*, 1976, 30(2), 20-33.

fore, the trainer's pre-workshop responsibilities include conducting a thorough needs analysis and obtaining management support for the classroom training and for the supervisors' use of the skills on the job.

Adults are more motivated to learn when they see that the skills being taught have immediate application, will enable them to overcome problems, and will have a "pay-off" in the real world. For example, supervisors will be more motivated to learn the skill of handling an employee complaint than the skill of effective listening. The former solves a specific supervisory problem, while the latter is "nice to know."

By conducting a thorough needs analysis prior to training, you can help ensure that the skills selected for the program are those of greatest "need" to the supervisors. In other words, the supervisors should consider the skills selected relevant to their problems and success on the job; communicated performance standards and negotiating performance goals are examples of such skills. While the proper selection of skills to be taught is no guarantee that skill transfer will occur, teaching skills for which the learners perceive no need is definitely a waste of time.

Supervisors will do those things their managers and the organization consider important and that are tied to the reward system. For example, when an organization introduces a new budgeting process, management must actively support the process, or it will fail. Likewise, when supervisors are learning new supervisory skills, management must actively support the use of the specific supervisory skills on

the job.

Management support will result only if management sees that the proposed training will produce specific benefits. For example, in a new budgeting process, the pay-off is improved planning and better management control. In supervisory training, the pay-off can be increased productivity, improved products and better employee/ supervisor communications. In each case, management must see specific benefits before it will support the training totally.

To gain management support, the trainer must give managers the opportunity to determine whether or not improved supervisory skills in these areas will provide a return on investment to the organization. Managers must also decide if they are willing to provide the required time, money and support essential to the success of the training endeavor. Obtaining the support of management prior to training can require a considerable time investment by the trainer. But the pay-off will be substantial in terms of long-term use of the skills on the job.

During training

The trainer controls the classroom learning experience. If the objective of the learning experience is to increase skill transfer and if the classroom training is designed to meet that objective, the extent to which supervisors actually will use the skills on the job will be considerable.

1. **Develop skill mastery.** Developing skill mastery in the classroom is essential. Until supervisors can successfully utilize the new skills in the classroom, they probably don't attempt to use them on the job. First attempts at using a skill are often discouraging because a person feels awkward and unsure. It is unrealistic, then, to expect a supervisor to utilize a skill such as conducting a performance appraisal if he or she has not previously mastered that skill in the classroom. The trainer can help supervisors master skills in the following ways.

- Demonstrate effective use of the skills. Allowing supervisors to learn by trial and error is neither cost effective nor efficient. Without an appropriate model, supervisors may stumble upon a better way of handling a situation, but this is unlikely. A person could not begin to fly an airplane without first observing an experienced pilot. Likewise, supervisors must see the correct way of handling a situation before they can develop the skills to do so themselves. Supervisors who witness an adequate demonstration of what they should be doing, rather than

REINFORCEMENT OF LEARNING HAS BIG PAYOFF

BY PETER JONES

It's time to take a hard, cold look at a classic training problem: How do we, as trainers, make sure that trainees employ their newfound knowledge and skills in actual on-the-job situations. How, in other words, do we ensure that training is a useful, not a wasteful, commodity? It's not easy. But strides are being made in the right direction.

After all, we've already come a long way toward eliminating one of training's original stigmas—that classroom sessions were irrelevant and meaningless in terms of nuts-and-bolts performance. Once we admitted to ourselves that *this* problem existed, it didn't take us long to tailor training sessions around knowledge and basic skills based on everyday situations our trainees faced. We began by developing better job descriptions, task analyses, behavioral objectives, and so on. Designing relevant course content is still hard work, of course, but nearly everyone recognizes it can be done and done well.

Once we started paying more attention to the worker in his job environment, we realized that the environment often has built-in obstacles that prevent the trainee from applying the knowledge and skills we helped him gain. So we began to think of effecting changes in job environments as part of our training job.

For many of us, this hurdle seemed more difficult to surmount than creating relevant course content. After considerable thought, discussions and research, we began to develop techniques to make these types of changes. But a lot of developmental work remains to be done in this area. In fact, it's unlikely that we will ever reach the stage where job environments always, or even often, produce ideal situations.

But that's no reason to give up. In our search for a solution, let's look in the classroom. This area has been thoroughly examined by practically everybody, but we'll do it a little differently this time. Ignoring everything up to the point where the student actually does what we've worked so hard to get him to do, we'll concentrate on how the trainee is rewarded, or not rewarded, for his response. Specifically, we'll consider how often this reinforcement occurs. Psychologists tell us that the frequency of reinforcement determines how fast the trainee will learn and how long he will remember a fact or perform a skill; they describe how often a reinforcement is delivered in terms of reinforcement schedules.

Basically, there are five kinds of reinforcement schedules. The one most commonly used in our business is probably the Continuous Reinforcement (CRF) schedule. Learning occurs faster with this schedule than with any other. Unfortunately, the CRF schedule also has the lowest retention rate. That means the trainee stops doing a learned behavior quickly if he stops receiving reinforcements for performing that behavior.

While trainers may use the CRF schedule frequently, the rest of the world marches to the beat of a different drummer. With any job there are periods of time when the employee receives no reward, feedback, or reinforcement of any kind. This erratic delivery of reinforcements is called the Variable Interval (V.I.) schedule. Psychologists usually agree that the V.I. schedule offers the slowest learning acquisition and the longest retention rate.

Hence, the problem. We take a trainee and put him on a schedule (CRF schedule) which has fast learning acquisition and low retention and then put him back in the real world, which is probably operating on the V.I. schedule of infrequent reinforcements. Nine chances out of ten, he will stop doing the learned behavior before he receives any feedback. Knowing this, how can we expect a trainee to take those newly learned skills back to his work environment and continue to use them?

One answer could be to start the learning process by using a Continuous Reinforcement schedule and convert to a Variable Interval schedule before the training is completed. But this answer raises some tough questions. How do we get each trainee to respond that many times in an abbreviated training session? How do we keep track of when the reinforcement is to be delivered and when it's not?

Another possibility is to train the trainees' supervisors in the art of delivering reinforcements. Now they can convert the trainee from the Continuous Reinforcement schedule used in the training session to the Variable Interval schedule their job environment requires. But this solution also poses problems. How do we get management to agree with us? How can we be sure the supervisors will do what they've been trained to do? Do we have to train the supervisor's supervisors?

Obviously, there is no panacea for the problem at hand. Even finding solutions which only create manageable problems is difficult. But then finding techniques to develop relevant course material and techniques to change job environments wasn't easy either. The initial reaction for many of us might be to declare this an impossible task, while some of the more stalwart members of our profession may accept the challenge. Somebody must if we ever want to reach the point where trainees are actually using the knowledge and skills they gained in our training.

Reinforcement Schedule	Topographical Description
Continuous Reinforcement Schedule (CRF)	Reinforcement is received after each appropriate response (i.e. response . . . reinforcement . . . response . . . reinforcement . . . etc.).
Fixed Ratio Schedule (FR)	Reinforcement is received only after a certain number of appropriate responses (i.e. 5 responses . . . reinforcement . . . 5 responses . . . reinforcement . . . etc.).
Variable Ratio Schedule (VR)	Same as the FR Schedule listed above but the number of responses before a reinforcement is received varies (i.e. 5 responses . . . reinforcement . . . 2 responses . . . reinforcement . . . 7 responses . . . etc.).
Fixed Interval Schedule (FI)	Reinforcement is received after the first appropriate response is made after a certain time period has elapsed (i.e. response . . . reinforcement . . . 2 hour time-out period . . . response . . . reinforcement . . . 2 hour time-out period . . . etc.). Any responses made during the time-out period are completely ignored.
Variable Interval Schedule (VI)	Same as the FI schedule listed above except the time-out periods vary in length (i.e. 2 hour time-out period . . . response . . . reinforcement . . . 5 minute time-out period . . . response . . . reinforcement . . . 1 day time-out period . . . etc.).

Reprinted from TRAINING, September 1977

what could go wrong, will make few initial errors in using the skills. Once they see that the new skills do work, training time will be reduced.

- Provide sufficient opportunity to practice the skills. But just seeing someone demonstrate the correct way of doing something isn't enough. Supervisors need an opportunity to practice the demonstrated skills often enough to become proficient at using them.

- Provide immediate feedback on effective and ineffective use of the skills. Positive reinforcement and suggestions for improving while practicing newly learned skills will increase the probability that supervisors will continue to use effective behaviors and that ineffective behaviors will gradually diminish. Effective football coaches provide specific feedback to the players immediately after each practice session. Likewise, the most effective supervisory trainers are those who provide specific feedback to the supervisors immediately after each skill practice.

- Strive for "over-learning." The more supervisors practice correct behaviors, the more likely they will be to apply the skills appropriately on the job. It's not difficult to use skills correctly in the comfort of the training room. Back on the job, however, anxiety or stress may inhibit use of the skills. For example, when supervisors learn the skill of introducing change to their work group, they often are able to handle this task with little difficulty—in the classroom. But when supervisors actually introduce on-the-job changes and employees raise difficult questions, the stress of the real-life situation can make supervisors nervous and ineffective. Supervisors who have over-learned skills in the classroom will be more likely to use them effectively under stressful on-the-job conditions.

2. **Build confidence.** Supervisors who develop confidence in their ability to use the new skills successfully will be more likely to use those skills on the job. But, too often, supervisors leave training programs feeling that the new skills are even more difficult and complicated than they had envisioned at the beginning of the program. The trainer can counter this by building supervisors' confidence through the following approaches.

- Coach for success experiences. Supervisors' confidence must be built through a series of successes rather than failures. Before the start of each skill practice, the trainer must discuss the situation to be handled to make sure the supervisor understands all the issues and information involved. In addition, the trainer must coach the supervisor on how to use the skills being learned so he or she can deal effectively with the situation in the skill practice exercise. This coaching assures that each skill practice attempt will result in a success, rather than a failure, experience for the supervisor.

- Provide an opportunity to practice using the skills in increasingly difficult situations. The trainer should structure the learning experience so that each practice situation becomes increasingly diffcult to handle. As supervisors discover that they can successfully handle the more diffcult situations, particularly those they previously had been unable to handle effectively, their confidence in their ability to use the skills will increase.

3. **Apply skills immediately.** The shorter the time between the training and the actual on-the-job use of the skills, the greater the probability that supervisors will continue to use those new skills. To facilitate immediate skill transfer, the trainer should gain the supervisors' commitment to use the skills.

While in the classroom, the supervisors should describe a situation in which they will use the new skills as soon as they return to the job. Once a supervisor has verbalized to his or her colleagues that he or she intends to handle a particular situation, the probability of actually doing it increases. For example, if Supervisor Smith indicates that he intends to handle a work habit problem with Employee Jones, Smith will feel more committed to tackle that problem.

The probability of skill transfer can be increased by having supervisors practice handling specific on-the-job situations in the classroom before applying the skills in real life. This rehearsal often provides the extra measure of confidence needed to confront a particularly difficult problem on the job.

The trainer also should follow up on skill use. In subsequent class sessions, time should be set aside to review the supervisors' experiences in using the new skills on the job. This provides a non-threatening environment in which supervisors can share their successes and discuss how to overcome the problems encountered in applying the skills.

When other supervisors hear that Jones did change his poor work habit after Smith discussed it with him, they will feel that they, too, can handle similar situations themselves. Those using the skills on the job can be coached by those who handled similar situations successfully. This mutual sharing of success experiences and coaching in problem areas will increase the use of the skills on the job.

After training

The success of supervisory training depends both upon the effectiveness of the classroom training and the reinforcement received on the job. Therefore, supervisors must be rewarded for using the skills on the job. This reinforcement can come from several sources, and, in each case, the trainer can increase the probability of it occurring.

1. **Self-assessment.** As supervisors begin to use their new skills on the job, the most readily available source of feedback and reinforcement is the supervisors themselves. Therefore, they must be able to assess their own effectiveness and then make the necessary adjustments for using the skills in the future. When supervisors determine that they have used the skill well, that behavior is reinforced. When supervisors judge that they used the skill ineffectively, they must be able to correct their behavior for future applications.

The trainer can help supervisors accurately assess their own skill levels by teaching them to discriminate between their effective and ineffective use of the skills. Often, supervisors don't know the difference between effective and ineffective behavior in handling a specific situation. They first must be provided with an effective model so they will have a standard with which to compare their own skill level. As supervisors observe others, as well as assess themselves in skill practices, their ability to distinguish between effective and ineffective behaviors gradually will increase.

Trainers also should encourage supervisors to assess their own skill level continually when they use the skills back on the job. To maintain skill proficiency, a person continually must analyze how he or she is doing compared with the established standard. Just as athletes compare their actual performance after each game with what they wanted to do, the good supervisor must analyze how a situation actually was handled compared with what he or she wanted to do. The supervisor then can determine what should be done differently next time.

2. **Peer reinforcement.** Supervisory training shouldn't be limited to new supervisors or to those "who really need it." When only some supervisors learn new skills, they return to work

with peer supervisors who may lack those skills. The reinforcement the trained supervisors receive from their peers will be directed primarily toward those skills that all the supervisors have in common. Consequently, the newly learned skills may receive no reinforcement and gradually may be extinguished.

The trainer can increase the likelihood that peer supervisors will reinforce each other's use of the new skills by having *all* supervisors within a functional group participate in the training. That way, supervisors who have successfully applied the skills will receive recognition from their peer supervisors. And supervisors who have been reluctant to use the skills will be encouraged to do so when they hear about other supervisors' successes.

3. **Management reinforcement.** If transfer is to occur and skill usage continue, supervisors must also receive reinforcement from their bosses for using the new skills. The trainer must make sure that managers assume three essential roles in reinforcing the skills their subordinate supervisors have learned in the classroom.

● Manager as a coach— Skill transfer will occur more often when managers coach their subordinate supervisors on how to use the newly learned supervisory skills. Unless managers are thoroughly familiar with the new skills, however, and can discriminate between effective and ineffective supervisory behavior, they will not be effective coaches. Therefore, the trainer must teach managers what specific skills the supervisors will be using. Once managers develop a thorough knowledge of these supervisory skills, they can coach their supervisors on how to use them on the job.

● Manager as a reinforcer— Managers may understand the theory of reinforcement but not be effective reinforcers, because they haven't been trained how to reinforce. For reinforcement to be effective, it must be directed toward specific behavior. Thus, managers must be trained to discriminate accurately between effective and ineffective behavior, as well as to utilize appropriate methods to reinforce the use of supervisory skills on the job. Trainers should provide managers with sufficient opportunities to develop the skills of discriminating between effective and ineffective supervisory behavior and of reinforcing effective supervisory behavior on the job. Thus, a manager will be able to recognize when a supervisor is correctly handling a situation, such as an employee's poor work habit, and positively reinforce the supervisor for doing so.

● Because managers are the most visible models for their subordinate supervisors, supervisors will tend to imitate their behavior. Consequently, to increase the probability that supervisors will use their new skills on the job, their managers must utilize supervisory skills compatible with those the supervisors learned in the classroom. In the classroom, for example, supervisors may learn to handle employee complaints effectively by listening to the employee and getting complete details about the complaint. When the supervisor then brings a complaint to his or her manager, he or she expects the manager to listen to all the details about *that* complaint. If the manager fails to do this, the supervisors will feel it's a waste of time to use those skills when handling complaints with his or her subordinates. The trainer must make managers aware of their impact as models upon their subordinate supervisors. In addition, the trainer must provide managers with classroom experiences that will enable them to develop the skills necessary to fulfill their roles as positive models.

Summary

Training provides skills, information, knowledge and the potential for successful application on the job. But only the actual transfer of those skills to on-the-job situations demonstrates the success of the training. And reinforcement of the use of skills on the job determines whether or not the acquired skills will be used in the future.

Trainers have the opportunity and the responsibility to use methods in the classroom that will increase skill transfer on the job. Through these methods, trainers can increase skill transfer, thus assuring on-the-job application of the potential developed in the classroom.

Reprinted from TRAINING, September 1979

TEN BENEFITS OF PARTICIPANT ACTION PLANNING

Why do experienced trainers run programs that work better than yours? For one thing, they're probably using PAPA

BY ROBERT B. YOUKER

The ultimate purpose of training employees is to improve an organization's results. The way training does this is by producing—or setting the stage for—a change in individual behavior on the job. As far as job-related training is concerned, "transfer of learning" from the classroom to the actual working situation is not just *an* issue, it's *the* issue. That's where PAPA comes in.

The Participant Action Planning Approach is a simple but powerful process that requires each trainee to prepare a list of concrete actions or changes he or she plans to make back on the job once the training program is over. A number of modifications or enhancements can be added to the basic PAPA model, and variations of the model itself go by a lot of names. But the intent is the same: to encourage changes in behavior back on the job.

What is a "concrete" action plan? In a 1978 article in *Management Review* titled "What Makes Sense in Management Training?" William G. Dyer had this to say:

"After the training-practice-feedback activities, each manager develops a detailed plan of action for implementing new behaviors in the back-home setting. The plan specifically includes what actions will be

taken, who will be asked to support the action, when it will start and how success or failure will be evaluated.

"If the program is held within a single company, all managers should review these plans with their bosses. In 'stranger groups,' participants should critique each others' plans, but are urged to share the plans with their supervisors back on the job."

Action planning is hardly a new concept. In the United States, the basic idea was proposed by Prof. James N. Mosel of the psychology department at George Washington University. In the late 1970s, Ruth Salinger and others in the U.S. Office of Personnel Management developed Mosel's idea into an organized process for action planning as a method of evaluating the success of training programs. When PAPA is used as a tool for evaluation, the organizer of a course follows up on the action plans at some later date (six months after the training is a popular choice) to see what changes actually have occurred.

What benefits does action planning offer the trainer? The accompanying figure shows a model or flowchart of a management training process, including the three key areas calling for evaluation: learning, behavior and productivity. Action planning provides benefits at all three levels.

Here are 10 of PAPA's benefits.

1 *Transfer of learning.* The plan of actions to be implemented back on the job starts the process of learning transfer. An action plan is a written list of goals similar to those negotiated in a management-by-objectives (MBO) format. The goal-setting process helps each trainee establish a level of aspiration for putting the training to work—for implementing the desired results of the program.

2 *Verbalization and commitment.* The process of discussing each participant's action plan in small groups leads to individual commitment. Talking about what you plan to do doesn't guarantee you'll do it, but it increases the likelihood.

3 *Practice for implementation.* During the small-group discussion, each trainee also works out some tentative strategies for putting the action plan to work. What problems might arise? How could those problems be overcome? This process of building confidence can be strengthened if there is time for rehearsal and role playing to simulate conditions back on the job.

4 *Contingency planning.* Once you start mapping out strategies for how you're actually going to accomplish something back in the "real world," some serious potential obstacles are likely to surface. The instructor can coach trainees and provide support in developing contingency plans.

5 *Commitment to action.* The process of preparing an action plan can create a self-fulfilling prophecy. In addition to focusing attention on post-training activities, the planning process also will generate commitment to action.

6 *Expectation of follow-up.* The commitment to action is reinforced by the trainees' knowledge that there will be some sort of follow-up to the actual training. Participants know that in six months somebody will be around asking about their progress and expecting answers.

7 *Reinforcement via follow-up.* The actual follow-up is also a powerful motivating force. First, it is a mechanical reminder of the action plan. The follow-up counters the ubiquitous "out of sight, out of mind" problem. In addition, it can generate a "Hawthorne Effect"—the phenomenon whereby desired behavior increases simply because employees know that somebody cares and is paying attention. The process of communication during the six-month check also is rewarding or reinforcing in the Skinnerian sense. This is particularly true if the trainee's supervisor is involved in the follow-up process.

To quote again from William Dyer, "Unless training is followed up and reinforced, it dissipates quickly. Follow-up procedures should include review sessions with the participant's boss, in-company support teams that meet regularly to review results of the action plan, reassembly of the instrumented data several months after the training program, direct consultation by internal training and development personnel, one-day follow-up training/practice/feedback sessions."

8 *Supportive post-training environment.* The six-month check on participants' progress with their action plans also can identify constraints in the environment that have prevented them from changing their behavior or achieving their goals. Ideally, the supervisor and/or the organization took steps before the training even began to ensure that trainees would return to a working environment that supported and reinforced the behavior they would be taught to adopt. The post-training interview provides an excellent opportunity to uncover any environmental factors that are blocking the desired behavior instead of encouraging it. These factors can involve anything from the way equipment is designed to the attitudes of superiors, subordinates and peers.

9 *Evaluation of behavior change.* The process of identifying and analyzing which behaviors in the action plans have been implemented is, of course, an extremely important step in evaluating the effects, and therefore the value, of the training program.

10 *A system for organizational change.* A major additional

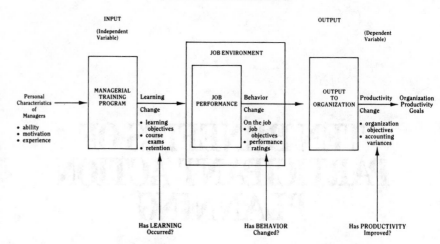

THE TRAINING EVALUATION MODEL

Source: Azevedo and Pinto in Determining the Payoff of Management Training, *Richard O. Peterson, editor (1978, American Society for Training and Development, Inc.).*

For Further Reading on PAPA

"A Guide to the Participant Action Plan Approach," U.S. Office of Personnel Management, Productivity Research and Evaluation Division, February 1980.

Dyer, William G., "What Makes Sense in Management Training?" *Management Review,* American Management Association, New York, June 1978.

Gast, Ilene, "Abstracts of Selected Management Training Evaluations," U.S. Civil Service Commission, Bureau of Training, Training Leadership Division, TLP-03-02, December 1977.

Hahne, C.E., "How to Measure Results of Sales Training," *Training and Development Journal,* November 1977.

Hamblin, A.C., *Evaluation and Control of Training.* McGraw-Hill Book Co., London, 1974.

Harmon, Frances L. and Albert S. Glickman, "Managerial Training: Reinforcement Through Evaluation," *Journal of the Public Personnel Association,* October 1965.

Kirkpatrick, Donald L. (ed.), *Evaluating Training Programs.*

American Society for Training and Development, Inc., Washington, DC, 1975.

Mosel, James N., "Why Training Programs Fail to Carry Over," *Personnel,* Nov-Dec 1957.

Peterson, Richard O. (ed.), "Determining the Payoff of Management Training," a series of research papers and discussions presented at the ASTD's First Annual Invitational Research Seminar, Pomona, CA, October 1978. American Society for Training and Development, Inc., Washington, DC.

Salinger, Ruth F. and Joan Bartlett, "Evaluating the Impact of Training: A Collection of Federal Agency Evaluation Practices," a publication of the U.S. Office of Personnel Management, Office of Training, Training Resources Management Division, Spring 1983.

Spitzer, Dean R., "But Will They Use Training on the Job?" *TRAINING,* September 1982.

Zemke, Ron and John Gunkler, "28 Techniques for Transforming Training into Performance," *TRAINING,* April 1985.

benefit from PAPA can be achieved if the trainee and his or her superior work *together* to define the objectives of the training, in behavioral terms, before the training starts. This not only helps to produce more realistic training programs, it also commits the supervisor to developing a

supportive post-training environment. In this way, PAPA can be expanded into a total system for encouraging organizational change, a system that exploits the Hawthorne Effect and many principles of learning transfer with happy results.

Reprinted from TRAINING, June 1985

ON-THE-JOB PERFORMANCE OBJECTIVES

The most a training course can promise is 'can do,' not 'will do.' Trainers who assume that learning equals job performance had better not offer any money-back guarantees

BY FRANK O. HOFFMAN

It happened again just the other day. A client inquiring about one of my standard supervisory training courses asked, "What are the learning objectives? How will supervisors' performance improve? What results will we get for our money?" All this before we had probed the problems to be solved, considered whether training might be part of the solution or identified the specific training activities which might help.

Two things are wrong with these questions: They are premature, and they confuse *learning* with *performance* and *results*. Although many trainers and human resources development (HRD) professionals have rightfully become dedicated to the idea of behavioral learning objectives, they forget that the most a course can guarantee is "can do," not "will do."

Expecting a course to offer you on-the-job performance improvements and payoff results as learning objectives shows naive faith in a simplistic equation:

Learning = job performance = results

Wouldn't that be nice? Unfortunately, once a trainee leaves the learning situation—no matter how solidly the learning has been implanted—many other factors influence whether or not on-the-job behavior will reflect that learning. And even if it does, results are often influenced by circumstances totally outside the realm of learning or job performance. Thus, a more accurate model is:

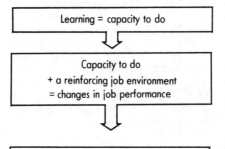

At best, a training course can provide only the first block of the model; the factors in the second and third blocks are beyond its scope. Learning objectives properly relate only to behavioral changes occurring within the confines of the course.

To guarantee performance or results, the course must become a training *program* that integrates all the factors necessary for the learning-performance-results process to occur. If all the factors are addressed, a training program can have objectives which extend beyond learning to the application of that learning and to the effects of that application. This involves several different types of objectives.

Learning objectives

Since Robert Mager first popularized the concept of behavioral learning objectives, much has been written about the need to spell out the behavioral changes which will occur if the targeted learning has been produced.

However, the changes in behavior that prove learning has been attained must occur *within* the training situation, not on the job *after* the training is over. Since the behavior you want to change occurs on the job, your natural tendency may be to state learning objectives in terms of job performance and results. This is where Mager and other proponents of behavioral objectives get misinterpreted. Typical learning objectives *misstated* in on-the-job terms are:

• "Using the Chi-analysis technique taught in the course, participants will correctly identify 98% of any improper loan forms submitted to them during the normal workweek."

• "Salespeople will use at least three of the five appropriate closing techniques in every sales call which goes beyond Stage 2."

Obviously, if the loan officers spot the improper forms and the salespeople apply the techniques, learning took place. But did the learning necessarily result from the course? Perhaps the behaviors are being demanded or taught by new influences in the job environment. If so, you could perpetuate a course which teaches nothing simply because its targeted behaviors are occurring on the job.

Worse yet, suppose the loan officers fail to spot the required percentage of improper forms. Does that mean they did not learn how to do so while they were in the training course? If on-the-job influences inhibit the application of learning, you could easily assume the course is at fault for not teaching. If so, you'll mistakenly modify or eliminate the course, rather than working on the job environment—an approach that can be likened to amputating the wrong leg.

Learning should be demonstrated while the training is going on, uncontaminated by outside factors which can give false signals as to whether or not it occurred. This way, you can still do something about it if the objectives are not being met. But keep in mind that when your training department offers a course, the most it can guarantee to produce is *learning*, not on-the-job change.

OTJ performance objectives

Job-performance objectives are not well understood. In the literature, they are rarely differentiated from end-of-course objectives. The technology for establishing and writing them is not at all advanced, probably because neither trainers nor managers have grasped whose responsibility they are.

If a course demonstrates that the students have learned, whose job is it to assure they apply their newly acquired knowledge? The same individual who is responsible for making sure employees know what they need to know in order to do their jobs properly. Obviously, their boss.

Bosses, not trainers or trainees, are accountable for developing and writing on-the-job performance objectives—and ensuring that their employees attain them. Therefore, it is also the boss who should see to it that employees use the targeted learning produced by a course.

As the technology of on-the-job performance objectives matures, it may take three different forms:

• Participant-initiated objectives for behaviors the trainee intends to apply.

• Boss-initiated objectives for trainee behaviors the boss intends to ensure.

• Boss-initiated objectives for activities the *boss* will perform to promote the application of learning by trainees.

From the trainee

Participant-initiated job-performance objectives are somewhat like standard MBO objectives, except that they describe activities as well as results. Remember, on-the-job performance objectives aim at changing *behavior*, therefore the behavior itself should be brought into focus. Rewritten from this perspective, the sample learning objectives would be:

• "I intend to apply the six-step checklist for troubleshooting on at least 90% of the problems I am assigned to diagnose. My goal is to catch 50% of the problems on the first pass."

• "I will apply at least three of the five closing techniques in each sales call which goes beyond Stage 2. My target is to increase the closings of such calls by at least 10% during the first six months and by 15% for the next six months."

To whom the trainee submits these objectives is a critical factor. Trainers who don't understand that line managers are accountable for the *application* of learning often encourage trainees to establish performance commitments with them (the trainers).

This posture assumes that trainees are totally in command of their job performance and that all they need is a sense of commitment: If they want to perform, they will. In the workaday world, however, output pressures, priorities, peer pressures, customer pressures and boss pressures can

easily drive out new behaviors.

Therefore, participant-initiated job-performance objectives should be a matter of commitment between trainees and their bosses. The trainer should stay out of it. The trainer's role in this process is to help participants understand *how* to meet their objectives, and to help bosses understand their responsibility for ensuring that the objectives are met.

From the boss

Boss-initiated objectives for the performance of trainees define what the boss would like to see the trainee doing on the job after the course is completed. Boss objectives might be phrased like this:

• "Salespeople will review the appropriate product descriptions and complete the Advantages Checklist prior to each sales call."

• Prior to setting up the job, foremen will review set-up plans with employees on at least 70% of the work orders.

Again, note that these are objectives for *behavior*, not just the effects of that behavior.

There is nothing magical about having both participant-initiated and boss-initiated performance objectives. These examples merely demonstrate that they can take either form. The ideal process would allow the boss and participant to develop objectives together.

Boss' responsibilities

Objectives initiated by bosses for their own activities should be aimed at creating a job environment that reinforces the newly learned behavior. Simply setting learning objectives or job-performance objectives is not going to change the pressures that caused employees to give low priority to quality, cost control, accurate record keeping or whatever in the first place. Without that crucial change in the job environment, performance probably will revert to the old patterns within a month or so after the training course ends.

Someone has to ensure a job environment that reinforces, rather than extinguishes, the targeted behavior—and that someone is the boss. Bosses must commit themselves to activities *they* will perform to assure that the desired on-the-job behavior will occur.

These objectives include reinforcing changed behavior and removing or reducing conflicting pressures in the job environment. Some sample boss-activity objectives:

• "Once a week I will spot-check at

least one salesperson's Advantages Checklists to see if they jibe with the product manual, and to be sure there is one for each sales call made."

• "I will relax output quotas by 5% for the next two months, so that employees can focus on practicing the quality-building skills taught in Course B."

The beauty of boss-activity objectives is that it doesn't take very many of them to work wonders. The boss doesn't need to develop an exhaustive list—just one or two commitments to action that will reinforce the training and one or two acknowledgements that conflicting counter-pressures will be dealt with.

Do we need 'em?

If you have any doubts that job-performance objectives are necessary, look at the effect learning objectives have had on the technology of course design and instruction. The same phenomenon will happen with job-performance objectives once the concept becomes well understood. No longer will trainers be forced into the untenable position of trying to guarantee that learning alone will produce the desired on-the-job behavior. No longer will we waste time and effort blundering down the false trails created by the notion that on-the-job behavior necesssarily proves or disproves that the intended learning took place in the classroom. If our purpose is to change job performance, we must focus on factors outside the classroom that control performance.

We will come to realize that any trainer who asks a course to produce on-the-job behavior change, without addressing boss objectives, is uninformed. Consultants who promote training courses on the basis of improved performance and results, without describing how they will influence job-environment factors under the control of bosses, will be recognized as charlatans.

The concept of on-the-job behavioral objectives—and especially of boss-initiated objectives—is in its infancy. I believe the next major frontier of training technology lies here. The concepts and techniques involved in things such as front-end analysis, criterion-referenced instruction, documented learning, behavior modeling, multi-image presentation, and computer-assisted instruction already are well advanced, but they don't solve the problem of on-the-job application. If you want to make a contribution to the training profession, experiment with job-performance objectives.

Reprinted from TRAINING, September 1983

FEEDBACK TECHNOLOGY AND THE GROWING APPETITE FOR SELF-KNOWLEDGE

Here's a report on what feedback is, and how you can improve your own programs by giving more of it

BY RON ZEMKE

If there is a universal concept in the diverse training and development field, it is feedback. It is common to all subspecialties. Performance management specialists work hard to ensure that people who produce widgets, serve meals, greet customers and tote barges receive accurate and timely information about the quantity and quality of widgets produced, meals served, customer greeted and barges toted.

Specialists in individualized and self-paced instruction pluck their chins over the best ways to use knowledge of results—feedback—to promote the mastery of concepts and ideas. Their academic cousins, the educational psychologists, have built prodigious literature around such issues as "the type and timing of questions and answers to promote retention of textual materials." Many theses—and careers—have been devoted to such specialized feedback issues.

Members of the team-building and organization-development branches of human resources development spend much of their energy helping work groups learn to communicate better and to collect, analyze and discuss data about both the means and ends of their unified efforts. Increasing organizational effectiveness through data-based feedback is the goal.

Management training and management development specialists

have a double-edged feedback blade in their razors. On the one hand they have the task of teaching managers to correctly read and respond to survey and other structured information from subordinates. At the same time, they must counsel managers in the delicate tasks of coaching, counseling and reviewing the goals and performance of subordinates in the

The technology to meet the demand for feedback exists—it's up to the HRD professional to implement it.

never-ending effort to be maximally effective.

And what sales trainer hasn't been delighted to discover yet another method his or her charges can use to read the reactions of their customers and to learn to obtain feedback from their prospects and clients? But ironically, the more we learn about feedback and the effects it can have on learning and performance, the more there seems to be to learn.

Simply put, feedback is "the process of giving data back for the purpose of bringing about change," according to David A. Nadler, a professor in the graduate school of business at Columbia University. Though not a new idea, the term feedback is of relatively recent vintage, owing coinage to engineer Norbert Wiener, formulator of cybernetic theory, the hot-button topic of the 1950s.

Though Wiener was thinking only of mechanical systems when he wrote that "for any machine subject to a varied external environment to act effectively, it is necessary that information concerning the results of its own action be furnished to it," it didn't take long for psychologists and communications researchers to see that "feedback, this property of being able to adjust future conduct by past performance" had application to human as well as strictly mechanical systems.

Nadler, in his book, *Feedback and Organization Development* (Addison-Wesley, 1977), reviews a broad body of research on exactly how feedback affects *human* performance, concluding that "Feedback affects behavior by performing two different types of functions ... First, feedback serves to create or generate energy. This generation of energy is frequently called the *motivating function* of feedback. Second, feedback serves to direct behavior where motivation already exists. This *directing function* is to a large extent similar to the error-correction model developed by the systems theorists."

Nadler goes on to describe three motivating and two directing feedback mechanisms that seem to account for the powerful effects of this information-sharing phenomenon.

Motivation by disconfirmation involves arousal through the creation of inconsistent perceptions. It includes information perceived as valid and accurate that tells the performer he or she is somehow "off target" and promotes actions to get back on target. ("Whoops! I thought the class went over better than *that*!" is an example of disconformation.)

Motivation by extrinsic reward expectation tells performers how well they are doing at meeting a goal that has a tangible reward pinned to it. Change occurs when the individual or group receiving the performance information believes there is a link between the feedback and the reward, that the reward has value and that the group or individual believes they can alter performance enough to meet the goal.

463

GETTING GOOD FEED-BACK—AND GIVING BACK IN KIND

BY RON ZEMKE

Training and development folks sometimes talk a better feedback game than they play. Our behavior often belies our lectures and admonitions and conveys a "Do as I say, not as I do" message.

If that accusation makes you edgy, you are not alone. William G. Dyer, professor of organizational behavior at Brigham Young University in Provo, UT, confesses, "As I observe my own behavior, I find the same tendencies—I have been writing and doing research on feedback for years and I don't engage in many feedback-gathering procedures. This has led to a not altogether brilliant, but certainly sound insight: Feedback is not fun! It is not easy to look at ourselves through others' eyes."

Even when we ask for feedback from others, we may not really want it, suggests Mathew Juechter, president of Wilson Learning Corp. in Eden Prairie, MN: "When someone who works for me says 'I want more feedback' or 'I want feedback on such and so,' I do two things: First I ask them to explain what they want a couple of different ways—until I can repeat back to them exactly what they want to know.

"Then I ask them 'How are you going to react and what are you going to do if the news is bad?' If they look shocked or surprised, I can be pretty sure that they were really looking for recognition and praise, not feedback."

We all probably ask for feedback with our fingers crossed. "Tell me *how* I'm doing" and "Tell me *how good* I'm doing" are really miles apart in meaning, but in conversation we frequently interchange them with cavalier abandon.

Asking for feedback

Frances Meritt Stern, director of the Institute for Behavior Awareness in Springfield, NJ, offers several guidelines for asking for or receiving feedback:

1. Ask for feedback only from people who have seen enough of your behavior that they can provide a balanced report. Make sure you trust and respect them enough to accept the feedback.

2. Tell your feedback source exactly what behavior(s) or performance(s) you want feedback on, why you want feedback, and what you will do with the information. Asking someone who was on a call with you "What did you think of that?" is asking for almost nothing.

3. Ask for feedback in a neutral fashion. To say "Some people think I'm pretty abrasive. I want to know whether that is true or not," is neither neutral nor behavioral. It is similar to asking someone to tell you whether or not you are short.

4. Tell the person how you will respond to the feedback report. Specifically, tell your resource that you won't take off his or her head if a clear, concise, honest report contains negative elements.

5. When receiving feedback, you can ask clarifying questions but do *not* put your resource person on the spot. To ask, "Could you say that another way?" or, "Could you give me an example?" is preferred to asking "What do you mean by *that*?"

6. Focus your attention on open-ended, future-oriented questions such as: "What could I do to keep that from happening next time?"

7. Tell the resource person what the "payoff" is for them. You must make the risk worth taking.

Giving feedback

If you get cornered into giving someone else feedback, and can't feign a sudden case of laryngitis, Stern has some guidelines that will help you through this event (which Dyer calls "most threatening and anxiety producing"). But above all else remember that the best kind of feedback is *about behavior*. It is nonjudgmental, unemotional and fair.

According to Stern, the following 10 ideas will maximize the chances you will help the asker and minimize the possibility of hurting the person and your relationship.

1. Good feedback is solicited, not imposed, and deals with a specific performance the "asker" wants feedback on.

2. Good feedback separates *perceptions* and *facts*. Fact: "I counted four interruptions while Jim was speaking." Perception: "The way I see this problem is..."

3. Good feedback is a balance of positives and negatives. A useful rule of thumb is to give two positives for each negative. It helps you keep a balanced view and avoids devastating the listener. The receiver *always* retains the option of cutting the feedback off. Do not override that option.

4. Good feedback is specific and clear. "The answer you gave to Jones' second price objection was very well worded. You said..."

5. Good feedback deals with things that can be changed. "The rabbit story may offend some listeners. Perhaps you could make it a little less sexist," is appropriate. "You're pretty short and your voice is nasal," is inappropriate.

6. Avoid emotion-laden, biased words. There is a world of difference between: "You're cheap!" and "I feel that you are a very money-conscious person."

7. Feedback should be given at an appropriate time. Don't give feedback on the run.

8. When giving feedback, check the message received to be sure it coincides with the message sent. People sometimes "miss the point" because of the emotional interference of receiving feedback.

9. Good feedback lets the receiver determine how to change. Don't tell the other person what to do.

10. Leave out anything you're unsure of. If the point is too important to leave out, check with another person who was present.

Remember, when someone asks you for feedback, they are showing trust and confidence in you. Respect both. If you feel complimented by being offered this role, tell the other person. Open, honest feedback is hard to give and hard to ask for. Acknowledge the risk the performer took.

Reprinted from TRAINING, April 1982

Motivation by intrinsic/internal reward expectation is similar to motivation through extrinsic expectation with the notable exception that the feedback itself is a rewarding event. In addition, the task must be challenging and the goal worth accomplishing. It also seems that a norm or reference standard is important for internal reward to be in effect. "I did well on a tough task, even better than a lot of others" seems to be the rewarding self-statement the feedback sets up here.

Directing through learning is the simple "Oops! That's wrong!" function feedback can provide when the individual can see an error but not a remedy. This sends the performer/learner on a search for new or different approaches or processes. This brand of feedback tells what happened, why and where the performance went awry; it provides a positive model against which to match the next effort.

Directing by cueing is what feedback is doing when it tells performers how close to plan they are in moving from A to B or achieving goal Z. This is the condition wherein the feedback must be specific and the performer must know already how to take corrective action. Think of driving a car from home to office; that's feedback as behavior directing through cueing.

Nadler's way of slicing feedback into smaller packages isn't the only one. Donald Tosti, vice president of Forum/Operants, Inc. in San Rafael, CA, finds it convenient to talk about the boss-subordinate interchange in terms of summative (motivational) feedback and formative (corrective) feedback.

Joseph A. Tucker, Jr., who teaches educational technology at the Catholic University of America in Washington, DC, discusses feedback in terms of eight feedback regimens or "explicit combinations of information sources used to form and set human performance repertoires."

But no matter how you cut it, one thing is clear: The idea of feedback as a simple playing back of information to the performer(s) who caused it to be generated is quaint and naive. Feedback is a powerful and subtle process, and pretty much a technology complete with vocabulary and a research base unto itself.

Growing appetite

It is really quite propitious that feedback technology is a growth industry, because one of the amazing phenomena of the last few years is the growing appetite for feedback trainers and others are noticing. This is especially true among vendors of training/feedback products and services.

John Geier, president of Performax Systems International, Inc., a Minneapolis, MN-based company that provides feedback instrument-based training programs, says that sales of his company's instruments and related systems have quadrupled since 1970. He estimates that by the end of the current fiscal year 3 million people will have received feedback using one of Performax's 20 instruments.

Mathew Juechter, president of Wilson Learning Corp., another Minnesota-based training company, gives a similar glimpse at the growth of feedback demand: "Last year we processed 30% more feedback instruments than the year before. The demand has been compounding for some time now. Six years ago we had one program that used a feedback instrument. Today all of our programs have feedback instruments or systems of some sort."

Why the high demand for this information? Geier attributes it to a combination of things: "It is part of the self-help, how-to movement, but it is also part of a deeper need. There is an element of control involved, I think. People want to know themselves better than anybody else knows them, so they can be in control and make informed choices about their lives."

Juechter, in another vein, cautions that the desire for information about "me" is not merely a holdover from the "Me Decade" of the 1970s. "The hedonists and self-seekers really couldn't have cared less about how they were seen by others," he says. "There is a sense of anxiety among people today about how they are doing and how they compare to others."

One feedback instrument developer, David W. Merrill, president of TRACOM Corp. in Denver, CO, sees the interest in feedback in general—and instrumented feedback in particular—more deeply rooted in human nature. "The human animal, as opposed to other species, is very much a 'norming' animal," Merrill suggests. "People want very much to know how they are doing relative to others.

"Think about golf and pars and handicaps," he continues. "Watch young people in the video arcades. They are norming—testing themselves against the way others have performed on the game machines. This process is essential if you want to be in control of your life. You need to know how you are doing compared to some standard to make reasonable judgments about what and how you can change. We are in a constant struggle trying to be both normal and unique. Feedback, especially instrumented feedback, helps people do that."

Does that mean instrumented feedback is *the* game? It's a big one, but certainly not the only one. Larry Miller, president of Tarkenton and Company in Atlanta, GA, finds that the demand for "How am I doing?" information has moved his implementation of instrument feedback systems from the assembly line to the executive suite. "CEOs are very eager to have clear, unfuzzy information about the organization and their impact on it," Miller observes. "They know how hard it sometimes is to get straight information from their people."

What's ahead for the application of feedback technology? What should we be doing to fill the demand for more feedback? Experts agree that feedback technology is maturing now, and that the real challenge is in helping people accept and learn to use the news—good and bad—for positive change and growth.

Growth and challenge

As Juechter sees it, "People say they want feedback of all sorts, but they really aren't prepared for information that doesn't simply confirm their positive expectations. I've seen people who I thought were psychologically very hardy get quite defensive over the data on how other people see them. Westerners have traditionally used information as a bludgeon. I think we have a lot of work to do in developing ways of helping people accept and use the information they can get from our technologies."

Miller sees a similar need, but with its own variations. "We have all been so concerned with getting CEOs and other senior executives to sit still and listen that we have forgotten that they need to be challenged to act on the data," he says. "When I'm giving them the news, they do all the right things, they reinforce me with attention and head nodding and ask the right questions. It's easy to believe they *are* processing the information and will take some action. In fact, they are just being good listeners. You have to negotiate a behavior change contract right then and there and hold them accountable to it."

The extreme case, adds Miller, is with entrepreneurs. "They have high energy and can say all the right things," he says. "They have read the latest management theory and are information sponges. But they have also been reinforced in a big way for having strong intuitions and sticking with them despite the opinions of others. Data-based change is hard for them."

Geier sees a big need for program development efforts to catch up with feedback instrument work. "In the early '70s," he says, "we were content to give people an awareness of how others saw them and how they compared to others. But the challenge today is to put learning and the opportunity to change together with the awareness. The IBM managers of yesterday who were content with the motto 'Know thyself' now want to merge that with performance improvement. They want a whole performance formula, and that's quite a challenge."

But lest you think the battle to get performance feedback into the hands of performers is won, consider a recent report by the Work In America Institute. In a survey of 360 managers in 190 institutions, the Scarsdale, NY, research group found that two-thirds of the sample had no idea where they stood in the organization. Moreover, the surveyed organizations collected insufficient data to make sound judgments on matters of compensation, promotion and general performance. Seventy-nine percent said performance data was not systematically collected and 50% said there were no performance reviews held in the organization.

The message is that there is a need and a want for feedback—information people can use to improve performance, change relationships and grow as individuals. The technologies for providing that information are ready and waiting. It is up to the HRD professional to bring the problem and solution together.

Reprinted from TRAINING, April 1982

USING CHECKLISTS AS AN AID TO TRANSFER OF TRAINING

If you're not sure your trainees are applying on the job what they've learned in training, perhaps a checklist can help

BY DON JOINSON

Training for transfer is essential if training is going to attain lasting balance-sheet respectability. If a training manager wishes to claim professional status, he must learn to mistrust end-of-course test scores as a valid criteria of the success of his training design. The only truly valid criterion is the extent to which trainees actively and accurately use on the job the behaviors they have learned in training.

How do you measure transfer? How do you design training to maximize the chance of transfer? These are both troublesome, but intriguing, questions. For our purposes here, we're going to focus on one small, but crucial aspect of the second question. The core answer lies in extensive simulation practice, ideally practice that continues until the learner feels comfortable, capable, and confident in making the learned responses to the stimulus situation.

Recent experience shows that the humble checklist provides an excellent transfer aid. At the end of the formal training course, the learner takes with him a step-by-step checklist of how he should apply his newly acquired concepts and ideas. And he makes a commitment to check his performance at specific intervals.

The checklist becomes, in effect, an over-learning schedule. It represents controlled learning by doing, with every rehearsal helping to consolidate and reinforce the behavioral sequence. After five or six such rehearsals, the checklist is withdrawn. The procedural chain of responses will have become a well-established behavioral pattern, and that elusive "transfer" will have been attained.

Contents of the checklist

A typical checklist, shown in Figure 1, comes from the supplementary material to a training-the-trainer program in the area of learning objectives, where transfer failure is notorious.

Trainers in training accept the concept of measurable objectives, and post-test analyses show us they can understand and describe the need to specify terminal performance in measurable terms, to specify the standards for such performance, and to state the conditions applicable to satisfactory demonstration of the performance. But, having learned how to write such objectives, some trainers still don't write them.

Instead, they will incorporate a film into a program "because it always gets a good reception." And they will run a mediocre supervision or sales training course "because it seems to meet our needs." Meanwhile, the concept of behavioral training objectives lies, dormant and unrealized, at the back of their collective skull.

We believe the solution to this transfer resistance may be extensive simulation practice, supplemented by the follow-through aid of the checklist. Simulation practice shows the importance of objectives (from a ten-minute lecturette to a whole semester of integrated learning activity) and helps develop the habit of constructing specific behavioral objectives for *every* designed learning activity. The checklist, a "process reminder" step-by-step aid, consists of 12 prime questions related to specific objectives.

Each question is so phrased that a "Yes" answer will signify that the original learning objective is being met in full. Wherever a "No" or "Partly" or "Not Sure" answer is recorded, the learner should check the "Action" column and commit himself or herself to remedy the deficiencies.

Build your own checklists

As an alternative to providing ready-made checklists and devices as transfer aids, why not have trainees design their own as the concluding exercise to a formal instructional course? We constructed such a checklist-building module as the final exercise in a two-day time-management training package, "The Time Machine," and found it has a significant effect on assisting transfer.

The training group receives guidelines in checklist construction and a sample checklist as a working model. The group then divides into teams, each of which develops a series of checklist questions for such areas as time-budgeting, delegation, handling paperwork, self-organization, and use of clerical support staff.

Later, the checklists are displayed, discussed, and synthesized into a commonly acceptable version. The course leader then has the final versions printed and distributed to members of the training group. Significantly, transfer tests and field surveys have shown the commitment to a series of self-developed checklists to be extremely high.

Reprinted from TRAINING, June 1977

**Sample
checklist on
following page.**

Figure 1.

Use the checklist as an essential step in your instructional design procedure. Whenever you check any column other than YES, also check the ACTION column. Ensure that appropriate action follows.	YES	NO	PARTLY	NOT SURE	ACTION
1. Have I stated exactly what the learner will be able to do as a result of successful completion of the learning?					
2. Have I stated the desired standard to which the learner will be able to carry out the desired end performance?					
3. Will it be possible to measure precisely that the learner can perform as required to the standard required?					
4. Have I specified what the learner will be allowed to use while he demonstrates he has reached the learning objectives?					
5. Have I specified what the learner will NOT be allowed to use while he carries out the desired end performance?					
6. Is all the above expressed in clear, concise, specific, and measurable terms as a Statement of Learning Objectives?					
7. Have I tested the Statement to ensure that it accurately and completely communicates the learning objectives to the learners?					
8. Have I divided each major learning objective up into a series of goals that may be used as reliable progress markers?					
9. Have I checked that the objectives provide adequate challenge to the learners, without appearing too difficult of attainment?					
10. Have I verified that I have, or will be able to obtain, all the resources needed to assist in objective attainment?					
11. Have I constructed a post-test which will adequately sample learner performance for each of the learning objectives?					
12. Have I constructed a transfer test which will adequately measure how well (if at all) the learning is putting learned skills to work on the job?					

TRAINING FOR SURVIVAL BACK ON THE JOB

Learn from these survey results

BY DON M. RICKS

Following their training, people should return to a work environment where their new performance skills will be recognized and rewarded. Trainers know that. Trainers also know that such an environment can be cultivated by including managers in the planning stages of training so that they become committed to looking for and supporting the subsequent.

But trainers in many organizations know some other things as well. They know, for instance, that a promising program can wither on the vine while months are spent searching for a "convenient" time for a group of managers to get together. They know that some managers have vaguely defined and ambivalent notions about training and are unwilling to discuss them openly. They know that some managers view training not as the road to improvement but to preservation — a way of perpetuating whatever level of mediocrity has become established as "the way we always do it." And to others, training, like janitorial services, is a necessary but essentially nonproductive part of organizational life, something best left to those who are interested in that sort of thing.

So while the average trainer may enjoy reading articles on the systematic design of programs — the ones with the diagrams of boxes and arrows arranged into neat feedback loops — he or she knows that "real life" is very different. A lot of guessing has to be done

concerning what results managers actually expect from training. Programs have to be designed or acquired in spite of unrealistic budgetary and constraints. Schedules have to be negotiated to assure that the training does not conflict with the important activities of the organization. And then trainees, having been put through the best program that management could be talked into approving, are sent back to work environments where their new skills, hardwon and still a bit tentative, are vulnerable to the clumsy criticism of the uninformed and the neglect of the indifferent.

We recently concluded a study that illustrates how little encouragement trainees can often expect "back at the office." From the records of writing workshops conducted, over an 18-month period, for a wide range of corporate and governmental organizations, we selected 150 people. The selection was random except for one variable: on the basis of their pre-course writing style scores, 75 people were chosen as the Study Group and another 75 as the Comparison Group.

The Study Group consisted of people whose pre-course scores indicated that they had entered the workshop with either "fair" or "deficient" stylistic skills. In other words, a substantial number of them could be expected to improve sufficiently to attract the notice of their superiors. The Comparison Group was made up of people whose pre-course scores indicated they entered the workshop with "good"

stylistic skills. So any improvements they took back to work were not likely to cause much comment.

The records on these people contained the pre-/post-follow-up scores from their writing style tests and their responses to a course critique form, completed four weeks after each workshop, that included questions about post-course feedback. In short, we were able to determine who had improved by the end of the workshop and who had retained that improvement until the follow-up testing point, as well as who had received feedback on their writing after the course and the nature of that feedback.

Q. Did the trainees receive post-training feedback from their superiors?

A. Some did, but not nearly as many as we would have liked. Exactly one out of three (only 50 of 150) people indicated that something had been said to them about their writing during the four weeks following the workshop.

Q. Was the feedback that was received consistent with measurable improvements in writing ability?

A. Apparently not. The above ratio applied (with only one percentage difference) to both groups. That is, one of every three people received post-training feedback, whether they were in the Study Group (which was expected to show visible improvements) or the Comparison Group (which was not). Moreover, the ratio held true within the Study Group itself. Of the 75 people in the group, 63 (84%) had achieved measurable improvement on the post-score test. Yet their feedback rate was only slightly higher that that of the 12 people whose test scores indicated no measurable improvement.

Q. Did post-training feedback from superiors affect the permanent acquisition of skills?

A. Again, apparently not very much. Of the 40 people in the Study Group who achieved measurably improved scores on the four-week follow-up test, only a moderately higher percentage (37.5% vs. 33.3%) indicated that they received feedback. In fact, the data contained one real surprise. Nine people who had pre-tested in the "deficient skills" range achieved "marked improvement" (a level of change that produces an almost new writing style) on the follow-up test, yet *all* of them indicated that no one had commented upon the improvement.

General conclusions

At this point, we had to arrive at three general conclusions:

1. We could expect the managers of

only one-third of our workshop participants to provide post-training feedback.

2. Those managers would provide feedback whether or not the individual actually improved.

3. The feedback would have little effect on whether the individual retained his/her improvement.

Then we turned to the critique form responses of those people who had indicated that they had received feedback. Of the 50 people, 40 characterized the feedback as "positive," and the written explanations of several suggested that their superiors had offered explicit comments on specific improvements. Of the remaining ten, none indicated the feedback was "negative," six said "mixed" (managers wondered if their writing had become "too direct"), and four checked the disturbing answer, "indifferent." (One written explanation: "Change was noticed but no reaction was evident.") On the surface, these figures suggested the conclusion that, of our participants who would receive feedback, 80% were likely to get positive responses, and the remainder would at least have a chance to discuss their training with their superiors.

But when we examined the written comments, another variable appeared. Nine of those 40 "positives" looked very much like *self-feedback*. Some examples: "My director signs my letters as I compose them; seldom now does he request changes"; "I received fewer inquiries as to what I have said and wanted in my letters and memos"; "I've been given more letter- and report-writing duties. The result has been great." In other words, these managers apparently did not *say* anything. But their behavior relative to the trainees' writing changed, and the trainees interpreted that change as evidence of their own improvement.

In short, the study suggested that our trainees, when they return to work, are pretty much on their own. Only a few will receive direct, positive encouragement to continue working at improving their writing. The rest will have to depend upon whatever self-teaching and self-feedback skills they gained in the course.

Implications for training

What do the results of this small study suggest for training generally? One pessimistic interpretation is that, except where it is feasible to prepare a receptive post-training environment, those who design workshops should assume that their trainees will return to a work situation in which few will understand what they are trying to do, fewer will care and some will feel threatened. On the other hand, the study also demonstrates that people can improve in a non-supportive work environment. Substantial numbers of the people did upgrade their writing skills, demonstrably and permanently, in spite of receiving little or no post-course feedback.

The key to training people for survival in the post-training environment is, of course, that foundation concept of adult learning — self-direction. Programs designed to provide people with the opportunity to define what skills they need, to measure their own strengths and deficiencies, and to set their own learning objectives will give them the tools they need to improve their performance in the absence of post-training support from others. The most positive result of our study was to illustrate, once again, that training is not something done *to* people, whether by the trainer alone or in collusion with management. It is something done *by* the individuals, who are the sole masters of their environment.

Reprinted from TRAINING, September 1979

BUT WILL THEY USE TRAINING ON THE JOB?

You conducted a dynamite course and set
trainees back to their jobs brimming
with new ideas and skills.
Think your job is over? It's just begun.
Add these techniques to your training
repertoire and prevent entropy

BY DEAN R. SPITZER

One of the trainer's most vexing problems is getting trainees to transfer what they learn in a training session back to the job. Most of us are confident in our ability to teach skills, but few of us can guarantee that these skills will be used when trainees leave the protected classroom environment and go back on the job.

The work environment has so many built-in factors that deter skill application and behavior change: productivity pressures (especially when trainees have been away for some time and work has been building up); pressure to do the job like everybody else ("Who do you think you are, Joe, with those new-fangled techniques!"); and the temptation to regress back to old, more familiar behaviors. But perhaps the strongest factor which works against change is simply that new learning takes time to integrate into existing behavior repertoires. Few employees are willing to make this extra effort unless there are some pretty obvious payoffs. Trainers rarely are in a position to offer tangible incentives for using new skills on the job.

However, the situation is not hopeless. Even without control over incentives, trainers can make on-the-job application of skills easier, provide motivational mechanisms and develop support systems for employees. Our responsibility as trainers does not end when trainees leave the classroom; that's actually only where it begins!

Try the following techniques and you will find that trainees *will* use the skills you have taught them. And this use will be much more effective and effortless than either you or they imagined.

1 Personal action planning is one of the most widely used methods to increase the likelihood of on-the-job follow-through. During the course, individual trainees complete an "action plan," which identifies the steps they plan to take to apply the new skills when they return to the job. As a result, trainees make a certain commitment to action, especially if they publicize their commitment by sharing their plans with others. Ask participants to complete part of their action plans after each segment of the course; then, at the end of the course, ask trainees to review and prioritize their action plan steps.

2 Group action planning follows the same format as personal action planning. Try to form groups of trainees who will either be working together or will have access to each other on the job. This technique develops the same sort of commitment as personal action planning, but also provides a support system for trainees when they return to the job.

3 Multi-phase programming involves running a training program in parts so that trainees immediately apply part of the lesson on the job. Often the lack of on-the-job skill application is caused by "skill overload." Participants just learn too much and feel overwhelmed. By dividing programs into parts, you can send your trainees back to the job with a manageable amount of new skill. They can apply these skills and return to the program to share their experiences and solve problems before progressing to the next skill area.

Multiphase programming is very successful in organizations flexible enough to permit this type of "commuter" training. However, many organizations are not receptive to the idea; they prefer the "all or nothing" approach. Try to sell this type of program within your organization. It is the best way to train.

4 The buddy system pairs program participants so that they can learn together and give each other support back on the job. Since lack of support back on the job is a major problem, train at least two people from each department at the same time. That way, some close interaction will exist after the training program ends.

When the "buddy system" is used along with small-group activities (involving people from other departments), you get the best of both worlds: trainees develop support systems *and* interact with people from other job categories.

5 Performance aids provide a meaningful transition from fully guided learning to independent skill application. Performance aids can include checklists, decision-tables, charts and diagrams; they give trainees a better chance to use new skills, since they provide the minimal guidance that is usually needed in the early stages of on-the-job application.

6 Recognition systems reinforce the value of new skill applications. Although few trainers have much control over major incentives, they can design meaningful recognition systems. Trainers can give certificates, letters of merit, "performance points" and publish newsletters, just to mention a few ideas. Recognition is a powerful incentive in a work environment that offers few other perks.

7 Training trainees as trainers takes the pressure off the training department; provides training in the performance environment; and motivates trainees to learn more, since they will be asked to teach others. This approach to training is a particularly effective way to expand

471

WHY IBM TRAINEES PRACTICE WHAT TRAINERS PREACH

The question of whether "soft" training for technicians and managers at IBM's home office in Endicott, NY, will be applied back on the job is anything but moot. Since 1982 week-long courses that cover subjects such as time management, listening skills and so on have concluded with each trainee providing a signed statement and videotaped description of an action plan that explains exactly how the new information will be used back on the job.

Participants are free to choose specific elements of the course which they feel will prove most useful to them, but they have to choose *something* and they must commit to using it.

The emphasis on application of new skills continues in follow-up sessions two months after the main programs. Entire classes are brought back together to discuss successes and failures, and experiences are compared with the original videotapes. The overall effect is noticeably persuasive in communicating the policy that training *will* be applied instead of forgotten, according to Steve M. Yourst, an IBM staff instructor in Endicott.

"In addition to providing a stimulus for the trainees to formulate solid action plans," Yourst writes, "these individual presentations significantly reinforce the key points made by the instructors by having them reiterated, along with applications, from the viewpoint of the students."

In order to prepare their statements and tapes, trainees obviously have to think about the material presented in the course. Yourst includes a 15-minute period for "reflection" at the end of each day's session for them to do that thinking. The process, he says, "significantly increases the probability that trainees will not only make a better mental connection between theory and practice, but will then go out and apply what they have learned."

Reprinted from TRAINING, August 1984

---

limited training resources, as well as increase the likelihood of on-the-job application.

8 **Contracting** with trainees is a useful motivational technique that increases the likelihood of skill application. The completion of a contract form increases commitment, especially when the trainee is reminded of it later. Some trainees may be reluctant to sign a contract, so this method can be used on a voluntary basis.

9 **Ample resource access** is an important follow-up to training that makes on-the-job application of skills easier. Trainers must never assume that initial training will be enough. Follow-up resources can include a hot-line phone number for asking questions, audiocassettes that will serve as a refresher, summary sheets, trainer visits to the work place and other methods. Resource provisions in the work environment will enhance skill application and demonstrate your continuing commitment to trainees' welfare.

10 **Follow-up questionnaires** should be sent to participants after they have had a week or two to try out new skills. Evaluation questionnaires completed immediately after a course ends are almost always biased by gratitude, relief (that the course is over) and forgetfulness (about all the worst aspects of the course). After all, it is only in application that any training course can be meaningfully evaluated. Additional information and "prodding" can be added to the questionnaire to increase the probability of application. It also shows trainees that you care and are still thinking of them. Send follow-up material to trainees on a regular basis (perhaps weekly) for the first month or two after a course.

11 **Follow-up contacts** such as telephone calls ("How are things going ... ?") or even personal visits serve the same purpose as a questionnaire, but do so more personally.

12 **Follow-up sessions** give participants an opportunity to come together again to share ideas and solve problems. This is particularly useful when the multiphase programming method is impractical. These sessions invariably produce a positive response, as well as provide the opportunity for follow-up course evaluation.

These methods will greatly enhance your effectiveness as a trainer. It will certainly increase the likelihood that trainees will use the skills you so expertly teach them. Program follow-up should not be viewed as an "optional extra." It is an essential part of any effective training course. A trainer must have an arsenal of techniques to avoid "training entropy" in the performance environment. The methods discussed in this article should give you just such an arsenal.

Reprinted from TRAINING, September 1982

PAYING FOR KNOWLEDGE

Looking for a way around
the Peter Principle?
Why not pay people for the skills they're
willing to learn and practice?

BY DALE FEUER

When employers talk about tinkering with the way they determine pay, employees listen.

In a growing number of U.S. organizations, people are listening very carefully as their bosses tell them that they won't be getting paid for what they do...and heaving great sighs of relief when they hear that they'll be paid instead for what they *know how to do.*

These people might even rejoice when they find out that this nontraditional form of compensation, known as skill-based pay, will reward them for learning new job knowledge and skills regardless of their position or length of service with the company.

Employees stand to benefit from a switch to skill-based pay in a variety of ways. First and foremost, they suddenly have a genuine, financial incentive for self-improvement. If they work hard and learn a lot, they'll be that much more valuable to any organization, especially the one that invested in their training. What's more, their earning potential likely will be greater than it would be under a conventional job-based pay plan. Finally, since pay raises are linked to mastery of certain knowledge or skill areas, employees can take the initiative and exercise some control over their financial fates.

But don't get the idea that companies are turning to skill-based pay solely out of the goodness of their hearts. Some American businesses see skill-based pay as a strategic weapon in an arsenal of workplace in-novations aimed at making offices and plants more productive and thus more viable in the world market. In a few companies, skill-based pay stands by itself as a nontraditional strategy in an otherwise conventional setting, but typically it is one element in a multifaceted approach to productivity improvement.

Just how does skill-based pay translate into productivity gains? Well, for starters, proponents claim that it will create a more competent work force. Employees in a skill-based system must demonstrate mastery in newly learned skills in order to receive pay increases. So, in effect, it provides a financial incentive for learning *and* performing.

Contrast this to traditional compensation plans in which pay raises tend to be more closely linked to annual staffing budgets than to individual performance. Frequently, the difference between the salary of the star performer and that of the average employee in the same job category is negligible. The only way to land a sizable pay hike is via promotion. And how many promotions are dictated by a seniority system that is blind to individual differences in job performance, or forced when employees hit the top of their salary ranges?

Not only do vertical promotions often fail as performance incentives, but they also are becoming scarcer in many companies currently cutting back their management staffs. Further, as management positions disappear, the number of employees vying for these positions is peaking, thanks to baby-boom demographics.

When skill-based pay is part of a broader scheme to encourage em-ployee involvement and teamwork, its adherents say, it will produce not only a more competent and motivated staff, but a more flexible and leaner one as well. A work force trained to take on any one of a number of jobs offers obvious advantages to manufacturers that have continuous production operations, or those that frequently change products and processes in response to market conditions.

The logic behind the leaner staffing argument takes two tacks: First, when employees are multiskilled, they can fill in when and where they're needed. The organization doesn't have to overstaff or hire temporaries to cover for sick or vacationing workers. Second, as workers acquire more knowledge and skill about the unit, the plant or the organization as a whole, they often can handle higher-level decision making and problem solving. As a result, the organization needs fewer supervisors and managers.

Gaining ground

From all indications, skill-based pay is a real comer. Business professors, researchers and consultants all report a surge in the number of inquiries on the subject. "I have no doubt it's catching on," says Gerald Ledford Jr., a research scientist at the University of California's Center for Effective Organizations. "I get more calls about that than everything else put together." Henry Tosi, professor of management at the University of Florida, concurs: "More and more companies are doing it. I get one or two calls a week from people wanting information about skill-based pay."

Two recently completed national studies, one on nontraditional reward systems in general and the other on skill-based pay in particular, provide hard data on the prevalence of skill-based pay: between 5% and 8% of all organizations use it to some extent.

One of these studies, "People, Performance and Pay," commissioned jointly by the American Productivity Center and the American Compensation Association, found that approximately 70% of all skill-based pay systems now in use were started within the last five years. The study's author, Carla O'Dell, adds that between one-third and one-half of all new plants—those built in the last 10

473

years—either use skill-based pay now or plan to do so in the near future.

Both studies found that production workers are covered by skill-based pay plans more often than any other type of employee, followed by administrative and clerical personnel, technical and professional people, managers, and service workers, in that order. While the companies that employ skill-based pay tend to be big ones (General Foods, Frito Lay, Sherwin Williams, Shell Oil, General Motors, Procter & Gamble, TRW, Westinghouse, Johnson & Johnson and Firestone, to name a few), the individual plants where it exists are generally small—about 500 employees on average.

More often than not, skill-based pay plans are found in "high-involvement" or "new-design" plants—facilities that encourage employee participation in a multitude of ways, ranging from job enrichment to self-managing work teams. Such plants also tend to have fairly flat organizational structures and minimize the trappings of status between levels.

From pet food to pastry

Probably the earliest reported case of skill-based pay* is that of General Foods' new-design pet food plant in Topeka, KS. As Richard Walton aptly describes in his classic *Harvard Business Review* article ("How to Counter Alienation in the Plant," November-December 1972), a rather bleak situation at the company's existing manufacturing facility paved the way for a bold experiment in human resource management:

"There were frequent instances of employee indifference and inattention that, because of the continuous-process technology, led to plant shutdowns, product waste and costly recycling. . . . Because of these pressures and the fact that it was not difficult to link substantial manufacturing costs to worker alienation, management was receptive to basic innovations in the new plant."

Taking what was deemed a radical approach at the time, management organized the new plant's 70 employees into six teams. "Processing" teams did the jobs of unloading, storing, retrieving and mixing materials, and putting together the final product. "Packaging" teams were responsible for packaging, warehousing and shipping the product.

Teams had much more far-reaching responsibility collectively than individual operators—as they were called in the new plant—would ever have had in a conventional factory. Making job assignments, screening and selecting new operators, conducting quality checks, maintaining equipment and keeping house all fell into the operating teams' domain. Each job assignment included tasks that demanded higher-level abilities, such as planning and problem diagnosis, as well as more mundane activities. This way, everyone was somewhat challenged and no one had to do a job that consisted solely of boring, routine work.

The new plant also was designed to achieve "status parity." It had one parking lot, one entrance shared by office and factory workers, and a common decor from the management offices to the operators' locker rooms.

The Topeka plant's skill-based pay system had four basic pay rates—a base rate and raises for three successive levels of skill mastery: learning the first job assignment, learning all of the job assignments within a team's jurisdiction and learning all of the jobs in the plant. Because everyone in the plant could theoretically earn top pay, operators had nothing to lose by training each other on job assignments they had already mastered.

Eighteen months after the new plant opened, its quality reject rate was 92% lower and its fixed overhead rate 33% less than at the old plant, Walton reports. Absenteeism and turnover were well below industry standards, and the safety record was laudable as well. But the most convincing testimony to the success of the new plant innovations, particularly the skill-based pay system, is the fact that today, 15 years later, plant employees are still paid according to how many job skills they have mastered.

Another pioneer in high-involvement plant design and skill-based pay was Procter & Gamble. P&G began to experiment with these innovations in the late '60s and also judged them effective. Says the University of California's Ledford, "The performance difference between their new and old plants was so great across the board that they decided that every new plant

they make has to be a new-design plant. It was clear that the new plants were making a lot more money than the old ones. In fact, they are now requiring existing plants to switch over."

While the team-based approach of new-design workplaces creates a climate conducive to skill-based pay systems, it is by no means critical for success. Organizations can benefit from a skill-based system even if it is a stand-alone innovation. At Au Bon Pain, a Boston-based manufacturer and retailer of bakery products, for instance, a fairly recent introduction of skill-based pay in a factory that is not organized around teams already has yielded several measurable gains.

Almost two years ago, Au Bon Pain set up a skill-based pay plan for its 60 (now 50) employees of a frozen-dough factory. Employees must master at least three "skill blocks" in the first year or they're out. But after that, they can pick and choose which, if any, of the seven additional skill blocks to tackle. Wages range from a base rate of about $6 up to $13 an hour.

The company's vice president and initiator of the skill-based plan, Leonard Schlesinger, notes that most of the plant workers don't want to learn all of the skill sets, that many are satisfied with the pay they get after mastering the requisite three. Schlesinger, a former Harvard Business School professor who has done a great deal of work on employee motivation, says that he's never seen this lack of interest in earning top dollar anywhere else and speculates that the pay hikes, in this case, may not be big enough to motivate workers to learn all of the new tasks. In any event, he says, low turnover and absenteeism rates suggest that workers are content with their jobs.

"We saw [skill-based pay] as an opportunity to develop depth much more quickly and to maximize flexibility," Schlesinger explains. "We have 19 different products, all processed differently. Now when someone is sick or out, others can fill in. We no longer have to hire temporaries to work during heavy vacation periods, because there are enough people who know how to do each job.

---

*Actually, Gerald Ledford claims to have traced the practice of skill-based pay back to the Roman Legion in the sixth century. According to Ledford, General Bella Sauris doled out pay, promotions and rations to his heavy cavalry based on how well they learned different armaments.

"It also allowed us to integrate our bread and pastry operations, which had been set up separately. Productivity in bread has increased 70% as a result. Another benefit is that our labor costs as a percentage of sales have been flat for almost two years."

All of these cases of skill-based pay represent the same type of system. However, there are variations on the theme. G. Douglas Jenkins Jr. and Nina Gupta, both management professors at the University of Arkansas, describe two fundamentally different forms of skill-based pay in "The Payoffs of Paying for Knowledge," (*National Productivity Review*, Spring 1985). The "multiskill-based pay system," as Jenkins and Gupta term it, is the one described thus far. Plans that fall into this category typically are used with production and clerical/administrative employees and reward employees for learning a wide variety of skills so that they can perform different job assignments.

"Increased knowledge-based systems," more commonly used with technical and professional employees, pay individuals for acquiring more skills or depth within their given speciality. Examples of this type of skill-based pay include dual career ladders, which attempt to compensate scientists, engineers, lawyers and other nonmanagement professionals on a par with upper level managers and the apprenticeship system in the skilled trades.

Success stories

From the perspective of both the organization and the employee, skill-based pay seems to work where it's been installed. In her study of nontraditional reward systems, O'Dell found that only four out of 55 companies that established skill-based pay systems in the last 15 years have since abandoned them. According to Ledford, this means that skill-based pay has one of the lowest "reject rates" of any workplace innovation.

Beyond that, O'Dell found that skill-based pay received better ratings in terms of its impact on performance than any of the other eight alternative reward systems. Eighty-nine percent of the companies using skill-based pay said that it had either a positive or a very positive impact on performance. "Part of the reason is that companies don't just do skill-based pay,

typically," O'Dell asserts, referring to the other employee-involvement and motivation strategies that often accompany skill-based pay.

Low rates of absenteeism and turnover in facilities that use skill-based pay suggest a high degree of job satisfaction. Researchers report high levels of satisfaction with pay as well.

Unfortunately, most of the evaluation of skill-based pay to date has been subjective and anecdotal. "The hard data's not there," Ledford says. "Since skill-based pay is just one of many different innovations, it's difficult to tease out its effects."

Still, the literature is replete with success stories, extolling the virtues and pointing out the pitfalls of skill-based pay, both as an ideology and as a practice. On the one hand, there are the academics and business theorists who write thought-provoking and often inspiring articles. They discuss the problems, the benefits and the larger ramifications of skill-based pay in the workplace, and they present well-conceived arguments for the feasibility of skill-based pay plans in all sorts of settings.

On the other hand, there are the business people who have attempted to start skill-based pay systems in the workplace. They've seen the results in real plants and offices with real employees. Their perceptions are based on firsthand experience and have very little, if anything, to do with theory. University of Florida's Tosi has found that "most managers try it and do it and work it out without much help from anyone except maybe a consultant who doesn't know much about it either." As one plant manager who oversaw the establishment of a skill-based pay plan recalls, "It worked in spite of itself. Management was together enough in its thinking and expectations were high enough to make it work."

What rises to the surface of this mixed sea of information are several points on which the professors and the practitioners agree, as well as several questions that no one can answer with assurance yet.

The known quantities include:
• *The success of skill-based pay hinges on a huge commitment to training.* For a skill-based pay system to work, all of the employees affected by the plan must have an equal opportunity to learn. In "Paying for Knowledge: Myths and Realities," (*National*

Productivity Review, Spring 1986), Gupta, Jenkins and Curington found that a typical skill-based pay plan includes about nine skill blocks, although plans range from having as few as four to as many as 90 skill blocks. In essence, this means that training must be going on all the time.

"Every time you turn around, someone else is in training," comments Au Bon Pain's Schlesinger. Since it's common for workers to train each other in skill-based pay facilities, lost production time can add up: You've not only taken a trainee off the line, but a "trainer" as well. "Because the whole system is built around training," Ledford says, "it's imperative to do the training well and cost-efficiently."

• *The "use-it-or-lose-it" phenomenon makes job rotation a must.* Employees have to practice the job skills they've mastered in order to keep them all reasonably well-honed, so they must continually change positions. The tendency, after awhile, is for employees to gravitate to the job assignments they like the most and do the best, and supervisors usually want it that way. Of course, this defeats the purpose of creating a flexible work force. "Companies that tend to be more disciplined about the rules do better with skill-based pay," says Richard Allison, a former manager at Cummins Engine who worked with skill-based pay plans at four separate facilities.

"Managers have to learn to work with it and support the system. You can't just put in a skill-based pay plan and let it hang," Tosi warns. "People begin to settle into their jobs, and if you have people settling into positions, why have skill-based pay?"

• *Business needs should dictate whether companies use a system of skill-based pay.* Skill-based pay systems are expensive. In addition to the hefty investment in training, direct labor costs and administrative expenses are typically reported to be higher in organizations that use skill-based pay. That's why any organization contemplating such a system should carefully weigh the benefits it hopes to gain against the additional costs.

"A company has to ask itself, 'Are there any economic advantages to increased flexibility?' If not, then skill-based pay certainly isn't a good idea," Schlesinger says. According to Allison, "You use skill-based pay when you want to change something and people need to be trained or educated. You start with the assumption that you've got to pay people. Then you design the system that's going to create the culture that will give you the results you need to compete in your industry."

• *Skill-based pay isn't every employee's cup of tea.* Results from the Gupta, Jenkins and Curington study support the widespread and rather commonsensical observation that people who have little desire to grow and develop on their jobs will not do well in a system that rewards this type of behavior. Some people simply like the stability of systems that pay one person for one job, Schlesinger points out. Allison found that while employees may be willing to learn new skills, they may back off from taking on the additional responsibilities that most skill-based systems foist upon them.

The message here is to take care in selecting and orienting new employees to work in a skill-based pay plant or office. Make it clear up front how the facility will operate and what will be expected of employees. Then, as Allison suggests, you can ask them to "deselect" themselves if they don't think they want to work in this kind of setting.

• *The evaluation of training and performance is more important than ever.* Evaluation is one of the toughest challenges of a skill-based pay system. Because employees receive so much training, and because pay raises are contingent upon some sort of sign-off that the employee has mastered the subject, evaluation is an ongoing activity, not to mention an ultrasensitive issue.

Concerns about who does the evaluation and how it is done are bound to arise. It is not uncommon for employees to have a say in their coworkers' performance evaluation in skill-based systems. For this reason, O'Dell says, "objective measures of training are even more important where skill-based pay is prevalent. No one wants to tell his coworker that he's not making it."

Allison stresses the need for good, objective measures of performance for a different reason. Without them, he says, "employees start to think that the name of the game is learning, not performance." He attributes the success of a skill-based pay system at one Cummins facility in large part to the fact that there was a "very strong, objective-setting performance system" in place.

Still unanswered questions about skill-based pay include:

• *What happens when employees master every skill block and reach the top level of pay?* Compensation expert Edward Lawler III, a professor in the Business School at the University of Southern California, refers to this problem as "topping out," and warns that it can create discontent among employees who have grown used to learning and getting paid for having new skills. And judging from reports from the field, he's right.

"The only problem with the system is when a really good person comes on. The employee advances through the skill blocks very quickly, and the system holds him back," says Schlesinger. According to Gupta, et al., the time it takes an employee to move through all of the skill blocks in the average skill-based system is five years.

Gain sharing and other forms of group-incentive bonuses are the most common solution to the problem. When all or most employees in a skill-based plan have topped out, then many organizations kick in with a gain-sharing plan. O'Dell explains that group incentives tend to encourage individuals to stay in the jobs they do best, and this is at odds with the goals of the skill-based plan. However, she goes on to say, "gain-sharing bonuses aren't typically strong enough to outweigh the desire for greater professionalism among employees. People who are selected for skill-based pay aren't run-of-the-mill individuals. They have aspirations to learn and improve themselves."

• *Can skill-based pay work with managers and professionals?* While several companies have had limited success with dual career ladders for their technical or professional specialists, precious few have even attempted a multiskill-based system for white-collar workers. Problems of defining and measuring skills are bound to become even more pronounced for these jobs.

Nevertheless, O'Dell claims, "it's a natural for the insurance industry. You could assign a client group to a claims group and all employees could eventually learn all parts of the job." Skill-based pay specialists also point to white-collar employees at banks and other businesses where teamwork and coordination are key as likely candidates for skill-based systems.

Information technology is another area where there is talk of trying skill-based pay with salaried employees. One manager of an information systems management group at a *Fortune 500* company explains that he is considering skill-based pay for his people because "the techniques and technology change rapidly in a professional organization. If we can forecast the capabilities we will need in the future, skill-based pay may provide the motivation for workers to prepare for the future." The biggest problems with introducing a skill-based system, he says, are deciding what skills to pay for and how much to pay for them, and getting the population to accept change.

• *Will skill-based pay ever replace traditional compensation systems?* Again, the question revolves around what American businesses need to compete in their markets today, and whether the benefits of a skill-based pay plan outweigh the costs. So far, unfortunately, no one has done a formal cost-benefit analysis of skill-based pay, probably because it would be difficult to tie benefits (i.e., productivity gains, improved employee morale, etc.) to one particular human resource management strategy.

If you listen to managers who have had direct involvement with skill-based pay, you'd probably think the chances were slim that it will ever catch on in a big way. Take the view of Schlesinger, for instance: "I think it will always have limited application and be an alternative to traditional systems. It requires such a huge investment in training and a commitment to stick with that investment."

If you talk to the researchers and theorists, on the other hand, you might think the future for skill-based pay is bright. The University of Southern California's Ledford certainly does: "Traditional pay systems provide an illusion of objectivity; they give managers a system for determining pay. But the way companies determine pay is just one of many things that you can make different assumptions about . . . . Skill-based pay shows employees in a tangible way that the organization values their development."

Reprinted from TRAINING, May 1987

20 WAYS TO ENERGIZE YOUR TRAINING

**The objective is to improve performance.
The obstacle is resistance to change.
The challenge to trainers? Jump the hurdle**

DEAN R. SPITZER

The goal of training is not training. The goal of all job-related training can be boiled down to one deceptively simple phrase: to achieve long-term improvements in the way employees do their jobs. Many excellent training programs fail to achieve this result because their excellence lies in the training and not in the performance improvement.

To design training processes powerful enough to produce results, it helps to keep in mind two concepts grounded in the physical sciences. The first is *inertia,* the tendency to resist change; the second is *entropy,* the tendency toward chaos, disorder and deterioration. Social systems, like physical systems, tend to resist change. They are inclined to stay just as they are, since the people who compose them have a vested interest in the status quo. Social systems, like physical systems, also tend to deteriorate over time unless energy is injected into them continuously.

This means that human-performance systems will resist efforts to improve them. They'll resist such efforts no matter how rewarding and worthwhile the efforts are understood—intellectually—to be. And even if you achieve some improvement in performance, it will deteriorate over time unless it is constantly reenergized.

Small wonder that most training

courses are too weak to combat the ubiquitous forces of comfort with the status quo, lack of management support for training, supervisor indifference, inappropriate trainee selection, lack of follow-up after training, low expectations for training, etc. But inertia can be overcome, entropy can be counteracted and training can be made a more powerful force for performance improvement in your organization. Here are 20 ideas to get you started.

1 *Run management-awareness seminars.* Most managers are woefully ignorant about training. It's not that they don't want training to succeed; they simply don't understand their role in the process. And trainers are at fault. We have failed to correct the tremendous number of misconceptions about training that exist throughout our organizations. Management-awareness seminars will give you the opportunity to explain the need for training and the essential role managers play in the success of training aimed at their subordinates. If you don't teach them, how are they ever going to learn?

2 *Define your own role in the performance-improvement process.* How many training departments do you suppose have a clear statement of their role in performance improvement? Very few. Managers

need to understand that the training department is not a course factory. Its function should be to improve performance by any means available—means that may include both training and non-training interventions. You also should make it clear that analysis of performance problems before training and follow-up after training are not peripheral activities but part and parcel of your job.

All training departments need a clear statement of purpose and a coherent set of unit objectives. It's better to clarify expectations up front than to correct them later. And don't simply file these statements and forget them; distribute them and keep them in front of your staff at all times.

3 *Develop a public-relations campaign.* Everybody in the organization should understand the role of your unit: what you can (and cannot) do for them and what cooperation you expect. To reiterate, if managers don't know what the training department's role is, how can they be effective allies? Develop a brochure that explains the training process, from project selection to follow-up and evaluation. Reposition training as a proactive function.

4 *Target training at key-result areas.* Rather than simply reacting to training requests, go out and find areas in your organization that are ripe for training. Areas likely to offer the greatest payoff for effort expended include purchasing, where considerable money can be saved; departments with high turnover; and any part of your organization where new technology, new procedures or new policies have created significant changes. Develop a cost-benefit model to help you select high-dollar, key-result areas.

5 *Adopt a training "process" approach.* Forget training "programs." They don't work in the long run. A "process" approach prepares people for training with a pre-course discussion with their supervisors and perhaps some preparatory exercises to create realistic expectations. It closes the course with an action-planning scheme. It follows up the training with action-plan reviews, including more discussions with supervisors. It provides for continuous evaluation. Training must use a process approach to build and maintain performance improvement.

6 *Encourage supervisors to talk about the course with subordinates before the training starts.* All too often, employees attend training courses without ever discussing the whys and wherefores with their supervisors—the key people in the performance system. Supervisors are the source of most rewards and punishments. If supervisors are uninterested in the training, why should trainees care about it?

If, however, the supervisor shows genuine interest in the course's objectives, then the trainee will likely take the course seriously. Obviously, management needs to establish a policy to make this a viable strategy. Once again, it's up to you to show managers how critical the supervisory role is.

7 *Focus training on relatively few key concepts.* Information overload is a common trainer trap. As long as they have a captive audience, many trainers burden trainees with every piece of information they can think of. Trainees emerge from such courses with their heads swimming. When they return to the job, they can't begin to apply what they learned because they remember only random bits and pieces. Learning psychologists refer to the problem as retroactive interference, which simply means that new information gets in the way of old information. Retroactive interference is a big part of the reason why loading up a training course to make it "a good value" often produces a course of no value.

8 *Give them practice, practice and more practice.* The most important elements in instructional design are practice and feedback. Practice builds competence and confidence. When you limit the information in your training courses, you will free up time for lots of practice.

Don't send trainees back to the job until you're certain that they really *can do.* "Overlearning" is a good strategy. Remember that when trainees return to their jobs, they will be working under tremendous pressure. If they can't perform the new skill almost as second nature, they probably will go back to the old, comfortable way of doing things.

9 *Substitute job aids for remembering.* Trainers who come from educational backgrounds tend to overvalue memory. A lot of what we call education is little more than a series of memory tests: Those who remember well excel; those who remember poorly do not. In the working world, performance rarely depends heavily on memory. In most cases, a simple set of printed instructions causes little inconvenience to a worker, especially in the early stages of learning. Whenever feasible, do not clutter trainees' minds with information. Give them some well-designed job aids, teach them how to use them, and they will naturally memorize the information on the job aid in a short time.

10 *Train intact groups.* Whenever possible, include "intact" work groups in your training courses. Unless there is a support system back on the job, deterioration of new skills is very likely. We tend to forget that work is a group activity, not an individual one.

Another concept from physics, critical mass, comes into play here. A "threshold" number of employees should be trained in any one job or unit in order to provide the support necessary for new skills to be applied back on the job. The threshold number depends on many factors that vary from job to job and organization to organization. But the point is that if only a few people are doing it the new way—especially if they are not supervisors or group leaders—they probably will revert to doing it the old way before long.

11 *Get trainees to complete end-of-course action plans.* Action plans encourage trainees to make a commitment. Although this technique doesn't ensure that trainees will use what they learn, it does force them to put the commitment in writing. This is bound to increase the likelihood that new skills will be used on the job.

12 *Schedule a discussion with the trainee's boss.* I always tell trainees that the first item on their action plans should be an immediate meeting with their bosses. Without a firm commitment to a meeting, the course is unlikely to be discussed at all. Trainees should take the initiative to set up a post-course meeting if their supervisors don't.

13 *Publicize the action plan.* With the trainees' approval, send copies of the action plans to their supervisors and keep copies yourself. The action plan not only gives the boss valuable information about the trainee's future performance, it also helps explain the value of the training course to the boss. The action plan serves as a guide for the trainee and the supervisor during their discussions of the course and its follow-up activities. Retain a copy to use for your own follow-up and evaluation. That way, when you contact the trainee later, you'll be able to inquire about specific items on the action plan.

14 *Use "multiphase programming."* By breaking a course into phases you give trainees a chance to try out a new skill on the job before learning other skills. When they return for the next phase of training, let them discuss problems they encountered in applying the skills. This approach builds in a support system among trainees during the difficult early stages of learning and application.

Too often, trainers overload learners with a huge number of skills and then expect them to use those skills under high-pressure conditions. Multiphase programming allows trainees to learn a little at a time, apply the skills, gain confidence, and receive feedback and support before learning more.

15 *Follow-up after training.* Follow-up may be the most important key to successful training. Performance-improvement efforts cannot just end when the course ends; there must be continuing efforts to upgrade, motivate, support and monitor performance on the job. Trainers who simply wash their hands of trainees when the course is finished give them a clear message with a clear implication: If the trainer doesn't care, who does?

The trainer must be perceived to care about the objective of on-the-job performance, not just about the training. Follow-up after training provides much of the additional energy necessary to counteract entropy. Without

MISCONCEPTIONS THAT PRODUCE BAD TRAINING

BY DEAN R. SPITZER

Some people collect coins and stamps, some baseball cards, and others miscellaneous household effects. I collect misconceptions about training.

These flawed ideas often lie at the root of failed training efforts. I trace them to a variety of unrealistic attitudes toward the field of training, organizations and people in general. But whatever the causes, their effects can devastate the most well-intentioned training activities.

As trainers, we want to produce measurable, long-term performance improvements; at least, that should be the goal of all our training efforts. To reach that goal, we need to adjust our mistaken views about the role of training in organizational life. Here are some sample misconceptions from my collection:

• *Training is the same as education.* Education (or "development"), with its vague, long-term goals, may be important to an organization's success, but it is not *training.* Training must be immediately applicable on the job. And it must be verifiable in terms of short-range, on-the-job performance improvement.

• *Training is a program.* Conventional wisdom holds that training should be a program, a well-defined course that begins on one day and ends on another. Actually, training should be a process that continues long after the employee has returned to the job.

• *Training is a fixed overhead expense.* Managers who view training as fixed overhead do not require performance-based accountability. Training should be a profit center, an accountable source of verifiable performance improvements and cost savings.

• *Everybody needs training.* Certainly, everyone can benefit from learning more, but not everyone needs immediate, job-relevant training. If limited training resources are spread evenly throughout the organization, many individuals are superficially trained, often in areas that are not directly related to their jobs. We should concentrate our training efforts on potential high-impact areas that really will pay off.

• *Trainers should be responsible for training.* Trainers are staff employees who are charged with helping to produce performance improvement. It is, and must be, line managers and supervisors who are *responsible* for the training and development of their subordinates. Managers love to delegate training to the training department. We should be ready and willing to help, but not to relieve them of responsibility.

• *Employees want to learn new skills.* Trainers tend to believe—idealistically—that all humans want to learn as much as they possibly can. But why should employees want to try new skills if there are no incentives to improve job performance? A business is not a school; it is a place where people work for a living, mostly because they have to work. As Abraham Maslow showed us so graphically, self-actualization needs rarely come into play until all other, lower-level needs are satisfied.

• *Trainers are the best people to do the training.* Actually, trainers tend to be *low credibility* instructors. They are not perceived as experts in the job, they often are young and inexperienced, and they lack the job knowledge that comes from years on the firing line. The best instructors usually are "exemplary performers" who are currently doing the best work on the job.

• *Quality training should be attractive, impressive and fun.* Many trainers spend their time designing courses that will be impressive and enjoyable. This creates the wrong expectations. Quality training is not "flash and splash," it is sharing knowledge and skills that will be used on the job. Let's put the emphasis on content, not on logistics, printing and catering arrangements.

• *The best training departments run the most courses.* Actually, the reverse often is more likely to be true. The best training departments are the ones that spend most of their time analyzing performance problems, providing appropriate training and non-training interventions, and following up after training. Training departments that are overloaded with courses to run don't have time to do the things that make for success. Don't show me your course catalog, show me your results.

• *Participation in training should be voluntary.* Voluntary participation in training gives you trainees who want to be in your class, but it does not contribute much to achieving high impact. Impact comes from training those who *need* training, not necessarily those who *want* training. Also, self-selecting volunteers often create a haphazard collection of trainees who have little in common except their desire to attend the course.

Reprinted from TRAINING, June 1985

adequate follow-up, most training efforts are doomed to ultimate failure.

16 *Use the "exemplary performer" as your model.* Many theorists have pointed out the wisdom of finding and studying the people who do the job best—exemplary performers who manage to do outstanding work within the same system constraints as others who do mediocre work. Why does this individual excel? Usually because of greater personal motivation. You can't teach that kind of motivation, but you can teach the knowledge and techniques this person uses. Identify and debrief your outstanding employees, and use their performance as the basis for training others. A word of caution here: They're great as models, but it may not be the best use of their talents to use exemplary performers as trainers.

17 *Involve managers and supervisors in the design of training.* Without a doubt, one of the best ways to get managers and supervisors on your side is to involve them in training design. People are always more committed to things in which they have been personally involved. You might not use every one of their suggestions, but by all means include representatives of management on your planning teams.

18 *Create a training committee.* Another good way to rally managers behind the training effort is to organize a committee composed of key opinion leaders in your organization. Ask for its guidance on policy matters. You'll probably get some valuable feedback and more support than you have in the past.

19 *Gain visibility in your organization.* Publish a newsletter describing your most successful projects. Highlight members of the training staff, managers who have been most cooperative, and trainees who have excelled in training and on the job after training. Present your training philosophy and objectives. Provide an open forum for feedback. Toot your own horn.

20 *Make a real attempt to evaluate performance.* Most "happiness-index" evaluations are not worth the paper they consume. Training departments need to assess the impact of training on subsequent job performance. I have found it useful to identify specific indicators, often the same indicators that helped identify the performance problem that gave birth to the training course in the first place: high turnover, waste, low morale, excessive costs, etc. Although it may be difficult and time-consuming initially, it will pay off in the long run to "objectify" these performance indicators and develop mechanisms for monitoring them regularly.

Reprinted from TRAINING, August 1985

CHAPTER 7

EVALUATING TRAINING AND MEASURING RESULTS

I ndustrial psychologist John B. Campbell wrote: "The recurring admonition to 'evaluate' training programs is a gross misrepresentation of the empirical question. It strongly implies a dichotomous outcome; to wit, either the program has value or it doesn't. Such a question is simpleminded, unanswerable, and contributes nothing to practical or scientific understanding. The phrase should be banished."*

That is a pretty stiff appraisal, but not a totally unfounded one. Measuring training as if it were an educational program is not really appropriate. Nor is it appropriate to look at training the way one looks at a depreciable machine, capable or not of so many welds per hour. Training is neither fish nor fowl. It requires its own ways of measuring results and interpreting outcomes.

The approach one takes to evaluating training and development activities is very much tied to the role those activities are assigned in the sponsoring organization. The philosophy of evaluation you adopt determines to a large extent the indicators you choose to measure, the instruments and methods you develop for data gathering, the criteria you apply to claiming success or failure, and the use you make of evaluation results. Author Dugan Laird suggested that there are three major philosophies of evaluation, any one of which we may choose to embrace as our touchstone for developing an organization's policy toward evaluating its training:

- contribution to goals
- achievement of learning objectives
- perception of worth.

The first approach is pretty much tied to the solving of organizational performance problems. The thrust of the evaluation effort is focused, therefore, on finding ways to determine whether training has affected the "bottom-line," or at least key operational results of an organization.

The "achievement of learning objectives" approach emphasizes comparing what trainees knew or could demonstrate before the training with what they know and can do after the training. Inherent in this philosophy is the belief that, "Our responsibility is to give them the skills and knowledge they need to do the job right. Whether they actually do the job right—that's someone else's problem." The effort becomes one of ensuring that the right objectives are being addressed, finding ways to measure gains in knowledge and skill, and making sure that the training increases rather than decreases the *likelihood* that trainees will perform better, faster, smarter or nicer back on the job.

The "perceptions" approach has at its core a belief that the trainer's responsibility is to create an environment where people can be exposed to useful information and ideas. The opinions they form about the utility of the material and the value of the training are held to be meaningful and important measures of a training activity. Essentially, if the trainees say it's good training, it's good training. The quest, then, becomes one of determining what opinions count, how they can best be expressed and what pattern of opinions represents a desirable outcome.

The obvious question is, "Shouldn't a good trainer use all of these approaches at one time or another?" The wise answer is, "Probably." But when push comes to shove and you're operating on a real-life time frame with a limited budget, which philosophy have you gone to bat with most frequently in the past? That is your primary evaluation method.

The sum, then, is that evaluation is the art of deciding which factors are important and the science of measuring them. Whether you focus on results, learning or opinion, the evaluation act is a tough one. The articles in this chapter are intended both to challenge your philosophies and to make your act easier to perform—regardless of how you and your organization approach the question, "What did we get in return for the time and money we invested in this training project?"

*Annual Review of Psychology, Vol. 22, p. 565, 1971.

TRAINING FOR IMPACT

Is your training department judged by the
number of bodies it runs through classrooms
or by the results it achieves?
Here's a step-by-step process to help you
create a more valuable role for HRD

BY DANA GAINES ROBINSON

Ever hear of "training for activity?" You may not call it that, but undoubtedly its characteristics will sound familiar: Trainers spend most of their time in the classroom delivering programs; accountability focuses on activity—the number of programs conducted, the number of participants and so on; the training function is *valued* for the same things for which the department is held accountable—the number and variety of its programs; having a large course catalog becomes a real barometer of success.

Those characteristics are common among training departments. It also is common for trainers in such departments to "burn out" from all the stand-up training and begin to wonder about the value of their efforts: Are people really using the skills being taught?

There is an alternative. A human resources development department may have:

• Trainers who spend less than half of their time in the classroom.
• Accountability that focuses upon *results achieved*, both in terms of on-the-job behavior change and the organizational impact of the training.
• A function valued for assisting management in resolving business problems and/or maximizing business opportunities.

This second set of characteristics describes a results-oriented training department that is "training for impact," and while they may not be the norm at present, they certainly are part of HRD's future. Neal Chalofsky, national vice president for professional development of the American Society for Training and Development, reinforced that notion plainly enough in his editorial comments on ASTD's competency study for trainers. In the future, Chalofsky says, "Trainers will be responsible not only for learning, but also for making sure that learning is applied on the job. Trainers will be responsible not only for identifying training needs, but also for evaluating whether those needs are met."

Line management *is* demanding increased accountability from all functions, particularly staff areas which traditionally have been the most difficult to evaluate. The HRD profession, as evidenced by the competency study, *is* moving toward results-oriented training as a standard. There can be no doubt that HRD departments which demonstrate a track record of results meaningful to management will be those most able to gain additional resources. The movement away from activity and toward impact appears irreversible. Where to begin?

The "training for impact" model in Figure 1 suggests one approach. Developed over the past six years, it has been validated through its use in determining the results of sales training, supervisory and managerial training, customer-relations training and technical-skills training.

In order to illustrate the steps involved in the model, let's use a fictitious organization known as Nu-Karparts, Inc. Nu-Karparts, we'll say, is a whole-sale company that supplies automobile parts to independent retail stores throughout the United States.

Step 1. Symptom or request for training

Training needs surface in many ways: Sometimes a line manager calls with a request; sometimes training is "mandated" from top management; often the HRD department itself uncovers a potential problem.

At Nu-Karparts, the director of distribution called the corporate training director to indicate concern over the growing number of customer complaints coming into his office from the retail stores (see Figure 2). These complaints suggested an increase in customer dissatisfaction and required a great deal of senior-level management time to resolve. The distribution director was certain that a training program he had heard about—one which instructed customer-service representatives in how to handle people—would be appropriate. He wanted to pilot-test the program in two distribution centers; granted positive results there, he would implement it in the other two centers.

Step 2. Identify client

Once a need has surfaced, the HRD department must determine the key decision maker for the project—the highest-level individual (or group of individuals) who has the power to make a go/no-go decision *and* has a need to be actively involved. This person or group becomes, in effect, the "client."

Generally, clients are people who a) are two or more levels above the learner, b) are in the learner's chain of command, c) approve any significant action regarding the training project and d) have the most to gain or lose from the success or failure of this effort.

Rarely is the client either the learner himself or the learner's immediate manager. It is also unusual for the client to be the company's training director. Together, the client and the trainer will be making many critical decisions regarding the training project. Ideally, they will arrive at these decisions in a collaborative, consensual manner.

At Nu-Karparts, the trainer assigned to the customer-relations project determined that the appropriate client group would be the director of distribution and the two distribution-center managers involved in the pilot. These were the people who had the most to gain or lose. After the training director discussed the advantages of a client team with the director of distribution, they decided to move forward with these three people as that team.

Step 3. Learner needs: Assessment #1

It is almost always unwise to respond to a training request based upon the input and perspective of just one person; the probability of an accurate diagnosis is very low. At best, the training department may wind up addressing some part of the true problem with modest results. At worst, the diagnosis may have been completely inaccurate, resulting in misplaced use of training resources and damage to the credibility of the training function.

A basic axiom of HRD is that before training resources can be appropriated effectively, a problem's *cause* must be determined. Only then can a decision be made as to whether the problem is something training can address. Information from multiple sources is critical to needs assessment to ensure that all relevant perspectives are included. Possible sources for data gathering might be:

Clients—Key decision makers already identified.

Learners—People who will participate in any training effort which results. Involving the prospective learners helps foster "buy-in" should training be identified as a solution to the problem.

Other interested parties—People who interact with the learners. They could be the direct managers or the employees of the learners. They also could be other staff or line personnel outside the chain of command of the learners. Finally, they might be customers or clients. Each situation determines what categories of people should be included.

State of the art—If someone requests a program in influencing skills, it is the responsibility of the HRD professional to research the field and identify the validated behaviors and skills required to become an effective influencer. We are not in the business of training others according to precepts and programs someone happens to *think* will work. We are in the business of identifying, building and delivering programs that produce behavioral skills which have been *proven* to work.

As Figure 1 illustrates, once information about the learners has been collected it must be analyzed, interpreted and readied for reporting to the client. During this meeting, the trainer and client must draw conclusions from the information. From these conclusions, implications must be determined: "Here's what we have concluded. So what?" The end result of the meeting should be an agreement between trainer and client as to what skills and knowledge, if any, will be taught to which groups of people within the organization.

At Nu-Karparts, the trainer conducted a needs assessment and reported back to the director of distribution and the two center managers. The data indicated the following:

1. Customer-service representatives (CSRs in the company's jargon) in the distribution centers were gathering information from customers in a variety of ways; there was no standard method.

2. About 12% of the calls taken each day were complaints. In a typical month, 22 of these complaint calls were escalated to the director and vice-president levels.

3. Most CSRs were not skilled in asking questions of customers and, therefore, were not getting complete and accurate information when they filled out complaint forms; 50% of the forms were filled out incompletely.

4. Seventy-five percent of the customers interviewed by the trainer during the needs assessment indicated that the CSRs seemed defensive when a complaint was made.

Based on this information, the clients and the training director agreed that CSRs should receive training in both telephone fact-finding skills and the use of empathy.

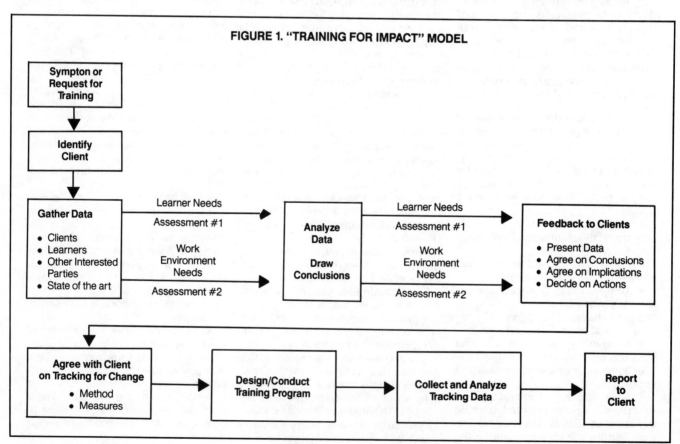

FIGURE 1. "TRAINING FOR IMPACT" MODEL

Work environment needs: Assessment #2

Once the client and the HRD professional have agreed upon specific training objectives, a second diagnostic effort is required if the goal is to produce long-lasting results on the job. Why? Because such results occur only as the product of a learning experience that is on-target and well-delivered, and a work environment that is *supportive* of the new skills. A zero on either side of the equation means long-term results will be impossible to achieve.

While the training department has a great deal of control over the learning experience, it has virtually no control over the work environment. This is where the client/trainer partnership becomes most critical and can really pay off. In order to ensure that skills will transfer to the work environment and persist over time, an analysis of that environment is necessary. In essence, the HRD professional will be attempting to answer these questions:

• What, if anything, about the learners themselves will inhibit or enhance the use of these new skills on the job?

• What, if anything, about the learners' managers will inhibit or enhance the use of these new skills on the job?

• What, if anything, about the organization will inhibit or enhance the use of these new skills on the job?

Once collected, this information again must be analyzed, interpreted and reported to the client. By painting this type of picture, the trainer shows management what will happen if the work environment does not support the new skills—the results management desires will not occur.

At Nu-Karparts, the trainer succeeded in convincing management of the benefits of a work-environment assessment. Even if CSRs had the skills to fact-find on the telephone and to use empathy, they might not use those skills for reasons relating to the organization: The problem would remain and the time and money spent on training would be flushed down the drain. Therefore, the trainer conducted a second assessment to determine whether anything *might* prevent CSRs who completed the training program from using the fact-finding and empathy skills they learned.

The study indicated that there were, indeed, organizational barriers. CSRs pointed out that their primary accountability involved the number of calls they took in a day; the effective handling of complaints was not a performance criterion. Obviously, it would require more time to handle a complaint well, meaning that fewer calls could be taken; in effect, a CSR could be punished for taking more time to handle complaints.

FIGURE 3. RESULTS FROM NU-KARPARTS TRACKING STUDY*

Behaviors	Prior to Training	After Training
1. CSRs will acknowledge the feelings of customers by labeling the feeling.	2.83	4.02
2. CSRs will rephrase what a customer has said before responding.	2.94	4.16
Scale: 1 = Behavior never used 2 = Behavior used about 25% of the time 3 = Behavior used about 50% of the time 4 = Behavior used about 75% of the time 5 = Behavior used 100% of the time		
Organizational Results Complaints per month escalated to director manager level of the organization.	22	5

*In a typical tracking study, dozens of behaviors may be observed. Only two are selected here for illustration.

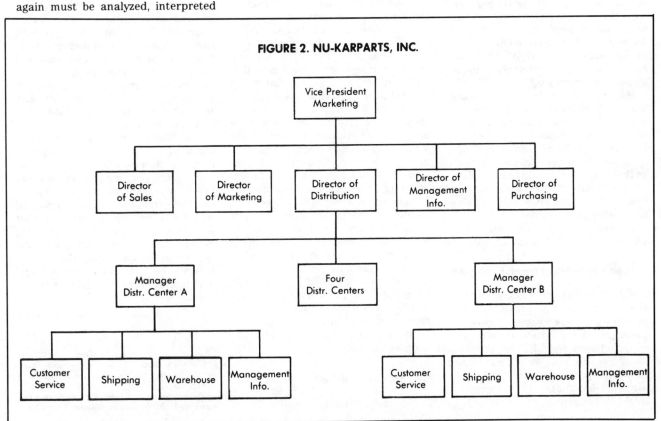

FIGURE 2. NU-KARPARTS, INC.

Management agreed to set up a new accountability system for CSRs that would evaluate the handling of complaints as well as the quantity of calls handled.

Agree with client on tracking for change

Once the program's outcomes have been clearly delineated, it is important to design a system that will monitor the results achieved both in qualitative and quantitative terms. The system must track both the behavior change which has occurred on the job *and* any resulting bottom-line impact to the organization. In order to accomplish this, the client and the trainer must agree on specific outcomes to be tracked.

The HRD professional must create the necessary survey process to gather the information. This usually requires collecting information about behavior both prior to training and at some point following the training. It also may be appropriate to compare the performance of people trained in the program against the performance of a similar group of people who have not received training.

At Nu-Karparts, the clients wanted to know if the CSRs were displaying behaviors such as "acknowledging the feelings of customers" and "rephrasing what the customer has said before responding." They also wanted to know if the number of complaints escalated to top management decreased over time. If complaints were being handled at the lowest level, avoiding the need for management involvement, customer satisfaction probably would increase—and that was another major goal of the training effort.

Information about CSRs' behavior was gathered prior to the training program and again four months later. In order to determine if the new behaviors were being used effectively, questionnaires were sent to the CSRs, to their supervisors and to customers. In this manner, information from the CSRs' self-assessments could be verified from other perspectives.

Information about escalated complaints also was collected.

Design and conduct training program

With the front-end work completed, the training department designs and delivers—or selects and buys—the program. Whether designed internally or purchased outside, the program should address the identified learner needs and proceed with an eye toward any work-environment barriers which might be present.

At Nu-Karparts, the training department designed a two-day program for the CSRs. Their supervisors were provided with an overview of this program and some skill-building in reinforcement behaviors.

Collect tracking data and report results to client

When the specified period has elapsed, post-training information is collected, tabulated, analyzed and reported to the client. This is truly where the "rubber meets the road" for the training department and the client team, for now we are looking at *results*. At this point, management and HRD either congratulate themselves on the program's success or decide on any actions to encourage results which have not yet appeared.

It is critical that the data which the HRD professional brings to this meeting paint an accurate picture so that appropriate decisions can be agreed upon. While HRD reports on the results, HRD *and* the client must determine the "So what?" and agree upon any required actions. If a study has been well constructed and presented, questions such as the following can be addressed:

• What behaviors are people using or not using on the job?

• What bottom-line impact, if any, did we have?

• If we have not achieved the desired results, why not?

• Should the training program be changed? If so, in what ways?

• Is additional training required?

• What must management do to create a work environment that will continue to support these new skills?

At Nu-Karparts, results indicated that behaviors *had* changed. As shown in Figure 3, CSRs who had been through the training program were using the behavior of "acknowledging feelings" at a mean frequency of 4.02, up from a mean frequency of 2.83; they were using the behavior of "rephrasing" at about the same frequency. The average number of escalated complaints dropped from 22 to five per month, providing a real organizational benefit. Most complaints were being handled at the lowest level possible. Because CSRs now were being evaluated on their use of the new skills in handling customer complaints, a reward system was in place to reinforce their *continued* use. All in all, the program appeared to be a success; the training had *impact*.

Can it really be done?

This description of "training for im-pact" may imply that an enormous—perhaps a prohibitive—amount of time is required. That is not the case. Knowledgeable trainers typically conduct some front-end work to clarify learner needs before launching their programs. The unusual parts of this process are the addition of a work-environment assessment and the design and implementation of a tracking system. Combined, these two activities require an additional five to seven days spread over the life span of the training project.

What *is* demanded here is skill: The HRD professional must be able to design good diagnostic systems; consulting skills are necessary both to forge the critical partnership with the client and to make that partnership work. Also required is a revised accountability system for the HRD department. Rather than being evaluated according to how many programs it offers in a year, the training department must be judged in light of the results it helps to achieve. Most HRD professionals probably will have to initiate this change by convincing management that significant benefits can derive from it.

And the benefits *are* significant, not only to management but to the training department: increased credibility in the eyes of management; the intrinsic reward that comes from knowing people are *really* using the skills learned in the classroom; allocation of limited training resources to assignments where results are relatively assured; creation of a work environment which supports these results; the education that management receives as to what training can and cannot do. With management viewing the training department as a partner in moving the organization forward, support for budgets and staffing becomes more probable.

The "training for impact" model is not appropriate for *every* training effort; but it is essential that at least some of the training projects in every calendar year follow this type of process. Only then can management and trainers be certain that skill transfer is occurring. Only then is the training department communicating its value as well as its cost. Only then can it honestly be said that we are working *with* management to achieve organizational goals.

Reprinted from TRAINING, February 1984

For Further Reading

Chalofsky, Neal, "Professionalism and Practicality," *Training and Development Journal*, p. 8 (June 1983).

Mager, Robert and Peter Pipe, *Analyzing Performance Problems*, Fearon, Belmont, CA (1970).

ROMANCING THE BOTTOM LINE

Suppose Cinderella *could* prove that
training returns measurable,
hard-dollar benefits:
Would she and the Prince really live
happily ever after?

BY JACK GORDON

A show of hands, please, for a quick reality check. How many can read the next two paragraphs and say, "Yep, that's pretty much the way life works in my organization"?

"You're the company training director and you want to run a program for first-level supervisors in Department X. But in order to get approval and/or funding for the course, you have to push your proposal past the "Hard-Nosed Financial Types" who control the company's purse strings. You explain the problems that you and the department's manager have painstakingly diagnosed and documented: The supervisors in Department X were promoted from the ranks and have never been taught how to function as managers. They have a number of shortcomings which, you believe, are largely responsible for the department's failure to meet its productivity goals and for an unusually high turnover rate among its hourly workers. You believe training is a big part of the answer. You have found a packaged program you think will do the job, and you know how much it will cost.

But these Hard-Nosed Financial Types (HNFTs) are tough cookies. Your analysis is persuasive, they say, but it fails to satisfy them. They demand to know exactly how many dollars the organization will save, due to increased productivity and reduced turnover, if they let you run this program. They want monthly financial-benefit breakdowns for the next two fiscal years. As for the

expense of this program, the HNFTs don't just want to know how much the package costs. They demand a report that factors in the salaries of the in-house trainers who'll do the actual teaching, the total value of salaries and benefits received by trainees during the time they'll spend in the course, the cost of the electricity you'll use to light the classroom and run the overhead projector, and the cost of janitorial services needed for a classroom that will be in use instead of sitting idle. If you can't come up with documented numbers for all this, the HNFTs say, then you can go hang, and so can the supervisors in Department X.

Can we see those hands now? Uhmmm, yes. Well, let's be charitable and call that a mixed response.

Strange as that scenario may seem, it describes—with pretty fair accuracy—the underlying assumption being made about the way your organization works by some of the people who present you with accounting formulas for calculating the return on investment (ROI) of a training program. You've encountered these formulas in books, in magazines (including this one) and in seminars.

A variation on this assumption—one that probably rings truer to most training professionals—is that the HNFTs are not demanding such precise numbers from you now, but they also aren't approving a lot of the programs you want to run. If, on your own initiative, you were to pin down those "hard numbers" and present them to the HNFTs, the scales would

fall from their eyes. "Hey!" the HNFTs would cry. "Training isn't just an expense after all! It's a superb financial investment! A low-risk, high-yield bonanza!" Funds hitherto unavailable for your projects would magically appear.

And if, after conducting that supervisory training program, you went back and evaluated its "bottom-line impact," again in hard numbers (meaning numbers with dollar signs in front of them), your credibility would skyrocket. Pushing your next proposal past top management would be a snap. Your power base would be assured. Training in your organization no longer would be "the first thing cut when times get tough."

Now *that* is a compelling vision. But a few skunks lurk in its rosebush. The most familiar problem is a long-standing and vociferous argument in the human resources development (HRD) business: Is it or is it not possible to isolate the final dollar benefits an organization receives purely as a result of a training program? And even if you do presume to have roped and branded those dollars, is it politically advisable to "claim" them on behalf of the training department? We'll come back to that argument in a minute.

There are some less well-hashed questions to be asked about the subject of tying training to bottom-line results. They turned up in conversations with directors of some of the most successful HRD functions in America—successful meaning that training in their companies is taken seriously by top management, that it is seen as a necessary and integral part of the business, that it is not "the first thing cut when times get tough." We talked to training managers in several of the companies identified by a 1984 poll of TRAINING readers as being the best in the country at training and developing their employees. And we talked to the top HRD people at a few other companies that since have been hailed as exemplars of what "management commitment to training" means.

Comments from these people certainly don't settle the issue of whether the quest for bottom-line results might be a genuine pathway to greater credibility for many training departments. But they suggest some interesting ways to think about the subject. For instance:

• Attitudes regarding the broader issue of rigorous program evaluation varied. But none of the training directors we spoke to credited their departments' success to efforts to document or claim specific dollars-and-cents returns on individual training programs or on the training division as a whole.

• None could recall offhand ever proposing a particular program and having it blocked by a HNFT who said, "No dice until I see hard-dollar projections of the bottom-line benefits." On the other hand, several did say that if they had a convincing way to come up with such projections, their jobs would be easier.

• Some feel that the whole controversy over claiming bottom-line results tends to overestimate the influence of "hard numbers" on business decisions in general. If a training department *could* prove an impressive ROI for its programs, they say, its credibility and its power to attract funding would increase—but not as dramatically as many trainers seem to think it would. Hard numbers play a role in funding decisions, but they aren't the whole ball game—not for training, not for any other business function.

• Everyone who expressed an opinion agreed that the impetus for tracking financial returns on training programs comes primarily from trainers, not from the executives and line managers to whom trainers answer. In other words, if you see an evaluation effort under way to isolate the results of a training program and hang a price tag on the benefits, chances are the training department is conducting the evaluation on its own initiative, not because a HNFT demanded the data. (This usually was an observation, not a criticism.)

• Several suggested that the legendary HNFTs—the ones who demand to see those hard numbers—are much more likely to rear their ugly heads when the training department is selling a "solution in search of a problem" rather than working with line managers to come to grips with a serious and "visible" business need. In other words, if you show up at the funding committee meeting with two division managers at your side, and they announce that unless this company does some customer-service training pronto it can kiss its repeat business good-bye, you probably

won't find a HNFT sitting on that committee. If, on the other hand, you walk in by yourself to propose that a six-week course in transcendental mud wrestling would imbue the organization's middle managers with a heightened sense of New Age awareness that will boost productivity like a Saturn rocket, you're likely to encounter a whole roomful of HNFTs.

• Sort of a corollary to that point: Whatever HRD people mean when they say "bottom-line results," the perceived need to get a better handle on training's connection to them applies almost entirely to management, sales and "soft-skills" training—rarely to technical training. You're less likely to need (or think you need) "hard numbers" to justify technical training. And if you do want them, they're easier to come up with.

• The issue does not boil down to just some academic squabble in the training world. It's seen as a potential powder keg. Several training directors were nervous about discussing this subject, and one refused to be quoted by name at all. "I can't win," he said. "If I tell you we don't measure bottom-line benefits, you run a headline that says, '____ Corp. doesn't evaluate its training.' If I say we do, you ask me how, and I can't answer because I don't believe you *can* hang dollar signs on the value of professional or management training."

Babel

Back up two points. "Whatever HRD people mean when they say bottom-line results . . . . " What is *that* about?

One trouble with this entire subject is that right off the bat, we run into a communication gap. When talk in the corporate training industry turns to "tying our programs to bottom-line results," the conversation starts out sounding as if it's about something as direct and unambiguous as hitching a horse to a post. Some say trainers should lay rightful claim to bottom-line benefits accruing to an organization as a result—or at least partially as a result—of training programs conducted for the organization's employees. Others argue that, for a variety of reasons, they shouldn't.

But it quickly becomes apparent that "training" and "bottom line" are words that go together like "Tower"

and "Babel." You don't get far into one of these arguments before you realize that the disputants have a basic problem.

When Trainer A is speaking, "bottom line" refers only to the number in bold type at the bottom of the company's annual profit-and-loss statement.

When Trainer B is talking, "bottom line" refers to a specific dollars-and-cents return on a particular training project: If you spend $10,000 to run your salespeople through a widget-selling course in April, and sales figures for widgets for the quarter ending in June are $100,000 greater than those for the quarter that ended in March, then the bottom-line benefit you're talking about (for this quarter alone) is $90,000. And tying training to it means claiming some or all of that $90,000 as your program's direct contribution.

Then we come to Trainer C, who uses "bottom line" as shorthand for a more or less particular orientation toward corporate training. A training department with a "bottom-line perspective" helps line departments solve problems that relate directly to boosting revenue or cutting costs. The training department is "hooked in" with operating departments, knowing and sharing their primary, driving concerns. But the question of claiming specific dollars-and-cents returns as a pure result of a training program is beside the point. For Trainer C, "bottom line" isn't a number, it's a philosophy.

Regardless of where they stood on the dollars-and-cents angle, every training director we spoke to stressed the importance of the approach Trainer C is describing. But in terms of the actual debate over the issue (can you/can't you, should you/shouldn't you claim bottom-line results), Trainer A and Trainer C are begging the question. As far as this article is concerned, Trainer B's definition is the key.

No you shouldn't

So what about that $90,000? One school of thought says it's essentially dishonest of you to try to claim any specific part of that sum as a sole result of your training program. Why? For one thing, your program probably would make little or no difference in how the salespeople did their jobs if the sales *managers* failed to follow through with support and coaching—and by insisting that their people actually use the skills they learned in class. Surely the sales managers, not the training department, deserve credit for that coaching.

"You can't get results from training without management reinforcement of the new skills," says consultant Dana Gaines Robinson, president of Partners in Change, Inc., of Pittsburgh and an authority on training evaluation. "And you can't isolate the effects of the training. It's like the wings on an airplane: You need both."

Even if you could separate those two factors (or lump them together and plant your flag on the whole bundle without having the sales managers at your throat), chances are almost nil that the training/support package was the only variable affecting widget sales between the first and second quarters of the year. What was the advertising department doing? What about consumer spending in general? Did your competitors' widget sales also increase?

And suppose you had run the training program and the next quarter's widget sales had *dropped*? Would you let your course take the blame? Regardless of other logical explanations for the problem, would you agree that training was solely responsible for a $90,000 loss?

In short, according to those on the "nay" side, too many forces are at work in the environment that creates that $90,000 result. You can't honestly claim it for training. "I don't believe you can say that because someone attended X course, the organization got a return of Y dollars," says Robinson. "First, I don't believe that cause-and-effect relationship exists. And second, I don't think people [HNFTs] would believe you if you claimed it did exist."

That sentiment is echoed—with a caveat—by Jack Bowsher, director of education for IBM, the company whose training and development program was the most admired in America in TRAINING's 1984 readers' poll. Bowsher is a former accountant and, like Robinson, a true believer in evaluating the results of training programs. "Measurements are the key to justifying education," he says.

But what *kind* of results should you measure? IBM uses four familiar levels of evaluation: *reaction* (the "happiness sheet" that asks trainees how valuable they found the course); *testing* (pre- and posttests that measure trainees' knowledge and skills before and after the course); *application* (are they using the new skills back on the job, and with what effects?); and *business results* (what does the organization get out of it in dollars-and-cents terms, or terms that can be converted to dollars and cents?).

It *is* possible to carry an evaluation to Level 4 (dollar impact), Bowsher asserts, but only in certain cases. And most of those cases involve technical or "hard skills" training. When IBM trains customer engineers to repair equipment, for instance, it can go back later and measure things like the number of calls the engineers make, the number of repeat calls they have to make because they failed to fix the right problem the first time, and how quickly they can repair machines.

'You can't isolate the effects of training.'

"We can clearly show that those factors have an impact on the business in dollars-and-cents terms," he says.

"But I think it's unrealistic to say you can do that with every course. Executive education? Sales training? So many things go into making a sale. You can't go to Level 4 with those types of programs.... And I certainly don't say I'm going to increase the total profit of the IBM Corp. by 1% or any shenanigans like that."

What about all the accounting formulas and cost-benefit work sheets offered by those who say you *can* isolate hard-dollar benefits deriving from soft-skills training? "The ones I've seen are flaky," Bowsher says. "You always wind up [building in] a lot of unsupportable assumptions no one believes. And if you become unrealistic, nobody will believe the good stuff you've got. Measure everything you responsibly can, but don't use unrealistic measurements."

Larry Doxsee, director of HRD for 3M Co., one of the top 10 companies in our 1984 poll, concurs. "For sales and management kinds of training, we've never successfully cracked the code of tying cause and effect together. If there were a proven scientific way to do it, that would be a welcome addition to my arsenal. And in general terms, it's certainly a serious concern; everybody I talk to about it says, 'Please call me when you find one.' "

However, Doxsee says, "The lack of a credible system doesn't stop you from tying training to business needs." On both the soft-skills and technical sides of the fence, there's such a thing as training you do simply because it makes sense for the business. And there's such a thing as getting silly in your attempts to nail down dollar benefits. Even when 3M evaluates technical-training programs, it generally doesn't try to tie them to bottom-line results in the sense that "an engineer goes out after the program and invents six new processes or something."

Another training manager at 3M says he struggled mightily with the cause-and-effect issue several years ago, combing academic literature for credible formulas, checking out the efforts of people in other companies and so on. His verdict: "I've since found more productive things to do."

Yes you should

In the face of such insistence on rigorous, provable measuring systems, is anybody out there asserting that you can and should claim bottom-line results for all sorts of training programs, and claim them every chance you get? Sure. Plenty of people. And nobody argues the other side of the case more forcefully than Jerry Peloquin, president of Performance Control Corp., a consulting firm in Media, PA.

"You *can't* measure the dollar value of training? You *have* to—if you want to keep your job," Peloquin asserts. "Otherwise, the classic cycle of the training department will get you as the economy rises and falls. When the cycle swings down, and managers start cutting budgets, they cut them in direct proportion to their perception of the value of the function.... Managers don't care about criterion-referenced instruction or whether your 'feel-good' surveys are positive. The only things they care about are things that bring them bonuses. That means better productivity, lower costs, more revenue—all of which mean higher profits.

"At some point, you've got to relate your activities to the profit of the company. Otherwise, when times get tough, it'll be the same old story: training, advertising and maintenance, first to go."

In fact, Peloquin declares, "You're a sucker if you don't claim bottom-line results." Profit comes from all sorts of complex, interwoven factors, so it's not legitimate for you to claim any of it? Curious how that moral delicacy seems to afflict only trainers, he notes, when in fact the same factors shed doubt on *anybody's* direct claim to the organization's profits.

"Actually, there's this pool of dollars out there, and everyone is competing for it and *everyone is claiming credit!* You're looked upon as valuable depending on the cogency of your argument."

Formulas for calculating specific ROI figures can be helpful, he insists. But actually, it's not so much a question of airtight formulas as a matter of negotiation. For example: "You claim that a sales increase was a result of your sales training program. Somebody else says, 'Nonsense, we hired better people,' or 'We ran a better ad campaign.' You say, 'Wait a minute, where was I during all this? Are you saying the training program didn't help at all? No? You're not saying that? Well then, how *much* came from the training?' You negotiate."

Also, he contends, there are situations in which a training program arguably was the only significant element that changed in a certain environment. In that case, you have a clear field: Stamp your name on the resulting dollars.

"Why are scythes cutting through the middle management ranks across the country right now?" Peloquin demands. "Because middle managers are not seen as contributing directly to the bottom line . . . . If you don't claim some impact on the bottom line, why in God's name are you there?"

Look, he says, "If we're doing relevant training, it's unreasonable to assume that some credit is not due us. So why not claim it? Why not negotiate for a piece of the bottom line that's

due to our efforts? The truth is, most trainers don't want to do it because they don't want to be held accountable for doing relevant training."

Ah, but this leads back to that point about accepting blame. What about the argument that if you're going to grab the credit when sales go up, you have to take the rap when sales go down—and that you'll be saddled with blame for a lot of factors that were honestly beyond your control?

Peloquin waves the objection aside. "Hey, when sales go down, nobody accepts the blame, sweetheart. Everybody explains why it's not their fault."

Dubious magic

Bowsher doesn't doubt the value of documented benefits: "Where we have the most measurements, we get the most resources. Where I've got education programs that don't have measurements, those are the ones that keep getting cut, where people cry that the company doesn't appreci-

---

'When sales go down, nobody accepts the blame, sweetheart.'

---

ate education. Programs with results I can measure, I have no trouble getting funding for."

But to his way of thinking, the answer is not to sabotage the credibility of those secure programs by arming yourself with dubious measuring tools and rushing out to claim hard-dollar benefits for the insecure ones. Ultimately, he says, gaining credibility for the training function is a matter of building a track record that allows you to establish in management minds that training is common sense.

"I'm driving toward, 'Do you want people trained to do their jobs, and what happens to the business if they're not trained?' " says Bowsher. "I'm driving away from the mind-set that relies on cost-benefit formulas full of unsupportable assumptions. I'm for saying, 'Here's my cost and here's the benefit—but not necessarily benefit down to precise dollars in ROI.' "

As far as that goes, says this former

accountant, "Trainers don't realize that lots of things in the business world are not nailed down to the last penny. [For example,] a company is building a new manufacturing plant. Management has to answer basic questions like 'Will we need this additional capacity?' and 'Have we chosen the right site?' A lot of that comes down to gut feel. The numbers don't play as important a part as people think."

For one thing, he says, plenty of the numbers that management sees in a situation like that will be "ginned up," i.e., unsupportable. And management knows it.

Bowsher is not alone in questioning the magic power of "hard numbers" to bend decision makers to one's will. Another doubter is Clifton Rhodes, director of corporate selection and training for Honeywell Corp. Says Rhodes, "In no way will bottom-line data ensure the survival of a training program—at least not in an organization like Honeywell. In no way is that all there is."

Real life

Honeywell is a company whose interest in the value of its management training is attested to by a landmark study on the various factors, including training, that contribute to a manager's long-term success. But according to Rhodes, painstaking analysis of cost-benefit calculations on a program-by-program basis is not a way of life at Honeywell. And training does not revolve around efforts to hang dollar signs on program benefits. Nor do HNFTs demand that it should.

But according to Rhodes, painstaking analysis of cost-benefit calculations on a program-by-program basis is not a way of life at Honeywell. And training does not revolve around efforts to hang dollar signs on program benefits. Nor do HNFTs demand that it should.

Indeed, he says, "Honeywell tends to pride itself to some degree on its informality. It's a 'roll up your sleeves and work' environment where people don't go overboard on paperwork or on monitoring and controlling things." The corporate training function works with a "key sponsor network" staffed by line managers who help determine training needs and the relevance of the department's programs. "The sponsors count on informal data—the feedback they hear,"

Rhodes says. "That's as impactful in their minds as more formal data."

In short, the data you need to justify training depends to a great extent on intangible factors—your organization's style, culture, call it what you will. "Training is not going to make any difference unless you have a clear indication of commitment from top management," says Rhodes. "If you don't have that, your numbers won't look good and training won't be around long. So it becomes a question of what people look to when judging the value of training. Here, they look at informal data."

A more dramatic statement of the cultural relativity principle comes from Ron Lessnau, dean of Hamburger University in Oak Brook, IL, nerve center of corporate training for McDonald's Corp. Speaking of the company's actual, annual "bottom-line" profit statement, Lessnau says: "We claim credit and accept failure right along with the operations people. The reason is that we're the same function. We report directly to operations, not to personnel or HRD. . . . All of our trainers have operations backgrounds. Here at H.U., they're just teaching to 50 people what they used to teach one-on-one as store managers and field supervisors."

Lessnau isn't claiming to have a cause-and-effect ROI formula that others don't, however. Actually, this is an example of the communications gap we saw earlier with Trainers A, B and C. He's not talking about tracking and measuring cost-benefit ratios on specific programs. Far from it.

"Cost sheets may be a way of life in companies that don't see training as an integral part of operations, but not here," he says. "We have a budget [$16.4 million for direct costs last year] and we're scrutinized, but if we can sell a [program] concept in a one-page memo, that's all we need."

At McDonald's, he says, the philosophy is, "Don't let the accountants run the business; do it because it makes sense." That philosophy applies to training as much as to the store manager who wants to buy, say, a new $800 toaster, Lessnau explains. The question isn't, "Where are the accounting sheets with your detailed cost-benefit analysis of the toaster?" The question is, "What happens if you don't have the toaster?" If the answer is, "Bad things happen," you buy the toaster.

By the same token, the training department eschews formal cost-benefit accounting on particular courses. Lessnau looks at what his direct costs will be, and makes the decision: "If we see something that needs doing, we do it."

And here's some cheering news for trainers who do feel singled out by HNFTs. At McDonald's, says Lessnau, the only notable exception to that corporate bias against bean counting is the marketing department. If a new advertising campaign is in the works, the operations people want to see hard numbers from the marketing people. "They need projections about what sales are going to do so they can staff up, stock buns and burgers, and so on." Also, he adds, store operators want to know what the "bang is going to be for their advertising dollars."

Not so with training. "They *know* what the bang is for the training buck because they've all been through it."

'You know deep inside that somebody's going to ask you to prove the benefits.'

Faith

Is support for training, then, ultimately a matter of faith (or common sense) on the part of management? Now that's a disturbing question for you. It fairly resonates with fatalistic overtones.

"I wouldn't want to trust management faith forever," says Dana Gaines Robinson. "Management changes, culture changes, charismatic training managers change." And when they do, she says, you'd better have "some nuts-and-bolts strategies" to prove that the things you do are valuable to the organization.

Sue Rye is starting to feel the winds of change, and the need for some of those nuts and bolts. Rye is manager of HRD at Walt Disney World in Florida, singled out by *Excellence* guru Tom Peters and others as the place to go if you want to know what outstand-

ing customer service looks like and how training supports it. The company's customer-relations training is driven, Rye says, by a rock-solid conviction dating back to Walt Disney that a "positive guest experience" is precisely what the business is all about. Comments from guests shape the training. Complaints from guests change and refine it.

"We don't do a lot of [numerical] tracking," she says. "I can tell you what the cost of putting a new person on board will be . . . . But we don't have any measurements like, 'We did X in July and saw Y impact in September.' " There has never been a need to spend the time, money and effort necessary to create and maintain such a tracking system.

The Disney organization changed ownership recently, but Rye says she sees no signs that the commitment to customer service will falter. The change she's concerned with isn't about personnel switches at the top. It has to do with her department's increasing involvement in management training.

"Management training is a whole new venture for us," she says. "We never used to do much of it. And you know deep inside that somebody's going to ask you to prove the benefits . . . . When you're proposing a program that costs thousands of dollars, and somebody's philosophy differs from what you're teaching, it's a lot more difficult to convince them."

Therefore, Rye is now among those "struggling to find a sharper correlation between training and the bottom line." But she doesn't expect it to turn into an obsession. "I'd hate to think we'd come to the point of spending days or weeks to come up with some percentage figure for our contribution. And I don't see us heading that way."

The cost of costing

When you think of rigorous "training technology"—needs analysis, instructional design, program evaluation, etc.—the name AT&T comes quickly to mind. It's a company that traditionally has run much of its training "by the numbers," in a lot of senses. According to Bill Luithle, division manager for the corporate training support group for AT&T in Basking Ridge, NJ, one current proj-

491

ect under development is a course on cost analysis that will be delivered to trainers and training managers company-wide.

You'd think that if anybody was claiming to have cracked the code on a direct cause-and-effect relationship between training and bottom-line benefits—or was devoting massive resources to the attempt—AT&T would be a good bet. Forget it, says Luithle.

"If you really wanted to set your mind to it," he supposes, you could *maybe* run a study isolating the contributing factors to, say, an increase in sales on a particular product, and come up with a defensible figure to assign to a training course. But would that study be worth the time and expense?

"I doubt it," Luithle says. The only way such a project would really pay off is if you could extrapolate the results to other sales training programs for other products in other sections of the corporation. And the trouble with those environmental factors you isolated in *this* project is that they won't be the same in the next one. It would be ridiculous, he says, "for me to run the study here and say to the rest of the organizations, 'This is how much benefit you get from a training program like this.'"

What about "meta-analysis," the process of evaluating a number of different studies and drawing general conclusions from them? Some claim the method is a convincing way to assign dollar values to various broad categories of training programs. (See, for instance, "The Dollars and Sense of Corporate Training" in last month's TRAINING.)

"It doesn't sound particularly convincing to me," says Luithle. One discouraging sign, as far as he's concerned: "I haven't seen anybody on my staff jumping at it, and they're the real technicians."

A similar view of the dubious value of running elaborate cost-benefit evaluations comes from Kenneth Hansen, manager of education and training for Xerox Corp. Xerox has tried it a few times with some specific programs, "but in general we don't try

to measure bottom-line returns on training investments."

The cost of a training program isn't too difficult to calculate, Hansen says. "But the return is so wrapped up in other environmental factors that it's impossible to separate and measure. You can spend a great deal of time and money trying to separate those things, and when you're done, nobody believes your story anyway; you still don't have a substantial answer."

So what about HNFTs? Conversations about ROI certainly go on at Xerox, he says, "but they go on at a different level—the level of the whole project the training is designed to support." Most of the training Hansen's group does is "locked to another business process—to an operational strategy or a product strategy or something." The question of dollar benefits applies to the entire project: "What's the payback for the process, the new product, or whatever?" Inside that calculation is an identified cost for training, and that cost affects the return the company can expect. Therefore, Hansen says, "Five percent of the cost of a new product introduction or something might be training. But there's no pressure to prove that 10% of the return is due to training or anything like that." Training is simply a recognized part of the operational process of bringing that product to market.

According to Hansen, "The real question is the focus with which you drive your training. If you focus on the operational needs of the organization, ROI isn't a big issue. Normally, managers understand they aren't playing just one card when they make an organizational change."

Messages

Remember Trainer A, Trainer B and Trainer C? The theme that threads its way through the comments of the leaders of some of the country's most successful HRD programs is that while Trainer B is technically correct about what the "dollars-and-cents" issue boils down to as an *issue*, it is Trainer C who points the

way toward greater credibility for corporate education. For training, "bottom line" really does work better as a philosophy than as a number.

Even Peloquin stresses that claiming credit for hard-dollar results is something you do only *after* you've made sure your training is focused on a relevant and pressing business need.

Robinson, who advises against claiming those hard dollars, nevertheless argues that trainers must measure and "articulate the outcomes" of their programs. The fact that they generally are not forced to do so by these quasi-mythical HNFTs is not a blessing but a curse. "We're *not* being asked to explain or document the benefits of our programs," she says. "So, being busy people, we don't. But this means we've colluded with management to allow ourselves to operate in the dark. Until that changes, management won't know what we're about. And that puts us at risk."

You can't evaluate a coherent outcome from a program with no specific objective, she points out. And you won't get an outcome you'd *dare* to articulate from a program that isn't focused on a real need. There's a vast difference, she says, between an organization that puts its people through a course on, say, "managing by influence" because it thinks the concept is neat, and an organization that is undergoing a major structural change and, knowing its managers will have to learn to operate in a "matrix" environment, puts them through the same course. In that second case, "the course is linked to a definite business need, and it will produce very different results."

Maybe the final message is this: If your proposals *do* keep getting blocked by HNFTs who can't understand how the organization would profit from them, step one is not to launch a search for a foolproof ROI formula for training programs. Step one is to ask yourself why nobody else seems to be suffering from the problem you want to solve.

Reprinted from TRAINING, June 1987

SIX GUIDING IMAGES TO MEASURE TRAINING RESULTS

It's so crucial—and yet often so difficult—to convince management that your training projects are worth it. Next time you need a boost, image results

BY JAMES F. McCAMPBELL

There's a story of an expert who fixed a very expensive machine just by tapping it with a hammer. The plant manager was very angry when a bill for $250 arrived. He asked that it be itemized. The expert's response read: Tapping machine, $1; knowing where to tap, $249.

Just like that hammer-bearing expert, trainers of the 1980's must know where to tap the machinery of the organization. More than that, they also must know how to itemize their bills to management to assure that their expert advice makes sense at the top.

During the past few years, I have found six images that can help us figure out how to do it, how to guide the uphill work toward education that produces measurable—and measured—results. These images can be the key to success for training managers, not only on the organizational level but on the personal, professional and political levels as well.

1 The businessman cartoon: A single concise goal, easily measured. My thoughts in this area began when I was on a committee of hospital educators interested in developing a common management information system so we could compare our respective labors and be both impetus and model for each other. When we read each others' final reports, we discovered that they were long and included many complicated catalogs: lists of methods of instruction, kinds of staff positions, varieties of courses, types of audiences and so forth. The combination of length and complexity made them difficult to read and impossible to comprehend.

After reading three such reports, I had no idea which of the three departments was doing the best job and which the worst. I had no idea how to compare them or where they were in relation to each other or in relation to any standard.

Later on, when I gave up and settled on the calming experience of reading the *New Yorker* magazine, the image of the businessman struck me. I saw that staunch, paunched, conservative codger planted at his walnut desk in front of a chart on the wall. The chart contained only one line—the bottom line. It went up or down according to the cartoonist's pleasure, but it was simple, direct, clear, and it communicated.

I set my heart on developing such a measure of my department—a straightforward measure that communicated so clearly that people could compare my department's performance to that of other departments or to a standard. With that vision came the nightmare of possibly disastrous success. What if I put a chart on the wall that measured my people's performance and they cared so much that they changed their performance for the better, making the chart run right off the top of the wall? Suppose the whole department went to hell because my chart influenced them to do the wrong thing?

Figuring it was worth the risk, I set out to find a simple measure that would influence the staff positively. At the second committee meeting, I said as much: "Who cares about all these catalogs of data? What we need is to measure our results." And one of my colleagues turned to me and said, "How?"

Thereby I developed a commitment. I would show them! So I went home to graph our departmental results. Somewhere in the files lies that first embarrassing attempt. But even though it graphed the wrong things and it misdirected staff, it was a beginning. Its content is insignificant, but the image of that businessman and his chart still guides my efforts as it did when I first went to my staff to convince them to measure results.

2 Numbers, not faith: Influencing staff and accepting honest feedback. Consider: of all the occupations, the teaching profession is least likely to measure results because teachers are creating lifelong patterns of learning and knowledge, and that is immeasurable. And of all the industries, hospitals are least likely to measure results because they deal with human life, and you can't put a price tag on that. In the matrix of occupations and industries, I am at the intersection of the least likely ... and the least likely.

So when the head of the X-ray department asked for our help in decreasing the discard rate in bowel X rays, I was elated. The number was known; here was a chance to measure results! My staff mounted an all-out campaign and retrained every nurse and nurse's aide in the hospital. Then each instructor wrote a report to me about how successful their part of the program had been.

In our next staff meeting I complimented their reports, and asked if they shouldn't wait until the numbers were in. But they were sure of themselves and proud and (just a little bit) sticking their collective tongue out at the new education director who wanted to measure things.

When the next month's results were reported, the error rate was up. That's right—up, not down. That failure has been a symbol for me ever since, because it exemplifies so practically the difference between intuitive faith and measured results.

Handed a problem with numbers attached, reports from the instructors predicted a change in numbers that

493

simply did not occur. The shock led them to focus on measures of results. They had lost faith, sullied by the numbers that failed to change. But the confrontation with reality made them more honest and humble and ready to learn.

3 **The classic training dialogue: Expanding the trainer's role.** The decision to seek measured results leads trainers beyond their usual role. My image of that role expansion—the need for new skills and new relationships—is captured in what I call the classic training dialogue. It presents the dilemma of training and organizational results.

We've all heard conversations like the following:

Trainer: Sir, we've just completed the course on waste control.

Manager: Fine. What were the results?

Trainer: The students rated the course 4.5 on a 5-point scale, and they know what operations cause the waste. They know the important facts about the process and they have been assessed on their ability to perform those operations up to standard.

Manager: Good. How much has waste been reduced?

Trainer: Unfortunately, not at all.

One resolution to the dilemma is for trainers to draw a firm line around training and its immediate results, and refuse responsibility for organizational results which are beyond both their authority and their training skills. Such a resolution is certainly defensible.

A second resolution is for trainers to accept responsibility for organizational results. To do so, they must become adept at analyzing problems and managing other ways of solving them besides training. If they are to focus on organizational results, they will have to extend themselves to places, relationships and skills which are not normally part of the training role.

The dialogue presents a dilemma: If you only train, you cannot be responsible for organizational results. If you accept responsibility for results, you cannot just train. It makes apparent the need for additional skills in the trainer's role.

4 **A final report format based on simplicity.** For me, a key image for results-oriented education is the final report. It reveals a great deal about the function of education in an organization because it must be selective. What it chooses to report and what it chooses to omit reflects what is and is not considered important.

My image of the final report is one that focuses on organizational results at the expense of the process used to get them. And it is elegant. Sometime children's talk is confused with poetry because it is effortless and simple. But real elegance is not the product of a child. It is the result of a level of skill and effort that is far beyond the average person's competence. The gem-cutter's skill, the dancer's leap are so well practiced and competent that they appear effortless. That's in the back of my mind when, out of all my struggle as an educator, I finally am so successful that I can produce a report so simple that it says only:

$$
\begin{array}{r}
\$5,000 \text{ benefit} \\
\underline{-1,000 \text{ cost}} \\
\$4,000 \text{ net benefit}
\end{array}
$$

It is this kind of hard result that reflects a great deal of effort, practice and skill compressed into a package that is so simple it seems natural and effortless. It reflects competence, and is equally appropriate for a project or a department. But it must be presented with its impact on clients clearly in mind.

5 **Fingerprints: Providing quiet leadership and appropriate credit.** Results-oriented education requires close work with administrators and department heads to influence how they view problems and what they do to solve them. At the same time, it does not carry the authority to demand.

On the contrary, because educators are stepping onto mangement's turf and finding out about their problems, the managers may be upset and difficult to work with—at the least nervous, at most downright hostile. Educators cannot threaten and cannot demand. They need to win cooperation and support in other ways. They need to exercise quiet leadership.

While there are many skills for quiet leadership, the one for reporting results has the strongest image—fingerprints. Fingerprints are the tracks you leave that let someone trace a project's success to you. The image was mentioned by Paul Chaddock, vice president, personnel, Lechmere Sales Co., Woburn, MA, in a presentation at the 1980 American Society for Training and Development (ASTD) conference: "When Duke Schmidt left corporate training at Ford ... his staff gave him a framed picture with five fingerprints in it, because Duke's management philosophy was that the training department never took credit for anything—never left its fingerprints on

any project. They put out a brochure at the end of the year and all the brochure contained were examples of the divisions in Ford solving performance problems."

In my reports, I might conclude with a sentence like this: "This project is a joint effort of staff in anesthesiology, business office, data processing, education, internal audit, operating room, pharmacy and purchasing." By giving appropriate credit, everyone shares in the success just as they shared in the project. And that makes it more likely that the educator will be invited back for another project, and another chance to exercise quiet leadership in getting measurable results. It's important to be invited back.

6 **Critical mass: Accepting the slow change to results-oriented projects.** Producing measurable results is difficult. In contrast to the educator's typical role, it sets new tasks, demands new skills and requires interaction with different parts of the organization. The hard work of change—retraining department members and restructuring clients' perceptions of what you can do for them—can be frustrating. But the concept of critical mass helps with the frustration.

Critical mass is the mass necessary for the job to do itself. Look at it this way: The first telephone salesman was in real trouble. No one wanted to buy a phone because there wasn't anyone to call—no one else had a phone. The salesman had a nearly impossible job. With each sale, he had to convince the customer that even though it wasn't true now, *someday* everyone would have a phone and there would be plenty of people to call.

After enough of those frustrating one-at-a-time sales, there came a time when many people had a phone. And at some point, the people without phones began to view themselves as outsiders rather than insiders. That was the point of critical mass—the point at which the selling started to do itself. Soon the phone salesman's problem was getting enough phones to fill his orders.

In results-oriented education, the early projects are hard to find and hard to do because the clients are hesitant and the staff unskilled. Success comes slowly at first, but eventually that will change. The time will come when the problem is filling the requests rather than selling the concept. That result—the critical mass—is worth the hard work during the slow change toward projects with measured results.

Reprinted from TRAINING, September 1981

QUALITY ASSURANCE AND CONTROL IN TRAINING

Here's how to minimize the risk of training failure, and ensure that your training accomplishes your objectives

BY J.B. CORNWELL

Quality is a word, like *professionalism*, that trainers tend to use with some abandon. The problem is that *quality* has a lot of definitions. So before I discuss how to assure and control quality, let establish a definition of that somewhat elusive word.

The bottom line on training quality is the degree to which trained personnel perform successfully on the job after training. Quality is the sum total of a number of contributing factors and can be seriously reduced by any one of them.

The major factors that affect quality are:

1. Accuracy in identifying the tasks that must be done on the job and in describing conditions and setting performance standards for those tasks

2. Accuracy in determining how existing performance capabilities of the student population differ from those needed

3. Accuracy in determining what knowledge, skills, tools, aids and attitudes must come together for acceptable performance to occur

4. Accuracy in determining the nature of the learning events best suited to producing needed knowledge, skills and attitudes

5. Effectiveness of any instructors, counselors, coaches, writers, producers or administrators involved in delivery of the learning system

6. Timeliness and frequency of opportunity to perform learned tasks after training

7. Timeliness, frequency and accuracy of feedback on the job

8. Accuracy in determining how available time, manpower, facilities and financial resources can best be applied to optimize quality

Rarely is it appropriate to pursue maximum possible quality. Optimum quality is the point of maximum value, or return on investment. In seeking to improve quality, a point will be reached in which cost increases faster than quality. On the other hand, in cost-cutting exercises, a point is reached when quality declines faster than cost. Quality should be maintained in the range between these points because that is where we get the best value. It is not the purpose of this article to explore value management but to explore quality, so enough said about financial matters.

Of the eight factors listed, all except 6 and 7 are the direct responsibility of the training function and item 8 is a training management responsibility. That leaves us five factors.

Quality assurance is what we do to minimize risk of error or failure in each factor before the training starts.

Quality control is what we do to measure each factor, independent of all others, and to correct for variances between actual and planned quality, which is the point at which management calculates optimum quality will occur.

Different methods of applying quality assurance and control are appropriate for different situations. Key differences are the nature of the job to be learned, the number of learners, the qualifications of the trainer(s) and the sophistication of the organization's management in controlling operations.

The range of methods is also great. In a small organization, where one person, an acknowledged master of the job to be learned, represents the training function and where decisions are made without gathering and analyzing a lot of facts, it is usually proper for the trainer to base these decisions on his/her own experience and knowledge and to accept subjective opinions of resulting quality. In this case, the costs of preventing or correcting low quality are usually greater than the costs of low quality, should it occur.

As organizations grow, however, it becomes less likely that a person responsible for preparing training is an acceptable source of answers about job content, learner characteristics and performance components (knowledge, skill, attitudes, tools, aids, and so on) and more likely that he/she is a good source of answers about the design of the learning process and is capable of delivering the learning system. It is also more likely that management controls operations on the basis of numbers rather than opinions and trust relationships.

In this situation, the larger number of learners makes systematic methods of quality assurance less costly than low quality. That means the job, the learners and the task components should be researched before defining and preparing the training. Research can range from interviewing selected master performers and job candidates to extensively testing and observing both and statistically analyzing the results. It is also proper in this case to ensure that trainers apply sound educational technology to the design and delivery of the learning system, rather than guesswork, intuition and popular mythology.

Regardless of the size and sophistication of the organization, it is necessary to find a valid way to determine how well people perform on the job after training. In other words, it is necessary to *control* quality. Though it is often done, it is risky to settle for a few randomly collected opinions about quality, no matter how credible the holders of those opinions. Too many factors, other than training

FEAR AND LOATHING ON THE EVALUATION TRAIL

You've just finished a training program. The sessions are over. The instructors—your own staffers or outside professionals of your choosing—are winding down. The evaluations are in. You go over the ratings and comments on each individual's effectiveness and notice that in and among the goods and acceptables, interwoven with the praise and plaudits, are some harsh words and critical reviews. How do you handle them?

It can be a tricky problem. You want to use the evaluations for their avowed purpose— as constructive feedback on what was done and how it might have been done better. But you also want to protect the professional pride, confidence and perhaps fragile personal egos of the people who've given their best on your behalf.

"If you ask for evaluations," says Bernadine Eve Bednarz, manager of organizational training and development programs in continuing educa-tion in mental health for the University of Wisconsin-Extension, Madison, "then I think you have to count them for what they are. When people put themselves out teaching, they also have to be prepared to take the brickbats with the roses."

That's not always as easy as it sounds, she points out, particularly when organizational politics is involved. In one case, Bednarz circulated the unedited evaluations on a training program considered successful overall. Among the comments on the faculty was this: "She is intelligent, yet has not found her own style— having become a poor carbon copy of the famous person who led the workshop." Another trainer on the program called to object to publication of such disparaging remarks, arguing that it would have been better to share the negative commentary with just the individual involved instead of opening her up to group scrutiny.

On another occasion, a participant wrote: "Due to (her) zero personality, I find it hard to concentrate on the information she has to offer from her apparently very effective program." That, says Bednarz, sparked three phone calls and one letter from members of the planning committee who felt the remark was impolitic, deadly and should have been edited (one suggestion— "zero personality" to "retiring personality").

"How do you handle it best?" Bednarz asks rhetorically. "How do you distinguish between criticism that may be personal and vituperative and an observation that is legitimately worthwhile? You might have 45 good comments and one lousy, but what will people pay attention to? The one lousy. All you can do is look at the positive stuff, too, to keep it in perspective."

Bednarz makes no distinctions between her own instructors and outsiders— both get a frank and unedited replay of all evaluations, with a cover letter or other suitable introduction pointing out the level of positive reactions overall. The only exception to her rule, says Bednarz, would be in the event a participant turned particularly hostile, using racist or sexist pejoratives obviously out of sync with the content of the training. In such a case, which has never yet arisen in her experience, Bednarz says she would edit out the remark completely rather than attempt to soften the wording.

"You know it can be demoralizing," she admits, "but I think you owe people the honesty and have to assume they will be professional enough to be able to put things in perspective."

Reprinted from TRAINING, March 1981

quality, influence those opinions, which, unfortunately, are rarely objective.

If opinions *are* to be collected from the graduates and from their supervisors, they should be collected by means of a questionnaire or survey that is designed to return numbers that can be averaged. This method eliminates much of the subjectivity and means that the results are more valid. It also allows rare cases to be discarded and individual differences in learners to have only "fair share" impact on results. The results should tell you approximately the quality of what you have done. If that final reading on quality varies above or below what you intended, you need additional data to suggest what to change.

You should measure the first five quality factors I listed at the beginning of this article separately because they are performed separately and will be adjusted, or controlled, separately.

1. Your post-training performance survey questionnaire should ask for demands of the job that the trainee couldn't perform after training and tasks that were learned but not needed. The data will show errors in item 1.

2. Test the learners, before training, for capabilities you assumed they had, as well as those you assumed they didn't have. The first is *prerequisite* testing; the second is *pretraining* testing. The results will show errors in item 2.

3. During the training, use quizzes, projects, problems and attitude surveys to compare knowledge, skills, attitudes, tools and aids to the performance achieved. For example, you've decided that Joe must be able to work differential equations to select the correct settings on a machine; if he fails the equations quiz but passes the performance test, you should question whether the equations are really necessary.

4. Examine the results of these quizzes, surveys and so on for the frequency of success for each item of learning. Low frequency, below 70%, suggests redesign of the learning event. Poor learner attitude toward the task or the learning event (from the attitude surveys) also suggests the need for a new approach.

5. In addition to using the degree to which learners achieve planned learning as an indicator of quality of delivery, we should collect feedback from the learners about delivery technique and style. Don't sit in on a classroom instructor's presentation in order to evaluate it. Instead, use results— that is, the way learners respond. Sure, there is some art to superior classroom instruction but not enough to justify evaluating the instructor's performance. Concentrate, rather, on the reactions and comments of those on the other side of the podium.

Exact, step-by-step procedures for each task of quality assurance and each task of quality control could fill a book— or several. And they have. If you want to read further about some specific techniques on quality assurance and control, often referred to in the literature as *evaluation* or *testing and measurement*, read books and articles on the research and design of training.

Reprinted from TRAINING, January 1980

SINS OF OMISSION

Want your HRD department to give more than lip service to your organization's strategic plan?

BY BARBARA BOWMAN

Your annual state-of-training report to management is a dazzler. You developed five new programs, attendance was up by 20% and trainees routinely rated sessions as "excellent." Your programs consistently met their objectives—you've documented the fact—and graduates are actually back on the job *applying* the skills they learned in class. All this and you're under budget, too.
back on the job *applying* the skills they learned in class. All this and you're under budget, too.

What more could you ask for? It's a training director's dream. . .or is it? Your assessment of this human resources development (HRD) department, which happens to belong to a hospital, might change if you also knew that:

• The hospital plans to introduce a new pediatric-rehabilitation program early next year. All the necessary governmental approvals have been obtained, funding is in place and publicity materials are ready. But there are no plans yet to train the staff to work with these complex new patients.

• The hospital was cited recently by its accrediting agency for failing to provide required ongoing infection-control instruction.

• Due to market shortages, it has been impossible to fill vacant medical transcriptionist positions. Several typists now employed by the hospital have expressed interest in the jobs, but no training is available to prepare them for the new assignments.

• An increase in the number of elderly, bedridden patients has resulted in more back injuries among the staff. There have been no classes on body mechanics or proper lifting techniques.

In other words, the programs of-fered by the HRD department were excellent, but what about the programs *not* offered? How do we evaluate needs not met, classes not taught, opportunities not realized?

The answer is, we don't. These sins of omission are blissfully ignored in typical evaluations.

Paths not taken

When they set out to determine, for themselves and for top management, how good a job they're doing, training departments focus on three aspects of evaluation: Participant reaction (Were trainees satisfied with the session? Did it meet their needs?), achievement of objectives (Did trainees master the information the program was designed to teach? Can they perform the skills?) and impact evaluation (Has a chronic problem been corrected as a result of the training? Has performance improved back on the job?).

Our hypothetical hospital training department performed beautifully according to all these evaluation measures. Programs were well received, they were cost effective and they produced behavioral changes both in the classroom and on the job. But, obviously, important training needs went unmet.

Quite logically, standard evaluation methods assess programs that have, in fact, taken place. It is another matter to evaluate the impact of a program that never happened. A ground swell of voices is exhorting organizations to tie training to their strategic plans. But using our usual methods, how can we evaluate the effectiveness of this linkage?
But using our usual methods, how can we evaluate the effectiveness of this linkage?

When HRD fails to support the strategic plan, it is generally because our evaluations fail to address our sins of omission. We need to take a different approach to evaluation, one that looks at how effectively the HRD department is meeting the *strategic* training needs of the organization. In other words, we need a system of total program evaluation.

The missing link

Total program evaluation links evaluation to needs assessment—the process of figuring out what employees need to know—rather than to program objectives. This is a fundamental change: Trainers customarily have been taught that when performance objectives are set, evaluation methods are automatically specified as well. We assume that the appropriate objectives have been established and that meeting those objectives will meet the needs of the organization. This approach fails to acknowledge those cases in which program objectives are met, but major needs are neglected. By linking needs assessment to the total program evaluation, however, we can avoid sins of omission—the programs that should have been offered but weren't.

Total program evaluation uses three major sources of data to identify missing programs and to evaluate the effectiveness of programs that did occur.

1. *A review of needs identified through a comprehensive needs assessment.* This implies, of course, that you have conducted a needs assessment and developed a prioritized list of training needs. Review these needs annually to determine which have been met and which have not. If the company's strategic plan calls for the launching of a new product line, for example, has training support for it been initiated? Is the accounting department ready for its new computers? Are managers prepared for the new performance appraisal system? Has training been completed to correct the safety violations on the factory floor?

2. *An assessment of employee satisfaction with programming.* No evaluation can afford to neglect the perceptions of trainees. Total program evaluation asks employees to consider the overall HRD effort, rather than just individual programs. Items from a questionnaire used in this year's needs assessment can help you

determine people's satisfaction with last year's programming. If you have collected good demographic information, you can correlate measures of satisfaction with departments, job classifications, shifts, seniority and other variables. This data also yields valuable information about whose needs are being met and whose are not.

Usually only employees who attend training programs are involved in evaluating them. Assuming these people attended voluntarily, they apparently felt that the program at least had the potential to meet their needs. Therefore, the results of a participant evaluation are inevitably skewed. What about employees who, for whatever reason, choose *not* to attend the program? This is your chance to find out why, and to determine whether you are neglecting the needs of some part of the organization.

3. *A comparison of the results of this year's needs assessment to those of last year's assessment.* Does the assessment conducted this year reflect a change in needs? Were problems identified last year resolved? Some needs, of course, are ongoing, but others should decrease in significance as a result of training.

If training is conducted to meet an identified need, but that need continues to appear in assessments year after year, something is wrong with either the training or the assessment. Maybe the needs are stated in such general terms that they are useless as guides for programming or evaluation. Maybe you're using inappropriate methods to deal with these needs. In either case, further study is in order.

Also compare employee satisfaction with this year's programming to that of previous years. Have problem areas been corrected? Has satisfaction decreased among any employee groups?

The fatal flaw

The potential flaw in total program evaluation is obvious: If it is based on a faulty needs assessment, it will be worthless. If your assessment missed important needs, the evaluation will fail to flag your sins of omission just as completely as one that considers only isolated programs. Here are a few points to keep in mind during the needs assessment process.

Be sure to review the type of material you will need in order to project long-term training needs. Consider the organization's goals and objectives, its business plan and, of course, its strategic plans. And don't forget the department-level counterparts of these plans.

Of course, not all organizations have strategic plans or other materials that lend themselves to this kind of analysis. They are far more common in some industries than in others. Even if your organization has a formal plan, you may find that changes are not reflected immediately in the written documents.

How do we evaluate needs not met, classes not taught, opportunities not realized?

---

ten documents.

Fill in the gaps with more informal sources of information. Interviews with managers at various levels will help you see the big picture. Senior executives will be more knowledgeable about long-term plans, whereas middle managers probably will be more aware of the effect of these plans on the day-to-day operations of their departments.

Don't ask line managers to describe their training needs; line managers don't always recognize training implications. Instead, ask them what new projects they'll be introducing, what changes they're anticipating, what kinds of people they'll hire and what problems they're encountering. It's your job to infer training needs from this information and validate them with the manager. Conduct these interviews at budget time if possible. Not only does this allow you to prepare your own budget more effectively, but managers are usually attuned to these issues when they are working on their own budgets.

In addition to its future plans, consider how the organization is functioning now. Identify performance indicators and use them as assessment tools. For example, production statistics, turnover rates, on-the-job injuries, quality assurance studies, reports from regulatory agencies and client comments may all point out potential training needs.

The key word here, of course, is *potential*. You may identify problems that are due to any number of causes; don't assume they automatically translate to training needs. This is especially important if you want the HRD function to be held accountable for meeting needs rather than just for providing instruction. The training department that confuses a procedural problem with a training need will not fare well in total program evaluation.

Use the employee needs-assessment questionnaire to verify managers' perceptions of needs and your own hypotheses rather than to present a laundry list of possible training topics. If you find a major discrepancy between managers' and workers' opinions, there may be poor communication between various levels of the organization. Again, this may be evidence of a training need requiring further investigation.

Considering these issues during the design and implementation of a needs assessment should result in data that can serve as the basis for a valid evaluation that addresses programs omitted as well as those actually offered.

Total program evaluation supplements rather than replaces the other three types of evaluation. It's still important to evaluate individual programs to identify strengths and weaknesses.

Let's go back to our hypothetical HRD department. What effect would total program evaluation have on our appraisal of its performance? A comprehensive needs assessment that followed these guidelines would certainly have identified such needs as preparing for a major new program, complying with regulatory agency requirements, meeting manpower needs by providing promotional opportunities and correcting unsafe techniques. Total program evaluation would have pinpointed several sins of omission and held the department accountable for meeting these needs.

Total program evaluation presents a new perspective on evaluation. It is a valuable technique for HRD departments that are serious about tying training to their organizations' strategic plans.

Reprinted from TRAINING, May 1987

MEASURE TRAINING RESULTS BACKWARDS

Start with the organization, not the students. Look for a problem that can be solved at least partly by training

BY STEPHEN P. BECKER

It's time for us, as trainers, to be much more specific when we discuss the value of our work. It is necessary for us to spend more time planning systems to measure trainer reinforcement, learner feedback, and organizational payoff.

One reason for this is that even within the HRD field, not everyone defines training measurement in the same way. Some believe a simple list of training activity is sufficient. Others, more statistically inclined, carefully evaluate program effectiveness, dollars saved or generated, or increases in employee proficiency on the job. Actually, all three approaches have their pluses.

The simple tally

The easiest kind of measurement is to tally training activity, either periodically or on a continuing basis. The list would include such things as programs conducted and the number of people who participate in each, new programs developed, publications generated, consulting days purchased, new audiovisual programs produced, etc. In addition to providing the basis for a rather specific departmental activity report, this process makes the trainers feel good. The exercise is likely to generate a very impressive list and you are guaranteed to be surprised at how busy you were. While this kind of measurement is recommended for its trainer reinforcement value, the major problem is that no information is provided about payoffs to individual learners, specific work groups, or the organization.

Measuring learning

A second type of measurement is aimed at determining what is gained by an individual as a result of specific educational experience. Here the training game starts to get a little complicated.

The best way to approach this subject is to ask three questions:

1. Are there valid learning objectives so the trainer and the learner know what is to be learned?
2. What does the trainee already know before entering the learning program?
3. What has been learned by each individual by the end of the course?

If we use this de facto definition, it is not possible to measure learning without first setting valid objectives. The word "valid" means the objectives should be properly written, and should reflect the intent of the program. That is, if the trainee achieves the stated objectives, then he or she ought to be able to use what was learned to solve job problems or make job improvements. Remember, it is quite possible to write excellent objectives that, when mastered, will not enable the learner to do what the course is designed to teach him or her to do. In that case the objectives (and the program) would be invalid. So when constructing objectives, ask yourself a question: If the learner achieves this objective, what difference could the application of the learned knowledge or behavior make in his or her job performance? If the answer is not much, then throw the objective out.

In addition to objectives, you must be able to measure the results of the training. This usually requires the construction of a pre-test and matched post-test. They must be reliable and valid. In other words, the tests must measure the same thing every time they are given and they must measure what you want to measure rather than something else. You can't simply compile a bunch of test items and assume they are telling you what you want to know. The tests must be tested. Since most of us are not statisticians, the least we can do is try out the test items with representative learners before we finalize the program design and materials.

Frequently the use of control groups will give a good indication about the validity of items, but simple mistakes can easily occur. For example, you might find that a majority of people tested interpret a particular item incorrectly. This could indicate they don't understand the question, so they all respond differently. If you don't try the test out in advance, you won't discover the problem until it's too late. If, on the other hand, the majority of the control group understands the item but consistently answers it incorrectly, most likely the trainees haven't learned what they were supposed to learn—the program hasn't done its job and needs to be revised.

One area of controversy in our profession revolves around the measurement problems in management development programs versus skill training programs. Some trainers say that while it's relatively easy to develop objectives for skills training, it's much harder to objectify and measure learning in management development programs. Frankly, I don't agree with this point of view. Such things as leading, planning, problem solving, deciding, listening, presenting, analyzing, budgeting, writing, interviewing, assigning, coaching, appraising, directing, selling, and goal setting are learnable, measurable managerial skills. While it's true that not every manager can attain the same level of judgment, it's also true that not every worker can produce the same number of widgets.

Organizational payoff

Even when there is much training activity and people are learning things they can use on the job, there may be no reason to believe that employees are applying what they have learned to job problems and opportunities.

To test this, you can use some basic sampling techniques. Since it's not possible to follow up on everybody, you can select at random a certain number of participants and follow a pre-designed system of measuring the dollar impact of new job behaviors. For instance, let's suppose you have a training program to help production planners learn new scheduling techniques. The intent is to reduce inven-

WHY PROGRAMS SUCCEED AND FAIL

BY JUDITH H. STEELE

If you want to guarantee that trainees will work toward their goals once they're back on the job, focus your training on what learners will do differently, not on what your lesson plan will cover. That's the advice of Scott Parry, president of Training House, a Princeton, NJ-based publishing and consulting firm.

Parry described specific ways to help implement trainees' performance change when he discussed "Why Training Programs Succeed or Fail" at TRAINING '78, TRAINING Magazine's annual conference and exhibition. According to Parry, the first step is to fill the classroom with key individuals, not just so many warm bodies. Unless you emphasize that, says Parry, bosses will "keep sending only the most expendable people to training—like 'good old Harry,' who's one year from retirement and doesn't supervise anyone anyhow."

The next step is to hold a pre-training briefing with the trainee's supervisors to kick off this essential partnership. "All too often, the organization's 'top dog' blesses a training program on the first day of class and then disappears," observes Parry. "Tell the bosses we can't train your people *for* you, but we can train them *with* you." Make sure the supervisors understand training's ground rules and accept their share of responsibility for staff development.

Go beyond an informal agreement, urges Parry. At the pre-training briefing, give the bosses a case study that underlines the need for their commitment. Clarify their understanding of your training goals and let them know what you require from them.

On the first day of class you can use the same case study to earn each participant's cooperation. When trainees learn that their bosses stand behind the guidelines, they'll heighten their own efforts to make training a success.

An Individual Action Plan is another tool that can help ensure successful training by changing trainees from passive learners to "doers." After the workshop session, each participant prepares a written plan detailing on-the-job follow-up activities. In the Action Plan, the trainee sets goals, anticipates possible problems, thinks through the applicable solutions, schedules the sequential steps that must be taken to reach particular goals and lists the yardsticks he'll use to measure accomplishments.

The Action Plan is the cementing link of the supervisor-subordinate-trainer team, and each boss/trainee team meets after the training session to review it. The two agree on ways to carry out the plan and schedule follow-up progress reviews. Then, at the next training session, participants break into small groups and report on how they've worked with their bosses to carry out the plans.

The Action Plan meeting between trainee and supervisor is so crucial, says Parry, that a participant should be "disenrolled" from a course if this meeting doesn't occur. He views this as an "adult" rather than "punitive" measure, evidence that the company won't waste its training investment. "There may be a perfectly good reason why the two couldn't get together, but we're not collecting excuses," he reasons.

Parry's system ensures continuous participation of the bosses. Toward the end of the course, each trainee integrates his separate Action Plan into a composite plan and timetable. Supervisor and trainee work together on the plans to check progress and make changes where needed. At a future agreed-upon date, trainees reassemble for a follow-up meeting, with their bosses sitting in the back of the room. Each trainee arrives prepared to report on how he has implemented his own Action Plan.

Both sides have something to gain through this process. "The bosses know in advance about this meeting, and no boss wants to have his or her people look bad," Parry points out. Similarly, ambitious trainees, hoping to be "discovered" by the group of superiors, strive to make a good impression.

But even this session shouldn't be the end-all of the training sequence, says Parry. To pave the way for the trainee's ongoing growth, he suggests that the training department organize a supervisory association for graduates of training courses. Once established, this becomes the trainees' own "swap shop" for continued professional development, a forum where real-life problems continue to be addressed.

With these tools, says Parry, trainers can give their company a return on investment. And the sooner we can get rid of the "Johnny Appleseed approach"—a scattering of training seeds here and there, hoping some of them take root—the better.

Reprinted from TRAINING, August 1979

tory levels and overtime labor hours. You might select a number of participants at random and monitor the way in which they apply the technique and the resulting dollar savings for their respective sections. The average savings could be projected for the year for all participants. The idea here is to measure dollars instead of training—to show that the participants in your training program have learned to make more money for the company.

Frequent testing during a program creates a continuous personal development chart, which can be highly motivational to a student. The true purpose of any test is to show success, not failure. It's the job of the trainer to help people successfully master and internalize the knowledge, attitudes, perspectives, skills, and behaviors necessary for more effective job performance.

There is still another kind of organizational measurement that behavior specialists should think about. Let's suppose you are asked to help your company become more safety conscious. The ultimate purpose is not to teach employees safe procedures, but rather to persuade people to use the safety knowledge they already possess. So we must consider the whole area of performance consequences, rewards, punishments, and reinforcement. There will probably be a significant investment in employee communication programs. But first we should measure the employees' existing attitudes toward safety. Then we'll know what needs to be done. We'll also be able to tell if progress gets off track and whether we have arrived at our goal.

One good way to get this broad-based information is to hire a professional survey firm to collect it. They have the statistical knowledge and experience to do a much better job than most trainers could do alone. Once you have the data, you'll know what your problems are and you'll be able to structure a change strategy that will be on target. If you don't take this approach you could spend a small fortune without ever knowing if you needed an organizational performance improvement effort in the first place, what objectives to set, what types of training and communication programs to develop, or whether or not you ever actually achieve your goal. Doing surveys will save you money, help you know what to do, and tell you what's happening. Without that kind of data, making any substantial expenditure is gambling—not investing—and the odds against success will be very high.

Reprinted from TRAINING, April 1977

WHY YOUR TRAINING-EVALUATION SYSTEM DOESN'T WORK

Of course you evaluate your instructors and your programs.
But is the information you gather used to improve things?

BY KENNETH E. CARLISLE

Everybody is in love with the idea of evaluating training programs. How effective was this course? Did it teach them what they were supposed to learn? Are they applying their new skills on the job? Are their efforts to apply the skills creating any unforeseen problems? How could we improve the program for the next group of trainees?

Articles about evaluation—in which we convince one another of its importance—are increasingly popular in training journals. Evaluation is a sacred word among top managers, training-department managers, instructional designers and classroom trainers. Every systematic training model includes an evaluation component. An efficient evaluation system is *the* most powerful way to improve training.

Evaluation provides essential feedback that can be used to "fix" poor training programs and to make good ones better. It can ensure that instruction is well-conducted, that a program's content is correct, that trained skills transfer to the work place, that the money the company spends on training produces measurable improvements in effectiveness, efficiency or safety—in short, that training is worth the trouble. And today's increasing emphasis on objective-based training makes it easier than ever to *conduct* a meaningful evaluation of most programs.

Why, then, do so many evaluation efforts fail to do what they're supposed to do? Why do our systems so seldom produce the desired changes in efficiency, effectiveness or safety? Why is it that the frequent product of an elaborate evaluation is a neatly typed report that is filed away and never referred to until management (or a regulatory or accrediting agency) asks about training-evaluation procedures—at which time the report is dusted off, used to make the predicted impressive impact, and refiled until called for again? How can all this be done without the evaluation ever affecting the quality of the organization's training programs?

Simple. We fail because, for all our enthusiasm about evaluating our training efforts, we miss the point. "Evaluation" is a term used to describe an organized feedback system in which evaluators collect information about trainees and—here's the important part—*give the data back to the people who provide the training*. The idea is that trainers then use the evaluative information to change their programs as needed to better meet the learning objectives or training needs.

Assuming they are technically sound (evaluators are competent and collect meaningful information, etc.) evaluation systems break down for two reasons. Either the data is not given to those who do the training, or the training environment does not allow change.

One of the prime criteria for useful feedback is immediacy. The evaluative data must be given to people who can change things while the training program and potential problems are still current. The passing of even one extra day can reduce the potential for significant changes. Both trainees and trainers forget which areas of a program need improvement once they begin dealing with new material or become involved in other job situations. Evaluation data must be collected in an ongoing flow throughout the training process, summarized immediately after the training and acted upon directly.

The intervention of "middlemen" often blocks evaluation data from reaching trainers in time to be of much use. A professional evaluator may be required by procedure to observe the training, hand out student surveys, interview workers, write summary reports, have the reports typed and review results with supervisors before giving any of the data to instructors. All of these activities increase the time and the number of people involved between the teaching situation and the feedback of information to the trainer.

The evaluator must fit observations into a busy schedule; therefore, some training sessions certainly will be missed. Students will fill out only a limited number of surveys before they rebel against the evaluation process. After training, employees return to their jobs and quickly forget the details that need improving. Writing a formal evaluation report takes time, as does typing the report. And supervisors' time is very limited—a real problem especially if supervisors are expected to meet individually with each trainer to share the evaluation data.

All in all, it may be weeks or even months before the results are given to the trainer. In the meantime, the course may have been taught to several other groups—or it may have been dropped from the curriculum. In the latter case, especially, the evaluation process has wasted the time of any number of people and produced only one effect: It fulfilled a bureaucratic requirement.

The solution to the problem of how to get immediate data back to trainers often is to eliminate the middleman. The trainer is the one whose job is most affected by the evaluation, who is most concerned with presenting the course correctly, is most knowledgeable about improvements that might be made, and is usually the individual responsible for changing the instruction. The trainer, therefore, should be the one to solicit and collect data.

Professional evaluators should help, of course, but their roles should involve providing evaluation forms, meeting with the instructor to plan alternative course changes or in-depth needs assessment and task analysis, ensuring that evaluations and changes are implemented, and writing required formal reports. The role of supervisors is to encourage trainers to follow through with changes, to provide trainers with adequate time and resources to *make* the changes, and to support trainers (if warranted) when the evaluations are negative. But the trainer must solicit, collect and act on the evaluation. When others get in the

501

way of the process, even if they want to be supportive by cushioning the blow of negative feedback, evaluation loses its effectiveness.

Environmental protection agents

The second factor that will demolish the effectiveness of an evaluation system is a training environment that doesn't allow change. This can mean a situation in which trainers are not obligated to improve training, one in which they lack the time, knowledge or skills required to change the training, or one where they lack management support for effective change.

A stagnant environment may affect the training staff in two different ways, depending upon whether the first problem—lack of timely feedback—also is involved. If both the "climate" and the evaluation system are poor, trainers will simply tend to become apathetic. It actually is harder on the training staff when they *are* receiving good evaluative feedback but are stopped by environmental factors from acting upon it. In the latter case, the results will be frustration, anger, apathy, withdrawal and, eventually, a search for new jobs.

When management recognizes that it has a problem in this situation, its frequent and completely inappropriate solution is to remove the efficient evaluation system by placing middlemen—professional evaluators and supervisors—between the trainer and the data. Problem one is thus created in a misguided attempt to solve problem two. A good evaluation loop is destroyed and problem two is not affected at all.

The correct solution, of course, is to change the training environment. Trainers must be given responsibility for evaluating and revising instruction immediately after training. Time must be allowed for this. Evaluation and instructional-development skills must be taught to trainers; in other words, trainers must be trained. Finally, management must provide the needed support—freedom to try new approaches, an atmosphere in which new approaches can fail without serious repercussions, adequate supplies of material and equipment, and so on.

Choices

As the accompanying figure shows, feedback factors and climate factors can combine in four basic patterns. An organization's approach to evaluation—and sometimes to training in general—is likely to fall into one of the figure's four cells.

□ **'Cover Your Rear' Approach (Cell 1).** The training department runs its evaluations of courses and instructors without giving instructors immediate feedback. This doesn't matter much, however, because due to environmental problems, the trainers couldn't or wouldn't do anything with the data if they had it. Evaluation records are kept to ensure that bureaucratic commitments are met, but training programs will not improve. Neither will the attitudes of trainers or trainees.

□ **'Try Your Best' Approach (Cell 2).** Courses and instructors are evaluated and data is returned promptly to instructors. But instructors lack the time, flexibility, responsibility, support or motivation necessary to change anything. Evaluation commitments are met better than in the 'cover your rear' approach, and training might slowly improve, but instructors probably will become very frustrated. Either they will force a change to a more open training climate (cell 4) or, as mentioned earlier, management will throw a monkey wrench into the efficient feedback machinery (cell 1).

□ **Unmanaged Approach (Cell 3).** Instructors have the time, flexibility and responsibility to improve training, but the evaluation system only documents the existing state of affairs without giving instructors immediate feedback. Proper documentation may ensure that evaluation *commitments* are met, responsible instructors probably will improve their courses, and instructor attitudes will be good. But those course improvements will be slow, and the lack of responsiveness probably will leave trainees unsatisfied.

□ **'Do It Right' Approach (Cell 4).** The training department evaluates its courses and instructors and provides trainers with immediate feedback as well as the responsibility, flexibility and time needed to change training. Not only will commitments be met completely, but trainers and trainees alike can become actively interested and involved in creating the best possible programs. Evaluation with this approach will continue successfully with only occasional monitoring to ensure that the feedback loop and training climate remain constant.

The best way to increase the value and impact of an evaluation system is to provide immediate feedback and an innovative training climate—to move to cell 4. Unless organizations—and training managers—recognize the importance of getting evaluation data quickly and directly to the people charged with delivering instruction, and of maintaining a supportive training environment which *allows* change, evaluation data will not be used in a valuable way and training programs will not improve.

Reprinted from TRAINING, August 1984

	Change not allowed by training climate	Training climate allows change
NO immediate feedback to instructors responsible for change	**CELL 1** *Result:* No improvement in training program, students unhappy, instructors apathetic *Solution:* Adjust climate to allow change, then provide immediate feedback	**CELL 3** *Result:* No improvement in training program without instructor initiative, students unhappy, instructors fine *Solution:* Provide immediate feedback
Immediate feedback to instructors responsible for change	**CELL 2** *Result:* Little improvement in training program, students apathetic, instructors very unhappy *Poor Solution:* Stop immediate feedback *Correct Solution:* Make climate allow change	**CELL 4** *Result:* Training undergoes constant improvement, students and instructors actively involved and interested *Solution:* Monitor to ensure that feedback and climate remain constant

FOUR APPROACHES TO EVALUATION

MEASURING THE IMPACT OF MANAGEMENT DEVELOPMENT

Management training is a billion-dollar business. But measuring its bottom-line payoff isn't a simple task

BY RON ZEMKE

Management development and management training are large and growing budget items. Large budget items inevitably provoke questions about cost justification and R.O.I. Many CEOs are beginning to ask about expected payoff and proof of tangible results. In short, management wants to know: "What are the measurable, bottom-line results of management training and development?"

The mandate is clear: "Get ye hence and measure the worth of management training." But to paraphrase the Bard's Hamlet, "To measure! Perchance to know; ay, there's the rub . . ." And the rub, of course, is to find a meaningful measure of the relationship between management training and that vaunted bottom-line.

To answer the question, "How do you evaluate the results of management development and training," we polled a number of activists in the management training and development field. Though we found differences in the way some approach the actual evaluation process, all preambled their answers with some specific qualifiers.

1. Management *development* and management *training* are two different topics. The difference became apparent as we talked with Malcolm Warren, director of manpower development, Dayton Hudson Corporation. Warren sees management development in holistic, big-picture terms. "For any organization," he contends, "management development relates to a set of costs and benefits accruing from the way it acquires human resources to fill positions or complete tasks.

"The organization has only two options: Hire already developed talent from the outside, or develop the talent inside. Obviously, one part of the organization's return is a consequence of choosing the best option. Cost reductions drop directly to the bottom-line. The out-of-pocket costs of the outside acquisition are easy to determine—search, relocation, orientation, etc. Also determinable is the risk cost. Outside acquisitions run a higher risk of failure than internal choices who are known by the organization and who know it."

Implicated in this global view of management development is the position that management training is only one management development activity. And while management development is hardly an optional activity, given the costs and risks of management personnel acquisition, management training is an activity about which decisions can be made rationally and outcomes weighed and evaluated.

2. Training is only one element of many which lead to job performance. Be it operating a derrick or directing operations, every individual's performance must be viewed in the context of the organization. Say, for example, that the organization teaches a management-by-objectives philosophy. But suppose that the organizational culture punishes mangers who try to decide, plan and mange by objectives, and rewards those who dramatically and successfully fight fires. Given these conditions, any new manager in his or her right mind will soon be reporting for work figuratively garbed in hard hat and red suspenders.

Larry Wilson, CEO of Wilson Learning Corporation, Eden Prairie, MN put it this way: "The idea, at least in part, is to train managers to manage, efficiently and effectively, the exisiting organization. It's not sensible to train a person to manage an environment or organization that doesn't exist. It's like training a pilot to fly a 747 and then sending him off to build the plane. It won't happen. He needs the skills *and* the plane to do the job."

Scott Parry, president of New York's Training House, makes a similar observation. "If training is to be effective, we must prepare the environment as well as the individual. We must take inventory of the *reinforcers* and *constraints* that will help or hinder supervisors and managers as they try to apply new concepts and skills gained in the classroom. We must then equip trainees with the tools and techniques for dealing with them."

3. The bottom line on the P&L statement is probably not the best measure of management training. While it may be an appropriate measure of the whole management-developement effort, it rarely assesses a specific management-training program.

Dayton Hudson's Warren makes the case for expecting a measurable relationship between management development and bottom-line results: "The costs of an effectively managed developement process must be found significantly lower than outside acquisition over time. The benefit to the organization from effectively investing in human resources is simple to figure. Simple, that is, if we accept the notion that the managerial work force of our organization contributes directly to its bottom line.

"Although we can argue about all the other variables—changes in the market, economic conditions, degree of contribution, etc.—ultimately the payoff will be a higher return on the investment in management resources. In my opinion, then, the bottom-line measure of management acquisition and development is the organization's earning before taxes, less the actual cost of management acquisition and development, divided by the compensation and benefit

503

costs for the management work force. If this margin improves over time, the acquisition and development process is paying off."

Dr. George Litwin, vice-president of the research and communications division of Boston-based Forum Corporation, basically agrees with this bottom-line-of-the-P&L opinion. "To me," he says, "the only sensible place to measure the results of a training effort is at the bottom line. By this I mean such things as growth in sales revenues and profits or the increase of market share, acceptance of products and services by customers, or the maintenance of a strong professional employee group which is reasonably stable and demonstrating the skills necessary for success."

But Litwin then points out a Catch-22 in depending on such a long-term measure: "Our experience with this kind of bottom-line measurement is that it is a lagging indicator of what's going on in the organization. That is, what the bottom line shows is the effectiveness of organizational units and their managers at an earlier time. We find that traditional bottom-line results lag by six months, a year or even two years behind the actual performance of the individuals involved. So, the first problem in measuring training results is to get some short-term indicators.

The trick, then, is to find something to measure—some indicator—which all parties will agree has a "known," or "logical," or "easily inferable" relationship to what the organization is trying to accomplish.

But what indicator?

As one would expect, all our respondents insisted that no management training activity, whether an internal training program, external management seminar or individualized development plan, should begin without first determining what changes or improvements the experience should provide.

Our experts offered no vehement opinions about the one best indicator to measure or how to measure it. As Richard Grote, president of Dallas' Performance Systems Corporation, explained, "It doesn't make much difference. The decision to measure, not the specific method of measurement, is the critical factor. When management makes the decision to measure the results of management development activities and follow that commitment with action, 80% of the job is done."

Once agreed that the organization's management must know and clarify what results they are trying to obtain, our respondents differed somewhat about which short-term indicators they preferred. Litwin, known for his research in climate and attitude, says trainee attitudes toward the organization and the job are worth watching. As he puts it, "The most immediate indication of change in an organization is revealed in the beliefs and expectations of the people in the organizational unit. The first place you would see change would be in people's beliefs and expectations about what they are doing and about the success they might have. The reason we know that's a short-term indicator is that these beliefs and expectations are subject to change as a result of an organizational program. We also know that beliefs and expectations really lead to the arousal of motivation. They kick off the motivational surge which is what often leads to a period of high performance."

Wilson offered another viewpoint "There is a difference between the objective and the purpose of a business. Usually the objective is to make a profit and stay in buiness. But the purpose of a business is to solve problems, or provide a service, or in some way help the customer. One way to really understand the impact of management training, or any training, is to clarify and measure that purpose or mission on an on-going basis. By continually measuring your impact with the customer, you develop an unbiased, third-party opinion of how your organization is doing and how the things you do internally impact that mission."

The third most frequently mentioned indicator and method of measurement was the individual-performance contract. Essentially this is an agreement between the training participant and his or her boss about which performance differences should occur following training and how these differences will be recognized and measured. As James R. Cook, Practical Management Associates, Woodland Hills, CA suggests, "No matter how good the training may be or how much learning occurs, the transfer of material from classroom to work is strongly influenced by actions and attitudes of the trainee's boss. Of course, other environmental elements, such as peer group expectations and organizational structures, are important, too. But the effect of these is often contingent upon, and mediated by the activities of the boss."

Scott Parry emphasises that by using the personal performance contract in conjuction with training, we take advantage of "that most basic law of learning: People learn, not by being told, but by experiencing the consequences of their action."

Grote notes two other advantages of a boss/subordinate agreement about what the training should provide and how the results will be measured. "First," he suggests, "the boss is more likely to support the subordinate's use of the new behaviors if he and the subordinate have discussed implementation beforehand. Second, management support of management development is likely to increase, since to measure the results of management development, management must heed it, must make the decision that it is worth measuring.

Alchemy or science?

A final, moderating viewpoint on the evaluation and measurement issue comes from Psychologist Chuck Bates, who teaches business and management courses at North Island College, British Columbia. Bates cautions that most current measurement and evaluation methods suffer from their susceptibility to the Halo or Placebo Effect. If you tell a manager that your seminar will make him a better manager and later ask him if you were right, you will invariably receive a positive answer. Often the manager will sincerely believe something good happened, but will be hard pressed to identify a specific change.

"What's the solution?," Bates asks rhetorically, and answers: "The alchemists provide a useful analogy. Most of them spent their lives trying to turn lead into gold, just as we squander our lives trying to turn bad managers into good ones. But a few alchemists had a better idea. Instead of shooting for the big prize, they limited themselves to studying only that which they could measure. They found the melting points of compounds and isolated a few elements. Their activity was mundane, but they laid the foundations for modern chemistry. The fellows trying for the flashy transmutations contributed nothing, and wasted their lives. Science has advanced only as fast as its measurement technology has advanced. "Someday, management development will be a science, too."

And as the opinions shared by our experts suggest, we aren't there yet, but we're getting closer.

Reprinted from TRAINING, October 1977

ARE SALES TRAINING RESULTS MEASURABLE?

A dozen experts offer their answers to this controversial question

BY RON ZEMKE

It is very "in" these days to talk a tough bottom-line game. But HRD people in general and sales trainers in particular have long been sensitive to the need to prove that their training and development efforts have a bottom-line payoff for their organizations.

Our 12 experts know full well that this concern is more than an academic interest or an ego trip for the sales trainer. There are jobs and budgets at stake. Big budgets. The total yearly sales training expenditure (counting direct expenses, indirect expenses, and missed sales opportunities) for most Fortune 500 companies runs easily into the millions. And as Homer Smith, President of the National Society of Sales Training Executives (NSSTE) reminded us, "During economic periods such as the one we've just come through, sales training departments that cannot prove their profitability invariably feel the austerity ax." It's a simple law of survival: In a crunch, the frills go. If sales training can't prove its profitability, it's a frill. When the sales training function isn't being effectively measured, the sales training budget is just as vulnerable as the advertising budget, suggests Sales Training Consultant Jack Snader, president of Systema Corporation. John Wolf, president of John Wolfe Institute, reminds us of the executive who complained that half of his advertising wasn't doing a damn bit of good;

but he didn't have any idea which half. A budget crunch makes his reduction formula easy: "Cut it by 50 percent." The only irrefutable way to combat this sort of whimsy is with hard data.

But measurement isn't easy

To be sure, a problem identified can be a problem solved. And, if a lack of measured results is the problem, the solution is to go measure some results. Right? Not necessarily, contended some of TRAINING'S panel of experts, who were quick to add that a lack of measured results doesn't necessarily point to a lack of effort or will power. "No trainer, in good conscience, could remain in his job if he didn't believe that his or her efforts made a contribution to the company's profitability," asserts George J. Lumsden, manager of sales training at Chrysler Corporation. But, Lumsden goes on, "measuring is often difficult or impossible. Do a lot of training in a bad market, and sales go down. Do a little training, and have a hot product, and sales go up. On a short-term basis, it is hard to evaluate training's relationship with profitability, except in those rare and unique circumstances where exceptionally rigid controls can be applied and the results carefully monitored."

And upper management is often uneasy with the call to spend money proving an already expensive program's worth. According to F.C. "Bud" Rebedeau, president of Kielty-Rebedeau and Associates, "Every sales trainer has had the experience of involving line management in the

program design to the extent they KNOW the process is excellent and won't allow the delay necessary to test it on a control group. 'It's good, they all need it now. Take it to the field,' is the mandate given."

In addition to this "permission to prove" problem, our experts point out two other make-or-break considerations. A measurement effort can go bust if the "what to measure" and "how to measure it" questions aren't attended to carefully from the outset.

As Russell Baker pointed out in one of his recent columns in the New York *Times,* when it comes to "bottom-line thinking," one person's bottom-line is often another's middle muddle. This sage counsel in hand, we looked to see exactly where *our* experts placed the bottom we're supposed to be measuring.

Each of our experts had a number of specific suggestions regarding measures of sales training effectiveness. NSSTE President Homer Smith and Jim Evered, manager of marketing education and development at Redman Industries of Dallas, together suggested 26 potential indicators of training impact (see short accompanying article). Of the more than 30 indicators suggested by the total panel, it's important to note that only five are strictly money measures.

How to look at it

The emphasis of panel members tended to be on the development of continuous measurement systems for obtaining input on the effectiveness of a sales training effort. *None* of our experts was willing to advocate measuring only one indicator or measuring results only one way. As Larry Wilson, CEO of Wilson Learning Corporation, puts it, "We've grown beyond the mentality that called for doing one big, mind-bending experiment or test which was supposed to prove that process or product A is better than process or product B. When someone asks if A is better than B we know that saying 'It depends' is really the most honest answer there is."

Bearing in mind this preference on the part of every panel member for multiple indicators and continuous measurement, it was still possible to find differences in preferred measures and methods among the experts we polled. Four basic tactics could be distilled: *Experimental, Critical Incident, Problem Solving* and *MIS.*

The Experimental approach

This emphasizes comparing trained and untrained, or pre- and post-trained people (or some combination of

505

both) on one, two, or more measures of sales performance. The indicators measured are usually agreed upon ahead of time by a joint sales management and training group, and the results are compared in some statistical fashion after a reasonable period of time has passed, during which the trained people have had a chance to show their "new stuff." While most of the panel members mentioned this quasi-scientific approach (which is the technically correct term for this sort of research), all were less enthusiastic than they would have been a few years ago, having become cognizant of the shortcomings of uncritically transporting the laboratory experimenter's tools into the "real world." There are so many possible variables in the sales situation that both positive and negative correlations can occur by chance, especially if you're only measuring a single outcome, such as sales closed, cautioned many of the panel. Put another way: You can't necessarily rely on statistical results to prove your program's worth.

Ian E. McLaughlin, president of Training and Education Consultants Inc., brings the point home with this story: "When I was Training Director for Del Monte Corporation, I once ran a before-and-after test to prove the value of a district training program. We did an outstanding needs analysis, put on a terrific program and the results were topnotch. The following three months saw this district move to the top third in sales of the item we wanted to see an improvement in. I turned in a report showing dollar increases and everything else I could think of.

"Then the deluge! The product manager claimed credit for his support of the effort. The local sales manager said he had concentrated *his* efforts on the item after our workshop, and he claimed credit. The regional sales manager said obviously if headquarters wanted a sales workshop on one item, it must be important, so *he* exerted pressure on the item. All in all, I learned several lessons from the episode:

"First, as Training Director I should never purport to take sole credit for increased sales results...and sometimes maybe not even a little bit of the credit. Second, profitability is never a one department or one action result. Training should be built into marketing plans just as are advertising and promotional activities. Training is *part* of the total action plan, not a poor relative and not a panacea. Third, a better measurement for me is having a trainee return home and a few weeks later write 'Hey, I followed your ideas

and I just closed the biggest sale of my life! Thanks!' "

George Lumsden's advice was a bit more blunt:

"Our training department would no more lay claim to the fact that we were responsible for Chrysler's resurgence in the current year any more than we would accept blame for our problems a year ago." A good touchstone, to say the least.

Another problem with treating a sales training program as an experiment is the hidden costs of such an evaluation. Although John T. Golle, president of Golle and Holmes Corporation, strongly recommended cost/benefit studies ("Proper evaluation/validation studies are crucial in helping top management decide where resources are best applied and what the ROI will be as a result"), he also emphasized that management must be aware of the costs which will be incurred: "There are two definite costs associated with the measurement of sales gains. One is the cost of analysis— EDP charges, time spent, and related out-of-pocket dollars. The second cost is the cost of opportunity loss. Sample and control groups have to be allowed to run at least six months. This means that the company is not benefiting in total should an improvement be validated. One of our clients discovered at the end of their six months' validation period that they were 'losing $75,000 per day' by not having the entire company trained."

"Scientific measurement may not be wholly necessary," argues John Wolfe of John Wolfe Institute. "Sales training is rarely an isolated activity. Usually it's employed—along with advertising, promotion, public relations, etc.—by management that is farsighted enough to recognize the value of *all* these marketing tools.

Take American Express as just one case in point, says Wolfe. "At one time, years ago, they almost went out of the credit card business because their competition seemed invulnerable. Then they decided (under new division management) to turn things around. So they hired a new top-flight ad agency; they upgraded their personnel; they embarked on an aggressive PR program; *and* they hired *me* to train their salesmen. Result? Within a year their billings had increased $53,000,000! What part of that $53,000,000 increase was I responsible for? Darned if I know!"

The Critical Incident approach

Some sales trainers prefer to solicit and collect specific incidents or stories of improved performance from the

trained population to show the effectiveness of their training efforts. At first blush, this may seem a self-serving, "war stories" ploy. It can, however, when applied under the proper controls, be most useful. Dr. John Flanagan developed the concept of the critical incident technique during WW II when he was looking for methods of improving Army flight training. When his approach (as improved by Industrial Psychologist Marvin Dunnette and others) is used, quite a bit of evaluative information is generated. Larry Wilson sees a well-designed sales indicator or incident collecting system as "one way to break out of the activity-reporting trap" and as "a potent way of systematically and logically tying results to objectives in an ongoing fashion."

Moreover, as Chrysler's George Lumsden believes, this collecting of apocryphal data can make an impression on management: "In 1975, when the automotive industry was struggling for each sale, we produced and put on a special training program for retail salesmen. One feature of this program was that each student, at the close of the conference, was given a textbook and a workbook. He was to read the text, complete the workbook, and send the final quiz in for evaluation. A certificate was promised.

"The student response was greater than we anticipated. We plowed through the papers and issued the certificates. And with each certificate we also sent a card asking two questions. 'How many cars have you sold since you attended the conference?' 'How many of these did you sell as a result of ideas you picked up at the conference?' This put a measurement of sorts on the program—a measurement we were happy to have.

"Salesmen would report, 'I have sold 32 cars since the training program. I sold 12 as a direct result of ideas I picked up.' Or, 'I have sold 12 cars since the program. All 12 were sold as a result of the training I got because I was brand new when I attended.' Or, 'I sold 16 cars since the training...maybe two of them as a result of what I learned.'

"We took them all—good and bad. The average net gain was 6½ cars per salesman. Multiply that by the nearly 2,000 salesmen who attended, and if that doesn't show up on the bottom line, we'll quit training. The data impressed us, and our management, too."

The Problem Solving approach

Many of the 12 experts interviewed take a very hard stand against generic training and the "training-for-training's sake" approach to sales training. Commensurate with that view of sales training, they see the attempt to evaluate a "training-'cause-it's-good-for-you" effort as just another piece of the cosmetic cover-up. "Bud" Rebedeau frames the philosophy of the problem-solving approach this way: "The contribution to profits is easily measured if the sales trainer is involved in identifying, quantifying, and solving high priority problems. These kinds of things easily lend themselves to pre- and post-measurement. A program specifically designed to correct one or two of these problems at a time—dramatically and with high visibility—contributes to bottom line. The 'rifle approach,' with pre- and post-documentation of facts, is impressive at budget time. Courses in general salesmanship or sales management can't compare."

J.D. Staunton, director of manpower resources development for National Starch and Chemical Corporation, expresses the view this way: "The key to measuring the results of sales training is the development of 'needs objectives.' If training programs are based on clear *objectives* that have been developed by careful *needs analysis,* and which are directly related to *profit-producing* performance or behavior, then the results of training will invariably be quantifiable."

The problem-solving approach is bound up with the concept of "front-end analysis." As Jack Snader puts it: "All too often, we find that many clients have requested our doing a training program for which there is no real training need. By doing a "front-end analysis" we find that we can frequently show a client that there is no real training problem and thus the performance problem can be solved by a change in the environmental or administrative systems and procedures or by re-evaluating some motivating factors affecting sales performance."

The most concise statement of how the problem-solving approach to sales training functions came from Paul H. Chaddock, director personnel development and management manpower planning at J.L. Hudson Company: "For a Sales Training department to make a measurable contribution in terms of bottom-line impact, it must be allowed—and willing—to accept the role of a performance problem analysis agency, not a purveyor of prepackaged programs. Within the context of this specific role, the contribution sales training makes to bottom-line *can* be measured. The measurement rests on five assumptions:

"1. Sales training as a function is most effective in impacting bottom-line results when it is aimed at changing behavior to create specific performances required by the organization;

"2. Some unsatisfactory human performance is caused because people do not know how to perform;

"3. When people do not know how to perform, some type of learning/training experience is appropriate. This assumes that the training is designed against performance objectives which, when operating, produce organizationally required results;

"4. If people in the organization know how to perform but are not performing, training them (as described in Assumption No. 3 above) will probably not change those results for any sustained period of time;

"5. However, if the sales training department does analyze organizationally required results in terms of current employee behavior and its causes, sales training is in a position to identify causes of undesirable or inappropriate performance. By recommending solutions for line management to consider, sales training can impact bottom line results.

"If these assumptions are valid, then sales training personnel can impact bottom-line results by designing learning/training experiences or by making operational recommendations to line management."

The Management Information System approach

A few of our experts suggest that measuring the effects of a single training program per se doesn't address the complete issue. This viewpoint holds that looking at the impact of sales training, or any other development activity, should simply be part of an ongoing performance tracking and feedback system. Clark Lambert, manager of professional development at Doubleday and Company sees measurement of bottom-line impact as simply part of such a personnel management philosophy: "The training department is no different from any other operating group of

---

WHAT TO MEASURE TO DEMONSTRATE THE EFFECTIVENESS OF SALES TRAINING

Making a hard-data connection between your training and the black ink on the P&L isn't easy but clearly necessary if your long-term goal is to have HRD efforts considered as integral parts of the company's or division's operating activities. Demonstrating that connection requires measuring the right activities. What to measure? TRAINING panel of top sales executives offered the following criteria as thought starters for deciding what you might measure to demonstrate the effectiveness of your training.

- sales force turnover
- sales volume
- absenteeism
- average commission per sale
- product mix
- average sale size
- number of calls
- calls-to-close ratio
- customer complaints
- reduced training time
- implementation of promotional activities

- new accounts per unit time
- percent of objections overcome
- volume increase for existing accounts
- volume of returned merchandise
- improvement of call quality
- improvement in rank position of the trained unit
- reduced cost of training
- sales-to-travel ratio

- new-to-old-account ratio
- competitive investigations
- sales-to-phone call ratio
- complaint letters
- compliment letters
- development of new product demand
- customer satisfaction
- ratings
- items per order
- credits-to-collections ratio

a company. Any worthwhile professional development program for sales personnel is probably doomed to failure, *unless* the basic principles of good management are observed.... *PLANNING, IMPLEMENTATION AND CONTROL.*

"Assuming you start with a carefully defined program based upon a sales *need*," says Lambert, "and all other factors have been considered (such as costs, training time required, degree of difficulty, etc.) it is now *mandatory* to build in new or revised measurement tools. The following short-term and long-term measurement factors are the sorts of things needed for tracking a program:

"1. *Attitude:* Observation of the trainees, both during the training period and several weeks afterward. Done through the Regional and District Managers, and reported to home office via call reports (a short-term measure).

"2. *Sales Performance During Sales Call* (after training): (A) *Observed Performance*: When manager makes a call with the salesperson, and later completes evaluation form for home office; (B) *Non-Observed*: Salesman reports *specifically* on success achieved using new training skill via call report.

"3. *Sales Conferences*: Through the use of role-playing at conferences, the new skills can be observed and positively reinforced.

"4. *Through Revised Call Reports*: When you build a sales training program with specific learning objectives, make certain that your weekly field call reports reflect this! If your forms are obsolete, redo them! Nothing is more motivating for a salesman who is becoming more proficient than to be able to report it and be *acknowledged* for it by the home office. You must know beforehand what types of measurement will be needed, then tailor your continuous and short-term control devices to provide yardsticks for performance analysis. In my book, that's how you look for a definite contribution towards the bottom line."

So where does that leave us?

Clearly, it is possible to measure bottom-line results of a training effort. Just as clearly, "the profitability of sales training *must* be measured if an organization conducts such an activity," summarizes Alan Master, general manager of the career training products division of Westhinghouse Learning Corporation. "Otherwise," says Master, "there exists no justification for the existence of a training function."

But just as surely, as Master and the other panelists admit, there is no one best way to do it, only the way that works best for what you are trying to accomplish. The thread that ties our experts' opinions most closely together is that the effort must be made if we want to get better at what we do. Performance doesn't improve without feedback, and that applies to sales training as well as to individuals.

Lest you take the challenge of measuring the bottom-line on next week's seminar too seriously, though, George Lumsden offers this important perspective: "Training is not like a paper napkin—use it, and it's used up. Training has a residual quality that makes it more valuable as time goes on. It's often stored away for a future use. It's often re-woven into a functional item far different from what was originally intended. If we train only for immediate and short-term results, we are missing some long-range potential. Training does show up on bottom lines—if not tomorrow, at least next year!"

Reprinted from TRAINING, October 1976

BUILD PLENTY OF EVALUATION INTO YOUR SALES TRAINING— EARLY

A demanding training schedule—with
frequent evaluations—can help
you determine the winners and losers
early in the game

BY BRIAN O'HARA

Sales trainees must be more closely evaluated during training than any other employees in a company. That's because it's often difficult to relate their performance the first few months to their potential energy and ability levels. And that's why you need a demanding training schedule—with frequent evaluations—to give you insight into what kind of a person you hired. If trainees perform poorly on tests, do not demonstrate an ability to learn, and prove to be more "takers" than "givers," fire them now and save yourself months of frustration and payroll costs. Regardless of their track records, these trainees may not be able to sell a particular product line, adapt to the new employment environment or relate effectively to the new boss.

Here, then, are some ideas that can help you successfully train and evaluate your next new salespeople. First, you must consider how you can convince the trainee of the importance of the skill to be learned. One way is to relate success stories of people the trainee has already met in your organization who are using this skill. Display the irresistible logic of the skill through role playing. Show materials your company has generated based on its belief in the utilization of this skill.

What approach is most likely to motivate the sales trainee to master various skills? You should impress on the trainee that skill competency will be closely evaluated and tested. Stress how mastering a particular skill will improve his or her chances of promotion.

The logical sequence for demonstrating the execution of a certain skill begins with outlining the necessary points involved in skill mastery. Test the outline. Teach all facets of product knowledge associated with the skill. Tell success stories that relate to the skill. Role play, with the trainee assuming the role of the salesman.

Show is better than tell

How, when, and where will you show the trainee how to perform this skill? The most widely used approach is videotaped role plays. Most trainees realize, however, that role playing sessions are, at best, simulated. Although the positive results of the sales presentation appear to be realistic, they do seem somewhat artificial. On the other hand, a successful sales call with the trainer has a strong impact on the trainee.

What will you look for when you work with your new salesperson? While experienced salespeople should be measured purely on results, the trainee should be measured solely on technique. Is he practicing proven techniques the way they were demonstrated? Does he follow the proper sequence you outlined? Is he attentive to detail, and does he react properly to changes from the prospect?

How will you determine if the trainee continues to perform adequately? The salesperson's reports should indicate both successes and failures. Occasional follow-up conversations with his prospects should indicate whether he is performing properly. Written tests in sales meetings will indicate if skills and techniques are being properly employed.

Stick to the basics

1. Keep in daily contact with the new trainee for at least the first six weeks. Get him to tell you about his sales calls in detail—what things worked and what things didn't. Review successes and failures and the reasons for each.

2. The most effective training occurs daily on the job. The salesperson employs the skills he has learned during training and grades his results after the sales call. He must constantly evaluate his own performance. To become a "pro" he must perform well and know why.

SALESMAN EVALUATION FORM

Sales Rep: _____ Date: _____
Supervisor: _____

	Satisfactory	Improvement Needed
Enthusiasm	___	___
Personal Appearance	___	___
Automobile	___	___
Samples & Briefcase	___	___
Qualifying Prospect	___	___
Building Rapport	___	___
Introduction	___	___
Probing	___	___
Selling to Needs	___	___
Product Knowledge	___	___
Use of Visual Aids	___	___
Summarizing Benefits	___	___
Isolating & Overcoming Objections	___	___
Trial Close & Close	___	___
Overall Presentation	___	___
Organization of Calls	___	___
General Record Keeping	___	___
Preparation for Follow-Up	___	___
Expense Control	___	___
Time Management	___	___

Comments: _____
_____

WEEKLY SALES REPORT

Sales Rep: _____ Week Ending: ___

1. Sales for Week—by Category _____
2. Projected Sales for Next Week _____
3. Number of Hours Spent on Phone _____
4. Number of Hours Spent in Field _____
5. Number of New Contacts _____
6. Number of Callbacks _____
7. Total Calls _____
8. Number of Accounts Sold _____
9. Percent of Accounts Sold (Divide total calls into the number sold for percent.) _____
10. Average Dollar Volume per Account Sold _____
11. Competitive Problems: _____
_____
12. Sales Suggestions: _____

509

YES, YOU CAN EVALUATE BOTTOM-LINE RESULTS

BY RON ZEMKE

One school of thought holds that training outcomes should be measured solely on the basis of in-class learning and trainee satisfaction. Those holding this viewpoint contend that the multitude of variables affecting bottom-line outcomes makes attempts to calculate return-on-investment from training an unrealistic effort. The opposing view, the "bottom-line results" school, holds that: a) the only training results important enough to measure are economic impact results and b) difficulty in measurement is no excuse for not measuring.

Which school of thought you adhere to depends a lot on the assumptions you make about management, appropriate staff-line relationships, accountability, teamwork, survival and what you think you can get away with—in that order.

Regardless of your allegiance, a recent study comparing evaluation measures should interest you. The study, conducted by Gary Rosentreter, manager of training and organizational development, Brown and Williamson (B&W) Tobacco Company, Macon, GA, compared the utility of four economic indices in evaluating the results of an interpersonal communication program.

The population for Rosentreter's study was 68 department managers, each of whom supervised a small first-line work group (16-38 people).

Managers were randomly assigned to *training* or *no training* conditions. The managers assigned to the *training* condition met in small groups (10-12 individuals) with an instructor three hours a day for a week and studied communications. The purpose of the training was to develop communication skills for goal setting. The specific objectives were to:

- increase self-awareness of personal communication style

- help identify effective responses in communication

- build a repertoire of responses to feelings and expressions of interpersonal communication

- build a response repertoire that was *specific, confronting* and *respectful*

The methods used to meet the objectives were filmed speakers and case studies, simulations, role plays, lectures and group discussions.

Rosentreter measured results using what Campbell and Stanley call a "pretest/post-test control group" design. Specifically, Rosentreter measured:

- employee turnover
- employee tardiness
- number of "level-two" employee grievances
- department manager's performance appraisal ratings

These measures were taken before training and six months after training for both the *trained* and *non-trained* groups. Rosentreter found:

- a *significant* difference in employee *turnover* between managers who received communications training and those who did not

- no significant difference in *hours of employee lateness, number of level-two grievances* or *managerial performance appraisal*

Rosentreter proceeded to test the economic benefit of the change in turnover. The Brown and Williamson personnel department calculated the cost of replacing an employee to be $62.33. Thus, the estimated total incremental cost savings to B&W from the lower turnover rate during the six months after the training was $3,429.80. The cost of the training was $1,300.00 The total incremental cost savings for the six-month period was, therefore, $2,129.80. Though the training was popular and had some significant performance outcomes—for example, decrease in turnover in the work groups of trained managers— the actual *economics* of cost versus savings give the "go/no-go" decision an added dimension.

The importance of Rosentreter's study is not, as he emphasizes, the actual outcome in terms of the change— or lack of it— in the four indices studied. It is, rather, the fact that both important managerial performance outcomes and economic criteria can be used to evaluate the benefit of a training program.

(Originally reported as "Evaluating Training by Four Economic Indices," in *Adult Education: A Journal of Research and Theory* Vol. 29, No. 4 Summer 1979.)

Reprinted from TRAINING, January 1980

---

3. Trainers can only partially solve training problems. Don't assume that the trainee's failure in a particular area is your fault. Remember, the burden for performance is on the trainee, who has to prove himself. Make it clear during training that he has an obligation to discuss any problem areas with you and that he's totally responsible for his own success.

4. Separate product training and sales training. Product training must revolve around features, advantages and benefits. It also emphasizes the technical aspects of the product. Sales training revolves around techniques, success stories, demonstrations and philosophy. Don't confuse the two; personality needs are entirely different.

Chart progress

Progress reports, like the one in the accompanying box, tell the salesperson exactly where he stands and what he must do to improve. Daily and weekly reports help you monitor activities and guide your trainees to success.

Don't be afraid to ask for the basics and to emphasize their importance. Such things as the number of calls, the number of appointments, the number of sales, total dollar volume of sales, and so on are essential to your evaluation.

Successful sales representatives are trained thoroughly in product knowledge and the philosophical aspects of sales and are able to employ dynamic sales techniques properly. And sound evaluation early in the training schedule helps you give appropriate career guidance.

Reprinted from TRAINING, November 1979

ONE MORE TIME: TEST TRAINEES BEFORE YOU TRAIN THEM

Pretests can be valuable in several ways,
not the least of which is their
ability to save your job by validating
your training's success

BY PAUL RAHN

We've all been enlightened by those trainers who advocate "testing trainees before training 'em." As another author wrote in these pages not long ago, all you have to do is sit everybody down before your show starts and ask each trainee some questions on the upcoming subject. Here's the rest of the scenario: Each participant probably feels that he already is an expert and will appreciate this little challenge. But, unfortunately for his ego, your test will succeed in pointing out his weaknesses. Then you give him the benefit of your years of experience—that is, your training session, which explains all of the important concepts. During this time, a red light pops on in the trainee's mind every time you mention one of his weak subjects. And finally, you repeat the test you gave at the beginning. This time, the trainee scores well because the few things he didn't already know are now clearly imprinted on his mind, thanks to those flashing red lights.

To validate the effectiveness of your training, you subtract scores of the pretest from the scores of the post-test to determine the real learning experience. After all, the training session was the only stimulus experienced by the trainees between the tests. Or could it be that the increase in test scores is merely a measure of the efficiency of the trainee's red light?

You can answer that question yourself, but it does raise another interesting possibility. Can pretests improve training effectiveness by sensitizing the participants to key concepts?

A comparison with the tried and true method— tell 'em what you're going to tell 'em, than tell 'em, and then tell 'em what you told 'em—uncovers an immediate similarity. Giving a pretest is just like telling what you're going to say, with emphasis.

It's difficult, of course, to give a pretest that covers all the subjects you feel are important but isn't so lengthy that the impact of individual items is diluted. Even the long test will help strengthen the learning experience for those concepts tested: if it's important enough to be in a question, it must be important enough to learn.

As frequent TRAINING contributor Joel Hochberger, a long-time advocate of "testing 'em before you train 'em" has correctly pointed out, another positive benefit of the pretest is that it can identify the participant's knowledge of the concepts covered in the tests. Training programs are usually attended by two groups. Group I knows everything you are going to say and shouldn't be in the sessions. Group II doesn't know enough to start at the level on which your program begins and shouldn't be there either. A third, but insignificantly small group, knows enough to follow you but not enough to be bored. They're the people you should be instructing.

Group I should be presented with more advanced material— if you aren't afraid of encouraging them to pursue your job. Group II should be started at a lower level. And you should tell your recruiting staff exactly what type of person you want.

Now, back to the original problem of validating the effectiveness of a training program. Hochberger has already told us about the problems of using only a final test. I also hope you see the bias introduced by using the same questions before and after on the same group. You can solve this problem without unnecessarily complicating your life simply by proving the statistical validity of the measured improvement in test scores. Any good statistician in your organization can do number crunching for you and provide more information on degrees of freedom, statistical significance, standard deviation, correlation and other equally undefinable sums than you would ever want to know. If you lack such talent in-house, the local college's business, statistics or psychology department will be happy to assist, expecially if you allow them to use the data as the basis for an article in a scholarly journal. If you still can't find someone with the skills, don't worry; if you can find an average, add and subtract, then you can do the number crunching yourself in the simple designs.

The problem originally caused by the pretest— testing bias— may be eliminated or at least controlled by any of several increasingly expensive and consuming methods. Provided you have a large enough group, the simplest procedure is to divide your participants randomly into two groups, "A" and "B." Group A is given a pretest. Group B, the control group, is not pretested. Recombine the two groups and put everyone through the training program. After the session is over, give everyone the test originally taken by Group A. The difference between the average of Group A's post-test scores and the average of the test scores of Group B results primarily because Group A was sensitized by taking the pretest. Thus, the true measure of the effectiveness of your training can be determined by subtracting Group A's pretest average from Group B's post-test average.

There is, unfortunately, a weakness to this approach. Groups A and B must be selected randomly from your participants. If your group is small, you will not be able to assume that random group assignment will ensure that the two groups are statistically "equal." With a small group, you must use the matching technique of pairing two people whom you think

WAIT TO CORRECT TRAINEES' TESTS

Common sense says you don't scold your dog tomorrow for the surprise it left on the rug today. Not if your objective is to prevent future unpleasant surprises. Psychologists would justify an on-the-spot scolding thusly: The effectiveness of a reinforcing stimulus is contingent upon the immediacy of the temporal relationship between the emission of the subject behavior and the presentation of the reinforcing stimulus. Verbiage aside, though, the principles of reinforcement do have a common sense sort of validation to them.

Learning is more effective when a reinforcer, called feedback, immediately follows the presentation and answering of test-like events. This proposal, a by-product of behavior modification and animal learning research, does indeed indicate that efficiency in learning and retention decreases the longer reinforcement is delayed.

There is increasing evidence that, when one is learning meaningful material, delayed feedback (of up to 24 hours) is reliably superior to immediate feedback, particularly when measured by delayed retention testing. And as you might guess, there are explanatory fictions (Skinner's term for theories) for this phenomenon also.

The two major theories that explain this "feedback-is-not-reinforcement" phenomenon are the **Rehearsal** and the **Interference** theories. The Rehearsal theory says the delay gives the trainee time to reflect and ruminate on the question(s) and the possible answer(s). The Interference theory says that during the delay between the test and feedback, the strength of the answers weakens; by the time feedback is available, the strength of a wrong answer has diminished sufficiently for it to be replaced by a correct answer. The answers are learned or practiced anew at the time of feedback without the interference of the testlike event. Immediate feedback to incorrect answers is low in effectiveness because the wrong answer is strong and interferes with the learning of the correct response.

J. M. Sassenrath of the University of California at Davis decided to find out which theory is more viable. Rather than run yet another study, Sassenrath re-analyzed data from a number of the original studies done by supporters of both sides of the question. His goal: to determine which sort of feedback, immediate or delayed, caused the greatest change in errors over time and which caused the most preservation of error.

Sassenrath is, by the way, a proponent of the rehearsal theory. Yet his re-analysis came down on the side of the Interference-Perseveration explanation of why delayed feedback to testlike events is more effective than immediate feedback in promoting superior performance on delayed recall tests. Translation: Delayed feedback of up to 24 hours is more effective than immediate feedback. This is most important if you are more concerned with long-term recall than with immediate performance. The delayed feedback situation is, in effect, another learning or practice opportunity.

—Reported in "Theory and Results on Feedback and Retention", *Journal of Educational Psychology,* Vol. 67, No. 6.

Reprinted from TRAINING, June 1976

will react (learn) in a similar manner and placing them in opposite groups.

Randomness or matching should take care of the selection biases that decrease design validity. But a multitude of other problems may be introduced in the form of history, mortality, experimental setting and some other "interactions" that statisticians working in the behavioral sciences have uncovered and have yet to devise a method for controlling— short of using a Solomon 4 Group 6 Test Design.** For those training managers under pressure to validate their programs and who also have extravagant budgets, a good statistician using the Solomon design will be able to crank out enough numbers to satisfy anyone in your organization who is questioning your effectiveness.

There are, then, three valuable uses of pretests. They can make classes more enjoyable because, no matter how often you get off the subject, your students will still remember the concepts on which you pretested them. You can start training the right people at the right level. And, finally, you can save your job by validating your training's success.

Incidentally, all three uses are only as good as the test happens to be in measuring what you think it's measuring. But that's a different subject, one that demands an even deeper understanding of multiple instrument or concurrent validity (the name depends on which statistician is describing it).

**The Solomon four group experimental design has been described as the "ideal model for controlled experiments" because of its ability to control for all sources of experimental error except measurement timing and reactive error, which are not subject to control by designs. The design is composed of four groups (two treatment and two control) and six measurements (two pretests and four post-tests). Although this design has many advantages, few instances of its use in applied experimentation have been reported. This is obviously the result of the increased cost of securing two additional control groups.

An excellent treatment of this subject may be found in D.S. Tull and D.I. Hawkins, *Marketing Research: Meaning, Measurement, and Method* (New York: MacMillan Publishing Co., Inc., 1976), Chap. 12

Reprinted from TRAINING, April 1980

SIX MORE BENEFITS OF PRETESTING TRAINEES

Traditional wisdom holds that pretests can help determine the benefit of your training program or discover that trainees already know what you intend to teach them. But that's not all

BY BOB MEZOFF

Are you willing to invest five or 10 minutes at the beginning of your training programs to get the most out of your training budget? If you adopt pretesting as a key component of your training programs, you can:

• dramatically increase your trainees' readiness to learn;

• help them learn far more from the training programs you conduct;

• get trainees to make a psychological investment in the training process;

• sensitize them to the key concepts you will present.

A pretest simply measures knowledge or attitudes related to the training session prior to the program. Traditionally, pretesting has been administered to determine the benefit of a training program and to determine whether, in fact, it is necessary. By measuring the difference between pretest and post-test scores, you can determine what trainees learned from the course. On the other hand, if the pretest shows that trainees already know what you plan to teach them, you can all save your time and effort.

These traditional rationales for pretesting are solidly based in learning theory and are reason enough to include it as a standard element in your training design. Yet the pretest's value as a learning tool does not stop there: The benefits of the method —accrue incrementally.

Benefit #1. Unfreeze your trainees

Unfreezing is the first phase of a three-step process of "change" (or learning) identified by Kurt Lewin in 1947. Following this phase comes "change" and then "refreezing." The unfreezing phase is an important, in fact essential, prelude to learning. In order for change (or learning) to occur, the individual must "let go" of his or her traditional perceptions, beliefs and behaviors. A properly constructed pretest is an effective unfreezing technique that can be administered in a matter of minutes.

Adults need to identify a purpose or personal motivation that will actively engage them in the learning process— otherwise they will have little incentive to learn. While some learning is purely "growth-oriented" (personally enriching yet not functionally critical), most organizational training attempts to teach people skills or information that the *organization* has determined they should acquire.

The trouble is that trainees often come to a training program without that sense of personal motivation. The question "What's in it for me?" needs an immediate answer if trainees are to be receptive to the program. If adult learners don't see a personal benefit to the instruction, they can maintain a complacent sense of "I'm doing just fine with what I already know" and the training program will have little impact.

A pretest, however, stimulates motivation by increasing anxiety and decreasing complacency. In our society there is so much pressure and anxiety inherent in testing situations that trainees often feel apprehensive about taking a pretest, despite your assurances that they are not expected to know the answers.

Although trainees cannot "fail" a pretest (again, pretesting simply determines their existing knowledge or attitudes), this anxiety can produce positive results. When trainees discover they do not know the answers, they can see for themselves how much they have to learn.

The unfreezing effect works better for some people than for others. Research indicates, for example, that a pretest is likely to have a greater impact on people with a field-attentive [or field-dependent] cognitive style (basically, people who are more sensitive to the way others perceive and judge them) and a lesser impact on those with a field-independent cognitive style (people who tend to be less concerned with the opinions of others).

Yet for those pretesting does influence, it dramatically increases their readiness to learn. And for those it does not influence, it doesn't diminish their learning in any way. Regardless of the differences in responses, a pretest that involves cognitive knowledge (where facts and skills are to be demonstrated) is an excellent way to get trainees "psyched up" to learn.

Even when a pretest takes the form of an attitude questionnaire, trainees may doubt their responses, asking themselves, "I wonder what the right answer is?" or "I wonder what the company thinks the proper attitude *should* be?" This uncertainty sets into motion an unfreezing process which, in turn, creates a readiness to learn.

A word of warning: Only a properly constructed pretest can nurture the unfreezing process and increase the trainees' appetite for learning. Ill-conceived or poorly constructed pretests can create resistance to learning, so it is crucial to take the time and effort to develop an effective pretest.

Benefit #2. Intrinsic value

In some cases, trainees may learn as much from taking a pretest as they do from the training process itself. For example, in *The Assessment of Change in Training and Therapy* (McGraw-Hill, 1969). J.A. Belasco and H.M. Trice demonstrated that some participants changed their attitudes about alcoholism *simply as a result of taking a pretest*. Using a sophisticated research design, they were able to determine the exact effects of the pretest. Although this study didn't show that every participant was affected similarly, on the average there was a significant impact.

The fact that a pretest occasionally can produce as much of an impact as

513

an entire training session dramatically illustrates its cost effectiveness.

Benefit #3. Ceremonial effects

Pretesting creates a "ceremonial effect" for the trainees. The higher the initial cost to trainees—in other words, the more effort they must put into the learning process—the more they will tend to value the training.

A difficult pretest (or a pretest on which the trainees are unsure of the "correct" answers) represents an initiation ceremony. Once they invest energy and effort into taking a pretest, trainees are motivated to find out what the answers really are. The pretest thus encourages a psychological investment in the training process.

A few minutes of pretesting pulls the trainees into the context and content of the training program—even before initial warm-up and introduction activities begin.

Benefit #4. Sensitizes trainees to key concepts

The pretest sensitizes trainees to the objectives and content of the course by enabling them to anticipate key points. Paul Rahn recommends this technique and compares it to the tried-and-true method of training: "Tell 'em what you're going to tell 'em, tell 'em, then tell 'em what you told 'em."

The 20 or 30 items on a pretest "flag" the most important concepts and help trainees establish a mental "checklist" to distinguish these key points from the other workshop materials. Don't include minor points in a pretest (or for that matter, the posttest); use it to focus trainees on the most important concepts.

Benefit #5. Focuses the trainer

Writing a pretest forces the trainer to conceptualize exactly what he or she intends to teach in the training session, a result similar to the effect of writing instructional objectives. In fact, it's only possible to develop an effective pretest if your instructional objectives are clearly defined.

A pretest cannot include all the objectives and therefore helps the trainer establish priorities among the various learning goals. When the trainer focuses on the most important goals, trainees are more likely to attain them.

The first time I developed instructional objectives and pretests for my training programs, I was amazed at how much easier it was to teach when I had an explicit idea of exactly what

the most important points were. And I was appalled at how fuzzy my course design was before I had developed and assigned priorities to my objectives. My training program benefited from the pretests I developed because I was clear on exactly how much effort and time I should be spending on the key learning points.

Benefit #6. Establishes a rigorous learning climate

The opening minutes (or even seconds) of any human interaction are critical to determining how the relationship develops. This is true in job interviews, counseling sessions, and certainly between trainer and trainees. At the beginning of a session, participants will be scouting for clues as to how to respond, how serious you are and what kind of expectations you have of them. The early signals you send will set the tone that determines the climate for the remainder of the session.

A pretest immediately makes trainees aware that: 1) your expectations are rigorous and serious; 2) there is an explicit body of information for the training course; 3) they are being measured and evaluated on their efforts to learn (at least as a group, if not individually); and 4) the company has seen fit to put an effort into measuring the effectiveness of its training programs. Effective testing (pre- and post-) suggests a high-quality training program.

By setting a rigorous learning climate, pretesting also helps overcome the problem of unmotivated trainees. Some trainees may be reluctant or

hesitant about attending a training session. As a result, they arrive as passive, rather than active, learners. In some companies, simply filling a chair and keeping one's eyes open are the only requirements for passing the course. This is especially true if training activities have earned a reputation as being a time to socialize with co-workers.

However, when the trainees arrive on the first day of the course and are greeted with a pretest, they immediately get the message that you are serious. Since there also will be a posttest, the trainee had better get serious.

Pretests provide an incentive to learn for both high and low achievers. The pressure of pre- and post-tests encourages reluctant or low-achieving trainees to search out the trainer for extra help, remedial work or at least individual coaching during the session. Achievement-oriented trainees want to learn even more because they know that they will have an opportunity to demonstrate their mastery on a competency test (if that is the case) at the end of the training program.

Reason enough?

The two traditional reasons to use pretesting should be enough to encourage most trainers to adopt it as a regular technique. For trainers who have not been so inclined to date, any one of these additional reasons should serve as an added payoff. Taken in total, these eight benefits form a forceful case for using pretests as a standard strategy to induce higher levels of learning.

Reprinted from TRAINING, August 1983

TRAINEES REACT TO A PRETEST
BY BOB MEZOFF

"This test brings out the realization that I am totally ignorant in this field. There is much to learn."

"I feel very inadequate and I hope I haven't started something I can't complete. I guess I'm just frustrated!"

"Trying to answer the questions on the pretest was frustrating, frightening and upsetting. Could the real purpose of this testing be to point out to us what we don't know so we'll be shocked into learning it?"

"This test leaves me feeling apprehensive, as though I should know data I'm totally unfamiliar with. If a failing mark on this test means expulsion, then I will bid the reader a fond adieu."

"This test has a tendency to be a little disconcerting."

"I found this test to be very frustrating and ego-deflating. I was not competent to answer the majority of the questions."

These comments are from a group of Canadian school administrators who had just taken a pretest for a course on leadership training.

I was surprised that so many of the comments referred to anxiety created by the test. Since all of the trainees were school administrators, I assumed they would understand the traditional purposes behind pretesting and realize that the test was not administered to make them feel inadequate. But apparently, even people who are familiar with educational environments find taking a pretest disconcerting.

Reprinted from TRAINING, August 1983

ADD 'THEN' TESTING TO PROVE TRAINING'S EFFECTIVENESS

How effective was your training program? Pre-Post testing is an old-reliable measurement method, but it can skew your evaluation. Here's a simple way to increase the accuracy of your measurements.

BY ROBERT C. PREZIOSI
AND LESILE M. LEGG

Would you like to improve the accuracy of your training program evaluations? Would you like to increase your bargaining position when negotiating your training budget? Would it enhance your department's power base to reduce the cost of evaluating your training programs, while demonstrating their high impact? If so, you should consider the advantages of "pre-then-post" testing over pre-post testing.

Pre-post testing is a familiar technique to most trainers. Before training begins, participants rate their ability, knowledge or skill using a Likert-type scale (see example). Once the training concludes, participants rate themselves again on the same factors. The two sets of scores are compared to determine the changes in the participants' self-ratings as a result of the training. While low in cost and easy to administer, this type of self-reporting can create some problems.

First, there's the "glowing estimate" problem. If trainees overestimate their ability, knowledge or skill on the pretest, score comparisons produce an inaccurate analysis of the effects of the training program.

A more serious problem is the "response-shift bias." This inaccuracy occurs, according to reseachers, because participants in a training program have a different frame of reference for a post-test than they did for the pre-test. The pre-post method does not take into account such changes in frame of reference.

For example, prior to training a participant's self-rating on a scale of one (low) to 10 (high) is six in the area of recognizing nonverbal communication cues; after the training session, the same subject rates herself as a seven. But that "seven" rating reflects the trainee's new understanding that there is a great deal more to the subject than she thought; she realizes now that the pre-test score of six was an overestimation—a lower score would have been more realistic—but it's too late to change the pre-test rating. Thus, the response-shift bias produces an inaccurate measure of the learning that has taken place, and the trainer cannot fully document the benefits resulting from his program.

To obtain accurate comparisons, participants must rate themselves using the same frame of reference. Pre-then-post testing makes this possible. After the program has concluded, participants are asked to think

EXHIBIT I
Likert-Type Scale

Using the following scale, rate yourself on the item listed below.

Low				Average					High
1	2	3	4	5	6	7	8	9	10

_____ My skill at listening attentively to other people.

FIGURE 1
PRE-POST RESULTS (N=20)
(Scale 1 - 10)

Item	Pre-Test	Post-Test	Pre-Post % Increase
Leadership	4.42	7.75	75%
Motivation	6.08	7.95	31%
Communication	5.96	7.64	28%
Supervisor Responsibilities	7.04	7.85	12%
Personal Strengths Awareness	5.90	7.92	34%

FIGURE 2
THEN-POST RESULTS (N=20)
(Scale 1 - 10)

Item	Pre	Then	Post	Then-Post % Increase
Leadership	4.42	4.00	7.75	94%
Motivation	6.08	4.93	7.95	61%
Communication	5.96	4.97	7.64	54%
Supervisor Responsibilities	7.04	5.37	7.85	46%
Personal Strengths Awareness	5.90	4.62	7.92	71%

back and rate their knowledge, skill or ability prior to training. This is the "then" measure. They are then asked to rate themselves in light of what they know now (the traditional post-test). The process eliminates response-shift bias because participants use the same frame of reference on the then-test as on the post-test. In addition, a traditional pre-test measure is taken at the normal time.

We can analyze the data from this testing approach in two ways: Pre-test and then-test scores can be compared so that the differences reflect the shift in frame of reference; the then- and post-test scores also can be compared and the differences analyzed based upon the same frame of reference. In our use of this testing technique, participants tend to overestimate their skills on the pre-test, and their "pre" scores are higher than their "then" scores.

Testing the method

In one application of this approach, we used two groups of participants in a management development program. The experimental group consisted of 20 people being trained in two separate sessions; the control group consisted of 20 people who would receive the same training at a future time. Both groups were given the pre-test before the experimental group began its eight-week training program. The

FIGURE 3			
CONTROL GROUP (N=20)			
Item	Pre	Then	Post
Leadership	5.42	5.41	5.42
Motivation	6.78	6.96	6.98
Communication	6.13	5.95	5.84
Supervisor Responsibilities	7.29	7.07	7.06
Personal Strengths Awareness	6.90	6.97	6.78

then- and post-tests were given to both groups at the conclusion of the experimental group's program. (The control group, in other words, took all three tests without receiving any training. As expected, the self-ratings did not change appreciably.)

The pre-then-post testing consisted of 22 statements covering the program content, such as "My ability to evaluate the most important factors in a leadership situation." Participants rated themselves on a Likert-type scale with values ranging from one to 10.

Figure 1 is a sample of the data collected from the experimental group, using pre- and post-test scores only. Figure 2 also reflects data from the experimental group, but includes the "then" scores. Scores from the control group are presented in Figure 3. The data in the first two figures speak for themselves: The response-shift bias is eliminated and a more accurate picture of learning changes is drawn.

The pre-then-post test scores also indicate that participants did indeed learn something as a result of the training program—significantly more than would have been documented by the traditional pre-post approach. This is a very important point when it comes to negotiating your training budget: You can precisely identify the impact your training is having. The percentage increases are significant enough to catch anyone's eye. (In a separate study of cross-selling training, the increases were even higher.)

Compared to direct observational techniques and other approaches, pre-then-post testing is an economical way to evaluate your training programs—an advantage that cannot be overemphasized at a time when costs and productivity are concerns of all organizations. HRD department resources used to implement this type of evaluation can certainly be justified by the benefits they produce.

Reprinted from TRAINING, May 1983

CONSTRUCTING TESTS THAT WORK

Here's a refresher course on how to construct tests that really measure whether trainees learned what they were supposed to learn from your training program

BY MARC J. ROSENBERG
AND WILLIAM SMITLEY

When the objectives of a training course demand a pencil-and-paper test of knowledge or appropriate job-like performance, the trainer confronts a deceptively difficult challenge: How do you write test items that effectively and accurately measure the extent to which trainees have learned the material you've been teaching them?

Like so many training tasks, this one looks easy until you try to do it. Constructing effective tests requires subject-matter expertise, clear and concise writing, and considerable time and effort. Above all, it requires that each test item be designed so that every student interprets it in exactly the way the designer intends.

The four most common types of written tests—multiple choice, dichotomous, matching, and short answer/completion—are all variations of the same basic, two-part format: first a *stem*, which is a statement or question that provides the stimulus to the student; then two or more alternatives, often called *distractors*, from which the correct response to the stem is selected. The alternatives may be provided directly, as in the case of multiple choice, dichotomous or matching items, or, as in the case of short answer/completion questions, they may be implied. In the latter case, the "distractors" are all of the imaginable answer choices the student must filter out in order to provide the correct response.

By looking at the four types of questions as variations of this universal format, our discussion of each type, including definitions, advantages and limitations, can be simplified. We should note at the start, however, that the advantages and limitations of each

Constructing an effective test looks easy—until you try to do it.

format *in a general sense* will not indicate which is best for a given testing situation. The format you choose should reflect your analysis of the specific content you wish to test and the learning objectives of the training course.

Multiple Choice

A multiple-choice test item consists of a stem, in the form of a statement or question, followed by more than two distractors. A key point in the design of multiple-choice questions is that all distractors should be plausible. Here are three acceptable examples:

Question format: What cartoon character was Walt Disney's first commercial success?

a. Donald Duck
b. Goofy
c. Jiminy Cricket
d. Mickey Mouse

Incomplete statement format 1: Walt Disney's first commercially successful cartoon character was:
a. Donald Duck
b. Goofy
c. Jiminy Cricket
d. Mickey Mouse

Incomplete statement format 2: The cartoon character _____ was Walt Disney's first commercial success.
a. Donald Duck
b. Goofy
c. Jiminy Cricket
d. Mickey Mouse

Major advantages of the multiple-choice format include:

1. Test scoring is simplified because possible bias by the test administrator cannot influence a student's score. And because all distractors are provided in the item, an answer key can be developed to allow anyone to grade the tests—you don't need a subject-matter expert to do the grading.

2. When more than two distractors are provided for each item, the trainee's chances of *guessing* the correct answer are reduced.

3. When enough plausible alternatives are available to be used as distractors, multiple-choice items are relatively easy to construct.

Major limitations of the multiple-choice format:

1. Since the answer is provided among the distractors, it *can* be guessed; you can't be certain that the student really knew the answer to a given question.

2. The format relies on recognition, rather than "production" of the answer by the student. It is generally agreed that recognition reflects a lower level of learning than does production.

3. When enough plausible distractors cannot be identified, the development of quality multiple-choice items can become very difficult.

4. Since several distractors must be provided for each item, the format uses more space than some of the others.

Dichotomous test items

The stem of a dichotomous, or alternative-response test item is typically a declarative statement but can be in the form of a question. The stem is followed by only two mutually exclusive distractors (yes/no, true/false,

TEST ITEM CHECKLIST

_____   _____
Reviewer's Name   Date

Directions: Indicate whether *all* test items meet each criterion by placing a check mark [ ] in the appropriate box. Write the number of any items that did not meet the criterion in the space marked "REVISIONS." Use only those criteria which apply to each particular item or test type.

Revisions: If any test item receives a NO, revise that item as needed.

I. GENERAL CRITERIA

	YES	NO	REVISIONS
1. Is the item grammatically correct?	[ ]	[ ]	_____
2. Have ambiguous statements/terms been avoided?	[ ]	[ ]	_____
3. Is the item written at the trainee's language level?	[ ]	[ ]	_____
4. Does it avoid giving clues that can be used to answer another item?	[ ]	[ ]	_____
5. Does the item contain only a single idea?	[ ]	[ ]	_____
6. Is only relevant information included?	[ ]	[ ]	_____
7. Has the use of a correct answer from another item as part of the stem for this item been avoided?	[ ]	[ ]	_____
8. Is there only one correct answer for the item?	[ ]	[ ]	_____
9. Are all parts of the item on the same page?	[ ]	[ ]	_____

II. MULTIPLE CHOICE TEST ITEMS

	YES	NO	REVISIONS
10. Have negative and double negative stems been avoided?	[ ]	[ ]	_____
11. Have grammatical clues been avoided?	[ ]	[ ]	_____
12. Is as much of the wording as possible in the stem rather than in the distractor?	[ ]	[ ]	_____
13. Are all distractors approximately the same length?	[ ]	[ ]	_____
14. Are all distractors plausible?	[ ]	[ ]	_____
15. Are enough distractors present in each item (4-5) to reduce guessing?	[ ]	[ ]	_____
16. Are distractors arranged in an orderly manner (alphabetically, numerically, logically)?	[ ]	[ ]	_____
17. Have distractors such as "none of the above," "all of the above," "A & B only," etc., been avoided?	[ ]	[ ]	_____

III. DICHOTOMOUS TEST ITEMS

	YES	NO	REVISIONS
18. Is the statement worded so precisely that it can be judged unequivocally?	[ ]	[ ]	_____
19. Have negative and double negative stems been avoided?	[ ]	[ ]	_____
20. Have clues which tend to qualify the "absoluteness" of the stem been avoided?	[ ]	[ ]	_____

IV. MATCHING TEST ITEMS

	YES	NO	REVISIONS
21. Are there more distractors than premises?	[ ]	[ ]	_____
22. Is the premise list short?	[ ]	[ ]	_____
23. Are distractors more concise than premises so that reading load is reduced?	[ ]	[ ]	_____
24. Are the distractor and premise lists related to the same central theme, concept or idea?	[ ]	[ ]	_____
25. Are all premises, distractors and matching rationale on one page?	[ ]	[ ]	_____
26. Are premises and distractors arranged in an orderly manner (alphabetically, numerically, logically)?	[ ]	[ ]	_____
27. Is there only one answer match for each premise?	[ ]	[ ]	_____
28. Have grammatical clues been avoided?	[ ]	[ ]	_____

V. SHORT ANSWER/COMPLETION TEST ITEMS

	YES	NO	REVISIONS
29. Is the item constructed so that only one briefly written answer is possible?	[ ]	[ ]	_____
30. For incomplete sentence items, does enough of the statement remain to convey the intent to the trainee?	[ ]	[ ]	_____
31. Does the main idea of the incomplete sentence precede the blank?	[ ]	[ ]	_____
32. Is the only omission a significant word, symbol or number?	[ ]	[ ]	_____
33. For numerical answers, has the degree of precision been included in the stem?	[ ]	[ ]	_____
34. Have negative and double negative stems been avoided?	[ ]	[ ]	_____
35. Has a list of acceptable responses (variations of the answer that are acceptable as correct) been specified?	[ ]	[ ]	_____

---

right/wrong, cold/warm).

Major advantages:

1. The dichotomous format is useful for distinguishing fact from opinion, right from wrong, or in any other situation where there are two, and only two, mutually exclusive alternatives.

2. As with multiple-choice items, scoring is simplified and unbiased.

Major limitations:

1. Since only two choices are provided, the student has a 50% chance of guessing the correct answer. Therefore, the dichotomous format usually requires more test items than other formats to measure the student's knowledge accurately.

2. Few important statements are *absolutely* right or wrong, true or false. Therefore, dichotomous test items can be difficult to construct. It usually is a mistake to try to "qualify" the stem with words such as "always," "usually," "never" and so forth; such qualifiers provide clues to the correct answer, as in these examples:

____T ____F An open style of supervision is always the better way to deal with subordinates.

____T ____F It never rains in California between the months of June and September.

If the test item doesn't fit the dichotomous format, don't force it; choose another format.

3. As with multiple-choice questions, the dichotomous format does not force the student to "produce" the correct answer.

Matching test items

In the matching format, a series of stems, usually called "premises," is listed in a single column, while the possible distractors are listed in a second column. All of the distractors in a matching series should be plausible answers for each stem or premise. In other words, all the premises and all the answer choices must be similar, or homogeneous.

In a matching exercise, stems should contain the majority of the information to be tested, while each distractor should be short, containing only a key word, number or phrase. This reduces the burden on the student of repeated reading of a long list of distractors.

Example of a matching format:
Match the type of frame joint with the correct method of nailing that should be used.

Frame Joint	Nailing Method
Soleplate to joist	a. Blind
Rafter to valley	b. Edge
Rafter to rafter	c. End
Header to joist	d. Face
	e. Toe

Major advantages:
1. Since the matching format allows all the distractors to be used as possible answers for all of the stems, a lot of test items can be covered on a single page. Matching tests also can be

USING 'DAILIES' TO KEEP TRAINING ON TARGET

Your organization has sunk a lot of money into this training program—design time, material and logistical expenses, perhaps travel and lodging expenses for the trainees, not to mention lost work time. As with any investment, you want to know whether or not this one is working out, and you want to know soon enough to correct any mistakes.

To protect your investment, one instructional designer recommends borrowing a technique from another fast-paced, high-budget industry: the movies. Kenneth A. Lawrence, chief of instructional design at the Veterans' Administration Medical Center in Washington, DC, points out that the film industry avoids expensive return trips to remote locations by processing film samples each day, so that any necessary reshooting can be done immediately.

Those film samples are called "dailies." If Steven Spielberg were a corporate trainer, he might refer to dailies as a type of formative evaluation. That idea occurred to Lawrence a few years ago when the VA switched from local to centrally conducted training for its medical center procurement specialists nationwide. The new arrangement called for eight to 10 five-day training sessions a year. Each session would cost more than $10,000. No room for second chances there.

Lawrence and his associates decided that what they needed was an evaluation form they could pass out at the end of each day's training—a form that would give them results they could process and interpret overnight. They rejected a daily content quiz as cumbersome to create and administer. Instead, they settled on an instrument very much like your standard, end-of-session evaluation form. It asks trainees to rate the program on such dimensions as relevance to their jobs, clarity and pace. It also asks them to list the most important things they learned in the session, and to make any other comments they wish.

The difference is that instead of filling out the questionnaire only at the end of the course, trainees are asked to complete it at the end of each of the first three days and occasionally on the fourth day—"for example, when a new or revised course is being tested, or when a new instructor is presenting training," says Lawrence.

The form uses Likert-scale questions ("Rate this characteristic from 1 to 5"). After each class, an evaluator plots the response distribution for each question, and categorizes the write-in comments by frequency. Then the evaluator reviews the results with the instructor.

They're looking for the usual things. For example, the distribution on "relevance," (1 = all the material was highly relevant, 5 = little or no relevance) should be toward the left end of the continuum. For "pace," rated from 1 (too fast) to 5 (too slow), the responses should be grouped near the center, with outliers evenly balanced between the two extremes. Trainees' comments about the most important things they learned should bear a reasonable resemblance to the intended content of the course.

Not long ago, Lawrence says, the usefulness of gathering this sort of data daily instead of only at course's end was illustrated when a regular instructor got sick on the third day of a session and had to be replaced. The day's subject—analyzing bidders' projected overhead costs—was one that often gave participants trouble anyway.

The evaluation showed that one of the classes taught by the substitute instructor had a particularly hard time with the lesson. For example, the "clarity" item, which normally turned up a leftward distribution (meaning most of the day's instruction was understandable), showed a nearly flat distribution for this particular class. That night the trainers developed a review sequence. The instructor presented it first thing the next morning. According to Lawrence, that day's evaluation indicated that the problem had been resolved.

One additional benefit of dailies, Lawrence adds, is that their cumulative information can be very helpful in evaluating an entire course. It may not be as glamorous as a Hollywood screening, he concludes, but it does the job.

Reprint from TRAINING, February 1987

completed more quickly than tests using other formats.

2. The format measures factual knowledge and the student's ability to recognize relationships and make associations.

3. As with multiple-choice and dichotomous items, scoring is simplified and unbiased.

Major limitations:

1. As students complete the items they know to be correct, the possibility of making a correct guess increases through the process of elimination. This limitation can be reduced by providing more distractors than stems.

2. Stems and distractors in a matching group must be homogeneous. That is, they must relate to the same concept and must be phrased in basically the same way. If the designer isn't careful, students will be able to reduce the number of plausible distractors.

3. Again, the matching format relies on recognition rather than production of the answer by the student.

Short answer/completion

Short-answer test items, also referred to as "completion" or "fill-in-the-blank" questions, have stems constructed in the same manner as multiple-choice items. But, instead of choosing from distractors supplied by the designer, students must come up with a specific word, number or symbol on their own.

Major advantages:

1. Short-answer items are relatively easy to construct since distractors do not have to be created.

2. They are very effective in measuring recall.

3. Unlike other formats, the short-answer item requires the student to produce the correct response rather than simply to recognize it. Thus, the possibility of guessing the correct answer is drastically reduced.

Major limitations:

1. The range of distractors depends upon the "mind-set" of the student at the time of testing. This mind-set may

be different from the trainer's without being "wrong." Thus, the student might produce an unanticipated response which is arguably correct.

2. Scoring is more difficult due to potential subjectivity in the interpretation of responses. A subject-matter expert may be required to determine whether the response is correct.

3. A short-answer format should be used only when the correct response is, indeed, a significant word, number, symbol or *short* phrase. Here are two *inappropriate* items:

1. A telescope is _____.
2. A tool used by astronomers to observe planets and _____ is a telescope.

Here is how the item might be improved:

3. A tool used by astronomers to observe planets and stars is a/an _____ .

4. Short-answer items that are poorly developed may measure the wrong things—by asking the student to recall an insignificant aspect of some important concept, for example.

Organization

Another important concern in the test-design process is that of layout. The organization of a written test centers around four major areas: the cover page, general test directions, specific directions and item groupings.

The cover page: At least two matters should be addressed clearly and concisely on the cover page of any written test: the *purpose* of the test itself, and a reminder of the *objectives* of the lesson or course which the test covers.

General test directions: These give the student any information necessary to complete the test. General directions should include: total time allowed; any resources the student is permitted to use during the test; whether any group work will be allowed; how to complete a separate answer sheet, if necessary; suggestions to help the student complete the test efficiently; scoring procedures and values for each test item; and instruc-

tions about what the student is to do at the conclusion of the test.

Specific directions: Each set of test items, multiple-choice, matching, dichotomous or completion, requires specific directions as to how the student is to respond. It also may be appropriate to provide practice items. If the procedures by which students indicate answers vary throughout the test (e.g., circle the letter, write in a number or write in an answer), those procedures must be explained.

Whenever possible, however, construct tests in a manner that relies on as few differing procedures as possible. Don't forget to repeat your directions if the same types of questions appear in more than one place in the test or if a given format continues on following pages.

Item groupings: The placement and grouping of test items is an important consideration. Some general recommendations:

1. If possible, group all items according to content.

2. Within each content area, group all items according to type (i.e., keep all multiple-choice items together, etc.).

3. Provide more space between items than within items.

4. Try to disperse the easier test items uniformly throughout the test.

Test item checklist

After your test has been constructed, a careful review by content and training specialists can identify potential problems, such as items that are ambiguous, poorly worded or incorrect. The accompanying checklist provides assistance in this process.

You also may save time and effort by reviewing the checklist *before* you begin writing test items. Remember, however, that the best "test of a test" is to try it out with typical students. Even the most knowledgeable reviewers cannot foresee all possible problems, since their "mind-sets" are inherently different from those of the students for whom the test is designed.

Reprinted from TRAINING, September 1983

IN YOUR NEXT CLASS, TRY THIS ALTERNATIVE TO HAPPINESS SHEETS

Here's a learner feedback form that
identifies specific strengths
and weaknesses in an instructor's
classroom technique

BY J.B. CORNWELL

Generally, most of us are uncomfortable with "happiness sheets" as feedback for performance improvement of classroom presentation skills. When they are "good" they provide an ego trip for the presenter. When they are "bad," well, maybe there was a personality clash between student and instructor.

An evaluation of the achievement of course objectives is, on the other hand, easier to ascertain. At least we can pinpoint what we didn't succeed in doing. We can't pinpoint *why* we didn't succeed, but we can identify which part of the job needs fixing.

Because it is so difficult to determine how to improve performance in presenting a course, we tend to leave presentation skills in the closet. To compound the problem, seminars designed to improve presentation skills are viewed suspiciously by some managers of classroom instructors.

The "bottom line" of performance measurement of training is the degree to which on-the-job performance matches the job needs—after the training. Also critical is the degree to which learners achieve course objectives during the course; this usually is represented as final exam scores. Any attempt to measure learner reactions to presentation techniques as an evaluation of overall trainer performance is bound to fail. Unless you are measuring merely the popularity of a so-called dog and pony show.

Interpreting trainee feedback about technique as a valid performance evaluation is a common error. One way to rectify it is to establish a hierarchy of evaluation. Three points should be considered. First, the degree to which the training course prepared the learner to perform the job should be the measure of success of the training program. It should also be the instrument to diagnose error in the front-end analysis.

Second, the degree to which learners achieve the objectives of the course is the instrument to diagnose error in the learning system design and to separate those errors from front-end analysis errors.

Finally, learner feedback about presentation technique should be recognized as only a diagnostic tool to identify how presentation techniques affected the success of achieving course objectives.

After struggling with a traditional "Was-the-instructor-adequately-prepared?" sort of happiness sheet, I decided to attempt a breakdown and analysis of the classroom presentation task. The idea wasn't to try to make subjective feedback look objective; it was to break down the subjective feedback into statements about what the presenter did and how the learner reacted to it.

The first step was to devise the task breakdown. That took several years of refining, adding, subtracting, modifying format, testing, and finally devising something that, based on unscientific evidence, works. It works, that is, to the extent that it suggests a learner feedback form that identifies specific weaknesses and strengths in an instructor's classroom technique. The results of that feedback correlate closely with the achievement of course objectives.

Initially, the major tasks identified were:
- open the presentation,
- conduct planned learning experiences, and
- close the presentation.

When I identified the sub-tasks, the major tasks were restructured as follows:

Open the presentation.

- Confirm mutual understanding of learner needs.
- Establish that the presentation objectives will meet some of those needs.
- Close a "contract" with the learners for mutual effort.

Conduct planned learning experiences.

- Sequence activities to allow successive approximations of objectives.
- Provide valid analogies and examples of applications of key points.
- Stimulate real or vicarious learner participation in the presentation.
- Provide a variety of learning experiences appropriate to the nature of the learning desired.
- Stimulate, analyze, and respond to learner feedback about their progress and understanding.
- Review and summarize at each milestone during and at the end of the presentation.

Communicate so that learners can perceive your meanings accurately.

- Word the presentation carefully so that learners are not confused.
- Use a presentation style that successfully communicates the nonverbal content of what you have to say.

Affect learner attitudes.

- Communicate attitudes that are inoffensive to all learners.
- Stimulate learners' enthusiasm for the objective of the presentation.
- Help learners enjoy the presentation.

After listing the tasks, I established criteria for their performance. The Presentation Analysis form (see accompanying box) was designed to measure the degree to which the tasks had been successfully accomplished. The form is completed by each learner at the end of the presentation, just as "happiness sheets" are. The boxes checked by the learners have point values, from one to five. Criterion for each task is a "score" of 4, averaged from all learner analyses of the question that relates to that task. Criterion for the presentation is a summed score of 60, the averaged analyses of all 15 questions.

There has been no scientific, statistically valid study of the correlation of Presentation Analysis scores to learner achievement of presentation objectives. The conclusions that follow, therefore, are tentative, based on several hundred learners and a few dozen presentations by a half dozen or so presenters of widely varying skill.

This much is fact: In every case in which average-learner final exam scores exceeded 85, Presentation Analysis scores exceeded 68. In every case in which Presentation Analysis scores exceeded 60, 80% or more of the learners achieved 80% or more of the presentation objectives. (80% is learner achievement criterion for learning system design.)

Generally, if P.A. scores fell below 60, learner achievement dropped below levels for the same presentation at or above criterion (60). Classroom presenters who have used the Presentation Analysis form to diagnose their own performances have achieved measurable improvement in learner achievement and learner satisfaction. In many cases, the performance improvement project included the validation of manuscript development materials for the how-to-do-it training manual.

Some predictable patterns occur in the analyses of a given presentation. Individual learners who are satisfied tend to rate every task above group average; disgruntled learners rate every task below the group average for that task. Even though the satisfied learner rates the presentation at a 70, let's say, and the disgruntled learner rates it a 55, each will identify the same tasks as having been bests—and leasts—accomplished. Feedback to the presenter, indicating where improvement opportunities exist, is, therefore, consistent. Not perfectly consistent, due to individual differences in learners, but consistent enough. When inconsistencies do show up, they suggest that the presentation did not serve all learners equally.

This system has produced results that, though not scientifically validated, suggest it can be a powerful tool in diagnosing and improving training program success.

Reprinted from TRAINING, May 1978

PRESENTATION ANALYSIS

KEY:
1. Absolutely no
2. Mostly no
3. Neutral (undecided)
4. Mostly yes
5. Absolutely yes

	1	2	3	4	5
1. Did the presenter have an accurate perception of what you wanted from the presentation, and why?	☐	☐	☐	☐	☐
2. Was it clear to you, from the beginning of the presentation, what the objectives were?	☐	☐	☐	☐	☐
3. Will the results of the presentation contribute to achieving your personal goals?	☐	☐	☐	☐	☐
4. Was the sequencing of the material logical?	☐	☐	☐	☐	☐
5. Were the concepts and principles discussed compared to real life situations that you identify with?	☐	☐	☐	☐	☐
6. Did the learning aids used assist your learning? Were they adequate?	☐	☐	☐	☐	☐
7. Did you get satisfactory opportunity to contribute your ideas?	☐	☐	☐	☐	☐
8. Did you get satisfactory answers to your doubts and questions?	☐	☐	☐	☐	☐
9. Do you feel that each step was satisfactorily achieved before the next step was started?	☐	☐	☐	☐	☐
10. Did the presenter use only language that is very clear to you—and inoffensive?	☐	☐	☐	☐	☐
11. Was the presenter's speech easy to listen to and understand?	☐	☐	☐	☐	☐
12. Do you feel that the presenter respects your point of view and your feelings?	☐	☐	☐	☐	☐
13. Would you describe the presenter as enthusiastic about the subject?	☐	☐	☐	☐	☐
14. Do you find the subject interesting?	☐	☐	☐	☐	☐
15. Did you, personally, enjoy the presentation?	☐	☐	☐	☐	☐

16. What changes would you suggest to make the presentation, or the presenter, more effective?

17. What other comments would you like to make?

WHY TRAINEES SHOULD *NOT* EVALUATE TRAINERS

Evaluation by trainees—the happiness rating—is, Broadwell suggests, worse than useless. What's needed? Something new . . . and truly helpful

BY MARTIN M. BROADWELL

Talking to a group of training specialists some time ago, I challenged them to come up with an acceptable reason for bothering to evaluate the training they were doing. It was an interesting thing for all of us to see the direction the brainstorming took. When honesty rose to the forefront—a sight to behold among trainers—most agreed that the main reason was pressure from the organization. Each had an idea that, deep down inside, he or she could really tell how good the instructing was without going through any formal evaluation activity. "But," came the conclusion, "management doesn't seem to be satisfied with that kind of evaluation anymore."

Finally, they decided that we should evaluate for two reasons: (1) to see if the time and effort were worth it in terms of return for the organization, and (2) to see if there was a way of improving the training in the future. There was general agreement that we are more often forced into the first and avoid the second once a course gets under way, especially if the "students all like it."

There's a good chance that many times we go down the wrong road in our evaluation techniques, especially in terms of how we interpret the results. For example, suppose we get very "financial." We figure the cost of the training right down to paper clips; then we figure out how much the improved behavior is worth to the organization. The difference—savings—is what the training is worth. Sounds simple enough, right? Not necessarily; if we stop there, we've done a poor job of evaluation.

Admittedly, not enough of us even go as far as the dollars-and-cents evaluation, but even when we do, it may be like measuring the mileage on a car without also knowing how well it was tuned up or how good the spark plugs were. Good, honest evaluation should say, "With the training we did, we got these results. We don't know how well the teacher was tuned or whether the class was really 'sparked up.'" In other words, we need to be careful that we don't accept the training as an invariable and measure its worth in light of whether this invariable gives us an organizational improvement. The real problems come when our efforts have proven that we actually are saving the organization a measureable sum of money (or time. or effort). We may ask, "Why worry about it when we know we're saving money

on it?" The answer is, "Worry about it because we might be able to save more money or time or effort." We shouldn't be satisfied with any training evaluation that doesn't take into account how efficiently the training was done, how well the instructor did, which instructors did better than others, and which are going to improve.

Let's see what assumptions we are making if we don't make any quantified evaluation of the trainer (and I don't mean students rating the teacher on a five-point scale!). First, we might be saying that the trainers are all perfect—or at least cut out of the same imperfect mold—when we say that they all will teach the same subject at the same rate and get the same results. For example, training directors often say, "We'll teach thus and so in this period of time." When asked who will teach it, they'll say that so far that isn't decided. This assumes that any instructor taking that material can teach it to the same degree of success as any other instructor in the same length of time. That becomes a strange conclusion when the question is asked whether some instructors are better than others. The answer always comes back that some *are* better than others, so our assumption is all wrong. To think that we'll get the same learning from different instructors or the same learning from the same instructor every time is false hope for sure!

When we do our evaluation on the dollars-and-cents basis alone, we're also running the risk of assuming that once the course gets underway we'll be getting the best possible instruction and have no need to improve it. None of us believe that, of course, but so often we let the instructing go after we've had some kind of instructor training class and gotten most of the instructors to take it. We make little effort to follow up on the instructors or sit in and help them catch their own weaknesses or build on their strengths. We make another false assumption by assuming that they will get better just because they are teaching all the time. There is little effort to support the idea that experience is

523

GOOD LEARNING VS. A GOOD RATING

BY DUGAN LAIRD

As a shameless eavesdropper, I naturally tilted my head. I wanted to hear every word between the couple at the next table. We were all waiting for the next conference session to start.

"This evaluation thing intrigues me," the fellow was saying. "Just once in my life I want to get perfect ratings from a class!"

His companion giggled. "Ernest, you've got to be joking! You've been in training long enough to know those numbers don't mean a thing."

Ernest seemed unconvinced. "You tell me that, Edith. Other trainers tell me that. I wish my boss would tell me that. He bases raises on ratings, and has even been known to drop a course because of low ratings...not to mention an instructor who got the ax for averaging less than 3.8 on a five-point scale."

The lady still giggled. "Ernie, you surely do better than 3.8."

The silence was embarrassing, but Edith rose to the occasion: "Then just let your old Aunt Edith tell you how to get superb ratings on any Happiness Index. First, say 'Yes' and 'Umhummmmm' and 'I see' and 'How interesting.' Say them a whole lot.

"Next—and this may be the most important part— look awfully pleasant all the time...pleasant, but concerned. We call it 'The Frown of Concern and the Smile of Sincerity.' A little practice with a mirror and any idiot can get it. Sorry, nothing personal. You know what I mean: you've seen it on all those conference leaders they send out from..."

"But that's so phony!" protested her pupil. "If I care sincerely about the people..."

"What's it got to do with caring? It's ratings you want, fella! True, chessy-cat grins don't guarantee success, but without them you haven't a chance! I'll tell you how to prove you care: laugh at every joke they tell you. No matter how vulgar, dull, or trite, you laugh. Quite loud, too! Else how will they know you're sincere?"

"But I don't like dirty jokes."

"So? Besides, you don't need to tell any yourself. But be sure to imply you're worldly. 'Imply' is the magic word. And be couth. Call them 'facilities' and 'boudoirs,' not bathrooms or bedrooms. Or just be simplistic; just manipulate the scale."

"You mean I should cheat?" Ernest was clearly shocked.

"It's not cheating...really. One government agency was getting lots of 2's on their four-point scale. So they shifted to a 20-point scale, and sort of hid words like 'Excellent' and 'Good' and 'Unsatisfactory' under the numbers. That way they had a four-point scale, but nobody knew it and their ratings went right up."

Just then a tall, toothsome fellow sat down. Edith introduced him as "Popular Perry, all-time ratings champ." It seems he even got an over-all 4.8 from training people..."And you know how low they always rate!"

Perry was full of tips. "Always steer clear of controversy. The fallacy of

---

Says Popular Perry: "Significant learnings force participants to re-examine their habits and values. Trainees won't give you a good rating for that."

---

teaching anything controversial is your assumption that people are there to change. Not true. They want to match their biases with yours. If there's no match, you get a 'Poor,' or even a 1. Once I got an 'Unsatisfactory' just because I said that behavior modification really existed!"

Ernie was distressed. "This makes the whole thing such a game."

"Well," consoled Popular Perry, "Then just concentrate on hygiene. You know: give 95 percent of your attention to the food and air conditioning. Be sure to dismiss early so they get to the bar before it gets crowded."

Edith was suddenly alert. "And, Perry, give us your theory about endings. Don't you think there's some-

thing special about the way you end?"

"Unquestionably! Endings are critical. Why, you can hoist ratings by more than half a point by what you do in the last 30 minutes. Stay away from any talk about applications. Nothing's so deadening as those 'What Am I Going To Do With What I Learned' routines.

"Use cliches. Just a few tried and trusty sayings from men like Franklin or Will Rogers. Use Drucker for the heavy stuff. But avoid anything cynical; keep your bromides upbeat...testimonies to participative management and the essential potential of the human spirit and the American system."

Edith was clearly turned on by all this. "That reminds me about certificates. We averaged almost half a point higher when we put them under glass and inside a frame. Do it. It helps."

But Ernest looked distressed again. He had the frown of concern, but not the smile of sincerity. "Certificates? Surely you don't give certificates without some kind of performance testing. And tests can be so threatening. Won't they lower the ratings?"

"Honey, you miss the whole point! It's ratings you want, not learning. In fact, that's Cardinal Principle Number One, isn't it Perry?"

Perry put on his Important Look. "Assuredly. As one who has mastered the ratings system, I have learned never to allow significant learnings. Significant learnings force participants to re-examine their habits ...even their values. You can't expect them to thank you for that by handing out a good rating."

"I'd say this," added Edith. "When you see a participant heading toward some major new insight (unless it's technical) just think '3.' Because '3' is the very highest those people are going to give you. For the sake of the rating, avoid those insights."

"But how? Tell me how," begged Ernest.

"Change the subject. Show a movie. Tell a joke," said Edith.

"Take a break. Back down on your position," counselled Perry, the old pro.

Just then the chairman introduced the speaker for our session. I could only hear Ernest utter mutely, "Well...okay, but..." as we started the workshop on "How To Evaluate Training."

Reprinted from TRAINING, September 1976

a good teacher for the teacher, especially if he isn't pointed in the right direction to start with.

I am sure there were several loud gasps from some reading the last paragraph, the part about not rating the instructors after the course gets under way. "But," they say, "we never close a class without an evaluation of the instructor!" Great! Done by a professional trainer, I hope. "Well, done by the students. After all they know good or bad instructing when they see it." Who says so? Where did we ever get the idea that students are the best judge of whether or not the teacher is doing a professional job of presenting material? That's like having a random sampling of patients give the medical exam to doctors (or, to be less kind, having a group of criminals give the bar exam for lawyers).

I'm now looking at an actual student evaluation card. It is on a five-point scale. The first question is, "How much interest did you have in this subject before you came?" The student has rated it 5. The second question is, "How well did this course meet your needs?" The rating is 4. Question three is, "What was the strong point of this course?" The answer, "The instructor." Question four, "What were the weaknesses?" The answer, "A little too long." Before talking about this as a help to the instructor, let's look at another student's view of the same course; again, these are actual cards. On question one, as to interest, the answer was 3. On question two, as to meeting needs, the answer was 4, the same as the first student. On strong points, "The instructor." On question four, about weaknesses, "Not long enough."

We're not going to talk about the whole field of students evaluating the course, but let's see what we would talk to an instructor about with this kind of information. To start with, each student rated the value of the course as the same: 4. But what does that tell the instructor about his presentation? Not much. The fact that one didn't expect much (3) and the other had great expectations (5) says that the 4 on question two

means quite different things to each of them, obviously. But what? What can I do as an instructor next time to change this? But what about the fact that both found the strength of the course to be the instructor? Since that's a good rating, we can sit back and say the instruction is all right; it's just the type of students we're getting. Or we might say that the instructor is all right, but the material isn't put together very well. Ironically, both of these might be right, but we haven't done much towards deciding the efficiency of the training program with the information we've gotten so far. Finally, one said it was too long, the other said it was too short. Rarely has a program ever been run that the students didn't just about equally divide on this question (except for the large number who like to rate it "about right"). What all of this says is that "happiness" ratings by the students don't give the instructors much usable information as to style, technique and approach to producing learning.

Where is all of this discussion leading us? It says that we need some concrete ways of evaluating the effectiveness and efficiency of our instructors. We all recognize that this is best done by looking at the student after he has returned to the world from whence he came and started to apply what we attempted to teach him. This is the true arena of evaluation, since it was a deficiency in this area that caused us (hopefully) to start thinking about the training in the first place. But there must be a better, earlier look we can take, not a dollar-and-cents measure but some real indicators as to how well the instructors are doing, while they're doing it. There are some ways, and they aren't all that complicated. We just have to get rid of some of our fuzzy thinking.

First, let's dispel some old-fashioned ways of evaluating instructors. It shouldn't happen, but every once in a while some old instructor-critique sheets crawl out of the woodwork and have to be stamped out all over again. The worst of these is the "public speaking" approach to evaluation. The form has a complete list of goods

and bads, all of which sound like they came out of an international-speech-training-club's manual: "How was the teacher's delivery? Did he lean on the podium? Did he hold your interest? Did he use visual aids (if any) well? Was he void of distracting mannerisms? Did he speak loudly enough?" Any time these types of critique sheets show up, they demonstrate clearly that the evaluator is looking for a substitute for effective teaching techniques. It also raises the question as to whether or not we really know what good instructing is.

There is little evidence to show that many students have failed to learn because the teacher failed to use an appropriate gesture at just the right time. There is serious doubt that any training programs have failed because the instructor leaned on a speaker's stand or turned his back on the audience while he wrote on the chalkboard. Not that it's a good practice to turn your back or fail to get eye contact or to talk too softly; it's just that we know more about teaching and learning than to think that a class will suddenly learn (and never forget) a point made with a raised arm or while being looked at directly by the teacher.

The important thing to remember in teacher evaluation is that learning is basically the result of something the learner does, usually—but not necessarily—having been provided the opportunity to do that thing by the teacher. The opportunity to learn does not result from a gesture or a word spoken during eye contact. It is an involvement process through which the learner is provided with some mental activity causing him to embed the material in his memory. And this should give us a clue as to what to look for when we critique a training program.

As we look at classroom activities, we should think of three major inputs: the student (and all his abilities and hang-ups), the teacher (and all his experience and knowledge), and the material to be learned. These inputs all converge in the teaching-learning environment (the classroom). How they come together is primarily under the control of the instructor. The instructor decides what the student will do, how the material will be handled and presented, and who will do all the talking. The instructor decides how much feedback will be obtained and how that feedback will be used, if indeed it will be used at all. As we evaluate the instructor we are also evaluating the instructing, which is the sum total of all the inputs plus the effect of the environment. A pretty good rule to follow is to avoid mind reading whenever possible: "I think the students were hostile because the chairs were uncomfortable," or "The students resented him because he had too many college degrees." When we do this kind of evaluation we're in trouble, because the answer sounds like, "Sorry, teacher, there's nothing you can do to look good so long as we have those hard seats or you have your college degrees." We need something more tangible to go on, and the instructor needs something that is behavior-oriented in order to know what to change if he's doing something wrong.

A good critique should have something about what the students are doing as well as what the instructor is or isn't doing. It should tell how much involvement there is in the classroom situation, not just the total number of times someone was involved. It should include the number of different students who were involved in any given period of time. An even better bit of information to discuss with an instructor is how many different kinds of involvement techniques were used and how well they were used: Were they forced? Were they effective? Did they have some reason for being used other than just making time go by faster? A critique sheet could easily track these things and be a valuable document for the instructor-evaluation session. A chart could easily plot the time used by the instructor in getting a point across compared to the amount of time students spent in "discovering" concepts. Those who use this type of evaluation process like to plot a graph of participation

but with more than just who's doing the talking. They carry it a step further by seeing whether the involvement was the regurgitation of old information or the generation of new conclusions. They put the instructor's remarks down one side and the student responses down the other, or at least they make enough notes to talk about later. A quick glance at these notes can immediately show how much responsibility the teacher is sharing with the students as far as learning is concerned.

Too often we tend to rate an instructor high just because he gets a lot of involvement. In fact, this is one of the real weaknesses of having students evaluate the instructor. They, too, think that if they participated a great deal the instructor did a fine job. What they may be saying is that time went by faster than it did when they weren't participating. They aren't necessarily saying they learned more. There ought to be a more noble reason for involvement than just to make time pass faster. In our critiquing, we should look at feedback as part of that noble purpose. We need all the information we can get on how the students are doing and how we are doing in getting the learning produced. Without feedback, it's hopeless, so we observe how many times feedback was obtained. We count how many times we get total feedback, that is, a response from everyone in the class that tells what they think, what they know, or what their problems are. This response may be in the form of a one-question quiz, a show of hands, writing down an answer, exchanging papers, calling out suggestions, etc. But we don't stop there. We not only find out how much feedback is obtained, but we all keep track of the way the feedback is used. Is an adjustment made by the teacher as a result of the feedback, or is the feedback left to die untouched? We should also find out how much feedback the students were allowed to get and use. Did they know they were heading down the wrong road early enough to react, or just in time to find out they have failed the course? We can rate the feed-

back as to how valid it was, that is, was it representative of everyone's thinking or was it from a vocal minority? Was it planned or accidental? Did the students force the information on the teacher, or was it obtained purposely by the instructor? These are necessary things to know, and things that can be observed with only a little training. They are behaviors; they can be discussed with an instructor. They give him meaningful information that he can use to change his behavior, if his behavior needs changing. Equally important in all of this is the fact that we are able to set a standard of performance for our instructors. We can do more than just tell them we think they should make their classes more interesting; we can tell them we expect some involvement and feedback, and then tell them how much. If we do our observing well, we can give them *quantified* information on these key techniques.

Where does all of this leave us? It all says that when we evaluate our training, we aren't doing a complete job if we don't give our instructors some measured feedback on their own performance. When we evaluate our overall training program, we aren't completely fair with management if we don't take a look at the efficiency of our instructors to see what we're getting for our training dollar. Instructors can be meaningfully measured and shown their strengths and weaknesses. A couple of easily observed and easily measured techniques of instruction are involvement and feedback. Both are necessary to producing efficient learning. Each is just as easy to see as poor writing on the chalkboard or a distracting mannerism. But to see them we have to watch the learner as well as the teacher, and this gets to be a problem. Our training in how to observe an instructor sometimes causes us to forget about the learner. Maybe someone should invent a classroom without students. It would surely simplify teacher evaluation!

Reprinted from TRAINING, October 1973

VALIDITY AND RELIABILITY

A very short course

BY DALE FEUER

Before I went to graduate school, validity and reliability were just a couple of awkward, academic-sounding words that I never dreamed of using in everyday conversation. By the end of my first year the terms had become common parlance, and I was calculating correlation coefficients in my sleep.

After three gut-wrenching courses in statistics, I understood that it's not just cars and people that are more or less reliable; the term takes on a whole new meaning with respect to test scores and survey data. As for validity, I figured out this much: If your assessment instrument (i.e., ability test, attitude survey, opinion poll, etc.) has any, you're golden.

It's a long, tedious story full of complications and qualifications, and unless you plan to become a statistician, industrial psychologist or some other kind of social-science researcher, you really don't want to hear it. However, when people tell you that their survey is "highly reliable" or that their job screening test is "extremely valid," it's nice to know, basically, what it is they're claiming.

In the most familiar sense, a test or survey is said to be *reliable* if it yields consistent results at two different points in time, assuming there have been no major changes in people or circumstances and no intervening treatments. Scores from an assessment instrument are judged to be *valid* if the instrument accurately measures what it's supposed to measure.

Let's say you take someone's temperature five days in a row and get consecutive Fahrenheit readings of 97°, 98.4°, 98.1°, 99° and 96.5°, when, in fact, the person's body temperature has been a normal 98.6° all along. What you have here is an unreliable measuring instrument, one influenced by *unsystematic* or random error. Since the thermometer is sensitive to some kind of irrelevant factors, it doesn't give a pure measure of body temperature, and the readings are not valid. In this way, a measurement instrument's reliability puts a ceiling on validity; that is, scores or readings from a particular instrument can only be as valid as the instrument is reliable.

What if the thermometer had registered 72° on all five days? (Assume the heat-sensing device is at the wrong end of the stick, so to speak, so that it actually measures room temperature, albeit accurately.) The *constant* error of 26.6° affects validity but not reliability. Because the thermometer gives consistent readings on repeated occasions, it is highly reliable. However, because it doesn't measure what it's supposed to measure—body temperature—its readings are not valid.

In order to get measurements that are reliable *and* valid, you need a thermometer that gives accurate and consistent readings of body temperature, undistorted by any kind of error, random or constant.

As one more example, consider the measurement of time. A watch that is sometimes fast, sometimes slow and sometimes on time (unsystematic error), is neither reliable nor valid, since it is affected by extraneous factors, such as humidity, a faulty battery, arm movement, etc. A watch that is always five minutes fast (constant error) is reliable but not valid. Only a timepiece that consistently gives the right time is both reliable and valid.

Measuring intangibles

As you move from the realm of physical properties to cognitive ones (attitudes, opinions and psychological characteristics), from thermometers and watches to surveys, tests and job-screening procedures, the concepts of reliability and validity get more complicated. Yet at the simplest level, the same basic principles apply.

Any test or survey that yields dissimilar results when given on separate occasions to identical or matched groups of people is neither reliable nor valid. Random fluctuations in scores across repeated administrations may be due to any number of variables—time, place, administrator, instructions, etc. In general, reliability tends to increase as the number of test items or survey respondents rises.

Tests and surveys that are subject to constant error are like watches that are consistently five minutes fast—reliable, but not valid. Response bias is one type of constant error that often affects surveys. Response bias occurs when people who feel a particular way about the subject of the survey (e.g., flexible benefits) are more likely to complete the survey than those who feel differently. Ratings of the popularity of flexible-benefit plans will be skewed as long as the response bias exists. Loaded questions and inappropriate rating scales also can introduce constant error.

With tests, both the individual and the instrument can be sources of constant error. In the former case, an individual's test anxiety, a constant but irrelevant source of variation in performance, may consistently lower the person's score on a mechanical aptitude exam by a certain number of points. As for the instrument itself, a test intended to measure math skills may actually assess verbal ability if it contains lengthy word problems. Again, validity suffers, while reliability is unaffected.

Half-truths

As threatened, the story gets more involved. For those of you who've already learned more than you ever wanted to know about reliability and validity, this is a good place to get off. But we've really only scratched the surface, and in the interest of warding off letters from indignant statisticians, I'll attempt to expand briefly on the half-truths told so far.

The concept of reliability described above is actually only one kind. Called *test-retest* reliability, it refers to how stable results are over time.

Reliability is always represented mathematically by a correlation coefficient ranging from zero (no correspondence) to one (total correspondence). You can calculate this coefficient of correspondence between *any* two sets of scores or measurements, not just those from a single test given on separate occasions. Scores can be from two similar tests, independently constructed to measure the same thing. Called *parallel forms* reliability, this type indicates the degree of equivalency between two separate forms of a test. Correlating scores from two or more judges or raters yields *inter-rater* reliability and indicates the degree of agreement among different raters.

Yet another kind of reliability is *split-half* reliability. Also known as internal consistency, it is computed by correlating scores from one half of the items on a test with scores from the other half. Jay Hall, president of the Woodlands, TX-based consulting firm, Teleometrics International, says that a split-half reliability coefficient tells you "whether or not the items in the first half of an instrument do as good a job of measuring the factor of concern as the items in the last half do—i.e., whether the items used do a pretty uniform job of measurement from start to finish."

Validity is an even more multidimensional concept than reliability. The three most common types of validity include *content, criterion-related* and *construct* validity. Content validity refers to the relevance and scope of the test or survey items. Criterion-related and construct validity deal with the relationship between test scores and other psychologically meaningful characteristics. Employers sometimes have to prove in court that their applicant-screening tests meet the requirements of all three types of validity.

Briefly, the content validity question asks whether the items on the test or survey adequately sample the entire content domain, be it spatial relations ability, reading comprehension, job satisfaction or whatever. Considerations of content validity, then, have to do with inferences about test construction.

Criterion-related validity involves inferences about test scores. The criterion-related validity of a test has to do with how well test scores correlate with existing or future attitudes or behavior. Organizations that use assessment centers to predict future managerial success are concerned about the criterion-related validity of the assessment procedure.

The third type of validity is the most important, encompassing the other two in its definition. In a nutshell, construct validity is an inference made on the basis of all the information relating to a given construct (i.e., trait, characteristic, aptitude or ability) and to the theory surrounding the construct.

The most common way of inferring the construct validity of a set of scores is to find out how those scores correlate with other measures of an identical or theoretically related construct. For instance, do people who score highly on your creativity test also score highly on other tests of creativity? If your theory holds that creative people are good problem-solvers and bad organizers, then correlations between measures of creativity and problem-solving should be positive while scores on tests of creativity and organization skills should be negatively correlated. What's more, there should be no correlation, positive or negative, between scores on tests of hypothetically unrelated constructs.

Hall sums it up like this: "An establishment of good construct validity requires both a sound theory base for new instrumentation and an understanding of 'to be expected' relationships between old and new measures."

Validity is a judgment made about a set of scores, based on both rational and empirical inquiry. Reliability, on the other hand, is an intrinsic property of a measurement instrument. Wayne Cascio probably said it as well as anyone in his classic text, *Applied Measurement Concepts for Personnel Decisions*: "Validity is . . . a complex and dynamic function of the sample chosen, the particular situation in which the procedure is used and, above all, the objectives of the user. Validity is *inferred*, not directly measured."

Reprinted from TRAINING, March 1986

HOW TO PROVE—AND REPORT—RETURN ON (TRAINING) INVESTMENT

Do yourself a favor and take the easy way out of situations where training clearly isn't the solution

BY STEPHEN P. BECKER

What line managers want most from trainers is proof of a training investment payoff. While nobody likes to spend money, everybody likes to invest it successfully. This is, after all, what the management game is about. The production manager minimizes his cost per unit by investing in a new equipment; the marketing manager invests in advertising to increase volume and reduce the cost per unit sold; the safety manager invests in protective devices and reduces both the frequency of personal injuries and the cost of insurance premiums. Professional managers spend their active careers making investment decisions and then proving that the resulting investments produce returns. When the returns are high compared to the investment, the manager wins respect, advancement, and rewards. Trainers must do the same.

It's not easy to prove the ROTI (return on training investment), but it can be done. Here's how.

Example 1. It will take an office clerk six months or longer to learn a fairly complex task by the trial-and-error method, even when help is available from the office supervisor or co-workers. The clerk's productivity progresses from zero to some acceptable level during those months. Yet a well-designed training program might easily advance that clerk to an acceptable (or better) performance level in a week or two. Of course, it may take three months and twenty thousand dollars to develop such a program; but if the job doesn't change much over time and there are many such clerks, the return during the first few years may be ten times the money invested. To prove the return, one measures both the error factor and the quantity of work produced by clerks during those early months. If the training time is reduced and the error rate as output increased, the total wages paid to the clerks is buying much more than the company was receiving prior to training.

Example 2. Experienced salesmen can be taught a new way to manage their territories and to prospect for new high-potential accounts. If, at the end of the training program, you select a small number of these salesmen and monitor their activity, they will be able to tell you what new accounts they secured as a result of the training program. Chances are, the first year's gained revenue from just one of these new accounts will pay for the entire training program many times over.

Example 3. A new production supervisor is not succeeding because he lacks the skills necessary to set performance objectives, keep performance records, and then use those records to conduct performance appraisal interviews with work crew members. After a one-week training program, the supervisor improves the performance of the shift by five percent within four months. If maintained, that five percent improvement may pay for the training program 50 times over.

Got the message? Training can have one of the highest returns on investment of any corporate function. The financial leverage of effective training is incredible. Unfortunately, many trainers don't know it. Why not? Because, as managers of training, they don't do the complete managerial job.

The most critical aspect of the management job generally ignored by trainers concerns control. Control here means getting specific measurements on a continuing basis to indicate the degree of return on investment. The management profession has developed elaborate control systems which generally express feedback on things like error factors, output per hour, sales volume, profit by line item, sales per square foot, etc. Essentially, the demand for control by most professional line managers supports the entire computer industry. Years ago, the management profession recognized the need for exact measurements that indicate *actual* performance against *planned* performance, but trainers haven't yet learned this basic principle. If we would only develop the control systems we need, training quickly would become one of the most important departments in any organization.

How can we have control over the training investment so that returns can be demonstrated? First, we must remember to measure the performance of people *after* they are trained. Of course, the before-training performance must also be measured to provide a baseline against which results are compared.

The performance being measured must be converted into numbers with organizational meaning. It's not enough to say that Sally or Tom does a better job after a program; performance measurements must be expressed in numbers. The ROTI might be stated like this:

1. 35 percent of the clerks are able to process 18 to 22% more applications with a 50 percent less error rate as a direct result of the training program conducted two months ago. We have been able to reduce the amount of clerical time by 120 hours per week, for an annual savings in labor cost of $60,000, including wages and fringe benefits. Program development and implementation, including the hidden costs of wages during training, travel, food, instructor salary, and course materials cost $30,000. Therefore, we will break even on the training investment within the first six months and realize a return on our investment of 100% within the first year.

2. Within a month after the training program, the average number of

prospecting calls, recorded on weekly call sheets, doubled. The average sales per person went from eight to 16 per week. In addition, new business secured from these calls increased by 10 percent; one out of nine prospects is now being closed. On an annual basis, the projected revenue from these additional accounts is currently estimated at one million dollars.

3. Measurements of shift productivity before and after the performance appraisal training demonstrated that:

a) 10 percent of our first line supervisors increased the productivity of their shifts between 15 and 25 percent.

b) 40 percent increased production between eight and 15 percent.

c) 25 percent increased between one and eight percent.

d) 20 percent had no change in shift productivity.

e) Five percent had some decline in shift productivity. In no case was the decline more than five percent.

If these levels are maintained, the net dollar benefit to the corporation is X amount per year. Considering the total cost of training, the return of the training investment is Y dollars per year.

In your own situation, you could, of course, make more specific statements. But until you do make such statements about your training, you aren't doing the total job. Only when you track your progress in terms of dollar payback against dollar objectives will you be in control of your training. And one side benefit of developing control systems is that you will be better able to make and justify trade-off decisions. For instance, if you have three alternative training programs that need development and implementation, you can calculate in advance the anticipated return from each.

Remember that nobody is going to measure the organizational return on training for you. Rarely does a department, plant, or division manager (or even a corporate executive) track improvements. Managers don't automatically relate improvements to training. It's up to you to incorporate the measurement or control system in your design. You or your department members must then collect, analyze, and present the data to those people who require proof of the return on the training investment. It's not enough that you know you are doing a good job; if you wish to be rewarded for results, prove your results to those who count.

One final point: training must be timely. If a manager has a problem which may be solved partially by training, provide the solution quickly. You cannot afford to spend six months analyzing, designing, and preparing, because sometimes no training is tremendously costly. In these situations, your front end analysis is mostly done, but you still have the responsibility to measure the return on the investment after the training. You must quickly select the baseline data you will use for comparison and determine, with the other managers involved, what dollar performance improvement is realistic within a specified period of time. You must also design a mechanism to collect the data necessary for your analysis and presentation.

Historically, trainers have tried to do their own thing, without recognizing the need for realistic controls. Now we know that one of the most critical aspects of training is to control the return on the training investment. The bottom line means we must do the managerial thing: get results we can prove.

Reprinted from TRAINING, May 1976

THE DOLLARS AND SENSE OF CORPORATE TRAINING

At last, there just might be a way to answer the question, "What is training worth?"

BY MICHAEL GODKEWITSCH

Sick and tired of waging an annual uphill battle for training budgets because you can't demonstrate a return on investment in strict, monetary terms? Discouraged by the age-old truth that training and development activities are the first to go when profits are down? Depressed because you have no hard numbers to back up the claim that training pays off?

Well, take heart. Just about everyone concerned with managing people cost-effectively has suffered from the same maladies. And there is at least a partial cure.

Most organizations invest in training because they are convinced that higher profits will result. And usually, this is what happens. Training improves workers' skills and often boosts their motivation, leading to better productivity and increased profitability. But to be certain and to be accurate about this causal relationship is seldom easy: How much profitability results from how many dollars invested in what kind of training?

One of the toughest challenges facing managers who are responsible for developing and training people is to clearly demonstrate the financial value of training. Trainers might nurse gut feelings that funding for corporate training will eventually translate into a healthy return. But that's not enough. In accounting language the question is: Does investing in corporate training add enough value to our human resources asset to make it a priority investment? In cost-accounting lingo: Does capital spent on training have a high return on invest-ment and a short payback period, coupled with high present value? In lay person's terms: Do we get our money's worth out of corporate training?

A question of financial utility

In the last decade quite a few economists and management and social scientists have tried to answer this basic question. One general and intuitively simple measure of the financial value of an intervention (e.g., a training program) is the resulting gain minus its cost. In turn, gain can be defined as the effect of the intervention times the monetary value of that effect. The complete equation, then, for calculating the financial utility of an intervention would look like this:

$F = N [(E \times M) - C]$, where

F = financial utility
N = number of people affected
E = effect of the intervention
M = monetary value of the effect
C = cost of the intervention per person

If we could only quantify these terms, we could evaluate any intervention (in this case, training courses) in financial accounting terms such as direct profit, present value, discounted cash flow and payback period. While costs and numbers of people affected are usually well known, the other two terms (effect of an intervention and monetary value of the effect) are much harder to pin down. But recent advances in industrial/organizational psychology have given us a way of quantifying these terms and thereby solving the equation.

To understand how these terms can be quantified, it is important to grasp the notion that any skill, attitude, etc., can be "measured" somehow and will show some distribution of scores. Even fairly unquantified skills such as "overall managerial skills" are "measured," when, for example, a group of senior executives rate that ability in a subordinate group of managers. So-called "normal" distributions of skills show a lot of scores at and near the middle, and fewer at the extremes. Just as every distribution has an average or mean, it also has what is called a standard deviation (SD). This is a measure of dispersion that describes how "bunched" the distribution is. In a normal distribution, about 70% of all scores fall within one SD from the mean.

To quantify the effect of a training course, we compare the distribution of a given skill among the participants before the training with the distribution after training. The shift, expressed in SDs, is the effect of that training course. Unfortunately, most organizations do not bother to or cannot measure skills before training, much less after, and so do not really know the impact of their training.

The good news is that Michael Burke of New York University's department of management, and Russell Day of the Illinois Institute of Technology and Chicago and North-Western Transportation Co., recently published "A Cumulative Study of the Effectiveness of Managerial Training" in the *Journal of Applied Psychology* (April-June 1986). Using a novel technique called meta-analysis, they summarized the effects of 70 published and unpublished studies on the effectiveness of corporate training. Burke and Day based their summary of the effectiveness of training content and methods on four criteria: subjective learning (judgments of course participants or trainers); objective learning (results on standardized tests); subjective behavior (changes in on-the-job behavior, as perceived by course participants, peers or supervisors); and objective results (tangible, bottom-line indicators such as reduced costs, improved quality or quantity of output).

The researchers provide hard data on the effects of different management training programs and teaching methods. Figure 1 shows some of Burke and Day's findings on the effects of corporate training.

While a training effect often can be quantified objectively, the notion of value is by definition tied into what stakeholders feel and think. Several industrial psychologists, including Wayne Cascio (University of Colorado at Denver), Frank Schmidt (U.S. Office of Personnel Management), and Jeff Weekly (University of Texas at Dallas), have come up with a practical way to quantify job performance. They frame the definition in terms of the standard deviation of job performance, which they agree is equivalent to roughly 40% of annual salary. In practical terms this means that for a given job or level of responsibility, a worker who performs one SD below the average worker (or at the 15th percentile) is seen to be worth 40% less than the average salary paid for that job. The reverse also holds: A worker who performs one SD above the average (or at the 85th percentile) is seen to be worth 40% more. This does not mean that workers who perform at different levels actually get paid (or even should be paid) such radically different salaries or wages; this political point is not at issue here.

How much is training worth?

Since the kinds of managerial training and the training techniques that Burke and Day reviewed are from a range of corporations, the findings can be generalized. This means that any given organization can calculate the financial utility of a given training course by plugging the appropriate numbers into the above formula—even if that organization has not done the internal research on the effect of a specific course. By using this formula, of course, you're assuming that course content, method and culture are comparable between the "norm group" and the one your organization wants to evaluate for financial utility, and that your company's trainers and trainees are not radically different from the norm group. On the whole, these assumptions will usually be safe.

In order to determine the overall worth of a corporate training course in—let's say—human relations for middle managers, you must first figure out the cost of the training per person. If, for each student, tuition costs $1,300, travel and living expenses amount to another $1,300,

---

FIGURE 1
EXAMPLES OF EFFECTS
OF TRAINING CONTENT AND METHOD

	Effect	No. of Effects Studied	No. of People Measured	Effect Size in Standard Deviations
CONTENT				
General managerial programs	On-the-job behavior	88	11,707	.40
Human relations leadership/ supervision communications, managing people	On-the-job behavior	118	6,537	.44
Problem solving and decision making	Objective tests	11	605	.17
Performance appraisal	Bottom-line results	46	1,326	.64
Overall corporate managerial training	Bottom-line results	60	2,298	.67
METHOD				
Lecture plus group discussion and role playing	Objective tests	20	1,708	.37
	On-the-job behavior	21	1,117	.34
Self-paced workbooks	On-the-job behavior	69	3,081	.40
Behavior modeling	On-the-job behavior	17	446	.78
Multiple techniques	On-the-job behavior	76	5,169	.51

FIGURE 2
FINANCIAL UTILITY OF TRAINING

Overall corporate business education in Company X:
$$F = N [(E \times M) - C]$$
N, number of persons trained in 1986 = 2,500
E, effect size (in standard deviations) = .67
M, monetary value of one standard deviation = .4 x $62,500 (average salary)
C, average cost per person = $3,000 (across all courses)
F, financial utility = 2,500 [.67 x .4 x $62,500 − $3,000] = $34,375,000.

---

and prorated salary plus benefits for the eight-day course come to $2,700, then the total cost per student (C) equals $5,300.

Next, assume that the size of the effect of the training on behavior on-the-job (E) is .44 SD, as judged by senior management. With the average annual salary of middle managers in this case at $60,000, the monetary value (M) of one SD of job performance (which, you'll recall, we're defining as 40% of annual salary) is 40% of $60,000 or $24,000. One final piece of information: 150 middle managers received the training.

By plugging in the appropriate numbers, you find that the financial utility of this training course is $789,000 in total, or $5,260 per person.

$$F = N [(E \times M) - C]$$
$$\$789,000 = 150 [(.44 \times \$24,000) - \$5,300]$$

Now, if you want to calculate the payback period in terms of years, simply divide the per-person cost of the training (C) by the gain (E × M):

$$\frac{\$5,300}{.44 \times \$24,000} = .5 \text{ years or 6 months}$$

And to get a figure for return on investment, just subtract cost from gain and divide by cost:

$$\frac{(.44 \times \$24,000) - \$5,300}{\$5,300} = \text{approx. } 100\%$$

An example of how to calculate the financial utility of a company's overall training effort is worked out in Figure 2.

Now that it is feasible to report the reaped profits from dollars spent on nontechnical training in corporations, human resource professionals have hard answers to the question that used to stop them in their tracks: What is training worth?

Reprinted from TRAINING, May 1987

HOW TO CALCULATE THE COSTS AND BENEFITS OF AN HRD PROGRAM

This one's exactly what it sounds like:
A step-by-step method for figuring out the
real cost of training and the dollar
value of its impact.

BY LYLE M. SPENCER, JR.

You don't really need an introduction, do you? For years the biggest boogeyman in the human resources development community has been the legendary difficulty of expressing the impact of HRD programs in cost/benefit terms: What can we tell top management about the "bottom-line" results of our efforts?

This article presents simple methods for calculating the costs and benefits of training, consulting and other HRD interventions in a variety of settings. So let's just get started.

PART I
CALCULATING COSTS

Two kinds of expenses are involved in any training effort: a) labor costs and b) direct costs, such as travel, per diem, materials, purchased services (e.g., consultants), equipment, facilities, (e.g., room rentals), and opportunity costs (e.g., the expense of hiring temporary workers or paying overtime to people attending a training program).

Labor costs—the value of the time spent by both HRD people and program participants—usually make up the largest part of the cost of any training program. Expenses in this category can be calculated in two ways: direct labor cost or full labor cost.

Direct labor cost is each person's salary divided by the number of days he or she works in a year (the U.S. average is 230 days). For example, a trainer earning $25,000 a year and

working 230 days would have a direct cost of $25,000 ÷ 230 = $108.69 per day.

Full labor cost is a person's salary plus fringe benefits (e.g., holidays, vacation, health benefits, pension costs), plus overhead (e.g., occupancy costs, support-staff salaries, equipment rental, etc.) and, if the person works in a profit center, the profit percentage the center is expected to earn—all of this divided by the number of days for which the person is *paid* (counting paid vacations, holidays and sick time, the U.S. average is 260 days). Figure 1 shows the calculation of the full cost of a person's time. (The

worksheet on page 43 allows you to calculate your own full cost per day.)

Full costs provide the best estimate of how much it actually costs an organization to deliver an HRD service. A good estimate of the full cost of a person's time is roughly three times his or her direct salary cost. This figure, called a "full-cost multiplier," provides a useful rule of thumb for estimating program costs. As we'll see, the full costing of people's time is the key to calculating the costs and benefits of training efforts.

Here's how to calculate the *labor costs* of an HRD project:

1. Identify all the steps of the project (e.g., curriculum development, trainer-training, delivery, evaluation).

2. Determine who is involved in each step, including both HRD people and the program participants, and how much of each person's time is involved.

3. Calculate the full cost of each person's time per day (or per hour, if appropriate). If several people with approximately equal salaries are involved, you can use averages.

4. To find the total cost of labor for each step, multiply the number of people involved times their cost per day (or hours) times the number of days they will spend on the project.

Follow these steps to determine the project's *direct costs*:

1. Identify the type of cost (e.g., materials, travel, per diem, computer time) involved in each step.

2. Determine the cost per unit (e.g., one workbook, one trip, one day's per diem).

3. Determine the total number of units involved.

4. Multiply the cost per unit times

FIGURE 1
Calculating the Full Costs of a Trainer's Time

The full cost of a person making the current HRD specialist's average salary of $25,000 and paid on the basis of a 260-day (2,080-hour) year is calculated as follows:

Expense	Calculation Formula	Amount
1. Salary	S	$25,000
2. Plus: fringe benefits @ 35% of salary	.35 x S = .35S	8,750
3. Subtotal	1.35S	33,750
4. Plus: overhead @ 125% of salary and fringe	1.25 x 1.35S = 1.69S	42,188
5. Total full cost/year	3.04S	$75,938
6. Total full cost/day	$75,938 (direct cost/year) ÷ 260 (days worked/year)	$292.07
7. Total full cost/hour	(direct cost/day) ÷ 8 (hours worked/day)	$ 36.51

the number of units to find the full cost for each direct expense.

Add full labor costs to direct costs to find the *total cost* for each step of the project. Add the step totals, and you have a project total.

This procedure is illustrated in Figure 2, which is a calculation of the cost of a management-training program for plant supervisors conducted by the training department of a large manufacturing concern.

Here's what's going on in Figure 2.

Step 1: Course Development.
Trainer Smith spent 10 days developing a 16-hour course on basic supervisory principles for plant managers. The course was delivered in eight two-hour segments. Smith's salary was $30,000 a year, so his *full* cost per day was $30,000 × 3 ÷ 260 = $346. Therefore, the full cost of his time for Step 1 was $3,460 ($346/day × 10 days). Direct expenses for

> **The full cost of a person's time is roughly three times his direct salary cost.**

this step were $260 for off-the-shelf training materials purchased from vendors. (Note that at five development days for each day of training delivered, this was particularly efficient course development. Industry norms range from 10 to 75 development days for each day of training. Note also that some common "steps" were not involved: discussion with "clients," needs assessment, etc.)

Step 2: Training Trainers.
Next, Smith conducted a five-day training session to teach plant supervisors from eight factories to deliver the program at their locations. The full labor costs for this step were the five days of Smith's time at $346/day, plus five days each of the plant supervisors' time at $288/day. Direct costs included Smith's per diem (consisting of meals at a local restaurant), materials for the eight trainees

FIGURE 2
COSTING WORKSHEET

Analysis Step*	Labor ("Who?")	(1) #	Full Cost/Time	(2)	(3) Time	(4) Cost (1)x(2)x(3)	Expense	(5) Cost/Unit	x (6) # Units =	(7) Cost (5)x(6)	(8) = (4)+(7) Totals*
1. Development of course	Smith (HR person)	1	S $30K x M 3 / T 260	$346/day	x 10 days	$3,460	Materials	$260	x 1	$260	$3,720
Step 1 Total						**$3,460**				**$260**	**$3,720**
2. Trainer training	Smith (Trainer)	1	S $30K x M 3 / T 260	$346/day	x 5 days	$1,730	Per diem	$20	x 5 days	$100	$1,830
	Plant Supervisors	8	S $25K x M 3 / T 260	$288/day	x 5 days	$11,520	Materials	$50/person	x 8 people	$400	$11,920
			S x M / T		x		Travel to training site	$350/person	x 8 people	$2,800	$2,800
			S x M / T		x		Per diem	$75/person/day	x 5 days x 8 people = 40	$3,000	$3,000
			S x M / T		x		Training room	$150/day	x 5	$750	$750
Step 2 Total						**$13,250**				**$7,050**	**$20,300**
3. Delivery of training	Plant Supervisors (Trainers)	8	S $25K x M 3 / T 260	$288/day	x 3 days (16 hrs delivery, 8 hrs prep)	$6,912			x		$6,912
	Head Foreman	80	S $20K x M 3 / T 260	$231/day	x 2 days	$36,960	Materials	$50/person	x 80 people	$4,000	$40,960
Step 3 Total						**$43,872**				**$4,000**	**$47,872**
4. Evaluation	Smith (HR Person)	1	S $30K x M 3 / T 260	$346/day	x 3 days	$1,038	Telephone & computer time	$100	x 1	$100	$1,138
Step 4 Total						**$1,038**				**$100**	**$1,138**
				Total Labor Cost $61,620				**Total Direct Costs**		**$11,410**	**$73,030**
											Total

*Fill in number and name of step; draw heavy horizontal line to show where one step ends and next begins; put step, labor, and direct cost subtotals on this line. Continue this procedure, and use as many costing worksheets as you need.

at $50 per course manual, travel to the training site for each of the trainees at $350 average per person, $75 per person a day per diem for eight people for five days, and $150 a day for the room in which the training was conducted. Total labor costs for Step 2 came to $13,250. Direct costs amounted to $7,050.

Step 3: Training Delivery. The eight plant supervisors trained 10 foremen in each of their factories. The full labor costs for the supervisors were their full costs of $288/day apiece times three days (16 hours of training, plus one hour of preparation for each of the eight sessions) for a total of $6,912. Full labor costs for the 80 trainees were their full costs of $231/day times two days for a total of $36,960. The direct costs for this step were $50 per person for course manuals times 80 participants for a total of $4,000.

Step 4. Evaluation. Smith subsequently spent three days contacting the eight supervisors and analyzing a reaction questionnaire given to each of the 80 foremen. Full labor costs for this step were Smith's three days times $346/day for a total of $1,038. The direct costs were $100 for telephone charges and computer time.

This plant-management training program cost a total of $73,030. It was a fairly typical case in that 85% of the cost was in people's time. Note that in Steps 2 and 3 the cost of participants' time was much greater than the cost of the trainer's time. This is true in most HRD interventions: The real cost of a training program is the participants' time.

This simple procedure (despite all the multiplying and dividing, it's not really any more difficult than preparing a budget) can be used to cost virtually any HRD project or program. The figures involved are not complex, but because people may not have kept accurate track of their time, calculating costs *after* a training program may require a probing inquiry strategy: What steps were involved? And for each step, who was involved? How much does each person make? For how much time (how many hours, days) was each involved? Finally, were any direct costs such as materials, travel and per diem involved in the step?

Most people, if asked the right questions, can readily come up with these figures. People know their salaries and can at least estimate the salaries of others. Your controller can tell you your organization's actual full-cost multiplier (it may not be "3") and the

number of days paid. "Best guesstimates" of time spent in various activities turn out to be surprisingly accurate—within three percent of actual time spent as monitored by time sheets, in most cases I've experienced.

PART II
CALCULATING BENEFITS

There are only two ways to dem-

WORKSHEET
Calculating Your Full Cost Per Day

Direct Rate
1. Your yearly salary = _____
2. Divided by the number of days you work a year _____
3. Your *direct cost/day* = _____

Full Cost Rate ×3
4. Multiplied by 3 is your *full cost/day*[1] = _____

Applied Rate
5. The number of days a month (e.g., use last month) you work on specific projects (be honest!) _____
6. Divided by 20 (days/month) ÷20
7. Your *applied rate* = _____

Cost per applied person day
8. Divide your *full cost/day* (4) _____
9. By your *applied rate* (7) _____
10. Equals your *cost/applied person day* = _____

This is how much you cost your organization/clients for each day of service.

_____

[1]A more precise calculation of your full cost can be obtained by:

(1) Your yearly salary (1a _____) divided by the number of days you are paid per year = (1b _____) (American Industry standard = 260 days) = your direct cost per day (1a ÷ 1b) _____ (1)

(2) Multiply (1) by your organization's *fringe-benefits rate* (American industry average = 35%) _____ (2)

(3) Fringe cost in dollars: (1) x (2) _____ (3)

(4) Subtotal: total compensation = (1) + (3) _____ (4)

(5) Multiply (4) by your organization's overhead rate (professional-service firm average = 125%) _____ (5)

(6) Overhead in dollars = (4) x (5) _____ (6)

(7) Subtotal: total labor cost = (4) + (6) _____ (7)

_____

OPTIONAL: if your organization breaks general and administrative (G&A) out separately

(8) Multiply (7) by your organization's *G&A rate* if calculated separately from overhead; _____ (8)

(9) G&A in dollars = (7) x (8) _____ (9)

(10) Subtotal: total cost with G&A = (7) + (9) _____ (10)

_____

OPTIONAL: if you are an external consultant

(11) Multiply subtotal (10) by your organization's *pretax profit rate* (American industry average = 10%): _____ (11)

(12) Profit in dollars needed/day on your efforts if organization is to meet its goal = (10) x (11) _____ (12)

(13) TOTAL: (7) + (10) + (12) _____ (13)

(14) Calculate your applied rate (see instructions (5) through (7) above). _____ (14)

(15) Calculate your *cost/applied person-day*: (13) ÷ (14) = _____ (15)

This is how much you cost/must return to your organization each day if it is to meet its profit goal.

onstrate benefits or increased profits in business: one can either increase revenues (by raising prices or by increasing volume or sales) and/or one can decrease expenses.

Rarely do HRD efforts affect pricing decisions. Training and consulting efforts *can* be shown to expand volume by increasing production or sales, but most "dollar" benefits which derive from training and development programs involve cost avoidance—such as reducing the cost of time, people, materials, equipment downtime, turn-over, or various expensive "people-problem events" such as grievances, accidents, disabilities and so on.

Time

Reducing the person hours or days needed to perform any organizational

---

FIGURE 3
Costing a Grievance

(1) Step (What happens 1st, 2nd, etc.?)	(2) Who is involved?	(3) How long? (hours)	(4) Salary/ year of each person involved	Full cost calculation (5) Cost/person/hour (4) x 3 (OHD factor) / 260 days ÷ 8 hours	Total (6) = (3) x (5) Total Cost Per Step	
1. The worker complains to the foreman.	Worker Foreman	.25 .25	$15K $20K	$21.64 $28.85	$5.41 $7.21	$12.62
2. Worker complains to shop steward.	Worker (Steward)	.50 .50	$15K (Paid by union)	$21.64	$10.82	$10.82
3. Local union rep. tells hourly how to write grievance.	Worker Union rep.	.50 .50	$15K $15K	$21.64 $21.64	$10.82 $10.82	$21.64
4. Hourly writes up grievance.	Worker	.50	$15K	$21.64	$10.82	$10.82
5. Union-plant mgmt. meeting.	Worker Union Pres. Plant personnel rep.	.75 .75 .75	$15K $16K $25K	$21.64 $23.08 $36.06	$16.23 $17.31 $27.05	$60.59
6. International union rep. writes division personnel; division staff calls plant, researches and writes response, decides whether or not to go to arbitration.	Div. staff	8	$32K	$46.15	$369.20	$369.20
If no arbitration						
7. Trip to meet with International rep. to deal with four grievances.	Div. staff Trip direct cost	16	$32K $400	$46.15	$738.40 $400.00 $1,138.40 ÷ 4 = 284.60 per grievance	
8. Implement agreement*	Plant personnel rep.	2	$25K	$36.06	$72.12	72.12
TOTAL PER GRIEVANCE IF NO ARBITRATION						$842.41
If arbitration (5% of grievances go to arbitration).						
9. Legal preparation	Corp. staff lawyer Div. staff Plant pers. director Labor lawyer	16 6 4 4	$45K $32K $25K $60K	$64.90 $46.15 $36.06 $86.54	$1,038.40 $276.90 $144.24 $346.16	$1,805.70
10. Arbitration meeting	Corp. staff lawyer Div. staff Plant pers. director Labor lawyer (arbitration fee)	4 4 4 4	$45K $32K $25K $60K	$64.90 $46.15 $36.06 $86.54	$259.60 $184.60 $144.24 $346.16	$934.60
						$2,740.30

*There is additional cost per grievance due to the expected value of arbitration:
• Expected value (E(v)) = probability (5%) of occurrence x cost ($2,740.30) per grievance = $137.02
• Total cost of grievance = $842.41 (no arbitration) + $137.02 (5% probability of arbitration) = $979.43

function (e.g., time wasted in useless meetings) is the easiest way to show dollar benefits from HRD efforts. Simply multiply the time saved (hours or days) times the *full cost* per hour or day. For example, if 10 people making $30,000 a year (each having a full cost per day of $346, or per hour of $43.25) can avoid a single one-hour meeting, it saves the organization $432.50. Is it a weekly meeting? Eliminate it for 50 weeks in a year, and you've saved the organization $21,625.

You may argue that this isn't a real savings because these people are still being paid. But if their time is freed from unproductive activities, they can either spend it performing more useful activities, which may increase revenues, or the organization may find it needs fewer people. The current reduction in middle management and staff personnel (who spend most of their time in meetings) to cut costs is one example of this trend. Time savings always add up to people savings, and the full cost of people's time is the best way to estimate where these savings can be made.

Materials

Benefits from savings on materials include reduced waste of inventory due to more efficient scheduling or better quality-control procedures. These savings are very easy to calculate. Simply multiply the number of units saved per day, week or month, times the cost per unit, times the number of days, weeks or months that the saving occurs. (A period of a year is a good standard for extrapolating savings.)

Equipment downtime

Significant benefits can be shown from increasing the use or preventing the downtime of expensive capital equipment—computers, for example. The dollar value of an hour of equipment time is calculated by dividing the equipment's cost by the number of hours it is expected to be used. For example, a $3-million computer system with a useful life of five years has an amortization value of $600,000 a year. If the system is expected to be used 20 hours a week or 1,040 hours a year, the dollar value of each hour is at minimum $600,000 ÷ 1,040 hours = $577 an hour. (Operator labor, maintenance and other overhead costs—occupancy and electricity, for example—will add to the equipment's value per hour.)

Anything HRD people can do to increase equipment utilization—conducting workshops that improve scheduling or maintenance of expensive equipment, recruiting or training key operators, teaching or helping people to "market" use of the equipment—enables them to claim the dollar benefits of each hour of increased usage or each hour of downtime saved.

Retention/turnover costs

The costs of recruiting and training new people to replace those who quit or are fired are, at minimum, equal to the direct salary of the people who leave. Recruitment, whether done in-house or by a search firm, usually costs one-third of the first-year salary for the job involved; training costs about 10% of the first-year salary; and "learning-curve" costs, which account for the fact that people take some time on the job before they become fully productive, amount to 50% of first-year salary. (Those figures can be found in the Gross and Flamholtz references mentioned at the end of this article.)

Any training program or consulting intervention which reduces turnover can claim the dollar value of each person saved. Retention benefits can be estimated on an organization-wide basis by multiplying the turnover rate times the total number of people in a given salary category to find the dollar

RED FLAG
BY JACK GORDON

Experienced HRD people will point to a hole in this argument for calculating the benefits of a training program and "claiming" those benefits as a direct result of training. In many cases, they will say, things such as job-turnover rates, improved sales figures, etc. are affected by any number of factors that have little or nothing to do with the training program.

Perhaps the economy has gone sour and jobs are harder to come by—therefore workers are staying longer whether they're satisfied or not. Perhaps sales improved simply because the economy *picked up*—or because sales managers realized that top management wanted to stress a particular product line and lit fires under their people independently of the training program.

Individual managers or superintendents may want to claim that their own efforts were partly responsible for the improvement you are crediting to your intervention, critics will say, and you will create enemies by trying to chalk up every dollar saved as a direct result of your program.

These concerns sometimes are valid and they cannot be dismissed lightly.

But the fact remains that your intervention was a response to a *problem*. Turnover was too high, regardless of economic conditions. Your training program was not the first indication sales managers got that the CEO wanted those widgets to move faster: If their "fire lighting" deserves the credit, why was there so little improvement in sales between the time they got the word and the time your program was delivered? And if the sharp upturn in office morale has indeed occurred not because of your participative-management seminars but simply because somebody painted the rest rooms, you either did an extremely poor needs assessment or somebody gave you extremely bad information about the problem to begin with.

Obviously, this is another reason why it's better to "cost" the problem, the solution and the benefits *before* you launch the intervention. If somebody has a better, cheaper or more effective solution to the problem, let him speak now; otherwise, it's your solution and you deserve to claim its benefits—or at least the lion's share of them.   Reprinted from TRAINING, July 1984

537

value of reducing turnover by, say, one percent.

People problems

The dollar value of any "people-problem event" (grievances, strikes, accidents, disability days) can be calculated using the same costing inquiry technique explained earlier. Figure 3, "Costing a Grievance," shows a case in which each grievance was found to cost the organization an average of $979.*

This same procedure can be used to cost accidents: What's the first (second, third) thing that happens? Who is involved? How much does each make? For how long is each involved? Are there any direct costs (e.g., disability claim costs) involved in the step?

Strategies for showing benefits

The opportunities are virtually unlimited for calculating benefits from interventions that save people's time, materials and equipment downtime, or that reduce turnover and "problem events." A simple strategy for calculating benefits in any training intervention is shown in Figure 4, a standard problem-solving sequence with three cost-benefit steps added.

First, always "value the problem" at the beginning of an intervention, when someone first requests your services. State in dollar figures what existing practices cost the organization. Go through the costing strategy with the "clients" to help them identify the dollar value of their problem, and hence the benefits of any training program or consulting you can offer them.

For example, if someone approaches you for a first-level management-training program, you might ask, "Why do you think this training is needed? What problems are the first-level managers' lack of ability currently causing?" The answer might be something like, "Poor morale, leading to high turnover." At this point you could ask, "How many people, at what salary level, are leaving?" This will give you a baseline cost of turnover against which you can show benefits if your training program results in decreased turnover.

Consider the costs and benefits of a training intervention *before* you begin. Valuing the problem will help you focus your efforts on those specific aspects which are most likely to pay off in dollar terms. For example, you can focus a management-training program on time management (directly translatable into the dollar value of time saved), retention of key people (translatable to the dollar value of reduced turnover), or reduced downtime of expensive equipment (directly translatable to the dollar value of equipment cost per hour).

Second, always "value the solution." Put a dollar figure on your program's benefit to the organization. You often can present this data in a way that makes the case for your program absolutely compelling. For example, $73,000 seems a lot to pay for the plant-management training program described in Figure 2, and cost-conscious executives might refuse to fund it. You could point out, however, that if turnover is reduced by just one $12,000 worker a year in each of the eight factories involved, the program

would save $96,000—and not only pay for itself, but return 30% on investment.

Finally, always "value the result." Follow up and evaluate the results of the intervention, and state in dollar terms (in a one-page final report, for instance) what the solution or program actually saved the organization. Circulate this memorandum widely—to your boss, to your peers and to other members of the organization.

Adding these three cost-benefit steps to any proposed intervention should also be considered as a means to market, as well as to justify, HRD services. You'll find that this simple calculation will quickly change the perception of the value of your HRD function.

*Note that a technique called "expected value" calculation is used to account for arbitration, an event that was quite expensive (it cost an additional $2,740) but occurred only once in a while (5% of grievances went to arbitration). An *expected value, E(V), is the probability or percentage (P) of an outcome multiplied by the amount (A) of the outcome: $E(V) = P \times A$, where A is the cost* (e.g., of an accident or a strike).

In Figure 3, the expected value of arbitration is .05 (one in 20 grievances go to arbitration) times the cost of arbitration ($2,740) = $137 per grievance.

Expected-value calculations are particularly useful in dealing with the probability of lawsuits, affirmative-action complaints and the like.

Obviously, anything an HRD person can do to reduce this probability will show an expected-value benefit.

FOR FURTHER READING

1. Flamholtz, E. *Human Resource Accounting*, (Dickinson Publishing Co., Encino, CA, 1974).
2. Gross, P.H. "Valuation of Intangible Assets" in Kelly, P.M. *The Economic Recovery Tax Act of 1981*, (AMA/AMACOM, New York, NY, 1982).

Reprinted from TRAINING, July 1984

Next, we must compute the standard cost for a contact hour by dividing the total contact hours into the actual training costs:

$$\frac{\text{Actual training cost}}{\text{Total Contact Hours}} = \text{Cost per Contact Hour}$$

In our example:

$$\frac{\$200,000}{14,000} = \$13.88 \text{ per Contact Hour}$$

To compute the standard cost for each individual course, we now multiply the number of contact hours by cost per contact hour. (Remember the number of contact hours is the length of the courses in hours multiplied by the number of trainees.)

The sales management course in our example is scheduled for 40 hours and will be attended by 25 trainees.

The standard cost of the course is:

1000 contact hours (40 course
    hours × 25 trainees)
× $13.88 cost per contact hour
$13,880 Standard Cost

Finally, we must add any additional costs associated with a particular course to the total standard cost for the course. For instance, if the training department must pay either the wages of trainees or the wages of other workers to replace the trainees on the job, those wage costs would also become part of the cost of the course. Other expenses such as the cost of an outside instructor, additional room rental or materials purchased specifically for the course would also be added at this point.

Let's say our sales management course is held in a local motel conference room at a cost of $750. A guest speaker is invited and paid $250. Trainees average $25,000 per year in salary and benefits or $12.02 per hour. That hourly wage of $12.02 is multiplied by 40 (the length of the course in hours) and that result is multiplied by 25 (the number of trainees) for a total of $12,020 in trainee costs. The total cost of the course is the standard cost plus the additional room rents, fee for the speaker and trainee costs.

$13,880	standard cost
750	rent for motel room
250	speaker's pay
12,020	trainee costs
$25,900	Total Cost

CALCULATING THE COST EFFECTIVENESS OF TRAINING

Cost effectiveness of training programs
is difficult to substantiate if you
haven't been compiling hard data.
Here's an interim solution

BY TRAVIS SHIPP

Recent trends in cost consciousness have put pressure on training directors to find ways to demonstrate the value training has for an organization. This emphasis on cost effectiveness has been troublesome, however, because training directors are not accountants and are usually so busy with training responsibilities they have little time to reconstruct the accounting data demonstrating the money-saving value of past training programs. Plans to accumulate data on future programs are now being developed by most training directors, but what is needed in the meantime is a quick, reasonably accurate method of estimating the value of training programs currently under way and of programs planned for the immediate future.

One way to arrive quickly and simply at a usable cost-effectiveness analysis is to estimate the cost effectiveness of training programs already under way. As a working example, let's follow a sales management course through all the necessary computations.

Computing the cost

The first task is to determine the total contact hours: how many courses will be offered during the budget year, the number of scheduled training hours for all courses offered during the budget year, and how many trainees will be taking the courses.

Multiply: total courses offered
    × total training hours
Result
    × total trainees
Total Contact Hours

In our example, an examination of the training schedule reveals that next year 36 courses will be offered. Some of the courses are as short as one day while others are as long as three months. The average length is 40 hours and the average number of trainees is 10 per course. Total contact hours:

Multiply: 36 courses
    × 40 hours/course
1440 course hours
    × 10 trainees/course
14,400 Contact Hours

Actual training costs start with the training department budget, less any costs for services performed in other functional areas. For example, the training department budget may be $215,000, but that may include $30,000 salary and benefits for a training director who spends one-half time as an assistant personnel officer on jobs having nothing to do with training. The actual training costs then would be:

$215,000	training department budget
−15,000	(half of $30,000 salary for work in personnel)
$200,000	Actual Training Costs

539

Estimating effectiveness

Once the costs of the course have been estimated, the savings associated with the course must also be determined. One method is to estimate potential savings. A panel of training personnel, supervisors and employees rates the potential of the course by examining the job descriptions and the training objectives to determine the potential for change that may be accomplished by training. The panel determines the potential for recovery of training costs by estimating the value of any resultant change in job performance over the next year.

Assume that a training department instructor, three sales managers who have taken the sales management course and three of their supervisors are asked to rate the value of job changes for a participant in the course. In examining the training objectives and the job descriptions, they isolate three potential areas of improvement. Each rater estimates the value of the improvement in efficiency or savings to the company. The raters are not told the costs of the training program, but they *are* told how savings or changes in costs may be calculated. Their estimates are listed in tabular form:

Rater	Area 1	Area 2	Area 3
1	$650	$150	$350
2	800	250	400
3	400	350	350
4	550	300	350
5	600	350	150
6	500	400	300
7	600	300	450
Modified mean =	$580	$310	$350

The potential value of the sales management course is calculated by discarding both the highest and lowest scores in each job area (circled) and using only the remaining scores in order to determine a *modified mean*. This method accounts for any individual bias toward the course, gross math errors and other variables, and levels the scores so that one wildly deviating figure does not exert an undue influence. The total of the modified means is the total estimate of the potential value of the course.

$$\begin{array}{ll} \$\ 1,240 & \text{(sum of modified means)} \\ \underline{\times\ 25} & \text{number of trainees} \\ \$31,000 & \end{array}$$

An alternative method for determining potential savings that provides even better estimates of the effectiveness of training programs is the use of historical accounting and other department records to document actual changes in performance owing to participation in a training program. If the data are available, they provide more precise information than the estimate method, and this precludes the necessity to use a rating panel. Unfortunately, usable data is seldom available at the beginning of a cost-effectiveness program. Every effort should be made, however, to begin accumulating hard data so that reliance on estimates can be reduced.

Comparing cost and effectiveness

The costs of the sales management course and the estimates of its effectiveness can now be compared to see if the course is cost effective. If the estimates of the potential savings (or increased revenues) exceed the costs, the course may be said to be cost effective. If costs exceed estimated value, then the course is not cost effective and must be analyzed further. The cost of the sales management course in our example is $26,900; the estimated potential value is $31,000. A comparison of the two indicates that the course, when considered independently of other factors, is cost effective.

Of course, other factors must be considered before allocating funds. The cost effectiveness of other courses must be compared. If a choice must be made about allocating training department resources, even a cost-effective course may be dropped from the schedule in favor of other courses or alternate uses of resources that promise a higher return. Conversely, a course that is not cost effective may remain in the schedule if it is mandated and must be conducted without regard to the returns on the training dollar, or if it provides a necessary service at less real cost (cost minus any savings or revenue increases) than an alternate source of training.

Estimates of cost effectiveness are adequate interim techniques for determining the relative value of training courses. But estimates cannot take the place of hard data planned for and specifically collected for cost-effectiveness analysis.

For example, when the Consortium for Human Resources, Inc. of Indianapolis implemented an employee assistance program at the Crawfordsville, TN, plant of R.R. Donnelley and Sons Company recently, this method was used to estimate the cost effectiveness of the program, which trains supervisors to salvage employees whose alcohol, substance abuse or family problems have affected such performance measures as production, absenteeism and accident rates. Employee assistance programs are considered socially desirable, but management usually views them as an expense of doing business rather than a sound financial investment.

After one year, the cost effectiveness of the Donnelley program was estimated by the above method at a ratio of $1.48 return for each $1 invested. When the *actual* cost effectiveness was determined by a computer using company accounting and personnel records, it was found that the employee assistance program yielded a $1.61 return for each $1 invested. Donnelley's foresight in training supervisors to help troubled employees was rewarded by salvaging valuable people who would have been terminated and by a healthy financial return on investment. The slightly conservative error of the estimate method as compared to the actual, computer-calculated, cost-effectiveness ratio enhances the credibility of the former method of estimating cost-effectiveness training programs.

Although this method relies on those in the organization who are in a position to exercise good judgment, the accuracy of the estimates depends largely on the precision of the instructions the raters are given for determining potential savings or revenue increases. The modified mean technique helps to overcome some errors caused by guessing or personal bias, but it will not eliminate problems created by inadequate instruction or imprecise methods of estimating potential values. For programs where hard data are not available, the estimate technique as described here can provide reliably sound analysis of the value of training and can substantiate the training director's contention that training is an investment rather than an expense.

Reprinted from TRAINING, November 1980

MEASURING BACK-ON-THE-JOB PERFORMANCE

To survive a recession or budget cut, find your dollar value

BY J.B. CORNWELL

The most foolproof way I know for a trainer to protect his or her job from the sometimes terminal effects of hard economic times is to document bottom-line results. Better yet, document the dollar value of those results, and show upper management a significant "profit" on investments made in training.

What are bottom-line results? For our purposes let's define the bottom line on training as the on-the-job performance of trainees *after* training. To document the actual influence your training program had on that performance, it's necessary to establish, and document, a baseline. What was the performance level *before*, or without, training? For those of you who protest that your training program was designed to change something other than on-the-job performance, I'll broaden the term "performance" to include manifestations of attitude, knowledge, appreciation or whatever intangible you sought to influence in the first place. (If you can't describe some visible, measurable evidence that would indicate that your training program works, stop reading—but figure out why the devil you wanted to do the program at all!)

The size and sophistication of your organization; the number, nature and accessibility of your students; and the nature of the job your students need to perform will all determine what methods you'll use to measure the final effects of your program. Regardless of differences in all those factors, however, there are some constants. There are certain questions that you will want answered, even though you may use very different techniques for gathering the answers.

Let's review some of the basic questions and some of the options for defining them more specifically.

1 **How accurately did the training program address the exact requirements of the job?** Assuming that the program was designed to train students how to do a job or how to do it better, how closely did it match the actual job the students were called on to do after the training? This question raises some sub-questions: Did the program address all the things the students needed to learn to be able to perform to standard? Were the things not addressed easy and convenient to learn on the job or to figure out when the need arose? Were things presented that weren't needed in the program? If so, weren't they needed because the student already knows

---

STUDENT'S POST-TRAINING SURVEY

Three to six months ago, you completed the Training Program, _____. The purpose of this survey is to determine how well the program prepared you for the job.

Attached is a list of the tasks covered in the program and a guide to code the answer sheet below. The information you provide will be kept in strictest confidence and will be used to improve the content and quality of training. Thank you for cooperation.

Coding instructions

For each task/learning objective for the program you attended, write in the number(s) of the appropriate statements under the letters designating the subject.

Example: If the task is #1— The learner will be able to adust a spark plug gap to the correct clearance— and if you do this routinely on the job but differently and with a different tool than that suggested in training, you would place a 3 in the box for task #1 under subject A (see code sheet) as below.

TASK #	A	B	C	D	E
1.	3				
2.					
3.					

A. I am doing this task regularly on the job.

1. After training I only needed practice.
2. After training I needed to learn this task on the job. I didn't learn it in training.
3. I am doing this task differently than I learned in training because:
   a) Work conditions don't allow me to do it as I originally learned it.
   b) It doesn't work the way I learned it.
   c) I figured out a better way.
   d) My supervisor told me to do it differently.

B. I rarely do this task on the job.

1. I learned it in training, but I don't get enough practice to keep sharp. Each time it comes up, I have trouble.
2. I get enough practice and stay sharp.
3. I didn't learn it in training. I had to learn it on the job.

C. I don't do this task on the job.

1. The job doesn't call for it.
2. I get help when it comes up because:
   a) I didn't learn it.

b) It's too difficult for me.
c) It comes up so rarely I forget how.
d) I was assigned a different job.

D. How I learned this task.

1. I could do it successfully before the training.
2. I learned it effectively in the training:
   a) Because it was taught well.
   b) But I could have learned it easier from a manual or instruction sheet.
   c) But I could have learned it just as well on the job.
3. I learned it with difficulty because:
   a) The training was confusing.
   b) There wasn't enough practice.
   c) There wasn't enough explanation.
   d) There wasn't enough reference material.

E. Because of attending this program.

1. I feel better about my job and the company.
2. I feel the same as I did before.
3. I'm impatient to get ahead.
4. I feel worse about my job and the company.

DECIPHER THE REAL FEEDBACK ON 'WHOOPIE SHEETS'

BY RON ZEMKE

Using participant end-of-course re-action forms, sometimes face-tiously referred to as "whoopie sheets," has been widely criticized as a method of evaluating training program effectiveness. The nay-sayers suggest that post-course reaction sheets are of dubious value because:

• Participants have difficulty making meaningful and unbiased assessments of the utility and effects of their participation.

• Participant-reaction forms invite overly generous ratings of the training experience.

• Reaction forms are usually administered to participants at the end of an exhausting training experience, when they'd rather go home than give thoughtful feedback.

But Dr. Kent Chabotar, a senior analyst with ABT Associates, Inc., and an associate professor of management at the University of Massachusetts, Boston, believes that reaction sheets can be effective evaluation tools. Chabotar accepts the fact that "... despite criticisms, the reaction form continues to be the evaluation instrument used most frequently." He points out that trainees and management *expect* rating sheets at the end of a program, and, for many trainers, the economics of a research design evaluation are insurmountable. "Where the choice is not between simple and sophisticated training evaluations but rather between simple evaluations and no evaluations at all, the reaction form is very attractive," Chabotar observes. "Since it seems likely that the participant-reaction form will survive, training evaluators must find ways to capitalize on its strengths and minimize its weaknesses."

Toward that end, Chabotar offers us five rules for the effective design and analysis

1. **Reaction forms should cover both training process and impact.** Some people argue that only impact on trainees and the organization should be measured. Others insist that the organization and delivery of the training are the major concerns. Chabotar tries to split the difference by suggesting that both be addressed. He suggests measuring the following three factors:

• *Training objectives*—the extent to which participants feel they were able to achieve pre-specified objectives calling for improvements in knowledge, attitudes, skills or job performance.

• *Training sessions*—a rating of the content and delivery of each training session or instructional unit, possibly including ratings of individual faculty.

• *Training components*—the overall reactions to training scope and goals, organization and administration, and content and delivery.

2. **Reaction forms should permit both essay and scaled responses.** Asking trainees to rate specific items using a Likert-like scale of some sort (e.g., 1 = poor/5 = excellent) is great for quantifying and comparing outcomes. But, Chabotar cautions, there's also much to be said for "... in-depth feedback not only on *what* happened during training but also *why* it happened, and *how* the program can be improved." This, of course, means that essay-type questions are invaluable. He goes on to suggest that such questions should focus on specifics and gives some examples:

• What were the stronger features of this training program?

• What were the weaker features? How would you improve them?

• Could you name two or three new ideas you gained from attending this program?

3. **Reliability of results can be increased by asking the participant's supervisor to complete similar reaction forms.** An abbreviated or slightly modified version of the reaction form can be used to measure the supervisor's impressions and observations of the extent to which participants from his or her unit have changed after the program.

4. **Results can be more meaningful if selected performance standards are used in interpreting data.** Interpretation of the data generated by the reaction form is often complicated by the lack of performance standards against which to compare the results of specific programs," says Chabotar. He suggests anchoring reaction questionnaires in either *norm-referenced* or *criterion-referenced* performance standards.

• *Criterion-referenced* standards define "success" as an absolute average score on a reaction form item or series of items. For example, it may be decided that each of the items relating to workshop components must have received an average score of at least four on a five-point scale in order for the program to be declared a success.

• *Norm-referenced* standards define "success" in relative, not absolute, terms. Scores on any item on a given program's reaction form can only be interpreted in comparison with scores on that same item achieved by other training programs. Comparisons are commonly made on a percentile basis. For example, training program X could achieve an average rating of 4.5 on the item: "The ideas and activities presented were (1 = dull/5 = very interesting)." This might seem impressive until compared with how other training programs did on that same item.

5. **Comparisons can be facilitated by accumulating a reaction-form-results data base.** By compiling a running record or data base of results from trainee-reaction questionnaires, comparisons among different training programs can be made. More importantly, though, historical trends can be tracked and future projections made. Using simple "eyeball projection," you can sense when classroom quality begins to deteriorate and take quality assurance measures before much damage is done. Specific program objectives can be tracked over time. And across-program quality can be assessed for instructors, *and* the efficacy of specific instructional strategies can be assessed across instructors.

Chabotar points out that this idea has become an actuality. As an example, he references the "workshop evaluation system," designed by Edward McCallon; the "system" has a national data base containing trainee reaction results from over 40,000 workshop participants. The results from any training program can be compared with the results of the programs represented in the data base in terms of organization, objectives, presenter, ideas and activities, scope, and overall effectiveness. A similar system can be developed fairly easily within a specific organization. It simply requires standardization of reaction forms and a central collection of reaction-form data.

Dr. Chabotar cautions that trainee reaction forms are not a be-all and end-all. Nor will behavioral and research designs be superceded by them as appropriate evaluation methodology. Rather, he concludes:

These recommendations are not intended to elevate the reaction form to undeserved status as a fully validated and reliable instrument. Its subjectivity and other defects prevent that. But the five rules are meant to acknowledge the remarkable persistence of the "whoopie sheet" as a principal assessment tool and the consequent need to improve it. The reaction form can provide valuable information about training process and impact for the ultimate consumers of training: participants and their employing organizations.

how to do it, the job doesn't require it or the student could have learned it quickly and easily on the job?

Note here that the answers to these questions shouldn't be "contaminated" by answers to later questions. At this point, all you want to know is whether or not you set proper specifications for the program, *not* whether it worked.

Probably the simplest way to obtain answers to this first question (and sub-questions) is to survey students and their supervisors by means of questionnaires. Where practical, one-to-one interviews, observations and statistical analyses of work-reporting data can be used to enhance your findings. If you've specifically defined performance objectives for the program, supply both students and supervisors with copies of those objectives along with the questionnaire so they can comment on the relevance of each item separately and specifically. The more specific the answers,

the easier it will be to determine what, if any, changes are appropriate.

2 How successfully are the students performing each item learned in the training program? Don't let answers to this affect your interpretation of answers to question 1. Here you want to learn whether or not your students are successfully doing the things they (should have) learned in the program and, if not, why not. Actually, the "why not" is of critical importance. Sub-questions are: Did the student learn the task in the program and then forget how to do it? Did the student not learn it successfully? Can the student do the task but isn't because of conditions, environment or management? Could the student do the job at first but didn't get enough practice to maintain his or her skill?

One pretty reliable way to determine if the students can do the tasks learned is to have them retake your final exam. There's some risk here, of

course, that your exam doesn't validly measure what you intend it to measure; performance tests are more reliable than paper-pencil tests to measure whether people can do things. Students frequently do things differently from the way they learned to do them because they lack management support and because they learned inappropriate techniques in training— that is, the way they learned to do it is exceedingly difficult or doesn't work in the real job environment.

Here again, well-designed questionnaires to students and supervisors, supplemented with observation, interviews and analysis of any available work-reporting data, usually provide as much reliability as you can get without a large budget dedicated to quality control. If you do have a large budget, actual observation of work as it's being done is probably the most reliable, time-consuming and expensive method of measurement available.

3 What consequences have occurred other than those intended? Training programs influence students in many ways, besides teaching new or improved ways to do defined tasks. Sometimes we specifically intend to apply some of these influences in order to, say, reduce attrition, grievances or accidents. If that's your intention, you'll want to know what happened. Did attrition decrease? How much? Is that more, less or the same as the target? Question 3, then, essentially asks, "What may have happened that we didn't expect— good or bad?" Training programs that have no goals related to morale, attrition, absenteeism, grievances, human and customer relations and so on quite often affect some or all of those factors. The changes they produce aren't always beneficial.

For example, a training program may provide necessary skills and stimulate ambitions for a more responsible and higher-paying job than the one the student supposedly is being trained for. The result may be that the trainee exhibits undesirable behavior stemming from his or her frustration. On the other hand, training programs can positively affect employee behavior, in addition to satisfying stated objectives related to job task skills.

It's important to find out, from supervisors, management, personnel records, or wherever you can collect evidence, what side effects the training program may be causing. If possible, try to get these sorts of data from two sources. The first will be the control group, people who did not attend the training program. The second source will be people who participated in the program. This information will be most useful when it reports on the behavior of a large number of people over the same time period— trained people versus untrained people during the same three month period, for example.

Accompanying this article is an example of a set of data collection instruments, including a post-training student questionnaire, supervisor questionnaire and supporting forms. The design of these instruments includes several assumptions, the most important being that the organizational climate will influence the students and supervisors to take the time to fill them out accurately. Unfortunately, in many organizations, the return rate would be less than 10%. Should you wish to vary this format, consider the possibility that the people you're attempting to survey won't take the time to fill out your questionnaires.

A far simpler format is more likely to get responses, but the information will be more general, harder to compile and analyze and less likely to suggest specific changes. A one pager that asks the following questions will give you less information than the examples, but general answers are always more useful than specific silence.

• What tasks do you need for the job that weren't presented or that you didn't learn successfully in the course?

• What tasks did you learn in the course that aren't needed on the job?

• What did you learn that has been most useful on the job?

• What did you learn that has been least useful on the job?

Finally, a word about expressing results in dollars. If your learners are sales reps, it's not too difficult to determine dollar value of results with this sort of model: Untrained sales reps average $100,000 per year in sales, and trained reps average $150,000 per year. Therefore, the return on the cost of training one sales rep is $50,000 in revenue. (That's income, not profit, but it is a net increase resulting from training.)

With a little creative accounting, any documented increase in productivity or decrease in nonproductivity, such as attrition, can be expressed as increased income or decreased cost to your organization. In other words, as bottom-line results of training. To reach that bottom line, you must find out how your students are performing on the job and how training influences that performance.

Reprinted from TRAINING, August 1980

ROI:
WHAT SHOULD TRAINING TAKE CREDIT FOR?

When calculating the return-on-investment for a training program, take the bows and accept the boos only for things you can control

BY JAMES R. COOK
AND CAROL M. PANZA

Statistics can be manipulated and used to prove almost anything. That disturbing little axiom comes to mind often these days as we follow the ubiquitous debate about the ultimate question: "Is training really paying off for our organization?" The reason it comes to mind is that the question often takes this form: "How do we get hard statistical data to prove that gains in organizational performance outweigh and justify dollars we invest?"

It seems to us that there are some dangerous assumptions underlying this whole line of thought. The question of return-on-investment (ROI) for employee training should be approached cautiously and judiciously. Otherwise, advocates of strong employee-development programs may be giving themselves "just enough rope," and wind up hanging from it.

That training should prove its worth is not to be argued. What training should take credit for and how to document its impact are the key issues.

Consider this scene:

Sales manager: "Welcome back. Did you have a good time in Atlanta?"

Life insurance agent: "Actually, we didn't get around the city too much. They kept us pretty busy with the training program. But it was terrific. We learned a lot about the company's target markets and using telemarketing to reach them. And I feel a lot more confident about getting leads because we did role plays and even practiced scripts with live calls."

Sales manager: "That's super! I knew you'd get a lot out of New Agent Orientation Week. But now that you're back here in the real world, I'll show you some unique things we do in this agency. Don't forget all that stuff you learned in Atlanta though. It may come in handy someday."

Agent: "Oh. . .okay. Uh. . .thanks, boss."

Let's say you're the corporate vice president who fought to establish New Agent Orientation Week, or the training director whose people built the program. Would you want to be responsible for the sales gain resulting in that manager's territory from the fact that his agents attended your course? Probably not. Unless you were looking for a quick way to get some quantifiable negatives on your track record, target-market sales increases for new agents wouldn't be *your* choice as a measure of ROI for training.

That's not to say that measurement of results isn't important. For very sound business reasons most of us would argue for looking at results as a function of the investment required to produce them. The trouble comes in determining which results a given organizational unit is really responsible for. What does each ultimately *control*?

Take a look at the diagram of ABC Insurance in Figure 1. We have highlighted the training department and agency operations. The labeled arrows tell us what is "flowing" between training and agency operations, and

between operations and the market. That is, they describe the basic inputs and outputs that link the functions together and to the external market. In ABC's scheme of things there is no direct link between the training department and the market; there is no way to *make* sales happen except through the direct actions of agency operations.

The figure does show, of course, that you can trace a connection from the market (and sales revenue) *through* agency operations to the training department. Training does play a role in sales performance. It helps line departments determine training needs, develops and delivers programs that cause learning, and suggests follow-up activities to ensure better performance. All of these are important outputs with a single bottom line: to support salespeople by influencing their skills and knowledge. Training is clearly a resource for improving or maintaining agency performance.

But don't warm up your calculator yet. The relevant term here is "resource." Training's outputs are inputs that contribute to line results. They do not determine line results. They do not make sales happen.

Certainly the results or outputs of a support function like training must link up with line results—in this case, sales dollars from the target market. But taking all the credit for a change in line performance is risky business. What, after all, can the training department control? Can it control the amount of time, if any, spent on telemarketing? The number of sales calls completed per week? The on-the-spot feedback (and consequences) delivered by a sales manager? No. Training can no more control these factors than agency operations can control product pricing, product features and benefits, agent sales commission schedules or conditions in the general economy and the financial markets.

So what about claiming the value of the change in line performance as a return for dollars invested in training? Willing to go for it now? What does that kind of ROI computation really say? It says that training, or the addition of specific skills and knowledge, is the only contribution to the changed results. How do you suppose the line organization is going to feel about that? What is the value of their management?

Further, are you willing to take the heat for the same ROI measurement in a case where performance does not improve or perhaps even gets worse in the months following your training program? More likely, your answer in such a situation would be something along these lines:

"The skills weren't applied properly on the job, or they weren't reinforced."

"Consequences weren't in place to reward desired behavior or even to discourage undesirable behavior."

"Resources weren't available to permit the salespeople to do their jobs properly."

"The market went sour."

In other words, if a training program that you had designed or championed failed to produce the sort of bottom-line ROI we're talking about, you'd stand up and howl that skills and knowledge are only one component of the performance system. No fair-minded, rational person could hold training solely responsible for lackluster market results. After all, "we" did our part. We provided our deliverables.

Care to wager on how far you'll get with that response if you've tried to grab all the glory for a change that *was* in the right direction? Think you might hear something about having your cake and eating it too?

Another route

Where does this leave training? If it can't take credit for results produced by line operations, how does it prove its contribution and justify its existence?

To begin, a company must define the results for which its training function is accountable, and then substantiate that the function produced quality outputs in those areas. In the cycle presented in Figure 2, the training department's accountabilities fall into two broad categories. One category, represented by the dotted lines, identifies the traditional staff role of advice, recommendations and support. The category represented by the solid line is the only "end result" that belongs entirely to the training department: The only result in this cycle for which training should have absolute accountability is the design and delivery of a training product that meets

the goals established by management.

We feel that the training function should improve documentation of the outputs for which it *is* accountable, and take credit for both successes and failures in those areas. Trainers should not look to the concrete results of line departments to prove their worth as a staff function. As Peter Block put it in his book *Flawless Consulting*, "If consultants really believe that they should be responsible for implementing their recommendations, they should immediately get jobs as line managers and stop calling themselves consultants."

Those dotted lines in Figure 2 represent the training department's "consulting" role. These are very important but different contributions that must be measured and substantiated differently.

The first step in the training cycle is to understand management's goals. The direction in which the organization is moving is the context for a needs analysis to determine if training is required to meet established goals. Training's accountability is to provide as much advice and support (including tools and resources) as necessary to help management make an informed decision on the need for training. When appropriate, that advice should include recommendations *not* to use training as a solution, plus viable alternatives to help produce the desired outcome. This advice function may require a strong and determined voice that must be heard above the din of quick-fix solutions. But like it or not, the final decision rests with the client, not the consultant.

Training must document its efforts, however, and prove that it provided quality service. This documentation should be in the form of memos to management, written reports of activities, examples of tools and instruments appropriate for the type of analysis to be conducted and any other documentation that could prove training provided quality output in helping line management determine its needs.

Once the decision to train some group of employees has been made, the content and training population must be determined. In the content area, the training department may find some of its most difficult work. This may include task analysis, por-

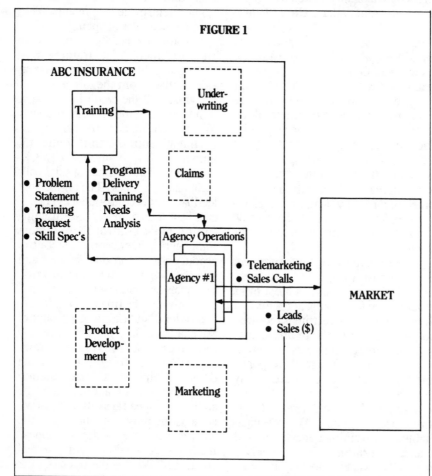

FIGURE 1

ing over job descriptions, looking at skills inventories and endless interviews with bosses, incumbents and subordinates. Again, the final decision on what will be taught belongs to line management. "But they don't understand what's needed!" trainers will cry. Well, convince them. But before you conduct any training, be sure that line management, not the training department, owns the content.

What does the training department use to show its contribution to the content decision? Documentation would include a description of the content-analysis process, along with the recommendations provided to management. Recommendations should be accompanied by all the supporting evidence the training department can muster.

To select trainees, repeat the process. The decision belongs to line managers. The training department must advise, recommend and provide data uncovered in the content analysis which would help the decision process. And again, it must document the fact that it has done so.

Results

All of this "soft" supporting evidence is getting a bit much? You're yearning for something more tangible? Don't despair. We come now to the part of the training cycle that *belongs* to the training department: the design and delivery of training that produces desired learning. The question that must be answered and documented is: "Did they learn what we intended?" Learning is the product of good training, and the training function must be able to show that the desired product was produced.

If we're talking about New Agent Orientation Week, some documentation should exist to prove that each trainee learned the techniques of telemarketing. In this case, taped recordings of the live calls or video records of the role plays would suffice. If neither of these is feasible in a given program, there at least should be a record of instructor observations regarding the performance of each student. Proof of effectiveness involves some recorded performance response or activity that shows that training produced its desired output: learning.

In addition to documenting the fact that students learned what they were supposed to, the training function

must be able to answer two other questions: "If they did not learn, why not?" and "Did they learn efficiently?" Both of these questions require proof that the content analysis was done correctly, that the program design followed acceptable industry standards and that the product was produced as efficiently as possible in terms of time and cost. That it's difficult to "prove" all this, we don't deny. But the importance cannot be overestimated. Trainers often are accused of taking too much time to deliver their product; if they can't prove otherwise, perhaps they deserve the criticism.

Traditional student evaluation sheets are only secondary documentation of good training. Have we stumbled on a fly in the ointment? Could it be that in some cases trainers don't have clear standards against which to measure whether or not they have delivered quality instruction? If the answer is yes, then this is an area in which training as a discipline needs work to better prove its worth. The same logic holds for the programs produced. If you can't show how your products meet established standards

of quality, you should expect criticism of those products.

Payoffs

Assuming you *can* document that the trainees learned, the next question is whether the learning transferred to the workplace—that is, are the trainees using the new skills on the job? Here again, the training department is accountable for advice and recommendations to line management on how to ensure this learning transfer. But it is the line manager, not trainers, who must *cause* new skills to be applied. Trainers are in the "can-do" business; line managers are in the "will-do" business. Training professionals should provide trainees' bosses with specific techniques on how to follow through on training. But they should not assume responsibility for the application of those recommendations.

To complete the training cycle, there must be a way for line management to determine if the training provided was worth the return. "Validation," in this sense, means sub-

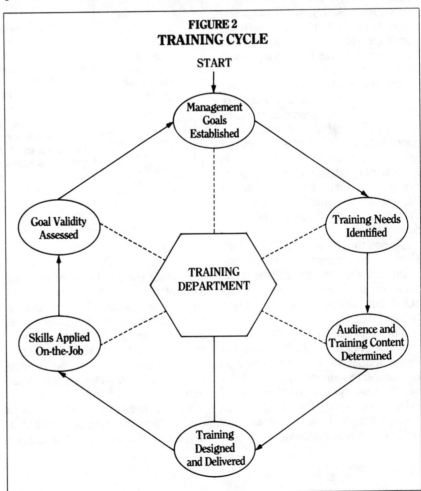

FIGURE 2
TRAINING CYCLE

START

Management Goals Established

Goal Validity Assessed

Training Needs Identified

TRAINING DEPARTMENT

Skills Applied On-the-Job

Audience and Training Content Determined

Training Designed and Delivered

stantiating that the instruction accomplished its original intent. The data that must be gathered will depend on that intent.

If training was done to improve performance in some specific job, then data must be gathered to see if performance gains have occurred. The training department, using interviews, observation, questionnaires and the like, may gather this information and provide a report for line management. Management must then decide on the value of the training. In their support role, trainers should help in interpreting the data and in suggesting ways to correct any problems that turn up in the performance study. The specific approach to data collection should be agreed upon before the training is conducted, with timetables and key people identified up front. Also, the training department's role should be clearly identified, with its "deliverables," if any, agreed upon beforehand. In this way the training department can prove that it met its responsibility by providing quality products.

This whole discussion assumes, of course, that training was done to improve specific performance. What about the validation of training that has no specific performance goals in mind? Here, management just has to determine whether the training met its original intent, whatever that may have been. The training department's accountability basically ends with good documentation that the desired learning occurred in the classroom. If a particular performance change is not an expected outcome, there is no need to collect performance data—unless, of course, you're experimenting.

To put things in perspective, let's drop the new agent orientation program into the context of the training cycle. Figure 3 shows some of the "results" that may be expected for a segment of that program.

The figure reiterates the theme that New Agent Orientation Week belongs to line managers. They are using it as one of the resources available to develop new agents. In the overall scheme of paying for this development, the formal training program is just one expense among many that

FIGURE 3

Steps	Management Actions	Training Department Actions
Management Goals	Management decides that it wants to reach certain target markets using telemarketing techniques.	No decision making. Should actively pursue up-to-date knowledge of management direction and key goals.
Training Needs Identified	Makes a decision that a segment of the new agent orientation program should cover target markets and how to use telemarketing techniques to reach those markets.	Suggests and recommends ways that training might best be used. May identify areas that could best be learned on the job, recommend ways for line managers to support desired performance, etc.
Audience and Training Content Determined	Hires new agents. Determines training schedule. Provides key people for training department to interview to determine training content.	Conducts a content analysis using interview and observation data. Recommends training content. Makes suggestions on prerequisite skills.
Training Designed and Delivered	Communicates expectations to trainees prior to program, including on-the-job application of skills to be learned.	Provides advice on how to conduct pre-course discussions with trainees. Designs and delivers a program that enables students to use telemarketing techniques to reach certain target markets.
Skills Applied On-the-Job	Gives specific assignments for new agents to use telemarketing techniques to reach certain target markets. Gives rewards for effort and results in this area.	Provides suggestions on how to follow through on and support the skills learned in the program.
Goal Validity Assessed	Determines if new agents are using the telemarketing techniques and if their performance shows that the techniques are helping them reach target markets.	Gathers specific data on the application of new skills. Provides feedback to management on revisions to training content, audience, pre-course preparation and/or supervision for application on the job.

constitute the total cost of creating top-notch agents. The return on the training investment is calculated in the total ROI for which agency operations is accountable. Training's exact contribution to that total ROI in terms of dollars and cents is unknown—and it will remain unknown despite all the statistical manipulation in the world.

Even if the training department could prove that the performance of new agents was due only to the train-

ing experience, the result belongs solely to agency operations, not to the training department. The risk of taking credit for positive results is evident in view of the multitude of variables that can cause negative results even when the training produced quality learning.

The message, then, is to prove your worth in those areas you can control and be cautious of taking credit for results that belong to others.

Reprinted from TRAINING, January 1987

SIX REASONS WHY TRAINING FAILS

When the evaluation says it didn't work, it may not be your fault

BY RUTH D. SALINGER

"Put that time [for training] in the bank as an investment of individual growth and development"—Manager

"There are just so many things you can get done in eight hours a day. And the job and training are slightly in conflict, because you've got the job to get done"—Supervisor

As a trainer, I'm sure you have encountered both types of managers—those supportive of training and development and those who feel that training comes second to getting the work out. You may even have tried to convince the second type of manager that training does not interfere with the job being carried out, but rather improves the quality and efficiency of the work. You've certainly been out on the "shop floor," seen the nature of people's jobs so that you can better advise supervisors on the type of training most suitable for individuals, or even recommend to supervisors that training in a particular case is *not* needed. Right?

Here's one manager's perception of the trainers in his organization:

"To my knowledge, and I've been in this job a little over eight years, I've never had anyone from the employee development branch of personnel come over and say, 'I'd like to go over your training plans with you and your ideas. Here's some ideas I have. Let's get together and make you a program.'"

I would like to propose that, in fact, many trainers do not have the contact with line people essential to being effective in their own jobs. I would also suggest that managers and trainers have a joint responsibility in providing training and development to employees—training that will actually change people's behavior in a way beneficial to both employee and organization.

In leading up to these conclusions, I will describe a process which seems to occur in many organizations and which prevents training programs from being properly planned, budgeted, and carried out. First, some background.

In 1973 a study * was completed by the Bureau of Training of the U.S. Civil Service Commission which investigated the factors preventing the occurrence of effective employee training and development—the *disincentives* to effective training. Research techniques used included analyzing findings from previous studies; surveying budget personnel in a number of Federal agencies; and conducting in-depth studies of three Federal agencies with varying missions,

* "Disincentives to Effective Employee Training and Development," Training Management Division, Bureau of Training, U.S. Civil Service Commission, Washington, DC, 1973.

sizes, structures, and range of occupations.

The findings obtained from the many interviews, the computer-analyzed supervisor/employee questionnaire, and the literature searches yielded a consistent pattern, a cause and effect system resulting in lowered chances of effective employee training and development occurring.

The following is a summary of the disincentives to effective training and development:

Disincentives process

1. *The benefits of training and development are not clear to top management.* This is especially a problem because of the lack of methods for demonstrating potential benefits to managers. Without the means to determine training and development benefits, top management is likely to concentrate its resources in areas where the returns are more evident.

This disincentive has two major effects, which become the next two disincentives on the list.

2. *Top management rarely evaluates and rewards managers and supervisors for carrying out effective training and development.* Obviously, if top management is not clear about the benefits of training and development and is clearer about the outcomes of other organizational efforts, its reward system will reflect such an attitude.

3. *Top management rarely plans and budgets systematically for training and development.* Lacking knowledge about the effects of training and development, and about long-range manpower needs, top management is neither likely to nor able to carefully consider training and development in formulating long-range plans and budgets.

Disincentives 2 and 3 lead to disincentives 4, 5, and 6.

4. *Managers usually do not account for training and development in production planning.* Without appropriate guidance from top management concerning training and development plans and budgets, managers are not able to systematically set aside time and money for the training and development of their employees. If resources were assigned to such a purpose, employees would be more

Training Climate Audit

The following items can be used as a check on the training climate in your organization. Employees and supervisors rate the statements on the extent to which they agree or disagree. Employees rate the first 15 questions only. Supervisors rate all 23.

	Yes	?	No
1. I am satisfied with the formal training I have received.	___	___	___
2. I would recommend that others in my position take advantage of the formal training programs offered by my organization.	___	___	___
3. I participated in selecting the courses I attended.	___	___	___
4. I am satisfied with the amount of participation I have had in selecting the courses I attended.	___	___	___
5. I have been able to attend the courses I planned to attend.	___	___	___
6. My supervisor is committed to my training and development.	___	___	___
7. Organizational policy promotes my training and development.	___	___	___
8. I am receiving the training necessary to do my present job properly.	___	___	___
9. I am receiving the training needed for my future advancement.	___	___	___
10. The purpose of the formal training I have received and will be receiving is clear to me.	___	___	___
11. The counseling I have received from my supervisor concerning my program of formal training is adequate.	___	___	___
12. The training programs made available at any given time were adequate to fulfill my specific needs.	___	___	___
13. The courses available at any time were adequate to fulfill my more general needs for future development.	___	___	___
15. The selection of employees for attendance in courses is fair and without bias.	___	___	___
16. As a supervisor, I feel that I could do a better job: a) in the counseling of employees with respect to their training plans. b) in the selection of employees for formal training.	___ ___	___ ___	___ ___
17. Supervisors in general do a good job: a) in the counseling of employees with respect to their training plans. b) in the selection of employees for formal training.	___ ___	___ ___	___ ___
18. The training specialists in my organization are knowledgeable with regard to the specific jobs within my jurisdiction.	___	___	___
19. Training specialists are helpful in performing task analyses.	___	___	___
20. Training specialists are capable of advising me when a particular problem is solvable through formal training.	___	___	___
21. I know what the objective of a particular training course is before it is given.	___	___	___
22. The desired objectives of formal training are met successfully.	___	___	___
23. The time spent in training by the employees under my jurisdiction is a good investment for the organization.	___	___	___

frequently sent to the training and development programs that are planned for them.

5. *Supervisors have difficulty meeting production norms with employees in training and development.* Without the appropriate planning discussed above, supervisors often find that production requirements preclude sending their employees to take training and development.

6. *Supervisors and managers train and develop employees unsystematically and mostly for short-term objectives.* Training is done unsystematically because of the lack of planning, and its purpose is mostly for short-term objectives because of the immediate return evident by training and development of this sort.

There are five additional disincentives which this study revealed. While not part of an interrelated system as with the previous six, these next disincentives are nonetheless influential in the reduced amount and quality of training and development that take place.

Behavioral objectives of training are often imprecise. People attending a training program may expect certain behavioral outcomes from the course, the course instructor may expect a different set of outcomes, the supervisor of the participant another set, and so on.

Training programs external to the employing unit sometimes teach techniques and methods contrary to practices of the participant's organization. For example, writing techniques are taught which may not be acceptable to standard organization writing practices, and hence the participant is discouraged from using the newly learned skills after returning to the job.

Timely information about programs external to an organization is often difficult to obtain. The lack of this information makes training and development plans difficult to develop.

Training and development effectiveness is impaired as a result of restrictions on travel funds. When an organization's travel funds are restricted, travel money is often reduced for training and development, rather than for other ongoing programs. Thus, even though the other monies for training and development are available, the lack of travel funds prevent the carrying out of this training and development.

Trainers provide limited counseling and consulting services to the rest of the organization. They do not carry out their consultant role in working with top management, with supervisors, or with individual employees. Yet all the information gathered in the disincentives to training study points to the consultant role as an essential component of the trainer's profession.

While there will be organizations, or units within organizations, where these disincentives are minimally present, we found the disincentives consistently in various types of agencies and in various types of settings. Feedback since the study was completed indicates that state and local governments, as well as private industries and businesses, are subject to similar factors impeding effective training and development.

Kinds of contacts

While the last five disincentives are not part of a system of disincentives, as are the first six, there is one which has an influence on that disincentives process and which helps create a dysfunctional cycle of its own. I am referring to the last on the list, "Trainers provide limited counseling and consulting services to the rest of the organization."

To understand more fully the impact created by this state of affairs, let's look at the roles of the trainer. While the roles a trainer plays have been discussed in different ways, using different phrases, we chose to summarize them with these three definitions. One role is that of "learning specialist," which refers to those activities concerned with instruction—the conducting of courses and the designing of training programs. "Administrator" refers to those activities concerned with planning, executing, coordinating, processing, approving, and classifying courses, arranging for training, assuring training funds, and implementing procedures. "Consultant" refers to those activities concerned with discussing training-related problems with top management, managers and supervisors, and employees. Within this role, "counseling" can

be used to refer to discussions with individuals, especially at the employee level, concerning their training and development needs and career plans.

The research study on disincentives showed that most of the time spent by a training office is in the performance of the first two roles (administration and instruction), with very little in the performance of the third (counseling). In fact, our questionnaire analysis revealed that supervisors have an average (median) of 2.0 contacts with their trainers per year.

Our study showed also that trainers are not prepared educationally or experientially to take on the role of consultant. Without the appropriate skills, the trainer does not and cannot provide consulting assistance. With this assistance rarely provided, top management and others in the organization do not *expect* the trainer to provide consulting services. And as long as these expectations do not exist, the trainer is not likely to make attempts to acquire the skills and knowledges needed. What we have found, then, is a vicious circle involving skills, performance, and expectations in regard to the trainer as consultant.

The question now is what can we do about the existence of the various impediments or disincentives discussed, and how can we break the two cycles identified—the influence of top management's attitude and actions throughout the organization concerning training (the disincentives process itself), and the limited role now played by the trainer as a consultant to management?

The following are some suggestions for actions which might minimize the impediments. First, trainers should compare the findings of the disincentives study to the climate and activities in their own organizations. Which of the impediments are present? Where? To what extent? What impact is the impediment having on the amount of training that occurs and on the effectiveness of the training? Are particular groups of people in the organization being less well trained than others?

"We have a woman that's a secretary, she's the only secretary we have and

she's got to go for two weeks of training. My normal reaction is, can I get somebody to fill in for two weeks, and generally, [the answer is] no. So it makes it kind of difficult . . . for the clerical level."—Supervisor.

Productivity measures

Disincentive 1, "The benefits of training are not clear to top management," presents a two-pronged problem. To address it, there need to be, first, measures of productivity in an organization and second, ways of measuring the influence of training and development on that productivity. It is only by productivity measures that executives will have a real and personal reason for knowing what benefits they are receiving from their agency's training and development. If the contribution of training to productivity *exceeds* the cost of training, then by training people they are going to look better as managers. If the contribution of training to productivity is *less* than cost, then training is going to make them look worse as managers.

In the absence of any productivity measure, executives' interest in the presumed benefits from training may tend to center around such questions as the personal happiness and satisfaction that their employees might or might not gain from the training. At best, their belief in the efficacy of training and development is based on faith rather than hard evidence. Based on productivity measures, decisions to train can be made as an investment in human capital, and in essentially the same terms as any other capital investment decision.

It should be emphasized that productivity measures need to be present in individual units, not just on an overall organization basis. In addition there should be measurable objectives for management and staff areas as well as line activities. With measurements at the unit level, a direct, specific relationship can be observed between training and outputs.

The second problem related to Disincentive 1 is the need for methods to determine the effect of training on productivity. The U.S. Civil Service Commission's Bureau of Training has developed and is continuing to develop systems for measuring the cost and benefits of training programs. The Training Cost Model, for instance, allows the prediction of the costs of training programs on an annual basis. Training Value Model I enables a person to determine the economic return on an investment in training, in terms of increased productivity, for those jobs with repetitive, measurable outputs of goods or services. Value Model II (nearing completion) will put a value on training where output measures are not readily available (e.g., for managerial and supervisory positions).

Disincentive 2 is "Top management rarely evaluates and rewards managers and supervisors for carrying out effective training and development."

We do not recommend that an organization plan to take any direct action for overcoming this disincentive since we believe it will be self-correcting if Disincentive 1 is overcome. Organizations could set up a requirement that managers be evaluated on the basis of whether or not they were carrying out training and development for their employees. But in the absence of any system to measure either the potential benefits of training and development or managerial performance based on objective goals, this requirement might turn into a numbers game with training done for training's sake alone. There would be no guarantee at all that it would be *effective* training and development, that the right people would be sent to the right courses, or even for that matter that too much training and development might not be carried out in some cases and still too little in other cases.

Therefore, we are proposing that managers *not* be directly evaluated and rewarded on their use of training and development, but rather that they be judged on successfully meeting both short- and long-range organizational goals. Training and development then becomes a consideration to the extent that it affects the achievement of those goals.

Trainer as consultant

Minimizing the other disincentives in the process, as well as

the additional impediments described, depends to a large extent on the expanded role of the trainer as consultant. What are some of the activities that trainers should take on if they are to have a real influence in improving training and development in their organization?

Assistance to managers and supervisors when they are determining their training activities for the upcoming year is one way that trainers can assure that the appropriate training for the right people is properly planned. This means that the trainer needs to understand the *work* of the organization, the nature of the *workforce,* and the special characteristics of a *work unit* (if there are peaks and valleys in the workload, for instance).

Trainers of course need to be aware of, or be able to find out about, training and development resources appropriate to the needs of employees. Of particular value for supervisors is the use of training technology resources which help reduce time away from the job—either total time or amount of time at any one stretch. Examples are programmed instruction, home-study courses, and individualized learning centers. In addition, employees should be able to attend only those portions, or modules, of a training program which are relevant to the participants' needs. Courses developed in-house could be put in this format as appropriate.

Often descriptions of training programs contain vague course objectives. Trainers, in helping to select external training programs for employees, can obtain information clarifying the objectives so that better decisions can be made concerning the usefulness of the course in any particular instance. With more precise behavioral objectives in hand, supervisors and employees can discuss the changes expected as a result of the employee's participating in the program. These kinds of discussions ahead of time will minimize the situations in which an employee returns to the organization after training and is expected to continue performing in the same way,

without application of the newly acquired knowledge or skill.

There really can be no excuse for in-house training programs not meeting the specific learning needs of employees, nor for their stated objectives to be imprecise. And the disincentives study did find that many of the problems we've been discussing stem from the improper use of external training programs.

Given the cycle of the trainer's not being able to act as a consultant, and the manager's not using the trainer as a consultant, a good place to break into this cycle would be for the trainer to start acquiring appropriate skills and try them out on a small scale in the organization. Once trainers can successfully demonstrate their skills in this area, and show managers the advantages of using their talents, the trainers' reputation can be built, the cycle broken.

While we don't necessarily expect all trainers to become consultants, the training office of an organization should have the personnel available not only to be ready when asked, but to make themselves known to the rest of the organization.

What happens when trainers discover problems through their analyses that are not solvable through training? At some point trainers may need to hand off the problem to others in the organization who, through expertise and organizational placement, are the more appropriate people to solve the problem.

With the trainer performing the role of consultant to supervisors and managers, the results will produce benefits of several types. The probability is increased that training and development programs will be attended by only those who have the learning needs, that the training will be appropriate for the particular situation, and that the organization will support the application of the skills and knowledge learned after the employee returns to the job.

Trainers will be thought of not as a unit isolated from the mainstream of organizational activities but as an essential group of professionals who have valuable skills to contribute.

Reprinted from TRAINING, February 1975

CHAPTER 8

TRAINING CLASSROOM INSTRUCTORS

The classroom is a great place to work—for those who love stand-up training and are good at it. But it's also a place where people come to get something and to get it as quickly and easily as possible. And that makes the difference between instruction and public speaking, between an instructor and a textbook, between a canned presentation and a facilitated learning experience.

Selecting and developing classroom instructors is an art—as much an art as the actual act of classroom instruction. It entails the subtle skills of finding people with the desire and temperament to teach others, and of helping them become effective and efficient without stifling the unique natural abilities you perceived in them in the first place.

We have all seen the finest of conversationalists grow pale when asked to "say a few words to the group." To borrow an old gag line, some of the finest wits and most knowledgeable people in the world couldn't lead a group in silent prayer. When you find an individual who not only *wants* to stand and deliver, but who has the raw talent and the technical background to become a good instructor, you have a rare breed of animal. The new trainer needs to be carefully selected, gently trained and emotionally supported.

Good classroom instruction is a rare combination of performing art and management—learning management. The instructor is expected to be interesting, knowledgeable, clear and concise. At the same time, he or she must be able to stand aside and watch for the telltale signs of progress and problem, of mastery and mystery.

And that is where the science of learning, as B.F. Skinner called it, comes to our aid and helps us help the helpers. By teaching the would-be trainer to test and sample trainee knowledge, to question and observe with skill, to match his or her approach to the needs of the students, we take training out of the realm of showmanship and move it toward that precise blend of art and science that we remember from our own peak learning experiences.

THE TRAINING OF CLASSROOM INSTRUCTORS

The would-be teacher has to go back to being a student again to see that not everything that looks like good teaching produces learning

BY MARTIN M. BROADWELL

A lot has been said about making good teachers; probably a lot will be said years from now. But just how much good is being done by the teacher training efforts in business and industry today?

Two extremes

There seem to two extremes, each equally harmful. First, there is the completely theoretical approach, akin to the college-type class, where learning theories are discussed, debated, and generally disposed of. Lectures are given on many subjects (including the importance of *not* lecturing) by very scholarly people. They may hear about Pavlov's dogs again, and even though they may not learn to spell it, they may learn the *gestalt* was not a man, but a German word.

The theoretical approach carries over to the area of teaching. The prospective teacher may have to read books on teaching, including the dynamics of personality; the impact of eye contacts; and numerous other subjects which at best may confuse him. If not confusing, they are certainly not very helpful when he faces a live class. The teacher-to-be is looking for help, not theory; answers to real questions, *not suppositions or hypothetical unrealities.*

Public speaking extreme

The other side of the coin from the theoretical is the ultra "practical" approach. Public speaking is taught by someone equivalent to a dramatist, and includes all of the proper gestures, facial expressions, body movements, etc. The student will learn not to distract the audience by jiggling his change, or tossing the chalk around. He will learn to organize his talk into an Introduction, Body and Conclusion. In short he will be trained in public speaking. He will be critiqued by the rest of the future teachers until he is convinced of his weaknesses, and knows where his strong points are. He will practice in front of them, and just may turn out to be a much better *speaker.*

He will be lectured to on the subject of advanced planning (not on objectives, necessarily, but on preparing leader's guide). The importance of self-preparation will be emphasized because "no speaker can be relaxed if he is unsure of himself."

But where does all of this lead? It may lead to the teacher-to-be's turning into some kind of superlecturer, with all the confidence of a Roman senator, but with no feel for the student's needs. The truth is, there may be no one on the receiving end of his presentation. With all the confidence he now has built up in himself, he may forget something more important than his own presentation: He may forget the real reason for the class in the first place. He may forget that there are some *students* who can't do something, who need to know something, or who are doing something wrong. His task is not to overwhelm them with oratory. He must see that they go away with

their training needs met.

If there were some way to suddenly remove all of the students every time the teacher forgets his purpose for being in the classroom, he would have a better prospective of his position in the classroom. The teacher who has been given a lot of theory about learning would be shocked if the students disappeared every time the theories didn't work. The teacher who has become so self-confident with his speaking ability that he forgets about the students' inability to remember words very long would be equally startled if the students evaporated every time they couldn't follow his every word.

Obviously we can't cause the students to disappear every time a bad learning situation arises, but our teacher training can include some built-in guarantees that the prospective teacher experiences (and knows the difference between) both good and bad examples.

Conventional teacher training not all bad

We found that what we were doing in both extremes—the theoretical and public speaking approaches—is necessary to some extent. It *does* help the teacher to know how and why students learn (even theoretically), and public speaking is a *prerequisite* for any teacher. The important thing, though, is that neither of these alone, nor both together, produced the kind of learning we desired. The situation looked pretty bad, but not completely hopeless. We found our emphasis was wrong. We were making teacher training an *end in itself.* We were looking at the teacher and making him the hero. We were directing everything towards him, and actually omitting the student altogether. We asked ourselves, finally, "Why are we training, anyway?" Suddenly it began to appear that the *student*—not the teacher-was the important person in the room.

This was heartbreaking, because most teachers feel pretty important. We told our prospective teachers they *are* important. But just remember, if it were possible for the students to learn better some other way, the teacher could be done away with altogether. This doesn't mean that the teacher is degraded. He still has all of the prestige and status he rightly deserves, but the student still comes first. We point out that the company is depending on the teacher to produce students who can perform specified tasks back on the job. At present the students can't do it, and the company is suffering from their inabilities. As a result of coming to a training class they should be able to do the tasks. Now the company is in better shape, partly because the teacher did his job well. But also because the students *learned well*.

What part does the teacher play?

The teacher's job is a means to an end. It is one of getting the necessary information (facts, skills, etc.) to the learner. The learner now accepts or rejects, absorbs or repel, learns or loses. Most likely the teacher is responsible for which of these the learner does.

It's not enough, just to tell the teacher this. He must experience it. He must go back and be a student again. He may have to experience enthusiasm, boredom, good pictures and poor lighting to develop empathy with his future learners. This focuses the attention on the learners instead of the teachers.

By being in a realistic classroom situation, *as students*, the teachers begin to see that not everything that *looks like good teaching* produces learning. A candidate from the class of prospective teachers is given some simple information to transmit. He does it to his satisfaction, then the class is *tested*. The results startle the volunteer and even the whole class. Each thought he was getting all of the information, but each may have gotten something different or each may have gotten only part of the information.

Here is another way we show that the teacher is responsible for the learning. Everyone has an overnight assignment which they are not to discuss with each other. Two of the people have *identical* assignments to cover the same four paragraphs of information. They are instructed not to go outside these paragraphs, and not to talk to anyone else about their presentations. When their time comes, half of the class is excused, including one of the two identical-assignment people, and the other makes his presentation. At the conclusion (8-minute time limit) the class is tested, and then sent on break. The other group returns and the procedure is repeated. When an error analysis is made and recorded on the board the results are always impressive.

Teacher blocks learning

Even though the scores may *average* to be close together, examination shows that the two groups got *different* information. All of one class may have gotten a certain question right, while all of the other half missed it. This may repeat itself on several questions. The two "experiment" teachers may fight the problem, but eventually even they will admit that where everyone in their group missed a certain question, it was the teacher's fault, not the learner's. As simple as this may seem, it is a major victory when the teacher finally realizes it is possible for him to *prevent* learning as well as *cause* it!

What about visual aids?

Most teacher training classes for years have stressed the importance of good visual aids. Ironically, many times the classes failed to *use* good visuals, only *telling* that they were important. How can you convince would-be teachers to use things that appeal to the sense of sight as well as the sense of hearing? Certainly not just by telling them how important visuals are. But just using good visuals may not convince them either. Somehow the would-be teacher must see the difference *in terms of learning*.

One way is to *show* them something, then *tell* them something of equivalent value, then later test them. For instance, show them a pie chart, well labelled, indicating that seventy-five percent of what they learn is through the sense of SIGHT. Then tell them that seventy-five percent of what they HEAR is forgotten in two days. Later test them on several items, including these two things which require "seventy-five percent" for an answer. Most often the majority will remember the pie chart and its story. Many will not remember what they *heard* about forgetting in two days.

Real or unreal objectives?

It is easy to get objectives written, even though most teachers prefer to write them *after* the course is prepared. Something as important as objectives cannot be treated superficially. On the other hand, a *theoretical* treatment is just as ineffective. There has to be an involvement on the part of the teachers, or they will not realize that a lot of what we call objectives really are not worth their weight in paper. Just getting teachers to "say words" isn't going to produce real, meaningful objectives. Yet, for years we have allowed objectives to be written which may sound good, but fail to describe when we are through with them. There are still many "appreciation" courses around, and all instructors have been told to see that the students "have an understanding" of something or other.

One way to get teachers to write (and think) better objectives is to have them first write (and think) some bad ones. Have them write the objectives for a *teacher training class* on the first day they appear to be teacher-trained. Don't give any advanced notice, just preboard, "What Are Our Objectives?" and let them start writing. Of course, tell them to write it from the instructor's point of view, not the student's.

After several exercises by these prospective teachers where they have failed to communicate, it's easy to get into the "behavioral" side of learning. When one member of the class attempts to get the class to draw a geometric figure he's looking at behind an easel, and the class makes a poor showing, ask him, "What did you want the class to be able to do?" Before long the class will see the importance of specifying some "terminal behavior" in their objectives. They will start to use such expressions as, "What do I want the student to be able to do when I get through with him?" Now it's time to go back and rewrite those objectives the class wrote which said, "Teach an understanding of the principles relating to proper evaluation of the various teaching techniques and methods as they are applied to the industrial classroom."

A real concern for the learner

Now we have left the student-teacher with a real concern for the learner and the learning in his classroom. How good it will be will be determined only by his conscientious effort to make it better. The teachers won't *leave* the teacher training class better; only time and experience can do that for them. But now they know which direction to head. Now they realize their responsibility in the learning process. Now they have a commitment to the learner. If they go into their classrooms with this attitude, they become the real hero in this little drama.

Reprinted from TRAINING, May 1967

EVALUATING TRAINERS: IN SEARCH OF THE PERFECT METHOD

Is there any such thing as an 'objective' way to rate something with as many intangibles as the performance of a classroom instructor? Southwestern Bell thinks it has come pretty close

BY ROBERT M. CALDWELL
AND MARVIN MARCEL

When you get right down to it, training has two major components: course development and course delivery. Development attracts a lot of attention, and rightly so; it is a complex and costly process. Delivery of content, however, is just as crucial in determining the ultimate effectiveness of training—and delivery depends upon the skills of the individual trainer.

To date, the art of trainer evaluation has been imprecise, to say the least. Criteria frequently are ill-defined or over-generalized. In many companies, supervisors evaluate trainers without actually observing them in classes or on the basis of infrequent or one-time observations. Southwestern Bell has been working on a "better mousetrap" for evaluating trainers. We have made considerable progress.

As in any major corporation, the training Southwestern Bell provides to its employees must be a high-quality service consistent with other corporate objectives. Employees must be knowledgeable and skilled to meet high standards of quality and cost efficiency. To ensure that its training efforts "work" as well as possible, the company's Interdepartmental Training Center (ITC) in Dallas has been developing a procedure to provide objective evaluations of trainers and the training process.

The ITC conducts training in management, network technical skills and marketing for employees in Missouri, Oklahoma, Texas and Arkansas. Instructors at the ITC are employees who work a two- to three-year rotation in training as part of a structured career path.

> **To date, the art of trainer evaluation has been imprecise, to say the least.**

Since their performance as instructors is critical to their future advancement in the company, proper evaluation of that performance is a major concern to management.

Adopt or build?

Many types of instructor-evaluation programs exist throughout the Bell System. Prior to building our own system, we tried to adopt one that had been developed by other Bell entities, but found none that met our precise needs. Some of the instruments were based on criteria other than AT&T delivery standards. Some used evaluation formats that provided no assurance that different evaluators would come up with similar results. Some depended too heavily on student feedback for instructor ratings.

In particular, few of these evaluation systems had been scientifically validated and proven reliable. The ITC wanted a format that would yield virtually the same evaluation results on an individual instructor *regardless of who did the evaluating*.

What we needed was an evaluation format that was credible, easy to use and would accomplish these objectives:

- Evaluate the instructor's performance against a well-known standard that was flexible enough to accommodate different teaching styles.
- Base evaluations on standards of instructor performance that both Bell and the instructor could agree were sound.
- Require the instructor's boss to observe the instructor's performance and do so frequently enough to produce a fair evaluation.
- Use the boss' input as the primary basis for the instructor's rating.
- Provide for specific documentation of critical incidents.
- Provide the basis for a joint boss-instructor improvement plan, not simply a one-shot rating.

We needed standards for instruction that would meet these criteria *and* Southwestern Bell's stated objective for the delivery of training: to "communicate to students the company's prescribed course content so they can retain and/or perform at levels as outlined in course objectives." After many meetings of instructors and their managers at the ITC, we developed a set of standards.

To validate them, we checked for similar experience with standards in other training groups. The most comprehensive teaching standards we found were developed for AT&T by a management-consulting firm, the Athena Corp. of Bethesda, MD. We decided that these standards had enough depth and breadth to cover many different teaching situations and gave us acceptable criteria by which to judge our own. In comparing ours with theirs, we adjusted our standards slightly to meet the broader AT&T standards.

Building the form

Next, we developed a form to guide evaluators while they observed instructors. We wanted an instrument that would be concise, convenient, weighted to the most important teaching skills and objective without being purely statistical. At the same time, we needed a rating system that could be translated easily to the company-wide management-appraisal system.

We used findings from research on teaching and evaluation design as the foundation for our evaluation form, and determined that a fair and un-biased form should have several characteristics.

☐ It should be descriptive, not evaluative. If an evaluation instrument is to have value in the training environment, it must provide feedback to instructors to help them identify the particular aspects of their teaching that need improvement.

If the evaluation is not to reflect merely the observer's value judgments of the relative "goodness" or "badness" of the instruction, it must describe what occurred and how specific teaching behaviors were used in the classroom in such a way that instructors can judge for themselves the effectiveness of their performance. Any other type of evaluation is a judgment instead of a step in the process of improvement.

Evaluation should be a process of analyzing data taken from multiple observations to determine the effectiveness or ineffectiveness of an instructor's particular behavioral patterns. The result is that the "evaluation" form is only one significant piece of data in an entire systematic process.

Data that reliably describes teaching performance depends upon identifying aspects of teaching that are under the instructor's control. These specific behaviors are not personality characteristics, but are observable, "low-inference" teaching behaviors.

☐ "Stated objectives of the lesson" and "asked divergent questions" are examples of low-inference behaviors that can be noted easily by observers with considerable reliability.

"High-inference" teaching behaviors, on the other hand, depend entirely upon an observer's subjective evaluations. The degree to which an instructor shows "enthusiasm for the subject" or "sensitivity to learners," for instance, is determined solely by the evaluator's ideas of "enthusiasm" and "sensitivity."

Since observers rarely agree on high-inference items, those items should be kept to a minimum on an evaluation instrument that aims for objectivity and reliability.

Low-inference criteria also tend to eliminate rating biases toward factors such as the instructor's sex or experience, class size, class level and other factors. They also reduce the "pygmalion effect," i.e., the expectations and biases the evaluator brings to an observation tend to be reflected in the evaluation itself.

☐ Criteria should be related to the training environment. Forms that include categories such as "dresses professionally" are evaluating criteria

---

INSTRUCTORS' PRESAGE VARIABLES

Presage variables are the characteristics that an instructor brings to the teaching situation. They influence the learning process but are not as much a part of the instructor's performance as process variables. Respondents indicated the following critical variables (listed in order of most frequent response):

☐ **Knowledge of subject matter**
☐ **Good speaking ability**
☐ **Enthusiasm, positive attitude**
☐ **Well prepared, good organization**
☐ **Depth of understanding**
☐ **Patience**
☐ **Poise, confidence**

INSTRUCTORS' PROCESS VARIABLES

Behaviors that are evident and easily observed in the actual presentation of a lesson are process variables. Respondents indicated the following critical variables (listed in order of most frequent response):

☐ **Control of class (does not allow students to get off the subject; adapts instruction to the level of the class; flexible, etc.)**
☐ **Gives feedback and positive reinforcement**
☐ **Fair and impartial (nonjudgmental, open, accepting, etc.)**
☐ **Communicates at the students' level (using language and examples appropriate to the level of the class)**
☐ **Involves students in the lesson (through questions, problem solving, simulations, etc.)**
☐ **Shows interest in each learner**
☐ **Attentive and responsive listener**
☐ **Has clear objectives**

STUDENTS' PRESAGE VARIABLES

ITC's students responded with the following presage variables (listed here in order of most frequent occurrence):

☐ **Understanding (willingness to listen to problems)**
☐ **Enthusiasm (positive attitude, genuine interest)**
☐ **Knowledge of subject matter**
☐ **Patience**
☐ **Sense of humor**
☐ **Neat appearance**

STUDENTS' PROCESS VARIABLES

ITC's students responded with the following process variables (listed in order of most frequent response):

☐ **Openness to suggestions (flexible, genuine interest in and respect for students)**
☐ **Gives positive feedback (respects student ideas)**
☐ **Controls class (doesn't allow meaningless discussion or individual students to dominate)**
☐ **Communicates at students' level (uses real-world examples)**
☐ **Well prepared**
☐ **Involves students in the learning process**
☐ **Has a depth of understanding beyond the planned content**
☐ **Has clear objectives and makes instructions clear**

that are not directly related to the training environment and have little impact on the effectiveness of a trainer's performance. Professional dress may or may not contribute to the trainer's effectiveness and, again, this judgment depends on the standards held by the observer. Great care must be taken to design criteria for evaluating teaching that relate to the objectives of the training program.

In short, evaluation should give instructors descriptive feedback that is based on objective, reliable standards. Anything else diminishes the validity of evaluation, particularly when it is used to make decisions about promotions, merit raises or job responsibilities.

Some research, in fact, indicates that evaluations that are not based on clear, objective standards may result in instructors changing their behavior in the opposite direction from that suggested by the evaluator. Not surprisingly, instructors become defensive toward evaluators who have no basis for judgment and yet attempt to tell them how to teach. Descriptive feedback, on the other hand, simply describes what occurred in a classroom and allows instructors to make decisions about their own performance.

The survey

To develop the evaluation form, we started by surveying the people who would be evaluated by it. We asked trainers in each of the ITC's four divisions to list five behaviors or characteristics that they considered essential to effective teaching. We analyzed and factored these findings, and came up with the list of "presage" and "process" characteristics in the accompanying boxes.

We also surveyed a large sample of students at the ITC (see boxes). Stu-

---

The criteria for evaluating teaching has to relate to the objectives of the training program.

---

dents and instructors agreed on many of the characteristics of effective teaching: knowledge of subject matter, enthusiasm, classroom control, openness and flexibility, and communication on a level students can understand.

The *emphasis* placed on each of these characteristics, however, depended on perspective. Students, for example, gave greater weight to factors such as fairness, open-mindedness and patience (a characteristic not mentioned by instructors at all), whereas trainers put more value on knowledge of the subject matter, class control and communication of ideas.

Putting our findings into perspective

Over the past decade, a number of studies have come up with measures of teacher effectiveness by establishing relationships between student achievement and the teaching behaviors that are part of the instructor's observable performance. In this type of correlational study, researchers observe teachers whose students are consistent high achievers and note the behaviors those teachers have in common. Through statistical correlation, researchers can conclude with a high degree of certainty that specific teacher characteristics strongly influence student achievement.

In 1975, Cornell University professors F.K.T. Tom and N.S. Cushman found 28 specific, low-inference teaching behaviors that correlated highly with student achievement on one or more general teaching objectives. Tom and Cushman classified those behaviors as effective at the college level (see Figure 1).

Student surveys also provide valuable information on the characteristics of effective teaching. Richard I. Miller summarized eight such surveys (see Figure 2) in *Developing Programs for Faculty Evaluation* (Jossey-Bass, 1974).

The differences in the types of teaching behaviors listed in the two figures are obvious. Those determined through research (Figure 1) are low-inference behaviors: They can be observed and recorded easily with little interpretation on the part of the ob-

---

FIGURE 1
LOW-INFERENCE TEACHING BEHAVIORS

Objectives and Planning

Pointed out what was important in each lesson.

Gave step-by-step instructions when needed by students.

Objectives of course.

Indicated when new topic was being introduced.

Summarized material presented in each class session.

Presented well-organized lectures.

Student-Centered Learning Activities

Promoted teacher-student discussion.

Encouraged silent students to participate.

Initiated conversation with student before and after class.

Addressed students by name.

Displayed concern that students learn.

Praised students during class.

Made written comments on papers.

General Learning Activities

Used a variety of teaching techniques.

Used a variety of teaching materials.

Made positive statements about the subject matter of the course.

Used understandable vocabulary.

Used examples to help make a point.

Provided Students with Practice (Experience) in:

✓ Recalling factual information.
✓ Recalling fundamental principles, concepts, theories.
✓ Logical thinking, problem solving.

✓ Developing skills in organizing ideas and presenting them.
✓ Providing opportunities to be creative.

From "The Cornell Diagnostic and Reporting System for Student Description of College Teaching," (*SEARCH: Agriculture Education 3*, Cornell University, 1975, Ithaca, NY) by F.K.T. Tom and H. R. Cushman.

server. Figure 2, on the other hand, lists behaviors with more emphasis on personality characteristics—dynamic and energetic person, sense of humor, rapport, pleasing personality and so on. While students obviously appreciate these high-inference characteristics, they are difficult to measure objectively and should be avoided in instruments used to evaluate how well individuals perform their jobs.

After further research into the characteristics of effective teaching, we presented a preliminary instrument to the instructors and managers of Southwestern Bell's ITC (see Figure 3 for an excerpt from the form).

We divided teaching skills into nine categories, and further divided them into "priority skills" and "secondary skills." Priority skills (knowledge of

subject matter, presentation skills, communications, receptivity, class control and classroom management)

Our validation process attempted to answer several important questions.

---

are those that appear to have the most direct impact on effective teaching, as well as the lowest levels of inference.

Secondary skills ("professional manner," "personalizes training," and "enthusiasm") are less important to teaching and more inferential, but nonetheless part of an overall evaluation.

Under each category of teaching skills, performance indicators are listed to aid observers. For example, one indicator for the skill "knowledge of subject matter" is "depth of understanding." Observers note the level of performance ("outstanding," "evident most of the time" and so on) and any anecdotal comments, and use them later as a basis for follow-up discussion with the instructor.

Even though we tried to avoid high-inference items and indicators of behavior that seem to have little correlation with learner achievement, the

---

FIGURE 2
CHARACTERISTICS OF GOOD TEACHING

Bousfield	Clinton	Deshpande	French	Gadzella	Perry	Pogue	Hildebrand
Fairness	Knowledge of subject	Motivation	Interprets ideas clearly	Knowledge of subject	Well-prepared for class	Knowledge of subject	Dynamic and energetic person
Mastery of subject	Pleasing personality	Rapport	Develops student interest	Interest in subject	Sincere interest in subject	Fair evaluator	Explains clearly
Interesting presentation of material	Neatness in appearance and work	Structure	Develops skills of thinking	Flexibility	Knowledge of subject	Explains clearly	Interesting presentation
Well organized material	Fairness	Clarity	Broadens interests	Well prepared	Effective teaching methods		Enjoys teaching
Cleanness of exposition	Kind and sympathetic	Content mastery	Stresses important materials	Uses appropriate vocabulary	Tests for understanding		Interest in students
Interest to students	Keen sense of humor	Overload (too much work)	Good pedagogical methods		Fair in evaluation		Friendly toward students
Helpfulness	Interest in profession	Evaluation procedure	Motivates to do best work		Effective communication		Encourages class discussion
Ability to direct discussion	Interesting presentation	Use of teaching aids	Knowledge of subject		Encourages independent thought		Discusses other points of view
Sincerity	Alertness & broad-mindedness	Instructional skills	Conveys new viewpoints		Course organized logically		
Keenness of intellect	Knowledge of methods	Teaching styles	Clear explanation		Motivates students		

Listed in order of importance by:

| 61 students, University of Connecticut | 177 students, Oregon State | 674 students rating 32 engineering teachers | students at University of Washington | 443 students, W. Washington State | 1,493 students, faculty & alumni, University of Toledo | 307 students, Philander-Smith College | 138 students, University of California, Davis |

From *Developing Programs for Faculty Evaluation* (Jossey-Bass, 1974), by Richard I. Miller.

results of our survey of instructors and students indicated that they wanted a few such items included. Any reliability problems with these items, we felt, would surface as we validated the instrument.

Our validation process attempted to answer several important questions.

□ *Do instructors accept the evaluation criteria as valid?*

Randomly selected trainers from Southwestern Bell's ITC took part in extensive discussions about the instrument's form, content and use. Most agreed that a form of this type could provide a basis for *describing* teaching performance so that improvement can be made easily. They also conceded that the form could act as an objective standard against which performance related to job responsibility could be measured and serve as a corresponding indicator to the company's management appraisal system.

But while trainers generally agreed that the performance criteria were valid, many were adamant about the procedures for using it, insisting that final evaluations of teaching performance should be made only after a series of observations and assessments. With this data, a composite profile of performance could be constructed, which would increase the evaluation's validity.

□ *Can the form be administered*

FIGURE 3: AN EXCERPT FROM SOUTHWESTERN BELL'S INSTRUCTOR-EVALUATION FORM

TRAINER EVALUATION FORM

DATE: _____   INSTRUCTOR _____

EVALUATOR _____

Performance Criteria		Knowledge of Subject Matter		Presentation Skills				Communications		Receptivity	
PRIORITY SKILLS											
Reference to where covered in AT&T standards		Section A	*	Sections C, D, E		*	*	Sections B, C, E	*	Sections B, C, E	*
PERFORMANCE INDICATORS	PRIMARY	Thoroughly familiar with content and objectives contained in Leader's Guide		Points out what is important in each lesson		Indicated when a new topic was being introduced		Uses language students can understand		Is an attentive and responsive listener	
		Reflects a depth of understanding		Makes objectives clear		Assessed learner understanding of each objective		Uses real-life examples to make points		Deals effectively with student questions	
				Presents material in well-organized fashion		Paced material according to student ability		Promotes student discussion by using open & closed questions		Is non-judgmental in response to student comments	
						Used variety of methods and materials				Is *PATIENT* and responsive to student concerns	
	SECONDARY			Uses a strong clear voice		Maintains eye contact and scans the room		Uses correct grammar and avoids jargon			
				Has a knowledge of and uses of AV materials							
COMMENTS											

*KEY:
4 = Outstanding
3 = Evident most of the time
2 = Evident some of the time
1 = Not present but needed
0 = Irrevelant to this lesson

561

fairly and objectively?

To answer this question accurately, we felt that *many* observers had to agree on an instructor's evaluation over a designated period of time.

The system we set up allowed each of the ITC's four managers to act as an observer, along with an educational consultant hired especially for this purpose. Each manager observed several classes with the consultant, and at least 90% agreement was achieved on each observation in every category. On this basis, we concluded that the evaluation instrument could serve as an objective tool for assessing teaching performance.

☐ *Can the form be used in classes where self-paced instruction is the primary delivery system?*

We made a special effort to test the evaluation form in the self-paced classes that the ITC uses extensively in the network maintenance division. We found that many of the same skills necessary for effective teaching in traditional instructor-led classes also are evident in one-to-one instruction.

Refinements

In order to base evaluations on a credible sample of an instructor's teaching, we developed a frequency formula for this instrument that requires the boss to observe an instructor for one to two hours per month, or a total of 15 hours per year. (A typical, experienced ITC instructor delivers about 500 hours of classroom training per year.)

Student evaluation of the program acts as a continuing validation check on the boss' evaluation. Student questionnaires are distributed (without the instructor present) and compiled. The summary is reported back to the boss. The overall rating from the student evaluations is not part of the instructor's rating in the management-appraisal system, but serves as a tool that bosses can use to double check their own ratings and plans for improving their instructors' skills.

The final product of the instructor-evaluation program will be a formal company appraisal, along with an assessment of the instructor's potential.

Southwestern Bell's management-development organization has recommended that "potential indicators" and "performance indicators" for an instructor's delivery work be one and the same.

The assumption is that student performance on the job cannot be attributed to the instructor with enough certainty to account for it in an appraisal. Instead, the trainers' performance as an instructor must measure potential as well as appraisal of performance. We feel that if the trainer demonstrates the appropriate training delivery standards, students will perform at the level the course intends.

This evaluation program is a fact-gathering plan only: It is not intended to advise or guide bosses on causes of problems, potential corrective actions or other methods to improve their instructors' performance. That is the boss' job. But we do think the evaluation program will help managers develop improvement plans that really pinpoint instructors' needs.

Reprinted from TRAINING, January 1985

REVIEWING YOUR STAFF'S PERFORMANCE

Simply put, your responsibility is to cause the performance of the people under your direction to improve

BY STEPHEN P. BECKER

Training mangers do not always practice what they preach. Most trainers have conducted programs for other managers and supervisors on MBO and performance appraisal. These concepts have met with wide interest in the world of professional training. That is, the trainers have been interested in getting all the other departments to adopt a managerial style based on performance objectives. In many cases we, as training managers, have not clearly thought through the implications of MBO and reviewing performance for our own departments.

Before setting up a performance review session with a subordinate, you should take some time to consider your own responsibility as a manager of other people. In this regard you have the same responsibility as any other manager. Simply put, your responsibility is to cause the performance of the people under your direction to improve.

Let's look at what this statement really means. First, it means that you, as a manager, have an obligation to help all people who report directly to you do a better job. You shouldn't consider only those who you feel aren't living up to your expectations. Even the good performers can get better, and it's your job to develop them, too.

Realistically, most of your staff will be somewhat below or above what you might consider to be average in terms of training knowledge, skill, and contribution. As is true with any population, only a small percentage of trainers are truly excellent performers. By the same token, only a small percentage are poor performers. The great majority lie somewhere in the middle or average range. Your great task, then, is to get the performance of your individual department members moving in the direction of excellence.

One point to keep in mind is that any trainer may be good at some things and not as good at other things. For instance, a trainer may be especially good as a classroom instructor and as a one-on-one coach. This trainer's great strength is in implementing a course that's already developed. If you think about all the trainers you know, chances are that you will find relatively few "general practitioners." In your performance appraisal planning for your staff, you will need to decide what your own philosophy is on this issue. Do you want generalists or do you want specialists?

The answer is important, because if you want generalists, you must be prepared to make a long-term investment in your individual staff members. Assuming that the people involved also want to be less specialized, you will have to be responsible for lengthy training of the trainers in the areas where there are needs for additional competencies. The specialist can apply his/her competencies immediately and even learn to be more specialized in a much shorter time than it takes to develop entirely new skills. New abilities may take months or years to develop and take much of your own time in the process.

Even if you're not training the trainer yourself, you will have to be highly involved in the planning, resource selection, measurement and application of the training. All this takes time. That doesn't mean that it shouldn't be done. You should carefully think about your staff and the pressure of your organization before you reach a conclusion about how specialized or unspecialized you want your staff.

Now that you've thought about your own responsibility as a manager (to cause individual performance improvement) and about your philosophy regarding specialization, you are ready to consider the performance of individual staff members. You should begin by sitting down and making some personal notes about results that have been achieved by the staff member over the past six months. As you think about the results, try to identify what the payoff has been for the organization, the training department and the staff member.

The idea is to be able to describe results to the subordinate in tangible terms as follows:

1. You developed and taught a sales training program on how to get more sales leads. Within two months, leads increased by twenty percent.

2. You completed the development of two audiovisual programs that are being used daily to teach new employees how to operate the widget machine. As a result training time has been cut by 50 per cent and is being done by the immediate supervisor on the shift rather than the area training assistant.

Once you determine the positive achievements, you should attempt to list the performance weaknesses of the individual. These might include things like:

1. The sales training program cost 25 per cent more than was projected because of poor control over expenses.

2. The AV programs were two months late in development because of inefficient use of time.

After you have done a lot of thinking about performance results in terms of strengths and weaknesses, you are prepared to conduct the actual interview. During the session, you should allow the staff member to do most of the talking. Your methodology should be to ask good questions so that the staff member has a chance to be heard by his or her "boss." You want to get the staff member to describe results in order to see if his or her perspective about performance achievement is the same as yours.

You should not voluntarily tell the interviewee what you wrote down about his or her performance. Rather, look for places where you can agree or disagree about what the staff member believes has been achieved. Where you agree, expand the point and recognize the value of the contribution. Where you disagree, let the discussion revolve around problems that came up and how effectively they were handled.

Where problems arise, you should attempt to get the staff member to identify the cause(s) of the problem. Remember that a problem can have more than one cause and that there may be a variety of solutions that could be applied to each cause. The staff member should be encouraged to create the solution(s) to whatever causes the problem.

The reason for this lies in the concept of dependency. If you, as the manager, identify causes of problems and the appropriate solutions, then the staff member could become dependent on you to deal with the same kinds of problems (or all problems) in the future. What you want is for your staff members to become more independent of you, more self-sufficient. The only way you can make people more independent of you is to allow or force them to take as much responsibility for solving

their problems as they can handle. They then can check out the quality of those solutions with you, their manager.

In essence, what you are doing is helping your staff members stay in touch with themselves. You are causing them to be confronted with their own behavior and performance in terms of the results they achieved. You are, in effect, holding up a mirror of their lives at work. While you are in the process of getting staff members to look at themselves, you are functioning like a manager.

Don't be naive about the kind of impact this type of session can have on people. It is quite possible that they will be overly critical of their performance in a negative sense. Most people are very critical of themselves. You, as manager, must be aware of this tendency and help keep a balance in the discussion. It is important that a person be proud of strengths. What you want is for a person to feel successful and at the same time be cognizant of areas where performance needs improvement.

As the staff members become more conscious of competencies, successes and areas for improvement, they will be more able to propose performance objectives for themselves. The word *propose* is appropriate here, because you still need to agree to these objectives. You may have knowledge about organizational needs that can influence the objectives as well as the methods of achieving them.

Receiving information about the development and needs of your organization is one of the benefits your staff members should get out of a performance review. It is always necessary for individual objectives to be congruent with organizational objectives.

Many managers think that every time they talk to a department member about work or progress toward objectives, they are conducting a performance review. This is not the case. A performance review should be formal, take about two hours and be done at least twice a year. When it's over, you and your staff member should better know where you've been and where you're going.

After the interview, you should write some notes to yourself about what took place—that is, what was discussed, what performance objectives were set and what things you (the manager) agreed to do before the next interview. The reason for the notes is that without them you probably won't remember all the points you should refer to in the follow-up session.

It's important that performance interviews be linked to each other. What you want to look at are patterns of performance. You want to see consistent and continuing development. It's not as valuable to your department or to the trainer involved to think of each interview as isolated. In a sense, you both should be able to graph performance improvement over a period of years. This type of mental graph can be done when objectives, and achievement against those objectives, are used as the basis of measurement.

One acid test of a performance review is to ask yourself if your relationship with your staff member is more productive as a consequence of the interview. If, after the interview has ended, the staff member feels that you were unfair, abusive, unwilling to listen or unwilling to help him or her be more successful as a trainer, then you have failed the test.

This is not to say that you can't be honest or give negative feedback about performance. In fact, you must be able to say what you feel and believe in order for the interviewee to value your comments. It is necessary for you to be sincere in order to have an effective interview. One key outcome of all such interviews should be that the working relationship between you and your staff person has been enhanced.

Like any other department head, we training managers usually recognize the need for formally reviewing the performance of department members. Our intentions are good, but somehow we forget to put this kind of activity on our schedule. If we work hard to teach others that this is the professional's way to manage, then it may be time for some of us to appraise our own performance.

Reprinted from TRAINING, August 1975

THE CARE AND FEEDING OF TRAINERS

It's not that trainers are always the last
to get any training.
But developing them and keeping them happy do
present special problems

BY BEVERLY GEBER

Nineteen training directors sprawl in a ragged circle around a couple of tables in a Florida resort and ponder a question: "What one thing would make a career in training more satisfying to you or your subordinates?" They give it all of four seconds thought, and no one wrinkles a brow or gazes reflexively into space. "A bigger office," one director says quickly. His joke a success, he quiets the laughter with his real answer: more respect and recognition by line managers.

Most of the others sober up and nod agreement. Nobody mentions money and nobody seriously pines for the trappings of success. True, it may be a mistake to extrapolate from that, since these are undoubtedly some of the best-compensated human resources development (HRD) people in their organizations. But it appears that the need for recognition never abates, even for many people at the top of the corporate-training pyramid. It's a need that drives some very good trainers out of the field altogether. And it helps explain why others, convinced that they cannot be prophets in their own land, seek respect by leaving salaried HRD jobs to become consultants.

Training directors know that. They know that the care and feeding of their own subordinates is one of the trickier challenges they face. It's also sometimes among the most neglected ones. In a recent survey of subscribers to the newsletter "Training Directors' Forum," 45 percent of the 172 respondents disagreed—11 percent of them strongly—with the statement that "development of my training staff is given high priority." Too often the Cadillac ideal becomes the Yugo reality that there may not be enough time and money to give those staffers as much training as they need.

It's hard enough to come up with an efficient development plan for "pass-through" trainers who come in from the line to spend a few years in HRD before moving on. The problems are often more acute with "career" trainers. If a company does employ career trainers, and if those professionals do get regular, high-quality training that lets them continue to hone their skills, the HRD director still is left with the problem of keeping them satisfied when promotion opportunities and pay hikes fizzle out.

Sometimes ambitious trainers are even frozen out of the top jobs within their own departments. One director of a 700-person corporate training function says bluntly that none of his subordinates will succeed him by advancing within the training department. In fact, say many training di-

rectors, the only promising career paths for an ambitious trainer lie beyond the training department's door.

It's a depressing thought for career trainers, the ones who invariably say they became trainers because they wanted to make a difference. Granted, their plights may not be measurably more severe than that of professionals in many other specialties; a technical writer at IBM, for instance, will climb the ladder only so far in his company, too. But if you want skillful trainers to turn down other opportunities in order to cling to their calling, you have to give them some reasons. They want fulfilling work. They want to be respected. They want to learn and grow. Hence the challenge for training directors.

Robert Saunders Jr., a vice president of the Northern Trust Co. in Chicago, is one training director who admits that there is a gap between the ideal and the reality of developing his staff. "We ought to do for ourselves what we do for other people [in the company]. But it's tough. I can see as a manager how easy it is to let those things slide," he says. He tries to send his subordinates through training as much as time and money allow—often to the neglect of his own continuing education. His attendance at the Training Directors' Forum in Boca Raton, FL, was his first formal attempt at self-development in two years.

The career-development issue sometimes influences the very structure of training departments. It's a factor that weighs in the basic choice between staffing the HRD function mostly with training careerists or with pass-through people.

Saunders intimately understands the difficulty of keeping career trainers satisfied in their jobs. He recently revised the department's hiring philosophy precisely because its design was making it difficult to keep people happy. Under his predecessors, the plan was to hire seasoned career trainers, individuals with experience in lecturing, group facilitation and instructional design who would need minimal training and could immerse themselves in the work immediately. "You can't go out and get experienced, highly paid individuals because if you don't have the resources to back them up, their satisfaction is going to run out very quickly," he says. "It's a problem, and I don't think it's unusual."

Now he hires only entry-level people, who tend to stay longer as they acquire skills and become proficient. Of course, when Saunders traded away experience, the result was a need to spend much more time on training those new trainers. He has created a formal development plan that includes orientation and outside courses in instructional design. Then the new employee observes expert trainers and undergoes a self-study course to become certified to teach his assigned courses. The next step is team-teaching before he finally teaches solo. It's a laborious process.

"With somebody who's really green, it could take six to nine months. That's tough in a small group," Saunders admits. In the meantime, the novice is producing minimally, and the others are sacrificing some of their own productive time to coach the newcomer along.

Then again . . .

There is, of course, a paucity of universal truisms in the training business. Edward Zobeck takes exactly the opposite tack in his HRD department and argues its wisdom strenuously. When he became manager of training and development for AAA Michigan in Dearborn, three-fourths of his trainers were subject-matter experts from line operations who had come into the training department, liked it and stayed.

For many training functions, that wouldn't be a problem. Early on, subject-matter experts contribute their specialized knowledge. Later, after training, they couple that knowledge with teaching skills and become valuable as experienced, stand-up trainers. But Zobeck found some of his subject-matter experts lacking instructional-design skills at the precise time that his company was decentralizing. It was a bad combination. "I'd like to reduce classroom time by about 50 percent in the next couple of years," Zobeck says. "So we need to find other, more cost-effective methods of getting the training out to the people. And that's dependent on tight instructional-design expertise."

His ultimate goal is to have a department that consults on specific training problems and designs courses that would be facilitated in the field by subject-matter experts.

So, he says, he'll only hire experienced, career trainers in the future.

But in the meantime, his staff of subject-matter experts is getting a big dose of training to meet the immediate need. Since it would have been too expensive to send them all away for training, Zobeck looked for something that could be done in-house. He selected a course on criterion-referenced instruction. "This one course won't make an instructional designer out of everyone but at least we'll all be speaking the same language," he says.

'We did zero for staff development; it was left up to the individual.'

With the help of additional training and practice, Zobeck's trainers should be able to cut the time they spend designing programs. He also hopes to see an increase in the quality of the programs.

Once the immediate need is met and the flurry of train-the-trainer instruction is finished, Zobeck isn't sure what the normal routine of trainer training will look like. He admits that he is limited by his budget and by the need to serve clients first, even if his own staff's development suffers. He doesn't consider that an unusual dilemma. "In my experience, there's very little done for trainers. I came from a government background. We did zero for staff development; it was left up to the individual. My experience with talking to my peers is that that's not always the case. But we do concentrate more on our clients than on ourselves," he says.

Generally, the people who get the most developmental attention are pass-through trainers. Their time is so short in the HRD function that it must be carefully planned if it's to be meaningful at all. In fact, if they don't learn quickly, they're liable to be millstones for their entire stints.

John Purcell, director of training at Ameritech Publishing in Southfield,

MI, has a model for developing trainers who are pulled in from the line and kept for two to three years before he shoots them back out again. He calls it "seeding" the organization with people who, he hopes, have become adept at developing others and will retain fond memories of the training department as they become more influential in the company.

Before he recruits them, Purcell carefully describes the training skills they'll acquire progressively. In the first year, they learn to be evaluators, group facilitators, instructors and individual development counselors. The second year finds them practicing instructional development, marketing, needs analysis and media development. The best ones stay for a third year and learn skills needed to be a lead trainer, program administrator and program designer.

Purcell admits that expecting people to learn all those skills—in essence, to become a well-rounded HRD professional—in three years is an imposing goal. Not all of his candidates succeed. But enough do to make the program an attractive career-development move at Ameritech. At least they're not bored in the HRD department, he says.

Off-the-shelf vs. customized

In the first year, Purcell's new trainers usually teach courses that relate directly to their previous experience. Salespeople, for instance, teach sales training. Also in that first year, Purcell sends them to an outside train-the-trainer course to learn platform skills and methodologies. In the second year, they do more instructional design and attend an outside course to learn related skills. In the final year, they may attend a national trainers' conference.

The flow of neophytes through the department puts a strain on the career trainers, who are expected to be coaches and to deliver on-the-job training, since there is no formal train-the-trainer instruction on-site. Three career trainers serve as team leaders for the rest, and an additional three are full-time course developers. The remaining 16 are rotational trainers. "It's tough to manage," admits Purcell, "but it's a working model and it's better than going at it willy-nilly."

Those career trainers don't get the same kind of development attention that the pass-throughs receive. But Purcell says that doesn't mean that the careerists have fewer opportunities to sharpen their skills. The pass-through trainers, he says, need a rigid format to adapt to new duties that might seem foreign. The difference between training for the pass-throughs and training for the careerists is akin to the difference between off-the-shelf programs and customized programs, he says. "You analyze their own needs," says Purcell of career trainers.

Unlike Northern Trust's Saunders, Purcell is satisfied with the training his subordinates receive. "I believe I'm doing as much as I want to do, and I really don't have trouble getting money for it," he says.

Michael Goodman, director of network operations education and training for AT&T in Bedminster, NJ, also uses a structured approach. He is trying to turn his function into one that is primarily rotational, and he is in the midst of revising the trainer-development program to make it more uniform across the company. The new plan will be based on specific competencies trainers must master. Currently, novices receive training in a stepped approach that calls for them to attend train-the-trainer courses, watch an experienced trainer teach a course, co-teach a course with an experienced trainer, then teach the course alone.

As for career trainers, Goodman aims to limit their numbers to just a small percentage of his 700 subordinates. That means forcing some people to leave, and Goodman is candid about the need for it. He says that during AT&T's pre-divestiture days, some deadwood types were dumped into training and retired there on the job. So he has drawn up some guidelines to determine their fates. From now on, those who are judged average on performance appraisals will be encouraged to leave the training department after three years. Those who are above average will be asked to stay for five years.

In most cases, five years should be the maximum stint, Goodman says. "If you're going to stay in training in this organization for more than five years, you'd better be one of the top people in your job or you better have a particular skill that's difficult to find on the outside."

The corollary to Goodman's phi-losophy is that there will be no appealing career path for training specialists. In fact, the transitory nature of the job makes it hard to argue that training is a legitimate profession within the company. HRD professionals at AT&T can't even reach the top of their own department.

"I don't think anybody will move into my position by staying in the training organization," says Goodman, whose one year in his current position equals his tenure in the HRD field. (It's telling, too, that there are no vice presidents of HRD at the company.) "I'm running a line organization, and the skills I need in my job are management skills, not training skills. We tell people who want to move forward in the company that they will find it tough to move to middle management and impossible to move beyond middle management by staying in a training job."

That sends a fairly brutal message to career trainers: The skills they acquire and the challenges they face in their chosen field are not the ones the organization values when it comes to advancement and compensation. But depressing or not, many training directors agree that the message holds truth.

In his 22-year career in the training industry, Arlan Tietel, a training manager at 3M Co. in St. Paul, MN, did some zig-zagging back and forth between the training function and other departments as he sought to advance. But he kept returning to training because it involved the kind of work he most liked to do.

The lack of advancement opportunities—and in most cases, the lack of a "dual career ladder" to provide status and fatter paychecks to key specialists, instead of just to managers—leads some career trainers to jump out of the corporation. They land in what they hope will be the greener pastures of the consulting world, where the money can be much better and respect is usually greater.

Tietel says a major allure of consulting is that consultants are often regarded as instant experts, who lend a fresh perspective and specific skills and knowledge the organization lacks. Deserved or not, that kind of respect suggests greater job satisfaction than trainers can glean in the corporation, butting their heads against a status ceiling.

Careers in training don't have to stagnate, of course. Zobeck, for one, considers it his responsibility to develop his people and groom someone to take his spot eventually. That means giving his subordinates as much management experience as possible within the training department. Yet he concedes that in many organizations, advancement means leaving the HRD world behind.

So how do you persuade good trainers to stay as long as possible? How do you keep them happy? One possibility, of course, is to follow the advice that HRD professionals sometimes give to managers of other departments that face the same sorts of problems: Create a dual career ladder. This is an arrangement that allows high-performing technical experts to receive perquisites and salary increases roughly parallel to those they'd get if they were moving up in the management ranks. The idea is to reward valuable performers who don't want to become managers, or who can't move into management because their organizations' hierarchies are flattening, or whose technical expertise the company doesn't want to lose by turning them into administrators.

Zobeck likes the idea but sees no mass rush to enact such systems. He thinks the ideal arrangement for developing trainers and keeping them happy would couple a dual career ladder with a developmental program based on the instructional design competencies prepared by the International Board of Standards for Training, Performance and Instruction. The former would provide satisfaction; the latter would provide specificity and uniformity in training.

Never enough TLC

Aside from a structured approach such as that, there probably aren't many special strategies training directors can use to keep their subordinates happy that wouldn't work equally well in any other department. Keep job assignments varied, for instance. And above all, give trainers strokes. Training specialists are probably little different from their bosses who attended the session in Boca Raton and voiced an overwhelming desire for greater recognition and appreciation, especially from line managers. The best way to get that respect, according to Saunders, is to make sure the department is perceived not as a supplier of training events but as an organizational problem solver.

Another important goal is to make sure trainers have the resources and authority to solve problems. "They should see themselves as contributing on an even par with other people in the organization," Saunders says. Eventually, "they have people coming back to them and considering them an expert."

David Brinkerhoff, president of Abbott-Smith Associates, a Millbrook, NY-based executive recruitment firm specializing in the human resources field, says he knew a training director who stumbled upon a useful trick for boosting morale among her 30 to 40 subordinates. She would pick trainers in turn to attend and evaluate a commercial training program. They would then report on it and recommend whether to buy the program for the organization. Within the department, the trainer would be viewed by colleagues as the expert on that particular program or subject.

The importance to the trainer of respect and recognition from colleagues or clients can't be underestimated, says Tietel. "I'm doing what I like to do and I'm getting feedback that matches my value set," he says of his own work. When he gets a thank-you from someone who was helped by his training he feels as though he's accomplishing the goal that prompted him to enter the training field: to make a difference. At times like that, money—or lack of it—doesn't matter as much, he adds.

But recognition alone does not job satisfaction make. One thing training directors can do is to ensure that job duties are rotated enough to provide challenge and limit ennui. "Nobody wants to keep doing the same thing over and over again," Purcell says. His department is fortunate in that it is constantly consumed by special projects.

To some trainers, it doesn't matter much if they aren't compensated lavishly and the training department is perceived as merely a funnel to another, more important place. There are those who understand their company's reward system and simply ignore it. These are the kind of people who get their satisfaction from internal reinforcers, rather than external reinforcers, says Tietel. They're the people who turn down promotions just to stay in the training department. And they aren't all that rare. Tietel suspects most training directors could cite at least one such lifer they've known.

Zobeck has one on his staff now. She has reached the top of her salary range. He can't give her a raise and was worried that he'd lose her. But when he sat down to talk to her, she said she had no interest in going into management. Her goal was to learn more about training.

Goodman says he has one subordinate who asked for a downgrade to a lower salary level because she misses hands-on work in her new position as a training manager. Another asked Goodman to take her out of the company's high-potential program because she knew it would mean promotion out of the training department. "She said, 'I like training. I'm making a choice between wealth, power and all this other stuff, and going home at the end of the day and feeling that I've done what I like to do.' "

Reprinted from TRAINING, August 1988

THE REGULATORS ARE COMING!

Should trainers be credentialed?
If so, by whom?
Here's a thought-provoking essay
on a looming issue

BY ROBERT F. MAGER
AND DAVID D. CRAM

The regulators are rolling their juggernaut in our direction. They have noted that training is beginning to exert a significant influence through its increasingly powerful technology and are getting ready to seize control of the craft.

Dozens of laws intended to regulate training and trainers are pending in Congress. The American Society for Training and Development (ASTD) has committed money to the cause. The National Society for Performance and Instruction (NSPI) has established a committee whose purpose appears to be to orchestrate the credentialing of practitioners.

Because we are in danger from those who would legislate where and how we can practice—even *whether* we can practice—and since we may be in danger of being controlled by those who least understand the practice of performance technology, an exploration of the issues is in order.

Concepts such as standards, ethics, certification and licensing are muddied, intermingled and used as if they mean the same thing. They don't. And unless the differences between these concepts are understood, it is difficult, if not impossible, to make sense of the issues. So let's take them one at a time.

The four main issues

Standards usually describe what competent professionals do when they are practicing a craft. They describe what the performance looks like when it's done well.

Standards therefore are useful

> **Concepts
> such as standards,
> ethics, certification
> and licensing
> are used as if
> they mean the same thing.
> They don't.**

guides for those trying to hire or train competent professionals and for those aspiring to learn a given craft. But standards raise a key question: Who gets to say what competence is?

A *code of ethics* prescribes conduct consistent with a set of values and sets the criteria by which conduct will be judged.

How does a code of ethics differ from a set of standards? Standards identify what practitioners actually *do* in the practice of their craft; a code of ethics describes the rules of conduct binding the craft to a particular set of values. A code of ethics protects clients in areas where they must trust vendors and often is proposed where inappropriate performance may endanger the health, safety or well-being of others.

Often a task may be performed in many acceptable ways, each of which is considered ethical because each is consistent with the set of values implied by the code. This latitude allows practitioners to innovate as well as to make adjustments to fit the immediate constraints on task performance. If, however, the task can be performed in ways that violate the values from which the code was derived, then those ways are considered unethical.

For example, suppose a consultant completes a performance analysis correctly and the analysis reveals one or more counterproductive management practices. It is possible that several consultants would come to the same conclusion even though the details of their processes differed. But if one of those consultants revealed the results of the analysis to anyone other than the client, it would be considered a breach of ethical conduct. Why? Because it would violate the ethical principle demanding minimum risk to the health, safety and well-being of others. If the consultant reported the findings only to the client, but went beyond the analysis to offer derogatory opinions of employees that were not supported by the analysis, that too would be considered unethical for the same reason.

A code of ethics has a judicial as well as an educative function; standards have only an educative function. Standards say, in effect, "This is how you are expected to perform the tasks of the craft." A code of ethics says, "If you don't perform these tasks according to these values, you violate the ethical code of the craft and action may be taken against you by other members of the craft."

Certification is the process of publicly attesting that a specified quality has been achieved or exceeded. When a side of beef is stamped "USDA Choice," it means that the beef has been attested to match the standards defined for that grade. When gold or silver bullion has been "chop-marked" by the minter, it has been attested to be of the purity stated.

If an instructional technologist were to be certified, the certification would imply a public confirmation that certain standards had been met. Standards of what? Standards of skill? Standards of performance? Standards of ability to recite theory? It doesn't matter. One who has been certified is one who has met a body of standards, however those standards are defined.

The catch is that unless one knows and understands the standards used as the basis for certification, it is not possible to evaluate the worth of the certification.

Suppose, for example, that certification were based on an ability to recite the role-play taxonomy (which, though it exists, is intended as a joke and adds no value to the craft). If we know what the basis of certification is, we understand that this certification is worthless as a yardstick. People who can recite the taxonomy may or may not be role-play experts—the certification doesn't tell us.

By the same token, if certification is based on an ability to recognize the correct answer to questions about the history or theory of training, that certification is of no value in identifying individuals who are competent in the *practice* of training.

Thus, for certification to be of any value, it must attest to an ability to *apply* skills that are relevant and valuable to the craft. People in any craft therefore should be wary of those who would design certification instruments, especially if the instruments are based on test items that measure ability to recall rather than ability to perform. We should have especially serious reservations about certification being conferred by those who do not practice the craft in the environment for which the standards were intended.

Licensing is a totally different issue. It has to do with passing laws that prescribe the means by which individuals will or will not be allowed to a) use certain words in describing what they do and b) practice a particular craft. For example, no one may legally call himself a clinical psychologist unless licensed by the state to do so, just as no one may

practice medicine unless licensed by the state to do so.

Licensing was initiated originally to protect the public from harm that might result from the incompetent practice of some craft. It was meant to protect laymen from hazards that they themselves could not be expected to detect or to protect themselves against. Licensing is supposed to minimize the potential hazards of things such as contaminated foods or

---

One thing is clear: We should not allow standards to be set by the clumsy hands of bureaucrats.

---

drugs, careless medical practice and unskilled airline pilots.

Over the years, however, the purpose of licensing has broadened. It is now used in some cases as a means of regulating the *number and nature* of practitioners as well as their alleged competence. In some states, for example, the licensing tests for dentists are scored so that only a "desirable" number of applicants are allowed to pass. Aspirants may have to submit to an examination several times (pay their dues) before they will be allowed into the inner sanctum. Licensed, practicing dentists who want to move their practice to another state often find that no amount of competence is enough to earn a license on the first examination. They must take the exam again, and possibly a third time, before they will be allowed into the "club."

The nature of licensing tests verifies the fact that licensing sometimes is a political rather than a professional issue. If the purpose of licensing were to "protect the public" from its inability to detect and avoid certain hazards, then it would be done on the basis of demonstrated competence. The only applicants licensed would be those who could demonstrate an ability to apply those skills of the craft which, if improperly applied, would put the public at undue risk.

This is hardly the case. Licensing examinations are generally multiple-choice tests that determine whether candidates can recall some esoteric points of theory rather than whether they can perform the tasks of the craft. FCC exams for licensing radio and television engineers are, for the most part, multiple-choice tests on the theory of electronics. Trick questions are included. The examinations used by the state medical and dental boards are similar. The items, in other words, are only marginally appropriate for testing anyone's ability to *practice* a given craft.

To get around this bureaucratic tangle, at least one medical school tells its students, "First we'll teach you the practice of medicine. Then, in your senior year, we'll give you a course on how to pass the state boards." This system has evolved because the skills needed for passing the boards are only tangentially related to the competent practice of medicine.

Are standards, codes of ethics, certification or licensing worthwhile to the craft of instructional technology? Will trainers perform better if we have them? Who will be harmed if we don't—or if we do? What reasons are given for regulating trainers?

Now that we have explored each of the four key concepts in the wrangle over regulation, let's examine the advisability of each—for instructional technologists.

Standards

Standards should be defined to reflect good practice, not merely good theory. That said, we ask, Who should define the standards of our craft? First let's look at who claims to be eligible to do so.

The impetus is coming from the government, in the guise of protecting the public from incompetents. This push appears to be motivated largely by the serious deterioration of the public schools and is supported by those who certificated public school teachers in the first place. Clearly something must be done to clean up the mess. The lawmakers' natural response is to pass a law and throw some money at the problem in an effort to make it go away. The fact that this hasn't worked very well elsewhere won't keep us from becoming the next target. If someone in the craft doesn't set the standards, the lawmakers will.

If we don't want lawmakers setting standards for us, who should do it? Two possibilities come to mind: the schools of education and instructional technology, or we ourselves—working trainers in the business world, probably as represented by the two major professional groups, NSPI and ASTD. Consider each alternative in turn.

Should the standards be set by universities? They appear to be prime contenders for the privilege, so their own practice should be examined. Unfortunately, there is ample evidence that the very nature of the university system severely discourages any attempt on the part of professors to function as competent practitioners. More to the point, there is a vast difference between how colleges teach and how they exhort students to teach. Their instructors tend not to model the procedures they tell others to use; they don't practice what they preach.

Examples abound. For every instructional technology course that is performance-based, there are dozens that aren't. For every course that tells students what they'll be expected to be able to *do* to be considered competent, there are dozens that don't. For every education course derived through analysis of a real-world need, 100 are subject-matter-driven. For every course that uses performance tests, 100 test the students' ability to memorize details of the topic—and those tests use an item format selected mainly for its ease of scoring. For every course in which students can get credit by proving their competence, there are 100 where students are required to sit through the entire curriculum regardless of how much knowledge or skill they already possess.

Would trainers in the business world heed standards set for them by people who think so little of those standards that they eschew them in their own classrooms? Unlikely.

Universities lose even more credibility as potential standard-setters when one remembers that they have been establishing the standards for the public schools for years. Presumably they must accept some responsibility for the current difficulties in that domain.

What about ASTD or NSPI—should they set the standards? As groups, they are as varied as any others. That is, not all instructional technologists in the business world practice as well as the technology permits. Far too many base their practice on models they've seen in college—except that there is no testing at the end and nobody ever gets away without a certificate. Someone who has never seen a jet should not be setting standards for how airplanes should be built.

What of those who have taken the trouble to learn the craft and who have insisted upon practicing it competently? They could certainly define standards for others to aspire to, but would they have any more credibility than the others?

Perhaps the question really is whether academicians and industrial trainers have anything in common for which standards can be set. For

TERMINOLOGY SUMMARY

TERM:	DEFINITION:	FUNCTION:	USED BY:	TO:
Standard	Description of performance considered to be competent; description of what competent people do when performing a task.	Educate	Recruiters	Select among candidates.
		Guide	Trainers	Develop competent practitioners.
			Learners	Provide learning targets.
Ethics	Description of conduct consistent with a set of values.	Educate	Practitioners	Guide their own performance toward the selected values.
		Judge		Judge other practitioners' conduct in relation to the values.
			Public	Judge practitioners regarding their adherence to the selected values.
Certification	Public assertion or acknowledgment that a given performer has performed according to prescribed standards.	Attest *(Stamp of approval)*	Recruiters	Discriminate among applicants.
			Performers	Establish credibility.
			Public *(Clients)*	Discriminate among possible vendors of services.
Licensing	Permission to perform granted to a given practitioner by an authoritative body.	Control	Regulatory Body	Control number & nature of practitioners.
			Existing Practitioners	Limit competition.
			Public	Identify legally endorsed practitioners.

THE KEY TO WHIZ-BANG TRAINING

A crack team of researchers recently published evidence that adds compelling proof to what we've all suspected for sometime: Instructor selection is the least-important variable in determining the success of a training program.

Over the past three years, the researchers rated 10,000 man-hours of training using nine criteria of trainer effectiveness. The experimental group, 50 randomly selected trainers, was compared to a matched control group including supervisors, managers, insurance agents and snake-oil salespeople. Unfortunately, only 7,000 hours of data from the experimental group could be analyzed. A total of 2,000 hours was labeled "unintelligible," while 1,000 hours were lost when raters couldn't stay awake.

Not unexpectedly, post-test assessments revealed significant increases in knowledge and skills among those who had contact with members of the control group. In contrast, participants in workshops conducted by the 50 trainers actually suffered a slight decrease in post-test knowledge and skills.

The trainers rated higher than the control group on only one variable—"pizzazz." However, consensus on a definition for this term could not be reached, and some evidence pointed to an inverse relationship between "pizzazz" and participant learning.

The researchers reported the following conclusion: "These findings provide overwhelming support for our original hypothesis that anyone can train. Therefore, the widespread practice of selecting trainers based on availability rather than credibility appears to be a viable one."

The following composite sketch of the 50 trainers used in this study provides a practical basis for instructor selection.

Instructor selection criteria

Organizational credibility: Perceived by self and others as a nonexistent entity. Is viewed as a resource by those who have contempt for resources. Mere presence evokes ambivalence.

Knowledge of managerial principles: Relates to and clearly represents unacceptable management principles, supervisory don'ts and antiquated managerial techniques. Makes the return of Theory X look like a panacea.

Knowledge of organizational norms: Thinks "norm" is a guy's name. Compulsively adheres to all policies, procedures, work practices and rules, especially if they've been replaced or never implemented.

Planning and organizing: Establishes elaborate, detailed, time-consuming plans toward the achievement of meaningless goals. Invariably arrives on time for meetings that were never scheduled. Comes to work but can't remember why. Gets lost on the way home.

Communication: Has no clear thoughts or ideas, talks to self but ignores what is said, interrupts self while talking. Expresses self in a manner that can be clearly misunderstood by self and others. Always repeats self, even when not talking.

Leadership: Inspires doubt in peers, subordinates, superiors and clients. Changes mind before making it up. Shows the way only when there's no place to go.

Sensitivity to others: Mislabels own and others' feelings. Offers congratulations for failure, condolences for success. Shares own feelings only when none exist. Thinks feelings are best left unfelt.

Ability to learn: Is suspicious of own and others' ideas. Combines acceptable ideas in ways that lead to rejection. Assimilates vast quantities of unusable information. Forgets more than originally was learned. Renders coherent thoughts incoherent.

Development of subordinates: Has never been introduced to subordinates. Makes arrangements for others to attend training but forgets to inform them. Asks for detailed summaries of training programs, even if cancelled or never attended.

Reprinted from TRAINING, December 1982

---

example, the priorities established and the procedures applied by instructional technologists in industry are quite different from those of teachers in the public schools. And were it not for the fact that the university claims to prepare instructional technologists for real-world practice, there would be little interaction between the university and the world of the industrial trainer.

It is entirely possible that each group should establish its own standards. One thing is clear: We should not allow standards to be set by default, by the clumsy hands of bureaucrats or by those who just happen to have the time to define them.

Ethics

As we defined it, a code of ethics describes how the tasks of a craft should be performed to protect the spirit of trust between client and practitioner and to minimize risk to the health, safety and well-being of others. Does instructional technology need such a code? The answer hinges on the word "risk." Is anyone at *risk* as a result of unethical practice? It would depend, of course, on how the code of ethics was formulated and on which principle was violated.

For example, if a consultant charged a client for services that were not performed, that act would be unethical because it violates a trust. On the other hand, if an instructor knowingly asserted that one or more students were competent to perform tasks when they were not, the act would not only be unethical, it might pose a significant risk to the public: Suppose the students were being taught to set dynamite fuses for blasting at the bottom of a mine shaft or to pilot a commercial airliner.

Since risk to the public from unethical conduct by trainers could be significant (in areas where the consequence of poor performance is serious), it is appropriate to support the development of a code of ethics.

Certification

Should training professionals be certified? As we have already seen, certification is merely the attestation by a second party that someone has completed a given procedure (such as attending a course) or has acquired a given set of proficiencies (such as accomplishing a set of objectives).

Informal certification is a fact of life. Whenever we make a recommendation to a client or colleague, we are informally certifying the competence of the person or company being recommended. Whenever a boss or a client asks us to take on an additional project, we are being informally certified. Whenever a manager who has attended one of our workshops sends his subordinates to attend it, we are being informally certified as an acceptable source of training.

Semiformal certification also is very much with us. Witness all the certificates trainers receive for courses attended and curricula completed.

So do we need formal certification of instructional technologists? Two issues rear their heads, both familiar by now. First, as long as the *basis* of the certification is clear and relevant, certification may be of some value in identifying those who have met the criteria upon which it is based. If a certificate is bestowed for reasons unknown, however, or for reasons unrelated to the attestation, then it is worthless for determining who can do what.

An even larger issue is that of who would do the certifying. Public school teachers have always been certified. (The fact that teacher quality has varied widely over the past few years does not speak well for certification.) University teachers have *never* had to be certified to teach at a university, nor are industrial trainers generally certified to do what they do.

Those who aspire to practice at the state of the art, either in academia or industry, would not accept certification from those who practice outdated methods. Furthermore, they would insist that the certification process be managed by those whose practice is consistent with prescribed standards. It is unlikely, in any event, that the universities would tolerate a requirement for certification, since the professors' definition of academic freedom appears not to include accountability.

Clearly an impasse would arise if certification of one group were to be proposed by another. And yet it appears likely that those working in the domain of higher education will set the standards for those working in industry.

Licensing

Should instructional technologists be licensed? Should some panel sit in judgment on who may and may not practice as an instructional technologist? The argument often offered for licensing is that it protects the public. And yet how many doctors who have been sued for malpractice were not licensed physicians? How many contractors who have botched a job were not licensed? Alas, whatever the motivation for licensing may be at the start, it almost invariably becomes a political instrument used to control the nature and number of people allowed to practice the craft.

Still, let's examine the argument. Is the public at risk from poor instructors? If so, what is the public being protected from?

The only members of "the public" who buy training are students who pay (through taxes) to attend public schools, and those who buy instruction from vocational and technical schools, universities and entrepreneurs. Protecting them would require certification and licensing of those who sell instruction *to* the public: university professors, music teachers, dancing instructors and so on. Such a proposal would be absurd. The public may be cheated by incompetent or unethical practitioners, with or without licensing. The alert buyer of instruction will check references (i.e., sources of informal certification).

Trainers practicing in the industrial arena do not provide services to the public. They provide services to corporate clients who are quite capable of looking out for themselves, since they are accustomed to evaluating the risks of hiring or dealing with any professional. They can, and do, protect themselves from whatever risk there is in selecting an incompetent to provide the services.

Another point. Licensing procedures usually involve testing, and since testing large numbers of people is invariably done in a way that permits machine scoring, one must ask which of the skills we use most on a daily basis could be fairly tested with multiple-choice questions. There's a big difference between deriving a good objective from an interview with a subject-matter specialist and merely *recognizing* a good objective on a multiple-choice test. Tests based on theory, history and taxonomies are completely misleading, since they are *about* instructional technology but not *of* it.

Without licensing, how can people tell if someone is competent or not? The same way they can tell *with* licensing: by checking references, questioning former customers and reviewing samples of actual work. In other words, licensing won't help the craft. It will only make work for more bureaucrats and create added cost for practitioners.

There are other disadvantages to licensing: It may constrain an employer's choice of applicants. It can freeze or slow advances in training technology—and surely the craft of instruction is not mature enough to justify any anchors on its progress. Furthermore, licensed practitioners can become leery of deviating from prescribed procedures. If they feel they will be "burned" for such deviation, they may be much more concerned with covering their backsides than in practicing as well as they know how.

A call for licensing of industrial instructional technologists is unreasonable. If licensing is based on risk to the public, then licensing would be indicated only for those who sell instruction to the public: schoolteachers, college professors and others who offer instruction directly to individuals rather than to the employees of organizations.

The summation

The regulators are looking over our shoulders. They want to tell us what constitutes good practice; they want to tell us who can call themselves instructional technologists; and they want to tell us who can and cannot practice the craft.

Licensing wouldn't help. It would be counterproductive, it wouldn't work as intended, and it would serve only to create a new bureaucracy and added expense for almost everyone. Let us resist all efforts toward licensing.

Certification may or may not be useful, depending on the relevance of the standards upon which the certification is based and on the need for additional safeguards to the public. Our craft hardly needs the shackle of certification, however, especially when standards and a code of ethics are being crafted (which are easier to change as the technology matures than are certification criteria). But however we decide (assuming we are given a choice), let us resist allowing those working in one domain to impose their standards on those working in other domains, whether they be academicians setting standards for industrial trainers or vice versa.

A code of ethics is needed mainly for those who work in professions that involve significant potential risk to the public—medicine, dentistry, law, law enforcement and so on—and whose practitioners accept legal responsibilities to their clients. Our craft can hardly be said to fit that description. Even so, a code of ethics for instructional practitioners can serve to highlight desirable and undesirable practices, reduce a client's risk of being cheated and protect the spirit of trust among practitioners. The development of a code is worth support, especially if it is derived from critical incidents collected from practitioners.

A set of standards could be helpful to those trying to hire competent performers, those aspiring to learn the craft and those trying to teach the craft to others. Let us support efforts to describe standards—provided that those doing the describing are competent and experienced practitioners, not just people who talk about training. Let us support a process of describing standards that involves the thinking and experience of the widest practical representation of practitioners, and of the clients who come into contact with them.

Reprinted from TRAINING, September 1985

LOOKING FOR THE 'IDEAL' INSTRUCTOR?

Choosing the best instructors depends
on your ability to judge their commitment
to produce good learning

BY MARTIN M. BROADWELL

Selecting the best instructors for your program can be difficult unless you know how to assess a teacher's ability to produce learning. Martin Broadwell offers some helpful insights to help you make the choice.

Q. What characteristics should I look for in selecting instructors?

A. Interestingly enough, and perhaps sadly enough, the one characteristic that is most often first is availability: Is the person available for the period of time the course will be run? Can the person be spared from the job for that period of time? At one time I was critical of people who used this as a criterion. But after thinking over the problems involved in keeping an organization going, I've decided this is a legitimate consideration.

If we're any good at instructor training, certainly we aren't required to accept only one person, no matter how busy or important to the organization that person is. But we do have to consider availability among the factors influencing our choice.

It is also important to note that we can't always judge an instructor's characteristics accurately. We don't get a chance to judge instructors under classroom situations until they get in the classroom, so we have to accept something that looks like the characteristics we want. Hopefully, our judgment will be good enough.

Q. How important is it that the person be open-minded about methods of instruction?

A. If the person hasn't had experience, we're going to have to do some teaching of techniques. The person who comes along and already has a set mind on teaching techniques is going to become a difficult problem. We want instructors who are committed to producing learning and who are willing to listen to ways of doing it.

This means finding people who have a respect for teaching technology and who believe there are good and bad ways of teaching, as opposed to those who believe teachers are born, not made. (It seems to me that the people who think this invariably believe that fortunately for everyone, they just happen to be among the people who were born lucky!)

Q. How can you recognize this attitude ahead of time?

A. An interview will tell much in a few minutes. Ask leading questions like, "What are your feelings about some of the different techniques now being used in the teaching field?" Unfortunately you may hear answers like, "I think that sooner or later we'll come back to the old ways, which were pretty good; after all, a lot of people learned a lot or this organization wouldn't be where it is today," or "I'm not really up on the latest techniques, but I'll bet there are some exciting things going on

now." Variations of these answers will tell us a lot. We can also find out how much motivation is going to be required in order to get newer techniques accepted.

Q. Will a good instructor be enthusiastic about his subject?

A. Yes, but that's only part of it. We want an instructor who can get excited over producing learning—any kind of learning. Sometimes we mistake enthusiasm for a subject as enthusiasm for teaching that subject. People who are enthusiastic about a subject will talk for hours on it. People who are enthusiastic about teaching a subject will spend hours finding ways of getting people to learn. We'd prefer to choose an instructor who is enthusiastic about getting learning to take place in the classroom, whatever the subject may be.

Q. What value do you place on the ability to communicate?

A. Two items you always see on teacher qualification lists are "empathy" and "ability to communi-

> ## "The teacher needs to keep the students thinking as long as possible."

cate." I'd like to amend, as well as combine, the two and say that what we really want is somebody who can think on the student level. Whatever we call that skill, those who have it are more likely to communicate with the empathy required. Many who seem to be good at communicating fail because they can't estimate the student level. (By the way, when we say "the student level" we aren't necessarily saying that we mean down at the student level. Those teachers who can believe that students know as much as they do are the real heroes.)

As for empathy, perhaps it's best described by the motto, "Don't judge a man until you've walked a mile in his shoes." Teachers may have a hard time thinking the way students do, but even trying will help.

TURNING SUBJECT MATTER EXPERTS INTO CLASSROOM TRAINERS

When using line personnel as trainers, the training director often derives one major benefit—field-learned expertise—at the cost of several methodological headaches. Jack Slagle, director of management development and training for Houston's Anderson, Clayton and Company, has been using line personnel for training and has some preventive medicine for those headaches.

First, Slagle suggests, find an approach that puts the line personnel at ease. Use learner-controlled instruction methods where a large number of learners must cover a broad area of subject matter. Invite line experts to speak to the trainees in groups and allow trainees to question them individually over a several-hour session. "We find the amount of learning that applies immediately is greater," Slagle says, "using the LCI approach than with using any other method."

Anderson, Clayton and Company also uses traditional lecture, but Slagle warns that this method relies heavily upon the skill of the presenter. By making the line person a discussion leader, however, some of the presentation problems are solved. The leader receives a guide and the training department gives him or her a list of questions, areas of interest and firm objectives.

The workshop technique, Slagle believes, is an easy one for line personnel. "They like the idea of working in a training situation with material taken from their own problems," Slagle adds, "and this technique gives the line person a non-threatening way to experiment with problems faced in the field. Also, it generates enthusiasm because the trainees are handling actual problems." But, he warns, line people tend to get so involved in the problem that they ramble far beyond the specific topic. So some limits must be set.

When using line personnel as trainers, problems arise in the areas of program material preparation and instructor preparation. "Materials must be prepared in great detail," Slagle advises, "because line people are usually more comfortable in free-wheeling discussions than in classroom settings. And they are more at ease with prepared visual aids rather than those that require writing on a chalkboard or pad."

Since line people are already content experts, the major job in preparing the instructor is in the area of presentation techniques. "Be sure to have material for a session available well in advance," he continues, "so the line person can prepare at his or her own pace and can add techniques or methods to personalize the presentation. And don't be afraid to criticize—most line people will welcome the opportunity to hone a new skill as a presenter."

Finally, Slagle says, be sure that the actual presentation of material goes smoothly by assisting the line person during the session and just before. The trainer should check all audiovisual equipment, organize any handouts and control the training environment. "Then place the line person in front of the room and pace the floor and chew your fingernails until the presentation is over," Slagle says.

After the presentation, Slagle advises, evaluate the training by relating it to the objectives set out at the beginning. "The first, but least valid, evaluation is the immediate feedback you get from a survey questionnaire," he insists, "because this may only reflect the rapport built up by the instructor." Rely, instead, on the way the training presentation solves the identified operating problems that required the training in the first place. In the case of Clayton, Anderson, Jack Slagle has found that the use of line personnel helps solve more problems than the use of untrained instructors creates.

Reprinted from TRAINING, August 1978

Q. If you could pick the one characteristic which would go farthest toward making the teacher a success, what would it be?

A. That's easy. For an answer, I'll borrow from Malcolm Knowles. He suggests that it is the subtle quality of evasiveness. The idea is that the teacher needs to keep the students thinking as long as possible. It means the ability to turn a question back to the learner or to the rest of the class in a subtle way. The skill lies in asking another question or giving just enough information so that the student stays in the conversation and keeps trying to get the answer. Ideally, the rest of the group will pitch in and collectively come up with the answer.

I like to think of it as letting the students keep as many of the *Aha*'s as they can. Inexperienced and self-centered instructors seem to covet these *Aha*'s and keep the juicy ones for themselves. Note the fallacy of the thinking here: If we've done such a good job of presenting information in a logical way, and the conclusion is very obvious, the student should be able to get it without any trouble. On the other hand, if we have to give the conclusion because we think the student will have trouble getting it, then there must be something wrong with our presentation.

There used to be a sign on the wall at the Kennedy Space Center in Florida that struck me as applying here: "Remember, a Confused Mind Is an Active Mind." The subtle quality of evasiveness is a matter of keeping the students' minds a little confused—but with light at the end of the tunnel—until enough activity has produced a genuine *Aha*.

Reprinted from TRAINING, September 1975

TONING DOWN YOUNG TRAINERS—WITHOUT TURNING THEM OFF

Troubles with novice trainers can
complicate your work as training director
and confuse trainees, too.
Here's how to be firm with new blood
without stifling creativity.

BY FRANK T. WYDRA
AND KATHLEEN WHITESIDE

Novice trainers can be the bane
of the training director. They
do not know, thus fail to follow,
the rules of the trade. Consequently,
they often cause problems for the unsuspecting training director.

Novice trainers are usually drawn
from the ranks of the technical experts, the upwardly mobile or the
newly graduated. Regardless of
where they come from, they view
their stay in the training department
as no more than a way station on
the track to their career objective.

Experts expect to move to other
opportunities that will provide an
even greater depth of knowledge.
High-potential, upwardly mobile line
managers expect to be awarded their
own lines. New grads, brimful of
theory, expect to find fame, and occasionally fortune, as consultants.
None expect to stay in the training
department. They are movers. Because they are transients, their actions, as they enter the training department, are predictable; they will
try to change things.

Novice trainers want to change
what is taught, how it is taught or
both. They are invariably impatient
with things as they are. Inexplicably,
they are usually given the chance to
make change. Accommodating their
quest for change may be a part of
our cultural heritage. Training departments have traditionally been
peopled by corporate nomads, or
those who, given the opportunity,
migrate from position to position. In
this environment the novice trainer

is unwittingly given license.

Ergo, the novice trainer who is an
expert will be permitted to demonstrate expertise and show the possession of "new" knowledge. The high-
potential person will try to bring the
"real world" into the Ivory Tower
and, incidentally, to make a visible
mark in that tower. Newly graduated
novices will try to implement labori-
ously learned theory, often without
regard to its utility in the situation.
It is what they know; it is what they
were hired to demonstrate. For all of
them, and for the unsuspecting training director, the code word is
innovation.

The altar of innovation

To innovate is to create. To innovate is to make the world a better
place in which to live. To innovate is
to make that mark, to garner that
reputation. But, in the end, to innovate is to initiate change.

In a discipline that prides itself on
innovation it is sometimes difficult
to insist on caution. Indeed, that
change may be counterproductive.
Innovation has such charm that
training professionals sometimes
make it an end in itself. Never mind
that the change is not needed; that it
has been tried before and has
demonstrated a failure to meet objectives. Never mind that it conflicts
with, or ignores, what is known
about the technology of learning.
Never mind that it is less effective,
more expensive or less efficient than
other approaches. And, never mind
that it is irrelevant to the task at

hand. For it is *innovative*. And so,
when trainers stand before the altar
of innovation, they ignore its faults.

Aside from the fact that novice
trainers are often encouraged to innovate, it usually is to their advantage to do so. The personal
agenda must be met; the track record
must be established; the expertise
must be displayed. These are significant incentives for novices who seek
change. And, being rational, they
respond to the incentive.

These circumstances make it difficult for training directors who on
one hand want to encourage innovation but who, on the other hand, are
responsible for generating effective,
efficient, validated instructional programs. How can you manage this
built-in conflict? How are you to
mediate between the bright, aggressive, articulate, on-the-way-to-the-top
course developer and the naive, vulnerable learner?

Accomplished training directors
will use their entire repertoire of
skills to manage the novice trainer
and protect the learner. They will
clearly specify outcomes, deliver assignments in manageable chunks,
provide timely and appropriate feedback and reinforce the novice as
mastery is successively approxi-
mated. But these are broad-sweep
strategies. On a scale less grand, the
training director can set down some
rules for the novice trainer to follow.

Rules of the road

Unfortunately, rules are anathe-
matic to the training professional. In
a permissive society, particularly one
that values creativity, rules are often
avoided. The rule makers are reluctant to develop them and the rule
followers ignore them. But without
rules progress is, at best, erratic.

The energy spent on activity is
greater than the result produced.
And it is this shortfall that so often
frustrates the training director
charged with the responsibility for
accomplishment. If we are to have a
training discipline, we must have
people following rules. The rules
must benefit those who make them
and those who follow them. The investment in rule making and the cost
of aborted creativity must produce
outcomes that clearly justify the
expenditures.

Like honest people, good rules are
hard to find. There are three, though,
that can be suggested to help you
manage novice trainers, for it is they
who most often violate them.

Rule 1: Follow established training
procedures until you have mastered

them; introduce change only when you can show, from your own experience, that the standard methods will not work.

This rule insists on rigid adherence to a model, any model. It matters not what model is used. Instead, it is important to follow a predefined course. For if the route is known, it is always possible to determine where the traveler strayed from the path. In the design of programs, and in their execution, there are often steps that do not make sense to novices.

To the neophyte designer, developing unambiguous objectives or validating tasks may seem like academic exercises. The creativity of writing a program is far more exciting than the routines of specification and evaluation. So they are skipped, or at best, glossed over. But when the program fails or is judged to be irrelevant, the culprit is usually found to be innovation without experience, change in the name of creativity. The novice, under the guise of innovation, has abandoned the model and strayed from the path.

When it appears that a process does not work, often it is the trainer and not the process that is deficient. Before jumping to conclusions about fault, both the training director and the novice trainer need to assure themselves that all steps of the program or process have been faithfully executed. Then, if the results are still unsatisfactory, the validity of the program (rather than the quality of its execution) can be legitimately questioned.

From time to time, though, the training program or process is in fact faulty. It doesn't work. It is then, having won their stripes through experience, that the novice trainer can rightfully take command of creation. They can revise with authority.

Rule 2: Remember that your program is not as important as the response of the learner.

The second rule requires novices to put the needs of the learner first. It shifts the focus from the process of training to its product, the learned person. Trainers become emotionally involved with programs they design or present. Programs seem to take on a life of their own.

This relationship is akin to that of parent and child. The trainer conceives the program, breathes life into it, shapes its character and takes pride as it develops to maturity. The presenter, through tryout after tryout, develops a style that could be mistaken for the personality of the program. Even in the naming of a program the deliberation is reminis-

cent of the naming of a newborn.

Given this emotional and intellectual investment, it is understandable why a trainer might resist changes that would be made solely to benefit an emotionally distant, impersonal learner. But, in reality, a program is not a person. It has no personality. There is no life, no death. It is the learner who has life and the need for the trainer's attention. It is the learner who needs to be nurtured, developed, strengthened and brought to maturity. If a learner suffers in an overzealous drive to keep a program or a presentation intact, then true harm has been done.

This rule reminds the novice trainer that the object of training is the learner's response. If the learner fails to make the expected response, the program is faulty and must be changed. The long-forgotten motto of merchandising can be paraphrased to read "The learner is always right." The learner is never at fault, only programs are.

The only direct control a trainer has is control over the program. Consequently, if the trainer is to change anything, it has to be the program. This second rule will keep the priorities of the novice trainer in proper perspective. In the process, the needs of both the training director and the learner will be served.

Rule 3: Measure your program by whether it does what you said it would do and not by what it actually does.

Obviously, to apply this rule, you must state performance expectations and measure performance outcomes. At issue is the standard used to gauge accomplishment.

Our technology is based on predictability. Although it is possible for great training programs to be created accidentally, it is not probable. Competent trainers are technicians more than they are artists. To move from artist to technician, the novice trainer needs to embrace the rigorous discipline of prediction, application, measurement and comparison.

In the act of comparison, you establish standards. If the standard is rigorous, you'll find a precise comparison of outcome to prediction. Lax standards, however, make for hazy comparisons. A dishonest standard yields a forced or fabricated comparison. The novice trainer who has not learned the differences between lax, rigorous and dishonest comparisons can easily employ a practice that would measure a program by what it does and not by what the trainer said it would do.

Standards vary from company to company. They come in all flavors;

some are lax; others are rigorous; most fall in between. You can achieve lax standards without effort or discipline. Although they are not very challenging, lax standards are basically honest. But it is both sloppy and dishonest to establish standards after you know the results of training.

And yet frequently, in testing a program, the objectives are gerrymandered to conform to the responses of the learner. Worse yet, sometimes the objectives of a program are developed after the program has been written and tested. These "standards" are phony, although they allow the trainer to state accurately that the outcome "matches" the objective. People who don't know better assume that the objective was specified before the outcome was known. This sleight of hand surely defeats the purpose of validation.

On the surface, the transgression seems minor. After all, the outcome being claimed for the program actually happened. It was an outcome demonstrated by a learner. But the comparison is not set up to test the response of the learner; it is the program and its predictability that is being validated.

If you can't predict the outcome of a program, it is poorly designed. Unpredictable results are unfair both to the learner and to the organization that requires the program. Both invested something in the product of the trainer: one, time; the other, money. Neither deserves to take a risk that could have been avoided. Neither deserves less than a predictable result.

By insisting that novice trainers follow the third rule, the training director will bring discipline to the training process and challenge rather than inhibit precision. In the process the novice trainer will learn that training is not an exercise in unbridled innovation, but rather a discipline for the effective and efficient transfer of skills and knowledge.

The novice trainer need not be the bane of the training director. Regardless of their background, experts, line managers and academically trained specialists can learn to become effective trainers. Converting the novice to the master trainer is the responsibility of the training director. The task is made easier if, in the process of conversion, the training director uses the rules of following process, regard for the learner and predictive validation. Once mastered, the time for creativity will have arrived.

Reprinted from TRAINING, June 1982

A TRAINING AID FOR SMALL GROUP SKILL DEVELOPMENT

If trainers need help perfecting "stand-up skills"—walk them through it with tent cards

BY GEOFFREY M. BELLMAN

Many trainers—especially new ones—need help to develop their own professional kit bags, their "stand-up skills" for working with groups. These skills range from simple, physical actions to perceptions and sensitivities which can be as difficult to describe as they are important.

What skills should training directors and managers build into their trainers? Some are physical (eye contact, volume, ennunciation, emphasis, speed, gestures, timing, and so forth). Others involve process (climate setting, contracting, decision-making, feedback, and others related to participative learning). Another set of skills relates to workshop design: objectives, knowledge of content, training techniques and methods, visuals, design continuity and unity, reinforcement of learning, and adult learning. All of these and more can be learned in a train-the-trainer setting, using the tent cards printed here. Each card focuses on one of eight areas of trainer skill development: content, design, methods, leadership, participation, adult learning, visuals, and time. These encompass most aspects of a trainer's performance, but you may want to construct cards of your own to better meet your special training needs.

Assume you are going to be training five new trainers in stand-up training skills for a supervisory training program. Before the session, cut out the cards along the solid lines. Select four (not five) of the eight skill areas you want to emphasize. (You pick four, since one of the trainers will be leading while the other four critique his performance.) Let's assume you select Design, Leadership, Participation, and Time. Fold each card along the dotted line. One side of the card shows the skill area in bold letters. Related questions are on the other side.

Tell your five trainer-trainees you will be concentrating on these four skill areas (as printed in bold type on the cards facing them). Discuss what these areas mean and ask the trainers to list likely indicators of skill and lack of skill in each area. Collect their responses and post them on the wall for later use.

Distribute the cards to four of the five trainers. The remaining trainer will be the first leader. Each of the observing trainers sits behind a tent card with its heading facing the leader, thus reminding the leader which behaviors to watch closely during the session.

Ask the observers to read the questions on the backs of their cards. This will tell the trainer in specific terms what is being reviewed. After the trainers finish reading their cards, tell them that they will be asked to evaluate the leader's presentation based on their cards' questions. For example, the observer with the Design card will later answer the questions on objectives, direction, instructions, and so on.

The leader begins leading. The observers observe, frequently participate, and take notes, if this is not too distracting to the session leader.

When the leader finishes, give the observers two to three minutes to write comments in response to their cards' questions. Ask the session leader to critique his presentation before hearing from the others. This will help the trainers become more competent and confident in self-evaluation.

After the leader has finished his self-evaluation, have the observers answer the questions on the backs of their cards. This helps them focus their critiques on specific questions. Give the leader a chance to ask for further clarification on comments and to add more self-evaluative statements. By now, you should have heard a fairly specific critique which you may want to supplement. Refer the group to their pre-session written comments, which you posted earlier.

Select a second leader. Rotate the four cards among the observers. This gives each observer something new to look for in the second presentation. Repeat the process until all five trainers have lead once and observed from four different viewpoints. It may take two hours or two days, depending on session length, depth of critique, and type of training involved. It can be repeated by folding the cards inside out and critiquing on content, methods, adult learning, and visuals. You may take as strong a leadership role as you like.

Design your own tent cards. Or, involve the new trainers in designing the cards. Talk with them about their needs and the kinds of behaviors they think are important for a trainer. Divide behaviors into a small number of evaluation areas and help trainers design questions in each area.

Questionnaires are another possibility that can be useful in situations when the new trainers are anxious about how others will see their initial performances. But use questionnaires carefully and only as a first step leading to group discussion of new trainer performance.

The cards also can be used by a group to evaluate another group in action. This is a fishbowl situation in which the inside group knows the kinds of actions and behaviors the outside group is considering as it observes the inside group perform. This can be especially useful in developing trainers' awareness of group processes. A group of four or five new trainers seated in the middle of a circle works together on a problem while four or five other trainers observe, using specific group process criteria. After the first group finishes its performance and critique, the outside group moves into the center and the process is repeated.

579

TRAINEES GIVE TRAINER A BEHAVIOR CHECKLIST

Will students learn *in spite of* the teacher? Dr. Charles F. Martinetz believes they will. In informal research conducted by Dr. Martinetz while serving as an instructional technologist for AT&T, student feedback indicates that he's right. And a study by Morsh and Wilder, published in *The Encyclopedia of Educational Research*, states that "no specific, observable, teacher act has yet been found whose frequency or percent of occurrence is invariably and significantly correlated with student achievement."

Martinetz decided to investigate what teaching behaviors students felt were important. He found, not surprisingly, that most of the classic dos and don'ts of training held true in the classroom. For instance, Martinetz's

Instructor's Checklist	
DOS	**DON'TS**
1. Make opening remarks	1. Don't break time agreements
2. Make the class comfortable	2. Don't waste time
3. State your objectives	3. Don't monopolize classroom conversation
4. Know your material	4. Don't lose them
5. Be prepared	5. Don't read your material
6. Use training aids	6. Don't fake it
7. Establish rapport	7. Don't interrupt students' answers
8. Show enthusiasm	8. Don't be pompous
9. Encourage participation	9. Don't lose your students' respect
10. Be flexible	10. Don't be undignified
11. Maintain control	11. Don't ridicule or intimidate
12. Answer questions	12. Don't bring your problems into class
13. Provide feedback	13. Don't display distracting mannerisms
14. Evaluate progress	14. Don't be a dictator
15. Be yourself	15. Don't lock horns

students felt that answering questions as they occurred to the students, rather than waiting for an established question-and-answer period, was a definite "do." And breaking time agreements concerning when to start, stop or take a break was just as definitely a "don't."

Based on his poll of students, Dr. Martinetz created an instructor's checklist. He recommends referring to the "dos" list prior to class, so the concepts will remain fresh in the instructor's mind. The "don'ts" list should be read after completing a class, when the behavior is still recallable.

Reprinted from TRAINING, March 1978

Strengths and Weaknesses

One weakness is that this process does not work well when trainers do not have a chance to display their skills frequently. Secondly, its structure turns off some people—especially experienced trainers—who see it as elementary game playing. Third, the questions and question areas tend to confine the observers' thinking to what is printed on the cards.

The strengths of the process are its visibility and simplicity. For new trainers who have not been through an evaluation of their skills before, a simple, down-to-earth process is not only attractive, it tends to reduce their anxiety because its main elements are readily apparent. It clarifies how they will be critiqued by putting before them—on the cards—the main elements of the critique. So, many elements of the process relieve the tension a new trainer naturally feels as he or she begins to demonstrate new training skills.

Process content and the process itself are adaptable. Reviewing the tent cards with the trainers helps them understand and appreciate the importance of these elements of their learning.

The cards before the new trainers constantly remind them of the skills they are developing. And, importantly, they get to hear the views of others on their work. The process also emphasizes the importance of self-evaluation. Since they have a chance to critique themselves first, the trainers can begin to learn to be their own best evaluators. And isn't that what training trainers is all about?

Reprinted from TRAINING, June 1976

PARTICIPATION

1. How did the leader affect the group? How aware was the leader of his effect?
2. Give examples of how the group responded to the session.
3. How many in the group participated? How long? In what ways?
4. How would you describe the group's behavior?

CONTENT

1. What is the primary content of this session?
2. How was this content made clear to you?
3. What does the leader do that causes you to believe he knows the content?
4. What does he do that causes you to doubt content knowledge?

DESIGN

1. Are the session objectives clear? Does the group share in them? How do you know?
2. How did the leader give the group a sense of direction?
3. Critique instructions the leader gave to the group.
4. How did the leader reinforce learning?
5. What gave unity to the design of the session?

METHODS

1. Write down every training method you see used in this session.
2. Which were most effective? Why?
3. Which were least effective? Why?
4. Name three alternative methods the leader could have used.

ADULT LEARNINGS

LEADERSHIP

1. How did the leader relate to or draw on the group's experience?
2. How did the leader relate content to group needs?
3. How did the leader acknowledge the variety of learning styles within the group?
4. What did the leader do to establish the learning climate?

1. How did the leader respond to group needs?
2. What decisions were made during the session? How?
3. How much control did the leader exhibit? The group?
4. What techniques did the leader use to move the group through the design?
5. How would you describe the leader's style?

VISUALS

TIME

1. Name all the visuals used during the session. Which were most effective? Why? Which were least effective? Why?
2. What other visual techniques could have been useful in this session?
3. How did the leader use himself as a visual aid?
4. What messages did this convey?

1. Keep track of the time spent on each major segment of the session.
2. Note how much time the leader talked or lead.
3. Describe the pace for each major segment.
4. How did the pace feel to you?
5. How could the leader have used the available time better?

HOW TO WRITE
—AND RECOGNIZE—
QUALITY
INSTRUCTOR MANUALS

**Whether you develop your own training
materials or buy them off-the-shelf,
one of the most important considerations
is the quality of the accompanying
instructor's manual**

BY RON ZEMKE

When your task is not only to train, but to design and develop program materials others can use to achieve reliable, predictable training outcomes, everything is important. So it is small surprise that the once lowly task of building the instructor's teaching guide—or manual—has experienced a rally in respect that would bring tears to Rodney Dangerfield's eyes.

At least that is one of the conclusions gleaned from conversations with seven instructional design experts TRAINING asked to explain how they design leaders' guides. And while the experts' advice may help you put together guides for your own training courses, it will also be valuable when you are in the market for somebody else's program.

Now more than ever, the leader's manual plays a dramatically important role in successfully implementing a training program, according to Dr. Peter Esseff, president of Educational Systems for the Future®, an instructional development firm in Columbia, MD.

"We didn't use to feel that way," Esseff says. "But experience has taught us that unless we offer a slip-proof track to run on, we can't take for granted the next instructor will get the course to do what we designed it to. And that is true even where the course is heavy in self-instruction materials."

William J. Payne, director of instruction and conference services at Wilson Learning Corp. in Eden Prairie, MN, agrees wholeheartedly,

adding: "Today's concept of a leader's guide is more than a simple list of 'what-to-do-to-kill-time-between-videotapes' activities. It is the quality control mechanism of the course."

Central to this new view of the humble instructor's manual is the realization that trainers need to know quite a bit more about the program designer's intent than was previously believed. Says Payne, "The instructor's guide is really the only place all the key concepts come together; where the instructor can see the whole concept map and the way the activities, examples and exercises support the key concepts." Moreover, adds Esseff, "The instructor's guide should contain just about everything the instructor might need."

Make no mistake, however; the effective leader's manual is not merely a junk drawer for instructional whatnots. It is a carefully conceptualized package, the most commonly prescribed element of which is the session or teaching outline.

The outline

In this regard, the instructor's manual serves the same purpose as a cookbook, says Victor Rosansky, vice president of Organizational Dy-

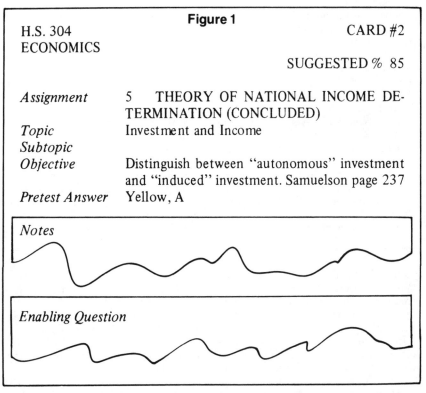

Figure 1

H.S. 304
ECONOMICS

CARD #2

SUGGESTED % 85

Assignment   5   THEORY OF NATIONAL INCOME DETERMINATION (CONCLUDED)

Topic   Investment and Income

Subtopic

Objective   Distinguish between "autonomous" investment and "induced" investment. Samuelson page 237

Pretest Answer   Yellow, A

Notes

Enabling Question

One way to present instructor information is illustrated here, *a sample page from Danny Langdon's* Instructional Design Library. *Using such a generic format, a trainer can fill in the assignment, topic, subtopic, objective and test answers while leaving room below for notes and questions.*

EXPERT ADVICE FOR MANUAL WRITERS

BY RON ZEMKE

Though experts TRAINING interviewed make it clear writing or evaluating an instructor's manual is more complex than you might think, each offers a few tips. The following thought-starters, along with the views expressed in the main article, should serve you well the next time you are called on to build, buy or revise an instructor' manual.

☐ **Peter and Mary Esseff are sticklers for detail**: Tend to the details, their message goes, and the reliability of the instructor's manual will be nearly taken care of. Some of their favorite detailing tips are:

• Include a comprehensive table of contents to the manual so the trainer can find what he/she needs without undue fumbling.

• Include a single list of all the resources needed to conduct each session.

• Give detailed instructions for use of "props" and alternative procedures, including the use of optional cases and roles plays. Also specify a back-up plan for malfunctioning props.

• If role plays or live simulations are used, provide details of not only the role play and case set-ups but detailed instructions on how to watch performance, and give feedback as a group as well.

• Give alternatives to all cases, examples, problems and group exercises. These could even be of varying difficulty.

☐ **Kandis Lange prides herself on being able to design** easy-to-use leaders' guides. The key to her success is a split-page technique she says yields easy visual access. Favorite tips to making it work include:

• Alternate blocks of information vertically as well as horizontally (content in the left column, methods and techniques to the right, time-frame information far right). Placing content and instructional technique side by side can be visually confusing.

• Make the instructor's manual complete, but encourage course leaders to write a personalized, condensed teaching outline, once they have shown mastery of the material.

• If you use special symbols to indicate activities or special media, use a few symbols, keep them simple and use them consistently.

• Put all chalkboard or flip-chart graphics in the instructor's guide just as they should appear on the board or newsprint.

☐ **When designing a leader's guide, Bill Payne walks a tightrope** between detail and completeness, leaving room for the instructor to personalize and be creative. He suggests several things:

• Include a leader's handbook, separate from the actual leader's guide. It is a good place for storing backup material and nice-to-knows.

• Put the leader's guide in a notebook that folds out into a free-standing lectern, frees the instructor's hands and brings the material closer to eye level.

• Use large, easy-to-see print.

• Include a one-page course outline that gives major topic headings and suggested time frames.

• When design calls for multiple video segments, include both the first two or three sentences and last two or three sentences of dialogue or narrative of each segment in the leader's guide. The instructor can then tell if she or he is at the right start and stop point.

• Recap all video segments on one page. Include running times, postage readings and reel numbers.

• Include a flowchart of the course's key concepts and supporting activities. Instructors *and* trainees sometimes profit from seeing the fit and flow of ideas in skeleton form.

• Prepare a page or two of "miniatures" of the charts and overheads used in the sessions. Trainees and beginning trainers ask for them and use them as memory aids.

☐ **Victor Rosansky and Stanley Wachs prefer the word "facilitate"** over "instruct." Among their tips are these:

• Keep sessions simple, clear and group-focused, not instructor-focused. If you can capture what you need for a session on a single 8½" × 11" page, you're on the right track.

• Highlight key transitional material. Take care to clarify the transitions from point to point or from theory to practice; the exercises and activities will take care of themselves.

• Highlight activities with distinctive headings in the leader's guide.

☐ **Danny Langdon has only one overriding rule**: Preplan or preprogram as much flexibility for the instructor as possible. One of his strategies calls for developing multiple, one-page lesson plans, each with a different or alternative method or "style" of achieving the instructional objectives.

There is no such thing as a perfect instructor's manual. Experience, background, subject matter and a dozen other variables preclude it. But the common theme is straightforward: Help the users do good, but don't keep them from doing even better. And that is the sort of goal best considered a journey and not at all a destination.

Reprinted from TRAINING, March 1982

---

namics Inc. (ODI) in Burlington, MA. "You can quickly find the key ingredients," he notes, "and the step-by-step, nitty-gritty back-up material."

In the outline, as well as in the entire manual, structure and format are important, according to Kandis Lange, director of program development with Practical Management Associates, in Canoga Park, CA. "We use a split-page format for our instructor manuals," she explains.

"Content is in the left column, teaching techniques in the center and time frames on the right."

But no matter what the content, she adds, "we don't consider the instructor's manual a tool for teaching. It is really a tool for preparing to teach. I encourage people to condense the content portion of the manual and prepare an abbreviated teaching guide that is comfortable for them and personalized."

Personalization of the outline is a theme many experts sounded. The most extreme view comes from Danny G. Langdon, manager of corporate training, Morrison-Knudson, Boise, ID, and editor of the 32-volume *Instructional Design Library* (Educational Technology Publications, 1978). Langdon says that "The extent to which one can personalize the teaching guide of a program—the lesson plan, really—is critically important."

Toward that end, Langdon espouses a technique he has dubbed the "Construct Lesson Plan," which calls for extensive pretesting of trainees. "I prefer making multiple resources available to instructors," says Langdon. "That includes media alternatives and letting the instructor set his or her own lesson plan, based on trainee pretesting and instructor preferences."

But regardless of how much or how little personalizing of the teaching outline the experts encouraged, all warned that the leader's guide be viewed as a springboard rather than a shackle.

"The facilitator's manual isn't designed to be taken literally," argues ODI's Rosansky. "Instead of giving the instructor three snappy jokes to lead into a discussion of motivation, it should get the instructor to face the issues the designer had in mind. New instructors have to discover their own awareness of the importance of the topic, their own insights into the material."

Stanley Wachs, director of training for ODI, piggybacks on that idea. "The trainees and their needs are the proper focus of a training session," he says. "The instructor's manual should contain everything needed to prepare you to do that. The teaching guide should just remind you of what you planned to do." Adds Payne: "The best guide is designed to be done away with. The more you use it, the less you should need it."

Although some designers prefer the teaching outline be closely scripted, most oppose that tack. "You can't expect the instructor's guide to do the teaching," says PMA's Lange. "It is not a book or procedures manual to be read aloud." Another danger of too precise scripting is that it encourages new trainers to talk too much, notes Payne.

But while scripting is considered taboo, the experts agree on the importance of including specific questions. "Don't just write 'Ask a feedback question here,' " says Lange. "Give the exact question to be asked, as well as the answers the instructor can expect and the ones he should accept. Don't make the instructor guess the proper question."

Payne, however, cautions against including too much about acceptable answers. "New instructors will lean on that," he says. "And once they start the 'Well-let's-see-what-answers-the-manual-suggests' routine, they are about to lose the class. Pretty soon the group just says, 'The heck with what we think. What does the manual say?' That isn't using the knowledge of the group."

Figure 2

All questions to the class are in CAPITAL LETTERS. This symbol in front of a question means that this is a very important question.

This symbol indicates a statement of some importance to make to the class.

The key symbol appears next to the concept which is the main point of the discussion. Be sure to drive this point home.

The TV symbol indicates that the appropriate video segment should be shown.

The material next to this symbol is best developed on the board.

If your students are doing what is stated in this circle, you have just accomplished one of the major learning objectives of the unit. Note that the objectives in this symbol correspond to the behavioral objectives stated at the beginning of each unit.

Graphics often help catch the trainer's eye *and draw quick attention to important aspects of a presentation. Use symbols such as these pictured here to keep your session on track. And look for some kind of graphics when you evaluate a training course–and its manual.*

To enhance their effectiveness, questions should focus on process rather than content, says ODI's Wachs. "The best questions are ones that open up to other questions," he says. "Compare-and-contrast questions, 'Have you ever seen this in your company?' questions are good. But the key is that questioning must help the group make the transition from theory to what's going on in real life. Those transitions into and out of the material should be personalized, developed by the instructor for his or her organization and written down. They are precious insights into the material. The task is to keep turning people inward to look at their own jobs in relation to the material."

The experts also disagree on the appropriateness of "time lining" a teaching outline, or specifying where an instructor should be and by when. Lange includes a "time-frame" column on her split-page format, but emphasizes "instructor discretion." Others argue the necessity of including an hour-by-hour agenda. "Instructors must know how they are progressing," insists Mary Esseff, vice president of Educational Systems for the Future®.

Wachs is less concerned about time and teaching points, recommending only that the instructor have a one-page-per-session summary of key points and transitions. "Keep in mind we are working with adult learners in a work-related situation," he says. "The trainer's job is to find out what they want to get out of the experience, and to help them think about their jobs in relation to the ideas being introduced. That takes the time it takes."

Payne prefers to keep time lines at arm's length. "We strenuously resist the urge to say, 'You have to be here by Wednesday afternoon coffee break and here by Friday morning.' When you do that, the instructor becomes a problem for himself. We even 'tab' our manuals by concept instead of day of the week, to avoid pressuring the instructor or implying that time and topic are more important than learning."

Formatting

Wilson Learning's format for manuals leads well into the general subject of how best to organize a leader's guide. While the experts have admittedly idiosyncratic approaches to the physical layout, all espouse a "chunking" or "organized-stimulus-field" approach. In essence, anything you can do to make it easy for the instructor to "glance and find" is appropriate.

In Langdon's Construct Lesson Plan system each unit is on a separate lesson plan card (see figure 1). The cards are chosen and assembled into a lesson plan after trainee pretesting. The lesson plan card contains all the key points plus critical questions to ask.

Both Lange and Payne use visual symbols to help instructors find their place on the teaching guide (see figure 2). Lange, Payne and the Esseffs say that any visual aids the instructor must use in class should be reproduced in the teaching guide.

Lange and Payne both advocate putting miniatures of the visuals within the outline. Both agree that trying to find chart 4 or overhead 33 is much slower than trying to find the visual that looks exactly like the one in the outline.

All the experts recommend packing the instructor's manual with lots of back-up and "just-in-case" materials. The Esseffs advocate including all visuals, all media scripts, optional or alternative forms, cases studies, role plays, performance checklists, test keys, instructions on the use of all materials, a checklist of necessary items, a list of references and a detailed table of contents.

Wachs and Rosansky suggest the inclusion of readings for the instructor. Particularly helpful, they say, are articles that take issue with the theories or viewpoints being taught. This arms the instructor for disagreements in class.

Flowcharts of the course concepts are also helpful, suggests Payne. "You need to know the core concepts and how the examples and parts fit when you are trying to transfer the concept to someone else," he says.

"By diagramming them in their conceptual relationship, you get the big picture. The instructor has to have the connections down pat."

Instructor training

But no matter how good the leader's guide, experts agree it can't be self-supporting: You have to train the trainer how to use it. "If you think you can write an instructor's manual and ship it out to the world, you are probably wrong," says Payne. In short, instructor training is an invisible but crucial part of the formula. "If you could do the training without the people, then *instructor* training would be a snap," ODI's Wachs says wryly.

Instructors should experience the program twice, say the experts: first as students, then as instructors in a "safe" environment. "They have to see someone else do it, have the opportunity to ask questions and then practice and get feedback on their own performance," suggests Payne. "That's when the instructor's guide takes on meaning."

Lange also sees instructor training

as the place where the actual teaching guide is prepared. "When they've seen the completed manual and understand the relationship between what happened in class and what is written in the manual, *then* they are ready to personalize and condense it."

The bottom line that attends this new interest in the art/craft of developing instructor manuals is the human factor training is ultimately aimed at. As Esseff sums up, "The well-developed, well-done instructor's guide *allows* the good instructor to put his or her energy into doing the human, interactive part of the course well. If you assume that programmed instruction and the like can do it all, you leave out the most important aspect of training, the human part of the equation.

"To do that is to misunderstand that new skills and new information have to be integrated into the individual's world of work and experience. And that takes both *good materials* and *well-trained instructors* that together can meet the needs of trainees in a truly individualized, personal manner."

Reprinted from TRAINING, March 1982

ARE THE BEST TRAINERS TEACHERS OR DOERS?

These are pros and cons for both sides of this knotty question

BY MARTIN M. BROADWELL

That perennial question about whether the teacher or the doer makes the better trainer is a knotty one. Martin Broadwell offers some guidelines that may point to an answer.

Q. Should a person have work experience in the subject being taught?

A. This is a perpetual argument which has strong advocates on both sides. Essentially, the argument is this—is it easier to make a teacher out of a technical expert, or make a technical expert out of a good teacher? There aren't any hard and fast rules, but there are a few general guidelines, although each of the guidelines has its own exceptions.

First, it's a general belief that the nearer the subject gets to being purely psychomotor, the greater the requirement for experience on the part of the instructor. If manual dexterity is involved, as opposed to theory or principle, it's much more important that the teacher have experience in the smells, the touch, the sounds of the job.

Job manuals rarely can express these things, although where there are good job standards, these things will be built into the job requirements. For example, if it's necessary for the trainee to know that pressure is to be applied slowly until there is a high-pitched whine from the hydraulic winch, this should be a part of the manual and the standard operating procedures.

Q. Should an instructor pretend to have work experience?

A. The answer to that is another guideline. The instructor without experience should never try to "fake it." Pretending to have experience is a dangerous game, and one that can have dire consequences when the truth comes out. Some have, admittedly, done a good job of pretending, but this doesn't remove the possible damage that can occur when the students find out that the instructor hasn't really been there after all.

Of course, this is a danger whether or not we're talking about purely psychomotor training. A

> **"A sales training program by an instructor who has never knocked on the first door isn't likely to produce the best sales force."**

training program conducted by an instructor who has never knocked on the first door isn't likely to produce the best sales force. However, a course based on a set of "six steps to selling" can be taught by a trainer without experience. The trouble comes when the student asks, "Yeah, but what do I do when the customer says he doesn't have room to store the stuff in his one-bedroom apartment?" Our just knowing the six steps isn't going to get us over the hump. It's going to be rough without the experience to back us up.

Q. Is there a substitute for experience?

A. There may be no substitute, but there are some things that can be done that will serve the instructor well in the absence of experience. For example, getting to know the manuals, the policies, the standard operating procedures is a great confidence-building factor. The instructor who knows what should be done—and knows it very well—will have a decided advantage over the person who's been there but doesn't really know the SOP very well.

Of course, the instructor should always know the standards. It's from these that the objective for the training course came. If the standards aren't available in good form, then the instructors trying to teach procedures will find themselves at a great disadvantage when facing a group of students who have years of experience.

Q. Is it helpful for an instructor who hasn't done the job himself to see how others do it?

A. Another thing that will serve the instructor well is getting some "substitute" experience. Sometimes a week at the work location can be equivalent to months or even years.

We should spend the time at the work location profitably by not only talking to people who've been there for a while, asking questions and investigating various aspects, but also by listening. We need to listen to the answers to our questions. We need to listen to the people on break—what do they talk about? what do they like and dislike? what would they like to have changed? what do they feel is working well for them? We don't have to ask questions about these things, either. If we just learn to listen, not respond nor challenge, we'll hear a lot.

But there is more to hear than just the comments of the people. We can hear the sounds of the

587

job. We can hear the customers. We can hear the bosses. We can hear the machines. We can hear the bells and the whistles and the traffic and the silence. If we stay conscious of these things, we'll come away with a great deal of first-hand information about what it's really like.

Of course, we don't want to spend our brief time just listening

textbook answer—which may be right—but find ourselves walking on pretty thin ice trying to sound convincing.

Worse yet, we may be too convincing, with the confidence gained in reading all the latest books on management principles. We may leave the trainees believing that we really have answered all their questions. We may have created a small monster in that these employees (managers) may go back fully expecting all these things to work and end up falling on their faces when they try to implement them back on the job.

It's true, of course, that there are a number of people out there teaching MBO, OD, TA, job enrichment and other management skills who have never managed anybody, and many who have managed but very poorly. They seem to get away with it, but maybe all the figures aren't in yet.

Q. Are you saying that course results depend only on the instructor?

A. We'd be remiss if we didn't point out that maybe this question about instructor competence is really missing the mark, missing the real question. The thing that's not being considered is the function of the instructors in the first place. Requiring them to be competent says that the course results are entirely dependent upon the instructor, not the design of the course.

We're getting a lot closer to the time when this question would be incongruous with an understanding of what constitutes good training. When we begin to think of the instructor's role as one of facilitating learning instead of "dishing it

out," we'll begin to look more at the way the course is designed than at what the teacher knows.

We'll also begin to ask questions about design instead of the teacher. We'll be more concerned with processes than people and their backgrounds. We wouldn't suggest that there isn't any direct contact between the student and instructor, so that experience isn't

a factor. But we would suggest that in a well-designed course—one aimed at overcoming specific deficiencies in a job where there are measureable standards, one in which the objectives are observable and match the standards, one in which the instructor has provided the students with appropriate learning maps and in which the students know that they are in the course to be trained to meet the specified standards—in such a course, the instructor's experience at training and facilitating learning is going to be a greater consideration than his previous experience in the material being taught.

Reprinted from TRAINING, August 1975

> ## "The instructor who knows what should be done will have a decided advantage over the person who's been there but doesn't know the SOP very well."

> ## "We should try to get in some actual work. We should try to deal with an unhappy customer, a cranky machine or a disgruntled employee."

and talking. We should try to get in some actual work. We should try to deal with an unhappy customer, a cranky machine or a disgruntled employee.

Q. Is experience necessary in management training?

A. Although management training isn't a psychomotor skill, it may be the exception that proves the rule. A management trainer who has never managed either people or money or materials is going to find it very difficult to come across convincingly with all the answers to the complex problems of management. If we've never had to deal with an irate employee who needs disciplining, we can give the

USING SUBJECT-MATTER EXPERTS IN TRAINING

A training director's guide to mining the
lode of specialized information
your program needs

BY TOM GOAD

Almost everything trainers do for the learning process requires working with or consulting the people who know most about the subject being taught—subject-matter experts. You may be part of a formal training unit within your organization, but the whole organization should be viewed as a pool of training talent in which every member is potentially a consulting or participating expert. Their roles can range from advisors to temporary staff members to long-term trainers. They can operate within the full span of training functions.

Experts often possess technical knowledge or skills too complex and specialized to be packaged and presented by a lone trainer. And for the numerous training projects that are short-term, straightforward and prepared on short notice, subject-matter experts can be invaluable.

These days it bears repeating that every minute is precious; a day or week is comparatively priceless. Unless you and your staff are unusually versed in technical fields, it is likely that you can use the help experts can provide. If the training is going to be automated, individualized or long-term, there is even more reason to rely on experts: The more control learners have over the instructional process, the more technically on-target the training must be.

How important is expert input? Take the case in which expert pilots

were developing, under a training specialist's guidance, a curriculum for jet pilot training. The trainer's idea was to place qualifications for night aircraft-carrier landing early in the curriculum. The prerequisite skills were there—on paper—and if feasible, the tactic would have made the curriculum more desirable than the competition's. But the experts pointed out an objection that had nothing to do with learning principles or training methods. A tremendous amount of pure, gut fear comes into play the first time a pilot tries to set an airplane down on a tiny, bouncing island in the middle of the ocean—in the dark. The more time "behind the stick," the easier it is to overcome this fear and do what has to be done. Night carrier landings were assigned later in the curriculum.

In another case, a sales training course had to be developed and delivered in too little time for things to be done "right." The program had to be successful, of course, success being measured by how quickly the learners could get into the field and secure qualified leads. The training specialist's natural desire to take the time to do a task analysis to identify and prioritize the program's key elements was thwarted. The demand was to get on with developing materials and do a dry run. Using their intuition and experience, expert salespeople came up with the handful of items they considered most important, and the course was born.

It isn't a question of whether the

subject-matter expert or the trainer is more vital to training. Both are important. The point is that, as "facilitators," we are continually called upon to facilitate *through* experts. Much of the training we do is classroom-oriented—an instructor interacting with learners—and it helps if the instructor knows more than the students. This places the expert in the most visible training element.

Experience has led me to believe that three steps can be decisive in making the most effective use of subject-matter experts—in helping them help you turn out good training programs.

1 Welcome yourself to the team. Some experts may be more extensively trained in their areas than you are in yours. Often their work is highly specialized. Recognize the pride and mindset that may accompany the experts when they step in .

The work they are about to do is an *extension of their regular work.* You may have to do a lot of convincing in some cases, but most will accept this notion readily. Help your experts see the training tasks as important in their own right—as important as work on the assembly line, in the field, behind the counter or in the cockpit. Their supervisors can help make the mission clear when the experts are initially recruited.

Serve up some positive strokes; let them know you value their expertise and that you are happy to have them as part of the training team. Why are you happy to have them? Consider this:

• They have been trained—presumably they know what does and does not work.

• With the proper approach, trainer-expert teams can determine quickly the essential issues to be covered in the proposed training.

• Other than by conducting expensive, controlled studies, you are unlikely to find better information than you can obtain from expert opinion.

• Subject-matter experts know tricks of the trade; they know what job elements are the toughest, what you can skimp on and what you can ignore altogether. These are the very things that will let you design an exceptional program.

When dealing with experts, however, remember:

• Sensitivities of team members will differ: The ego drives of a jet pilot or a salesperson with a six-figure salary tend to be different from those of an administrator or computer programmer.

• Respect the years of experience standing behind your chosen experts.

• There's a natural tendency for some "old pros" to look down on novices. But if you penetrate the crust, you'll generally find that they want to share their wealth of knowledge and skills.

2 **Identify roles.** When members know their roles and are willing to perform them, the "team" becomes an extremely effective unit for getting things done. Identify everyone's role before doing any work. Each member of the team will have strong and weak points. If you can discover these, you'll be able to fill in gaps.

One way to do this is through exploratory, fairly informal meetings in which members will begin to show where their individual abilities and interests lie.

Role identification probably should be your first order of business. For example, in one program whose objective was to identify every task required to operate and maintain a particular computer system, the new team promptly determined that a group of programmers and engineers would be responsible for technical documentation. The trainer's role was to provide a standard, easy-to-use format for documenting the task and skills analysis, and to do the editing and production work necessary to come up with a finished program. This clear division of labor yielded tasks easily translated into learning objectives and training materials for several courses.

3 **Complement one another.** It is vital that you accept responsibility for the role of manager. This role begins when you start planning for the task of working with experts. Even with willing, able partners and well-defined roles, adjustments will be needed. Your responsibility—like any manager's—is to see that the work gets done.

One of your first jobs is to define the expert's level of training awareness and skills. Ask respectful questions. Find out what he or she has done in the way of analysis, instructing and testing.

If nothing else, your experts probably have attended courses and workshops. Relate elements of their experience to training functions. Based on this, begin a process of *training them to be trainers*. This may or may not involve formal training. In any case, give them as many down-to-earth examples as possible. There's a threshold beyond which the expert neither needs nor wants to know about esoteric theories or principles or techniques. You must know when to stop the process.

If the training ability of your experts needs shoring up and you can't send all of them through a formal training pipeline, don't despair. In-house training can be done informally. You can try discussion groups, do-it-yourself courses and assignments from among the treasure trove of reading materials in the training field. But avoid highly technical expositions, especially those that are full of jargon.

On the other hand, you should try to learn all you can about your experts' field. The idea is to create an environment in which knowledge and skills are shared freely.

It helps if you and your team can speak a common language. You may have to give a lot here, so try to pick up on the buzzwords. Language peculiar to the subject may be critical. If you're training Navy people, for instance, and you keep referring to the right-hand side of the boat, little round windows and floors, you'll be a joke, not an effective trainer.

Confronting problems

You can expect to hit snags now and then. An expert may, for instance, insist on teaching a certain work procedure as part of a course, even though you know it isn't feasible or shouldn't be done (e.g., the procedure violates company policy). What do you do in a case like this? If it is a vital point, you may have to press hard. Use win/win negotiating techniques. Compromise if necessary.

Suppose your expert insists that role playing is the only way to present a vital segment in a sales-training course, while experience has convinced you that classroom discussion mediated by an experienced salesperson is a faster and more effective way to go. The solution may be to do it both ways.

When it comes down to it, however, you have to run the team and that means giving direction to your experts. Since you're unlikely to have line authority in the situation, you can only do this in an atmosphere of mutual trust and respect. It is up to you to build this trust early to avoid confrontations.

The right subject matter, in the right amount, is what training is all about. If your delivery methods are also effective, then you have all the ingredients for a top-quality product. Maybe it's time for you to mine a new lode of expertise.

Reprinted from TRAINING, March 1983

THE WHATS, WHYS AND HOWS OF TEACHING MANAGERS TO BE TRAINERS

Tips on choosing, using and training line managers to teach others

BY GEOFFREY M. BELLMAN

Many of us in the training profession labor under the assumption that all the skills we have are needed to perform an adequate job in a learning setting. Our own control needs, our need for recognition, and perhaps our need to be "certified" professionals all contribute to the notion that it takes considerable skill to lead a training session.

To some extent this is true. A great deal of experience in working with groups in a particular content area is helpful in advancing a group from where they are to where you and the design want them to be.

But what if you, or someone like you, is not available? What if you can't be in 15 places in two weeks? What if the client can't afford to pay your expenses to visit all its locations? What if you get bored with doing the same session over and over again? What if the client would really rather do the training himself? Answers to these questions point to the possibility that someone with great motivation but less skill than you possess might be capable of group training.

This notion has been widely accepted in technical areas. On-the-job training and job-instruction training emphasize putting training skills in the hands of the supervisor. Indeed, the same thing can be done in the area of supervisory skills. That is, many managers can assume the task of training supervisors.

Where it appears that line managers are going to train their supervisors, four significant differences can be noted. First, in doing the needs analysis you must determine whether the skills needed can actually be taught by line managers. After all, to teach skills, the teacher must possess them. Second, you must make clear to top management how you intend to have line managers do supervisory training. Third, acknowledge that in the actual design of the program—objectives, methods, and medium — a considerably different structure will emerge than if you were doing the program yourself. And fourth, consider that the evaluation of the program is

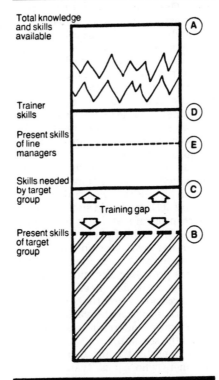

effected significantly because those teaching it are so closely involved in carrying it out.

The above chart is a simplified linear portrayal of the situation we're discussing. If line A represents the amount of knowledge and skills presently available and line B represents the amount of knowledge and skills presently possessed by the target group, you must ask: How much do you want the target group to learn of what is available? Your needs survey should help you determine both present resources and resources needed to perform as expected.

The resources needed are represented by line C. Ordinarily a trainer would look at the gap between the resources needed and the present resources of the target group. If he decided training was appropriate, he would then insert his own knowledge and skills into the picture that is represented by line D on the chart. Occasionally, such an action is appropriate. Actually, there is yet another line that ought to be considered (line E) — the present resources of the line managers of the target group. Do their skills equal or exceed the amount needed to deliver the expected performance? If the answer to that question is "yes" or "maybe," the alternative of using line managers as trainers presents itself.

The consultant involved now must identify the present skills of the line managers, and decide whether these individuals are capable of actual training. Remember, some coaches are poor players, but can help others be good players. Managers frequently say, "How can I teach people to do something when I don't always do it right myself?" or "I'm not an expert in this area, and the trainees will recognize this." Your task is to reduce the demands on the manager/trainer through good design.

That is, you must design a training program that allows participants to meet the content without the manager/trainer getting in the way. This means more emphasis on structured experiences, group discussions, and canned (film, tape or type) experts and less reliance on weighty lectures, question-and-answer sessions, and other methods that assume the session leader is an expert.

How do you know whether a line manager will be a good trainer? First, assume that most people could do a satisfactory job of training if they were properly prepared. A crucial quality to look for in a line manager is a strong but flexible personality. The manager should be able to vary his or her presentation; this can be discerned rather quickly in the course of a conversation.

If a personality is present in the form of facial expressions, gestures, and variation in voice level, probably this person could handle the presentation and maintain interest throughout.

A second item to be aware of with potential managers/trainers is motivation. Do they consider training an effective way of helping people perform more effectively? How have they demonstrated this belief in the past? Are they willing to alter some of their own behaviors? Are they asking others to alter theirs? Are they interested in helping people learn?

A third area to consider is the individual's experience. How much experience does he or she have in the areas that will be trained? Does he know the terminology of the people involved? How long has she been at this location? Is he familiar with its special problems?

Fourth, consider respect. An individual may possess all the skills needed to be an outstanding trainer but not have the respect of fellow employees. To gather impressions about the manager's status, talk with others in the plant or office.

A positive aspect of using managers as trainers is that it converts a training effort into an organization development effort. When you use managers to train line supervisors, you are intervening in the way the organization operates. You are making more obvious and formal a responsibility all line managers have. In so doing, you bring work dynamics into the classroom. The likelihood of real problems being discussed and acted upon increases and should be incorporated in the design itself. Much time should be set aside to discuss real work problems in relation to the content of the session. If, after a session, a participant says something like, "Gee, I didn't feel like I was in a training session; it felt more like a project committee meeting," you'll know you're on the right track.

When line managers are being trained as trainers, they should consider how they are going to deal with the real work issues that come up in the session. Such issues should be collected and acted upon; begin with the action that happens in the session itself and extend it back to the work place.

The manager/trainers must understand that to be good trainers they don't have to do everything right themselves. By the same token, they shouldn't expect their trainees to do everything right either. Instead, the manager/trainers should expect their trainees to be willing to adopt new behaviors that are more effective than those they presently use.

The actions managers take can be models for supervisors, but the actions are not necessarily the same that supervisors take. For example, a manager may expect supervisors to hold work-performance discussions with their trainees within two weeks of the session. The manager, on the other hand, may meet with each of the supervisors within two to four weeks of the session to ask how their work-performance discussions went and to offer counsel, if necessary. This represents a change of behavior on the manager's part, and thus is a model for the supervisor.

By involving a number of line managers as trainers — perhaps four or five in a two-day session — you can reduce the amount of responsibility for learning that each one needs to as-

---

Line managers who act as trainers are also trainees learning new skills in group leadership.

---

sume. One manager could be responsible for three hours of a two-day session and could be a back-up for another manager/trainer for another three-hour session. Thus, the task of training is reduced to manageable proportions, and a manager's fears of the training situation are lessened.

Whenever a line manager is leading the session, a colleague should be on the scene to offer assistance. To help not just in case of difficulties, but to add another perspective to what's being said. If four managers are involved in one two-day training session, all of them should sit through the entire program at least once. Subsequently, each of them should lead his or her own session and act as back-up for another manager/trainer. Besides providing the moral support that session leaders need and giving them occasional breathers, this team approach also provides variety for the participants and reinforces the content of the session.

An important point to note: Line managers who act as trainers learn more from sessions than participants

do. As one line executive said, "This whole training effort was worth it because of what my five key people learned as trainers. Even if the participants hadn't learned anything, I would've gladly spent time on this. Put another way, being a trainer is a very good way to train my managers to manage. After all, they're just carrying out a role they've already been assigned."

Another advantage of using line managers as trainers is that you will, in effect, multiply yourself many times— if you do it correctly. You will, of course, spend a little more time designing and significantly more training trainers than if you were to do the session yourself. But the two extra days in design and three to five days in training can free you for the weeks it would take to do the sessions yourself. Another benefit: As line managers become trainers, they get a significantly better understanding of what can realistically be accomplished in a classroom environment. They know more about how people actually learn and how much effect classroom activity has on their behavior. Line managers are in a better position to observe this than you because they shift from the classroom setting to the job and back again.

Eventually, manager/trainers will realize that people are in learning situations, in training all the time. A program that is designed to emphasize a discussion of and work on an application of skills in real work situations should produce a healthy confusion in the manager/trainer's mind. He finds it more difficult to separate training from the real situation than he did in the past— and that's as it should be.

Using line managers as trainers frequently results in less polished, less professional presentations. But the significant question is: Does it result in less learning? While I haven't studied this scientifically, I would say "no." Not only do trainees generally benefit from this approach, but manager/trainers also gain individual growth. They acquire more knowledge in the area they are training and they learn new skills in group leadership that are transferable to many work-group situations. They also learn to evaluate themselves more accurately and immediately in group situations.

Finally, I'm not suggesting that we always use line managers as trainers. Rather, that we seldom use them when we could. Remember: the purpose of training is to get results. Often the less "glamorous" approach of using manager/trainers places the focus on such results rather than on content presented in a slick, "professional" way.

Reprinted from TRAINING, June 1978

WHO SHOULD DO THE SALES TRAINING?

In this corner, the pass-through paragon
with credibility to burn.
In that corner, the career trainer,
weighing in with stability and expertise

BY BEVERLY GEBER

In a perfect world, the kind that suffers no wars, harbors no criminals and brooks no tooth decay, the perfect sales training program might resemble this: Headed by a career trainer, a former sales pro, the department is staffed with experienced, gung ho salespeople who were pulled out of the field to serve two- or three-year stints as trainers.

Grateful for this lucky opportunity, they arrive exuberantly, fit in immediately, perceive the department's goals telepathically and become the very models of trainer excellence. Later, saddened by their leave-taking, they're promoted out of the department to climb to the top of the corporate ladder, there to remember fondly the training department and look kindly on its budget requests. For its part, the training department has been enriched by the presence of these pass-through paragons.

A rosy picture. Here's another: The sales training division is filled with former salespeople—the best and brightest—who clawed their ways in as soon as they heard of openings. They, too, fit in immediately. Perfectly. What's more, they keep getting better at their new profession—training. The department isn't burdened with constant turnover. And no trainee would dare accuse these trainers of lacking real-world experi-ence, of being too isolated from sales-people and their problems. After all, these trainers aren't only seasoned sales reps, they're still out in the field, continually tagging along on sales calls and learning just exactly what the customers and salespeople need.

Unfortunately, the world is imperfect. Reaching even rough approximations of either ideal is a difficult proposition that requires continuous work and a bit of luck. In the meantime, the debate continues on the relative merits of the two different approaches to sales training. Adherents mightily defend their method against the other. And some people, of course, occupy a position in the middle of the continuum; they use a hybrid approach that they say exploits the strengths and minimizes the problems of both approaches. At the heart of the argument is a question familiar to all trainers: What's the best way to deliver the training?

David Brinkerhoff, president of Abbott Smith Associates, of Mill-brook, NY, an employment service specializing in the human resources field, says that most sales training managers prefer to have salespeople pass through the department.

That's an impression echoed by Robert Whyte, vice president of Por-ter Henry Company, Inc., a New York City consulting firm that specializes in sales training. Even though the pass-through program takes consider-ably more effort to run and may not be feasible at all for small organizations, Whyte estimates that 30% to 50% of companies prefer that method.

Instant trainer

It's appealing to think you can take a subject-matter expert who has instant credibility with trainees, thorough product knowledge and current experience with the customer base, then put it all to work by making the expert a trainer. Some see this method—done right—as sales training's highest life form. Still, the pass-through program is hard to do right and the training manager can suffer migraines trying to make it work.

Isabel Kersen is one who chooses not to cycle salespeople through the training department. As director of sales training at Cosmair Inc., a New York City-based cosmetics and fragrance firm, she recruited her trainers from the sales ranks, but not for temporary stints. They had the option of returning to the field if they didn't like training, but they were encouraged to stay—and all stayed. A move into the Cosmair training department isn't considered a way station on the path to a promotion. It *is* a promotion: a promotion into management, accompanied by a boost in salary.

"If I find someone who is good, why on earth would I want that person to leave?" Kersen asks. What's more, she says, pass-through programs that are used as management development tools mean the training manager can be saddled with a person who's good management material but lousy trainer material: "Once you pull someone out of the field, you're stuck with him for a couple of years no matter what he's like."

Kersen says her trainers spend about 80% of their time in the field delivering training and going along with salespeople on their calls. That's designed to keep them fresh and attuned to the trainees' needs. Not that she believes that one absolutely must have recent sales experience to be able to teach salespeople. "There's a lot of this, 'If you can't do it, you can't teach it.' That's a lot of crap. If I can observe you doing it and break it down into its components, I can teach it. I have never sold cosmetics and fragrance. Everybody knows that. Guess who has the most credibility in my department?"

Actually, Kersen doesn't understand why training managers think the pass-through approach benefits anyone but the short-timer who's passing through. "The area of least concern is the quality of the training," she says. "They take a supersalesman and expose him to training and then send him out to be a supermanager. There's little concern about whether he was a supertrainer for those two years."

Kersen, however, is bucking the tide. Most training managers seem to prefer the pass-through method. If registrations for a train-the-trainer course offered by the National Society of Sales Training Executives provide a clue, every year more salespeople see a need to learn how to train.

'There's a lot of this "If you can't do it you can't teach it." That's a lot of crap.'

Chuck Harper, administrative manager for the Orlando, FL-based society, says demand for the semiannual train-the-trainer course has been so strong in the past two years, he is considering offering a third session. Although the course is geared for sales training, it concentrates on basic principles: adult learning theory, how to write objectives, how to evaluate training and instructional techniques.

That would seem to indicate a lot of rookie instructors coming into sales training departments. To Kersen, the trend in that direction is a mystery, because there are greater administrative headaches involved in moving streams of people through the training department. Recently, too, recruiting has gotten tougher because salespeople in many companies are reluctant to cycle through the training department during an economic environment made uncertain by mergers and downsizing.

The on-deck circle

Nevertheless, advocates of the pass-through approach think it's the best way to run a sales training pro-

gram. They argue that everyone benefits—trainees, training department and, not least, the salesperson plucked from the field. In many cases, the training department is a rung on the corporate ladder. In companies in which the pass-through program works smoothly, the salesperson gets a few years of training experience, then usually is promoted into some kind of management job.

Pitney Bowes, Inc. hews strictly to the pass-through philosophy—so strictly that national training manager Charles Kinney is the only full-time career sales trainer in the company's Peachtree City, GA, department. Salespeople vie for the training positions, he says, because there's plenty of evidence that his department is the bull pen for the next open management spot.

Some companies don't just put the salesperson in a specific training position for the duration of the rotation. They carefully manage the experience to give the individual a well-rounded exposure to the training department.

At Lederle Laboratories in Wayne, NJ, for instance, the young promotables don't just "cycle through" the training department on their way to other jobs. According to Robert J. Burns, Lederle's manager of educational services, they learn about all facets of the department, taste-testing most of its jobs. Before their two-year rotation is up, they've been exposed to a smorgasbord of trainerly functions, including communications training, management training and hospital oncology training.

The whole pass-through concept is a management grooming strategy that helps achieve a worthwhile goal even if there weren't advantages for the trainees and the department, says Tom Hartley, Union Carbide's manager of sales education services. "You're making that person more valuable to the company. It's good business to do that."

What about the trainees and the department? What do they gain? Pass-through advocates like to cite the credibility factor. Salespeople who were recently in battle, they say, carry more authority with trainees than do training professionals who have never sold anything, or even former salespeople who are years removed from cold calls and recalcitrant clients.

Deanne Hannibal, a training con-

sultant with Metropolitan Life Insurance Company who has never been a saleswoman, sees it firsthand. "There's skepticism about anything you say," she says. To avoid being challenged by trainees, she's careful to preface her remarks with qualifiers such as, "When I talk to people in the field, they say. . . . "

Former salespeople project instant credibility, and offer other advantages as well, she says. "They have a better feel for what the market is and how skillful you need to be as a salesperson. We do role playing and they're better customers."

They can bring fresh ideas to the training department. Their enthusiasm is likely to be high, especially if they know they're on a promotion

---

When the revolving door whirls so often, what happens to continuity? Quality?

---

path. And their knowledge of the product is intimate.

But managers who prefer the pass-through scheme all admit there are numerous pitfalls to beware. It takes a great deal of a manager's time just to keep the program going—to recruit the best and brightest salespeople who might pan out as trainers. Hartley says he spends half his time just recruiting and administering the program. There's also a definite time lag as rookies enter the department and are expected to learn quickly how to be effective trainers so they can make a worthwhile contribution during their short stint.

Just passing through . . .

There's some question, too, about whether the process enhances the training department's operations. When the revolving door is whirling as often as is necessary to cycle people through for two-year terms, what happens to continuity? What happens to quality? And doesn't it demean the profession to imply that just about any high achiever in some other line of work can become a successful trainer?

Burns acknowledges there are occasional problems with continuity. If a salesperson who has been working on a project reaches the end of the rotation, the project is suspended until the next person picks up the thread. "Things can slip a little bit in the interim," he says.

Kinney echoes that problem and adds another. Pass-through people are there learning the rudiments of the trainer's art. In two years, they can't be expected to pick up all the finer points. When it comes to things like program development in the Pitney Bowes sales training department, Kinney must call upon management trainers—career trainers—to help.

Overall, then, what happens to the quality of instruction if all those problems gang up on the department—if the actual training becomes secondary to the career development of the up-and-comers?

Kermit H. Boston, vice president for marketing development and training at McGraw-Hill Book Co., New York City, has operated his department according to both philosophies. "One of the problems of having people cycling through is that you've got to watch the level of presentation in terms of the quality. Some people coming in know they'll be there for a short time and they may not dig in and get to a level at which you want them to be."

Whyte agrees. "The question is, 'Is this a real job or is it just a route to another opportunity?' " he says. "Here we have the job of training salespeople, which is one of the most important jobs in the company, and it's just a position for somebody to warm their rear while they wait for another job."

But Whyte isn't adamantly against the idea of pass-through. "Properly done, it's a marvelous opportunity for everyone," he says. Whyte prefers a hybrid system. Ideally, a staff of career trainers, all of them former salespeople, is supplemented by a number of young recruits, fresh from the sales force, who stay several years. Some may go on to management jobs; others, who find they like training, may stay. Management should make it clear that reaching the training department is a promotion in its own right that may lead to more promotions; it's not a purgatory on the way to heaven.

Of course, that's the ideal. The problem is that in companies where training departments aren't highly respected, it's difficult to recruit the prize salespeople unless there's the incentive of promotion—and not just to the training department. Even in the best of situations, it's sometimes a hard sell to recruit top salespeople who are living high on commissions, getting perks like a company car and enjoying a lot of personal freedom on the job.

Some companies try to surmount that obstacle by ensuring that salespeople won't lose anything in a move to the training department. When the transfer is a genuine promotion and the financial compensation is equal or greater, the training unit stands a

---

Sales training isn't a purgatory on the way to heaven.

---

better chance of attracting the top performers. . .except that in the past couple of years, recruitment has gotten even tougher.

"I think companies would very much like to have line salespeople come in and train, but it's getting more and more difficult to do that," says Brinkerhoff. Recently, he's been asked to find career sales trainers for companies that previously only recruited for those positions from their own sales ranks.

The dark side

In a time of corporate instability from mergers, downsizing, hiring freezes and fewer promotions, some salespeople are reconsidering the wisdom of jumping to the bottom of the totem pole in a different department. Even if they believe that the company really wants to promote them and wouldn't consider firing them, they worry they'll get "stuck" in the training department during corporate cutbacks. Or, worse yet, the training department will be one of those cutbacks.

"It all depends on the way the company views training," says Whyte. "If you're in a company that has a pass-

through program and you hear that the first thing they cut [in a financial squeeze] is training, why would you want to come in?"

McGraw-Hill's Boston is among those coping with problems caused by economic uncertainty. The lack of predictability made so many salespeople reluctant to enter the training department that Boston has been forced to scale back his pass-through program dramatically in the past few years. He is now deciding whether it's worth the effort to resurrect it.

Hannibal also is finding it hard to staff her department with the experienced salespeople she'd like to have, but for a different reason. Metropolitan Life, she says, is growing so fast and promoting so rapidly that salespeople don't "need" to work in the training department as they await promotions.

"We used to say, 'Come in for two years and you'll walk out an account executive,' " Hannibal says. "Now they don't need that because we're promoting people so fast. We now have 28- and 29-year-old sales managers."

As if to underscore the point, some companies have had a hard time beginning a pass-through program precisely because management wouldn't promise promotions. "We've been trying to get pass-through but it's just been recently that we've been able to get them promoted," says David Mehl, manager of sales education programs for General Electric's major appliance business group in Louisville, KY.

Other reasons combine to inhibit the move by top salespeople into training. Even if the training department can match or exceed their current salaries, the move to corporate headquarters is likely to put them in an area where the cost of living is higher. The family has to move, an added hassle. And for some, the thrill of the chase in sales is addictive.

"In contrast, the environment we offer them is too mundane," Hannibal says.

Without experienced salespeople, she says, the training department is lacking. She combats the problem by bringing in salespeople to teach classes for a day or two. She also formed an advisory committee of salespeople to help her develop curricula.

Others seeking to fill the void have

videotaped courses taught by their subject experts and sent the tapes out to the troops. And some, such as Mehl, have begun grooming salespeople in the field. Instead of making one-on-one presentations to customers, they get up in front of large groups of customers to explain the product. Those who enjoy the experience may more easily be persuaded into the training department he says.

Perish the thought

In some cases, the situation has become so desperate that sales training directors are reaching outside their walls. Brinkerhoff says companies have recently begun coming to his firm for career trainers when they can't grow their own inside the company. That, however, is considered the least attractive option.

Pitney-Bowes' Kinney, who has operated with both philosophies, explains why. "It's easier for us to teach people who know our business how to train than to teach trainers our business," he says.

Of course, some trainers are raising a brow at all this. They agree with Kersen, who figures you don't have to do it to be able to teach it. They wonder at all this worry about the lack of trainer fodder out there in the sales ranks and the schemes to entice them into the training department. Why not dispense with the time-consum-

ing bother of pass-through? Why not "professionalize" the department?

Boston speaks for many pass-through advocates when he argues that sales training is different from other kinds of training. "I think you can be a very effective trainer and do management training okay, but in sales training I don't think you can do it unless you have been in sales. You

---

'When someone leaves the department, you usually have a supporter of training.'

---

have to be able to cite situations that are real to these people. . . . When we have an acquisition, before I can do any sort of training, I have to make sales calls to find out what the product is, who the customers are and what their needs are."

Actually, the discussion about who should do the sales training doesn't necessarily imply polar opposites between career trainers and salespeople "moonlighting" as trainers for a couple of years. You won't find too many training managers preferring a strictly pass-through sales training depart-

ment. Nor do many want nothing but career trainers in that department. Most prefer a point on the continuum that's somewhere in between.

Most managers would like to select their sales trainers—short-term or long-term—from within the sales ranks to get that savvy and product knowledge. They'd like to entice those who would make great trainers and they'd prefer to keep them if they're good. After all, most sales trainers can keep up with the field and maintain credibility easily enough by tagging along or making their own sales calls.

Despite all the headaches involved with pass-through, advocates feel there's one good—and sly—reason to pursue it. According to this theory, it doesn't matter if the revolving door is spinning.

GE's Mehl explains. He recently added some lower-level training positions in his department, the kind tailor-made for a pass-through program. Mehl is willing to endure the administrative problems to make it succeed. And he won't weep to see the good ones go. "When someone leaves the department, you usually have an ally and supporter of training," he says. "That's important because one of the things training departments have to do all the time is maintain support for something you can't always fully justify."

Reprinted from TRAINING, May 1987

HOW TO SELECT GOOD TECHNICAL INSTRUCTORS

Okay, so the best performer won't necessarily make the best trainer. That doesn't mean you can't find good trainers among your organizations' technical experts

BY RUTH C. CLARK
AND PHYLLIS KYKER

Even in sports it's a cliché. The best athletes often make lousy coaches. In the training business it's axiomatic that people with the best technical skills, be they mechanics, power-line troubleshooters or computer programmers, do not necessarily make the best instructors, Technical skills don't guarantee communication skills, and communication is the essence of training.

In fact, ample evidence suggests that those with the highest levels of expertise often make poor instructors. Their wealth of experience makes it difficult to appreciate the learning needs of novices. The depth of background knowledge that for experts has become automatic or self-evident tends to lure them into several traps: They leave gaping holes in the information they present. They fail to sequence topics from simple to complex. They become impatient with trainees, who, in turn, feel intimidated and fail to ask questions.

All of which is why trainers have been telling managers for years that "You can't just pick out the best technicians and tell them they're now classroom instructors."

That said, if a company is seeking technical trainers, a good place to start looking is among the ranks of the company's own technicians. The fact that subject-matter expertise is not sufficient doesn't mean it isn't necessary. Yes, you can hire professional trainers and teach them the subject matter, but you also can teach technicians to be trainers. And technical experts have an advantage in that they gain automatic credibility with trainees by virtue of their expertise. The experts themselves may benefit from the experience as well. In Southern California Edison's customer service division, for example, the instructor position serves as a grooming opportunity for potential supervisors.

Many skilled technicians can become perfectly good classroom instructors—provided they have the prerequisite abilities to benefit from the train-the-trainer help you can provide. The challenge is to identify those prerequisites and then come up with a valid and reliable way to select technicians who have them. Here is a step-by-step approach based on a process we have found useful at Southern California Edison.

Getting started

The first step is to define the entry-level skills you're looking for. These have to be determined on the basis of your instructors' job requirements. Some skills, such as "effective verbal communication," are likely to be on everyone's list, but others will depend on the specific job. For example, if instructors are responsible for developing written materials—manuals, job aids, etc.—you'll have to screen for writing skills. If they aren't, you won't—and for legal reasons, you probably shouldn't.

Begin by examining the job's major responsibilities. If they haven't already been defined, spelling them out will not only improve your selection process but will help you set performance standards and appraisal guidelines. Books, articles and published research are helpful in outlining the skills instructors need in order to meet various responsibilities, but don't rely on them alone. "Validate" your list by going to your current and past instructors, former students and supervisors of those students. Ask them to identify behaviors or describe incidents that characterize effective or ineffective instruction in your organization.

Once your list is complete, you'll have to decide which skills you can feasibly develop in new instructors by training and which ones need to be entry level. Your selection process will be designed to identify these entry skills.

But your process also has to be reliable. That is, you want a procedure in which different people or panels screen a given candidate and arrive at similar ratings. Reliability is best achieved by evaluating each candidate according to very specific behaviors. It isn't enough to say, for example, that you want instructors who "show enthusiasm." You need a checklist that allows screeners to rate that trait in specific behavioral terms, e.g., "moves around the room during presentation; varies voice modulation and pace; uses verbal and visual clues to emphasize important points," etc. All of your desired entry-level skills will have to be broken down into such checklists.

Designing the selection process

Obviously, there are a lot of ways to set up a procedure that helps you evaluate each candidate's skills against your selection criteria. At Southern California Edison, we rely on a combination of technical qualification, simulation and interviews. Figure 1 summarizes our list of skills and selection procedures.

Technical competence. We draw

FIGURE 1
TECHNICAL INSTRUCTOR SELECTION SKILLS AND PROCEDURES

1. **Job-Related Technical Competence**
   - Has reached top promotional level
   - Supervisory recommendation
   - Performance appraisals
   - Screening of technical behaviors/products

2. **Written Communication Skills**
   - Simulation: Develop written lesson
   - Evaluation of prior writing samples

3. **Individual and Group Verbal Communication Skills**
   - Simulation: Present lesson developed to panel
   - Role Play: One-on-one communication skills
   - Interview: Evaluation of presentation style and content

4. **Ability to Relate to Supervision, Peers and Students**
   - Supervisor recommendation
   - Interview: Look for evidence of teamwork and cooperation

5. **Ability to Work With Minimal Supervision**
   - Supervisory recommendation
   - Interview: Look for willingness to make decisions, set priorities

FIGURE 2
INSTRUCTIONAL SIMULATION RATING CRITERIA: WRITTEN LESSON

Candidate's Name _____   Date _____

Company Division _____   Instructional Topic _____

CRITERIA	POINTS	
1. Contains no more than one grammatical/punctuation error	Essential	_____
2. Sentences are complete	Essential	_____
3. Information sequenced from simple to complex	2	_____
4. Information chunked into short sections	2	_____
5. Mager-style behavioral objectives included	1	_____
6. Content effectively communicated using definitions, examples, procedure tables	1	_____
7. Information mapping formatting techniques used appropriately	1	_____
8. Practice exercise included that matches objective(s)	2	_____
9. Evaluation items included to measure acquisition of objective	1	_____

candidates from a pool of employees who have reached top promotional status via a combination of seniority, promotional tests and supervisory recommendations. Any employee who reaches the top level is eligible to apply for an instructor's job.

In-house evaluation of performance over a period of time provides an effective screening device for technical capabilities. If you were to hire trainers from outside your organization, you'd need a process to rate both their instructional skills and the entry-level *technical* competence you decide they would need.

Simulation. Because our instructors write training materials, they are evaluated for basic writing skills as well as oral presentation ability. We have found simulations very useful in evaluating both types of skills.

Each candidate is given one hour to write a lesson on a familiar nontechnical topic such as "How to Write a Check" or "How to Use a Pocket Calculator." Figure 2 illustrates the weighted checklist used by our training specialists to score the lessons. Note that the checklist includes both basic and advanced skills. Because we initially appoint instructors on a six-month trial basis (a "temporary upgrade"), we generally interview both inexperienced and upgraded candidates for permanent positions. Typically, candidates who have been serving as instructors on an upgraded basis fill the permanent job openings. The temporary upgrade positions are then filled by lower-ranked, inexperienced candidates.

Following the written simulation, each candidate is given 15 minutes to present his or her lesson to a panel consisting of an instructional specialist and two training supervisors. The panel uses the checklist shown in Figure 3 as a guide to rate each presentation. Again, the list includes both basic and advanced skills.

To increase reliability, the panel watches a videotaped presentation by an experienced instructor and uses the video as a model for rating each candidate. In other words, candidates are evaluated against the model video performance, not against one another.

Interviews. Following the simulation, each candidate is interviewed by the panel, which uses questions with "correct answer" guidelines, such as the ones in Figure 4. The questions emphasize job dimensions not captured by the simulations, such as the

598

FIGURE 3
INSTRUCTIONAL SIMULATION RATING CRITERIA: LESSON DELIVERY

Candidate's Name _____   Date _____

Company Division _____   Instructional Topic _____

Start Time _____   Finish Time _____

CRITERIA	POINTS	
1. Speaks in clear, understandable English	Essential	_____
2. Presents information conversationally rather than reading it	1	_____
3. Presents and clarifies lesson objectives	½	_____
4. Moves around room, varies voice modulation, uses natural and animated hand gestures, maintains eye contact	½	_____
5. Uses written materials, board, flip chart, lecture and discussion to present information	½	_____
6. Gives a demonstration of procedures	1	_____
7. Includes practice exercise directly related to objective(s)	1	_____
8. Gives clear directions for practice exercise(s)	½	_____
9. Monitors practice by checking individual student responses	½	_____
10. Gives feedback on practice at conclusion of exercise(s)	1	_____
11. Asks students questions to check understanding	½	_____
12. Evaluates learner acquisition of skill objective(s)	1	_____
13. Gives learners positive reinforcement for questions/responses	1	_____
14. Learners are actively involved for at least 50% of lesson	½	_____
15. Completes lesson in time allowed with appropriate allocation of time to all major portions	½	_____

Other Comments:

_____

candidate's time-management strategies and teamwork experiences. Candidates are rated both on what they say and how well they say it.

Choosing instructors

The entire process takes about two hours of the candidate's time (an hour to develop the written lesson and an hour for the presentation simulation and interview) and one hour of the panel's time. Summary scores for each candidate are entered on the weighted worksheet shown in Figure 5. The criteria and associated weights shown were developed during a number of validation trials. The worksheet reflects the major criteria we have found related to job success. If several candidates wind up with high, closely grouped scores, the training supervisor does the final rankings.

Following up

No selection process is foolproof, which is why we initially select candidates only for a six-month trial period. During those six months, "upgraded" instructors receive formal training on teaching skills and are closely evaluated on the job. Supervisors sit in on their classes to rate their skills using the same checklists as in the selection process, interview their students and evaluate student performance. Instructors on temporary assignment who have not performed satisfactorily are returned to their former jobs after six months.

We have found that employees whose technical skills are good, rather than expert, often *do* make better instructors. But that doesn't mean that the experts can't be useful in training. It's not unusual for the top technical expert in some area to wind up serving as a consultant to the instructor.

Reprinted from TRAINING, December 1985

GROWING YOUR OWN TECHNICAL EXPERTS

One high-tech firm hopes to cling to the cutting edge by cultivating old-fashioned master-apprentice relationships

BY DALE FEUER

A little over a year ago, John Tsotsos and Fred Cheyunski embarked on a journey into a new frontier of human resources development and rediscovered a bit of HRD history along the way. Their mission: to clone six prized individuals. The only acceptable outcome: a quick and successful replication. The whole future of inertial systems analysis at Honeywell Corp.'s avionics division in Clearwater, FL, hung in the balance.

Gratuitous dramatization? All right, yes. While Tsotsos, a technical education specialist, and Cheyunski, an HRD professional, did have a difficult training challenge on their hands at Honeywell, test tubes had nothing to do with their solution.

The problem, in brief, was this: Over 70% of the engineers in the military avionics, space systems and strategic guidance operations in Clearwater were at least 35 years old. And many of the most experienced employees, particularly in the critical area of inertial systems analysis (i.e., research and development work on navigational systems for military planes) would soon be retiring. As for qualified people to fill their spots, well, long-running open requisitions for the positions tell the story.

"We have a lot of older engineers here for a few reasons," says Tsotsos. "What they know isn't really taught in schools; it's too specific. There aren't that many inertial systems analysts out there in industry, and where they are is with our competitors, who do their best to keep them."

Because the position is so highly specialized and requires a great deal of on-the-job experience, colleges and vocational schools cannot equip students with all of the knowledge and skills they will eventually need to perform competently on the job. What's more, systems are unique to the organizations in which they are developed, so the longer an analyst has been with the company, the more indispensable he or she is.

In a nutshell, the academic community can start but not finish the job of producing qualified inertial systems analysts. Since the chance of hiring experienced specialists away from other companies was negligible, the only viable option left for Honeywell was to grow its own experts in-house, as quickly as possible.

Reviving a lost tradition

Harkening back to one of the oldest forms of on-the-job training—apprenticeships—Tsotsos and Cheyunski decided that the best approach to this experiment in accelerated employee development was to pair up young engineers who demonstrated the greatest aptitude and interest in inertial systems analysis with senior people valued for their technical expertise.

On June 17 of last year, six "apprentices" and six "masters" began an intensive, six-month program. Apprentices spent about half of their time in formal classroom instruction and the other half working closely with their mentors on actual job assignments.

What systems analysts do is a lot like what systems engineers do, except that it involves more theoretical and mathematical analysis. "Systems analysts are more analytical in their approach to problems," Tsotsos explains. "They have to find out what the product has to do, whether the hardware will be capable of doing what it's supposed to do, and how the hardware and software will relate. We left it up to the engineering directors [at the three operations] to handpick two apprentices each."

Since systems analysts are a highly respected bunch at Honeywell—the "crème de la crème of engineers," according to Tsotsos—apprentices were delighted at being chosen for the program. "It was like Christmas for them," he says.

However, Tsotsos continues, "It meant taking them out of their previous career and putting a label on them that precluded them from going back. People were going to know what they were being trained to do. It was an identity thing, a transformation from an old position to a new one."

As for choosing the mentors, Tsotsos says there wasn't all that much to it. "It was pretty clear who to pick. They were indeed masters. We knew we needed a clone of this guy or that guy.

"At first, they were a little skeptical, but they knew something had to be done. They realized that no one was groomed to step into their shoes, but they saw it as a lot of work for themselves. People tend to think in terms of short-term needs instead of long-term gains. Devoting time to coaching and mentoring is a long-term strategy.

"It was something that went against the system here. Normally, we've had lots of low-level, subliminal OJT [on-the-job training]. Now, it was going to be a full-time, intense, mentor-apprentice relationship. Usually systems analysts work on projects independently. Now they had to work closely with someone else."

"They agreed with the objectives and perhaps the approach," concurs Harry Gaines, technical coordinator of the program and the individual in charge of recruiting the masters. "But they were concerned that the program might interfere with their own job responsibilities, that there would be too much competition for their time. To some extent, that turned out to be the case."

Getting the program off the ground was difficult not only because the masters were worried about the time commitment, but also because apprentices were highly valued in their previous positions. Predictably, their managers didn't want to give them up. As it turned out, the key to a successful start-up was getting the operations' vice presidents and directors of engineering to see the long-term need and actively demonstrate their support. "Once we were able to convince these guys that this is what was necessary, the middle managers had to go along. All the pieces then fell into place," Tsotsos recalls.

"We knew that after six months we wouldn't have experienced inertial systems analysts, but it was easier to sell that way," he adds. "We did have the labels in place, and apprentices could take on some assignments independently after the six-month period. The main thing was, we had the option to modify the program as needed."

Surprises

The original program is now over, and the primary goal has been achieved. The six apprentice engineers have made the career switch to systems analysis and are handling their new jobs competently. The master-apprentice link, though no longer a formal tutoring relationship, is expected to continue until the masters retire.

"We've established a certain camaraderie," says Tsotsos. "Apprentices go to their masters or any of the others when they have problems. Each master has a specialty, and apprentices soon figured out who was the real expert on what."

Even though the masters had spent their entire careers working pretty much on their own, Tsotsos says, "We found that these guys were very congenial. They fell into the program quite easily. Maybe the personal interaction was something they'd been missing."

Some of the bonds between master and apprentice were stronger than others. Variations had to do with personality differences and with how easy it was for a given master to incorporate an apprentice into his current job assignment. If the mentor was working on learning a new technology or software system, for instance, he had little difficulty getting the apprentice involved, says Gaines. On the other hand, some mentors were immersed in projects totally unrelated to anything an apprentice could understand.

Once the program was complete, the HRD department conducted for-mal interviews with all of the participants as well as apprentices' previous and current supervisors. The overall response was thumbs up, notwithstanding a few specific criticisms.

For the most part, negative reactions focused on the classroom curriculum chosen for the six apprentices. "It seems that some of the material was targeted a little low," says Tsotsos. "Some of the apprentices we chose were so versed in their subjects that part of the classroom training was redundant. We should have shot a little lower in terms of work experience . . . . Selection is probably the most critical factor. We could have gotten more out of the time invested if there had been more commonality of needs among the apprentices."

In retrospect, he suggests, "A good way of doing that would be to advertise a program that will be taking place and have all interested employees apply. Then select from the applicants a group that would be at more or less the same level." This approach, as opposed to having the engineering directors select participants, also would be more equitable from the engineers' point of view.

Derivative programs

The initial apprenticeship program may be over, but Honeywell, like so many high-tech companies these days, still has urgent needs for hard-to-find technical specialists. Tsotsos thinks that formal mentoring programs will soon become a trend in technical training. "What's needed is company-driven, very tailored training. Companies are doing their own thing; their needs are so specific. Universities are dealing with training in a generic manner. You also need someone identified as responsible for calling the shots on what courses these people should take—not necessarily someone from HRD or education."

In response to its immediate staffing needs, Honeywell's avionics division has launched two more apprentice programs, one for on-board data processing employees (i.e., software people who have experience with on-board computers) and the other for "real-time" computer programmers working in avionics applications. Still based on the mentoring concept, the new programs are "less condensed" derivatives of the original, says Tsotsos.

"Participants [in the original program] felt it would be more appropriate to have one master working with two or three apprentices. Also, instead of apprentices in training on a full-time, dedicated basis, they will still be involved in their old jobs. I'm not convinced this more diluted version will be as effective, but it is easier to administer and easier for everyone to handle."

Other options for the future might include sending young engineers on residency-type programs to study with experts in different Honeywell divisions, and designing less formal apprenticeships, in which experienced employees would be viewed more as coaches and mentors than as masters. "In certain areas of technical expertise, the apprentice-master relationship is optimal. In others, there is more need for classroom training," Tsotsos points out.

Drawbacks?

Over the years, apprentice training programs, like OJT in general, have been criticized on several grounds. Some say the "masters" typically provide little systematic guidance. Also, they may pass along a lot of irrelevant idiosyncrasies and shortcuts that become sloppy ways of getting things done in the hands of trainees. Other arguments against apprenticeship programs focus on the fact that on-site training is inevitably disrupted by day-to-day operational pressures and other distractions. As one technical training manager points out, "In manufacturing, at least, you're almost always operating in an eleventh-hour function. You just don't have the luxury to take people off the job."

Proponents, on the other hand, point out that apprenticeships can provide employees with more challenging job assignments than they might otherwise get. In addition to teaching their charges about the technical aspects of the job, mentors may also enlighten them as to the political ins and outs of getting things done in the organization. Maybe the best argument for apprentice programs is that after years of formal education and training, the last thing a new hire wants is to be shoved right into another structured, book-oriented learning experience.

Reprinted from TRAINING, July 1986

TAKING THE MONOTONY OUT OF THE TECHNICAL INSTRUCTOR'S JOB

Trainers need job enrichment too

BY RICHARD REAGH

One of the greatest occupational hazards for the classroom technical instructor is an overdose of his or her own specialty. After a technical trainer has conducted a particular program for several months, he or she begins to commit to memory electrical sequences, mechanical adjustments, and so forth. On the surface, this can make the instructor appear quite a subject matter expert. He can lecture eloquently and at length on the material without referring to notes.

Very impressive. But familiarity can *also* breed contempt. And contemptuous familiarity can lead to problems which adversely affect the learning situation.

One way a training manager can minimize these problems is by rotating training assignments, one of the several solutions explored later in this article. But first, some needs analysis. It's important for training managers to be able to recognize at least these danger signs:

Battle fatigue. This leads to boredom. The instructor tends to cover material too fast. He knows the information so well he touches only the high points, or what he considers to be the most pertinent information. The instructor has forgotten what it's like to be a beginner.

The learner suffers, too. Unable to grasp the relevancy of these high points because he requires basic, building-block information as a foundation, he becomes frustrated. The instructor suddenly "discovers" that the students lack understanding of what is transpiring in the classroom. Obviously, that should be a signal to the trainer that he or she is not giving good information. Instead, the instructor very often resorts to...

"Attacking" students. Frustration-based oral attacks on the trainees can take several forms. The instructor may be impatient or curt when responding to questions. You'll hear him say, "You know that. You aren't thinking." "You're not listening. If you paid more attention, you would get this." "I can't hold up the class for an unimportant point. See me later." Or, worst of all, the instructor cops out by calling on his "star" trainee to tell the others trainees how it all works.

After the attack occurs and the students discover that the consequence for trying to pick the instructor's brain is a personal or general attack, they'll quit asking questions and the learning process stops.

Too many details. Another problem can evolve when the instructor has been teaching the same class for too long. Over the years, he has accumulated a huge reservoir of facts and is anxious to tell them all. He assaults the class with *every* detail and provides so much information that most students can't differentiate between important and "nice to know" information. Very soon the learner begins to doubt his ability to absorb this mountain of information. He asks fewer questions because he doesn't feel he can handle any more data. Again, the learning process breaks down, and again the instructor may not be aware that he has created the problem.

A negative attitude. Example: After a year or so, the course outline "Joe" has been tied to becomes not just routine, it becomes a tedious classroom agenda that he wants to escape. His manager can't understand why Joe, who has been an enthusiastic, cooperative producer, has become a thin-skinned grouch who is constantly complaining about his pay, his lack of opportunity, his "stupid" students, and the lousy way that the training center and the company in general is run.

Management has the responsibility to monitor the instructor's participation in any given program. Training management cannot simply assume that the department is staffed by totally dedicated professionals who will maintain a high interest level, despite the fact that they lack new challenges and change in their routine.

Part of the manager's MBO should be a plan for rotating instructors at least every six months. Rotation can be accomplished through a program of cross-training and the assignment of new projects on a regular schedule.

The knowledge an instructor has gained in a particular program is not lost through rotation or new assignment. The instructor can always be tapped as a ready resource or "backup" when the need arises. Most instructors demonstrate a high degree of pride and cooperation when they are called upon to show their expertise when they know that they are not going to be "stuck" with the program indefinitely.

In training departments where expansion has stopped and the department is simply maintaining, it might not be possible to rotate instructors on a regular schedule, but it is still possible to break the instructor's routine. Staff development for the staff development staff *is* legitimate. Management feedback to the instructor concerning classroom conduct and post-training problems add to personal development efforts.

Breaks should be created in class schedules and the instructor encouraged to use this extra time to devise new methods of implementation and audiovisual support to constantly improve the quality of his program. Inside and outside programs of instructor training should be organized for the instructor so that he knows he is always learning and growing and that management is interested in that growth.

Most important, training managers should realize that an instructor is usually at the peak of effectiveness between the second and the sixth months of involvement in a training program. During this period, he is involved in his *own* learning process, and because he is still learning himself, he is able to relate to the needs of the student. He has a fresh approach to teaching and the subject.

But after six months, the program tends to become monotonous, and this monotony is reflected in the instructor's attitudes and methods of instruction. The instructor loses sight of the students' needs and starts to impede instead of facilitate the learning process. The students suffer, the company suffers.

Reprinted from TRAINING, July 1977

LET THE 'ACADEMICS' TRAIN—AFTER THEY PAY THEIR DUES

BY DON M. RICKS

Much of the work we do in training and development is necessary because certain academicians failed to do it when they should have. That's why we have to spend considerable time helping many university-"educated" people become productive employees who can read and write competently; who have the skill needed to work with and lead others; who can utilize information and make sound decisions. Sometimes we even have to teach them the basic technical skills they need to do the jobs they were supposedly trained to do.

Now the academics, faced with dropping enrollments and shrinking budgets, have taken a new interest in assisting us with those tasks. Universities are expanding and redirecting their continuing-education programs to meet what they see as the training needs of business and government. Individual "moonlighting" is becoming a common practice, even in academic departments where it was previously unheard of.

But I question whether we can afford all this "help." We are never allocated enough training time and money. Dare we gamble what we do have on the academics' assumption that they can now accomplish (usually in a short program) what they failed to accomplish in four or more years? More importantly, can our new credibility support more "interesting and informative" courses that produce little recognizable skills improvement?

Using academics, in both individual and institutional form, can be temptingly easy and inexpensive. Managers are usually agreeable to sending people to a course taught by a professor, especially since such courses often have to be offered after hours (when the "real" work of the suppliers is finished). And the costs tend to be attractive, usually because they are, in effect, subsidized by capital, operating and salary expenditures that have been made for public education purposes.

Also, the academics seem more flexible than before. Only a few years ago, the trainer who turned to them for help was likely to be told, "Here's what we offer. Therefore, it must be what you need." Now they are going to considerable lengths to find out what business and government actually need. And they are adapting their schedules and programs to training requirements.

Such changes are only superficial, however. Having worked "both sides of the street" (I was an academic for 12 years and have been in training for 10), I seriously doubt that the time has yet come for the wide gap between training and academia to be bridged. Those involved in the latter operate from a foundation of assumptions that we feel— with very good reason, I think— is invalid. And we have learned too many things about learning that most of them neither know nor are ready to accept.

I feel we face a serious threat from those who, working either on behalf of institutions or as individual consultants, see training and development as a vast new market for their offerings. It appears that they are trying to exploit that market without investing the time and effort required to find out what it's all about.

In essence, the academics offer various versions of a pedagogic system that was developed in the Middle Ages for teaching small numbers of elite students and that has since been adapted, with clearly questionable results, to teaching masses of average students.

That system presumes that exposure to content, in both spoken and written form, somehow produces learning. It presumes that the teacher knows almost everything and the learner almost nothing. It does not recognize the vast differences between cognition and behavior; between instructional objectives and learning objectives; the vast difference, in fact, between teaching (as the instructor's external behavior) and learning (as the student's internal behavior).

Its understanding of motivation is primitive, being limited to threats of punishment and withholding of rewards. It does not provide for the asking of open-ended questions, for the generation of positive group dynamics or for the individual pursuit of self-determined learning goals. It is very effective at teaching people that they are uninformed and incompetent but of little use in helping them become informed and competent.

We in training have worked hard at establishing our credibility, at proving to management that we can generate performance improvements that make direct and valuable contributions to the effectiveness of the organizations we serve. Let's not forfeit that credibility by putting our opportunities to train into the hands of those who have already demonstrated their inability to do the job.

Instead, let's insist that the academics who want to serve training "pay the dues" that we paid. That is, let's require that they learn about learning. Once they have become as competent as we are in delivering learning, the special expertise they can offer will be a valuable resource we can use in helping people develop the abilities needed for effective and rewarding work.

Reprinted from TRAINING, September 1980

CHAPTER 9

UNDERSTANDING THE ADULT LEARNER

How do people learn? The question has no ultimately satisfying answer. Long before educational psychologists existed, philosophers puzzled over the meaning of "to know" and "to learn." The puzzle remains unsolved.

There is no absence of effort. Names such as Watson, Hull, Skinner, Brunner, Gagne, Maslow and Rogers pepper a distinguished literature of research and thought. The ancient "nature vs. nurture" argument continues unabated, weighted with all its questions about the extent of training's power to change behavior: Are humans almost infinitely malleable, infinitely capable of change? Or are many behavioral and personality patterns "wired in" to the individual and extremely difficult to alter in any significant way?

Then there is the more recent fascination with the computer as a model for studying the human brain. Will research in artificial intelligence give us dramatic new insights into the human thinking process? Will it produce revolutionary improvements in our ability to teach and learn?

Of particular interest to corporate trainers is the matter of the adult as a special learner with special needs, an issue brought to our consciousness by Malcolm S. Knowles. With his books *The Adult Learner: A Neglected Species, The Modern Practice of Adult Education, Self-Directed Learning* and others, Knowles helped destroy two myths. The first was the assumption that adults learn—and can be taught—the same way small children, monkeys and pigeons learn. The second myth, covert but real, was that there is something deficient, odd or lacking in an adult who needs any formal learning.

Andragogy, the study of how adults learn, has produced a wealth of new ideas for working with men and women who need to know things that they didn't learn in school.

How important is all this adult-learning information to designing and developing training? In one sense, it is totally dispensable. Any one of us could "get by" designing and developing training programs on intuition or by mimicking learning experiences we have found personally likable. Untrained trainers do it every day. But the belief in progress, the idea that things can always be done better, is central to what trainers do for a living. The better we are at modeling that belief, at seeking improvements in the effectiveness and efficiency of what we do, the better we become at encouraging others to do the same.

30 THINGS WE KNOW FOR SURE ABOUT ADULT LEARNING

The body of knowledge on the subject is just beginning to accumulate, but there are some truisms (we think)

BY RON AND SUSAN ZEMKE

We don't know a lot about the mechanisms of adult learning. At least, not in the "What are the minimum—necessary and sufficient—conditions for effecting a permanent change in an adult's behavior?" sense of knowing.

In that, we're not alone. Dr. Malcolm Knowles came to much the same conclusion in *The Adult Learner: A Neglected Species*. Eight years ago, he equated his efforts to summarize what was then known about adult learning to a trip up the Amazon: "It is a strange world that we are going to explore together, with lush growth of flora and fauna with exotic names (including fossils of extinct species) and teeming with savage tribes in raging battle. I have just made a casing-the-joint trip up the river myself, and I can tell you that my head is reeling." Today Knowles says, "The river is much tamer. We are beginning to understand what we do that works and why it works." But as we listen, we have the distinct impression that what our point man Knowles sees as tame travel can still be white-water rapids for the rest of us.

While there are hundreds of books and articles offering tips and tricks for teaching adults, the bulk of that knowledge is derived from three relatively limited spheres. The first is "My life and times in teaching," wherein one teacher/trainer of adults shares his or her career's accumulation of secrets with others. Though intriguing and interesting, this literature focuses more on teacher survival than anything else, and while we learn much about living, we learn relatively little about learning.

The second common source is the "Why adults decide to study" research. Here we learn some interesting, even fascinating, things about the conditions and incidents that motivate adults to engage in a "focused learning effort." But in most of this research, the adult seems assumed to be a learning machine who, once switched on, vacuums up knowledge and skill. It is more indicative than instructive, suggestive than substantive. A cynic would call this body of knowledge about adult learning a form of market research.

The third source is extrapolation from theory: both adult learning theory and research and that derived from work with children and nonhuman subjects. The adult learning theories in question are really holistic treatments of human nature: the Carl Rogers/Abraham Maslow sort of theory from which we can only infer, or guess at, rules of practice."Would you rather learn from a lecture or a book?" or "On your own or with direction?" are interesting questions, but ones that beg the issue of results or learning outcomes. A trainee may prefer listening to lectures but learn best by practice and application exercises.

The nonadult theory and research is a broad lot—everything from child development studies to pigeon training. The tendency seems to be to draw guidance from the B. F. Skinner/behavior modification/programmed instruction, and the Albert Bandura/behavior modeling/social learning schools of thought. While both schools are generating research and results, they are still shorter on proven practices than pontification and speculation. No single theory, or set of theories, seems to have an arm-lock on understanding adults or helping us work effectively and efficiently with them.

Still and all, from a variety of sources there emerges a body of fairly reliable knowledge about adult learning—arbitrarily 30 points which lend themselves to three basic divisions:
- Things we know about adult learners and their motivation.
- Things we know about designing curriculum for adults.
- Things we know about working with adults in the classroom.

These aren't be-all, end-all categories. They overlap more than just a little bit. But they help us understand what we are learning from others about adult learning.

Motivation to learn

Adult learners can't be threatened, coerced or tricked into learning something new. Birch rods and gold stars have minimum impact. Adults *can* be ordered into a classroom and prodded into a seat, but they *cannot* be forced to learn. Though trainers are often faced with adults who have been sent to training, there are some insights to be garnered from the research on adults who seek out a structured learning experience on their own; something we all do at least twice a year, the research says. We begin our running tally from this base camp.

1 Adults seek out learning experiences in order to cope with specific life-change events. Marriage, divorce, a new job, a promotion, being fired, retiring, losing a loved one and moving to a new city are examples.

2 The more life-change events an adult encounters, the more likely he or she is to seek out learning opportunities. Just as stress increases as life-change events accumulate, the motivation to cope with change through engagement in a learning experience increases. Since the people who most frequently seek out learning opportunities are people who have the most overall years of education, it is reasonable to guess that for many of us learning is a coping response to significant change.

3 The learning experiences adults seek out on their own are directly related— at least in their own perception— to the life-change events that triggered the seeking. Therefore, if 80% of the change being encountered is work related, then 80% of the learning experiences sought should be work related.

4 Adults are generally willing to engage in learning experiences before, after, or even during the ac-

NEW RESEARCH ON ADULT "STYLES"

Most trainers know that STYLE is one of the hottest buzz words for 1977. There's a renewed interest in leadership style. There's a communication style, conceptual style, and behavioral style. Confused by all this stylish babble? You needn't be, as the concept behind it is pretty straightforward.

Suppose you have two teenagers, Susan and Sam. Susan moves slowly and languidly. When she speaks, she does so evenly and quietly. When Sam walks, he runs. He speaks at a machine-gun pace and often with .45 caliber concussiveness. His tone and volume run radio-dial ranges. Sam and Susan are different.

A personality theorist would look at them and wonder about the antecedents of their behavior and their cognitive structures. Was Sam punished for being idle as a tot? Was Susan scolded for making noise as a baby? What pathologies might they develop as they grow into adulthood?

Different learners, styles

Style theorists, on the other hand, would ask how Frenetic Sam and Dreamy Susan live together in the same house without producing a constant state of undeclared sibling warfare. Could Sam and Susan ever learn to work together? Where do their differences complement; where do they collide?

Personality theorists are interested in the whole person—all the interests, attitudes, temperaments, needs, physiology, aptitudes, and morphology which they consider necessary to fully describe and explain a person. Those who study style have different fish to fry. They try to:

1. determine and codify those observable behavioral aspects of individuation referred to as Style;

2. develop a theory of interpersonal one-to-one relations and communications based on style differences;

3. determine and codify interpersonal style factors which lead to effective and ineffective interpersonal relations and communications; and

4. develop a body of knowledge which will yield a technology for improving interpersonal relations and communications utilizing the concept of style.

Are you a relational?

Now a group of adult education researchers from the Ontario Institute for Studies in Adult Education have added a fifth concern—developing a theory of differential instruction based on cognitive style differences between learners.

Researchers Richard W. V. Cawley, Sheila A. Miller, and James N. Milligan have done preliminary work that supports the conjecture that there are a limited number of cognitive styles among adult learners. Their research indicates that these styles are pretty evenly distributed in the population and, therefore, may be critically important to understand in the design of training for adults. Based on research conducted with a small group of graduate students, Cawley, Miller, and Milligan are convinced that there are at least two major cognitive or adult information processing styles: the *Analytical* and the *Relational*.

The *Analytical* learner is field-independent and able to select relevant stimuli imbedded in a larger context. Analyticals seem able to resist interfering signals when working on technical tasks. They have long attention spans, are highly reflective, and can concentrate deeply. In tasks, the Analytical prefers complexity. In

learning environments, he or she prefers the formal learning situation, sees the instructor strictly as an information giver, and conceptualizes learning as a non-social experience.

The *Relational* learner is field-dependent. He or she sees things in global terms and tends to understand learning experiences as wholes or Gestalts. A short attention span, distractability, and hyperkinesis characterize the *Relational*. Simple tasks and concepts appeal. The Relational values learning which is centered in the self, has relevance for his or her life, relates to his or her feelings, ties into other, prior experiences. The Relational prefers the informal learning setting and sees the instructor first as a person, then as a facilitator of learning.

Ah, congenial company

Two supplemental findings tend to tie Cawley's, Miller's, and Milligan's work with other style research. First, they noticed that the Relationals who had difficulty with one particular analytically oriented test tended to be apologetic for taking so much time and doing so poorly. The Analyticals, on the other hand, responded to a similar situation without apologies.

The second incidental finding pertained to the life styles of the graduate students studied. Analyticals tended to live alone, while the Relationals tended to live with a group or in a family. The Analyticals believed that a family obligation would detract from the tasks of student life and interfere with the goal of attaining a graduate degree. The Relationals rationalized their life-style selection thusly: You only go around once in life, and without congenial company, the trip is not worth taking.—Reported in "Cognitive Style and the Adult Learner," *Adult Education*, 1976, Vol. 26, No. 2.

Reprinted from TRAINING, May 1977

tual life-change event. Once convinced that the change is a certainty, adults will engage in any learning that promises to help them cope with the transition.

5 Although adults have been found to engage in learning for a variety of reasons— job advancement, pleasure, love of learning and so on— it is equally true that for most adults learning is not its own reward. Adults who are motivated to seek out a learning experience do so primarily (80-90% of the time) because they have a

use for the knowledge or skill being sought. Learning is a means to an end, not an end in itself.

6 Increasing or maintaining one's sense of self-esteem and pleasure are strong secondary motivators for engaging in learning experiences. Having a new skill or extending and enriching current knowledge can be both, depending on the individual's personal perceptions.

The major contributors to what we know about adult motivation to learn have been Allen Tough, Carol Asla-

nian and Henry Brickell, Kjell Rubenson and Harry L. Miller. One implication of their findings for the trainer is that there seem to be "teachable moments" in the lives of adults. Their existence impacts the planning and scheduling of training. As a recent study by the management development group of one large manufacturer concluded, "Newly promoted supervisors and managers must receive training as nearly concurrent with promotions and changes in responsibilities as possible. The longer such training is delayed, the less impact it appears to have on actual job performance."

Curriculum design

One developing research-based concept that seems likely to have an impact on our view and practice of adult training and development is the concept of "fluid" versus "crystallized" intelligence. R. B. Catell's research on lifelong intellectual development suggests there are two distinct kinds of intelligence that show distinct patterns of age-related development, but which function in a complementary fashion. Fluid intellect tends to be what we once called innate intelligence; fluid intelligence has to do with the ability to store strings of numbers and facts in short-term memory, react quickly, see spatial relations and do abstract reasoning. Crystallized intelligence is the part of intellectual functioning we have always taken to be a product of knowledge acquisition and experience. It is related to vocabulary, general information, conceptual knowledge, judgment and concrete reasoning.

Historically, many societies have equated youth with the ability to insatiably acquire information and age with the ability to wisely use information. Catell's research suggests this is true—that wisdom is, in fact, a separate intellectual function that develops as we grow older. Which leads to some curriculum development implications of this concept:

7 Adult learners tend to be less interested in, and enthralled by, survey courses. They tend to prefer single-concept, single-theory courses that focus heavily on the application of the concept to relevant problems. This tendency increases with age.

8 Adults need to be able to integrate new ideas with what they already know if they are going to keep—and use—the new information.

9 Information that conflicts sharply with what is already held to be true, and thus forces a re-evaluation of the old material, is integrated more slowly.

10 Information that has little "conceptual overlap" with what is already known is acquired slowly.

11 Fast-paced, complex or unusual learning tasks interfere with the learning of the concepts or data they are intended to teach or illustrate.

12 Adults tend to compensate for being slower in some psychomotor learning tasks by being more accurate and making fewer trial-and-error ventures.

13 Adults tend to take errors personally, and are more likely to let them affect self-esteem. Therefore, they tend to apply tried-and-true solutions and take fewer risks. There is even evidence that adults will misinterpret feedback and "mistake" errors for positive confirmation.

Dr. K. Patricia Cross, author of *Adults As Learners*, sees four global implications for designing adult curriculum in Catell's work. "First, the presentation of new information should be meaningful, and it should include aids that help the learner organize it and relate it to previously stored information. Second, it should be presented at a pace that permits mastery. Third, presentation of one idea at a time and minimization of competing intellectual demands should aid comprehension. Finally, frequent summarization should facilitate retention and recall."

A second neat new idea that impacts curriculum design is the concept of adult developmental stages. Jean Piaget, Lawrence Kohlberg and others have seen children as passing through phases and stages for some time. It is only recently, thanks to Gail Sheehy, Roger Gould, Daniel Levinson and others, that we've come to acknowledge that there are also adult growth stages. A subset of this concept is the idea that not only do adults' needs and interests continually change, but their values also continue to grow and change. For that insight, we can thank Clare W. Graves and his pioneering work in value analysis. The implications, though still formative:

14 The curriculum designer must know whether the concepts and ideas will be in concert or in conflict with learner and organizational values. As trainers at AT&T have learned, moving from a service to a sales philosophy requires more than a change in words and titles. It requires a change in the way people think and value.

15 Programs need to be designed to accept viewpoints from people in different life stages and with different value "sets."

16 A concept needs to be "anchored" or explained from more than one value set and appeal to more than one developmental life stage.

A final set of curriculum design guides comes from the research on learning media preference. Researchers have for years been asking students if they preferred learning XYZ from a book, a movie experience or another person. Though there are limitations to the value of this sort of data, enough of it is accumulating to be of some help to the design effort.

17 Adults prefer self-directed and self-designed learning projects 7 to 1 over group-learning experiences led by a professional. Furthermore, the adult learner often selects more than one medium for the design. Reading and talking to a qualified peer are frequently cited as good resources. The desire to control pace and start/stop time strongly affect the self-directed preference.

18 Nonhuman media such as books, programmed instruction and television have become popular in recent years. One piece of research found them very influential of the way adults plan self-directed learning projects.

19 Regardless of media, straightforward how-to is the preferred content orientation. As many as 80% of the polled adults in one study cited the need for applications and how-to information as the primary motivation for undertaking a learning project.

20 Self-direction does *not* mean isolation. In fact, studies of self-directed learning show self-directed projects involve an average of 10 other people as resources, guides, encouragers and the like. The incompetence or inadequacy of these same people is often rated as a primary frustration. But even for the self-professed, self-directed learner, lectures and short seminars get positive ratings, especially when these events give the learner face-to-face, one-to-one access to an expert.

Apparently, the adult learner is a very efficiency-minded individual. Allen Tough suggests that the typical adult learner asks "What is the cheapest, easiest, fastest way for me to learn to do *that*?" and then proceeds independently along this self-determined route. An obvious tip for the trainer is that the adult trainee has to have a hand in shaping the curriculum of the program.

In the classroom

We seem to know the least about helping the adult maximize the classroom experience. There are master performers in our trade who gladly pass along their favorite tips and tricks, but as Marshall McLuhan observed, "We don't know who discovered water but we can be pretty sure it wasn't a fish." In other words, the master performer is often a poor judge of how one becomes a master performer. There certainly are volumes of opinion and suggestion, but by and large they rest more on theory than hard data. Ironically, some of the strongest data comes from survey studies of what turns off adults in the classroom. Likewise, there is a nicely developing body of literature on what makes for good and bad meetings that has implications for training:

21 The learning environment must be physically and psychologically comfortable. Adults report that long lectures, periods of interminable sitting and the absence of practice opportunities are high on the irritation scale.

22 Adults have something real to lose in a classroom situation. Self-esteem and ego are on the line when they are asked to risk trying a new behavior in front of peers and cohorts. Bad experiences in traditional education, feelings about authority and the preoccupation with events outside the classroom all affect in-class experience. These and other influencing factors are carried into class with the learners as surely as are their gold Cross pens and lined yellow pads.

23 Adults have expectations, and it is critical to take time up front to clarify and articulate *all* expectations before getting into content.

Both trainees and the instructor/facilitator need to state their expectations. When they are at variance, the problem should be acknowledged and a resolution negotiated. In any case, the instructor can assume responsibility only for his or her own expectations, not for that of trainees.

24 Adults bring a great deal of life experience into the classroom, an invaluable asset to be acknowledged, tapped and used. Adults can learn well—and much—from dialogue with respected peers.

25 Instructors who have a tendency to hold forth rather than facilitate can hold that tendency in check—or compensate for it—by concentrating on the use of open-ended questions to draw out relevant trainee knowledge and experience.

26 New knowledge has to be integrated with previous knowledge; that means active learner participation. Since only the learners can tell us how the new fits or fails to fit with the old, we have to ask them. Just as the learner is dependent on us for confirming feedback on skill practice, we are dependent on the learner for feedback about our curriculum and in-class performance.

27 The key to the instructor role is control. The instructor must balance the presentation of new material, debate and discussion, sharing of relevant trainee experiences, and the clock. Ironically, we seem best able to establish control when we risk giving it up. When we shelve our egos and stifle the tendency to be threatened by challenge to our plans and methods, we gain the kind of facilitative control we seem to need to effect adult learning.

28 The instructor has to protect minority opinion, keep disagreements civil and unheated, make connections between various opinions and ideas, and keep reminding the group of the variety of potential solutions to the problem. Just as in a good problem-solving meeting, the instructor is less advocate than orchestrator.

29 Integration of new knowledge and skill requires transition time and focused effort. Working on applications to specific back-on-the-job problems helps with the transfer. Action plans, accountability strategies and follow-up after training all increase the likelihood of that transfer. Involving the trainees' supervisor in pre-/post-course activities helps with both in-class focus and transfer.

30 Learning and teaching theories function better as a resource than as a Rosetta stone. The four currently influential theories—humanistic, behavioral, cognitive and developmental—all offer valuable guidance when matched with an appropriate learning task. A skill-training task can draw much from the behavioral approach, for example, while personal growth-centered subjects seem to draw gainfully from humanistic concepts. The trainer of adults needs to take an eclectic rather than a single theory-based approach to developing strategies and procedures.

Study of the adult as a special species of learner is a relatively new phenomenon. We can expect the next five years to eclipse the last fifty in terms of hard data production on adult learning. For now, however, we must recognize that adults want their learning to be problem-centered, personalized and accepting of their need for self-direction and personal responsibility. When you think of it, that's quite a lot to work with right there.

Reprinted from TRAINING, June 1981

THE ADULT LEARNER IS A SPECIAL SPECIES

Malcolm Knowles, often credited as the Father of Adult Learning Theory, speaks out on self-directed learning

An interview with Malcolm Knowles is a delightful experience. Less an interview than a conversation with a self-professed and bona fide lifelong learner.

For the record, Malcolm S. Knowles is a professor of Adult and Community College Education, North Carolina State University, Raleigh. Three of his books, The Modern Practice of Adult Education, The Adult Learner: A Neglected Species, *and* Self-Directed Learning *are cornerstones in the adult learning field. He is credited by many as The Father of Adult Learning. In truth, Malcolm Knowles seems a bit too unpretentious for so ponderous a title. People who wear the title "Father of..." seldom exhibit the good humor, rapacious wit and open eagerness of a Malcolm Knowles.*

But beware. Malcolm Knowles is, by his own report, a man with a mission: "I have been so impressed with the joy my students have found in self-directed learning that I want to spread the gospel. My motives are the motives of the missionary—so beware, I'll try to convert you."

Knowles, like the true believer he professes to be, has a rather broad witness. He can be found consulting with a medical college in Canada one day and a company in Colombia, South America the next. Somewhere between his various pulpits and parishes, Philip Jones and Ron Zemke, managed to buttonhole this trainer of 40 plus years long enough to ask . . .

TRAINING: What has changed in your thinking about adult learning since publication of your excellent 1973 book, *The Adult Learner: A Neglected Species?*

KNOWLES: The major changes or breakthroughs in my thinking deal with implementation processes. For example, I have found that the use of learning contracts is the magical answer to many of the problems that we were running into in helping adults organize and structure their self-directed learning. I use learning contracts in all of my course work here on campus, in all of my in-service training work with professional associations, and in the management development work I do in industry.

TRAINING: Aren't learning contracts increasingly popular in public education also?

KNOWLES: Yes, they are. For example, the reason public school educators ran into a lot of problems with alternative schools, open schools and ungraded classrooms is that they tossed out *content structure* without supplying a *process structure* in its place. Kids would come in and the teachers would say "what would you like to learn today" and not much would happen. Now the youngsters develop learning contracts which specify what the learning objectives are, what the resources and strategies are for accomplishing the objectives, and what evidence they will collect to demonstrate that they accomplished the objectives. This turns out to be a structure that the kids can use to have a systematic, articulated, sequential set of learning experiences. Well, the same thing's true with adults.

TRAINING: Isn't this "new concept" of learning contracts just another version of the behaviorist's "If... Then," "Behavior...Reinforcer," "First work...Then play" performance contract idea?

KNOWLES: There are similarities, but that's all. Allen Tough's* research is pretty clear about what a learning contract needs to be to respond to the adult's needs. Those requirements distinguish the learning contract from the behavioral performance contract. One of the things he found is that when adults decide they want to learn something, they start organizing their thinking in terms of a project; not in terms of behaviors to be acquired. And so, the form of the learning contract is really the identification of a set of projects for accomplishing a particular set of learning objectives.

The objectives *may* be stated in terms of behavior, particularly for simple, motor kinds of learning, but I don't find terminal behavior statements to be very appropriate for the complex kinds of learning that involve the combining of a number of behaviors into a performance. What I do in my own practice is to give a lot of freedom to the learner to state the objectives in terms that are meaningful to him, and to use a variety of forms. As a result, some of the objectives might be behaviorally stated while others may simply be in terms of improving one's ability to do something.

TRAINING: When you don't state the performance change in behavioral terms isn't there an evaluation problem; simply stated. the problem of "knowing one when you see one"?

KNOWLES: The new thing in education in general, but particularly in professional education and management education, is competency based education. The competencies that are required for performing a particular role are described and evaluated in holistic terms. The problem the competency model approach avoids is the fragmenting and isolating of behaviors which must be seen in interaction with one another for the performance to make sense. In other words, a given performance might require a combination of knowledge, understanding, skill, attitude and value—and so the competency statement combines all the behaviors that are relevant to that particular performance.

Now to your specific question, "Isn't it hard to measure competencies?" Of course it is, but the device that is being found most appropriate is what is rather awkwardly being called a criterion-referenced performance test. For example, a critical incident is presented, the learner shows how he would solve that critical incident making use of the knowledge and skill a particular competency contains. Development of the criterion-referenced

*See Harry Levinson: "Adult Growth Stages Affect Management Development," TRAINING, May 1977.

performance test is difficult, but for most competencies it makes evaluation very reliable and fairly easy.

TRAINING: "For most competencies" doesn't mean for all competencies then?

KNOWLES: No. For complex human behaviors we must often base attainment of competency on data from subjective judgments. For example, in assessing whether a person has in fact developed a certain competency, having a panel of judges observe him doing the performance and rating him according to a prescribed set of criteria on that performance is really better data than we get from paper and pencil tests that give a quantified score.

TRAINING: Where are people doing what you'd like to see done with adult learners?

KNOWLES: There are two institutions that have carried these ideas that we've just been talking about to the furthest degree. One is a little liberal arts college on Prince Edward Island, Canada—the name of it is Holland College, in Charlottesville. The president there is Don Glendenning. He's been the catalytic agent for converting their entire curriculum away from a course structured program to a competency based modular program.

TRAINING: The curriculum is completely by contract?

KNOWLES: By contract. They don't have any "classes" as we know them. They've identified the competencies that are required for a wide variety of roles, vocational and general. They have seriously addressed the question of what exactly it means to be a well-educated person. And they've constructed learning packages for each competency. The individuals write personalized contracts toward developing the established competencies they want to develop.

The other place, that has done a tremendous job of developing a self-directed learning environment is the School of Medicine at McMaster University in Hamilton, Ontario. The key person there is Dr. Victor Neufeld. I've been a consultant to both of those institutions on faculty development, which is why I know them so well. The McMaster School has developed what they call a problem-centered approach to medical education. They've identified a large number, a couple hundred, of the most common problem situations that doctors confront. For each problem situation they have developed modules that contain in them what a doctor needs to know about anatomy, pathology, pharmacology, prognosis, diagnosis, etc.

necessary to handle that kind of problem situation.

TRAINING: Are they completely away from the bio-systems approach?

KNOWLES: Yes, except of course, where the problems have to do with intersystemic problems. But on the main, the learning is in terms of developing competencies for dealing with this wide variety of problems.

TRAINING: From our experience, it's pretty hard to bring people in professional education to agreement on process issues. They tend to agree on the goals and objectives, but disagree on the most appropriate steps for getting there.

KNOWLES: You're really getting to

the problem of validation of the competency model. The process by which both Holland College and McMaster School of Medicine validated their models was a two-step process. First they involved experts from the field as well as experts on the faculty, former students and present students on a series of task forces, each assigned to develop a specific competency model. The second step was to field test that model through a jury system. These juries were comprised of a broad spectrum of people across the country. Ultimately, of course, the model can only be validated by the performance of the graduates. And that's what both colleges are now in the process of

WHAT RESEARCH SAYS ABOUT ADULT LEARNING

BY RON ZEMKE

How do adults learn? On their own mostly, or so suggests Allen Tough, professor of adult education, Ontario Institute for Studies in Education, Toronto. In an adult learning research review that appeared in a recent issue of *Adult Education*, Tough suggests that most adults are a) continually involved in some sort of a major learning project and b) involved alone.

According to Tough, "Adults spend a remarkable amount of time each year at major efforts to learn. In fact, a typical learning effort requires 100 hours. The typical adult conducts five such efforts a year; 500 hours altogether. Some of these learning projects rely on instructors and classes, but over 70% are self-planned and others rely on friends and peer groups."

The 20-plus studies Tough reviewed were conducted within the last 10 years, tended to be survey or semistructured interview in nature, and used the same general definition of an adult learning project. "A learning project," says Tough, "is a highly deliberate effort to gain and retain certain definite knowledge and skill, or to change in some other way. To be included, a series of related learning sessions (episodes in which the person's primary intention was to learn) must all add up to at least seven hours." Tough suggests that this definition includes all media and methods— reading, listening, observing, attending class, reflecting, practicing, getting answers to questions.

The term "knowledge and skill" in-

cludes such matters as changed awareness, competence, habits, attitudes, sensitivity and confidence. Self-planned learning, classroom learning, learning guided by a friend or a group of peers and learning guided by programmed instruction are all included. Non-credit learning as well as degree or certification-aimed learning are included, as are learning for practical reasons and learning motivated by curiosity, interest, puzzlement and enjoyment.

Some of Tough's other conclusions based on his literature review are:

1. Probably 90% of all adults engage in at least one major learning effort a year, though the range of studies is from 70% to 100%.

2. About 20% of all adult learning projects are planned by a "professional"— someone trained, paid or institutionally designated to facilitate the learning. The other 80% is planned by an "amateur"— the learner (73%), a friend (3%) or a group of peers (4%).

3. The *most* common motivation for a learning project is some anticipated use or application. The person has a task— raising a child, writing a report, handling a case, teaching a class, fixing or improving something around the home, sewing a dress— and acquires certain knowledge and skill to perform successfully. The *least* common motivation (5%) is learning for credit for some sort of certification— degree, certificate, driver's license. An only slightly more common motivator is curiosity, or knowledge for knowledge sake.

4. Surprisingly, studies in Jamaica, Ghana and New Zealand revealed the same general pattern of results as did studies in the U.S. and Canada; that is, 70% of all adults participate in at least one major learning project per year.

5. Males, professionals and the more highly educated tend to need

doing. Systematically collecting data about the performance levels of the graduates as compared to pre-graduation predictors.

TRAINING: When a jury of experts begins discussing a competency model, isn't there a danger that the discussion will degenerate into arguments of specific processes rather than outcome—that how the students should look during the performance will become the topic rather than what result should be achieved?

KNOWLES: Absolutely. And the only way out of that is through negotiation. I had an experience as a consultant to the Hoffmann-LaRoche Drug Company helping to develop their multimedia system for training cardiological nurses. What they did was to assemble a panel of the country's outstanding cardiologists, sit them down and say, "We're not going to let you out of the room until this is settled." The panel simply had to argue through the taught criterion issues and come to a consensus. In a few cases consensus was achieved by majority vote. Going with the best judgment available at the moment is sometimes about all you can do. Incidentally, the meeting was held in Scottsdale, in the winter, so there was some additional motivation to resolve things within the allotted time period.

TRAINING: Are other medical schools showing an interest in McMaster's approach to training?

KNOWLES: Yes. In fact they're experiencing some problems due to the heavy number of outside consulting requests their faculty members receive. An interesting thing: They opened in 1969, so they've had a few graduating classes. Still, they had quite a hard time getting their first graduating class into internships. They had to go out and do a heavy sales job. They had much less difficulty getting their second class placed. Now, as I understand it, they have more applications from hospitals and clinics for interns than all the other medical schools in Canada put together. And there's great competition for McMaster's graduates. When the McMaster people ask, "Why do you want our people?" the answer they get is, "Well, your graduates come into an internship behaving like doctors. The graduates of other places come in behaving like graduate students."

TRAINING: If industrial trainers take this message to heart, the message that adults need lots of options and they need to be able to organize the learning environment in their own idiosyncratic fashion, shouldn't they then stop being trainers, accountable for learning, and become information presenters and communicators? Maybe they should revise their roles and just become brokers and librarians for various kinds of learning aids and materials.

KNOWLES: I see the required functions here being more than just brokering. In fact the new brokering agencies that are being established have found that more is needed than just giving the person information about where the resources are. Help is needed in structuring and planning the learning strategies. Help is needed in getting evidence as to accomplishment of the learning objective.

What I see happening is the redefinition of the role of teacher *away* from that of the transmitter and controller of knowledge and skills. I would describe that role as facilitator and resource person to self-directed learners. That's not a passive, permissive role. It's an active role that includes such functions as helping the learner diagnose his needs for learning. There are all sorts of strategies, tools and methods for helping the learner get some objective data about the competence he needs to learn to become what he wants to become. The facilitator needs to have a big repertoire of tools and devices and procedures for aiding the learner in self-diagnosis.

Then, too, he needs to have a broad repertoire of strategies that he can

more help in setting goals, locating expert assistance, finding information and materials, dealing with difficult parts of their projects, and finding sources to assist in evaluation. Blacks tend to be more involved in formal courses and whites in self-planned learning.

Tough emphasizes, however, that demographic variables, such as age, race, sex, income and occupation, tend not to account for much of the difference between the "life-long learners" and the "non-learners." The learners seem to represent every imaginable demographic set. While professionals tended to do more projects per year (11) than others, they were by no means dominant in the studies. One study showed that 86 of 100 unemployed adults interviewed had engaged in at least one learning activity. Learning efforts of the latter group ranged from coping skills to preparation for a new job.

6. People who prefer learning on their own to learning in courses do so for the following reasons: a) desire to set own learning pace, b) desire to keep learning style flexible and easy to change, c) desire to use own style of learning, d) desire to put own structure on learning, e) didn't know of an available course, f) wanted to learn immediately, g) lack of time to engage in group learning programs, h) not enough money for a course or a class, i) transportation to a class is too hard to obtain or too expensive.

In the same vein, one study suggested that group projects were the preferred method for those attempting a religious learning project (47% of all religious projects) and academic learning: one to one was most common for self-development (29%); self-planned for current events (96%); and vocational learning (79%).

7. The number of vocational oriented learning projects varied by vocational group. Eighty-four percent of learning projects by college and university administrators were job related; 62% of learning projects by parish ministers were job related. (Specifically, ministers reported engaging in learning projects that would lead to Sunday sermon grist.) A general professional group—managers to engineers— reported 55% of all projects to be job related. A study of Atlanta pharmacists found that 30% of the group's learning projects were vocationally related.

8. Self-learners tend to follow a general pattern in planning and organizing their learning projects: a) clarifying a general problem or issue; b) becoming aware of the need to learn or deciding to begin a learning project; c) generating long-term objectives and identifying resources.

Self-learners report the most difficulty in "knowing how to start their learning projects (setting objectives); finding or making time to learn (setting objectives and scheduling); and knowing whether or not they were progressing or had accomplished what they had set out to do."

9. And finally, one study reports that while the learner retains control of the project, he or she characteristically seeks help from a mean of 10.6 persons, largely acquaintances.

Tough ends his fascinating trip through the frontiers of adult learning by suggesting that we have much to learn about the adult learner and how the "professional" can be a better facilitator. Clearly, the pontifical information giver is low on the list of resources sought by the adult learner. Perhaps Alvin Toffler was right when he suggested that the life-long learner, the future shock survivor, won't be the person with a superior font of facts but the person who can learn, unlearn, and relearn effectively, and independently.

Reprinted from TRAINING, January 1979

give to the learner: how to make use of material resources, what strategies to use to go to various multimedia and print resources, how to make use of human resources. One of the greatly underused resources in a corporation are *peer* resources, other human beings in the environment. In my little book on self-directed learning, for example, you will see that I give quite a bit of attention to how one learns from another person. These are just examples of the kinds of tools and strategies and skills and knowledge that a learning facilitator and resource person needs to have. They're different from that of the simple transmittor

TRAINING: Is another of the facilitator's roles to give me good evaluative feedback before I build my own?

KNOWLES: Oh, absolutely. I don't think of self-directed learning as isolated learning. In fact, a more descriptive phrase would be interdependent self-directed learning.

TRAINING: What impact is the adult life stages research, the sort of data reported in Gail Sheehy's *Passages* having on adult learning theory and practice?

KNOWLES: The adult developmental studies are having a tremendous impact. For example, there is a new section in the American Psychological Association called "The Life Span Developmental Psychology Section," which is indicative of the importance of this new field of study.* Until recently, we only had data on adult growth up through adolescence and after 65. There was a big void in the middle. In the last five years there's been a growing body of knowledge about the in-between period. *Passages* is a popular version of some of that research. A much more scholarly work is a book by Baltes and Goulet called *Life Span Developmental Psychology*. What we're finding out from that work, of course, is that there are various kinds of developmental tasks people face at different stages of their lives. Education or training has to be geared to those developmental tasks.

By the way, one of the early insights that we got from research on adult learning was that readiness to learn is a product of an adult confronting the need to know something or to be able to do something in order to perform a life task that he is about to undertake or to cope more effectively with a life problem. The point *Passages* makes clear is that crises are dramatic manifestations of the confronting of life tasks. So, in a sense, *Passages* is saying, "If you want to engage an adult in a learning program in which he'll be highly motivated, highly ready, then find out what his life crises are, and build your learning around his life crises."

TRAINING: Is anyone doing that tailoring in an applied setting?

KNOWLES: Not in terms of the kind of crises Sheehy talked about, but there are a couple of parallels. One of them is what I think of as the most significant development in history in regard to the education of the under-educated, the illiterate, and the semi-illiterate. I'm referring to the work on coping done by Northcutt at the University of Texas. What Northcutt found in his initial study of the coping skills was that 39 percent of the adult American population is coping inadequately with typical life problems. The problems of getting work and holding a job, the problems of buying things and managing one's economic life. The problems of parenting. All kinds of problems. Given that finding, Northcutt and friends organized a curriculum for helping adults learn to cope better. The curriculum is exclusively based on those life situations people seemed to have the most trouble with.

For example, the Northcutt people no longer teach reading, writing and arithmetic to adults as subjects. They have a whole sequence of units on coping with the world of work. In one unit they ask "What's the first thing you need to be able to do to get a job?" Well, you need to be able to read a classified ad. The next task is to be able to fill out a job application form. Well, let's learn how to read the words in that. Then one has to learn to write on the application form. So, you see they're teaching survival skill content but only in relation to life tasks and problems.

TRAINING: That's a good example, though generally a public education example. It sounds as if you're saying that educators in business and industry don't yet see any relevance in the life stages/adult development work.

KNOWLES: I don't think it's had the impact on industrial trainers that it has had on some of the more public-serving institutions for the simple reason that most of the crises addressed in Roger Gould's research on life stages (reported in *Passages*) tend to be non-occupationally oriented. The most comprehensive attempt to gear a total, continuing self-development program to the concept of developmental stages that I know of is the program Walt Storey has worked out at General Electric. His career development program. That program starts with the new worker, the new exempt worker coming into GE. Right off, they engage him or her in a continuing process of career planning and career competency development. It moves through his whole career with GE. It's organized according to levels, and those parallel personal developmental stages.

TRAINING: Any final words of wisdom or wit?

KNOWLES: Let me make one point final that sort of gets at the feeling and tone of our conversation. In the 40 years that I've been in the business of training and educating adults I've seen a lot of innovation. But, I have seen more innovation, more new knowledge, more ferment in the last five years than in the previous 35. If that is any indication, the next 20 years are simply going to be revolutionary. We're on the verge of coming up with a whole new way of organizing our national educational enterprise. I believe the organizing concept for that enterprise will be lifelong education and the training and development of lifelong learners.

In terms of my own practice, the single most important innovation has been the bringing together of the new knowledge about adult development and adult learning into a comprehensive theory which we've labelled androgogy. A concept quite differentiated from the traditional comprehensive theories of learning that went under the label of pedagogy. Initially, I defined androgogy as the art and science of helping adults learn and I put that in opposition to pedagogy which I was defining as the art and science of teaching children. But in the last five years there's been enough experimentation with the application of the concepts of androgogy to the teaching of children and youth, that I am ready to assert pretty firmly that they also learn better when they're involved actively in the process. I'm now defining androgogy as the art and science of helping people learn, period!

We seem to be developing a general comprehensive theory, which yields guidelines for making decisions about organizing learning experiences and selecting methods and materials that are appropriate for learners in different stages of development, and under different environmental and personal conditions. Before that, before we had a comprehensive theory, we only could deviate from classical pedagogy by the intuition in the seat of our pants. Until we began formulating androgogy, adults in fact were taught as if they were children. Now that we've begun to treat adults like adults, it's making an enormous impact.

Reprinted from TRAINING, August 1977

FROM WHENCE THE THEORY?

A look at six theorists who made significant contributions to the management profession

BY LESLIE A. BRYAN, JR.

How many times have you dropped the name of a famous theorist in the course of, say, a management-development workshop, and drawn only blank stares from your participants? How often have you then backed up to explain the reference only to realize—perhaps because of an unexpected question—that you don't really know all that much about the person you cited?

If you're talking management theory, names like Maslow, McGregor, Taylor, Herzberg, Mayo and Drucker pop out almost inevitably. Perhaps some trainees would find the theories associated with these names a bit more meaningful—and our instruction a bit more interesting—if we provided some background information about the theorists themselves.

The list of "big guns" whose lives are sketched here obviously could be expanded. But the ideas and work of these six are almost invariably included in textbooks about managing people. If you want to build your own list, this ought to give you a good start.

Peter F. Drucker

Born: 1909, Vienna, Austria

Peter Drucker's ancestors were book publishers in Holland and the family name means "printer" in Dutch and German. Drucker has achieved his position as perhaps the preeminent management consultant and author on the scene today by living up to the heritage of his name: While one biography (by John J. Tarrant) calls Drucker "The Man Who Invented the Corporate Society," he is known more for the prolific volume and range of his writings than for any specific theory.

After his 1927 graduation from a college preparatory school in Vienna, Drucker worked in Hamburg and London as a junior clerk for an export company. He moved to Frankfurt, Germany in 1929 and received a LL.D. degree in 1931. It was while teaching law and history at the University of Frankfurt that he began his writing career—with a bang.

In 1933, shortly after the publication of his first book, *Friedrick Stahl, Conservative Political Theory and Historical Change*, he was forced to leave Germany. The book was an attack on Nazism and the concept of absolute monarchy. It had slipped by German censors and was published two months after the Nazis came to power. Much to Drucker's delight, the book became the subject of instant and widespread attention; it was banned quickly.

After his hasty departure from Europe, Drucker worked in England as a bank economist until 1937, when he sailed for the United States with the half-finished manuscript of his second book, *The End of Economic Man*. He took a job as American correspondent for a group of British newspapers, and in 1941 worked for the U.S. government on wartime intelligence studies.

In 1942 Drucker moved his family to Bennington College in Vermont, where he taught philosophy, government and religion until 1949. His reputation as a management expert started with a 1943 consulting job with General Motors. He was retained to study the corporation's top-management structure and policies, and worked closely with GM officers including Alfred Sloan and Charles Wilson. GM was said not to be happy with his findings, but the experience generated another book, *Concept of the Corporation*.

In 1950 he returned to New York City and became professor of management at New York University. It was during this period of his life, the 1950s and '60s, that he wrote the books and magazine articles that brought him international fame as *the* management expert.

During the Kennedy administration, Drucker served on management advisory boards to the U.S. Department of Defense. Since 1971 he has held the chair of Clarke Professor of Social Science at Claremont Graduate School in California.

Frederick I. Herzberg

Born: 1923, Lynn, MA

Frederick I. Herzberg's "two-factor motivational theory" has probably appeared in almost all organizational-behavior textbooks since the 1950s. Now a professor of management at

> **Herzberg is universally recognized as a behavioral scientist who has profoundly influenced management thinking on the motivation of workers.**

the University of Utah, Herzberg is universally recognized as a behavioral scientist who has profoundly influenced management thinking on the motivation of workers; but he probably would prefer to be called a humanistic scientist rather than a behaviorist.

Herzberg's initial fascination with the question of what motivates people probably arose during his stint as a World War II patrol leader in the 63rd Infantry and as a member of the occupational forces at the Dachau Concentration Camp. After the war he obtained a bachelor's degree from City College of New York and an M.S. and Ph.D. from the University of Pittsburgh, the latter in 1950.

Herzberg's research on the two-factor theory was conducted while he served as Douglas McGregor Distinguished Professor of Psychology at Case Western Reserve University. Herzberg proposes that there are certain job factors which, if absent, tend to make workers dissatisfied, but if present, will not produce higher levels of motivation. These he calls "hygienic" or "maintenance" factors, and they include such things as good relationships with supervisors and co-workers, fair salary, job security and working conditions.

On the other hand, Herzberg says, there is another category of factors whose absence will not cause dissatisfaction, but whose presence will motivate. These "motivational" factors include challenge, recognition, opportunity for growth and development and a chance for increased responsibility.

Since 1972, Herzberg has held a seat as Distinguished Professor of Management at the University of Utah.

Abraham Maslow

Born: 1908, Brooklyn, NY
Died: 1970

Few individuals have had anything approaching Maslow's impact on human-relations training. His concept that individuals are motivated by fulfilling a "hierarchy of needs" developed slowly during the 1940s and seems to have appeared originally for public consumption in his 1954 text, *Motivation and Personality.*

After graduating from high school, Maslow tried several colleges, including City College of New York and Cornell, but he ended up in an unlikely spot for a Jewish boy from Brooklyn: the University of Wisconsin. There he received his B.A. in 1930, an M.A. in 1931 and a Ph.D. in 1934. His academic career began at Columbia University, where he stayed from 1935 to 1937.

From there it was back to Brooklyn, and the bulk of Maslow's research on the hierarchy of needs was done while he taught at Brooklyn College between 1937 and 1951. In 1951 he became chairman of the Department of Psychology at Brandeis University in Waltham, MA. He died at the age of 62 while on leave from Brandeis, serving as a resident fellow at the W.P. Laughlin Charitable Foundation of Menlo Park, CA.

Maslow is regarded as the founder of humanistic psychology, a branch distinct from Freudian psychology and from the behaviorist school associated with B.F. Skinner. Throughout his career, Maslow maintained a vision of man as an essentially good creature whose behavior suggests otherwise only because of life's pressures and frustrations. Put very simplistically, this view contradicted the Freudian vision of humanity as naturally wicked or selfish, and the be-

> **Maslow maintained a vision of man as an essentially good creature whose behavior suggests otherwise only because of life's pressures and frustrations.**

haviorist view that man is neither good nor bad but essentially neutral— a being whose behavior will be determined by the sort of actions that are reinforced.

According to Maslow, people behave badly only when some of their fundamental needs go unmet—especially needs for security, love or affection and self-esteem. The hierarchy proposes a rank order of needs beginning with basic physiological requirements and progressing upward to "self-actualization." Higher-ranking needs do not become concerns, Maslow suggested, until lower-ranking needs have been satisfied.

Although basically a researcher, teacher and writer, Maslow's leadership in the field also led him to the presidency of the American Psychological Association. His impact is summed up by Dr. James Klee, a colleague at Brandeis, who said: "For psychology, the work of A.H. Maslow is one of the great bodies of accomplishment in the 20th century. His ideas are now major factors in education, business management, religious thought, sociology and psychology."

George Elton Mayo

Born: 1880, Adelaide, Australia
Died: 1949

The name of Elton Mayo will always be identified with the famous Haw-

thorne Experiments conducted in the Hawthorne Plant of the Western Electric Co. in Cicero, IL.

Mayo and his colleagues at the department of industrial research of the Harvard Business School originally designed their Hawthorne Experiments to study the influences of physical and environmental factors, such as lighting, on the productivity of industrial workers. However, the studies culminated by demonstrating that group affiliation, interaction and the personal relationship of management to employees had much more influence on production than did the original variables—thus the origin of the "Hawthorne Effect." Although subsequently criticized for his research design and control, the fact remains that the Hawthorne Effect offers much that appears to be true about the interaction of human relations and work productivity.

Mayo graduated from Adelaide University in 1899 and received an M.A. in 1917. He served as a lecturer and later as a professor of logic and philosophy at Queensland University from 1911 to 1923. Migrating to the United States in 1923, he became an associate in research at the University of Pennsylvania. He joined the Harvard faculty in 1926. It was during the period from 1927 to 1932 that Mayo and his Harvard associates conducted their studies at Hawthorne. In 1947, Elton Mayo retired to England where he died in 1949.

Douglas McGregor

Born: 1906, Detroit, MI
Died: 1964

If there is one universal starting point for discussing how managers and supervisors behave, it is probably Douglas McGregor's Theory X and Theory Y. McGregor believed that the styles and climates of organizations are determined according to the basic philosophy which filters management's view of the way people behave. At the Theory X extreme, man is viewed as being lazy, stupid and without ambition. At the Theory Y extreme, man is viewed as industrious and responsible—a creature who wants and responds to challenges. Managers will tend to use supervisory techniques that match their view of subordinates. McGregor felt that promoting the Theory Y philosophy among managers would produce more satisfied and productive workers.

McGregor graduated from Detroit's Wayne State University in 1932. He received an M.A. and Ph.D. from Harvard in 1933 and 1935, respectively, and taught at Harvard before accept-

WILL THE REAL MOTIVATIONAL THEORY PLEASE STAND UP?

Just say "motivation theory," and you'll conjure up a whole gamut of half-baked approaches and pseudo-scientific methods. That's unfortunate, say the authors of a recent book, because there are concrete and practical ways to motivate employees.

Sheila Murphy and Kenneth Carlisle try to sort out the confusion in *Practical Motivation Handbook* (John Wiley & Sons, 1986). They begin by describing a few of their favorites in the category of soft-headed motivational theories:

The Drill Sergeant Approach. Similar to good, old-fashioned, behind-the-woodshed performance conditioning, it relies on a loud voice and gruff manner. Short-term results are fabulous but long-term results? Sorry.

The Pep Rally. This is what happens when a supervisor gets religion in an off-site motivational program, then comes back to enlighten the heathens. After the dust settles. . .no significant difference.

The Nice Guy Approach. If only supervisors are pleasant and empathic, this method promises better performance. It can actually reduce productivity by overemphasizing appearances at the expense of real motivational goals.

The More Training Approach. This one assumes that people don't do their jobs because they don't know how to do them properly. It encourages us to throw training at performance problems in hopes they'll go away. Of course, the problems are usually more complicated than that.

The Pavlovian Approach. The Pavlovian manager rewards small, increasingly correct behavior changes, presuming they will lead to overall improvement. It works adequately when job tasks are simple and discrete, but breaks down in complex situations.

> **Too often the supervisor says "work harder or else," and the employees plunge fearfully into unproductive busy work.**

Participative Approach. Typically, a supervisor confers with employees about problems, encouraging them to apply their own solutions. It works well for high-level, creative jobs but is impractical for low-level, simple jobs.

So what are the components of practical motivation? The authors say they combine the best elements of the approaches above and are based on these six assumptions:

- *Motivation must focus narrowly on individual skills.* Start with specific skills you want your employees to acquire, such as handling problems and complaints, remembering names, self-discipline, better grooming and appearance.

- *Employees must understand how to perform correctly.* They may know what you want them to do but not how. Too often the supervisor says "work harder or else," and the employees plunge fearfully into unproductive busywork. This motivates them to work harder all right but not smarter.

- *Employees must be able to solve problems and make decisions.* They have to be treated as adults if it's going to work. The "defiant dictator" ignores this and defines the problem only as he sees it. He plans the rewards he feels are appropriate, administers the improvement program himself and almost always fails to improve performance.

- *Employees must want to perform well.* Motivation may result from external forces, such as a drill sergeant supervisor. But commitment grows out of an individual's personal decision. Supervisors can't force their employees to be committed to good performance. But supervisors can suggest how commitments are made and how they can help a person succeed.

- *Rewards and consequences must be linked directly to performance.* Incentives must be tied to *correct* performance. If they aren't, they can sabotage a motivational program. For instance, it makes little sense to reward typists for producing more if their rush to produce causes more mistakes.

- *Motivation requires patient, persistent follow-up.* It's a mistake to sacrifice follow-up planning in the haste to improve productivity during a crisis. The crackdown may yield immediate improvement but the team spirit is damaged. Follow-up meetings allow supervisors to review with the employees their progress on a certain skill.

Reprinted from TRAINING, December 1987

ing a professorial post at MIT in 1937. In 1949 he became President of Antioch College in Ohio and stayed there until he returned to MIT in 1954 as a professor of industrial management, a position he held until his death at the age of 58.

McGregor was a psychologist by education, but his 1960 book, *The Human Side of Enterprise*, in which he presented his Theories X and Y, indicated that he probably would like to be remembered as a philosopher of human relations. Some of the non-academic experience that helped form his ideas included work as a labor analyst and arbitrator for the U.S. government in World War II and as director of industrial relations for the Dewey and Almy Co., a chemical firm now a division of the W.R. Grace Co.

Frederick W. Taylor

Born: 1856, Philadelphia, PA
Died: 1915

The most historically prominent figure in this group is undoubtedly "the father of scientific management." Taylor's study of management practices developed during the period when factory managers embraced hard-driving, authoritative, often physically and mentally abusive supervision, and when 11- and 12-hour days were the rule rather than the exception.

Born to socially prominent and well-to-do Philadelphians Franklin and Emily Winslow Taylor, Frederick was an unlikely candidate to reform the 19th-century system. His last two high school years were spent at Phillips Exeter Academy in New Hampshire in preparation for a Harvard education in law or finance. In 1874 he was accepted by Harvard, but headaches and vision problems, later diagnosed as astigmatism and corrected with eyeglasses, caused him to drop out during the first year.

Taylor returned to Philadelphia and became an apprentice machinist and patternmaker at the Enterprise Hydraulic Works. Apparently neither he nor his parents viewed the Harvard episode as a social failure or embarrassment; apprenticeship was not an unusual way to become a practical engineer. While serving as an apprentice Taylor became a noted cricket and tennis player. In 1881, at the age of 25, he and a partner won the National Doubles Championship.

After completing his apprenticeship in 1878, he took a job as subforeman in the machine shop of the Midvale Steel Co. During his 11 years at Midvale, he progressed to machine-shop foreman, master mechanic and chief engineer while obtaining, apparently through correspondence, a mechanical engineering degree from Stevens Institute of Technology. During the 1880s and '90s, Taylor developed more than 40 patentable inventions pertaining to machine-tool grinding, boring and cutting.

In 1889, seeing future progression at Midvale blocked by management changes, Taylor launched into an engineering and management-consulting career. His consulting required numerous moves, and although he generally prospered because of wise financial investments, often in client companies, his work did not keep him as busy as he had foreseen—partly because of the severe industrial depression of that era.

In May 1898, Taylor began a three-year consulting job at the Bethlehem Iron Co. in South Bethlehem, PA. During his years there, he not only instituted his scientific management procedures, but expanded his world-wide reputation as an inventor and innovator of steel-cutting tools.

The most famous of his many publications, *The Principles of Scientific Management*, was published in 1907. In it, Taylor explained that his reforms centered on four basic categories of managerial activities: 1) the substitution of scientific methods for "rules of thumb" in production control, inventory purchase and management, tool standardization, and accounting procedures to identify costs of production by item; 2) the scientific selection and training of workmen; 3) functional foremanship, in which supervisory authority is divided by function, rather than centralized in an individual person; 4) stopwatch time study for the development of job methods and a differential piece-rate incentive wage plan.

Reprinted from TRAINING, June 1983

THE HAWTHORNE EFFECT: ORWELL OR BUSCAGLIA?

The act of training people builds their
self-esteem and that leads to
improved job performance

BY BEVERLY GEBER

Chameleon words are those shifty-eyed little lizards of the language that assume multiple definitions over the years without ever straying too far from their roots. They come about as close as possible to being all things to all people without compromising themselves in the process.

The word "marriage" is a chameleon. (Remember "open marriage"? Remember "till death do us part"?) In the training world, the "Hawthorne Effect" is a chameleon. Ask several trainers and you'll probably get several definitions, most of them legitimate and all of them true to some aspect of the original experiments in Chicago that produced the term.

Jerome Peloquin, for instance, describes it as the rewards you reap when you pay attention to people. Peloquin, president of Performance Control Corp. of Westchester, PA, says that the mere act of showing people that you're concerned about them usually spurs them to better job performance. That's the Hawthorne Effect.

Suppose you've taken a management trainee and given her specialized training in management skills she doesn't now possess. Without saying a word, you've given the trainee the feeling that she is so valuable to the organization that you'll spend time and money to develop her skills. She feels she's on a track to the top, and that motivates her to work harder and better. The motivation is independent of any particular skills or knowledge she may have gained from the training session. That's the Hawthorne Effect at work.

In a way, the Hawthorne Effect can be construed as an enemy of the modern trainer. Carrying the theory to the edges of cynicism, some would say it doesn't make any difference *what* you teach because the Hawthorne Effect will produce the positive outcome you want.

How do you respond to executives who denigrate training and credit the Hawthorne Effect when productivity rises? Peloquin recommends that you say, "So what?" Effective training performs a dual function: It educates people and it strokes them. And there's nothing wrong with using the Hawthorne Effect to reach this other training goal, Peloquin says. In fact, he contends that about 50% of any successful training session can be attributed to the Hawthorne Effect.

Scott Parry, president of Training House, in Princeton, NJ, calls the Hawthorne Effect the "Somebody Upstairs Cares" syndrome. It's not as simplistic as the idea—popular during the human relations craze 10 years ago—that you just have to be nice to workers. It's more than etiquette. When people spend a large portion of their time at work, they must have a sense of belonging, of being part of a team, Parry says. When they do, they produce better. That's the Hawthorne Effect.

Dana Gaines Robinson, president of Pittsburgh, PA-based Partners in Change, says she often hears a different interpretation of the Hawthorne Effect. George Orwell would understand this version; it has a Big Brother ring that's far less benign than other definitions. Robinson says people use it when they talk about workers under the eye of the supervisor.

She'll hear it when she suggests that someone should subtly observe workers on the job to see if they truly apply new procedures they've learned in a training course. Occasionally, managers object, saying that observation isn't a valid test. "Of course they'll do a good job if you're watching them," they tell her. "Isn't that the Hawthorne Effect?"

Well. . .not exactly.

The Hawthorne Studies (or Experiments) were conducted from 1927 to 1932 at the Western Electric Hawthorne Works in Chicago, where Harvard Business School professor Elton Mayo examined productivity and work conditions.

The studies grew out of preliminary experiments at the plant from 1924 to 1927 on the effect of light on productivity. Those experiments showed no clear connection between productivity and the amount of illumination but researchers began to wonder what kind of changes *would* influence output.

Specifically, Mayo wanted to find out what effect fatigue and monotony had on job productivity and how to control them through such variables as rest breaks, work hours, temperature and humidity. In the process, he stumbled upon a principle of human motivation that would help to revolutionize the theory and practice of management.

Mayo took five women from the assembly line, segregated them from the rest of the factory and put them under the eye of a supervisor who was more a friendly observer than disciplinarian. Mayo made frequent changes in their working conditions, always discussing and explaining the changes in advance.

He changed the hours in the workweek, the hours in the workday, the number of rest breaks, the time of the lunch hour. Occasionally, he would return the women to their original, harder working conditions. To his amazement, he discovered a general upward trend in production, completely independent of any of the changes he made.

His findings didn't mesh with the current theory of the worker as motivated solely by self-interest. It didn't make sense that productivity would continue to rise gradually when he cut out breaks and returned the women to longer working hours. Mayo began to look around and realized that the women, exercising a freedom they didn't have on the factory floor, had formed a social atmosphere that also included the observer who tracked their productivity. They talked, they joked, they began to meet socially outside of work.

Mayo had discovered a fundamental concept that seems obvious today: Workplaces are social environments and within them, people are moti-vated by much more than economic self-interest. He concluded that all aspects of that industrial environment carried social value. When the women were singled out from the rest of the factory workers, it raised their self-esteem. When they were allowed to have a friendly relationship with

---

Mayo stumbled upon an important finding about human involvement.

---

their supervisor, they felt happier at work. When he discussed changes in advance with them, they felt like part of the team. He had secured their co-operation and loyalty; it explained why productivity rose even when he took away their rest breaks.

The power of the social setting and peer group dynamics became even more obvious to Mayo in a later part of the Hawthorne Studies, when he saw the flip side of his original experiments. A group of 14 men who participated in a similar study *restricted* production because they were distrustful of the goals of the project.

The portion of the Hawthorne Studies that dwelt on the positive effects of benign supervision and concern for workers that made them feel like part of a team became known as the Hawthorne Effect; the studies themselves spawned the human relations school of management that is constantly being recycled in new forms today: witness quality circles, participative management, team building, et al.

Incidentally, the Hawthorne Works, the place where history was made, is history now itself. Western Electric closed it in 1983.

Reprinted from TRAINING, November 1986

SELF-FULFILLING PROPHECY: BETTER MANAGEMENT BY MAGIC

The lesson is as important to managers
as it is to trainers:
One of the most powerful tools for
influencing the performance of others is
your own expectations

BY LEN SANDLER

In 1911 two researchers with the unlikely names of Stumpt and Pfungst began an investigation of an even more unlikely horse named Clever Hans. The unlikely thing about Hans was that he could add, subtract, multiply, divide, spell and solve problems involving musical harmony.

Any number of animals had been taught to perform such tricks before, but they all had to be cued by their trainers. The really clever thing about Clever Hans was that he could run through his repertoire even when his owner, a German mathematician named Von Osten, was not present. The horse would answer questions for anyone. Von Osten swore he was mystified by the whole thing.

In *Teachers and the Learning Process* (Prentice-Hall, 1971), Robert Strom describes what Stumpt and Pfungst learned:

"Among the first discoveries made was that if the horse could not see the questioner, Hans was not clever at all. Similarly, if the questioner did not himself know the answer to the question, Hans could not answer it either. . . . A forward inclination of the head of the questioner would start Hans tapping, Pfungst observed. . .as the experimenter straightened up, Hans would stop tapping. . .he found that even the raising of his eyebrows was sufficient. Even the dilation of the

questioner's nostrils was a cue for Hans to stop tapping."

In other words, unwittingly, people were giving the horse the correct answers by communicating their expectations to him via physical signals. Hans was able to pick up on those signals—even subtle ones. He was clever only when people expected him to be.

As it is known and taught today in management and education circles, the notion of the self-fulfilling prophecy was conceptualized by Robert Merton, a professor of sociology at Columbia University. In a 1957 work called *Social Theory and Social Structure*, Merton said the phenomenon occurs when "a false definition of the situation evokes a new behavior which makes the original false conception come true."

In other words, once an expectation is set, even if it isn't accurate, we tend to act in ways that are consistent with that expectation. Surprisingly often, the result is that the expectation, as if by magic, comes true.

Magic certainly was involved in the ancient myth from which the idea of the self-fulfilling prophecy takes its other common name. As Ovid told the story in the tenth book of *Metamorphoses*, the sculptor Pygmalion, a prince of Cyprus, sought to create an ivory statue of the ideal woman. The result, which he named Galatea, was so beautiful that Pygmalion fell desperately in love with his own creation.

He prayed to the goddess Venus to bring Galatea to life. Venus granted his prayer, and the couple lived happily ever after.

That's where the name originated, but a better illustration of the "Pygmalion Effect" is George Bernard Shaw's play *Pygmalion*, in which Professor Henry Higgins insists that he can take a Cockney flower girl and, with some rigorous training, pass her off as a duchess. He succeeds. But a key point lies in a comment by the trainee, Eliza Doolittle, to Higgins' friend Pickering:

"You see, really and truly, apart from the things anyone can pick up (the dressing and the proper way of speaking and so on), the difference between a lady and a flower girl is not how she behaves, but how she's treated. I shall always be a flower girl to Professor Higgins, because he always treats me as a flower girl, and always will; but I know I can be a lady to you because you always treat me as a lady, and always will."

It boils down to this: Consciously or not, we tip people off as to what our expectations are. We exhibit thousands of cues, some as subtle as the tilting of heads, the raising of eyebrows or the dilation of nostrils, but most are much more obvious. And people pick up on those cues. The concept of the self-fulfilling prophecy can be summarized in five key principles:

● We form certain expectations of people or events.

● We communicate those expectations with various cues.

● People tend to respond to these cues by adjusting their behavior to match them.

● The result is that the original expectation becomes true.

● This creates a circle of self-fulfilling prophecies.

Does it really work?

A convincing body of behavioral research says it does. In 1971 Robert Rosenthal, a professor of social psychology at Harvard, described an experiment in which he told a group of students that he had developed a strain of super-intelligent rats that could run mazes quickly. He then passed out perfectly normal rats at random, telling half of the students that they had the new "maze-bright" rats and the other half that they got "maze-dull" rats.

The rats believed to be bright improved daily in running the maze—they ran faster and more accurately. The "dull" rats refused to budge from the starting point 29% of the time, while the "bright" rats refused only 11% of the time.

This experiment illustrates the first of a number of corollaries to our five basic principles.

Corollary #1: High expectations lead to higher performance; low expectations lead to lower performance.

Rosenthal concluded that some students unknowingly communicated high expectations to the supposedly bright rats. The other students communicated low expectations to the supposedly dull ones. But this study went a step further. According to Rosenthal, "Those who believed they were working with intelligent animals *liked* them better and found them more pleasant. Such students said they felt more relaxed with the animals, they treated them more gently and were more enthusiastic about the experiment than the students who thought they had dull rats to work with."

Corollary #2: Better performance resulting from high expectations leads us to like someone more; lower performance resulting from low expectations leads us to like someone less.

Rats aren't good enough for you? In another classic experiment, Rosenthal and Lenore Jacobson worked with elementary school children from 18 classrooms. They randomly chose 20% of the children from each room and told the teachers they were "intellectual bloomers." They explained that these children could be expected to show remarkable gains during the year. The experimental children showed average IQ gains of two points in verbal ability, seven points in reasoning and four points in overall IQ. The "intellectual bloomers" really did bloom!

How can this possibly work? In *Pygmalion in the Classroom* (Holt, Rinehart and Winston, 1968), Rosenthal replies:

"To summarize our speculations, we may say that by what she said, by how and when she said it, by her actual facial expressions, postures and perhaps by her touch, the teacher may have communicated to the children of the experimental group that she expected improved intellectual performance. Such communication together with possible changes in teaching techniques may have helped the child learn by changing his self-concept, his expectations of his own behavior, and his motivation, as well as his cognitive style and skills."

There was no difference in the amount of time the teachers spent with the students. Evidently there was a difference in the quality of the interactions.

Expectations, as if by magic, come true.

The teachers also found the "bloomers" to be more appealing, more affectionate and better adjusted. Some students gained in IQ even though they had not been designated as "bloomers," but they were not regarded to be as appealing, affectionate or well-adjusted. Apparently, the bloomers had done what was expected of them and the teachers were comfortable with them. The other students who did well surprised the teachers; they did the unexpected and the teachers were not as comfortable with them. It may be that they were thought of as overstepping their bounds or labeled as troublemakers.

Corollary #3: We tend to be comfortable with people who meet our expectations, whether they're high or low; we tend *not* to be comfortable with people who don't meet our expectations, whether they're high or low.

As for our expectations of what will happen or how someone will behave, we form them in a thousand ways, many preconceived. We all are prejudiced in the literal sense of the word; we "prejudge" either positively or negatively. We like to think we know what's going to happen before it happens, and we don't like to be proven wrong. We want to feel that we can control things. The impulse has given rise to religion, which says we can influence the gods with prayer; magic, which says we can manipulate events with secret powers; and science, which says we can understand the logic behind events and use it to predict similar events.

Corollary #4: Forming expectations is natural and unavoidable.

And the simple truth is that almost all of us behave pretty much according to the way we're treated. If you keep telling a teenager, for example, that he's worthless, has no sense of right or wrong and isn't going to amount to anything, he'll probably respond accordingly. If you keep telling him (sincerely) that he's important to you, that you have every confidence in his judgment as to what's right or wrong and that you're sure he's going to be successful in whatever he decides to do, he'll also tend to respond accordingly. You transmit those expectations to him and he'll begin to reflect the image you've created for him.

Corollary #5: Once formed, expectations about ourselves tend to be self-sustaining.

Exactly how do we communicate the expectations responsible for the Pygmalion Effect? The process works in very similar ways with people as it did with Clever Hans. In *Educational Sociology: A Realistic Approach* (Holt, Rinehart and Winston, 1980), Thomas Good and J. Brophy list a dozen ways in which teachers may behave differently toward students. Figure 1 shows their list.

Does it work at work?

It doesn't take much of a leap to see how Good and Brophy's list of teacher behaviors might apply to managers and subordinates in the business world, let alone to adult education and training. Figure 2 shows some obvious parallels. And research into the impact of self-fulfilling prophecies has not been limited to the classroom.

In one study a group of female applicants for a machine operator position was tested for intelligence and finger dexterity. Their supervisors were told that some of the women (actually chosen at random) had scored high on the tests. The results? The foremen gave more favorable evaluations to those workers whom they had been led to believe had higher test scores. And there's more: The actual production records of these women were substantially better.

Another example is the work of Albert King, a professor of business administration at Kansas State University. King randomly picked some novice welders, mechanics, presser machine operators and assembler trainees, and told their supervisors that these workers showed special potential for their jobs. Trainees from whom supervisors expected better job performance delivered just that. They were rated higher by their peers, scored better on objective tests and had lower absence rates. The average performance rankings for the high-expectation group were substantially higher than for the control group.

One dramatic illustration of the Pygmalion Effect achieved notoriety in the 1960s when it was reported in *Look* magazine as "Sweeney's Miracle." Jim Sweeney taught at Tulane University and was responsible for the biomedical computer center. He insisted that he could teach a janitor named Johnson to become a computer operator. The University required a certain score on an IQ test to

qualify a person to become an operator trainee. Johnson failed the test miserably. Sweeney threatened to quit unless the administration allowed him to give Johnson a chance. After much work, Johnson not only became an operator but wound up running the main computer room and being responsible for the training of new operators.

Sweeney's story brings up an important point. The Pygmalion Effect really begins with a belief in your own ability to manage yourself and others. The best managers share this belief.

Warren Bennis, a professor of management at the University of Southern California who has written extensively on the subject of leadership, recently interviewed 90 successful business leaders and their subordinates to determine what traits the leaders had in common. One of the characteristics that came through loud and clear was a positive self-image.

Why are the best managers able to create high performance expectations while weaker managers cannot? For decades theorists have pointed to the manager's self-confidence. In a 1969 *Harvard Business Review* article called "Pygmalion in Management," J. Sterling Livingston, a professor of business administration at Harvard

and president of the Sterling Institute, put it like this:

"If he has confidence in his ability to develop and stimulate them to high levels of performance, he will expect much of them and will treat them with confidence that his expectations will be met. But if he has doubts about his ability to stimulate them, he will expect less of them and will treat them with less confidence."

Why is it that subordinates whose managers have low expectations of them tend to produce lower performance? Livingston uses the example of salespeople to make the point:

"Unsuccessful salesmen have great difficulty maintaining their self-image and self-esteem. In response to low managerial expectations, they typically attempt to prevent additional damage to their egos by avoiding situations that might lead to greater failure. They either reduce the number of sales calls they make or avoid trying to 'close' sales when that might result in further painful rejection, or both. Low expectations and damaged egos lead them to behave in a manner that increases the probability of failure, thereby fulfilling their managers' expectations."

Corollary #6: Good managers pro-

FIGURE 1
HOW TEACHERS COMMUNICATE EXPECTATIONS

- Seating low-expectation students far from the teacher and/or seating them in a group.
- Paying less attention to lows in academic situations (smiling less often, maintaining less eye contact, etc.).
- Calling on lows less often to answer questions or to make public demonstrations.
- Waiting less time for lows to answer questions.
- Not staying with lows in failure situations (e.g., providing fewer clues, asking fewer follow-up questions).
- Criticizing lows more frequently than highs for incorrect responses.
- Praising lows less frequently than highs after successful responses.
- Praising lows more frequently than highs for marginal or inadequate responses.
- Providing lows with less accurate and less detailed feedback than highs.
- Failing to provide lows with feedback about their responses as often as highs.
- Demanding less work and effort from lows than from highs.
- Interrupting lows more frequently than highs.

From *Educational Sociology: A Realistic Approach*, T. Good and J. Brophy, Holt, Rinehart and Winston, New York, 1980.

FIGURE 2
HOW MANAGERS COMMUNICATE EXPECTATIONS

- Seating low-expectation employees in low-prestige office areas far from the manager.
- Paying less attention to lows in business situations (smiling less often and maintaining less eye contact). Giving them less information about what's going on in the department.
- Calling on lows less often to work on special projects, state their opinions, or give presentations.
- Waiting less time for lows to state their opinions.
- Not staying with lows in failure situations (i.e., providing less help or giving less advice when subordinates really need it).
- Criticizing lows more frequently than highs for making mistakes.
- Praising lows less frequently than highs after successful efforts.
- Praising lows more frequently than highs for marginal or inadequate efforts.
- Providing lows with less accurate and less detailed feedback on job performance than highs.
- Failing to provide lows with feedback about their job performance as often as highs.
- Demanding less work and effort from lows than from highs.
- Interrupting lows more frequently than highs.

duce employees who perform well and feel good about themselves; bad managers produce employees who perform poorly and feel badly about themselves.

Pygmalion in action

One of the critical tools a manager uses to influence employees is the performance review. Most managers underestimate its importance. Certainly the review is used as a report card, as a means of calculating the size of raises, as a way to introduce areas needing improvement and as a permanent record of what someone has accomplished. Much more importantly, though, reviews influence future performance. They offer a good example of how self-fulfilling prophecies work, for good or ill.

Take the case of a bright, young, aggressive employee. Let's assume she is abrasive, disruptive and disrespectful at times. However, she can also be creative, hard-working and full of enthusiasm. Given proper channeling, she can produce excellent results.

Some managers, required to assign her to a performance category, would call her "excellent." They're impressed by her strengths. Others, focusing on her weaknesses, would call her "poor." Still others, weighing the pluses and minuses, would call her "average."

Even with the scant information you have, you can see that any of these ratings could be justified. But what these managers are doing, probably unknowingly, is helping to determine the young woman's future performance. If she's rated "excellent," what will happen? She'll tend to be even more abrasive, disruptive and disrespectful. She'll also probably be more creative, enthusiastic and hard-working. She will do more of what she believes her manager wants.

What if she's rated "poor?" She'll likely be less abrasive, but she'll also be less creative and enthusiastic.

Suppose she's rated "average?" Depending on what her manager says about the rating and why she got it, she may adjust her behavior slightly.

The variable here is the manager's rating. It is based on the manager's values, prejudices and feelings. Most employees will take the cues and alter their future behavior accordingly.

Corollary #7: Performance ratings don't just summarize the past, they help determine future performance.

Communication

A manager cannot avoid communicating low expectations because the messages are often nonverbal and unintentional. As with observers communicating to Clever Hans and teachers communicating to students, managers nod their heads, prolong or shorten eye contact, express themselves in a certain tone of voice, etc.

Some managers refuse to admit they communicate negative expectations: "I never said anything negative to him. I hardly spoke to him at all." (As if that doesn't send a powerful message.) The key is not what managers say, but the way they behave.

Corollary #8: The best managers have confidence in themselves and in their ability to hire, develop and motivate people; largely because of that self-confidence, they communicate high expectations to others.

A manager increases or decreases initiative by the frequent or infrequent use of praise, criticism, feedback, information, etc. The manager, therefore, plays a highly significant role in the success or failure of an employee.

Robert Rosenthal breaks down the various ways in which teachers communicate expectations to students into four general categories. The same categories suggest ways by which managers can influence the success of subordinates.

- *Climate.* Managers create a warmer social and emotional mood for high-expectation employees. They smile more, nod their heads approvingly and look into subordinates' eyes more often. They are generally more supportive, friendly, accepting and encouraging.

- *Input.* More assignments and projects are given to high-expectation employees. In addition, these assignments are more challenging and afford higher visibility.

- *Output.* Managers give high-expectation employees more opportunities to speak at meetings, to offer their opinions or to disagree with the manager's opinions. They pay closer attention to their responses, and give them more assistance or encouragement in generating solutions to problems.

- *Feedback.* Managers give more positive reinforcement to high-expectation employees. They praise them more for good work and criticize them less for making mistakes. Consequently, confidence grows.

Like the teacher with the student and the trainer with the trainee, the manager has a profound impact on the success or failure of the subordinate. To quote Livingston once more, "If he is unskilled, he leaves scars on the careers of the young men (and women), cuts deeply into their self-esteem and distorts their image of themselves as human beings. But if he is skillful and has high expectations of his subordinates, their self-confidence will grow, their capabilities will develop and their productivity will be high. More often than he realizes, the manager is Pygmalion."

Reprinted from TRAINING, February 1986

BEHAVIOR MODIFICATION PRINCIPLES FOR TRAINERS

The basic laws of human behavior and learning are deceptively simple. Here's how to make sure you don't forget them

BY CHARLES F. SCHULER

As far as I'm concerned, the basic laws of human behavior are deceptively simple. So simple, in fact, and so deceptive in their simplicity, that it's possible to lose the flavor of their simplicity in the morass of overly complex academic explanation that characterizes much of the behavioral sciences. My own technique for keeping learning theory straight in my mind is, well, pretty simple. When in doubt about what I'm listening to or reading, I simply reflect on three little sentences:

- 99-44/100% of all behavior is learned.
- S.O.C. it to 'em.
- Behavior is a result of its consequences.

No matter how cloudy the writing or obscure the speaker, I can sort out what's being said using these three simple sentences.

The first of the three sentences says 99-44/100% of all behavior is learned. Yes, I stole my numbers from a box of Ivory soap; and, of course, I don't know if the figure is actually correct but I don't care. The point is that *almost* all behavior is learned behavior and the over-statement helps me remember that we learn to do most of the things we do; behavioral genetics be damned! The "almost but not quite" figure of 99-44/100 cues me to remember that in fact.

There are two categories of behavior; operant and respondent. Respondent behaviors are those few that we are born with. Nobody has to teach a baby to cry. No one needs to train us to quickly pull our hand away when we touch a hot burner on a stove. These behaviors are respondent, or reflex behaviors. We are born with them but they represent only a very small portion of the total number of things that we know how to do.

The other category, the operant behaviors, contains all of the things that we do when we operate within our environment. These are learned behaviors. No one necessarily taught them to us, but we did learn them and we learned them because of the natural laws of behavior. For all intents and purposes, almost all behavior is learned behavior. Certainly the behaviors that trainers deal with are operant, or learned, behaviors.

S.O.C. it to 'em!

S.O.C. is actually an acronym for *specification, observation* and *consequation*. These are the three steps one performs to produce a behavior change.

The specification step sometimes takes place on paper in the form of writing goals or objectives for a formal training program. It also may take place in the mind of the trainer, supervisor or manager in working directly with an employee. If you're going to cause someone to be able to do something new, then you must be able to clearly specify exactly what that new behavior is to be. Our purpose here is not to go into an essay on behavioral objectives, but if you can't clearly define the new behavior, how are you going to know when the trainee has learned it? The first step is the precise specification of what you want the trainee to be able to do. Oh yes, sharing that expectation with the performer is part of the system. Both trainer and trainee must know what the expected behavior is.

Observation is the second step. The effective trainer, or manager or supervisor, must be able to determine what the employee is doing now in order to be able to tell when the behavior is changing. Researchers call this gathering baseline data. I just call it a part of good common sense. Suppose that you are a sales manager and you want each of your salespeople to get at least one new referral from each existing client. It's only logical that you have to know how many referrals they're getting now, in order to be able to measure any change or improvement. There are lots of ways of gathering this information and, of course, that depends upon what business or industry you're in and what new behaviors you're trying to teach.

Consequation step is the final one. It's the payoff that will actually cause the change to occur. As a trainer, you must arrange the consequences of what the employee is presently doing so that the desired change, that is, the new behavior that you have specified, begins to replace the present, or old behavior, that is taking place. In the case of the sales referrals, a positive consequence might be extra commissions, a bonus, a day off or just some highly complementary recognition from the regional manager. Start with the latter, interpersonal stroking; it's cheap and often effective. Best bet of all is to *ask* the performer what he or she would *like* as a payoff. Different strokes for different folks and all that.

Behavior is the result of its consequences

This particular principle is really the only one that ever confuses anyone. The consequence of a behavior is that event which happens after you do something. Most behaviors have rather immediate consequences. Sometimes, however, the consequence, or payoff, doesn't come until sometime later. We are most influenced by that which happens to us after we perform the desired behavior. If good things happen to us after we exhibit some behavior, then we will be likely to exhibit that behavior again. Likewise, if bad things happen, then we probably won't exhibit that behavior again in the near future. For example, if a restaurant owner switches to a new brand of coffee and he finds that coffee sales increase, then he will probably continue to serve that type of coffee. On the other hand, if sales dropped, he would be likely to stop serving the new coffee and change back to the old brand.

In general, there are two major categories of consequences, good things and bad things. In more sophisticated terms, the good things are called reinforcers, and bad things are called punishers. By definition, a reinforcer is any event, or consequence, that increases the frequency or duration of the behavior that it follows. A punisher is any event, or consequence, that decreases the frequency or duration of the behavior that it follows. Remember, it is the *function* of the event, not the intent, that determines whether it is a reinforcer or a punisher. To determine if a consequence has reinforced or punished a behavior, you must look at what happened *after* it was applied.

Now comes the twist that sometimes confuses. There are two subcategories of reinforcement and two of punishment, giving us a total of four techniques that can be used to effectively change behavior. It is within these subcategories that misunderstandings and misuses are generally found. In designing training programs or materials, all four techniques can be effectively used under the appropriate circumstances. It is important that we understand the differences in the four processes.

Reinforcement

The two types of reinforcement are positive reinforcement and negative reinforcement. Remember that by definition *all* reinforcers *increase* the behaviors that they follow. Positive reinforcers are those events that add something good to the employee's life. A pat on the back, a smile, a bonus, an extra commission or a prize for selling the most widgits could all be examples of positive reinforcers. Most company incentive programs try to deal in positive reinforcement.

Negative reinforcement is the proc-ess of removing something bad from the employee's life. Suppose that your labor crew was told that all of those who had perfect on-time attendance for 30 days would be excused from some particularly distasteful job that is usually done on the last day of the month; for instance, shoveling grindings in a steel mill. You would be negatively reinforcing good "on-time" attendance by removing a distasteful event. This is still a *reinforcer* because it will *increase* the frequency of the target behavior, on-time attendance.

Punishers also fall into two subgroups. Although it sounds rather unusual, the two types are positive punishment and negative punishment. Both types of punishers are designed to *decrease* the behavior that they follow. Positive punishment is the process of adding something bad to the employee's environment. Examples of positive punishment might include a negative comment or harsh words from the boss, a poor employee rating, or extra work to do (such as doing a job over if it wasn't done correctly the first time).

Negative punishment decreases the target behavior by removing something good from the employee's environment. A fine (i.e., removal of some portion of your wages), or the loss of a privilege might be examples of negative punishment.

In almost all instances, reinforcement techniques are far superior to punishment techniques in producing lasting changes in behavior. Research supports this feeling and also substantiates some other negative results of the use of punishment.

Well, that's it in a nutshell. And, as promised, these underlying principles of human behavior, principles I believe need to be in the professional trainer's toolbox, are indeed fairly simple—at least in concept. Application is another "horse," so to speak. The best way to learn application is from the experiences of others. Read TRAINING and other professional magazines. Whatever you read, ask yourself, "How do the principles apply here? What little things did the writer have to do to apply the principles effectively?"

And talk to people. Talk to people who are trying to apply sound learning principles to their training. Talk to people who are applying the principles of learning to the management of people. Find out what they learned, where they made mistakes, what they would do differently next time.

Finally, look about yourself for opportunities to apply these simple but powerful concepts systematically. Start small, but think big. Apply them in your own office with your own staff. Then find a situation, a good win-win situation with a supervisor or manager who is doing well and who wants to do better. Help him or her use these simple learning principles to enhance the organization's operation.

Behavioral psychology has brought us a set of very simple but very powerful tools we can use in the human resources development effort. Conceptually they are pretty easy to understand. But like any other "deceptively simple" set of ideas, they are worthless unless they are used. We must not only understand these principles but we must be prepared to apply them and apply them well. For that part of the story to have a happy ending, we must continually be looking for opportunities to succeed. And we must be willing to share our successes—and failures—with others.

Reprinted from TRAINING, November 1978

SO LONG, SKINNER . . . HELLO COG SCI?

Is behaviorism on its ways out as the profession's theory of choice? And if so, will the baby exit with the bathwater?

BY RON ZEMKE

The craft of training has derived many of its key principles and practices from the science of psychology. As the fancies of psychology go, so often go the fascinations of training. And when psychologists, particularly those who interpret and popularize the concepts of research and academic psychology, "get hot" on the concept, it invariably becomes a hot topic in training as well.

Stress management, transactional analysis, team building, personal growth, leadership, management styles and feedback technology are but a sampling of training and development *content* topics that arose—in part or whole—from the pop-psych impetus.

Likewise, assessment centers, criterion-referenced testing, needs assessment, task analysis, programmed instruction, learning contracts, feedback instruments, computer-aided learning, group process and climate surveys are but a smattering of the many *process* contributions the various psychological and behavioral science specialities have made to the training and development craft.

More subtle, but equally as important, is the effect of psychology on the theories and philosophies of the training and development field. In short, the view of human nature espoused by academic psychologists has a tremendous impact on the view of human nature that influences the approaches favored by trainers.

The "rub," as Shakespeare would have said, is that the winds that disturb the bay disturb all boats anchored therein. For the past few years, the science of psychology has been swept by a tide of fundamental change. This "cognitive revolution," as some call it, could well throw the Good Ship Training into a tumult of painful reassessment as well.

From the time of the Greek philosophers, psychology has been popularly defined as the study of mental life: of the mind. But the 20th century, the century of science and experimentation, found that definition operationally wanting. Wilhelm Wundt, in his laboratory experiments with self-reported perceptions, quickly ran afoul of statistical reliability, not to mention Sigmund Freud and the concept of the unconscious. The development of psychology as a science was in question. A new approach to the study and understanding of the "nature of man" clearly was called for.

The stalemate in the status of experimental psychology was broken by the seemingly simple act of refocusing attention from the world of mind to the world of behavior. The simplicity is apparent, of course, only in retrospect; the process of redefining psychology as the study of human behavior required 30 to 50 years of research and the combined genius and enthusiasm of Ivan Pavlov, Edward L. Thorndike, John B. Watson, B.F. Skinner and an army of other behavior-obsessed researchers.

By the mid-1960s, behaviorism was

the psychology of choice in industrial training. And the fit has been appealing: Trainers are charged with causing people to perform, and behavior is a sure measure of performance. Behavior became the focus of most training "modules," and changes in behavior the desired result of all training practices and procedures. That which could not be defined in measurable, observable terms was deemed inconsequential. Trainers who failed to use behaviorist jargon in describing their work were immediately suspect.

The most strident form of behaviorism was that of the Skinnerian school. B.F. Skinner's followers insisted that the focus of training (and learning) must be on behavior change. Period. Concepts such as thinking, problem solving and creativity tended to be viewed as, at best, imprecise descriptions of secondary behavior—explainable, ultimately, in terms of the reinforcement or punishment the behavior had engendered in the past, and the developed generalizations and discriminations of stimuli closely associated with the behavior. It was primarily the Skinnerian school that gave us programmed learning, behavioral objectives and the first practical behavior-modification concepts.

The "social learning" or "behavior-modeling" school, generally associated with the work of Albert Bandura, was less hard-nosed in its attitude toward "mind." The social learning school contends that people can learn by observing "models" (the behavior of others) without receiving an immediate, observable reward. Further separating the two behaviorist approaches is the social learning view that "cognitive control"—the ability of an individual to guide and maintain his or her behavior through self-reinforcement—plays an important role in human learning.

The behavior-modeling/social-learning form of behaviorism has led to a new precision in the production and use of film and videotape in training, and promising new strategies for long-term support of learned behaviors.

Although battered by behaviorists of all shades, the notion of "mind"—that invisible, unmeasurable and, to the behaviorist, irksome concept—has been neither expelled from psychology as a useless hobgoblin nor relegated to the "iffy" status of witchcraft and pseudoscience. On the contrary, the concept of mind has been alive and well among clinical psychologists all along. Even those who adopted behavior-modification technology have continued to use the concepts of mind, thought, emotion, motivation and other "outlawed" lingo to explain their work to clients and colleagues.

Not so in educational, industrial, experimental and general academic psychology. In these disciplines, "mentalism" has been taboo. Institutionalized taboos, however, tend to produce backlashes, and there has been simmering, for the last 20 years or so, a "pro-mind" revolt—a revolution in search of a season. At one time or another the work of child psychologist Jean Piaget, psycholinguist Noam Chomsky and mathematician John Von Neumann have been proposed as the right spark for igniting the antibehaviorist backfire.

In actuality, the push that has come to shove is neither an elegant counter-theory nor a critical research refutation. It is instead the advent of what science historian Thomas S. Kuhn calls a paradigm shift: an alternative view of reality that cuts the ideological Gordian knot and is robust enough in it's own right to encourage researchers and theorists to spend time and energy proving and defending it—a back-turning on the old and exhausted in favor of the new, unknown and untried.

This cognitive revolution—the return from exile of the concepts of mind and thinking—is being led by an interdisciplinary hybrid of psychology, computer science, psycholinguistics and psychobiology referred to by science writer Morton Hunt (*The Universe Within: A New Science Explores the Human Mind*) as "cognitive science" or just Cog Sci.

The corpus of Cog Sci research often resembles a page out of a brain-teaser puzzle book. For instance, when asked, "What was George Washington's phone number?" we immediately recognize the inconsistencies in the question. "But how?" asks the Cog Sci researcher. Likewise, most of us recognize that "adult" fills the blank in the IQ-test analogy, "Acorn is to oak as infant is to   ." But how?

A favorite tool of the cognitive researcher is the cryptarithmetic problem. In the following example, each letter stands for a one-digit number. When decoded, the first line added to the second will equal the third. Your task is to find the correct numerical substitutions for the letters:

LET'S
+ WAVE
= LATER

The researcher's task is to explain how you did it. Solutions to these sorts of problems require mental rather than behavioral gymnastics. The mental variety is the focus of concern for Cog Sci researchers. Given the kinds of problems they work on, it is understandable why Cog Sci people feel that observable behavior comes up short in the meaningful-data department.

Among those now flying the Cog Sci colors is Susan M. Markle, professor of educational psychology at the University of Illinois and, until recently, an influential name in the behaviorist camp. Her concluding statement in a recent *Journal of Instructional Development* article is a nice summation of the expectations held by many advocates of the evolving Cog Sci approach:

"There is a small but increasingly voluble chorus across the country opposing the viselike grip of content coverage and calling for cognitive development—i.e., thinking—as the valuable outcome of liberal arts education. When we become the majority, instructional designers will have to be ready with the skills and models for reaching these important new objectives."

Driving forces

Two of the leaders of the problem-solving side of the cognitive revolution are economist Allen Newell and political scientist Herbert A. Simon. They and others who have studied human problem-solving strategies have found it provocative to model the descriptions of their findings on computer analogies. Their work has stimulated new thinking and research into the areas of problem solving, decision making, strategic thinking and negotiation.

To the many enthusiasts of this approach, the mind-as-computer analog is less repugnant than the behaviorist man/rat or man/pigeon analogies. A mechanical mind, it appears, is better than no mind at all.

"So powerful, pervasive and compelling is this tool, the computer," admits City University of New York psychologist Stanley Milgram, "that psychology [is] hard put to avoid its seductive, metaphorical impact."

A second important force behind the cognitive revolution is the effort to decode the mysteries of brain-mind dualism. The effects of mind on body a la psychosomatic illness and wellness have become well-publicized, as has brain lateralization (right-brain/left-brain) research. At the same time, correlations have been found between gross brain characteristics—such as density and number of neurons—and such psychological and behavioral characteristics as aggressiveness,

nurturance, mathematics skills, spatial reasoning, language skills and sex roles.

California Institute of Technology physiologist Roger Sperry won a Nobel Prize for his work on brain lateralization, which automatically lent a lot of credibility to the study. Psychologist Robert Ornstein has done much to popularize brain concepts among trainers and educators. Much of the work on learning styles originated from research on brain differences.

The final force that seems to be propelling the cognitive revolution is Harvard University entomologist Edward O. Wilson's controversial "sociobiology," which suggests that human behavior is genetically controlled to a startling degree. In his Pulitzer Prize-winning *On Human Nature* (1978), Wilson argues that our general patterns of altruism, worship, love, sexuality and aggression spring from a genetic inheritance dating back to the Ice Age.

In *Genes, Mind and Culture,* Wilson and Charles Lumsden contend that behaviors as specific as marriage customs, ethical considerations and religious beliefs are genetic at base. Xenophobia, nurturing behaviors and specific cognitive skills are painted with the same genetic brush. In other words, Wilson and Lumsden argue that to a tremendous degree, social structures and human behavior are based on biological imperatives, fixed and relatively unchangeable—a direct contradiction of the fundamental behaviorist axiom that most behavior is highly malleable.

Sociobiological dictums already are being used to explain away the failures of many massive social-engineering programs. This return to "trait thinking," some speculate, also accounts for the renewed interest in selection testing in evidence today.

The combined impact of these triumvirate forces—the computer, brain/mind research and sociobiology—has been both trivial and basic. It has been trivial, for example, in the sense that articles in scholarly journals now use cognitive buzzwords in their titles instead of behavioral buzzwords: The same piece that once might have been titled "Problem-Solving Behavior in Three-Year-Olds," now will appear under the heading "Cognitive Strategies for Problem-Solving in Three-Year-Olds."

The impact has been basic in the sense that those who take theories and research seriously, and who must stand and deliver human services, are being forced into uneasy reexamination of both the assumptions and consequent practices of their trades.

IT'S ALL IN THE IMAGE

How do you *know* that your doctor is competent? That your mechanic is honest? That your spouse is faithful? The ultimate answer is, you don't, says Chet Wright. But on the other hand, you do—or at least you live as if you do. And the reason is that they behave in ways that match certain stereotypical assumptions you make about competent doctors, honest mechanics and faithful spouses. In short, they look the part. If they didn't, you'd trade them in for models that did.

Such stereotypes may be superficial and certainly can be misleading, but they're useful, says Wright, a senior analyst with Information Spectrum Inc., an Arlington, VA, consulting firm. And in any case, we rely on them to make judgments about one another.

For as long as you've been dressing for success and learning interpersonal communication techniques designed to build empathy and trust regardless of the message you're communicating, you've been aware of the principle that what really counts is not who you are but how you come across. Wright subscribes to the theory that the race goes not to the most skillful or knowledgeable, but to the one with the best image. He also subscribes to the theory that image training—how to look and act the part—ought to be a key ingredient of any corporate management-training curriculum.

Image training is, of course, what his company sells, and we wouldn't be telling you any of this except that Wright brings something new to the game, something near and dear to the trainer's heart: a conceptual model. At the National Society for Performance and Instruction's annual conference in April, he outlined a simple and convenient classification system. It's called "image matching," and it has to do with how closely an individual's appearance and behavior match our stereotype of how such a person ought to look and act. Images fall into three categories.

Almost right. Here you're aware that the person is trying to present some particular image: George Bush trying to act macho, for instance, or Dan Rather trying to smile like kindly Uncle Walter. If you can see the strings, you know it's a puppet show. It doesn't work.

Exactly right. The person comes across as precisely what he or she is supposed to be. Very little mud sticks to Ronald Reagan, the Teflon president, regardless of the scandals in his administration. Why? Because, Wright says, Reagan mirrors perfectly our stereotype of how a president ought to look and sound. Another example of "exactly right" is Margaret Thatcher in the role of prime minister of England.

Better than right. This is the person who shatters the mold and redefines the role, going beyond the stereotypical ideal. Lee Iacocca as corporate chieftain. Eleanor Roosevelt as first lady.

"Better than right" can't be taught, Wright maintains. It's just something particular individuals show us from time to time, to our surprise and delight. Image training, therefore, should focus on teaching managers to do their roles "exactly right." But this is not just a matter of teaching each person to play one particular role. Trainees have to be taught to "scan the environment," he says, so they can adjust their images to a variety of situations.

Getting your image exactly right won't assure success, Wright admits, "but failure to do it will ensure failure."

Reprinted from TRAINING, June 1988

The effects on training and development

Again, the specific effects on the training scene have been relatively minor in one sense. "Brain training" is a hot topic right now, and has been for a year or two. Seminars that promise to tell all about "The Impact of Brain Research on Training" tend to draw crowds, and articles on the topic draw readers. But the same has been true for every brighter bauble that has ambled down the T&D pike since P.T. Barnum introduced the world to the Egress.*

Beyond the hype, however, lies a real possiblity that the new paradigm will have considerable and lasting impact on the basic premises and practices of the field. Paul Harmon of Harmon Associates in San Francisco sees this as inevitable. "When things are very procedural," he says, "the classic task analysis form—look at the behavior, look for an algorithm, draw some arrows and boxes—is fine. But when the important data is about the way the performer processes information, develops strategies and makes decisions—when you are working with what researchers call 'expert systems'—then you are talking about heuristics and cognition."

Harmon is cautious, however, about going overboard for the cognitive sciences. "We are practicing a technology, not a science," he warns, "and we ought to be more concerned with understanding what a master performer does, thinks and says, not with being able to explain which school of psychology we adhere to."

Richard Scudder, a former training director who now is an assistant professor of management at the University of Denver, believes that brain research, cognitive psychology, information science and artificial-intelligence research portend a period of great growth in knowledge about human learning and great changes in the practices of education and training.

Harmon and Scudder already have seen their prophecies fulfilled in a limited fashion. The widespread use of algorithms and decision tables as job aids, for instance, owes much to the cognitive approach. Expatriate Russian educational psychologist Lev Landa, one of the more sophisticated algorithm builders, initially developed his use of this flow-charting technique to model and study mathematical thinking skills in children.

Geary A. Rummler of The Rummler Group in Summit, NJ, is among those who doubt that the popularity

---

*In 1871, P.T. Barnum opened "The Greatest Show on Earth" Museum in Brooklyn. Problem: The show was so good that people lingered in the building for hours on a single 10-cent ticket. He was being killed at the turnstile by poor traffic flow at the exits. Solution: Barnum hung signs reading, "This Way to the Egress" and "Don't Miss the Egress." Faithful sign-followers wound up outside the museum, learned that egress and exit are synonymous, and solved the traffic-flow problem.

of cognitive lingo heralds a significant change for training and development. He cites two reasons: the slowness of "real" change, and the bottom-line orientation of modern training.

"I like to use the ocean as an analogy," Rummler says. "The waves at the top are very busy, but the sand and the bedrock shift very slowly. Yes, there is a lot of cognitive rhetoric, but not much impact so far. Eight years ago we were talking a lot about behavior and used a lot of behavioral rhetoric, but things actually changed very slowly. We really are just now seeing widespread understanding of the behavioral approach.

"Training isn't actually as much behavior-oriented as it is performance-based," Rummler continues. "That, I don't think will change." He adds that a successful performance model has to adapt to new information while avoiding the whimsy of changing theoretical orientations for fashion's sake.

Karl Albrecht, author of *Brain Power* (Prentice-Hall, 1980), says he is glad to see "a fair number of people throwing off the yoke of Skinnerian orthodoxy" in favor of an approach oriented more toward cognitive science. But Albrecht is equally happy to see Cog Sci replacing "the cult of the hypothalamus," his term for emotion-centered, "touchy-feely" training.

He sees the cognitive concern as "low on weirdness level" to the man in the street and, therefore, much more acceptable. "This approach is more rational than either the Skinnerian demand that 'If you can't see it, touch it and measure it, it doesn't exist,' or the touchy-feely claim that 'You are your emotions.'"

Bob Mezoff, an associate professor on the business faculty at the University of Connecticut in Stamford, conducts research on cognitive style and the implications for human relations training. Although a Cog Sci enthusiast himself, Mezoff worries that trainers will go overboard in their eagerness to adopt it.

"If practitioners discard everything that has been learned from the behavioral approach, it would be a terrible mistake," he says. "It would be a classic situation of throwing the baby out with the bathwater. I hope that doesn't happen."

Are Mezoff's fears unfounded? If past is prologue, unfortunately, his concern about a wave of overenthusiasm is all too well-grounded. Advocates of the Neurolinguistic Programming (NLP) variant of the brain/mind research findings already have distinguished themselves through conspicuous zealotry. According to true believers, all else pales in the face of NLP; why use any other approach? The words have changed a little, but the refrain is painfully familiar.

The effects are being felt at levels beyond those of the new convert, the new company, the new trainer. Already, one major purveyor of training programs has taken a giant step back from the assumption that training is, by definition, to change behavior, declaring in a recent client newsletter: "We recognize that people don't really learn 'how to's' in seminars—at least they don't learn how to do what the seminar purports." The chairman's editorial goes on to redefine the company's stance as "teaching them [trainers] how to learn a skill out of their own experiences."

Asked whether this meant the company was eschewing behavioral for cognitive aims, an insider confided that the issue is far from resolved internally and that heated discussions have been commonplace. The situation is likely to face most established vendor firms and consulting groups as their "cognitive bases" are challenged by wave-rider clients.

There are chapters yet to be written. But as "mind" once again emerges as a legitimate topic of concern, those who would be guided less by trends and more by results might find their sanity served if they try to think of the issue as a reevaluation rather than a revolution.

The behaviorists chose to ban the concept of mind because of its inextricable association with soul, spirit, the unconscious and any number of other poetically appealing but operationally inconvenient images of humanness. The mind became a "black box" whose workings did not have to be understood in order for mankind to be understood—and manipulated. As principles emerged from the self-imposed myopia of behavioral analysis, however, the need to do *something* with the black box became too obvious to ignore. Cognitive science, at its best, is a rational attempt to introduce thought, choice and mental life in a reasoned, measured and non-phenomenological way.

Consider it a step forward. Consider it progress. Consider it important and appropriate. But take care to consider it within the context of performance, achievement and helping others become as much as they can be. Most of all, consider it carefully.

Reprinted from TRAINING, February 1983

SELF-DIRECTED LEARNING: A MUST SKILL IN THE INFORMATION AGE

The high achievers of tomorrow—even more than today—will be marked by their ability to learn, unlearn and relearn. We all have the innate ability, these researchers say, we just have to hone it

BY RON ZEMKE

In our rapidly changing, high-technology world, skill and knowledge are perishable commodities. By one estimate the half-life of the knowledge base of today's graduating Massachusetts Institute of Technology (MIT) engineer is from five to seven years. Another expert reports the number one fear and fate of the technical manager is informational obsolescence. All in all, Alvin Toffler's *Future Shock* assessment that the illiterate of the year 2000 A.D. will not be the individual who cannot read and write, but the one who cannot learn, unlearn and relearn, seems wrong only in its too generous timeframe.

How does one swim upstream, or just stay afloat, in this modern raging river of constantly changing facts and concepts? According to Lucy M. and Paul J. Guglielmino, of Florida Atlantic University in Boca Raton, "There is mounting evidence to suggest that workers of the future will need to be able to take more responsibility for the management of their learning," says Paul. And the key to our successfully accepting responsibility for our own learning, say the researchers, is our ability to develop a self-directed learning style.

If that gives you a shudder and an impulse to reach for a security blanket or an early retirement application form, hold on a moment, for the prognosis is brighter than the problem is grim. According to the Guglielminos,

developing the skills and attitudes that lead to a self-directed learning style isn't that difficult. In fact, many successful people already acknowledge self-directed learning to be a key to personal success.

Paul Guglielmino, director of the Center for Management and Professional Development at Florida Atlantic, surveyed managers in a nationwide sample of Fortune 500 companies. He found that many believe success today and tomorrow requires managers to become more creative and innovative, and they credit success in the transition to the skill of learning in a self-directed way.

"Today's successful managers," he explains, "can't spend valuable time in unproductive seminars that are 60% old stuff or sit around waiting for someone to offer just the right course. Nor can they expect much from a mentor. The rapid rate of change rules out the existence of wise old heads to lead the way. Only those who can design their own learning can cope with that kind of constant change."

In his most recent study, conducted for a major communications company late last year, Paul discovered even more evidence that self-directed learning is both a necessary and a learnable skill. His findings, based on administration of the Self-Directed Learning Readiness Scale (SDLRS) to 421 management and 318 nonmanagement employees, suggest successful management and non-

management employees in high-tech companies both understand the need for, and attempt to practice, self-directed learning.

He also found that outstanding performers in jobs requiring a very high level of creativity, jobs requiring a high level of problem-solving skill and jobs involving a high degree of change, all scored significantly higher in self-directed learning readiness than the others tested. In addition, he found slight tendencies for women to outscore men and for people with higher levels of educational accomplishment to score high on the same readiness measure.

Lucy Guglielmino, who developed the SDLRS, believes that research is beginning to show links between self-directed learning, creativity and right-brain, or holistic, thinking. "We think managers who are good problem solvers are also self-directed learners," she says. "They question assumptions, set objectives and assess alternatives on merit."

Her research indicates that self-directed learners are distinguished by several factors. "Highly self-directed learners exhibit initiative, independence and persistence in learning; they accept responsibility for their own learning and view problems as challenges, not obstacles; they are capable of self-discipline and have a high degree of curiosity; they have a strong desire to learn or change and are self-confident; they can organize their time, set an appropriate pace for learning and develop a plan for completing work; and they enjoy learning and have a tendency to be goal-oriented. In short, the self-directed learner is one who takes charge, accepts responsibility and is not stopped by problems."

How does one go about developing these skills or fostering them in others?

STEP 1. Find out how you, or your trainees, rate as self-directed learners right now. The Guglielminos have provided a modified version of the SDLRS you can test yourself against (see accompanying box). Be cautioned, however, not to overinterpret the results of this mini-quiz. You would need to take the full-scale SDLRS to have a 100% accurate assessment of your self-directed learning readiness.

The next four steps come right out of the systems approach model, with a dash of "Stand up, talk back" thrown in for seasoning.

631

STEP 2. Do a needs assessment on yourself. Figure out what it is you want/need to learn. You may be able to do that alone, or you may want to do it in consort with someone who knows your professional strengths and weaknesses; given, of course, that your goal is professional or job knowledge improvement.

STEP 3. Set objectives. Decide exactly what you want to get out of a self-directed learning experience, when and how you'll learn it and how you'll know that you've got what you want.

STEP 4. Do it! Sometimes politely referred to as the implementation phase, this step simply says stop planning and get about the business of attacking your self-admitted ignorances.

STEP 5. Evaluate. When you're done with the project, ask whether you got where you were planning to go, learned what you were planning to learn. If you didn't, go back and see why and how you fell short of your goal.

In addition, the Guglielminos advise that you will have to be proactive to get what you want when and how you want it. "You have to be pretty aggressive about getting exactly what you want. Self-directed learners don't—can't—just settle for a seminar," they caution. And it might not hurt to develop some group support. Some people, especially those of us with more *want* than *will* (we're probably in the mid-range on Guglielmino's instrument), find a little pressure from our peers helps us get into the personal-learning-project mood a bit faster.

And, finally, pat yourself on the back for completing a self-directed learning project. Odd as it may sound, the Guglielminos report that people tend to undervalue the outcomes of learning projects they design and implement themselves. And that is probably another good argument for leaning on a support group at first—a source for strokes and feedback for a job well done.

If breaking out of the other-directed learning mode sounds like a bit too much work, take heart from Lucy Guglielmino's developing hunch that self-directed learning skills probably are innate in most of us, but are unused primarily because of social conditioning.

"The research is very clear," she says. "Our traditional approach to education stifles self-directed learning and decreases the desire to learn. We've been trained to undervalue our own independent learning and overvalue that which we get from authority figures."

The good news is that her work with the gifted and in professional schools convinces her that people can reawaken. "Once we point out the importance of self-directed learning, show people what self-directed learning looks like and reinforce the value of their efforts, people begin to take responsibility for their learning," she says. "It's exciting to watch."

Reprinted from TRAINING, August 1982

How Self-Directed Are You in Your Learning?
To what extent do you agree with these statements?
(Check the appropriate column).

	Strongly Disagree	Disagree	Agree	Strongly Agree
1. I usually can generate highly creative solutions to problems I encounter.	☐	☐	☐	☐
2. I prefer learning on my own—usually I accomplish what I set out to learn.	☐	☐	☐	☐
3. I'll never get tired of learning new things.	☐	☐	☐	☐
4. Much of my time is spent on *future* issues.	☐	☐	☐	☐
5. I know that I am responsible for my own learning. If I don't learn something, it's my own fault.	☐	☐	☐	☐
A. Number of checks per column	☐	☐	☐	☐
B. Multiply	×1	×2	×3	×4
C. Total	☐	☐	☐	☐

Add totals on line C for your score and compare to the chart below:

Total Score	Indication of SDL Readiness*
4-10	Low
11-15	Medium
16-20	High

*For a valid indication of self-directed learning readiness, individuals are cautioned to use the Self-Directed Learning Readiness Scale. To obtain a sample copy, contact Dr. Lucy Guglielmino or Dr. Paul Guglielmino, 734 Marble Way, Boca Raton, FL 33432.

BLOOD AND BLACK BILE: FOUR-STYLE BEHAVIOR MODELS IN TRAINING

The best way to judge the effectiveness of a behavior-modification program based on inner 'style' is to sit down and watch one in action

BY ROGER T. O'BRIEN

Since the Middle Ages, sages have taken delight in dividing human behavior into four clearly defined styles. The only problem with the medieval version of the Four-Style Behavior Theory (called the Four Temperaments) was that it was based on the questionable assumption that each temperament was determined by which particular humor (inner juice) dominated an individual: yellow bile = choleric; blood = sanguine; black bile = melancholic; phlegm = phlegmatic. Not very appetizing—or accurate.

However, the *specific characteristics* of the Four Temperaments made eminent sense then and have been taken seriously in some quarters even in this century. They are summarized in Figure 1 and bear an amazing resemblance to modern theories.

For the past half-century, human behavior has been divided into quadrants in increasingly compelling and useful ways. (For a listing of the 15 most prominent modern systems, see sidebar.) Some of the authors, to be sure, would disagree with this broad categorizing of their systems, but the similarities to the ancient styles are nonetheless striking.

Four-Style Behavior Theory has been a most helpful training tool, and you can use it with measurable success in a number of subject areas.

- Interpersonal communication.
- Improving meeting skills.
- Conflict resolution.
- Team building.
- Performance appraisal.
- Time management.
- Situational leadership.

Teaching the Four-Style Behavior Theory

Ask your trainees to fill out the form, "How Do You Describe Yourself?' (Fig. 2); give no explanation other than directions on how to fill it out. The whole group should wait until everyone has finished one step before going on to the next.

After your group members have tallied their responses (step 2) but before going on to the next step, you can present some background to the Four-Style Behavior Theory.

Consider:

A Middle-Age sage would have described Sally as phlegmatic and Charlie as sanguine; the late William M. Marston would have said that she shows Compliance behavior while he shows Inducement behavior; David Merrill and Roger Reid would call her Analytical and him Expressive; Stuart Atkins would claim she is Conserving/Holding and he is Adapting/Dealing. The labels, of course, are not as important as the underlying concepts.

If you view "Assertiveness" as a continuum with "Asking" at one end and "Telling" at the other, you will be able to place yourself somewhere along that line, based on your perception of your behavioral style. Are you more of an asker or a teller? Or are you just about in the middle?

If you take another continuum, call it "Responsiveness" with the extremes marked "Closed" and "Open," you will again be able to place yourself on that continuum at a particular point, based on your knowledge of yourself.

The Four-Style Behavior Questionnaire is designed to help you do that. Returning to Figure 2, transfer the totaled figures under columns a, b, c and d to the circles in the corresponding quadrants. You have now identified your own perceived predominant behavioral style.

If one of the four numbers is significantly higher than the others, it represents your most characteristic style; if two or three of the high numbers are the same or very close, it simply means that you tend to share two or even three styles.

Figure 3 presents descriptive words that characterize each style. For a full explanation of the four styles, refer to any of the sources in the accompanying reading list. Merrill and Reid, in particular, have written a very detailed account of personal styles.

Sally sits tensely at the far end of a conference room. She glances at her watch, restacks the neat pile of papers in front of her, and says to herself: Where's that damn Charlie, anyway?... Seventeen minutes late— again!... I put a note on the seat of his chair....His desk is so messy, he'd never find it there....Said specifically on the note that we were to meet at 1:30 today....He knows we have to finish the first draft of the Emerson report by close of business today....He's downright thoughtless! ... Twenty minutes now....

"Oh, hi, Charlie. Hey, let's get down to work."

Charlie peeks in at the front door of the conference room, adjusts his bow tie, smiles broadly as he makes his way to Sally's corner, thinking to himself: Uh oh, Sally looks peeved.... Well, George just had too much of a problem to unburden at lunch.... First things first....Besides, I'm sure we can get an extension on the Emerson report, anyway—whenever that deadline may be....

"Hi, Sally! Sorry I'm a couple of minutes late. That Lazy Bee Restaurant service is getting worse by the day!"

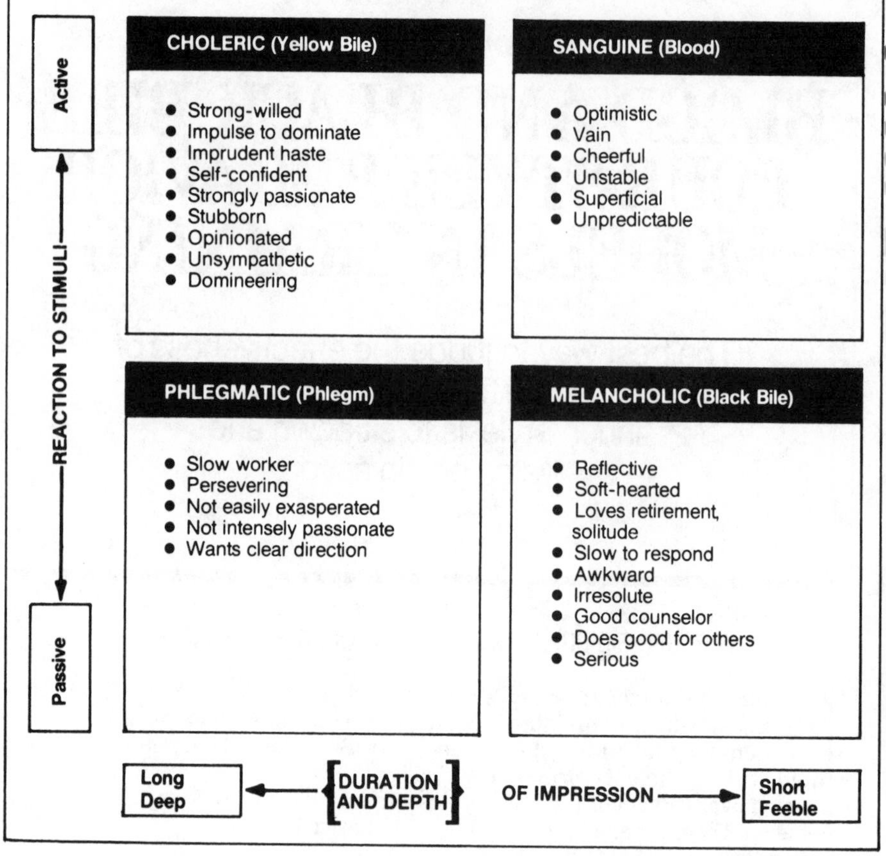

An important contribution Merrill and Reid have made to the Four-Style Behavior Theory is a third dimension, *Versatility*. They define it as that "dimension of behavior that indicates the extent to which others see us as adaptable, resourceful and competent....It reflects the effort that a person makes to have a relationship succeed, the skill shown in this effort, and, finally, the endorsement that he or she earns as a result of it."

Atkins' *The Name of Your Game* uses the unfortunate analogy of game playing (which extends even to the book's title), but his volume is probably the most practical of the lot. Chapter Six, "Overplaying Our Game," is alone worth the effort of reading the book. In it, Atkins develops the observation that "our so-called weaknesses are nothing more than strengths pushed to an excess."

John G. Geier rightly points out that there is no "best" or "ideal" behavioral style. Our style (which may be a combination of more than one quadrant) is not rooted as physically and rigidly in us as the Four Temperaments were thought to be. Nevertheless, our style represents *a manner of dealing with life's tensions* which we have learned to use from early childhood. It's our characteristic way of coping.

Learning to adapt

What is important, therefore, is learning to adapt, modify and harness negative aspects of our style and build on the positive aspects.

The tri-dimensional model in Figure 3 is an attempt to highlight the need for developing versatility. The receding dimensions of the four quadrants indicate the negative characteristics of each style. As you learn to adjust and modify those qualities, you can move forward on the scale of versatility.

For instance, a "Steady," by learning to set clear priorities, can begin to say "no" to the unimportant requests of others without feeling guilty. On the other hand, a "Dominant" would have little trouble saying no, but might have to work on softening the harsh tone of "Bug off, buddy!" responses.

The Four-Style Behavior Questionnaire as an assessment instrument obviously is limited and superficial. But in many cases it has helped people attain a very real "aha!" in understanding how their behavior affects others and vice versa. You can distribute extra copies of the questionnaire so that trainees can fill them out with respect to one another—

Figure 1
The Four Temperaments:
Medieval Four-Style Behavior Theory

to check self-perceptions against the perceptions of others. Merrill and Reid—in fact most of the experts—insist on the primary need for others' descriptions. Geier, however, has de-

---

The Four-Style Behavior Questionnaire may seem simplistic, but it can help people attain a very real 'aha!'

---

signed his form for self-description.

If the needs of the training session require it, such as in team building, you can use a comprehensive format such as Geier's Personal Profile System.

Seven applications

Interpersonal communication. The most obvious use of the behavioral style concept comes in helping people understand why they act the way they do and helping them learn to modify their communication styles (without denying their basic style-orientation) to become more effective communicators. To understand the fullness of the theory and to test it out, participants should use a commercial program.

Improving meeting skills. If you are conducting a skill-based course and want to help the participants understand and practice specific task and maintenance functions, then it helps a "Compliant," for example, to realize that he or she may not have a problem giving information or clarifying what has been said, but needs to "stretch" in order to initiate or gate-keep. A "Dominant" will easily summarize and give opinions, but may have to work hard on harmonizing and encouraging. Exercises can thus be tailored to the needs of individual participants.

THE MANY FACES OF THE FOUR-STYLE GRID

One of the most popular kinds of feedback instruments trainers use is based on the so-called four-style behavior grid, which divides human behavior into four distinct styles. With such instruments, trainees use a self-scored inventory, the results of which indicate where they fit in a four-part grid of behavior adjectives such as Dominant, Compliant, Influential or Steady.

The variety and proliferation of four-style grids is illustrated in the chart below, compiled by Roger T. O'Brien. The chart portrays the common elements among the various instruments. As you can see, the behavior styles used in today's instruments align well with the "Four Temperaments," used to delineate behavioral differences in the Middle Ages.

	High Assertiveness Low Responsiveness	High Assertiveness High Responsiveness	Low Assertiveness High Responsiveness	Low Assertiveness Low Responsiveness	Combination
1. BASIC SYSTEMS					
Medieval Four Temperaments	Choleric	Sanguine	Melancholic	Phlegmatic	
William M. Marston, *Emotions of Normal People*	Dominance	Inducement of Others	Steadiness	compliance	
John G. Geier, Personal Profile System	Dominance	Influence	Steadiness	Compliance	
Thomas C. Ritt, Jr., Personal Concepts	Dominance	Influence	Steadiness	Compliance	
Leo McManus, AMA's Management and Motivation	Dominance	Influence	Steadiness	Compliance	
David W. Merrill- Roger H. Reid, *Personal Styles and Effective Performance*	Driver	Expressive	Amiable	Analytical	
Personnel Predications and Research, Style Awareness Training	Driver	Expressive	Amiable	Analytical	
Wilson Learning Systems, Managing Interpersonal Relationships	Driver	Expressive	Amiable	Analytical	
Stuart Atkins, LIFO® (Life Orientations)	Controlling-Taking	Adapting-Dealing	Supporting-Giving	Conserving-Holding	
2. CONFLICT RESOLUTION					
Thomas-Kilmann Conflict Mode Instrument	Competing	Collaborating	Accommodating	Avoiding	Compromising
Allen A. Zoll, III, *Explorations in Management,* quoting Mary Parker Follett	Domination	Integration	Suppression	Evasion	Compromise
Donald T. Simpson, "Conflict Styles: Organizational Decision-Making"	Power	Integration	Suppression	Denial	Compromise
Jay Hall, Conflict Management Survey	9/1 Win-Lose	9/9 Synergistic	1/9 Yield-Lose	1/1 Lose-Leave	5/5 Compromise
3. PERFORMANCE APPRAISAL					
Robert E. Lefton et al., *Effective Motivation Through Performance Appraisal*	Q1 Dominant-Hostile	Q4 Dominant-Warm	Q3 Submissive-Warm	Q2 Submissive-Hostile	
Dimensional Training Systems. Dimensional Appraisal Training	Q1 Dominant-Hostile	Q4 Dominant-Warm	Q3Q2 Submissive-Warm	Submissive-Hostile	

Reprinted from TRAINING, November 1982

Conflict resolution. One of the essential points stressed in the Thomas and Kilmann Conflict Mode Instrument is that the four modes that correspond to the four styles—as well as "Compromise," a combination of two modes—all have their place and specific uses in peace-keeping. It is a genuine insight for "Dominants" to realize they have a natural tendency to use the Competing mode in cases where, say, an Accommodating mode would be more effective. Zoll and Simpson use slightly different terminology, but the quadrants are almost identical. Learning to deal with conflict is one of the hallmarks of versatility, but first one has to learn to deal with oneself. That is why I suggest that the Four-Style Behavior Theory

---

> ### What is important is learning to adapt, modify and harness negative aspects of our style and build on the positive aspects.

---

should be the foundation for training in conflict resolution.

Team building. Depending on the identified team-building needs, it is probably better to use a comprehensive approach, such as Merrill and Reid's Style Awareness Training, Wilson Learning Corporation's Managing Interpersonal Relationships, Leo McManus/American Management Association's Management and Motivation, or Stuart Atkins' LIFO®. John Geier's Personal Profile System is relatively easy and extremely effective to use in team-building workshops. His program can be adequately covered in a half-day, with an equal amount of time applying the learning to specific team problems such as poor communication or ineffective leadership.

Performance appraisal. Robert E. Lefton, president of Dimensional Training Systems, has coauthored a very interesting book that outlines four styles of management. The book deals comprehensively with each style's characteristics and concludes the Q4 (Dominant-Warm) is the most productive style for appraising employees'

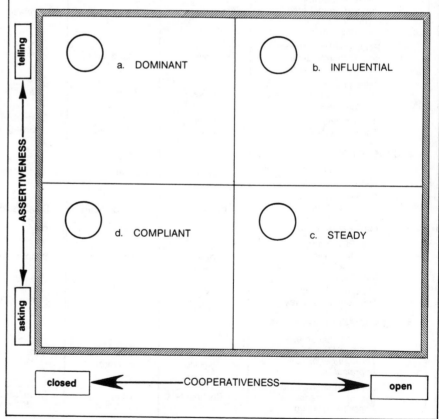

Figure 2
Four-Style Behavior Questionnaire and Model

Step One

In each of the five boxes below, examine the four descriptive adjectives as they may or may not describe you. In each box, rank the adjective that most nearly describes you as "7," the next closest adjective as "5," the next closest adjective as "3," and the word that *least* closely describes you as "1." Each box should have four adjectives ranked 7, 5, 3 and 1 (no ties).

1.
    _____ a. stubborn
    _____ b. persuasive
    _____ c. gentle
    _____ d. humble

2.
    _____ a. competitive
    _____ b. playful
    _____ c. obliging
    _____ d. obedient

3.
    _____ a. adventurous
    _____ b. life-of-the-party
    _____ c. moderate
    _____ d. precise

4.
    _____ a. determined
    _____ b. convincing
    _____ c. good-natured
    _____ d. cautious

5.
    _____ a. assertive
    _____ b. optimistic
    _____ c. lenient
    _____ d. accurate

Step Two

Transfer your responses to this answer sheet, and then total columns a, b, c and d.

	a.	b.	c.	d.
1.				
2.				
3.				
4.				
5.				
Total:				

Step Three

Transfer the totals for each column to the circles in each corresponding quadrant marked a, b, c and d.

a. DOMINANT   b. INFLUENTIAL   d. COMPLIANT   c. STEADY

ASSERTIVENESS — telling / asking

COOPERATIVENESS — closed / open

performance.

Leadership. Knowledge of your own behavioral style will add insight into why you may tend to gravitate naturally toward one particular quadrant or corner of the grid. If you concede that no single style works best in every management situation, it obviously is helpful to be aware of the style you are likely to adopt "automatically" so that you can modify it when the situation demands.

Time management. While teaching this old standby, you can emphasize the golden rules of time management (write a daily to-do list, set goals and priorities, bunch telephone calls, hold stand-up meetings, etc.). But a "High-Dominant" probably does not need to make a to-do list, while "High-Influentials" and "High-Steadies" certainly do! By knowing your own basic behavioral style, you can deal more easily with the underlying problems of your own management of time. You can, for instance, examine Kahler's list of the major

> It obviously
> is helpful to be aware
> of the style
> you are likely to adopt
> "automatically"
> so that you can modify
> it when the
> situation demands.

types of compulsive behavior (Be Strong, Be Perfect, Please Me, Hurry Up and Try Hard) and personalize an action plan with specifics instead of soporifics.

Which system is best?

No one has produced an ideal theory of behavioral style that can fit all needs. To select one suitable for your needs, good starting points would be Marston's *Emotions of Normal People*, Merrill and Reid's *Personal Styles and Effective Performance* and Atkins' *The Name of Your Game.*

You will find that some commercial programs include computerized and personalized printouts; some have excellent video examples; a few have sales-oriented versions. But the best way to examine the effectiveness of a behavioral-style program is to sit in, if possible, on a workshop offered in-house by a nearby com-

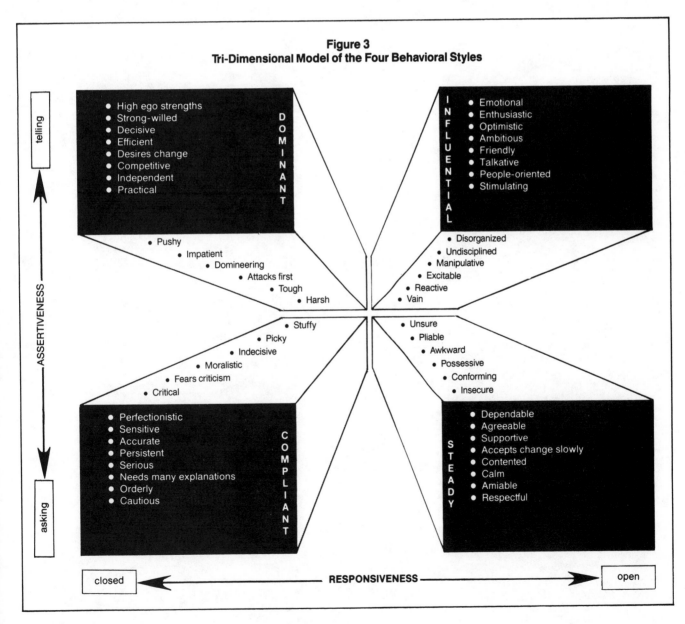

Figure 3
Tri-Dimensional Model of the Four Behavioral Styles

telling

ASSERTIVENESS

asking

DOMINANT
- High ego strengths
- Strong-willed
- Decisive
- Efficient
- Desires change
- Competitive
- Independent
- Practical

- Pushy
- Impatient
- Domineering
- Attacks first
- Tough
- Harsh

INFLUENTIAL
- Emotional
- Enthusiastic
- Optimistic
- Ambitious
- Friendly
- Talkative
- People-oriented
- Stimulating

- Disorganized
- Undisciplined
- Manipulative
- Excitable
- Reactive
- Vain

- Stuffy
- Picky
- Indecisive
- Moralistic
- Fears criticism
- Critical

- Unsure
- Pliable
- Awkward
- Possessive
- Conforming
- Insecure

COMPLIANT
- Perfectionistic
- Sensitive
- Accurate
- Persistent
- Serious
- Needs many explanations
- Orderly
- Cautious

STEADY
- Dependable
- Agreeable
- Supportive
- Accepts change slowly
- Contented
- Calm
- Amiable
- Respectful

closed ◄——— RESPONSIVENESS ———► open

pany. It is an excellent way to catch the flavor of a program, to see how participants react to it, and how they pick up and apply the principles.

If that can't be done, then call *several* training directors of companies that use a particular program. Ask hard and concrete questions. Only you can be the judge of how well the program would work in your own environment.

If you were a knight or a lady in the Middle Ages, you would have had to guess at your bile or phlegm levels to identify your predominant behavior style. The means for identifying that style today are much more accurate, scientific and helpful in promoting self-understanding and improving your relations with others.

Reprinted from TRAINING, January 1983

READING LIST AND SOURCES

American Management Assns., 8655 West Higgins Rd., Chicago, IL 60631.

Atkins, Stuart Inc., LIFO® Division (9301 Wilshire Blvd., Beverly Hills, CA 90210); *The Name of Your Game* (Beverly Hills, CA: Ellis and Stewart Publishers, 1981).

Blake, Robert R. and Jane Srygley Mouton, *The Managerial Grid* (Houston, TX: Gulf Publishing Co., 1964).

Davidson, Jim, *Effective Time Management* (New York: Human Science Press, 1978).

Geier, John G., "A Manual for Using the Personal Profile System," Performax Systems International (12805 State Hwy. 55, Minneapolis, MN 55441).

Hersey, Paul and Kenneth H. Blanchard, *Management of Organizational Behavior: Utilizing Human Resources*, 3rd ed. (Englewood Cliffs, NJ: Prentice-Hall, 1977).

Hock, Conrad, *The Four Temperaments* (Milwaukee, WI: Bruce, 1934)

Lefton, Robert E., et al, *Effective Motivation Through Performance Appraisal* (New York: John Wiley and Sons, 1977).

Marston, William M., *Emotions of Normal People* (New York: Harcourt, Brace, 1928). The book, long out of print, is now available from Performax Systems International, Persona Press.

Merrill, David W. and Roger H. Reid, *Personal Styles and Effective Performance* (Radnor, PA: Chilton Book Company, 1981).

Scott, Dru, *How to Put More Time in Your Life* (New York: Rawson, Wade Publishers, 1980).

Simpson, Donald T., "Conflict Styles: Organizational Decision Making," in *1977 Annual Handbook for Group Facilitators* (La Jolla, CA: University Associates, 1977).

Thomas, Kenneth W. and Ralph H. Killmann, *Conflict Mode Instrument* (Xicom, Inc., Sterling Forest, Tuxedo, NY 10987).

Wilson Learning Corporation, 6950 Washington Ave. So., Eden Prairie, MN 55344.

Zoll, Allen A., III, *Explorations in Managing* (Reading, MA: Addison-Wesley, 1974).

FOUR STYLES OF ADULT LEARNING

Ever wonder why your supervisory-skills workshop goes over like a lead balloon with one group of trainees, then gets rave reviews from the next?
The trainees' preferred style of learning could be the answer

BY LANE D. WARD

Why has your brilliantly planned and executed training session just been savaged on the evaluation forms turned in by several of your trainees? Why is it that no matter how you set up the workshop, some participants always are dissatisfied with their learning experiences? Take, as examples, these not-so-uncommon statements from four trainees who attended the same training session:

Trainee #1: "I'm an adult and there's certainly a better way than what this training offers. Let's look at the 'big picture' and come up with some better conclusions."

Trainee #2: "How do I know that all this training will work outside this classroom? Let's try it where the action really is, on the job."

Trainee #3: "Listen, quit beating around the bush. Tell it like it is. Let me know what I have to do, show me how to do it and I'll get it done."

Trainee #4: "I like what you're telling me in this training session. It makes sense. But I think I have some ideas that will work just as well. Let's look at what we're all doing on our jobs, discuss the positive points of each individual and get the job done according to our own best talents."

Every one of these participants wants to be trained differently. How can you overcome these problems and give better training to more people for less money? By addressing the fact that adults have particular learning styles with which they are most comfortable and to which they tend to be most receptive.

To fine tune training programs—and make them effective for adult learners—trainers must do a better job of understanding these individual differences. Although the identification of distinct learning styles, like behavior styles or leadership styles, is not a recent discovery (see editor's note), much of the literature on adult education or andragogy might lead you to think that all mature-thinking individuals like self-paced, self-governed learning strategies. This is not always the case. Adult-learning styles differ and your methodological decisions will meet with greater acceptance if they reflect those differences.

Typical adult-learning styles can be broken down into four profiles: idealistic, pragmatic, realistic and "existentialistic." Careful analysis of these characteristics can help you match your trainees' learning styles with the appropriate training methodology.

The idealistic learner

The *idealistic* adult learner is the builder, the thinker, the reasoner, the one who likes to discover the important characteristics of job or performance competencies. Idealistic learners are typically offended by training programs that are restrictive, struc- tured in nature, or "tell" them what must be done. In general, they feel that they are being treated like children when they have to submit to step-by-step detail. They also typically balk in trainer-centered environments, especially those that hint at being autocratic and manipulative or those in which the trainer comes across as a "know-it-all."

Therefore, the idealistic learner is most receptive to self-paced training that allows time for discovery and expansion of the training content (see Figure 1). These people tend to like group discussion, sharing, self-appraisal and evaluation, goal setting and democratic involvement. They enjoy

FIGURE 1
SAMPLE TRAINING METHODOLOGIES FOR THE IDEALISTIC LEARNER

- Discussion
- Democratic Planning Groups
- Case Study
- Problem-solving
- Goal Setting
- Discovery
- Inquiry Training
- Interactive Video Instruction
- Role Play
- Lecture
- Quality Circles
- Critical Incident
- Brainstorming
- Debate
- Reading Assignments
- Parables

identifying and discovering for themselves the skills necessary to do a job.

This type of training typically will be based on deductive reasoning which is stimulated through methodologies such as case studies, interactive video, and somewhat controversial situations requiring intense problem-solving and resolution skills. This does not mean that an idealist-based workshop should have unidentified objectives or job competencies. But it does mean that adults with idealistic learning styles should be allowed to discover those skills for themselves.

The pragmatic learner

"I'll believe it when I see it" is the credo of the *pragmatic* learner. This person assumes that relevant learning takes place only when it occurs in the environment where it is to be applied. That is, "Unless you teach me the skills of my job where my job really takes place, I am not sure that the laws, rules and information you give me will really be applicable."

As far as pragmatic learners are concerned, the situations in which they work are unique. Therefore, training programs which require them to leave their job environments and to retreat to a classroom setting are generally perceived as foreign to the "real world." Pragmatic learners also tend to have significant difficulty in "transferring" skills from one setting to another. This tends to make them uncomfortable with off-the-job training sites, packaged training programs and statements such as, "Here's how it worked in Department B," or "This is how they do it in Organization Z."

The best training methodologies for these learners include a heavy dose of hands-on experience (see Figure 2). Their confidence, trust and eventual

---

FIGURE 2
SAMPLE TRAINING METHODOLOGIES FOR THE PRAGMATIC LEARNER

- Custom-designed, Job-specific Training Materials
- Simulation
- Role Play
- Value Clarification
- Job-related Games
- Individualized Instruction
- On-the-job Demonstration and Practice

---

application of job skills will increase with on-the-job training, coaching and mentorship programs, custom-designed development programs and simulations that are specific to their jobs.

FIGURE 3
SAMPLE TRAINING METHODOLOGIES FOR THE REALISTIC LEARNER

- Goals Identification
- Programmed Instruction
- Behavior Modeling
- Job-description, Competency Identification
- Simulation
- Role Play
- Video and Computer-Assisted Instruction
- Off-the-shelf Training Materials
- Examples/Non-Examples
- Question/Answer
- Audiovisual (showing "how to" procedures)
- In-class Demonstration and Practice
- Reading Assignments (emphasizing "how to" procedures)
- Testing/Feedback

The realistic learner

Learners with the *realistic* profile are very "time-efficient." They want fast-paced programs that are void of "warm fuzzy" human-relations activities. To realistic learners, getting-acquainted and team-building exercises are time consuming and difficult to tolerate. These people are often low in interpersonal skills, but highly motivated in doing what they are told or what they have been trained to do. Discovery experiences, intellectualization, long hours with others in problem-solving or group developmental-

type activities are generally ineffective in getting their attention and genuine cooperation. If your training approach is not in tune with realistic learners' style, you will hear comments like, "Let's get on with it. Just tell me what needs to be done and let's do it."

The training design best suited for realistic learners (see Figure 3) is straightforward and based on "hard, fast data." They are most receptive to structured, programmed instruction that has explicit goals and well-defined outcomes. For these learners, "how-to" workshops, computer-assisted instruction and behavior modeling are generally very effective approaches. Typically, programs that are systems- or procedure-oriented and competency-based, with logical cause-and-effect relationships, also will be warmly received.

The existentialistic learner

The people I choose to call *existentialistic* learners demonstrate high regard for their own and others' peculiar strengths and abilities. Their learning style is based on the belief that there are many effective ways to produce the same results. They learn best from training experiences that rely on inductive reasoning, are based on situational or contingency theory, and that support the assumption that no one way is the "right" way.

Existentialistic learners are typically products of the '60s generation—people who demand a voice in the decisions that affect them. These are the individuals who most appreciate training sessions that stress human relations—programs which show understanding, sensitivity and respect for others' ways of doing things.

FIGURE 4
SAMPLE TRAINING METHODOLOGIES FOR THE EXISTENTIALISTIC LEARNER

- Team Building
- Group Dynamics
- Value Clarification
- Personal Goal Setting
- Expectation Theory
- Interpersonal Games
- Inductive Reasoning
- Contingency or Situational-based Competency Design
- Transactional Analysis
- Quality Circles
- Individualized Instruction
- Participant Presentations

In designing training programs for these learners, you should perform extensive needs analyses and base your programs on clearly defined outcomes and expectations. Let existentialistic learners share experiences (see Figure 4). Allow them to identify and

develop their own particular strategies for best accomplishing job objectives.

If you are careful to identify the objective that existentialistic learners should shoot for, they will reach it in their own ways. When given the freedom, these learners do well at achieving goals: They like to "prove themselves."

These learners also prefer training programs that encompass the "whole" individual. A training program directed at overall professional development, career development or quality of work life is likely to produce a better response than a program which focuses on on-the-job competencies.

Now what?

Naturally, very few learners will fit snugly and entirely into a single category; there are qualities of each of these learning styles in everyone. Nevertheless, people feel most comfortable with a training approach that deals to their long suit.

From this brief description of the four adult-learning styles, you will be able to identify the group represented by each of the trainee statements quoted at the beginning of this article. (If you are an *idealistic* learner, you probably are tempted to go back and do so immediately, unwilling to risk the possibility that if you keep reading, it may be spelled out for you.)

A few commercial instruments are available to help you identify trainees' learning profiles (see editor's note), though not the specific profiles outlined here. A review of adult-learning literature and research will help prepare you to "spot" individuals who demonstrate particular styles. A thorough preassessment can determine the dominant learning style of each participant in your training programs.

Obviously, the degree to which the trainer's sensitivity toward individual learning styles can produce more effective training will depend upon the flexibility and options available to the trainer: *Can* you split up this group of trainees and assign them different learning tasks? If not, is the group small enough that you can give individual attention to its members? Do you have a real choice of media and methods with which to handle the training task at hand?

In the long run, however—regardless of your options for any *particular* training challenge—the better you understand these adult-learning styles and match them to your training designs, the sooner you will improve your programs and "do better, for more, for less."

Reprinted from TRAINING, November 1983

UNDERSTANDING TRAINEE COMMUNICATION STYLES: DIFFERENT STROKES FOR DIFFERENT FOLKS

Why, when and how to use each of four communicating styles

BY JOHN L. BLEDSOE

Have you sometimes wondered why it seems so difficult to communicate with some people? And why at other times you instantaneously hit it off with someone you have just met? There seems to be a basis of understanding that is more than could be explained by a common background or related profession.

Or perhaps you've been surprised by an abrupt breakthrough in understanding when talking to a friend or business associate. You may have spent several minutes presenting what you see as relevant information — background material, pertinent facts, logical options. Your friend or associate has been growing progressively more restless. Then you decide to tell him how it *feels,* and, suddenly, you have instant communication.

What accounts for this change? And why do we seem to relate better with some people than with others?

The secret was unlocked by Carl Jung, a Swiss psychoanalyst. In a monumental work, *Psychological Types,* written in the 1920's but not translated in its entirety and published in the U.S. until 1974, Jung articulated a theory of personality so revolutionary in its divergence from so-called modern psychology that most personality theoreticians have, at this writing, refused to rebut it, much less assimilate it. To do so would involve nothing less than scrapping fifty years' worth of accumulated "psychological laws and truth."

What really accounts for personality differences, Jung said, is that every individual develops a primacy in one of four major behavioral functions:

Intuiting: speculating, imagining, envisioning, daydreaming, creating, innovating.
Thinking: rationally deducting, analyzing, ordering facts, identifying and weighing options, reflecting.
Feeling: empathizing, perceiving, associating, remembering, relating.
Sensing: acting — doing, relying on sensory data, combating-competing, striving for results, living in the here and now.

Behavior patterns, Jung claimed, are genetically determined and are reflected by infants during their first day of life. Study young children, he said, truly observe them and you must discover that they process experience on different primary channels. The truth is that children in elementary school can be validly classified as intuitors, thinkers, feelers, and sensors.

The *intuitor* child sits alone, apparently daydreaming. In reality, he is forming global concepts, integrating experience in a constant quest to determine the *why* of things. Knowing something because the teacher says it's true is not sufficient. He must discover why a thing is true. In the absence of such discovery, he will summarily reject your premise.

The *thinker* child prides himself

on being correct. He demonstrates a structured and systematic approach to learning. He gathers facts, not ideas. His concern is to systematize, to collect and infer but not to dream. His approach is information-centered.

The *feeler* child responds to mood, to affect — his own as well as the emotions of others. He learns through his emotions, his visceral

641

responses. He is empathetic, sentimental. He demonstrates keen interpersonal radar. Whether or not he engages in an activity with true commitment depends upon its perceived meaning in terms of past experience — not future possibilities or book-learned facts. His touchstone of reality is meaningful memories.

The *sensor* child is the doer, the fast-mover, the restless jack-in-the-box, the learner who must grab the rock or the frog in his own hands to know its reality; the child who is sent to the principal's office today and who emerges as the corporate president of one of Fortune's 500 tomorrow. He dissipates anxiety through action, he knows by *doing* — not by imagining, thinking, or feeling.

So what does this have to do with training in U.S. corporations today? Perhaps a great deal more than you may imagine.

Consider these concepts:

1. Every one of us, trainer and trainee (yes, even you), uses a blend of the four behavioral styles. No one is a walking "pure style" or cardboard creature.

2. Despite using a blend or style-mix, each person relies most heavily on a primary or dominant style.

3. An individual's weaknesses — or areas of key behavioral difficulty — often represent an over-extension of his strengths.

4. An individual's style is reflected in his behavior and is therefore *observable* and *identifiable.*

Psychologist Paul Mok saw the need to translate Jung's theories into *action* terms, to make the theory "see-able" and "do-able." Mok figured that if people do use these four main styles to process data (re-ceive) and to broadcast data (send), then it follows that one of their primary functions is to serve as communication channels.

No style should be considered good or bad. No one style is more "right" or "wrong" than another. The communicating styles we have developed over the years have little to do with intellectual abilities, aptitudes, performance, or concerns about mental health or illness. You use four main channels of communication; so do I. So does every boss and every subordinate, every salesman and every customer, every husband and every wife, every teacher and every pupil.

Transactional analysis, based on the Freudian model of personality, suggests that if you and I are communicating in our adult ego states, we will be engaged in adult-adult communication, ergo a parallel transaction. Not necessarily so.

Why? If you are a primary sensor functioning in your adult ego state, you want to know *immediately* what

Primary Communicating Style	TYPICAL TELEPHONE BEHAVIOR	TYPICAL OFFICE DECOR OR SURROUNDINGS
INTUITOR	Wordy but aloof. Impersonal. Goes off on tangents. Not mindful of your time or his.	Intuitors are likely to demonstrate their imagination in their selection of new-wave furnishings and decor. Those in "think" occupations and professions have offices resembling mini think-tanks: round conference tables, inspiration-pads on walls, offbeat periodicals. Add citations for idealistic work, community service and pet causes.
THINKER	"Business like" but lackluster. Little voice inflection. Ticks off specifics. Ordered, measured manner. Sometimes suggests ground-rules for phone conversation, i.e., "Shall we begin with your agenda or mine?"	Thinkers like their work surroundings to be correct and non-distracting. They select furnishings that are tasteful but conventional. Likely to have charts for business use, reports, and reference works nearby. Few touches of informality and color.
FEELER	Warm and friendly, sometimes seemingly too much so. Doesn't seem to distinguish between business and personal calls in the sense that he's likely to be quite informal. Interjects humor, personal associations, questions about one's well-being, etc. Likes to "gossip." Talks incessantly. Feels rude if hangs up fast.	Feelers tend to personalize their surroundings, make their offices informal and somewhat "homey." They like warm colors, antiques; big, live plants, mementos, snapshots rather than formal photographs of family. Papers and files, etc., are likely to be messy on the surface, "organized" underneath in a personal way only they can understand.
SENSOR	Abrupt. Staccato. Gets to the point, expects others to do the same. Interrupts. Needs to control the conversation.	Sensors generate atmosphere of hard-charging clutter. Mementos, if any, connote action: heads of animals hunted, golf trophies, mounted fish, racing prints. Desk is likely to be big, messy. Sensor is too busy to be neat, too action-oriented to be concerned with image unless he has a strong thinker back-up style.

I'm proposing, what the *upshot* or *bottom line* is that I'm suggesting.

If I'm a primary thinker functioning in my adult ego state, and I want you to *know all the facts* and insist on giving you a *long-detailed run-down* on my *fact-finding* and *historical review* of the situation, we are not effectively interacting, not communicating in parallel!

Certainly, there are applications for the teacher. It's very hard to have a successful education experience if the trainee is trying to learn on one wavelength and the trainer is trying to teach on another.

Mok designed a Communicating Styles Survey which, in a few minutes, can give an individual valid data on his primary communicating style, his back-up style, and his short-suit (or less typically relied upon) styles which he uses under everyday normal conditions. The same instrument also provides data feedback on the individual's *style-shifts* under stress (e.g., the normally fast-moving, hard-charging sensor who becomes, under stress, a conservative, cautious, weighing thinker).

The accompanying tables will demonstrate. First, try to pinpoint the positive characteristics associated with your primary style. Then, imagine situations in which you would be apt to over-extend these positive characteristics (see table of characteristics). Do you realize how your positive characteristics can, as a result of over-reliance and a lack of self-monitoring, become negative or dysfunctional?

For example, if you are a primary thinker, you probably tend to be analytical. But you must be careful not to over-extend this characteristic and become rigid and overly serious.

The point is, individuals *can* learn to read their communicating styles more accurately, and to read and assess the styles of other individuals with whom they do business on a daily basis.

Once they accept this concept and relate it to increased personal awareness, it's time to learn to *style-flex*. Style-flexing means communicating with another individual on *his* primary channel rather than communicating with all people as though they were all, say, primary thinkers. Is this really possible?

Absolutely.

Is it easy?

Certainly not.

Jung indicated that individuals rarely outgrow or discard their primary styles. In other words, a person's communicating style tends to be very stable through time.

It would be difficult, if not impossible, for you or me, even as professional trainers, to style-flex continuously over a 24-hour period. That is, if you're a primary thinker, it would be unrealistic to expect you to be able to communicate effectively as a feeler for an entire day. But most transactions are much shorter in duration. How long is an average sales call — 45 minutes to an hour and a half? How long is a

TYPICAL STYLE OF DRESS	CHARACTERISTICS ASSOCIATED WITH THE COMMUNICATING STYLES	
	Effective Application	**Ineffective Application**
Hard to predict. May be like "absent-minded professor," more into ideas than image, a la Howard Hughes. May be too wrapped up in future goals to think about daily appearance. Alternatively may have imaginative self-concept that may reflect in clothes from stunning to outlandish.	original imaginative creative broad-gauged charismatic idealistic intellectually tenacious ideological	unrealistic "far-out" fantasy-bound scattered devious out-of-touch dogmatic impractical
Conservative, "proper." Unassuming, understated. Dress invariably appropriate to circumstance. Business-like in office; well tailored, "correct" in non-work atmosphere. Color-coordinated, but not colorful.	effective communicator deliberative prudent weighs alternatives stabilizing objective rational analytical	verbose indecisive over-cautious over-analyzes unemotional non-dynamic controlled and controlling over-serious, rigid
Dress is more according to own mood than to suit others' expectations. Likes colorful, informal clothes. Often has sentimental, favorite articles of clothing. Sometimes shows a hankering for old-fashioned touches or "costume" effects.	spontaneous persuasive empathetic grasps traditional values probing introspective draws out feelings of others loyal	impulsive manipulative over-personalizes sentimental postponing guilt-ridden stirs up conflict subjective
Informal, simple, functional clothes are the order of the day. Wants to be neat but not fancy. Tends to categorize: everyday or dress-up. If sensors see the occasion as being "special," they throw simplicity to the winds; their competitive zeal then rises to the surface and they may "outclass" everyone.	pragmatic assertive, directional results-oriented objective — bases opinions on what he actually sees competitive confident	doesn't see long-range status seeking, self-involved acts first then thinks lacks trust in others domineering arrogant

typical boss-subordinate performance review session — an hour or two? Most people can, with practice, learn to style-flex for limited periods of time.

And style-flexing is, in itself, not the only key. Sometimes just asking a person the "right question" can thaw a difficult communication transaction. For example, if you're dealing with a primary intuitor, ask him, "How do you feel about the basic *concept* underlying this proposal?"

To a thinker, ask: "Based on your own *analysis,* how would you evaluate the relevance of the facts I've presented?"

To a feeler: "I've given this a lot of consideration but I'd like to know *how you feel we're tracking.*"

To a sensor: "I hope I haven't bored you; what's your reaction to the *main point* here?"

If you take the time and trouble to learn the technology presented here and to apply it by style-flexing, will people regard you as a phony? That's a common fear, but experience by thousands in industry proves quite the contrary. People will say, "Now you're on *my* wavelength!" Or, "I appreciate your being open enough to share some of your doubts and apprehensions." Or, "Thanks for boiling it down and respecting the fact that I really don't have a hell of a lot of time!"

A few weeks ago, Bob Baker, regional administrator of a Fortune 500 listed corporation and a very hard-nosed, competitive person, made this comment: "I've seen it all — sensitivity training, TA workshops, team-building, you name it. But in the three months since I learned style-flexing and began applying it, I've realized for

the first time that I'd been treating certain types of subordinates like dirt under my shoe. One subordinate whom I was convinced had to be terminated has now emerged as my most promotable assistant."

Eighteen hundred miles away in Atlanta, a 44-year-old Coca Cola account executive wrote: "Yesterday I approached a new prospect, a VP of purchasing for 300 fast-food chain stores, about Coke syrup. In eight minutes, I read him as a primary feeler, so I style-flexed, shifting my presentation from my natural thinker style to his major receptivity channel. He placed an initial order of $150,000 and thanked *me!* Why? I spoke *his* language!"

Are you a doubting Thomas?
You might be missing the best bet of your life!

Reprinted from TRAINING, March 1976

HOW TO TEACH TECHNICAL SUBJECTS TO NONTECHNICAL LEARNERS

It takes more than expertise in the subject matter

BY JIRI BEZDEK

Most instructors of technical subjects are extremely knowledgeable in their areas of expertise. But when it comes to expertise in teaching, they often leave a lot to be desired—especially if the audience is filled with nontechnical learners.

Technical instructors at one end of the spectrum come off like comedian Professor Irwin Corey, rattling off a baffling barrage of technical terms. Those at the other extreme assume the saintly forbearance of children's show host Mr. Rogers, oversimplifying to the point of patronization. In the middle of the road is Mr. Wizard, the technical expert or instructional specialist who can clearly and effectively communicate with the nontechnical learner.

Professional trainers, instructional designers and subject-matter experts can use the same techniques to prepare technical presentations or materials for nontechnical learners. It's not hard to be a real Mr. Wizard, but it does take a little planning and an understanding of some basic rules for designing training.

What's different about technical subject?

Many technical instructors mistakenly believe that content is all important. A science instructor once said, "If you don't understand it, just memorize it. Maybe you'll understand it later." Acquiring facts is important, of course, but *learning* also involves understanding concepts, seeing relationships and applying knowledge.

If you, the technical instructor, are not there to help the student understand, what *are* you there for? The instructor (or instructional material) should present information in a way

---

Adult learners need to understand what they are going to learn and why it is important.

---

that promotes both learning (retention) and understanding (the ability to apply knowledge). To accomplish this goal, instruction must be carefully designed. That means you must decide what to teach and how—how to organize the lesson, what sequence should be followed, what examples and supporting materials should be used and so on.

Nontechnical learners are usually unfamiliar with technical terminology and, more importantly, they do not have a common frame of reference with which to approach the subject matter. Instruction has to compensate for these shortcomings. A poorly designed message only complicates the problem and increases the learner's handicap. While you can use the following techniques to develop almost any kind of training, they are particularly important in teaching technical subjects to nontechnical learners.

☐ **Understand the audience.** Before you do anything else, your first task is to understand the learners' backgrounds and needs. How familiar are they with the subject matter? Is there any material they need to know before instruction in the actual subject can even begin? How much detail do they need? A number of well-established techniques such as audience analysis and needs analysis can help you answer these kinds of questions.

☐ **Set objectives.** Adult learners are task oriented. They are usually interested in solving a particular problem or learning a specific skill. They need to understand what they are going to learn and why it is important.

Set learning objectives or goals based on what the audience *needs* to know. Be sure participants understand what they are going to learn and why. Above all, don't be overly ambitious. It's better to cover less material well than to cover a great deal of material too hastily.

☐ **Get organized.** Organization is probably the most important characteristic of good instruction. Well-organized material is easier to learn and teach. Organization can also help the learner form mental constructs that will serve as a frame of reference for future learning.

To check the organization of your instruction, look at the content outline. At least one major topic subhead should appear on each page. If not, the content is probably poorly organized.

Next look at the construction of your outline. The outline should not contain too many parallel items— items that do not have a strong relationship to each other. In Figure 1, each item is related only to the parent above. This kind of outline ends up being a simple laundry list of subtopics with no apparent reason for one item to follow the next. Parallels make it too easy to overlook intermediate points.

A better outline, with nonparallel structure (Figure 2), illustrates the relationship between items and clearly defines the categories. These organizational categories help learners structure the material in their minds.

☐ **Follow a logical sequence.** The content of an outline should present information in a careful sequence and each point should serve as a foundation for later points. Information can be sequenced in many logical ways:

- *Empirically* or according to physical characteristics. For example, in a lesson on basic computer systems, you might categorize processors in terms of size (microcomputer, minicomputer and mainframe).

- *Conceptually*, with the sequence showing relationships among objects or concepts. Continuing with the computer example, you might associate each of those processors with its appropriate operating systems.

- According to *origin*—how objects or concepts were formed. With this approach, you would discuss processors in terms of chronological evolution, i.e., mainframes appeared first, micros last.

- According to *utilization*, with information and skills presented in the order in which they will be used by the learner. In a lesson on loading a computer printer, instruction might go through the procedure step-by-step, providing information as needed.

- The last category, *instructional sequencing*, includes a number of possible schemes, each used for a different purpose. Depending on the audience and desired result, you might teach from general to specific, familiar to unusual, easy to difficult, exotic to common, rule to example or example to rule.

Here is a portion of an outline that flows from general to specific. It deals with IBM's Systems Network Architecture (subtopics have been omitted).

- Functional definition of SNA
- Why SNA is an important concept
- Why you need to know about SNA
- Introduction to SNA layers
- Discussion of first SNA layer
- Discussion of second SNA layer, etc.

"Rule to example" means that a rule is presented, followed by several specific examples of that rule. If you wanted learners to "synthesize" or combine previously learned information into new rules, however, you might use the opposite sequence—"example to rule."

Inherent in all these forms of sequencing is the concept of progressive revelation: Material is revealed in small segments, each building on the next.

☐ **Provide meaningful transitions.** If a

FIGURE 1
POOR OUTLINE STRUCTURE

I. IBM mainframe computers
   A. S/360
   B. S/370
   C. 303X
   D. 43XX
   E. 308X
II. IBM Operating systems
   A. DOS/VS
   B. DOS/VSE
   C. VS1
   D. MVS
   E. MVS/XA

---

lesson is well organized, transitions from one topic to another generally will be natural and logical. If they are not, your organization may be at fault.

Consider three transition statements. "Now let's talk about. . ." is a poor transition. It suggests no relationship between one point and the next. "Another component of. . ." is better—at least we know the instructor is talking about components in the same category. "The next step in the process. . ." is usually the best choice because we *know* the next step will be closely related to the overall process under discussion.

The transition functions to reorient learners, or to remind them where they are in the sequence of the course and why. An effective instructor should introduce, summarize and relate new material to what has already been studied. This way,

---

FIGURE 2
BETTER OUTLINE STRUCTURE

I. IBM mainframe computers
   A. Non-virtual storage
      1. S/360
   B. Virtual storage
      1. S/370
      2. 303X
      3. 43XX
      4. 308X
II. IBM Operating systems
   A. Dos-type
      1. DOS/VS
      2. DOS/VSE
   B. OS-type
      1. VS1
      2. MVS/370
      3. MVS/XA
   C. VM

---

learners always know what road they're on and where they're headed.

☐ **Use illustrations.** Concepts are invisible. When you describe them with words alone, they become subject to individual interpretation. Learners are much more likely to see what you mean if you draw them a picture.

However, complex illustrations need lots of explanation. Figure 3 illustrates the major types of software that might be used on a large computer under IBM's MVS operating system. Software categories (systems software, auxiliary systems software, etc.) are shown in boxes. Arrows are used to illustrate relationships. Two kinds of relationships are shown: who uses different programs (programmer, user), and how each program relates to others.

This illustration is too complex for learners to absorb all at once. It should be presented instead as a series of four or five illustrations, starting with the basic structure (the box categories), then revealing progressive levels of detail.

☐ **Use analogies.** Since many nontechnical learners have a limited frame of reference, you should provide one for them. Compare the material with familiar objects, concepts or experiences. Once information is put in a familiar context, it is easier to understand and remember.

Figure 4 illustrates IBM's "families" of mainframe computers by showing the relationships among different models in terms of physical size, year and processing power. One measure of processing power is MIPS (millions of instructions per second), or the number of program instructions the computer can process in one second.

To make the concept of MIPS more accessible to nontechnical learners, one MIP is equated to 100 miles per hour. The right-hand column shows in familiar terms the awesome increases in processing power over the last two decades. The visuals in the second column from the left associate each computer with a similar model of automobile, designed to suggest decreasing size and increasing efficiency.

☐ **Use examples.** Analogies are helpful but they're not enough. It may seem obnoxiously obvious to suggest that you use examples in instruction, but maybe it isn't. A former colleague of mine was a data-base expert temporarily involved in training. He was very good at explaining highly technical concepts because he frequently used analogies. Sitting at a table in the cafeteria, he would use saltshakers, ashtrays and anything else at hand to construct his analogous model. The problem was he never got to specifics; he assumed that his nontechnical audience would not understand anyway. When he was finished, his audience knew a lot about saltshakers, but little about the purpose of the RES library in an IMS data-base system.

Analogies are great for explaining what something is like. But sooner or later, you have to explain what that something *is*. Go slowly, be patient, and avoid or explain unfamiliar technical terms.

☐ **Point out exceptions and unusual situations.** Nontechnical learners may not have the experience they need to see exceptions or inconsistencies, so you have to point them out.

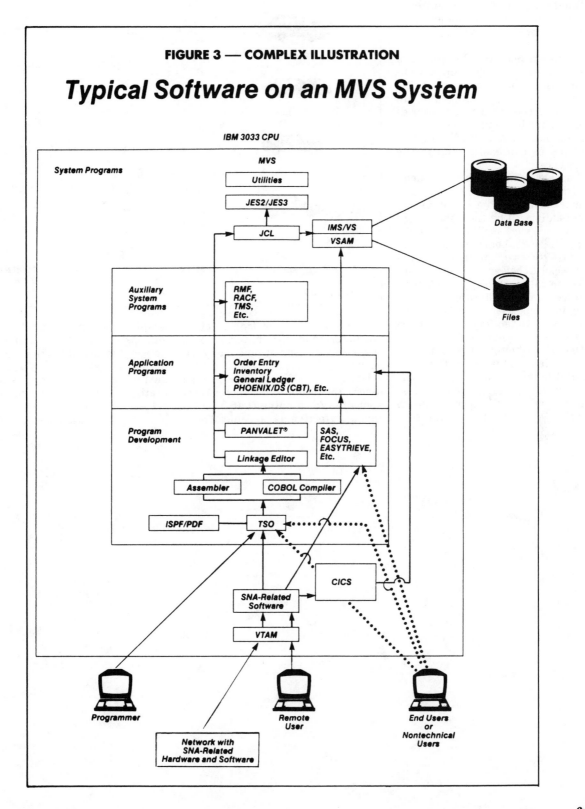

FIGURE 3 — COMPLEX ILLUSTRATION

Typical Software on an MVS System

For example, an operating system is a complex program that controls the operation of the computer. IBM has developed three types of operating systems for mainframe computers: DOS, OS and VM. Each type has different architecture and functions. But VM is unique in that it can be used to control *other* operating systems functioning on the same computer.

When you point out exceptions, you not only clarify the subject, you make it more interesting.

☐ **Anticipate questions.** Nontechnical learners can easily develop misconceptions and not even know it. Remember, their experience is limited. They are actively building categories and stuffing bits and pieces of information into them. Any of those bits and pieces can easily land in the wrong box.

Another computer example demonstrates the point. A popular data-management program for microcomputers, dBase II by the Ashton-Tate Co., sounds very similar to IBM's DB2 (Data Base 2). Learners can easily confuse the two, and that's a problem because they are very different.

Technical terminology is rife with subtleties and similarities, particularly in computer-related fields. The wise instructor anticipates questions and areas of possible confusion.

One trick is to role play the part of the student. This is particularly helpful in instructional writing. After writing a passage, review it as though you were a student reading it for the first time. Try to find sentences that raise questions. Try to misunderstand the material. You might be surprised at how many assumptions you make.

Like anyone charged with training others, the technical instructor is responsible for making that instruction as effective as possible. These simple techniques can help you design instruction that is understandable and memorable. You may even become a real-life Mr. Wizard. And best of all, you can experience the gratifying "Aha!" of the nontechnical learner.

Reprinted from TRAINING, April 1985

FIGURE 4 — VISUAL ANALOGY

IBM Mainframe Computers

		Model	Year	MIPS	Equiv. MPH
S/360		360/65	1965	.68	**68** MPH
		360/85	1968	2.4	**240** MPH
S/370		370/168-3	1972	2.7	**270** MPH
303X		3033	1977	4.7	**470** MPH
43XX		4341-2	1980	1.1	**110** MPH
308X		3084-Q	1982	26	**2600** MPH (3.5 times speed of sound)

1 MIP = 100 MPH

CHANGING WHAT TRAINEES SAY DOESN'T ALWAYS CHANGE WHAT THEY DO

Studies of human behavior bring to light a startling gap between attitude and action

BY JOE SEACRIST

Fire-and-brimstone preachers exhort their flocks to repent. Feminists hold consciousness-raising sessions. Training directors conduct training programs. Does all this organized brainwashing work? Can attitudes and beliefs be changed? In adults? A growing body of scientific research indicates that the preachers, feminists and training directors are right. Attitudes and beliefs can be changed. And in a relatively short time. Since it's also been proved that existing attitudes determine behavior, it's logical to assume that if you change a person's attitude, you'll change his behavior. It's logical, but it isn't true.

New scientific studies of human behavior bring to light a startling gap between attitude and action, behavior and belief. One of the most interesting of these studies was done in an industrial setting by a team of Ohio State University researchers. They set out to measure the behavior changes in a group of plant foremen who were about to undertake a two-week course in human relations. The course emphasized ways and means of dealing with subordinates. The plant foremen were exposed to lectures, group discussions, visual aids and role plays—all the techniques used in highly sophisticated training programs. The general purpose of the program was to persuade foremen that mutual trust, warmth and consideration are desirable in dealing with subordinates.

The foremen filled out questionnaires before taking the course, and afterwards. The results of the questionnaires indicated that after taking the course, foremen were sold on mutual trust, warmth and consideration.

Had the study stopped here as most studies do, it would not have turned up a surprising fact. When the researchers went into the plant and measured the behavior change of the trained foremen against a group of untrained foremen—a control group that had not taken the course—they found *no discernable difference in behavior*. In other words, attitudes which were changed in the training sessions did not cause changes in behavior in the factory. Why? This is a question which is probably not asked often enough.

Arthur R. Cohen, renowned researcher and author of social psychology texts, points out this disinclination in his book, ATTITUDE CHANGE AND SOCIAL INFLUENCE. He says, "Attitudes are always seen to be a precursor to behavior, a determinant of what behaviors the individual will actually go about doing in his daily affairs. However, though most psychologists assume such a state of affairs, very little work on attitude change has explicitly dealt with the behavior that may follow upon a change of attitudes. Most researchers in the field are content to demonstrate that there are factors which affect attitude change

and that these factors are open to orderly exploration, without actually carrying through to the point where they examine the links between changed attitudes and changes in learning performance, perception and interaction."

Attempting to examine these links, let's go back to the plant foremen. Whatever happened to them in the training program aimed at changing attitudes evidently worked. It changed their beliefs and attitudes. Then they left the training environment and went back to the factory, where a different set of stimuli worked on them. Instead of a training director, there was a boss and a quota. Instead of lectures and films there was work to get out. Instead of an approving peer group, there was derision. In short, whatever pressures had formed their original opinions—before training—were alive and well and operative.

Another example can be seen in the salesman who believes in high-pressure closes as the best way to make sales. He's developed the opinion over the years. He's been successful with the technique. He's seen other salesmen succeed with it. After hours, he's heard fellow salesmen brag about their ability to make high-pressure closes and the benefits they've reaped because of this ability. When he manages a high-pressure close himself, he gets a lot of satisfaction out of it. Nobody has ever complained, and once when he used a high-pressure close, two people came up to him afterwards and commented on how forceful he was in the final minutes of his presentation. Surely, this man feels, high-pressure closes must be desirable.

At this point, the salesman has a discussion with his newly-appointed sales manager who tells him that he does not approve of high-pressure closes, that he, himself, has never needed them. The sales manager tells many success stories proving that soft sell works better. The salesman knows many of the stories are true. He respects the sales manager and is impressed by his sales record and actually begins to believe that high-pressure closes aren't desirable. Now, if the salesman were asked on a questionnaire if high-pressure closes were desirable, he would probably answer no. He might even decide that on his next sales call, he would try a different approach. However, when he actually makes the call, what happens? The salesman remembers how important this sale is, to his record, income, ego. He finds it easy to go back to his tried-and-true high-pressure tactic. Some other time, he tells himself, he will try soft sell. But now, because he really needs this sale, he'd better nail it down the best way he knows. So he uses his usual high-pressure close. He is still not convinced it's the best way, but the environment makes it too convenient for him to use it.

As these examples demonstrate, psychologists are coming to see that when opinions and attitudes are changed through the impact of a persuasive communication, the change is likely to disappear unless it is supported by an environmental change as well. Before we can provide these changes, we need to know what they should be and we need to know more about how people receive and maintain attitudes and beliefs and translate them into behavior. Currently, there are a number of intriguing pieces to this puzzle.

1. Attitudes frequently function to meet psychological needs. It's useless to try and change an attitude without knowing the psychological need it is meeting.

2. The old punishment-reward idea is still valid. People do develop favorable attitudes towards objects associated with satisfaction of needs and react unfavorably toward objects or events which thwart.

3. The clarity, consistency and nearness of rewards and punishments as they relate to the individual's activities and goals are important factors in the development of attitudes. For example, management seeks to increase production by convincing workers that the plant is a good place to work, assuming that production will correspondingly rise. Management succeeds in convincing the workers that the plant is a good place to work. But production rates do not climb.

4. A hard-to-fit piece of the puzzle is the fact that when human subjects in research are invariably rewarded for correct responses, they do not tend to retain their learned responses as well as when the reward is sometimes skipped.

5. Many attitudes function to protect self-image. In these instances, external rewards and punishments are less important than the subject's own deep feelings. Satisfactions also accrue from the expression of attitudes which reflect cherished beliefs. The reward in these instances is not so much a matter of gaining social recognition or money as of confirming the subject's notion of the sort of person he seems to be.

6. People acquire attitudes and beliefs not only to satisfy needs, but also to give meaning to what would otherwise be an unorganized chaotic universe. To the educator's dismay, people are not too often seekers-after-knowledge-in-general. They *do* want to understand the events which impinge on their lives. Developing attitudes and beliefs about these events gives them order and clarity. Giving up these attitudes and beliefs threatens what Walter Lippman has called "the ordered more or less consistent picture of the world to which our habits, our tastes, our capacities, our comforts and our hopes have adjusted themselves."

One thing is clear. What Arthur Cohen has called "the links between changed attitudes and changes in learning performance, perception and interaction" need a lot more study. When it comes to training programs, the hard fact is: training programs which change attitudes and beliefs without forcing changes in the environment will result in workers talking a better game but doing the same old thing. Is that what we want?

Reprinted from TRAINING, February 1976

ENHANCING SKILLS ACQUISITION THROUGH ACHIEVEMENT MOTIVATION

Helping trainees behave like high achievers has another payoff: Trainees learn complex technical skills faster—and better

BY LAWRENCE HOLPP

Skills training, whether it involves complex or routine tasks, can become boring and arduous work both for trainee and trainer. Seldom is all the information you teach in the classroom used on the job, and the excitement and urgency of the actual work environment is rarely present in training seminars.

Some of the reinforcing properties of on-the-job learning can, however, be built into skills training. One way is to base training on a theoretical model that has been shown to produce trainees motivated by a need for high achievement. That need—a powerful psychological drive—causes people to work harder at doing things better.

Research by David C. McClelland and his associates indicates that individuals who have a high need to achieve (n Achievement) approach goal setting, problem solving, planning and organizing— all key management processes— with a degree of creativity and energy significantly greater than that of their peers. Direct training for n Achievement is effective in motivating owners of small businesses, corporate executives and students to behave in a more aggressive, entrepreneurial manner in their work. Can an approach to skills training that uses an achievement-motivation design have a similar effect?

Work in training underwriters to be better negotiators suggests that it can. Experience also suggests that n Achievement training can help them master, on the job, many complex technical areas with minimum cost to the organization. An n Achievement design can also produce measurable changes in the climate of an organization, resulting in higher morale, lower turnover rates, increased confidence and specific, quantifiable improvements in sales-related activities.

The need for achievement is a drive. Henry Murry, who first named n Achievement, described it in the following way: "To accomplish something difficult. To master, manipulate, or organize physical objects, human beings or ideas. To do this as rapidly and as independently as possible. To excel oneself." (From *Explorations in Personality*, 1938.)

Overall, this drive produces highly efficient, goal-directed people. However, the nature and strength of drives are variable and subject to competing psychological interpretations. To be measurable, a drive must activate behavior— it must cause the individual to operate on the environment, not merely respond when conditions call it forth. An individual who has operant n Achievement characteristics thinks about achievement and structures his life accordingly. The *respondent* individual may show an interest in achievement, but only when prompted from outside. This is a key difference. The individual high in n Achievement scans the environment for opportunities; the respondent individual waits for opportunity to knock.

We measure this characteristic by qualitative, not merely quantitative, behavior. High n Achievers may or may not contemplate achievement more often than those low in n Achievement, but they will more frequently focus their achievement-related imagery *toward goals*.

McClelland and his colleagues used Murry's Thematic Apperception Test (T.A.T.) to measure the degree to which n Achievement thinking was present in their subjects. By comparing pre-training and post-training T.A.T. scores of latent n Achievement, McClelland showed that it was possible to increase the number of operant verbal responses indicating n Achievement through training his subjects to think and act in more goal-directed ways. This is important because such increases lead directly to better performance on a variety of tasks. Since organizations are interested in performance, not "operant verbal responses," let us focus on the specific behaviors and conditions research has indicated will increase performance.

N Achievement skills training is based on observed behaviors of individuals high in n Achievement. These behaviors show interest in goal setting, responsibility, feedback and activity— all of which indicate that an n-Achievement design is well suited to organizational development.

- **Goal setting:** N Achievers set goals of moderate difficulty that are challenging but attainable. Moderate goals tell the n Achiever more about how he or she is doing than goals that are either too hard or too easy.

- **Responsibility:** Individuals high in n Achievement like to take responsibility for their actions. They gravitate to jobs that allow them maximum control over the means of attaining their goals.

- **Feedback:** N Achievers select goals and milestones which are concrete and readily measurable. Because profit and loss statements tend to fall in this category, business people often show considerable n Achievement.

- **Activity:** N Achievers are very active. They have high energy levels, and they apply their energy to solving business problems, bringing them closer to their goals.

Training designed around these four characteristics will promote frequent goal setting, encourage and reward people to take responsibility for new ideas, provide a mechanism for

651

feedback and create organizational channels so that activity in new areas is encouraged.

In a program to train underwriters, technical material was structured in a series of cases, or practice sessions, followed by role plays. Scripts were not written for the role plays, but careful directions were given. After every practice session, each participant developed a personal plan for the role play, going back to the technical information presented in the practice session to retrieve needed facts and figures. How well a person did this depended, in part, upon his or her level of *n* Achievement.

In order to develop a plan for the role play, an individual must set moderate but challenging goals, devise his or her own way of reaching those goals, assume responsibility for success or failure (saying "the boss told me so" is not allowed), devise a system for obtaining feedback and engage in systematic planning that includes anticipating problems and developing flexibility to accommodate changing situations. The effects of this kind of training are significant. Participants' confidence and energy levels increase, along with sales calls.

Using coaches

In the underwriter training program, line managers were designated coaches, and the responsibility for creating a positive climate was put in their hands. Their jobs were carefully spelled out to include helping employees set goals and get feedback for their efforts, maintaining an organizational climate conducive to testing new ideas at a line level, facilitating the acquisition of vital skills in product areas and cross-training between departments.

To ensure that the coaches (first- or second-level supervisory managers) kept their people on track, they were in turn supervised by a business development manager who reported directly to the branch manager. Overall team success became an element in measuring the coaches' performance, making it worth their while to give feedback and keep things going.

Climate

Changing the climate in an organization to facilitate high achievement is usually an expensive and complex organizational development effort conducted from the top down. When line managers are used as coaches in skills training and given clear authority to keep organizational channels open, their team members gain access to new challenges and oppor-

tunities for growth and experimentation. This produces an organizational climate conducive to *n* Achievement from the bottom up. Not only is the coach responsible for advocating or running interference for team members, he or she is able to get a payoff at appraisal time for doing so.

Cross-training

In any industry, the more people trained to do several different jobs, the more useful they are and the better they are able to represent their organization. This can be accomplished by forming coaching groups across departmental lines. Any skill which is common to most of the members of an organization can be taught interdepartmentally, with cross-training results.

Summary

Strong evidence suggests that organizations that demonstrate a favorable climate to *n* Achievement are more productive, show increases in sales, decreased turnover, lower rates of absenteeism, healthier employees, greater geographic growth— even more suggestions in the suggestion box. By using a training design shown to be effective in getting employees to behave like high achievers, and by creating a climate that will encourage their efforts, the human-resource professional can help carry the motivating influence of the bench, shop or work unit into the classroom and back again.

This system is good for the organization because it minimizes time off for centralized training and because it has many characteristics of on-the-job learning. In the long run, the success of this approach will earn the trainer valuable support within the organization for infusing new and different ideas— which is, after all, the final purpose of education. And the trainee, to paraphrase a very old saying, has been given not a fish, but a fishing rod and a clear map to a well stocked stream.

References

Litwin, G.H. & Stringer, R.A. *Motivation and Organizational Climate.* Boston. Division of Research, Graduate School of Business Administration, Harvard University, 1968.

McClelland, D.C. (1962) "Business Drive and National Achievement," *Harvard Business Review,* 40:July-August, 99-112.

McClelland, D.C. & Winter, D. *Motivating Economic Achievement.* New York, N.Y. The Free Press, 1969.

McClelland, D.C. (Ed.) *Human Motivation.* Morristown, N.J. General Learning Press, 1973.

Reprinted from TRAINING, June 1980

THEORY X OR THEORY Y?

Should managers crack the whip, foster self-actualization, or find some middle ground?

BY BEVERLY GEBER

Theory Y: A form of participatory management. You really do have a say in how things are run. Sure you do.— Business Week

The editors at *Business Week* were having a little fun with the lingo in their January 20, 1986, cover story "Business Fads—What's In-And out." Of course, Theory Y is a perfect target because thoroughly modern managers like to talk a good game about how they used to be Theory X but then they saw the light and now they're so Theory Y their spouses and children barely recognize them anymore. Some things just *beg* to be satirized, you know?

The trouble is, *Business Week* got it wrong, confusing the theory with its common extension in practice. The writers were exercising poetic license, no doubt, but it's a mistake lots of people make. After all, as people in this society are wont to ask, what good is a theory if it doesn't have any *practical* application? It's probably the same reason business schools spit out MBAs at supercomputer speed while cobwebs grow in the philosophy department.

But because this is a column on definitions, we're going to give short shrift to the practical applications (Do you really want to read another article telling you that participative manage-

ment is the best thing that happened to this country since Donny and Marie broke up?) and go straight to the theory of Theory X and Theory Y.

Strictly speaking, Theory X and Theory Y merely represent philosophies, two different ways that managers typically interpret the motivations and character of workers. Although the concepts had been around for awhile—at least since the 1920s, when Elton Mayo tinkered

---

Theory Y: Motivated people are the rule, not the exception.

---

with worker motivation at Western Electric's Hawthorne Works in Chicago—it wasn't until 1960 that Douglas McGregor defined and named them in his book, *The Human Side of Enterprise* (McGraw-Hill, New York).

McGregor's thinking drew heavily upon the ideas of Abraham Maslow, who published his theory of human motivation in 1954 (*Motivation and*

Personality, Harper and Row, New York). Maslow, a clinical psychologist, classified human needs into five categories and asserted there is a definite order (a hierarchy) in which those needs must be satisfied. The order: 1) physiological needs, 2) safety and security, 3) love and belonging, 4) self-esteem, 5) self-actualization.

One assumption generally made when applying Maslow's theory to the modern worker, especially by Theory Y managers, is that physiological, safety and belonging needs already have been met. So the workers are searching for something that will fulfill higher-level needs involving self-esteem or self-actualization. The job is one such source.

Along came McGregor, a professor at the Massachusetts Institute of Technology and former president of Antioch University, to define the self-actualization view a bit more completely and place it within the context of the workplace. He argued that most managers fall into one of two camps, defined by their assumptions about workers, and that those assumptions have a profound effect on their supervisory styles.

Theory X managers (that is, managers holding Theory X assumptions about people) believe that workers are essentially lazy, spend most of their time avoiding work and responsibility, want security above all, have little ambition and need to be threatened with punishment before they'll do what they're supposed to do. Therefore, managers who see their subordinates through the Theory X prism tend to be crack-the-whip types. McGregor's observations led him to believe that most managers adhered to the school of scientific management; they were Theory X types who severely underestimated the capabilities of their workers and, consequently, their organizations.

Theory X serves as a nice polar opposite (some would say straw man, because it is so extreme) to the theory of the worker McGregor preferred. Theory Y managers, he said, believe that the effort people expend at work is as natural and self-rewarding as play or rest. They believe that work is not inherently a source of dislike and can instead be a source of satisfaction. If you proceed from this theory, it follows that management control and threats aren't necessary to get people to do their jobs because workers are controlled internally—people will be self-directed toward goals to which they are committed.

What's more, commitment to those goals comes about because self-esteem and self-actualization are gained through a sense of accomplishment. McGregor holds that under Theory Y conditions, people seek responsibility as a means of achieving satisfaction in their work. Moreover, he argues, these motivated people are the rule, not the exception; most would love to use their imagination and ingenuity to serve the organization. Sadly, McGregor concluded, modern industrial life is so deeply imbued with Theory X assumptions, it hinders the individual's intellectual achievement.

If the Theory Y model were instituted company-wide (here it comes, practical application fans), it probably would lead to things like elimination of the time clock, flextime, job enrichment programs and . . . yes . . . participative management. McGregor's ideas captured a lot of managers' imaginations in the 1960s and 1970s, when the Theory Y bandwagon got rolling. Today, most managers seem to be Theory Y in theory (see *Business Week*'s definition again). It has become common wisdom that people produce better in a developmental environment than in a punitive one.

While that may be true, McGregor himself sort of backed away from the trend he inspired. He quickly grew distressed with the interpretation given his theories, objecting to the simplistic "either/or" configuration of Theory X/Theory Y that implied polar opposites with no middle ground.

In *The Manager's Motivation Desk Book* (Ronald Press Publications, New York, 1985) Thomas L. Quick argues, "These two views were not at opposite ends of the spectrum but were two points on a continuum extending through all perspectives of people." McGregor simply observed a management style common at the time and suggested another way—not *the* way—to do things, Quick says.

Quick's view is that the either/or approach to Theory X/Theory Y is just one more example of our tendency to oversimplify things into black and white generalizations. The fact is, some people need and want direction while others chafe under the slightest bit of control. Some people live to work; others work to live.

"In short," concludes Quick, "some people in the work force justify Theory X assumptions about them, just as there are those who make Theory Y assumptions legitimate. And there are many people at various other points along the continuum." Wise are the managers who can recognize the difference and mold their management styles to fit the employees.

Reprinted from TRAINING, January 1987

THEORY X	THEORY Y
Assumptions about People	**Assumptions about People**
Most people . . . • Dislike work and want as little as possible to do • Are lazy • Dislike responsibility • Resist change • Are indifferent to organizational goals • Are self-seeking • Are primarily motivated by money • Prefer to be directed	Most people . . . • Enjoy and want meaningful work • Will work hard to accomplish worthwhile goals • Like responsibility • Will adapt to change • Will become committed to meaningful organizational goals • Are able to seek team goals • Are primarily motivated by challenging work • Prefer self-direction
Supervisory Practices	**Supervisory Practices**
A supervisor should . . . • Plan, organize, direct and control closely the efforts of people • Make most of the important decisions • Punish mistakes • Not get too close to employees • Assume that his or her authority is unquestionable • Push people to keep them motivated	A supervisor should . . . • Let employees become involved in planning, organizing and controlling their own efforts • Delegate the authority to make decisions • Focus on resolving problems, not punishing mistakes • Know each employee personally • Rely on earned, not formal, authority • Motivate people by giving challenging assignments

From *Supervisory Management* by D.D. Warrick and Robert A. Zawacki (Harper and Row, 1984). Reprinted by permission.

WHAT TRAINERS NEED TO KNOW ABOUT BOTH HALVES OF THE BRAIN

Recent findings about the head provide a gauge for designing development programs, judging these programs and improving their results

BY THOMAS S. ISAACK

A head is like a house. When it's crammed full and no regular order is observed, it's only littered, not adequately furnished. It may be like a crow's nest, full of every shiny object that attracts the collector's attention; no use to the crow, perhaps, but an inspiration to an abstract painter. Recent findings about the head deserve the attention of human-resource developers.

In essence, the evidence demonstrates that there are two hemispheres for thinking in the brain. One is the intuition; the other is the intellect. Each is specialized for a different purpose, but it is essential that they work in tandem to provide the ore and to refine it in problem handling and decision making. Since management is, primarily, a drama of the mind and the human resource developer is a director of that drama, it is expedient that we note what research tells us about the intuition and the intellect. I will serve as a guide, summarizing the research findings and then demonstrating their relevance to commonly used development methods.

Research on the organization of the brain has a pretty long history. Originally, much of this was done with stroke victims who had brain lesions and with soldiers injured in battle. More recently, the *corpus callosum* has been severed surgically to treat severe epileptics. The *corpus callosum* provides an important connection between the two hemispheres of the brain; in severing it, the hemispheres are isolated and their individual specializations examined.[1] It is almost like slitting the throat of the songbird in order to understand where the beautiful notes come from. However, the results of this radical procedure give us some good ideas about the nature of specialization of each hemisphere of the brain.

The left hemisphere

The left hemisphere of the brain, which I call the "intellect," controls the right side of the body in normal right handers, about 90% of our population. It handles linguistic activities and is efficient through thinking in language. It does linear and sequential processing of materials, integrates materials in a linear fashion, and is the source of analysis and logic.

This hemisphere operates by taking ideas apart, and relies on using artificial measuring tools, (i.e. inches, pounds) and conventional time frames (i.e. hours, weeks). Intellect works with a series of still shots to achieve the impression of movement. Note how much we rely on graphs or curves to give us a lineal picture of facts. We speak of a line of trees, of "getting a line on things," or "getting people into line." Logical arguments are manifestations of the work of the left hemi-

1. For a survey of the research on brain organization see: Gardner, Howard, *The Shattered Mind*, New York: Alfred A. Knopf, 1975; Gazzaniga, Michael S. *The Bisected Brain*, New York: Appleton-Century-Crofts, 1970; Levy-Agresti, Jerre and Sperry, R. W., "Different Perceptual Capacities in Major and Minor Hemispheres," *Proceedings of National Academy of Sciences*, Vol. 61 (1968), p. 1151; and Ornstein, Robert E. "Right and Left Thinking," *Psychology Today*, Vol. 6 (1973), No. 12, pp. 87-93.

sphere. One might have a lesion of the right hemisphere but speak so logically there is no evidence in conversation of the lesion.

The right hemisphere

The right hemisphere of the brain, the intuition, controls the left side of the body for normal right-handed persons. It is specialized for Gestalt perception (seeing the pattern of things), for grasping the whole of circumstances, for orientation in space, for body awareness, recognition of faces, and for artistic talents. The right hemisphere handles spatial processing, visual imagery, creativity, and intuition.

A lesion of the right hemisphere can abruptly end the career of an artist, but not interfere with the work of a bookkeeper. It may be quite difficult for a witness of a crime to verbally describe the criminal, but the same witness may easily recognize the offender from a number of pictures. It seems that the language of the left hemisphere is inadequate for the rapid, complex syntheses achieved by the right hemisphere. When we say "One picture is worth a thousand words," we refer to the functioning of the right hemisphere.

Alloying the two hemispheres

This article is an example of the unity of the two hemispheres of the brain. At first, I had a general picture of what I wanted to do. This "stewed" in my intuition below levels of conscious thought, for about a week, and, eventually, the central idea became clear. At this point, I had to determine the breakdown of parts and their organization to convey my intentions. My left hemisphere had taken over from the right one. To be successful, this article must create images and ideas in *your* intuition which has a grasp of *your* circumstances. The process, then, starts over for you.

Such a process has been observed in persons credited with great innovations. Arthur Koestler concludes that a review of the letters and autobiographies of such innovators as Louis Pasteur, Henri Poincaire and Ben Franklin shows, "The themes that reverberate through their intimate writings are: the belittling of logic and deductive reasoning (except for verification after the act); horror of the one-track mind; distrust of too much consistency; (and) skepticism regarding all-too-conscious thinking."[2] Our intuitive knowledge is neither precise nor too explicit. But when the intellect processes our intuitive insights, it tests the soundness of the insights and makes them operational.

This same process is followed by someone responsible for the development of human resources. Intuitively, the problem as a total picture is grasped. This, then, must be broken into parts and the method selected for presenting the different parts to trainees. In the process, the trainees should intuitively sense the whole pattern and not just concentrate on the separate parts at the risk of missing the whole picture.

We often refer to the latter as the synergistic effect: The whole is more than the sum of the parts. For example, in teaching about organization structure, we want the learner to see beyond the neatly laid out boxes and lines of an organization chart; we hope that he or she also senses the complexity of relationships, too difficult to present on a chart. Many a teacher and executive have been frustrated by this apparently simple problem, which seems to be one of logic but which relies on the intuitive grasp of the right hemisphere.

Now, let's take a precursory look at how the intuition-intellect process fits into some common training methods.

The *lecture* method is frequently used in training. However, it is difficult to present the whole pattern in a lecture; the teacher too often teaches separate segments as though they were separate chapters in a textbook and tests periodically to learn if the student has command of these compo-nents. The last step—assisting the student to grasp the whole pattern—can be missed this way. Almost certainly the total pattern will be missed if testing is confined to objective methods which reinforce accumulating knowledge of separate parts without demanding that the whole subject be put together.

Programmed learning or forms of *self-paced* methods can produce the same problems unless the trainer introduces his own methods of testing with these approaches to be sure that trainees grasp the whole picture. The temptation is to rely on standardized, small-piece tests in order to learn about the relative progress of the trainees; knowledge may be accumulated in the process, but ability is not enhanced. It's like giving the trainee the jumbled pieces of a jigsaw puzzle without requiring them to be assembled. The trainer mistakenly believes that the trainee learned the parts in a nice, *logical* fashion.

Case method, incident approaches, in-basket techniques and similar methods appear to place greater demand on utilizing the intuition-intellect process. A trainee is required to intuitively grasp the whole picture, speculate, and test his speculations analytically, logically, and realistically against the circumstances with which he wrestles. Then, that intuition must be checked to learn if the total picture fits neatly, with minimal contradictions of analysis and recommendations. A human-resource devel-oper might also be able to identify trainees who break with the common mould and present results that are innovative, yet realistic—different, in other words, from the general pattern of the training group. Such trainees just might have exceptional creative potential.

Conclusion

Research on brain organization which identifies general functions of the right and left hemispheres—the intuition and the intellect—provides us with another dimension to incorporate into training methods. If we want to train a parrot to be a salesman, we might well concentrate on methods which utilize only the intellect. But if we're engaged in management development at any level of organization, we'd better be aware of the operations of both the intuition and the intellect.

Our emphases on quantification and quantitative decision-making techniques lure us into thinking that management is a logical process. But, even after all the alternatives are neatly laid out for the decision maker, he still relies on an inexplicable "feel" to make his decision. Science has had such an impact on our society that we're often tempted to rely on "rational" methods alone in development programs. In doing so, we might be guilty of "half-brained" training.

2. Koestler, Arthur, *The Act of Creation*, London: Hutchinson, 1964, p. 146.

Reprinted from TRAINING, January 1978

RIGHT BRAIN VS. LEFT BRAIN: HOW TO SORT FACT FROM FICTION

Experts still have more questions than answers

BY RON ZEMKE

I f you've ever heard someone say, "They may be brothers, [sisters, cousins, Yalies, etc.] but they're different as night and day," then you already know plenty about the split-brain psychology fad. People are different.

"Split-brain psychology is the fad of the year," declared Editor/writer Daniel Goleman in a recent *Psychol-ogy Today* editorial. We suggest his time frame is conservative; "fad of the 70s" may be more accurate. Look at the evidence.

Exhibit One. Since 1970, *Scientific American* has carried three major articles on brain dichotomy, *Psychology Today* four, *Harvard Business Review* three, *American Psychologist* one, and *Human Behavior* and *Saturday Review*—both fad-maker magazines—have done special editions on "the brain." Add to that paper flow the 14 or so best-selling books either dedicated to the brain and its dual nature (e.g., Ornstein's *The Psychology of Consciousness*) or devoting lengthy sections to the topic (e.g., Sagan's *The Dragons of Eden*).

Exhibit Two. Take the case of one of the aforementioned *HBR* articles, McGill University Management Professor Henry Mintzberg's lengthy piece, "Planning on the Left Side and Managing on the Right," (July/ August 1976). In it, Mintzberg declares that "which hemisphere of one's brain is better developed may determine whether a person ought to be a planner or a manager."

So far this year, we've counted an even dozen training conferences where the topic "implications of right brain, left brain psychology on management development" have essentially been discussions of Mintzberg's thesis. General Electric's Manager of Management Development, William E. Herrman, started collecting research and writings on right brain/left brain psychology strictly as a personal interest; recently, he has been swamped with requests for speeches, panels and presentations.

Exhibit Three. Medical Psychologist Robert Ornstein and Neurosurgeon Joseph Bogen, two of the most vocal split-brain scientist types, decided to do a modest symposium this fall titled "Educating Both Halves of the Brain." They played to standing-room-only crowds in Chicago, Philadelphia, Minneapolis and Boston. During a break in one session, Dr. Bogen gazed out at the milling throng, shook his head in disbelief, and declared, "I would never have dreamed that this many people would know or give a darn that the brain has two hemispheres."

The state rests. Split brain is indeed the hottest fad going.

It's terrific...but what is it?

A friend of ours cautions us about jargon and psychobabble with an apocryphal tale. Professor Far-Out of Big Deal University was holding forth to a group of first-line supervisors from XYZ Manufacturing. About 15 minutes into his intrepid trek through modern motivation theory and application, a voice from the back of the room drawled, "Sir, ya wanna rein in there a second?" Unaccustomed to stopping, the irritated Far-Out crossly queried, "Yes. What is it?" "Well, sir," the voice continued, "it'd help a mite if you was to 'splain some of those four-bit words. Like, I got a purty good idie what a cog-no-tive dissonance is, but I

TABLE A

LEFT HEMISPHERE (RIGHT SIDE OF BODY)	RIGHT HEMISPHERE (LEFT SIDE OF BODY)
Speech/verbal	Spatial/musical
Logical, mathematical	Holistic
Linear, detailed	Artistic, symbolic
Sequential	Simultaneous
Controlled	Emotional
Intellectual	Intuitive, creative
Dominant	Minor (quiet)
Worldly	Spiritual
Active	Receptive
Analytic	Synthetic, Gestalt
Reading, writing, naming	Facial recognition
Sequential ordering	Simultaneous comprehension
Perception of significant order	Perception of abstract patterns
Complex motor sequences	Recognition of complex figures

Reference: Science News, April 3, 1976

'spect some of the boys ain't never rode in one even."

That's just about how the brain psychology jargon sounds to us—clear as split-pea soup. Hence, the following trip back to the basics in an attempt to comprehend the current uproar.

1 The dual nature of things and stuff. The idea that nature is split into opposites is as old as recorded history. In *The Psychology of Consciousness,* Ornstein catalogs 20 of these dichotomous pairs and their origins. Start with I Ching's Yin vs. Yang, Light vs. Dark, Time vs. Space; work through Bacon's Argument vs. Experience, Jung's Causal vs. A Causal, Blackburn's Intellectual vs. Sensuous; move on to Lineal vs. Nonlineal, Sequential vs. Simultaneous, Analytic vs. Gestalt. Obviously, people have been talking about separate modes of understanding and perceiving for a long time.

A second twist is the belief that seemingly opposite ways of perceiving and processing experience and the world exist together in the same person. "There's good and bad, saint and sinner in all of us" is an age-old shibboleth. In fact, Frederick Herzberg, in *The Motivation to Work,* calls on the dual or dichotomous nature of man to explain the differences between dissatisfaction and satisfiers. "In each of us," he suggests, "there exists both an Abraham and an Isaac."

2 The brain is the thing. Stage set, enter the brain. Almost forever, philosophers have debated over something called mind/body dualism. Are mind and body the same thing, or is the mind a separate nonphysical entity? Do thoughts, emotions, motives have real, physical existence, or are they ethereal? Concerning mind/body dualism, there are lots of logical, metaphorical and esoteric arguments but only a few facts.

Fact one. Early in this century, neurosurgeons were able to electrically stimulate the physical brain of patients, causing old images, tastes, smells and thoughts to surface in the consciousness of the subjects. Pretty good evidence that thinking and remembering take place in the physical head.

Fact two. In the 1960s, Neurosurgeon Joseph Bogen was looking for a way to relieve severe epileptics of their seizures. Bogen severed the corpus callosum—the bundle of nerves which joins the two hemispheres, or right and left sides, of the brain—of some of his patients. Psychologist Roger Sperry, who worked with Bogen's patients, and others since Sperry, who have worked with split-brain patients, found some interesting things about the functioning of these split-brain or cerebral commasurotomyzed patients. While blindfolded, they could answer questions about objects held in their right hands but not in their left hands. Patients reported that they "knew" what the answers were but couldn't verbalize them. This jibed with the physiological theory that the neural pathways from each side of the body cross over and connect with the opposite side of the brain.

Information from a person's right hand is relayed to the patient's language center in the left hemisphere of the brain. Information from the left hand is relayed to the right hemisphere. Since the connector between left and right hemispheres, the corpus callosum, was cut, right hemisphere (left hand) information or sensations could not reach the language center and become verbalized. In addition, these same people could "find" the original object in a bag of objects, although they were not able to name it or any of the others.

These experiments and a few more became a substantial basis for claiming that the two halves or hemispheres of the brain, right and left, have distinct and separate functions.

3 Open the flood gates. Excited brain researchers and their groupies—especially their groupies—have sprinted out in front of actual research to claim that split-brain psychology could explain all those heretofore unexplained sweet mysteries of life. Sound familiar? Remember transactional analysis?

Current pop claims for split-brain significance run from silly to ridiculous.

• Marshall McLuhan claims that "bureaucracy is left hemisphere...The generation gap of the 1960s was a conflict between right-hemisphere kids and left-hemisphere parents."

• Some educators are suggesting that truth, beauty, justice, and love are rooted in the right brain.

• In the *New York Times Magazine,* a dream researcher suggests that dreaming is the function of the right brain.

• A media-research psychologist claims that newspapers and magazines are left-brain media and television is a right-brain medium.

• The right brain synthesizes patterns from diverse-looking data; the left brain analyzes the nature and lawfulness of such patterns.

• Invention is a right-brain function, production a left-brain function.

• People with analytical cognitive styles are left-brain dominant. People with intuitive cognitive styles are right-brain dominant.

4 Separating fact and fiction. How do we sort the hope and the just plain humbug from the real and reliable? In a word, carefully. William Herrmann of General Electric, who has a feel for the differences between fact and fantasy, referenced Table A during the seminar he conducted at TRAINING '77 entitled " 'Whole Brain' Approaches to Education and Training." The table originally appeared in the April 3, 1976 issue of *Science News.* It claims to represent the general sorts of findings which can be somewhat supported with data.

5 Some modifiers. Claims for any new panacea generally obliterate the fact that the discoverers never claimed that the new gadget would be a cure-all, end-all, be-all. *P.T.*'s Goleman offered these modifiers to the wild claims abroad in the land.

• University of Chicago's Jerre Levy cautions that the popularly accepted brain-hemisphere data tend to apply only to "right-handed males, right-eye dominant, with no left-handed relatives," which, at most, includes 25% of the population.

• The brain has more than a right side and a left side. It could just as easily have been "cut up" from front to back or top to bottom.

• The right side of the brain is *not* idle or out of gear when you're writing a letter or doing something linear. It simply is *less* active than the left side of the brain. Every mental operation, according to E. Roy John of NYU Medical College, requires many parts of the brain to be active.

• There may be important sex-linked differences and hormonal-balance differences which account for many of the things now attributed primarily to differences in brain physiology.

Let us add a final caution. By all means keep an open mind as you are engulfed with new views on the right brain/left brain dichotomy. Open your right-brain creative, intuitive self and accept the possibility. But before diving into right brain/left brain training, do some left-brain processing of the facts and possible fictions and make the data pass the tests of reason and logic.

A runaway right brain never proves anything or makes much happen. A lone-wolf left brain never finds new facts to process. With this in mind, keep your head *together* when exploring the newest psycho-fad—split-brain psychology.

Reprinted from TRAINING, January 1978

TRAINING BOTH SIDES OF THE BRAIN TO WORK TOGETHER

Here's how trainers (and learners) can boost their right-brain thinking

BY GEORGE PRINCE

There is a growing body of evidence suggesting neglect of a marvelous human resource: the right hemisphere of the brain. Dr. Gorgi Lozanov in his Research Institute of Suggestology in Bulgaria, teaches a three-year course in French in 20 half days; graduates know the language as well as three-year students. D. Paul Watzlawick helps patients achieve behavior changes with a speed that was unthinkable to psychiatrists just a few years ago.[2] Dr. W. C. Ellerbroek experimented with 36 subjects suffering from acne, a disease notoriously resistant to treatment. Six of the subjects dropped out of the experiment, but the remaining were judged 80% improved within eight weeks. After 16 weeks, 17 patients had clear skin, while the rest were 80% to 90% improved.[3] A group of people are working on a tough problem, which they have attacked before without success. Then, using some special procedures, they develop not one but three solutions to the problem.[4]

The common thread running through these experiments is that the experimenters were able, in one way or another, to get the subjects to establish cooperation between the right and left hemispheres of their brains. With this internal cooperation, remarkable things happen.

My own experience with this phenomenon comes from studying groups attempting to solve difficult problems. The difference between a successful group and one that isn't appears to lie in right-hemisphere involvement. In a successful group people are able to engage their right hemispheres in the action. In addition, the other members of such groups are able to tolerate support and build upon this thinking.

I believe that we all come into the world able to use both hemispheres of the brain comfortably and effortlessly. Because of this easy cooperation that nature engineered and intended, we learn and grow at phenomenal rates. We learn with such incredible skill that, without anyone telling us

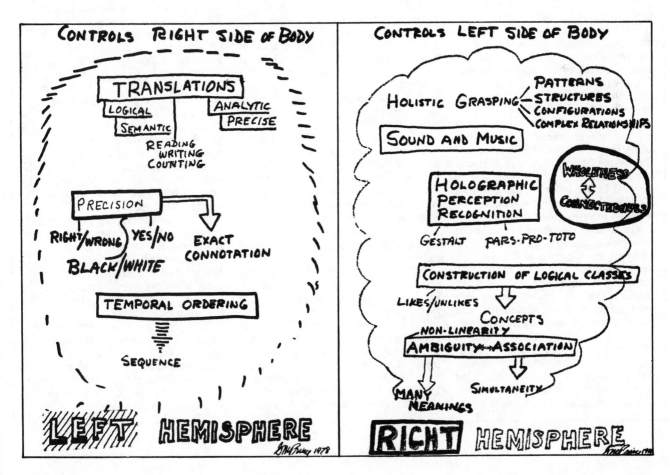

ARE YOUR PROGRAMS DESIGNED FOR WHITE RATS?

Any speaker in the field of adult education and training can ensure audience applause and adulation through the forceful utterance of the single, simple declarative sentence: "Adults are not white rats!" But once said and applauded, what exactly does the statement mean?

Are we expected to conclude from this pronouncement that the principles about learning and performance culled in the rat and primate labs are null and void when the target population is composed of relatively normal John and Jane Doe adults?

"No," insists Patricia McLagan, president of McLagan and Associates, an HRD firm specializing in developing educational experiences for adults. "To embrace the slogan and then jump to the conclusion that reinforcement or modeling or C.A.I. doesn't work for adults is to miss the whole point," she continues. "The real issue here is how one goes about structuring adult learning opportunities for maximum benefit to the individual learner. The adult learning specialist doesn't argue that reinforcement is or isn't necessary for learning—behavior change—to occur. We do argue that, at best, it is not—by itself—sufficient for learning to take place."

Some detractors of the adult learning movement imply that the new adult learning specialist is afraid of the systematic approach to training and education and the accountability implied in the model. Other skeptics see the adult learning specialist as a warmed over-remnant of the defunct T-group and sensitivity training movements, sheep in wolves' clothing, lobbying for a return to the good old days of touch and feel training.

McLagan believes that the adult learning specialist viewpoint actually asks us to be *more* systematic and *more* pragmatic than we already are. Take the issue of a working definition of learning. "In the laboratory, learning is defined as a relatively permanent change in behavior resulting from experience and not attributable to maturation or physical changes in the organism. Now that's functional and adequate for the lab, but it doesn't help trainers much. I need a bigger, broader definition, so I've had to build my own. To me, learning is a change in knowledge, behavior, attitudes/values/priorities or creativity that can occur when learners interact with information. It occurs to the extent that learners are motivated to change, and it is applied in the real world to the extent that they take successful steps to integrate learning into the real-world situation. Now that's something I can work with, get guidance from."

Nor does the adult learning specialist shy from the concept of instructional objectives or evaluating the results of a learning program. He or she simply attacks these issues from a different perspective.

The difference is in who does what in the learning design process. "I believe that the instructor or curriculum designer has the responsibility for doing a good needs analysis, determining whether a problem exists and whether a training solution is appropriate. I have no problem with the instructor creating guide objectives and being responsible for really designing a well-organized program aimed at specific objectives. But I don't believe that the instructor can write terminal objectives. The instructor's role is one of co-designer, co-author, at best. To me the *real* terminal objectives have to be written by the learner."

Implicated in this co-design concept is an explosion of problems for the evaluation of the learning effort, the measurement of bottom-line impact. "To me," McLagan continues, "evaluation is tied to application. The instructor doesn't own the performance problem; the learner does. Only the individual learner can solve the problems. It's their world, their environment. For me to assume ownership is off base. But pointing to the individual as responsible for solving the problems doesn't divest the teacher-trainer-facilitator of all responsibility. Learner and trainer are mutually responsible."

The trainer is responsible for correct needs and problem analysis, information finding and organizing; for communicating the information clearly, correctly and in a way that makes it important to the learner; for helping the learner to learn. The learner is responsible for analyzing his own needs, for setting goals, for customizing the learning to his own situation, and, ultimately, for designing an application plan and using it.

We need to have those responsibilities clear before we talk evaluation. That's because the evaluation must address all the responsibilities. "What did you learn?" is an important question to ask trainees...although it usually isn't. It's important because the overlap between this self-report and what you, the trainer, intended is very telling. For example, if the overlap is 100 percent most of the time, you're doing something wrong. The learners don't feel free to pick and choose and they don't feel free to be creative. They are taking, holding, and giving back, but that may not be enough. And you have to look at behavior. Did they do what they said they'd do in their application plans? And to organizational outcome the questions "Did the problem get solved?" and "Was money made or saved?" have to be answered. Evaluation is a lot tougher when dealing *with* adults, *as* adults, *from* an adult learning perspective.

The design orientation of the new adult learning specialist is most at variance with traditional pedagogy. This difference is characterized in the title of McLagan's own book, *Helping Others Learn: A Handbook for Adult Educators*. To McLagan, helping others learn involves designing at least some extra degrees of "learnability" into courses, workshops and seminars. McLagan's approach to analyzing the adult learnability of a program has three touchstones we can apply to any adult learning program:

1. Is the learning experience problem centered, as opposed to curriculum-, concept- or subject-matter oriented?

2. Is the experience personalized, reflective of the learner, the learner's world and the learner's needs?

3. Does the learning experience ask the learner to share his or her examples, ideas and experiences and, in general, share responsibility for the learning experience?

If your training program or educational experience *does not* lead you to answer "yes" to each of these three questions, then you should ask yourself *one more question:* "Is my program designed for adult learners or for white rats and pigeons?"

Reprinted from TRAINING, August 1977

NINE WAYS TO
DEVELOP YOUR RIGHT BRAIN

For trainers and for learners in general, there is a goldmine in finding ways to systematically increase right-hemisphere thinking. Below are 9 suggestions, outrageous and otherwise, with which you might experiment, using students, subordinates and self as subjects.

• When presenting information, have a musical background that occasionally drowns out the presentation.

• Give everyone in meetings colored pens and ask them to mix their notes with doodles.

• Give each participant in a meeting a lump of modeling clay.

• Give a 30-second explanation of something, and ask people to guess what you're getting at.

• At the beginning of every third meeting, set this ground rule: We can explain a point only a single time. No repeating. No "in other words." If someone wants to ask a question, he does; but before getting an answer, he guesses what it will be.

• In every meeting where old solutions are not working, have everyone leave his or her shoes at the door. This is a signal that we will welcome confused, beginning ideas, and use ourselves to build on them rather than shoot them down.

• When it is a shoes-off meeting, have the person presenting the problem limit his explanation to two minutes. Then ask each participant to connect the problem with an experience that is *approximately* relevant.

• At every third meeting, institute the ground rule that the chairman will randomly interrupt to ask a member to describe the images going through his or her mind at that instant. Other members listen to see if they can use this image to give them a beginning idea, one that does not yet work.

• One day a week, make it a rule that *no one* in the office or plant can use the word no. (The right hemisphere has no equivalent of no.) If something is not acceptable, the person must deal with it by saying, "yes, if...."

directly, we somehow become convinced that we must limit our speed of learning. Our left hemispheres, being in charge of the operation, become expert at shutting down right-hemisphere action. By the time we reach 15 or so, we are suitably shut down and behaving like normal grown-ups. Which is to say we are using somewhere between 5% and 20% of our potential.

What is it that makes this right hemisphere so magical? According to Dr. Watzlawick, our two hemispheres have very different functions. "In the typical right-handed person, the left hemisphere, which controls the actions of the right side of our bodies, is the dominant one. Its main functions appear to be translating perceptions into logical, semantic and phonetic representations of reality and communicating with the outside world on the basis of this logical-analytical coding of the surrounding world. It is competent for all that has to do with language (grammar, syntax, semantics), with thinking, ... reading, writing, counting, computing and, generally, digital communication.

"The function of the right hemisphere is very different. It is highly specialized in the holistic grasping of complex relationships, patterns, configurations and structures." It is

suggested that this ability is somehow akin to holography. This part of the brain can reconstruct a whole pattern out of only a small piece. It also sees in three dimensions. We all enjoy this quite remarkable talent. For example, I can reconstruct a friend's face from just seeing a small portion of it, and I can rotate the face and imagine it from almost any angle.

The right hemisphere is competent for the construction of logical classes and, therefore, for the formation of concepts. Its associations are non-linear, and time appears not to be a factor for it. Two mutually exclusive concepts can be entertained at the same time. Its language is archaic and undeveloped. It lacks prepositions and practically all the other elements of grammar, syntax and semantics. I think it may be responsible, though, for connotations. Its concepts are ambiguous; it draws illogical conclusions; confuses literal and metaphorical meanings; uses condensations, composite words, puns.

I believe that because we operate in such a sequential-seeming world and because the logical thought of the left hemisphere is so honored in our culture, we gradually damp out, devalue and disregard the input of our right hemispheres. It is not that we stop using it altogether; it just

becomes less and less available to us because of established habit patterns. Thus, we inadvertently put a damper on two important capacities: the ability to understand deeply and learn speedily and the ability to retrieve and use experiences that are only approximately relevant to the matter at hand. I will discuss understanding and learning speed first.

As children, we were blessed with the willingness to jump to conclusions. This practice is widely thought to be sloppy thinking that leads to error and misunderstanding. After observing thousands of people as they work to understand and solve problems, I am convinced that jumping to conclusions is the natural and efficient way to understand, learn and invent. It is the way the right hemisphere uses its talent for holographic reconstruction.

The traditional way we are taught to think (actually, few of us are directly taught how to think—we learn it by indirection and inference) is an effective block to developing holistic (holographic) skill. The "good" thinker is careful to avoid jumping to conclusions. He waits until all the data are in. He asks questions to fill in any apparent gaps. Finally, he draws the appropriate conclusion. His right hemisphere is discouraged from making contributions.

In contrast, as a child, I do not hobble myself that way. I hear the first few words of an explanation, and an image appears full-blown in my mind's eye. The completeness is supplied from similar experiences I have stored in my head. I instantly "understand" the concept being explained. In truth, because my understanding consists mostly of information from my *own* experience, it will be only approximately "right." As the explainer gives me additional data, I modify my image, leaping to a new conclusion. Through these successive approximations, I arrive at the intended "truth." And I believe I arrive there faster and with a more authoritative ownership of the understanding than if I hold back until all the returns are in (if that ever happens).

To be more explicit, I will make up a play-by-play description of a process that is, of course, really unknown. Let us say that a trainer is teaching me a problem-solving process called Synectics, one element of which is called a goal/wish. As soon as he says the words, I see a soccer goal complete with goalie and a fairy godmother with a wand who stands ready to grant me a wish. This is the work of my right hemisphere, which takes a fraction of the data and jumps to a complete conclusion. It is also the work of my left hemisphere, which keeps me aware that these conclusions are useful but temporary. Through training, my left hemisphere does not (as a traditionally trained one might) reject these images as incorrect and, therefore, not to be entertained. As the full explanation of goal/wishes emerges, there is a kind of dialog between the hemispheres in which the earlier images are transformed into new ones, but the old images are not thrown out or devalued. They are kept as background aids to more complete understanding of the whole concept of goal/wishing.

In this mode of operating, the two hemispheres cooperate to produce an understanding and learning synergy that equals much more than the sum of the two parts.

We know that this synergy occurs from experiences in our creative problem-solving course, which is designed around the participants' problems. Each person takes a turn being client, the owner of a problem who presents it to his group for their help. Early on, the group spends 15 minutes or more making sure that the members understand enough of the problem to begin to help with it. Typically, the client is bombarded with questions to add to the information. After four days of training, most participants understand enough after the first minute of explanation to begin to work on the problem. At the end of three minutes, nearly all feel that they understand it sufficiently. There are few questions because each participant has jumped to enough conclusions and drawn from his own experiences enough to have a satisfying approximate knowledge of the problem.

My conclusion, jumped to a couple of years ago, is that understanding and learning speeds can be multiplied (and the quality improved, too) if we can relearn to involve our right hemisphere more fully.

The other capacity we damp is the ability to retrieve and use experience (and observations) that are only approximately relevant to the matter at hand. Somehow, perhaps in the service of precision, accuracy and positive discrimination, we develop a strict internal censor. We give it the power to make instant decisions on whether or not a given thought or observation is relevant to an enterprise. When I am doing a routine task— one where tested answers work, such as filing, driving or tying my shoe— it is appropriate to repress as irrelevant any interrupting thought that might disrupt my performance. But when I am problem solving or learning, it is efficient to welcome any retrieval and check out its relevance in a tolerant way.

The great thinkers, who share an openness to everything they think or observe, can teach us something here. It is as though they have trained themselves to believe that *anything* is relevant until proved otherwise. For example, Archimedes and his overflowing bath (displacement), Fleming and his culture that was spoiled by an alien mold (penicillin), Goodyear and his spilled latex (vulcanization), Pasteur and the patch of green grass (source of Anthrax) and so on and on. In every example, lesser thinkers had dismissed the observations as irrelevant or erroneous.

The very heart of creative thinking and of learning is the willingness to honor approximate and seemingly irrelevant thinking. This gives our right hemisphere a chance to exercise its enormous power to connect, to see a pattern, to grasp a complex relationship, to construct a whole out of a tiny hint of an idea.

When we permit our domineering left hemisphere to eliminate instantly that which seems irrelevant, the enterprise had better be routine. Otherwise, we are reducing our ability to learn something new and to invent or improvise by between 5% and 20% of what we are really capable.

For me, the moral is clear: If I wish to enhance my learning and problem-solving abilities, I will cultivate activities and attitudes that encourage my right hemisphere to contribute aggressively to my thinking—and learn to *value what it presents me.* What this requires is re-evaluating such things as illogical thinking, guessing at causes, guessing in general, making up patterns from small amounts of data, leaping to conclusions, occasionally cultivating ambiguity and confusion, making puns, looking for double entendres and, in general, playing around.

These activities, which are characteristic of right hemisphere thinking, tend to be associated with mistakes and wrongness, which is why they have dubious reputations. If we can reframe them, perhaps we can make them easier to tolerate. This messy, approximate and seemingly careless kind of thinking is not supposed to stand on its own; its job is to develop beginning raw possibilities, which are then refined in cooperation with the analytic, logical and precise powers of the left hemisphere. The full, cooperative involvement of *both* hemispheres is what gives the synergy that produces great thinking.

REFERENCES

1. For more information on suggestology, see "Suggestology: Trainers combine relaxation techniques, music and suggestion to boost learning speed and efficiency dramatically" in the January 1977 issue of TRAINING.
2. Paul Watzlawick, *The Language of Change*, New York: Basic Books, Inc., 1978.
3. W. C. Ellerbroek, "Language, Thought, and Disease," *The Co-Evolution Quarterly*, Spring 1978, p. 30.
4. George M. Prince, "The Mindspring Theory: A New Development from Synectics Research," *The Journal of Creative Behavior*, Volume 9, Number 3, Third Quarter 1975, p. 159.

Reprinted from TRAINING, November 1978

CHAPTER 10

SELECTING AND USING OUTSIDE RESOURCES

Employer-sponsored training has been called the "shadow education industry." If you've ever tried to explain to a taxi driver what you do for a living, you know why. Relatively few people outside the corporate-training profession are aware that there is such a thing as a corporate-training profession. And as for the existence of a training *industry*—a whole segment of the economy that makes its living selling goods and services to other segments of the economy for the purpose of employee training—the average taxi driver is completely in the dark.

Oh, your driver has heard of management consultants. But book publishers, film producers, computer-based training suppliers, companies that "package" classroom programs on everything from basic time management to esoteric technical subjects? A commercial industry that includes executive-education courses run by Ivy League universities as well as gunnery simulations for Army tank crews made by custom-software shops that specialize in interactive video? No, of these things your driver knows nothing.

But that multi-billion-dollar industry is there, all right. And if you're in charge of providing training to your organization's employees, you will almost certainly tap into it from time to time.

Build or buy? The question confronts HRD professionals whenever a need for training arises. Can you (and should you) design and deliver the instruction yourself? Or would it make more sense to go shopping for a video or a computer-diskette or a public seminar or whatever—a "packaged" instructional program that somebody else has already designed and, presumably, tested? How about incorporating some packaged "pieces"—a commercial film, say—into a program you design yourself?

The articles in this chapter were selected with two goals in mind. Some will give you useful perspectives on the whole build-or-buy issue: Under what circumstances and for which kinds of training challenges does it make more sense to go shopping for programs or expertise than to try to tackle the project on your own? Other articles zero in on the nuts and bolts of specific transactions between buyer and seller, offering practical advice on everything from negotiating with a consultant to hiring a producer for a training video whose content will be dictated by your company's technical experts.

The point of it all: to help you cope more effectively with the resources at your disposal. After all, it's a jungle out there.

THE CASE FOR BUYING PREPACKAGED PROGRAMS

There are, of course, several reasons to consider going shopping for a program rather than inventing it yourself. Here's how to make sure what you get is what you need

BY JUDITH E. FISHER

Habits die hard; and training habits are no exception. When faced with a newly defined training need, some trainers respond habitually in one of two ways. Either they rally the troops in the training development department to "crank out" a course, or they dial the nearest development company to invent a course to meet the need. Obviously, there is nothing inherently wrong with either of these responses, but trainers can often be blinded by the "development habit." In the automatic rush to invent, create, and develop training materials, trainers often overlook a third alternative—the prepackaged, commercially available training course.

From motivation to management awareness, from sales to clerical skills, from assertiveness to decision-making— you name it; there's a course for it! The pages of training periodicals are brimming with advertisements for programs, courses, seminars, and workshops which are ready and waiting to be put to use. Perhaps it's time to take a closer look at the idea of including ready-made courses in your training repertoire.

As with any issue, there are two sides to the question of using packaged courses or programs. Some trainers are enthusiastic and positive about commercial programs, based on the success they've had using them. Others, mainly those who have used a commercial program with miserable results, remain steadfastly negative. However, there remains another group— the skeptics. For those dissenters and skeptics, this discussion of commercial programs focuses on the potential value of such courses. For those already positively disposed toward off-the-shelf programs, this discussion offers some new guidelines to help you select the best of the commercial offerings.

Accentuating the positive

In general, commercially available educational programs offer several potential benefits. First, and perhaps foremost, packaged programs may save both time and money.

Choosing a commercial program instead of developing a custom program may have striking financial benefits. To the trainer with limited financial resources, commercially packaged programs offer an excellent, cost-effective alternative to custom development. Quite often the initial investment required to purchase ready-made materials is substantially lower than the total cost of developing materials from scratch. In some cases, packaged materials can be used repeatedly for several years, thus easily paying back the initial investment. In addition to saving on development costs, packaged programs also offer the advantage of being ready when you are. Faced with a pressing training need, purchasing and implementing a commercial program can usually be accomplished quickly. Where development time is a problem, an off-the-shelf program may be the answer.

Another beneficial effect of using packaged programs is evidenced in how training development personnel are utilized. By making use of commercial programs to handle part of the training load, training development personnel can be put to work where they can do the most good— creating materials which are not already available on the open market.

It may come as a surprise to you, but today's commercial programs offer excellent quality in both content and presentation format. They've come a long way from the dull fine print of the technical manual. Many of today's packaged courses utilize the most advanced knowledge of the subject matter and present the information and skills in accordance with the best learning and communication theory. Thus, packaged programs— once regarded as second-class education— now offer the distinct advantage of high quality. In fact, some commercial packages are so carefully designed and tested that it would be virtually impossible for the average training department with limited resources to develop materials of comparable quality for the same cost.

Finally, packaged programs offer the advantage of many implementation options. From the traditional stand-up lecture to self-study, to group encounters—commercial offerings provide implementation alternatives to suit every imaginable preference. Moreover, today's educational products also accommodate nearly every conceivable delivery system including print, video, audio, film, filmstrip, film loop, overhead projection, and slide/tape shows, to mention but a few. Indeed, the flexibility of commercial programs and the ease of adapting them to various training environments is a definite advantage. There's likely to be a ready-made program in existence somewhere which will not only meet your training objectives, but will meet your implementation requirements as well.

In summary, prepackaged programs offer advantages related to savings in time and money, to utilizing program development personnel efficiently, and to facilitating high-quality instruction in a myriad of environments and formats. Commercially available programs appear to be an excellent alternative to a full-blown development effort. Why, then, isn't everyone making use of the resources packaged courses offer? That's a good question, and the answer takes us back to the idea of training habits.

A look at the opposition

Although commercial training programs offer some important, broad benefits to the potential user, many trainers continue to voice objections to them. In discussing the use of packaged programs with many training managers and HRD specialists, three objections seemed to crop up frequently. As you'll discover in an analysis of the typical objections, the objections themselves appear to be based on "habits of thinking" rather than on the nature of packaged programs.

First, every organization likes to believe it is absolutely unique. Thus, many trainers object to packaged programs on the basis that the programs are generic and *their* training needs are somehow special or unusual. On the surface, this objection appears to have some validity. Organizations do differ in some ways, and training needs may require some specific or highly unusual skills. However, underneath the differences and specifics, there is a common core of knowledge and skills which is the domain of the packaged program. The habit of thinking of an organization or an environment as totally unique often leads the trainer to overlook the common denominator— the realm of the packaged program.

Take, for example, the case of the training manager who is faced with preparing "new" managers recently promoted from the rank and file work force. Instead of rushing to invent management training materials, it may be more efficient to sort out the training needs, leaving the general managerial skills to be handled by the commercially available programs and concentrating development efforts on the unique managerial tasks associated with the organization. Commercial programs need not replace customized development efforts. As a matter of fact, the two are not mutually exclusive, rather, they are complementary.

A second common objection to the use of prepackaged programs takes the form of textual nit-picking. Many trainers examining commercial training packages tend to search zealously for small areas of conflict— an example which may not exactly fit, one or two statements which may not reflect precise company policy, or technical jargon which varies. Finding such examples of conflict, some trainers will reject the whole program outright in favor of creating a program which is "just right." Again, this line of thinking may be counterproductive. In many cases, the small areas of conflict may be easily resolved with a bit of customizing on the spot. It isn't necessary to reinvent the proverbial wheel...modification may be the simple answer.

Commercially prepared programs, because they are designed to apply to a wide potential marketplace, will invariably include some examples, ideas, or techniques which may not be suitable in a specific situation. But, if the overall thrust of the program is useful— if it meets the major training objectives— minor adjustments and adaptations can be made rather painlessly.

Finally, there's a third typical objection to packaged programs which rests on the connotations associated with "canned" training materials. The assumption here is that training courses must be "new," "fresh," and "exciting"; the old stand-bys— the packaged core knowledge and skills— have gone stale. True, there are some "has-beens" among commercial training packages on the market. But, by and large, training programs— like textbooks— undergo constant revision and modernization to meet changing educational needs. Furthermore, as new skill areas emerge, more and more new training programs are introduced to meet those needs.

Upon close scrutiny, the objections cataloged here and other similar objections to using packaged materials appear to be ways of rationalizing the habit of "original" course development. Like those who resisted the advent of cake mixes and automatic transmissions, the opponents of commercially available programs tend to cling to the vague notion that "doing it yourself" is somehow always better. With due respect to the loyal opposi-

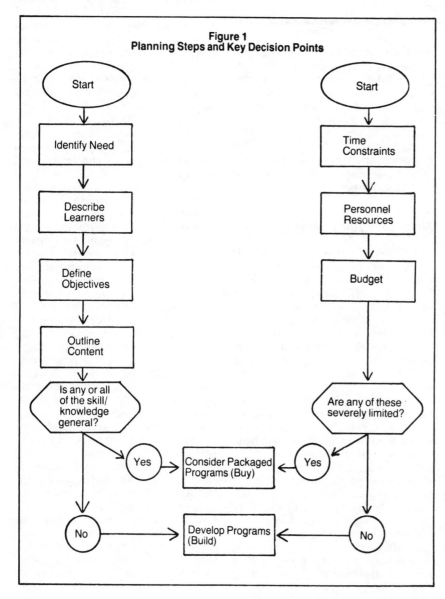

Figure 1
Planning Steps and Key Decision Points

tion, "letting the other guy do it" can be an excellent alternative.

Prepackaged training courses, with or without modification, can be a vital part of the trainer's repertoire. The multitude of professionally designed prepackaged programs offers considerable potential. The trick lies in choosing and using them correctly.

When are packaged programs applicable?

Determining whether packaged programs may be suitable in a specific training situation requires a series of planning steps. In fact, the potential usefulness and success of any packaged program will depend, to a great extent, on the solidarity of preliminary planning. To begin, one must go through the conventional planning tasks of identifying the training need, describing the learning audience, defining performance objectives, and outlining key topic areas to be included in the learning.

Once these initial decisions have been made, it is possible to take a critical look at the proposed training effort to determine if *all or part* of the skills and knowledge to be learned can be considered general. If all or a substantial part of your training need could be described as generic, then prepackaged programs are definitely worth considering. Next, one must also consider the key external factors which may realistically influence the decision to buy or to build. Primary concerns here are limited training resources—time, personnel and money. If time schedules are short, if development or implementation personnel are limited, or if budget restrictions preclude a full-blown developmental effort, once again prepackaged programs are worth serious consideration. (These basic planning steps and key decision points are diagrammed in Figure 1.)

Seeking suitable programs

Assuming that a packaged program appears to be a potential way of solving a specific training need, the next step is finding existing programs which might possibly fit the defined parameters. This step sounds relatively simple, but it may require some extensive searching the first time around. Many training managers maintain a file of descriptive brochures and catalogs which they have received from education and training firms, publishing houses, and professional organizations. If such a file exists, it is a good place to

---

Figure 2
Key Questions for Evaluating Commercial Programs

Yes	No	Evaluation Questions
		1. Are the majority of learning objectives consistent with those defined in the plan?
		2. Are the majority of key topics from the plan included in this course?
		3. Is the material suitable for the intended audience?
		a. Are directions and content information presented clearly?
		b. Is the tone of voice or style of writing appropriate?
		c. Is the material at an appropriate level of difficulty?
		d. Do learners have the required entry skills?
		e. Are cases, examples, and activities appropriate?
		f. Is the material well-organized?
		g. Can the material be used without modification? (If not, estimate the % of revision ____)
		4. Is the format (e.g. self-study, group, etc.) appropriate to the audience and to the existing training environment?
		5. Are audiovisual requirements consistent with existing hardware?
		6. Is pacing lively and is there sufficient variety in activities to prevent boredom?
		7. Are learners *actively* involved in the program?
		8. Are concepts and skills transferable to the learner's job duties?
		9. Are print materials designed to foster learning?
		a. Is there some means of quickly accessing information (table of contents, index, etc.)?
		b. Is the print typeface large and clear enough for easy reading?
		c. Are advance organizers used (previews, graphic cues, lists, etc.)?
		d. Is there adequate "white space" for visual relief and for notetaking?
		e. Are illustrations or photographs used to help convey information or build skills?
		f. Are key ideas repeated and emphasized?
		g. Are key terms of ideas emphasized graphically by italics, boldface type, boxes, second color ink, etc.?
		h. Are summaries or reviews included periodically?
		i. Is space provided to respond to exercises?
		j. Is there enough immediate feedback for tests, exercises, or drills?
		k. Is the binding sturdy and suited to its use?
		l. Are print materials attractively packaged?
		10. Are audiovisual materials designed to foster learning?
		a. Are audio or visual segments tied directly to content and objectives?
		b. Are dramatized scenes presented with suitable realism?
		c. Is humor (if any) consistent with good taste?
		d. Are audio tracks of good recording quality?
		e. Are visuals clear and color-consistent?
		f. Do actors in audio or visual productions fairly represent racial groups and minorities?
		g. Can the voices of characters be easily distinguished from one another?
		h. Are segments clearly identified and titled?
		i. Are transitions or interfaces provided among audio, visual, and print materials?
		j. Are graphic displays, titles, drawings, charts, etc. clear and readable in visual segments?
		k. Do audio or visual segments make use of advance organizers and/or summary devices?

---

start the search. If a file does not exist, it may be time to get one started!

Training periodicals carry numerous ads for courses, and following up on ads is another possibility. In pursuing the search for programs through ads, be sure to describe the present training need and ask about any programs which might be suitable. But, also ask for a complete catalog of courses, inquire as to the existence of a mailing list for new product announcements, and consider the possibility of meeting with a salesperson for more detailed information on courses available.

Another avenue of search is through friends or colleagues. Often peers may suggest programs of potential value or make referrals to respectable specialty houses. Finally, don't overlook the possibilities of conventions, meetings, and professional shows as resource banks for identifying current offerings in the education/training market.

When a market survey of available training courses is finished, the selection process begins. A review of the market offerings related to a specific training need requires some seri-

TEST PROGRAMS *BEFORE* BUYING

An occupational hazard encountered by many sales training people is a tendency on the part of the non-trainer manager to react too rapidly to fads in both training methods and tools. It is a healthy sign, of course, that both training and non-training people are constantly looking for new solutions to the problems of changing human behavior. But too often the layman may embrace a new concept without fully understanding its application . . . or its implications for the company as a whole.

How can the training director bank the fires of overzealousness, slow down the premature buying decision and introduce some reflection and reason into the process? By requesting that new products or tools be subjected to a pilot test, said T. G. Sheftall, assistant vice president, marketing and training services for Metropolitan Life in a speech he gave recently to marketing executives. Using test vs. control groups, prior to springing upon trainees the most recently touted sales training "discovery," the training director can gain time for reason to set in as well as gain some information valuable to the decision-making process. Saving one manager from an embarrassing training purchase has added many a chevron to many a training sleeve.

According to Sheftall, a pilot test can be done effectively by splitting into two groups, test and control, a reasonable number of sales representatives. *Statistically,* 25 people in each group is the minimum requirement, but most organizations can't go that route. The test group might consist of several new people, some in the formative stages of their sales careers, and some grizzled veterans. The test group is exposed to the new tool or method. The control group is not. The latter would represent a similar mix of sales representatives and would be trained the time-tested way.

Take the sales records of both groups, by individual, before the tool is introduced and after the new training is implemented. Track these individuals for a reasonable period of time and attempt to measure the effect of the new tool or method on the test group as compared with the control group. If *significant* improvement in sales results occurs in the test group, attempt to quantify the improvement as applied to the total sales force to determine the ROI expected from utilizing the new tool or technique.

Simplistic as this procedure may sound, it is often ignored. Instead, some trainers and managers obtain approval for the expenditure of enormous sums of money on the basis of "Company X is using such-and-such a training program (or machine or whatever), and they love it." Others will "field test" the item by introducing it in one or two sales offices and request reports on whether the sales reps responded positively or negatively to it. The resulting "puff" letter file usually indicates that the sales representatives thought it was "super'" ...but never say compared with what?

A true test-vs.-control-group experiment serves a dual purpose. First, it will test management's commitment to go with and the trainer's ability to utilize effectively, a new tool or technique. And, second, it will indicate whether a reasonable rate of return can be anticipated from a substantial investment of time and money.

Reprinted from TRAINING, September 1977

ous analysis and evaluation.

The selection process

Selecting a single program from the multitude of those discovered during a market review can be a difficult task. If many courses are available, a preliminary review will probably be necessary to eliminate some of the choices. When the field of choices has narrowed to a few "best bets," sample programs should be requested for evaluation. Once sample materials are on hand, an in-depth evaluation of each program should be conducted to make the selection process systematic. Whether the evaluation is conducted by an individual or by a committee, it is absolutely essential to have a firm set of criteria to guide the evaluation process. This is often the point where the going gets tough. Evaluators have a tendency to leaf through materials without really knowing just what they are looking for. Or, they may merely focus on the obvious factors of objectives and content. To make the evaluation process a bit easier, try using the guidelines suggested in Figure 2. It provides some important questions to consider in evaluating prepackaged programs. Although the list of questions is by no means exhaustive, it will help to focus on some of the key aspects of concern for evaluation. To use the guide, simply answer "yes" or "no" to each question as you review a program. Then, the program with the most "yes" responses will be the likeliest choice!

Reprinted from TRAINING, March 1979

BUILD OR BUY?

Should you design a training course
in-house or go shopping for a
packaged program?
Some thoughts for trainers and managers
new to the game.

BY TOM COTHRAN

The dilemma is an increasingly common one in organizations large and small. You've diagnosed a problem and decided that the answer will involve training for some group of employees. You've determined who needs to be trained and what it is they need to be trained to do, or do better.

The question is: Where do you get the training itself? Is it better to build your own instructional programs, or should you buy one "off-the-shelf" from one of the many training and consulting companies to be found around town—or around the country?

The build-or-buy issue is rarely a simple, clear-cut question. More often it's a dilemma. On the one hand, the cost of designing, administering, evaluating and continually fine-tuning a training program, regardless of its nature or complexity, is both time-consuming and expensive. On the other hand, the idea of simply buying something in a box—one size fits all—doesn't always inspire comfort or confidence.

What do you need?

Many experienced corporate trainers say that the answer often lies in combining the two alternatives: Buy a basic package from a training vendor, then develop your own tailor-made supporting parts—often in cooperation with the vendor—to make the purchase suit the needs of your organization and your trainees. It still takes time and money to sift through the growing array of packages in the busy training marketplace to find the right one, and then follow through to come up with a finished program that does the intended job. But even when you add the cost of the package itself, this route usually is less expensive (if you figure time as an expense) than building a good training program from scratch.

"I think the basic factors that determine what is best are, first, what exactly do you need?" says Amelia D. Rego, director of training at American Savings Bank in New York City. "After that, you look at what's out there [in the marketplace], how easily it can be customized to your needs and, finally, whether you have the budget."

If you find a packaged program that meets your needs, if it can be customized easily, and if you have the money in your budget, Rego says, then you're better off buying. "If you don't have the money or there isn't anything available, then you're probably better off building rather than buying something that isn't exactly what you want." But in some cases, she adds, you may *have* to buy—even if you don't like all the material—because it will turn out to be less expensive than creating the program in-house.

Going outside

"Many times the main consideration is time," says Marshan Mason, manager of training design for Avon Corp. If you're building your own program, "you have to allow for research, development, creating a pilot, evaluating the pilot, revising and evaluating again. It takes a lot of time."

If the training you need falls into a generic subject area, packaged programs can be significant time savers. "A lot of generic programs have proven to be very effective," Mason points out. "For example, if I'm putting together some general supervisory training, I would probably purchase it on the outside. Someone else has already invested the time needed to create and evaluate the program, and I can also talk to people who have used the program to benefit from their experience."

In terms of cost, going outside is frequently cheaper—although sometimes the savings are not immediately obvious. Charles J. Wolfe, assistant director of management education for the Hartford Insurance Group in West Hartford, CT, says the key for the Hartford was determining that eight hours of research and development were required for just one hour of quality instruction. (And plenty of instructional designers would say that 8:1 is remarkably quick.) Wolfe figures he saved a lot of money by buying a packaged program called "The Supervisor's Survival Kit" at $15 per trainee. "It's almost impossible to beat that doing it internally," he says.

"When we go with a vendor," Wolfe adds, "the only additional cost we incur is the time needed to develop our wrap-around for the package, which we see as a necessary investment." The program's content may be fine on its own merits, he notes, but it still has to be well-suited to the company and its people.

Custom jobs

Many situations are best addressed by a combination of internal and external resources, a tactic that allows a company to extend its own subject-matter expertise by taking advantage of a training vendor's design experience. To develop your own training, you often need experts within the corporation to design and teach the program. If they're not readily available, or if they're unwilling or unable to spare the time, company materials can instead be given to a consultant to use in creating a more specifically tailored program than might otherwise be possible.

"We're a financially oriented company," says John Corridan, director of personnel development for W.R. Grace & Co.'s Industrial Chemical Group in New York, "but we're not an organization with a huge training staff. There's a basic requirement in our group that everyone be able to talk about finance. To meet that training need, we contracted with an outside organization to develop a finance course for our nonfinancial personnel."

Corridan turned to a Boston consulting firm for Grace's two-week, executive-level program. Using Grace's own balance sheets, the vendor, Harbridge House, developed a course that includes case studies from the company's actual experiences. "It emphasizes finance," says Corridan, "but in our own way."

For similar reasons, but for a radically different audience, American Savings Bank combined internal and external resources for a course in basic English. The target group in this case, explains Rego, was entry level employees who did not speak English as a first language. The bank combined on-the-job materials and experience with the involvement of an English teacher from Bow-Manhattan Community College to develop a two-day course, but with the days about a month apart. In the interim, the employees were asked to study materials and write an autobiography in English.

"They learned parts of speech, vocabulary, how to put your thoughts down on paper," says Rego. "Like many large corporations, we found that sometimes our people can speak fairly good English, but can't write it. In our kind of a service business, our people need to have those skills."

Whether you're working exclusively with outside programs or combining internal and external re-sources, there can be a risk in using more than one package or vendor, cautions Wolfe of the Hartford. "There are a lot of different theories out there," he explains. "If you use one now and come back in a month with another theory, people will question your value to the group."

Wolfe uses an internal quality-control panel made up of people who work in the area targeted for training. The group screens new material and helps determine whether it's compatible with what has been taught before.

Working from the inside

Sometimes resources or the training situation itself dictate a reliance on internal sources of training.

"When I'm trying to train employees on something peculiar to our business," says Mason, "such as performance appraisal training, I develop it in-house." The culture of the company, she explains, is a primary consideration in such cases; an internally developed program is more likely to reflect key organizational values, and lend consistency and continuity to the company's appraisal practices.

Calling in an outsider can be a sensitive matter, especially in a smaller, privately held company faced by larger competitors, or one with industrial secrets to safeguard. Such companies often display an understandable reluctance when it comes to divulging tightly controlled information to a consultant or vendor.

A case in point: Before she went to Avon, Mason was manager of curriculum development for sales and systems training at Data General Corp. In that job, she much preferred developing programs internally to bringing in people from outside the organization. On several occasions, she says, she bit the bullet and built her own, even when she knew the marketplace contained programs similar to the ones she was developing.

"The sensitive nature of the company's business was the issue," she says. "For example, we built our own communications protocols so we could protect our information and make it specific to our audiences."

When outside consultants were hired to develop or deliver a training program, she adds, the arrangement was under a tight contract: "They were under oath, if you will, and had to sign for all documents given to them."

Mason also worked for the American Management Association, an organization with a number of proprietary materials. When an outside consulting firm was brought in at one point to help develop a computer-based simulation, she recalls, "every step of the way they had to sign and re-sign nondisclosure statements."

"A consultant becomes in some ways an organizational therapist," observes Wolfe. "If you're training for skills, there's no issue. But when you're consulting at a high level in the organization, you find yourself becoming a sounding board."

In those cases, according to Wolfe, the consultant must have the experience and maturity to know when to listen, when to respond with a question or recommendation—and when to admit that he or she is not the right person to solve the problem.

"That kind of consulting," he maintains, "is what earns and justifies the client's confidence and respect."

Adaptability, both in the organization and in the outside vendors with which it deals, may be the ultimate consideration in resolving the build-or-buy dilemma. Whether developed internally, externally or through a combination of inside and outside resources, the training program in question must be able to meet very specific needs in ways directly appropriate to the organization.

Reprinted from TRAINING, May 1987

> **Research, development, creating a pilot, evaluating the pilot. . . . It takes a lot of time.**

WHICH OFF-THE-SHELF SALES PROGRAM IS BEST FOR YOU?

Here's one approach to choosing a commercially prepared program

BY NORMAN R. TICE

"Yes, Ralph, Apex has a big organization which means plenty of back-up in case someone gets sick. On the other hand, I'm not quite sure they understand our type of selling. Ya' know, that teacher, Bill, really was good, but then again, he was teaching a group of salesmen selling to retail stores. Wonder if he could switch gears to industrial products? Rick, I know you liked what you saw at Fargo Institute, but they would have to start from scratch and we'd be looking at a quarter of a million dollars. I say let's go with George. He seems to have most of what we want. But no back-up there, damn! How in heck are we ever going to decide

who will do the best job? Ya' know, guys, what we really need is a system to sort this out."

That's the way it went. Johns-Manville, a billion-dollar multi-divisional company, parted ways with its out-of-house sales training company (the reasons are irrelevant) and we were looking for a replacement.

We knew generally what we wanted. We knew also that there were many sales training companies ready, willing and able to fill our needs. The problem was becoming obvious: How could we make a final selection of an out-of-house sales trainer with peace

of mind, knowing that right then and there the decision was the best one—without question?

A listing of *premises* and *objectives* was developed as follows:

PREMISES

1. Use of Johns-Manville product case studies exclusively. No generalized, non-relating selling situations.
2. Approach of program should be learner-centered as opposed to instructor-centered. Subject matter should be remembered—*not* the instructor!
3. Sales managers, i.e., general and district must be involved from a training/coaching standpoint.
4. Advanced sales training must be on a divisional or homogeneous group basis.
5. All programs must incorporate videotape recording equipment for roleplay.
6. Learning should be through workshop activity (learn-by-doing) as opposed to the lecture and parable approach.

OBJECTIVES

1. To improve selling skills.
2. To assure that district sales managers and other immediate supervisors of sales representatives become an integral part of J-M's sales training effort.
3. To provide training in "selling through secondary distribution."
4. To foster consultant/client rather than seller/buyer relationships in sales territories.

CHART A

COMPARISON RANKING

RANKING	APEX	HAMILTON	FARGO	JONES
Course Content	2	1	2	3
Trainer Capacity	2	3	1	4
Content Depth	2	1	1	3
Cost	3	1	4	2
Design	1	2	1	3
Train-Trainer	1	2	1	3
Flexibility	1	1	1	2
Industrial	2	1	3	2
Tie-in training	2	2	1	3
J-M Input	1	2	1	2
Trainer Depth	1	3	1	2
Accessibility	2	3	1	4
References	1	1	1	2
Copyright	1	2	2	2

671

5. To assist each sales representative in becoming a "business manager" in his territory.

6. To provide specialized training units as necessary, e.g., pre-contract bid strategy, key account penetration, team selling, etc.

7. To train in a manner acceptable to women, minorities, beginners and experienced sales representatives.

8. To develop J-M's in-house sales training capability.

9. To meet J-M's commitment to continuing sales training.

marketing training department: Ralph, the director of marketing training, Rick, the staff manager, and me, the manager for sales training.

With three of us concurring, a list of ingredients we thought should constitute a sales training program was developed.*

Once this listing of ranked ingredients was determined, we put together a series of columns with the ingredients and four finalists, as shown in Chart A. The values (numbers) were assigned on the basis of who

Capacity—15 percent, Content Depth—13 percent, etc., all adding up to 100 percent.

Our next matrix (Chart B) incorporates all of the elements to provide a solution to our original problem. Multiplying the percent weight of each ingredient by the RANKING from Chart A, a value is obtained. Adding up these values for each candidate indicated which company was the best—based on everything we could throw into the pot. Upshot: Hamilton won, based on a low score of 162.5.

CHART B
WEIGHTED EXTENSIONS

RANKING	% WT.	APEX RANK	APEX	HAMILTON RANK	HAMILTON	FARGO RANK	FARGO	JONES RANK	JONES
Course Content	20	2	40	1	20	2	40	3	60
Trainer Capacity	15	2	30	3	45	1	15	4	60
Content Depth	13	2	26	1	13	1	13	3	39
Cost	12	3	36	1	12	4	48	2	24
Design	10	1	10	2	20	1	10	3	30
Train-Trainer	7	1	7	2	14	1	7	3	21
Flexibility	6	1	6	1	6	1	6	2	12
Industrial	5	2	10	1	5	3	15	2	10
Tie-in Training	4	2	8	2	8	1	4	3	12
J-M Input	3	1	3	2	6	1	3	2	6
Trainer Depth	2	1	2	3	6	1	2	2	4
Accessibility	2	2	4	3	6	1	2	4	8
References	.5	1	.5	1	.5	1	.5	2	1
Copyright	.5	1	.5	2	1	2	.5	2	1
TOTALS			**183**		**162.5**		**166**		**288**

Our next step was to search the market for sales training organizations capable of fulfilling the *premises* and *objectives* as listed.

Twenty-one sales training companies were identified as first-round candidates.

Four companies were selected as final candidates. For purposes of illustration, we'll name them Apex, Hamilton, Fargo and Jones.

There were three of us in the

did the best job (all three of us agreeing) for each ingredient: 1 for best, 2 for second best, etc. If there were a tie for any place (as in the first row across), the same value was assigned.

No decisions were made based on this matrix. It had to go one step farther—*weighting* each ingredient. Again, collectively we agreed that Course Content was to be weighted 20 percent of the total, Trainer

Hamilton is now our out-of-house sales trainer specialist.

*How can ingredients be ranked easily? Let's say five favorite foods were listed—steak, ice cream, candy, potatoes, and peas—and a selection of the best was needed, second best, etc. Start at the top and decide between steak and ice cream and place a mark next to the winner. Then decide between steak and candy and place another mark. Steak and potatoes, then steak and peas. Now start with the second food from the top (ice cream) and select the best choice, going down the list as before.

Reprinted from TRAINING, March 1977

TAILORING PURCHASED PROGRAMS TO FIT YOUR OWN NEEDS

The key is finding a program that is flexible enough to allow you to take it apart, customize it and put it back together again—without losing content, time or money

No off-the-shelf T&D program, regardless of how good it is, will address all the particular problems and situations your organization faces. But if you can purchase a program that's flexible enough, you can adapt or add elements to meet unique needs. In the long run, this method may be less expensive than struggling to design an in-house program.

Merle Barnes, manager of training and development programs at HON INDUSTRIES, a Muscatine, IA-based manufacturer and marketer of office furniture and material-handling equipment, recently learned the value of this concept. When a systems analysis revealed career concerns among younger HON employees, Barnes was assigned to select an integrated program to train personnel in career advancement and self-improvement. In March 1979, after four months of investigating over a dozen assessment center and custom programs, HON ran a pilot on Sterling Institute's "Careers in Management" program.

Sterling's program revolves around videotaped vignettes that dramatize and illustrate various career-planning problems and possible responses or solutions. In addition, the program uses videotaped discussions, a viewer's guide, a self-assessment guide and an action-planning guide.

Three-part structure

The program is aimed at three levels within the corporate structure. Series I is for those who are not yet supervisors but who would like to become better supervisory material. Series II is for first-line supervisors and managers. And Series III is for top managers and executives, up to and including the CEO. The content and the language are the same for all three series; the difference is in the emphasis.

In July 1979, Sterling prepared HON trainers to administer the pro-

gram, which was officially introduced in August.

First, 35 vice-presidents and general managers from seven of HON's ten locations in six states were called to the Muscatine headquarters. A person at this level has usually reached a career goal, so Series III emphasizes developing subordinates, assessing personal managerial style and developing action plans to increase effectiveness.

Next, 233 first-level supervisors and managers at those seven plants were put through a one-week course on company time. Series II training is aimed at helping them develop *their* subordinates. It helps them perceive their managerial and developmental styles, and they, too, learn action planning.

Series I, which is voluntary, teaches self-assessment and self-development. People are drawn into group discussions and are encouraged to react to videotaped vignettes. They examine their managerial profile. Here, again, action planning is emphasized; participants are taught to develop plans (as illustrated) with an objective, action steps, evaluation methods, review dates, potential obstacles and sources of help. To date, 180 people have gone through Series I, and another 125 are already scheduled.

Eventually, one series or another will be available to all of the firm's 3,000 plus employees. Each course lasts 24 hours; the instructor can choose to administer 8 three-hour sessions, 5 four-and-a-half-hour sessions, or 3 eight-hour sessions.

Room for adjustments

Although T&D manager Barnes is generally satisfied with the "Careers in Management" program, he recognized early on where adjustments should be made for HON's particular situation. For instance, he now involves the personnel department at each location so that a corporate administrator and a local personnel staffer can team teach. "It shows individual participants that their loca-

tion is committed. The personnel department at each location is there to provide resource help. And people get to know their personnel manager as more than someone who just hires them. They're willing to come to that person and ask for help."

Another weakness Barnes perceived was that all action planning was done at the end of the training period, following the group discussions and vignettes. He now teaches action planning with the tapes, thus reducing that last spurt of individual activity from six hours to two.

The third adjustment Barnes made to the original program involved smoothing the transition between Series I and Series II. Series I teaches people how to summarize their talents, strengths and so on; Series II prepares participants to meet with Series I subordinates. "But the supervisor does not learn in the program how really to work with those subordinates. So we've developed a career counseling program, which is a follow-up to Series II. About six weeks to two months after they've completed the Series II, the supervisors come back and review it." At that time, they learn counseling techniques.

The six-hour career counseling session teaches how to deal with questions such as "How do I manage differences when they arise?" and "How do I help a subordinate prepare for a position when neither one of us knows what's available?"

On the basis of these sessions, Barnes has developed a workbook that deals with self-assessment from the standpoint of "What are my interests?" "Not skills," says Barnes. "We can get skills. But 'What are my likes and dislikes?' " (HON is currently printing copies of Barnes' workbook, which takes about two and a half hours to complete.)

Final analysis? Positive

Overall, Barnes is enthusiastic about the value of the "Careers in Management" system. Besides being able to document several thousand dollars that have already been saved,

he says, "I've received almost 400 evaluation forms; of all the participants, only three haven't been satisfied with the program. That's less than 1%.

"Going into the program, probably 25% to 30% of the top managers were somewhat skeptical. But once they participated, they became totally supportive, which explains, to some degree, our success."

In retrospect, Barnes admits that the company probably tried to do too much too soon. In five months, he and one other trainer gave 46 programs of 24 hours each. Now he must go back to pick up the HON-designed career counseling segments.

HON has decided to follow up less formally than the Sterling program suggests. It allows Series I individuals to initiate contacts with their supervisors on action items. Barnes has found about 25% do follow up, compared to around 35% of the pilot group. He expects it will take three to six months before many submit action plans; perhaps half never will. Among the half that have already, however, results are startling. Barnes cites the following examples:

• A Series I employee who was regularly tardy or absent improved at least 75%.

• A supervisor in the paint department submitted an action plan that radically cut rejects.

• Changes in shipping procedures reduced late shipments; and shipments of present orders actually increased.

The program expanded the horizons of several participants. For example, a woman moved from the advertising department to customer service, where she was better able to use her talents.

All in all, HON personnel in general and Merle Barnes in particular are pleased with the off-the-shelf program they purchased and tailored to their needs. In two important ways, it delivered what it promised: sound training and a flexible format that permitted alterations.

Reprinted from TRAINING, April 1980

WAYS TO MAKE YOUR TRAINING DOLLAR COUNT

This system can help you buy the best program within your budget

BY DAVID CHESNUT

When you are in the market for AV equipment and software, you might be able to save yourself and your organization a bucket full of frustration—and cash—by following this simple yet widely unused routine:

1. Define the training objective;
2. Obtain a trainee profile;
3. Establish the curriculum level;
4. Establish the training methodology;
5. Construct a purchasing-cost-estimate matrix; and
6. Develop procurement specification sheets and cover letter.

When followed, these operations (shown in Figure 1) will result in a request-for-quote package to be sent to vendors. This package describes exactly what the training program is to accomplish, its time frame, budget restrictions, and any other pertinent information. Ideally, both training director and vendor will be able to make better decisions when this systematic approach to purchasing is used. Let's take a hypothetical case to illustrate the practical application of this system. Assume that you, as a training director of an electronics company, are asked to establish a

40-hour elective program to train 25 electronic technicians in a basic knowledge of minicomputer programming. Your budget is $7,000. The performance or training objective is: The trainee should be able to write a simple minicomputer program upon completion of training. With this understanding of the objective and your given budget, you are ready to prepare a request-for-quote.

Defining the **training objective** is your first responsibility. Without fully understanding this objective, trying to decide on purchase requirements will be futile. First, study the trainee profile. What kind of student will be trained? Note such things as special learning requirements as indicated by the physical, mental, and skill abilities of the trainee. Training techniques for those persons with "disadvantaged" backgrounds may differ markedly from those with so-called normal socio-economic backgrounds. This kind of trainee behavioral information will be useful in establishing the level of instruction and the kind of equipment to be used.

Procedure Two is the determination of a **trainee profile.** In the case of the hypothetical training program, it has been established that the typical trainee has a two-year technical

school background beyond high school, with at least two years electronic industrial experience.

Next, the **curriculum level** must be established. Based on the profile information, you realize that instruction must be given at a junior college level. It should include considerable illustrative material, and theoretical discussion should be minimized. Analysis of the trainee profile also helps determine the kind of hardware and software needed. Consideration must also be given to the amount of time available for instruction and whether on-the-job, spare-time, or full-time classroom instruction is anticipated. The hypothetical computer programming course will run for 40 hours. Add to this the time needed for the instructor to prepare visuals and other teaching aids and your own time as advisor for a total of 120 man hours.

The next step in the system, the **training methodology** decision, requires the development of techniques to help the trainee comprehend the instruction. Here, class size, number of instructors, AV material, simulation techniques, and other devices pertinent to the subject are considered. The idea is to develop a training methodology that specifically fits the trainee. Ultimately, you and the program instructor decide to purchase a textbook on computer fundamentals, a 2 by 2 slide projector, and an overhead projector. The instructor will develop all software, the materials and services for which (film processing, transparencies, etc.) must also be purchased.

Now it is time for Procedure Five, the design of a **cost estimate matrix.** Figure 2 shows such a matrix, based on the proposed training program in minicomputer programming. Along the top are those items you will use in teaching each subject listed at the left side. The last line across is a rough cost estimate of the various items; it provides an idea of how close you are to your budget restrictions.

Using the matrix gives the training director the flexibility necessary in adjusting purchases to budget. Be sure that you include your overhead expenses in this estimate. In our fic-

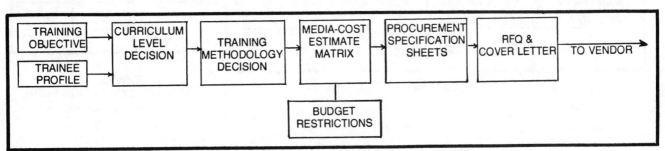

FIGURE 1 — RFQ PREPARATION FLOW DIAGRAM

tional case, the overhead percentage rate of 60 percent presumably will be obtained from your controller's office. As with most new training programs, there may be media that can be used from an existing program; therefore, in the cost estimate, list only those items you intend to purchase.

You are now ready to write up your **procurement specifications** sheets, defining the details of each item to be purchased. Each specification sheet needn't be lengthy, but it should contain details necessary for your particular requirements. If it will help in clarification, include a rough sketch of your classroom or any facility data you think will assist the vendor in understanding your requirements, including your price limits.

After you have developed a specification sheet for each item, you are ready to make up a **vendor list**, preferably at least three vendors for each item. Along with the specification sheets, each vendor should be sent a cover letter containing the parameters of your training program—time and budget restrictions and other pertinent data that will allow the vendor to make a more intelligent selection of what he has to sell you. In each request-for-quote include only those item specification sheets that pertain to the vendor's particular specialty; the same cover letter, of course, goes to all vendors.

After the quotes have been requested, you must decide how you will evaluate them. Here is one simple **quote evaluation system** found quite adequate for evaluating training items. First, eliminate those vendors who quote on equipment that obviously does not meet your specifications. The evaluation form shown in Figure 4 illustrates how you would gauge the quotes submitted for the AV projector and overhead projector. Along the top of the matrix are listed the items to be purchased; in the vertical column is the name of each vendor. The squares are divided diagonally; and each vendor's quote is weighted on a one-to-five scale. A vendor's rating is placed in the upper half of the square; his "weight," indicating his ability to meet the item specifications, is placed in the lower half. After all of the quotes have been weighted and listed, it is easy to make vendor comparisons and selections. Referring to Figure 4, Vendor B is the winning vendor for the AV projector and Vendor F wins the purchase order for the overhead projector.

This flexible system approach to purchasing media permits you to obtain items that fit your training requirements more precisely, prevents overbuying, and provides you with back-up material should you be asked to justify certain purchases. When you purchase within the requirements of both the training program and your budget, you are purchasing cost-effectively. And, that, after all, is what we set out to do.

SUBJECT MATTER / MEDIA & OTHER COSTS	Text Book	A-V Slide Projector	Overhead Projector	Software Prep. & Materials	A — Total Media Cost	B — Instructor & Training Dir. (120 man hours)	Overhead Expense (60% of A & B)	Total Cost Estimate
Computer Fundamentals	X		X	X				
Minicomputer Architecture	X	X		X				
Minicomputer Software	X	X		X				
Assembly Level Programming		X	X	X				
Cost Estimate (In Dollars)	300	400	300	1500	2500	1740	2544	6784

FIGURE 2 — COST ESTIMATE MATRIX

PROCUREMENT SPECIFICATION   DATE 10-9-77

ITEM	A-V 2 x Slide Projector
CAPABILITIES	— Super Slides — Automatic Focus — Forward and Reverse — Auto-Timed Advance — 80-140 Slide Tray Capacity — 300-Watt Lamp
WARRANTY	Parts & Labor 1 Year
PRICE RANGE	$300 - $400
REMARKS	— Firm delivery before Jan. 1, 1978 — Quote due date Nov. 15, 1977

FIGURE 3 — PROCUREMENT SPEC. SHEET

Vendor / Media	A-V Projector	Overhead Projector
Vendor A	4 / 3	
Vendor B	4 / 5	2 / 5
Vendor C	NC	
Vendor D		4 / 4
Vendor E	3 / 5	3 / 4
Vendor F		5 / 5

**FIGURE 4 —
VENDOR EVALUATION FORM**

Reprinted from TRAINING, April 1977

EVALUATING, BUYING AND CUSTOMIZING OFF-THE-SHELF PROGRAMS

Torn with doubt between buying off-the-shelf and going custom? Ask for a field test, a pilot study or a sneak preview by the vendor to determine what meets your needs

BY JUDITH E. FISHER

Undoubtedly, the most difficult task facing the potential user of commercial courses is deciding which available course best meets the defined training need. Of course, one would attempt to compare available offerings by examining content, design, and structure. However, W. Larry Petcovic, manager of training products at Radiation Management Corporation, reminds us how valuable a field test or pilot study can be. Petcovic suggests that even professional trainers cannot always accurately predict the results of a proposed training program; thus, he strongly recommends a field trial of any prepackaged course before it is actually purchased. "Unless the trainer has knowledge of the program working for other similar facilities," says Petcovic, "I would always test before purchase."

A serious field test should be run on a sample group which represents the real training audience. It should attempt to make concrete measurements of the learning which transpires during the course, and it should also assess the overall appeal of the course to the trainees. Based on measurable test results, the trainer is in a much better position to predict the potential success or failure of any off-the-shelf program. According to Petcovic, many firms are willing to rent their courses for a field test or pilot study, and often the rental fees may be applied to eventual purchase of the course. Other vendors may even be willing to conduct a field test *for* you to demonstrate how

their courses apply to your training needs. However, in such cases, one must take extra care to be sure the test results are objective.

Although a controlled field test is always desirable, it is not always possible. If you don't have the time and talent on hand to conduct such a test, James Page, manager of Radnor Training Facility of Burrough's Corporation, has another idea. Page reports that some vendors will provide a "sneak preview" of a course in the form of a closed-workshop session. The workshop session, in effect, allows potential buyers to actually take the course. Naturally, this approach would not yield the same kinds of concrete data you'd get from a field test, but the firsthand experiences it provides can offer some valuable insights for further course evaluation.

Field testing or participating in a course session will help identify the strengths and weaknesses of proposed programs. These methods also will allow you to make a good estimate of how much revision might be necessary to adjust an existing course to suit your particular training environment.

Tailoring off-the-shelf programs

Aware that commercial courses are designed for a broad spectrum of applications, many trainers are willing to consider tailoring an existing course to make it apply more directly to specific training needs. The practice of modifying or adapting commercial courses is quite common, and, in some cases, it appears to be virtually essential. Tom

Manning, training manager at Honeywell Information Systems, states that he has used some off-the-shelf programs "as is," provided that content and skills to be learned are generic. However, he adds that his instructors usually attempt to enhance the prepackaged programs with specific examples, problems, and discussions which make the materials directly relevant to the Honeywell business environment.

Similarly, at Burroughs, Page reports that his best successes have been with "tailored" programs. Indeed, he now assumes that tailoring is essential to make any prepackaged program truly suitable to Burroughs' specific needs. "Without tailoring," says Page, "learners lose interest quickly." By adjusting case studies, exercises, and examples, a generic course can be made more applicable to the trainee's frame of reference. Because tailoring makes a purchased program more relevant to the trainee's real job environment, motivation and interest are likely to increase with tailored material.

It is possible to give a commercial course the "custom touch" through minor modifications. Such tailoring can often be accomplished rather easily by in-house staff. However, if large-scale revisions are necessary or if in-house resources are limited, you might consider another approach—customizable training packages.

Customizable training packages

Customizable training packages (CTPs) offer a middle ground between purchasing an off-the-shelf program and developing a custom course. Dr. Lewis Stern, president of Focus Consulting Company, points out, "It is rare to find a prepackaged program which fits all of your requirements and is specifically aimed at the target audience in your organization." Stern suggests that CTPs might solve that problem. He defines a CTP as a foundation or core program around which specific programs can be built to meet the unique needs, priorities, and characteristics of your organization. One could, for example, begin with a CTP core program in a given skill area, then work with a consultant to adapt such program components as role play exercises, discussion topics, language/jargon, and media presentations in order to meet your specific needs. Stern adds that the cost of a CTP program is likely to be a bit more than an off-the-shelf course, but substantially less than a full-blown custom development effort. The CTP approach, according to Stern, may allow you to get the best of both training worlds—a package

HOW TO PLUG EXISTING MATERIALS INTO NEW PROGRAMS

BY GARY BRAGA

Existing industry or other commercially available generic reference materials sometimes may be effectively utilized as primary ingredients in new training packages.

This is particularly attractive under the following circumstances:

1. The subject matter is comparatively lengthy and somewhat complex;

2. The existing material covers the subject adequately (but perhaps without direct application to your own particular products, services, philosophies, markets, etc.);

3. Existing materials cost less than the expense of creating your own versions or lack of time or facilities preclude ground-floor development;

4. Future changes are likely and the required updating exceeds your capabilities.

The challenge, of course, is to adapt or supplement such materials in order to create a thorough, effective training package.

One simple approach is to provide an attachment that may be read (or listened to, if in cassette form) after completing the basic materials. This will merely point out ways that your own products, services, philosophies, etc., differ from those presented in the generic forms. It's also a way to include additional information you may wish to offer.

There is a more professional approach, used successfully by trainers in the past, that consists of these four steps:

1. Divide the program into five or more manageable segments.

2. Preface each segment with a cassette overview of content and variations from the generic.

3. Assign reference materials for each segment.

4. End each segment with a PI-type test and reinforcement of what has been covered.

Don't panic. There's actually less to this technique than initially meets the eye.

Step one, for example, may be brief. Each cassette segment introduction may run for as little as five to ten minutes. And you needn't be an "expert" to prepare it. Its purpose is to paint a broad, understandable picture of *what* is in the segment, *why* it's important, *which* points are critical or on which ones there may be variations and *how* the information may be used. The student is thus aware of what lies ahead and is better prepared to take the second step. Keep this overview general, however, so that future changes may be avoided here or limited to the reference materials.

Step two involves informing the student of what reference page should be covered in the segment. Single or multiple reference sources may be utilized.

Step three is to test and/or reinforce, and there are many ways to proceed. One popular route is through a PI-type question-and-answer approach that focuses on key points in each segment. An example:

Four types of bonds are generally used. These include all the following *except* _____.

(Individual/Standard/Name Schedule/Position Schedule/ Blanket)

In a self-testing program, the answer will appear covered on the page or on the following page. The questions should not appear in a random sequence but should flow logically, one to another.

The cassettes, along with the assignment and testing pages for this four-step technique, may be packaged together in a binder, if desired. The reference materials probably would be supplied separately.

Reprinted from TRAINING, February 1980

which is both customized and cost-effective.

Shopping tips

When considering prepackaged programs for purchasing, most trainer agree that careful planning and decision making are required. Manning recommends a precise identification of training needs before beginning to survey the market for available courses. When needs are defined, he takes a careful look at what's available and follows up with a thorough examination of competitive offerings. That evaluation process typically includes collecting information about the courses, reviewing samples, and often attending demonstrations or tests of the courses. Manning's best advice: "Don't be stampeded into buying." Snap decisions—desperation purchases—usually give disastrous results!

Page follows a similar plan for analyzing the market and evaluating potential programs. However, he observes that good commercial programs are not exactly cheap. Although one can justify a high price for excellent quality materials, there is still a wide variance in price among vendors with similar products. To be practical, Page advises, "Shop around."

Prepackaged, commercially available training programs—off-the-shelf courses—are, it seems, here to stay. Prepackaged courses and customizable training packages appear to be gaining wide acceptance as cost-effective ways of teaching basic skills within a variety of disciplines. Indeed, such courses offer viable alternatives to custom program development, but they must be chosen and implemented wisely.

Reprinted from TRAINING, September 1979

THE CASE FOR AND AGAINST HIRING AN OUTSIDE CONSULTANT

THE CASE AGAINST

BY FRANK T. WYDRA

Some time back, at the national convention of a respected training society, a panel discussion was held to argue the pros and cons of using consultants. Panelists who advocated the use of consultants were easy to find: Several consultants volunteered. During the discussion, the arguments favoring the use of consultants were delivered with wit, charm, and overpowering, documented logic. Room-sized visuals punctuated pertinent points. And handouts, suitably monogrammed, captured the message for future reference. By contrast, a lone dissenter, pale and colorless, devoid of handouts and lacking visuals, argued against the use of consultants. Therefore, in the American tradition of fair play, this article, based on the notes of that discussion, focuses on the case against using consultants.

Consultants, as we have come to know them, sell knowledge. We, as users, share our problems with them and they, in turn, give us the benefit of their long and intensive academic preparation. Sometimes, to tide them over the rough spots of meeting a monthly payroll, they sell services. They perform work. But the principal stock-in-trade of a consultant has always been the specialized knowledge he or she possesses.

In times past, the consultant was often a university professor. The consultant's role was then but a brief interruption from the teaching and research tasks. The primary role of that expert was to maintain, expand and transfer knowledge.

Over time, the demand for specialized knowledge exceeded its availability and, true to the laws of supply and demand, its price escalated. To take advantage of the high price and fill the demand, a consulting industry was born that sold a "process" instead of knowledge. The process was usually a fixed set of procedures that could be applied to a broad range of situations. The most marketable schemes of that one-time professorial consultant were packaged and sold to a hungry public like so many loaves of air-filled bread. The "process," whatever its discipline, became the solution to a whole generation of problems yet unborn. The "process" allowed the mass production of answers to meet the increasing demand for technical assistance by the multiplying clients. It was but another small step that led to the marketing of the "process" by non-experts. Today, amateurs are peddling processes, the origins of which they only vaguely comprehend, to an unsuspecting cadre of gullible clients.

If the process or product is worth the price, it should be purchased. But, too often, the client has become less than objective in the selection and evaluation of consultants. The absence of objectivity often leads to practices that make the snake-oil peddler look honest by comparison. To encourage objectivity in the selection and evaluation of consultants, the first rule should be: Don't use them unless they're absolutely necessary. And an absolute necessity is difficult to justify when several other factors are considered.

1. Consultants are expensive. Pound for pound, they cost you more than an employee. The promise is usually that the results are less costly than using in-house staff because of the efficiency of the consultant. But that's not always true.

Money spent on consultants cannot be spent on increasing either the number or the competency of your own staff. Short-term money should not be equated with long-term money.

2. The use of consultants inhibits development of in-house expertise. If somebody from the *outside* is doing the *thinking,* your people are not. The outside people are not smarter or brighter than yours; they are just more experienced. They're more experienced *because* people have hired them to do their research and thinking. If you want your people to be as experienced as consultants, let them do their own research and thinking.

3. What is sometimes mistaken for expertise is actually the application of a standard technique to non-standard situations. The result is that the output of the project is less than expected. Consultants are human, and they are also creatures of habit. Consequently, the path of least resistance is to use what they have used before on *your* problem, whether or not it is appropriate. I have yet to find the consultant who, after getting all the facts, says, "My technique won't work."

4. Worse than the use of standard techniques is the use of trainees. Most consultant work is done by the novices, the people who are just getting started. Sure, they're bright, but *your* company and *your* problems are being used to train *them*. Why not use the money, time and problems to train your *own* people?

5. After you have shared your problems and trained your consultant's people, you will suddenly realize that you are addicted to them. Because they have the knowledge and you have a need for the details of that knowledge, you are *dependent* on them. The dependency is even more insidious because the knowledge gap often prevents you from making routine changes that are needed to maintain the system. Consequently, you call in the consultant again.

6. Finally, consultants have their own agendas. Even the best consultants aren't there when you need them. During and after the project, they will be out hustling other projects. When you need a fast answer or when their solution breaks down, they invariably are somewhere else. And since they *aren't* your employees, there is nothing you can do about it.

To recap, there are at least six factors you should consider when you are tempted to use a consultant:

- Consultants are expensive.
- Using them inhibits development of in-house expertise.
- Standard techniques are applied to non-standard problems.

- Trainees are used.
- Use builds dependency.
- They are absent or unavailable at crucial times.

In spite of all the reasons against the use of consultants, there are times when they should be used. Here are five situations when the use of consultants seems appropriate:

- When only an "outside bias" will serve.
- Where the necessary expertise is needed to solve a unique problem, one that probably won't recur.
- Where the solution or project will need no maintenance (for example, legal matters).
- Where the urgency is so great that time prevents the development of an in-house capability.
- Where the *long-term* cost of developing an internal resource is greater than the long-term cost of developing an outside consultant.

If, because of these reasons, you do hire a consultant, then hire a person you know and trust, someone who has demonstrated expertise in similar situations. Then make sure he or she *personally* works on your project.

THE CASE FOR

BY STEPHANIE F. JACKSON

Everything you've just read about consultants is true (almost). It's also largely true of doctors, lawyers and auto mechanics. The description of the consulting panel at the beginning of the article seems a bit biased, but let's ignore the pleas for sympathy ("pale and colorless voice," indeed!) and look at each of the points made.

1. Consultants are expensive. Sure, they are. If you hire consultants at a daily rate, most will charge more than comparable employees are earning. But those rates begin to look a lot lower if you consider that you don't have to provide consultants with office space, support or fringe benefits.

Nor must you find ways to continue to support them once a project's over.

2. They inhibit in-house development. Used properly, consultants actually can *expand* in-house development of your employees. Before bringing in a consultant, decide if your staff really needs the expertise. If not, forget it. If you *do* need the expertise in-house, use the consultant to work with your staff in developing it, just as you'd ask a doctor to help you learn to control hypertension.

3. They apply standard techniques to nonstandard situations. Some consultants will do that sometimes. And some lawyers will crank out standard wills with little or no modification to fit your situation. Check out consultants before hiring them. Ask what they plan to do. If a consultant sounds as if he or she's got the answer *before* probing your situation, find another one. If the consultant starts by asking intelligent questions about your situation, give him or her a closer look.

4. Consulting firms use trainees on you. True again— sometimes. Lawyers and auto mechanics are luckier here than consultants; they usually do their work off-premises. And doctors frequently do theirs while you're under anesthesia. Everyone uses trainees sometimes— even clients. Ask about the training and experience of those who'll be working on your project. If they don't seem adequate to you, ask who'll be supervising. Ask for a contract with review and approval options at several critical stages in the project. Or ask for a fixed-price contract specifying the outcomes you want; thus, you put the burden of worrying about the trainee's output on the consulting firm.

5. Consultants foster dependency. Maybe. But not if you carefully specify what you want from the consultant, including the transfer system maintenance skills to your staff.

There are at least two ways to get "hooked" on a consultant. One is to hire one to put in a program or system— and then find that your people don't have the skills and knowledge to maintain it successfully. You can reduce or eliminate the problem by insisting that any agreement with the consultant include providing your organization with the necessary materials, skills and knowledge to maintain the consultant's program.

The other way to get hooked is to use a consultant who's done good

work for you several times in succession. The consultant begins to learn things about the organization that make it faster and easier to work with you— and you begin to dread the thought of having to bring another consultant "up to speed." Such relationships can be very comfortable— and potentially dangerous— for both consultant and client. Try to familiarize yourself with several consultants with more or less comparable expertise whom you can call on.

6. Consultants have their own agenda. True. Consultants aren't constantly available to any one client, any more than are the aforementioned doctors, lawyers and auto mechanics. If you genuinely need constant availability of the consultant's expertise, there are several options:

- Hire the consultant through a long-term contract or as a full-time employee;
- Hire the consultant to develop the level of expertise you need in your own organization, or develop it yourself;
- Familiarize yourself with a number of consultants with comparable expertise.

The problems cited in dealing with consultants aren't unique to consultants and the practice of consulting. Nor are they insurmountable. Careful selection and use of consultants can provide clients with programs, systems and solutions to problems that they themselves couldn't develop because of time and staffing constraints. Furthermore, consultants can simultaneously upgrade in-house capabilities.

The final set of guidelines in the first half of this article— when and how to choose consultants— is certainly useful. Here are a few additional suggestions:

- Use some of the same care in choosing a consultant that you'd use in choosing any other professional: ask others who've used consultants; check the consultant's reputation, experience and track record.
- Make sure the consulting agreement clearly specifies the outcomes you want and the expectations of both parties.
- Look for consultants who'll help you develop your organization's capabilities.

Finally, remember that the client is the buyer. It may be possible for clients to survive without consultants—but not vice versa. And, now, a little sympathy for the consultants, please. Can you imagine someone setting out to write an article titled "A Case Against Clients"?

Reprinted from TRAINING, June 1980

TIPS FOR HIRING AN OUTSIDE CONSULTANT

When consultants bomb, they're not always the ones at fault. Here's how to ensure a successful consulting relationship

BY ROBERT N. LANDAUER
AND PAMELA J. NEWMAN

At 11:30 a.m., the training consultant shrugged his shoulders and cast a "What can I do?" looks of helpless exasperation at his program manager host. He then told his 30 participants gathered from middle-management ranks at a major bank, "I quit, I'm leaving, Obviously, you people aren't interested in what I have to say."

It may sound like a nightmare, but this scenario happened recently. Moreover, unsuccessful seminars, conducted by outside consultants, are a common event. Unfortunately, the impact of a training program is so powerful that a bad experience can leave a bitter taste—and can even dangerously erode the efficacy of the training department—in the company. We suggest that adherence to the following Do's and Don'ts can make use of the outside consultant a worthwhile, rather than a nightmarish, experience.

DO'S

1. Continually read current literature to learn the names of prominent resources. Good reading includes *Psychology Today, MBA Magazine, The Wall Street Journal* [Ed.'s note: and, of course, TRAINING] and publications of various schools and businesses. Good people tend to be published and are likely to provide your audience with up-to-date material.

2. Develop a network of friends who will share their references with you. Finding a good consultant is much like finding a good television repairman, so check with others. There is no mileage in being shy. If you need to know who's good, ask the people you work with.

3. Always ask for— and check out— references from the consultant. Many consultants list clients on their biographies even if they are no longer serving them. If this is the case, you might want to check what happened. Ask the clients if they have collected participant evaluations, and, if so, will they release them for your review. Most consultants have a handy package of "love letters" that they're willing to supply at a moment's notice. But it often is necessary to dig deeper than these into the consultant's past performance.

4. When interviewing a potential resource, evaluate the individual for his or her compatibility with your organization. Remember to consider such subtle factors as the consultant's dress, interpersonal style (hard sell or soft sell), organization style (use of agenda) and his or her ability to think about business in a broad sense. The success of any training consultant depends upon the consultant's ability to "speak the language" of the organization. This includes being able to adapt to your organization's culture.

5. Ask the consultant to conduct a "pilot" session for you or ask to observe an "open" session. Explain to the participants and to the consultant that this open session will simply be a pilot. (You might want to take your boss to this session.) Be sure to tell the consultant after the initial session what materials you would like modified or expanded. There's no sense making a "marriage" between the firm and the consultant if it isn't going to be a successful one.

6. Make sure you fully counsel and help the consultant. Work as a team. Give your consultant an organization chart. Share "war stories," the experiences of previous consultants used and the exact reasons why this particular consultant was selected.

7. Provide classroom participants with a biography describing the consultant's background. This minimizes confusion about why the consultant was selected. Put the biography in the course materials for the participants. While it might seem like "window dressing," we've found that participants like to have the credibility of an outside consultant established.

8. Have a member of your organization make a formal introduction. The enthusiasm generated by the person making the formal introduction sets the tone for the consultant, who must get up and work with the group. These few minutes are critical in determining whether or not the consultant has a positive or negative effect on the group.

9. Have participants evaluate the consultant after the seminar. A formal evaluation procedure helps determine how participants reacted to an outside consultant. Exhibit 1 shows a sample evaluation form.

10. Make sure to update the outside consultant continually on current company and professional events. Make sure your consultant is privy to the company's house organ. Let your consultant know about related planned projects or task forces within the organization.

DON'TS

1. Don't get into a lengthy discussion with an outside resource until you have determined if that person is available for the dates needed. We once met with an excellent consultant for three hours before we asked about dates. Unfortunately, the consultant was completely booked for the times we were discussing. Most outside consultants attempt to work on a six-month to one-year advance schedule, so be sure to check out availability before determining suitability.

2. Don't trap yourself into a fixed-fee and/or cancellation-date constraint that you may later regret. Organizations and budgets have a way of changing with the wind. While you may be quite convinced that you now have enough

WHAT MAKES A CONSULTANT TICK?

It's just as important for a training director to know the motivations and psychological makeup of his or her free-lance consultant as it is for the consultant to know about the trainer. So says Allen Harrison, a principal in California-based Bramson, Parlette, Harrison and Associates. But, Harrison found, little research has been done to determine what qualities make for a successful consultant.

So Harrison conducted an informal survey of a number of professional consultants in the Berkeley/San Francisco area. Harrison interviewed 10 men and two women, with a median age of 41 and a median experience of five years. He asked them three questions: What were their three most important motivations for going into private consulting? What were the three biggest problems? And what were the three most important rewards?

Not surprisingly, respondents rated "Independence and Autonomy" and "Money and Income" as important motivators. But Harrison also found "Use of Self and Skills" very important to consultants as a motivator and reward. "The responses from these consultants," Harrison concludes, come close to the responses one might expect from "self-actualizing people."

Based on Harrison's survey, training directors can paint a partial picture of most free-lance consultants. They are people who are motivated in large part by the desire to be free from the constraints of formal organizations. They have a willingness to take risks, and an enthusiasm for experimentation. Usually they have a high tolerance for ambiguity and an eagerness to grow and learn. Their motivation is not financial, but rather to make the best possible use of their time and skills.

Harrison suggests that the professional consultant is a product of the '60s and '70s, when large numbers of highly-trained people wanted a change in life and a chance to use their skills outside the boundaries of a formal organization. In the latter part of this decade, Harrison says, the role of consultant seems to be changing again, moving away from the consultant as technical expert toward the consultant as a facilitator to problem solving.

"This is the kind of role," Harrison explains, "that most of the practicing consultants in my survey would choose. It fits their value system and suggests that the consultant has certain expectations of the client. Rather than seeing himself or herself as an expert problem-solver, rescuing a floundering client, the consultant values autonomy and self-actualization in the client."

"If the client assumes that consultants are motivated and rewarded primarily by financial gain," Harrison warns, "and can be dealt with as hired hands rather than as independent contractors, the relationship is likely to hit snags."

Reprinted from TRAINING, June 1978

participants to arrange for a fixed-fee or cancellation-date arrangement with your outside consultant, you may later wish you had not been so helpful. What seems like a bargain may become very expensive.

3. Don't accept an agreement that prohibits you or others from observing the outside consultant at training programs or seminars. Lately, we've met consultants who insist that the nature of the program requires complete isolation from the "management" of the organization. We believe you have a right to see what is going on unless your appearance at such a seminar inhibits the confidentiality of what is being discussed.

4. Don't be impressed if the outside consultant "confidentially" criticizes someone else's shop. Remember, next week, he or she might be attacking your shop. You may want to state that your name, or the name of your organization, should not be used in any other context without your expressed permission.

5. Don't let the outside consultant distribute any written material that you have not approved prior to the seminar meeting. This caution will allow you to make sure that the language is suitable for your organization. For example, some organizations talk about "non-exempt" and "exempt" employees; others talk about "management" and "staff." If you review all written material, you can spare the consultant an awkward situation.

6. Don't allow the consultant to send a substitute unless you have previously agreed to this arrangement. Make sure that you get whom you hired. It may well be that the consultant's associates are as good as, if not better than, the consultant you have hired. But you have a right to the individual you've paid for.

7. Don't accept a retainer-fee arrangement unless you're certain this is a person your company wants to live with for some time. It may seem cheaper, initially, to go with a retainer arrangement. But it can become very expensive if the person does not work out satisfactorily. And it's hard to get rid of the individual once you're financially committed.

8. Don't give consultants carte blanche use of your office space; they'll often take you up on it. Many consultants will ask you for office space, and it often will be mutually beneficial if you can accommodate them. On the other hand, you might find it a bit uncomfortable if the consultant makes a regular practice of using your space for his or her other business endeavors. It pays to outline telephone and secretarial usage and mail room and coffee policies before "giving away the key."

9. Don't make the consultant use somebody else's material. This technique invariably dooms a program to failure. People talk best about what *they* know and where *they* have been.

10. Don't judge too quickly if the consultant doesn't have a successful set of evaluations and participant reactions the first few times he or she conducts a seminar. It often takes time for a consultant to adjust to a particular audience. This "acclimation time" should be respected.

Using an outside consultant is not only an economically sound way of "breathing fresh air" into an organization, but it also promotes synergistic learning. Heeding these tips will ensure that the consultant you hire serves your company with maximum effectiveness.

Reprinted from TRAINING, August 1979

HOW TO MANAGE AN OUTSIDE CONSULTANT

Proper management of the consulting relationship can save your organization time and money

BY STEPHEN P. BECKER

A lot of training directors find it easy to contain their enthusiasm for hiring consultants. Two reasons:

1. They've been burned and believe they've learned their lesson.

2. They haven't been burned and aren't willing to take a chance.

The first reason is understandable. The second is unforgivable and is exemplified by a comment made to me by a training director acquaintance: "Right now, my staff and I are considered the training authorities in our organization. We have top management snowed into believing we know everything about HRD. If we bring in consultants, the jig is up. And there goes my job."

Right?

Wrong. At least most of the time. The measure of an effective training director is not that he is superior in all aspects of his field, but rather that he has the ability to supplement his skills and those of his staff. The training director who hires consultants could very well be demonstrating strength, not weakness, displaying sophistication, not ineptness.

And yet, training departments that need consultant help the most are often the least likely to hire it. And that's just plain dumb. Effective use of outside training consultants can make a training department more productive and can actually cut the cost of training. In small training departments, where much of the manager's time is spent implementing training programs and systems, consultants can be used productively to develop programs and materials. If trainers spend months developing programs and doing all the "dogwork" personally, they won't have the time necessary for proper implementation, which is at least as important as development.

In medium-sized training departments, consultants can be effectively used both for development and implementation on projects that are important but perhaps not top priority. These might be projects that, without consultant help, would wait forever because the training staff is fully employed already. You can do the projects when funds become available. You can start, stop, and then continue building a course over several months or even years. Consultants can supplement your staff and bring fresh points of view at the times of the year when the budget loosens. Using consultants this way makes it easy for you to tighten your cash outflow when corporate revenues decline. In effect, the arrangement can provide financial flexibility.

So, what's the problem?

Murphy's Law lives. Anything that can go wrong will go wrong. This is a fact of life in project management and in consultant relations, because the core of any project plan is communications. And communications are especially hard with people who come in cold from the cold. Larry Wilson, chairman of the board of Wilson Learning Corp., calls it the two-tunnel problem. Back in the 1800s, when the first transcontinental railroad was being built and the line from East to West came to an especially big mountain, the chief engineer gathered his crew and announced: "Half of you start digging from the West side and half of you start from the East. If you don't meet in the middle, you will have dug two tunnels." We often dig two tunnels when we are trying to communicate with our consultants.

Part of the solution probably rests in the same nest as all communications problems—getting the interpersonal relations into a comfortable and trusting mode. But task-oriented communications can be greatly improved by structuring what you are doing with some common sense and precision. Jack Hayes, president of the La Jolla, CA-based Innovative Group, suggests seven tips for getting the most bump for your consulting buck:

Do some homework. First, it's a good idea to collect the inputs on what people think the problem is—and then boil them down to an initial problem definition before you talk to a consultant. Second, define the end result you want. That is, decide how you'll recognize if the problem has been resolved.

Evaluate on specifics. Tell the consultant what the problem is and what you want as an end result. Let him ask questions and respond to your specific problem. It's a lot easier to evaluate a consultant on a subject familiar to you than it is on what he's done for someone else.

Have decision makers participate. Decision makers are particularly interested in solutions. They help keep the discussions solution-oriented. More than that, decision makers who are involved are very good insurance that your work with the consultant will be effectively put to use.

Put the budget on the table. If the work is currently non-budgeted or if restrictions exist, let the consultant know that up front. He'll adjust his efforts and you'll get a better result. In other words, if you have a "Toyota" budget, let him design a useful, complete Toyota rather than half a Cadillac.

Decide who does what — and when. Define responsibilities. Make it clear what the consultant is to do and what you are going to do. Distinguish, for example, between "activities" and "deliverable items." A written time schedule is a natural means of combining meetings, trips, reports, and other deliverable items, as well as the names of responsible parties. Be sure to identify the consultant's project leader and your own right away to assure a clear-cut contact for coordination, information, and problems. Good schedules help make good projects.

Agree on a measure of performance. Together with the consultant, select

MAKE BETTER USE OF YOUR CONSULTANTS

BY MARTIN M. BROADWELL

The primary and most obvious reason for using a consultant at all is the desire to obtain objective expertise. Ideally, a consultant is someone who has years of experience in the field of our deficiency. The person may be quite inadequate in some fields and only mediocre in others, but he or she does possess skills in a specialized field.

A first-rate professional consultant is proficient at presenting programs, conveying information, and changing behavior in one particular area. He or she is keenly aware of student reactions—how far can trainees be "pushed," how much controversy can they handle. Familiarity with different approaches to a problem and examples from other organizations with similar problems are also part of a consultant's stock-in-trade.

A final reason for using a consultant may be less convincing, but it's worth considering. Many times an outsider can come in, say the same things we've been saying, and get the point across where we have failed. Perhaps this is because a consultant commands a certain respect. It may be because he or she brings in experience and prestige from the outside. Or it may be that the consultant is afforded more freedom to work than is the inside instructor who is restricted by the organization.

How to use one

Once we decide to contract a consultant, how can we get the best, most efficient use of that individual's time and efforts? First and foremost: Use the consultant only in his or her field of expertise. As we've indicated, the consultant offers experience and study in certain specialized fields. Our decision to use this person should be based on *our* problem in his or her field of expertise. Obviously, there is no consultant who can do everything well. When we tax a consultant beyond his or her field of expertise, we pay an exorbitant price for a professional "presenter," who must study and learn a new field. This could have been done, of course, more economically by someone in our own organization.

A consultant ought to be involved in the planning or needs-analysis stage of the training. Some time spent here may reveal that the problem can be solved without training, or it might result in the training being directed to other areas. In order words, when the consultant is involved in the planning stage, the overall picture will be clearer, the consultant's commitment will be greater, and the presentations will be more credible because they are done directly by the consultant.

In the name of economy, a consultant's time should be used fully and efficiently. For example, if we hire a consultant to begin a program at ten o'clock Tuesday morning, we shouldn't let our own discussions run overtime. The program should begin and end on schedule. Prior to the program, room arrangements should be made, the right visual-aid equipment secured, and the housekeeping items attended to, so the consultant can be productive immediately.

A sense of trust, but not blind faith, should develop between ourselves and the consultant. This allows us to make constructive suggestions which won't be perceived as restrictive. It fosters an environment that lets the students know we are confident in the skills of this person. If top management is familiar with the consultant's program and endorses it in front of the students, so much the better.

Perhaps the best way to use a consultant is to have our own people work directly with the individual so they eventually may assume the responsibilities he or she has borne during the training. This working arrangement should be part of the original agreement; the consultant may even be reimbursed for the training necessary to bring our people up to an acceptable standard of performance. Sometimes a consultant is paid a royalty for the number of students trained, or the organization may agree to purchase certain training materials from the consultant.

As we cautioned earlier, a consultant should operate only in his or her area of expertise. It's easy to get "hooked" on a consultant and ask for programs slightly outside of that expertise area. Of course, an ethical consultant will not accept an assignment for which he or she lacks the knowledge and/or experience to complete successfully.

Another pitfall is to ask a consultant to work in his or her particular area and then gradually to change the requirements of the original assignment. Recognizing that we've engaged someone who communicates well with our students, we take advantage of the situation by "suggesting" that the consultant say something about related topics that actually are beyond his or her sphere of influence. Eventually, the consultant is working outside the area for which the agreement was made, and everyone concerned is on thin ice.

Another role we mustn't be tempted to ask the consultant to play is that of "housemother" to the students. A consultant shouldn't be asked to see that the group spends a limited time on break or otherwise adheres to certain company regulations. Most consultants will do these things, feeling they are part of the contract, but it is an abuse of the consultant's time—and the company's money. Nor should a consultant ever be charged with checking to see if lunches are ready and where or arranging for coffee breaks.

Even the way we evaluate the consultant's contribution to our program can represent a misuse of time and budget. Remember, these are professionals who make their living by presenting programs to impart knowledge. We must not, therefore, measure their success by how much they *pleased* the students. If we evaluate on the basis of some kind of "happiness scale" at the end of class, we create a number of inequities. Many unscrupulous consultants know how to get high popularity ratings by altering their presentations during the last 30 minutes of the program. To evaluate these individuals favorably gives students the wrong idea of what we consider quality.

Selecting the right one

How do we know, once we've decided to use a consultant, that we're talking to the right one? Let's look at some simple measuring devices. First, is the selected individual busy? That's a simple test, but often a sure one. If he or she is available next week, how come? Next, does the consultant have experience in the field or job area we're concerned with? Has he or she consulted with others in this area? Can references be furnished?

Then there are the questions the contenders should ask us. Are *they* the right ones? Do the would-be consultants probe to find out what our organization's deficiencies are? Do they want to know how many people are performing below standard? Do they want to know how *we* know we've got a problem?

Finally, there are the promises. First, do they offer any? Do they present some behavioral objectives and give reasons why they think these are valid? Do they promise too much, claiming to be able to do everything for everybody all the time? The promises of competing consultants are remarkably telling.

Reprinted from TRAINING, June 1977

measurable items from the end result you want. Establish by mutual agreement how these items will be used as a "yardstick." This way both you and your consultant will start with an objective measure of the consultant's performance.

Make it a cooperative effort. Get into the work with the consultant. Do it from the outset and stay with it.

Using consultants for fun and profit

To prevent a rip-off, decide exactly what it is you want the consultant to do for you. Do this before you go looking for a consultant. Your objective should be clear enough to write down. For example, you should be able to state that "At the end of the consulting assignment you will deliver to me a printed, self-instructional text on how to control sales costs. This text will be used with all sales supervisors and managers in our consumer products division." If you don't determine what you want in advance, you won't know what kind of consultant to hire. You won't know what kinds of skills to look for.

Let's say you know you need somebody who is a writer skilled in developing self-instruction. These are the basic qualifications. If you went looking for sales training consultants, you might not find the working skills you really need. Once you have located a possible consultant, arrange an interview. If the consultant has to travel to the interview, he should be willing to pay the travel cost. But, be sure to clarify this in advance. Usually, consultants are willing to make at least one trip at their own expense. If you need to invite them back for additional discussions you might be charged for it, so be well prepared for the initial interview.

During the interview, specify all aspects of the task. Many seemingly small things must be considered and agreed upon.

Some trainers who have used consultants specify the job and the end product and state a maximum budget. What happens is that a contract is signed indicating that the job will be done within the budget. Later everybody discovers that the consultant's fees, and perhaps travel expense, use up the budgeted amount. While the trainer was thinking of the entire project costing the budgeted dollars, the consultant was thinking only in terms of personal income. Don't rip yourself off in this way. Think through all of your costs and then indicate a portion specifically for consultant fees. Break down all other items in great detail and estimate or get quotes on

every item to determine the total investment for the project.

Another way you can cause your own rip-off is by supplying the consultant with the wrong subject matter experts. Insist that the best subject matter experts make the necessary time available to the consultant. If you settle for less, it will take longer to do the job and your cost will go up. And watch out for personality clashes between consultants and those supplying information. It's better to switch than have a fight sap productivity.

If you're an inexperienced consultant user, you should think about what you'll be doing while the consultant is at work. You might hire a consultant to save your time—but end up not saving time. If you have to spend a great deal of time explaining problems, systems, solutions, and benefits, then perhaps you should have done it yourself, assuming, of course, that you have the skill and ability. If you're using consultants on small projects, then the consultant should be able to carry the ball and you should be spending your time on other things. On large projects, much more of your personal time may be legitimately required.

How to "rip-off" consultants

Don't be afraid to negotiate. As a training director at Motorola put it recently: "My people were aghast when I offered a consultant half of his published daily fee for counselling with us. But they were dumbfounded when he blinked twice and accepted

the offer." The consultant will respect you for being concerned with the corporate cash box.

If you foresee a long-term use (three months or more) of a consultant's time, you will save money by negotiating a quantity discount. Consultants will work at substantially lower prices if they are assured of longer contracts. The consultant doesn't always have to be working on the same project, but make sure he or she is competent to work on all the projects you have planned.

Another thing you can do to save money on a specific project is to ask the consultant for an "introductory special." That is, ask the consultant to demonstrate competence at a lower than usual rate on this project with the promise that if performance is good, there will be future projects. This may appear like you're ripping off the consultant, but in fact, it's simply good management. It's really just another form of a performance contract where the consultant could end up with much more business than originally anticipated. Besides, the consultant always has the right to refuse.

One thing consultants really dislike is when you change the specifications of the contract after the work has been started. If you do this, the price for their services will skyrocket. They lose respect for you, feel they have been misused, and believe you owe them extra compensation for allowing them to waste their time, which is, in effect, what they're selling. It's clearly in your best interest to be certain that you want what you said you wanted.

SO WHO ARE
TRAINING CONSULTANTS, ANYWAY?

Most training consultants are individuals or very small firms of fewer than 20 people. There are a few consulting companies of 20 to 100 people specializing in training. Then, too, a few large publishing companies which have been producing training programs using a wide variety of media think of themselves (sometimes justifiably) as training consultants. One outfit I'm familiar with is a subsidiary of a company which makes trophies and designs sales incentive promotions. And, of course, several big companies have training consulting subsidiaries which package and sell generic versions of programs the companies have produced and used in-house.

Perhaps the best way to classify consultants is to break them down into

two groups. The first group is made up of those who want to sell you products, packages, courses, workshops, seminars, materials, films, tapes, books, modules, units, machines, and other tangible items that you may be able to plug into your training program. For an additional cost, these con*sell*tants will customize their materials and products to fit your particular situation. The second group is made up of those who perform services and sell advice. They can collect data, analyze it, make recommendations, design curriculums, write objectives, write materials and scripts, produce media, evaluate results, and conduct training sessions. Most of these consultants can't do it all, so they specialize.

Reprinted from TRAINING, July 1976

An interesting and fun way to get ripped off by consultants is to buy their specialty because your organization can probably use it. What this means is that some consulting firms are basically offering one particular thing such as MBO, job enrichment, communications systems or grid training, or transactional analysis, etc. Even though you may be able to achieve something useful with these approaches, it's wrong to buy them simply because they exist. Specific training should be a solution, or part of a solution to a problem. Use specialized consultants only because you have determined that you need them and getting their services is high priority in relation to other training needs.

Working with "conselltants"

Except in very large organizations, it's almost always cheaper to buy training materials than to make them. But don't, for example, buy a good film and then build a training session around it. Finding or building the right materials or courses is one of the last things to do when developing a training program. Off-the-shelf courses and materials should be carefully reviewed to make sure the way the needed ideas are presented is a way that will ring true for the participants in your training sessions. If you don't actually go through the entire program yourself, you won't really know what you're buying. This process takes precious time, but not to investigate materials thoroughly is just sticking your head in the mouth of a rip-off.

How to pay consultants

Payment schedules, too, are negotiable. As long as consultants can plan their finances and can count on your

keeping to the agreed upon payment schedule, they are usually willing to make almost any arrangement. My preference is to pay the bulk of the money near the end of the contract and after the work is completed. Many consultants will ask for partial payment in advance for working capital. I will do that only on rare occasions. Normally I will make a small payment upon completion of a first draft or phase. I will then make a second payment after the program or materials have been reviewed and corrections have been made. I will then make several periodic payments after final completion. In effect, I am still making payments for development while the materials are being implemented and people are learning from them. In summary, don't blame somebody else if all of a sudden you find yourself deep in quicksand. You should have been looking for it. The way to spot such a trap is by planning in detail before any work is started. A written contract can be less detailed. In any event, every aspect of the total project should be thoroughly discussed. Remember that consultants get burned, too. They lose reputation and customers when performance is not what was expected. Some consultants have very strong ethics and will walk away from poorly planned contracts. Others will do anything for a buck. But in the beginning, the money belongs to you. You must develop the skill of using consultants so that those dollars will be well invested. Never forget that the consultants can always walk away when things get too messy, but you have to stay behind and live with the result. If you manage the consulting relationship and activity properly, you can significantly increase and improve the value of training in your organization.

Reprinted from TRAINING, July 1976

CUSTOMIZED TRAINING

When a consulting firm offers you
a customized training program, how much
customizing will really go into it?
And how much do you really want?
Here's a look at some options

BY HAROLD SCHARLATT

So the outside consultant has promised you a customized training package. Sounds great. But what does "customized" mean?

Sometimes it means simply that the consulting firm is going to stick your logo on one of its standard packages. That probably is not what you had in mind. But in the consulting business, "customized" can mean any number of things.

As long as you are dealing with a reputable person or firm, you may be fairly well assured that a customized training program will involve more than the printing of your company's name on a glossy cover; or, if that's what the consultant means by "customizing" the package for you, it will be explained that that's what you're buying.

But pragmatically, "customized" rarely means that the consultant will start from scratch and come up with entirely original material. You hire these people, after all, for their knowledge, resources and expertise; part of that expertise involves the ability to draw upon knowledge and resources to avoid reinventing the wheel—at your expense. If standard material will suit your needs for some sections of the program, why pay to have those sections customized?

Once you have decided you need a customized program rather than something straight off the shelf, therefore, the challenge becomes one of finding your way through the vast gray area that falls between complete originality and "customization" in name only.

Five types

Basically, customized training programs come in five varieties. The consultant may offer to: 1) allow you to pick a module; 2) modify a core program; 3) fill the gaps in your present curriculum; 4) work with industry content experts; 5) conduct what I'll call "prescriptive activity sessions." Generally, the more work the consultant puts into custom-tailoring the program, the more you pay.

The "pick-a-module" approach used by many large consulting firms allows you to select one or more packages out of a number the firm has to offer. One advantage of this option is that you usually get a polished, well-tested, moderately priced training package with which the consultant is very familiar. Another benefit, if you want professional-looking audiovisual support for the program, is that these modules often include AV materials.

The disadvantage, of course, is that the package is "customized" to your needs only in the loosest sense of the word. Often the objectives are not completely in sync with yours, the content may have little face validity (they talk about using machine X, instead of the Y machine you use), and the instructional level may be too basic or too advanced for your people.

In the second approach to customization, the consultant has a core package but offers to revise it for your special needs. The objectives can be tailored, the content changed to provide greater face validity, the language of reading material elevated or lowered depending upon the educational level of your trainees, and so on. This avoids most of the disadvantages of the "pick-a-module" approach, but even when tailored, the package may produce training that does not fit snugly into your curriculum. And if you are looking for slick, expensive AV support, you probably will be better off picking a module.

By offering to "fill the gaps in your curriculum," the consultant is promising to take a long, hard look at what you are already teaching and devise a training package that teaches new skills by building upon the training your people have already received. This may lead to the creation of entirely original material and has the obvious advantage of addressing your special needs precisely.

But here the disadvantage may lie in the very extent of the customization. Every time a consultant creates something genuinely new just for you, you are paying for training that is, essentially, field-testing. Also, it is entirely possible that the program you really need to plug a gap in your curriculum cannot be designed by someone unfamiliar with the idiosyncrasies of your particular operation, which means the consultant will have a lot of learning to do—learning you'll have to pay for. And it is not unusual (or out of line) for consultants to charge more for this kind of work, since they probably will not be able to use much of the resulting product elsewhere. Finally, the cost of videotapes and films to support training custom-built to this extent can be almost prohibitive except to the largest and most development-minded companies.

If your business or industry has unique and highly specialized training problems, you might choose the fourth option, in which your consultant develops a customized program in conjunction with (or after picking the brains of) content experts. In this team approach, the experts familiarize the consultant with the problems and identify the course content. The consultant's role is to shape the content into learnable packages and, often, to teach those packages. In other words, you are paying the consultant primarily for his or her skills in the areas of instructional design and teaching.

This approach has the same advantage as "filling the gaps" in that it addresses your needs precisely, but it avoids some of the disadvantages of that approach. The experts can speed and improve the consultant's learning process by steering him only to those areas he really needs to study. Since the consultant does not have to work as hard learning all about your business, you should pay less. In addition, the resulting training package is likely to field-test better because of the experts' input. The only drawback is that, again, AV materials probably will have to be produced from scratch.

The fifth approach incorporates what we'll call "prescriptive activity sessions" to combine a standardized package with customized training. The consultant begins the training session with a core program that may or may not be modified and tailored to the particular audience, as in approach number two.

After absorbing the basic program—on conflict resolution, for example—participants meet with the consultant individually to discuss their own interests and needs and to select specific material they would like to work on further—conflict styles, nonverbal communication, resolution methods or whatever. The consultant then groups participants with similar desires and gives them predesigned activities and exercises. If the consultant lacks a packaged program to suit the needs of a given group, or even an individual, he may customize one. The advantages and disadvantages of such customization, of course, are the same as those outlined earlier: The nearer you approach genuinely original material, the more you pay and the closer you come to field-testing an unproven program.

Questions for the consultant

When you talk to a consultant, it is not always evident exactly what is meant by, "We'll customize it for you." Here are some questions you might ask to get a clear fix on what the consultant is promising to do.

• *How will the program's objectives be generated?* Will they be tied into the results of a needs analysis? Selected from a list of options? Written from scratch?

• *Who else have you customized*

for? Ask for company names and specific people to contact. Question the contacts about what "customization" meant in their cases. Ask to see the materials generated for some former clients.

• *Why should I choose your firm?* You need to find out what the consulting firm sees as its particular strengths. You'll get a sales pitch, of course, but what areas does that pitch stress? Are they the areas with which you are concerned? How does this firm differ from others you're considering?

• *Will there be pilot tests?* Without pilots, customizing that results in effective training is hardly possible. Extensive customizing produces a product that is more or less new. To avoid a hit-or-miss training effort, it must be tried out.

• *Who will be running the program?* Sometimes you will be approached by a salesperson who knows a lot about sales and zilch about training. Other times you may be approached by honchos who have forgotten everything they ever knew about training. You need to talk to the people who will be designing and conducting the program.

This is a crucial point and deserves some elaboration. As the trainer gets better, the customized programs he or she produces obviously get better; but they also may get cheaper. Why? Because the more knowledgeable the trainer—the more extensive his mental "library" of effective programs and of situations similar to yours—the less time he will spend reinventing wheels in an effort to meet your particular, but not necessarily unique, needs.

A customized program wrapped around a solid, proven core probably will require fewer adjustments, and therefore less field-testing to ensure its validity. And in many cases a trainer who can tailor sections of a program effectively "on his feet"—who can anticipate special problems, answer questions authoritatively and create variations on the spot—does not have to be paid for the time it would take to go back to the drawing

board.

• *Will training your trainers be part of the design?* You probably do not want to be dependent on your outside consultant for so long that he becomes part of the office furniture. There are exceptions to this rule (e.g., you want the consultant to come in and run the program two or three times a year instead of burdening your staff), but by and large you want a training program your people can take over and run.

Questions to ask yourself

• *Are you listening or talking?* You should be talking. The consultant should be drawing you out regarding your needs. You should not be listening to a sales pitch (at least not for long) if what you are looking for is customized training.

• *How fast does the consultant have an answer?* The consultant who listens to you and mulls over your problems is more likely to customize than is the consultant who has a quick solution to everything. If you're convinced that you need more than a thinly disguised "package," the consultant who offers to go away and think about your training needs may well be the one to go with.

• *Does the consultant offer to do a needs analysis?* Training cannot be tailored to your particular needs unless those needs are identified.

• *Does the proposal show developmental steps?* Field-testing is essential for effective customized materials, but so is your input along the way; there ought to be resting places to reevaluate the program's progress. Customizing is a process that, in plowing new ground, is likely to turn up the unexpected. Developmental steps with built-in time for thinking and rethinking are a must.

Customizing is, as the expression goes, great work if you can get it. You can get it by knowing up front what kind of customizing you are looking for, and by asking the consultant—and yourself—the right questions.

Reprinted from TRAINING, August 1983

STRATEGIES AND TACTICS FOR MANAGING TRAINING

If the training and development function is to have an impact on the organization, it has to be well managed. How do you tell a well-managed training function from a poorly managed one? Easy. If the titular head of training walks around whining that, "Nobody ever listens to me," or "They always cut my budget first," or "Those darn line managers don't appreciate the value of our courses," then you've found a poorly managed training function.

Effective training managers realize that every support group, like human resources development, has an equal parochial interest in getting a slice of the pie—that is, of the organization's limited resources. The "doting parent" approach to training and development ("Eat! It's good for you!" or "If a little is good, a lot is better") gains neither credibility nor budget dollars.

As some of the authors in this chapter argue, a strategically managed training department has to battle for resources, as does every other key function. But the negotiation is over "what kind and how much?" It is not over whether "we can afford any of that stuff at this critical time." A well-managed HRD function is in the business of offering the organization tactical options to help it achieve its strategic goals.

Shall we heed advice that urges us to be "internal consultants to management?" Certainly sounds good. But as a training director once told us, "I tried that line about internal consultant, and my boss's boss came back with, 'Consultant my foot. You're on the payroll with the rest of us. We all sink or swim together.' " A good training manager may use a lot of consulting skills, but to be effective, you have to be a part of the organization. You must have a stake in the action. And you must be good at making the organization work for you.

There is also the matter of behavior modeling. How you act will always speak louder than what you say. Is the training department itself a well-managed entity or is it riddled with performance problems? If you run the kind of ship other managers can respect, they are more likely to listen when you talk about performance and how to improve it.

In this chapter, you'll find a lot of sound advice from a lot of knowledgeable people. But you'll also find a number of different perspectives. So here's a key bit of counsel to keep in mind as you sift through these ideas: Know thyself. When the training function is clearly defined, and everyone in the organization knows what business you are—and are not—in, you have the foundation not only for a well managed training operation but for a key partnership role in driving the organization toward its strategic ends.

10 MANAGEMENT MUSTS FOR HRD DIRECTORS

Which is the best-managed department in your organization? It should be yours, thanks to the special opportunities and responsibilities that HRD directors have

BY GEOFFREY M. BELLMAN

Managers of HRD (human resources development) functions have many of the same problems that all other managers face. And they also have a special opportunity as custodians of human resources development within their organizations. Because of their special responsibilities, they usually have more formal knowledge of how to develop human resources and, more specifically, of the techniques of management.

The following ten suggestions come from my own experience as an HRD manager and as a consultant to HRD managers in other organizations. They contain obvious biases, but these biases have been useful to me and may well stimulate your thoughts in related areas.

1 First and Foremost, Manage. When you are consulting with a client, you are not managing. When you are training supervisors, you are not managing. You may consult or train well, but when you do, you aren't managing.

Management may not be a full-time responsibility for you because of the size of your department or your organization. But there are times when you must put on your manager's hat and concentrate all your energies on deciding where this function is going to go and how you are going to take it there.

2 Delegate. If you spend more time managing, someone else is going to have to do much of the training and consulting you normally do. You say they don't have the skills to do that work? Or they don't have the time? Or you don't have confidence in them? Have you ever heard those same complaints from line managers who won't let go of their technical work to do their managerial jobs?

Learn about how difficult it is to delegate by delegating yourself. Learn about the problems line managers face as they move from being individual contributors to being managers.

3 Establish Ideals. What do you want your HRD department to be in the long term? What are your hopes for it? What are the HRD ideals that you want to serve? Consider these questions with your staff, and together write a statement of ideals that your department will constantly work toward. Further, measure your department against these ideals on a project-by-project, objective-by-objective basis, always asking, "Does this project or objective serve the ideals we're reaching for?" You will find that much of the work you undertake doesn't move you toward your ideals, but don't punish yourself for this. If, however, you feel that few projects are moving you in the direction of your ideals, then stop to reconsider what your purposes are and whether you, individually or as a de-

partment, can get what you want through continuing to work in this organization. It's also a good idea to reconsider your ideals to see if they are the same guides you want to continue to follow.

4 Be a Model for Your Clients. If your department trains people in performance appraisal, use performance appraisal within your HRD group. If you work with others on meeting skills, use meeting techniques in your own group meetings. If you encourage line managers to be more open regarding organization information, risk being open with information in your own group. If you teach MBO (management by objectives) in workshops, use MBO in planning in your group. If you believe managers should build teams, then build a team within HRD.

In HRD, we too often ask for changes from others in areas that we don't want to change ourselves. As a general rule, don't ask clients to try new supervisory or interpersonal skills or systems that you haven't tried first in your own organization. As you try these new skills or systems, pay attention to your own comforts and discomforts and use these feelings to adjust your approach to your line clients. When clients see that you believe enough in what you say in your workshop and consultation to use certain techniques, they will be more likely to use them as well. In the process, you will learn how to manage better and more realistically.

5 Risk Managing Innovatively. What new management process or technique have you tried out in the last three months? What have you tried within the last year that didn't work?

In HRD, we have access to much knowledge on alternative ways of managing. We should be trying out these alternatives, just as we expect our clients to be open to new ways of managing. Even an occasional failure lets us know that we are testing management limits rather than operating too conservatively within management boundaries. When a new approach to managing doesn't work, discuss it in the group and move on to something that you hope will be more successful.

6 Manage in Ways Respected Within Your Organization. Innovation is fine, but most of your management practices should be along established lines within your organization. "Established" not in the sense of what is

691

done, but in the sense of what people say should be done in a particular organization. When you show a healthy respect for the "establishment," other managers will realize that you know how to do well on their terms. Your success at managing according to the "mores" of an individual organization will make it easier for clients to trust you.

7 Don't Rely On Promoting From Within. For many HRD functions (especially in larger and more technical organizations), the day is past when you can promote well-intentioned and motivated people who do what makes sense. There is a rapidly expanding body of knowledge and skills in human resources development. Many of those skills should be practiced by your staff, especially if yours is a corporate-level staff. If you don't hire talent from outside to supplement your well-intentioned and motivated internal people, your staff may rely entirely on its own past experience. It also takes you much longer to develop the skills you need in a staff inexperienced in HRD than it does to hire someone with HRD experience from without. In addition to hiring people with HRD talents (full-time or part-time), encourage reading, attendance at workshops, the practice of skills within your group and the use of outside experts.

8 Multiply Yourself. Long before HRD departments came into formal existence, training and consulting were done between line and staff departments. In fact, most training and consulting are still done without your involvement, and that's how it should be. Seek out the line personnel who are operating as HRD consultants and trainers as a part of their regular responsibilities as managers. Help them build their human resources skills, so they can do the work they're already doing more effectively. This approach allows you to multiply yourself and to demonstrate the importance of human resources development across the line organization.

9 Insist On a Line Review. Too many of us spend too much time avoiding contact with management. Our fear of them stems from the possibility that they won't like what we're doing or that they won't understand the importance of what we're doing or that they might take some drastic, irreversible action.

Although it's difficult to operate with people outside our control and of greater organizational power, that's exactly what we must do. We shy away from being measured, but if management doesn't see fit to measure us, how important are we? Remember, management keeps a close eye on anything it considers important to the organization. So if we expect management to think of us as important, we should expect them to hold us accountable. Insist, or at least work toward, being reviewed regularly by the line management of your organization. Use that review time to report on what's happened in the past and what you plan to do in the near future. Use that time to get management's commitment.

10 Don't Worry About Working Yourself Out of a Job. Many HRD managers are working hard toward the day when they no longer will be needed. In fact, many of us use that as a kind of slogan for ourselves as we talk to the people around us. But I think "working ourselves out of a job" is an unfortunate expression.

The HRD function is a legitimate and continuing one, as real and important as the law, accounting or personnel. Ideally, there is no *way* for you to work yourself out of a job; your function will always be needed. True, your own or your organization's performance can result in the HRD department being trimmed down or eliminated, but the need for human resources development will continue.

The notion of "working ourselves out of a job" is based on a problem-centered image of HRD; that is, once we solve these few problems, we'll no longer be needed. But that's not the way the world of work really is. Problems are not the exception waiting to be resolved so we can return to a more idyllic workplace. Instead, what we call problems are the rule, the very essence of our work and work life. The HRD function exists because of the natural day-in and day-out occurence of situations between people who are trying to complete a task together. As you use your own and your department's resources more effectively within your organization, more work will come to you as organization managers begin to understand how HRD can help them be even more successful.

Reprinted from TRAINING, October 1979

USEFUL STRATEGIES FOR MANAGING THE HRD DEPARTMENT

Few trainers will dispute the fact
that strategy—doing the right things—and
tactics—doing things right—are
the keys to success

BY GERALD A. MICHAELSON

Just as Machiavelli's *The Prince* has become a standard text in many business schools, so has Clausewitz' *On War* become a weapon in the arsenal of many sales and marketing organizations. And some of the tactics, strategies and concepts codified by the early 19th century soldier and philosopher can also be adapted to training.

If this talk of warfare leaves your hair standing on end, you're not alone. For a group as humanistic as HRD professionals, the idea of combat in a training session seems especially heretical. However, the warfare analogies are not those of combat but, rather, the broader strategies of command. Trainers who have frequently linked their training sessions to sporting events will find that the proven strategies of military success offer interesting analogies that help get the point across on the battleground of the mind.

If you're confused about the enemy, it's clearly explained by General Pogo of Okefenokee Swamp fame who said, "We have met the enemy and they is us." If you can consider that your own mind and the minds of others are battlefields, it makes sense to use the principles of military strategy to win on those fields.

The basic idea that strategy—doing the right thing—and tactics—doing things right—are keys to successful training is one that few will

dispute. And nowhere have strategies and tactics been refined and tested as successfully as in humankind's long history of armed conflict.

Jack Trout and Al Ries, co-directors of the Marketing Warfare seminars, have expanded this concept into a successful one- and two-day business strategy session. Best known for their development of the "positioning" concept that's revolutionized modern advertising, Ries and Trout have now teamed with Tony Whyte of Advanced Management Research to bring battlefield techniques into the business office.

The idea of converting military knowledge into business tools isn't a new one, of course. Business leaders often come from various officer training schools and bring to their business organizations many of the basic tools learned in the military. Look no further than the standard division between staff and line responsibilities for evidence of that fact.

But what about those trainers who have never served in the Armed Forces? How familiar must they be with the military to translate those tactics into training tools? Well, the answer is the same for those trainers who never swallowed mud in pursuit of a piece of pigskin. Military terms like "objectives," "targets" and "strategies" are as much a part of everyone's vocabulary as are sports terms like "huddling," "passing" and "quarterbacking."

Trainers sometimes talk about

"bringing up the big guns" to get across a difficult training objective. It's often more effective to "keep our forces concentrated on a single objective" than to spread ourselves too thin. And it often pays to make a "flank or rear attack" instead of meeting a major problem head on. These, and countless other cliches, come from Clausewitz. In his study of the battles of history, he developed many basic lessons for trainers as well as warriors.

Clausewitz' studies led him to conclude that "the superiority in numbers is the overwhelming factor in the result of a combat." Napoleon said it this way, "God is on the side of the heavier artillery." How, then, can a smaller company's training director help the firm win battles against the giants?

Long ago, military commanders found numerically superior forces could be defeated by an opponent with some kind of relative superiority. This is a key principle for both military and business strategists. In training terms, the concept suggests that the training director of a small computer firm shouldn't pattern the firm's training program after IBM's. As Alfred Lord Tennyson wrote, immortalizing the battle of Balaclava, "Into the valley of death rode the 600," referring to 600 Lancers facing the overwhelming odds of 27,400 enemy troops. How can a company that can afford 600 minutes of training compete with one that provides 27,400? The smaller organization must develop a relative superiority.

For example, 11,000 Athenians defeated 15,000 Persians at Marathon in 490 B.C. because the Athenians fought from a phalanx, which required special training so that in the fight the shield of each soldier would overlap that of the neighboring soldier. This was an entirely new concept for men accustomed to fighting one to one. The phalanx secured the victory, and the principles of training and concentration of forces to achieve relative superiority were firmly established. The results of this battle have a parallel when you compare the high failure rate of independent business to the relatively low failure rate of well-trained operations, such as the modern-day franchises. Every business can develop its own phalanx of relative superiority. Training focused around the relative superiority can, in turn, assure victory.

"Where absolute superiority is not obtainable, "wrote Clausewitz, "you must develop a relative superiority at the decisive point by making skillful use of what you have." The classic

693

COMMAND STRATEGIES FOR TODAY'S TRAINER

Organizing the grand strategy

Everything is very simple in war, but the simplest thing is very, difficult—*Clausewitz*
  Translation: The solution is easy, it's just hard to find.

Keep forces concentrated in an over-powering mass. The fundamental idea, always to be aimed at before all and as far as possible—*Clausewitz*
  Translation: Conquer one training objective at a time.

Where absolute superiority is not attainable, you must produce a relative one at the decisive point by making skillful use of what you have—*Clausewitz*
  Translation: Get your act together…now.

Fools say that they learn by experience. I prefer to profit by others' experience—*Bismark*
  Translation: Steal all the good ideas you can.

A great battle has never been an unprepared, unexpected, blind, routine service—*Clausewitz*
  Translation: Miracles don't happen; they are planned.

Theory can give no formulas with which to solve problems. It lets the mind take a look at objects and their relations, and then the mind goes to the higher regions of action *there to act—Clausewitz*
  Translation: Concepts train the mind for action.

Marshalling your forces

Knowledge begins with practice, and theoretical knowledge, which is acquired through practice, must then return to practice—*Chairman Mao*
  Translation: Practice makes perfect; repetition works.

The soldier is levied, clothed, armed, exercised; he sleeps, eats, drinks, and marches, all merely to fight at the right time and place—*Clausewitz*
  Translation: All training is for the result.

Our attitude toward ourselves should be "to be insatiable in learning" and, toward others, "to be tireless in teaching."—*Chairman Mao*
  Translation: We learn—to teach.

Our slogan in training troops is: Officers teach soldiers, soldiers teach officers and soldiers teach each other—*Chairman Mao*
  Translation: Trainees train the trainer.

Our kingdoms lay in each man's mind—*Laurence of Arabia*
  Translation: Train the mind—and own the world.

Developing your plan of action

Many assume that half efforts can be effective. A small jump is easier than a large one, but no one wishing to cross a wide ditch would cross half of it first—*Clausewitz*
  Translation: Half efforts lead to half results.

Weapons are an important factor in war, but not the decisive factor. It is people, not things, that are decisive—*Chairman Mao*
  Translation: Nothing works unless people do.

A great battle is a grand act which partly itself and partly from the aim of the Commander stand out from amongst the mass of ordinary efforts—*Clausewitz*
  Translation: Heroes are made by their deeds.

The whole secret of the art of war lies in the ability to become the master of the lines of communication—*Napoleon*
  Translation: If the orders you issue are carried out, you're in charge.

It may be in the future that I will lose a battle, but I shall never lose a minute—*Napoleon*
  Translation: Do it now; there may be no tomorrow.

For winners only

Only great battles can produce great results—*Clausewitz*
  Translation: Forget the molehills; it's the mountains that count.

Knowledge must be converted to real power. This is the reason why—with distinguished men— everything is ascribed to natural talent—*Clausewitz*
  Translation: Winning only looks easy.

Victory has a thousand fathers; defeat is an orphan—*J.F. Kennedy*
  Translation: Lose and you lose alone; win and you're part of the team.

---

military example is the battle of Agincourt in 1415 A.D., where 5,000 English defeated 20,000 French. The English were armed with a superior weapon called the longbow, which required years of training to assure proper use. Every business has an available longbow that can deliver a well-aimed arrow of relative superiority.

These superior battlefield tactics are only a few examples of how the trainer can develop relative superiority. The grand strategy may be a flank or rear approach that doesn't meet the opposition head on. MacArthur's landing at Inchon is a modern warfare classic. His July 23rd, 1950, radiogram to Joint Chiefs outlining his proposal could be readily paraphrased in modern business communiques: "Operation planned mid-September is amphibious landing of a two-division corps in rear of enemy lines . . . The alternative is a frontal attack, which can only result in an expensive and protracted campaign."

Chief executive officers can find an interesting lesson in the command strategy differences of Napoleon and Churchill. While Napoleon was running around Europe fighting battles, the politicians back home were planning his downfall. On the other hand, while Churchill constantly gave advice to the military, he delegated the actual field command to the appropriate field commanders.

The military analogies are endless. History proves that well-trained troops have an edge in battle and that new weapons require new training. The same concepts hold true for trainers. The strategies and tactics proved in battle are fertile brain food for trainers seeking new approaches. The lessons of warfare can indeed help HRD professionals achieve success in peaceful pursuits.

Reprinted from TRAINING, October 1979

THE TRAINING WHIRL (AND HOW TO KEEP IT FROM SUCKING YOU UNDER)

Ever get the feeling that management's esteem for training shifts according to some mysterious pattern that has nothing to do with the training department's performance?

BY GAYLE COATES WIGGLESWORTH

The training world is a victim of a seemingly inevitable cycle, an evolutionary whirlpool. The whirlpool spins at varying speeds in different companies, different industries and under different economic conditions, but it spins relentlessly.

We trainers, sucked up in the whirl, have not always been noted for managing our environment successfully over long periods of time. The well-known risks of this business, especially for those of us who ply our trade in large organizations, are the periodic political upheavals and reorganizations to which training and development departments are subjected.

How often do we hear the lament that the training department has lost its credibility and therefore has been disbanded, reorganized or shunted aside and ignored? And how often does that cry issue from a training department that only a few months or years before was crowing its success? Having observed this phenomenon over several years in different organizations, I have concluded that the rise and fall of training departments does not *necessarily* have to do with their performance so much as with the inexorable movement of a certain cycle from one stage to the next.

Details of the cycle I describe may differ in specific instances, but I believe the basic pattern will look all too familiar to most experienced trainers.

I see it as a "wheel" composed of six stages which can vary in duration.

The cycle can move only clockwise. Its revolution starts at the bottom, in Stage 1, and the training department picks up steam in Stages 2 and 3 until reaching the pinnacle of success in Stage 4. Then comes the regression, with the department's status deteriorating through Stage 5 and hitting bottom in Stage 6, from which point the cycle is ready to begin again. Only from the position of strength represented by Stage 4 is it possible to break the cycle by skipping any of its phases.

Here's how the training whirlpool works.

Stage 1: Identification of training as a solution

Severe problems are identified and training becomes perceived as part or all of the solution. This stage is placed at the extreme low point of the wheel because severe problems involving training usually result from the downward movement of the last training cycle.

A company moves into this critical stage slowly, all the while feeling pain from the situation and suffering for some time before management (or someone) identifies training as the solution. Stage 1 generally is the shortest phase of the cycle because upon recognizing the critical need, management can be expected to want the solution applied immediately, thereby propelling the company into the next stage.

Stage 2: Allocation of resources

Management's attention brings sponsorship. Sponsorship produces the people, money and other resources deemed necessary to do the job. The critical need usually is found to be "only the tip of the iceberg," and the company now is willing to assign its fair-haired boys and golden girls to the problem. Management isn't kidding around now. The dormant training function receives a quick infusion of credibility, power, dollars—and instructions to "fix it."

Stage 3: Building expertise

The training effort gathers momentum. The wisdom of developing internal resources is generally accepted, but outside experts are called in to provide quick solutions for mini-icebergs that lend themselves to fast fixes (and often for a few icebergs that don't) and to add immediate expertise to attempts to solve critical problems.

Now the training department is really flying its colors. It's a winner. Even the Hawthorne effect contributes to its success. Indeed, success is self-perpetuating because it suddenly becomes possible to convince management of the value of preventing future problems *now* rather than fixing them later.

The longevity of this stage will vary depending on how much needs to be done. When the major effort is no longer directed to recruiting and providing basic resources but rather to looking toward future development, continuity and revisions, you can assume you have entered Stage 4.

> **Once the training department is no longer backed by the power structure, it becomes an easy target for blame.**

695

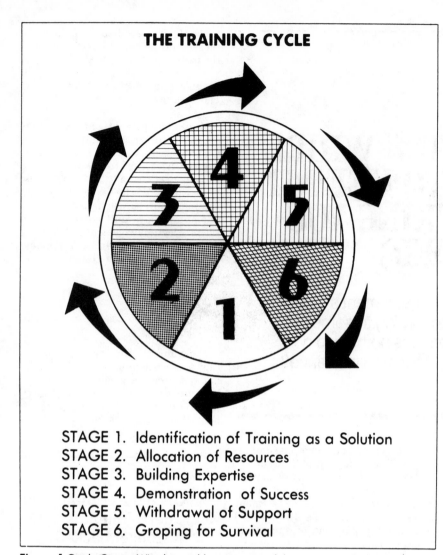

THE TRAINING CYCLE

STAGE 1. Identification of Training as a Solution
STAGE 2. Allocation of Resources
STAGE 3. Building Expertise
STAGE 4. Demonstration of Success
STAGE 5. Withdrawal of Support
STAGE 6. Groping for Survival

Figure 1.Gayle Coates Wigglesworth's conception of the training cycle. Regardless of your department's performance, the wheel spins.

Stage 4: Demonstration of success

The training department is riding the crest of the wave. Not only has it solved the original problems, it has identified and defused many more.

Training may come to be viewed as a panacea for virtually any situation; suddenly every project manager and department head perceives a need for training to ensure success. If your biggest headache as a training manager is that you have to keep saying, "...but this isn't a training problem," cheer up: You're in Stage 4.

Being the "in thing" in an organization can be difficult with limited resources—and there always are limits. There is only so much time in a day and any single function can command only so much attention from management, to say nothing of dollars and staff. Almost in spite of itself, the training department becomes a power, able to pick and choose among the projects and departments it identifies as likely to receive the most benefit from its services.

Stage 4 usually is the longest phase of the cycle, since the training manager's major goal is to reach this state of grace and maintain it. It also appears to be the only stage of the cycle where an option exists as to the next movement: clockwise to Stage 5 or, with the right combination of management, circumstances and luck, directly across the circle to begin again at Stage 1 (see Figure 2).

Stage 5: Withdrawal of support

In the previous phase, the training department was riding the wave. In Stage 5 the wave breaks and foams onto the beach.

By now, the original pain of Stage 1 is long gone. Frequently the company's top managers don't even remember how it hurt. For a variety of reasons, management redirects its attention and allocates its resources to more visible problems. Once the training department is no longer backed by the power structure, it becomes an easy target for blame should anything anywhere go wrong—and the high-riding trainers are sure to have made enemies during their heyday, what with the picking and choosing of groups upon which to bestow their attention.

It's often difficult to determine exactly when a company moves into this phase, as the transition from Stage 4 can be gradual. Like a cyclist who

> ## An organization may linger for years in a single phase of the cycle before moving on.

has been pedaling furiously, the training department can coast for awhile. But unless the cyclist begins pedaling again, the bike keeps slowing down. Eventually it stops. Then it falls over.

Unlike the coasting cyclist, however, a training department that has slipped into Stage 5 *cannot* begin pedaling again; the muscle is gone. Once into Stage 5, the only way out leads through Stage 6.

The only real key to recognizing the onset of Stage 5 is to spot the moment when management's attention and sponsorship begin to wane. By the time the withdrawal starts in earnest, it's too late. And the sooner you recognize you're *in* Stage 5, the easier it is to begin moving to Stage 6.

Stage 6: Groping for survival

If Stage 5 is hard to identify, this one is hard to miss. You'll probably see a major turnover of staff, changes in reporting structures and delegation of duties, constant budget planning, and an avalanche of "analysis." Nothing much gets done, mainly due to the lack of resources and sponsors. The training department's contribution to the company comes under intense scrutiny, as does the cost of maintaining it. And whatever may go wrong during this stage, it is always training's fault:

"If it was fixed right, why hasn't it stayed fixed?"

"The expense of ongoing training

isn't necessary. The problem has gone away."

Meanwhile, gremlins begin to emerge from the vacuum where the trainers used to be. After a respectful period of confusion, indecision and neglect, the problems turn into critical needs and the company returns to Stage 1.

None of this is to say that critical needs and problems are not identified during Stage 5 or early in Stage 6. But while the training department may be blamed for the problem, training is not seen as the solution during these phases. When management *does* decide that training is the answer, the

---

The best alternative during Stages 5 and 6 is wholesale desertion by the training staff.

---

company has moved into Stage 1 of the next cycle.

An organization may linger for years in a single phase of the cycle before moving on. For instance, some companies reorganize several times and shuffle their staffs completely before moving into Stage 1. Each new group of trainers optimistically renames the department (attempting to divorce themselves from past blame) and sets out to collect support and resources from management. If the support is not allocated, the company remains in Stage 6. If you find yourself in this position, you have two viable alternatives: Initiate the transition to Stage 1 by gathering data and exposing problems, or get out as soon as you can.

Why are we stuck in this cycle? I believe the underlying reason involves a crucial difference in philosophy between managers and trainers. Fundamentally, the training and development industry is dedicated to proactive problem solving. While trainers become heroes to the business world by resolving existing problems, our *real purpose for being* is to prevent future problems by preparing people through training and development.

Managers, on the other hand, have been schooled for decades in a reactive philosophy. "If it's not broken, don't fix it," is typical of sentiments expressed by perfectly good managers. You will argue that "really good" managers *are* proactive; and in truth, sometimes they are. But genuinely

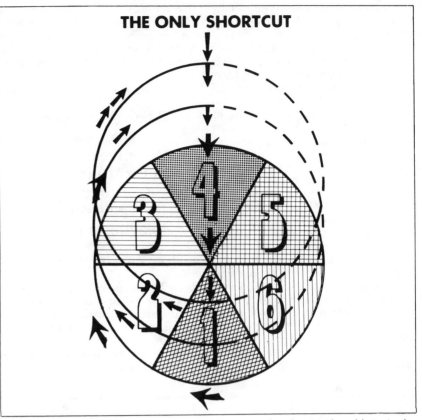

Figure 2. Astute training managers in Stage 4 may identify critical problems in the company that training can solve, and persuade management they're right, thereby cutting across the circle to begin a new cycle at Stage 1.

proactive management would never allow its training department to spiral into Stages 5 or 6 in the first place, because it would understand the ultimate consequences.

The truth is that when the pressure is on, even the best managers tend to revert to reactive styles under the guise of "taking action" or "playing hardball." The predominant reactive style shows up clearly in Stage 5 when, forgetting the pain of the past, management directs its attention and resources—quite understandably—to the most obvious current problem.

What is really ridiculous about this situation is that we trainers have been promoting and perpetuating this style by *teaching* many well-established management concepts that reflect reactive rather than proactive values.

In addition to the philosophical problem, some tangible factors cause the cycle to evolve from one stage to the next. The upward swing is based on need: Momentum builds, beginning in Stage 1, and carries the company to Stage 4. How long it remains there depends on the style and skill of management, both in the executive suites and in the training department itself. In some companies this may be years, in others months.

The downward swing usually begins with a "push" from some condition or

event: an economic reversal, a change in management, a need to diversify the business, or a problem within the training department. It is worth looking at these factors separately.

The economic environment can have a profound effect on the company's attitude toward its training effort. Any reversal will spur management to seek ways to cut costs and improve productivity. If the training department is in Stage 5, this is bad news because training is regarded as expensive overhead. If the cycle is in either Stage 4 or 6, the same economic reversal could be good news: Perhaps this is the critical need that catapults the organization into Stage 1 of the next cycle.

A change of management frequently pushes a company from Stage 4 to Stage 5. The new management team does not regard training as the hero that solved a critical problem 18 months ago. In fact, the new group may be unaware that there was a problem.

New managers are *always* looking for ways to justify their existence and prove their value to the organization. They need to make an impact by solving problems and/or increasing profits. An established, well-run, Stage 4 training department is of no obvious value in accomplishing these goals. Stage 4 trainers may maintain a number of existing programs, but they usually concentrate most of their "change" efforts on the future—developing programs aimed at eliminating problems before they occur. Their contribution to profit margins tends to be long-range and subtle. If training's demand for attention and resources begins to compete with the demands of a project the new manager can use to show immediate benefits, training loses.

Diversification frequently forces a company's training cycle from one stage to another, or even causes the cycle to leapfrog several stages.

In this day of deregulation and varying market demands, companies sometimes need to diversify to stay alive. If training is in Stages 3 or 4 when the company decides to diversify, it will be seen as a force and utilized to make the transition into another market successfully. A Stage 5 or 6 department, with little or no credibility, will be left out of the diversification process.

The performance of the training department can play a very important role in the cycle. The department that misuses its power, forgets the reasons for its existence, dabbles in the esoteric at the expense of the practical (runs programs that please trainers,

---

When the pressure is on, even proactive managers revert to reactive styles under the guise of 'playing hardball.'

---

for instance, instead of pleasing managers, supervisors and employees), or the department that is simply incompetent will erode its own value to the company.

Our greatest disservice to ourselves seems tied to an inherent predilection

of our industry. As a whole, we are a group more dedicated to intangible benefits than to tangible ones. Our rewards and indicators of success tend to come from the response to our programs and the "development" of our "students." The companies we work for, on the other hand, measure success through tangible benefits which are best depicted as numbers. Although we're making progress, the training industry has not developed the science of providing supporting numbers to the same degree that other industries have developed it over the past few decades.

While riding the upward swing of the cycle, trainers usually don't need these figures—everyone feels good about what's happening; gut feelings, "observed" behavioral changes and other intangible benefits are enough justification for what we do. But comes the swing from Stage 4 to Stage 5 and "bottom-line" management concepts get us every time. (Next time you hear two trainers arguing the importance of "measurable, bottom-line impact,"

THE CYCLE AND YOU: TRAINING MANAGERS

It is to the training manager that the cycle offers the greatest chance for glory—and the lion's share of the risks.

The ultimate proof of your skills lies in Stages 4 and 6. In Stage 4, the astute training manager has the opportunity to maintain the status quo or leap directly to Stage 1 by uncovering and "selling" the next critical need.

But if you are managing a training department as it revolves into Stage 5, you're in a no-win situation. Leave. Leave as fast as you can. Yes, you could continue to manage through Stage 6, but you will never be able to relive your past glories, nor will you be able to recapture enough of the old credibility to carry you through the cycle again.

There are two reasons for this. One, the once-successful manager loses her self-respect as she watches her successes disintegrate. She knows what the consequences will be, but is allowed to do less and less to ward off the coming storm.

Two, as the cycle nears bottom, any training manager participating in the downward plunge will be a target for blame regardless of his contribution or guilt. The captain who goes down

with his ship as it sinks through Stage 5 gets no respect from upper management. He simply loses its confidence.

New training managers have most to gain by entering the cycle at Stage 6 or Stage 1. Stage 6, when accepted consciously, can provide the fuel needed for a good manager to propel the department into Stage 1. There is the risk that you might not be able to break through to the next stage, but the benefit is that you can control and direct the company's attention to the correct critical need.—G.C.W.

THE CYCLE AND YOU: CONSULTANTS AND VENDORS

It pays for consultants and other "outside" providers for training materials and services to track these cycles in various companies.

It pays for consultants and other "outside" providers of training materials and services to track these cycles in various companies.

Invariably, opportunities arise to provide expertise and products needed to address problems in a company during Stages 2 and 3. As the company nears the end of Stage 3, and certainly once it enters Stage 4, you probably

will find that its demand for your services wanes—by this time, the internal staff is expected to have developed the expertise to handle most projects in-house.

During Stage 4 you should be networking throughout the company, ensuring that line managers who request and sponsor training are aware of the role you played in taming the once-critical problem. Maintain friendly relations with the training department, but establish with others in the company your separate status as an outsider. In other words, don't get caught in the blame blizzard likely to hit the training department when it cycles into Stage 5.

Outside providers owe it to themselves and their clients not to get caught up in company politics. Avoid that trap, and you can be there again to assist during the next upswing of the cycle. This sounds ruthless, but it really works out best for you and the company you're serving. Part of your value to the organization is your detachment from its day-to-day activities, your ability to come and go as needs indicate, and your ability to provide expertise garnered from exposure to many different organizations.

Your survival and prosperity often may depend upon your ability to work concurrently with several companies

ask a few questions designed to reveal their companies' positions in the training cycle.)

Managers have long been taught that resources have to be allocated where they do the most good. In the absence of cold, hard facts from the training department, they eventually will be allocated elsewhere.

Beating the game

While the training profession may be victimized by this cycle, the individuals caught up in it—training managers, consultants and vendors, internal subject-matter experts, and staff trainers—can learn to manage their own destinies within the whirl. Individual strategies and considerations for each group are outlined in the four short sidebars that accompany this article.

Acknowledge the existence of the cycle I describe (or of something very much like it), consider the thoughts in those sidebars about consciously assessing your moves in relation to

the cycle, and I believe you will find yourself managing your career more successfully. To do so, however, you may have to make some tough-minded decisions. For example, read the indi-

---

> ## The performance of the training department can play a very important role in the cycle.

---

vidual strategies for training managers and training professionals, and you'll notice that I advocate wholesale desertion by the staff in Stages 5 and 6.

It is not necessary for anyone to staff a training department in Stage 6. The only reason for all the reorganizing, needs-analyzing and budget shuf-

fling that occurs during this phase is that the trainers have not recognized or accepted the fact that they're in Stage 6, and so keep acting as if they're in Stage 4. It's an exercise in futility. In fact, if no one remained in the training department during Stages 5 and 6, the deterioration and resulting problems would escalate and the company would cycle back into Stage 1 that much faster.

Participating in the two downswing stages of the cycle can confuse even the strongest of us as to our real value and contribution. You will spend too much time analyzing your own short-comings, and undermine your self-confidence for no good purpose—because unless you can determine what you did wrong and come away with a lesson you can use next time, that type of introspection is useless. If you *are* trapped in a company during a downswing, recognize instead that you were valuable when needed and will be again—if not to the same organization, then to others.

What actions can we take as an

---

in various stages of the cycle, minimizing the dangers of an uneven cash flow caused by cyclical demands for your services. When major economic shifts—such as this last recession—come into play, only the strongest cycle managers will weather the storm. They will locate and attach themselves to industries in Stage 1 and offer training as part of the solution to combat the dismal economy. And they will prosper despite the many companies that will be moving into Stages 5 and 6 as a result of the same conditions.—G.C.W.

THE CYCLE AND YOU: PROFESSIONAL TRAINERS

As a career trainer, you understand that in order to advance in your field you probably will have to move from company to company: With the exception of consulting firms and training vendors, most organizations provide limited promotional opportunities in their support departments as opposed to their line functions.

The professional trainer in a company at Stage 4 has a good thing going for the time being, but should be on the lookout for companies that are beginning (or appear ripe to begin) an upswing in their cycles. Keep track of

how things develop. When opportunity knocks, answer it—especially if you suspect your present organization is headed into Stage 5.

Sticking with a company through Stage 5 can be heartbreaking. It is fairly "safe" for a professional trainer to hang around during this phase—after all, your value is predicated on certain skills and expertise, and the loss of the *department's* credibility in one organization probably won't affect your chances with another employer. But you'll be in a deteriorating situation which you are powerless to control. The psychological effects will not be pleasant. If you can get out, do it.

Even if you choose to stay through Stage 5, *do* leave before Stage 6. There is a very real risk of losing your job during the reorganization-and-survival stage, and nobody needs that kind of trauma. Keep your network alive, and look for organizations that will be desperate for your expertise in their upward swings.—G.C.W.

THE CYCLE AND YOU: INTERNAL EXPERTS

During Stages 2, 3 and 4, subject-matter experts often are assigned to the training department to add line expertise to the design of programs. In

return, the company tells you, the tour of duty in training will broaden your skills by exposing you to a variety of techniques and styles.

It's not unusual for this kind of assignment to turn into a high point in your career. People from various line functions frequently become very enthused with training and development; some think about career changes.

But internal experts who understand that their futures lie in the company's particular business (as opposed to the training profession) should keep one thing in mind: Their career success and their value to the company dictate that they limit their training assignment to one or two years—and only while the training department is in Stages 1 through 4. To stay longer is to be perceived as a trainer, not a line expert.

And woe be unto the expert who is perceived as a trainer when the company cycles into Stage 5. You'll find yourself in limbo, lacking the schooling and specialized skills you'll need to compete in the job market as a trainer, and unable to break back into your old line function at your present company. The final nail in the coffin: Experts who fail to return to the line by the end of Stage 4 end up carrying much of the blame during Stages 5 and 6.—G.C.W.

Reprinted from TRAINING, May 1984

industry to combat the negative effects of this cycle?

Those of us who specialize in management development can increase our emphasis on proactive management styles and clarify the long-range benefits (to the bottom line) of this style over the reactive style.

The entire industry can get deadly serious about developing the science of attaching meaningful numbers to the behavioral changes resulting from our training. A lot of work already has been done in this field. With proper attention, enough generic information could be compiled so that even the smallest training operation could justify its existence and demonstrate its successes in a way that hits managers where they live.

We can identify truly proactive managers and solicit their sponsorship for proactive management-development programs. And we can keep track of these people, because wherever they are in control we can be assured that training will be in Stages 1 through 4 and the company will welcome competent professional help.

We can learn to recognize the cycle and identify its stages. Even in cases where we can't control the flow from one stage to another, we *can* control our reaction to the flow.

We can take care of ourselves by trying to work only in environments that can benefit from our talents and where we can make the greatest contributions.

As the training wheel turns, we can take comfort in knowing that we do not have to be its victims. With knowledge comes the ability to exercise some control over the cycle itself and a great deal of control over our movements within it. And remember that the continuous spinning can be a blessing as well as a sorrow, for while Stages 5 and 6 are painful, Stage 1 will always be coming around, starting that upward swing again.

Reprinted from TRAINING, May 1984

WHAT THEY DON'T TEACH YOU ABOUT BEING A TRAINING MANAGER

Some things you just don't learn until you're in the job

BY JACK GORDON

In the bad old days, company training departments were looked upon (when they were noticed at all) as necessary evils. Little red schoolhouses staffed by little red schoolmarms or disgraced line managers, they were simply an unavoidable expense. They existed in a sort of void, divorced from the crucial issues that affected the business and the gut-level action that made it run.

Training careerists argued incessantly that the training function needed to become more "visible." They seized eagerly upon the term "human resources development" to underscore the point that the tools of their trade—behavioral and motivational theories, and instructional, diagnostic and performance technologies—had to do with far more than just running people through classes to teach them basic technical skills, or company policies, or generic subjects like interpersonal communication. Management, trainers argued, ought to view employee development as a vital strategic opportunity, and the HRD department as the prime agent for capitalizing on that opportunity.

Most of this arguing they did among themselves, since the only people who wanted to hear about it were other trainers.

Today, though skirmishes still are being fought in plenty of companies, the war for visibility for HRD as an issue is pretty much over. For a lot of social, economic, technological and political reasons having little directly to do with the arguments of trainers, training got visible. In the lip-service department, certainly, the victory is complete. You can't throw a brick over your shoulder without knocking a CEO off-stride in the midst of a speech about his company's most valuable resources being its human ones. And the same brick will ricochet off two business reporters taking notes and a college professor writing a book on the subject. Over the past few years, HRD has become outstandingly noticeable as a management concern.

The issue for trainers, however, is not just HRD as a laudable idea, but HRD as a specific function and as a professional calling. When they languished in the backwaters of management neglect and cried for more visibility for the training *department*, what nobody told them was that the sudden glare of management attention could be a mixed blessing.

For the president or assorted senior managers to take a profound and active interest in your activities is a wonderful thing—if you are as ready, willing and able as you think you are to deliver the goods these worthies perceive as valuable. If you're not, it can be a disaster.

It's cheering to know, for instance, that top-level HRD managers are now actively pursued by corporate head-hunters. But it's sobering to stop and ask just which jobs—or, more precisely, whose jobs—some of these managers are being recruited to fill.

As president of Abbott Smith Associates of Millbrook, NY, an executive recruitment firm specializing in the HRD and personnel fields, David Brinkerhoff's job is to help organizations and training managers get together. One current client is a major company that hired a new CEO a few years ago. The CEO brought in six new vice presidents and developed a new strategic plan for the company. "It's a whole new ball game," Brinkerhoff says. "But some people in the training department haven't awakened to that fact, even though it's been three-and-a-half years. They've been having a hell of a time adapting to it. So heads are going to roll. We're bringing in new people who can work with the new top team."

In the days of the little red schoolhouse, when the idea of working with the top team was only a forlorn dream, inability to do so wouldn't have become an issue in more than a handful of companies. Today, Brinkerhoff says, situations like the one he described aren't unusual. "I've seen it happen before. It's gotten worse over the past three years, and it's going to get worse yet. When you have companies cutting back, decentralizing, taking new tacks and strategies, a training manager who isn't plugged into what's going on is going to be in big trouble. . . . Sometimes it isn't even a matter of a major change. Sometimes it's just failure to look up from the day-to-day role."

As an example of how times have changed, consider how Geoff Bellman, now an independent HRD consultant who heads GMB Associates of Seattle, recalls his experience 10 years ago as corporate director of development for G.B. Searle, a Chicago-based pharmaceutical company. He remembers that one of the biggest surprises he ran into when he became a training manager was loneliness—a sense of isolation. "Nobody tells you how alone you are in that position. No other manager in the company has a job like yours. Your [subordinates] understand training technology, but they don't have company-wide responsibility, and they don't appreciate the burdens that come with that responsibility." Managers who do have such responsibility—the training manager's peers—don't relate very closely to HRD, he says.

No doubt some of today's training managers would empathize. But when we mentioned Bellman's comment to Linda Novotney Kemp, director of HRD for Dayton Hudson Department Stores of Minneapolis, it struck no chord at all.

"I don't feel that way, and I don't know if [Bellman] would feel that way today," she says. "So much of what we're all about is helping our organization change. Part of the technical

---

'No significant contribution we've made has resulted from a pure conversation about training.'

---

training we do involves new systems. Part of management development involves trying to change the culture and the structure of the company to position ourselves for growth. Because we're trying to change as a company, and the direction is coming from the top, I'm linked in. I'm very much involved. And I view other managers as having the same mission—just different pieces of the pie. I don't feel at all as if I'm out here as the Lone Change Agent."

What do HRD managers have to say to the training professional who aspires to move up to the management ranks? They mention many factors about their roles that aren't fully appreciated, and perhaps can't be, until one is actually in the job. They talk about the classic difficulty of making the switch from "individual contributor" to someone whose job it is to get work done through others. They speak of the surprises one gets when one tries to manage trainers. But no subject comes up more often or more emphatically than the need to "plug in" to the driving concerns of the company.

Plugging in

"A lot of trainers and even training managers have no idea what the real

GIVING IT UP

BY JACK GORDON

Remember the classic anguish of the dedicated professional who gets promoted to a management job? All the stuff you've read, and maybe even taught, about how hard it is for many people in fields like engineering to give up the immediate rewards of doing the actual work and concentrate instead on the less tangible achievement of getting work done through others?

Well, one thing they don't teach you about becoming a training manager is that it all applies to you. And knowing about it in the abstract doesn't necessarily make it any easier.

"The hardest thing for me was to give up the active, daily participation in design and development," says Steve Floyd, former manager of Coca Cola's bottler training group and now head of Floyd Consulting and Design in Atlanta. "To be a good manager, you can't be overly involved in projects. But then you produce no [immediate] tangible results. You have no class to run, no program to design. It's classic Peter Drucker: You're doing more long-term planning, people positioning, looking at the strategic implications of actions and inactions, not just for yourself but for others.

"It becomes an ethical problem. I could have done it all at Coke, but then I wouldn't have been a good manager. One of the reasons I left was because I missed the involvement in designing and developing projects."

Geoff Bellman of GMB Associates of Seattle, another former training manager turned consultant, felt similarly. "Budgets, affirmative action reports, performance appraisals. . .suddenly there's this huge amount of paperwork and administrative crap you've got to take care of so your people can work—so they can go out and do what you're good at but no longer get to do because you're a manager."

The syndrome doesn't apply to everyone. Training professionals who have become bored or restless with their roles as "individual contributors" and are genuinely eager to move on to broader responsibilities probably won't suffer the same sense of loss. But the absence of anguish about leaving hands-on training behind raises the issue again from a different perspective.

As you rise up the management ladder and "learn the business you're in," says Melinda Bickerstaff, director of management education for American Express Travel Related Services of New York City, "you back yourself away" not just from direct involvement with training but from the training profession as a whole. Bickerstaff serves on a task force for the American Society for Training and Development that is studying the issue of "how you keep the vice president of HRD, say, involved in the profession."

On the other hand, titles are tricky in the HRD game. A "training manager" can be anyone from the executive director of a massive corporate education function to a one-person training-and-personnel department. And some training managers, even those in their companies' top HRD positions, don't have to give up active participation in training. But if you are the top dog in a corporate training department and still get to do a significant amount of classroom work, it's probably because you have a very small staff.

Ellen Kamp, director of training and development for Home Life Insurance Co. of New York City, has only two subordinates, and considers herself lucky that she still gets to do some presenting. "I don't choose to take myself completely out of training," she says. But even when you don't have a large staff to worry about, the press of management responsibilities makes it tough to find time to keep your hand in, Kamp adds. "You have to commit time to remaining a polished trainer; you can see those skills slip away very easily. It requires extra work. The classroom planning has to happen outside the office."

Reprinted from TRAINING, June 1986

business of their company is. They don't know what the critical issues are. They don't know who the major competitors are. They don't know why and how the business makes a profit. That's what line managers care about, and if you can't deal with a line manager on his level, there's no way you can apply instructional technology to his problems, because you don't understand his problems. . . .

"We had our training professionals ride with the drivers and spend time in the terminal on the day shift and the night shift. We wanted them to understand that our business is moving freight from point A to B without breaking it into a thousand pieces. That's why people pay us. That's how the business makes money."—Jack Zigon, former manager of corporate HRD at Yellow Freight System, Overland Park, KS.

"If I knew eight years ago what I know now, I'd get into some marketing and business programs. . . . Trainers come in with the idea of keeping training separate from the rest of the organization. As a profession, we have built-in rewards that promote that view. We measure how well we do what we do by looking to academia for standards. We buy into the academic reward system; we look for ways to label and identify things. We spend all our time trying to write the best behavioral objective instead of stepping back and asking how that objective relates to this particular business. . . .

"The biggest mistake I could make would be to go to the senior management team of my company with [an academically perfect] proposal for a training program and fail to demonstrate in the proposal how it would impact the company and tie into the strategic plan for 1986-'87."—Melinda Bickerstaff, director of management education for American Express Travel Related Services, New York City.

In *TRAINING Magazine's Industry Report, 1984* (October), we listed our readers' rankings of the 10 best training organizations in the country (IBM, Xerox, Hewlett-Packard, AT&T, McDonald's, the U.S. military, General Electric, General Motors, 3M and Procter & Gamble). When we asked the training directors of several of those organizations what made their efforts successful, we heard a similar refrain again and again. Ken

Hansen, Xerox's manager of corporate education and training, put it most succinctly: "Training [at Xerox] is linked directly to business objectives. The training function is not something separate from the management function. Training is seen as an enabling process to meet goals."

Among the training managers (and former managers) interviewed for this article, being hooked to the heart of the business is by far the greatest pride of those who perceive their departments to have achieved that status. And it is the number-one goal of those who don't.

'Generic programs help, but you reach a point where that ground has been pretty well covered.'

Ellen Kamp is director of training and development for Home Life Insurance Co. of New York City. The position is only five years old; Kamp has held it for the last three. Her staff consists of one training professional and an administrative assistant. "We're a 125-year-old company with a five-year-old training function," she says.

For Kamp, the battle for HRD visibility is still a long way from being over. "It really surprised me that management had such a limited view of our function," she says. "They saw our role as just running classes. And they figured that just running classes would solve problems." Kamp sees her major challenge as "educating management in terms of how we could help meet their business needs. Some [managers] are saying, 'Aha!' Others still see us [as belonging] in the classroom."

According to Robert Harloe, director of training and development for Dunkin' Donuts of America, Inc., there's a deceptively simple secret to plugging in—and to gaining power and influence for the training function in general. "The key is, you've got to listen. You can't sit in your ivory tower and come up with pronouncements about how to solve problems."

But there's a little more to it. Even

when training people do go out to listen to the troops—while conducting a needs analysis, for instance—the mistake they make is to "tune out" until the conversation turns to training. "No significant contribution we've made to our organization has resulted from a pure conversation about training," Harloe says. "You find the opportunities in conversations about the business—where it's going, where it's hurting."

It's in conversations like those that you'll pick up other key pieces of information, as well, he says. For instance, "Unless new training people come in from other management roles, they don't pay attention to how things are measured. What does the company really care about? What do managers get rewarded for? Is it return on investment? Earnings per share? If you can impact that, people are going to be all ears when the conversation does turn to training."

Bickerstaff makes a similar point. "You have to understand how your organization determines its performance not only from the [human] performance standpoint, but from the marketing and financial standpoints. . . . How does your organization decide how it's doing? If you're going to create effective training, you've got to know that. Do you know how to read a financial report?"

Training specialists typically aren't inherently interested or formally educated in subjects like marketing and finance, she says. And at the specialist level, most don't have to worry much about those areas. But for training managers, it's a different story.

Lest this all sound like just one more rehash of the frequently repeated admonition to link training to "bottom-line results," Harloe raises a yellow flag. In evaluating his programs, he says, "We use the measures operating departments use, not pure training measures. And we measure what goes on back on the job. But we don't take credit for [bottom-line results]."

That way lies danger, he says, because if you claim full credit for benefits that follow on the heels of your training programs, "you've got to take the rap for the failures, too." Rarely or never will training be the single cause of something like a quarterly increase in revenue, for instance. "You can have an impact, but you're no more solely responsible than the marketing department that placed the ads or whatever."

Walter Wells, corporate manager of training and development for the Boston-based Gillette Co., is among those still struggling to plug in. But he views the battle from a different perspective than does Home Life's Ellen Kamp, partly because he thinks his department is tantalizingly close to the main socket. For Wells, it's not a question of opportunity or of obtaining some kind of sanction from upper management to expand the scope of his role. Instead, it's a matter of knowledge and resources. He senses that the transition from a training function that is more or less peripheral to the driving forces of a company to one that is genuinely integrated requires a sort of leap—a fundamental change not only in perspective but in the types of training done.

"When I started here nine years ago," Wells says, "a lot of generic management programs were in place—how to use MBO [management by objectives], time management, conflict resolution, communication skills and so on. [Generic programs] help, but you reach a point where that ground has been pretty well covered. To get to that next plateau, where your training is hooked straight to the business, you need something else."

As one does more and more generic training, one's clients—line managers—get more and more sophisticated, Wells notes. "Their expectations become higher. The things they want become more complex, more technical, more functional, more specific." When managers in areas like production, finance and marketing start asking for narrowly focused training that will help them or their subordinates perform esoteric, specialized tasks that might relate exclusively to the ways their particular departments run, "you're into things you don't know about," Wells says. "That's where we are now—at the edge of that transition."

The going gets tough because the HRD professional's subject-matter expertise, and the resources available to him in the form of packaged programs, consultants, etc., tend to be limited to generic topics. What do you do when the marketing manager stops asking for time-management seminars and starts asking, "How do I get better at analyzing financial

sheets?"

Skilled needs analysts and instructional designers are supposed to be able to respond to such requests by picking the brains of subject-matter experts, but Wells doesn't have a cadre of such specialists. Under Gillette's decentralized training setup, his corporate HRD staff consists of one professional and a secretary. Each major Gillette facility has someone in charge of training, but it's usually a personnel manager with other responsibilities, who reports to Wells only indirectly.

"With limited resources, you get

'I don't feel at all as if I'm out here as the Lone Change Agent.'

---

spread thinner and thinner," Wells points out. He can recite along with everyone else that "the hints you get about what line managers are doing and what their real problems are come from the relationships you build with them." But then what?

A plethora of information and advice is offered to training managers via conferences, books, magazines and other resources, but Wells finds something missing. What's needed, he says, is something that would help training managers put their understanding of the organization's business needs to work in developing specific, targeted programs. "It's easy to say. It's hard to make it happen."

Line managers

Melinda Bickerstaff has resources that Walter Wells doesn't. She spent the last two years heading up the development of a 33-module management education curriculum for six levels of American Express managers—about 4,000 people worldwide. The implementation phase will send those managers to six domestic and five international training centers, each of which has a professional HRD staff. Counting her 10 subordinates in New York, about 60 people currently report to Bickerstaff either directly or

via dotted lines on the organizational chart.

But the reason the curriculum is able to include specific modules on topics such as advertising, marketing and competitive analysis, she says, is not just because she has a number of trainers at her command. It's because the whole thing was codesigned by training professionals and line managers. Many modules also will be cotaught.

The key to plugging training into the company, Bickerstaff suggests, is to plug line managers into the training. Somebody wants a course on analyzing financial sheets? Find a line manager who is expert in the subject and get her to teach it together with a training specialist.

Line managers are magic. They are a bottomless resource for the training director. They have direct authority over trainees. They have subject-matter expertise in all sorts of specific topics, which can make for better, more focused instruction. They lend instant credibility to training programs. They make wonderful marketing aids and political henchmen.

"A staff job is probably the most difficult role to be stuck in if you want to make a real difference in the organization. You get no respect in a staff job. In some ways, I'll probably never have a better job than the four years I spent as a line manager. In the line, I got my budget, I spent it the way I wanted, and if I wanted somebody to do something, they did it. It was wonderful.

"But as a training manager, the biggest mistake you can make is to try to legislate training. People have got to want to come to training, line managers have got to want to send them, and people have got to want to apply it on the job. When you're a line manager you can tell people to do things. In training, even if you could, you can't. It doesn't work."—David Barkemeyer, director of training and development for Dow Chemical-U.S.A., Midland, MI.

"Nothing you could do yourself would have the impact of three or four line managers who have bought into what you're doing," Bickerstaff says. "There's nothing like the accounting manager team-teaching with a management-development professional .... Trainers can't learn everything about the business. They can't be credible in every area. But they can cooperate with line people."

The reason they sometimes have trouble doing so, Bickerstaff opines, comes back to the peculiar, quasi-academic reward system of the training world. "We reward individual contributors. We don't reward training people for cooperating with other personnel functions or with the company at large. Our reward system is: 'I have this bag of tricks, and the things in my bag make me valuable to the organization. I'm not going to share them with line managers.'. . . Trainers don't want to give up center stage."

By center stage, she mostly means the limelight of the classroom. The trainer wants to be the one up front with the microphone. That, after all, is one of the things trainers are supposed to be particularly good at. But Bickerstaff argues that the training director's goal ought to be "to provide tools and ways for other managers to be successful. Keep your eye on that. It's, 'How do *they* look good to their employees?' It's not, 'How can I look good?' When you look at it that way, all sorts of opportunities arise." It's almost like a Zen paradox, she suggests: "You have to give up your power in order to get it."

Bickerstaff says she sees management education as a "shared responsibility" of the training function and the line. "But it's true that when you try to implement [that idea], you get resistance from both sides: from line managers because they have to do something in addition to their jobs, and from trainers because they have to give up some of what they're good at and learn the business."

Why not go a step further and recruit all trainers from among the ranks of line managers and technical specialists? Indeed, a familiar question for many training directors (and their organizations) is whether it's easier and more effective to teach training skills to a subject-matter expert or subject matter to a training expert.

Harloe comes down solidly in favor of turning managers into trainers. Every instructor at Dunkin' Donuts' national training center in Braintree, MA has run a store, he says. "We want somebody who understands our business; we'll teach them how to train." He adds, however, that it takes six to eight months to train the trainers before they are given full responsi-

bility for classes of their own.

Barkemeyer says Dow Chemical's decentralized training function runs primarily on a pass-through basis, meaning that personnel specialists and line managers rotate through the training department on two- to five-year assignments. Barkemeyer himself got into training that way. "When I came in," he says, "I believed in that system." He still does, he says, but his belief has become less fervent as he gains a deeper appreciation for the HRD tool kit. "The more I learn about training technology, the more I realize that it's hard to pass it along."

Bickerstaff proposes that the ideal

Line managers are magic.

---

training department would include "a combination of professional trainers and people from line positions who float in and out."

That's exactly what Jack Zigon put together at Yellow Freight before he left the company a year ago to launch his own consulting business, the Zigon Performance Group of Overland Park, KS. "We hired four high-powered instructional technologists and taught them trucking. We brought in 10 high-performing line managers and taught them training." The former line people did the actual classroom work, with the professional "performance engineers" serving as their project managers on specific programs. Zigon used the line managers as presenters "for the same reason other people do—credibility. I just added a level of training expertise behind them."

Playing politics

"As a [first-level] training manager who reported to the director of HRD, I was shielded from politics. As I matured in this position [i.e., director of HRD], I learned that the most important thing in getting the department's work accomplished is to establish personal relationships with people throughout the company whom you're going to need to get the job done. That's how I define politics."—Linda Novotney Kemp.

"A big surprise to me was the positive aspects of politics in organizations. In HRD we have a bias against politics. It's a dirty word. Well, you have to accept and understand the realities of the way things work. You need to learn to see politics as a way to get things done.

"My bias at first was to run from it—to distance myself. Fortunately, a vice president took me aside and told me I had to understand *how the political game was played in the organization. Then I could choose whether to play or not. But I could not choose not to understand.*—Geoff Bellman.

If politics is a dirty word in organizations, it's mostly because the term tends to call up images either of empire building or of rear ends—kissing them or covering them. In the best sense, however, politics for the training manager is nothing more than a way to plug in and stay plugged in.

Everything Zigon and Harloe and Bickerstaff say about focusing on the key problems of the business, and about recruiting and using line managers in training, has plenty to do with effective training. But it clearly has to do with politics, too.

One thing advice-givers tell you ad nauseum about being a training director is that you need top-management support—as in, "Your training efforts will never be successful unless you get top-management support." The axiom often pops up in connection with griping about recalcitrant line managers who don't want to play along with the training manager on some project. And it suggests a scenario like this: Training director determines that program X would be a good thing. Goes straight to CEO. Convinces CEO that program X is vital. CEO leans on relevant line managers. Line managers allow training director to run them and/or their subordinates through program X.

Several of the training managers we spoke to suggested that this top-down power model is backwards. "I've modified my view of 'getting top-management support,' " says Home Life's Kamp. "You get support where you can. Where can I have influence? If it's in the middle-management ranks, I want the middle ranks. Initially, I work with people who are willing to work with me."

In training—more, perhaps, than in any other function—support is something you have to build among the sergeants and lieutenants and colonels, not something you seize from the general and then ram down the troops' throats. "It's a slow process," Kamp says. "It doesn't necessarily start from the top. But it can end there, because now the president isn't just hearing about [program X] from me. When we wanted to start our executive development course, we went first to the president's direct reports. By the time we took it to the president, we had powerful allies."

Zigon makes a related point. "Nobody ever told me how handy a marketing and sales background was going to come in when I became a training manager, and how important it is to know the difference between the two. When I talked to my peers in other companies, the conversations centered on how to convince top management to let us do what we wanted to do—a fancy needs assessment or whatever. That's selling: having a product and looking for ways to sell it. Marketing starts with a need and creates a product to satisfy it.

"Trainers have a technological orientation: 'I want to use my technology.' Instead of a selling role, you need to adopt a marketing role. I found myself primarily in marketing, then in selling, then in training."

The very concept of top-management support means different things to different people in different types of organizations. On the one hand, Zigon and Harloe argue strenuously that what you want is not just support from the top, but active participation. "Trainers mistake assent for support," says Harloe. "Allowing you to run a program is just permission to operate. In essence, you're being told to run along and play. That's not support, and it shows in budget cuts when training goes out the door."

Roger O'Brien, a regional training officer for the U.S. Department of Housing and Urban Development, takes an opposite view. Based in Glenview, IL, O'Brien heads up HUD's training efforts in a six-state region. "I get a lot of support from the organization—to the extent that they leave me alone to do things," he says. HUD directors "don't give me a lot of detailed information about what they want done," which suits O'Brien fine. Every 18 months he conducts "a relatively formal needs assessment" that involves all managers and some non-management employees in the region.

MANAGING TRAINERS: HOW WELL-SHOD

BY JACK GORDON

There are two kinds of training managers in the world: those who come to training from other line or staff management roles, and those who start as trainers and work up to management. Among the latter group are many people in the singular position of having taught management skills to others before getting a chance to practice those skills themselves. And regardless of which route they take to reach the job, training managers often have the dubious pleasure of managing people who teach management. Everybody still here?

The whole thing raises two interesting questions. First, how hard is it to translate skills you have taught into skills you practice?

"Companies [hiring training directors] are looking for management capability first and training knowledge second. I have trouble finding people who know the HRD field and can also manage a staff. That involves politics, budgets, performance evaluations, benefits—everything trainers have talked about for somebody else. The 'Shoemaker's Children' syndrome comes into play: 'I'd rather talk about it than do it.' I'd say about 80% of trainers don't really want to be training managers. They like what they're doing."—David Brinkerhoff, Abbott Smith Associates.

"I'm not sure that [teaching management and 'doing management'] are transferable skills. You just don't know until you're there. I think a lot of it depends on things like individual style, drive and adaptability. Managers are a special breed. You can have all the book learning and theoretical understanding in the world, but unless there's some 'X' quality to help you transfer that, it doesn't work. It's almost a passion; there has to be an emotional hook. Teaching management can help prepare you to become a good manager, but it doesn't guarantee anything."—Paul A. Ross, personnel manager for the internal field service group of Digital Equipment Corp.

"You could be a hell of a trainer and fail totally as a director of training. There's a world of difference between teaching management and doing it. Take the difference between constructive feedback and criticism. Oh, boy, do we ever talk about that well. We conduct role plays, we give trainees lots of terrific feedback—it's easy as long as nobody's emotions are really involved. But you take a trainer who has taught constructive criticism, and give him a big board presentation to make and a secretary who forgot to make his plane reservations. It's amazing how fast constructive feedback goes out the window."—Robert Harloe, Dunkin' Donuts of America.

"If you came up through the management training ranks, [you'll be in for a big surprise] when you come face-to-face with your own needs for authority and control. You've been telling managers for years to be participative; you may find you don't do that well yourself. And it's especially hard when you've got a staff of [management and organization development] experts watching your every move and seeing how inconsistent it is with what you've been preaching. . . . After years of preaching shared responsibility, I still feel embarrassed about my need for authority."—Geoff Bellman, GMB Associates.

"One pleasant surprise to me was that practicing what you preach really works. It's one thing to talk about selecting employees based on a systematic analysis of the job, about giving them proper feedback and incentives, about trying to 'catch them doing something right' and so forth. It's another thing to find out that when you do all that, it really does make your job easier. Some things that sound like platitudes really work. [Once you learn that],

ARE THE SHOEMAKER'S CHILDREN?

your confidence in selling training to line managers goes up tremendously. And they're more likely to listen to you because now you sound like you know what you're talking about. . . . Line managers notice if you don't practice what you preach. If you're having trouble selling training, that may be part of the reason."—Jack Zigon, Zigon Performance Group.

What about managing people who teach management? Unusually easy? Unusually tough?

"Managing trainers is hard. They supposedly know how it's all supposed to be done—how you're supposed to motivate, communicate and give a reprimand—so their expectations of managers are higher. . . . Also, trainers often are less flexible, less willing to adapt to the needs of the organization, than people elsewhere in the company. Trainers want to stand apart, and sometimes that's valuable. But sometimes it makes them reluctant to roll up their sleeves and get in there with the other managers and workers. . . .

"I was surprised at the amount of resistance to change you find among training professionals. The heart of our profession is the idea of the change agent, the change manager. But when it comes to changing ourselves to meet current needs, we're just as guilty as the line manager who doesn't want to automate or doesn't want to delegate authority. For example, I see far too much belief in the classroom as an effective training vehicle. Why is it that we're just now beginning to see that we can embed training through technology—job aids, software that coaches, hardware that eliminates some training needs?"—Steve Floyd, Floyd Consulting and Design.

"Trainers tend to be prima donnas. They value the individual and individual contributions above all. They expect their own contributions to be valued highly, but they have trouble working within the organizational structure. [For example, take the participation issue.] Sometimes you can't come to consensus. When the [participative decision making] ends, somebody's got to be the boss. A lot of times, people just have to move forward under the guidance of their manager. That becomes a real test for you as the manager.

"It's also hard to get trainers to stick with projects they start. People in HRD are creative types who like to move on to new things. Well, it usually takes two to four years in the implementation phase of a project to bring about real change."—Geoff Bellman.

"I think it's easy to manage training professionals. [At Yellow Freight System] I said, 'Hey, I'm human, I make mistakes. You people are trained in this technology [i.e., management theory]. If you catch me not giving you clear expectations or not giving you enough feedback, ask. If you're punished in some way for doing a good job, tell me. If you notice something missing that keeps you from doing a good job, I'm holding you responsible for telling me now."—Jack Zigon.

"I find that training people in general are very critical of how management manages. It applies both to their own managers and to company management. That's a caution to trainers as they move up in the organization: You need to make that leap from critiquing management to being part of it. You need to be able to identify with upper management. As managers, we have to pay attention to the progress we're making toward the ideal. Maybe because we [trainers] are so conscious of trying to fix things, we tend not to look for what people are doing right."—Linda Novotney Kemp, Dayton Hudson Department Stores.

Reprinted from TRAINING, June 1986

"That gives us all sorts of opportunities to meet needs."

In one important sense, many training managers say, their political challenge boils down to a balancing act. On one side of the scale is the desire to "do training right," to apply instructional and performance technology the way they believe it ought to be applied. And on the other side?

"The training manager's role is a classic case of being caught in the middle," says Steve Floyd, former manager of Coca-Cola's bottler training group and now head of Floyd Consulting and Design of Atlanta. "It's critical to maintain good relationships with line managers in sales, production or wherever, and to try to satisfy their legitimate day-to-day operating needs. But it's also critical to have a high regard for your own profession—not to leave that behind. It's always a tough sell to do the right thing in training, because most problems wind up being systemic [and therefore not conducive to a quick fix, which is what line managers want]. Finally, you have to try to satisfy some long-term missions or visions for the organization. The real challenge is to achieve harmony among those three things."

Dayton Hudson's Novotney sees it as a question of where you draw your lines. Sometimes the textbook models for doing training right just don't apply in the real world. For example, she says, if you adhere to the principle that 150 hours ("or whatever the textbook figure is now") of design time is supposed to go into each hour of actual instruction, "you wouldn't be able to do any MIS training at all." Typically, she points out, computerized management information systems "aren't finished until they come on-line," meaning that the bugs aren't worked out and some details of how the system actually will work aren't final until people are supposed to begin using it. That gives you an immediate need for training with zero time to plug any gaps in the instruction you were able to develop beforehand. So where do you make your stand in terms of doing training the way it "ought" to be done?

"You've got to decide what's negotiable and what's not," she says. "What won't you give up?" As far as Novotney is concerned, "You can compromise on how to get something done, but not on what you're doing. If

707

we're going to do any training, I want to be sure we're really teaching somebody something they don't know how to do. I don't want to go in with training to fix a non-training problem. So we won't do a program until we've done some type of analysis to determine what the problem is and how we'll know if we fix it."

That's where Novotney draws her line, but she draws it quietly and tactfully. "I don't play it up, because we'll get accused of analysis paralysis or of being too research-based."

What if you do discover that the situation a line manager presents to you is not a training problem—that something else is needed? "You need negotiating skills, and you have to be able to recommend what that something else is," she warns. "You can't just say, 'Training won't fix it.'"

Bickerstaff attacks the same issue with entirely different tactics. "Go with what managers want to do instead of telling them you know better," she advises. If the financial group has done its own kind of needs analysis and the manager wants financial training, give him financial training—or at least start the wheels in motion. "You don't think it's a training problem? Well, that's what they want. Do it first, then come back and talk about how maybe we can do some other things, too."

There's a catch to her method. You have to have a policy that says you only launch training projects on request, and that somebody from the

---

The trainer's reward system is: 'I have this bag of tricks and I'm not going to share them'

---

line department making the request has to help you design and implement the training. The line manager, in other words, must be actively involved in the process from the word go so that he's hooked into *your* analysis of the problem and, ahem, your efforts to figure out what kind of training program would solve it.

"If managers are involved in the design and implementation, and it doesn't work, they know it doesn't work and now they know *why* it doesn't work. Hopefully, they find out in the design process [and you

never have to run the poorly conceived program]." If they aren't involved and the program fails, Bickerstaff says, "they just blame training. We've been caught in that trap too many times in this profession."

What if managers request training but refuse to participate in creating and delivering it? "You probably ought not to do it," she says. "But you can only say no if it's standard practice for training to be a joint responsibility."

In a nutshell, says Geoff Bellman, politics means building relationships with key people in the organization who can provide you with both information about the business and support for your activities. First you have to cultivate the relationships. But then you have to keep them. And there's a secret to doing that.

"Maintain your relationships with these people *especially when you don't need them* [e.g., to support some specific project]," Bellman says. "Develop a web out there and tend it regularly, as a spider would, so when they see you coming it's not just a sudden appearance that means you want something. Be around when you don't want something. That allows you to find out what's going on."

Reprinted from TRAINING, June 1986

TEN WAYS TO UNDERMINE YOUR HRD EFFORT*

You may not agree that each of these errors is fatal, but at least be aware that some heavy-hitters see potential danger in them

BY RON ZEMKE

Call these "learnings"—lessons garnered from seven years of interviewing the best and the brightest in the field. Call this a primer of surefire ways to blunt the organizational effectiveness of your training and human resource development HRD effort. Consider it a Christmas present from the heavy-hitters and go-getters—those individuals who have raised their training and/or HRD efforts to positions of prominence and impact in their organizations and who have, over the years, been willing to take time to tell TRAINING how they did it.

Warning! You won't necessarily—and needn't—agree that every one of these "ways to whiff it" is a devastating policy or a fatal faux pas. You may even see one or two as *success* principles rather than blunders. Fine. But be aware that someone sees a down side or potential danger in the idea you cherish.

In truth, none of the pros we have talked with would decry all 10 as disastrous ideas. But each is a practice that has been cited, convincingly and frequently, as having imbedded within it some seed of organizational self-destruction. Each has, at the very least, stood the test of remaining intriguing to us over time. Stitched together, we feel, the 10 make up a thought-provoking sampler of ways to turn an effective training and HRD effort to mud.

ERROR 1: *Fail to define the role of HRD in your organization.*

Ben Tregoe of Kepner-Tregoe, Inc. in Princeton, NJ, and Geary Rummler, who heads The Rummler Group of Summit, NJ, both have argued that to be optimally effective, the head of the HRD function must understand and agree with top-management's concept of what the organization is trying to become. And the HRD effort must be structured in such a way as to help accomplish *that* mission. Should your department function as a corporate university? As a performance-problem-engineering team? The answer lies not in some mystical measure of right and wrong, but in discovering the most appropriate tactical fit with organizational strategy.

Being strategic and effective in your HRD efforts, knowing who you are and are not, what business you are and are not in, requires that you take the time to think through and publish a clear-cut mission statement and a menu of responsibilities. Without such a charter you will never be able to evaluate and modify your HRD function, and you will dilute your chances of becoming a key part of the organization.

ERROR 2: *Allow HRD to report to middle management.*

Some of the finest people in the world—some of our best friends—are middle managers. But when it comes to clout, the kind needed to ensure a long-term involvement in HRD, you need positive support at the highest level. The chief executive officer (CEO) is ultimately responsible for attracting, developing and retaining talent in the organization. To whom the HRD unit reports is the choice, ultimately, of the CEO. If, by design or neglect, the unit reports to middle management, with little or no access to upper management, it shows something important about the CEO's concern for and interest in developing people. At best, the top dog has an impoverished idea of the contribution people-development efforts can make to the development of the organization.

Under these conditions, the HRD manager will never attain the posture necessary to be really effective in the organization. The least the HRD manager should settle for is reporting to a senior officer close to the executive office. The ideal setup, of course, has the HRD officer reporting to the president, managing director or CEO.

At Olin Corp. in Stamford, CT, president John M. Henske considers centralized control of HRD an operating necessity. To ensure proper attention to the area, Henske established a corporate HRD team, headed by the vice president of administration, that reports directly to him. Team members include the employee relations directors from each operating group and from the corporate staff, the medical director, compensation chief, management staff and personnel services director and the director of development and training.

As a result, training director Boris "Bo" Sichuk is accountable for the quality and effectiveness of programs run by every operating group of the corporation. He is directly responsible to the HRD committee and, through it, to Henske. That's pretty good positioning: good enough that Sichuk was able to budget an unheard of 80,000 hours of start-up training for a new plant opening a few years ago.

Obviously, Sichuk has access to

---

*The concept of cataloging particularly effective ways to "screw up" owes its origin to Dr. Olaf Isachsen, president of the Institute for Management Development, Oakland, CA. It was spawned during a 1978 interview when Isachsen was vice president-management development for Wells Fargo Bank in San Francisco. Since then he has had a great influence on their shape and number.

more resources and influence than HRD people whose direct reporting level is significantly lower. In addition, training and HRD results are highly visible.

ERROR 3: *Claim measurable bottom-line results for HRD efforts.*

The contention that training and HRD efforts can prove their bottom-line results may be the greatest myth ever concocted by the profession. Someplace along the way, we in HRD have convinced ourselves that our efforts can show a direct, measurable contribution to profits. Some suggest we aren't doing our jobs if we don't try to claim so many cents of profit per share for our activities. It's a fantasy that can rise up and bite us.

Ian E. McLaughlin, president of Training and Education Consultants, Inc., brings the point home with this story: "When I was training director for Del Monte Corp., I once ran before-and-after tests to prove the value of a specific training program. We did an outstanding needs analysis, put on a terrific program and the results were top-notch. The following three months saw this district move to the top third in sales of the item we wanted to see improvement in. I turned in a report showing dollar increases and everything else I could think of.

"Then the deluge! The product manager claimed credit for his support of the effort. The local sales managers said they had concentrated their efforts on the item after our workshop, and claimed credit. The regional sales manager pointed out that if headquarters wanted a sales workshop on one item, it obviously must be important, so he had exerted pressure on the item.

"All in all, I learned several lessons from the episode. First, as training director I should never try to take sole credit for increased sales results ... and sometimes maybe not even a little bit of credit. Second, profitability is never a one-department or one-action result. Training should be built into marketing plans just as are advertising and promotional activities; training is part of the total action plan, not a poor relative and not a panacea. Third, a better measurement for me is having a trainee return home and a few weeks later write, 'Hey, I followed your ideas and I just closed the biggest sale of my life! Thanks!' "

Question: How many other staff people make such an absurd claim? The controller? The treasurer? The

janitor? The typing pool? Research and development? Of course they don't. HRD, like every staff function, exists to support people on the line; to help line management and line operatives attain superior performance. Self-aggrandizement only squelches the motivation of line personnel and contributes to unproductive conflict.

Answer one final question: If the organization has an unprofitable, over-budget year, how many cents per share of that outcome are you willing to be accountable for? We can't have it both ways.

If this one upsets you and you still feel the need to show bottom-line results, perhaps you'll appreciate the view of Jay Beecroft, who until his recent retirement was top trainer at the giant 3M Company. "No training group can expect to gain influence without committing to operational results," he says. But, he adds quickly, "A training manager has a responsibility to realism. Management must know what is and is not possible through training, even if it detracts from the image."

**CEN WAYS CO BLUNC
CHE HRD EFFORC**

FAIL CO DEFINE CHE ROLE OF HRD
IN YOUR ORGANIZACION.

ALLOW HRD CO REPORC CO A
MIDDLE-MANAGER.

CLAIM MEASURABLE BOCCOM-LINE
RESULCS.

"PLAY" LINE MANAGER.

USE 'OCHER-DIRECCED' ASSESSMENC
CECHNIQUES.

PERFORM IN CHE CLASSROOM.

CRACK AND REPORC ACCIVICIES.

HIRE A LARGE IN-HOUSE PROGRAM
DEVELOPMENC SCAFF.

BUY FADS.

EXEMPC HRD FROM HRD.

© PERFORMANCE RESEARCH

ERROR 4: *Allow the HRD staff to 'play act' as line managers.*

When still a corporate HRD officer, Olaf Isachsen characterized his job as that of an extra head and hands for line managers to use in solving problems. "My job, like the job of every staff manager, was to be a resource to line management. They make the profit, we don't. Their profitability pays for our luxury of being able to take some time, step back and help them grapple with unknown concepts."

The problem is, we sometimes confuse thinking *with* and thinking *for* line management. If the HRD staff is making decisions for line managers or making unilateral moves that usurp the time line people budgeted for productive pursuits, the staff is "playing" line manager.

This indicates that performance criteria for both line and staff are inadequate, which puts the HRD director in a no-win situation. Line managers are almost universally gifted at withholding commitment from decisions to which they have had no input and for which they were not responsible. Facilitating a line manager's decision-making is appropriate; accepting responsibility for making decisions the line manager would prefer to abdicate is inappropriate.

A humiliating personal example may make the point. As an eager-beaver training director for a major New York financial institution, I had the bad sense to tell a senior personnel VP that he needed a certain genre of supervisory training because his turnover rate of 17.5% was too high. His response: "It is my job to decide when turnover is too high or just right. It is your job to find and focus the data. Don't ever attempt to usurp my responsibility again."

From there, he proceeded to get nasty. But he was 100% right. I had attempted to do his job, to play line manager, and that was *not* what I was getting paid for.

Frequently, trainers are asked to decide if training is needed. The real job is to work with management to determine whether training—or any other intervention—might be an appropriate response to a given problem. But in the end, the decision belongs to line management.

Tregoe suggests that the HRD job at its best is a data-gathering job: a search for information in and outside the organization about conditions that will have an impact on its long- and short-term existence. And how can you resist this line from Beecroft: "Our most critical task is to help line managers spot the problems, to sort real problems from perceived problems. Once the problem is identified, most people can find a reasonable solution."

ERROR 5:
Use 'other-directed' assessment techniques.

According to Allen Tough of the Ontario Institute for Studies in Education, the typical adult engages in five learning projects a year. These projects or, as Tough defines them, "highly deliberate efforts to gain and retain certain definite knowledges and skills or to change in some other way," typically consume 100 hours of work or study. Eighty percent of the time they are planned and executed by the individual on his own; 73% of the time they are job-related. The most common motivation is a desire to get better at, or develop new skills for, a specific task. In short, people learn because they want to, and they most frequently want to

when they find they need to improve their ability to do something related to their jobs.

Assessment by a superior, an assessment center or a battery of standardized tests is "external" or "other-directed" assessment. The individual "judged" in this manner to be in need of learning is likely to reject the assessment as inaccurate.

Self-assessment tends to be more credible. The individual must be able to respond to an authentic situation and interpret his or her performance without an assessor's aid. While "other-directed" assessment can be perfectly valid from a technical standpoint, self-assessment tends to result in the instigation of a learning project more frequently than does external assessment.

A condemnation of the assessment-center concept? It might sound like it, but it isn't. Nor does assessment-center guru William C. Byham of Development Dimensions International in Pittsburgh interpret it as such. Says Byham, "Developmentally oriented or career-planning assessment centers do combine self-evaluation with the assessment-center process itself. This is especially true in diagnostic centers where the individual is there only for his or her own benefit and there is a greater level of trust and openness."

ERROR 6: *Spend a large percentage of your time in the classroom.*

The head of HRD is a manager first and a specialist second—or third. Like every other manager in the organization, the training director is responsible for the total performance of a unit or department. If the HRD chief insists on being the star classroom performer, he or she eventually will jeopardize his or her image with peers as a "fellow manager." Worse yet, senior management may come to regard the HRD department as "Sam/Samantha and his/her band of classroom crusaders" rather than as a group of people capable of making a meaningful contribution to the company's goals.

Isachsen wrestled with the problem of whether or not to take the stage and chose to demur: "My mission when I was at Wells Fargo was to create conditions that would cause line managers to improve, but without putting HRD in the limelight. I had to forego the pleasures of the classroom-trainer role."

A different view is taken by Ray Crapo of the education and training branch of the New York State Office

of Court Administration. "The training director," he says, "should be a teacher/participant/facilitator of instruction, not just a management expert. And it is up to training directors to 'sell' this idea to top management so that management will respect them as much as it would a consultant who brings in the same program and expertise." Consequently, Crapo does train in the classroom from time to time.

Two knowledgeable people, two different opinions. But consider a final question: What one thing do managers and executives fear most? Give up? Time and again, surveys have shown that executives are most fearful of speaking in public. Trainers *live* to be on their feet talking. Unless you can find a way to turn the difference to your advantage, why risk being judged "not like us" by executives with chronic flop-sweat syndrome?

ERROR 7:
Track and report activities.

If your year-end report to senior management reads, "... 892 people attended 2,489 hours of instruction in 1982 through 103 course offerings ..." you probably are blowing it. You would be better off tracking and reporting on change. Changes in performance, productivity, even attitudes, would be more meaningful than a tabulation of classroom hours.

Reporting that "the HRD unit assisted the word-processing department in efforts to decrease employee absences and the percentage of return work" would be an improvement. Asking program participants, their subordinates and superiors to evaluate changes in the participants' behavior over time—and summarizing those changes when reporting to senior management—would be better still. The tracking and reporting of *activities* suggests a belief on your part that being busy counts. In fact, only results count.

Paul H. Chaddock, vice president of Boston-based Lechmere Stores, a division of Dayton Hudson Corp., uses the concept of critical ratios to measure his management development efforts in the belief that "we should make our measurements as parallel to the accounting measures used in the organization as possible. The senior management of most companies is taught to understand reports that talk of inventory expenses, capital, costs and so on. Our measures should at least parallel those. And we should report information in ratio form. Management is used to looking at percentages and ratios. We should adhere to that approach. It is comfortable and has credibility as well."

Chaddock has found five measures useful in his work at Lechmere and elsewhere in the Dayton Hudson organization.

• **Placement ratio:** comparison of promotable or placeable internal talent with talent brought in from outside.

• **Backup continuity:** comparison of available, qualified managerial backups to the number of slots for which backup is judged appropriate.

• **High performer-retention ratio:** comparison of people evaluated as better-than-average who leave the company to those who stay.

• **High potential-usage ratio:** comparison of the percentage of managers rated as capable of two levels of advancement in five years, to the percentage of those who are, in fact, moved up.

• **Management effectiveness ratio:** a set of fairly flexible comparisons—top-management payroll vs. total payroll, exempt vs. nonexempt employees, payroll vs. cost of sales or net sales and other measures for tracking management effectiveness.

ERROR 8: *Hire and maintain a large, in-house program-development staff.*

As we mentioned earlier, most adult learning takes place at the adult's pace, in the adult's own mode of preference and at the adult's own direction. Aside from our contention that mandatory classroom training struggles against these facts, the in-house development of programs has five other potential problems.

• In-house productions generally are limited by the resourcefulness of in-house employees. Their skills and abilities alone determine the quality of their programs.

• Sooner or later, activities become important "track and measure" items because of the constant need to justify a large in-house staff. This moves the focus away from helping others perform better.

• Internal programs become predictable, safe and boring as the ceiling of internal talent is reached.

• If you build a program internally and it bombs, a crisis ensues. If you buy a program, try it out and discard it, your liability is limited.

• Keeping the in-house staff busy eventually tends to become the pre-

eminent HRD management concern, and training programs come to be seen as the only solution to performance problems. If you are zero-base budgeted, as you should be, most management time will be spent talking others into attending your programs and authorizing the development of new ones.

Isachsen recommends thinking of the data-processing and information-management functions as analogous to the training function. "The computer-systems people don't do a systems analysis and then go out in the garage and build the organization a computer. Of course not. They buy a computer, adapt it to the system they designed and move on. "Why shouldn't training people be allowed to follow the same model?" the crafty Norwegian asks.

A corollary: If you don't have an internal development staff, you will have to buy or lease programs when you have a problem that can be addressed through training. The temptation is to work with the last vendor who brought in a winner for you. Take care. No vendor can possibly have the best answer to all problems. But beyond expertise, becoming a captive of a given vendor damages one's organizational credibility. Once you begin hearing comments like, "Well, Harry, what XYZ program are you pushing this year?" there is no need to ask for whom the bell tolls.

In Beecroft shorthand, this rule reads: "No training department can be all things to all people. We have to bring in outside talent and help continually just to stay even with progress. The future is in problem analysis, not program building. To sell to the need, you have to know the need."

ERROR 9: *Follow the fads and fancies of the field.*

The sign on your door should read: "Vendors with dubious products beware." Current "in" things should be investigated rather than dismissed out of hand, but the HRD director who goes in search of "some of that behavior-modeling or right brain-left brain or assertiveness-training stuff" simply because everyone else is doing it, has fallen into a trap.

There are no shortcuts to performance improvement. The job is to create conditions within the existing reward-and-punishment systems that will foster lasting improvement. Sometimes that requires knowledge and

skill programs; sometimes it requires change in the system and/or culture. Usually it requires investigation and consultation.

A corollary is that the HRD group, to be most effective, must avoid the appearance of having pet social causes as well as pet training programs or training solutions. As Olin's Sichuk puts it, "You can have all kinds of great social values, and you should. But if you're interested in selling those values and not in problem solving, then perhaps you're better off as a consultant outside the organization."

ERROR 10: *Exempt HRD from HRD.*

If the HRD department does not take its own medicine, others will be skeptical. Aside from the embarrassment of the "cobbler's children syndrome," professionals in HRD must be aware of the intellectual and emotional impact of HRD efforts on the client organization. And, of course, HRD units need performance improvement as much as do other units. Sometimes they even need to bring outsiders in to facilitate their internal development.

If you have a professional staff, when was the last time one of your people was hired away by a line manager impressed by that person's talent and promise? Do you have formal, written development plans for your department? If you believe that career development and career planning are conservation measures—that they keep us from squandering valuable resources—how would you explain an HRD staff without internal development plans?

To drop one final Beecroftism, "People who don't grow continually become inefficient, then ineffective and finally obsolete." That's just as true of trainers as it is of managers, CEOs and engineers.

A last word

The HRD function can have a significant impact on organizational effectiveness, efficiency and long-term survival. Without the right people with the right skills in the right places at the right times, that survival is in serious jeopardy. To ignore the wisdom implicit in these 10 little land mines is to put the development effort, and ultimately the organization's survival, in jeopardy.

Reprinted from TRAINING, December 1982

CRASH TRAINING

Suddenly, you have to train a lot of
people in very little time.
When the sky is falling, how do you
avoid getting flattened?

BY BEVERLY GEBER

I t's tax time, that grisly time of
year when fear and loathing over-
take most Americans as they settle their bills with their government.
At Arthur Andersen & Co., Michelle
Landow and her fellow trainers must
endure the annual chore just like everyone else. Yet Landow would probably tell you that dealing with the IRS is
a day at the beach compared with
what she and her colleagues faced
when Congress passed the Tax Reform Act of 1986, a move that up-
ended most of the old tax rules.

President Reagan had no sooner
pressed ink to the bill than Arthur
Andersen accountants across the
country—spurred on by their anxious
clients—began clamoring for the low-
down on the new tax rules. Landow,
senior education manager at Arthur
Andersen's Center for Professional
Education in St. Charles, IL, had all
of six months to completely overhaul
the public accounting company's
basic tax curriculum. Meanwhile,
others had to see to it that the company's accountants had some broad-
brush information to tide them over.

Or take this situation. Eighteen
months ago, when customer service
training was starting to sizzle as the
latest hot item on the national business menu, a vice president of a major retailing chain decided that every

single employee in the company's 37
department stores needed eight
hours of customer service training.
Twenty-thousand people in all. Linda
Novotney Kemp's eyes still widen
when she describes the assignment.
As director of human resources development for Dayton Hudson Department Stores, it was her job to
make sure those 20,000 employees
received their training before the onset of the Christmas season in October. That was a bare four months
from the time the vice president conceived his idea.

Although these situations arose in
two very different industries, the
trainers involved had something in
common. Sheer panic, for one. The
kind of panic that eventually strikes
any trainer who's been in the field
awhile. You can give such situations
any number of names: instant training, crisis training or, particularly
evocative, *crash* training. Whatever
you call it, it means that you have to
react to a sudden training need. You
have much less time than you need to
prepare a training program from
scratch, and a lot more people than
you'd like to train.

Fortunately, not all of the rush orders are as daunting as the ones at Arthur Andersen and Dayton Hudson.
Like so many other things, crash
training comes in various sizes.

Usually, outside forces bring about

the crisis. The precipitating event
might be the introduction of a new
product, which must be veiled in se-
crecy until the final moment due to
the highly competitive nature of the
market. Perhaps there's a strike, and
the company decides to hire a whole
new set of replacement workers to
keep the business operating. Maybe
it's a sudden merger or acquisition.
Or a new government regulation.

But the curious thing about crash
training, the thing that doesn't seem
obvious in the initial horror at the
size of the project, is that it often offers a wonderful opportunity to people in the human resources development (HRD) business. Crash training
offers the ultimate challenge for contributing to the bottom line. This is
the training manager's big chance to
show line managers that she's not
paralyzed by process, that she can
think on her feet and do the job that
needs to be done—now.

In the process, she might find a
better way to conduct her training, or
she might cement relationships with
other departments. And ultimately, if
she's successful, there's a supreme
payoff. She could gain the admiration
and gratitude of top management because she has contributed nimbly
and decisively to the bottom line.

Denial, bargaining, acceptance

Though Dayton Hudson's Kemp
says now that the vice president's request for customer service training
was an opportunity for her 12-person
department at the company's Minneapolis headquarters, she didn't feel
that way at the start. Once she absorbed the initial shock of having to
train 20,000 people within three
months with a course that hadn't
been conceived yet, she counted
backward from the deadline. She realized that if she left enough time to
deliver the training, she had only six
weeks to develop the eight-hour
course. She put everything else on
hold.

She envisioned how she wanted
the finished product to look and
quickly pulled together a small planning team that included in-house advertising and video specialists. "We
wanted a professional-looking package and we needed video to deliver
it," she explains.

For the first few weeks, Kemp's
team met daily for four hours merely

to decide what they wanted to include in the eight-hour course and how to structure it. During this process, Kemp realized she had a rare chance to achieve a long-held goal—developing a formal orientation program.

She knew that good customer service training is far more than smile training. Employees need to understand the business, their role in its success and the importance of the customer to that business. Translated into a course, that meant half a day devoted to the history of the business, emphasizing the 1984 merger of the Dayton and Hudson companies, and four additional hours on customer service. Together, the two segments became the company's new orientation program.

Within six weeks, the planning team had created the program, which included five videos from three to 15 minutes long, printed materials and leaders' guides. They may have been quick, says Kemp, but they weren't dirty. "We didn't just throw it together. We felt proud at the end of it," she says.

In order to deliver the program to all company employees, the HRD department had to hand off delivery to the stores. Nearly 350 store managers and supervisors received two days of train-the-trainer sessions before they fanned out to the stores.

The evaluation sheets told Kemp that the employees liked the new program. Most important, it was a hit with top management. The executive who originally requested the course asked Kemp to present an overview to top executives, each of whom then asked her to brief their divisions. Because the HRD department delivered a polished product, quickly, on a topic with direct impact on profits, HRD's stock rose, Kemp says.

It was consuming work, especially for the first six weeks, but Kemp thinks she came out of it with a recipe for trainer bliss. The ingredients are an important assignment that matters deeply to top management combined with an impossible deadline. "It was a peak experience," she says.

A taxing challenge

The Dayton Hudson experience was unusual in that the essential training challenge came down from top management. More often, it sneaks in from the outside. The train-ing department may or may not see it coming. And even if there is some foreshadowing, the actual training need often fails to take shape until the last minute. Trying to plan for it early is like trying to lasso fog. That was the case for Arthur Andersen's Michelle Landow. Throughout the summer of 1986, Congress debated the details of tax reform legislation, changing its mind frequently. In Oc-

---

What do these situations have in common? Sheer panic.

---

tober, the president signed the sweeping reform bill.

Instantly, executives from the accounting firm's 70 U.S. offices were asking for preliminary interpretations of the new law so they could tell their clients how to restructure their finances before 1987 began. First, the new laws had to be understood. Then, the accountants needed briefings. Finally, nearly 300 hours of course instruction had to be revised before the following May, when training would begin for the following tax season. It was the most taxing challenge the education center had ever faced.

Luckily, Landow had a head start on her project. "We knew something was going to happen. So [we tried] to get as much information as soon as possible," she says. Arthur Andersen lobbyists in Washington kept track of the legislation throughout the spring and summer. By fall, an instructional designer and a tax expert had been dispatched to Washington so they could quickly develop the informational updates that would go to the firm's accountants and the slide show that would be shown to clients after the bill became law.

Meanwhile, Landow was in St. Charles, IL, deciding how she and her staff of trainers would tackle the revision of the tax curriculum. Normally, she called upon subject-matter experts in the company to interpret each year's tax law changes, then asked the instructional designers to blend the new information into the courses. Using statistics from past years that showed the number of changes they had to make and the number of tax experts they had needed to accomplish the task, Landow devised a formula that told her she needed nearly 100 subject-matter experts to make this project work. In addition, she would need to lean heavily on "specialty teams"—groups of experts in specific areas of tax law who could interpret the law's gray areas.

"It was a much greater request than we had ever had before. But top management thought it was extremely important and they made the requests for the people to serve in training," Landow says. "And people came through."

In addition to specialty teams, Landow assembled an advisory committee of Arthur Andersen partners to make sure that she was including the right information and inserting it into the proper places in the tax course curriculum. To show how the entire project would work, she created a flowchart that gave time lines, and showed who would be working on what subjects and when they'd be doing it.

Then the grind began. From November through May, the tax experts, instructional designers and support staff spent 30,000 man-hours writing new material. Not everyone was working all the time because the office could hold only 30 subject-matter experts at a time. Some of them needed a brief orientation because they had never before worked with the training department.

By the time the annual training courses were to begin, Landow's division was ready. Her initial estimate of the resources she would need was accurate. Top executives were pleased that the new information was ready in time, correct and logically placed in the curriculum.

"Initially, in the early summer, I thought, 'How are we ever going to do this?' We had to reorganize our whole shop," Landow says. "But once we got into it and it was going fairly smoothly, it was a wonderful feeling to realize we really could do it."

The rock-and-hard-place syndrome

Sometimes, you know what you

TEN TIPS FOR TEAM LEADERS

Project teams undertake tasks that range from planning the company picnic to turning out the next generation of computers. But they all face the same challenges: Get the job done on time, within budget and according to the required quality standards.

While individual members often work independently throughout a project, they also count on the project's manager or leader to provide unity and direction. W. Alan Randolph, senior associate of San Diego-based Blanchard Training and Development Inc., and Barry Z. Posner, authors of *Effective Project Planning and Management: Getting the Job Done* (Prentice-Hall, 1987), suggest 10 tips that will help project leaders manage effectively.

• *Set a clear goal.* The more clearly you and your team can visualize the results, the more effectively you can plan how to achieve them.

• *Determine the project objectives.* Now that you've established a goal, break it down into smaller steps. Make sure the team members understand their individual roles in each step.

• *Establish relationships, time estimates and checkpoints.* Identify the relationships among the various project activities. Estimate the time needed to complete each one. Set checkpoints to monitor their progress.

• *Create a picture of the project schedule.* Get those relationships and checkpoints down on paper. Use GANTT, PERT or other project-management charts to help team members visualize the overall plan.

• *Direct people individually and as a team.* Know each person's unique skills and talents, and work to build the group into a strong team of contributors. Bone up on theories of team building and group dynamics. Apply them.

• *Reinforce commitment and excitement.* Keep the goal of the project in front of the group throughout the process. Be sure to praise team members for their accomplishments along the way.

• *Keep everyone informed.* Regularly update everyone involved with the project. Keep yourself informed by listening and learning from the rest of the team.

• *Use conflict creatively.* Conflicts are part of the game. Use the energy they generate to promote innovative solutions to problems.

• *Empower yourself and others on the project team.* You may have limited authority, but use your personal power to get the job done. Encourage team members to do likewise.

• *Encourage risk taking and creativity.* New ideas and breakthroughs will come to the forefront if team members know they will not lose face for taking risks.

Reprinted from TRAINING, April 1988

---

need to do, but you can't do it because a crucial piece of the puzzle is missing. Dennis Schmidt, director of methods and training for Delta Airlines, was in that spot late last year. The Federal Aviation Administration had just issued a new regulation requiring that all airplane cockpits be fitted with new breathing devices that not only give the pilots oxygen but protect them from smoke fumes if fire breaks out on board. Pilots had to be trained to don the new breathing equipment and continue flying the plane.

Time was tight, even though the new regulation was issued last September and won't take effect until July 1988. That's because each month Delta puts a batch of new pilots through training. So in order to minimize the number of pilots who would have to come back after completing their training to learn how to use the breathing equipment, management wanted the new training segment ready as soon as possible. Schmidt agreed to prepare the segment by January.

Tough deadline to meet, especially when the protective breathing devices didn't even exist when the FAA decided airplanes needed them. Complicating things further was the fact that the training design itself had to gain FAA approval because it dealt with a federal regulation.

By late fall, Schmidt got prototype equipment and started marathon sessions with the FAA to gain approval of his training design. When he and the FAA had reached "90 percent agreement," he began to train the trainers, as he awaited final approval. All of a sudden, it was December.

"We had to bring five weeks of work in at 10 days," Schmidt recalls.

As much as trainers like to be perfectionists, there is seldom room in crash training for such niceties. An immediate need exists and it must be met. "Any time you start a new course, you're going to have rough edges," Schmidt says. "We get the very best course we can in the time we have and then we just begin modifying it."

Ellen Foley, vice president and director of training and development for BayBanks Inc., in Boston, also has felt the shock of crash training brought on by the federal government. She was a trainer in the bank when deregulation hit the banking industry in the early 1980s. Her deadlines were even more pressing than Schmidt's. The bank felt it had little choice but to release new financial products as soon as regulators allowed.

Foley would have liked more time to train employees on the new products, but competition was too fierce. "Everyone was out there on the same day with their products and we couldn't wait," she says.

Even though many deregulation directives took effect on Jan. 1 each year, the details of the decisions wouldn't be known until December. "A lot of Decembers were pretty busy," Foley remembers. She discounts the thrill of adrenalin surges when the crises are unending. "It was exciting at first, but when you're into your tenth product rollout, you begin to wonder if it will ever stop."

Eventually, training for the new-product rollouts formed a pattern. As soon as managers defined the product, the HRD division created documents describing it, along with the supporting materials. The department always prepared a videotape on how to sell the new product, but that was just a stopgap measure. Foley and her bosses would have preferred classroom role plays to teach employees those methods, especially since the idea of selling was foreign to the banking business. But time constraints forced them to settle for the tapes.

Some branch managers and supervisors, however, managed to include role plays in the training sessions they conducted. They were the ones responsible for delivering the training in the 13 branches. In preparation, they went to the main office for train-the-trainer sessions, which included classroom instruction and role plays.

Foley realizes that the plan didn't foster deep understanding of each product. Nor was there much follow-up to evaluate whether the training stuck. But she maintains that the training did what it had to do.

"We made the best of a tough situation," she says. "In an ideal world, we would have been able to do more follow-up on what we were doing. But we were living day-to-day."

Go get 'em

With time to reflect, all these training managers who delivered crash training had advice for the uninitiated. Naturally, advice is cheap because the very nature of a crash training situation means that the trainer must be resourceful and creative. No two situations are alike.

But the theme heard most often is that you shouldn't be chintzy with the initial planning. Landow says that was key to the success of Arthur Andersen's revamped tax training. Be-

---

When a project is recognized as crucial, executives tend to loosen the purse strings.

---

yond that, she adds, it's crucial to monitor developing situations closely. But if you know training will be needed, don't wait until every last detail is known before you start to devise a program.

There was little opportunity for Dayton Hudson's Kemp to be proactive, since she couldn't read the mind of the vice president who wanted the customer service training. But she was careful to focus on her deadline, taking into account the most efficient way to deliver the training. Also, she made sure there was enough time for planning a quality product. "We knew that if we were going to do it, we

wanted to do it right," she says.

Although none of these trainers used consultants heavily during their crises, that is one way to stretch your resources to meet a deadline. In Kemp's case, she sought outside help in scripting videos, something she ordinarily wouldn't be able to purchase outside. That's an incidental benefit of crash training. When a project is recognized as crucial, executives tend to loosen the purse strings.

Kemp and Landow also agree that it's good to involve other departments that can help you get the job done more quickly. With Kemp's project, it was the video and advertising departments; with Landow's assignment, it was the accounting types and the firm's partners, who could help make sure the information was right.

In situations like these, of course, it's easier to get that kind of help, mostly because the training projects tend to be highly visible. But such visibility is not self-sustaining. When executives rely on the training department to—in some cases—"save" the company, and the training department fails to come through, top management support withers.

"I think that's what we're here for," says BayBanks' Foley. "If we can't respond in a way that's useful to the company when things like this happen, then it doesn't make sense to have us around."

Reprinted from TRAINING, March 1988

USING POWER TO CREATE HRD CHANGES

Power doesn't have to be a bad word. Yet reluctance to use it can keep you from doing what you do best

BY FRANK T. WYDRA

It's not that human resources development (HRD) practitioners are opposed to causing change. To the contrary, most enter—and stay in—the field to cause it. Seldom do they say, "I don't want anyone to do things differently because they attended my course." They say instead, "Because of this course you'll be able to . . . " or "With this information you can . . . " or "When this program is implemented people will . . . " The reason most HRD professional are in this trade is precisely because they want to cause change. They want to impose values on others. They want other people to do things differently. They want to create programs that will allow the exercise of power by the organization and by the individuals within it. In short, they want to be change agents.

But since HRD practitioners have traditionally operated from a minimal power base, causing change has been difficult. The jargon of the trade is replete with phrases attributing saintliness to the powerless state. "Our job is to act as consultants to the organization." "We attempt to be nondirective." "We're service-oriented." "That's the way production (or sales, or operations, or accounting) wants it." Accommodation, cooperation, facilitation, collaboration are our key words. Confrontation, directives, competition are to be avoided.

And then HRD professionals wonder why they have so little impact on the fortunes of the organization. They wonder why programs are discarded, budgets cut, resources diminished at will. They wonder why they're ignored. A little reflection would reveal that all of these things happen because the HRD practitioner has little skill in exercising power. When others exert pressure, the equilibrium is upset—but how few of us know how to exert power to counteract that pressure.

The irony is that we, the ostensibly powerless, so often attempt to train others in the use of power, in "how to get things done." We are often the pushers of the corporate power process, but seldom the users. We have never learned to apply the lessons of power to our own interests. Can it be that those who would be change agents understand neither the parameters of power nor its use? Or is it that we think it inappropriate to use to our own advantage those tools we have helped shape? In either case the result is the same: Those who would cause change are its victims.

Change is caused by those who have power. Power is the ability to cause others to do or act. It is the ability to cause change. It is a neutral force, neither good nor evil. If a person, if a group, if a profession or a mob is to cause others to do, to act, to change, it must have power. If the change is to have direction and purpose, the managers of that power must have control over the force at their disposal. They must understand its motive and its use, its limits and its scope. Unfortunately power has taken on a negative connotation. It is discussed only in hushed tones. And the victims of the hush are those who lack power. Because they fail to explore power, they fail to understand either its nature or its use. To cause change, power is needed. To use power wisely, its nature not only must be explored but understood.

The first step in understanding power is to decide why it is needed. Granted its object is to change something, but what? Some would say the question is irrelevant. They see power as its own end. If you have enough power, they reason, you can change anything.

Aside from the fact that this amount of power is rarely available, the reality is that such absolute power is not needed if the object of change is known. In most cases change is determined by relative, not absolute power. Before change, all forces are at equilibrium, all elements are in balance. If nothing changes, everything will continue as before. But if pressure is reduced at one point or increased at another, the equilibrium is upset and change occurs.

This phenomenon is not unique to the organizational world. It happens day-to-day in the more physical, social and political worlds in which we live. In all cases the amount of change is determined by the amount of power invoked, withdrawn or held constant relative to the force of power opposing it. Great damage can be initiated through the application of a very small amount of pressure. To effectively use even small amounts of power, it is crucial to know your objective.

And who sets the objective? Why not the HRD pro?

To believe that a particular management approach, philosophy or technology makes a difference in the success or failure of an enterprise is to be concerned with who, if anyone, makes the decision to use the technology within the organization. There is a myth that alleges management philosophies are the result of clear-eyed direction from above. More likely is that an organization's way of doing things is the result of "philosophical Darwinism"—over the years bits and pieces of a hundred philosophies have survived and merged into "our way of doing it."

Of course, this poses a problem for the trainer charged with introducing the neophyte supervisor to the nuances of "our way," since "our way" may be an incoherent philosophy. While incoherent or difficult-to-define topics are not inherently bad, it is understandable that the HRD practitioner, whether reduced to desperation or with malice aforethought, frequently attempts to substitute a coherent—though not necessarily valid or acceptable—philosophy for an incoherent one. In the process the complexities of the organization's philosophical Darwinism are compounded. Yet in this wonderland in which we all work, the values of the HRD pro are as good as those of any other. If this be Darwinism, in other words, make the most of it. Your concept may indeed be the fittest, but you will never know unless you attempt to implement it.

For the farseeing, rational HRD professional, concepts of the good life will in all likelihood be logical and systematic. And were this a perfect world, the HRD professional would be lauded for bringing order from chaos. After all, even flawed order can be analyzed and altered; chaos cannot.

But organizations functioning in imperfect worlds occasionally reject order imposed, and not without reason. Sometimes the order is truly flawed—HRD practitioners are in no way certifiably omniscient. What's more, the structure as imposed by the change agent may not be perceived as valid—or worse, relevant—by others in the organization. Galileo found this out when he proposed a new structure to explain the universe. While he was, to the best of our knowledge, correct, his peers did not agree. They rejected both Galileo and his new order.

Finally, there are those within organizations who benefit from incoherence and disorder. Often it is the source of their power; frequently it is the reason for their jobs. They can be expected to resist the new order. If they have power, their resistance will be powerful. As a result, bringing order to management practice may not only be difficult, it may also have some danger attached to it in the unpredictable response of opposing forces. Specifically, the initiator of change may not survive the effort. An HRD pro's tenure is thus imperiled when he or she is sponsoring truths perceived to be invalid, irrelevant or threatening. In bringing personal values to the organizational scene, the HRD practitioner can expect to be applauded, eliminated, or anything in between.

Which brings us back to power and the HRD pro. Both the chance of success and immunity from extinction are enhanced if the change agent has power. The question is not whether your values should be imposed on the organization. Rather it is how you can acquire the power to impose them—and once gained, how that power can be employed

Let's not confuse power with authority, by the way. Your authority, or what you are permitted to do, is directly related to the power the organization has delegated to you. It may be great or it may be minimal, but in any case it is not yours. It is something the organization has loaned you and can take back at any time. Your power, on the other hand, is your ability to get things done regardless of organizational permission.

The distinction is important because many HRD professionals crave authority and ignore the power they

---

THE HRD POWER TEST

BY RON ZEMKE

Power," said Jimmy Breslin, "is relative. If you think you've got it, you've got it. If you don't think you have it, even if you have it you don't have it." How do you feel about power in general? What is your power quotient? Take this power skills and power perception test and find out.*

A. Your Power Attitude

1. Power and politics is nasty business. Only the untalented, incompetent and perverse partake. **T F**
2. The higher you go in an organization, the more power you have. **T F**
3. Power is a one-way street. Those above use it to intimidate those below. **T F**
4. Only people in line management are in a position to gain and keep power. To succeed in the HRD business it is prudent to avoid power and politics. **T F**
5. Being power conscious is destructive and denotes a desire to manipulate others. **T F**
6. People who stoop to playing power and politics are usually lazy or incompetent and have something to hide. **T F**
7. On balance, hard work is more important to success than are power and politics. **T F**
8. The appraisal of one's work has nothing to do with power and politics. **T F**
9. People are fired or asked to resign from a job for political reasons as often as for performance reasons. **T F**
10. Power is unfair. **T F**

What your score means

● **0 - 3:** Your attitude toward power is both negative and a little naive. You fail to see compromise, negotiation and interpersonal skill as having anything to do with fulfilling your needs and wants.

● **4 - 7:** You are aware of but not obsessed with power. You are probably cognizant of power and its implications, but place value on both means and ends, not just ends.

● **8 - 10:** You are aware of and sensitive to power. You must be careful not to get carried away with the concept of winning the game. Don't press every point to win/lose resolution. Exercising power for power's sake can be as boring as not seeing power as an issue in the work place.

B. Your Power Skills

1. Keeping the boss happy should be considered an A priority. **T F**
2. Company functions such as staff parties and dinners are important political and power occasions. **T F**
3. It isn't necessary to curry favor and give out strokes to get cooperation from other staffers. Fellow professionals know what they are being paid for and don't need that sort of treatment. **T F**
4. The closer you get to colleagues, the more involved you become in their goals and needs, the more likely you are to get cooperation from them when you need it. **T F**
5. Your professional skills and knowledge are an important political and power tool. **T F**
6. Courtesy is one of the most effective tools for getting ahead. **T F**
7. You must be scrupulously fair to your employees to get ahead and have them on your side. **T F**
8. Criticizing subordinates' mistakes *is* a mistake. **T F**
9. Being cordial to influential and important people is more important than being highly skilled. **T F**
10. Finding ways to package your ideas so they don't clash with others' opinions and prejudices is a cop-out on your integrity. **T F**

Scoring

● **0 - 3:** You have a disdain for power and politics that needs reexamining. Disraeli called every human action a political act, and Nietzsche dubbed "the will to power" man's common motivator. A group exists for mutual, not exclusive, benefit. You can no more expect your thoughts and ideas to go uncontested than you can expect to live a mistake-free life. If you walk about believing people will do things because they are *right*, you are bound to live a life of disappointment if not ulcerous righteous indignation.

● **4 - 7:** You understand power and its imperatives but choose to be flexible in your approach to applying it. That's fine as long as you don't expect others to play by your rules.

● **8 - 10:** You are power-sensitive and aware, as well as knowledgeable about the ways of the world. If you choose to use that knowledge to benefit yourself and others but adhere to a benign amusement about the whole thing, great. Your live-and-let-live attitude should work to your advantage. If, however, you use your superior knowledge and sensitivity to crush opposition and turn peers and subordinates into quivering jelly, you don't understand the goals of power, only that the game exists.

---

*The grist for the HRD Power Test comes from four sources: *Machiavelli and Management* by Anthony Joy; *Office Politics, Seizing Power Wielding Clout* by Marilyn Moates Kennedy; *You Can Negotiate Anything* by Herb Cohen; and *John Malloy's Live for Success* by John T. Malloy.

UNDERSTANDING THE DIFFERENCE BETWEEN POWER AND AUTHORITY

BY FRANK T. WYDRA

A common lament among trainers is that they are impotent to cause change. Yet HRD professionals are often the keepers of the management theory of an organization. They are the high priests of process. They lecture on motivation, design evaluation programs and establish succession plans. They explore, analyze, teach and sometimes preach concepts of getting things done through people. How can they argue over whether or not they can control change rather than being controlled by it?

Can it be that they do not understand the forces that direct change, even though they deal so often with those very forces? Or is it that they confuse power and authority? Perhaps they, along with other managers, assume that authority is power, or that the presence of power confers authority, or that the absence of authority is the absence of power. Power and authority are not synonymous. An understanding of the distinction is necessary to effectively manage the acquisition and use of either.

Basic to the confusion is our unwillingness to explore power as a topic of management science. Authority is considered legitimate, but evil connotations abound whenever power is discussed. Machiavelli and his Prince come readily to mind, along with a lot of familiar power pejoratives: "Power corrupts," "power monger," "hungry for power." Unfortunately this emotion-laden prejudice against confronting and understanding the nature and legitimate uses of power minimizes our ability to master and manage it. The consequence is that power often goes to those least able to manage it and frequently is absent for those who legitimately need it.

Authority, on the other hand, has long been an acceptable topic in management theory, and the connotations surrounding it are generally positive. "Delegate authority," "Give responsibility with authority" and "Have respect for authority" are frequent organizational admonitions. Classes are taught on the proper use of supervisory authority. Policies are written establishing authority.

Organizational charts are drafted to delineate authority. Authority is a legitimate concern. Power is not. Both should be.

Contrary to popular belief, power is relatively easy to attain. In human organizations it flows from three sources: consequences, knowledge and collaboration. Consequences are those things, planned or unplanned, related or unrelated, that follow an event. Knowledge is the compendium of facts and figures, processes and programs, skills and arts that surround a discipline or an industry. Collaboration is people working together, their efforts focused on a common goal and their actions synchronized to minimize friction and disharmony.

Consequences can be managed. Knowledge can be brokered. Collaboration can be engineered. Those who have the ability and opportunity to do these things have the capability of acquiring power in organizations. But the acquisition of power does not imply the automatic acquisition of authority. A common mistake of novice supervisors is to overstep the bounds of their authority. They soon learn, through reversal of their decisions and public embarrassment, the lesson of organizational humility.

Since authority relies on power for its force, it will be only imperfectly understood until power is analyzed and the knowledge disseminated. HRD pros need to know about authority. So do managers. But both need to understand power, too. They need to know how to recognize it, acquire it, use it, conserve it, counter it and control it.

Power, like authority, is neither positive nor negative. It is neutral. It is simply the ability to do or act. It is possession of control over other people or things, with or without their permission. The force of power exists without social sanctions. Its limits are defined, not by society or the people in it, but rather by the ability to do or act.

In social situations, permission comes into the power picture. Sometimes social power is vested in a group. At other times it is placed in the hands of one individual. In each case, people give others permission to make decisions that will affect their actions, even their lives.

Authority is that social permission in delegated form. It is usually limited by the terms of the delegation and the ability of the recipient to do or act. As opposed to the absolute characteristics of natural power, authority is inherently unstable. It is only as strong as others perceive it

to be. It can be withdrawn at any time. And challenges to authority will quite often cause its very legitimacy to be reviewed and perhaps modified.

Authority is a social concept. It is an invention of man used to allocate power. Authority is a tool used to restrain power. It exists only in group situations because it assumes power over people rather than things or natural events. The primary difference is therefore the aspect of social permission. With power, you can do anything you have the ability to do. Authority simply allows you to do it without social reprisals.

Power is not authority. But it can lead to authority. Organizations cannot give a supervisor the ability to do something he or she is incapable of doing. What they can give is the permission to do those things the supervisor is qualified and able to do.

Management critics are quick to attack the promotion of the best technician to supervision. They point out, and properly, that such an individual may know nothing about the techniques called for in the supervisor's role. What they fail to recognize is that the technician already has a power base: knowledge. By providing the sanction of authority, the organization seeks to increase the possibility that such knowledge will be used to direct and control the outputs of others.

In a similar vein seniority is often criticized when it is used as a basis for promotion. Once again, however, the organization is recognizing a pre-existing power base. Senior people often have the best knowledge of the organization's culture. They may have the ability to call on diverse, even obscure, resources to engineer collaboration. By granting authority to its senior people, the organization hopes to capitalize on power that can be productively employed.

All managers, including HRD pros, can cause change. To do so, they must recognize the sources of power and master the techniques for tapping the resources already available to them. Power will not ordinarily come as delegated authority. That may happen in time, but first there must be sufficient evidence that such confidence is deserved.

Power begets authority. Until HRD pros demonstrate their command of the former, they can't expect to be given the latter. The sooner we get about the business of making subtle power obvious, covert power overt, obscure power clear, the sooner we will be in a position to manage change.

Reprinted from TRAINING, August 1981

have at their disposal. Consequently, in the absence of delegated authority they sense an absence of power. This is a mistake. The power is there. It needs only to be employed. If you have authority, it should certainly be employed to champion your values. But lack of authority should not be used as an excuse for surrendering those same values. Power is available to those who wish to take it. The acquisition of this power requires no sanction or permission.

Power as it applies to organizational settings springs from three sources: events, interactions and information. In the workaday world, these are transformed into consequences, collaboration and knowledge. The person or organization seeking power must first gain control over the processes that can produce one or more of these effects, becoming in the process a consequence manager, collaboration engineer or knowledge broker.

The most common perception of power is a vision of *managing consequences*. X is powerful because he can decide to continue or scratch a program. Y is powerful because she can give or withhold a raise. Z is powerful because he can hire or fire. All are considered powerful because they control the delivery or dispensation of rewards and punishments.

Yet while this is an important source of power, it is usually delegated within organizations, so gaining increased ability to control consequences—particularly as they affect superiors—is at best a difficult task. There are some consequences available to HRD professionals that lie outside organizational delegation, but their affect is relatively mild in relation to both power delegated organizationally and power available from other sources.

In addition, where causing change through the decisions of others is concerned, the consequences that would have to be managed are those that impact the decision makers. While it is possible for the HRD practitioner to acquire this type of power, it is also unusual. Rather than focus on it, our purpose is served by acknowledging the force of consequence management and then moving on.

By contrast, the power inherent in *engineering collaboration* is right up the HRD pro's alley. To engineer collaboration is to get people working together as a team. This is done through clarifying objectives, opening communications, identifying group consequences. These are the very skills we teach in negotiation classes, conflict resolution seminars,

objective setting workshops and the dozens of other programs that focus on building interactive skills.

While they work effectively in line management and on-the-job situations, they also work for HRD pros who develop and use them for their own ends. By bringing agreement where there was disagreement, by developing teamwork where there was competition, by analyzing and identifying payoffs for a particular course of action, the collaboration engineer acquires the ability to influence, shape and eventually direct. These controls over action are, in fact, the application of power. When applied to the objectives the HRD practitioner holds dear, they can have the effect of changing the values and processes of the organization. When the HRD pro is able to impose his or her values on the organization, power is being exercised.

To *broker knowledge* is also to deal in power. Through acquisition, analysis and application, data are transformed into information, then knowledge and finally change. Those who control the process of transforming data into action hold power. HRD practitioners have a unique opportunity within organizations to collect, review and apply data-generated information. If the organization is the sum of its people, their capabilities and actions, then typically the greatest resource for knowledge of these people is the HRD department.

Too often, though, information is collected and then forgotten. It never moves from bits of information into knowledge that could prompt action. From employment application to exit interview, from discipline reports to performance evaluation, from work history to promotion record, the data are available. Properly analyzed they can lead to knowledge that can help shape the management philosophy of the unique organization you serve. But to acquire that power the HRD pro must search and think, working with knowledge to find meaning, then utility.

Power is available to the HRD practitioner, although not in the form normally associated with it. The HRD pro can't expect to be delegated great authority to manage the consequences that lead to evolutionary or revolutionary change. Instead this professional will have to depend on developing his or her own sources of power. Normally these will be forces beneficial to practitioner and organization alike. They will be the result of employing the processes that are taught on a day-to-day basis in the most familiar of arenas, those

of human enterprise.

If you believe that your view of the world, or any part of it, is correct, then you have a responsibility to communicate it. Whether your view is about the technology of the organization, its economic goals, its social values or its management style, you have every right to impose it on the organization if you can. Most can't. Most never try. Most don't know how, since to do so requires power. But that power is available to the HRD pro.

POWER KEYS: MANAGING CONSEQUENCES

Many people identify power as the ability to manage consequences. When organizations delegate authority, it is often the power to reward or punish that is being delegated. Each is a type of consequence. And when nothing at all happens, that too is a consequence. The reasons these events are called consequences is that they follow behavior: They are consequences of an action. Scientists have come to believe that it is the events that follow a behavior that determine whether that behavior will be repeated.

For consequences to become a major source of power, however, they must be timely, predictable and consistent. A reward or punishment does not have to be large to be effective, but it must follow the behavior closely enough, and predictably enough, and consistently enough that the worker can see a relationship between his or her behavior and the consequence.

As consequence managers, HRD pros will most likely follow a three-step process. First they will identify the consequences available for managing performance. They will next make sure that the consequences being managed are compatible with objectives; that desirable actions are rewarded instead of punished, and vice versa. Finally they will take care to deliver consequences on a timely and consistent basis—as soon after the behavior as possible and compatible with past consequences.

Of course, it isn't always that simple. Sometimes the authority delegated is not adequate to the task. Here again, though, power can be augmented through effective management of the consequences available. Systematically and strategically applied on a consistent and timely

Answers to Part A of the HRD Power Test

1. False. Herb Cohen defines power as "the capacity to get things done...to exercise control over people, events, situations and oneself." To manage, to get things done through others, you must be willing to help others get things done. Power is an economic process based on the law of psychological reciprocity and transacted through the commerce of support, favor and trust.

2. True and False. The higher up the pyramid you go, the greater your *formal authority*. But most power is personal, not official. No one can give you power. You can be handed the reins, but you have to make the horses go by yourself. You have to acquire power as you go. Just as goods and services acquire value as they are perceived to be of value, your personal influence grows in value as you gain in ways to be helpful to your own and others' ends. (*You* decide if your answer was right.)

3. False. Power in action is the exchange of help and favors. You ask a favor, you owe a favor— debits and credits. If your credit rating is in good shape, you've got power. Abuse the system, exploit the people involved, and they take your credit card away from you.

4. False. Line people are in the worst position to develop and wield internal or in-company power; staff people must develop their own power to survive and succeed. Ideas are boundless, resources less so.

HRD is not a solo act, it is a group dance. Involvement in your projects begets commitment to them. Commitment begets power. By definition, the group must empower you to orchestrate. You *play* politics to *gain* the power to *use* your skill and knowledge for mutual benefit. To get participation and involvement in your projects, you must give commitment and involvement to other people's plans. That is a political activity.

5. False. Knowing how to get things done is in no way destructive. Suppose you need to get 50 student workbooks to Cheyenne overnight. Maybe you've been giving the folks in the mailroom a tough time. Maybe you've done some little things to make their lot easier. Which gives you a better chance of getting those workbooks to Wyoming?

6. False. People who play power and politics games are more often than not people with a zeal for accomplishment and a beloved project near and dear to their hearts in the offing. They are ambitious enough, and confident enough in their skills, to work the levers and pulleys necessary to get a shot at the thing they really believe in or believe needs doing. By contrast, those who borrow power to paper over performance potholes show themselves as weak and inadequate.

7. False. Marilyn Moates Kennedy is adamant on this issue: "Hard work depends on what your boss says it is. This is true whether productivity is easy to measure or difficult. There is no way to measure hard work outside the context of the specific work

environment defined and managed by a specific boss." Hard work equals style plus results, both of which are defined by someone other than yourself.

8. False. Performance appraisal is the ultimate act of power. The textbooks usually talk about motivation, productivity and objective assessment when they explain performance appraisal. That's the theory. In practice performance appraisal is feedback on your political acumen. What is being appraised is how well you are able to match the style-and-results picture your boss had in mind when you were hired. If you've advanced his or her ends through acceptable means, you win. Miss on either and you're out. Not clarifying the real expectations you're working under is a critical error.

9. True. As many people are let go for political as for competence reasons. Aligning yourself with a losing cause or faction, playing the wrong card at the right time or failing to comprehend and play by the local political rules are quick trips to the unemployed life. "Inability to get along with others," "bad attitude," and "personality clashes" are smoke-screened ways to say that a released employee didn't make the grade politically.

10. True. Life is unfair. Some people are six-foot-five, some are five-foot-six. So it goes. Power comes to those who work at the process of accumulating the commodities needed to barter for success. But unfair does not equal unjust. A thing can be unfair and just, just as easily as it can be fair and just. Power is unfair but neutral.

Answers to Part B of the HRD Power Test

1. True. Any time a substantial difference of opinion between boss and subordinate develops, the smart money bets on things being resolved in the boss' favor. When your best arguments and most compelling logic have failed to communicate the need for a video network, drop the idea. The boss— like the house— wins all ties. The boss doesn't have to be right to win, only the boss. Consider such losses as setbacks, not total defeats. Try again later when the odds seem more favorable.

2. True. And how! The worst thing you can do at a company party is party. Come late and leave early, advises John Malloy— company parties and occasions are see-and-be-seen affairs. Malloy also advises against becoming the life of the party. You are always being sized up at a company function so treat it like an interview. Do *not* use it as an opportunity to sell your pet idea or bring up your biggest problem; the time and place are inappropriate. A special note to women from Malloy: Be extra careful of conduct. Avoid "touch football" games. You have to spend too much time and effort building your professional image to risk it for a frolicsome time at the Christmas party.

3. False. We all need stroking to exist and we all need allies to succeed. The best allies are those who can help or hurt the accomplishment of your job. If the word-processing people, or the print shop, or shipping have been able to "do it *for* you" in the past, make sure it is in their best interest not to "do it *to* you" in the future. Threats won't work, but strokes will. Same with colleagues and superiors. Good relations at least keep the results channels greased for when they are needed.

4. False. Don't get so close to people that you can be expected to "understand" why they don't feel obliged to pay their debts when they are called in. You need distance to remain the cool, calm, rational problem-

solving person you need to be. Success and failure, cooperation and obstruction are impersonal. Your mental health depends on keeping the game a game and people at a decent arm's length.

5. True. Your skill, along with your personal style, got you hired. Your image as an expert— real or perceived— is what brings people to your door. Use your expertise as an asset, something of high value worth trading for. Don't give it away. And don't hesitate to defer to others who claim expertise in an area— not yours of course. Even though others may be less skillful or knowledgeable in their area of expertise than you are, it is helpful in the long run to leave the illusions of their expertise intact. It's no different than letting people think you can't type when, in fact, you do 60 wpm. The favor is always returned in kind.

6. True. There is a world of difference between tough and testy. Your goal is to get ahead, to win, not to become the scourge of the office. You can be political and power-oriented and still be viewed as a decent human being. It's a combination of the iron hand in the velvet glove and picking your spots that brings power. Make it your goal to give everyone you deal with an opportunity to "save face" and keep self-esteem intact if at all possible.

7. False. "Fair," like "good job," is a relative term. The first rule of power and survival as a manager of people is to be in charge. Even in a participative structure, somebody is in charge and accountable. To a highly aggressive subordinate, being fair may mean rolling over and playing dead when he or she reaches for your piece of the action. To a dependent, unassertive person it may mean not enforcing standards or applying pressure to produce. You can't accept either definition of fair and be effective. Managers are paid to run departments and critical organizational functions, not T-groups or popularity contests. The HRD function is still a function. If your shop doesn't hold to the locally accepted standards of conduct and

production, you may not have a department one of these days.

8. False. People need to know what's expected and how they are doing relative to those expectations. The more clear and behaviorally concise the feedback, the more likely the subordinate is to change in the direction desired. Discounting error and problems, sugar-coating bad news is a mistake. We all work very hard at justifying our behavior and performance. To change we need to know unequivocally that change is needed and expected. However criticism in the pejorative sense is the opposite of tact and courtesy. Lambasting poor performance brings about defensiveness, fear and hostility. That won't do. On balance remember one thing: data clearly show that over 50% of the people who are fired for poor performance cannot state what it was they were doing that was wrong or different from expectation. That smacks of managerial malpractice.

9. True. Mark Twain said "the hardest challenge parents face is teaching their children to be nice to the truly unlikable." People with status and power expect to be deferred to by those of lower station. Who hasn't laughed at an unfunny joke told by the boss' boss? The trick is to understand and accept the fact of power and develop the skills and strategies that will keep you from being inordinately jostled about by it.

10. False. This is where we invariably separate those who see HRD as a form of home economics from those who see it as a corporate strategy. We are always in competition for the organization's limited resources. To call for support on the basis of what is "right" or the "good thing to do" is to position what we do as a form of social work. Getting funding for something as soft and squishy— and nontangible— as training and development requires allies. Attending to their vested interests and prejudices increases the likelihood that you will get the permissions and resources you need to do the job you were hired to do.

basis, the ability to dispense rewards, deliver punishments or do nothing at all—but for good reason—can become a management tool far more effective than might be expected from outward appearances.

ENGINEERING COLLABORATION

It is not by accident that most organizations stress teamwork. Experience has taught us that we can accomplish more by working together than by working alone. HRD pros who can show managers and supervisors how to build collaboration into the work team—and who use the same techniques in their own departments—tend to be more effective. They are able to control the production of results. They have increased power.

We gain power through collaboration by engineering situations in which collaboration will occur. Think like the producer of a Broadway show—the resources, the players, the objective and the process must be brought together to produce a desired result.

Collaboration occurs naturally in social organizations. That is, if enough people are brought together, some will work together. But to gain power the HRD pro must develop an ability to increase or decrease collaboration. There are three variables in this process: clarity of objectives, open communication and group consequences.

By clarifying objectives, making them commonly understood, the HRD pro sets the stage for increased collaboration. Conversely, vague objectives can be used to decrease collaboration. A team pulling in all directions is unlikely to move in any one direction. In the heat of debate, the members of a work team can lose sight of the common goal.

Clear objectives provide the work team with a target, a focus and a direction that will allow it to channel its energy into the production of the desired result. It is therefore the responsibility of those—including the boss—who would gain influence to both decide and communicate the objective.

But collaboration engineering, like knowledge brokering, involves more than a single action. Clarifying an objective is a worthy step, but by itself will not necessarily result in collaboration. The vision needs to be supported by building, with open communication, toward group con-

sequences. It truly is engineering.

Open communication permits information to flow freely among team members, allowing a pooling of the group's resources. While this builds a mutual dependency, it also can lead to true synergy: an interaction that can generate cooperative ideas no one individual would be capable of producing independently.

Open communication is enhanced by consistent and accurate feedback. It is strengthened by rewarding rather than ignoring or punishing divergent views. It is facilitated by making the process easy instead of difficult. HRD pros, and the people they train, who can develop the ability of team members to communicate openly increase the potential for collaboration. In the process, they begin to collect the power to impact outcomes.

The third concern is the degree to which consequences impact the group. The self-sufficient person, the team member who neither needs nor wants anyone else's aid, is unlikely to be an active collaborator. Those who find they gain the greatest rewards by being "the star," regardless of whether their success is earned at the expense of other team players, will try to continue to be stars.

If, however, the only route to individual reward is through group accomplishment, members will learn to support each other. By linking each individual's outcome directly to the group outcome, the probability of collaboration is increased. To be an effective collaboration engineer, the HRD pro must construct or at least identify group consequences. What's more, these must be perceived as significant enough to provide an incentive for the members of the group to work toward a common goal.

BROKERING KNOWLEDGE

In the early 1960s, Peter Drucker predicted that the American work force would soon be composed largely of knowledge workers, people who were effective because of what was in their heads as opposed to the strength of their backs. As prophecy, it has proven to be pretty heady stuff. Increasing numbers of modern workers are now white-collar or knowledge workers—computer programmers, medical technologists, word processing operators,

quality control engineers and HRD professionals to name but a few. To understand the potential of knowledge is to open up one of the three avenues to power: The brokering of knowledge.

Knowledge derives its power from enabling someone to do something others cannot do. To enhance power, knowledge must therefore be both useful and used. It may be knowledge about a process or technique used in an operation. It may be a management skill. Or it may be totally unrelated. But if it provides the ability to do something others cannot do, it becomes power.

Knowledge is processed into power through *acquisition*, *analysis* and *application*. Supervisors who assume the role of the broker may or may not perform these activities personally. They may acquire knowledge directly or through a surrogate. Their analysis may be made directly or through researchers. And application may be self-directed or accomplished through activities initiated by subordinates. But throughout the process the supervisor brokers the various elements that transform knowledge into power.

Acquisition, however, is not enough. Knowledge for the sake of knowledge may be nice, but it is not in itself power. The graveyard of ineffectiveness is abundantly populated with knowledgeable but inactive people. Knowledge acquired needs to be analyzed. Only when knowledge takes on meaning does it begin to become powerful. Sometimes the analysis will be aided by collaboration, but the basic question is always: "What does it mean?"

This is a root cause of supervisory ineffectiveness, a disease to which HRD professionals are far from immune. Some people spend their entire worklife acquiring knowledge without ever analyzing it. The accountant who only puts together numbers, the production foreman who only collects scrap data, the school administrator who only compiles test results: All of these people and countless others are merely collectors of knowledge. Until they start to analyze, they will not begin to acquire power

There is a third step, too. Knowledge acquired and analyzed is still a dormant resource. Like a lump of coal, the energy of knowledge is not released until ignited through use.

There is one additional consideration in the effective brokering of knowledge. Information in the form of knowledge is a perishable commodity. The longer it remains unused, the less valuable it is likely to become.

Reprinted from TRAINING, August 1981

POWER BROKERING IN TRAINING

Here's an eight-point strategy for training managers who want to increase their budgets, broaden their power bases and save money for their organizations

BY LARRY WINTERS
AND JO DIMINO

Training departments have a power problem. The problem is that most of them have no power—or so little that distinctions between "some" and "none" become hard to draw. And the reason this *is* a problem, regardless of your attitude that organizational politics is a shabby subject, it that "power," in and of itself, means nothing more nor less than the ability to get things done.

In most business environments, power is associated with budget size and control of expenditures—with how much money you've got and your authority to decide what to do with it. If the organization invests in a specific department or activity, it is committing itself to making that activity successful.

Although most competent training and development (T&D) managers could more than justify their contribution to any operation, their departments tend to be viewed as staff support, with little or no impact on the organization's bottom-line profits. Resulting budgets (and policy commitments) are meager in comparison to those given the majority of line functions.

Historically, T&D managers have tried to defend their expenditures by demonstrating "back-end" behavioral changes and productivity improvements. But these contributions are extremely difficult to document, especially when operating managers are likely to cite non-training factors (such as salary increases, incentive plans and work-place adjustments) as contributing to those improvements.

Suppose that, instead, you practice a bit of classic, solid management strategy: Focus your attention on a budget line item—in this case, training—and document how you could reduce expenses without reducing the quality or quantity of service.

How can you, as manager of training and development, increase the size of your budget and use the resulting power boost to increase your company's profitability? You can do it by gaining control of all T&D expenditures throughout the entire organization. Within 12 months, the eight-point program we'll outline here will produce a strategic shift in your organization's balance of power—a shift toward the training department—and will solidify certain changes within the organization to sustain that shift.

What we're talking about is a power play, carried out on the organization's own terms. And yes, we're speaking of empire building. A disreputable term, that, but only because it is associated with managers whose determination to build empires outweighs (or negates) their desire to serve the interests of the organization as a whole. In short, empire building is a negative force only when it produces negative consequences or fails to produce positive ones.

If you can build an empire that serves the company—and everyone in the company—better than they are served by existing empires, you are not Darth Vader.

With no apologies for the term, therefore, we'll explain that this power play is made possible by the simple fact that employee training in this country currently represents a $3-billion business: According to TRAINING Magazine's *U.S. Training Census and Trends Report, 1983*, that is the approximate figure budgeted each year by organizations—excluding the federal government—to be spent "outside" on hardware, materials, programs and services for use in training and development.

If your organization is at all sizable, chances are that thousands of dollars are spent every year by various department managers for seminars, films, books, consultants, computer software and other training-related items. Each manager, restricted by departmental boundary lines, is unable to purchase in volume and therefore unable to negotiate the best price available from vendors. In other words, if vendors are selling directly to individual operating managers, the dollars spent by those managers probably are undiscounted.

What's happening under this all-too-common arrangement? Not only has the T&D specialist lost control over the quality of many company training programs, he or she also lacks the power to negotiate potentially substantial savings for the organization as a whole.

The strategy outlined here is challenging and may not appeal to the faint of heart. But it can be tremendously rewarding for those not afraid to broker in the elusive commodity of power.

Step 1. Network

Interview a representative sample of profit-center managers. Your task at this point is not to convert skeptics, but simply to gather information on how they spend training dollars. The trade-off for their cooperation is your promise to save money for their operating units while increasing training opportunities for their people.

If you can get them to support your concept of stretching their budgets through volume purchasing of training, so much the better. But trying to argue your way through all possible objections is exhausting. Concentrate, instead, on managers willing to help make the concept work, or on likely converts. Effort spent with these people is well worth the time.

But for heaven's sake, exercise some tact. You're talking about taking money out of this manager's "pocket" and putting it into yours. You needn't present your idea as something you are determined to do regardless of what this particular person thinks. You simply have an idea that may work out extremely well for everybody.

If the information you gather from the skeptic and from other managers indicates that you *can't* make good on your promises, you will, of course, drop the plan. And this is true. Unlikely, if they're all buying training individually, but true.

Once you have chosen your network of contacts, what's the best way to gather the vital information? You might want to conduct a person-to-person survey or use a questionnaire. Written questionnaires about financial matters tend to make people nervous, however, so explain at the outset that your main desire is to understand the *intent* of the expenditures, as well as the sums per se.

But make it clear that you do need the sums. And you'll need to know the *actual dollars* spent on training for a selected 12-month period, as opposed to the amounts that have been budgeted. Be sure to have the managers indicate exactly what they purchased: cassette programs, seminars, outside consultants for in-house programs, college courses, periodicals, newsletters, correspondence courses and so on. Travel and living expenses should not be included in the totals.

Step 2. Analysis

Start by segmenting your responses. List the types of training purchased, the dollars spent, and the vendor or provider of the service. Begin to look for patterns in purchasing—similar categories of topics or needs, recurring vendors, etc. If certain responses need qualifying, especially if the survey was in the form of a written questionnaire, follow up with a personal visit to the manager.

Keep in mind that your data represents only a sample of the total training dollars your organization spent. You do not have a categorical picture of your company's expenditures for the previous year. But if you have sampled responsibly, you ought to be able to make some pretty good projections.

Step 3. Decide

Question yourself. If the power to disburse all of this money were indeed in your hands, what would you do? Based on your operating managers' expressed needs, how would you allocate the dollars most effectively for them and for your company's balance sheet? Be especially careful here, because the decisions you begin to make now will be prime contributors to the ultimate power you broker for yourself.

Step 4. Contact

Get in touch with reputable outside training vendors, including the ones selected by your sample managers. Suppliers will be more than willing to discuss training programs and packages with you, make suggestions about the most economical way to use your designated budget and, most importantly, outline any discounts available to you as a volume purchaser.

Don't be satisfied with reading about these programs or listening to sales people describe them. Attend seminars yourself, wherever possible, and get your hands on samples of other products to test in your company.

Step 5. Organize

Now that you've done your homework, put your facts in order. Document the actual training dollars spent during the last 12 months and compare this amount to the number of employees trained. Highlight your discoveries about how volume discounts would affect the total price tag in relation to the number of people trained.

Make sure you have a good, strong story to tell and that the approach you've developed is efficient, effective, timely and, above all, economical. As a precaution, show your proposal to a financially astute colleague; he or she may be able to spot any questionable assumptions or statistical holes in your presentation.

Step 6. Meet

Arrange a meeting with your company controller or, if appropriate, with the chief executive officer. Explain that you have identified an area in the corporate budget which you feel can be reduced by 15%, 40% or whatever figure applies.

Start by sharing the results of your survey. Then outline your findings concerning the potential savings with volume purchasing. Your primary goal at this point is to present facts and figures objectively. Let the figures open the door for the revelation of your intent to save the company money by becoming the sole purchasing agent for training.

Step 7. Follow-up

Don't let a good idea wither on the vine. Any suggestions brought up by the controller (or CEO) should be incorporated into your proposal immediately. If necessary, reevaluate any items or approaches which met strong objections during the meeting, and search for alternate methods. You won't want to compromise your goal, but as in any realistic situation, a few adjustments may be needed to push the proposal over the corporate hurdle.

When you draft the final copy of your plan for the controller, send a copy to your immediate superior. Power building is by nature a play of strengths against weaknesses, and at this juncture you're negotiating from a position of strength. It may take some courage (and some tiptoeing) to keep your research to yourself until you're ready to relate it to dollars-and-cents benefits, but you'll have to try; it's too easy for a charge of "empire building" to be hung around your neck *before* you've accomplished anything. In this case, time is your leverage, so use it to your best advantage.

Step 8. Publicize

As soon as you've gotten any positive feedback on your completed plan from top management, start sharing your results with line managers. Recruit their cooperation and support. Emphasize the fact that they're not losing funds, they're gaining better-trained staffs—both quantitatively and qualitatively—and they're making a greater contribution to the profit picture their operating units present.

These eight steps definitely will require hard work, initiative, imagination and, perhaps, a thick skin. But many training managers who have tried this strategy have accomplished considerably more than the enhancement of their power bases within the organization. They also have achieved some or all of the following objectives:

• The ability to contribute—on a continuing basis—to the profits of their companies.

• Increased respect for their training and development expertise from line managers.

• A better understanding of the training needs of *all* company employees.

• The ability to report to upper management on the *exact* training activities going on within the organization.

• Access to the type of data necessary for planning future training programs in line with company growth projections.

In other words, the training empire you build with this strategy is going to be one that serves the needs of the organization and its people. Your increased ability to *get things done* will pay off for everybody. And if, in the process, bigger budgets and greater commitments from upper management accrue to you, these are simply the results of well-performed power brokering at work.

Reprinted from TRAINING, May 1984

HOW TO MARKET TRAINING INTERNALLY

To be successful, HRD pros must be marketers as well as trainers and performance engineers

BY CHIP BELL

A friend once told me that all human resources development managers would do well to have either marketing experience or a marketing planner on their HRD staff. At the time, I mentally labeled the comment an "egotistical pearl of wisdom;" my friend was a marketing planner. But considering recent demands for results in our adversary economy, I know my marketing friend was on the right track: The successful HRD manager should be able to think in marketing.

Training pros have for years recognized the need to be able to sell their ideas, proposals, budgets, and requests for additional human and material resources to decision makers. While the words selling and marketing are both cut from the same cloth, they involve different activities and, more importantly, different ways of viewing the act of influencing an outcome. Philosophically, selling is like a solo played by a violinist, while marketing is more like a symphony performed by an orchestra.

The model below includes four phases in the marketing of training process — assessment, marketing strategy, presentation, and decision. Effective marketing requires awareness of each phase and skill in managing the forces incumbent in each phase. Contained in the explanations that follow are questions designed to help tailor the model to the users' needs. All the component parts may

not be appropriate to all situations; parts not explored in this article may occur to the reader just in the process of experiencing the concept. In a sense, the model represents a penciled beginning rather than an engraved capstone.

Assessment Phase. A fellow HRD manager had an outstanding training proposal shot down in the boardroom because he failed to assess that the company was on the verge of reorganization. His proposal referred only to the existing organization when it could have been subtly arranged to provide a transition into the emerging structure.

The assessment phase incorporates research and analysis and is analogous to preparatory work in the generic marketing function. Assessment includes a comprehensive diagnosis of the major elements in the marketing situation—the buyer (decision maker), the seller (HRD manager), the setting (organization), and the user (learner). Each of these elements hold characteristics which restrain and assist the ultimate decision. Minimizing the restraining characteristics and optimizing the assisting characteristics requires accurate assessment and adroit action by the HRD manager.

What appears to be the top concern at the moment among decision makers? Will there be a near-term shift in objectives, markets, products, services, people? Why should a decision maker do something differently? Why

should a training program be proposed? Assessing the needs of the organization should be a critical event in the development of all training programs. This same assessment done for design can be used again when the HRD proposal is placed on the docket for vote by decision makers.

Ultimately, decisions regarding a training proposal will be "business decisions" which reflect the value system of the organization. The organizational value system, reflecting the degrees to which form and substance factors are appreciated—like long run, short run, aggregation, integration, proaction, reaction—are by-products of the sum influence produced by key clout people. Thus, the needs of the organization (and concomitantly, the organizational response and direction) are in part shaped by the personal psychological needs and values of major decision makers.

Knowledge of the decision makers and their psychological needs can be vital when anticipating the reaction to the training proposal and when structuring the proposal presentation—its promotional form and HRD substance. Frequently, effective sales people size up the potential buyer during the opening of a sales presentation.[1] The HRD manager has an advantage over the outside salesperson—sizing up can be done before the pitch, thereby tailoring it in advance to a tune to which the buyer enjoys dancing.

How does the HRD manager assess the personality makeup of the decision makers? All people act out certain psychological needs. While we each have basically the same needs, they have different weights or priorities in different people. My high need to be liked may be only a moderate need of yours; your high need to achieve may be a low need of mine. Since people tend to act (behave) to satisfy the high needs, diagnosis can occur by observing the chosen actions in a given situation and hypothesizing what high need precipitated a certain action. If a person has a high need for power, even a small opportunity for power will likely evoke action toward that opportunity.

Think of the actions or behaviors you have seen or heard a decision maker emitting. Ask yourself, what sort of need would cause a person to engage in those actions? For instance, the decision maker who requires lots of documentation might be operating out of a high need for order, control, or power. This could provide a clue about how to structure your proposal presentation.

Coupled with diagnosis of the decision makers' needs is what one might call personal psych-out—assessing the psychological needs of the HRD manager. We are all guilty of occasionally letting our own needs get in the way of our effectiveness. Our intense need to win, for example, might cause us to choke on the road to victory. Our need to be liked may cause us to delay following up with an associate because the follow-up might include negative evaluation—a risk we are unwilling to introduce into the relationship. And our need to be perfect might cause us to fail to meet deadlines while continuing the pursuit of "perfection." The point is, our own needs can doom a training proposal to a negative decision unless we recognize that possibility and take steps to counteract it.

If your training proposal is for a program which has occurred successfully in the past, either in your organization or another organization to which you have access, the previous users' responses could represent a valuable resource to marketing assessment efforts. User response may be in the form of pre-test post-test measurement, post-workshop reaction sheets, observable behavior change, improved productivity, and reduced turnover—each credibly linked to the training program.

We have all been bored with those repetitious user response advertisements which tell us why Ms. Anita Break from Muddywater, MT swears by a certain brand. Despite their vanilla quality, these ads are reinforcing; buyers gain some measure of confidence in knowing that others found the product satisfactory. The confidence produces new customers and at the same time increases brand loyalty among old customers.

The possession of hard, irrefutable proof that the proposed training program worked elsewhere in a similar setting can sometimes mean the difference between a go and no-go decision. As will be explored in the next phase of the model, previous users can also be helpful when designing the marketing strategy, personally influencing individual advocates or decision makers, and providing supporting data useful in the presentation of the training proposal.

Marketing Strategy Phase. The development of the marketing strategy starts with analyzing the mar-

keting situation defined in the assessment phase in order to derive certain assumptions. These assumptions are further scrutinized and ultimately lead to tactics of maneuvers for obtaining specific results (in this case, a favorable decision). The creativity required of the marketing planning unit in a generic marketing function is typically rivaled only by the advertising unit which communicates the result.

The accompanying conceptual model includes four activities for formulation and implementation of the strategy for marketing a training proposal—generating and selecting proposal attributes for marketing, winning individual advocates prior to the proposal presentation, assembling supporting data, and structuring the proposal presentation. From the standpoint of creativity, attribute generation and selection is likely to be the most taxing of the four activities. This activity requires viewing the proposal from a variety of perspectives in order to generate attribute alternatives responsibly. The knowledge acquired in the assessment phase then becomes the criteria for ultimate attribute selection.

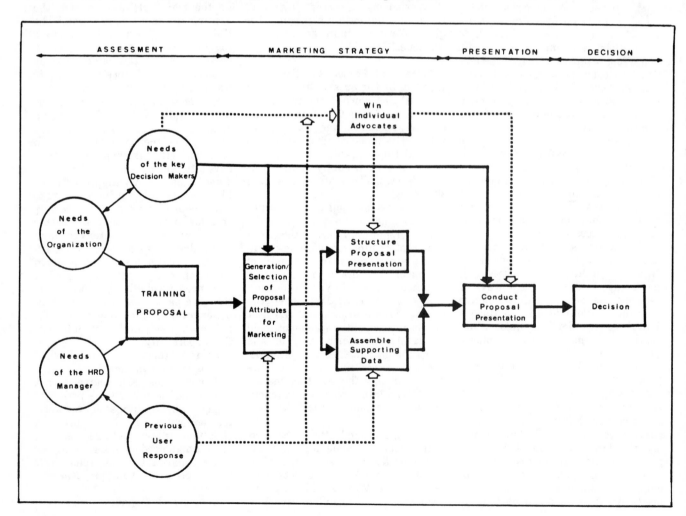

Why generate and select proposal attributes for marketing? Shouldn't the pure, ostensive altruism of the proposal be sufficient? In some cases it may be. But as Theodore Levitt stated in *Marketing for Business Growth* ,"It is not so much the basic central thing we are selling that counts, but the whole cluster of value satisfactions with which we surround it. It does little or no good to make a better mousetrap when 'betterness' now has a new, more subtle meaning."[2] In clothing, it is not dresses or suits one sells, but fashion; it is not cosmetics, but hope. People buy quarter-inch drill bits, not because they want drill bits, but because they want quarter-inch holes.[3]

The task of attribute generation is accomplished by multiplying perspective; the task of attribute selection is accomplished by matching the attributes with the assessment. The process is useful for escaping from the thought pattern prisons of conventionality. By defining the training proposal differently than one traditionally defines it, it is possible to "see" new aspects—opportunities—which could be useful for internal marketing. The railroads failed to do this and almost stopped growing because they assumed they were in the railroad business rather than the transportation business; the movie industry was practically overrun by television because Hollywood defined their business as movies rather than entertainment.[4] HRD could be perceived as "programs to produce behavior change." It could also be seen as "an experience to facilitate learning how to learn." As you plan the marketing strategy for your training proposal, think of at least four different ways of perceiving or defining the proposal.

Another activity in the marketing strategy phase is the winning of individual advocates. Advocates are important influence allies. We have all heard the line, "it's not *what* you know, but *who* you know that counts."

Are there individuals you can influence who could in turn influence the decision makers? Are there previous program participants or colleagues who could be persuaded to put in a good word? Once advocates have been solicited and signed, the HRD manager can tap the advocate's knowledge of and experience with the decision makers and/or channel the advocate to influence the decision makers. A training manager I know is convinced her proposal was approved by top management because she had her friend, the dean of the local university business school, review the training

proposal and then favorably mention it to the company president at a cocktail party. Secretaries can also be highly effective down-field blockers! Their ability to manage the timing and exposure of correspondence regarding the proposal can enhance the development of a positive proposal image.

Once proposal attributes for marketing have been selected and individual advocates influenced, the HRD manager is now in a position to structure the proposal presentation.

What in your proposal appeals to accounting, operations, maintenance, the stockholder, and the public? Often, by shifting perspective, new dimensions will come to mind.

Another key point to remember in structuring the presentation, whether it is a formal "event" with a group or an informal dialogue with a single decision maker, is to couch the request in the language and style appropriate to the buyer and setting. Many excellent proposals have been disapproved because the presenter failed to accurately assess and deliver the form and substance which the decision makers preferred. Sellers have oversold, undersold, used figures and graphs before a non-figures oriented audience, used excessive buzz words and technical language, and used dog and pony showmanship when it wasn't showtime. What supporting data might be expected by the decision makers? What and how the buyers need to see and hear can be as important as what the buyers need to know—a subtle distinction which can turn the tide in the affairs of the seller!

The critical issues in need of prepresentation resolution can be distilled. Here are some suggestions to increase the chances of covering all the bases:

1. Anticipate resistance and then plan the necessary steps ahead to ensure success. There are risks involved with most proposal presentations. To assume tacitly your proposal will be approved is foolhardy.

2. Analyze the successes and failures which you and others experi-

enced in the past to determine why they occurred.

3. Consider coupling your proposal with another proposal which you know to be a sure winner.

4. Plan a fall back or compromise position. Consider recommending a longer program, a shorter program, a more expensive program, a less expensive program, et al.

5. Consider selling to decision makers individually rather than as a group. Decision makers rarely enjoy surprises.

6. Consider changing the principal presenter.

7. Consider selecting a different time, place, or method to make the proposal presentation.

8. Consider the organization's budgeting methodology and its impact on the proposal. Would a zero-base approach be more appropriate? Could the proposal be financed in a different manner (e.g., a grant, marketing the program externally, budgets from other units, going over budget, changing the rules)?

9. Consider changing the program methodology, length, materials, timing, instructor(s), target market.

10. Consider whether risking a disapproval on this proposal will start a chain of events which multiplies the loss to the HRD unit. Better to lose a battle—win the war!

Before leaving this section, take an HRD proposal which was not approved at some time in the past. Using your present knowledge of the needs and values of the decision makers, the presenter, the organization, and the 10 considerations listed above, try to figure out why the proposal failed to be approved. Done inclusively, this is a productive way to develop advocate involvement. Now think of a training proposal you plan to present some time in the future. What supporting data should you collect which might be expected by the potential buyer? Like saving canceled checks for that one-in-100 chance of a tax audit, consider every training program and activity as someday requiring cost justification to top management.

Presentation and Decision Phases. I once heard a highly effective marketing executive say, "When it comes to selling, if you've done your homework, the final exam is a piece of cake!" Admittedly overstated, it holds a measure of truth. If the HRD manager has mapped the mental terrain of the decision makers, maintained cognizance of his/her own needs and those of the organization, and constructed a marketing strategy with the assessment as mortar between the bricks, the actual presentation or promotion should include few surprises. Trump cards may be represented by advocates who are members of the decision-making body—stacking the deck in favor of approval. One should remember, however, that advocates represent reserve power, not core power. They are rarely kamikaze pilots. Unless the proposal is itself meritorious, when the curtain is drawn the HRD manager may find the audience devoid of supporters.

Keep in mind that the approval decision will occur only if the majority of the decision makers perceive (consciously or subconsciously) some direct or indirect personal benefit. The presentation should be made around the diagnosed personal needs of the audience. As the presentation proceeds, ask yourself, "What can I say or do to assist Mr./Ms. X in feeling that approval will be to their advantage?"

Maintain awareness of where you stand or sit, how you dress, the words you use, the material you present, and how each might be perceived by those present.

The marketing process continues beyond the achievement of a favorable decision. The HRD manager should "romance the sale"—selling advocates and the decision makers on the correctness of their decision. This prevents the onslaught of "buyers' blues." A way to nurture the process is to have those affected by the decision—the learners—voice favorable reaction in a way which filters to the top. Individual advocates should be continually won. Periodic status reports, while in some cases a requirement, can also serve to intensify decision correctness.

Each success brings greater likelihood of subsequent approval decisions; nothing breeds success like success. And perhaps nothing facilitates success more than awareness. Formal and informal feedback will serve to identify problems and opportunities for the HRD manager. A post-process critique of the marketing effort—assessment through decision—is critical for improved future endeavors. Objective appraisal of ongoing programs will help in making proposal changes which enhance the credibility of the entire HRD function.[5]

1. Bell, Chip R.. "Selling: Persuasion or Manipulation?" Xchange (Xerox Learning Systems). 1976, No. 3, p. 5.

2. Levitt, Theodore. Marketing for Business Growth. N.Y.: McGraw-Hill, 1974, p. 47.

3. Ibid. p. 8.

4. Levitt, Theodore, "Marketing Myopia," Harvard Business Review, (Sept-Oct. 1975), p. 26.

5. Appreciation is expressed to Bruce W. Fritch, Director of Marketing Planning, NCNB Corporation, for his editorial suggestions.

Reprinted from TRAINING, February 1977

PR THAT WORKS

If you really want to polish training's image
in your company, use what you know about
instructional technology

BY THOMAS PETRO
AND DONALD P. DUROCHER

If you ask some corporate training directors how their departments use public relations to anticipate training needs, to mold management perceptions of training and to market courses, you'll get a predictable response.

Most will recite a shopping list of communication vehicles they use to help sell their programs to the rest of the organization. They print catalogs, posters and brochures. They contribute stories to the company newsletter. Things like that.

In other words, they'll answer your question by telling you how they market courses. Chances are they'll ignore the parts about anticipating training needs and molding management perceptions.

Probe a little further and most training directors will readily admit that they're still fumbling in the dark about how to use public relations to do anything *but* market courses.

What if trainers could apply their own methodology—instructional technology—to develop an ongoing public relations program within their companies: a program designed to "train" all levels of management in how they should view both the concept of training and the training department itself.

Well, class is in session. What follows is a blueprint, based upon some basic principles of instructional technology, for building an effective public relations program for training in your own corporate environment.

We'll walk through the six steps of a public relations plan for training de-

partments: image analysis, quantifiable benchmarks, goal and objective setting, program design, implementation and measuring results. Sound familiar?

A good way to start is to review the main lessons learned over the last decade or so by people in other professions, such as accounting and law, who have tried successfully—and unsuccessfully—to position themselves and market their services. These lessons are fully translatable to corporate training departments, because training departments are, in fact, internal consulting organizations of professionals who provide services to their organizations.

Why PR fails

Many professionals in various industries (including training vendors and consultants) have been able to control the way their markets perceive them. Others have tried and failed. If a professional firm's public relations effort bombs, it's generally due to one or more of these five reasons:

1. *The firm thinks public relations means trying to tell the world how excellent it is.* This is the biggie, the fundamental mistake repeated *ad nauseum*, even by many people who bill themselves as PR professionals. The trouble with telling the world how wonderful you are is that nobody but you—and maybe your mother—cares. Successful public relations efforts concentrate on *demonstrating* excellence by communicating your insights into solutions to problems plaguing your markets.

A good example is a program oper-

ated by Arthur Andersen & Co. Every year, the Big Eight accounting firm interviews top executives of auto-supply companies about industry problems, possible solutions and what they think the future holds. The firm then produces a report and shares it with auto-supply companies. In other words, Arthur Andersen provides valuable information for this industry, and they update it each year. By doing this—not by trumpeting its own self-proclaimed virtues—Arthur Andersen has created the perception among auto-supply executives that it is the most knowledgeable CPA firm serving their industry.

People pay attention to messages in which they recognize value to themselves. The people who control your budget dollars don't want to listen to the sound of you patting yourself on the back. The gatekeepers of company communication vehicles (newsletters, annual reports, etc.)— and especially of outside vehicles such as newspapers and magazines— will "let you in" only if they think your message benefits the audiences they serve. Editors aren't press agents. It's not their job to help you promote yourself or to "give" you publicity.

Even if it worked from a strategic viewpoint, which it doesn't, the approach that views public relations as self-congratulatory puffery produces an immediate tactical problem: How in the world do you justify the company dollars you spend on a program that serves no one but you?

2. *The firm is not really good enough to deserve a better reputation.* Every major city has a professional firm or two that provides mediocre service but attracts a heavy flow of new business because it is excellent at promotion. These characters typically end up with a rapid turnover of clients who have been lured by silk-purse promises, only to find a sow's ear. A firm that deals with the general public can survive this way for a while. A company training department can't; it's dealing with a closed universe of customers—people who talk to each other.

3. *The firm doesn't really believe it provides excellent services.* Therefore, it doesn't believe it deserves a better reputation. Therefore, it pursues its public relations program halfheartedly. The inferiority complex is "confirmed" when the effort fails.

729

One of the nation's oldest law firms hired a public relations firm to try to reverse its declining growth rate. After spending several months interviewing the partners about their practice areas, the PR experts designed a program. But the law firm did not think highly enough of its calibre of service to implement the most important parts of the program. It authorized a brochure and some personnel releases ("Joe Writsandtorts has been promoted to the position of . . . . "). At year's end, revenues were down again.

4. *The firm expects change to occur too quickly.* When things don't improve immediately, it loses its will to continue to build what must always be a long-term effort.

5. *The firm mistakes the vehicles of public relations for a program of public relations.* Scattered publicity attempts and quasi-programs that ignore critical steps do not constitute a strategic public relations program and can't be expected to produce a significant change in perceptions. A shotgun approach won't do when a rifle is needed. Most training departments should be very familiar with mistake number five.

Now that we know something about public relations programs that don't work, let's design one that does.

Image analysis

Since you are the training expert here, no doubt you have a strong sense of your organization's training needs. You also have a sense of the image training enjoys in your company—the way both the concept of training and your department in particular are perceived by managers and others who interact with your group or make decisions important to its status and future.

But don't be guided solely by instinct, no matter how deeply grounded in experience. Methodical self-analysis, checked against what your customers say about their needs and perceptions, is the most frequently skipped step in developing a public relations program. And skipping it is comparable to skipping a front-end analysis in responding to a manager's diagnosis of what he or she considers a training problem. You can wind up designing a useless program to deal with a wildly erroneous perception of reality.

What you need is a public relations audit. If you can tap your company's public relations department or hire a PR consulting firm to help you conduct it, by all means do. Their expertise and outsiders' perspective will be invaluable. But if you have to go it alone, your familiarity with instructional technology will serve you well.

There are two steps to the public relations audit. First you need to clarify the training department's perception of itself. Then you examine the way it's perceived by its clients.

A model self-analysis starts with a rigorous look at how your department operates: how it works with senior, technical and operations managers; how it solves problems; how it handles course offerings, enrollments and marketing; and how it identifies and serves the broader training needs of the company and its various units.

A portrait also should emerge of your department's vision or mission for training. If your mission is to help the company achieve its goals, how do you think you can best fulfill that mission? A clear sense of corporate direction, or any anticipated change in that direction, needs to be identified in order to set the direction for training.

Much of this information should come from interviews with training staff members, individually and in groups. In these same interviews, gather impressions of how the department thinks it is perceived by its various customers within the organization. Something vital to nail down: Exactly who do you think those customers are? Try to identify and segment your markets.

In short, the self-analysis phase of a public relations audit tells you how you perceive yourself and how you *think* you are perceived by the rest of the company. Now you have to check those findings against the way your "markets" actually perceive you.

You'll want to use a variety of techniques to do the external study, similar to the lines of inquiry in a training needs analysis. But here you're coming from an image and marketing standpoint. The information-gathering process might include:

• Face-to-face interviews with key decision makers and people of influence throughout the organization, including those who rely heavily on training and those who don't. Probe their attitudes toward training in general and your department specifically. How often do they use your services? Can they cite examples when training made a difference in their operations?

• Phone or written surveys of middle and lower-level managers who make decisions about training for their subordinates. Go for their perceptions of strengths and weaknesses in your course offerings. Any performance improvements noted from specific courses?

• Reviews of your recent course evaluations. What do the trainees think of your programs?

Obviously, the list could go on. But once you feel you have a good handle on actual market perceptions, compare the internal and external studies to see where your perceptions square with your customers'—and where they don't.

It's possible at this point to get more than you bargained for. The results of your audit may tell you that what you need first is not a public relations program but a reorganization of your operation. The training department of one of the Big Three automakers was already studying its operations when it commissioned a public relations audit. The result was a total restructuring. The department transformed its primary role from that of a direct provider of classroom training to that of an internal consulting firm.

In fact, if you combine a public relations audit with a large-scale training needs analysis (What are the company's most pressing training needs?) and a marketing study (How can we deliver the right training "products" at the right price to the right markets at the right time and promote them effectively?), the results are quite likely to spur your department into a structural shake-up or a significant change in its service emphasis.

This raises a crucial point. Your customers perceive you for what you actually are, not in terms of what you may perceive as your greatest strength or potential. If you look like an orange and act like an orange, they'll see an orange—never mind that you want them to see you as an apple. This discovery can shed new light on some of your old frustrations. For example, why *should* your company's managers think their training department can help them improve performance, reduce costs and meet the demands of changing market imperatives when its course offerings don't seem any different than they were a decade ago?

Most effective public relations programs aim at changing *misperceptions*, not correct perceptions. If you want to be perceived as an apple, *you* probably will have to change until you resemble an apple. An orange who manages to get quoted in the company newsletter calling himself an apple should not be baffled by the continuing failure of the powers-that-be to envision him as one.

Benchmarks and measurements

Your audit findings will help you develop an itemized profile of where you stand right now. The elements in that profile will help define how you will position training, what your messages should be and to what misperceptions you will be directing heaviest attention.

State as many of those elements as possible in quantifiable terms. This will help you identify your program's goals and allow you to monitor progress. Establishing meaningful, quantifiable benchmarks can be as difficult in public relations as it is in management training, but if you don't do it, you're teaching a class with no pre- or posttesting to see if anyone learned anything.

Measurements that tell you whether you're succeeding in changing perceptions are not necessarily the same as those that tell you whether you're doing effective training. Quantifiable benchmarks for your public relations campaign might include things like growth in enrollment levels for key courses; an increase in course fees you're able to charge, without corresponding drops in enrollments; direct responses to promotional activities aimed at specific courses or company units; increased use of training courses and consulting help by particular units or managers; and changes in management attitudes toward training, as measured by periodic surveys. More subjective measures might include improvements in your working relationships with managers, changes in senior management's use or characterization of training and, last but not least, the gut feelings of the trainers who are regularly in contact with the customers.

Goal and objectives

The only measurements worth monitoring are those that directly or by inference serve as indicators of change. This might seem obvious, but its corollary is that many prospective measurements for a public relations program simply will not be central to the challenge *you* face.

State one overall goal such as, "Establish broad management recognition of training as the primary tool for change in corporate culture, policy and directions," or "Establish broad management recognition of training as a crucial tool in helping the corporation accomplish its goals."

Set objectives in areas that will demonstrate progress in addressing your long-term goal. Express them in quantifiable ways whenever possible, and state them in terms that can be measured against your benchmark findings. For example:

• Increase course head count by 15 percent by the end of the first year.

• Increase positive response from 33 to 40 percent by the end of the first year to the management-survey item: "Staff training has played a critical role this year in helping my unit accomplish its goals."

• During the first year, get three of the 10 division managers to explain, in stories for the company newsletter, the role training has played in making their units successful.

Other objectives might involve getting the company to establish an executive training committee, a company training policy, mandatory management courses or a requirement that training be included as a line item in all departmental budgets. Your public relations effort will be directed at cultivating an atmosphere in which such things can happen.

Design and implementation

Establish an underlying message. The benchmark data helped define the objectives your public relations program must address to accomplish your ultimate goal. The messages you need to communicate should now flow naturally out of those objectives, all directed toward your goal.

A simple statement of the underlying theme you want to communicate will guide you in setting priorities for your PR activities and help you determine the actual content of your messages. Just as you won't be telling the world directly how great your department is, you won't be overtly stating your message. The idea is to demonstrate the message in action. Show, don't tell.

On the other hand, it is perfectly acceptable to arrange for company managers to state your message for you. For example, the message you want to communicate might be something like, "Training helps our company improve performance," or "Training has a direct impact on the bottom line," or "Training can speed your climb up the corporate ladder."

Trainers have been hollering these things for years. The only receptive audiences they find are at training conventions. The challenge for your public relations program is how to demonstrate these messages through people and accomplishments in other operations in your company. You need actions that speak louder than your words.

Plan strategically. You want to demonstrate your message and chip away at accomplishing your objectives among certain audiences within the corporation, some of whom will be more important to your public relations program than others.

Start with what you most want to communicate and pinpoint the markets. Then forget—for now—about the conventional communication vehicles within your company and force the planning onto a strategic, innovative level. What would be the most powerful communication action you could take with each audience and with each objective to firmly implant your message in the receiver's mind?

Only run-of-the-mill public relations programs are carried out entirely within the boundaries of newsletters, brochures and the like. If you study an exceptional PR program, you'll find at least one component—one "big idea"—that forms its foundation. In almost all cases, the big idea has these five characteristics:

• It is ongoing or periodic; it's not a one-shot deal.

• It is indirect, providing a genuine service to its audience. This is not just the difference between a "hard sell" and a "soft sell." Remember Arthur Andersen's annual report to auto-supply companies? Had the accounting firm set out with purely altruistic motives—no PR agenda in mind—to offer a service to those companies, it might be producing that same report.

• It successfully interacts with a very well-defined audience, involving hard-to-reach individuals in two-way communication that benefits them.

• It is compelling to the audience because it provides them with personally useful information or participation unavailable in any other way. As a result, it overcomes the individual's natural inclination to resist "being sold."

• It positions the sponsoring organization over the long term in precisely the role it wishes to project, without the organization ever having to say it should be perceived in that manner.

Another good example of a "big idea" was conceived by a regional office of Arthur Young & Co., another Big Eight accounting firm. It wanted to be invited to submit bids to do financial audits of publicly traded companies, so the office adapted the *Fortune 500* concept to its local region by reporting annually on the performance of the area's largest publicly traded companies. It continued to add new components over the years: an annual survey of CEOs and CFOs on the economy, a ranking of the area's fastest-growing publicly traded companies and another of the fastest-growing private companies.

The small, elite prospect audience of CEOs and CFOs loved it. In the late 1970s, when the program began, the Arthur Young office averaged less than one bidding invitation a year. Today it averages more than four a year. It also became known as the auditing firm most knowledgeable about the area's publicly traded companies.

You may come up with a big idea for your operation quite easily if there is an obvious opportunity or need within a certain market in your company. But you may not arrive at it in your initial program development. A big idea can come as often from luck as from inspiration.

But in the process of forcing your thinking onto the creative level required to identify a big idea, you will probably create a number of "little" big ideas that are exciting in themselves.

Once you have mapped out several powerful actions—whether little or big ideas—that look like they'll move you toward your objectives and your ultimate goal, assess the existing communication vehicles under your direct control or available within the company. There are a lot of them. Consider course catalogs, training department newsletters, brochures, posters, fliers, direct mail pieces, training displays, electronic mail, company publications, meeting presentations, audiovisual profiles of the training department or blocks of courses, internal company television networks, speeches before company groups, cafeteria placemats, the corporate annual report—the possibilities go on and on.

Who is the audience for each of these vehicles? How important is each audience to your effort? How can you best use each vehicle to demonstrate your message or address a specific objective? Answer these questions and you've set your priorities.

That third question also prompts you to make intelligent tactical decisions. For example, your interests are better served by a story in the company magazine in which an executive credits training for part of his operation's success than by a profile of the training department written by you.

Remember, however, to drive these communication vehicles—don't be driven by them. The vast majority of public relations efforts exhaust almost all of their time and money communicating almost anything to almost anyone in the company through almost every vehicle possible. Look at the time many companies' PR departments spend writing and distributing "news releases" announcing every minor personnel change in the organization. That's an example of wasting time to communicate something simply because it's there.

Monitoring results

Monitoring and evaluating the results of a public relations program is an ongoing activity. This isn't to say that you scrap an element of your program if the phones don't immediately start ringing. You need to establish realistic expectations for each activity. And realism includes accepting the fact that changes in attitudes and behavior result from the cumulative impact of many "messages" over time. Arthur Young's miniature *Fortune 500* program didn't begin to generate new business inquiries or changes in executive attitudes toward the regional office until it had been operating for several years.

But if a particular tactic is directed at a very specific objective—increasing the engineering department's participation in a certain course, for example—response to that tactic needs to be monitored closely. If what you're doing clearly isn't working, change what you're doing. The problem may lie in the way you're presenting your message, the basic premise in which the tactic is grounded, the communication vehicles you're using or changes occurring in your marketplace.

After carefully diagnosing what is right and wrong about every aspect of your program, you may load more effort into the most effective activities, fine-tuning the campaign now that you know what works and what doesn't. You may have to redesign the entire program. Or your evaluation may indicate that you just have to sit back and be patient.

While you may not want to survey your audiences more than once a year, feedback mechanisms have to be designed to address each of your attitudinal-change objectives. You can't afford to wait 12 months to find out whether an element of your program is on target.

How do you measure changes in attitudes? The same way you do when you evaluate the results of a training program targeted at attitudinal change.

In the program's first year, you probably will find that the quantitative objectives you set at the start were either too aggressive or too pessimistic. This is to be expected since, with no experience to guide you, you probably established your measures on a best-guess basis.

If you discover that your program's results are falling far short of reasonable goals, you may need to reevaluate your overall expectations, the basic capabilities of the program design, or the amount of time and money you're spending on the effort. And don't forget to take a hard look at the operational changes you made (or failed to make) as a result of your original public relations audit. Remember: If you want to be perceived as an apple, your best bet is to look and act like an apple.

Reprinted from TRAINING, June 1988

BREAKING THE NEWS TO MANAGEMENT

Whether your findings are good, bad or somewhere in between, you have to know how to communicate them effectively

BY RON ZEMKE

Better you should *be* the bad news than have to deliver it," advises Susan E. Murray, training specialist for New York-based American Express Co. And that sentiment about sums up the way many trainers, organization development people and other HRD specialist feel about having to present disappointing program evaluation outcomes, uncomplimentary survey findings and sticky needs analysis results to their organizations management, or even to their departmental peers and bosses.

We recently asked a number of HRD research consultants, evaluation specialists and communication experts to share some words of wisdom on two key show-and-tell questions: "What is the best way to present research results to management?" and "Is there any special knack to presenting bad news outcomes?"

As you would expect of a question containing the phrase, "What is the best way to...," we received a lot of "it depends" answers. The most frequent "it depends" we heard revolved around the issues of purpose and audience.

Define the purpose first

John F. (Jack) Anderson, Anderson and Berdie Research, Minneapolis, puts the issue of purpose in a handy perspective: "When you're commissioned by an organization to do an evaluation or any kind of program or personnel research, it's because someone wants an answer to a question. But beyond that, we have an obligation to present the results of our work in a way that allows the decision makers in the audience to determine some course of action. If six months after you've presented your findings nothing has changed, you haven't really done the job you were commissioned to do."

Though others said it differently, the "cause some action" focus seems to be a good touchstone. To paraphrase Anderson and the others interviewed, the purpose of any presentation of field research findings, such as an evaluation study or needs analysis, is to communicate in a manner that allows others to formulate and instigate a course of action. Another way to say that is when we report findings to a sponsor or client, our one and only goal should be to cause someone to do something. Until you can answer the questions, "Who do you want to have do *what* and *how* do you get them to do it?," you can't start planning a presentation. At least not a presentation with a chance of communicating something specific to someone.

Even if you are reporting that everything is okay in a program, work group, system or whatever it is you are studying, there is an action goal. The desired action may be to gain consensus that the program should continue unchanged or uninterrupted. It could also be that your goal is to keep the program funded. It might even be that you want to demonstrate your competency and worth. Regardless of specifics, every presentation needs a clearly conceived action goal.

Eight ways to make it work

Beyond the "define a purpose" message, our respondents had some definite "how to's" to pass along. Their counsel can be divided into eight key points or rules— small r, please—to bear in mind when preparing a results or findings presentation for delivery to the study sponsor.

1 Know thy audience. When you develop training, you do your best to make it audience sensitive. The same treatment should be afforded the planning of an evaluation or research results presentation. Some of the obvious audience questions to ask and answer are:
- Is the audience all decision makers?
- How do they like results communicated?
- What sorts of presentations have they given "10s" to in the past?
- How do they respond to displays of numbers? Tables? Graphs? Charts?

As a rule of thumb, it's safe to say that decision makers are more receptive to "big picture" results reports than they are to reams of charts and correlations. The further removed the decision maker is from the problem, the more concerned he or she is with broad results and findings. Of course there are data-cruncher decision makers to be dealt with, but they tend to be a minority. The best rule of thumb is, "Ask 'em how they like their eggs." No one expects the fry cook to guess how you want your eggs; they won't fault you for asking how they want their results cooked and served. Don't, under any circumstance, try to outguess the audience. Find out how they want their results packaged and then do it.

2 Communicate as you go. Communicating results is not a one-shot affair. Douglas R. Berdie, the other half of Anderson and Berdie, believes that part of the communication job is to keep the client posted on everything that's happening. Send the sponsor and/or key decision makers copies of surveys, schedules and your routine field communiques about the project. Pen some sort of FYI on their copies. As results accumulate, share bits and pieces with your key person or persons.

Four reasons for continuous communication:

• The sponsor is paying for your time and effort and needs to see energy being expended; action builds credibility and trust.

• The results of your study will be more easily accepted by those who have ownership feelings toward the study. Asking the sponsor for advice and making brief informal interim reports help build that ownership.

• Sponsors and key decision makers can give valuable feedback. An unexpected, unusual or especially damning finding needs validation. Sponsors can tell you if your findings make sense and they can tell you how others are going to respond when your findings are made public. Both these bits of information help you tailor the presentation of results to your audience.

• Sponsors don't like public surprises, especially bad ones. By giving key decision makers or sponsors an advanced look at results, you give them time to think about implications and prepare their response to the public presentation of results. If results are good, they need time to see implications and get excited about them. If results are bad, they need time to plan response strategies. Sponsors and key decision makers want to be on your side— they hired you— and they want to appear calm and in control. A tactical information leak gives them the lead time they need to look good *and* be on your side.

3 Dope out the best "media-time-style" mix for clients. Most results presentations follow the rule of tradition: We do what we've seen others do and hope it works. If our organization traditionally writes 200-page reports, *we* write 200-page reports. If most presentations are verbal, to small groups, we follow this organizational family formula as well. In reality, a two-day presentation and a 200-page report may be too little for some groups and studies; a two-hour presentation and a 20-page report too much for other circumstances.

The trick is to tailor. If your report is to be made to six people, find out as much as you can about the communication and organizational needs of those six people. What issues are sensitive to them? What vested interests do they have that relate to your study? What are their communication styles? What outcomes do they expect, and what unexpected results might be rejected out of hand?

Regardless of what you deduce about your client's needs expectations and communications comfort zone,

there are some overriding style points or tips and tricks for effective client communication.

• If you find you must prepare a written report, do so in English, not thesis. The objective is to communicate, not to overpower.

• In both written and oral communications to mixed audiences of decision makers and technical people, use a *Wall Street Journal* or pyramidal format. Basically, that means begin the report with a brief statement of the problem under investigation, findings and, if appropriate, conclusions and recommendations. In written form this Executive Overview, as it is sometimes dubbed, will take two to five pages tops. In oral presentation it should take less than an hour to establish rapport, set a workable climate and get to the punch line. The subsequent parts of the report simply elucidate the executive overview and, if necessary, explain study methods, data reduction procedures and the like.

• Most audiences prefer a *descriptive* results report to correlational or complex tabular presentations. If you are an in-house or trusted investigator, you are probably respected as an expert and expected to be competent. Spare your audience the details of your design and analysis steps if you can. Keep your computer runs to yourself.

• Clearly separate findings, interpretations, conclusions and recommendations. Dr. Darwin Hendle, University of Minnesota measurement services center, suggests that clients do want to hear your ideas on possible problem solutions, but they need to know what is supportable fact or finding and what is conjecture. After all, you'll probably never know as much as the client about the fit of your finding with the area under study.

• Accuracy is another key to credibility. Spelling and title errors, tables that don't total 100%, wrong dates and misattributions interfere with the building of credibility. When in doubt, use phrases such as "It is our understanding" or "It is our perception of the situation" rather than "The problem is" or "Since the goal of your division is to." Being wrong but aware that you might be inaccurate is forgivable; cocksureness is not.

• Think your way through the media use and choreography of the presentation. Use the same media-method savvy you use when designing training, a sales presentation or a media show of any sort. "Why," Anderson asks provocatively, "do we assume that a report is a written

minithesis or that an oral presentation requires an armful of unreadable tables on mylar sheets? How about presenting results in skit form, or poetic, or cartoon or a straight slide show? People somehow have gotten the idea that an evaluation results report must be dull and dry."

4 Pilot test the presentation. We pilot test training, don't we? Isn't an evaluation study or a needs analysis just as important to our success? Get your research team, your department's two biggest nitpickers and the coordinator from your client department together and do a dress rehearsal. Only during a dry run will you find out that your findings aren't as crystal clear as you thought or that "MBO" or "TA" or "Behavior Mod" are taboo words in the client organization while "goal setting," "interpersonal communication" and "performance management" are not. You'll also get a test of the sell-power of your presentation from the client rep.

5 When you have bad news—deliver it first. Research by Linda Marshall and Robert Kidd of Boston University suggests that people prefer to hear bad news first, followed by good news. Though they aren't sure, they suspect the contrast between the bad and the good makes the good seem better, while the bad placed a bit further back in "history" seems not quite so bad.

Whatever the case, bad news is still bad news and must be delivered with care. Don't begin with, "Good morning. Your course really stinks. Now for the good news..." Steve Mayer of Rainbow Research, another Minneapolis research firm, cautions that bad news should be delivered directly and not unnecessarily minimized or sugar coated. "If you minimize bad news," he says, "you rob your sponsor of an important learning opportunity."

Anderson cautions not to overblow the good news either. "You might get away with one of those 'This is the finest program of its kind we've ever had the inestimable pleasure to evaluate' evaluations once— or twice— but people get awfully suspicious of that sort of syrupy thing," he says.

A good model for delivering bad news is the fine arts review. People who review books, movies, plays, art shows and the like know that a bad review is a more difficult review to write, but often a more interesting review to read. The reviewer must compare and contrast, use examples and analogies, and generally construct a more persuasive argument than is necessary for complimentary reviews. Edward F. Kelly, Syracuse University center for instructional development, believes that the literary criticism approach to evaluation is useful because it demands a public demonstration of justification on two fronts: "These claims are, in the first place, that the object either met or failed to meet a particular norm or set of norms and, in the second place, that these norms were themselves appropriate to the judgment." Where data-testing techniques give a false sense of authority to a finding, the literary criticism approach requires argued defense of value judgments.

6 Leave nothing to chance. Nitpick your presentation— and all the components— to death. You may have conducted the best study in the world and developed strong, compelling results and findings, but you won't gain a grain of favor if your presentation has halitosis.

Using sharp word-processed copies of written materials instead of poor photocopies or mimeos, packaging written materials in attractive binders and the like, and using professionally prepared visuals gains points— important credibility points. Likewise, making certain that presentation rooms are the right size for the group, appropriate AV equipment is on hand and functioning, chairs and tables are appropriate to the group, and the room itself is clean and temperate are examples of nitpicking that gain credibility points for a face-to-face presentation. Apologizing for report misspellings or smudges, overhead projectors that don't work, and a pile of party hats and empty champagne bottles doesn't gain back lost credibility points.

7 Expect to be rejected. A client once did us a great favor by explaining that we should be prepared for rejection by his group. "We won't believe much of what you tell us right now. But in a few months, you'll see a lot of action." This same client, a bank senior vice-president who had seen the results in preview— the tactical leak at work— and knew them to be potentially unsettling, went on to compare his group's acceptance of bad news results to Dr. Elisabeth Kubler-Ross' stages of death acceptance. And oh how right he was! In the intervening years we have observed about seven steps or stages in the "Acceptance of Bad News" syndrome.

- *Wrong*
  The client believes your findings are wrong and should be dismissed summarily.
- *Right, but a bad sample*
  The client believes *you* believe your findings, but thinks they are based on bad sampling and are a statistical accident.
- *Right, but trivial*
  The results and findings are right, but out of context. Seen in the proper perspective, the *insider's* perspective, the bad news results are not important.
- *Right, but we like it this way*
  The results are correct and important. However, we don't consider the situation bad; on reflection we really *like* things this way.
- *Right, but we can't change*
  Okay, so things are bad. That's the nature of the business. We would have to change all of society to make any impact on our situation.
- *Okay, let's do something*
  The problem is real and probably manageable. Let's do something about it.
- *Problem! What problem?*
  The client accepts the problem, solves it, and goes on. In instances of especially sensitive organizational problems, repression of or denial of the original problem takes

---

NEWTON'S LAWS APPLY TO COMMUNICATION

BY RON ZEMKE

According to Edgar B. Wycoff, associate professor of communications, University of Central Florida, Orlando, most of the research and writing on communication can be encapsulated in three basic underlying principles strikingly similar to Newton's three basic laws.

Law 1. Newton— For every action, there is an equal and opposite reaction.

Law 1. Wycoff—For every communication action, there will be some internal receiver reaction.

"With every utterance you make, with every sign or symbol you display, if it is perceived, there will be a response by someone," says Wycoff. The most important analogy to draw from Newton's first law is that "in both the physical as well as the social realms, we cannot escape consequences. Our lives are made up of a continuous stream of consequences or reactions to our actions," he explains. Wycoff contends the first law applies as relentlessly to communication as it does to baseballs and concrete walls.

Law 2. Newton— Every particle of matter attracts every other particle of matter with a force that varies directly as the product of their masses and inversely as the square of the distance between them.

Law 2. Wycoff— One person's thoughts are attracted to another person's thoughts with a force directly proportional to the similarity of their experience.

"Not only do 'birds of a feather flock together,' but researchers have found that when the average person has a choice, he will tend to choose someone like himself with whom to communicate," Wycoff explains. "And the more alike two people are, according to research, the better they communicate. They call it 'homophily' as opposed to 'heterophily.' "

Law 3. Newton— A body at rest will tend to remain at rest until acted upon by some outside force.

Law 3. Wycoff— The clarity of your communication is dependent on your willingness to dramatize the important points of your message.

Newton's third is sometimes referred to as the law of inertia. "The 'body' which tends to remain at rest, from the standpoint of communication, is the other person's interest or the focus of their concentration," says Wycoff. "We might think of the mind as a high flywheel. The ponderous weight is at rest and needs an ever-so-powerful force to set it rolling in the direction of our topic."

Whether you find good Dr. Wycoff's analogy between Newton's Laws and the principles of communication germane or gibberish is beside the point. When we begin to consider and look for behavioral principles as potentially powerful as the laws of physics and chemistry, we begin to see our realm of interest from a new perspective.

Wycoff's concept of Newton's Laws for communication appeared as "Canons of Communication" in the March 1981 issue of *Personnel Journal.*

Reprinted from TRAINING, August 1981

place; like the ex-smoker who, having become a nonsmoker, can't really remember having any difficulty quitting.

The importance of this syndrome is in its preparatory value. Knowing the possibility of this reaction helps us keep our mental health and patience intact. Knowing of the syndrome can also help the client maintain a measure of composure when the client team trips off into it.

8 Evaluate. How do you evaluate an evaluation? Or any other research effort for that matter? One way is simply to stand back and watch. If you see activity taking place around the neighborhood of the problems and opportunities you elucidated, that's a nice indicator. After some time has passed, a more direct indicator is to ask what's happened as a result of the study, report and presentation. If the answer is, "Oh, a few things" — which of course is a euphemism for nothing— you have just inherited a new study. What study? The study you're going to have to do in order to find out why your study didn't produce the results you planned, or any results at all. After all, if your study was on target and your presentation followed these guidelines, it *should* have had an effect.

Reprinted from TRAINING, August 1980

THE PLUSSES OF A WRITTEN POLICY

A training policy statement can be the
vehicle for putting
everyone—management, trainers
and trainees—on the right track

BY STEPHEN P. BECKER

"Write it down." That's good basic advice for any kind of manager. Your job is to manage the training work of others rather than do it all yourself. What you want others to do remains clear over the period it takes to do it when it is written down and available for reference.

Similarly with the basic training policy of your company: In many cases you'll want to write it down. A clearly written statement of general training policy explains to all concerned—management, trainers and trainees alike—the agreed-upon direction, procedures, expectations and limitations of the company training program.

A written training policy clarifies the training needs of your organization, focuses attention on the ability of the training department to meet those needs and, as the policy is developed, provides you with an opportunity to examine your career goals and managerial style. The exercise of writing a training department policy should be approached seriously and conscientiously, since it can have significant impact on the organization's development and your own.

The first decision you will have to make is whether a written policy statement is called for in your company's case. This decision will depend on the environment of your organization and on how you plan to use the policy statement.

The best use you can make of a policy is as a basis for planning training department strategy and programs. A policy should give you long-range direction so that your activities are continually becoming more important to the health of your organization and its individual members. If you intend to "whip out" your policy to justify not developing or conducting a program, you are heading for failure. It would be better to have no policy at all than to use it that way and lose respect for yourself; no trainer can afford that.

Some organizations do not want a written policy. This is particularly true of many smaller organizations. They think that written (public) policies limit flexibility. They want to make individual decisions about individual employees rather than be forced through policy to do the same thing for many people.

The fact is that the top management of some organizations hate to obligate themselves in a general way. The obligation, they feel, could be very costly. If this is the case in your situation, you can still develop a private policy statement for use in developing plans for the future and as a guideline for your department.

Once you are committed to writing a training policy you will need to decide if you are going to do it alone, or with some other members of your department or organization. I'd suggest trying it alone first, then checking it out with others. This approach forces you to describe what you believe is the role of training and encourages you to clarify the responsibilities of the training department. To accomplish this you will have to rethink your original "contract" with the organization. You will also need to decide if the assumptions and expectations made about training in the organization really fit real training needs.

Once you write the statement, the checking-out process will match your perceptions about training, in that environment, with those of other people. Be sure to ask people who are in a position to support and utilize training to review the policy. It's also a good idea to review your policy with managers who represent powerful organizational functions.

You may find at this point that you have a responsibility to help the organization decide or know what it needs or wants from a training department. It may be reasonable for you to do a comprehensive needs or performance analysis prior to establishing a training policy. In fact, if you intend training to have a major impact on improving the performance of your organization, it is probably essential to conduct this kind of survey.

It may not be necessary to spend the time and money for a complete analysis. If your training responsibilities are limited to a single area—sales training or orientation programs, for example—there is a question of the extent of analysis necessary. Just how much detail is called for is a management decision you will have to make. If you have a large charter from an organization ready to support it, then a performance analysis prior to writing a training policy is definitely advisable.

A policy which has been agreed upon (at least in principle) by all the significant people who will be involved with the training department will do many things for you. It will identify the scope of training in the organization. Training may be seen as skills training,

---

---

management development, organization development, media services, sales training, management by objective, adult basic education, on-the-job training, college recruiting, orientation programs, or a wide variety of other activities. It may be seen as all of these or a combination of some of them. Whatever the case, at least you and your organization will agree on what your training operation is all about.

A second benefit of your policy statement is that it will help you plan your individual programs. In order to breathe life into a policy, there must be programs or systems working. Making decisions about what those programs ought to be will be easier because they will have to support the policy. For example, your policy may state that the training department will provide a continuing supply of well-trained first-line supervisors. If this is the case, then you, and everybody else, are pretty clear about the kind and number of programs the organization needs.

Another benefit is that once programs are planned with regard to policy, it is much easier to prepare a budget or to justify expenditures. If the policy is a good one that

meets the organizational needs and is generally acceptable, and if certain programs are required to fulfill the policy, then the need for the necessary budget to get the job done becomes reasonable.

A training policy will help you, and everybody else, determine whether the training department is on track. It is a way to measure training success. If there is in fact a continuing supply of first-line supervisors available who are well trained, then the department will be succeeding. If there is not, you won't.

Because a policy statement makes the success or failure of training visible, it is important that you take as much time as possible to develop the statement. You must make sure that both you and your organization can realistically live up to the policy on a day-to-day basis. In addition, you must want to be visible. If you are proud of your work and want some "positive strokes," a written policy may be a good thing for you. If you are a manager who prefers not to be too visible, then don't write a training policy.

Your training policy statement should be revised periodically to reflect changing priorities in your organization and changing capabilities in your training department. Your policy should be reviewed at least every two years. This interval will give you time to develop and implement some major programs and systems. When that has been accomplished, it becomes appropriate for you to re-evaluate the role of training.

Since you are a manager, your personal style and goals can have an impact on training policy. If you are an innovator, creator, and developer of programs and systems, then the organization must need that kind of person to manage training. That means there must still be an organizational need for new kinds of training. If there is, then you are the person to make it happen—you're in the right place at the right time. If, on the other hand, the organization basically has all the training sys-

tems and programs it needs, the training manager's job is in a *de facto* way one of departmental administration and maintenance. If this is the case, there is probably a mismatch between you and the job.

This kind of gap can develop over a two-year period and could

---

---

certainly happen over five years. The point here is that there must be consistency between the training needs of the organization, the written training policy, and your career goals and managerial style as the training manager.

If this consistency does not exist, then there will be some lack of efficiency. You may sacrifice your personal needs and ambitions in order to serve the organization and be true to the policy. You may also begin behaving in a way that satisfies your own needs at the expense of the organization and its training policy. Either situation is bad.

By periodically reviewing your own aspirations and performance in terms of your decisions and the way you spend your time, you should be able to determine if a change is necessary. You may be ready for a new challenge or the policy may require improvement because the training needs of the organization have changed. Whatever the outcome, you will be in a better position to make decisions about your own development and the role of training in your organization if you base your thinking on a written training policy.

Reprinted from TRAINING, January 1975

DEFINE AND BROADCAST YOUR TRAINING PHILOSOPHY

How do you solve the problems of standardizing training in a decentralized organization? Put your goals and beliefs down on paper

BY BARRY LASTRA
AND MAURICE B. NICHOLS

My company made a major change in organization design last year. Four autonomous operating companies headquartered in different geographical areas and responsible for their own marketing efforts became one company headquartered in San Francisco with responsibility for all U.S. operations.

This reorganization had a dramatic effect on our sales training organization. In two of the "old" operating companies, training was centrally controlled from headquarters, with trainers reporting to training supervisors. In the other two companies, training was decentralized, with trainers reporting to line field sales managers and taking only functional guidance from staff training units at headquarters. Each of the four operating companies had its own management style and training approach. With the advent of our newly reorganized company, this all had to change.

In the new company, Chevron U.S.A. Inc., training is now a decentralized function, with trainers reporting to line sales managers. Our headquarters training staff provides overall direction for training programs and gives policy and functional guidance to field trainers.

The problem we were—and are still, to some extent—faced with was: How do we determine a central theme, while still allowing field trainers to be responsive to their own— and their managers' —unique styles?

The headquarters marketing training staff spent the first 15 months, until April of this year, working individually and in small groups with field managers and trainers. Most of our time was spent determining the program structure and style of presentation. We didn't try to change the basic content, because the needs of our target groups (mostly dealers, distributors, or jobbers) really hadn't changed. The only change was in our internal management style. We finally put together—with considerable pain— programs that are consistent and uniform. The pain was caused, quite naturally, by each of the four (now extinct) training groups "knowing" their program was exactly right and that any change would just "screw things up." During all this time, our focus was primarily geared toward the mechanical efforts of drawing people and programs together.

Suddenly we realized that we'd been working so hard on meeting new people and program mechanics that we'd overlooked a potential solution to many of the questions in the minds of both our field managers and trainers. We overlooked a well-defined training philosophy.

I can now say—in hindsight—that we probably should have started here. However, because of new management and the traumatic experience of a major reorganization, we might not have received immediate acceptance of the meaning behind an overall phi-

---

THE ROLE OF TRAINING AND DEVELOPMENT AT CHEVRON U.S.A. INC.

Philosophy

The purpose of training and development is to maintain and improve effectiveness and efficiency of individuals within the organization. This can only have sustained effect if it influences the actions and practices of line managers so as to serve better both the self-interest of employees (personal return, both tangible and intangible) and the needs of the corporation (profit return, both short and long range).

All training and development within the company is based on the firm belief that:
1. Employees have a need for growth and self-fulfillment which can be compatible with the goals of the organization for the benefit of both.
2. Learning is a self-activity; all employee development is self-development.
3. The primary job of a trainer is not to train; it is to manage the learning process for those individuals with whom the trainer interfaces.
4. Training, to be effective, must be a function of line management.

Characteristics

A training and development system should have the following characteristics:
1. It requires management commitment and follow-up. This only comes about when training helps individuals accomplish:
   - Their established objectives;
   - The changes they desire; and
   - The mission of their organization.
2. It recognizes that most performance problems are not caused by lack of skill but are execution problems—caused by lack of feedback, either positive or negative.
3. If no measurement can be developed, training is not undertaken. Measurement can be either objective or subjective but is based on observable data, preferably in dollars of cost reduction or productivity increase.
4. Programs are tested both on the job and in the classroom before publication—and they are revised until they meet standards.
5. It is based on the fact that new employees learn how to do most jobs very quickly. Therefore, training concentrates only on major payoff areas of what they are not performing after some time on the job. (This is in sharp contrast to the organization that believes new employees must be formally taught everything.)
6. As company goals change, the training system adjusts to meet the new goals of the company.
7. It recognizes the difference between:
   - Training (improve performance in current job);
   - Education (improve competency in a specified career direction); and
   - Development (prepares employee to move with the job as it changes and grows).
8. It has qualified individuals who:
   - Maintain both knowledge and skill, in depth, to identify and formulate concepts and implementation techniques which will strengthen management at all levels;
   - Stay abreast of and evaluate changes in managerial practices;
   - Stay abreast of training and development techniques and procedures; and
   - Recommend and/or adopt changes as appropriate.

SHOULD TRAINING DIRECTORS INSTRUCT? SOMETIMES

BY JUDSON SMITH

"Many training directors consider instructing to be one of the last things they wish to do," says Ray Crapo, from the Education and Training Office of Court Administration. Crapo suggests that many directors believe being stereotyped as an instructor makes it more difficult for them to move into decision-making areas within the company. In addition, he says, some firms hire directors who lack experience in their firm's field and who are not qualified to instruct. In this situation, the director is a resource consultant and administrator who simply happens to work in the area of education and training.

When, then, should training directors instruct? Crapo lists several times:

1. Some instruct due to their high degree of specialization and knowledge. But there are psychological barriers to this form of instructing. The training director must avoid those areas of specialization that the chief executive officer has already usurped; usually he or she does this by bringing in a well-known consultant who will reflect favorably on the CEO and the firm. The only safe time to instruct, Crapo says, is when the training director can do so in specialized areas that require elaborate preparation.

2. Sometimes training directors must put out fires in crisis situations. Here the training director earns the firm's gratitude for support during the crisis and is considered the best source available to solve an immediate problem. But this situation can lead to a "Catch 22" nightmare: If the TD is asked to instruct whenever a crisis occurs, then refusal to instruct during a crisis means refusing to be part of the crisis-solving team. But by choosing to instruct, the TD risks being thought of as an instructor rather than a manager.

3. Many TDs operate in a "mixed mode" environment, which offers several advantages to instructing. First, the director learns about the response to a training program by teaching it. Second, staff development is enhanced through example, and no one can accuse the director of failing to be involved with the real-life world of training. Third, it improves the director's credibility with vendors and staff. And, fourth, it forces the director to improve his or her professionalism in the craft of program delivery.

Crapo says, "The director who instructs ought to ask himself or herself questions such as Time Management Expert Alan Lakein's classic 'What's the best use of my time right now?' The director also should determine to what extent being a practitioner is helpful to his or her own growth and development as well as that of the training department."

Training implications

The multifaceted implications of all this for training professionals raise questions such as: "Is the delivery of training little more than a stepping stone in the training director's growth?" and "Is training best left to lower-paid, less experienced people, or should the director participate as an instructor?" Crapo believes that those who consider the training director to be a highly proficient manager who just happens to have grown through the training route are undermining the whole rationale of the training profession.

"What makes the training profession unique," he explains, "may be found in the process during which one or more human beings is exposed to new information in an environment carefully constructed so as to motivate the absorption of new information. And that translates into one word— instruction. But the training director should be a teacher/participant/facilitator of instruction, not just a management expert. And it is up to training directors to 'sell' this idea to top management so that management will respect them as much as it would a consultant who brings in the same program and expertise."

Reprinted from TRAINING, September 1979

THREE CATEGORIES OF TRAINING

The total context of training can be subdivided into three categories:

Training can be defined as those activities designed to improve performance on the job the employee is presently doing, is being hired to do, or is being promoted into (provided the promotion is to a position having the same basic area of activity—merely greater responsibility, more authority, a larger scope, etc.).

Education includes those activities which are designed to improve the overall competence of an employee in a specified direction beyond the job now held. The employee is being prepared for a different place in the organization from that he now holds. Education includes preparation for promotion into a position with new areas of activity; it also includes learning inputs for long-range career advancement.

Development activities are those which increase the competence and ability of an employee to move with the organization as it changes and grows. Development is concerned with the future of the organization and the individual and usually has goals which cannot be stated in specific behavioral terminology. The current job is evolving and changing and what it will be in the future probably has not been identified; the future conditions and standards of proficiency are not today's reality. Employee development is designed to produce a viable and flexible work force as the organization moves into the future.

losophy. By working together, we gained some understanding of each other's points of view. I'll use that as the reason (or excuse) why we waited until April of this year to formalize the philosophy.

At this point, our philosophy is too new for me to evaluate its use by managers. However, several have told me that it has helped them gain a better understanding of training. They also see its value for their performance planning sessions with the trainers who report to them because it gives them an overall goal direction. My guess is that, after a year or so, we'll want to re-examine our philosophy and perhaps make it more "complete." The principles won't change, of course. But we'll try to make things clearer and more explicit for our managers.

Reprinted from TRAINING, November 1978

THE ONE-PERSON TRAINING DEPARTMENT

Running a one-person training department
calls for a variety of skills.
Before you hang up a hatrack, find out how
many hats you'll have to wear

BY JUDITH H. STEELE

Congratulations! As the new training director, you're in a one-person training department, you *are* the whole show. You serve as training designer, training coach, training accountant and training publicist, as well as training director.

You don't have to be "Supertrainer" to conquer the one-person training department challenge, says one expert who did it. But, according to Rosalie Hakker, it's not enough just to work harder. Instead, you must invest your energy where it can have maximum effect. To do more than just survive, you need to enlarge your resources and increase your visibility.

Hakker offered her tips at a recent New York City ASTD workshop attended by one-person training department heads from diverse companies. Now the head of her own consulting firm, Ms. Hakker told the group how she set up a one-person training department at Suburbia Federal Savings and Loan in Garden City, NY. After three years, she had expanded her staff to include two trainers and— no easy feat— a full-time secretary.

Hakker, who boasts an advertising and marketing background, stresses the importance of using a sales approach. While any trainer needs to weave a sales strategy into the training process, she said, it's especially crucial for the trainer who's forced to work alone.

These are her practical hints for multiplying your training impact when you carry the training burden singlehandedly.

Look before you leap

Since mistakes can be extra costly for those who face the training music alone, do your homework. And do it before you prescribe training panaceas, perhaps even before you set up shop in your new firm.

When you pore over the company's annual reports and organization charts, read between the lines. Take the pulse of the organization to find out where it is right now. But don't limit yourself to the standard needs-analysis tools— questionnaires, attitude surveys and interviews. If your organization deals with the public, survey the customers directly, suggests Ms. Hakker, who tried this approach at Suburbia Federal.

Do you want to find out how secretaries answer the phone? Call up all the vice-presidents' offices and record the secretaries' responses. Armed with concrete data to pinpoint training needs, you'll be better able to sell your ideas, as well as demonstrate the improvements your training activities produce.

Get out from behind your lonely desk

You can hardly expect recognition for training if you're hiding behind a pile of papers. Burst out of your cocoon and take a purposeful stroll around your company.

Have lunch with a different person each week. In one lunch hour, you may learn more about the organization's needs than you'd learn in a week of formal interviews.

In the course of amiable conversations, you're developing a training cheering section, identifying the key people who will help your training programs succeed. Later on, several of them may become part of a formal training advisory committee to give you feedback, guidance and support.

Use the principle behind "man in the street" interviews to help you lay your training foundation. Notes Hakker, "Marketing companies don't spend all that money just to ask people foolish questions. They really conduct survey interviews to spread a product's name around." The name of your product is *training*. Make sure it's heard loud, clear and often. Tell your coworkers what you're there for and what you intend to do.

"You may not have done anything concrete yet," says Hakker, "but you'll soon have a whole force out there talking up how great you are and expecting you to succeed."

If you can't count on anyone else to promote training, you'll just have to double as your own public relations agent.

Decide how your single small voice can gain the impact of a powerful roar. For a starter, there's the company newspaper. Its editors would probably welcome a pithy paragraph or two. For added impact, highlight your article with photos of smiling trainees "graduating" from one of your successful training courses.

But don't wait patiently for the organization to wake up and take notice. Herald your achievements by issuing your own "training newsletter," in which you document your training department's great strides. Afraid your publicity release will never reach senior management? "There's no reason you can't drop it off in person at a board meeting," suggests Hakker.

Remember another advertising gem—the testimonial. Invite a representative of senior management to drop in at the start of every training class. "This tells the trainees that someone very important has put money behind you and wants to get results," says Hakker. While you might begin this strategy to enhance your status, it could yield an unexpected payoff. Perhaps your senior official will linger, ask questions and become truly involved in the training session.

Emphasize training's payoff

Avoid the shotgun approach when you're all alone on the training team. A round of training here and a round of training there may add up to an impressive body count— but few results you can document.

To keep from spreading yourself too thin, consider your needs analysis carefully. Focus on those few areas where you will be able to demonstrate tangible improvements.

Listen to the organization, but don't let it dictate your function. Use pro-

SHOULD YOU MANAGE YOUR OWN BOSS

BY RON ZEMKE

It may sound a little nutsy at first—the idea that you should manage your boss. But, according to John J. Gabarro, professor of organizational behavior at Harvard Business School, and John P. Kotter, also of Harvard Business School, your organizational survival—not to mention your effectiveness—may depend on your skill at consciously managing the ebb and flow of superior-subordinate relationships. The pair reports that "recent studies suggest that effective managers take time and effort to manage not only relationships with their subordinates but also those with their bosses." Gabarro and Kotter emphasize that active management of boss-subordinate relations is not only characteristic of highflying managers but is also a significant factor in organizational success and profitability.

How does one manage one's manager? According to Gabarro and Kotter, there are three general areas to consider.

1. **Understand your boss and his or her context.** To work effectively for someone, you need to understand clearly his or her goals, pressures, strengths, weaknesses, blind spots and preferred working style. Suppose that your new boss likes formal meetings, complete with agendas and required background reading. You, on the other hand, favor informal idea-spinning, free-flowing forums. Guess who'd better give in and learn a new style?

If that sounds like a cop-out, the researchers caution, take your pulse again. You'll never know how effective—helpful to you—your new boss can potentially be until you do everything you can to help him or her put a best foot forward and operate from his or her strengths and within his or her comfort zone.

How do you go about *understanding* the boss? You can ask about objectives, personal agendas and issues. Many bosses, however, can't state explicitly where they're coming from. In that instance, say Gabarro and Kotter, accept a strategy of:

• Never taking information from the boss at face value; look for a hidden meaning in the speech or memo.

• Making no assumptions until the data are overwhelming. Remember the old Red Motley line, "When you *assume*, you make an *ass* out of *u* and *me*." Silly, but in this case probably good advice.

• Continually seeking clarification of the boss's goals.

2. **Assess yourself and your needs.** This simply means knowing as much about yourself as you know about, or need to know about, your boss. Gabarro and Kotter emphasize the importance of understanding your attitude toward authority figures. If you can admit that authority makes you testy, you can try harder to hold yourself in check when the boss gets "bossy." If, however, the boss likes a good fight but you're a pacific sort, you've got to learn to be more aggressive when the situation demands it.

3. **Develop and maintain a relationship.** This is the toughest and most complex bit of advice Gabarro and Kotter offer. First, work out a style that is comfortable for both but that also meets your needs. Next, develop mutual expectations, based on agreed-upon targets and ultimate goals. Meeting the boss's informational needs is also critical. Some hate bad news and react adversely to it. Others can stonewall a complete debacle. There's no excuse for delivering only "good news" to your boss, but you *can* learn to give bad news in a way that won't cost the messenger his or her head.

Finally, the researchers stress that dependability and honesty are critical to your boss's perception of how much room he can allow you to "do your thing." If you accept bad delivery dates time after time and if your rationalizations for errors sound like a string of "the check is in the mail" jokes, you're in bad trouble.

Gabarro and Kotter conclude their report by acknowledging that boss management may not be a lot of fun: "No doubt, some subordinates will resent that, on top of all their other duties, they also need to take time and energy to manage their relationships with their bosses. Such managers fail to realize the importance of this activity and how it can simplify their jobs by eliminating potentially severe problems. Effective managers recognize that this part of their work is legitimate. Seeing themselves as ultimately responsible for what they achieve in an organization, they know they need to establish and manage relationships with everyone on whom they are dependent, and that includes the boss."

(Gabarro and Kotter's report appeared in abbreviated form in the January/February 1980 issue of the *Harvard Business Review* under the title "Managing Your Boss." A more detailed account of some aspects of their work appeared in the Fall 1979 issue of *Organizational Dynamics*, in an article by Gabarro titled "Socialization at the Top: How CEOs and Their Subordinates Develop Interpersonal Contracts" and in Kotter's 1979 book, *Power in Management*.)

Reprinted from TRAINING, April 1980

---

ven results to expand your job definition and to ensure that your services will be needed long after you solve the first training problem.

When Hakker first began the training department at Suburbia Federal, the bank's teller turnover rate was high, and management expected her to spend all her time with "teller training."

"My job was cut out for me, but it wasn't what I wanted to do," Hakker recalls. "If I trained tellers who'd be leaving in three months, where was my impact on the organization? I decided that if I was going to stay, my emphasis would have to be not only on reducing the teller turnover rate through training but also on credi-bility, visibility and clout." Combining these objectives, Hakker wrote a statistical report on how training reduced the turnover rate and distributed it directly to upper management.

But your credibility mission extends beyond top management. You have to cultivate trainees' favor as well, showing them why it's worth their while to "get trained." Emphasize training's payoff—having the right skills when those skills are most valued.

That's what Hakker did when she learned that her bank aimed to double the existing number of savings accounts. She openly linked this goal to her training course objectives. "I wanted to make sure the branch managers knew what the president wanted. That way they'd see what would help them get ahead. They'd become 'sold' on learning what they needed to move up."

Watch the bottom line

A few final words from someone who's been there and knows whereof she speaks. Even the most resourceful head of a one-person training department can't afford to become complacent. Organizational needs change and so do the players. So stay as dynamic as the organization you work for. Keep observing. Be visible. Toot your horn. And keep watching that bottom line.

Reprinted from TRAINING, July 1980

ORGANIZING THE ONE-PERSON DEPARTMENT

Going it alone is seldom easy.
Here are some thoughts on how to match
your skills most effectively with
the organization's needs

BY STEPHEN P. BECKER

If you're a one-person training department, your most common mistakes probably don't revolve around the "how" to train, but rather the "what" and the "why." It's surprisingly easy for a lone trainer to misapply himself. When this happens, the trainer wastes valuable time and the organization does not receive the real benefits the trainer could be delivering.

Whatever the size of your organization, there are two key variables in the role a single trainer can play. The first is what an organization needs from a trainer, and the second is the qualifications of the trainer.

In most small organizations, the trainer is part of the personnel staff. Unfortunately, this is a very vulnerable position. The trainer who reports directly to the chief operating executive of the organization will have better control over the training budget.

In the small organization there can be justification for both the personnel director and the training director to report to the top man or woman. An advantage of this reporting relationship is that you'll be able to speak for yourself to the most important decision maker at the most important times. Another plus: Being a member of the executive staff helps at salary review times. If you're under personnel, your pocketbook may suffer even if there is no economic crisis.

As for that precious commodity—your time—it would be a mistake to spend two-thirds of it planning programs and then developing fancy materials such as programmed instruction or synchronized cassette-slide audiovisuals. These things aren't bad, but they require specialized skills and time to prepare. It's not necessary that you be an excellent writer or a technical expert in media. The skills you need are basically classroom and coaching skills. In addition, you should be expert at writing instructional objectives.

Chances are, the smaller the organization, the more skills training you'll be doing. A high degree of "trustability" with people—regardless of their organizational level—pays off in motivational dividends. You, as a person and as a personality, will determine your success. People will seek your instruction, coaching, and advice, or they will want to avoid it, and that's that.

As for funding, let me reemphasize the advantage of a reporting relationship in which the trainer reports to the CEO or to the executive vice president. In terms of financial record keeping, the training budget can be lumped under the general personnel funds, but to get budget approvals, the trainer must have access to the key decision maker.

In a larger organization, the biggest payoff is probably in the area of supervisory training and management development. Almost of necessity, the one-person training department can best spend the majority of its time designing, developing, and conducting a few excellent, highly valuable seminars and workshops for middle managers. In addition, the trainer will probably need to function as coach and advisor to the same group. This is normally done when you visit students after the workshop to help them apply on the job what they learned in the classroom.

At this point, you may be faced with all the environmental constraints. The standard excuses are: There hasn't been time; I'm waiting for everybody to go to the workshop so we can all start together; or, I'm planning to begin next week. Now is the time to use some of that authority you have because you report to the CEO. Banging people over the head is not the way to exercise your authority. But what you say will make a difference because you will be perceived as speaking for the corporation. If you don't have that reporting relationship, you still have the obligation to help the middle manager "see the light," but you'll have to rely on your interpersonal skills and personal powers mixed with a touch of salesmanship.

One way for a one-person training department to save time is to take advantage of AV instructional techniques and commercially available software programs. If you buy outside programs, the risk is that you'll get married to them. So make sure you really want the program and that it's aimed at the same needs you are attempting to help the organization meet. What you can do is buy learning modules or packages from outside sources that will fit into your own designs. This is not too expensive and can save you time while making you look more professional. And to make sure you *stay* more professional, a certain amount of your time must be allocated to your own continuing education.

The larger the organization the less training in the traditional sense and the more the one-person training department, of necessity, must restrict its activities to internal organization development consultation to the president. For example, high-level OD sessions can help the top management team solve organizational performance problems better.

A trainer in this capacity needs to be skilled in performance analysis techniques and OD technology. He or she must have a sound philosophical and theoretical base which probably required some advanced university study in adult education and organizational behavior. This individual needs a mastery of group process skills and a significant amount of personal

HOW TO HANDLE THE OFFICE BAD GUYS

BY RON ZEMKE

According to consultant Robert M. Bramson, approximately 10% of the people we work with are "relentlessly difficult" or just plain troublemakers. He also suggests that 70% of us are unable to cope effectively with these troublemakers. But by studying the behavior of the 20% of us who *can* cope with the professionally difficult, Bramson has been able to both classify the troublemakers into several basic types and identify strategies and tactics for dealing with each.

Hostile-aggressive

There are actually three of these:
- **Sherman Tanks—** Straight-ahead brash and brassy, pushy, opinionated, loud and "right" about everything. Use "It seems to me..." openers. The remedy is to stand up to them but not fight with them. Adapt an unflappable pose and don't respond to Sherman's attempts to turn your resistance into war games.
- **Snipers—** The potshot artist. Snide semi-humor is his or her ploy. The remedy is to call the bluff. Don't antagonize, but do call them on the cutting remark.
- **Exploders—** This style screams, yells, cries and otherwise throws a tantrum. The remedy is to do nothing. When the tirade ends, they usually apologize. If worse comes to worse, excuse yourself and leave the scene of the fire.

Indecisives

Never a decision: "I need to go over these figures again," "We don't have enough data" and "We don't want to alarm people unnecessarily" are standard for the indecisives. Get them to talk; be gentle and low key; don't push but give firm deadlines for work.

Unresponsives

These are the glowering rocks. They sit and stare, too scared, confused or upset to respond. Outwait them. Be pleasant but quiet. Try to provoke them to sound by using nonverbals yourself. Lean toward them; look directly at them or raise an eyebrow. Force them to speak first.

Know-it-alls

Some of these are generally right; some are generally wrong. All are genuinely annoying. Dogmatic, stubborn and infuriatingly superior acting. Bramson advises questioning them in an "extensional fashion." "How will that work for our South American customers?" is the kind of question he recommends. When they become too overbearing, firmly make your "minority opinion" known and let it go at that.

Bramson insists that the key is to "manage your own behavior." Even getting away from the scene is acceptable if it can be accomplished practically. The goal, he says, is to get the job done in spite of the craziness and destructiveness of the small percentage of real troublemakers.

Bramson's work was originally reported on in the March 17, 1980 issue of *Time*.

Reprinted from TRAINING, August 1980

security as a foundation for the advocacy role. In addition, an ability to visualize change and to communicate that change to others is required. A long-range view together with an appreciation for statistics and research methodology is essential.

Remember, we have been discussing a single full-time trainer in an organization. If a staff of trainers were available in the organization, the way the work would be organized could be very different. With staff support, the qualifications of the training director and the way that individual spends time would also be altered.

Trainers who function alone must give serious thought to how their qualifications as trainers fit the needs of their organizations. It's possible to be over or under qualified in relation to the size of the organization. Then, too, a trainer may be in the right-sized organization with respect to his or her skills, but spending too much time on the wrong activities. If, after analyzing your own situation, you discover you've been making this mistake, you can reorganize some of your activities so both you and your organization achieve greater training efficiency.

Reprinted from TRAINING, December 1976

SURVIVAL HELP FOR NEW TRAINING DEPARTMENTS

At Corning, a simple, three-step process
buys time so new training departments start
off on the right foot

BY JOEL D. RAMICH

Imagine that you've just been asked to set up and supervise a plant's first training department. Now it's time to determine what approach you'll take in organizing training. Don't be surprised if you find yourself being pulled in opposite directions.

On the one hand, various people in the organization are clamoring for training for themselves or their departments. Perhaps their insistence on the need for effective training is one of the reasons you're being asked to organize a training department in the first place. Obviously you want to accommodate these people with effective programs as soon as possible.

On the other hand, the literature you've read on industrial training consistently emphasizes the importance of performing training needs diagnosis, analyzing the job, deciding on an appropriate training design and developing an effective means of evaluating the training— all before any training is done in an area.

Clearly, you're going to have to select one of two approaches. Either begin immediately to develop training programs and forget about all those other time-consuming steps. Or tell those clamoring for training that they'll just have to wait while you complete all the preliminary work required to do the job right.

A tough choice? Definitely. Especially when you consider that choosing *either* of these approaches may cause failure in your training efforts. After all, a training department must be both responsive to the needs of the organization it services *and* must base its activities within the framework of sound training principles. Therefore, the most effective approach is the one that meets both these requirements.

At Corning Glass, we use a three-step approach to aid new training directors who face this organizational dilemma. Although designed to meet our specific needs, the approach can benefit other trainers and organizations in a similar quandary.

1 **Assessing the training situation.** For the past few years, Corning Glass has been moving to establish a training capability within each of 39 domestic plants; at this time, we're approximately halfway there. The plants and corporate training department have worked together in developing joint standards for a solid training program, including training director selection criteria.

The typical training director selected is a salaried Corning employee with production supervision experience and demonstrated skills in communication, planning and interpersonal relations with both management and hourly employees. Experience in teaching and knowledge of training theory are considered pluses but are not required. A combination of internal and external "train the trainer" programs is used to provide the necessary tools.

In a Corning plant, the training director may report directly to the production superintendent, the personnel manager, a manufacturing engineer or even the plant manager. However, the training director always has a dotted-line relationship to the corporate training department. The training director function is expected to offer a career path to personnel manager, staff training or other staff positions in the HRD sector.

Our experience has taught us that new training directors are seldom provided by the plant with all the information needed to set up training departments from scratch. Required information might include the purpose of the training department as perceived by management, the history of training in the plant, the key interfaces, and the resources and facilities available to accomplish the training.

As a preliminary challenge, it is imperative that the training director gather the required information so that he or she can assess the situation in which the new department will operate. Without doing so, a training director may start out knowing neither where to go nor how to get there. We have found it useful for the new director to ask supervisors and other appropriate people in the plant the following questions in order to assess the training situation and start in the right direction:

Purpose
- Why is a training department being created now?
- What is the department's charter within the plant?
- What problems is training expected to address?

History
- What training has been done in the past in the plant?
- Who did the training? Who were the participants?
- Was the training effective? Why or why not?
- Are outlines of any of the earlier training programs available?
- Are any training records available?

Interfaces
- Which departments and individuals represent the key interfaces?
- What is the general attitude in the plant toward training?

Resources
- What people resources are available to the department?
- Are any additional resources available if needed?
- What external resources have been used in the past?

Facilities
- What facilities and equipment are available, both internally and externally?
- On what basis are the facilities and equipment available?

Once the training director is satisfied that he or she has a reasonably clear picture of the situation in which the department will operate, it's possible to take the next step in the approach.

2 **Establishing a training philosophy.** It may *seem* easy to make philosophy statements regarding training and its role in a plant or organization. We find, however, that it is quite another matter to ask a production department head, for example, to take such statements on faith alone and commit people and machine time to training. Not until that reluctant department head has experienced a dramatic increase as the result of training, will he or she realize that training is indeed valuable and deserving of the department's support.

Therefore, the establishment of a training philosophy is an evolutionary process within the plant, and the training director is responsible for bringing about this evolution through positive results. Nevertheless, the training director should begin immediately to espouse and "sell" certain training ideas within the plant.

Our training directors have found the following four statements useful in beginning to establish a basic training philosophy. Although they may seem somewhat trite, the statements should be written in order to support training activities.

1. Training, like any other plant activity, is expected to help achieve the goals of the organization. Training has no value unless it helps eliminate deficiencies and achieve the organization's goals.

2. Training should never be regarded merely as an "activity" but rather as a management tool for changing individual behavior and improving plant efficiency.

3. The effectiveness of a plant's training effort depends upon the extent to which management is committed to support it; the proper assignment of responsibility to line managers and training specialists; and the skill with which the training is planned, implemented and evaluated.

4. Both line managers and the training director have important roles in and responsibilities for the training effort. Each manager must accept the development of his or her people as a prime responsibility, include it in objectives and be willing to be appraised on the basis of how well the goals have been achieved.

In addition to stating the basic training philosophy, we find it necessary to develop specific training approaches related to the particular plant involved. The training director must develop these on the basis of in-formation gathered when the training situation is assessed. Each addresses the particular problems unique to the environment in which the training department will operate — for example, "After training programs are in place, no new employee will be allowed to work in production before undergoing training."

3 **Setting priorities.** The training director must ensure that members of the plant understand several things about the priority-setting procedure:

• Priorities are systematically determined.

• Inputs from all departments are used in determining priorities.

• Priorities are applied in a logical manner.

• Despite priorities, the training department will consider requests and be flexible to respond to other needs.

The first step in conveying these messages is to meet with heads of the various plant departments. These meetings serve both to explain the concept of priority setting and to gather information needed for the process. By asking the department heads for specific department goals for the coming year in which training can play a part, the new director can glean pertinent priority information.

Once meetings have been completed with all the appropriate plant people, the priority-setting process can proceed. First, some objective method of establishing priorities must be identified. In one case, we determined priorities by applying the following four criteria to each production department unit:

• Actual year-to-date performance versus budgeted rates.

• Actual year-to-date performance versus budgeted selections.

• Actual year-to-date employee turnover rate.

• Impact of department unit on the plant.

After the resulting data was compiled, each unit was compared in order to determine relative priorities, and a priority number was then assigned. The department with the highest priority number was the first to be scheduled for a needs diagnosis. If training in this department was shown to have good cost/benefit potential and was approved by the department head, it was implemented. We then moved on to the department unit with the second highest priority, continuing down the list until initial training programs were completed for all departments.

This approach helped us convince people that the priorities were sys-tematically determined, that inputs from all departments were utilized and that the priorities would be applied in a logical manner. We went on from there to emphasize that the priorities were not etched in stone and that the training department would consider requests outside of the priority list. For example, one plant training department found it necessary to completely alter priorities in order to provide training for 45 new employees hired as a result of unexpected business. Although the initial priorities could not be completed on time, the training department response had greater overall value to the plant.

Feasibility

We have found that the use of this three-step approach provides a new training director with a number of significant benefits. Foremost among these is the elimination of the conflict between responding to the plant's needs and applying sound training principles. Because the three-step approach provides the opportunity to do both, it prevents the two major causes of training director failure: a) attempting to accommodate every training request at once and thereby accomplishing little in any area; and b) keeping an entire plant waiting while the principles outlined in the training literature are learned and applied.

Of course, the application of sound training principles is an important element in setting up and initiating training. However, applying these principles may prove to be very time-consuming, particularly for a new trainer unskilled in their use. The three-step approach helps "buy time" for new trainers deluged by requests for training. At the same time, the tasks involved in following this approach encourage new directors to use sound training principles by providing many of the very elements necessary to perform needs diagnosis, analyze jobs, decide on an appropriate design and develop an effective means of evaluating the training.

Plant members have reacted very favorably to this approach. Even those whose departments end up low on the priority list are supportive. They may not be happy about having to wait for training, but they accept the priority-setting approach and are grateful to have an idea of when to expect training department attention. As a result, the training director is recognized early on as being a competent professional as well as being responsive to the plant's needs.

Reprinted from TRAINING, March 1981

THE NEW HRD MANAGER: HOW TO HIT THE GROUND RUNNING

You've just been named director of training and development for the Acme Widget Corp. What's your first move?

BY WILLIAM R. TRACEY

People who manage the training and development functions in organizations go by a lot of titles, from "yard foreman" to "chief executive officer." More commonly, they answer to tags like "training director" or "vice president-human resources development."

Regardless of the title, the fundamental challenge to any HRD manager is identical to that faced by all other managers: to deliver what the organization needs—to produce *results*—in the fastest and most cost-effective manner possible.

To do that, training directors must think and act like managers—they must be action-oriented. The keys to that kind of performance are few but crucial.

• Focus on managing results—on bottom-line outcomes.

• Demonstrate the skills and behavior of an effective manager.

• Evaluate systems, programs and services to determine accomplishments and shortfalls.

• Communicate the department's accomplishments up, down and laterally in the organization.

• Identify significant problems and barriers to progress, and explain them to top management.

• Help build an environment of openness, trust, confidence and mutual respect throughout the organization.

If those are your goals, how do you go about reaching them? For the new HRD manager, the first order of business obviously is to get up to speed. But how shall we define that phrase?

'WHAT'S GOING ON AROUND HERE?'

BY WILLIAM R. TRACEY

When you examine your organization systemically, you always learn some surprising things and you usually identify a few key opportunities.

When I took over as director of teacher training at Fitchburg State College in Massachusetts, my initial survey resulted in some unexpected findings. The most confounding was the discovery that faculty members responsible for supervising student teachers had no training for that role (although they were master teachers), received no orientation to their duties, and were provided no written policy or procedural guidance such as might be found in a supervisors' handbook.

The most critical semester of the teacher-education program, the one during which student teachers worked directly with pupils in the classroom, was largely a trial-and-error process. The 28 supervisors developed their own policies, procedures, requirements and standards. The consequences? Inconsistencies, discontent and erratic progress among student teachers, frustration and dissatisfaction among supervisors.

We attacked the problem (over a period of months) by working with supervisors and student teachers to articulate workable and equitable policies, procedures and standards. The products of that effort were published in a *Supervisors' Handbook* and a companion *Student Teachers' Handbook*. Both documents also were used as a basis for discussion during orientation programs for new supervisors and student teachers.

A second example. Shortly after I became director of training at the U.S. Army Security Agency Training Center and School at Fort Devens, MA, I worked with a group of civilian-education specialists to plan and conduct the first full-scale internal audit of a military school—Project MINERVA.

MINERVA was a systematic study of all aspects of training for officers and enlisted personnel, including the students themselves, their living conditions and recreational opportunities, curricula and their development, and training facilities, strategies and materials. The purpose was strictly functional—to identify areas in need of improvement.

Over a period of 11 months, all members of the staff and faculty, representative officers and enlisted students, and the cadre of the Training Regiment became deeply involved in the project. Although everyone learned a great deal about the school—its strengths and shortfalls—MINERVA's most significant product was the development and testing of a systematic approach to the design, validation, implementation and quality control of instructional systems.

Our system was described in a procedures manual, *The Development of Instructional Systems*, which was a forerunner of *Interservice Procedures for Instructional Systems Development*, today's "bible" for the design and conduct of military technical training.

But again, the most important products of this or any other system are the *gains* it produces. MINERVA resulted in better-trained personnel—people who were more confident, flexible, responsive and competent than graduates of earlier systems. The system reduced on-the-job training time, cut trainee attrition, enabled earlier identification and remediation of learning difficulties, and improved the motivation of trainers and trainees alike. MINERVA also made it possible to provide greater and more effective attention to individual differences among trainees.

All of this became possible because we asked a simple question, "What's going on here?" and set out to answer it in a systematic way.

Reprinted from TRAINING, April, 1984

Suppose I suggest that "getting up to speed" involves the use of specific, practical and tested techniques for learning about the organization—collecting, assimilating, evaluating and using information to create a firm basis for developing plans to improve things, and putting those plans into action. Am I still talking only to *new* HRD managers? Well, decide for yourself.

The thesis of this article is simple. Regardless of their skills and motivation, training directors cannot manage the HRD function competently and achieve outstanding results before studying their organizations in detail. The manager must determine:

- What the organization is and what it does.
- How it does it.
- Where the organization wants to be in the future.
- How it plans to get there.
- How it will determine when it *does* get there.
- Who the players are.
- Where the power centers are.

Gathering information

Obviously, all of the information you will need cannot be collected in a day, a week, a month, or even, perhaps, a quarter. And all of the information you collect in the first weeks cannot be fully assimilated, let alone used.

But in fact, the process started before you got the job—you acquired *some* information about the organization before you were hired. Other data must be collected in the first few days, and *most* of it within the first few weeks. In any event, the information must be gathered quickly, systematically and in the proper sequence. And it must be obtained from the proper sources.

Here are some suggestions for getting the collection process under way:

- Identify and categorize the information you need.
- Start collecting it before you get the job.
- Establish a filing system for the data.
- Commit everything important to writing; use a notebook or file cards.
- Accumulate all of the organization's key documents.
- Burn the midnight oil.

The type of information you're after falls into three general categories.

The current organization. See how much you can learn about the company's origins, history, missions, functions, products and services; its formal structure, informal structure, goals and objectives, policies and rules. What

Information	Sources
Origins and history	Organization manual Employees' handbook Supervisors' handbook Interviews Records and reports
Mission and functions	Organization and functions manual Policy manual Employees' handbook Supervisors' handbook
Products and services	Catalogs Brochures Price lists Advertising copy
Formal structure	Organization and functions manual Organization chart Interviews Staff meetings
Informal structure	Observation and visits Meetings and conferences Interviews
Goals and objectives	Planning documents Forecasts Interviews Policy manual MBO documents Staff meetings
Policies and rules	Policy and procedures manual Employees' handbooks Supervisors' handbooks Collective bargaining agreements Contracts
Collective bargaining agreement	Contracts Policy manual Interviews Staff meetings
Physical layout	Visits Maps Plot plans and floor plans Photographs
Budget	Budget documents Interviews Quarterly reports Staff meetings
External relationships	Policy manual Catalogs and brochures Employees' manuals Annual reports Interviews
Key personnel	Biographical sketches Interviews Observation Job descriptions Staff meetings

Figure 1. Information you need about the *CURRENT ORGANIZATION* and where to find it.

collective bargaining agreements are in force or pending? How about its physical layout, its budget, its external relationships? Who are the key players?

The future organization. Identify projected changes in the firm's mission and functions, its products and services, formal structure, goals, objectives and physical layout. Any plans for new equipment or systems? Any

changes in the wind regarding external relationships or key personnel?

The current HRD organization. Zero in on the training and development function—its mission, its activities, its position in the organizational structure, its goals and objectives, programs and services, policies and rules. What about its budget, facilities, significant accomplishments, critical problems and issues, current projects and key personnel?

Where do you look for all of this information? The three figures accompanying this article list some obvious and not-so-obvious sources.

Tabulating, analyzing and interpreting

Once the information has been collected, it must be summarized, analyzed and interpreted before it can be useful.

The difficulty of summarizing and tabulating the results of your observations, interviews, reading and so on depends upon the type of information you're working with. Where the data are quantitative, the problems are relatively simple; the tabulation of non-quantitative descriptive data is much more difficult. But you will find it easier to get a handle on your "subjective" data if you recognize that the basic problem is one of selecting appropriate summarizing categories.

The steps in tabulating data are:
- Review your notes.
- Establish summarizing categories.
- Determine the treatment to be applied to each category; that is, mathematical (rank order, mean, range and the like) or other (listings, key words and so on).
- Make the appropriate entries in each summarizing category.

Once you have worked the data into manageable form, you are ready to tackle the most demanding and crucial step in the entire process: analyzing and interpreting it. This is the stage that depends most heavily on the competence of the HRD manager.

You must be able to examine the information you have gathered and answer two basic questions: What does the information reveal? What do these revelations mean? You must be able to identify significant strengths and weaknesses in the organization, in its plans for the future, and within the HRD department. And you must be able to draw conclusions upon which to base recommendations.

Logical steps in analyzing and interpreting data are:
- Review the summaries for each category of information in turn.
- Draft statements of your conclusions for all areas of strength.
- Identify weaknesses. Then identify their direct and underlying *causes*. The latter effort begins by 1) isolating the part of the process or situation that is the probable source of the problem, and 2) determining when and where the problem started and how long it has existed.
- Draw conclusions and state them in simple and concise language.

The ultimate purpose of everything you have done is to improve HRD pro-

Information	Sources
Projected changes in:	Enterprise planning documents
Mission and functions	Forecasts (political, economic, technological, social, demographic, industry)
Products and services	
Formal structure	Long-range plans for expansion, contraction or diversification
Goals and objectives	Long-range financial plans
Physical layout	Mid- and long-range plans for construction, rehabilitation, equipment and facilities—
New equipment and systems	including automation, robotics, computer-aided design and manufacturing (CAD/CAM) systems
Key personnel	Interviews with key personnel (CEO, executives, line managers, staff officers)
External relationships	

Figure 2. Information you need about the *FUTURE ORGANIZATION* and where to find it.

grams, services and activities in order to make them more efficient and to be sure they provide real, recognizable benefits to the organization. The value of the whole process, then, depends upon the quality of your conclusions and recommendations, and upon what is done with them.

Your first step is to establish a priority listing of all problems to be

---

The point of your job— first, last and always—is to produce results.

---

addressed, ensuring that weaknesses most critical to the organization's goals and objectives are attacked first. Then, for each problem you decide to address, go on to the following steps, taking them in sequence.

Identify and evaluate alternative solutions. Canvass all methods and procedures that could conceivably solve or help to solve the problem. Withhold judgment about the value of any solution until as many alternatives as possible (let's make that, "as feasible") have been identified. It *is* important to identify several solutions to a problem rather than just the one that first comes to mind. It is even more important to subject each alternative solution to rigorous analysis and/or testing so that the most promising one can be identified.

Therefore, you'll have to formulate criteria for judging possible solutions—

some sort of yardstick against which alternatives can be measured. When establishing those yardsticks, consider: 1) the end results to be achieved, 2) the time and other resources required to implement the solution, and 3) other limitations or consequences.

Select and outline the solution. Basically, you're looking for the solution that is most likely to fix the problem and least likely to produce negative side effects while doing so. Once you have identified it, outline it. Your outline should include:
- A description of the problem (a list of the defects in the system or process revealed by your analysis).
- A description of the proposed major changes.
- Advantages and disadvantages of each change.
- Costs of the solution (personnel, time, money, materials, etc.).
- Steps required to put the solution into effect.

Seek support and, if necessary, approval. Develop a strategy to obtain support for your solution from top management, middle management, line supervisors and any union that may be involved. Go to as many levels of the organization as possible, but be sure to enlist those most affected by the solution. And if you lack the authority to implement the solution without higher-level approval, get that approval formally.

Develop an action plan. Once the decision has been made and approved to try the solution, develop a detailed action plan, covering the following topics as a minimum:
- The specifics of what will be done. (What changes in systems or procedures are to be made?)
- Who is to make each of the changes.
- When the changes are to be made.

Information	Sources	
Mission and functions	Organization manual Employees' manual Supervisors' manual Interviews Records and reports	
Department structure	Organization and functions manual Organization chart Interviews	
Goals and objectives	Policy manual Planning documents Interviews Staff meetings MBO documents	
Programs and services	Catalogs and brochures Policy manual Employees' manuals Supervisors' manuals Collective bargaining agreements Contracts Records and reports Surveys and audits Interviews	
Policies and rules	Policy and procedures manuals Employees' handbooks Supervisors' handbooks Collective bargaining agreements Contracts	
Budget	Budget documents Financial reports and records Audit reports Quarterly reports Interviews Staff meetings	
Personnel resources	Organization and functions manual Job descriptions Personnel surveys and audits Reports and records Interviews	
Facilities	Visits and inspections Floor plans Interviews	
Significant accomplishments	Annual reports Historical reports Quarterly reports	House organs Interviews Briefings
Critical problems and issues	Annual reports Historical reports Quarterly reports Reports of audit Financial reports Personnel records Training and development reports Briefings and correspondence Interviews Observation	
Current projects	Planning documents MBO documents Briefings	Interviews Staff meetings Project boards
Key personnel	Biographical sketches Interviews Observation	

Figure 3. Information you need about the *HRD FUNCTION* and where to find it.

- How the changes are to be made.
- Who is to supply the needed resources and when.

Implement the action plan and follow up. Obtain the necessary resources, assign people to various tasks, delegate authority as appropriate, provide guidance and assistance—put the idea to work. This is your plan and its success or failure reflects directly on you, regardless of who was "supposed to be responsible" for what.

Finally, it is your job to review progress, make modifications to the solution if required, and report the results to all concerned.

The new HRD manager must hit the ground running if he or she is to win the confidence and support of superiors, peers and subordinates. You cannot manage the HRD function competently unless and until you know the organization thoroughly: what it is and what it does, how it does it, where it wants to be, how it plans to get there and how it judges success.

Having acquired that information, you must identify the organization's strengths and weaknesses. Finally, you must develop and implement plans to exploit the former and remedy the latter.

Reprinted from TRAINING, April 1984

WHERE DOES TRAINING BELONG?

Should training be centralized at corporate HQ?
Or should it be spread out in the field?
The answers to both are yes—and no

BY CHRIS LEE

Attend any gathering of trainers and you'll find at least one seminar, panel of experts or discussion group examining the merits of decentralizing the training department. Or centralizing it. Or the disadvantages of decentralizing. Or centralizing.

It may be that to those charged with making the training function best serve the company's needs, the subject itself is endlessly fascinating. It's also possible that the debate keeps surfacing because one or the other approach becomes *de rigueur* for a variety of economic and organizational reasons. Thanks to corporate staff slashing, high-tech delivery media and a pervasive stay-close-to-the-customer mentality, the trend today seems to be toward decentralization.

A recent discussion by a group of high-powered training directors provides a case in point. Nearly 30 of them got together to ponder some of the abiding questions in this debate: When does it make sense to decentralize training and what are the biggest challenges you face in switching from centralized to decentralized training, or vice versa? A show of hands indicated which way the pendulum is currently swinging. About half were steering their departments toward decentralization; most of the rest were already wrestling with the problems of managing a decentralized function.

During the discussion, these training directors kicked around many of the standard pros and cons of moving a corporate support function out to the field.

On the plus side: Training conducted by line managers or employees with part-time training responsibilities may be imbued with greater immediacy, credibility and sense of ownership; it may be cheaper to conduct training sessions locally; and, in these days of lean corporate staffs, it may seem an attractive alternative to home-office training departments operating with skeleton crews.

Opponents of decentralization, however, argued that each advantage has an equal and opposite disadvantage: line "ownership" of training programs may produce inconsistencies and, eventually, poor quality; locally conducted training sessions may appear to save money initially, but poor quality can create a time bomb with steep clean-up costs; and line managers in many slimmed-down companies already have a full plate without taking on tasks formerly handled by a corporate department.

Before the meeting ended, the group reached two sensible conclusions: 1) It does not have to be an either/or decision. 2) Decisions about structure should be based on the content and function of the training, rather than a single, overriding philosophy.

Form follows function

Think of it as a continuum. At one end you have a training department at corporate headquarters that provides all the organization's training. Training needs are determined by the HQ staff. Training programs and materials are developed, delivered and evaluated by HQ staff trainers at HQ's training center. All training budgets are controlled solely by the HQ training department. At the other extreme, you have no corporate training staff—and thus no centralized budgeting for the development, delivery or evaluation of employee training programs.

There probably are companies that employ one or the other of these extremes, but we couldn't find them. Most fall somewhere in the middle of the continuum, choosing their struc-

> **Structure should be based on the control and function of the training in question.**

ture from the perspective that form follows function. Often, technical training is developed with plenty of help from the workers and may be delivered by trainers who report to line managers or by those managers themselves. On the other hand, management and executive development, succession planning and the like tend to rest with the corporate training staff.

Loews Corp., a diversified *Fortune 500* company that includes Bulova Watch Co., Lorillard Tobacco and a hotel division, takes this tack. "Our training function combines both centralized and decentralized approaches," explains Alan Momeyer, director of manpower planning and development at Loews' headquarters in New York City. "Our centralized training department works for Bulova, the hotels and Lorillard. Satellite offices for Lorillard that provide sales training are part of [Lorillard], but they have a dotted-line reporting relationship to corporate. The director of training in [a particular] hotel works for hotel operations, but also has a dotted-line relationship to corporate."

Generally, the home office provides all management training while the field offices handle technical training, says Momeyer. The reasoning is simple: "Good management is based on universal principles—it doesn't matter if you're making watches or selling hotel rooms. But technical training, employee job-skills training, is industry specific. Lorillard sales reps, for example, have merchandising jobs. They are trained in the field to use sales display materials, [create] customer interest and so on. It's technical training that is better done by field experts.

"It would be very expensive to try to equip field training operations with the degree of management-training expertise they would need to have credibility," he continues. "Those who have it are part of the home-office training department." Momeyer's management trainers, many of whom worked in one of Loews' divisions before coming to corporate training, already know the industry, or they can learn enough about it to be credible, he says.

To Momeyer, the centralize-decentralize argument boils down to a simple question: "What are you trying to train people to do? Both [approaches] are the right way, but usually both are right in different situations."

Passion for autonomy

Ed Baron is the director of training and development for Gannett Co. Inc., the media conglomerate that owns newspapers, broadcasting operations and outdoor billboard businesses scattered across 40 states and Canada. He offers an anecdote to explain the extremely decentralized nature of his company. "It happened again this morning in a meeting with a prospective supplier [of training materials]. They look us up in some directory and see we've got $3 billion in sales and 37,000 employees and think, 'Wow, this is a hot prospect.'

They find out the training director is [in Arlington, VA] and come to call.

"Then I have to tell them, 'Yes, we're all those things, but we're so decentralized.... There's almost a passion here for local decision making....'" At that point, Baron laughs, he often gets "an earful" from a salesperson who can't quite believe that Gannett's training director doesn't

---

Each business unit decides what—if anything—to budget for training.

---

buy training materials for the whole corporation.

So what does the corporate training director do at a company that is really more a collection of small businesses than a corporate behemoth? The approximately 125 operating units—newpapers and television and radio stations—"rely on us for guidance, for in-house consultations, knowledge about available programs and so on," Baron explains. His department handles registration and coordination for industry-association seminars and subscribes to a computerized seminar service to stay on top of program offerings. "We also operate a lending library of films and packaged programs. They can borrow them, but we absorb the costs."

Each property of the Gannett corporation operates much like an independent business. That tradition began within the newspaper side of the business, where local autonomy is a must if the newspaper is to cover the local community as it sees fit. Each business unit is responsible for its own profit and loss, and each decides what—if anything—to budget for training. As small businesses—Baron estimates that an average Gannett newspaper has around 300 employees, a medium-size television station about 200 and a big radio station no more than 60—most have no full-time trainer, although the newspaper and television divisions handle some

training for their numerous units.

As a result, virtually no training is mandated from headquarters, Baron says. Instead, it plays an advisory role. "For example, we think Employee Assistance Programs are a good idea—we have one here—and we tell operating units they should have one, but not which one to have or how much to pay. If they don't, we can jawbone at them, or put in a good word for it at budget time, but that's it. Our culture is such that we can tell them what we think they should do, but we can't run 90 newspapers from Arlington, VA."

Recently Baron's staff, which consists of an instructional designer, a secretary and an administrative assistant, created its first packaged programs. The two courses, one on basic selling skills for space sales reps and one on circulation for district sales managers, were distributed free to Gannett's newpapers. The programs were designed to be flexible; they can be delivered by line managers or, at newspapers with specialized staff, personnel people or trainers.

Baron has a few more programs in the works, but he says he harbors no secret inclination for empire building. "What we do is designed to fit with the cultural and geographical diversity of our business. I sometimes wonder, if I had the power to mandate a program, would it even make sense? The employees and their needs vary so much."

Control central

It's a whole different story at Johnson Controls Institute, the employee and customer training center for Johnson Controls Inc. For one thing, there's a much narrower scope of cultural diversity to consider: The Milwaukee-based manufacturer of building management systems and industrial control equipment is an engineering-oriented company. For another, the nature of the training lends itself to a centralized structure.

While management training often is taken on the road, most of the company's technical training is conducted at the institute. "Because of the technical nature of much of our training, it's usually easier to bring people to Milwaukee to use our lab equipment," explains institute manager Dave Podeszwa.

The institute provides 55 courses

for employees and 22 for customers. Employees go through orientation at individual plants but attend the institute for skill-development courses, Podeszwa says. Customers follow a similar path, but for different reasons. "We'll often take the basic stuff to customers so they can get a feel for our quality—so they'll know what they don't know—before they come to the institute." Since the systems save energy when used properly, training for customers will help them get the best payback on their equipment investment. Costs for training may be built into a customer's purchase price, or he may pay tuition outright.

Podeszwa says that because he is able to control the transportation and housing costs for students attending the institute in Milwaukee, Johnson Controls' centralized system has made good economic sense. "Management tends to feel it would be cheaper to decentralize—we'd save airfares, for example—but, in my opinion, a blend of centralization and decentralization is more efficient for the students as well as the company."

He began testing his theory last month, when Johnson Controls opened a Los Angeles office, complete with classrooms and labs for customer training. The decision to open a West Coast office was not made overnight. "We were out there so often, we finally got a place to call home," he says. "It won't be as cost-effective, but we're going after convenience for the customer."

After conducting a needs assessment among customers, employees and managers, Podeszwa discovered that Californians don't want to "go back East" for training—and they consider anything east of the Rockies "back East." He's now committed to a three-year experiment in decentralized technical training (the length of the L.A. lease), but he thinks it will pay off in increased revenues from customer training.

"I don't think there's any cut-and-dried answer to this centralize-decentralize question. At least I haven't found one and I've been looking for 10 years," he says. "I think you have to be flexible."

Making a move

When do organizations decide to decentralize? Often when, like Johnson Controls, they sense a chance to attract or better serve more customers—both the ones who buy the company's products and services, and the company's own employees.

Three years ago, Gene Drumm, manager of training and development at Silverado Banking in Denver, looked around and observed an industry that was introducing new products at breakneck speed, a rap-

---

Californians don't want to 'go back East' for training.

---

idly expanding organization, and a vast reservoir of in-house expertise waiting to be tapped. With the help of line managers and their subordinates, he began to develop a system that would put the bank's technical training into the most capable hands he could find: the subject-matter experts themselves.

The Silverado training department approached decentralization with a certain amount of trepidation. "We struggled with centralization vs. decentralization, line vs. staff-driven training," Drumm says. "We ended up with a matrix listing the pluses and minuses of both."

On the minus side, they anticipated that decentralization would create problems with selection of good line trainers, control and continuity. With a centralized approach, however, there would be a time lag while the training staff boned up on technical changes. In the end, they decided to trade coordination headaches for speed and subject-matter expertise.

Silverado's approach to decentralization evolved into a highly structured—and effective—technical training system. The team of "unit trainers" are subject-matter experts with part-time training responsibilities. They go through a rigorous selection process, which includes a 20-minute "audition" presentation on a topic of their choice, before they are assigned technical training duties.

Their relationship to the training department is far from casual. "Their job descriptions [specify] that they dedicate 10 percent of their time or 16 hours a month to training and development," Drumm explains. Since unit trainers take on a variety of training tasks—needs assessment, development and delivery—their performance evaluations cover training responsibilities, as well as their regular job duties. Unit trainers who are in sales are paid 5 percent of their salary every six months to compensate for the 10 percent of time spent training.

After three years, Drumm says the system has proven effective on several counts. "We've got a good delivery system with subject-matter experts from the field who face the same problems [their trainees do] every day. Over three years we've provided a population of 170 people with more than 8,000 hours of training through five unit trainers at a direct cost of less than $15,000. That's less than $2 per training hour."

Another company that is making a concerted effort to push certain training functions out to the field, albeit on a much grander scale, is Control Data Corp. Why? Michael Hopp, director of human resource development and research, offers a succinct answer: "We want the decision-making capabilities closer to Control Data's customers."

To reach that goal, CDC is decentralizing its training functions and, at the same time, creating a corporate-wide management academy whose mission is to support decentralization.

Training always has been somewhat decentralized at CDC. Some divisions, for instance, have handled their own unique types of technical training. "That's continuing," Hopp says. "What's changing is that we're getting more clear about the role of the corporate training function vs. the role of division training functions."

Formerly, corporate HRD would have supplied the bulk of the training programs for all the divisions. Today, the staff of three professionals and three support employees has a much narrower mandate. It will provide only training that is truly corporate-wide in nature; it will consult with divisions to help them find appropriate outside suppliers for local training needs. Since the corporate HRD staff has been radically cut over the last two years, this move owes as much to necessity as preference.

Hopp and his staff also will develop the curriculum for the Control Data Management Academy. "The academy was established to maintain the glue—the philosophy of management—that holds the organization together," says Hopp.

The academy has two missions. The first is to establish a clear understanding of the company's values and commitment to its customers, marketing, quality and people. (If that sounds a bit vague, remember that the curriculum is still in the development stage. "Our initial efforts will focus on putting content around those words," says Hopp.) The second is to ensure that managers have the fundamental skills they need to do their jobs. That may mean helping individual business units identify their needs, as well as helping them plan training strategies to address those needs. It also means helping them audit the results of training programs.

To Hopp, the discussion about centralization vs. decentralization eventually becomes a red herring. "We're talking less about it as a concept and more in terms of what training needs

---

Endless discussion about centralization vs. decentralization becomes a red herring.

---

to be centralized and what needs to be decentralized so we can get closer to our customers and our market."

The red herring

Certainly, there's no *right* way for an organization to structure its training and development function. As these examples demonstrate, a laundry list of idiosyncratic factors determines how a training department will be organized in a given company: products, internal organization, culture, as well as training needs and priorities.

As these factors change, the training function tends to evolve into a different—and complementary—shape. Eventually, however, many organizations that wrestle with different approaches to organizing the training function end up taking a simple position: Let's do what works for us.

Perhaps the most important consideration to keep in mind is best summarized by John Humphrey, chairman and CEO of The Forum Corp., a Boston-based management-training company: "Does a company see training as a key element in creating its competitive advantage? If it does, training will be in close proximity to the core activities of the business. If it doesn't, it will screw around with [questions of] whether training should be centralized or decentralized."

Reprinted from TRAINING, February 1988

DESIGNING CENTRALIZED TRAINING FOR A DIVERSE ORGANIZATION

Here's some practical advice on determining *how much* centralization—and how to achieve it

BY DAVID C. HON

As corporations expand and move into new ventures and new areas, the central corporate headquarters often assumes a service, rather than a directive, role. Branches of the corporation become almost autonomous, and the corporate headquarters must tailor its services to accommodate a wide diversity of products, markets, and methods.

Because of this diversity, a corporate training department may seem overwhelmed by the task of uniting elements of the company. Certainly, the exigencies of certain methods may demand specialized training in each area, on site, to keep pace with the specific demands of each diverse business. But the fact remains that generally there are standards and methods that pervade a corporation. And corporate unity may depend on a particular style of management or marketing being accepted by the whole organization. This is why centrally created training can not only increase corporate unity and efficiency but can make people more mobile within the corporation because they have more in common with all its parts.

The training manager in such a situation is faced with both the philosophical problem of how much centralization is good and the pragmatic problem of how to achieve centralization of training that would be valuable to all personnel. In such areas as purchasing, personnel administration, order-entry systems, information systems, supervisory practices, management practices, financial planning, and production planning, there are often seven or eight variations of practices in each. While these practices may actually vary little, the result of the differences is useless segmentation of the organization, wasted duplication, and, ultimately, a withering of synergy throughout.

Obviously, centralized training can be an important unifying agent, but only if its designers: 1) realize exactly what its advantages are to the corporation; 2) know what the obstacles are to its existence; and 3) know how to pull the diverse elements together.

Once a training manager knows these, he is in a position to contribute greatly to corporate unity and efficiency. Surprisingly, some corporate training managers aren't certain about the advantages of centralized, standardized training packages. Here are the four key pluses:

● **Lower cost per head** — especially if trainees are not instructed at a central location.

● **Consistency of terminology and concepts** — The strength of many companies is due, in large part, to the consistency of an internal culture shared by management and workers. Being a member of a total culture produces a feeling of belonging and a resultant ease of communication.

● **Cross-fertilization of techniques and ideas** — This occurs naturally when people feel they are speaking the same language. But such interchange becomes inhibited if they feel their backgrounds are different. One semantic inconsistency can cost millions: "I told him we don't make lorries here. How was I to know he meant trucks?"

● **Exceptionally good training materials** — These standardized materials —films, slides, manuals— can be used to achieve greater communication in less time and to enhance the self-image of employees.

However well-intentioned its motives, the corporate training department may encounter two obstacles: autonomy and local thoroughness.

Autonomy — This is usually the result of the small-business mentality of many successful divisions. The top manager who turns over several million dollars in annual profits to the corporation must, by the nature of his job, be a strong-willed person; and one indicator of his success is that he receives less direction from corporate headquarters.

Local thoroughness — Quite often, a training unit in one division points with pride to the "thoroughness" of its training program. Frequently, however, those programs are "thorough" only for a few people, only in certain subjects, or at a high cost of time off the job.

Aware of the advantages of and obstacles to centralized training, the training manager can perform a critical role for the corporation— unifying it and stimulating the interaction and efficiency of its parts. Often this does not happen, however, because the obstacles of autonomy and local thoroughness thwart the development process. To help circumvent these, we offer a few "how to's" to accomplish the desired goal of corporate-wide training.

The best way is with a mandate issued by a top executive who believes that training is more than simply bringing a new production operator up to a performance standard. It is preferable if this mandate does not come from the corporate director of personnel but from an individual with a profit-oriented job, which must be accomplished across the corporation. A marketing vice-president or a director of finance could and probably would respond to a dollars-and-cents proposition regarding centralized training.

As a trainer, you will meet with these individuals to discuss bottom-line figures and present back-up data. You must have firm estimates of the numbers of people who would be reached by the proposed program and of the funds needed to implement it. These should always be simplified with a cost-per-student projection, in volume and over a "product" life-year. (For instance, if 1,000 managers per year are trained in essentials of purchasing and you estimate the information/skills life-span of the training program to be five years and the cost of the program to be $10,000 to create and $40 per student to administer, the cost-per-student over 5,000 students will be $60. Then, if you wish, the cost

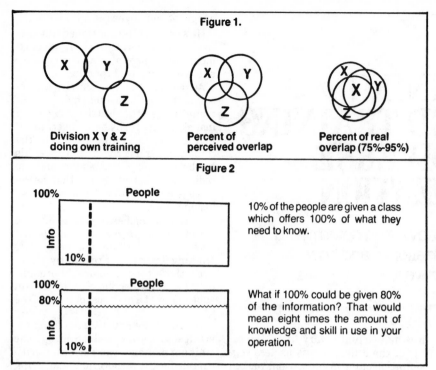

Figure 1.

Division X Y & Z doing own training

Percent of perceived overlap

Percent of real overlap (75%-95%)

Figure 2

100% | **People**
Info | 10%

10% of the people are given a class which offers 100% of what they need to know.

100% / 80% | **People**
Info | 10%

What if 100% could be given 80% of the information? That would mean eight times the amount of knowledge and skill in use in your operation.

of an average purchasing error of one percent can be brought up as return on investment. Remember, money derived from those efficiencies is as good as profit — but not as taxable.) This cost-per-student projection is essential, since the funds you'll request will look extremely large as a front-end cost, and your strongest return-on-investment case will be money saved by volume.

A central mandate alone is not going to convince the successful individuals who feel — and can prove —they've done quite well on their own. Their very success allows them to ward off most mandates, if they wish. So just having a mandate to do corporate training is no guarantee that you'll accomplish it. As a matter of fact, if the mandate appears to be a dictate from corporate headquarters, it may be detrimental to your chances.

What the mandate should give you is the power to call meetings with top executives from the diverse divisions. What you do with those meetings will determine whether you develop a corporate-wide program of real value. These early meetings, their composition and their progress, are critical; once the heads of divisions have planned a common program, they'll back its implementation. Too often, corporate-wide programs, created in a vacuum and then presented to divisions, are greeted with a chorus of objections and ingenious stalling. But if the corporate training manager has been firm in handling those early stages of development (when the product is murky but the mandate is fresh), the path to implementation will be strewn with palm leaves.

By every strategy possible, make sure either a top officer or an influential and trusted proxy for each of the strongest divisions attends the early planning sessions. Your mandate can help you get the key people to a meeting, and you should use it— along with every other trick you know. If there is to be a catered lunch, make sure it's the best one available. If you have sample movies, let prospective attendees know.

Don't try to proceed unless all influential divisions are represented. You may need to call on your mandate— or corporate clout — here. And if the former doesn't get you the people you need in those first few meetings, it isn't firm enough.

If you generate enthusiasm here, you'll have it for the other three major meetings. But here, in the first meeting, is where you will probably encounter the obstacles of autonomy and local thoroughness and where you'll have to translate your corporate advantages into *their* division advantages.

Let us look first at how *autonomy* might surface: "We do things a bit differently in X division." In this case, ask what percent of practices and methods X division has in common with the corporation as a whole. You'll usually get figures of 75% to 95%, if your appraisal of the need has been correct. Then, agree with X division's spokesman that you foresee handling only this 75%-95% *commonality* and leaving the unique variations of his division untouched. Now you can point out that, by "commonizing" that 75%-95%, you will save them and the corporation time and money in train-

ing. You can bring in the lower cost per head, using a visual like Figure 1.

The "X"ed portion of the third set of circles in Figure 1 is an area where corporate handling of the commonality can have advantages in terms of lower cost per head, common terminology, cross-fertilization, and better materials.

Existing *localized training* may be an obstacle if the division head has participated in its development. He may ask: "But we give our people the 100% course, so isn't that better?" Usually, you can point out that only 10% to 20% of potential trainees are actually getting the thorough course, and the rest are getting nothing until there is more time (or money) available. A visual like Figure 2 might help.

Once the advantages of a commonality of training are agreed upon, you can work out objectives of the course with division heads. To reach that point, you may have to bargain a bit. Tell them they could integrate their course with yours, that you'd run yours as a trial with them; suggest whatever is necessary to move them from the "obstacle" frame of mind to that of defining common objectives.

No matter how well your group defines common objectives, don't dismiss that first meeting without making psychological contracts for the participants' assistance at three other points. Be prepared to tell them what other commitments you require of them. And secure their consent to participate in future planning meetings.

Your plan for planning should be clear and concise and call for as little — but as *definite* — a use of the attendees' time and efforts as possible. After these first three meetings, you should be able to incorporate the proposals of division managers into your design and they should be able to schedule many of the in-between reviews. But be sure to inform them that they will be expected to review the final product before its implementation.

Obviously, you have lots of work to do between these meetings. And the division heads will have to formulate plans to decide among in future meetings. Only in the first meeting should anything be vague or visionary; from then on, you and the division managers will be focusing on a definite, tangible course of action.

If you rely upon a firm mandate early on and then follow these suggested procedures, you stand a good chance of enhancing the corporate service role in training and, thus, uniting the diverse parts of a large corporation.

Reprinted from TRAINING, April 1979

THE CASE FOR CORPORATE COLLEGES

If 'sheep-dip'training is so bad, why are
some companies able to use it so well
to develop their managers?

BY JACK GORDON

The corporate management academy. The centralized, "building block" approach to training managers. The core curriculum of long-lived courses that most or all managers at particular levels of an organization are encouraged or required to attend. With this whole concept, the human resources development (HRD) community has a love/hate relationship that seems almost bizarre.

Love? Let a company open a new, multimillion-dollar training center, and listen to the cheers. The investment is hailed as proof of top management's sincere commitment to training. And in the HRD world, nothing is held in higher regard than top-management commitment.

Love? Ask professional trainers which companies they most admire for the way they handle management training. You'll hear about IBM, General Electric, Xerox, McDonald's—all organizations with campus-like training centers. And all of those centers exist, at least in part, to teach standardized courses.

Hate? How often have you heard standardized courses derided as "sheep-dip"? How many times have you heard the phrase, "Don't measure the value of your training by the size of your course catalog"? In how many ways, from how many experts,

have you received the message that individual employees or departments or business units are all unique entities with unique training needs that are not served by generic training programs? How often have you been warned that the course you teach at corporate headquarters in Chicago will just waste the time of people who will return to the Kansas City plant, where *things don't really work like that?*

Hate? Maybe this sounds familiar: Never design or conduct a training program unless it's aimed at a specific, pressing problem in a specific area of the organization, and a needs analysis has convinced you that the problem is caused by some discrete group of employees who lack some specific skills or knowledge. Never use training to try to fix anybody or anything that isn't visibly, demonstrably broken.

A company that establishes and supports an ongoing management curriculum draws the envy of the rest of the training world. But after bowing their heads respectfully, a lot of people in the field go back to talking about HRD as if the only useful and legitimate training function is one that cruises through the corporate waters like a shark on an eternal seek-and-destroy mission for bleeding fish. It chews up bite-sized performance problems and excretes solutions—preferably solutions whose

impacts are measurable in dollars and cents. Then it swims on, in search of the next wounded tuna, the next department with a performance hemorrhage.

This ambivalence in our attitudes toward the fixed-curriculum approach to training is real. But it is also largely a straw man. Most directors of corporate management academies are happy to agree that the cruising shark is an essential feature of an effective training effort. They just don't think it's the only feature. To say, "A thick course catalog does not effective training make," is not the same as to say, "Don't have a course catalog." You aren't designing a core curriculum to handle all the training you're going to do—just the training you want *every* manager to get.

"The premise that everybody needs to get something unique out of an educational experience is probably valid," says John Murphy, director of executive and management education at GTE's management development center in Norwalk, CT. "But that doesn't invalidate offering them the same educational experience. To say they need unique outcomes and applications is not to say they need unique input. If [the curriculum] is relevant to real business issues, people can grab hold of the elephant in different places and get unique things out of it."

Sheep dip? Defenders of the curriculum approach are not necessarily intimidated by the term. "Sheep dip has its place in life," says J. Robert Carleton, former manager of executive development at Southland Corp. (7-Eleven stores) and now a consultant with the Vanguard Group of San Francisco and London. "You dip sheep when they need to be dipped—when there are particular diseases you're trying to avoid or specific innoculations everybody needs."

The problem sheep-dip training runs into, Carleton continues, is that "you can start to think it does things it doesn't." Again, a core curriculum is not a *substitute* for the roving shark that seeks out training needs indigenous to particular areas in the organization. And indeed, a management academy can jump the track and drift into irrelevance for any number of reasons.

But at the same time, advocates say, a standard curriculum can do things that the find-it-and-fix-it approach can't. Different companies design their core courses to achieve different goals, but three major objectives tend to emerge: 1) Build generic management skills. 2) Build skills and knowledge uniquely applicable to managing in this particular organization. 3) Forge and maintain a cohesive corporate culture.

Even if a company has all three goals in mind—and many don't—the distinctions among them are by no means clear-cut. Where does a company-specific management skill leave off and a generic (universally effective) management skill begin? Where is the line between delivering information about how the company works, and indoctrinating people into a certain value system or culture? In practice, the same course can cover all three bases. In fact, some argue that it must. Says Kenneth Hansen, manager of education and training for Xerox Corp., "Value systems are interpreted through the policies and procedures you have in place, and policies are carried out through the skills you teach people. You can't separate those things. It's critical to have them locked together."

Nevertheless, if you want to compare and contrast some different approaches to designing a management academy, those three goals offer a useful frame of reference.

Generic skills

Most companies structure their core curricula in building-block style. As people advance up the career ladder, from first-level supervisor to middle management to the executive ranks, they are urged or required to take certain standard courses that prepare them for their new responsibilities.

In some organizations these courses are heavily customized and loaded with cultural indoctrination. Virtually everything they teach refers specifically to "how we do things *here*." At IBM, for example, every entry-level manager who joins the company is sent to its Armonk, NY, training center for a one-week course. Everyone who reaches the midmanagement level goes back for another one-week course. Newly promoted executives go to Armonk for two weeks. These core courses, representing only a fraction of the formal training a typical IBM manager receives, concentrate entirely on "people skills," as opposed to functional responsibilities such as marketing, engineering or finance. But they don't teach you (as it were) "how to supervise people effectively" or "how good executives deal with subordinates and peers" in general. They teach you how supervisors and middle managers and executives *at IBM* are expected to supervise and deal with people.

None of this is to say, however, that IBM believes there's no such thing as people-management skills that are more or less universally effective. Elements of various packaged training programs are folded into some of the company's courses, says corporate education director Jack Bowsher. It's just that you'd be hard pressed to recognize them. All generic material has been thoroughly IBMed.

In most other companies, skill-building courses tend to take a more universal approach to developing managers as they move up the ladder. At The Hartford Insurance Group, a core management curriculum was launched just two years ago at the company's Hamilton Heights Conference Center in West Hartford, CT. "We started with the assumption that there are certain skills associated with different levels of management in virtually any organization," says Charles Wolfe, director of management development. "A number of people have gone out and done massive studies that categorize the skills that come into play when you become a supervisor, a middle manager, an executive." For instance, he points out, researchers keep finding that at the midmanagement level, artful interaction with peers is vital. At the executive level, you have to "understand the external environment and be able to respond internally.

"Nobody has to spend millions of dollars to find that out," Wolfe says. "It's all been well spelled out in the literature. . . . We built an approach you could basically use in any company."

The Hartford's core curriculum includes courses recommended—not mandated—for all employees at four levels: pre-supervisor (that is, supervisory candidates), supervisor, manager and executive. Much of the material refers specifically to The Hartford's policies and operations, but to a large degree, the skill-building elements in these programs are deliberately generic, using packaged material from various training vendors.

In other words, says Wolfe, "Our core curriculum is not just about doing things The Hartford way." At the same time, he acknowledges that the next challenge, now that the basic curriculum is up and running, is to integrate parts of it with the peculiar needs of various company divisions. The training department is now working with The Hartford's commercial insurance division, for instance, "to overlay their particular career ladder on our programs." But Wolfe does not intend to retreat from the curriculum's basic structure. "Ten years from now," he says, "there will be more specific courses for each division. But there will still be core programs for the whole company. The core stuff may change, but it will be there and it will be pretty generic."

In 1984, First Bank System launched three parallel building-block curricula: one for management, one for consumer banking and one for commercial banking. All are centrally operated from the 15th floor of the bank's Minneapolis headquarters building, although trainees are not necessarily sent to Minneapolis to attend all courses. Sometimes trainers deliver the programs in branch offices spread over a six-state region.

"When we designed the [management] curriculum, we had no clear and immediate presenting problems," says Susan Zemke, former director of the management academy and currently manager of training consulting services for First Bank. (She is now, in effect, the cruising shark of the company's training function, working on problems in individual divisions and units.) "There was no huge hue and cry about specific needs, no major turnover problems or anything. But we knew that we had excellent managers, medium managers and poor managers. We started by asking, 'What would excellent managers have to be able to do?' and we built from there."

The result is a core curriculum that offers 12 to 15 courses to people at each of three levels: supervisor, middle management and senior management. At every level, the courses are grouped in clusters under the headings, "Managing Personal Effectiveness," "Managing People," "Managing Results" and "Leadership." What changes as people move up the career ladder is the scope and complexity of the building-block courses. At the supervisory level, for instance, "Managing People" translates into courses on how to hire, manage, delegate to and evaluate the performance of nonexempt employees. At the senior management level, modules teach the same sorts of skills, but with regard to managing and developing other managers.

That basic strategy—keep the same themes but broaden the scope as people move up the ladder—is fairly common to building-block curricula, although variations in structure and focus are endless. For example, General Electric Co.'s Crotonville Management Development Institute in Ossining, NY, operates on six levels. All newly hired college graduates, be they salespeople, accountants or chemists, go to Crotonville for a three-day orientation course within six months of being hired. After three years with the company, they go back for a week. Every first-time manager at GE goes to Crotonville for six days. Then there are the "advanced functional curricula" for senior people in functions such as marketing, engineering and finance. Executive programs kick in for people under consideration for one of the top 400 jobs in the company. Finally, "officers workshops" are for incumbents in the top 100 or so jobs at GE.

According to James Baughman, manager of corporate management development, all six programs are organized along three "dimensions." He calls them personal stretch (raising your own standard of knowledge and expertise), business stretch (where you "wrestle with the realities of GE's competitive situation") and leadership stretch. What changes from level to level is the scope and focus of the training. A lower-level leadership course, for instance, might deal with "how to get your own act together with maybe a three-person team." In a top-level course, Baughman says, "you might be talking about leading a $6 billion business with 25,000 employees."

Managing here

Baughman estimates that the Crotonville courses represent only about 20 percent of the core training a typi-cal GE manager receives. Fourteen major businesses reside under GE's umbrella, and each operates its own building-block curriculum. "Crotonville's job is to integrate," he says. "Eighty percent of the job is to differentiate. . . . We're so diverse, it would be foolish to have a central sales training function, for instance. Sales in aircraft engines is different from sales at NBC."

In GE's "personal stretch" courses—and even in IBM's heavily customized skill-building programs—a manager who had been through some other company's academy might well recognize many of the basic principles and skills being taught. When it comes to matters like how to give effective performance feedback to a subordinate, for instance, nobody completely reinvents the wheel. As The Hartford's Wolfe points out, many tried-and-true people-management techniques tend to be universal, whether you customize your programs or not.

But in some corporate academies, people-management skills and basic orientation to company policies make up only part of the core curricula. Other parts have to do with specific issues currently facing the company. In many of GE's "business stretch" courses, an outsider would be much more at sea. "We have people in there working on real problems in real time," Baughman says. Sometimes with their actual coworkers, sometimes in heterogenous groups, GE managers in some Crotonville courses wrestle with actual business issues and make real recommendations about how to handle them. "This is the element GE includes that 90 percent of the [management academies] I've seen don't," Baughman says.

Another academy that *does* is GTE's. John Murphy explains that quality improvement has been tagged by top management as the No. 1 goal of all of GTE's 35 "strategic business units." Accordingly, the Norwalk management development center is running a quality course for the senior managers of all 35 units. Four units at a time, in groups of about 40 people, these executives gather in Norwalk for three days. About half the time is spent discussing quality-improvement strategies. The other half is spent developing implementation plans for each business unit.

"They leave with an actual strategic plan and roughed-out action plans," Murphy says. And 30 days after they get back to their offices, they're expected to turn in final quality plans to corporate headquarters. Those plans will represent their actual goals for the next two years.

"The reality is that the most productive management training you can do is to have real teams working on real issues at the time they're actually dealing with those issues," Murphy says.

That GTE quality course, like some of General Electric's "business stretch" programs, obviously is "standardized" only in the sense that everyone goes in with the same general goal in mind. When real teams wrestle with real problems, most of the course "content" will vary from group to group. But the fact that Murphy views this as the ultimate type of management training does not mean he sees no value in more generic skill-building programs. GTE's building-block management curriculum, which operates in conjunction with two parallel curricula, one in finance and another in sales and marketing, uses elements from packaged programs in some supervisory modules.

Even in its core building-block programs, however, GTE is not necessarily trying to shape a specific type of manager. "We've made a conscious transition away from that idea over the past five years," Murphy says. When the company opened its $35 million management center in 1982, the initial strategy was indeed to come up with a model of the perfect manager and try to build him through training. "But we gave up on that," he says.

"Nobody really knows what a perfect manager is. Trying to build perfect managers through some model may be a waste of time—and maybe it's something you wouldn't want to do even if you could." So now, he says, "Most of our core courses are heavily strategy-driven. In the director-level course, the question is, 'What's your role in driving the business' strategy? In the executive course, the content is determined each year by the participants. We don't use [these courses] primarily for skill building."

In some companies, the core curriculum focuses entirely on teaching people the ins and outs of *this partic-*

ular business. Little or no attention is devoted to people-management skills. At Dunkin' Donuts of America's national training center in Braintree, MA, the closest thing in the core curriculum to a people-skills program is a course for district sales managers on how to run an effective meeting—the Dunkin' Donuts way. No, at Braintree, the point is to teach donut-shop franchise owners—and a lot of corporate-level employees—all about how Dunkin' Donuts operates.

"We do a program for all new franchise owners," says Robert Harloe, corporate director of training and development. "Now there's a sheep-dip course if ever there was one; everybody gets exactly the same information. But you cannot operate the business unless you know the nuts and bolts of how it works."

Also, the company feels its corporate marketing people, real estate specialists and even internal auditors cannot do their jobs effectively—their jobs being to support the franchise owner—unless they understand the owner's world and how it works. Therefore, the support troops are "dipped" right along with the owners in the basics of lease arrangements, legal considerations and various arcane donut concepts such as "yield and usage."

Forge a culture

Most management-academy directors agree that a centralized core curriculum can be helpful in building and maintaining a homogenous culture or value system in an organization—a standard way of doing things. There is considerable disagreement, however, as to how the academy should approach this role. Is culture—or cultural change—something you identify and teach directly? Or does a culture evolve from the needs of the business and the training you do to support those needs?

IBM is famous for addressing cultural issues explicitly: This is what IBM believes, this is how we do things here, and this is the only way we do things here. Personnel policies—the performance evaluation system, for instance—are consistent throughout the entire mammoth organization.

General Electric also takes the head-on approach, but in a somewhat different way. Once noted for a culture nearly as homogenous as IBM's, GE has changed considerably since chairman John F. Welch Jr. took the helm in 1981 and embarked on an ambitious campaign of acquisitions, swallowing such disparate companies as RCA and Kidder, Peabody & Co.

"We're not trying to build a single, IBM-like culture," says GE's Baughman. "We have 14 very different types of businesses, and we want their cultures to be different. But we do want them all to share some common standards, values, purposes and behaviors . . . . It's like, you don't want to try to turn Texas into Rhode Island, but they're both part of the United States."

GE has developed an "evolving" 18-page value statement that trainees at Crotonville study and talk about directly. "We have very explicit, heated discussions of what we want to be, how we want to behave and what we value," Baughman says.

Xerox, too, addresses cultural issues right out loud in its corporate-wide building-block programs. The company runs a five-level curriculum, starting with "pre-management" programs and ending with courses for top corporate officers. A major purpose of the entire curriculum, says Ken Hansen, is to "instill our values and expectations of managers across all units and divisions—to institutionalize values across the corporation."

But the decision to use training to institutionalize a culture was not automatic, Hansen says. "When we put the building blocks in place, we discussed whether we *wanted* a corporate-wide value system. Our operating companies do business in the same environment to a great extent. That's why a common value system made sense for us."

GTE's Murphy agrees that a core curriculum can be an engine for cultural change ("It's at least a secondary objective of every course we've got"), and some of the company's programs used to hit the subject head-on. But now Murphy is taking a different tack. "I think that establishing a company culture or a corporate 'religion' as an avowed purpose of training is a mistake in most places. It doesn't fit us, and it doesn't fit most companies. At IBM and maybe GE, it might make sense; IBM has been very clear about what its management philosophy is for 35 years or whatever. But unless you *are* IBM, trying to ram a culture down people's throats doesn't work."

A better approach for most companies, Murphy argues, is to focus training on major strategic business goals—quality, productivity, customer service—and "let a culture evolve out of how you meet them."

By addressing the need for cultural change explicitly, he says, "We tended to deal with the issues in too generic and broad a way. Everybody at GTE understands that the telephone industry has been deregulated, but so what? It wasn't clear enough what we wanted managers to do about it—the payoff for changing wasn't clear." After going through GTE's quality-improvement program, on the other hand, managers go back to work and "realize that in order to implement specific quality strategies, they've got to change the way the organization is managed. Well, guess what: That's what we meant all along by cultural change."

As a result of the quality program, says Murphy, "We have new compensation plans, new management structures and new communication strategies already out there happening. We've achieved more than we did in five years of having [guest experts] come in and talk about culture change."

Robert Harloe of Dunkin' Donuts has no patience at all with the notion of spending classroom time on explicit discussions of the company culture. "It seems ludicrous to me that you go get some training program and that's going to establish or change your value system. We have a strong culture, but it's just a result of the way we manage. 'Dunkin' Donuts 101' wouldn't make a culture or change it.

"In the old days," Harloe continues, "our training center was called Dunkin' Donuts University. That smacks of a certain kind of lunacy to me. . . . A lot of our franchisees quit their jobs and took out second mortgages on their homes in order to go into this business. They need to know how to run the shop. They don't want to hear about the philosophy of donuts."

Reprinted from TRAINING, March 1988

HOW TO BUILD A TRAINING STRUCTURE THAT WON'T KEEP BURNING DOWN

Task: Create a coherent training curriculum—a 'curriculum architecture'—that will pay off for your entire organization.
Recommended construction method: Group process

BY D. DOUGLAS McKENNA,
RAYMOND A. SVENSON,
KAREN M. WALLACE
AND GUY WALLACE

Fire fighting is a familiar routine for training departments. The company president gets wind of the latest participative-management program and wants all senior executives run through it—pronto. The vice president of marketing suddenly decides the sales staff needs an emergency dose of telemarketing training. Before you know it, the training department is racing around in circles, attempting to douse these flare-ups with its limited resources.

As a result, training efforts are not directed at problems that have the largest impact on the organization's performance. Instead, resources are allocated and rushed to the scenes of various conflagrations according to the importance of the person who spotted the fire. If the fire ranger was the CEO, those executives *will* get that program.

Your training department can escape this reactive mode by designing a "curriculum architecture" that organizes the company's various training needs into a logical sequence of courses or modules. With this coherent design in hand, you will have a blueprint to help you plan and assign priorities to developing and maintaining your training programs. You'll also have a weapon to stave off raids on your resources by well-meaning but ill-advised fire rangers.

The group-process method

Just as an architect designs a building so that each piece considers and contributes to the entire structure, an "architectural" approach to training aims at building a curriculum with individual parts that add up to a logical whole within the context of a given job, a department or an entire organization.

There are a variety of ways to approach this task, but the group-process method will help you achieve three key objectives:

• It will produce a performance-based curriculum that focuses specifically on what trainees *need to know* to perform effectively on the job.

• It is much faster and less expensive than other methods, so it will meet time and budget constraints.

• It is particularly effective in situations where the relationship between the training department and the rest of the organization is less than wonderful. When you involve line managers and employees in curriculum design, you begin to break down the "we-they syndrome." An additional benefit: Employees who have a sense of ownership in the final product will see the training department as responsive to their needs.

As we're using the term, "group process" means simply that you enlist the aid of subject-matter experts (people who know how to do the jobs you're training for), potential trainees and their managers in the design of the training curriculum.

STEP 1 DETERMINE THE SCOPE

Before you get these people actively involved in the process, however, you must determine the scope of the curriculum you intend to build. Will you focus on a single job? A department? The whole organization? Since your primary purpose is to provide a framework for planning course-development activities, be sure to select a scope that will represent the training needs of your major "client groups."

One approach is to follow your organization's existing structure or functions. For example, you might develop a separate curriculum for the marketing, engineering, manufacturing and management functions. Likewise, if your company is involved in a variety of different businesses (e.g., microprocessors and radios) or is highly decentralized, you can probably save yourself some time and effort in the long run by developing a curriculum for each business or location. It usually will be easier to build a variety of curriculums than to try to "sell" a single version to distinctly different units or divisions.

To further define the scope of your curriculum, you must zero in on a target population of trainees. For example, if you decide to focus on the needs of new and/or experienced personnel, you also might address basic, advanced or change-driven training needs. Obviously, you will want to consider the level of competence in the work force, your organization's current business plans and strategies, and existing training programs.

Two rules of thumb should guide your decision on the scope of the project. First, as employees' training needs become more diverse, a narrower scope usually will produce a more accurate and comprehensive curriculum. Second, since the curriculum must be accepted by employees before it can be implemented successfully, consider whether a group is willing to "own" the design before you decide on a target population.

STEP 2 ESTABLISH PARTICIPANT GROUPS

The next task is to identify and recruit the people who will participate in the curriculum-design effort. Typically, three groups are established.

761

To guarantee employees' participation in the process, recruit key middle- and upper-level managers to serve on a curriculum committee. This committee oversees the design portion of the project—it reviews, critiques and approves all recommendations. The committee also identifies subject-matter experts who help analyze performance and construct the curriculum.

Generally, the curriculum committee meets twice during the project: once to review the project plan and select the group-process participants, and again at the end of the project to critique the results and set priorities for training activities.

The subject-matter experts (SMEs) the project committee selects will provide information for performance analysis, identify job knowledge and skill requirements, critique the existing curriculum (if any), and build the new curriculum. SMEs should be expert in the work itself, able to describe that work articulately, and representative of the departments or locations that ultimately will use the training.

SMEs are critical to the group-process method: They provide the basic information on work performance and the skills necessary to support that performance. They should be prepared to commit four to six days to attending meetings; no outside work is required of group members.

If you intend to address the training needs of new employees, you'll need a third group composed of recent hires, preferably with six to 12 months of experience. Because new employees lack experience and perspective, however, it's a good idea to ask the expert group to review the performance-analysis data they produce.

STEP 3
ANALYZE WORK PERFORMANCE

During a two-day meeting, the expert group systematically analyzes the work. The goal of this meeting is to come up with a performance analysis (see Fig. 1) that defines these elements.

• A mission statement for the job or function.

• A list of *major* accomplishments or responsibilities for the job or function.

• A list of the major "outputs" or results produced by each accomplishment or responsibility.

• A list of the major tasks that must be performed to achieve each result.

• Measures by which the results are evaluated (e.g., accuracy, timeliness, etc.).

• Typical and/or critical deficiencies in the results.

• Perceived causes of those deficiencies (e.g., lack of knowledge or feedback).

The 'fire spotter's' position tends to determine the resources allocated to fighting the fire.

Performance analysis establishes *effective work performance* as the criterion for all training activities. It becomes the foundation for task-oriented training modules because it defines the major accomplishments, outputs and tasks of the job.

Analyzing deficiencies and their causes allows you to pinpoint performance problems for which training is a likely solution (e.g., workers lack certain skills), as opposed to non-training problems (e.g., substandard equipment, poor performance-appraisal system, etc.). This also is a terrific opportunity for teaching people that training is not a panacea for solving all performance problems.

The expert group's next task is to develop knowledge/skill matrices. A good way to start is by showing the group a list of categories into which various skills might fall. With engineering groups, for example, we have used categories such as introduction/background information, policies/procedures, tools/resources, product technologies, process technologies, technical engineering skills, generic professional skills, management skills and theories/concepts. The categories you use are not critical, but they should stimulate the group's thinking about relevant knowledge and skills.

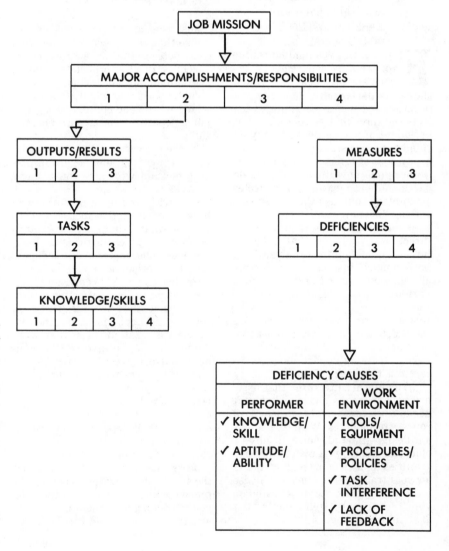

FIGURE 1
Elements of Performance Analysis

The specific knowledge and skills in each category are generated by tracing back through the performance analysis. Pay particular attention to deficiencies that seem to call for training solutions. When the group is satisfied that all major knowledge and skill

needs have been captured in at least one of the categories, each item is cross-referenced to the major accomplishments or responsibilities identified in the performance analysis. The result is a knowledge/skill martix like the one in Figure 2.

This cross-referencing of knowledge and skills to accomplishments serves three purposes.

☐ It ties particular knowledge or skills directly to the work itself.

☐ It provides specific direction for those who ultimately will develop a training program to teach the skill. Rather than using a generic program on oral presentations, for example, the training developer, knowing from the beginning that presentation skills are needed only in certain aspects of the job, can build (or buy) a program that teaches the specific types of presentation skills the work requires.

☐ The knowledge/skill matrices also

help when it comes to developing curriculum modules and a strategy for delivering the training. If some specific knowledge or skill is used in all of a job's major accomplishments, it may be appropriate to develop a single course to cover all its applications on the job. Where a skill is relevant to only one or two accomplishments, however, it might be more efficient to include it in a module built around that particular goal.

Once the expert group has developed the performance analysis and knowledge/skill matrices, the new-employee group can meet, if necessary, to review the materials and suggest additions based on their needs.

STEP 4 DESIGN THE CURRICULUM

The expert group reconvenes for a two- or three-day meeting to review the work of the new-employee group and to design the curriculum. At this point, you probably will want to add members of the training staff to the group. Their role is to contribute information on existing training programs, potential or existing delivery systems, and forecasts about when the training can be delivered.

First, the group must decide upon the general structure of the curriculum architecture. One useful outline that can be adapted to a wide variety of jobs and functions begins with orientation and progresses to increasingly specific skill/knowledge modules.

The top level in this four-level structure contains training courses designed to introduce employees to the company, its divisions, product lines, procedures, policies, etc. The modules

at the third level provide overviews of the major accomplishments, responsibilities and tasks identified in the performance analysis. Second-level courses teach the steps or procedures involved in completing each of the tasks. Finally, first-level modules sup-

port the entire structure by providing instruction on basic or advanced knowledge and skills. These knowledge/skill programs are linked to the task and task-overview programs according to the group's knowledge/skill matrices.

Once the general structure has been set, the group must organize all the training content into modules and identify logical sequences. Creating the modules is a demanding task that requires the group to juggle many variables simultaneously. Variables related to training delivery—considerations such as the number and location of trainees, optimal timing of the training, the existing budget and staff—are likely to be the trickiest problems.

If you are designing a curriculum architecture for a target population that is scattered across remote locations, cannot be taken away from the job for significant periods of time, and is not accustomed to on-the-job coaching, what might you do? One solution would be a curriculum architecture containing short, mentor-delivered modules. Another might be a structure that relies heavily on computer-based training.

Once the group has pounded out a modular curriculum architecture, it identifies the subgroups who will need each module, the potential impact of each module on job performance and the time necessary to complete each module. The group is now prepared to recommend priorities for module development.

Risks vs. benefits

Certain risks are involved in using the group-process method for developing a curriculum design. Without a leader who has a clear understanding

FIGURE 2
Sample Portion of Design Engineering Knowledge/Skill Matrix

Knowledge/Skill	Major Accomplishments			
	Product Definition Developed	Project Plan Completed	Prototype Built and Tested	Pilot Run and Production Supported
1. Second order effects	✓		✓	✓
2. Grounding and shielding	✓		✓	✓
3. Human factors engineering	✓	✓	✓	✓
4. Modeling and simulation			✓	
5. Testing and measurement theory and practice			✓	✓

of what data must be generated, the method probably will not succeed. And even with a knowledgeable leader, group process can run into trouble if there are serious disagreements within the group that can't be resolved.

For example, if group members in a software-development function disagree on whether a particular new computer language will become the standard in their work, they may not be able to produce a curriculum that will be widely accepted. But keep in mind that this type of problem is not unique to the group-process method. If clients can't agree on the nature of the work, it will be extremely difficult to design a satisfactory curriculum regardless of the method you use.

The speed with which a curriculum can be built using the group-process method is one of its key benefits. But even this has a drawback: If the performance analysis is—or is perceived to be—superficial, you've got a problem. When the comprehensiveness of the analysis is a key concern, more group or individual interviews are certainly an option. For a training department with no overall plan for course development, however, a timely and relatively inexpensive curriculum blueprint that identifies 80% of the target population's training needs may be worth much more than a delayed, expensive design that covers 98% of all needs. An overall plan that gives you a place to begin is more important than a perfect one that never gets off the drawing board.

Regardless of the method used to produce a curriculum architecture, the design itself provides a valuable, broad-based survey of an organization's training needs. It is a "client-driven data base" that can help estimate the resources needed to develop and deliver training. And that means you can approach senior management with a budget request based on solid data rather than a laundry list of training needs.

One more benefit: Once potential clients have been involved in a curriculum-design project, they are liable to line up behind the training department in support of its budget requests. These are now *their* needs, and they want to see them met.

Reprinted from TRAINING, September 1984

FOR FURTHER READING
Gilbert, T. *Human Competence*, (McGraw-Hill, New York, NY, 1978).
Svenson, R. A. *Planning a curriculum*, (Training and Development Journal, October 1978).
Ulschak, F. L., Nathanson, L., & Gillan, P. G. *Small Group Problem Solving: An Aid to Organizational Effectiveness*, (Addison-Wesley, Reading, MA, 1978).
Zemke, R. & Kramlinger, T. *Figuring Things Out: A Trainer's Guide to Needs and Task Analysis*, (Addison-Wesley, Reading, MA, 1982).

CONDUCT A FRONT-END ANALYSIS ON YOUR OWN CAREER IN HRD

'Physician heal thyself!' said the trainer to the mirror

BY JOAN WACKERMAN
AND NANCY MARCUE

Looking for an effective way to clarify your career goals? Seeking new ways to get ahead, move up the managerial ladder, increase your salary or find the right niche within your own company? Sure, you say. Who isn't.

We, too, had hazy career goals—until we began to use our expertise as instructional designers to clarify them. When we began to treat them the way we do the goals of our clients, we met with positive results. And now we'd like to share the process and the results with you, so you can do the same.

The purpose of this article is to show how you, as an experienced trainer, can do a front-end analysis on your own career. In other words, you can do a needs assessment and task analysis and set goals and objectives for your own life, much as you would for a training project. Moreover, this front-end analysis can help you move up, move laterally or do whatever you wish with your career.

The process

Developing career goals is, of course, a method of focusing one's energies in a specific desired direction. We found that before we could list our goals, we needed to identify just what we really wanted to do. To help us clarify our needs, we used the following checklist. Perhaps you'll want to use it for your own needs assessment.

Our next step was to refine our needs to reflect one-year, two-year and five-year goals. By focusing on our five-year goals first and working backwards, we could set one-and two-year goals that would serve as stepping-stones to the more difficult, long-term goal.

The following sample goals show how we projected into the future and eventually established more immediate, present-tense objectives.

- 5-year goal: To acquire a line position in upper management in an instructional design firm.
- 2-year goal: To manage an instructional design project within the company.
- 1-year goal: To obtain a position as an instructional designer in an instructional design firm.

Next, we performed a task analysis in order to clarify exactly what we had to do to attain these goals. Essentially, this consisted of analyzing the skills of successful business men and women across all fields. More specifically, we read articles about people who had either 1) successfully acquired high-level management positions, or 2) made successful career changes. In other words, we read about people who had done what we wanted to do. Then we selected and analyzed those tasks they performed that we needed to learn.

In addition, we observed and

Personal Job Needs Assessment

Do you want or need...

___ 1. to manage people?
___ 2. to become more technically competent?
___ 3. a salary increase?
___ 4. a more prestigious job?
___ 5. more interface with clients?
___ 6. less interface with clients?
___ 7. a position with less pressure?
___ 8. more freedom on the job?
___ 9. a position where you are more closely involved with the end product?
___10. more responsibility?
___11. more free time?
___12. more tangible rewards for accomplished tasks?
___13. a chance to travel?
___14. less travel?
___15. a job with security?

interviewed people who now held the jobs we hoped to attain, and we identified the abilities and skills necessary to perform those jobs. In other words, we looked at the corporate structure and asked, "How do I get there from here?"

If you've decided to take our tack toward career planning, you're now ready to write your own behavioral objectives. To do so, you'll have to take the skills identified in your task analysis and subtract from those the skills you already possess. What remain are the skills you need to obtain and those you want to convert into objectives.

Here, for example, is how one of us stated a goal and then spelled out specific behaviors for attaining it.

As you articulate your goals and objectives, share them with family and close friends. We found that it was important to discuss our career ambitions with people who cared and whom we could trust. Remember, your family will be more supportive of your upward mobility, or any changes you make, if you share your plans with them.

Finally, establish a feedback mechanism. One of the most useful steps in the instructional design process is that of validation and revision. The same applies to our lives: valid feedback on our performance tells us how we're doing and helps us improve our product.

One way to establish a feedback mechanism is to encourage capable people around you to comment on your performance. Identify someone— probably a boss or a peer— who's in a position to provide specific feedback and solicit his or her comments.

Reaping the benefits

We found that once we wrote down our objectives, opportunities to realize our goals surfaced immediately. Probably the opportunities had always been there, but we were never aware of them before. We concluded, therefore, that the front-end analysis did for us personally what it often does in the training setting.

- It puts you through a *clarifica-*

> **GOAL:** To increase my credibility and visibility within corporate management within the next six months
>
> **OBJECTIVES:**
> 1. I will telephone at least one member of corporate management once a week.
> 2. I will write memos once a month to the corporate program director to keep him informed of my efforts.
> 3. I will deliver at least four confident, well-organized presentations to corporate management within the next six months.
> 4. I will solicit feedback and criticism of my work as a means of improving my capabilities as often as practicable.

---

tion process that forces you to be more precise about what you really want to do.

- It makes you more aware of *using present resources and opportunities* to reach your goals.

Of course, not everyone wants to move up within his or her company. But even if you're satisfied where you are, the front-end analysis process can still be of value to you. Do you want a position with less client contact? Do you want to move from design analysis to production? Do you want a raise? If you answered yes to any of these queries, then we suggest you systematically approach your wants and needs. The figure illustrates how.

An equal time share

If you're still not convinced that a front-end analysis is worth all the time and effort, consider please the staggering amounts of time, energy and money you spent to earn your college degree. And what about all those night classes you took? Remember the exams, the papers, the projects?

All of us spent many hours learning design skills. But how many hours did we put into learning how to negotiate for salary, move up the managerial ladder, or identify our special niche in the company where we can be happiest and contribute the most? Virtually none. Did we do our homework in the areas that would provide us with a more satisfying job? No, most of us didn't give an equal time share to job preparation, career planning and job satisfaction.

But that shouldn't prevent us from doing it now. A front-end analysis on our own lives can help us do whatever we wish with our careers. We know design. We know the systematic process works for our clients. Let's make it work for ourselves.

Reprinted from TRAINING, November 1980

TRAINING HERE MEANS LISTENING AND THINKING

How should you manage at the country's best-managed bank?

BY RON ZEMKE

S an Francisco-based Wells Fargo Bank is *not* the country's largest bank. It's number 11. Wells Fargo Bank is, however, one of the nation's most profitable banks—an acknowledged top performer in per-share-earnings gross. Many industry analysts suggest that Wells is the best-managed financial institution in the country.

What do you do if you find yourself in charge of management development in one of the better-managed organizations in your industry? According to Dr. Olaf Isachsen, vice president of human resources development, Wells Fargo Bank, N.A., the first thing you do is decide who you are, what business you're in, and what your company's management philosophy is or should be. And since Isachsen firmly believes that "If an organization has no management philosophy, there can be no management development," much of the work of the Wells Fargo HRD unit is aimed at helping managers clarify their management philosophy. That belief is strongly reflected in the Wells Fargo HRD group's own mission statement. (See accompanying box.)

From this mission statement spring a number of significant ramifications for the way the HRD group "does business." This is especially true of the role Isachsen plays. "Our mission dictates that my role be that of a manager first and foremost," he asserts. "Equally important, our posture has to be very low key, and our ultimate purpose is to assist in creating conditions which will cause line managers to improve performance — without putting HRD in the limelight. One ramification of this position is that we must forego the pleasures of the classroom trainer role."

This was an especially tough decision for a man like Isachsen, who holds an MBA from Harvard and a Ph.D. in interpersonal communications from Michigan, and who teaches business policy at Stanford. Obviously, it was a decision based on organizational need, not personal preference. "Of course I like to teach very much," the Norwegian-born Isachsen admits, "but the minute I play teacher in my job, I'm no longer a manager and no longer effective. My job, like the job of every staff manager, is to be a resource to line management. They make the profit, we don't. In HRD our job is to think through various human resources situations and people problems with the line managers when they ask us to. Their profitability pays for our luxury of being able to take some time, step back and help them grapple with unknown concepts."

The decision to make the HRD group somewhat of an in-house management consulting firm meant making quite a dramatic change in the organization Dr. Isachsen inherited. "We went from over 50 to 15 people in my area," he comments, "and we got out of the training development business and into the listening, thinking and problem-solving business."

While this may seem an antithetical move to those who have grown up thinking that management development is equivalent to management training, Isachsen defends the change with a compelling analogy. "Look, the people in computer systems don't spend their time building computers.

**WELLS FARGO BANK
HUMAN RESOURCES DEVELOPMENT GROUP
MISSION STATEMENT**

The purpose of the Wells Fargo Bank Human Resources Development Group is to develop and install an integrated system for improving human effectiveness to specified standards in an organizational setting.

Conceptually, the approach differs from traditionalized-training efforts in three dimensions:

1. It takes heavily into account the culture and technology within which an organization functions and designs approaches to performance improvement to uniquely fit organizational needs, and not vice versa.

2. A common concept of required management work to achieve organizational purpose is developed with officers of the organization— it is not imposed upon them.

3. Conditions are created where key individuals are afforded opportunities for professional growth through action learning in actual work situations, as well as provided with individualized approaches to performance improvements in administrative, people-oriented, and technical tasks.

In order to determine specific standards of performance, key managers, along with their immediate subordinates, are asked to develop a statement of purpose for respective organizational units. Major areas of responsibility are determined, and specific action plans for designated positions are conceived.

Managers at all levels learn and are aided in planning for and determining approaches for the professional development of subordinates by having access to the most effective learning techniques available.

When the above processes are installed and functioning, a system is provided for performance evaluation, based upon attainment of individual action plans to achieve organizational purpose, and where individuals are recognized for their improved administrative abilities.

They leave that to IBM, NCR, Burroughs and the others. Instead they spend their time with the users, the line managers, making sure that they get the best solutions to the problems they're trying to solve."

The overlay of this analogy to HRD is that Isachsen sees his most appropriate training-related role to be that of a wise buyer. "First of all, if we waste our time and money building training programs, we can't be problem solving with line managers on a day-to-day basis. And what if we build a program that doesn't work so good or doesn't compare in polish to the programs that big vendors produce? We're stuck with it and we waste more time and energy defending the indefensible. If I see a Forum, or Sterling Institute or Wilson or Louis Allen course that I like and that I think our line managers have a need for, I buy it. If in our evaluation process we find that it doesn't measure up, well, we drop it. The size of the mistake is minimal that way."

Isachsen's insistence that he and the HRD staff consultants not be branded as trainers extends to the actual running of the training programs he uses. "Sure, it's more expensive to have a super pro like Ralph Bettman or Dick Johnson or Buzz Bainbridge or Tony Athos do the actual training, but we want to avoid that type casting internally and ensure that our top people have top learning experiences."

Isachsen insists that the Well's HRD approach is the essence of simplicity and, therefore, highly efficient. "Look," he argues, "I'm just this little guy who landed in Boston 10 years ago with very little money and a beat-up Volvo. I learned the value of simplicity and I get nervous with grandiose, complex processes." Isachsen suggests

---

Isachsen: "The staff's on one side, the line on the other. My job, like the job of every staff manager, is to be a resource to line management. They make the profit, we don't. Their profitability pays for our luxury of being able to take some time, step back and help them grapple with unknown concepts."

---

that there are only four rules to developing a successful HRD/MD unit.

1. Never claim bottom-line results — profit and loss results — for a staff function like HRD. The line has responsibility for profit and loss. If you take *credit* for profit, you must accept *responsibility* for loss. That doesn't make sense.

2. Earn credibility but do not demand authority. The only way to earn trust, respect or credibility is by responding to the needs of line management and doing so effectively. In Norway we say, "If it's raining on the minister, it drips on the guy who rings the bell, too."

3. Keep learning and changing, avoid being complacent with what you're doing. Go out and see what other people are doing — challenge yourself to be better. I take trips to General Electric, Ford, IBM, anyplace they'll let me visit. It keeps me fresh and humble.

4. Don't get enmeshed in power and budget and territorial struggles. Use your energy to do what you're paid for — helping others do what they need to do more effectively.

A final "rule" Isachsen suggests is: "Be lucky enough to have a good boss." Isachsen suggests that a good boss is simply someone who understands and personally believes in what you're trying to accomplish. "Just the other day," Isachsen proudly reports, "he came into my office and there I sat with my feet up, shoes off, looking out across the Bay thinking about something or other. And do you know what he said? He said, 'I'll talk to you later. I didn't know you were working.' And he meant it. That's really a fine understanding of what we're trying to do here."

Reprinted from TRAINING, March 1978

EIGHT STEPS TO STRATEGIC PLANNING

Here's a guide to HRD strategy and planning
that advises training managers to
incorporate the latest findings
in political, social, technological and economic research

BY LANE D. WARD

Corporate officers increasingly are requiring department heads to sharpen their entrepreneurial edge. More and more of us—training directors included—are required to manage according to the big corporate picture. It is evident that each department is expected to develop its own top management skills and essential abilities and to *think corporate*.

This is especially true for human resources development (HRD) professionals who interface with most, if not all, departments throughout the corporate structure. Professionals in HRD are pressed to demonstrate a keen understanding of corporate policies and objectives and to do their part to affect the bottom line.

It is evident that many top managers want HRD programs to be as much profit-oriented as they are people-oriented. Studies and literature are full of top-management responses asking for improved, corporate thinking among their HRD managers—especially in strategic planning.

There are essentially eight steps to a good corporate strategy. They represent efficient and effective means by which HRD managers can increase the likelihood of success.

1 The strategic profile is the first step to a strategic plan. The profile helps HRD departments identify their philosophy, mission, competitive posture and fundamental goals and objectives. The criteria to be met and developed in the profile are to:
• Identify what HRD is about and why it exists.
• Identify HRD expertise and how it can be used to advantage to promote full appreciation and applica-

tion of HRD throughout the company.
• Establish HRD's self-concept as being proactive, rather than reactive.
• Identify the broad goals and essential outcomes that the HRD department is trying to achieve.

2 The strategic forecast is the second step in formulating an effective HRD strategy. The latest findings in political, social, technological and

economic research pertinent to HRD must be used to help focus training practices and programs. Naturally, you should ensure that the changes made in HRD programs will continue to contribute to profits.

3 The resource audit is a crucial step in the development of your HRD department strategy. It helps make the strategy practical for implementation. The chief difficulty in auditing is summoning the required objectivity in evaluating one's own environment and competencies, including the operational, financial and people resources of the HRD group. To help determine the relationship between resources and successful implementation of strategy, outside or unbiased resources (professional consultants) can greatly help in establishing and developing an objective audit.

It is also essential to determine the availability of outside materials, supplies and services that will be needed to carry out the strategies, plans and objectives. The HRD manager-auditor will need to:
• Know what is happening to the

CHECKLIST FOR HRD STRATEGY AND PLANNING

THE STRATEGY	Yes	No
*Can HRD management define what an organizational strategy is?	☐	☐
*Does HRD have a "strategic profile"?	☐	☐
*Has a "strategic forecast" been completed?	☐	☐
*Has a "resource audit" been completed?	☐	☐
*Has a "test of consistency" evaluation been completed?	☐	☐
*Have alternative strategies been developed?	☐	☐
*Has a "strategic choice" been based on facts, results, and experience?	☐	☐
*Is the strategy identifiable and has it been made clear either in words or practice?	☐	☐
*Does the strategy take full advantage of resources and opportunities?	☐	☐
*Is the strategy consistent with HRD competence and resources, both present and projected?	☐	☐
*Are the major provisions of the strategy and the program of major policies of which it is comprised internally consistent?	☐	☐
*Is the chosen level of competency feasible in institutional and personal terms?	☐	☐
*Is the strategy appropriate to the personal values and aspirations of the key participants?	☐	☐
*Is the strategy appropriate to the desired level of contribution to the main organization?	☐	☐
*Does the strategy constitute a clear stimulus to HRD effort and commitment?	☐	☐
*Are there any early indications of the responsiveness of the company to the strategy?	☐	☐

need for HRD's services.

• Identify HRD's distinctive competencies in operations, finance, organization, personnel, materials and programs.

• Understand how HRD strengths and weaknesses relate to corporate objectives. Wise managers will obviously build into their strategies the necessary tasks to overcome department weaknesses.

4 Formulating strategic alternatives or options will plumb the real genius and entrepreneurial spirit of the HRD manager. Realistic options require broad vision and insight into the relationship between HRD's services and the organization's product. Alternative plans must be developed to meet "what if" situations and to stay abreast of changing conditions. Information gathered in the strategic forecast will allow the HRD department to take advantage of any new and exciting opportunities in the field.

Strategic alternatives always:

• Are identifiable and clear in words and writing.

• Exploit opportunities brought about by change.

• Are consistent with personal values and aspirations of key individuals in the department and company.

• Are implemented through systems that are sensitive to HRD's results or outcomes.

Laying out options requires some system of indicators to identify when strategic-specific alternatives are to be implemented. More and more HRD programs are using computers and mathematical models, as well as systematic information gathering, to help in these kinds of management decisions.

5 The test of consistency helps make sure that a strategy is practical. This step helps influence management's strategy decisions by evaluating what the HRD department is actually able to do, rather than what it might like to do. The test of consistency relies heavily on the resource audit as well as HRD's past results.

A strategy encourages change and improvement, but it nevertheless should be harmonized with realistic competencies and demonstrated achievements. If the HRD strategy requires unrealistic quantum leaps beyond the professional and financial resources of the HRD department, the strategy will be doomed to failure. This is a fine line; you need to achieve a balance between where you are and where you want to go.

Top management in many organizations expects HRD programs *to be as much profit-oriented as they are people-oriented. This checklist and plan for implementing an HRD strategy can help HRD managers do their part to affect the bottom line.*

6 The strategic choice constitutes the decision, in concert with others, on the strategy most likely to improve the department's contribution to the company, its profits and its overall objectives. Selection can begin when all important and significant individuals have been involved in the strategy planning. The chosen HRD strategy must be consistent with HRD competence and immediately available resources and with the limitations of external and internal company conditions.

7 Specific plans and policies are a natural outcome of choosing a strategy. The strategy is used as the framework for specific plans and policies. They should be consistent with short- and long-term objectives and supporting policies. After time frames are outlined, the entire HRD organization, as well as all other appropriate departments, are geared up for implementation. In other words, the action plan is defined and carried out. This, of course, involves the necessary interventions with people, operations and company systems. This is where organizational development works best in synchronizing the strategy, systems, people, plans and policies.

You will know this step has been effectively addressed when:

• Policies and plans are consistent with each other and with the overall HRD strategy.

• Plans and policies have corporate approval.

• Plans and policies are clearly expressed and communicated.

• All information and measurement systems have been correlated with the HRD strategic planning and are prepared to measure the results that are produced by the strategy.

8 Constant strategic reevaluation and update help prevent one of the biggest mistakes an HRD manager can make: failure to look at the strategy again until time lines have expired. To be successful, a strategy must have constant updating and reevaluation. Initially, this should be done on a weekly or monthly basis. Eventually, yearly monitoring should be sufficient. This constant review enables management to know what is happening in response to the strategy and what options might need to be considered.

An HRD strategic plan, in short, is flexible, moves with the times and is established on the premise that every opportunity for contribution to profits will be seized by the HRD department. In addition, there are measurable goals and outcomes and the objectives of the company constitute the nucleus for all HRD actions.

When these eight steps of strategic planning are practiced and implemented in an HRD department, managers will begin to understand the advantage of *thinking corporate.*

Reprinted from TRAINING, November 1982

STRATEGIC THINKING: A CRITICAL HRD SKILL

Your role—and success—in the years to come may depend on your ability to align your actions with the organization's driving force

Increasing, trend articles in leading business magazines, personnel and industrial relations journals, as well as the popular press, nominate the 1980s as the era of "Progress Through People." The popular wisdom is that we have entered a decade in which the finding, developing, utilizing and managing of superior human resources is expected to play a key role in forging a competitive edge, improving productivity and curing or preventing any number of other current and impending organizational ills. Human resources development is becoming viewed as one of a family of new organizational silver bullets; for better or worse, the latest panacea is us.

Many HRD specialists are as unprepared as they are surprised to be facing the tough demands and stringent accountabilities that accompany the spotlight of organizational stardom. True, HRD practitioners, consultants and theorists have long- and loudly-declared our speciality underutilized, undervalued and capable of significant contribution to organizational goal attainment. But politicking for a turn at bat and whacking the ball from the park require different skills.

Drs. Ben Tregoe and Geary Rummler, of Kepner-Tregoe Inc., contend that many, if not most, HRD people are ill-equipped for the challenge. The cobblers, it seems, are poorly shod. What are the critical skills for playing organizational hardball they feel many HRDers lack? According to Tregoe, coauthor with John Zimmerman of an important new book on organizational strategy, Top Management Strategy, *most HRD people are pretty good at the operational aspects of their work – at applying learning technologies, solving performance problems, developing organizational interventions and the like – but pretty bad at deciding when, where and to what end they can best apply those skills. In essence, Tregoe sees many HRD specialists as short on the strategic conceptualization and planning skills necessary to make a human resources development function an effective organizational force.*

Intrigued by the idea of trainers going into the strategic thinking/organizational planning business, and having Tregoe and Rummler cornered in their Princeton, NJ corporate lair, we pressed on.

TRAINING: How exactly are you using the word "strategy"?

TREGOE: There is a lot of confusion on the word. You hear people talk of a marketing strategy, or a personnel selection strategy, but that's not strategy to us. When we speak of strategy, we are talking about a management vision of *what* the organization should be, not *how* the organization will get there. We purposely separate whats and hows; the hows are the plans. First, before doing any planning, you need a framework that can guide the choices that determine the nature and direction of the organization. A plan is the result of weighing possible actions and allocations. Strategy, as we define it, is the framework for guiding those choices of action and resource allocation.

A lot of organizations do long-range planning and think that means they know where they are going. A delusion. Long-range planning without a solid strategy statement is simply financial and market projection, business goals perhaps, but not a statement of where the company or organization is headed, what it is trying to become. Without that strategy touchstone, the long-range plan is relegated to the comptroller's office. It doesn't give anyone else any guidance on how to positively impact the organization.

TRAINING: In your book, you've added a novel and pretty elegant idea to the notion of developing a strategy: the idea of Driving Force. What is it? How does it help in setting strategy?

TREGOE: In our basic look at the field, we talked to people in about 200 companies. We asked them to tell us how they did planning, how they developed strategy. What we observed was that people *did* do their strategic homework. They collected all sorts of information with strategic implications: assumptions about the environment, the competition, technology, sociopolitics. They would list these assumptions, inventory their strengths and weaknesses, and then do nothing with the information. They would go directly from listing assumptions to their financial projections.

It seemed to us that this information could impact and should impact the planning. We knew that sort of information was important, but that it had to be filtered through markets, products, who was being served and why. And the more research we did, the more convinced we were that there was indeed an implicit concept of some sort guiding most strategic positions. So, we sifted through these implicit concepts looking for commonalities and came to the conclusion that there are basically nine strategic areas or, as we've come to call them, Driving Forces. Every organization we've encountered seems to be driven by—that is, the primary determinant of the scope of its products and marketing seems to be— one of the nine Driving Forces.

TRAINING: And those Driving Forces are?

TREGOE: Two focus on the organization's products or services; these are Products and Services Offered and Market Needs. Five have to do with the organization's capabilities: Technology, Production Capability, Method of Sale, Method of Distribution and Natural Resources. The final two are results areas: Size/Growth and Return/Profit.

Don't misunderstand. All of these nine areas are important to every company. However, in every organization we've worked, we've found that only one of these is the Driving Force for the total organization. When it comes down to a final decision about a product or market or allocation of resources, one of these nine strategic areas turns out to be the Driving Force for the decision.

TRAINING: And you believe individual organizational units— marketing, finance, personnel, whatever—should have a Driving Force?

TREGOE: Absolutely.

TRAINING: Exactly how would that translate for an individual HRD unit?

TREGOE: We've worked with the HRD function of a large organization, $4 billion or so in sales, and found just what your question implies—that the concepts of strategy and Driving Force are just as useful at that level as they are at the organizational policy level. One of the things that makes the concept of Driving Force very useful is that it forces to the surface various issues that need to be discussed and resolved if you are going to set up sensible strategy.

We got into great debate in that organization, not about what the future strategy should be, but about what the current Driving Force of the HRD function was. Some people felt it was Market Needs, that their job was to respond to any expressed need of the employees or management of the organization. But others were convinced that the Driving Force was Products and Services Offered. These people felt that it was their job to convince the organization that their products and services should be utilized; they saw themselves as selling a specific set of products and services to the organization. Even though there was pretty good agreement on what they were offering, there was quite a disagreement on the markets being served and the appropriate approach to those markets. The point is, without the focus on Driving Force these substantive issues would not have surfaced and been resolved.

TRAINING: Geary, you've been known to hold some pretty strong views about exactly what businesses a training and development function should be in. How does this strategy development approach fit?

RUMMLER: Well, in my other life, before becoming president of K-T Strategy Group, I worked with a number of clients around the model of training as a performance engineering function. A performance engineering model is basically Market Needs-driven. You have to look at the organization as a series of markets and market segments. Manufacturing, engineering, marketing and so on have very different needs, so you have

to treat each uniquely. You have to profile each, gather data on each and have different use profiles and sales goals for each. You have to know what the particular business mission and Driving Force of each is.

Key to the success of a Market Needs-driven approach is data. You need continual feedback and access to management information. The thing, then, that distinguishes the HRD unit using a performance engineering approach, or any Market Needs-driven unit, is that you can't sit on your butt and wait for people to ask you to do things. You've got to anticipate where the organization is going and be prepared to support it when it gets there.

TRAINING: Let's try a reverse example: the HRD unit with an edifice complex. The organization builds a corporate university, and hires a "faculty," who in turn publish a yearly or quarterly catalog of courses, invest in state-of-the-art audiovisual equipment and recruit a top-notch program development staff. Does this approach suggest or imply a certain Driving Force and HRD strategy?

TREGOE: At least on the surface there seems to be a Method of Distribution Driving Force leading the HRD decision making of your hypothetical company. The implications, of course, are interesting. An HRD unit like this one might be tempted to do only those things that can be done through the delivery mechanism, that in-house university. It strikes me that this approach has some important disadvantages. For instance, if there is an extensive field force or decentralized structure, there could be an argument from the field that the field-training needs are not being met.

RUMMLER: There is a real-world example at Western Electric's Hopewell facility. It appears to me that one of the major reasons they have three- and four-week residential engineering technology courses is because it contributes to keeping the beds full. The "let's have a school" decision really does continue to influence many other decisions.

But every Driving Force decision has continuing ramifications. Take, for example, a Technology Driving Force decision. Suppose an organization decides to go with a small group-centered organizational development approach to HRD. It's not hard to see that there will be some problems that won't get handled. And the same would apply to an organization that goes with a Method of Delivery Driving Force and focuses on audiovisual systems such as a video network: If you can't put it on tape, it can't be a solvable problem. Every Driving

Force has positives and negatives.

TREGOE: It would be fair to say that with a subject as complex as strategy and Driving Force, there are risks associated with every approach. To minimize risk, you have to understand the organization's strategy and Driving Force, and what the best response strategy for the HRD function might be. Our feeling is that if there is some knowledge of where the organization is going and what its strategy is, then the HRD function has to be responsive to that and develop a complementary strategy. The HRD function should be supportive of where the organization is going. But if there is a vacuum, if there is no formal statement of where the organization is going, there has to be a thoughtful effort from HRD to think through its own strategy and use that as a way of forcing the issue.

TRAINING: The idea that HRD managers need to be involved in strategic thinking and planning seems to be part of a larger concern with human resources and human factors in general. Senior managers are starting to ask personnel-related functions to be proactive, anticipating rather than responding to the organization's people needs. What do training and development people have to do to meet these new demands?

TREGOE: Whether you're talking about HRD or the whole organization, you cannot do a sensible job of setting strategy if you lack information about what's going on in and around the organization. The information-gathering job is perhaps harder for an HRD function than for the organization as a whole. Part of the external environment HRD people have to track is the whole organization external to the HRD unit. At the same time, HRD people have to be on top of the "external" external environment— government regulations, immediate economic trends, long-term social trends and the like.

I think it is safe to say that there isn't a company we've worked with that is satisfied with the way it tracks the latter external environment. If an HRD director wanted to make a tremendous impact on the organization, the identification and tracking of critical aspects of the external environment would be ideal.

RUMMLER: First, you have to decide that you're willing and capable of doing things in a different, more proactive way. *Then* you have to make a concerted effort to change the organization's perceptions and expectations of your unit. Where I've seen real success in the last four years has been where the HRD function has been managed in an out-and-out opportunistic fashion. They set a conscious strategy or had a clear idea of what they wanted to accomplish, and they waited and watched for just the right opportunity to move.

For example, the HRD function of one of the top 10 American organizations is going through a massive worldwide reorganization. But the shake-up is planned, the result of some tough HRD people jumping into a vacuum. The organization's patents— its monopoly— ran out about three years ago. People who had been waiting to jump into the business did, with both feet, and "Big Company's" worldwide dominance came unglued. The HRD people risked standing up and saying, "We're really committed to helping meet the goals of improving the product and regaining preeminence. We're not going to run one more program or carry out another activity that doesn't relate to that goal." This same group had been guilty of setting some pretty unrealistic expectations of HRD in the past, but senior management heard the new message, bought it and is backing it up.

TRAINING: What changes have the HRD people experienced?

RUMMLER: They have become an active part of the organization's management. For years they were the last to know that a new product was coming out or that a plant was being phased out or a whole product line cut. Now they have demanded and won more advance warning on change. They said, "Look, we've got to be on those long-range committees and task forces and groups if we are going to do long-range planning." For instance, the company has a full employment policy. The HRD people argued, successfully, that if the company was going to commit to retraining and relocating the technologically displaced, then HRD people needed early warning if they were going to be able to make that policy work.

TREGOE: I guess another way to say it is that if HRD has been a doormat, or simply content to assume a reactive role, nothing is going to change. One tactic for being perceived as more proactive is to begin alerting those who set corporate strategy to external factors that can impact those deliberations. There's not a top management group we have worked with that hasn't expressed a need for more information about their environment. They know that good sound information is key to their deliberations about the future. It's doubly important if they are contemplating a dramatic strategic change. If the HRD

function can be very proactive and provide information just about likely events that will affect the skills people will need to develop or new capabilities the organization will need, they will have demonstrated their right to be a part of the organization's strategic deliberations.

TRAINING: We haven't said much about the management of training in the classical sense. Where do concerns with cost effectiveness of training, good needs analysis, transfer of learning to the job, evaluating behavior change and that myriad of things that go with managing the technology of training fit in HRD strategy?

TREGOE: What you are describing are what I call the operational aspects of the HRD function. HRD managers and the HRD function have, in the past, been primarily concerned with the operational improvement of human resources. And most HRD people and managers and functions have become damned good at the operational aspects. They can spot problems, put out fires and run a top-notch department. But they are like a lot of good operational managers who are suddenly thrown into the position of having to think strategically. They are no longer rewarded for doing good work; that's assumed. They suddenly find they are being rewarded for clear thinking, and they haven't had much practice at being visionary and may not even understand that the demand exists.

To meet today's demands it is extremely important for the HRD manager to clearly recognize the difference between the strategic and operational aspects of the job. Even if all you really want to do is improve operational effectiveness, you've got to know something about where the organization is going. But that's not maximizing HRD's potential. I think those in the HRD function have to be concerned with how you develop strategic thinking capability in others. You've got to be able to think strategically yourself if you are going to take on that charge.

The head of the organization or corporation has to think strategically for the corporation. The head of a division has to think strategically about the division. If you are going to be head of HRD, *you* have to be able to think strategically.

TRAINING: But managers and others in HRD are still going to get those phone calls from executive vice-presidents, who just read a story in *Business Week* or *Fortune* about quality control circles, asking, "How come we aren't doing that?"

RUMMLER: If I received a call like

that, I would consider it a symptom, an indication that there is some perceived problem with the current plans. On the one hand, I would want to know what problem, if any, he or she is trying to solve using quality circles as a tactic. On the other hand, I would want to know what that need is telling me about my strategy. If there *is* a legitimate need, how did I miss it? How does this over-the-transom request fit with the strategy I'm trying to develop for my HRD function? I would definitely want to review what I think I understand about that individual's plant or division and where he or she or they are trying to go. I certainly wouldn't panic. I would consider it an opportunity to work with someone who thought enough of my expertise to call me and ask my counsel.

TRAINING: What skills are HRD people going to have to develop to work in a more strategic fashion?

TREGOE: Not a simple question to answer. Obviously, they are going to have to develop strategic thinking skills. You absolutely have to start looking at the organization the way the organization looks at the world: in terms of markets, services, priorities and strategic needs. Once again, let me emphasize the point: There is absolutely no excuse for not doing strategic thinking for your HRD unit. Even if top management doesn't now consider HRD part of the strategic effort, you can force the issue by doing your own homework and asking the right questions of the right people.

Another thing, and this is a point George Odiorne has been making for some time, is that HRD people are going to have to learn more about the business they're in. They need to know the products, the markets, the manufacturing process— more about the business in general. If HRD is going to impact an organization, those managing the function have to know the organization's business. There's also data gathering. I can't think of a single thing that will impress top management faster than a dependable source of critical information about the organization's environment.

TRAINING: How do I know it's time to get involved in strategic thinking and how do I get started?

TREGOE: There is a distinction between when *you* are ready and when you and the organization need to make HRD part of the strategic process. Some signs of organizational readiness are when you find yourself surprised by new products, new markets, new acquisitions. When people ask you questions you can't answer, you're ready. A federal agency on your doorstep telling you about a personnel guideline violation and serving a summons is an indicator. Slipping margins, high turnover, all the classics are indicators. But the most important indicator is when you look yourself over and conclude, "Damn it! I can be contributing a lot more than I am." That's a personal readiness test. It's conceivable that you will be ready before the organization is ready for you. Test the water. Can you find someone with a five-year plan? Does it give you any guidance? Do they understand why you are asking questions about the future?

RUMMLER: It would be great if the chairman of the board suddenly asked you to come to lunch to discuss the future of the organization. That won't happen to most of us. Start by getting your own house in order. It's important to have your own strategy clear in your mind. You might not be able to get answers to all the questions we

think should be asked, but you can do a first approximation. Sit down and go through the Driving Force drill in your own shop.

I'm a firm believer that people have models in their heads that they use for decision making. Once you have developed that model for your HRD function, you can go to corporate and say, "Tell us what your strategy is so we can interface with it." If that's unrealistic, concentrate on where you want your group to go and goal set from there. There's no law that says you and your staff can't go off into the woods and get your own act together.

TREGOE: Let's try to end this with some perspective. Right now there is a tremendous push to solve this country's productivity and other problems by operational means, by doing things better. The push for wholesale importation of things Japanese— Quality Circles, national planning, Ringi management and the like— may be important, and there may be things

we *can* learn about operations from the Japanese, the Germans, the whoevers. But let me suggest that operational improvement is only a partial answer for our current problems. Historically we, the United States, have been in the catbird seat: unlimited resources, market dominance, little competition. In that environment coping with competitive threats through operational improvements worked well. Being efficient was all it took for an organization to succeed. Becoming *more* efficient was all it took to beat out the other guys.

Those days are gone. We are not going to cope today by tending only to the "do things better" aspect of business. We are going to have to spend time thinking about "doing better things," thinking strategically. And that's why we believe that this is a tremendously opportune time for those involved in human resources development to get with it— strategically.

Reprinted from TRAINING, April 1981

THE ART OF CRAFTING STRATEGIC PLANS

Getting information isn't the problem.
Sorting the worthwhile from the
worthless-that's the problem

BY GEORGE S. ODIORNE

Strategic planning is no longer a game played strictly by major leaguers. In fact, large numbers of small and mid-sized firms are taking a longer look into the future, trying to prevent it from crashing about them. Too often in the past, organizations found themselves enmeshed in crises that might have been averted by anticipating and preparing for an uncertain future.

One of the newest tools in the strategic planner's repertoire is the "environmental scan." This is the method planners use to try to spy the threats just over the horizon, the risks that must be faced in the next five to 10 years, and the opportunities waiting to be exploited by those with foresight. Strategic planners scan the gamut of environmental factors: governmental changes caused by elections or shifts in administration philosophies, demographic changes brought on by fluctuating population characteristics, social changes in taste and morals, and many more.

By studying demographics, for example, we can project that in 10 years there will be 7 million fewer workers between the ages of 18 and 24, and almost 20 million more between 34 and 59. The fastest-growing segment of the population will be the elderly, whose middle-aged offspring will face the problem of parental care. Age discrimination laws now enable people to work longer, which guarantees that employers' health-care costs will keep rising.

At the other end of the spectrum,

> **What you need
> to plan
> strategically
> is more information
> and less data.**

the birthrate is resurging. Phoenix already is planning a dozen new elementary schools and half-a-dozen new high schools to cope with the current baby boom. As the number of working women continues to rise, demand for employer-supported child care is bound to increase as well.

Data overload

Unless you are a newspaper editor, you probably struggle just to stay abreast of current events, much less sort out issues that might affect your business in the future. One shortcut is to do what professional strategic planners do: Subscribe to information services. Commercial information and data-bank companies such as Lockheed Dialog and ABI Inform can find you everything that has been written on any known subject—at least that's how it will appear to you. You simply send them the key words that interest you, and they return abstracts of every article on that topic from a vast assortment of publications.

Or, if you want to simplify things, you can subscribe to a service that distills information into periodic reports. The Bureau of National Affairs, Commerce Clearinghouse and other companies provide monthly updates on topics ranging from tax laws to personnel practices. Newsbank, another monthly data service, provides an index to every story in every issue of more than 100 U.S. daily newspapers. Subscribers can order the complete text of any story on microfiche.

Yes, it's easier than ever to collect mounds of data. But how do you keep from being inundated with the stuff? As consultant Thomas Gilbert, founder of Performance Engineering in Hampton, NJ, puts it: "Data comes in stacks like hay, each straw pointing in a different direction. Information, on the other hand, is like a needle; it points in one direction and has a point."

What you need to plan strategically, then, is more information and less data. With information you can create policies and goals. With information you can turn your analysis into actions that advance your business. The problem remains: How do you turn data into information?

Critical issues

Pop sociologists and journalists like to create monumental trends out of isolated incidents. Managers are ill-advised to listen indiscriminately; we can't interpret each new eruption of media hype as a dire warning of imminent disaster lying square in our path. If we read today's headlines and extrapolate them into the future, for example, we would have a world of cocaine-crazed arbitrageurs using inside information to pull off a leveraged buy out of the entire Milky Way galaxy. Half our employees would be donating urine samples, while the other half would be jumping at early retirement.

Instead, we must find the few critical issues that must be faced in the future. How do we define the ones we should be prepared to address in our own organizations?

STEP 1: First, examine your organization's major problems. What might they be in the future, given recent trends? If your earnings have been flat for four years, you have a problem. If your turnover of key people such as engineers, accountants or other skilled employees is too high, you have a problem. Where are you now and how did you get there? If you

---

If there is a difference between where you are headed and where you want to be, you have defined the problem.

---

didn't do anything differently, where would you be in one year? Two years? Five years? Ten years? Do those answers please you? If not, where would you like to be at the end of those periods?

If there is a difference between where you are headed and where you want to be, you have defined the problem: It is the gap between the desired and the projected outcomes. Strategic planners call this exercise "gap analysis." You can use gap analysis to examine your organization's markets, products, customers, employees, finances, technology and community relations.

You're unlikely to find all of your organization's problems in a single department or in a single sitting. Problems are bound to surface in several areas of the organization. Similarly, it's naive to expect some central staff guru to proclaim the best or even a realistic definition of all of them.

People's Bank in Bridgeport, CT, has an innovative method for identifying such problems, the first step in finding the critical strategic issues. It has established "cabinets" or task

forces of managers and staff experts from each area of the business. Their mission: to define the critical long-range problems facing the bank—deregulation, competition and the like.

STEP 2: Next, you're ready to examine outside influences that are important to your organization. When is a change, trend or event important? When it relates to a key problem you have or anticipate having.

While it may be intellectually stimulating to try to keep tabs on the whole world, you have to be selective when it comes to strategic planning. You must focus on those few major issues that could reach inside your business and create problems.

If the cost of energy is crucial for your business, the outcome of the war between Iraq and Iran could be of keen interest, along with the outcome of OPEC's next meeting. Or, if you are being ravaged by Japanese competition, the relative value of the dollar and the yen will be important; a falling dollar against the yen will raise the prices of imports, leaving you in a better competitive position.

Fast-food operations, such as Burger King and McDonald's, should be interested in the projected decline in the number of 18- to 24-year-olds by 1990, since this group has supplied most of their store workers in the past. School superintendents, too, should track birthrates and immigration of young families into their regions. They must gauge fluctuations in their clientele if they want to do any long-term strategic planning. Facility planning, teacher staffing, budgetary planning, tax requirements and a host of other operating details five years from now will be affected by today's birthrates.

STEP 3: Now you're ready to list the critical issues. As you consider candidates, keep in mind that critical issues used for strategic planning have several distinguishing features:
- They usually affect the entire organization, rather than one department.
- Their impact is usually long-term. Operational issues must be faced next quarter or next year; strategic issues gradually spin out over five or 10 years.
- They are based upon information that is "protracted and robust," to use the jargon of the strategic plan-

ner. This simply means that the trend or condition is supported by irrefutable evidence and has been under way for a long time. Strategic planners can't afford to be stampeded by media hype or a single current event, no matter how surprising it may be.

STEP 4: There are several sorting techniques you can use on your list. First, rank the critical issues according to their importance to your organization. Top priorities are issues that must be turned into programs or operating objectives within the next year. You probably will want to include them in your next budget plan.

Divide your list into categories of

One way to practice the art (of defining critical issues) is to try applying it to your own career.

---

urgency such as "must do," "need to do," and "important, but not urgent." The most urgent are the issues that should command management attention now in order to exploit an opportunity that may be five years down the road. For example, if the company doesn't start a research program in a promising area immediately, it won't have a product to meet the competition in five years. This list may also include some areas in which the company has fallen behind and needs to play catch-up.

Divide the items on your list into "success producers" and "failure preventers." Success producers are the top few items that offer chances for big scores in the future. Failure preventers are issues that, allowed to slide, may cause us to stumble.

STEP 5: Describe these critical issues to your organization's management. Make it clear that these are organization-wide goals that should be reflected in the annual operating objectives of every department or division.

At Tenneco, this communication took the form of a letter from the company president. Recently at General Motors, every company manager received a film from the president, who described what he saw as the critical human-resource issues: getting more minorities into dealerships, making factory work more human and promoting more women into managerial ranks.

This downward communication is necessary if critical issues are going to be converted into long-term corporate objectives for the operating managers. It's an article of faith in management-by-objectives programs that corporate objectives must be set at the top and passed downward before operating objectives for the coming year are fixed. Similarly, in strategic planning top management must define the critical issues so that line management can figure out how they should be addressed.

STEP 6: Timing is an important element in communicating the critical issues. April or May usually is a good time—issues can be clarified and defined far in advance of budget time. Once critical issues have been "wired into" budgets, they become part of the operating objectives for the following year.

Starting small

Most people don't define critical issues as part of their daily activities, and learning to do so takes some training. One way to practice the art is to try applying it to your own career.

STRATEGIC PLANNING WITH A PEOPLE FOCUS

Involving human resources development in strategic planning is easy. Just let HRD study whatever demographics you happen to have on hand, scan the organization's strategic plans for the past few years, gather a few colleagues, and two flip-chart pads, and—presto—integrated objectives and strategies appear. Right?

Wrong, says Frank Basler, president of Basler Associates, a Westport, CT-based consulting firm. In his opinion, the crucial missing ingredient is information about what will be expected of *people* in order to reach the organization's goals. He proposes a strategic planning process for HRD based on seven considerations:

• *What does the organization want to be best at?* Basler stresses that this is a qualitative question that goes beyond standard mission statements based on percentage of market, sales or profit growth. "The question asks for *competencies* that will distinguish the organization from its competitors," he explains. "What will this organization be *able* to do that no one else can, that will assure those numerical gains?"

To answer this question, Basler encourages HRD and management jointly to examine the organization's past competitive edge, the values and beliefs that shaped its development, the market it can target and the product or service it can provide.

• *Internal measures of success.* Basler points out that this factor is more than a vague philosophy statement about values and ideal behaviors. It must answer the question, "How will we *know* if our philosophy is being implemented?" As examples of such measures, Basler lists "employees who can describe specifically what [the organization is] striving to become (who share a common vision or image of quality); entry-level development positions filled by capable, energetic people who can grow with the business; specific agreements between each manager and employee on the objectives and standards against which work will be evaluated; [and] frequent, ongoing coaching, encouragement and positive feedback."

• *What does it take to get there?* The "content" side of this question concerns the way the organization will perform differently in relation to its customers, creditors, competitors, vendors, etc. The "process" side involves the skills and knowledge that will be required for key groups within the organizaton to bring about these changes in performance.

When both parts of the question are answered, Basler says, it becomes possible to estimate how many people with what kinds of competencies are needed in specific parts of the organization. "This then becomes the central, long-range objective for the HRD group: ensuring that the right people with the right skills are available and willing when the organization needs them."

• *Recruiting and growing the needed talent.* A number of questions must be answered to carry out this process: How many of the present employees have skills that are becoming obsolete? Can they be retrained or transferred? How many people will have to be recruited and what skills must they have? How can the organization find and attract them? Who will need what kind of training and what is the best way to provide it? How will employees' managers and peers be rewarded for their efforts as mentors, coaches and instructors?

• *Communicating the organization's expectations to employees.* HRD and management need to consider what types of systems, especially performance planning and review systems, they will develop to clarify the organization's expectations for each employee.

• *Rewards for meeting and exceeding performance standards.* This factor includes both monetary compensation and nonmonetary rewards such as recognition and support for good work.

• *How will we be sure it's all working?* According to Basler, HRD and management need to decide what systems, surveys, data and corrective action will be used to monitor and maintain success once it is achieved. "Success" includes both external success in the marketplace and internal success—effectively building the desired norms, practices and capabilities in the organization.

"If HRD can help organizations discover and articulate the ways in which they can and will be uniquely competent, then the requirements for an HRD strategy become clear," he concludes. "It is a strategy for enabling the organization to find, grow, challenge and reward the talent its 'best' requires."

Reprinted from TRAINING, May 1985

First, define the major problems in your job and career. If you don't do anything differently, where would you be in five or 10 years? Do you like your answer? Where would you really like to be? The gap between the two answers is your personal career management problem.

Second, look at your environment. What are some of the threats, risks and opportunities in your world? Examine it from a variety of perspectives: personal, financial, social and cultural.

Next, list the critical issues that must become part of your long-range career development strategy. Rank them according to urgency. Of the things you might do, do differently or refrain from doing, which would be success producers? Which would be failure preventers?

You now have your critical issues list for your career. You are ready to choose actions that will help you close the potential gaps in your future.

You also might practice strategic planning in counseling subordinates. Let's say you have an employee who shows star potential, but is unable to manage her career. Try going through a critical-issues exercise with her. Have her define her problems, environment and critical career issues. Have her rank them, and ask her to define the success producers and failure preventers in her life. The end result just might be a developmental plan that accelerates her achievements and enhances her value to the organization.

These career exercises are good ways to study and practice strategic planning. Having mastered the art of defining critical issues in your career and that of a promising protégé, you are ready to apply the same steps in defining the critical strategic planning issues for your organization.

Reprinted from TRAINING, October 1987

CONTRIBUTORS

Readers of TRAINING Magazine will notice that most articles have an author ID listing the writer's title, affiliation and location. Rather than reprint out-of-date information, we've listed here the current data (current at the time of this book's publication!) about each contributor.

KARL ALBRECHT
Management and OD Consultant
San Diego, CA

DAN E. ANDERSEN
Manager, Marketing
Communications
Semiconductor Division,
Raytheon Co.
Mountain View, CA

ELLEN BALL
Marketing Assistant
AT&T
South Plainfield, NJ

BARBARA BAKER
Regional Vice President
Mohr Development
Stamford, CT

MICHAEL J. BASHISTA
Freelance Scriptwriter
Santa Cruz, CA

MAUREEN M. BEAUSEY
Eastman Kodak Company
Rochester, NY

ARTHUR C. BECK, JR.
Retired
Richmond, VA

STEPHEN P. BECKER
President
Learncom, Inc.
Cambridge, MA

FORREST BELCHER
President
MEGA Consultants
Sand Springs, OK

CHIP R. BELL
Independent Consultant
Charlotte, NC

GEOFFREY M. BELLMAN
Principal
GMB Associates, Ltd.
Seattle, WA

JIRI BEZDEK
Senior Writer
Deltak
Naperville, IL

JOHN L. BLEDSOE
President
Mok-Bledsoe International
Dallas, TX

GEORGE W. BLOMGREN
President
Organizational Psychologists
Chicago, IL

A.E. BLOOMWELL
Manager, Development & Training
Merck & Co.
Rahway, NJ

BARBARA BOWMAN
Corporate Director of Human
Resources
Children's Hospital of Wisconsin
Milwaukee, WI

ALAN P. BRACHE
Principal
Rummler-Brache Group
Warren, NJ

GARY BRAGA
Des Moines, IA

KAREN BRETHOWER
Brethower Associates
Wilton, CT

MARTIN M. BROADWELL
General Manager
Center For Management
Services
Decatur, GA

P. CAROL BROADWELL
Associate
Center for Management Services
Marietta, GA

LESLIE A. BRYAN, JR.
Assoc. Professor, Dept. of
Supervision
Purdue University School of
Technology
West Lafayette, IN

MARGARET MORGAN BYNUM
Managing Editor
Learn Inc.
Mt. Laurel, NJ

DAVID CALDWELL
Associate Professor
Leavy School of Business &
Administration,
Santa Clara Univ.
Santa Clara, CA

ROBERT M. CALDWELL
Assoc. Prof., Dept. of Allied
Health Ed.
University of Texas Health &
Science Ctr.
Dallas, TX

KENNETH E. CARLISLE
Senior Training Representative
Morton Thiokel, Inc.
Logan, UT

JANET HOUSER CARTER
Director, Educational Services
St. John's Regional Medical
Center
Joplin, MO

DAVID CHESNUT
Deceased

RUTH COLVIN CLARK
Manager of Training Information
Services
Southern California Edison
Rosemead, CA

JAMES R. COOK
Vice President, Instruction
Practical Management, Inc.
Calabas, CA

MICHAEL J. COPPOLINO
President
Computer Tutor Corp.
Wellesley, MA

J.B. CORNWELL
Technical Training & Management
Consultant
Mound, MN

TOM COTHRAN
Freelance Writer
Minneapolis, MN

DAVID D. CRAM
Manager, Instructional
Technology
Apple University
Cupertino, CA

MARILYN DARLING
Management Consultant
Charlestown, MA

ROBERT P. DELAMONTAGNE
President
Personnel Management Systems
Princeton, NJ

ROBERT W. DOBLES
Retired
Rochester, NY

JO DOMINO
Senior Editor, Education Services
Dun & Bradstreet
New York, NY

DIANE DORMANT
President
Dormant and Associates
Bloomington, IN

PATRICIA M. DROST
Law Clerk
Eastman Kodak
Rochester, NY

DONALD P. DUROCHER
President
Durocher & Co.
Detroit, MI

ROBERT C. EIMERS
Medina & Thompson
Chicago, IL

JOE FARACE
Farace Photography
Englewood, CO

DALE FEUER
Contributing Editor
TRAINING Magazine
Minneapolis, MN

CAROL FEY
Sales Representative
Honeywell
Denver, CO

JEFF FIERSTEIN
Training Consultant
Time Systems Inc.
Phoenix, AZ

JUDITH E. FISHER
President
Education and Training
Consultants, Inc.
Riverview, FL

P. JEFFREY FLOOD
Information Specialist
Esso Resources Canada Ltd.
Calgary, Canada

BEVERLY GEBER
Associate Editor
TRAINING Magazine
Minneapolis, MN

JAMES C. GEORGES
Chairman
ParTraining Corp.
Tucker, GA

PATRICK J. GERMANY
Dir. of Management Development
The Western Co. of North
America
Ft. Worth, TX

THOMAS GILBERT
Morristown, NJ

TOM W. GOAD
Training Specialist
Logicon San Diego, CA

MICHAEL GODKEWITSCH
Industrial Psychologist
Canada Imperial Oil LTD., HRD
Division
Toronto, Canada

JACK GORDON
Editor
TRAINING Magazine
Minneapolis, MN

EDWARD GUBMAN
Consultant
Hewitt Associates
Lincolnshire, IL

DAVID G. GUEULETTE
Professor, Instructional
Technology
Northern Illinois University
De Kalb, IL

PAT BURKE GUILD
Pat Guild Associates
Seattle, WA

JOHN GUNTHER
Principal
Decision Futures
St. Louis Park, MN

JOE HARLESS
Harless Performance Guild, Inc.
Newman, GA

PAUL HARMON
Harmon Associates
San Francisco, CA

EDWARD HARRISON
Professor of Management
College of Bus. & Mngmnt.
Studies,
University of South Alabama
Mobile, AL

WILLIAM W. HARVEY
Boise, ID

STANLEY S. HAZEN
Training Counselor
Eastman Kodak Company
Rochester, NY

JESSE M. HEINES
Senior Staff
Digital Equipment Corp.,
Educational Services
Bedford, MA

MATTHEW J. HENNECKE
Corporate Training Manager
Helene Curtis
Chicago, IL

MURRAY HIEBART
Sr. Organization Effectiveness
Advisor
Esso Resources Canada Ltd.
Calgary, Alberta

TED C. HILL
Supervisor, Technical Training
Rubbermaid
Wooster, OH

ELLIS D. HILLMAR
Associate Pro., Management
Institute
University of Richmond
Richmond, VA

ROBERT C. HINKELMAN
Educational Consultant
Eastman Kodak Company
Rochester, NY

FRANK O. HOFFMAN
Frank O. Hoffman Organization
Woodland Hills, CA

LAWRENCE HOLPP
Director of Training and
Development
McNeil Consumer Products
Fort Washington, PA

DAVID C. HON
President
Ixion, Inc.
Seattle, WA

ROBERT E. HORN
President
Information Mapping
Waltham, MA

RUTH SIZEMORE HOUSE
President
The Paradigm Corp.
Kenesaw, GA

DANNY E. HUPP
Partners In Change
Pittsburgh, PA

HANK HUTSON
Corporate Staff Personnel
Director
Cummins Engine Co., Inc.
Columbus, IN

JOHN D. INGALLS
President
Competency Development Corp.
Arlington, MA

JOHN R. INGRISANO
President
Custom Communications
Maizomanie, WI

THOMAS S. ISAACK
Professor of Management
West Virginia University
Morgantown, WV

STEPHANIE F. JACKSON
Senior Partner
Vanguard Consulting Group
Larkspur Landing, CA

DON JOINSON
Managing Director
Instructa Pty. Ltd.
Cremorne, Australia

PETER JONES
Manager/RAC Products
Carrier International Corp.
Syracuse, NY

HELEN KELLY
Consultant
New Haven, CT

MALCOLM KNOWLES
Knowles Enterprises
Raleigh, NC

THEODORE J. KREIN
Senior Manager
Ernst & Whinney
Cleveland, OH

ROBERT E. KUSHELL
President
Dunhill Personnel System, Inc.
Carle Place, NY

PHYLLIS KYKER
Manager, Customer Service
Training
Southern California Edison
Rosemead, CA

DUGAN LAIRD
Deceased

ROBERT N. LANDAUER
Retired
Houston, TX

LINDA LASH
Director, Training
Avis Rent A Car
Bracknell, Berkshire, England

BARRY LASTRA
Senior Planning Consultant
Chevron USA, Inc.
San Francisco, CA

CHRIS LEE
Managing Editor
TRAINING Magazine
Minneapolis, MN

LESLIE M. LEGG
Staff Development Specialist
American Savings & Loan Assoc.
of Florida
Miami, FL

JAMES M. LEWIS
Independent Training Consultant
Washington, DC

LESLIE P. LIMON
Chairperson, VAX New Products
Comm.
Digital Equipment Corp.
Tewksbury, MA

ANTONI A. LOUW
President
Louw's Management Corp.
Fort Lee, NJ

GEORGE T. LYNN
Principal
Optimax
Kirkland, WA

JO ANNE BARRIE LYNN
Principal
Optimax
Kirkland, WA

PATTY MACK
Manager, Industrial Training
Coca Cola Foods
Houston, TX

ROBERT F. MAGER
President
Mager Associates
Carefree, AZ

MICHAEL MAGINN
Vice President
The Forum Corporation
Boston, MA

STEVE MANGUM
Ohio State University
Academic Faculty of Mngmnt. &
Human Resources
Columbus, OH

MARVIN MARCEL
Expert Marketing Witness
Southwestern Bell
St. Louis, MO

NANCY MARCUE
Technical Assistant/Sr. Training
Analyst
Veda Inc.
Orlando, FL

FREDRIC MARGOLIS
Independent Consultant
Washington D.C.

PETER MARTIN
UDATA
Morristown, NJ

MARK J. MARTINKO
Ass't Prof. of Management
Florida State University
Tallahassee, FL

JAMES F. McCAMPBELL
Director of Education
Little Company of Mary Hospital
Evergreen Park, IL

CHARLES R. McCONNELL
Ontario, NY

D. DOUGLAS McKENNA
Research Psychologist
Personnel Decisions Research
Institute
Minneapolis, MN

PATRICIA A. McLAGAN
Chief Executive
McLagan International, Inc.
St. Paul, MN

J. REGIS McNAMARA
Associate Professor of
Psychology
Ohio University
Athens, OH

BOB MEZOFF
President
ODT Associates
Amherst, MA

PAUL J. MICALI
Barclay Personnel Systems
Boston, MA

GERALD A. MICHAELSON
V.P. Sales, Special Markets
NAP Consumer Electronics
Knoxville, TN

RICHARD MIRABILE
President
Behavioral Systems Management
Group
Half Moon Bay, CA

ALEX MIRONOFF
Manager of Corporate Training &
Education
Provident Life and Accident
Insurance Co.
Chattanooga, TN

WILLIAM F. MOLLOY
Vice President, Western Region
Development Dimensions
International
Los Angeles, CA

CARL C. MOORE
Associate Dean
College of Bus. & Mngmnt.
Studies,
U. of South Alabama
Mobile, AL

PAUL NASMAN
Sr. Vice President
Omega Performance Group
San Francisco, CA

ANDRE NELSON
Training Officer
California Youth Authority
Ventura, CA

PAMELA J. NEWMAN
Managing Director
Marsh & McLennan
New York, NY

MAURICE NICHOLS
Retired
Belmont, CA

STEVEN D. NORTON
Chief Research Psychologist
Department of Defense
Dayton, OH

ROGER T. O'BRIEN
Regional Training Officer
Midwest Region,
U.S. Dept. of Housing & Urban
   Devel.
Glenview, IL

TERENCE O'CONNOR
Dir. of Personnel & Community
   Relations
St. Patrick's Home
New York, NY

TERRI O'GRADY
Freelance Writer
Minneapolis, MN

BRIAN O'HARA
Libertyville, IL

CHARLES O'REILLY
Professor of Management
School of Business,
University of California
Berkeley, CA

GEORGE S. ODIORNE
Professor of Management
Eckerd College
St. Petersburg, FL

H. ADRIAN OSBORNE
Director, Placement Systems
   Division
Department of Defense
Dayton, OH

CAROL M. PANZA
Management Consultant
CMT Associates
Convent Station, NJ

JEFFREY W. PARIS
Producer, Director & Scriptwriter
Memorex
Santa Clara, CA

PAUL H. PETRI
Director of Management
   Development
College of Bus. & Mngmnt.
   Studies,
University of South Alabama
Mobile, AL

THOMAS PETRO
Account Manager
Creative Universal Inc.
Detroit, MI

JACK J. PHILLIPS
Senior Vice President, Human
   Resources
Alabama Federal Savings & Loan
Birmingham, AL

CARL E. PICKHARDT
Consulting Psychologist
Organizational Life Management
Austin, TX

ROBERT C. PREZIOSI
V.P. Staff Planning & Development
American Savings & Loan Assoc.
   of Florida
Miami, FL

RALPH PRIBBLE
Freelance Writer
Minneapolis, MN

GEORGE PRINCE
Synectics Inc.
Cambridge, MA

PAUL RAHN
Product Manager
Union Camp Corp.
Griffin, GA

JOEL RAKOW
Executive Vice President
American Training International
Manhattan Beach, CA

JOEL D. RAMICH
Manager of Total Quality
Corning Glass Works
Corning, NY

RICHARD REAGH
Addressograph Multigraph Corp.
Field Operations Division
Schaumberg, IL

LILLITH REN
U.S. Army
ERADCOM
Adelphi, MD

ANGUS REYNOLDS
Senior HRD Consultant
Education Technology Center
Washington D.C.

DON M. RICKS
President
IWCC—Training In Writing
Calgary, Canada

DANA GAINES ROBINSON
President
Partners in Change
Pittsburgh, PA

JAMES C. ROBINSON
Chairman
Partners in Change
Pittsburgh, PA

LINDA E. ROBINSON
Instructional Technologist
The Contact Group
Pittsburgh, PA

ROSALIND L. ROGOFF
Senior Instructional Designs
Hughs Aircraft
Culver City, CA

BERNARD L. ROSENBAUM
President
Mohr Development
Stamford, CT

MARC. J. ROSENBERG
Staff Manager
AT&T Data Systems Education
   Center
New Brunswick, NJ

NATE ROSENBLATT
President
NPR Marketing
Cherry Hill, NJ

WILLIAM J. ROTHWELL
Special Services Officer
Illinois Office of the Auditor
   General
Springfield, IL

GEARY A. RUMMLER
Principal
Rummler-Brache Group
Warren, NJ

TOM SALEMME
Consultant
Organization Consulting Group
Concord, MA

RUTH SALINGER
Employee Development
   Specialist
Department of Health & Human
   Services
Washington D.C.

RAYMOND E. SANDBORGH
Staff Consultant
Sperry Univac
St. Paul, MN

LEN SANDLER
Independent Consultant
Boston, MA

DICK SCHAFF
Writer
Minneapolis, MN

HAROLD SCHARLATT
President
Training & Development
   Associates
Lexington, KY

CHARLES F. SCHULER
Executive Director
Palm Beach Regional
   Achievement Center
West Palm Beach, FL

IRVING R. SCHWARTZ
Boston, MA

JOE SEACRIST
V.P. Human Resource
   Development
The Continental Corp.
New York, NY

JAY SEDLIK
President
Jay Sedlik Enterprises/
National Training Systems
Encino, CA

TRAVIS SHIPP
Program Area Head
Adult Education,
Indiana University
Bloomington, IN

KENNETH SHORT
Wichita, KS

DAN SIEMASKO
Supervisor of Writing,
A/V Services
Fisher Scientific Co.
Pittsburgh, PA

W. NORMAN SMALLWOOD
Senior Human Resources
   Advisor
Esso Resources Canada Ltd.
Calgary, Canada

JUDSON SMITH
Business Communications
   Specialist
Minneapolis, MN

WILLIAM SMITLEY
Staff Manager
American Bell
Orlando, FL

LYLE M. SPENCER, JR.
Sr. Vice President
McBer Co.
Boston, MA

JOSEPH SPINALE
Sr. Operations Analyst
Taco Bell
Irvine, CA

DEAN SPITZER
Associate Professor
Boise State University
Boise, ID

LINDA STANDKE
Consultant
McLagan International, Inc.
St. Paul, MN

JUDITH H. STEELE
Senior Program Director
Learning International
Stamford, CT

TERESA S. STOVER
Training Supervisor
National Semiconductor
Puyallup, WA

PATRICK SUESSMUTH
Managing Director
Cantra Training Ltd.
Ontario, Canada

SUSAN HAKE SURPLUS
Management Consultant
Glastonbury, CT

RAYNOLD A. SVENSON
President
Svenson and Wallace, Inc.
Wheaton, IL

VAN SYMONS
Manager, Training & Development
General Products Division, IBM
San Jose, CA

EMILIA SZAREK
Program Specialist
Department of Health & Human
   Services
Philadelphia, PA

NORMAN R. TICE
Sales Representative,
Engineered Products
Manville Sales Corp.
Defiance, OH

WILLIAM R. TRACEY
President
Human Resources of Cape Cod
South Yarmouth, MA

BEN TREGOE
Kepner-Tregoe, Inc.
Princeton, NJ

CHARLES UTT
Asst. Superintendent for
  Administration
Clarks Summit State Hospital
Clarks Summit, PA

C.W. VON BERGEN, JR.
Director, Manpower Development
Western Company
Ft. Worth, TX

JOAN WACKERMAN
Instructional Systems Designer
Logicon Inc.
San Diego, CA

GUY WALLACE
Associate
Svenson and Wallace, Inc.
Wheaton, IL

KAREN M. WALLACE
Vice President
Svenson and Wallace, Inc.
Wheaton, IL

LANE D. WARD
General Manager
Shipley Associates
Bountiful, UT

KATHLEEN WHITESIDE
Corporate Director
Harper-Grace Hosptial
Detroit, MI

**GAYLE COATES
WIGGLESWORTH**
Independent HRD Consultant
Foster City, CA

CAPT. JEROLD W. WILEY
Director of Training &
  Development
Air Defense Weapons Center
Tyndall Air Force Base, FL

LARRY WINTERS
Manager
Dun & Bradstreet
New York, NY

GARY AUSTIN WITT
Media Design Inc.
Austin, TX

HAROLD WOLFE
Principal
Helios Custom Training, Inc.
Haydenville, MA

FRANK T. WYDRA
Executive Vice President
The Chi Group
Ann Arbor, MI

ED YAGER
President
Yager Associates
Park City, UT

ROBERT B. YOUKER
Management Training Specialist
The World Bank
Washington D.C.

RON ZEMKE
President
Performance Research
  Associates
Minneapolis, MN

SUSAN ZEMKE
Human Resources Officer
First Bank System
Minneapolis, MN